WELCOME TO

EXPLORING STRATEGY

Strategy is a crucial subject. It's about the development, success and failure of all kinds of organisations, from multinationals to entrepreneurial start-ups, from charities to government agencies, and many more. Strategy raises the big questions about these organisations – how they grow, how they innovate and how they change. As a manager of today or tomorrow, you will be involved in shaping, implementing or communicating these strategies.

Our primary aim with *Exploring Strategy* is to give you a comprehensive understanding of the issues and techniques of strategy. We can also help you get a great final result in your course. You can make the most of the text by:

- Exploring hot topics in cutting-edge issues such as competition, corporate governance, innovation and entrepreneurship and strategy in practice.

- Engaging with the 'Key Debates' and the different strategy 'lenses' to get new perspectives and set you on your way to better grades in your assignments and exams.

- Pursuing some of the recommended readings at the end of each chapter. They're specially selected as accessible and valuable sources that will enhance your learning and give you an extra edge in your course work.

After you've registered with the access code (either in the back of this book or available separately online), visit *Exploring Strategy* at **www.mystrategylab.com** to find essential student learning material including:

- The **Strategy Experience simulation**, which gives you practical hands-on experience of strategic decision making in organisations. As a Director of the Board, you must deal with opportunities as they arise, and your decisions will affect the company's performance. Choose wisely!

- A **personalised study plan** based on feedback that identifies your strengths and weaknesses, then recommends a tailored set of resources that will help to develop your understanding of strategy.

- **Video case studies** on organisations including Eurostar, Sony Pictures and the British Heart Foundation that put a spotlight on strategy in practice.

We want *Exploring Strategy* to give you what you need: a comprehensive view of the subject, an ambition to put that into practice, and – of course – success in your studies. We hope that you'll be as excited by the key issues of strategy as we are!

So, read on and good luck!

Gerry Johnson
Richard Whittington
Kevan Scholes
Duncan Angwin
Patrick Regnér

Gerry Johnson, BA, PhD, is Emeritus Professor of Strategic Management at Lancaster University School of Management. He has also taught at Strathclyde Business School, Cranfield School of Management, Manchester Business School and Aston University. He is the author of numerous books and his research has been published in many of the world's foremost management journals. He is also a partner in the consultancy partnership Strategy Explorers (see **www.strategyexplorers.com**), where he works on issues of strategy development and strategic change.

Richard Whittington, MA, MBA, PhD, is Professor of Strategic Management at the Saïd Business School, University of Oxford. He is author or co-author of nine books and serves on several editorial boards. He has had full or visiting positions at the Harvard Business School, HEC Paris, Imperial College London, the University of Toulouse and the University of Warwick. He is a partner in Strategy Explorers and active in executive education and consulting. His current research focuses on strategy practice.

Kevan Scholes, MA, PhD, DMS, CIMgt, FRSA, is Principal Partner of Scholes Associates, specialising in strategic management. He is also Emeritus Professor of Strategic Management and formerly Director of the Sheffield Business School. He has extensive experience of teaching strategy internationally as well as working in the private and public sector. He is a Companion of The Chartered Management Institute.

Duncan Angwin, MA, MPhil, MBA, PhD, is Professor of Strategy at Oxford Brookes University. He is author of six books and 38 journal articles and serves on several editorial boards. He sits on the advisory board of the M&A research centre, Cass Business School, London and on the Academic Council of ENPC Paris. He is active internationally in executive education and consulting, His current research focuses on mergers and acquisitions, strategy practice and international management.

Patrick Regnér, BSc, MSc, PhD, is Associate Professor of Strategic Management at Stockholm School of Economics. He serves on several editorial boards and has published numerous articles in leading academic journals. He has extensive experience of teaching strategy internationally. He conducts executive training and consulting with organisations worldwide. His research interests are in strategy creation and change and international management.

Follow the authors' latest comments on the strategy issues of this book at **https://twitter.com/ExploreStrategy**.

ASKHAM BRYAN
COLLEGE
LEARNING RESOURCES

EXPLORING STRATEGY

TENTH EDITION

GERRY JOHNSON
Lancaster University Management School

RICHARD WHITTINGTON
Saïd Business School, University of Oxford

KEVAN SCHOLES
Sheffield Business School

DUNCAN ANGWIN
Oxford Brookes University

PATRICK REGNÉR
Stockholm School of Economics

With the assistance of Steve Pyle

PEARSON

Harlow, England • London • New York • Boston • San Francisco • Toronto • Sydney • Auckland • Singapore • Hong Kong
Tokyo • Seoul • Taipei • New Delhi • Cape Town • São Paulo • Mexico City • Madrid • Amsterdam • Munich • Paris • Milan

Pearson Education Limited
Edinburgh Gate
Harlow CM20 2JE
United Kingdom
Tel: +44 (0)1279 623623
Web: www.pearson.com/uk

First edition (print) published under the Prentice Hall imprint 1984
Fifth edition (print) published under the Prentice Hall imprint 1998
Sixth edition (print) published under the Financial Times Prentice Hall imprint 2002
Seventh (print) edition 2005
Eighth (print) edition 2008
Ninth edition (print) 2011
Tenth edition published 2014 (print and electronic)

© Simon & Schuster Europe Limited 1998 (print)
© Pearson Education 2002, 2011 (print)
© Pearson Education Limited 2014 (print and electronic)

Text only
ISBN: 978-1-292-00255-2 (print)
       978-1-292-00694-9 (PDF)
       978-1-292-00693-2 (eText)

Text and cases
ISBN: 978-1-292-00254-5 (print)
       978-1-292-00689-5 (PDF)
       978-1-292-00688-8 (eText)

British Library Cataloguing-in-Publication Data
A catalogue record for the print edition is available from the British Library

Library of Congress Cataloging-in-Publication Data
A catalog record for the print edition is available from the Library of Congress

10 9 8 7 6 5 4 3 2 1
16 15 14 13 12

Front cover design by Dan Mogford

Print edition typeset in 9.5/13.5pt Photina MT Std by 35
Print edition printed and bound by L.E.G.O. S.p.A., Italy

NOTE THAT ANY PAGE CROSS-REFERENCES REFER TO THE PRINT EDITION

BRIEF CONTENTS

CONTENTS

PART I
THE STRATEGIC POSITION

PART III
STRATEGY IN ACTION

CASE STUDIES

ILLUSTRATIONS AND KEY DEBATES

ILLUSTRATIONS

KEY DEBATES BY CHAPTER

FIGURES

TABLES

PREFACE

As a newly enlarged team of authors, we are delighted to offer this tenth edition of *Exploring Strategy*. With sales of previous editions now over one million, we believe we have a well-tried product. Yet the strategy field is constantly changing. For this edition, therefore, we have thoroughly refreshed each chapter, with new concepts, new cases and new examples throughout. Here we would like to highlight five particular changes, while recalling some of the classic features of the book.

The tenth edition's principal changes are:

- An **increased focus on ownership:** reflecting the growing importance of family, entrepreneurial and state-owned businesses around the world, this edition addresses the implications of different ownership models for strategy.

- A **new treatment of performance:** given that business is so diverse today, this edition also introduces a substantial discussion of how to assess the success of strategies.

- An **enhanced analysis of the non-market aspects of the environment:** with politics and regulations so important to business nowadays, we now give more space to analysing these complex but vital elements of the environment.

- **More discussion of entrepreneurial strategies:** with so many undergraduate and graduate students interested in entrepreneurial careers, we have extended our discussion of entrepreneurship, with more focus on actual strategies.

- **Recognition of the need for organisational ambidexterity:** in a world in which both efficiency and innovation are so important, we stress now the need to exploit current capabilities with one hand, while exploring for new capabilities with the other.

At the same time, *Exploring Strategy* retains its longstanding commitment to a comprehensive and real-world view of strategy. In particular, this entails a deep concern for:

- **Process:** we believe that the human processes of strategy, not only the economics of particular strategies, are central to achieving long-term organisational success. Throughout the book, we underline the importance of human processes, but in particular we devote Part III to processes of strategy formation, implementation and change.

- **Practice:** we conclude the book with a chapter on the practice of strategy (Chapter 15), focused on the practicalities of managing strategy. Throughout the book, we introduce concepts and techniques through practical illustrations and applications, rather than abstract descriptions.

The Strategy Experience simulation gives students a chance to apply the frameworks of the book to a dynamic, realistic simulation of strategy in the advertising industry.

Many people have helped us with the development of this new edition. Steve Pyle has taken leadership in coordinating the case collection. We have consulted carefully with our Advisory Board, made up of experienced adopters of the book. Many other adopters of the book provide more informal advice and suggestions – many of whom we have had the pleasure of meeting at our annual teachers' workshops. This kind of feedback is invaluable and we hope you will keep the comments flowing. Also, our students and clients at Lancaster University, Oxford University, Oxford Brookes, Stockholm School of Economics, Sheffield Hallam and the many other places where we teach are a constant source of ideas and stimulus. We also gain from our links across the world, particularly in Ireland, the Netherlands, Denmark, Sweden, France, Canada, Australia, New Zealand, Hong Kong, Singapore and the USA. Many contribute directly by providing case studies and illustrations and these are acknowledged in the text.

Finally, we thank those organisations that have been generous enough to be written up as case studies. We hope that those using the book will respect the wishes of the case study organisations and *not* contact them directly for further information.

Gerry Johnson (gerry.johnson@lancaster.ac.uk)
Richard Whittington (richard.whittington@sbs.ox.ac.uk)
Kevan Scholes (KScholes@scholes.u-net.com)
Duncan Angwin (dangwin@brookes.ac.uk)
Patrick Regnér (patrick.regner@hhs.se)
April 2013

ADVISORY BOARD

Special thanks are due to the following members of the Advisory Board for their valued comments:

Dr Martin Friesl	Lancaster
Peter Smith	University of Auckland
Robert Wright	Hong Kong Polytechnic
Frédéric Fréry	Professor in the Strategy, Organisational Behaviour and Human Resources Department of ESCP Europe Paris campus and Dean of the European Executive MBA
Clive Choo	Nanyang Technological University
David Oliver	HEC Montreal
Emiel Wubben	Wageningen University
Eric Cassells	Oxford Brookes University
Erik Wilberg	BI Norwegian School of Management
Professor Heather Farley	University of Ulster
Kenneth Wiltshire	University of Queensland
Ludovic Cailluet	IAE Toulouse
Professor Martin Lindell	Hanken School of Economics
Dr Moira Fischbacher-Smith	University of Glasgow
Shigefumi Makino	The Chinese University of Hong Kong
Michael Mayer	University of Bath

EXPLORING STRATEGY

This tenth edition of *Exploring Strategy* builds on the established strengths of this best-selling textbook. A range of in-text features and supplementary features have been developed to enable you and your students to gain maximum added value from the teaching and learning of strategy.

- **Outstanding pedagogical features**. Each chapter has clear learning outcomes, practical questions associated with real-life illustrations and examples which students can easily apply to what they have learnt.

- **Flexibility of use**. You can choose to use either the Text and Cases version of the book, or – if you don't use longer cases (or have your own) – the Text-only version. The provision of Key Debates, Commentaries and Strategy 'Lenses' allow you to dig deeper into the tensions and complexity of strategy.

The two versions are complemented by a concise version of the text, *Fundamentals of Strategy*, and instructors also have the option of further customising the text. Visit **www.pearsoned.co.uk/CustomPublishing** for more details.

- **Up-to-date materials**. As well as a new chapter on mergers, acquisitions and alliances, we have fully revised the other chapters, incorporating new research and updating references so that you can easily access the latest research.

- **Encouraging critical thinking**. As well as the Strategy Lenses, we encourage critical thinking by ending each chapter with a 'Key debate', introducing students to research evidence and theory on key issues of the chapter and encouraging them to take a view.

Our 'three-circles' model – depicting the overlapping issues of strategic position, strategic choices and strategy in action – also challenges a simple linear, sequential view of the strategy process.

- **Case and examples**. A wide range of Illustrations, Case examples and (in the Text and Cases version) longer Case studies are fresh and engage with student interests and day-to-day experience. The majority of these are entirely new to this edition; we have extensively revised the remainder. Finally, we draw these examples from all over the world and use examples from the public and voluntary sectors as well as the private.

- **Teaching and learning support**. You and your students can access a wealth of resources at **www.mystrategylab.com**, including the following:

For students

- **The Strategy Experience** simulation, which puts the students in the driving seat and allows them to experience the real world of strategic decision making.

- A personalised study plan that helps students focus their attention and efforts on the areas where they're needed the most.

- Flashcards and a multilingual glossary.

For instructors

- An Instructor's Manual which provides a comprehensive set of teaching support, including guidance on the use of case studies and assignments, and advice on how to plan a programme using the text.

- PowerPoint slides.

- A test-bank of assessment questions.

- Classic cases from previous editions of the book.

In addition to the website, a printed copy of the Instructor's Manual is also available.

- **Teachers' workshop**. We run an annual workshop to facilitate discussion of key challenges and solutions in the teaching of strategic management. Details of forthcoming workshops can be found at **www.pearsoned.co.uk/events**.

GUIDED TOUR

→ Setting the scene

The **'three-circles' navigational diagram** shows where you are in the three-part structure that underpins the book.

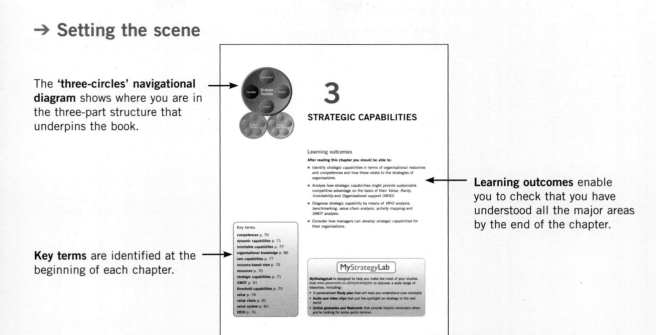

Learning outcomes enable you to check that you have understood all the major areas by the end of the chapter.

Key terms are identified at the beginning of each chapter.

→ Strategy in the real world

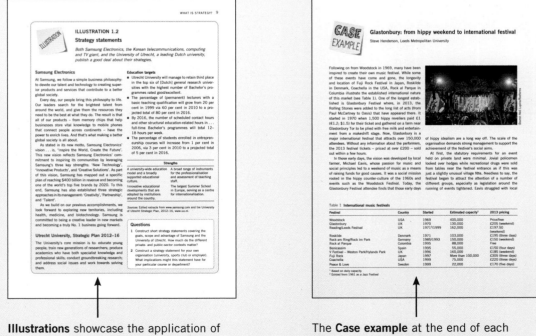

Illustrations showcase the application of specific strategic issues in the real world so you can identify and relate theory to practice.

The **Case example** at the end of each chapter allows exploration of topics covered in the chapter.

→ **Critical thinking and further study**

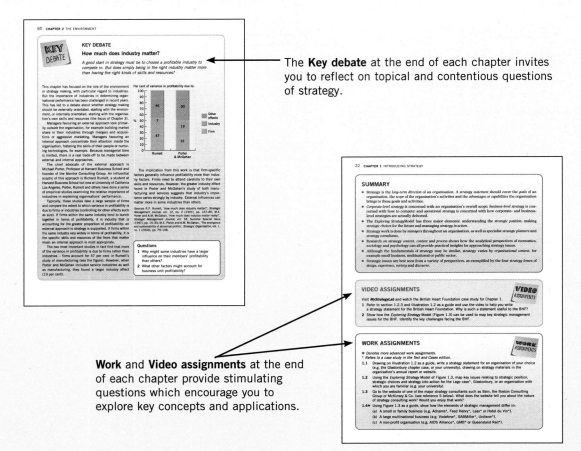

The **Key debate** at the end of each chapter invites you to reflect on topical and contentious questions of strategy.

Work and **Video assignments** at the end of each chapter provide stimulating questions which encourage you to explore key concepts and applications.

Commentaries at the end of each part of the book present a view of strategy through four 'lenses' to help you see strategic issues in different ways.

→ Check your understanding with MyStrategyLab

All key terms are included in the **Glossary**, found in **MyStrategyLab**. (The Glossary is also translated into Chinese, Dutch, French, Norwegian and Swedish.) You can also test your understanding of these key terms using **Flashcards**.

Need a little extra help? **Self-assessment tests** will help you to identify the areas where you need to improve . . .

. . . and the **Personalised study plan** will direct you to the specific resources that can help you achieve a better grade.

Video cases give you a glimpse at real people in real organisation.

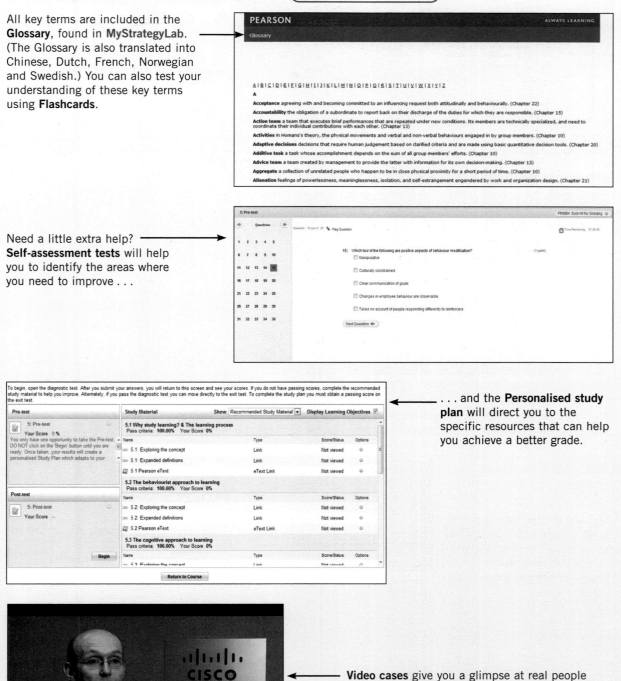

www.mystrategylab.com

The **Strategy Experience simulation** included in **MyStrategyLab** puts you in the position of a strategic decision-maker. You are the Director of the Board at WRSX Group, a global advertising and marketing communications business.

Multimedia resources and briefing documents help you to build an understanding of the WRSX Group's strategic position, as well as the choices that are available to the organisation.

You apply your knowledge in the boardroom, where you are faced with a number of scenarios. Here you must make tough decisions that will shape the company's future.

Success will depend on how well you understand and can apply the concepts that are covered in *Exploring Strategy*. Choose wisely!

EXPLORING STRATEGY

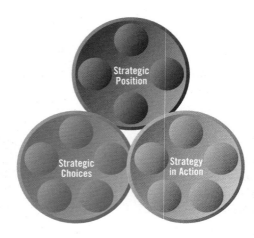

1

INTRODUCING STRATEGY

Learning outcomes

After reading this chapter you should be able to:

● Summarise the strategy of an organisation in a '*strategy statement*'.

● Distinguish between *corporate*, *business* and *operational* strategies.

● Identify key issues for an organisation's strategy according to the *Exploring Strategy* model.

● Understand different people's roles in *strategy work*.

● Appreciate the importance of different *organisational contexts*, *academic disciplines* and *theoretical lenses* to practical strategy analysis.

MyStrategyLab

MyStrategyLab is designed to help you make the most of your studies. Visit **www.pearsoned.co.uk/mystrategylab** to discover a wide range of resources, including:

● A personalised **Study plan** that will help you understand core concepts

● **Audio and video clips** that put the spotlight on strategy in the real world

● **Online glossaries and flashcards** that provide helpful reminders when you're looking for some quick revision.

(1.1) INTRODUCTION

Strategy is about key issues for the future of organisations. For example, how should Apple, primarily a devices company, compete in the computer and tablet market with Google, primarily a search company? Should universities concentrate their resources on research excellence or teaching quality or try to combine both? How should a small video games producer relate to dominant console providers such as Microsoft and Sony? What should an arts group do to secure revenues in the face of declining government subsidies?

All these are strategy questions, vital to the future survival of the organisations involved. Naturally such questions concern entrepreneurs and senior managers at the top of their organisations. But these questions matter more widely. Middle managers also have to understand the strategic direction of their organisations, both to know how to get top management support for their initiatives and to explain their organisation's strategy to the people they are responsible for. Anybody looking for a management-track job needs to be ready to discuss strategy with their potential employer. Indeed, anybody taking a job should first be confident that their new employer's strategy is actually viable. There are even specialist career opportunities in strategy, for example as a strategy consultant or as an in-house strategic planner, often key roles for fast-track young managers.

This book takes a broad approach to strategy, looking at both the economics of strategy and the people side of managing strategy in practice. It is a book about 'Exploring', because the real world of strategy rarely offers obvious answers. In strategy, it is typically important to explore several options, probing each one carefully before making choices. The book is also relevant to any kind of organisation responsible for its own direction into the future. Thus the book refers to large private-sector multinationals and small entrepreneurial start-ups; to public-sector organisations such as schools and hospitals; and to not-for-profits such as charities or sports clubs. Strategy matters to almost all organisations, and to everybody working in them.

(1.2) WHAT IS STRATEGY?[1]

In this book, **strategy is the long-term direction of an organisation**. Thus the long-term direction of Amazon is from book retailing to internet services in general. The long-term direction of Disney is from cartoons to diversified entertainment. This section examines the practical implication of this definition of strategy; distinguishes between different levels of strategy; and explains how to summarise an organisation's strategy in a 'strategy statement'.

1.2.1 Defining strategy

Defining strategy as the long-term direction of an organisation implies a more comprehensive view than some influential definitions. Figure 1.1 shows the strategy definitions of three leading strategy theorists: Alfred Chandler and Michael Porter, both from the Harvard Business School, and Henry Mintzberg, from McGill University, Canada. Each points to important but distinct elements of strategy. Chandler emphasises a logical flow from the determination of goals and objectives to the allocation of resources. Porter focuses on deliberate choices, difference and competition. On the other hand, Mintzberg uses the word 'pattern' to allow for the fact that strategies do not always follow a deliberately chosen and logical plan, but can emerge

Figure 1.1 Definitions of strategy

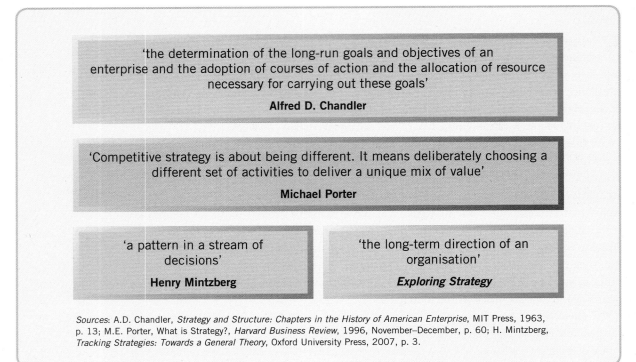

'the determination of the long-run goals and objectives of an enterprise and the adoption of courses of action and the allocation of resource necessary for carrying out these goals'

Alfred D. Chandler

'Competitive strategy is about being different. It means deliberately choosing a different set of activities to deliver a unique mix of value'

Michael Porter

'a pattern in a stream of decisions'

Henry Mintzberg

'the long-term direction of an organisation'

Exploring Strategy

Sources: A.D. Chandler, *Strategy and Structure: Chapters in the History of American Enterprise*, MIT Press, 1963, p. 13; M.E. Porter, What is Strategy?, *Harvard Business Review*, 1996, November–December, p. 60; H. Mintzberg, *Tracking Strategies: Towards a General Theory*, Oxford University Press, 2007, p. 3.

in more ad hoc ways. Sometimes strategies reflect a series of incremental decisions that only cohere into a recognisable pattern – or 'strategy' – after some time.

All of these strategy definitions incorporate important elements of strategy. However, this book's definition of strategy as 'the long-term direction of an organisation' has two advantages. First, the long-term direction of an organisation can include both deliberate, logical strategy and more incremental, emergent patterns of strategy. Second, long-term direction can include both strategies that emphasise difference and competition, and strategies that recognise the roles of cooperation and even imitation.

The three elements of this strategy definition – the long term, direction and organisation – can each be explored further. The strategy of Vice Media illustrates important points (see Illustration 1.1):

● *The long term*. Strategies are typically measured over years, for some organisations a decade or more. The importance of a long-term perspective on strategy is emphasised by the 'three-horizons' framework in Figure 1.2 (below). **The three-horizons framework suggests organisations should think of themselves as comprising three types of business or activity, defined by their 'horizons' in terms of years.** *Horizon 1* businesses are basically the current core activities. In the case of Vice Media, Horizon 1 includes the original *Vice* magazine. Horizon 1 businesses need defending and extending but the expectation is that in the long term they will likely be flat or declining in terms of profits (or whatever else the organisation values). *Horizon 2* businesses are emerging activities that should provide new sources of profit. For *Vice*, that might include the new China business. Finally, there are *Horizon 3* possibilities, for which nothing is sure. These are typically risky research and development

ILLUSTRATION 1.1

Vice pays

Beginning in 1994 as a government subsidised free 'zine' in Montreal, Vice Media now pursues an ambitious strategy of diversification and globalisation.

Vice Media is a global business, with a declared ambition to be the largest online media company in the world. But at its heart is still the original print magazine, *Vice*, specialising in fashion, music, lifestyle and current affairs. With a good deal of nudity, satire and violence, the magazine is regarded as edgy by some, puerile by others. An early spin-off book, *The Vice Guide to Sex, Drugs and Rock and Roll*, gives an idea of its market position. *Vice* magazine is paid for by advertising and distributed free via style-conscious clothing retailers.

However, since the late 1990s, the company has steadily diversified into a number of businesses, including clothing retail, web video, a record label, book publishing, live events, an advertising agency, television and film production, and even a London pub. By 2012, Vice Media was operating in 34 countries around the world. Revenues were approaching $200 m, with an estimated company value of around $1 bn (€750 m; £600 m).

The magazine had been started as a government work-creation scheme by three friends with no publishing experience, Suroosh Alvi, Gavin McInnes and Shane Smith. The magazine had originally been *The Voice of Montreal*, a newspaper for the local community. It soon drifted from its mission, and the three founders each borrowed $5,000 Canadian (€4,000; £3,000) to buy it out. It was said that the magazine got its title '*Vice*' because the *Village Voice* magazine of New York threatened to sue them over its name. True or not, *Vice* was a very good fit with the magazine's provocative content and style.

Outside investors were soon attracted to the magazine's strong connection with its youth audience. The first investor was the Normal Network, which in 1998 bought one quarter of the group for $1 m (US), implying a total value of $4 m. This injection of capital allowed *Vice* to move its base to New York and helped its diversification into clothing retail. When Normal Network went bust in 2000, another investor, Barrontech, stumped up more capital. In 2007, the media giant Viacom helped *Vice* into video. This partnership was said to have provoked the departure of co-founder Gavin McInness, distrustful of corporate constraints on creative freedom. In 2011, a consortium of external investors that included the world's largest advertising agency, WPP, injected a sum rumoured at between $50 and $100 m. These new funds helped launch *Vice* in China and India. New ventures were also envisaged in gaming and sports.

Co-founder Suroosh Alvi explained to the *Financial Times* the advantages to advertising partners of Vice Media's wide range of businesses and territories: 'Diversification of our media and pushing quality content through it on a global level has played massively for us. It's created a deep engagement with our audience and made a compelling story for brand partners as well, who are signing up platform-wide and doing international buy-ins. It's a bit better than publishing a magazine in a single territory.'

Vice's approach is informal, however. Another co-founder, Shane Smith, recalled the early days: 'We didn't have a business plan or any idea of what we were doing. We just loved magazines and loved making the magazine. And we didn't have anything else to do, so we kept doing it.' As for *Vice* today: 'It's a totally insane working environment. It's like an incestuous family. It's a weird culture and we love it. Keeping that culture is one of our big challenges going forward.'

Sources: National Post, 19 July 2000; *Financial Times*, 19 November 2009; *Forbes*, 1 January 2012.

Questions

1 How does Vice Media's strategy fit with the various strategy definitions of Alfred Chandler, Michael Porter and Henry Mintzberg (see Figure 1.1)?

2 What seems to account for Vice Media's success and is it sustainable?

Figure 1.2 Three horizons for strategy

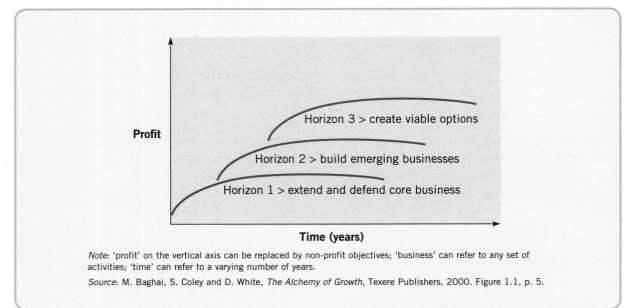

Note: 'profit' on the vertical axis can be replaced by non-profit objectives; 'business' can refer to any set of activities; 'time' can refer to a varying number of years.

Source: M. Baghai, S. Coley and D. White, *The Alchemy of Growth*, Texere Publishers, 2000. Figure 1.1, p. 5.

projects, start-up ventures, test-market pilots or similar: at Vice Media, these might be the gaming and sports initiatives. For a fast-moving organisation like Vice Media, *Horizon 3* might generate profits only a couple of years from the present time. In a pharmaceutical company, where the R&D and regulatory processes for a new drug take many years, *Horizon 3* might be a decade ahead. While timescales might differ, the basic point about the 'three-horizons' framework is that managers need to avoid focusing on the short-term issues of their existing activities. Strategy involves pushing out Horizon 1 as far as possible, at the same time as looking to Horizons 2 and 3.

● *Strategic direction*. Over the years, strategies follow some kind of long-term direction or trajectory. The strategic direction of Vice Media is from the original print magazine to diversified youth media services. Sometimes a strategic direction only emerges as a coherent pattern over time. Typically, however, managers and entrepreneurs try to set the direction of their strategy according to long-term *objectives*. In private-sector businesses, the objective guiding strategic direction is usually maximising profits for shareholders. However, profits do not always set strategic direction. First, public-sector and charity organisations may set their strategic direction according to other objectives: for example, a sports club's objective may be to move up from one league to a higher one. Second, even in the private sector profit is not always the sole criterion for strategy. Thus family businesses may sometimes sacrifice the maximisation of profits for family objectives, for example passing down the management of the business to the next generation. The objectives behind strategic direction always need close scrutiny.

● *Organisation*. In this book, organisations are not treated as discrete, unified entities. Organisations involve complex relationships, both internally and externally. This is because organisations typically have many internal and external *stakeholders*, in other words people and groups that depend on the organisation and upon which the organisation itself depends. Internally, organisations are filled with people, typically with diverse, competing and more or less reasonable views of what should be done. At Vice Media, the three co-founders had clashed over corporate partnerships, leading to the departure of Gavin McInness. In strategy, therefore, it is always important to look *inside* organisations and to consider the people involved and their different interests and views. Externally, organisations are surrounded by important relationships, for example with suppliers, customers, alliance partners, regulators and investors. For Vice Media, relationships with investors and advertisers were crucial. Strategy therefore is also crucially concerned with an organisation's external *boundaries*: in other words, questions about what to include within the organisation and how to manage important relationships with what is kept outside.

Because strategy typically involves managing people, relationships and resources, the subject is sometimes called 'strategic management'. This book takes the view that managing is always important in strategy. Good strategy is about the practicalities of managing as well as the analysis of strategising.

1.2.2 Levels of strategy

Inside an organisation, strategies can exist at three main levels. Again they can be illustrated by reference to Vice Media (Illustration 1.1):

- **Corporate-level strategy is concerned with the overall scope of an organisation and how value is added to the constituent businesses of the organisational whole.** Corporate-level strategy issues include geographical scope, diversity of products or services, acquisitions of new businesses, and how resources are allocated between the different elements of the organisation. For Vice Media, diversifying from the original magazine into retail, publishing and video are corporate-level strategies. Being clear about corporate-level strategy is important: determining the range of businesses to include is the basis of other strategic decisions, such as acquisitions and alliances.

- **Business-level strategy is about how the individual businesses should compete in their particular markets** (for this reason, business-level strategy is often called 'competitive strategy'). These individual businesses might be standalone businesses, for instance entrepreneurial start-ups, or 'business units' within a larger corporation (as the magazine is within Vice Media). Business-level strategy typically concerns issues such as innovation, appropriate scale and response to competitors' moves. In the public sector, the equivalent of business-level strategy is decisions about how units (such as individual hospitals or schools) should provide best-value services. Where the businesses are units within a larger organisation, business-level strategies should clearly fit with corporate-level strategy.

- **Operational strategies are concerned with how the components of an organisation deliver effectively the corporate- and business-level strategies in terms of resources, processes and people.** For example, Vice Media had to keep raising external finance to fund its rapid growth: its operational strategy is partly geared to meeting investment needs. In most businesses, successful business strategies depend to a large extent on decisions that are taken, or activities that occur, at the operational level. Operational decisions need therefore to be closely linked to business-level strategy. They are vital to successful strategy implementation.

This need to link the corporate, business and operational levels underlines the importance of *integration* in strategy. Each level needs to be aligned with the others. The demands of integrating levels define an important characteristic of strategy: strategy is typically *complex*, requiring careful and sensitive management. Strategy is rarely simple.

1.2.3 **Strategy statements**

David Collis and Michael Rukstad[2] at the Harvard Business School argue that all entrepreneurs and managers should be able to summarise their organisation's strategy with a 'strategy statement'. **Strategy statements should have three main themes: the fundamental *goals* (mission, vision or objectives) that the organisation seeks; the *scope* or domain of the organisation's activities; and the particular *advantages* or capabilities it has to deliver all of these.** These various contributing elements of a strategy statement are explained as follows, with examples in Illustration 1.2:

- *Mission*. This relates to goals, and refers to the overriding purpose of the organisation. It is sometimes described in terms of the apparently simple but challenging question: '*what business are we in?*'. The mission statement helps keep managers focused on what is central to their strategy.

- *Vision*. This too relates to goals, and refers to the desired future state of the organisation. It is an aspiration which can help mobilise the energy and passion of organisational members. The vision statement, therefore, should answer the question: '*what do we want to achieve?*'.

- *Objectives*. These are more precise and ideally quantifiable statements of the organisation's goals over some period of time. Objectives might refer to profitability or market share targets for a private company, or to examination results in a school. Objectives introduce discipline to strategy. The question here is: '*what do we have to achieve in the coming period?*'.

- *Scope*. An organisation's scope or domain refers to three dimensions: customers or clients; geographical location; and extent of internal activities ('vertical integration'). For a university, scope questions are twofold: first, which academic departments to have (a business school, an engineering department and so on); second, which activities to do internally themselves (vertically integrate) and which to externalise to subcontractors (e.g. whether to manage campus restaurants in-house or to subcontract them).

- *Advantage*. This part of a strategy statement describes how the organisation will achieve the objectives it has set for itself in its chosen domain. In competitive environments, this refers to the *competitive* advantage: for example, how a particular company or sports club will achieve goals in the face of competition from other companies or clubs. In order to achieve a particular goal, the organisation needs to be better than others seeking the same goal. In the public sector, advantage might refer simply to the organisation's capability in general. But even public-sector organisations frequently need to show that their capabilities are not only adequate, but superior to other rival departments or perhaps to private-sector contractors.

Collis and Rukstad suggest that strategy statements covering goals, scope and advantage should be no more than 35 words long. Brevity keeps such statements focused on the essentials and makes them easy to remember and communicate. Thus for Vice Media, a strategy statement might be: 'to build the world's largest online media group, focused on youth and with competitive advantages in terms of the diversity and international range of our businesses and the strength of our relationships with key partners'. The strategy statement of American financial advisory firm Edward Jones is more specific: 'to grow to 17,000 financial advisers by 2012 by offering trusted and convenient face-to-face financial advice to conservative individual investors through a national network of one-financial adviser offices'. Of course, such strategy statements

ILLUSTRATION 1.2

Strategy statements

Both Samsung Electronics, the Korean telecommunications, computing and TV giant, and the University of Utrecht, a leading Dutch university, publish a good deal about their strategies.

Samsung Electronics

At Samsung, we follow a simple business philosophy: to devote our talent and technology to creating superior products and services that contribute to a better global society.

Every day, our people bring this philosophy to life. Our leaders search for the brightest talent from around the world, and give them the resources they need to be the best at what they do. The result is that all of our products – from memory chips that help businesses store vital knowledge to mobile phones that connect people across continents – have the power to enrich lives. And that's what making a better global society is all about.

As stated in its new motto, Samsung Electronics' vision . . . is, 'Inspire the World, Create the Future'. This new vision reflects Samsung Electronics' commitment to inspiring its communities by leveraging Samsung's three key strengths: 'New Technology', 'Innovative Products', and 'Creative Solutions'. As part of this vision, Samsung has mapped out a specific plan of reaching $400 billion in revenue and becoming one of the world's top five brands by 2020. To this end, Samsung has also established three strategic approaches in its management: 'Creativity', 'Partnership', and 'Talent'.

As we build on our previous accomplishments, we look forward to exploring new territories, including health, medicine, and biotechnology. Samsung is committed to being a creative leader in new markets and becoming a truly No. 1 business going forward.

Utrecht University, Strategic Plan 2012–16

The University's core mission is to: educate young people; train new generations of researchers; produce academics who have both specialist knowledge and professional skills; conduct groundbreaking research; and address social issues and work towards solving them.

Education targets

- Utrecht University will manage to retain third place in the top six of [Dutch] general research universities with the highest number of Bachelor's programmes rated good/excellent.
- The percentage of (permanent) lecturers with a basic teaching qualification will grow from 20 per cent in 1999 via 60 per cent in 2010 to a projected total of 80 per cent in 2016.
- By 2016, the number of scheduled contact hours and other structural education-related hours in . . . full-time Bachelor's programmes will total 12–18 hours per week.
- The percentage of students enrolled in entrepreneurship courses will increase from 1 per cent in 2006, via 3 per cent in 2010 to a projected total of 5 per cent in 2016.

Strengths	
A university-wide education model and a broadly supported educational culture.	A broad range of instruments for the professionalisation and assessment of teaching staff.
Innovative educational developments that are adopted by institutions around the country.	The largest Summer School in Europe, serving as a centre for internationalisation.

Sources: Edited extracts from www.samsung.com and the University of Utrecht Strategic Plan, 2012–16, www.uu.nl.

Questions

1 Construct short strategy statements covering the goals, scope and advantage of Samsung and the University of Utrecht. How much do the different private- and public-sector contexts matter?

2 Construct a strategy statement for your own organisation (university, sports club or employer). What implications might this statement have for your particular course or department?

are not always fulfilled. Circumstances may change in unexpected ways. In the meantime, however, they can provide a useful guide both to managers in their decision making and to employees and others who need to understand the direction in which the organisation is going. The ability to give a clear strategy statement is a good test of managerial competence in an organisation.

As such, strategy statements are relevant to a wide range of organisations. For example, a small entrepreneurial start-up can use a strategy statement to persuade investors and lenders of its viability. Public-sector organisations need strategy statements not only for themselves, but to reassure clients, funders and regulators that their priorities are the right ones. Voluntary organisations need persuasive strategy statements in order to inspire volunteers and donors. Thus, organisations of all kinds frequently publish materials relevant to such strategy statements on their websites or annual reports. Illustration 1.2 provides published materials on the strategies of two very different organisations: the technology giant Samsung from the private sector and the Dutch University of Utrecht from the public sector.

(1.3) THE *EXPLORING STRATEGY* MODEL

This book is structured around a three-part model that emphasises the interconnected nature of strategic issues. The *Exploring Strategy* Model includes understanding *the strategic position* of an organisation; assessing *strategic choices* for the future; and managing *strategy in action*. Figure 1.3 shows these elements and defines the broad coverage of this book. Together, the three elements provide a practical template for studying strategic situations. The following sections of this chapter will introduce the strategic issues that arise under each of these elements of the *Exploring Strategy* Model. But first it is important to understand why the model is drawn in this particular way.

Figure 1.3 could have shown the model's three elements in a linear sequence – first understanding the strategic position, then making strategic choices and finally turning strategy into action. Indeed, this logical sequence is implicit in the definition of strategy given by Alfred Chandler (Figure 1.1) and many other textbooks on strategy. However, as Henry Mintzberg recognises, in practice the elements of strategy do not always follow this linear sequence. Choices often have to be made before the position is fully understood. Sometimes, too, a proper understanding of the strategic position can only be built from the experience of trying a strategy out in action. The real-world feedback that comes from launching a new product is often far better at uncovering the true strategic position than remote analysis carried out in a strategic planning department at head office.

The interconnected circles of Figure 1.3 are designed to emphasise this potentially non-linear nature of strategy. Position, choices and action should be seen as closely related, and in practice none has priority over another. It is only for structural convenience that this book divides its subject matter into three sections; the book's sequence is not meant to suggest that the process of strategy must follow a logical series of distinct steps. The three circles are overlapping and interdependent. The evidence provided in later chapters will suggest that strategy rarely occurs in tidy ways and that it is better not to expect it to do so.

However, the *Exploring Strategy* Model does provide a comprehensive and integrated framework for analysing an organisation's position, considering the choices it has and putting strategies into action. Each of the chapters can be seen as asking fundamental strategy questions and

Figure 1.3 The *Exploring Strategy* Model

providing the essential concepts and techniques to help answer them. Working systematically through questions and answers provides the basis for persuasive strategy recommendations.

1.3.1 **Strategic position**

The **strategic position** is concerned with the impact on strategy of the external environment, the organisation's strategic capability (resources and competences), the organisation's goals and the organisation's culture. Understanding these four factors is central for evaluating future strategy. These issues, and the fundamental questions associated with them, are covered in the four chapters of Part I of this book:

● *Environment.* Organisations operate in a complex political, economic, social and technological world. These environments vary widely in terms of their dynamism and attractiveness. The fundamental question here relates to the *opportunities* and *threats* available to the organisation in this complex and changing environment. Chapter 2 provides key frameworks to help in focusing on priority issues in the face of environmental complexity and dynamism.

● *Strategic capability.* Each organisation has its own strategic capabilities, made up of its *resources* (e.g. machines and buildings) and *competences* (e.g. technical and managerial skills). The fundamental question on capability regards the organisation's *strengths* and *weaknesses* (e.g. where is it at a competitive advantage or disadvantage?). Are the organisation's capabilities adequate to the challenges of its environment and the demands of its goals? Chapter 3 provides tools and concepts for analysing such capabilities.

- *Strategic purpose.* Most organisations claim for themselves a particular purpose, as encapsulated in their *vision*, *mission* and *objectives*. But often this purpose is unclear, contested or unrealistic. The third fundamental question therefore is: what is the organisation's strategic purpose; what does it seek to achieve? Here the issue of *corporate governance* is important: how to ensure that managers stick to the agreed purpose? Questions of purpose and accountability raise issues of *corporate social responsibility* and *ethics*: is the purpose an appropriate one and are managers sticking to it? Chapter 4 provides concepts for addressing these issues of purpose.

- *Culture.* Organisational cultures can also influence strategy. So can the cultures of a particular industry or particular country. These cultures are typically a product of an organisation's *history*. The consequence of history and culture can be *strategic drift*, a failure to create necessary change. A fundamental question here, therefore, is: how does culture fit with the required strategy? Chapter 5 demonstrates how managers can analyse, challenge and sometimes turn to their advantage the various cultural influences on strategy.

The *Exploring Strategy* Model (Illustration 1.1) points to the following positioning issues for Vice Media. What is the future of *Vice* magazine given the environmental shift from print to internet media? Are its distinctive capabilities in youth media sustainable, given the ageing profiles of its two remaining founders? Is Vice Media's dedication to rapid growth funded by corporate partners consistent with the kind of creativity defended by departing co-founder Gavin McInness? Is the original 'weird' culture, as championed by Shane Smith, still a source of advantage, or is it now a constraint on what is fast becoming a diversified, global media conglomerate?

1.3.2 Strategic choices

Strategic choices involve the options for strategy in terms of both the *directions* in which strategy might move and the *methods* by which strategy might be pursued. For instance, an organisation might have a range of strategic directions open to it: the organisation could diversify into new products; it could enter new international markets; or it could transform its existing products and markets through radical innovation. These various directions could be pursued by different methods: the organisation could acquire a business already active in the product or market area; it could form alliances with relevant organisations that might help its new strategy; or it could try to pursue its strategies on its own. Typical strategic choices, and the related fundamental questions, are covered in the five chapters that make up Part II of this book, as follows:

- *Business strategy.* There are strategic choices in terms of how the organisation seeks to compete at the individual business level. For example, a business unit could choose to be the lowest cost competitor in a market, or the highest quality. The fundamental question here, then, is how should the business unit compete? Key dilemmas for business-level strategy, and ways of resolving them, are discussed in Chapter 6.

- *Corporate strategy and diversification.* The highest level of an organisation is typically concerned with issues of corporate scope; in other words, which businesses to include in the portfolio. This relates to the appropriate degree of *diversification*, with regard to products offered and markets served. Corporate-level strategy is also concerned both with internal relationships, both between business units and with the corporate head office. Chapter 7 provides tools for assessing diversification strategies and the appropriate relationships within the corporate portfolio.

- *International strategy*. Internationalisation is a form of diversification, but into new geographical markets. Here the fundamental question is: where internationally should the organisation compete? Chapter 8 examines how to prioritise various international options and key strategies for pursuing them.

- *Innovation and entrepreneurship*. Most existing organisations have to innovate constantly simply to survive. Entrepreneurship, the creation of a new enterprise, is an act of innovation too. A fundamental question, therefore, is whether the organisation is innovating appropriately. Chapter 9 considers key choices about innovation and entrepreneurship, and helps in selecting between them.

- *Acquisitions and alliances*. Organisations have to make choices about methods for pursuing their strategies. Many organisations prefer to build new businesses with their own resources. Other organisations develop by acquiring other businesses or forming alliances with complementary partners. The fundamental question in Chapter 10, therefore, is whether to buy another company, ally or to go it alone.

Again, issues of strategic choice are live in the case of Vice Media (Illustration 1.1). The *Exploring Strategy* Model asks the following kinds of questions here. Should Vice Media compete predominantly with cheap web video or move up market with film and TV? How far should it widen the scope of its businesses: does the London pub really belong in the portfolio? How should Vice Media manage its partnerships with the various corporate giants, already the cause of disputes over creativity? And should Vice Media be allowed to continue to innovate in its 'insane' free-wheeling style?

1.3.3 **Strategy in action**

Managing strategy in action is about how strategies are formed and how they are implemented. The emphasis is on the practicalities of managing. These issues are covered in the five chapters of Part III, and include the following, each with their own fundamental questions:

- *Strategy performance and evaluation*. Managers have to decide whether existing and forecast performance is satisfactory and then choose between options that might improve it. The fundamental evaluation questions are as follows: are the options *suitable* in terms of matching opportunities and threats; are they *acceptable* in the eyes of significant stakeholders; and are they *feasible* given the capabilities available? Chapter 11 introduces a range of financial and non-financial techniques for appraising performance and evaluating strategic options.

- *Strategy development processes*. Strategies are often developed through formal *planning* processes. But sometimes the strategies an organisation actually pursues are *emergent* – in other words, accumulated patterns of ad hoc decisions, bottom-up initiatives and rapid responses to the unanticipated. Given the scope for emergence, the fundamental question is: what kind of strategy process should an organisation have? Chapter 12 addresses the question of whether to plan strategy in detail or leave plenty of opportunities for emergence.

- *Organising.* Once a strategy is developed, the organisation needs to organise for successful implementation. Each strategy requires its own specific configuration of *structures* and *systems*. The fundamental question, therefore, is: what kinds of structures and systems are required for the chosen strategy? Chapter 13 introduces a range of structures and systems and provides frameworks for deciding between them.

- *Leadership and strategic change.* In a dynamic world, strategy inevitably involves change. Managing change involves *leadership*, both at the top of the organisation and lower down. There is not just one way of leading change, however: there are different *styles* and different *levers* for change. So the fundamental question is: how should the organisation manage necessary changes entailed by the strategy? Chapter 14 therefore examines options for managing change, and considers how to choose between them.

- *Strategy practice.* Inside the broad processes of strategy development and change is a lot of hard, detailed work. The fundamental question in managing this work is: who should do what in the strategy process? Chapter 15 thus provides guidance on which *people* to include in the process; what *activities* they should do; and which *methodologies* can help them do it. These kinds of practicalities are a fitting end to the book and essential equipment for those who will have to go out and participate in strategy work themselves.

With regard to strategy in action, the *Exploring Strategy* Model raises the following kinds of questions for Vice Media. Should the firm move towards a more disciplined strategy development process rather than continuing with the unplanned processes of the early years? Does the 'insane' environment of Vice Media need more structure and systems? How should the surviving co-founders lead any changes that may be necessary as Vice Media grows?

Thus the *Exploring Strategy* Model offers a comprehensive framework for analysing an organisation's position, considering alternative choices, and selecting and implementing strategies. In this sense, the fundamental questions in each chapter provide a comprehensive checklist for strategy. These fundamental questions are summed up in Table 1.1. Any

Table 1.1 The strategy checklist

Fourteen fundamental questions in strategy		
Strategic position	**Strategic choices**	**Strategy in action**
• What are the environmental opportunities and threats?	• How should business units compete?	• Are strategies suitable, acceptable and feasible?
• What are the organisation's strengths and weaknesses?	• Which businesses to include in a portfolio?	• What kind of strategy-making process is needed?
• What is the basic purpose of the organisation?	• Where should the organisation compete internationally?	• What are the required organisation structures and systems?
• How does culture fit the strategy?	• Is the organisation innovating appropriately?	• How should the organisation manage necessary changes?
	• Should the organisation buy other companies, ally or go it alone?	• Who should do what in the strategy process?

assessment of an organisation's strategy will benefit from asking these questions systematically. The frameworks for answering these and related questions can be found in the respective chapters.

The logic of the *Exploring Strategy* Model can be applied to our personal lives as much as to organisations. We all have to make decisions with long-run consequences for our futures and the issues involved are very similar. For example, in pursuing a career strategy, a job-seeker needs to understand the job market, evaluate their strengths and weaknesses, establish the range of job opportunities and decide what their career goals really are (positioning issues). The job-seeker then narrows down the options, makes some applications and finally gets an offer (choice issues). Once they have chosen a job, the job-seeker sets to work, adjusting their skills and behaviours to suit their new role (strategy in action). Just as in the non-linear, overlapping *Exploring Strategy* Model, experience of the job will frequently amend the original strategic goals. Putting a career strategy into action produces better understanding of strengths and weaknesses and frequently leads to the setting of new career goals.

WORKING WITH STRATEGY

Strategy itself is a kind of work, and it is something that almost all levels of management have to engage in, not just top decision-makers. Middle and lower-level managers have to understand their organisation's strategic objectives and contribute to them as best they can. Managers have to communicate strategy to their teams, and will achieve greater performance from them the more convincing they are in doing so. Indeed, as responsibility is increasingly decentralised in many organisations, middle and lower-level managers play a growing part in shaping strategy themselves. Because they are closer to the daily realities of the business, lower-level managers can be a crucial source of ideas and feedback for senior management teams. Being able to participate in an organisation's 'strategic conversation' – engaging with senior managers on the big issues facing them – is therefore often part of what it takes to win promotion.[3]

For many managers, then, strategy is part of the job. However, there are specialist strategists as well, in both private and public sectors. Many large organisations have in-house strategic planning or analyst roles.[4] Typically requiring a formal business education of some sort, strategic planning is a potential career route for many readers of this book, especially after some operational experience. Strategy consulting has been a growth industry in the last few decades, with the original leading firms such as McKinsey & Co., the Boston Consulting Group and Bain joined now by more generalist consultants such as Accenture, IBM Consulting and PwC, each with its own strategy consulting arm.[5] Again, business graduates are in demand for strategy consulting roles.[6]

The interviews in Illustration 1.3 give some insights into the different kinds of strategy work that managers and strategy specialists can do. Galina, the manager of an international subsidiary, Masoud, working in a governmental strategy unit, and Chantal, a strategy consultant, all have different experiences of strategy, but there are some common themes also. All find strategy work stimulating and rewarding. The two specialists, Masoud and Chantal, talk more than Galina of analytical tools such as scenario analysis, sensitivity analysis and hypothesis testing. Galina discovered directly the practical challenges of real-world strategic planning, having to adapt the plan during the first few years in the United Kingdom. She emphasises the importance

ILLUSTRATION 1.3
Strategists

For Galina, Masoud and Chantal, strategy is a large part of their jobs.

Galina

After a start in marketing, Galina became managing director of the British subsidiary of a Russian information technology company at the age of 33. As well as developing the strategy for her local business, she has to interact regularly with the Moscow headquarters: 'Moscow is interested in the big picture, not just the details. They are interested in the future of the business.'

The original strategic plans for the subsidiary had had to be adapted heavily:

'When we first came here, we had some ideas about strategy, but soon found the reality was very different to the plans. The strategy was not completely wrong, but in the second stage we had to change it a lot: we had to change techniques and adapt to the market. Now we are in the third stage, where we have the basics and need to focus on trends, to get ahead and be in the right place at the right time.'

Galina works closely with her management team on strategy, taking them on an annual 'strategy away-day' (see Chapter 15): 'Getting people together helps them see the whole picture, rather than just the bits they are responsible for. It is good to put all their separate realities together.'

Galina is enthusiastic about working on strategy:

'I like strategy work, definitely. The most exciting thing is to think about where we have come from and where we might be going. We started in a pub five years ago and we have somehow implemented what we were hoping for then. Strategy gives you a measure of success. It tells you how well you have done.'

Her advice is: 'Always have a strategy – have an ultimate idea in mind. But take feedback from the market and from your colleagues. Be ready to adjust the strategy: the adjustment is the most important.'

Masoud

Aged 27, Masoud is a policy advisor in a central government strategy unit in the United Kingdom. He provides analysis and advice for ministers, often on a cross-departmental basis. He typically works on projects for several months at a time, continuing to work with responsible service departments after the delivery of recommendations. Projects involve talking to experts inside and outside government, statistical analysis, scenario analyses (see Chapter 2), sensitivity analyses (see Chapter 11), hypothesis testing (see Chapter 15) and writing reports and making presentations. As he has progressed, Masoud has become increasingly involved in the management of strategy projects, rather than the basic analysis itself.

Masoud explains what he likes most about strategy work in government:'I like most the challenge. It's

of flexibility in strategy and the value of getting her managers to see the 'whole picture' through involving them in strategy making. But Masoud and Chantal too are concerned with much more than just analysis. Chantal emphasises the importance of gaining 'traction' with clients, building consensus in order to ensure implementation. Masoud likewise does not take implementation for granted, continuing to work with departments after the delivery of recommendations. He sees strategy and delivery as intimately connected, with people involved in delivery needing an understanding of strategy to be effective, and strategists needing to understand delivery. For him, strategy is a valuable stepping-stone in a career, something that will underpin his possible next move into a more operational role.

Strategy, therefore, is not just about abstract organisations: it is a kind of work that real people do. An important aim of this book is to equip readers to do this work better.

working on issues that really matter, and often it's what you are reading about in the newspapers. They are really tough issues; these are problems facing the whole of society.' He thinks people should get involved in strategy: 'I would encourage people to do strategy, because it gets to the heart of problems. In all organisations, having some experience of working on strategy is very valuable, even if it is not what you want to major on your whole career.'

Masoud is considering moving into service delivery as the next step of his career, because he sees knowledge of strategy and knowledge of operations as so interconnected: 'Part of doing strategy is you have to understand what can be delivered; and part of doing delivery is you have to understand the strategy.'

Chantal

Chantal is in her early thirties and has worked in Paris for one of the top three international strategy consultancies since graduating in business. Consulting was attractive to her originally because she liked the idea of helping organisations improve. She chose her particular consultancy because 'I had fun in the interview rounds and the people were inspiring. I pictured myself working with these kinds of topics and with these kinds of people.'

Chantal enjoys strategy consulting: 'What I like is solving problems. It's a bit like working on a mystery case: you have a problem and then you have to find a solution to fit the company, and help it grow and to be better.' The work is intellectually challenging:

'Time horizons are short. You have to solve your case in two to three months. There's lots of pressure. It pushes you and helps you to learn yourself. There are just three to four in a team, so you will make a significant contribution to the project even as a junior. You have a lot of autonomy and you're making a contribution right from the start, and at quite a high level.'

Consulting work can involve financial and market modelling (see Chapters 2 and 11), interviewing clients and customers, and working closely with the client's own teams. Chantal explains:

'As a consultant, you spend a lot of time in building solid fact-based arguments that will help clients make business decisions. But as well as the facts, you have to have the ability to get traction. People have to agree, so you have to build consensus, to make sure that recommendations are supported and acted on.'

Chantal summarises the appeal of strategy consulting: 'I enjoy the learning, at a very high speed. There's the opportunity to increase your skills. One year in consulting is like two years in a normal business.'

Source: Interviews (interviewees anonymised).

> ### Questions
> 1 Which of these strategy roles appeals to you most – manager of a business unit in a multinational, in-house strategy specialist or strategy consultant? Why?
> 2 What would you have to do to get such a role?

(1.5) STUDYING STRATEGY

This book is both comprehensive and serious about strategy. To understand the full range of strategy issues – from analysis to action – it is important to be open to the perspectives and insights of key disciplines such as economics, sociology and psychology. To be serious about strategy means to draw as far as possible on rigorous research about these issues. This book aims for an evidence-based approach to strategy, hence the articles and books referenced at the end of each chapter.[7]

This book therefore covers equally the three main branches of strategy research: conventionally, these are known as strategy *context*, strategy *content* and strategy *process*. In terms of

Figure 1.4 Strategy's three branches

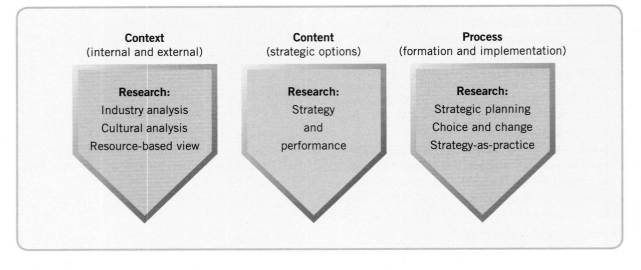

the *Exploring Strategy* Model (Figure 1.3), context broadly relates to positioning, content to choice and process to action. Each of these branches contains various research streams whose lessons can be readily applied to practical questions of strategy issues. Figure 1.4 shows the three branches and their respective research streams: these are listed in the approximate historical order of their emergence as strong research streams, the arrows representing the continuously developing nature of each. In more detail, the three branches and the characteristic analytical approaches of their main research streams are as follows:

- *Strategy context* refers to both the internal and the external contexts of organisations. All organisations need to take into account the opportunities and threats of their external environments. *Industry analysis* took off as a research tradition in the early 1980s, when Michael Porter showed how the tools of economics could be applied to understanding what makes industries attractive (or unattractive) to operate in.[8] From the 1980s too, *cultural analysts* have used sociological insights into human behaviour to point to the importance of shared cultural understandings about appropriate ways of acting. In the internal context, cultural analysts show that strategies are often influenced by the organisation's specific culture. In the external context, they show how strategies often have to fit with the surrounding industry or national cultures. *Resource-based view* researchers focus on internal context, looking for the unique characteristics of each organisation.[9] According to the resource-based view, the economic analysis of market imperfections, the psychological analysis of perceptual or emotional biases, and the sociological analysis of organisational cultures should reveal the particular characteristics (resources) that contribute to an organisation's specific competitive advantages and disadvantages.

- *Strategy content* concerns the content (or nature) of different strategies and their probability of success. Here the focus is on the merits of different strategic options. *Strategy and Performance* researchers started by using economic analysis to understand the success of different types of diversification strategies. This research continues as the enduring central core of the strategy discipline, with an ever-growing list of issues addressed. For example, contemporary Strategy and Performance researchers examine various new innovation strategies, different kinds of internationalisation and all the complex kinds of alliance and networking strategies that organisations adopt today. These researchers typically bring a tough economic scrutiny to strategy options. Their aim is to establish which types of strategies pay best and under what conditions. They refuse to take for granted broad generalisations about what makes a good strategy.

- *Strategy process*, broadly conceived, examines how strategies are formed and implemented. Research here provides a range of insights to help managers in the practical processes of managing strategy.[10] From the 1960s, researchers in the *Strategic Planning* tradition have drawn from economics and management science in order to design rational and analytical systems for the planning and implementing of strategy. However, strategy involves people: since the 1980s, *Choice and Change* researchers have been pointing to how the psychology of human perception and emotions, and the sociology of group politics and interests, tend to undermine rational analysis.[11] The advice of these researchers is to accept the irrational, messy realities of organisations, and to work with them, rather than to try to impose textbook rationality. Finally, *Strategy-as-Practice* researchers have recently been using microsociological approaches to closely examine the human realities of formal and informal strategy processes.[12] This tradition focuses attention on how people do strategy work, and the importance of having the right tools and skills.

From the above, it should be clear that studying strategy involves perspectives and insights from a range of academic disciplines. Issues need to be 'explored' from different points of view. A strategy chosen purely on economic grounds can easily be undermined by psychological and sociological factors. On the other hand, a strategy that is chosen on the psychological grounds of emotional enthusiasm, or for sociological reasons of cultural acceptability, is liable to fail if not supported by favourable economics. As underlined by the four strategy lenses to be introduced later, one perspective is rarely enough for good strategy. A complete analysis will typically need the insights of economics, psychology and sociology.

 # **DOING STRATEGY DIFFERENTLY**

So far we have stressed that strategic issues are typically complex, best explored from a number of points of views. There is no simple, universal rule for good strategy. This section introduces two ways of exploring strategy differently: one depending on context, the other depending on perspective.

1.6.1 Exploring strategy in different contexts

Although the basic elements of the *Exploring Strategy* Model are relevant in most circumstances, how they play out precisely is likely to differ according to organisational context. To return to Illustration 1.2, both Samsung and the University of Utrecht share some fundamental issues about how to compete and what activities they should have in their portfolio. However, for a Korean electronics company and a Dutch university, the role of the government, the freedom to choose and the ability to change all vary quite widely. In applying the *Exploring Strategy* Model, it is therefore useful to ask what kinds of issues are likely to be particularly significant in the specific context being considered. To illustrate this general point, this section shows how issues arising from the *Exploring Strategy* Model can vary in three important organisational contexts:

- *Small businesses.* With regard to positioning, small businesses will certainly need to attend closely to the environment, because they are so vulnerable to change. But, especially in small entrepreneurial and family businesses, the most important positioning issue will often be strategic purpose: this will not necessarily just be profit, but might include objectives such as independence, family control, handing over to the next generation and maybe even a pleasant lifestyle. The range of strategic choices is likely to be narrower: it is rare for a small business to make an acquisition itself, though small businesses may have to decide whether to allow themselves to be acquired by another business. Some issues of strategy in action will be different, for example strategic change processes will not involve the same challenges as for large, complex organisations.

- *Multinational corporations.* In this context, positioning in a complex global marketplace will be very important. Each significant geographical market may call for a separate analysis of the business environment. Likewise, operating in many different countries will raise positioning issues of culture: variations in national culture imply different demands in the marketplace and different managerial styles internally. Strategic choices are likely to be dominated by international strategy questions about which geographical markets to serve. The scale and geographical reach of most multinationals point to significant issues for strategy in action, particularly those of organisational structure and strategic change.

- *Public sector and not-for-profits.* Positioning issues of competitive advantage will be important even in these contexts, but have a different flavour. Charitable not-for-profits typically compete for funds from donors; public-sector organisations, such as schools and hospitals, often compete on measures such as quality or service. The positioning issue of purpose is likely to be very important too. In the absence of a clear, focused objective such as profit, purpose in the public sector and not-for-profits can be ambiguous and contentious. Strategic choice issues may be narrower than in the private sector: for example, there may be constraints on diversification. Strategy-in-action issues often need close attention, leadership and change typically being very challenging in large public-sector organisations.

In short, while drawing on the same basic principles, strategy analysis is likely to vary in focus across different contexts. As the next section will indicate, it is often helpful therefore to apply different lenses to strategy problems.

1.6.2 Exploring strategy through different 'strategy lenses'

Exploring means looking for new and different things. Exploring strategy involves searching for new angles on strategic problems. A comprehensive assessment of an organisation's strategy needs more than one perspective. We introduce 'the strategy lenses' as distinct, theoretically informed ways of thinking about strategy. **The strategy lenses are ways of looking at strategy issues differently in order to generate additional insights.** Looking at problems in different ways will raise new issues and new solutions. Thus, although the lenses are drawn from academic theory, they should also be highly practical in the job of doing strategy.

The four lenses are described fully at the end of Part I, after you have had a chance to take on board some key strategy frameworks for analysing strategic position. We shall return to them as well through brief *commentaries* at the end of Parts II and III. This section is therefore just a brief introduction to the lenses, as follows:

- *Strategy as design.* This takes the view that strategy development can be 'designed' in the abstract, as an architect might design a building using pens, rulers and paper. The architect designs, and then hands over the plans for the builders actually to build. Thus the design lens encourages a detached approach to planning and analysis, valuing hard facts and objectivity. It tends to exclude improvisation in strategy development and gives little credit to the unpredictable, conservative or political aspects of human organisations. Taking a design lens to a strategic problem means being systematic, analytical and logical.

- *Strategy as experience.* The experience lens recognises that the future strategy of an organisation is often heavily influenced by its experience and that of its managers. Here strategies are seen as driven not so much by clear-cut analysis as by the taken-for-granted assumptions and ways of doing things embedded in people's personal experience and the organisational culture. Strategy is likely to build on and continue what has gone on before. Strategic dilemmas will be resolved not simply through rational analysis, as in the design lens, but also by rules of thumb, appeals to precedent and standard fixes. The experience lens suggests that the biases and routines of key decision-makers need to be understood. It sets low expectations of radical change.

- *Strategy as variety.*[13] Neither of the above lenses is likely to uncover radical new ideas in strategy. Design approaches risk being too rigid and top-down; experience builds too much on the past. How then are radical new ideas discovered? The variety lens sees strategy not so much as planned from the top as emergent from within and around organisations as people respond to an uncertain and changing environment with a variety of initiatives. New ideas bubble up through unpredictable selection processes. The variety lens therefore emphasises the importance of promoting diversity in and around organisations, in order to allow the seeding of as many genuinely new ideas as possible. Somebody with a variety lens would look for future strategies at the bottom and the periphery of organisations. They should be ready for surprises.

- *Strategy as discourse.* Managers spend most of their time talking, persuading and negotiating. They are always using language, or what is here called 'discourse'. Adopting the discourse lens focuses attention on the ways managers use language to frame strategic problems, make strategy proposals, debate issues and then finally communicate strategic decisions. Strategy discourse becomes a tool for managers to shape 'objective' strategic analyses in their favour and to gain influence, power and legitimacy. For believers in the discourse lens, strategy 'talk' matters. The discourse lens tries to look under the surface of strategy to uncover the personal interests and politicking in organisations. Taking a discourse lens encourages a sceptical view.

None of these lenses is likely to offer a complete view of a strategic situation. The point of the lenses is to encourage the exploration of different perspectives: to look at the situation first from one point of view (perhaps design) and then from another. These lenses help in recognising how otherwise logical strategic initiatives might be held back by cultural experience; in checking for unexpected ideas from the bottom or the periphery of the organisation; and in seeing through the formal strategy discourse to ask whose interests are really being served.

SUMMARY

- Strategy is the *long-term direction* of an organisation. A *strategy statement* should cover the *goals* of an organisation, the *scope* of the organisation's activities and the *advantages* or *capabilities* the organisation brings to these goals and activities.

- *Corporate-level strategy* is concerned with an organisation's overall scope; *business-level strategy* is concerned with how to compete; and *operational strategy* is concerned with how corporate- and business-level strategies are actually delivered.

- The *Exploring Strategy* Model has three major elements: understanding the *strategic position*, making *strategic choices* for the future and managing *strategy in action*.

- Strategy work is done by *managers* throughout an organisation, as well as specialist *strategic planners* and *strategy consultants*.

- Research on strategy *context*, *content* and *process* shows how the analytical perspectives of economics, sociology and psychology can all provide practical insights for approaching strategy issues.

- Although the fundamentals of strategy may be similar, strategy varies by *organisational context*, for example small business, multinational or public sector.

- Strategic issues are best seen from a variety of perspectives, as exemplified by the four *strategy lenses* of *design, experience, variety* and *discourse*.

VIDEO ASSIGNMENTS

Visit **MyStrategyLab** and watch the British Heart Foundation case study for Chapter 1.

1 Refer to section 1.2.3 and Illustration 1.2 as a guide and use the video to help you write a strategy statement for the British Heart Foundation. Why is such a statement useful to the BHF?

2 Show how the *Exploring Strategy* Model (Figure 1.3) can be used to map key strategic management issues for the BHF. Identify the key challenges facing the BHF.

WORK ASSIGNMENTS

✱ *Denotes more advanced work assignments.*
* *Refers to a case study in the Text and Cases edition.*

1.1 Drawing on Illustration 1.2 as a guide, write a strategy statement for an organisation of your choice (e.g. the Glastonbury chapter case, or your university), drawing on strategy materials in the organisation's annual report or website.

1.2 Using the *Exploring Strategy* Model of Figure 1.3, map key issues relating to strategic position, strategic choices and strategy into action for the Lego case*, Glastonbury, or an organisation with which you are familiar (e.g. your university).

1.3 Go to the website of one of the major strategy consultants such as Bain, the Boston Consulting Group or McKinsey & Co. (see reference 5 below). What does the website tell you about the nature of strategy consulting work? Would you enjoy that work?

1.4✱ Using Figure 1.3 as a guide, show how the elements of strategic management differ in:

    (a) A small or family business (e.g. Adnams*, Feed Henry*, Leax* or Hotel du Vin*).

    (b) A large multinational business (e.g. Vodafone*, SABMiller*, Unilever*).

    (c) A non-profit organisation (e.g. AIDS Alliance*, GMB* or Queensland Rail*).

RECOMMENDED KEY READINGS

It is always useful to read around a topic. As well as the specific references below, we particularly highlight:

- Two stimulating overviews of strategic thinking in general, aimed particularly at practising managers, are C. Montgomery, *The Strategist: Be the Leader your Business Needs*, Harper Business, 2012; and R. Rumelt, *Good Strategy/Bad Strategy: the Difference and Why it Matters*, Crown Business, 2011.

- Two accessible articles on what strategy is, and might not be, are M. Porter, 'What is strategy?', *Harvard Business Review*, November–December 1996, pp. 61–78;

and F. Fréry, 'The fundamental dimensions of strategy', *MIT Sloan Management Review*, vol. 48, no. 1 (2006), pp. 71–5.

- For contemporary developments in strategy practice, business newspapers such as the *Financial Times*, *Les Echos* and the *Wall Street Journal* and business magazines such as *Business Week*, *The Economist*, *L'Expansion* and *Manager-Magazin*. Several of these have well-informed Asian editions. See also the websites of the leading strategy consulting firms: www.mckinsey.com; www.bcg.com; www.bain.com.

REFERENCES

1. The question 'What is strategy?' is discussed in R. Whittington, *What Is Strategy – and Does it Matter?*, International Thomson, 1993/2000; and M.E. Porter, 'What is strategy?', *Harvard Business Review*, November–December 1996, pp. 61–78.

2. D. Collis and M. Rukstad, 'Can you say what your strategy is?', *Harvard Business Review*, April 2008, pp. 63–73.

3. F. Westley, 'Middle managers and strategy: microdynamics of inclusion', *Strategic Management Journal*, vol. 11, no. 5 (1990), pp. 337–51.

4. For insights about in-house strategy roles, see D. Angwin, S. Paroutis and S. Mitson, 'Connecting up strategy: are strategy directors a missing link?', *California Management Review*, vol. 51, no. 3 (2009).

5. The major strategy consulting firms have a wealth of information on strategy careers and strategy in general: see www.mckinsey.com; www.bcg.com; www.bain.com.

6. University careers advisors can usually provide good advice on strategy consulting and strategic planning opportunities. See also www.vault.com.

7. For reviews of the contemporary state of strategy as a discipline, J. Mahoney and A. McGahan, 'The field of strategic management within the evolving science of strategic

organisation', *Strategic Organisation*, vol. 5, no. 1 (2007), pp. 79–99; and R. Whittington, 'Big strategy/Small strategy', *Strategic Organisation*, vol. 10, no. 3, (2012), pp. 263–8.

8. See M.E. Porter, 'The five competitive forces that shape strategy', *Harvard Business Review*, January 2008, pp. 57–91.

9. The classic statement of the resource-based view is J. Barney, 'Firm resources and sustained competitive advantage', *Journal of Management*, vol. 17, no. 1 (1991), pp. 91–120.

10. A recent review of strategy process research is H. Sminia, 'Process research in strategy formation: theory, methodology and relevance', *International Journal of Management Reviews*, vol. 11, no. 1 (2009), pp. 97–122.

11. Psychological influences on strategy are explored in a special issue of the *Strategic Management Journal*, edited by T. Powell, D. Lovallo and S. Fox: 'Behavioural strategy', vol. 31, no. 13 (2011).

12. For a review of Strategy-as-Practice research, see E. Vaara and R. Whittington, 'Strategy-as-practice: taking social practices seriously', *Academy of Management Annals*, vol. 6, no. 1 (2012), pp. 285–336.

13. In earlier editions, this lens was called the 'ideas lens'.

Glastonbury: from hippy weekend to international festival

Steve Henderson, Leeds Metropolitan University

Following on from Woodstock in 1969, many have been inspired to create their own music festival. While some of these events have come and gone, the longevity and location of Fuji Rock Festival in Japan, Roskilde in Denmark, Coachella in the USA, Rock al Parque in Colombia illustrate the established international nature of this market (see Table 1). One of the longest established is Glastonbury Festival where, in 2013, the Rolling Stones were added to the long list of acts (from Paul McCartney to Oasis) that have appeared there. It started in 1970 when 1,500 hippy revellers paid £1 (€1.2; $1.5) for their ticket and gathered on a farm near Glastonbury Tor to be plied with free milk and entertainment from a makeshift stage. Now, Glastonbury is a major international festival that attracts over 150,000 attendees. Without any information about the performers, the 2013 festival tickets – priced at over £200 – sold out within a few hours.

In those early days, the vision was developed by local farmer, Michael Eavis, whose passion for music and social principles led to a weekend of music as a means of raising funds for good causes. It was a social mission rooted in the hippy counter-culture of the 1960s and events such as the Woodstock Festival. Today, the Glastonbury Festival attendee finds that those early days

Source: Neil Lupins/Redferns

of hippy idealism are a long way off. The scale of the organisation demands strong management to support the achievement of the festival's social aims.

At first, the statutory requirements for an event held on private land were minimal. Jovial policemen looked over hedges while recreational drugs were sold from tables near the festival entrance as if this was just a slightly unusual village fête. Needless to say, the festival began to attract the attention of a number of different groups, especially as legislation around the running of events tightened. Eavis struggled with local

Table 1 International music festivals

Festival	Country	Started	Estimated capacity[1]	2013 pricing
Woodstock	USA	1969	400,000	Price/free
Glastonbury	UK	1970	130,000	£205 (weekend)
Reading/Leeds Festival	UK	1971[2]/1999	162,000	£197.50 (weekend)
Roskilde	Denmark	1971	103,000	£195 (three days)
Rock am Ring/Rock im Park	Germany	1985/1993	150,000	£150 (weekend)
Rock al Parque	Colombia	1995	88,000	Free
Benicassim	Spain	1995	55,000	£150 (four days)
V Festival – Weston Park/Hylands Park	UK	1996	160,000	£185 (weekend)
Fuji Rock	Japan	1997	More than 100,000	£305 (three days)
Coachella	USA	1999	75,000	£220 (three days)
Peace & Love	Sweden	1999	22,000	£170 (five days)

[1] Based on daily capacity
[2] Existed from 1961 as a Jazz Festival

residents who hated the invasion of their privacy; with hippy activist groups whose contribution in helping at the festival gave them a sense of ownership; with drug dealers carrying on their activities on the fringes of the festival; and with fans climbing over the fences to get free access.

The continued expansion has resulted in a festival with over ten stages covering jazz, dance, classical, world music and other genres. Added to this, there is comedy, poetry, circus, theatre and children's entertainment alongside more esoteric street theatre performances. Much of this is organised into specific grassy field areas where, for example, the DanceVillage uses a number of tents dedicated to different types of dance music. Indeed, such is the range of entertainment on offer that some attendees spend the whole weekend at the festival without seeing a single live music act. Though the Eavis family remain involved with the main programme, much of the other entertainment is now managed by others. Reflecting this shift towards more diverse entertainment, the name of the festival was changed from Glastonbury Fayre (reflecting the ancient cultural heritage of the area) to the Glastonbury Festival for Contemporary Performing Arts.

In some years, like 2012, the festival is forced to take a year off to allow the farmland to recover from the trampling of thousands of pairs of feet. Not only is this wise for agricultural reasons but it also gives the local residents a rest from the annual invasion of festival goers. Despite this, the festival has met with a number of controversies such as when a large number of gate-crashers spoilt the fun in 2000. This caused the festival to be fined due to exceeding the licensed attendance and excessive noise. Furthermore, health and safety laws now impose on event management a 'duty of care' to everyone on the festival site. To address these health and safety concerns, support was sought from Melvin Benn who ran festivals for the Mean Fiddler events organiser. With a steel fence erected around the perimeter, Melvin Benn helped re-establish the festival in 2002 after a year off.

In 2006, Mean Fiddler was taken over and renamed Festival Republic by major music promoters, Live Nation and MCD Productions. In a worrying move, Live Nation announced that it would entice a number of major artists to appear on the weekend normally used by Glastonbury at a new festival called Wireless. Based in London, this seemed set to offer a city-based alternative to Glastonbury. Later, in 2010, Live Nation acquired Ticketmaster in a controversial move that extended its control over the ticketing of its own and other events.

This shift among the major music promoters indicated not only their interest in the ownership of key events but their desire to control income streams and the customer interface.

Elsewhere in the world of live entertainment, the success of Glastonbury had not gone unnoticed and the music festival market showed considerable growth. Some of the other festivals tried to capitalise on features that Glastonbury could not offer. For example, Glastonbury was famous for its wet weather with pictures of damp revellers and collapsed tents being commonplace. Live Nation's city-based Wireless Festival offered the opportunity to sleep under a roof at home or hotel, as opposed to risking the weather outdoors. Alternatively, Benicassim in southern Spain offered a festival with an excellent chance of sunshine and top acts for the price of a low-cost airline ticket. Other festivals noted that Glastonbury attendees enjoyed the wider entertainment at the event. In doing this, they realised that many festival goers were attracted by the whole social experience. So, sidestepping major acts and their related high fees, smaller festivals were created for just a few thousand attendees. These offered entertainment in various formats, often in a family-friendly atmosphere. Freddie Fellowes, organiser of the Secret Garden Party, describes this 'boutique' type of festival as a chance 'to be playful, to break down barriers between people and create an environment where you have perfect freedom and perfect nourishment, intellectually and visually'. Festival Republic, the rebranded Mean Fiddler, created a boutique festival on a larger scale with its Latitude Festival. Similarly, Rob da Bank, a BBC DJ, put together Bestival on The Isle of Wight where the attendees are encouraged to join in the fun by appearing in fancy dress. Quite clearly, audiences are now being presented with a wide range of festivals to consider for their leisure-time entertainment.

Many of these festivals attract sponsors with some becoming prominent by acquiring naming rights on the festival, e.g. the Virgin brand's support of V Festival. Others have low-profile arrangements involving so-called 'contra' deals as opposed to sponsorship payments. For example, Glastonbury has official cider suppliers who typically boost their brand by giving the festival a preferential deal on their products in exchange for publicity. Though these commercial relationships are sometimes spurned by the smaller festivals that see the branding as an intrusion on their social environment, larger festivals often need such relationships to survive. In order to attract sponsors, large festivals are turning to radio and television broadcasters as a means to expand the audience and offer wider exposure for the sponsor. Indeed, in 2011, the BBC sent around 250 staff members down to Glastonbury for broadcasting aimed at satisfying the interest of the armchair viewer/listener.

With such huge demand for their talents, artists can have a lucrative summer moving between festivals. Similarly, audiences can make lengthy treks to their favourite festivals. For some, this has caused environmental concerns with Glastonbury's rural location, poor transport links and large audience being cited as a specific problem. On the other hand, artists are not only finding that the festivals offer a good source of income but that private parties and corporate entertainment have emerged as alternative, often greater, income opportunities. One newspaper claimed that George Michael pocketed more than £1.5 m to entertain revellers at the British billionaire-retailer Sir Philip Green's 55th birthday party in the Maldives. Hence, for major artists, the summer has become a case of 'cherry picking' their favourite festivals or seeking out the most lucrative opportunities.

Over time, the shift from small, homespun event to corporate-controlled festival has provided awkward situations for Michael Eavis – from the difficulties with establishment politicians who felt the event was out of control to the demands of counter-cultural groups such as the travelling hippies. However, along the way, the festival has maintained its aim of supporting charities like CND and, later, Greenpeace, Oxfam and a number of local charities. In the mind of the audience, this helps position the festival as a fun event with a social conscience.

In recent years, Glastonbury has sold all its tickets and is relatively highly priced to many competitors (Figure 1). Indeed, since 1979, Glastonbury has been moving its prices up significantly faster than both inflation and the comparable Danish Roskilde Festival (see Case Example Figure 1). At the same time, it continues to make donations to favoured causes, confirming the financial viability of the current business model. Indeed, the festival's iconic status has helped it to become a rite of passage for many young music fans. Yet, in 2008, Eavis publicly registered concern over the ageing nature of the Glastonbury audience and announced that Jay-Z, an American rap artist, was to headline in order to help attract younger people. Reflecting on the 2008 festival, Michael Eavis displayed concerns over the future, saying: 'Last year I thought that maybe we'd got to the end and we'd have to bite the bullet and fold it all up. A lot of the bands were saying Glastonbury had become too big, too muddy and too horrible.'

Audiences and artists are the two key factors that underpin financial success at these events, as successful festival promoters are well aware. Despite the fact that Michael's daughter, Emily Eavis, and her husband were taking on more of the workload and Michael himself has become more of a figurehead for this event, these comments from the festival's founder highlight worries in key strategic areas that would be troubling for management. Others pointed to the strong relationships Live

Figure 1 Glastonbury ticket price trend, 1979–2013, relative to Roskilde festival prices and inflation (all rebased to 1979)

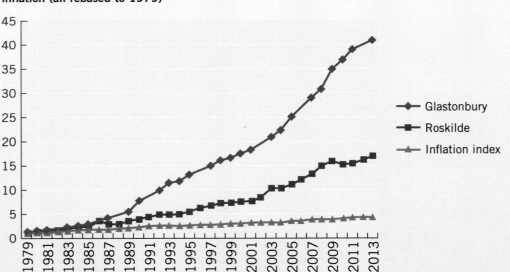

Nation were developing with artists via 360 degree deals that meant both parties would profit not only from live performances but from some combination of merchandise, publishing and recordings too. Both Jay-Z in 2008 and U2 who headlined in 2011 had such relationships and encouraged some observers to accuse the festival of adopting corporate elements that took them away from their core social image.

In 2012, the year of the London Olympics when Glastonbury took a break, Melvin Benn and Festival Republic amicably parted company with the festival. Citing the demands of expanding international festival responsibilities on Benn, the separation of the two seems aimed at re-establishing independence and removing some of the more recent corporate aspects to the festival. Thanking Melvin Benn for his efforts, the Eavis family find themselves firmly back in control and planning the way forward for this iconic festival in a market that is facing difficult recessionary times.

Sources: The history of Glastonbury is charted on the website, www.glastonburyfestivals.co.uk/history, while details of ownership and finances are available through Companies House; most of the background to the festival and related market has been drawn from online news resources such as the BBC, *Times Online*, *the Independent* and *the Guardian*, or industry magazines such as *Music Week*. See also: *Watchmojo: The History of the Glastonbury Festival*: https://www.youtube.com/watch?v=b2bXzuB7sZw.

Questions

1 Sticking to the 35 word limit suggested by Collis and Rukstad in section 1.2.3, what strategy statement would you propose for the Glastonbury Festival?

2 Carry out a 'three-horizons' analysis (section 1.2.1) of the Glastonbury Festival, in terms of both existing activities and possible future ones. How might this analysis affect its future strategic direction?

3 Using the headings of environment, strategic capability, strategic purpose and culture seen in section 1.3.1, identify key positioning issues for the Glastonbury Festival and consider their relative importance.

4 Following on from the previous questions and making use of section 1.3.2, what alternative strategies do you see for the Glastonbury Festival?

5 Converting good strategic thinking into action can be a challenge: examine how the Glastonbury Festival has achieved this by considering the elements seen in section 1.3.3?

PART I

THE STRATEGIC POSITION

This part explains:

- How to analyse an organisation's position in the external environment.

- How to analyse the determinants of strategic capability – resources, competences and the linkages between them.

- How to understand an organisation's purposes, taking into account corporate governance, stakeholder expectations and business ethics.

- How to address the role of history and culture in determining an organisation's position.

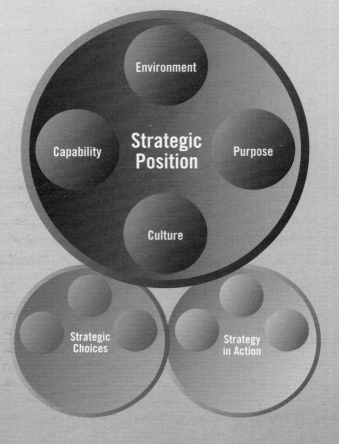

INTRODUCTION TO PART I

This part of the book is concerned with understanding the strategic position of the organisation. There are four chapters, organised around two themes. The first theme is the organisation's strategic *potential*, in other words, what it *can* do. The second theme is the organisation's strategic *ambitions*, what it actually *seeks* to do, sometimes deliberately and sometimes not so deliberately (see Figure I.1).

Strategic potential is addressed as follows:

- Chapter 2 considers how different environments can be more or less rich in opportunities or hostile, imposing threats and constraints.

- Chapter 3 considers how each organisation has its own particular strategic capabilities (resources and competences), and how these can enable or constrain strategies.

Organisational ambitions are addressed in the following two chapters:

- Chapter 4 is about ambition in terms of the organisation's fundamental purpose, often expressed in terms of vision and mission statements for example.

- Chapter 5 examines how an organisation's history and culture may shape the ambitions of an organisation, often in taken-for-granted and hard-to-change ways.

There is an important strategic dilemma that runs through Chapters 2 and 3. How much should managers concentrate their attention on the external market position and how much should they focus on developing their internal capabilities? On the external side, many argue that environmental factors are what matter most to success: strategy development should be primarily about seeking attractive opportunities in the marketplace. Those favouring a more internal approach, on the other hand, argue that an organisation's specific strategic capabilities should drive strategy. It is from these internal characteristics that distinctive strategies and superior performance can be built. There can be a real trade-off here. Managers who invest

Figure I.1 Strategic position

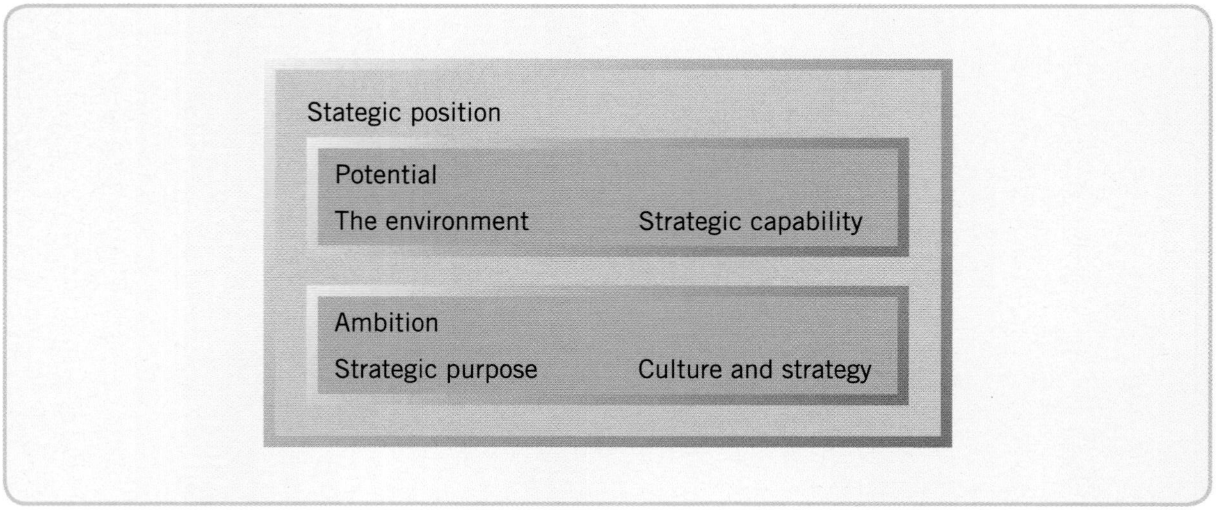

time and resources in developing their external market position (perhaps through acquiring companies that are potential competitors) have less time and resources to invest in managing their internal capabilities (e.g. building up research and development). The same applies in reverse. This trade-off between the internal and the external is discussed explicitly in Chapter 2's Key Debate at the end of that chapter.

Chapters 4 and 5 raise another underlying issue. To what extent should managers' ambitions for their organisations be considered as free or constrained? Chapter 4 explains how the expectations of investors, regulators, employees and customers can often influence strategy. Chapter 5 raises the constraints on managers exercised by organisational history and culture. Managers may be only partially aware of these kinds of constraints and are often in danger of underestimating the hidden limits to their ambitions.

Understanding the extent of managers' freedom to choose is fundamental to considering the issues of strategic choice that make up Part II of this book. But first Part I provides a foundation by exploring the question of strategic position.

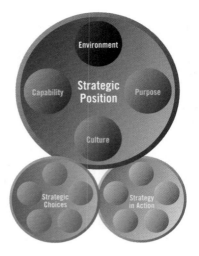

2

THE ENVIRONMENT

Learning outcomes

After reading this chapter, you should be able to:

- Analyse the broad macro-environment of organisations in terms of political, economic, social, technological, ecological and legal factors (*PESTEL*).

- Construct alternative *scenarios* in order to address possible environmental changes.

- Use *Porter's five forces* analysis in order to define the attractiveness of industries and markets and to identify their potential for change.

- Analyse strategic and competitor positions in terms of *strategic groups*, *market segments* and '*Blue Oceans*'.

- Use these various concepts and techniques in order to recognise *threats* and *opportunities* in the marketplace.

Key terms

Blue Oceans p. 58

complementor p. 49

critical success factors p. 58

industry p. 41

market p. 41

market segment p. 56

PESTEL framework p. 34

Porter's Five Forces Framework p. 41

strategic groups p. 54

strategy canvas p. 58

value net p. 49

MyStrategyLab

MyStrategyLab is designed to help you make the most of your studies. Visit **www.pearsoned.co.uk/mystrategylab** to discover a wide range of resources, including:

- A personalised **Study plan** that will help you understand core concepts
- **Audio and video clips** that put the spotlight on strategy in the real world
- **Online glossaries and flashcards** that provide helpful reminders when you're looking for some quick revision.

$\left(2.1\right)$ INTRODUCTION

The environment is what gives organisations their means of survival. It creates opportunities and it presents threats. For example, the success of Facebook's platform created rich market opportunities for online games publishers such as Zynga. On the other hand, the rise of online encyclopaedias such as Wikipedia forced the traditional market-leader *Encyclopaedia Britannica* to cease publishing its print editions after nearly two-and-a-half centuries of production. Although the future can never be predicted perfectly, it is clearly important that entrepreneurs and managers try to analyse their environments as carefully as they can in order to anticipate and – if possible – influence environmental change.

This chapter therefore provides frameworks for analysing changing and complex environments. These frameworks are organised in a series of 'layers' briefly introduced here and summarised in Figure 2.1.

● *The macro-environment* is the highest-level layer. This consists of broad environmental factors that impact to a greater or lesser extent on almost all organisations. Here, the PESTEL framework can be used to identify how future issues in the *political, economic, social, technological, ecological and legal* environments might affect organisations. This PESTEL analysis provides the broad 'data' from which to identify *key drivers of change*. These key drivers can be used to construct *scenarios* of alternative possible futures.

● *Industry*, or *sector*, forms the next layer within this broad general environment. This is made up of organisations producing the same sorts of products or services. Here the *five forces*

Figure 2.1 Layers of the business environment

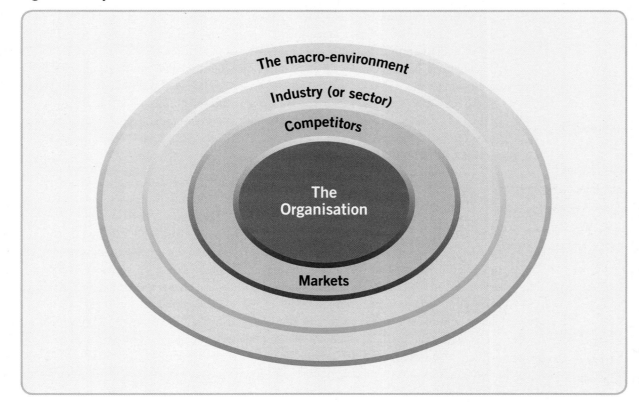

framework is particularly useful in understanding the attractiveness of particular industries or sectors and potential threats from outside the present set of competitors. The Key Debate at the end of this chapter addresses the importance of industry factors, rather than business-specific factors, in determining success.

- *Competitors and markets* are the most immediate layer surrounding organisations. Here the concept of *strategic groups* can help identify different kinds of competitors. Similarly, in the marketplace, customers' expectations are not all the same, which can be understood through the concept of *market segments*. Finally, competitors' relative positions can be analysed using the *strategy canvas*, helping also to identify '*Blue Ocean*' opportunities in the marketplace.

This chapter works through these three layers in turn, starting with the macro-environment.

(2.2) THE MACRO-ENVIRONMENT

This section introduces two interrelated tools – PESTEL and scenarios – for analysing the broad macro-environment of an organisation. PESTEL provides a wide overview and scenarios build on this in order to consider how the macro-environment might change. Both PESTEL and scenarios, however, can be overwhelming in the amount of issues and possibilities that they uncover. So throughout this section we shall emphasise techniques and concepts that help focus the analysis on what is likely to matter most.

2.2.1 The PESTEL framework

The **PESTEL framework** is one of several frameworks (including the similar 'PEST' and 'STEEPLE' frameworks) which categorises environmental factors into key types.[1] PESTEL highlights six environmental factors in particular: political, economic, social, technological, ecological and legal. This range of factors underlines that the environment is not just about economic forces: there is an important *non-market* environment. Organisations needs to consider both market and non-market aspects of strategy (Illustration 2.1).[2]

In practice, political, economic, social, technological, ecological and legal factors are often interconnected. Nevertheless, going through each of the six PESTEL factors helps raise a wide range of potentially relevant issues, as follows:

- *Politics* highlights the role of the state and other political forces. The state is often important as a direct economic actor, for instance as potential customer, supplier or owner of businesses. But there are also influences from various political movements, campaign groups or concerned media. Figure 2.2 (p. 36) is a matrix that helps identify both the relative importance of the state as direct economic actor and exposure to other political influences. Thus the defence industry for instance of course faces highly involved states that are both customers and often owners of key companies, while also being exposed to political groups campaigning against the arms trade, for instance. Food companies are mostly privately owned and operate in private-sector markets, but are still be exposed to great political pressures from fair trade, labour rights and health campaigners. Canals are often state-owned but nowadays are not usually politically sensitive. Industries can rapidly change positions: thus after the financial crisis of 2008, banks moved towards both greater state ownership and increased political criticism.

ILLUSTRATION 2.1
Oil's troubled waters

In 2013, the controversial oil giant BP faced a complex environment.

BP is one of the world's largest oil and gas companies. It operates right across exploration, production, refining, distribution and marketing. It has about 21,000 service stations worldwide, half in the United States, 40 per cent in Europe. The largest sources of its oil production are Russia (about 45 per cent) and the USA (20 per cent); the USA accounts for about a quarter of its natural gas production and Russia about 10 per cent. Since 2005, BP has had a small alternative energy business, active in biofuels and windpower. In 2010, BP's Deepwater Horizon oil rig exploded, causing 11 deaths and an oil slick in the Gulf of Mexico covering 180,000 km². In 2012, the US government fined BP more than $4 bn. (about £2.5 bn; €3 bn) for the disaster, and many court cases are still pending.

Some headline features of BP's environment include:

Political: More than 80 per cent of the world's oil reserves are owned by state-controlled enterprises, the largest being Saudi Aramco and the Iranian National Oil Company. In 2013, BP's oil business in Russia was transferred from a controversial alliance with a group of leading Russian businessmen to a partnership with Rosneft, the state-controlled Russian oil company, in which BP would hold 18 per cent of the shares.

Economic: *Forbes* magazine reports predictions of economic growth between 2012 and 2020 of 7 per cent per annum for China, about 2 per cent for the United States and 1 per cent for Europe. Oil prices peaked at about $120 a barrel in 2008, before dropping to around $30 as recession took hold in 2009, and recovering to around $100 in 2012. New extractive technologies led natural gas prices in the USA to fall 30 per cent between 2011 and 2013.

Social: Car usage is falling in many European economies. After having doubled in the preceding 30 years, miles travelled in the United Kingdom by motor vehicles have fallen by about 1 per cent between 2008 and 2012; miles travelled by train reached a record in 2012, having increased by 50 per cent since the mid-1990s. From 2008 to 2012, the number of driving tests taken in the United Kingdom fell by about 17 per cent.

Technology: New technologies include the exploitation of 'fire ice' (gas hydrates under the sea) and 'fracking', the extraction of gas by fracturing underground rock to produce 'shale gas'. Fire ice might eventually equal 4,000 times all the natural gas consumed in the US in 2010; fracking offers the prospect of doubling the world's available natural gas supply by 2020.

Ecological: Fracking is liable to pollute local water supplies and even trigger small earthquakes. According to Cornell University, about 8 per cent of the gas extracted by fracking is released direct into the atmosphere, potentially a major contribution to global warming. In the USA, natural gas costs about $50 per megawatt hour to produce; wave $500; tidal $450; biomass $130; on-shore wind $80.

Legal: The Deepwater Horizon disaster has led to new safety regulations for deepwater drilling. The European Union, where 90 per cent of oil extraction is from the sea, has imposed stricter exploration licensing procedures, risk assessment and financial guarantees against the costs of accidents. New regulations in the USA are estimated to increase costs by $1.5 m per oil well. In 2012, the USA banned BP from tendering for all government contracts.

Sources: BP Annual Report, 2012; *Business Week*, 7 March 2013; *Forbes*, 26 March 2012.

Questions

1 Which of the above PESTEL factors offer the most important opportunities to BP, and which the most important threats?

2 Which of the above factors spill over from one PESTEL category to another? Does this matter?

Figure 2.2 The political environment

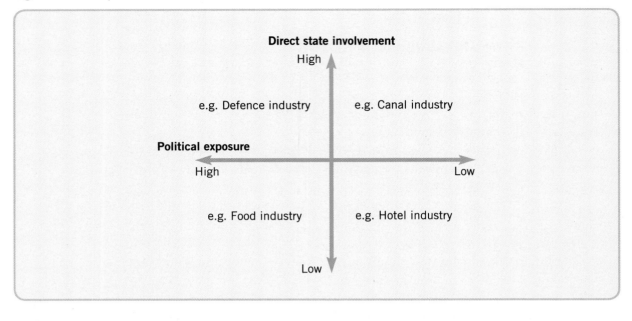

- *Economics* refers to macro-economic factors such as exchange rates, business cycles and differential economic growth rates around the world. It is important for a business to understand how its markets are affected by the prosperity of the economy as a whole. Managers should avoid over-confidence at the top of the business cycle, and excessive caution at the bottom. They should have a view on how changing exchange rates may affect viability in export markets and vulnerability to imports.

- *Social* influences include changing cultures and demographics. Thus, for example, the ageing populations in many Western societies create opportunities and threats for both private and public sectors. Changing cultural attitudes can also raise strategic challenges: for example, new ethical attitudes are challenging previously taken-for-granted strategies in the financial services industry.

- *Technological* influences refer to influences such as the internet, nano technology or the rise of new composite materials. As in the case of the internet in retailing, new technologies open up opportunities for some (e.g. Amazon), while challenging others (traditional stores).

- *Ecological* stands specifically for 'green' environmental issues, such as pollution, waste and climate change. Environmental regulations can impose additional costs, for example with pollution controls, but they can also be a source of opportunity, for example the new businesses that emerged around mobile phone recycling.

- *Legal* embraces legislative and regulatory constraints or changes. For example, legal changes might include restrictions on company mergers and acquisitions or new tax treatments of profits earned overseas. On the other hand, legal changes can provide opportunities, as for example the liberalisation of foreign investment in India.

As can be imagined, analysing these factors and their interrelationships can produce long and complex lists. Rather than getting overwhelmed by a multitude of details, it is necessary to step back eventually to identify the *key drivers for change*. Key drivers for change are the environmental factors likely to have a high impact on the future success or failure of strategy. Typical key drivers will vary by industry or sector. Thus a retailer may be primarily concerned with social changes driving customer tastes and behaviour, for example forces encouraging out-of-town shopping, and economic changes, for example rates of economic growth and employment. Public-sector managers are likely to be especially concerned with social change (e.g. rising youth unemployment), political change (e.g. changing government priorities) and legislative change (new training requirements). Identifying key drivers for change helps managers to focus on the PESTEL factors that are most important and which must be addressed most urgently. Without a clear sense of the key drivers for change, managers will not be able to take the decisions that allow for effective action.

Three concepts are useful for focusing on change while at the same time avoiding too much detail:

- *Megatrends* are large-scale social, economic, political, ecological or technological changes that are typically slow to form, but which influence many other activities and views, possibly over decades.[3] A megatrend typically shapes other trends. Thus the megatrend towards ageing populations in the West influences other trends in social care, retail spending and housing. The megatrend towards rapid economic growth in Asia drives employment patterns in the advanced economies and commodity prices worldwide. It is important to identify major megatrends because they influence so many other things.

- *Inflexion points* are moments when trends shift in direction, for instance turning sharply upwards or downwards.[4] For example, after decades of stagnation and worse, in the early twenty-first century sub-Saharan Africa may have reached an inflexion point in its economic growth, with the promise of substantial gains in the coming decade or so. Town-centre retailing may also have reached an inflexion point, where the rise of internet shopping and out-of-town retail parks has put urban shopping on a path to significant decline in advanced economies. Clearly it is valuable to grasp the inflexion point at the moment when trends just start to turn, in order either to take advantage of new opportunities early or to act against escalating decline as soon as possible.

- *Weak signals* are advanced signs of future trends and are particularly helpful in identifying inflexion points.[5] Typically these weak signals are unstructured and fragmented bits of information, often perceived by observers as 'weird'. A weak signal for the worldwide financial crisis that began in 2008 was the rise in mortgage failures in California the previous year. An early weak signal foreshadowing the current success of Asian business schools was the first entry of the Hong Kong University of Science and Technology into the Financial Times' ranking of the top 50 international business schools in the early 2000s. It is important to be alert to weak signals, but it is also easy to be overwhelmed by 'noise', the constant stream of isolated and random bits of information without strategic importance. Some signs of truly significant weak signals (as opposed to mere noise) include: the repetition of the signal and the emergence of some kind of pattern; vehement disagreement among experts about the signal's significance; and an unexpected failure in something that had previously worked very reliably.

2.2.2 Building scenarios

When the business environment has high levels of uncertainty arising from either complexity or rapid change (or both), it is impossible to develop a single view of how environmental influences might affect an organisation's strategies – indeed it would be dangerous to do so.

Scenario analyses are carried out to allow for different possibilities and help prevent managers from closing their minds to alternatives. Thus scenarios offer plausible alternative views of how the business environment might develop in the future.[6] Scenarios typically build on PESTEL analyses and key drivers for change, but do not offer a single forecast of how the environment will change. The point is not to predict, but to encourage managers to be alert to a range of possible futures. Effective scenario-building can help build strategies that are robust in the face of environmental change.

Illustration 2.2 shows an example of scenario planning for the global fashion industry to 2025. Rather than incorporating a multitude of factors, the authors focus on two key drivers which (i) have high potential impact; (ii) are uncertain; (iii) are largely independent from each other. These two drivers are the extent to which the world becomes more interconnected and the speed with which society, and fashion, changes. Both of these drivers may produce very different futures, which can be combined to create four internally consistent scenarios for the next decade and a half. The authors do not predict that one will prevail over the others, nor do they allocate relative probabilities. Prediction would close managers' minds to alternatives, while probabilities would imply a spurious kind of accuracy.

While there are many ways to carry out scenario analyses, five basic steps are often followed:[7]

- *Defining scenario scope* is an important first step. Scope refers to the subject of the scenario analysis and the time span. For example, scenario analyses can be carried out for a whole industry globally, or for particular geographical regions and markets. While businesses typically produce scenarios for industries or markets, governments often conduct scenario analyses for countries, regions or sectors (such as the future of healthcare or higher education). Scenario time spans can range from a decade or so (as in Illustration 2.2) or for just three to five years ahead. The appropriate time span is determined partly by the expected life of investments. In the energy business, where oil fields, for example, might have a life span of several decades, scenarios often cover 20 years or more.

- *Identifying the key drivers for change* comes next. Here PESTEL analysis can be used to uncover issues likely to have a major *impact* upon the future of the industry, region or market. In the fashion industry, key drivers range from demographics to technology. However, the scenario cube suggests two additional criteria are relevant (see Figure 2.3): *uncertainty*, in order to make different scenarios worthwhile; and *mutual independence*, so that the drivers are capable of producing significantly divergent or opposing outcomes. In the oil industry, for example, political stability in the oil-producing regions is one major uncertainty; another is the capacity to develop major new oil fields thanks to new extraction technologies. These could be selected as key drivers for scenario analysis because both are uncertain and regional stability is not closely correlated with technological advance.

- *Developing scenario 'stories'*: as in films, scenarios are basically stories. Having selected opposing key drivers for change, it is necessary to knit together plausible stories that incorporate both key drivers and other factors into a coherent whole. Thus in Illustration 2.2, the 'Techno-chic' scenario brings together in a consistent way a more global and integrated culture with a rapid rate of social, technological and economic change. But completing the story of 'Techno-chic' would also involve incorporating other consistent factors: for example, rapid development in China and India where low cost becomes supplanted by technological sophistication as source of advantage; free markets to allow rapid growth and international trade; and the creation of an under-class whose cheap labour and outdated technological skills are no longer needed.

Figure 2.3 The scenario cube: selection matrix for scenario key drivers

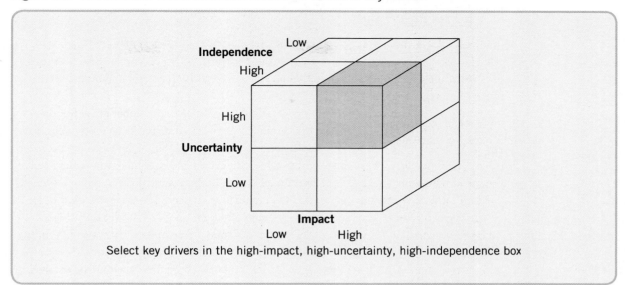

Select key drivers in the high-impact, high-uncertainty, high-independence box

- *Identifying impacts* of alternative scenarios on organisations is the next key stage of scenario building. 'Techno-chic' might have a very negative impact for many traditional fashion labels and retailers who could not keep up with hi-tech clothing and distribution. On the other hand, 'Community couture' could see the strengthening of local craft producers. It is important for an organisation to carry out *robustness checks* in the face of each plausible scenario and to develop *contingency plans* in case they happen.

- *Establishing early warning systems*: once the various scenarios are drawn up, organisations should identify indicators that might give early warning about the final direction of environmental change, and at the same time set up systems to monitor these. Effective monitoring of well-chosen indicators should facilitate prompt and appropriate responses. In Illustration 2.2, indicators of a 'Slow is beautiful' trend might be low wage growth and rises in religious observance.

Because debating and learning are so valuable in the scenario-building process, and they deal with such high uncertainty, some scenario experts advise managers to avoid producing just three scenarios. Three scenarios tend to fall into a range of 'optimistic', 'middling' and 'pessimistic'. Managers naturally focus on the middling scenario and neglect the other two, reducing the amount of organisational learning and contingency planning. It is therefore typically better to have two or four scenarios, avoiding an easy mid-point. It does not matter if the scenarios do not come to pass: the value lies in the process of exploration and contingency planning that the scenarios set off.

ILLUSTRATION 2.2

Scenarios for the global fashion industry, 2025

Levis uses students to investigate alternative futures.

During 2009–10, the clothing company Levi Strauss & Co., known worldwide for its jeans, worked with Masters students at the London College of Fashion to produce four scenarios for the global fashion industry in the coming 15 years. Levi Strauss knew that fashion was facing massive changes in fabric technologies, manufacturing locations, retailing and much more. It wanted to understand what kinds of futures it might have to deal with.

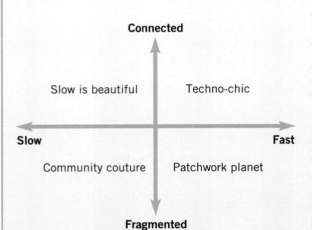

The students identified many important drivers that could simply be taken for granted: for instance, an ageing population and increasing natural resource constraints. However, they highlighted two key drivers that involved high uncertainty and that were largely independent of each other, and so could create divergent scenarios: interconnectivity and speed of change. The first driver offers two extreme points: on the one hand, a highly connected world with low trade barriers, integrated communications internationally and a homogenisation of cultures; on the other hand, a fragmented world with falling long-distance trade and strengthening regional identities. The second driver offers a range between fast change

and slow change: a fast world would be one in which media and communications are increasingly instant, capital moves easily and people live hectic lives; a slow world would imply less emphasis on consumption and more conservatism in cultures.

The divergent directions of the two key drivers define four scenarios for 2025. The first is 'Slow is beautiful', based on a slow world with high interconnectivity. In this scenario, durability and sustainability would be highly important, but interconnectivity would allow people to swap and refurbish old clothes very easily: 'vBay' (like eBay) would emerge as a hugely popular website dedicated to vintage clothing. The second scenario, 'Community couture', would also be slow because of growing resource constraints, climate change and poverty, while political barriers would reduce interconnectivity in the form of international trade: new, fashionable clothes would only be for the privileged. 'Techno-chic' on the other hand would be the product of a fast-paced interconnected world: clothes would be 'smart', changing colour, carrying embedded media and even controlling bodily health. Pharmaceutical companies could be in the clothing business. Finally, the 'Patchwork planet' scenario imagines low interconnectivity but rapid change. In a 'Patchwork planet', fast-growing emerging economies would be culturally confident, so that national rather than global fashions would prevail: Western clothes might even be banned in some countries.

Source: http://www.forumforthefuture.org/project/fashion-futures-2025/overview.

Questions

1 Which scenario would Levi Strauss most desire and which would it most fear?

2 What are the implications of these fashion industry scenarios for other industries, for example hotels or retail?

(2.3) INDUSTRIES AND SECTORS

The previous section looked at how forces in the macro-environment might influence the success or failure of an organisation's strategies. But the impact of these general factors tends to surface in the more immediate environment through changes in the competitive forces surrounding organisations. An important aspect of this for most organisations will be competition within their industry, sector or market. **An industry is a group of firms producing products and services that are essentially the same.**[8] Examples are the automobile industry and the airline industry. Industries are also often described as 'sectors', especially in public services (e.g. the health sector or the education sector). Industries and sectors are often made up of several specific markets. **A market is a group of customers for specific products or services that are essentially the same (e.g. a particular geographical market).** Thus the automobile industry has markets in North America, Europe and Asia, for example.

This section concentrates on industry analysis, starting with Michael Porter's *five forces framework* and then introducing techniques for analysing the *dynamics* of industries. However, while the following section will address markets in more detail, this section will refer to markets and most of the concepts apply similarly to markets and industries.

2.3.1 Competitive forces – the Five Forces Framework

Industries vary widely in terms of their attractiveness, as measured by how easy it is for participating firms to earn high profits. One key determinant of profitability is the extent of competition, actual or potential. Where competition is low, and there is little threat of new competitors, participating firms should normally expect good profits.

Porter's Five Forces Framework[9] **helps identify the attractiveness of an industry in terms of five competitive forces: (i) threat of entry, (ii) threat of substitutes, (iii) power of buyers, (iv) power of suppliers and (v) extent of rivalry between competitors.** These five forces together constitute an industry's 'structure' (see Figure 2.4), which is typically fairly stable. For Porter, an attractive industry structure is one that offers good profit potential. His essential message is that where the five forces are high, industries are not attractive to compete in. Excessive competitive rivalry, powerful buyers and suppliers and the threat of substitutes or new entrants will all combine to squeeze profitability.

Although initially developed with businesses in mind, the five forces framework is relevant to most organisations. It can provide a useful starting point for strategic analysis even where profit criteria may not apply. In the public sector, it is important to understand how powerful suppliers can push up costs; among charities, it is important to avoid excessive rivalry within the same market. Moreover, once the degree of industry attractiveness has been understood, the five forces can help set an agenda for action on the various critical issues that they identify: for example, what can competitors do to control excessive rivalry in a particular industry? The rest of this section introduces each of the five forces in more detail. Illustration 2.3 on the evolving steel industry provides examples.

Competitive rivalry

At the centre of five forces analysis is the rivalry between the existing players – 'incumbents' in an industry. The more competitive rivalry there is, the worse it is for incumbents. *Competitive rivals* are organisations with similar products and services aimed at the same customer group

Figure 2.4 The Five Forces Framework

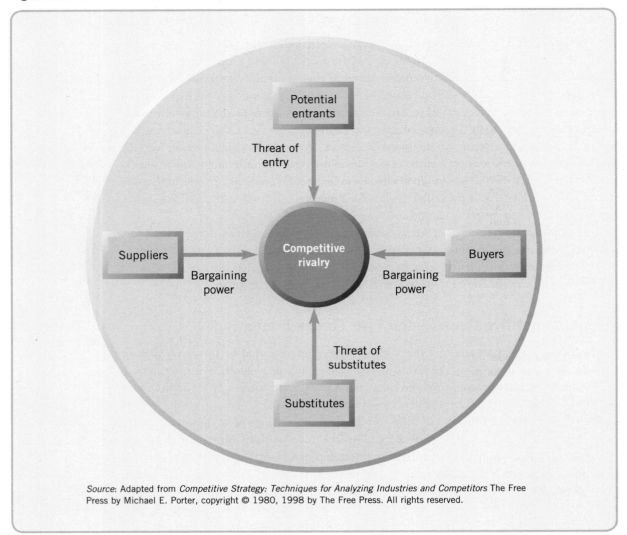

(i.e. not substitutes). In the European airline industry, Air France and British Airways are rivals; high-speed trains are a 'substitute' (see below). Five factors tend to define the extent of rivalry in an industry or market:

- *Competitor balance*. Where competitors are of roughly equal size there is the danger of intensely rivalrous behaviour as one competitor attempts to gain dominance over others, through aggressive price cuts for example. Conversely, less rivalrous industries tend to have one or two dominant organisations, with the smaller players reluctant to challenge the larger ones directly (e.g. by focusing on niches to avoid the 'attention' of the dominant companies).

- *Industry growth rate*. In situations of strong growth, an organisation can grow with the market, but in situations of low growth or decline, any growth is likely to be at the expense of a rival, and meet with fierce resistance. Low-growth markets are therefore often

ILLUSTRATION 2.3

The consolidating steel industry

Five forces analysis helps understand the attractiveness of an industry.

For a long time, the steel industry was seen as a static and unprofitable one. Producers were nationally based, often state-owned and frequently unprofitable – the early 2000s saw 50 independent steel producers going into bankruptcy in the USA alone. But there then followed a surge in confidence. During 2006, Mittal Steel paid $35 bn (€24.5 bn) to buy European steel giant Arcelor, creating the world's largest steel company. The following year, Indian conglomerate Tata bought Anglo-Dutch steel company Corus for $13 bn. But these acquisitions were made just before the onset of the Great Recession in 2008 and further turmoil in the world steel industry.

New entrants

In the last two decades, China has become a major force in the world steel industry. Between the early 1990s and 2011, Chinese producers increased their capacity seven times. Although the Chinese share of world production reached over 45 per cent by 2011, most of this was directed at the domestic market. None the less, China was the word's largest steel exporter in 2011, and there were fears that any slowdown in domestic demand would lead to a surge into international markets. The Chinese companies Herbei and Baosteel are ranked number two and number three in the world.

Substitutes

Steel is a nineteenth-century technology, increasingly substituted for by other materials such as aluminium in cars, plastics and aluminium in packaging and ceramics and composites in many high-tech applications. Steel's own technological advances sometimes work to reduce need: thus steel cans have become about one third thinner over the last few decades.

Buyer power

The major buyers of steel are the global car manufacturers. Car manufacturers are sophisticated users, often leading in the technological development of their materials. In North America at least, the decline of the once dominant 'Big Three' – General Motors, Ford and Chrysler – has meant many new domestic buyers, with companies such as Toyota, Nissan, Honda and BMW establishing local production plants. Another important user of steel is the metal packaging industry. Leading can producers such as Crown Holdings, which makes one third of all food cans produced in North America and Europe, buy in large volumes, coordinating purchases around the world.

Supplier power

The key raw material for steel producers is iron ore. The big three ore producers – Vale, Rio Tinto and BHP Billiton – control about 70 per cent of the market for internationally traded ore. Iron ore prices had multiplied four times between 2005 and 2008, and, despite the recession, were still twice 2005's level in 2012.

Competitive rivalry

World steel production increased by about 50 per cent between 2000 and 2008, dropped about 10 per cent in 2009, before recovering to reach a record in 2012. Despite acquisitions by companies such as Mittal and Tata, the industry is fragmented. The top five producers still accounted for only 17 per cent of world production in 2012, up only 3 per cent since 2000. The world's largest company, ArcelorMittal, accounted for just 7 per cent of production. Over-capacity in the European steel industry was estimated at 25 per cent in 2012, but when ArcelorMittal tried to close down its Florange plant, the French government threatened to nationalise it. After a cyclical peak in 2008, the world steel price was down 40 per cent by 2012, basically the same as in 2005.

Questions

1 How attractive is the world steel industry? What accounts for this?

2 In the future, what might change to make the steel industry less attractive or more attractive?

associated with price competition and low profitability. The *industry life cycle* influences growth rates, and hence competitive conditions: see section 2.3.2.

- *High fixed costs.* Industries with high fixed costs, perhaps because they require high investments in capital equipment or initial research, tend to be highly rivalrous. Companies will seek to spread their costs (i.e. reduce unit costs) by increasing their volumes: to do so, they typically cut their prices, prompting competitors to do the same and thereby triggering price wars in which everyone in the industry suffers. Similarly, if extra capacity can only be added in large increments (as in many manufacturing sectors, for example a chemical or glass factory), the competitor making such an addition is likely to create short-term over-capacity in the industry, leading to increased competition to use capacity.

- *High exit barriers.* The existence of high barriers to exit – in other words, closure or disinvestment – tends to increase rivalry, especially in declining industries. Excess capacity persists and consequently incumbents fight to maintain market share. Exit barriers might be high for a variety of reasons: for example, high redundancy costs or high investment in specific assets such as plant and equipment which others would not buy.

- *Low differentiation.* In a commodity market, where products or services are poorly differentiated, rivalry is increased because there is little to stop customers switching between competitors and the only way to compete is on price.

The threat of entry

How easy it is to enter the industry influences the degree of competition. The greater the threat of entry, the worse it is for incumbents in an industry. An attractive industry has high barriers to entry in order to reduce the threat of new competitors. *Barriers to entry* are the factors that need to be overcome by new entrants if they are to compete in an industry. Five important entry barriers are:

- *Scale and experience.* In some industries, *economies of scale* are extremely important: for example, in the production of automobiles or the advertising of fast-moving consumer goods. Once incumbents have reached large-scale production, it will be very expensive for new entrants to match them and until they reach a similar volume they will have higher unit costs. This scale effect is increased where there are high *investment requirements* for entry, for example research costs in pharmaceuticals or capital equipment costs in automobiles. Barriers to entry also come from *experience curve* effects that give incumbents a cost advantage because they have learnt how to do things more efficiently than an inexperienced new entrant could possibly do (see section 6.3.1). Until the new entrant has built up equivalent experience over time, it will tend to produce at higher cost.

- *Access to supply or distribution channels.* In many industries manufacturers have had control over supply and/or distribution channels. Sometimes this has been through direct ownership (vertical integration), sometimes just through customer or supplier loyalty. In some industries this barrier has been overcome by new entrants who have bypassed retail distributors and sold directly to consumers through e-commerce (e.g. Dell Computers and Amazon).

- *Expected retaliation.* If an organisation considering entering an industry believes that the retaliation of an existing firm will be so great as to prevent entry, or mean that entry would be too costly, this is also a barrier. Retaliation could take the form of a price war or a marketing blitz. Just the knowledge that incumbents are prepared to retaliate is often sufficiently discouraging to act as a barrier.

- *Legislation or government action.* Legal restraints on new entry vary from patent protection (e.g. pharmaceuticals), to regulation of markets (e.g. pension selling), through to direct government action (e.g. tariffs). Of course, organisations are vulnerable to new entrants if governments remove such protection, as has happened with deregulation of the airline industry.

- *Differentiation.* Differentiation means providing a product or service with higher perceived value than the competition; its importance will be discussed more fully in section 6.3.2. Cars are differentiated, for example, by quality and branding. Steel, by contrast, is by and large a commodity, undifferentiated and therefore sold by the tonne. Steel buyers will simply buy the cheapest. Differentiation reduces the threat of entry because of increasing customer loyalty.

The threat of substitutes

Substitutes are products or services that offer a similar benefit to an industry's products or services, but have a different nature. For example, aluminium is a substitute for steel; a tablet computer is a substitute for a laptop; charities can be substitutes for public services. Managers often focus on their competitors in their own industry, and neglect the threat posed by substitutes. Substitutes can reduce demand for a particular type of product as customers switch to alternatives – even to the extent that this type of product or service becomes obsolete. However, there does not have to be much actual switching for the substitute threat to have an effect. The simple risk of substitution puts a cap on the prices that can be charged in an industry. Thus, although Eurostar has no direct competitors in terms of train services from Paris to London, the prices it can charge are ultimately limited by the cost of flights between the two cities.

There are two important points to bear in mind about substitutes:

- *The price/performance ratio* is critical to substitution threats. A substitute is still an effective threat even if more expensive, so long as it offers performance advantages that customers value. Thus aluminium is more expensive than steel, but its relative lightness and its resistance to corrosion give it an advantage in some automobile manufacturing applications. It is the ratio of price to performance that matters, rather than simple price.

- *Extra-industry effects* are the core of the substitution concept. Substitutes come from outside the incumbents' industry and should not be confused with competitors' threats from within the industry. The value of the substitution concept is to force managers to look outside their own industry to consider more distant threats and constraints. The higher the threat of substitution, the less attractive the industry is likely to be.

The power of buyers

Buyers are the organisation's immediate customers, not necessarily the ultimate consumers. If buyers are powerful, then they can demand cheap prices or product or service improvements liable to reduce profits.

Buyer power is likely to be high when some of the following three conditions prevail:

- *Concentrated buyers.* Where a few large customers account for the majority of sales, buyer power is increased. This is the case on items such as milk in the grocery sector in many European countries, where just a few retailers dominate the market. If a product or service accounts for a high percentage of the buyers' total purchases their power is also likely to increase as they are more likely to 'shop around' to get the best price and therefore 'squeeze' suppliers more than they would for more trivial purchases.

● *Low switching costs*. Where buyers can easily switch between one supplier and another, they have a strong negotiating position and can squeeze suppliers who are desperate for their business. Switching costs are typically low for weakly differentiated commodities such as steel.

● *Buyer competition threat*. If the buyer has the capability to supply itself, or if it has the possibility of acquiring such a capability, it tends to be powerful. In negotiation with its suppliers, it can raise the threat of doing the suppliers' job themselves. This is called *backward vertical integration* (see section 7.5), moving back to sources of supply, and might occur if satisfactory prices or quality from suppliers cannot be obtained. For example, some steel companies have gained power over their iron ore suppliers as they have acquired iron ore sources for themselves.

It is very important that *buyers* are distinguished from *ultimate consumers*. Thus for companies like Procter & Gamble or Unilever (makers of shampoo, washing powders and so on), their buyers are retailers such as Carrefour or Tesco, not ordinary consumers. Carrefour and Tesco have much more negotiating power than an ordinary consumer would have. The high buying power of such supermarkets is a strategic issue for the companies supplying them. It is often useful therefore to distinguish '*strategic customers*', powerful buyers (such as the retailers) towards whom the strategy should be primarily orientated. In the public sector, the strategic customer is typically the provider of funds, rather than the consumer of services: for a pharmaceutical company, the strategic customer is the hospital, not the patient.

The power of suppliers

Suppliers are those who supply the organisation with what it needs to produce the product or service. As well as fuel, raw materials and equipment, this can include labour and sources of finance. The factors increasing supplier power are the converse to those for buyer power. Thus *supplier power* is likely to be high where there are:

● *Concentrated suppliers*. Where just a few producers dominate supply, suppliers have more power over buyers. The iron ore industry is now concentrated in the hands of three main producers, leaving the steel companies, still relatively fragmented, in a weak negotiating position for this essential raw material.

● *High switching costs*. If it is expensive or disruptive to move from one supplier to another, then the buyer becomes relatively dependent and correspondingly weak. Microsoft is a powerful supplier because of the high switching costs of moving from one operating system to another. Buyers are prepared to pay a premium to avoid the trouble, and Microsoft knows it.

● *Supplier competition threat*. Suppliers have increased power where they are able to cut out buyers who are acting as intermediaries. Thus airlines have been able to negotiate tough contracts with travel agencies as the rise of online booking has allowed them to create a direct route to customers. This is called *forward vertical integration*, moving up closer to the ultimate customer.

Most organisations have many suppliers, so it is necessary to concentrate the analysis on the most important ones or types. If their power is high, suppliers can capture all their buyers' own potential profits simply by raising their prices. Star football players have succeeded in raising their rewards to astronomical levels, while even the leading football clubs – their 'buyers' – struggle to make money.

Types of industry

Five forces analysis helps to identify four main types of industry structure. In practice, particular industries are typically not pure representatives of these types, but none the less it is helpful to have these broad categories in mind in order to compare the attractiveness of industries and likely broad patterns of competitive behaviour within them. These four types are:

- *Monopolistic industries.* A monopoly is formally an industry with just one firm and therefore no competitive rivalry. Because of the lack of choice between rivals, there is potentially very great power over buyers and suppliers. This can be very profitable. Firms can still have monopolistic power where they are simply the dominant competitor: for example, Google's 66 per cent share of the American search market gives it price-setting power in the internet advertising market. Some industries are monopolistic because of economies of scale: water utility companies are often monopolies in a particular area because it is uneconomic for smaller players to compete. Other industries are monopolistic because of 'network effects', where a product is more valuable because of the number of other people using it: Facebook and Microsoft Office are so powerful precisely because so many friends and colleagues are already users.[10]

- *Oligopolistic industries.* An oligopoly is where just a few firms dominate an industry, with the potential for limited rivalry and great power over buyers and suppliers. The iron ore market is an oligopoly, dominated by Vale, Rio Tinto and BHP Billiton (see Illustration 2.3). Where there are just two oligopolistic rivals, as for Airbus and Boeing in the civil airline industry, the situation is a duopoly. In theory, oligopoly can be highly profitable, but much depends on the extent of rivalrous behaviour, the threat of entry and substitutes and the growth of final demand in key markets. Oligopolistic firms have a strong interest in minimising rivalry between each other so as to maintain a common front against buyers and suppliers.

- *Hypercompetitive industries.* Hypercompetition occurs where the frequency, boldness and aggression of competitor interactions accelerate to create a condition of constant disequilibrium and change.[11] Under hypercompetition, rivals tend to invest heavily in destabilising innovation, expensive marketing initiatives and aggressive price cuts, with negative impacts on profits. Hypercompetition often breaks out in otherwise oligopolistic industries. Thus the global mobile phone industry has some oligopolistic characteristics, with Nokia holding 27 per cent market share, Samsung 23 per cent and Apple 9 per cent in 2012. However, the industry is very dynamic: Apple only entered the industry in 2007, and Nokia has lost around 8 per cent of the market since then. Competitive moves under conditions of hypercompetition are discussed in section 6.4.2.

- *Perfectly competitive industries.* Perfect competition exists where barriers to entry are low, there are many equal rivals each with very similar products, and information about competitors is freely available. Few markets are absolutely perfectly competitive, but many are highly so. In these conditions, firms are unable to earn more profit than the bare minimum required to survive. Competition focuses heavily on price, because competitors typically cannot fund major innovations or marketing initiatives. Minicab services in large cities often come close to perfect competition. Entrepreneurs should beware entering industries with low barriers to entry, as these are liable to be perfectly or highly competitive and good profits will be very hard to earn.

Implications of Five Forces analysis

The Five Forces Framework provides useful insights into the forces at work in the industry or market environment of an organisation. It is important, however, to use the framework for more than simply listing the forces. The bottom line is an assessment of the *attractiveness* of the industry. The analysis should conclude with a judgement about whether the industry is a good one to compete in or not. Here it is important to note that just one significantly adverse force can be enough to undermine the attractiveness of the industry as a whole. For example, powerful buyers can extract all the potential profits of an otherwise attractive industry structure by forcing down prices.

The analysis should next prompt investigation of the *implications* of these forces, for example:

- *Which industries to enter (or leave)?* The fundamental purpose of the five forces model is to identify the relative attractiveness of different industries: industries are attractive when the forces are weak. Entrepreneurs and managers should invest in industries where the five forces work in their favour and avoid, or disinvest from, markets where they are strongly against. Entrepreneurs sometimes choose markets because entry barriers are low: unless barriers are likely to rise quickly, this is precisely the wrong reason to enter.

- *What influence can be exerted?* Industry structures are not necessarily fixed, but can be influenced by deliberate managerial strategies. For example, organisations can build barriers to entry by increasing advertising spend to improve customer loyalty. They can buy up competitors to reduce rivalry and to increase power over suppliers or buyers. Influencing industry structure involves many issues relating to *competitive strategy* and will be a major concern of Chapter 6.

- *How are competitors differently affected?* Not all competitors will be affected equally by changes in industry structure, deliberate or spontaneous. If barriers are rising because of increased R&D or advertising spending, smaller players in the industry may not be able to keep up with the larger players, and be squeezed out. Similarly, growing buyer power is likely to hurt small competitors most. Strategic group analysis is helpful here (see section 2.4.1).

Although originating in the private sector, five forces analysis can have important implications for organisations in the public sector too. For example, the forces can be used to adjust the service offer or focus on key issues. Thus it might be worth switching managerial initiative from an arena with many crowded and overlapping services (e.g. social work, probation services and education) to one that is less rivalrous and where the organisation can do something more distinctive. Similarly, strategies could be launched to reduce dependence on particularly powerful and expensive suppliers, for example energy sources or high-shortage skills.

Key issues in using the five forces framework

The five forces framework has to be used carefully and is not necessarily complete, even at the industry level. When using this framework, it is important to bear the following three issues in mind:

- *Defining the 'right' industry.* Most industries can be analysed at different levels, for example different markets and even different segments within them (see section 2.4.2 below). For example, the airline industry has different geographical markets (Europe, China and so on) and it also has different segments within each market (e.g. leisure, business and freight). The competitive forces are likely to be different for each of these markets and segments and can be analysed separately. It is sometimes useful to conduct industry analysis at a dis-aggregated level, for each distinct segment or market. The overall picture for the industry as a whole can then be assembled, while particular market or segment opportunities can be highlighted.

- *Converging industries.* Industry definition is often difficult too because industry boundaries are continuously changing. For example, many industries, especially in high-tech arenas, are converging. Convergence is where previously separate industries begin to overlap or merge in terms of activities, technologies, products and customers.[12] Technological change has brought convergence between the telephone and photographic industries, for example, as mobile phones have come to include camera and video functions. The camera company Kodak was driven into bankruptcy by mobile phone producers such as Apple and Samsung.

- *Complementary organisations.* Some analysts argue that industry analyses need to include a 'sixth force', the existence of organisations that are complementors rather than simple competitors. **An organisation is your complementor if it enhances your business attractiveness to customers or suppliers.**[13] Thus McAfee computer security is a complement to Microsoft because its Windows software is more attractive to customers when protected. Even competing airline companies can be complementary to each other because for a supplier like Boeing it is more attractive to invest in particular improvements for two customers rather than one. Complementarity implies a significant shift in perspective. While Porter's Five Forces sees organisations as battling against each other for share of industry value, complementors may *cooperate* to increase the total value available.[14] If Microsoft and McAfee keep each other in touch with their technological developments, they increase the value of both their products. Opportunities for cooperation can be seen through a **value net: a map of organisations in a business environment demonstrating opportunities for value-creating cooperation as well as competition.** In Figure 2.5, (p. 51) Sony is a complementor, supplier and competitor to Apple's iPod. Sony and Apple have an interest in cooperating as well as competing.

2.3.2 The dynamics of industry structure

Industry structure analysis can easily become too static: after all, structure implies stability.[15] However, the previous sections have raised the issue of how competitive forces change *over time*. The key drivers for change are likely to alter industry structures and scenario analyses can be used to understand possible impacts. An illustration of changing industry structure, and the competitive implications of this, is provided by Illustration 2.4 on the UK charity sector. This section examines two additional approaches to understanding change in industry structure: the *industry life-cycle* concept and *comparative five forces analyses*.

The industry life cycle

The power of the five forces typically varies with the stages of the industry life cycle. The industry life-cycle concept proposes that industries start small in their development stage, then go through a period of rapid growth (the equivalent to 'adolescence' in the human life cycle), culminating in a period of 'shake-out'. The final two stages are first a period of slow or even zero growth ('maturity'), and then the final stage of decline ('old age'). Each of these stages has implications for the five forces.[16]

The *development stage* is an experimental one, typically with few players, little direct rivalry and highly differentiated products. The five forces are likely to be weak, therefore, though

ILLUSTRATION 2.4

Chugging and the structure of the charity sector

Industry structure contributes to inefficiency and aggression in the United Kingdom's charity sector.

The charity sector has become controversial in the United Kingdom. The aggressive fund-raising of some charities is epitomised by workers soliciting donations from shoppers on a commission basis. Such is their perceived aggression that these charity workers are known as 'chuggers', compared with the violent street-crime of 'muggers'.

In 2008, there were 189,000 charities registered in England and Wales, 95 per cent having annual incomes of less than £500,000. However, about 80 per cent of all charity income is raised by the largest 20 charities, headed by Cancer Research UK (2008 income, £355 m (~€390 m; ~$532 m)). According to *Charity Market Monitor*, in 2008, the top 300 charities averaged a 0.9 per cent increase in income, but the largest 10 managed income growth of 2.3 per cent (excluding impact of mergers).

The United Kingdom government introduced the 2006 Charities Act with the specific intention of assisting mergers between independent charities. This had followed a report of the Charity Commission, the regulator for charities in England and Wales, which had commented on the charity sector thus:

'Some people believe that there are too many charities competing for too few funds and that a significant amount of charitable resource could be saved if more charities pooled their resources and worked together ... The majority of charities are relatively small, local organisations that rely entirely on the unpaid help of their trustees and other volunteers. They may have similar purposes to many other charities but they are all serving different communities. The nature of these charities suggests that there are less likely to be significant areas of overlap ... It is the much larger, professionally run, charities which, because of their size, tend to face charges of duplication, waste and over-aggressive fund-raising. While there are some clear advantages to be had from a healthy plurality of charities, which are constantly refreshed by new charities pursuing new activities, there are also big benefits of public confidence and support to be had from showing collaborative, as opposed to over-competitive, instincts.'

Local authorities in particular were frustrated by duplication and waste, as they increasingly commission local charities to deliver services. With respect to small charities, local authority budgets are relatively large. One charity sector chief executive, Caroline Shaw, told *Charity Times* as she pursued more cooperation between local charities:

'Without a doubt there is increased competition when it comes to [local authority] commissioning ... Our driving force has really been to try to create a more effective service for front line organisations; to offer more projects, more diverse services, more effective services. There's a huge amount [of charities] all fighting for funding. I really think that people should be looking at working more closely together.'

During 2008, more than 230 charity mergers were registered with the Charity Commission. As the recession began to put pressure on charitable donations throughout the sector, early 2009 saw the merger of two well-established charities helping the elderly in the United Kingdom, Help the Aged and Age Concern. The new charity, Age UK, has a combined income of around £160 million, including £47 million a year raised through fund-raising, and over 520 charity shops.

Sources: 'RS 4a – Collaborative working and mergers: Summary', http://www.charity-commission.gov.uk/publications/rs4a.asp; *Charity Times*, 'Strength in Numbers', August 2007; *Charity Market Monitor*, 2009.

Questions

1 Which of Porter's five forces are creating problems for the United Kingdom's charity sector?

2 What type of industry structure might the charity industry be moving towards? What would be the benefits and disadvantages of that structure?

Figure 2.5 The value net

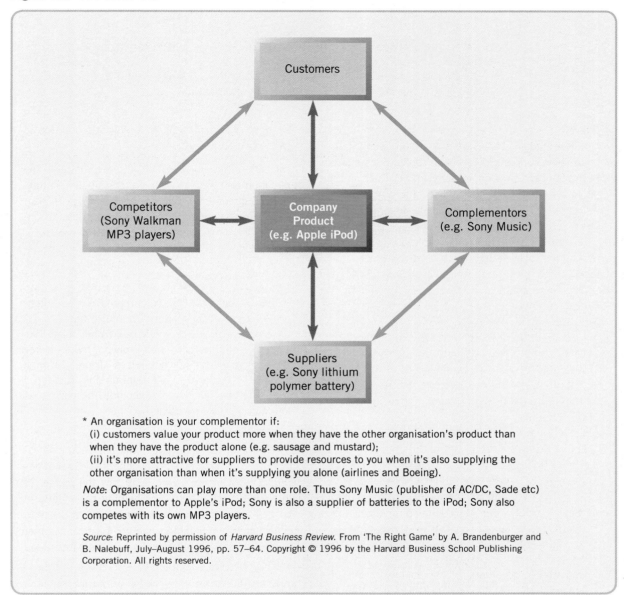

* An organisation is your complementor if:
  (i) customers value your product more when they have the other organisation's product than when they have the product alone (e.g. sausage and mustard);
  (ii) it's more attractive for suppliers to provide resources to you when it's also supplying the other organisation than when it's supplying you alone (airlines and Boeing).

Note: Organisations can play more than one role. Thus Sony Music (publisher of AC/DC, Sade etc) is a complementor to Apple's iPod; Sony is also a supplier of batteries to the iPod; Sony also competes with its own MP3 players.

Source: Reprinted by permission of *Harvard Business Review*. From 'The Right Game' by A. Brandenburger and B. Nalebuff, July–August 1996, pp. 57–64. Copyright © 1996 by the Harvard Business School Publishing Corporation. All rights reserved.

profits may actually be scarce because of high investment requirements. The next stage is one of *high growth*, with rivalry low as there is plenty of market opportunity for everybody. Low rivalry and keen buyers of the new product favour profits at this stage, but these are not certain. Barriers to entry may still be low in the growth stage, as existing competitors have not built up much scale, experience or customer loyalty. Suppliers can be powerful too if there is a shortage of components or materials that fast-growing businesses need for expansion. The *shake-out stage* begins as the market becomes increasingly saturated and cluttered with competitors. Profits are variable, as increased rivalry forces the weakest competitors out of the business. In the *maturity stage*, barriers to entry tend to increase, as control over distribution is established and economies of scale and experience curve benefits come into play. Products or

Figure 2.6 The industry life cycle

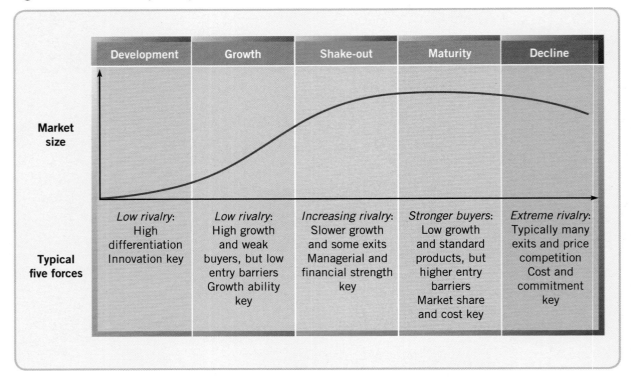

Development	Growth	Shake-out	Maturity	Decline

Market size

Typical five forces

| *Low rivalry*: High differentiation Innovation key | *Low rivalry*: High growth and weak buyers, but low entry barriers Growth ability key | *Increasing rivalry*: Slower growth and some exits Managerial and financial strength key | *Stronger buyers*: Low growth and standard products, but higher entry barriers Market share and cost key | *Extreme rivalry*: Typically many exits and price competition Cost and commitment key |

services tend to standardise, with relative price becoming key. Buyers may become more powerful as they become less avid for the industry's products and more confident in switching between suppliers. Profitability at the maturity stage relies on high market share, providing leverage against buyers and competitive advantage in terms of cost. Finally, the *decline stage* can be a period of extreme rivalry, especially where there are high exit barriers, as falling sales force remaining competitors into dog-eat-dog competition. However, survivors in the decline stage may still be profitable if competitor exit leaves them in a monopolistic position. Figure 2.6 summarises some of the conditions that can be expected at different stages in the life cycle.

It is important to avoid putting too much faith in the inevitability of life-cycle stages. One stage does not follow predictably after another: industries vary widely in the length of their growth stages, and others can rapidly 'de-mature' through radical innovation. Thus the telephony industry, based for nearly a century on fixed-line telephones, rejuvenated rapidly with the introduction of mobile and internet telephony. Anita McGahan of Toronto University warns of the 'maturity mindset', which can leave many managers complacent and slow to respond to new competition.[17] Managing in mature industries is not necessarily just about waiting for decline. However, even if the various stages are not inevitable, the life-cycle concept does remind managers that conditions are likely to change over time. Especially in fast-moving industries, five forces analyses need to be reviewed quite regularly.

Comparative industry structure analyses

The industry life cycle underlines the need to make industry structure analysis dynamic. One effective means of doing this is to compare the five forces over time in a simple 'radar plot'.

Figure 2.7 Comparative industry structure analysis

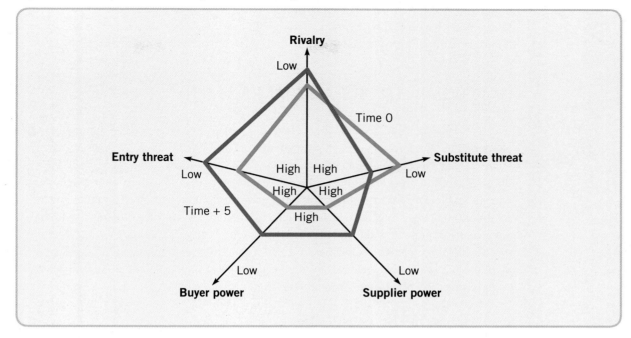

Figure 2.7 provides a framework for summarising the power of each of the five forces on five axes. Power diminishes as the axes go outwards. Where the forces are low, the total area enclosed by the lines between the axes is large; where the forces are high, the total area enclosed by the lines is small. The larger the enclosed area, therefore, the greater is the profit potential. In Figure 2.7, the industry at Time 0 (represented by the light blue lines) has relatively low rivalry (just a few competitors) and faces low substitution threats. The threat of entry is moderate, but both buyer power and supplier power are relatively high. Overall, this looks like only a moderately attractive industry to invest in.

However, given the dynamic nature of industries, managers need to look forward, perhaps using scenario analysis. Figure 2.7 represents five years forward by the dark blue lines. Managers are predicting in this case some rise in the threat of substitutes (perhaps new technologies will be developed). On the other hand, they predict a falling entry threat, while both buyer power and supplier power will be easing. Rivalry will reduce still further. This looks like a classic case of an industry in which a few players emerge with overall dominance. The area enclosed by the blue lines is large, suggesting a relatively attractive industry. For a firm confident of becoming one of the dominant players, this might be an industry well worth investing in.

Comparing the five forces over time on a radar plot thus helps to give industry structure analysis a dynamic aspect. Similar plots can be made to aid diversification decisions (see Chapter 7), where possible new industries to enter can be compared in terms of attractiveness. The lines are only approximate, of course, because they aggregate the many individual elements that make up each of the forces into a simple composite measure. Notice too that if one of the forces is very adverse, then this might nullify positive assessments on the other four axes:

for example, an industry with low rivalry, low substitution, low entry barriers and low supplier power might still be unattractive if powerful buyers were able to demand highly discounted prices. With these warnings in mind, such radar plots can none the less be both a useful device for initial analysis and an effective summary of a final, more refined analysis.

(2.4) COMPETITORS AND MARKETS

An industry or sector may be too high a level to provide for a detailed understanding of competition. The five forces can impact differently on different kinds of players. For example, Hyundai and Porsche may be in the same broad industry (automobiles), but they are positioned differently: they are protected by different barriers to entry and competitive moves by one are unlikely to affect the other. It is often useful to disaggregate. Many industries contain a range of companies, each of which has different capabilities and competes on different bases. Some of these competitor differences are captured by the concept of *strategic groups*. Customers too can differ significantly and these can be captured by distinguishing between different *market segments*. Thinking in terms of different strategic groups and market segments provides opportunities for organisations to develop highly distinctive positionings within broader industries. Competitor differences, both actual and potential, can also be analysed using the strategy canvas and '*Blue Ocean*' thinking, the last topic in this section.

2.4.1 Strategic groups[18]

Strategic groups are organisations within an industry or sector with similar strategic characteristics, following similar strategies or competing on similar bases. These characteristics are different from those in other strategic groups in the same industry or sector. For example, in the grocery retailing industry, supermarkets, convenience stores and corner shops each form different strategic groups. There are many different characteristics that distinguish between strategic groups but these can be grouped into two major categories (see Figure 2.8).[19] First, the *scope* of an organisation's activities (such as product range, geographical coverage and range of distribution channels used). Second, the *resource commitment* (such as brands, marketing spend and extent of vertical integration). Which characteristics are relevant differs from industry to industry, but typically important are those characteristics that separate high performers from low performers.

Strategic groups can be mapped onto two-dimensional charts – for example, one axis might be the extent of product range and the other axis the size of marketing spend. One method for choosing key dimensions by which to map strategic groups is to identify top performers (by growth or profitability) in an industry and to compare them with low performers. Characteristics that are shared by top performers, but not by low performers, are likely to be particularly relevant for mapping strategic groups. For example, the most profitable firms in an industry might all be narrow in terms of product range, and lavish in terms of marketing spend, while the less profitable firms might be more widely spread in terms of products and restrained in their marketing. Here the two dimensions for mapping would be product range and marketing spend. A potential recommendation for the less profitable firms would be to cut back their product range and boost their marketing.

Figure 2.9 shows strategic groups among Indian pharmaceutical companies, with research and development intensity (R&D spend as a percentage of sales) and overseas focus (exports

Figure 2.8 Some characteristics for identifying strategic groups

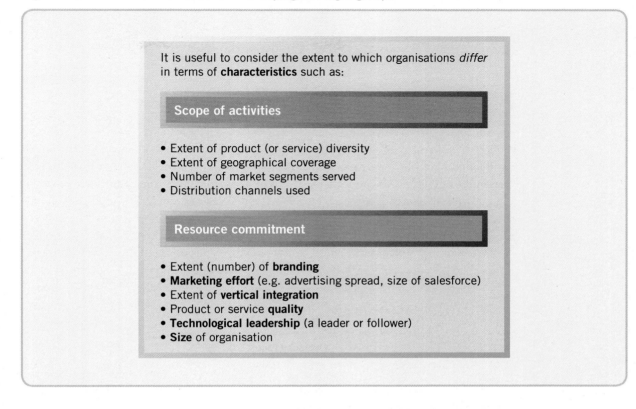

It is useful to consider the extent to which organisations *differ* in terms of **characteristics** such as:

Scope of activities

- Extent of product (or service) diversity
- Extent of geographical coverage
- Number of market segments served
- Distribution channels used

Resource commitment

- Extent (number) of **branding**
- **Marketing effort** (e.g. advertising spread, size of salesforce)
- Extent of **vertical integration**
- Product or service **quality**
- **Technological leadership** (a leader or follower)
- **Size** of organisation

and patents registered overseas) defining the axes of the map. These two axes do explain a good deal of the variation in profitability between groups. The most profitable group is the Emergent globals (11.3 per cent average return on sales), those with high R&D intensity and high overseas focus. On the other hand, the Exploiter group spends little on R&D and is focused on domestic markets, and only enjoys 2.0 per cent average return on sales.

This strategic group concept is useful in at least three ways:

- *Understanding competition.* Managers can focus on their direct competitors within their particular strategic group, rather than the whole industry. They can also establish the dimensions that distinguish them most from other groups, and which might be the basis for relative success or failure. These dimensions can then become the focus of their action.

- *Analysis of strategic opportunities.* Strategic group maps can identify the most attractive 'strategic spaces' within an industry. Some spaces on the map may be 'white spaces', relatively under-occupied. In the Indian pharmaceutical industry, the white space is high R&D investment combined with focus on domestic markets. Such white spaces might be unexploited opportunities. On the other hand, they could turn out to be 'black holes', impossible to exploit and likely to damage any entrant. A strategic group map is only the first stage of the analysis. Strategic spaces need to tested carefully.

- *Analysis of mobility barriers.* Of course, moving across the map to take advantage of opportunities is not costless. Often it will require difficult decisions and rare resources. Strategic groups are therefore characterised by 'mobility barriers', obstacles to movement from one strategic group to another. These are similar to barriers to entry in five forces analysis.

Figure 2.9 Strategic groups in the Indian pharmaceutical industry

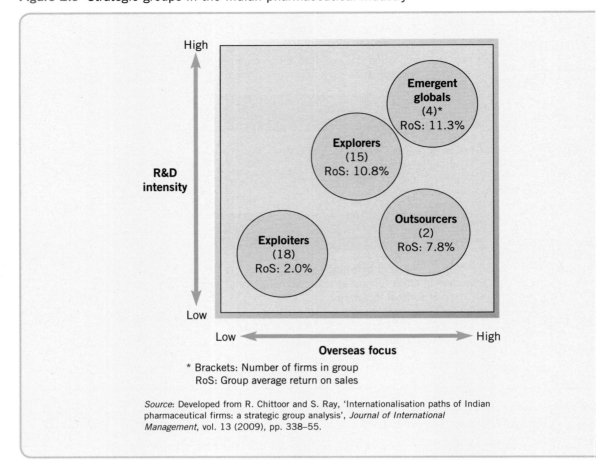

* Brackets: Number of firms in group
  RoS: Group average return on sales

Source: Developed from R. Chittoor and S. Ray, 'Internationalisation paths of Indian pharmaceutical firms: a strategic group analysis', *Journal of International Management*, vol. 13 (2009), pp. 338–55.

Although movement from the Exploiter group in Indian pharmaceuticals to the Emergent global group might seem very attractive in terms of profits, it is likely to demand very substantial financial investment and strong managerial skills. Mobility into the Emergent global group will not be easy. As with barriers to entry, it is good to be in a successful strategic group protected by strong mobility barriers, to impede imitation.

2.4.2 Market segments

The concept of strategic groups discussed above helps with understanding the similarities and differences in terms of competitor characteristics. The concept of market segment focuses on differences in *customer* needs. A **market segment**[20] **is a group of customers who have similar needs that are different from customer needs in other parts of the market.** Where these customer groups are relatively small, such market segments are often called 'niches'. Dominance of a market segment or niche can be very valuable, for the same reasons that dominance of an industry can be valuable following five forces reasoning.

For long-term success, strategies based on market segments must keep customer needs firmly in mind. Two issues are particularly important in market segment analysis, therefore:

Table 2.1 Some bases of market segmentation

Type of factor	Consumer markets	Industrial/organisational markets
Characteristics of people/organisations	Age, gender, ethnicity Income Family size Life-cycle stage Location Lifestyle	Industry Location Size Technology Profitability Management
Purchase/use situation	Size of purchase Brand loyalty Purpose of use Purchasing behaviour Importance of purchase Choice criteria	Application Importance of purchase Volume Frequency of purchase Purchasing procedure Choice criteria Distribution channel
Users' needs and preferences for product characteristics	Product similarity Price preference Brand preferences Desired features Quality	Performance requirements Assistance from suppliers Brand preferences Desired features Quality Service requirements

- *Variation in customer needs.* Focusing on customer needs that are highly distinctive from those typical in the market is one means of building a long-term segment strategy. Customer needs vary for a whole variety of reasons – some of which are identified in Table 2.1. Theoretically, any of these factors could be used to identify distinct market segments. However, the crucial bases of segmentation vary according to market. In industrial markets, segmentation is often thought of in terms of industrial classification of buyers: steel producers might segment by automobile industry, packaging industry and construction industry, for example. On the other hand, segmentation by buyer behaviour (e.g. direct buying versus those users who buy through third parties such as contractors) or purchase value (e.g. high-value bulk purchasers versus frequent low-value purchasers) might be more appropriate. Being able to serve a highly distinctive segment that other organisations find difficult to serve is often the basis for a secure long-term strategy.

- *Specialisation* within a market segment can also be an important basis for a successful segmentation strategy. This is sometimes called a 'niche strategy'. Organisations that have built up most experience in servicing a particular market segment should not only have lower costs in so doing, but also have built relationships which may be difficult for others to break down. Experience and relationships are likely to protect a dominant position in a particular segment. However, precisely because customers value different things in different segments, specialised producers may find it very difficult to compete on a broader basis. For example, a small local brewery competing against the big brands on the basis of its ability to satisfy distinctive local tastes is unlikely to find it easy to serve other segments where tastes are different, scale requirements are larger and distribution channels are more complex.

2.4.3 **Competitor analysis and 'Blue Oceans'**

Any environmental analysis should also include an understanding of competitors. As Michael Porter's five forces framework underlines, reducing industry rivalry involves competitors finding differentiated positions in the marketplace. W. Chan Kim and Renée Mauborgne at INSEAD propose two concepts that help think about the relative positioning of competitors in the environment: the strategy canvas and 'Blue Oceans'.

A strategy canvas **compares competitors according to their performance on key success factors in order to establish the extent of differentiation.** Figure 2.10 shows a strategy canvas for three electrical components companies. The canvas highlights the following three features:

- Critical success factors (*CSFs*) are those factors that either are particularly valued by customers (i.e. strategic customers) or provide a significant advantage in terms of cost. Critical success factors are therefore likely to be an important source of competitive advantage or disadvantage. Figure 2.10 identifies five established critical success factors in this electrical components market (cost, after-sales service, delivery reliability, technical quality and testing facilities). Note there is also a new sixth critical success factor, design advisory services, which will be discussed under the third subhead, value innovation.

- *Value curves* are a graphic depiction of how customers perceive competitors' relative performance across the critical success factors. In Figure 2.10, companies A and B perform well on cost, service, reliability and quality, but less well on testing. They do not offer any design advice. They are poorly differentiated and occupy a space in the market where profits may be hard to get because of excessive rivalry between the two. Company C, on the other hand, has a radically different value curve, characteristic of a 'value innovator'.

Figure 2.10 Strategy canvas for electrical components companies

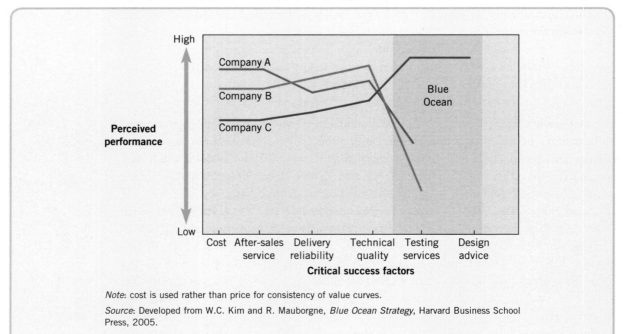

Note: cost is used rather than price for consistency of value curves.

Source: Developed from W.C. Kim and R. Mauborgne, *Blue Ocean Strategy*, Harvard Business School Press, 2005.

- *Value innovation* is the creation of new market space by excelling on established critical success factors on which competitors are performing badly and/or by creating new critical success factors representing previously unrecognised customer wants. Thus in Figure 2.10, company C is a value innovator in both senses. First, it excels on the established customer need of offering testing facilities for customers' products using its components. Second, it offers a new and valued design service advising customers on how to integrate their components in order for them to create better products.

A value innovator is a company that competes in 'Blue Oceans'. Blue Oceans **are new market spaces where competition is minimised.**[21] Blue Oceans contrast with 'Red Oceans', where industries are already well defined and rivalry is intense. Blue Oceans evoke wide empty seas. Red Oceans are associated with bloody competition and 'red ink', in other words financial losses. The Blue Ocean concept is thus useful for identifying potential spaces in the environment with little competition. These Blue Oceans are *strategic gaps* in the marketplace.

In Figure 2.10, company C's strategy exemplifies two critical principles of Blue Ocean thinking: *focus* and *divergence*. First, company C focuses its efforts on just two factors, testing and design services, while maintaining only adequate performance on the other critical success factors where its competitors are already high performers. Second, it has created a value curve that significantly diverges from its competitors' value curves, creating a substantial *strategic gap*, or Blue Ocean, in the areas of testing and design services. This is shrewd. For company C, beating companies A and B in the areas where they are performing well anyway would require major investment and likely provide little advantage given that customers are already highly satisfied. Challenging A and B on cost, after-sales service, delivery or quality would be a Red Ocean strategy, increasing industry rivalry. Far better is to concentrate on where a large gap can be created between competitors. Company C faces little competition for those customers who really value testing and design services, and consequently can charge good prices for them. The task for companies A and B now is to find strategic gaps of their own.

(2.5) OPPORTUNITIES AND THREATS

The concepts and frameworks discussed above should be helpful in understanding the factors in the macro-, industry and competitor/market environments of an organisation (see the Key Debate: just how much do such industry and market factors affect successful strategic outcomes?). However, the critical issue is the *implications* that are drawn from this understanding in guiding strategic decisions and choices. The crucial next stage, therefore, is to draw from the environmental analysis specific strategic opportunities and threats for the organisation. Identifying these opportunities and threats is extremely valuable when thinking about strategic choices for the future (the subject of Chapters 6 to 10). Opportunities and threats form one half of the Strengths, Weaknesses, Opportunities and Threats (SWOT) analyses that shape many companies' strategy formulation (see section 3.4.4). In responding strategically to the environment, the goal is to reduce identified threats and take advantage of the best opportunities.

The techniques and concepts in this chapter should help in identifying environmental threats and opportunities, for instance:

KEY DEBATE

How much does industry matter?

A good start in strategy must be to choose a profitable industry to compete in. But does simply being in the right industry matter more than having the right kinds of skills and resources?

This chapter has focused on the role of the environment in strategy making, with particular regard to industries. But the importance of industries in determining organisational performance has been challenged in recent years. This has led to a debate about whether strategy making should be externally orientated, starting with the environment, or internally orientated, starting with the organisation's own skills and resources (the focus of Chapter 3).

Managers favouring an external approach look primarily *outside* the organisation, for example building market share in their industries through mergers and acquisitions or aggressive marketing. Managers favouring an internal approach concentrate their attention *inside* the organisation, fostering the skills of their people or nurturing technologies, for example. Because managerial time is limited, there is a real trade-off to be made between external and internal approaches.

The chief advocate of the external approach is Michael Porter, Professor at Harvard Business School and founder of the Monitor Consulting Group. An influential sceptic of this approach is Richard Rumelt, a student at Harvard Business School but now at University of California Los Angeles. Porter, Rumelt and others have done a series of empirical studies examining the relative importance of industries in explaining organisations' performance.

Typically, these studies take a large sample of firms and compare the extent to which variance in profitability is due to firms or industries (controlling for other effects such as size). If firms within the same industry tend to bunch together in terms of profitability, it is industry that is accounting for the greater proportion of profitability: an external approach to strategy is supported. If firms within the same industry vary widely in terms of profitability, it is the specific skills and resources of the firms that matter most: an internal approach is most appropriate.

The two most important studies in fact find that more of the variance in profitability is due to firms rather than industries – firms account for 47 per cent in Rumelt's study of manufacturing (see the figure). However, when Porter and McGahan included service industries as well as manufacturing, they found a larger industry effect (19 per cent).

Per cent of variance in profitability due to:

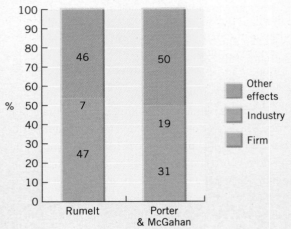

The implication from this work is that firm-specific factors generally influence profitability more than industry factors. Firms need to attend carefully to their own skills and resources. However, the greater industry effect found in Porter and McGahan's study of both manufacturing and services suggests that industry's importance varies strongly by industry. External influences can matter more in some industries than others.

Sources: R.P. Rumelt, 'How much does industry matter?', *Strategic Management Journal*, vol. 12, no. 2 (1991), pp. 167–85; M.E. Porter and A.M. McGahan, 'How much does industry matter really?', *Strategic Management Journal*, vol. 18, Summer Special Issue (1997), pp. 15–30; M.E. Porter and A.M. McGahan, 'The emergence and sustainability of abnormal profits', *Strategic Organisation*, vol. 1, no. 1 (2003), pp. 79–108.

Questions

1 Why might some industries have a larger influence on their members' profitability than others?

2 What other factors might account for business unit profitability?

- *PESTEL analysis* of the macro-environment might reveal threats and opportunities presented by technological change, or shifts in market demographics or such like factors.

- Identification of *key drivers for change* can help generate different scenarios for managerial discussion, some more threatening, others more favourable.

- *Porter's five forces analysis* might, for example, identify a rise or fall in barriers to entry, or opportunities to reduce industry rivalry, perhaps by acquisition of competitors.

- *Blue Ocean* thinking might reveal where companies can create new market spaces; alternatively it could help identify success factors which new entrants might attack in order to turn 'Blue Oceans' into 'Red Oceans'.

While all these techniques and concepts are important tools for understanding environments, it is important to recognise that any analysis is likely to be somewhat subjective. Entrepreneurs and managers often have particular blinkers with regard to what they see and prioritise. Techniques and concepts can be helpful in challenging existing assumptions and encouraging broader perspectives, but they are unlikely to overcome human subjectivity and biases completely.

SUMMARY

- Environmental influences can be thought of as layers around an organisation, with the outer layer making up the *macro-environment*, the middle layer making up the *industry or sector* and the inner layer *strategic groups* and *market segments*.

- The macro-environment can be analysed in terms of *PESTEL factors*, from which *key drivers of change* can be identified. Alternative *scenarios* about the future can be constructed according to how the key drivers develop.

- Industries and sectors can be analysed in terms of *Porter's five forces* – barriers to entry, substitutes, buyer power, supplier power and rivalry. Together, these determine industry or sector attractiveness.

- Industries and sectors are dynamic, and their changes can be analysed in terms of the *industry life cycle* and *comparative five forces radar plots*. In the inner layer of the environment, *strategic group* analysis, *market segment* analysis and the *strategy canvas* can help identify strategic gaps or opportunities.

- *Blue Ocean* strategies are a means of avoiding *Red Ocean*s with many similar rivals and low profitability.

VIDEO ASSIGNMENTS

Visit *MyStrategyLab* and watch the Nationwide and Pearson case study for Chapter 2.

1 Using the PESTEL framework as a starting point, discuss the main elements of the external environment that shape strategy at the Nationwide Building Society.

2 How is the nature of Pearson's competitors likely to change with the evolving nature of the textbook industry, and what critical success factors are likely to become important?

WORK ASSIGNMENTS

✽ *Denotes more advanced work assignments.*
* *Refers to a case study in the Text and Cases edition.*

2.1 For an organisation of your choice carry out a PESTEL analysis and identify key drivers for change. Use Illustration 2.1 as a model.

2.2✽ For the same organisation as in 2.1, and using Illustration 2.2 as a model, construct four scenarios for the evolution of its environment. What implications are there for the organisation's strategy?

2.3 Drawing on section 2.3, carry out a five forces analysis of the pharmaceutical industry* or Vodafone's position in the mobile phone industry*. What do you conclude about that industry's attractiveness?

2.4✽ Drawing on section 2.3, and particularly using the radar plot technique of Figure 2.7, choose two industries or sectors and compare their attractiveness in terms of the five forces (a) today; (b) in approximately three to five years' time. Justify your assessment of each of the five forces' strengths. Which industry or sector would you invest in?

2.5 With regard to section 2.4.1 and Figure 2.8, identify an industry (e.g. the motor industry or clothing retailers) and, by comparing competitors, map out the main strategic groups in the industry according to key strategic dimensions. Try more than one set of key strategic dimensions to map the industry. Do the resulting maps identify any under-exploited opportunities in the industry?

2.6✽ Drawing on section 2.4.3, and particularly on Figure 2.10, identify critical success factors for an industry with which you and your peers are familiar (e.g. clothing retailers or mobile phone companies). Using your own estimates (or those of your peers), construct a strategy canvas comparing the main competitors, as in Figure 2.10. What implications does your strategy canvas have for the strategies of these competitors?

Integrative assignment

2.7 Carry out a full analysis of an industry or sector of your choice (using for example PESTEL, scenarios, five forces and strategic groups). Consider explicitly how the industry or sector is affected by globalisation (see Chapter 8, particularly Figure 8.2 on drivers) and innovation (see Chapter 9, particularly Figure 9.2 on product and process innovation).

RECOMMENDED KEY READINGS

● The classic book on the analysis of industries is M.E. Porter, *Competitive Strategy*, Free Press, 1980. An updated view is available in M.E. Porter, 'The five competitive forces that shape strategy', *Harvard Business Review*, vol. 86, no. 1 (2008), pp. 58–77. An influential development on Porter's basic ideas is W.C. Kim and R. Mauborgne, *Blue Ocean Strategy: How to Create Uncontested Market Space and Make Competition Irrelevant*, Harvard Business School Press, 2005.

● For approaches to how environments change, see K. van der Heijden, *Scenarios: The Art of Strategic Conversation*, 2nd edn, Wiley, 2005, and the work of Michael Porter's colleague, A. McGahan, *How Industries Evolve*, Harvard Business School Press, 2004.

● A collection of academic articles on PEST, scenarios and similar is in the special issue of *International Studies of Management and Organisation*, vol. 36, no. 3 (2006), edited by Peter McKiernan.

REFERENCES

1. PESTEL is an extension of PEST (Politics, Economics, Social and Technology) analysis, taking more account of ecological and legal issues. PEST is sometimes called STEP analysis. PESTEL is sometimes called PESTLE and is also sometimes extended to STEEPLE in order to include Ethical issues. For an application of PEST analysis to the world of business schools, see H. Thomas, 'An analysis of the environment and competitive dynamics of management education', *Journal of Management Development*, vol. 26, no. 1 (2007), pp. 9–21.

2. D. Bach and D. Allen, 'What every CEO needs to know about nonmarket strategies', *Sloan Management Review*, vol. 51, no. 3 (2010), pp. 41–8; and J. Doh, T. Lawton and T. Rajwani, 'Advancing nonmarket strategy research: institutional perspectives in a changing world', *Academy of Management Perspectives*, August (2012), pp. 22–38.

3. R.A. Slaughter, 'Looking for the real megatrends', *Futures*, October (1993), pp. 823–49.

4. A. Grove, *Only the Paranoid Survive*, Profile Books, 1998.

5. S. Mendonca, G. Caroso and J. Caraca, 'The strategic strength of weak signals', *Futures*, 44 (2012), pp. 218–28; and P. Schoemaker and G. Day, 'How to make sense of weak signals', *Sloan Management Review*, vol. 50, no. 3 (2009), pp. 81–9.

6. For a discussion of scenario planning in practice, see R. Ramirez, R. Osterman and D. Gronquist, 'Scenarios and early warnings as dynamic capabilities to frame managerial attention', *Technological Forecasting and Strategic Change*, vol. 80 (2013), pp. 825–38. For how scenario planning fits with other forms of environmental analysis such as PESTEL, see G. Burt, G. Wright, R. Bradfield and K. van der Heijden, 'The role of scenario planning in exploring the environment in view of the limitations of PEST and its derivatives', *International Studies of Management and Organization*, vol. 36, no. 3 (2006), pp. 50–76.

7. Based on P. Schoemaker, 'Scenario planning: a tool for strategic thinking'. *Sloan Management Review*, vol. 36 (1995), pp. 25–34.

8. See M.E. Porter, *Competitive Strategy: Techniques for Analyzing Industries and Competitors*, Free Press, 1980, p. 5.

9. An updated discussion of the classic framework is M. Porter, 'The five competitive forces that shape strategy', *Harvard Business Review*, vol. 86, no. 1 (2008), pp. 58–77. C. Christensen, 'The past and future of competitive advantage', *Sloan Management Review*, vol. 42, no. 2 (2001), pp. 105–9, provides an interesting critique and update of some of the factors underlying Porter's five forces. A critical overview of Porter's thinking is also provided in R. Huggins and H. Izushi (eds), *Competition, Competitive Advantage, and Clusters: The Ideas of Michael Porter*, Oxford University Press, 2011.

10. D. McIntyre and M. Subramarian, 'Strategy in network industries: a review and research agenda', *Journal of Management*, vol. 35 (2009), pp. 1494–512.

11. This definition is from R. D'Aveni, *Hypercompetition: Managing the Dynamics of Strategic Manoeuvring*, Free Press, 1994, p. 2.

12. See for example A. Malhotra and A. Gupta, 'An investigation of firms' responses to industry convergence', *Academy of Management Proceedings*, 2001, pp. G1–6.

13. A. Brandenburger and B. Nalebuff, 'The right game', *Harvard Business Review*, July–August 1995, pp. 57–64.

14. See K. Walley, 'Coopetition: an introduction to the subject and an agenda for research', *International Studies of Management and Organization*, vol. 37, no. 2 (2007), pp. 11–31. On the dangers of 'complementors', see D. Yoffie and M. Kwak, 'With friends like these', *Harvard Business Review*, vol. 84, no. 9 (2006), pp. 88–98.

15. There is a good discussion of the static nature of the Porter model, and other limitations, in M. Grundy, 'Rethinking and reinventing Michael Porter's five forces model', *Strategic Change*, vol. 15 (2006), pp. 213–29.

16. A classic academic overview of the industry life cycle is S. Klepper, 'Industry life cycles', *Industrial and Corporate Change*, vol. 6, no. 1 (1996), pp. 119–43. See also A. McGahan, 'How industries evolve', *Business Strategy Review*, vol. 11, no. 3 (2000), pp. 1–16.

17. A. McGahan, 'How industries evolve', *Business Strategy Review*, vol. 11, no. 3 (2000), pp. 1–16.

18. For examples of strategic group analysis, see G. Leask and D. Parker, 'Strategic groups, competitive groups and performance in the UK pharmaceutical industry', *Strategic Management Journal*, vol. 28, no. 7 (2007), pp. 723–45; and W. Desarbo, R. Grewal and R. Wang, 'Dynamic strategic groups: deriving spatial evolutionary paths', *Strategic Management Journal*, vol. 30, no. 8 (2009), pp. 1420–39.

19. These characteristics are based on Porter, reference 4 above.

20. A useful discussion of segmentation in relation to competitive strategy is provided in M.E. Porter, *Competitive Advantage*, Free Press, 1985, Chapter 7. See also the discussion on market segmentation in P. Kotler, G. Armstrong, J. Saunders and V. Wong, *Principles of Marketing*, 3rd European edn, Financial Times Prentice Hall, 2002, Chapter 9.

21. W.C. Kim and R. Mauborgne, 'How strategy shapes structure', *Harvard Business Review*, September 2009, pp. 73–80.

Global forces and the advertising industry

Peter Cardwell

This case is centred on the global advertising industry which faces significant strategic dilemmas driven by the rise of consumer spending in developing economies, technological convergence and pressures from major advertisers for results-based compensation. Strategy in this industry is further explored in **The Strategy Experience** *simulation (http://www.mystrategylab.com/strategy-experience).*

In the second decade of the new millennium, advertising agencies faced a number of unanticipated challenges. Traditional markets and industry operating methods, developed largely in North America and Western Europe following the rise of consumer spending power in the twentieth century, were being radically reappraised.

The industry was subject to game-changing forces from the so-called 'digital revolution' with the entry of search companies like Google and Yahoo as rivals for advertising budgets. Changing patterns in global consumer markets have impacted on both industry dynamics and structure. Budgets being spent through traditional advertising agencies were being squeezed as industry rivalry intensified.

Overview of the advertising industry

Traditionally, the business objective of advertising agencies is to target a specific audience on behalf of clients with a message that encourages them to try a product or service and ultimately purchase it. This is done largely through the concept of a brand being communicated via media channels. Brands allow consumers to differentiate between products and services and it is the job of the advertising agency to position the brand so that it is associated with functions and attributes which are valued by target consumers. These brands may be consumer brands (e.g. Coca-Cola, Nike and Mercedes Benz) or business-to-business (B2B) brands (e.g. IBM, Airbus Industrie and KPMG). Some brands target both consumers and businesses (e.g. Microsoft and Apple).

As well as private-sector brand companies, governments spend heavily to advertise public-sector services such as healthcare and education or to influence individual behaviour (such as 'Don't drink and drive'). For example, the UK government had an advertising budget of £285 m (€325) in 2012. Charities, political groups, religious groups and other not-for-profit organisations also use the advertising industry to attract funds into their organisation or to raise awareness of issues. Together these account for approximately 3 per cent of advertising spend.

Advertisements are usually placed in selected media (TV, press, radio, internet, etc.) by an advertising agency acting on behalf of the client brand company: thus they are acting as 'agents'. The client company employs the advertising agency to use its knowledge, skills, creativity and experience to create advertising and marketing to drive consumption of the client's brands. Clients traditionally have been charged according to the time spent on creating the advertisements plus a commission based on the media and services bought on behalf of clients. However, in recent years, larger advertisers such as Coca-Cola and Procter & Gamble have been moving away from this compensation model to a 'value' or results-based model based on a number of metrics, including growth in sales and market share.

Growth in the advertising industry

Money spent on advertising has increased dramatically over the past two decades and is estimated in 2012 at over $165 billion (€127 bn, £102 bn) in the USA and $483 billion worldwide. While there might be a decline in recessionary years, it is predicted that spending on advertising will exceed $560 billion globally by 2015. Over 2011–12, the Dow Jones stock price index for the American media agencies sector (of which the leading advertising agencies are the largest members) rose about 15 per cent ahead of the New York Stock Exchange average (sources: bigcharts.com and dowjones.com).

The industry is shifting its focus as emerging markets drive revenues from geographic sectors that would not have been significant 5 to 10 years ago, such as the

BRIC countries and Middle East and North Africa. This shift has seen the emergence of agencies specialising in Islamic marketing, characterised by a strong ethical responsibility to consumers. Future trends indicate the strong emergence of consumer brands in areas of the world where sophisticated consumers with brand awareness are currently in the minority. (See Table 1.)

In terms of industry sectors, seven of the top 20 global advertisers are car manufacturers. However, the two major fmcg (fast-moving consumer goods) producers Procter & Gamble and Nestlé hold the two top spots for global advertising spend. Healthcare and beauty, telecommunications companies, food and beverage manufacturers, retailers and the entertainment industry are all featured in the top 20 global advertisers. The top 100 advertisers account for nearly 50 per cent of the measured global advertising economy.

Competition in the advertising industry

Agencies come in all sizes and include everything from one- or two-person 'boutique' operations (which rely mostly on freelance outsourced talent to perform most functions), small to medium-sized agencies, large independents to multinational, multi-agency conglomerates employing over 150,000 people. The industry has gone through a period of increasing concentration through

acquisition thereby creating multi-agency conglomerates such as those listed in Table 2. While these conglomerates are mainly headquartered in London, New York and Paris, they operate globally.

Large multi-agency conglomerates compete on the basis of the quality of their creative teams (as indicated by industry awards), the ability to buy media more cost-effectively, market knowledge, global reach and breadth and range of services. Some agency groups have integrated vertically into higher-margin marketing services. Omnicom, through its Diversified Agency Services, has acquired printing services and telemarketing/customer care companies. Other agency groups have vertically integrated to lesser or greater degrees.

Mid-sized and smaller boutique advertising agencies compete by delivering value-added services through in-depth knowledge of specific market sectors, specialised services such as digital and by building a reputation for innovative and ground-breaking creative advertising/marketing campaigns. However, they might be more reliant on out sourced creative suppliers than larger agencies.

Many small specialist agencies are founded by former employees of large agencies, such as the breakaway from Young & Rubicam to form the agency Adam + Eve. In turn, smaller specialist agencies are often acquired by the large multi-agency conglomerates in order to acquire specific capabilities to target new sectors or markets or

Table 1 Advertising expenditure by region. Major media (newspapers, magazines, television, radio, cinema, outdoor, internet) (US$ million, currency conversion at 2009 average rates)

	2009	2010	2011	2012	2013
N America	156,556	160,386	164,516	169,277	175,024
W Europe	100,143	104,225	107,520	111,300	114,712
Asia Pacific	99,746	106,021	113,345	122,000	130,711
C & E Europe	25,402	27,095	29,243	32,284	35,514
Latin America	25,711	29,315	31,673	34,082	36,836
Africa/ME/ROW	21,220	22,654	24,150	25,941	28,044
World	**428,778**	**449,696**	**470,447**	**494,884**	**520,841**

Source: ZenithOptimedia, September 2012.

Table 2 Top five multi-agency conglomerates: 2011, by revenue, profit before interest and tax, number of employees and agency brands

Group name	Revenue	PBIT	Employees	Advertising agency brands
WPP (UK)	£10.2 bn	£1.429 bn	158,000	JWT, Grey, Ogilvy, Y&R
Omnicom (US)	$13.9 bn	$952 m	70,600	BBDO, DDB, TBWA
Publicis Groupe (France)	€5.8 bn	€600 m	53,807	Leo Burnett, Saatchi & Saatchi, Publicis, BBH
IPG (US)	$7.0 bn	$520 m	43,500	McCann Erickson, FCB, Lowe & Partners
Havas Worldwide (France)	€1.65 bn	€220 m	15,186	Havas Conseil

Source: Ad Age, Omnicom, WPP, Publicis Groupe, IPG, Havas.

provide additional services to existing clients, like WPP's acquisition of a majority stake in the smaller ideas and innovation agency AKQA for $540 m 'to prepare for a more digital future'.

Recent years have seen new competition in this industry as search companies such as Google, Yahoo and Microsoft Bing begin to exploit their ability to interact with and gain information about millions of potential consumers of branded products.

Sir Martin Sorrell, CEO of WPP, the world's largest advertising and marketing services group, has pointed out that Google will rival his agency's relationships with the biggest traditional media corporations such as TV, newspaper and magazine and possibly even become a rival for the relationships with WPP's clients. WPP group spent more than $2 bn with Google in 2012 (over double the $850 m the group spent on the internet company just four years previously) and $400 m with Facebook. Sorrell calls Google a 'frenemy' – the combination of 'friend' and 'enemy'. Google is a 'friend' where it allows WPP to place targeted advertising based on Google analytics and an 'enemy' where it does not share these analytics with the agency and becomes a potential competitor for the customer insight and advertising traditionally created by WPP.

With the development of the internet and online search advertising, a new breed of interactive digital media agencies, of which AKQA is an example, established themselves in the digital space before traditional advertising agencies fully embraced the internet. These agencies differentiate themselves by offering a mix of web design/development, search engine marketing, internet advertising/marketing, or e-business/e-commerce consulting. They are classified as 'agencies' because they create digital media campaigns and implement media purchases of ads on behalf of clients on social networking and community sites such as MySpace, Facebook, YouTube and other digital media.

Online advertising budgets are increasing faster than other traditional advertising media as search companies like Google generate revenues from paid search as advertisers discover that targeted ads online are highly effective (see Table 3). By mid-2011 Google had a 40 per cent market share of the $31 bn spent on online advertising in the USA, with Facebook also increasing its share.

The disruptive change in the advertising industry at the beginning of the twenty-first century started with the internet. Many industry experts believe that convergence of internet, TV, smart phones, tablets and laptop computers is inevitable, which in turn will have a further

Table 3 Advertising expenditure by medium (US$ million, currency conversion at 2009 average rates)

	2009	2010	2011	2012	2013
Newspapers	97,237	94,199	93,019	92,300	91,908
Magazines	43,844	43,184	42,644	42,372	42,300
Television	165,260	180,280	191,198	202,380	213,878
Radio	31,855	31,979	32,580	33,815	35,054
Cinema	2,104	2,258	2,393	2,538	2,681
Outdoor	28,120	29,319	30,945	32,821	34,554
Internet	54,209	61,884	70,518	80,672	91,516
Total	**422,629**	**443,103**	**463,297**	**486,898**	**511,891**

Note: The totals in Table 3 are lower than in Table 1, since that table includes advertising expenditure for a few countries where it is not itemised by medium.

Source: ZenithOptimedia, September 2012.

major impact on the advertising industry. Advertising on mobile devices, such as smart phones and tablets, is still in its infancy but accounted for 8 per cent of all search advertising in the last quarter of 2011 and is forecast to reach 15 per cent by 2016, which has attracted Google to make acquisitions in this sector.

Factors that have driven competitive advantage to date may not be relevant to competitive advantage in the future. Traditionally this industry has embodied the idea of creativity as the vital differentiator between the best and the mediocre. Individuals have often been at the heart of this creativity. With the emergence of Google, Yahoo, Facebook and Bing, influencing and changing the media by which advertising messages are being delivered, a key question is whether creativity will be more or less important in the future, in relation to breadth of services and global reach.

Sources and references

ZenithOptimedia, September 2012; Advertising Age; Omnicom Group http://www.omnicomgroup.com; WPP Group http://www.wpp.com; Publicis http://www.publicisgroupe.com; Interpublic Group of Companies http://www.interpublic.com; Havas Conseils http://www.havas.com/havas-dyn/en/; http://www.financialcontent.com. *See also* **The Strategy Experience**: the Strategy Simulation designed for *Exploring Strategy*: http://www.mystrategylab.com/strategy-experience.

Questions

1 Carry out a PESTEL analysis of the advertising industry in 2012, with particular attention to megatrends, inflexion points and weak signals.

2 Carry out a five forces analysis of the advertising industry in 2012. Which forces are becoming more negative or positive for the major advertising agencies?

3

STRATEGIC CAPABILITIES

Learning outcomes

After reading this chapter you should be able to:

● Identify *strategic capabilities* in terms of organisational *resources* and *competences* and how these relate to the strategies of organisations.

● Analyse how strategic capabilities might provide sustainable competitive advantage on the basis of their *Value, Rarity, Inimitability* and *Organisational support (VRIO)*.

● Diagnose strategic capability by means of *VRIO analysis, benchmarking, value chain analysis, activity mapping* and *SWOT analysis*.

● Consider how managers can *develop strategic capabilities* for their organisations.

MyStrategyLab

MyStrategyLab is designed to help you make the most of your studies. Visit **www.pearsoned.co.uk/mystrategylab** to discover a wide range of resources, including:

● A personalised **Study plan** that will help you understand core concepts

● **Audio and video clips** that put the spotlight on strategy in the real world

● **Online glossaries and flashcards** that provide helpful reminders when you're looking for some quick revision.

(3.1) INTRODUCTION

Chapter 2 emphasised the importance of the external environment of an organisation and how it can create both strategic opportunities and threats. However, it is not only the external environment that matters for strategy; there are also differences between organisations that need to be taken into account. For example, manufacturers of saloon cars compete within the same industry and within the same technological environment, but with markedly different success. BMW has been relatively successful consistently; Ford and Chrysler have found it more difficult to maintain their competitive position. And others, such as Rover in the UK and SAAB in Sweden, have gone out of business (even though the brands as such have been acquired by others). It is not so much the characteristics of the environment which explain these differences in performance, but the differences in their company-specific *strategic capabilities* in terms of the *resources and competences* they have. This puts the focus on variations between companies within the same environment and industry and how they vary in their strategic capabilities and arrangements. It is the strategic importance of such capabilities that is the focus of this chapter.

The key issues posed by the chapter are summarised in Figure 3.1. Underlying these are two key concepts. The first is that organisations are not identical, but have different capabilities; they are 'heterogeneous' in this respect. The second is that it can be difficult for one organisation to obtain or copy the capabilities of another. The implication for managers is that they need to understand how their organisations are different from their rivals in ways that may be the basis of achieving competitive advantage and superior performance. These concepts

Figure 3.1 Strategic capabilities: the key issues

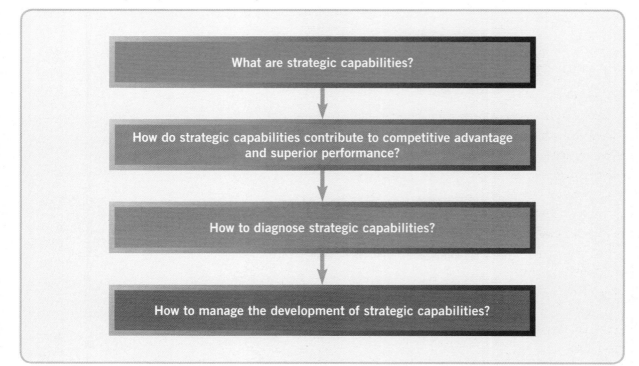

underlie what has become known as the resource-based view (RBV) of strategy[1] (sometimes labelled the 'capabilities view') pioneered by Jay Barney at Ohio State University: **that the competitive advantage and superior performance of an organisation are explained by the distinctiveness of its capabilities.** Resource – or capabilities – views have become very influential, but it should be borne in mind that while the terminology and concepts employed here align with these views, readers will find different terminology used elsewhere.

The chapter has four further sections:

- Section 3.2 discusses the foundations of *strategic capability*; in particular what is meant by *resources*, *competences* and the related concept of *dynamic capabilities*. It also draws a distinction between *threshold capabilities* required to be able to compete in a market and *distinctive capabilities* that may be a basis for achieving competitive advantage and superior performance.

- Section 3.3 explains the ways in which distinctive capabilities can contribute to the *developing and sustaining of competitive advantage* (in a public-sector context the equivalent concern might be how some organisations sustain relative superior performance over time). In particular, the importance of the *Value, Rarity, Inimitability and Organisational support* (VRIO) of capabilities is explained.

- Section 3.4 moves on to consider different ways strategic capability might be analysed. These include *benchmarking, value chain analysis, VRIO analysis* and *activity system mapping*. The section concludes by explaining the use of *SWOT* analysis as a basis for pulling together the insights from the analyses of the environment (explained in Chapter 2) and of strategic capabilities in this chapter.

- Finally section 3.5 discusses some of the key issues in managing the *development of strategic capabilities* through internal and external development and the management of people.

(3.2) FOUNDATIONS OF STRATEGIC CAPABILITY

Given that different writers, managers and consultants use different terms and concepts, it is important to understand how concepts relating to strategic capabilities are used in this book. Here strategic capabilities are **the capabilities of an organisation that contribute to its long-term survival or competitive advantage.** However, to understand and to manage strategic capability it is necessary to explain its components and the characteristics of those components.[2]

3.2.1 Resources and competences

There are two components of strategic capability: resources and competences. Resources are the assets that organisations have or can call upon and competences are the ways those assets are used or deployed effectively. A shorthand way of thinking of this is that resources are 'what we *have*' (nouns) and competences are 'what we *do well*' (verbs). Other terms are common and 'capabilities' and 'competences' are sometimes used interchangeably. For example, Gary Hamel and C.K. Prahalad refer to *core competences* and many writers use the term *intangible assets* as an umbrella term to include competences and capabilities as well as intangible resources such as brands.

Table 3.1 **Components of strategic capabilities**

Strategic capability		
Resources: what we have (nouns), e.g.		**Competences: what we do well (verbs), e.g.**
Machines, buildings, raw materials, products, patents, databases, computer systems	Physical	Ways of achieving utilisation of plant, efficiency, productivity, flexibility, marketing
Balance sheet, cash flow, suppliers of funds	Financial	Ability to raise funds and manage cash flows, debtors, creditors, etc.
Managers, employees, partners, suppliers, customers	Human	How people gain and use experience, skills, knowledge, build relationships, motivate others and innovate

Long-term survival and competitive advantage

Typically all strategic capabilities have elements of both resources and competences as Table 3.1 shows. Resources are certainly important, but how an organisation employs and deploys its resources matters at least as much. There would be no point in having state-of-the-art equipment if it were not used effectively. The efficiency and effectiveness of physical or financial resources, or the people in an organisation, depend not just on their existence, but on the systems and processes by which they are managed, the relationships and cooperation between people, their adaptability, their innovative capacity, the relationship with customers and suppliers, and the experience and learning about what works well and what does not. Illustration 3.1 shows examples of how executives explain the importance of the resources and capabilities of their different organisations.

3.2.2 **Dynamic capabilities**[3]

If they are to provide a basis for long-term success, strategic capabilities cannot be static; they need to change. University of Berkeley economist David Teece has introduced the concept of **dynamic capabilities**, by which he means **an organisation's ability to renew and recreate its strategic capabilities to meet the needs of changing environments**. He argues that the capabilities that are necessary for efficient operations, like owning certain tangible assets, controlling costs, maintaining quality, optimising inventories, etc., are unlikely to be sufficient for sustaining superior performance.[4] These '*ordinary capabilities*' allow companies to be successful and earn a living now by producing and selling a similar product or service to similar customers over time, but are not likely to provide for long-term survival and competitive advantage in the future.[5]

In other words Teece acknowledges the danger that capabilities that were the basis of competitive success can over time be imitated by competitors, become common practice in an industry or become redundant as its environment changes. So, the important lesson is that if capabilities are to be effective over time they need to change; they cannot be static. Dynamic capabilities are directed towards that strategic change. They are dynamic in the sense that they can create, extend or modify an organisation's existing operational capabilities. Teece suggests the following three generic types of dynamic capabilities:

ILLUSTRATION 3.1

Strategic capabilities

Executives emphasise different strategic capabilities in different organisations.

The Goddard Space Flight Center

Flight Center NASA's Goddard Space Flight Center manages many aspects of the space agency's missions and lays claim to some unique resources. For example, its 42-foot-tall acoustic test chamber can produce sounds of up to 150 decibels to allow technicians to expose payloads to launch noise. The high bay clean room, which can accommodate two Space Shuttle payloads, circulates 9 million cubic feet of air every minute through its filters to prevent contaminants damaging spacecraft components – essential to space missions since cleaning of such contaminants in space is highly problematic. And its 120-foot-diameter high-capacity centrifuge with two 1250-horsepower motors can accelerate a 2.5-tonne payload up to 30Gs.[1]

Royal Opera House, London

Tony Hall, Chief Executive of the Royal Opera House:

' "World-class" is neither an idle nor boastful claim. In the context of the Royal Opera House the term refers to the quality of our people, the standards of our productions and the diversity of our work and initiatives. Unique? Unashamedly so. We shy away from labels such as "elite", because of the obvious negative connotations of exclusiveness. But I want people to take away from here the fact that we are elite in the sense that we have the best singers, dancers, directors, designers, orchestra, chorus, backstage crew and administrative staff. We are also among the best in our ability to reach out to as wide and diverse a community as possible.'[2]

Infosys

The Indian company Infosys is a global leader in information technology, outsourcing and consulting. It is listed as one of the world's most reputable companies with close to 150,000 employees worldwide. Infosys has developed from providing business process outsourcing services including call centres and back office IT operations to offering IT infrastructure management, system integration services and IT consulting. Today its 'Infosys 3.0 strategy' is taking a further step to provide more advanced IT products and services.

The new strategy emphasises innovation and focuses on higher-value software. Innovation abilities are central for this, as stated on the website: 'The foundation of our innovation capability is our core lab network – Infosys Labs – and the new thinking that our team of over 600 researchers brings to the table.' The new strategy thus requires human resource and training capabilities including the ability to attract, employ, educate and retain new high-quality engineers. As Srikantan Moorthy, Senior Vice President and Group Head explains: 'We are currently hiring and developing talent in the areas of cloud, mobility, sustainability and product development. In addition, a key focus is consultative skills. All of these are in line with our Infosys 3.0 strategy. We place significant value on continuous learning and knowledge sharing.'

Infosys CEO S.D. Shibulal explains Infosys capability build-up: 'We continue to make focused investments in our organisational capabilities.' 'Our Infosys 3.0 strategy requires us to focus on our acquisition strategy to enhance our capabilities. . . .' Accordingly, Infosys acquired the Swiss management and IT consultants Lodestone in September 2012: 'A key plan of our Infosys 3.0 strategy is to expand our consulting and systems integration business. This acquisition fits perfectly into that strategy.'[3]

Sources: (1) Goddard Space Center website. (2) Annual Review, 2005–6, p. 11. (3) *Financial Times*, 13 August 2012; *Financial Times*, 11 September 2012; http://www.infosys.com © Infosys; http://www.skillingindia.com/.

Questions

1 Categorise the range of capabilities highlighted by the executives in terms of section 3.2 and Table 3.1.

2 To what extent and why might these capabilities be the basis of *sustained* competitive advantage?

3 For an organisation of your choice undertake the same exercise as in questions 1 and 2 above.

- *Sensing.* Sensing implies that organisations must constantly scan, search and explore opportunities across various markets and technologies. Research and development and investigating customer needs are typical sensing activities. For example, companies in the PC operating systems industry, like Microsoft, have clearly sensed the opportunities in and threats from tablets and smart phones.

- *Seizing.* Once an opportunity is sensed it must be seized and addressed through new products or services, processes, activities etc. Microsoft, for example, has started to seize opportunities by developing its own tablet device and software and by acquiring the mobile company Nokia.

- *Reconfiguring.* To seize an opportunity may require renewal and reconfiguration of organisational capabilities and investments in technologies, manufacturing, markets, etc. For example, Microsoft's inroad into tablets and smart phones requires major changes in its current strategic capabilities. The company must discard some of its old capabilities, acquire and build new ones and recombine them.

This view of dynamic capabilities above relates directly to the framework for this book: strategic position, strategic choices and strategy in action (see Figure 1.3). Sensing capabilities are to do with understanding an organisation's strategic position; seizing opportunities relate to making strategic choices; and reconfiguration is to do with enacting strategies. Illustration 3.2 provides an example of dynamic capabilities in the context of mobile telephones.

New product development is a typical example of a dynamic capability and strategic planning is another. They both involve activities that can sense and seize opportunities and that are intended to reconfigure capabilities. Outlet proliferation by chain retailers such as Starbucks is another example of a dynamic capability as it extends operational capabilities.[6] Dynamic capabilities may also take the form of relatively formal organisational systems, such as recruitment and management development processes and cooperating with others through alliances or acquisitions, by which new skills are learned and developed.[7]

As Teece acknowledges, however, dynamic capabilities are likely to have 'microfoundations'[8] in people's behaviour of organisations, such as the way in which decisions get taken, personal relationships, and entrepreneurial and intuitive skills. This puts the focus on behaviour and the significance of beliefs, social relationships and experience in capability management, which is discussed in the very last section of this chapter on managing capabilities (see section 3.5).

In brief, strategic capabilities include both operational capabilities and dynamic capabilities that can change operational capabilities in case the environment changes. However, as dynamic capabilities are focused on finding solutions beyond and outside current operational capabilities there is a trade-off and tension between the two that can make it difficult to achieve an optimal balance between them within a single organisation or unit. This is sometimes referred to as exploration/exploitation trade-offs and they are further discussed in Chapter 14.

3.2.3 Threshold and distinctive capabilities

A distinction also needs to be made between strategic capabilities that are at a threshold level and those that might help the organisation achieve competitive advantage and superior performance. **Threshold capabilities are those needed for an organisation to meet the necessary requirements to compete in a given market and achieve parity with competitors in that market.** Without such capabilities the organisation could not survive over time. Indeed many start-up businesses find this to be the case. They simply do not have or cannot obtain the resources or competences needed to compete with established competitors. Identifying

ILLUSTRATION 3.2

Dynamic capabilities (and rigidities) in mobile telephone companies

Dynamic capabilities can help firms sense and seize opportunities and reconfigure operational capabilities in changing environments.

Companies in the mobile telephone industry have built on their dynamic capabilities in their effort to adapt to environmental changes and dominate the market. They have identified and evaluated new opportunities (sensing); addressed these opportunities with new products (seizing) and renewed and redeployed their capabilities accordingly (reconfiguring). This is illustrated in the table.

The pioneers in mobile telephony, Ericsson and Motorola, managed to sense and explore an entirely new mobile telephony market. They satisfied and captured value in that market by recombining and redeploying telecommunication and radio capabilities. However, they got stuck in these early mobile telephone capabilities and were followed by Nokia. Nokia sensed new opportunities as it realised that mobile phones' awkward design and functionality was not suited to what had become a mass consumer and fashion market. The company seized and addressed these new opportunities, offering improved design and functionality, building on design and consumer

behaviour capabilities. Finally, Apple, with a long legacy in consumer products, explored even further opportunities. Apple realised that most phones, even the new smart phones, still maintained a complex and unintuitive interface with limited multimedia functionalities. Apple addressed this by introducing an upgraded multimedia platform smart phone with an intuitive and simple interface combined with complementary services like the App Store and iTunes Music Store. Apple built on a recombination of its prior design, interface and consumer behaviour capabilities and new (for them) mobile phone capabilities.

While the dynamic capabilities of the mobile phone companies helped them adapt, they are no guarantee for keeping ahead permanently as the operating capabilities they developed risk becoming rigidities as markets and technologies change even further. If dynamic capabilities do not manage to detect and alleviate rigidities, competitors may emerge over time with more appropriate dynamic capabilities for the constantly changing environment.

---

threshold requirements is, however, also important for established businesses. There could be changing *threshold resources* required to meet minimum customer requirements: for example, the increasing demands by modern multiple retailers of their suppliers mean that those suppliers have to possess a quite sophisticated IT infrastructure simply to stand a chance of meeting retailer requirements. Or they could be the *threshold competences* required to deploy resources so as to meet customers' requirements and support particular strategies. Retailers do not simply expect suppliers to have the required IT infrastructure, but to be able to use it effectively so as to guarantee the required level of service.

Identifying and managing threshold capabilities raises a significant challenge because threshold levels of capability will change as critical success factors change (see section 2.4.3) or through the activities of competitors and new entrants. To continue the example above, suppliers to major retailers did not require the same level of IT and logistics support a decade ago. But the retailers' drive to reduce costs, improve efficiency and ensure availability of merchandise to their customers means that their expectations of their suppliers have increased markedly in that time and continue to do so. So there is a need for those suppliers continuously to review and improve their logistics resource and competence base just to stay in business.

Companies	Approximate time period	Product	Sensing	Seizing	Reconfiguring
Ericsson (primarily Europe) **Motorola** (primarily the US)	Mid-1980s– late 1990s	Mobile phones	Need for mobile telephones: Fixed telephony did not offer mobility	Creating the first mobile telephone systems and telephones	Creating a new mobile telephone market Acquiring and building mobile telephone capabilities
Nokia	Late 1990s– early 2000s	Mobile phones with improved design and functionality	Need for well-designed and fashionable mobile phones: Existing mobile phones were close to their car-phone origins and maintained their awkward design and functionality	Upgrading the mobile phone to provide a richer experience in design, fashion and functionality	Entering the mobile telephone market Acquiring and building mobile telephony capabilities Building design and marketing capabilities
Apple	Late 2000s–	Mobile phones with perfected design, functionality and interface	Need for smart phones with multimedia functionality: Existing smart phones maintained a complex and unintuitive interface with limited functionalities	Upgrading the mobile phone to include an intuitive interface and multimedia functionalities containing the App store and iTunes	Entering the mobile telephone market Acquiring mobile telephony capabilities and recombining them with existing design and interface capabilities Cooperating with the music and telephone app industries

Questions

1 What type of dynamic capabilities could help companies avoid becoming stuck in their old capabilities?

2 a What are the possible future opportunities in mobile telephones?

   b How could they be sensed and seized?

   c What type of ordinary capabilities could possibly address them?

While threshold capabilities are important, they do not of themselves create competitive advantage or the basis of superior performance. **Distinctive capabilities are required to achieve competitive advantage.** These are dependent on an organisation having distinctive or unique capabilities that are of value to customers and which competitors find difficult to imitate. This could be because the organisation has *distinctive resources* that critically underpin competitive advantage and that others cannot imitate or obtain – a long-established brand, for example. Or it could be that an organisation achieves competitive advantage because it has *distinctive competences* – ways of doing things that are unique to that organisation and effectively utilised so as to be valuable to customers and difficult for competitors to obtain or imitate. Gary Hamel and C.K. Prahalad argue that distinctive competences typically remain unique because they comprise a *bundle* of constituent skills and technologies rather than a single, discrete skill or technology (they refer to this as a 'core competence').[9] The emphasis is thus on the linked set of skills, activities and resources.

Bringing these concepts together, a supplier that achieves competitive advantage in a retail market might have done so on the basis of a distinctive resource such as a powerful brand, but also by distinctive competences such as the building of excellent relations with retailers. The distinctive competences that are likely to be most difficult for competitors to match and form the basis of competitive advantage will be the multiple and linked ways of providing products, high levels of service and building relationships. Section 3.3 that follows discusses in more depth the role played by distinctive resources and competences in contributing to long-term, sustainable competitive advantage. Section 3.4 then explores further the importance of linkages between activities.

(3.3) 'VRIO' STRATEGIC CAPABILITIES AS A BASIS OF COMPETITIVE ADVANTAGE

As explained above, distinctive capabilities are necessary for sustainable competitive advantage and superior economic performance. This section considers four key criteria by which capabilities can be assessed in terms of their providing a basis for achieving such competitive advantage: value, rarity, inimitability and organisational support – or **VRIO**.[10] Figure 3.2 illustrates these four fundamental criteria and the questions they address.

3.3.1 V – value of strategic capabilities

Strategic capabilities are valuable when they create a product or a service that is of value to customers and if, and only if, they generate higher revenues or lower costs or both. There are three components here:

- *Taking advantage of opportunities and neutralising threats*: the most fundamental issue is that to be valuable capabilities need to provide the potential to address the opportunities and threats that arise in the organisation's environment, which points to an important complementarity with the external environment of an organisation (Chapter 2). Capabilities are valuable if they address opportunities and/or threats and generate higher revenues or lower costs or both compared to if the organisation did not have those capabilities. For example, IKEA's cost-conscious culture, size and its intricate configuration of interlinked activities lower its costs compared to competitors and addresses opportunities of low-priced furniture that competitors do not attend to.

Figure 3.2 VRIO

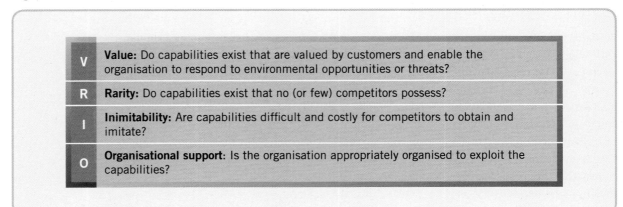

- *Value to customers*: it may seem an obvious point to make that capabilities need to be of value to customers, but in practice it is often ignored or poorly understood. For example, managers may seek to build on capabilities that *they* may see as valuable but which do not meet customers' critical success factors (see section 2.4.3). Or they may see a distinctive capability as of value simply because it is distinctive, although it may not be valued by customers. Having capabilities that are different from other organisations' is not, of itself, a basis of competitive advantage.

- *Cost*: the product or service needs to be provided at a cost that still allows the organisation to make the returns expected of it. The danger is that the cost of developing or acquiring the capabilities to deliver what customers especially value is such that products or services are not profitable.

Managers should therefore consider carefully which of their organisation's activities are especially important in providing such value and which are of less value. Value chain analysis and activity mapping explained in sections 3.4.2 and 3.4.3 can help here.

3.3.2 R – rarity

Capabilities that are valuable, but common among competitors, are unlikely to be a source of competitive advantage. If competitors have similar capabilities they can respond quickly to the strategic initiative of a rival. This has happened in competition between car manufacturers as they have sought to add more accessories and gadgets to cars. As soon as it becomes evident that these are valued by customers, they are introduced widely by competitors who typically have access to the same technology. Rare capabilities, on the other hand, **are those possessed uniquely by one organisation or by a few others**. Here competitive advantage is longer-lasting. For example, a company can have patented products or services that give it advantage. Service organisations may have rare resources in the form of intellectual capital – perhaps particularly talented individuals. Some libraries have unique collections of books unavailable elsewhere; a company can have a powerful brand; or retail stores can have prime locations. In terms of competences, organisations can have unique skills developed over time or have built special relationships with customers or suppliers not widely possessed by competitors. However, it can be dangerous to assume that resources and capabilities that are rare will remain so. So it may be necessary to consider other bases of sustainability.

3.3.3 I – inimitability

It should be clear by now that the search for strategic capability that provides sustainable competitive advantage is not straightforward. Having capabilities that are valuable to customers and relatively rare is important, but this may not be enough. Sustainable competitive advantage also involves identifying inimitable capabilities – **those that competitors find difficult and costly to imitate or obtain or substitute**. If an organisation has a competitive advantage because of its particular marketing and sales skills it can only sustain this if competitors cannot imitate, obtain or substitute for them or if the costs to do so would eliminate any gains made. Often the barriers to imitation lie deeply in the organisation in linkages between activities, skills and people.

At the risk of over-generalisation, it is unusual for competitive advantage to be explainable by differences in the tangible resources of organisations, since over time these can usually be

Figure 3.3 Criteria for the inimitability of strategic capabilities

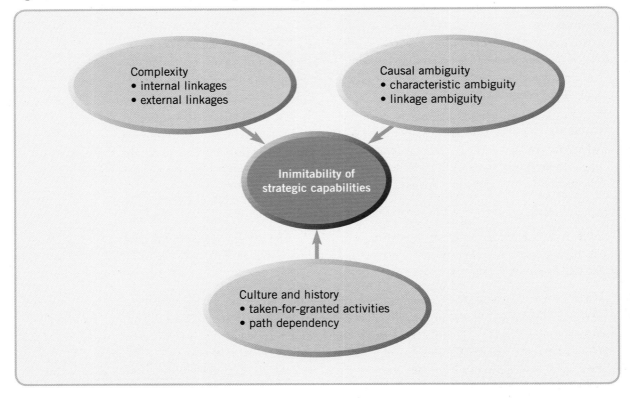

acquired or imitated (key geographic locations, certain raw material resources, brands, etc., can, however, be exceptions). Advantage is more likely to be determined by the way in which resources are deployed and managed in terms of an organisation's activities; in other words on the basis of competences.[11] For example, as indicated above, it is unlikely that an IT system will improve an organisation's competitive standing in itself, not least because competitors can probably buy something very similar on the open market. On the other hand the competences to manage, develop and deploy such a system to the benefit of customers may be much more difficult and costly to imitate. Compared to physical assets and patents, competences, then, tend to involve more intangible imitation barriers. In particular, they often include *linkages* that integrate activities, skills, knowledge and people both inside and outside the organisation in distinct and mutually compatible ways. These linkages can make capabilities particularly difficult for competitors to imitate and there are three primary reasons why this may be so. These are summarised in Figure 3.3 and are now briefly reviewed.

Complexity

The capabilities of an organisation can be difficult to imitate because they are complex and involve interlinkages. This may be for two main reasons:

- *Internal linkages.* There may be linked activities and processes that, together, deliver customer value. The discussion of activity systems in section 3.4.3 below explains this in more detail and shows how such linked sets of activities might be mapped so that they can be better understood. However, even if a competitor possessed such a map, it is unlikely that it would be able to replicate the sort of complexity it represents because of the numerous interactions between tightly knit activities and decisions.[12] This is not only because of the complexity itself but because, very likely, it has developed on the basis of custom and practice built up over years and is specific to the organisation concerned. For example, companies like IKEA and Ryanair still enjoy competitive advantages despite the availability of countless case studies, articles and reports on their successes.

- *External interconnectedness.* Organisations can make it difficult for others to imitate or obtain their bases of competitive advantage by developing activities together with customers or partners such that they become dependent on them. This is sometimes referred to as *co-specialisation.* For example, an industrial lubricants business moved away from just selling its products to customers by coming to an agreement with them to manage the applications of lubricants within the customers' sites against agreed targets on cost savings. The more efficient the use of lubricants, the more both parties benefited.

Causal ambiguity[13]

Another reason why capabilities might be difficult and costly to imitate is that competitors find it difficult to discern the causes and effects underpinning an organisation's advantage. This is called *causal ambiguity.* Causal ambiguity may exist in two different forms:[14]

- *Characteristic ambiguity.* Where the significance of the characteristic itself is difficult to discern or comprehend, perhaps because it is based on tacit knowledge or rooted in the organisation's culture. For example, the know-how of the buyers in a successful fashion retailer may be evident in the sales achieved for the ranges they buy year after year. But it may be very difficult to comprehend just what that know-how is, so competitors will find it difficult to imitate.

- *Linkage ambiguity.* Where competitors cannot discern which activities and processes are dependent on which others to form linkages that create distinctive competences. The expertise of the fashion buyers is unlikely to be lodged in the one individual or even one function. It is likely that there will be a network of suppliers, intelligence networks to understand the market and links with designers. Indeed in some organisations the managers themselves admit that they do not fully comprehend the linkages throughout the organisation that deliver customer value. If this is so it would certainly be difficult for competitors to understand them.

Culture and history

Competences that involve complex social interactions and interpersonal relations within an organisation can be difficult and costly for competitors to imitate systematically and manage. For example, competences can become embedded in an organisation's culture. Coordination between various activities occurs 'naturally' because people know their part in the wider picture or it is simply 'taken for granted' that activities are done in particular ways. We see this in high-performing sports teams, in groups of people that work together to combine specialist skills as in operating theatres; but also, for example, in how some firms integrate different activities in their business to deliver excellent customer service. Linked to this cultural embeddedness is the likelihood that such competences have developed over time and in a particular way. The origins and history by which competences have developed over time are referred to as *path dependency.*[15] This history is specific to the organisation and cannot be imitated (see section 5.2.1). As explained in Chapter 5, there is, however, a danger that culturally embedded competences built up over time become so embedded that they are difficult to change: they become rigidities.

3.3.4 O – organisational support

Providing value to customers and possessing capabilities that are rare and difficult to imitate provides a potential for competitive advantage. However, **the organisation must also be suitably organised to support these capabilities** including appropriate organisational processes and systems. This implies that to fully take advantage of the capabilities an organisation's structure and formal and informal management control systems need to support and facilitate their exploitation (see sections 13.1 and 13.2 for further discussions of organisational structure and systems). The question of organisational support works as an adjustment factor. Some of the potential competitive advantage can be lost if the organisation is not organised in a way that it can fully take advantage of valuable and/or rare and/or inimitable capabilities. The supporting capabilities have been labelled *complementary capabilities* as, by themselves, they are often not enough to provide for competitive advantage, but they are useful and effective in the exploitation of other capabilities that can provide for competitive advantage.[16] In brief, even though an organisation has valuable, rare and inimitable capabilities some of its potential competitive advantage may not be realised if it lacks the organisational arrangements to fully exploit these.

In summary and from a resource-based view of organisations, managers need to consider whether their organisation has strategic capabilities to achieve and sustain competitive advantage. To do so they need to consider how and to what extent it has capabilities which are (i) valuable, (ii) rare, (iii) inimitable and (iv) supported by the organisation. Table 3.2 summarises the VRIO framework of capabilities and shows that there is an additive effect. Strategic capabilities provide sustainable bases of competitive advantage the more they meet all four criteria. Illustration 3.3 gives an example of the challenges in meeting these criteria in the context of an internet-based company. If capabilities for competitive advantage do not exist, then managers need to consider if they can be developed. How this might be done is considered in section 3.5 below.

3.3.5 Organisational knowledge as a basis of competitive advantage

A good example of how both resources and competences may combine to produce competitive advantage for an organisation is in terms of organisational knowledge.[17] **Organisational knowledge is organisation-specific, collective intelligence, accumulated through formal systems and people's shared experience.**

The reasons why organisational knowledge is seen as especially important illustrate many of the points made above. As organisations become larger and more complex, the need to share what people know becomes more and more important but increasingly challenging.

Table 3.2 The VRIO framework

| Is the capability . . . | | | | |
valuable?	rare?	inimitable?	supported by the organisation?	Competitive implications
No	–	–	No	Competitive disadvantage
Yes	No	–	↑	Competitive parity
Yes	Yes	No	↕	Temporary competitive advantage
Yes	Yes	Yes	Yes	Sustained competitive advantage

Source: Adapted with the permission of J.B. Barney and W.S. Hesterly, *Strategic Management and Competitive Advantage*, Pearson, 2012.

ILLUSTRATION 3.3

Groupon and the sincerest form of flattery

When a firm identifies a new market niche it must also make sure its strategic capabilities are valuable, rare, inimitable and supported by the organisation.

Chicago-based Groupon was launched in 2008 by Andrew Mason with the idea to email subscribers daily deals of heavily discounted coupons for local restaurants, theatres, spas, etc. Groupon sells a coupon for a product and takes up to half of the proceeds, which represent a big discount on the product's usual price. In return, Groupon aggregates demand from the customers who receive its emails and this provides exposure to and increased business for the local merchants. The venture rapidly became the fastest-growing Internet business ever and grew into a daily deal industry giant. In 2010 Groupon rejected a $6 bn (€4.5 bn) takeover bid by Google and instead went public at $10 bn in November of 2011.

While Groupon's daily deals were valued by customers – the company quickly spread to over 40 countries – they also attracted first hundreds and later thousands of copycats worldwide. Investors started to question Groupon's business model and to what extent it had rare and inimitable strategic capabilities. In 2012 the CEO Andrew Mason denied in *Wall Street Journal* (*WSJ*) that the model was too easy to replicate:

> 'There's proof. There are over 2000 direct clones of the Groupon business model. However, there's an equal amount of proof that the barriers to success are enormous. In spite of all those competitors, only a handful are remotely relevant.'

This, however, did not calm investors and the online coupon seller's shares promptly fell by 80 per cent to its all-time low. The question thus remained – to what extent were Groupon's capabilities rare and inimitable? One significant asset Groupon had that is rare and possibly difficult to imitate is its impressive customer base of more than 50 million customers. The more customers, the better deals and this would make customers come to Groupon rather than the competitors and the cost for competitors to acquire customers would go up. Critics argued, however, that other companies such as Facebook, Google and Amazon had even broader user bases and could possibly

become competitors. Further defending Groupon's competitiveness the CEO emphasised in *WSJ* that it is not as simple as providing daily deals via email, but that a whole series of things have to work together and to imitate Groupon competitors would have to replicate everything in its 'operational complexity':

> 'People overlook the operational complexity. We have 10,000 employees across 46 countries. We have thousands of salespeople talking to tens of thousands of merchants every single day. It's not an easy thing to build.'

Another resource that Andrew Mason stressed was Groupon's advanced technology platform that allowed the company to 'provide better targeting to customers and give them deals that are more relevant to them'. Part of this platform, however, was got via acquisitions – a route competitors possibly could take as well.

If imitation is the highest form of flattery Groupon has been highly complimented. Hundreds of copycats have, however, left the business and Groupon has also beaten back more serious competitors, but the company continues to be under considerable pressure. In February 2013 founder and CEO Andrew Mason was forced to step down, which was a sign that many changes would come at Groupon.

Sources: All Things Digital, 2 November 2012, *Wall Street Journal*: http://allthingsd.com/20121102/groupon-shares-dive-to-new-low-a-year-after-the-ipo/; *Financial Times*, 14 May 2012; *Financial Times*, 2 March 2013; *Wall Street Journal*, 31 January 2012.

Questions

1 Andrew Mason admits that Groupon has thousands of copycats, yet his assessment is that imitating Groupon is difficult. Do you agree?

2 Assess the bases of Groupon's strategic capabilities using the VRIO criteria (Figure 3.2 and Table 3.2).

3 Which is the most important strategic capability that provides, or could provide, Groupon with sustainable competitive advantage?

So organisations that can share knowledge especially well may gain advantage over those that do not. Computerised information systems are available or have been developed by organisations to codify technological, financial and market data that are *valuable* to them; indeed without which they probably could not compete effectively. However, the technology that forms the basis of information systems is hardly *rare*; it is widely available or can be developed. It is therefore less likely that organisations will achieve competitive advantage through such resources and more likely that it will be achieved through the way they manage and develop organisational knowledge more broadly. This may be to do with the competences they employ to utilise and develop information technology. But it is also likely to be about how they draw on and develop the accumulated and dispersed experience-based knowledge in the organisation.

The distinction between *explicit* and *tacit organisational knowledge* made by Ikijuro Nonaka and Hiro Takeuchi[18] helps explain why this is important in terms of achieving competitive advantage. Explicit or 'objective' knowledge is transmitted in formal systematic ways. It can take the form of a codified information resource such as a systems manual or files of market research and intelligence. In contrast, tacit knowledge is more personal, context-specific and therefore hard to formalise and communicate. For example, it could be the knowledge of a highly experienced sales force or research and development team; or the experience of a top management team in making many successful acquisitions. It is therefore not only distinctive to the organisation, but likely to be *difficult to imitate* or obtain for the reasons explained in section 3.3.3 above. Such knowledge may have been developed over the years by '*communities of practice*'[19] developing and sharing information because it is mutually beneficial to them. It may also be continually changing as their experience changes. It will also be difficult for competitors to comprehend precisely because it is context specific, experiential and dispersed (and therefore complex and causally ambiguous).

Many organisations that have tried to improve the sharing of knowledge by relying on IT-based systems have come to realise that, while some knowledge can usefully be codified and built into computer-based systems, it can be very difficult to codify the knowledge that truly bestows competitive advantage.

(3.4) DIAGNOSING STRATEGIC CAPABILITIES

So far this chapter has been concerned with explaining concepts associated with the strategic significance of organisations' resources and capabilities. This section now provides some ways in which strategic capabilities can be understood and diagnosed.

3.4.1 Benchmarking[20]

Benchmarking is used as a means of understanding how an organisation compares with others – typically competitors. Many benchmarking exercises focus on outputs such as standards of product or service, but others do attempt to take account of organisational capabilities.

Broadly, there are two approaches to benchmarking:

- *Industry/sector benchmarking.* Insights about performance standards can be gleaned by comparing performance against other organisations in the same industry sector or between similar service providers against a set of performance indicators. Some public-sector organisations have, in effect, acknowledged the existence of strategic groups (see section 2.4.1) by benchmarking against similar organisations rather than against everybody: for example, local government services and police treat 'urban' differently from 'rural' in their benchmarking and league tables. An overriding danger of industry norm comparisons (whether in the private or the public sector) is, however, that the whole industry can be performing badly and losing out competitively to other industries that can satisfy customers' needs in different ways.

- *Best-in-class benchmarking.* Best-in-class benchmarking compares an organisation's performance or capabilities against 'best-in-class' performance – from whichever industry – and therefore seeks to overcome some of the above limitations. It may also help challenge managers' mind-sets that acceptable improvements in performance will result from incremental changes in resources or competences. For example, Southwest Airlines improved refuelling time by studying the processes surrounding Formula One Grand Prix motor racing pit stops.[21]

The importance of benchmarking is, then, not so much in the detailed 'mechanics' of comparison but in the impact that these comparisons might have on reviewing capabilities underlying performance. But it has two potential limitations:

- *Surface comparisons.* If benchmarking is limited to comparing outputs, it does not directly identify the reasons for relative performance in terms of underlying capabilities. For example, it may demonstrate that one organisation is poorer at customer service than another, but not show the underlying reasons.

- *Simply achieving competitive parity.* Benchmarking can help an organisation to develop capabilities and create value in the same way as its competitors and those best-in-class. However, the best performance that can be expected out of this exercise is to achieve threshold capabilities and/or competitive parity. For organisations with competitive disadvantage this can be highly rewarding, but to achieve competitive advantage an organisation needs to move further and develop its own distinctive capabilities.

3.4.2 The value chain and value system

The **value chain** describes the categories of activities within an organisation which, together, create a product or service. Most organisations are also part of a wider **value system, the set of inter-organisational links and relationships that are necessary to create a product or service.** Both are useful in understanding the strategic position of an organisation and where valuable strategic capabilities reside.

The value chain

If organisations are to achieve competitive advantage by delivering value to customers, managers need to understand which activities their organisation undertakes that are especially important in creating that value and which are not. This can then be used to model the value generation of an organisation. The important point is that the concept of the value chain invites the strategist to think of an organisation in terms of sets of activities. There are different frameworks for considering these categories: Figure 3.4 is a representation of a value chain as developed by Michael Porter.[22]

Primary activities are directly concerned with the creation or delivery of a product or service. For example, for a manufacturing business:

Figure 3.4 The value chain within an organisation

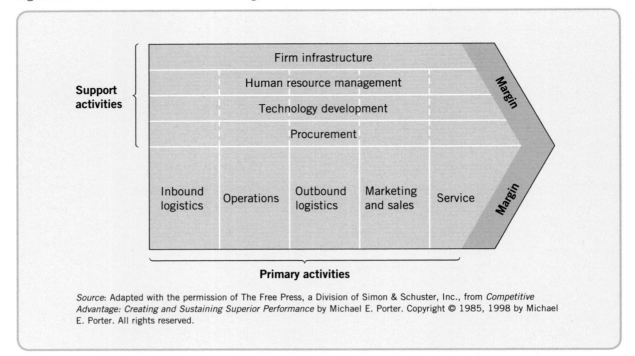

- *Inbound logistics* are activities concerned with receiving, storing and distributing inputs to the product or service including materials handling, stock control, transport, etc.

- *Operations* transform these inputs into the final product or service: machining, packaging, assembly, testing, etc.

- *Outbound logistics* collect, store and distribute the product or service to customers; for example, warehousing, materials handling, distribution, etc.

- *Marketing and sales* provide the means whereby consumers or users are made aware of the product or service and are able to purchase it. This includes sales administration, advertising and selling.

- *Service* includes those activities that enhance or maintain the value of a product or service, such as installation, repair, training and spares.

Each of these groups of primary activities is linked to *support activities* which help to improve the effectiveness or efficiency of primary activities:

- *Procurement.* Processes that occur in many parts of the organisation for acquiring the various resource inputs to the primary activities. These can be vitally important in achieving scale advantages. So, for example, many large consumer goods companies with multiple businesses none the less procure advertising centrally.

- *Technology development.* All value activities have a 'technology', even if it is just know-how. Technologies may be concerned directly with a product (e.g. R&D, product design) or with processes (e.g. process development) or with a particular resource (e.g. raw materials improvements).

- *Human resource management.* This transcends all primary activities and is concerned with recruiting, managing, training, developing and rewarding people within the organisation.

- *Infrastructure.* The formal systems of planning, finance, quality control, information management and the structure of an organisation.

The value chain can be used to understand the strategic position of an organisation and analyse strategic capabilities in three ways:

- As a *generic description of activities* it can help managers understand if there is a cluster of activities providing benefit to customers located within particular areas of the value chain. Perhaps a business is especially good at outbound logistics linked to its marketing and sales operation and supported by its technology development. It might be less good in terms of its operations and its inbound logistics.

- In analysing the competitive position of the organisation using the *VRIO criteria* as follows:

    V Which *value*-creating activities are especially significant for an organisation in meeting customer needs and could they be usefully developed further?

    R To what extent and how does an organisation have bases of value creation that are *rare*? Or conversely are all elements of its value chain common to its competitors?

    I What aspects of value creation are difficult for others to *imitate*, perhaps because they are *embedded* in the activity systems of the organisation (see section 3.4.3 below)?

    O What parts of the value chain support and facilitate value creation activities in other sections of the value chain? For example, firm infrastructure support activities including particular formal and informal management control systems can be necessary to fully exploit value creation in the primary activities.

- To *analyse the cost and value of activities*[23] of an organisation. This could involve the following steps:

    - *Identifying sets of value activities.* Figure 3.4 might be appropriate as a general framework here or a value chain more specific to an organisation can be developed. The important thing is to ask (i) which separate categories of activities best describe the operations of the organisation and (ii) which of these are most significant in delivering the strategy and achieving advantage over competitors? For example, it is likely that in a branded pharmaceutical company research and development and marketing activities will be crucially important.

    - *Relative importance of activity costs internally.* Which activities are most significant in terms of the costs of operations? Does the significance of costs align with the significance of activities? Which activities add most value to the final product or service (and in turn to the customer) and which do not? It can also be important to establish which sets of activities are linked to or are dependent on others and which, in effect, are self-standing. For example, organisations that have undertaken such analyses often find that central services have grown to the extent that they are a disproportionate cost to internal sets of activities and to the customer.

    - *Relative importance of activities externally.* How does value and the cost of a set of activities compare with the similar activities of competitors? For example, although they are both global oil businesses, BP and Shell are different in terms of the significance of their value chain activities. BP has historically outperformed Shell in terms of exploration, but the reverse is the case with regard to refining and marketing.

    - *Where and how can costs be reduced?* Given the picture that emerges from such an analysis it should be possible to ask some important questions about the cost structure of the organisation in terms of the strategy being followed (or that needs to be followed in the

ILLUSTRATION 3.4

A value system for Ugandan chilled fish fillet exports

Even small enterprises can be part of an international value system. Analysing it can provide strategic benefits.

A fish factory in Uganda barely made any profit. Fish were caught from small motorboats owned by poor fishermen from local villages. Just before they set out they would collect ice and plastic fish boxes from the agents who bought the catch on their return. The boxes were imported, along with tackle and boat parts. All supplies had to be paid for in cash in advance by the agents. Sometimes ice and supplies were not available in time. Fish landed with insufficient ice achieved half of the price of iced fish, and sometimes could not be sold to the agents at all. The fish factory had always processed the fillets in the same way – disposing of the waste back into the lake. Once a week, some foreign traders would come and buy the better fillets; they didn't say who they sold them to, and sometimes they didn't buy very much.

By mapping the value chain it was clear that there were opportunities for capturing more value along the chain and reducing losses. Together with outside specialists, the fish factory and the fishing community developed a strategy to improve their capabilities, as indicated in the figure, until they became a flourishing international business, the Lake Victoria Fish Company, with regular air-freight exports around the world.

You can see more of their current operations at http://www.ufpea.co.ug/.

(The approximate costs and prices given represent the situation before improvements were implemented.)

Questions

1 Draw up a value chain or value system for another business in terms of the activities within its component parts.

2 Estimate the relative costs and/or assets associated with these activities.

3 What are the strategic implications of your analysis?

---

future). For example, is the balance of cost in line with the strategic significance of the elements of the value chain? Can costs be reduced in some areas without affecting the value created for customers? Can some activities be outsourced (see section 7.5.2), for example those that are relatively free-standing and do not add value significantly? Can cost savings be made by increasing economies of scale or scope; for example, through central procurement or consolidating currently fragmented activities (e.g. manufacturing units)?

The value system

A single organisation rarely undertakes in-house all of the value activities from design through to the delivery of the final product or service to the final consumer. There is usually specialisation of roles so, as Figure 3.5 shows, any one organisation is part of a wider *value system* of different interacting organisations. There are questions that arise here that build on an understanding of the value chain itself:

● *What are the activities and cost/price structures of the value system?* Just as costs can be analysed across the internal value chain, they can also be analysed across the value system: Illustration 3.4 shows this in relation to fish farming. Value system analysis was used by Ugandan fish farmers as a way of identifying what they should focus on in developing a more profitable business model.

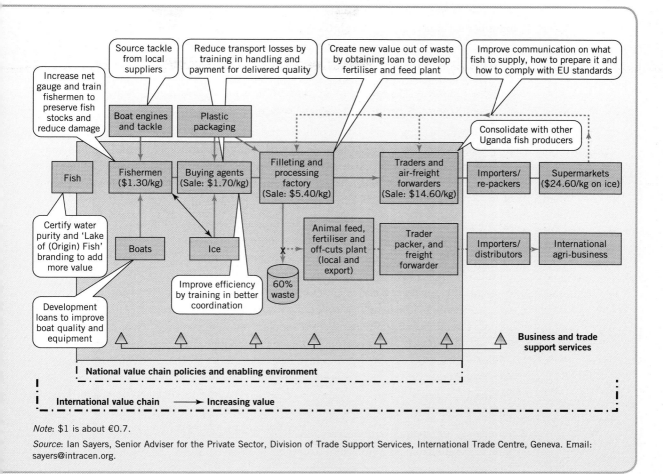

Figure 3.5 The value system

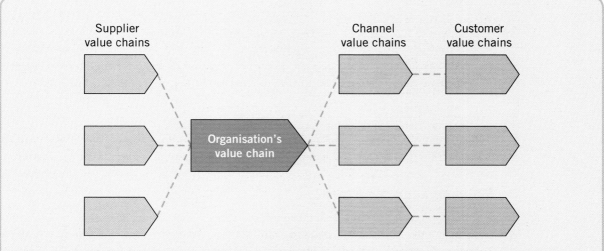

Note: $1 is about €0.7.

Source: Ian Sayers, Senior Adviser for the Private Sector, Division of Trade Support Services, International Trade Centre, Geneva. Email: sayers@intracen.org.

● *Where are the profit pools?*[24] **Profit pools refer to the different levels of profit available at different parts of the value system.** Some parts of a value system can be inherently more profitable than others because of the differences in competitive intensity (see section 2.3.1). For example, in the computer industry microprocessors and software have historically been more profitable than hardware manufacture. The strategic question becomes whether it is possible to focus on the areas of greatest profit potential. Care has to be exercised here. It is one thing to identify such potential; it is another to be successful in it given the capabilities an organisation has. For example, engineering firms may recognise the greater profit potential in providing engineering consulting services in addition to or instead of manufacturing. None the less many have found it difficult to develop such services successfully either because their staff do not have consultancy capabilities or because their clients do not recognise the firms as having them.

● The *'make or buy'* decision for a particular activity is critical given some of the above questions. This is the *outsourcing* decision. Increasingly outsourcing is becoming common as a means of lowering costs. Of course, the more an organisation outsources, the more its ability to influence the performance of other organisations in the value system may become a critically important capability in itself and even a source of competitive advantage. For example, the quality of a cooker or a television when it reaches the final purchaser is influenced not only by the activities undertaken within the manufacturing company itself, but also by the quality of components from suppliers and the performance of the distributors. There is, of course, the converse question: which activities most need to be part of the internal value chain because they are central to achieving competitive advantage? There may also be activities that do not generate competitive advantage in themselves, but which the organisation needs to control as they enable the exploitation of competitive advantage in other parts of the value chain, as indicated in section 3.3.4.

● *Partnering.* Who might be the best partners in the various parts of the value system? And what kinds of relationships are important to develop with each partner? For example, should they be regarded as suppliers or should they be regarded as alliance partners (see section 10.4)?

3.4.3 Activity systems

The discussion so far highlights the fact that all organisations comprise sets of capabilities, but that these are likely to be configured differently across organisations. It is this variable configuration of capabilities that makes an organisation and its strategy more or less unique. So for the strategist, understanding this matters a good deal.

Value chain analysis can help with this, but so too can understanding the activity systems of an organisation. As the discussion above in section 3.3 has made clear, the way in which resources are deployed through the organisation actually takes form in the activities pursued by that organisation; so it is important to identify what these activities are, why they are valuable to customers, how the various activities fit together and how they are different from competitors'.

Mapping activity systems

A number of writers,[25] including Michael Porter, have written about the importance of mapping activity systems and shown how this might be done. The starting point is to identify what Porter refers to as 'higher order strategic themes'. In effect these are the ways in which the organisation meets the critical success factors determining them in the industry. The next step is to identify the clusters of activities that underpin each of these themes and how these do or do not fit together. The result is a picture of the organisation represented in terms of activity systems such as that shown in Illustration 3.5. This shows an activity systems map for the Scandinavian strategic communications consultancy, Geelmuyden.Kiese.[26] The core higher-order theme at the heart of its success is its knowledge, built over the years, of how effective communications can influence 'the power dynamics of decision-making processes'. However, as Illustration 3.5 shows, this central theme is related to other higher-order strategic themes, each of which is underpinned by clusters of supporting activities. Three points need to be emphasised here:

- *Relationship to the value chain.* The various activities represented in an activity map can also be seen as parts of a value chain. The in-house methodology is, in effect, part of Geelmuyden.Kiese's operations; its recruitment practices are a component of its human resource management; its stance on integrity and insistence on openness rather than suppression of the information part of its service offering; and so on. However, activity systems mapping encourages a greater understanding of the complexity of strategic capabilities – important if bases of competitive advantage are to be identified and managed.

- *The importance of linkages and fit.* An activity systems map emphasises the importance of different activities that create value to customers pulling in the same direction and supporting rather than opposing each other. So the need is to understand (i) the fit between the various activities and how these reinforce each other and (ii) the fit externally with the needs of clients. There are two implications:
  - The danger of *piecemeal change* or tinkering with such systems which may damage the positive benefits of the linkages that exist.
  - The consequent *challenge of managing change.* When change is needed the implication is that change to one part of the system will almost inevitably affect another; or, put another way, change probably has to be managed to the whole system.

- *Relationship to VRIO.* It is these linkages and this fit that can be the bases of sustainable competitive advantage. In combination they may be *valuable* to clients, truly distinctive and therefore *rare.* Moreover, while individual components of an activity system might be relatively easy to imitate, in combination they may well constitute the complexity and causal ambiguity rooted in culture and history that makes them *inimitable.* Finally, there can be activities in the system that in themselves do not provide for competitive advantage, but that provide *organisational support* for other activities that do.

However, it is not just at the conceptual level that activity maps are important; they can also be directly helpful in the management of strategy:

- *Disaggregation.*[27] Useful as an activity map is, the danger is that, in seeking to explain capabilities underpinning their strategy, managers may identify capabilities at too abstract a level. If the strategic benefits of activity systems are to be understood, greater disaggregation is likely to be needed. For example, managers may talk of 'innovation' or 'putting the customer first' as a basis for 'good service'. These terms are too generic; they are umbrella descriptors of activities that exist at an even more operational level. If an activity map is to be useful for the purposes of managing activities then specific manageable activities need to be identified at an operating level. To take an example from Illustration 3.5, there is the recognition that the mentoring of junior staff by partners is important; but the map itself does not show specifically how this is done. Managers need to delve further and further into explanations of how specific activities support other activities so as to eventually 'deliver' customer benefit.

ILLUSTRATION 3.5

Activity systems at Geelmuyden.Kiese

The strategic capabilities of an organisation can be understood and analysed in terms of linked activities (an activity system).

Geelmuyden.Kiese is the largest Scandinavian strategic communications consultancy – an extension of what has traditionally been known as public relations services (PR). Its clients include organisations in the financial, oil, energy, pharmaceuticals and healthcare sectors. These clients typically approach Geelmuyden.Kiese when they have a problem, the solution of which critically depends on effective external or internal communication. In this context, its services include facilitation of contacts with public agencies, officials and government, investor relations, media relations, communication campaigns for new product launches, crisis management and in-company communication on key strategic issues.

At the heart of the company's success is the knowledge it has built up since its founding in 1989 of the dynamics of decision-making processes, often within influential bodies such as government and, linked to this, 'how effective communication may move power within those decision-making processes'. This knowledge is underpinned by some key aspects in the way in which it does business (see also Figure 3.6 below).

- The company seeks to *work at a strategic level* with its clients, prioritising those clients where such work is especially valued. Here it employs its own in-house methodology, developed on the basis of years of experience, and systematically reviews the assignments it undertakes both internally and on the basis of client surveys.

- The company takes a clear stance on *integrity of communication*. It always advises openness of communication rather than suppression of information and only deals with clients that will accept such principles. It often takes a stance on this approach in controversial and high-profile issues in the public domain.

- Staff are given high degrees of *freedom* but with some absolute criteria of *responsibility*. In this regard there are strict rules for handling clients' confidential information and strict sanctions if such rules are broken.

- *Recruitment* is based on ensuring that such responsibility can be achieved. It is largely on the basis of values of openness and integrity but also humour. The emphasis tends to be on recruiting junior personnel and developing them. Geelmuyden.Kiese has learned that this is a better way of delivering its services than recruiting established 'high-profile' consultants. Combined with its mentoring system for competence development of junior staff, it therefore believes that it offers the *best learning opportunities* in Scandinavia for young communications consultants.

- Geelmuyden.Kiese also offers *strong financial incentives* for top performance within the firm. Such performance includes rewards for the development of junior personnel but is also based on the internal evaluation of leadership qualities and performance.

- *Superfluous activities.* Just as in value chain analysis, but at a more detailed level, the question can be asked: are there activities that are not required in order to pursue a particular strategy? Or how do activities contribute to value creation? If activities do not do this, why are they being pursued by the organisation? Whether Ryanair used activity mapping or not, it has systematically identified and done away with many activities that other airlines commonly have. It is also continually seeking further activities that can be eliminated or outsourced to reduce cost.

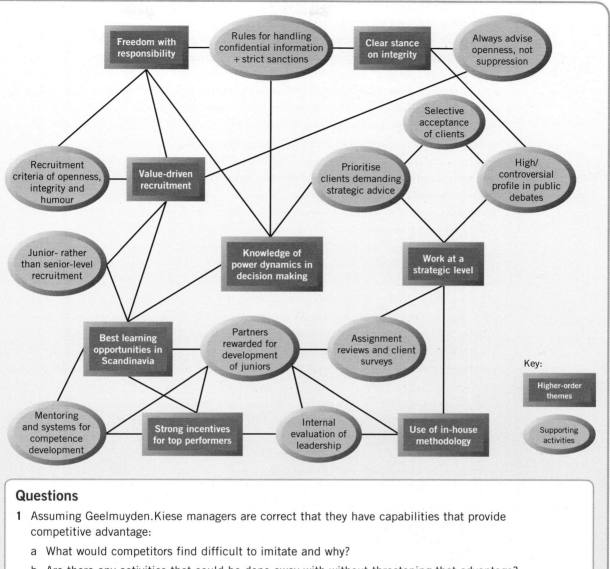

Key:

Higher-order themes

Supporting activities

Questions

1 Assuming Geelmuyden.Kiese managers are correct that they have capabilities that provide competitive advantage:

  a What would competitors find difficult to imitate and why?

  b Are there any activities that could be done away with without threatening that advantage?

2 If disaggregation (see section 3.4.3) is important, suggest what even more specific activities underpinning those in the activity map might be important.

3.4.4 SWOT[28]

It can be helpful to summarise the key issues arising from an analysis of strategic capabilities discussed in this chapter and the analysis of the business environment discussed in Chapter 2 to gain an overall picture of an organisation's strategic position. **SWOT provides a general summary of the Strengths and Weaknesses explored in an analysis of strategic capabilities** (Chapter 3) **and the Opportunities and Threats explored in an analysis of the environment**

(Chapter 2). This analysis can also be useful as a basis for generating strategic options and assess future courses of action.

The aim is to identify the extent to which strengths and weaknesses are relevant to, or capable of dealing with, the changes taking place in the business environment. Illustration 3.6 takes the example of a pharmaceuticals firm (Pharmcare).[29] It assumes that key environmental impacts have been identified from analyses explained in Chapter 2 and that major strengths and weaknesses have been identified using the analytic tools explained in this chapter. A scoring mechanism (plus 5 to minus 5) is used as a means of getting managers to assess the interrelationship between the environmental impacts and the strengths and weaknesses of the firm. A positive (+) denotes that the strength of the company would help it take advantage of, or counteract, a problem arising from an environmental change or that a weakness would be offset by that change. A negative (–) score denotes that the strength would be reduced or that a weakness would prevent the organisation from overcoming problems associated with that change.

Pharmcare's share price had been declining because investors were concerned that its strong market position was under threat. This had not been improved by a merger that was proving problematic. The pharmaceutical market was changing with new ways of doing business, driven by new technology, the quest to provide medicines at lower cost and politicians seeking ways to cope with soaring healthcare costs and an evermore informed patient. But was Pharmcare keeping pace? The strategic review of the firm's position (Illustration 3.6a) confirmed its strengths of a flexible sales force, well-known brand name and new healthcare department. However, there were major weaknesses, namely relative failure on low-cost drugs, competence in information and communication technology (ICT) and a failure to get to grips with increasingly well-informed users.

However, in the context of this chapter, if this analysis is to be useful, it must be remembered that the exercise is not absolute but relative to its competitors. So SWOT analysis is most useful when it is comparative – if it examines strengths, weaknesses, opportunities and threats in relation to competitors. When the impact of environmental forces on competitors was analysed (Illustration 3.6b), it showed that Pharmcare was still outperforming its traditional competitor (Company W), but potentially vulnerable to changing dynamics in the general industry structure courtesy of niche players (X and Y).

There are two main dangers in a SWOT exercise:

- *Listing.* A SWOT exercise can generate very long lists of apparent strengths, weaknesses, opportunities and threats, whereas what matters is to be clear about what is really important and what is less important. So prioritisation of issues matters. Three brief rules can be helpful here. First, as indicated above, focus on strengths and weaknesses that differ in *relative* terms compared to competitors and leave out areas where the organisation is at par with competitors. Second, focus on opportunities and threats that are directly *relevant* for the specific organisation and industry and leave out general and broad factors. Third, summarise the *result* and draw concrete conclusions.

- *A summary, not a substitute.* SWOT analysis is an engaging and fairly simple tool. It is also useful in summarising and consolidating other analysis that has been explained in Chapters 2 and 3. It is not, however, a substitute for that analysis. There are two dangers if it is used on its own. The first is that, in the absence of more thorough analysis, managers rely on preconceived, often inherited and biased views. The second is again the danger of a lack of specificity. Identifying very general strengths, for example, does not explain the underlying reasons for those strengths.

ILLUSTRATION

ILLUSTRATION 3.6

SWOT analysis of Pharmcare

A SWOT analysis explores the relationship between the environmental influences and the strategic capabilities of an organisation compared with its competitors.

(a) SWOT analysis for Pharmcare

	Environmental change (opportunities and threats)					
	Healthcare rationing	Complex and changing buying structures	Increased integration of healthcare	Informed patients	+	−
Strengths						
Flexible sales force	+3	+5	+2	+2	12	0
Economies of scale	0	0	+3	+3	+6	0
Strong brand name	+2	+1	0	−1	3	−1
Healthcare education department	+4	+3	+4	+5	16	0
Weaknesses						
Limited competences in biotechnology and genetics	0	0	−4	−3	0	−7
Ever lower R&D productivity	−3	−2	−1	−2	0	−8
Weak ICT competences	−2	−2	−5	−5	0	−14
Over-reliance on leading product	−1	−1	−3	−1	0	−6
Environmental impact scores	+9	+9	+9	+10		
	−6	−5	−13	−12		

(b) Competitor SWOT analyses

	Environmental change (opportunities and threats)				
	Healthcare rationing	Complex and changing buying structures	Increased integration of healthcare	Informed and passionate patients	Overall impact
Pharmcare *Big global player suffering fall in share price, low research productivity and post-mega-merger bureaucracy*	−3 Struggling to prove cost-effectiveness of new drugs to new regulators of healthcare rationing	+6 Well-known brand, a flexible sales force combined with a new healthcare education department creates positive synergy	−3 Weak ICT and lack of integration following mergers means sales, research and admin. are all underperforming	−2 Have yet to get into the groove of patient power fuelled by the internet	−2 Declining performance over time worsened after merger
Company W *Big pharma with patchy response to change, losing ground in new areas of competition*	−4 Focus is on old-style promotional selling rather than helping doctors control costs through drugs	−4 Traditional sales force not helped by marketing which can be unaccommodating of national differences	+0 Alliances with equipment manufacturers but little work done across alliance to show dual use of drugs and new surgical techniques	+4 New recruits in the ICT department have worked cross-functionally to involve patients like never before	−4 Needs to modernise across the whole company
Organisation X *Partnership between a charity managed by people with venture capital experience and top hospital geneticists*	+3 Potentially able to deliver rapid advances in genetics-based illnesses	+2 Able possibly to bypass these with innovative cost-effective drug(s)	+2 Innovative drugs can help integrate healthcare through enabling patients to stay at home	+3 Patients will fight for advances in treatment areas where little recent progress has been made	+10 Could be the basis of a new business model for drug discovery – but all to prove as yet
Company Y *Only develops drugs for less common diseases*	+3 Partnering with big pharma allows the development of drugs discovered by big pharma but not economical for them to develop	0 Focus on small market segments so not as vulnerable to overall market structure, but innovative approach might be risky	+2 Innovative use of web to show why products still worthwhile developing even for less common illnesses	+1 Freephone call centres for sufferers of less common illnesses Company, like patients, is passionate about its mission	+6 Novel approach can be considered either risky or a winner, or both!

Questions

1 What does the SWOT analysis tell us about the competitive position of Pharmcare with the industry as a whole?

2 How readily do you think executives of Pharmcare identify the strengths and weaknesses of competitors?

3 Identify the benefits and dangers (other than those identified in the text) of a SWOT analysis such as that in the illustration.

Prepared by Jill Shepherd, Segal Graduate School of Business, Simon Fraser University, Vancouver, Canada.

Figure 3.6 The TOWS matrix

	Internal factors	
	Strengths (S)	**Weaknesses (W)**
Opportunities (O)	**SO Strategic options** Generate options here that use strengths to take advantage of opportunities	**WO Strategic options** Generate options here that take advantage of opportunities by overcoming weaknesses
Threats (T)	**ST Strategic options** Generate options here that use strengths to avoid threats	**WT Strategic options** Generate options here that minimise weaknesses and avoid threats

External factors is labelled to the left spanning the Opportunities (O) and Threats (T) rows.

SWOT can also help focus discussion on future choices and the extent to which an organisation is capable of supporting these strategies. A useful way of doing this is to use a TOWS matrix[30] as shown in Figure 3.6. This builds directly on the information in a SWOT exercise. Each box of the TOWS matrix can be used to identify options that address a different combination of the internal factors (strengths and weaknesses) and the external factors (opportunities and threats). For example, the top left-hand box prompts a consideration of options that use the strengths of the organisation to take advantage of opportunities in the business environment. An example for Pharmcare might be the re-training of the sales force to deal with changes in pharmaceuticals buying. The bottom right-hand box prompts options that minimise weaknesses and also avoid threats; for Pharmcare this might include the need to develop its ICT systems to better service more informed patients. Quite likely this would also help take advantage of opportunities arising from changes in the buying structure of the industry (top right). The bottom left box suggests the need to use strengths to avoid threats, perhaps by building on the success of the healthcare education department to also better service informed patients.

(3.5) MANAGING STRATEGIC CAPABILITY

The previous section was concerned with diagnosing strategic capability. This section considers what managers might do to manage and improve resources and capabilities to the strategic benefit of their organisation.

One lesson that emerges from an understanding of the strategic importance of capabilities is that it can be difficult to discern where the basis of competitive advantage lies. Hence, if managers are to manage the resources and capabilities of their organisation, the sort of analyses explained here, especially VRIO, value chain analysis and activity systems mapping, are centrally important. If capabilities are not understood at these levels, there are dangers that managers can take the wrong course of action. For example, managers in an industrial cleaning company undertook an activity mapping exercise. It revealed that the way their van drivers dealt with collecting often filthy garments from industrial premises was especially valued by customers. This had developed through custom and practice, competitors did not do it and the managers themselves were not aware of it explicitly until they did the exercise. The irony was that they were just about to outsource the van delivery service! They were about to lose control of one of their potential bases of competitive advantage for the sake of cost reduction. This demonstrates the significance of diagnosing strategic capabilities. However, developing strategic capabilities that provide for competitive advantage can be extremely challenging as indicated by the strict criteria they need to fulfil in section 3.3 above. The question, then, is what can managers do to create, extend or upgrade an organisation's strategic capabilities after having diagnosed them?[31]

There are several different ways in which managers might develop strategic capabilities:

- *Internal capability development.* Could capabilities be added or upgraded so that they become more reinforcing of outcomes that deliver against critical success factors? This might be done, for example, by:

  - *Building and recombining capabilities.* Creating entirely new capabilities that provide for competitive advantage requires entrepreneurship and intrapreneurship skills. Managers can build managerial systems and a culture that promote capability innovation or form new venture units outside the rules of ordinary R&D and product development.[32]

  - *Leveraging capabilities.* Managers might identify strategic capabilities in one area of their organisation, perhaps customer service in one geographic business unit of a multinational, that are not present in other business units. They might then seek to extend this throughout all the business units. While this may seem straightforward, research has demonstrated that it can be rather difficult.[33] The capabilities of one part of an organisation might not be easily transferred to another because of the problems of managing change (see Chapter 14).

  - *Stretching capabilities.* Managers may see the opportunity to build new products or services out of existing capabilities. Indeed, building new businesses in this way is the basis of related diversification, as explained in Chapter 7.

- *External capability development.* Similarly, there may be ways of developing capabilities by looking externally. For example, this could be by developing new capabilities by acquisition or entering into alliances and joint ventures (see Chapter 10).

- *Ceasing activities.* Could current activities, not central to the delivery of value to customers, be done away with, outsourced or reduced in cost? If managers are aware of the capabilities central to bases of competitive advantage, they can retain these and focus on areas of cost reduction that are less significant.

KEY DEBATE

How useful is the resource-based view?

Although the resource-based view (RBV) of strategy has been highly influential during the last couple of decades it has been questioned by some academics.

Three recurring critiques have been considered as particularly damaging:

1 *The risk of tautology.* The underlying explanation of RBV is that the resource or capability characteristics that lead to competitive advantage are those that are valuable and rare. Richard Priem and John Butler argue that since competitive advantage is defined in terms of value and rarity this verges on tautology. To say that a business performs better than another because it has superior resources or is better at some things than other businesses is not helpful unless it is possible to be specific about what resources are important, why and how they can be managed.

2 *The lack of specificity.* A second and related critique centres on RBV's axiomatic definitions and that resources are not specified. The definitions of resources have been overly inclusive and can include virtually every asset of a firm. However, if everything can be a resource, nothing strategically useful can be associated with the firm that is not a resource. The specifics of resources and capabilities have, however, rarely been defined in RBV. Priem and Butler suggest this is particularly so with regard to the argued importance of tacit knowledge in bestowing competitive advantage: 'This may be descriptively correct, but it is likely to be quite difficult for practitioners to effectively manipulate that which is inherently unknowable.' Others agree that RBV has to come to grips with this as 'the practical assessment and valuation of resources involve subjectivism, knowledge creation and entrepreneurial judgement' (Kraaijenbrink et al.), something RBV largely ignores.

3 *The lack of dynamics.* Critics argue that RBV may only hold in relatively stable conditions where 'the rules of the game' in an industry remain relatively fixed. In more unpredictable environments the value of resources can easily and quickly diminish. Also, to keep up with dynamic environments resources must change, but RBV does not explain the origins of resources that provide for competitive advantage.

Jay Barney, one of the main proponents of the RBV, rejects most of the critique above even if he admits that we need to know more about how resources provide for sustainable competitive advantage:

1 Barney defends the view's practical value as it emphasises that managers must identify, evaluate and develop critical resources even if RBV does not specify exactly how. According to him, many strategy theories becomes tautological if restated in the way the RBV critics do and many of them are of a descriptive rather than prescriptive type in their early stages. Although he does not agree with the tautology critique, he concurs that the value of resources has to be exogenously determined on a market.

2 Barney admits that resources are defined to be all-inclusive, but he rejects that this lowers RBV's managerial relevance. On the contrary, he argues, this enhances its applicability. According to him, it is not possible to provide a comprehensive list of all resources that provides sustained competitive advantages. What RBV does is to clearly define the specific attributes required and then managers can apply this logic when evaluating and developing resources.

3 RBV proponents argue that, contrary to the dynamics critique, the view explicitly acknowledges that changes in environmental conditions might undermine the competitive advantage of a particular resource. Barney admits, however, that dynamic issues of resource change and creation are not covered by RBV and that it needs to be integrated with the dynamic capabilities approach.

Sources: R. Priem and J.E. Butler, 'Is the resource-based view a useful perspective for strategic management research?', *Academy of Management Review*, vol. 26, no. 1 (2001), pp. 22–40; J. Kraaijenbrink, J.-C. Spender and A.J. Groen, 'The resource-based view: a review and assessment of its critiques', *Journal of Management*, vol. 36, no. 1 (2010), pp. 349–72; J.B. Barney, 'Is the resource based view a useful perspective for strategic management research? Yes', *Academy of Management Review*, vol. 26, no. 1 (2001), pp. 41–56.

Questions

1 How easy do you think it would be to identify and imitate the strategic capabilities that give firm competitive advantage?

2 What roles do you think imagination and creativity play in identifying new and valuable strategic capabilities and combinations?

3 Is RBV useful?

- *Monitor outputs and benefits when it is not possible to fully understand capabilities.* There are organisations where managers may know that there are activities that have a positive impact on competitive advantage, but may not fully understand just how such positive impact arises. For example, the delivery of value can be dependent on highly specialised skills as in a cutting-edge hi-tech firm, or on complex linkages far down in the organisation. Here managers may have to be careful about disturbing the bases of such capabilities while, at the same time, ensuring that they monitor the outputs and benefits created for customers.[34]

- *Awareness development.* One of the lessons of this chapter is that the bases of competitive advantage often lie in the day-to-day activities that people undertake in organisations, so developing the ability of people to recognise the relevance of what they do in terms of how that contributes to the strategy of the organisation is important. This suggests that staffing policies, training and development including developing employee's awareness of how they contribute to competitive advantage are all central to capability deployment and development. Together with organisational learning these issues are discussed in later chapters on organising for success and leading strategic change (Chapters 13 and 14).

Much of the discussion in this chapter builds on research and the writing of scholars who take a resource-based view of strategy. They therefore emphasise the central importance of managing resources and capabilities for competitive advantage. The Key Debate summarises the arguments for and against the practical value of such an approach.

SUMMARY

- *The competitive advantage* of an organisation is likely to be based on the strategic *capabilities* it has that are valuable to customers and that its rivals do not have or have difficulty in obtaining. Strategic capabilities comprise both *resources and competences*.

- The concept of *dynamic capabilities* highlights that strategic capabilities need to change as the market and environmental context of an organisation changes.

- Sustainability of competitive advantage is likely to depend on an organisation's capabilities being of at least *threshold value* in a market, but also being *valuable*, relatively *rare*, *inimitable* and *supported by the organisation* and consequently fulfilling the *VRIO* criteria.

- Ways of diagnosing organisational capabilities include:
  - *VRIO analysis* of strategic capabilities as a tool to evaluate if they contribute to competitive advantage.
  - *Benchmarking* as a means of understanding the relative performance of organisations.
  - Analysing an organisation's *value chain* and *value system* as a basis for understanding how value to a customer is created and can be developed.
  - *Activity mapping* as a means of identifying more detailed activities which underpin strategic capabilities.
  - *SWOT analysis* as a way of drawing together an understanding of the strengths, weaknesses, opportunities and threats an organisation faces.

- Managers need to think about how and to what extent they can manage the *development of strategic capabilities* of their organisation by internal and external capability development and by the way they manage people in their organisation.

VIDEO ASSIGNMENTS

Visit **MyStrategyLab** and watch the CISCO case study for Chapter 3.

1 Using the video, identify the distinctive strengths and capabilities that give CISCO a competitive advantage.

2 Using Figure 3.2 and Table 3.2 from the text and referring to the VRIO criteria, explain how CISCO may be able to sustain its competitive advantage over time.

WORK ASSIGNMENTS

✱ *Denotes more advanced work assignments.*
* *Refers to a case study in the Text and Cases edition.*

3.1 Using Table 3.1 identify the resources and competences of an organisation with which you are familiar, your university or school for example. Alternatively, you can answer this in relation to, H&M* or Formula One* if you wish.

3.2✱ Undertake an analysis of the strategic capabilities of an organisation with which you are familiar in order to identify which capabilities, if any, meet the criteria of (a) value, (b) rarity, (c) inimitability and (d) organisational support (see section 3.3; Figure 3.2 and Table 3.2). You can answer this in relation to H&M* or Formula One* or the end case, Rocket Internet, if you so wish.

3.3✱ For an industry or public service of your choice consider how the strategic capabilities that have been the basis of competitive advantage (or best value in the public sector) have changed over time. Why have these changes occurred? How did the relative strengths of different companies or service providers change over this period? Why? Did dynamic capabilities play any role? Which?

3.4 Undertake a value chain or system analysis for an organisation of your choice (referring to Illustration 3.4 could be helpful). You can answer this in relation to a case study in the book such as Ryanair* or the end case, Rocket Internet, if you wish.

3.5✱ For a benchmarking exercise to which you have access, make a critical assessment of the benefits and dangers of the approach that was taken.

Integrative assignment

3.6 Prepare a SWOT analysis for an organisation of your choice (see Illustration 3.6). Explain why you have chosen each of the factors you have included in the analysis, in particular their relationship to other analyses you have undertaken in Chapters 2 and 3. What are the conclusions you arrive at from your analysis and how would these inform an evaluation of strategy (see Chapter 11)?

RECOMMENDED KEY READINGS

- For an understanding of the resource-based view of the firm, an early and much cited paper is by Jay Barney: 'Firm resources and sustained competitive advantage', *Journal of Management*, vol. 17 (1991), pp. 99–120. An overview of RBV research is written by Jay B. Barney, David J. Ketchen Jr and Mike Wright; 'The future of resource-based theory: revitalization or decline?', *Journal of Management*, vol. 37, no. 5 (2011), pp. 1299–315.

- A comprehensive book on dynamic capabilities is written by C. Helfat, S. Finkelstein, W. Mitchell, M. Peteraf, H. Singh, D. Teece and S. Winter, *Dynamic Capabilities: Understanding Strategic Change in Organisations*, Blackwell Publishing, 2007. The concept of dynamic capabilities is reviewed in Barreto, I., 'Dynamic capabilities: a review of past research and an agenda for the future', *Journal of Management*, vol. 36, no. 1 (2010), pp. 256–80.

- For a discussion of micro-foundations and dynamic capabilities see D.J. Teece, 'Explicating dynamic capabilities: the nature and microfoundations of (sustainable) enterprise performance', *Strategic Management Journal*, vol. 28, pp. 1319–50 (2007) and his book *Dynamic capabilities and strategic management – organising for innovation and growth*, Oxford University Press, 2009.

- Michael Porter explains how mapping activity systems can be important in considering competitive strategy in his article 'What is strategy?', *Harvard Business Review*, November–December 1996, pp. 61–78.

- For a critical discussion of the use and misuse of SWOT analysis see T. Hill and R. Westbrook, 'SWOT analysis: it's time for a product recall', *Long Range Planning*, vol. 30, no. 1 (1997), pp. 46–52.

REFERENCES

1. The concept of resource-based strategies was introduced by B. Wernerfelt, 'A resource-based view of the firm', *Strategic Management Journal*, vol. 5, no. 2 (1984), pp. 171–80. The seminal and most cited paper is by Jay Barney, 'Firm resources and sustained competitive advantage', *Journal of Management*, vol. 17, no. 1 (1991), pp. 99–120. There are now many books and papers that explain and summarise the approach: for example, D. Hoopes, T. Madsen and G. Walker in the special issue of the *Strategic Management Journal*, 'Why is there a resource based view?', vol. 24, no. 10 (2003), pp. 889–902; and J. Barney and D. Clark, *Resource-Based Theory: Creating and Sustaining Competitive Advantage*, Oxford University Press, 2007.

2. The literature most commonly differentiates between 'resources' and 'capabilities'. See, for example, an early article by Raphael Amit and Paul Schoemaker: Amit, R. and Schoemaker, P.J.H. 'Strategic assets and organizational rent', *Strategic Management Journal*, vol. 14 (1993), pp. 33–46; and Jay Barney's book: J.B. Barney, *Gaining and sustaining competitive advantage*, Addison-Wesley, 1997. The term 'core competences' was promoted by Gary Hamel and C.K. Prahalad in the early 1990s: G. Hamel and C.K. Prahalad, 'The core competence of the corporation', *Harvard Business Review*, vol. 68, no. 3 (1990), pp. 79–91. 'Capabilities' is, however, a more common term today, but it is sometimes used interchangeably with 'competences' in the literature. Later 'capabilities' has been distinguished into 'operational capabilities' and 'dynamic capabilities'. David Teece and his co-authors were first to introduce 'dynamic capabilities': D.J. Teece, G. Pisano and A. Shuen, 'Dynamic Capabilities and strategic management', *Strategic Management Journal*, vol. 18, no.7 (1997), pp. 509–533. Sid Winter later explained the differences between

'ordinary' and 'dynamic capabilities': S.G. Winter, 'Understanding dynamic capabilities', *Strategic Management Journal*, vol. 24 (2003), no. 10, pp. 991–5.

3. For summary papers on dynamic capabilities see I. Barreto, 'Dynamic capabilities: a review of past research and an agenda for the future', *Journal of Management*, vol. 36, no. 1 (2010), pp. 256–80; C.L. Wang and P.K. Ahmed, 'Dynamic capabilities: a review and research agenda', *International Journal of Management Reviews*, vol. 9, no. 1 (2007), pp. 31–52; and V. Ambrosini and C. Bowman, 'What are dynamic capabilities and are they a useful construct in strategic management?', *International Journal of Management Reviews*, vol. 11, no. 1 (2009), pp. 29–49. The most comprehensive book on dynamic capabilities is written by C. Helfat, S. Finkelstein, W. Mitchell, M. Peteraf, H. Singh, D. Teece and S. Winter, *Dynamic Capabilities: Understanding Strategic Change in Organizations*, Blackwell Publishing, 2007.

4. David Teece has written about dynamic capabilities originally in D.J. Teece, G. Pisano and A. Shuen: 'Dynamic capabilities and strategic management', *Strategic Management Journal*, vol. 18, no. 7 (1997), pp. 509–34. More recently he has expanded his explanation in D.J. Teece, 'Explicating dynamic capabilities: the nature and microfoundations of (sustainable) enterprise performance', *Strategic Management Journal*, vol. 28, vol. 1 (2007), pp. 1319–50; and in the book *Dynamic capabilities and strategic management – organizing for innovation and growth*, Oxford University Press, 2009.

5. Sid Winter has explained the differences between ordinary and dynamic capabilities in S.G. Winter, 'Understanding dynamic capabilities', *Strategic Management Journal*, vol. 24, no. 10 (2003), pp. 991–5.

6. For a discussion of outlet proliferation as dynamic capability see S.G. Winter, 'Understanding dynamic capabilities', *Strategic Management Journal*, vol. 24, no. 10 (2003), pp. 991–5.

7. For a list of examples of dynamic capabilities see K.M. Eisenhardt and J.A. Martin, 'Dynamic capabilities: what are they?', *Strategic Management Journal*, vol. 21, no. 10/11 (2000), pp. 1105–21.

8. For a discussion of microfoundations of capabilities and managerial beliefs see G. Gavetti, 'Cognition and hierarchy: rethinking microfoundations of capabilities development', *Organization Science*, vol. 16 (2005) pp. 599–617.

9. Gary Hamel and C.K. Prahalad were the academics who promoted the idea of core competences. For example, G. Hamel and C.K. Prahalad, 'The core competence of the corporation', *Harvard Business Review*, vol. 68, no. 3 (1990), pp. 79–91. This idea of driving strategy development from the resources and competences of an organisation is discussed in G. Hamel and C.K. Prahalad, 'Strategic intent', *Harvard Business Review*, vol. 67, no. 3 (1989), pp. 63–76; and G. Hamel and C.K. Prahalad, 'Strategy as stretch and leverage', *Harvard Business Review*, vol. 71, no. 2 (1993), pp. 75–84.

10. The VRIO criteria were introduced by Jay Barney in J.B. Barney, *Gaining and sustaining competitive advantage*, Addison-Wesley, 1997. Originally the acronym *VRIN* was used to also emphasise Non-substitutability and how competitors must not be able to substitute a valuable, rare and inimitable capability for another, but this is now encompassed in the inimitability criterion (see 1 above; Barney, 1991).

11. This is borne out in a meta-study of research on RBV by S.L. Newbert, 'Empirical research on the Resource Based View of the firm: an assessment and suggestions for future research, *Strategic Management Journal*, vol. 28 (2007), pp. 121–46.

12. For an explanation of how complex capabilities and strategies contribute to inimitability see J.W. Rivkin, 'Imitation of complex strategies', *Management Science*, vol. 46, no. 6 (2000), pp. 824–44.

13. The seminal paper on causal ambiguity is S. Lippman and R. Rumelt, 'Uncertain imitability: an analysis of interfirm differences in efficiency under competition', *Bell Journal of Economics*, vol. 13 (1982), pp. 418–38. For a summary and review of research on causal ambiguity see A.W. King, 'Disentangling interfirm and intrafirm causal ambiguity: a conceptual model of causal ambiguity and sustainable competitive advantage', *Academy of Management Review*, vol. 32, no. 1 (2007), pp. 156–78.

14. The distinction between and importance of characteristic and linkage ambiguity is explained by A.W. King and C.P. Zeithaml, 'Competencies and firm performance: examining the causal ambiguity paradox', *Strategic Management Journal*, vol. 22, no. 1 (2001), pp. 75–99.

15. For a fuller discussion of path dependency in the context of strategic capabilities, see D. Holbrook, W. Cohen, D. Hounshell and S. Klepper, 'The nature, sources and consequences of firm differences in the early history of the semiconductor industry', *Strategic Management Journal*, vol. 21, nos 10–11 (2000), pp. 1017–42.

16. For an extensive discussion about complementary assets and capabilities see D. Teece, 'Profiting from technological innovation', *Research Policy*, vol. 15, no. 6 (1986), pp. 285–305.

17. The knowledge-based view was pioneered by B. Kogut, and U. Zander, 'Knowledge of the firm, combinative capabilities, and the replication of technology', *Organization Science*, vol. 3, no. 3 (1992), pp. 383–97. The importance of analysing and understanding knowledge is discussed in I. Nonaka and H. Takeuchi, *The Knowledge-creating Company*, Oxford University Press, 1995. There are also collections of articles on organisational knowledge: e.g. the Special Issue of the *Strategic Management Journal* edited by R. Grant and J.-C. Spender, vol. 17 (1996) and the *Harvard Business Review on Knowledge Management*, HBR Press, 1998. More recently Mark Easterby-Smith and Isabel Prieto have explored the relationships in: 'Dynamic capabilities and knowledge management: an integrative role for learning', *British Journal of Management*, vol. 19 (2008), pp. 235–49.

18. See I. Nonaka and H. Takeuchi, reference 17 above.

19. E.C. Wenger and W.M. Snyder, 'Communities of practice: the organisational frontier', *Harvard Business Review*, vol. 73, no. 3 (2000), pp. 201–7; and E. Wenger, *Communities of Practice: Learning, Meaning and Identity*, Cambridge University Press, 1999.

20. See R. Camp, *Benchmarking: the Search for Industry Best Practices that Lead to Superior Performance*, Quality Press, 2006.

21. See A. Murdoch, 'Lateral benchmarking, or what Formula One taught an airline', *Management Today* (November 1997), pp. 64–7. See also the Formula One case study in the case study section of this book (Text and Cases version only).

22. An extensive discussion of the value chain concept and its application can be found in M.E. Porter, *Competitive Advantage*, Free Press, 1985.

23. For an extended example of value chain analysis see 'Understanding and using value chain analysis' by Andrew Shepherd in *Exploring Techniques of Analysis and Evaluation in Strategic Management*, edited by Veronique Ambrosini, Prentice Hall, 1998.

24. The importance of profit pools is discussed by O. Gadiesh and J.L. Gilbert, 'Profit pools: a fresh look at strategy', *Harvard Business Review*, vol. 76, no. 3 (1998), pp. 139–47.

25. See M. Porter, 'What is strategy?', *Harvard Business Review*, Nov.–Dec. (1996), pp. 61–78; and N. Siggelkow, 'Evolution towards fit', *Administrative Science Quarterly*, vol. 47, no. 1 (2002), pp. 125–59.

26. We are grateful for this example based on the doctoral dissertation of Bjorn Haugstad, *Strategy as the Intentional Structuration of Practice: Translation of Formal Strategies into Strategies in Practice*, submitted to the Saïd Business School, University of Oxford, 2009.

27. 'Disaggregation' is a term used by D. Collis and C. Montgomery, 'Competing on resources', *Harvard Business Review*, July–August (2008), pp. 140–50.

28. The idea of SWOT as a common-sense checklist has been used for many years: for example, S. Tilles, 'Making strategy explicit', in I. Ansoff (ed.), *Business Strategy*,

Penguin, 1968. See also T. Jacobs, J. Shepherd and G. Johnson's chapter on SWOT analysis in V. Ambrosini (ed.), *Exploring Techniques of Strategy Analysis and Evaluation*, Prentice Hall, 1998. For a critical discussion of the (mis)use of SWOT, see T. Hill and R. Westbrook, 'SWOT analysis: it's time for a product recall', *Long Range Planning*, vol. 30, no. 1 (1997), pp. 46–52.

29. For background reading on the pharmaceutical industry see, for example, 'From vision to decision Pharma 2020', PWC, www.pwc.com/pharma, 2012; 'The pharmaceutical industry', Scherer, F.M., *Handbook of health economics*, vol. 1 (2000), part B, pp. 1297–336; 'A wake-up call for Big Pharma', *McKinsey Quarterly*, December 2011; and Gary Pisano, *Science Business*, Harvard Business School Press, 2006.

30. See H. Weihrich, 'The TOWS matrix – a tool for situational analysis', *Long Range Planning* (April 1982), pp. 54–66.

31. For a fuller discussion of how managers may manage strategic capabilities, see C. Bowman and N. Collier, 'A contingency approach to resource-creation processes', *International Journal of Management Reviews*, vol. 8, no. 4 (2006), pp. 191–211.

32. For a discussion of how the periphery in organisations can build radically new capabilities see P, Regnér, 'Strategy creation in the periphery: inductive versus deductive strategy making', *Journal of Management Studies*, vol. 40, no. 1 (2003), pp. 57–82.

33. See C.A. Maritan and T.H. Brush, 'Heterogeneity and transferring practices: implementing flow practices in multiple plants', *Strategic Management Journal*, vol. 24, no. 10 (2003), pp. 945–60.

34. This observation is made by Veronique Ambrosini in her book (see reference 23 above).

Rocket Internet – will the copycat be imitated?

Introduction

Rocket Internet is a very successful Berlin-based start-up incubator and venture capital firm. It starts, develops and funds e-commerce and other online consumer businesses. It has 25 offices around the world with over 700 employees and an additional 15,000 in its portfolio companies. It has helped create and launch over 100 start-ups and is currently active in more than 50 portfolio companies across more than 40 countries.

The company was founded by the Samwer brothers, Alexander, Oliver and Marc. After going to Silicon Valley in the late 1990s they became inspired by the Californian entrepreneurial culture and especially eBay. The brothers offered eBay to create a German version of the online auction house, but they received no reply from eBay. Instead they launched their own eBay clone, Alando, and adapted it to German conditions. A month later they were acquired by eBay for $50 m. This was to be their first great online success, but far from the last.

Next the brothers created Jamba, a mobile phone content platform. It was sold to VeriSign, a network infrastructure company, for $273 m in 2004. Since then they have become experts in spotting promising business models, especially in the USA, and imitating and scaling them internationally quicker than the originals. This model is the basis of Rocket Internet, which was founded in 2007. Several of their ventures have been acquired by the company with the original idea (see table). Two of their most high-profile ventures after

The Samwer brothers

Alando were CityDeal, which was sold off to American Groupon, and eDarling sold to American eHarmony.

The company's has frequently been criticised for simply being a copycat machine without any original ideas and some have even claimed it is a scam that rips off the originals. However, the question remains: if Rocket Internet has been so incredibly successful and what it does is simply copying, why has no one successfully imitated Rocket Internet yet? The brothers, through Oliver Samwer, defend their model in *Wired*:

'But look at the reality. How many car manufacturers are out there? How many washing-machine manufacturers are there? How many Best Buys? Did someone write that Dixons copied Best Buy, or did anyone ever write that Best Buy copied Dixons, or that [German electronics retailer] Media Markt copied Dixons? No, they talk about Media Markt. They talk about Dixons.

Company	Founded	Business	Buyer	Founded	Price, $m	Transaction date
Alando	1999	Online marketplace	eBay	1995	50	1999
cember.net	2005	Online business network	Xing	2003	6.4	2008
eDarling	2009	Online dating	eHarmony	1998	30% stake*	2010
GratisPay	2009	Virtual currency for online games	SponsorPay	2009	na	2010
CityDeal	2009	Discount deals for consumers	Groupon	2008	126†	2010
viversum	2003	Online astrology	Questico	2000	na	2010

*With option to buy more   † Including a stake in Groupon
Source: Gründerszene.de

They talk about Best Buy. What is the difference? Isn't it all the same thing?'

Source: http://www.economist.com/node/21525394#

Finance and expert teams

Rocket Internet has strong financial backup from its main investor globally, Kinnevik, a Swedish investment company. Kinnevik also contributes with its long-time experience from investing in new businesses and its global network of contacts. Many other investors invest directly in the start-ups and in the later growth stages, among them the American investment bank J.P. Morgan. To work with the investors and structure the financial solutions Rocket Internet has a team of about 35 experts in finance at the Berlin headquarters.

While Rocket Internet has the financial skills needed for an incubator and venture capital firm, it also develops the concepts of new ventures, provides the technology platforms and combines various skills necessary for setting up new ventures. It has about 250 specialists working at the Berlin head office. These specialists are part of diverse expert teams. Engineering including IT software, programming and web design skills are of course essential for product development. At head office there are around 200 engineers who have access to state-of-the art technologies and tools.

There are several other expert teams as well, not least in marketing, including experts in customer management, customer relationship marketing and online marketing. Other teams include Operations, Business Intelligence and HR. Apart from this expertise Rocket Internet has a Global Venture Development programme that includes a global mobile task force of entrepreneurial talents that can bring further know-how to all international markets. This task force includes venture developers with functional skills in product development, supply management, operations and online marketing. They rotate every 4–6 months to a new venture in another part of the world.

Human resource management and culture

The HR team recruit not only regular staff support for Rocket Internet, but specialists for the expert teams and Global Venture Development programme and, not least, the founders of the ventures. Based on their Silicon Valley entrepreneurial spirit they emphasise personal drive rather than good school grades. Head of HR, Vera Termuhlen, explains to VentureVillage.com:

'All in all, it doesn't matter if an applicant is from an elite university. For the area of global venture development, we look for applicants that are hands-on, first-class, have analytical skills, describe themselves as entrepreneurs, have a passion for the online start-up scene along and a willingness to work internationally, often in exotic locations like the Philippines or Nigeria.'

The co-founders and managing directors of the individual ventures establish all operations, build the team around a venture, and develop the business. They act as entrepreneurs and hold personal stakes in a venture's equity. Recruiting them is central and Rocket Internet normally recruits extraordinary, ambitious MBA-level graduates with high analytic skills from within the local regions where the venture is set up. As Alexander Kudlich, Managing Director of Rocket Internet, says:

'We are looking for those who from an analytical point of view understand the beauty of the business model, understand the rationale and understand what a huge opportunity is. Sometimes we say we are looking for analytical entrepreneurs rather than accidental billionaires.'

The company emphasises not only strong expertise, but 'a close cultural connection to Rocket Internet'. Rocket Internet has an intense entrepreneurial working culture that is highly performance driven including high pressure, long working hours, often from 09.00 to 23.00, and little job security. While this is attractive to some, the culture has also been criticised for being too tough and aggressive. Rocket Internet's Managing Director Alexander Kudlich comments on the culture:

'I would describe our culture as very focused, we have young teams – the average age is below 30. There is no place where you get more freedom and where you can take as much responsibility as you want. The only thing we want back is accountability.'

Identification of business models and execution

While some of Rocket Internet's skills are common among other Berlin incubators and indeed incubators throughout Europe, the company is more of an international venture builder compared to most. Expertise is shared throughout the portfolio of ventures globally and its best practice can be applied across the diverse business models (ranging from online fashion to payments to deals to social networking). Compared to many other incubators, the function of the headquarters is central. While entrepreneurs are hired to oversee individual ventures, overall strategy for Rocket Internet is largely shaped at the head office. In particular, this is the case in the identification of new ideas, concepts and business models. The four managing directors at head office lead the scanning for and identification of novel and proven online and mobile transaction-based business models that are internationally scalable. Former Managing Director Florian Heinemann explains in *Wired*: 'We take a pretty systematic look at business models that are already out there and we basically try to define whether a model suits our competence and is large enough that it's worth it for us to go in there.'

Another significant aspect of Rocket Internet's centralised model is the speed at which it can launch novel business models internationally. This is different compared to many US counterparts, but also European ones. Rocket Internet has an international infrastructure and distribution network that build ventures on an international scale in just a few months. The capacity for multiplying business models has been demonstrated repeatedly for diverse types of online business models. As Managing Director Kudlich explains in *Wall Street Journal*:

'When we identify a business model we can, within a few weeks, build a platform out of our central teams. In the meantime the local Rocket offices will have hired or allocated the people who will execute on the ground . . . That gives us the speed. The combination of access to the best talent in each country combined with highly standardised or modular approach in terms of platform and systems which are rolled out by our headquarters.'

In brief, Rocket Internet specialises in execution rather than innovation. This is also how the management defend their model when they are blamed for simply being a clone machine. Oliver Samwer says that they are 'execution entrepreneurs' rather than 'pioneering entrepreneurs'. Managing Director Kudlich explains to *Inc. Magazine*: 'Which is harder: to have the idea of selling shoes online or to build a supply chain and warehouse in Indonesia? Ideas are important. But other things are more important.'

Paradoxically, even though Rocket Internet often builds on others' ideas it prefers to keep its own ideas for itself as explained by Marc Samwer in the *New York Times*: 'We really don't like to speak about our investments since our track record encourages people to set up competing sites . . . Ideas travel much faster these days.'

The future

Rocket Internet's success has continued. Zalando, which initially mimicked the online shoe retailing business in the USA by Zappos, now part of Amazon, has expanded into clothing and jewellery. Sales are rising rapidly; annual revenues for 2011 were $650 m and Rocket Internet claim $130 m in revenue per month. Recently it has also launched an Amazon clone, Lazada in South East Asia and a mobile payments company, Payleven, inspired by American Square.

Rocket Internet has, however, started to attract imitators of its own. One of the operations is Wimdu, a copy of the American Airbnb, which allows individual home and apartment owners to list their properties as holiday accommodation. However, Airbnb quickly formed a partnership with another Berlin incubator, Springstar, and they have since been rolling out Airbnb globally. Similarly, the original company responded swiftly when Rocket Internet imitated Fab.com, a designer deal site, with its Bamarang. Fab acquired Casacanda, a parallel European site, and quickly relaunched it as a Fab internationally and Rocket Internet had to close down Bamarang. Rocket Internet is even facing imitators from within. Two of its managing directors have together with other former employees left to set up the Berlin incubator 'Project A Ventures'. There are thus signs that Rocket Internet may eventually be imitated itself.

Questions

1 Based on the data from the case (and any other sources available) use the frameworks from the chapter and analyse the strategic capabilities of Rocket Internet:

   a What are its resources and competences?

   b What are its threshold, distinctive and dynamic capabilities?

2 Based on your initial analysis and answers to question 1, carry out a VRIO analysis for Rocket Internet. What do you conclude? To what extent does Rocket Internet have strategic capabilities with sustained competitive advantage?

3 What is the importance of the Samwers brothers? What would happen if they left or sold the company?

References
1. Joel Kaczmarek, 'An inside look at Rocket Internet', *VentureVillage.com*, 18 November 2012.
2. Max Chafkin, 'Lessons from the world's most ruthless competitor', *Inc. Magazine*, 29 May 2012.
3. Ben Rooney, 'Rocket Internet leads the clone war', *The Wall Street Journal*, 14 May 2012.
4. Gerrit Wiesmann, 'Zalando to set foot in seven new countries', *Financial Times*, 26 March 2012.
5. Tim Bradshaw, 'Facebook backers to take stake in Zalando', *Financial Times*, 2 February 2012.
6. Matt Cowan, 'Inside the clone factory', *Wired UK*, 2 March 2012.
7. Robert Levine, 'The kopy kat kids', *Cnnmoney.com*, 2 October 2007.
8. *New York Times*, 3 December 2006.
9. *The Economist*, 'Attack of the clones', 6 August 2011.

Suggested video clip

http://www.youtube.com/watch?v=Tq7WnzY89KE

4

STRATEGIC PURPOSE

Learning outcomes

After reading this chapter you should be able to:

● Assess the *strategic purpose* of an organisation in terms of *mission*, *vision*, *values* and *objectives*.

● Analyse the strategic significance of different *ownership models* for an organisation's purpose.

● Evaluate the implications for strategic purpose of the *shareholder* and *stakeholder models* of corporate governance.

● Undertake *stakeholder analysis* as a means of identifying the influence of different stakeholder groups in terms of their power and interest.

● Relate *corporate responsibility* and *personal ethics* to purpose and strategy.

MyStrategyLab

MyStrategyLab is designed to help you make the most of your studies. Visit **www.pearsoned.co.uk/mystrategylab** to discover a wide range of resources, including:

● A personalised **Study plan** that will help you understand core concepts

● **Audio and video clips** that put the spotlight on strategy in the real world

● **Online glossaries and flashcards** that provide helpful reminders when you're looking for some quick revision.

(4.1) INTRODUCTION

In Spring 2012, Sir Stelios Haji-Ioannou, founder of the easyJet airline, took his former company to court as part of his campaign to curb what he saw as its excessive growth. Although he had retired from a management role, Sir Stelios and his family were still major shareholders in easyJet, with 38 per cent ownership, and they had become fierce critics of the company's growth strategy. According to Sir Stelios, easyJet's current management were investing in growth at the expense of dividends for shareholders. At stake in the clash between founder and managers were crucial issues about the purpose of business – long-term growth or immediate dividends – and who has the right to control strategy – owners or management.

The previous two chapters have looked at the importance of the external environment and internal capabilities for an organisation's strategic position. This chapter examines how external pressures and internal aspirations interact in the setting of organisational purpose. The chapter warns that organisational purpose can rarely be reduced to a simple formula such as 'profit maximisation'. Organisational purposes are typically complex and diverse. It is important to be clear about what purposes drive strategy, who influences such purposes and who monitors performance against them. These are the concerns of this chapter.

An important concept here is that of **stakeholders, those individuals or groups that depend on an organisation to fulfil their own goals and on whom, in turn, the organisation depends**. An underlying question is whether the strategic purpose of the organisation should reflect the expectations of a particular stakeholder, for example shareholders, or incorporate broader stakeholder interests, such as employees, customers and the local community. Figure 4.1 summarises the different influences on strategic purpose discussed in the chapter:

- The chapter begins in section 4.2 by developing the discussion in Chapter 1 about different ways in which organisations express *strategic purpose*, including statements of *mission, vision, values* and *objectives*.

- Section 4.3 considers the *ownership* structures and the *corporate governance* framework within which organisations operate. The concern is with the way in which formally constituted bodies such as investors or boards influence strategic purpose through the formalised processes for supervising executive decisions and actions.

Figure 4.1 Influences on strategic purpose

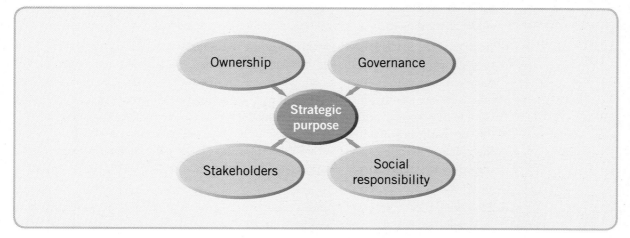

- In determining purpose, it is important to understand how different *stakeholders* may be involved in strategy. Section 4.4 addresses the different power and interest of various stakeholders through *stakeholder analysis*.

- Section 4.5 is concerned with issues of *social responsibility* and *ethics*. Here the question is which purposes an organisation *should* fulfil. How should managers respond to the expectations society has of their organisations, both in terms of *corporate responsibility* and in terms of the *behaviour of individuals* within organisations, not least themselves?

(4.2) MISSION, VISION, VALUES AND OBJECTIVES

Harvard University's Cynthia Montgomery[1] argues that defining and expressing a clear and motivating purpose for the organisation is the core of a strategist's job. Even for private-sector organisations, this purpose is typically more than simple profit maximisation. Long-term prosperity and employee motivation usually require expressions of purpose that go beyond just profits. According to Montgomery, the stated purpose of the organisation should address two related questions: *how* does the organisation make a difference; and *for whom* does the organisation make that difference? If the stakeholders of an organisation can relate to such a purpose it can be highly motivating. Indeed, research by Jim Collins and Jerry Porras suggests that the long-run success of many US corporations – such as Disney, General Electric or 3M – can be attributed (at least in part) to the clear guidance and motivation offered by such statements of purpose.[2]

There are four ways in which organisations typically define their purpose:

- A **mission statement aims to provide employees and stakeholders with clarity about what the organisation is fundamentally there to do.** This is often expressed in the apparently simple but challenging question: 'What business are we in?' Two linked questions that can clarify an organisation's 'business' are: 'What would be lost if the organisation did not exist?'; and 'How do we make a difference?' Though they do not use the term 'mission statement', Collins and Porras[3] suggest that understanding the fundamental mission can be done by starting with a descriptive statement of what the organisation actually does, then repeatedly delving deeper into the organisation's purpose by asking 'why do we do this?' They use the example of managers in a gravel-and-asphalt company arriving at the conclusion that its mission is to make people's lives better by improving the quality of built structures. At the University of Utrecht (see Illustration 1.2), the mission includes educating students, training the next generation of researchers and addressing social issues.

- A **vision statement is concerned with the future the organisation seeks to create.** The vision typically expresses an aspiration that will enthuse, gain commitment and stretch performance. So here the question is: 'What do we want to achieve?' Porras and Collins suggest managers can identify this by asking: 'If we were sitting here in twenty years what do we want to have created or achieved?' They cite the example of Henry Ford's original vision in the very early days of automobile production that the ownership of a car should be within the reach of everyone. For the Swedish music site Spotify, the vision is to become 'the Operating System of music', a universal platform for listening just as Microsoft is for office software.

- **Statements of corporate values communicate the underlying and enduring core 'principles' that guide an organisation's strategy and define the way that the organisation**

should operate. For example, Google famously includes in its values 'you can be serious without a suit', 'fast is better than slow' and 'don't be evil'. It is important that these values be enduring, so a question to ask is: 'Would these values change with circumstances?' If the answer is 'yes', then they are not 'core' and not 'enduring'. An example is the importance of leading-edge research in some universities. Whatever the constraints on funding, such universities hold to the enduring centrality of research. On the other hand, as Google has grown and diversified, some critics wonder whether the company still abides by its principle of 'don't be evil' (see Chapter 12 end case).

- **Objectives are statements of specific outcomes that are to be achieved.** These are often expressed in precise financial terms, for instance the level of sales, profits or share valuation in one, two or three years' time.[4] Organisations may also have quantifiable market-based objectives, such as market share, customer service, repeat business and so on. Sometimes objectives focus on the basis of competitive advantage: for example, low-cost airlines such as Ryanair set objectives on turnaround time for their aircraft because this is at the core of their distinctive low-cost advantage. Increasingly organisations are also setting objectives referred to as 'the triple bottom line', by which is meant not only economic objectives such as those above, but also environmental and social objectives to do with their corporate responsibility to wider society (see section 4.4.1 below).

Some critics regard vision, mission and values statements as liable to become bland and too wide-ranging.[5] Objectives can seem attractively precise by contrast. However, vision, mission and values statements provide a longer-term view of the organisation and its underlying strategy. While objectives are useful for guiding and monitoring performance in the short term, visions, missions and values can offer more enduring sources of direction and motivation. But it remains crucial to make vision, mission and values statements meaningful.

Three principles are helpful in creating meaningful vision, mission and values statements:[6]

- *Focus*: statements should focus attention and help guide real decisions. Effective vision, mission and values statements should define what is excluded from the organisation's strategy as much as what is included. At Apple, the visionary founder Steve Jobs regarded as crucial the ability to say 'no' to non-core activities. Statements should also be practical decision-making tools. Google's value of 'fast' can guide choices between strategic options with different levels of complexity: Google's product development managers will cut product features which slow down its essential search and advertising functions, even if they might be nice to have.

- *Motivational*: statements should motivate employees to do their best. Here it is important that they not be so bland as to be applicable to nearly all organisations, but rather be distinctive and authentic to the particular organisation in question. To motivate, they should stretch organisational performance to higher levels, but at the same time the targets must be credible. Thus Apple's vision of making computers available to everybody inspired Steve Jobs' employees in the early years of the company.

- *Clear*: the third important principle in such statements is clarity. In order to motivate employees in their day-to-day work, visions, missions and values should be easy to communicate, understand and remember. Here it is often useful to be crisp and simple. Thus founder Mark Zuckerberg identified three of Facebook's values as 'move fast', 'be bold' and 'be open': these are clear, memorable and actionable.

ILLUSTRATION 4.1

Mozilla's mission: beyond Firefox

Can the Mozilla Foundation's mission and principles guide and motivate it into a new generation of products beyond its Firefox browser?

The Mozilla Foundation is a non-profit organisation that originated in the late 1990s from the old web-browser company Netscape. Mozilla's best known product is the Firefox open source web-browser, produced largely for free by a community of volunteer software developers. In 2012, Firefox had about 25 per cent share of the world's browser market, recently over taken by Google's Chrome. About 85 per cent of Mozilla's revenue is a contract with Google, renewed for three years in 2011, which pays the Foundation in return for using Google as Firefox's default search engine.

Mozilla says the following about itself:

'Mozilla's mission is to promote openness, innovation and opportunity on the web.

What we do
We do this by creating great software, like the Firefox browser, and building movements, like Drumbeat [the community of software developers], that give people tools to take control of their online lives.

What we strive for
As a non-profit organisation, we define success in terms of building communities and enriching people's lives instead of benefiting shareholders. We believe in the power and potential of the Internet and want to see it thrive for everyone, everywhere.'

Mozilla also publishes what it calls a 'Manifesto', containing a set of principles intended 'to make Mozilla contributors proud of what we're doing and motivate us to continue'. Principles of the Manifesto include:

- The internet is a global public resource that must remain open and accessible.
- The internet should enrich the lives of individual human beings.
- Individuals' security on the internet is fundamental and cannot be treated as optional.

- Individuals must have the ability to shape their own experiences on the internet.
- Free and open-source software promotes the development of the internet as a public resource.

In 2012, Mozilla was developing a range of new initiatives. The most notable is 'Pancake', a cloud-based framework that allows users to carry and manage their personal data wherever they go. One objective of Pancake is to counter the way mobile apps are fragmenting the internet. Mozilla's President, Mitchell Baker, explained to the BBC: 'The internet was meant to be connected – not siloed. We really do want to encourage developers to develop across devices, using the same kind of power and explosive innovation and freedoms that the web has given us over the last 15 years.'

For Mitchell Baker, 'the reason for [these] initiatives is not driven by revenue. It is driven because we cannot fulfil the Mozilla mission unless we have a presence in these other spaces.' She continued, referring particularly to Mozilla's users and developers: 'Our stakeholders – we don't have shareholders – are not looking for a financial return on investment. The return on their time and energy and goodwill that they're looking for is the product that they like, and an internet that has a layer of user sovereignty in it.'

Sources: Mozilla website, 2012; and www.bbc.co.uk, 'Life after Firefox', 10 April 2012.

Questions

1 Mozilla does not produce a formal vision statement. Based on the materials here, what do you think Mozilla's vision would be?

2 How do Mozilla's mission and principles influence its approach to new initiatives? Is there any danger in its apparent priorities?

Whatever statements of mission, vision and values are employed, or whatever the objectives which are set, it is important to understand who influences what they are. The following sections examine key influencers.

(4.3) OWNERS AND MANAGERS

Purpose is typically set by the organisation's owners and managers. Owners and managers are not always the same and their interests can diverge. This section explores different kinds of ownership models and the governance issues involved in reconciling owners and managers.

4.3.1 Ownership models

There are many types of ownership, and the boundaries between them often blur.[7] However, it is useful to distinguish four main ownership models, each with different implications for strategic purpose. Figure 4.2 ranges these four models along two axes. The horizontal axis describes the dominant modes of management, ranging from wholly *professional* (with managers employed for their professional expertise) to wholly *personal* (with management determined by personal connections to ownership). The vertical axis describes the extent to which purpose is focused on profit as an exclusive goal or on profit as just one of a mix of motives. In each case, there is a range along the axes: organisations vary in their relative positioning and sometimes organisations do not conform to the typical behaviour of their ownership model. None the less organisations with different ownership models do tend to bunch together in distinctive ways.

Figure 4.2 Ownership, management and purpose

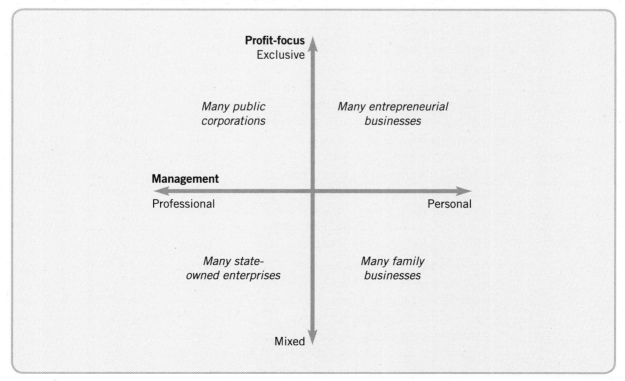

The four main ownership models are as follows:

- *Public companies* (often called publicly traded companies or public limited companies) are the most important ownership model in economies such as these of the USA, northern Europe, Japan and many others. These companies sell their shares to the public, with ownership typically in the hands of individual investors or, frequently, institutions such as pension funds, banks or insurance companies.[8] Usually owners do not manage public companies themselves, but delegate that function to professional managers. In principle, company managers work to make a financial return for their owners – that is why the public usually buy the shares in the first place. If shareholders are not satisfied financially, they can either sell the shares or seek the removal of the managers. In terms of Figure 4.2 therefore, most public companies focus strongly on profit. However, profit maximisation is rarely a simple goal for companies. There is often a delicate balance to be struck between the short-run profits and long-term survival, for example. Short-term profits might be improved by cutting research budgets or taking advantage of loyal customers, but such action may well be at the expense of the long run. In relation to the vertical axis in Figure 4.2, public companies may therefore vary in how extremely they focus on profit objectives.

- *State-owned enterprises* are wholly or majority owned by national or sometimes regional governments. They are very important in many developing economies: about 80 per cent of stock market value is accounted for by state-owned companies in China, 60 per cent in Russia and 40 per cent in Brazil.[9] Privatisation has reduced the role of state-owned enterprises in many developed economies, but quasi-privatised agencies such as hospital trusts and school academies in the United Kingdom operate in a similar way. In state-owned enterprises, politicians typically delegate day-to-day control to professional managers, though they may intervene on major strategic issues. State-owned enterprises usually have to earn some kind of profit or surplus in order to fund investment and build financial reserves, but they are also likely to pursue a range of other objectives that are in keeping with government policy. For Chinese state-owned enterprises, for example, securing access to overseas resources such as minerals and energy is an important objective.

- *Entrepreneurial businesses* are businesses that are substantially owned and controlled by their founders. Lakshmi Mittal remains chairman and chief executive of his creation, Arcelor Mittal, the largest steel company in the world. Sir Richard Branson is chairman of the Virgin Group, founded as a record store in 1972 and now including airline, train and sports businesses. None the less, as they grow, entrepreneurial businesses are likely both to rely more on professional managers to cope with increasing complexity and to draw in external investors in order to fund new opportunities. Typically entrepreneurial companies need to focus heavily on profit in order to survive and grow, and the presence of external investors is likely to increase the pressure for financial performance. However, entrepreneurial businesses may also be partly directed by personal missions, for instance developing a particular technology to its full potential.[10]

- *Family businesses* are typically businesses where ownership by the founding entrepreneur has passed on to his or her family, on account of the founder's death or retirement for instance. Typically family businesses are small to medium-sized enterprises, but can be very big: Ford, Fiat, Samsung and Walmart, the largest retailer in the world, are all under family ownership and retain significant family involvement in top management roles. Quite often the family retains a majority of the voting shares, while releasing the remainder to the public on the stock market: thus half of stock market-listed companies in the 10 largest Asian markets are effectively family-controlled.[11] Also, management may be partly profession-alised, even though top management remains ultimately under family control: thus the Chief Executive of Ford is a non-family member, but the Executive Chairman is still William Ford Jr. For family businesses, retaining control over the company, passing on management to the next generation and ensuring the company's long-term survival are often very important objectives, and these might rule out profit-maximising strategies that involve high risk or require external finance. Thus a family business might diversify into lots of small businesses rather than engage in one large one, because that would minimise risk and give a chance to younger family members to work in distinct areas of activity.[12]

As well as these four main types of ownership model, there are several other variants which play smaller but still significant roles in the economy.[13] *Not-for-profit* organisations, such as Mozilla (Illustration 4.1), are typically owned by a charitable foundation: they may need to make some kind of surplus to fund investment and protect against hard times, but they fundamentally exist to pursue social missions. The *partnership* model, in which the organisation is owned and controlled by senior employees (its partners), is important in many professional services such as law and accounting. There are also *employee-owned* firms, which spread ownership among employees as a whole. The most famous example of this in the United Kingdom is the retailer John Lewis, but this model is also being promoted for hospitals in the British National Health Service. Typically these not-for-profits, partnerships and employee-owned firms are restricted in their ability to raise external finance, making them more conservative in their strategies.

Clearly everybody should know how the ownership of their own organisation relates to its strategic purpose: as above, strategy for a state-owned business is likely to be very different to that of a public company. However, it is also important for managers to understand the owner-ship of other organisations with which they engage, for example competitors and partners. Different ownership models will shape their purpose and drive their strategic decisions as well. Without understanding the relationship between ownership and purpose, it is easy to be sur-prised by competitors and partners with different priorities to your own. For example, Western public mining companies have often found themselves outbid for overseas mining opportuni-ties by Chinese state-owned companies keen to secure supplies.

4.3.2 Corporate governance

The varying roles of owners and professional managers raise issues of corporate governance.[14] **Corporate governance is concerned with the structures and systems of control by which man-agers are held accountable to those who have a legitimate stake in an organisation.**[15] Key stakeholders in corporate governance are typically the owners, but may include other groups such as employee representatives. Connecting stakeholder interests with management action is a vital part of strategy. Failures in corporate governance have contributed to calamitous strategic choices in many leading companies, even resulting in the complete destruction of global companies such as the energy giant Enron in 2001 and the leading investment bank Lehman Brothers in 2008. With the survival of whole organsations at stake, governance is increasingly recognised as a key strategic issue.

Managers and stakeholders are linked together via the governance chain. **The governance chain shows the roles and relationships of different groups involved in the governance of an organisation.** In a small family business, the governance chain is simple: there are family share-holders, a board with some family members and there are managers, some of whom may be family too. Here there are just three layers in the chain. In large public corporations, however, influences on governance can be complex. Figure 4.3 shows a governance chain for a typical large, public corporation. Here the size of the organisation means there are extra layers of management internally, while being publicly quoted introduces more investor layers too. Individual investors (the ultimate beneficiaries) often invest in public corporations through investment funds, i.e. institutional investors such as unit trusts or pension funds, which then invest in a range of companies on their behalf. Funds are typically controlled by trustees, with day-to-day investment activity undertaken by investment managers. So the ultimate beneficiaries may not even know in which companies they have a financial stake and have little power to influence the companies' boards directly.

Economists analyse the relationships in such governance chains in terms of the *principal–agent model*.[16] Here 'principals' pay 'agents' to act on their behalf, just as homeowners employ estate agents to sell their homes. Classically, the principal is simply the owner and the agent is the manager. However, the reality for large public corporations is usually more complex, with principals and agents at every level. In Figure 4.3, the beneficiaries are the ultimate principals

Figure 4.3 The chain of corporate governance: typical reporting structures

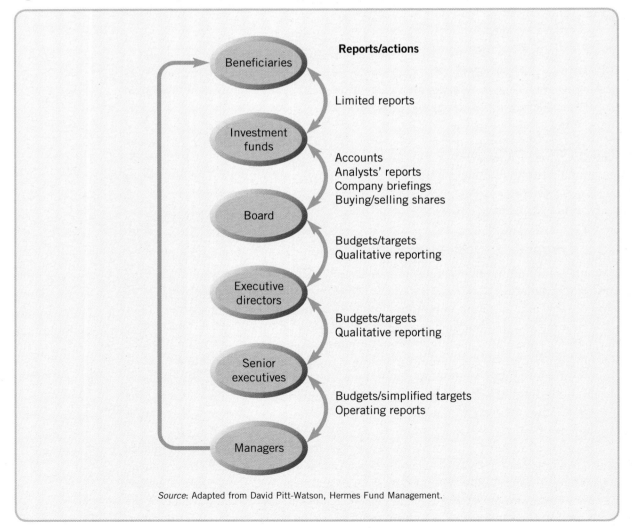

Source: Adapted from David Pitt-Watson, Hermes Fund Management.

and fund trustees and investment managers are their immediate agents in terms of achieving good returns on their investments. Further down the chain, company boards can be considered as principals too, with senior executives their agents in managing the company. Thus there are many layers of agents between ultimate principals and the managers at the bottom, with the reporting mechanisms between each layer liable to be imperfect. Weak links in the governance chain at several levels is what led to the scandals at News Corporation for example (see Illustration 4.2).

The governance issues in principal–agent theory arise from three problems:

- *Knowledge imbalances*: agents typically know more than principals about what can and should be done. After all, it is they who are actually doing the job and they have presumably been hired for their expertise.

- *Monitoring limits*: it is very difficult for principals to monitor closely the performance of their agents. This limit is made worse because principals usually have many investments, so their attention is likely to be split several ways.

- *Misaligned incentives*: unless their incentives are closely aligned to principals' interests, agents are liable to pursue other objectives that reward them better. Principals might introduce bonus schemes in order to incentivise desired performance, but then agents may game the system: for example, they might use their superior knowledge to negotiate bonus targets that are in reality easy to meet.

Principal–agent theory therefore stresses the importance of knowledgeable principals, effective monitoring systems and well-designed incentives in order to make sure that large organisations actually pursue the purposes that their owners set for them.

4.3.3 Different governance models

The governing body of an organisation is typically a board of directors. Although the legal requirements vary in detail around the world, the primary responsibility of a board is typically to ensure that an organisation fulfils the wishes and purposes of those whom it represents. However, who the board represents varies. In the private sector in some parts of the world it is primarily shareholders, but in other parts of the world it is a broader or different stakeholder base. In the public sector, the governing body is accountable to the political arm of government – possibly through some intermediary such as a funding body. These differences have implications for organisational purpose and strategy as well as the role and composition of boards.

At the most general level there are two governance models: the shareholder model, prioritising shareholder interests; and the stakeholder model, recognising the wider set of interests that have a stake in an organisation's success.[17] These two models are pure types, and there are many variants on each. The question for managers, therefore, is where their organisation is positioned on the range between the pure shareholder and pure stakeholder models of governance.

A shareholder model of governance

The shareholder model is dominant in public companies, especially in the USA and UK. Shareholders have priority in regard to the wealth generated by the company, as opposed to employees for example. The shareholder interest in a company is assumed to be largely financial. Shareholders can vote for the board of directors according to the number of their shares and, in the

ILLUSTRATION 4.2

A family affair? News Corporation's governance crisis

The governance chain at News Corporation seems to have failed at several levels, putting at risk family control.

In 2012, Rupert Murdoch was 81 years old and still Chairman and Chief Executive of News Corporation, the international media conglomerate that he had launched in Australia in the 1950s. News Corporation's assets included Fox News, the *Wall Street Journal* and the movie studio 20th Century Fox. The company also owned several leading British newspapers, including the *Sun*, *The Times* and the *Sunday Times*, and a 39 per cent holding in the dominant United Kingdom pay-TV broadcaster, BSkyB. The Murdoch family owned 39 per cent of the corporation's voting shares and a family friend, Prince Al Waleed bin Talal, held a further 7 per cent. Other important shareholders included the Bank of New York, the investment management company Invesco, and Calpers, the Californian teachers' pension fund.

News Corporation was run as something of a family fiefdom. Rupert Murdoch's son Lachlan had been Deputy Chief Operating Officer until 2005, when he resigned abruptly for unexplained reasons. Murdoch's daughter Elisabeth had been Managing Director of BSkyB before setting up her own television production company, Shine, with backing from BSkyB itself. In 2011, Shine was bought by News Corporation for £290 m (€350 m; $440 m): Elisabeth personally received more than half this sum, at the same time as retaining her role as Shine's Chairman and Chief Executive and joining the News Corporation main board. Some News Corporation shareholders accused the company of paying too much for Shine. Another of Rupert's sons was James, who was News Corporation's Deputy Chief Operating Officer. At the start of 2012, James was also Chairman of BSkyB and Chairman and Chief Executive of News Corporation Europe and Asia, overseeing a range of international assets including the group's British newspapers.

This last position placed James Murdoch in the front line of the telephone hacking scandal that engulfed News Corporation's British newspapers during 2011–12. In a fiercely competitive market, News Corporation's tabloid newspaper editors had encouraged journalists to get the most sensational stories they could, and this often led them to break into people's mobile phone and email accounts. It was unclear when James Murdoch became aware of these practices: he claimed in a British Parliamentary inquiry that he did not know of them until much later. If James was unaware, he appeared not to be in close control of his own newspapers and to be very lax in investigating accusations of lawless behaviour by his employees.

In early 2012, James Murdoch resigned all his British responsibilities. But James continued as Deputy Chief Operating Officer of News Corporation globally, while retaining responsibilities for the company's Continental European interests. Shareholders were deeply unhappy with the Murdoch family's management, despite the strong performance of News Corporation's shares relative to competitors' since 2009. In October 2011, more than half the independent shareholders had either voted against or abstained on the re-appointment of Rupert Murdoch as Chairman and a similar proportion had voted against the reappointment to the board of James. Of course, the family controlled enough shares to win the overall majority. However, Anne Simpson, Head of Corporate Governance for Calpers, said of the hostile votes: 'This sends a strong signal to the News Corp board that investors are looking for robust independence. It's a vote in favour of board rejuvenation.'

Main sources: *Financial Times*, 25 October 2011 and 3 April 2012.

Questions

1 Referring to Figure 4.3, at what levels did the governance chain at News Corporation seem to fail?

2 Given that News Corporation's share price was outperforming competitors', why would shareholders vote against the Murdochs' management at News Corporation? What else could they do?

pure model at least, there are many shareholders so that no single shareholder dominates. Shareholders can also exert control indirectly through the trading of shares. Dissatisfied shareholders may sell their shares, leading to a drop in the company's share price and an increased threat to directors of takeover by other firms.

There are arguments for and against the shareholder model. The argued advantages include:

- *Higher rates of return.* The unambiguous focus on shareholder interests means that investors typically get a higher rate of return than in the stakeholder model. Managers are not distracted by the interests of other stakeholders.

- *Reduced risk.* Shareholders face less risk in the shareholder model, especially if operating within an economy with an efficient stock market. Shareholders can diversify their risk by using the stock market to buy shares in many different companies. They can also use the stock market to sell the shares of companies that look in danger.

- *Increased innovation and entrepreneurship.* Since the system facilitates higher risk-taking by investors, the shareholder model should promote entrepreneurship, innovation and higher growth. It is easier to attract capital investment where investors know that they can easily diversify their shareholdings and trade their shares.

- *Better decision making.* Arguably the separation of ownership and management makes strategic decisions more objective in relation to the potentially different demands and constraints of financial, labour and customer markets. If the shareholders are well spread, no one shareholder is likely to exercise undue control of management decisions.

Potential disadvantages of the shareholder model include:

- *Diluted monitoring.* Where there are many shareholders, each with small stakes and often with many other investments, the principal–agent problem is exacerbated. Any single shareholder may not think it worthwhile monitoring performance closely, and simply hope that other shareholders are doing so. This may allow managers to sacrifice shareholder value to pursue their own agendas. For example, CEOs may further their own egos and empires with mergers that add no value to shareholders.

- *Vulnerable minority shareholders.* On the other hand, especially where corporate governance regulation is weak, the shareholder model can be abused to allow the emergence of dominant shareholders. Such dominant shareholders may exploit their voting power to the disadvantage of minority shareholders. This is the *principal–principal problem*: the dominant shareholder (principal) may appoint managers, make acquisitions, guarantee debts or sell assets contrary to the interests of the other shareholders (also principals).[18] Minority shareholders do not have enough votes to control abusive majority shareholders.

- *Short-termism.* The need to make profits for shareholders may encourage managers to focus on short-term gains at the expense of long-term projects, such as research and development. Some high-technology public companies such as Google and Facebook have deliberately adopted a dual-class shareholder structure, where the original founders and their associates have larger voting rights in order to protect these companies' commitment to long-term innovation.

The stakeholder model of governance

An alternative model of governance is the stakeholder model. This is founded on the principle that wealth is created, captured and distributed by a variety of stakeholders. It is not just shareholders who have a stake in the future of a business. Important stakeholders may include employees, local communities, local governments, major suppliers and customers, and banks. Shareholders are also stakeholders, of course, but in the stakeholder model they are likely to take larger stakes in their companies than in the pure shareholder model and to hold these stakes longer term. Thus in the stakeholder governance model, management need to be responsive to multiple stakeholders. In some governance systems, some of these stakeholders, for example banks and employees, may be formally represented on boards.

The argued advantages for the stakeholder model of governance include:

- *Long-term horizons.* It is argued that when shareholders hold large blocks of shares, they are likely to regard their investments as long term. It is harder to dispose of large shareholdings when business is going wrong, and the incentive to get involved in order to maintain the value of the stake is proportionately greater. Thus the predominance of large investors in the stakeholder model reduces the pressure for short-term results as against longer-term performance.

- *Less reckless risk-taking.* Many stakeholders are more risk-averse than diversified shareholders. Employees fear for their livelihoods. Large-scale shareholders have more to lose, and find it harder to exit in the case of difficulty. Local government bodies may face the loss of major employers in their regions. The stakeholder model therefore discourages excessive risk-taking.

- *Better management.* Given stakeholders' concern for the long-term prosperity of the company, there may be a closer level of monitoring of management and greater demands for information from within the firm. Management are under greater pressure to perform. Further, because power may reside with a limited number of large shareholders, it is easier to intervene in the case of management failure.

There are also possible disadvantages to the stakeholder model of governance:

- *Weaker decision making.* Close monitoring by powerful stakeholders could lead to interference, slowing down of decision processes and the loss of management objectivity when critical decisions have to be made.

- *Uneconomic investments.* Due to lack of financial pressure from shareholders, long-term investments may also be made in projects where the returns may be below market expectations.

- *Reduced innovation and entrepreneurship.* Because investors fear conflicts with the interests of other stakeholders, and because selling shares may be harder, they are less likely to provide capital for risky new opportunities.

The stakeholder model recognises that organisations typically operate within a complex set of relationships, going beyond simple economic ones. As discussed in section 5.3, organisations participate in *organisational fields* in which *legitimacy* matters, not just profits.[19] Legitimacy typically means more than sticking to the letter of the law; it involves following norms of appropriate conduct in the eyes of key members of an organisation's institutional field (e.g. governments, regulators, trade unions and customers, as well as shareholders). Legitimacy is an overarching concept of purpose, where profits, ethical conduct and fairness to stakeholders all play a role. Even if an organisation does not operate explicitly according to a stakeholder model, it is typically important that strategies be legitimate in this wider sense of satisfying all key stakeholders' expectations of appropriate conduct. Firms operating on a shareholder model also need to maintain legitimacy in their field if they are to avoid interference by regulators, consumer boycotts and demoralised employees.

4.3.4 **How boards of directors influence strategy**

A central governance issue is the role of boards of directors and of directors themselves. Since boards have the ultimate responsibility for the success or failure of an organisation as well as the benefits received by shareholders or wider stakeholders, they must be concerned with strategy.

Under the shareholder model there is typically a single-tier board structure, with a majority of 'non-executive' directors, outsiders who do not have day-to-day managerial responsibilities but provide oversight on behalf of shareholders. The emphasis on outside directors is intended to bring greater independence to the primary role of the board, protecting shareholders' interests. However, as explained above, this is not without its problems since the choice of non-executives is often influenced by the executive directors themselves.

The stakeholder model can involve a two-tier board structure. For example, in Germany for firms of more than 500 employees there is a supervisory board (*Aufsichtsrat*) and a management board (*Vorstand*). The supervisory board is a forum where the interests of various stakeholder groups are represented, including shareholders and employees but also banks with a long-term involvement in the company. Strategic planning and operational control are vested with the management board, but major decisions like mergers and acquisitions require approval of the supervisory board. Two-tier boards also exist in other European countries, notably the Netherlands and France.

Two issues are especially significant here:

- *Delegation*. Strategic management can be entirely delegated to management, with the board receiving and approving plans and decisions. Here it is important that an organisation's strategy is not 'captured' by management at the expense of other stakeholders. The two-tier board system seeks to prevent this. It is less clear how this occurs in the single-board structure typical of the shareholder model.

- *Engagement*. The board can engage in the strategic management process. This has practical problems concerning the time and knowledge level of non-executive directors in particular to perform their role this way. This problem can be especially pronounced in organisations such as charities or public bodies with governing boards or trustees of people committed to the mission of the organisation, keen to become involved but with limited operational understanding of it.

In the guidelines increasingly issued by governments[20] or advocated by commentators there are some common themes:

- Boards must be seen to *operate 'independently' of the management* of the company. So the role of non-executive directors is heightened.

- Boards must be *competent to scrutinise the activities of managers*. So the collective experience of the board, its training and the information available to it are crucially important.

- Directors must have the *time* to do their job properly. So limitations on the number of directorships that an individual can hold are also an important consideration.

However, it is the *behaviour of boards* and their members that are likely to be most significant whatever structural arrangements are put in place.[21] Important, therefore, are respect, trust, 'constructive friction' between board members, fluidity of roles, individual as well as collective responsibility, and the evaluation of individual director and collective board performance. Board behaviour was a problem at ENRC (see Illustration 4.3).

ILLUSTRATION 4.3

ENRC's boardroom – City or Soviet?

After spectacular dismissals, this Kazakhstan multinational seeks to shake off doubts about the operations of its board.

The Eurasian Natural Resources Company (ENRC) originated in the 1990s, with the bulk of the assets acquired by three entrepreneurs – Patokh Chodiev, Alijan Ibragimov and Alexander Machkevitch – during the privatisation of Kazakhstan's heavy industries from 1994 to 1996. All three men are now billionaires, owning between them 35 per cent of what has become a multinational company headquartered and listed in the City of London. With 70,000 employees, ENRC is one of the world's largest producers of ferrochrome, one of the world's biggest exporters of iron ore and the world's ninth largest producer of traded alumina. It has substantial interests in Brazil and Africa as well as back home in Kazakhstan. The Kazak state owns 12 per cent of the company, and another Kazak entrepreneur controls a further 26 per cent through his company, Kazakhmys.

However, since 2008, when ENRC listed on the London Stock Exchange, the company has had a significant proportion of ownership by ordinary external investors. The listing had raised £1.4 bn (€1.7 bn or $2.1 bn) in additional capital, intended to fund international expansion: the Kazakh government was keen on creating a 'national champion'. The listing had also provided an opportunity to tidy up the company's corporate governance arrangements in order both to meet Stock Exchange requirements and to improve acceptability as an acquirer of businesses internationally. It also offered Chodiev, Ibragimov and Machkevitch a convenient means of realising the value of their shareholdings, which could now be easily traded in the market should they want to.

The three entrepreneurs were not, however, allowed to sit on the main board of ENRC, because of an ongoing prosecution by the Belgian authorities regarding alleged money-laundering. Nevertheless, the company recruited some highly respected non-executive directors to its board, including Ken Olisa and Sir Richard Sykes. Olisa had had a distinguished career at IBM and Wang Laboratories, before entering investment banking in the City of London. Sykes is a former chairman of pharmaceuticals giant GlaxoSmithKline and former rector (head) of Imperial College, London.

The board chairman was Dr Johannes Sittard, a German executive who had formerly worked for the Mittal international steel group.

Not all went well for the non-executives. After long-standing rumours about disagreements over governance and international strategy, Sir Richard Sykes and Ken Olisa were voted off the board in 2011 by the three founding entrepreneurs and allied shareholders. Ken Olisa wrote to *The Times* newspaper immediately afterwards: 'Although the founding shareholders had signed Representation Agreements committing them to support an independent board, it soon became obvious that the original owners' informal historical links with Directors and senior management meant that their influence would be ever-present... The chairman frequently played the part of founders' messenger – not always accurately – rather than as leader of an independent board.' Olisa went on to describe his dismissal as 'more Soviet than City'.

ENRC responded by reviewing its corporate governance. In February 2012, a new chairman was appointed: Mehmet Dalman, formerly with the leading German company Commerzbank. In his first official meeting with investors, Dalman commented on the ENRC board: 'We have continued to review board composition, mindful of the need to progressively refresh the board, with a view to affording it with talented and dedicated directors exhibiting, among other qualifications, domain knowledge, long experience of best-in-class corporate governance practices, as well as corporate finance and strategy.'

Sources: Financial Times, 8 June 2011; 3 February 2012; Daily Telegraph, 21 March 2012.

Questions

1 Ideally, what sort of companies and roles might Dalman's new non-executive directors have worked in previously?

2 Should ENRC's governance not improve, what could (i) independent investors and (ii) the London Stock Exchange do?

(4.4) STAKEHOLDER EXPECTATIONS[22]

It should be clear by now that managers' decisions about the purpose and strategy of their organisation are influenced by the expectations of stakeholders. Even in a shareholder model, managers cannot entirely ignore stakeholders such as employees or local communities: whether or not they are represented on the organisational board, their support is important for long-term success. This poses a challenge because there are likely to be many stakeholders, especially for a large organisation (see Figure 4.4), with different, perhaps conflicting, expectations. This means that managers need to take a view on: (i) which stakeholders will have the greatest influence; (ii) which expectations they need to pay most attention to; (iii) the extent to which the expectations of different stakeholders vary.

4.4.1 Stakeholder groups

External stakeholders can be usefully divided into four types in terms of the nature of their relationship with the organisation and how they might affect the success or failure of a strategy:

Figure 4.4 Stakeholders of a large organisation

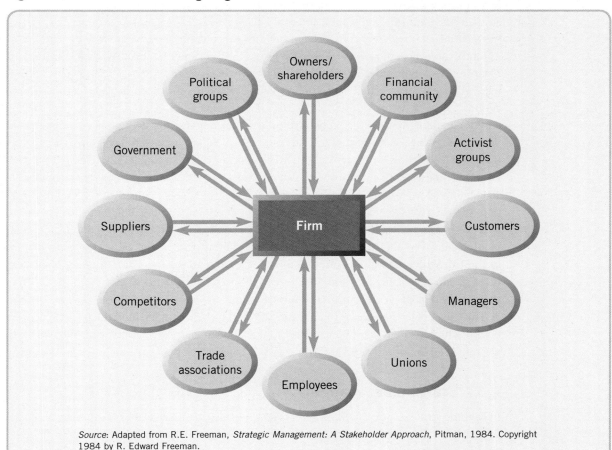

Source: Adapted from R.E. Freeman, *Strategic Management: A Stakeholder Approach*, Pitman, 1984. Copyright 1984 by R. Edward Freeman.

- *Economic stakeholders*, including suppliers, customers, distributors, banks and shareholders.

- *Social/political stakeholders*, such as policy-makers, regulators and government agencies that may influence the strategy directly or via the context in which strategy is developed.

- *Technological stakeholders*, such as key adopters, standards agencies and ecosystem members supplying complementary products or services (e.g. applications for particular mobile phones).

- *Community stakeholders*, who are affected by what an organisation does; for example, those who live close to a factory or, indeed, the wider society. These stakeholders typically have no formal relationship with the organisation but may, of course, take action (e.g. through lobbying or activism) to influence the organisation.

The influence of these different types of stakeholders is likely to vary in different situations. For example, the 'technological group' will be crucial for strategies of new product development, while the 'social/political' group is usually particularly influential in the public-sector context or for companies operating in different countries with different political and legal systems.

There are also stakeholder groups internal to an organisation, which may be departments, geographical locations or different levels in the hierarchy. Individuals may belong to more than one stakeholder group and such groups may 'line up' differently depending on the issue or strategy in hand. Of course, external stakeholders may seek to influence an organisation's strategy through their links with internal stakeholders. For example, customers may exert pressure on sales managers to represent their interests within the company.

Since the expectations of stakeholder groups will differ, it is normal for conflict to exist regarding the importance or desirability of aspects of strategy. In most situations, a compromise will need to be reached. The more companies globalise, the more they add further complications as they operate in multiple arenas. For example, an overseas division is part of the parent company, which will likely have expectations about consistent global behaviour and performance, but is also part of a local community, which may well have different expectations. Table 4.1 shows some typical situations which give rise to conflicting stakeholder expectations. It may, however, also be possible in developing a strategy to look for compatible stakeholder expectations. For example, managers of the English conservation tourist attraction, the Eden Project, looked for 'synergies around purpose' among different stakeholders to obtain support and funding for it. Both the European Union and the local economic development agency were interested in developing the economy of Cornwall, one of the poorest areas in the UK, while the Millennium Commission, a government-sponsored funding body, was interested in developing iconic architecture in the area. The synergies between the three led to the success that the Eden Project has since become.

The stakeholder concept is, then, valuable when trying to understand the political context within which strategy develops. Indeed, taking stakeholder expectations and influence into account is an important aspect of strategic choice, as will be seen in Chapter 11.

4.4.2 **Stakeholder mapping**[23]

In defining strategic purpose, it is useful to identify and categorise all the various stakeholders. Stakeholder mapping **identifies stakeholder interest and power and helps in understanding political priorities.** The focus is on the *power* different stakeholders have to influence strategy and the *interest* each stakeholder has in particular issues.

Table 4.1 **Some common conflicts of expectations**

- In order to grow, short-term profitability, cash flow and pay levels may need to be sacrificed.

- 'Short-termism' may suit managerial career aspirations but preclude investment in long-term projects.

- When family businesses grow, the owners may lose control if they need to appoint professional managers.

- New developments may require additional funding through share issue or loans. In either case, financial independence may be sacrificed.

- Public ownership of shares will require more openness and accountability from the management.

- Cost efficiency through capital investment can mean job losses.

- Extending into mass markets may require a reduction in quality standards.

- In public services, a common conflict is between mass provision and specialist services (e.g. preventative dentistry or heart transplants).

- In large multinational organisations, conflict can result because of a division's responsibilities to the company and also to its host country.

These two dimensions form the basis of the power/interest matrix shown as Figure 4.5. The matrix classifies stakeholders in relation to the power they hold and the extent to which they are likely to show interest in supporting or opposing a particular strategy. The matrix allows different stakeholders to be plotted either according to the simple either – or dichotomy of low or high, or more subtly according to their relative positions along the continuous axes from low to high. The positions of different stakeholders on the matrix are likely to vary according to each issue, especially to the amount interest they have. Stakeholder groups are also likely to vary in their power according to the governance structures under which they operate (see section 4.3) and the stance taken on corporate responsibility (section 4.5.1). For example, in some countries unions may be weak but in others they may be represented on supervisory boards; banks may take a 'semi-detached' view of strategy in some countries, but be part of the governance structures in others.

In order to show the way in which the matrix may be used, take the example of a business where managers see themselves as formulating strategy by trying to ensure the compliance of stakeholders with their own assessment of strategic imperatives. In this context the matrix indicates the type of relationship that managers might typically establish with stakeholder groups in the different quadrants. Clearly, the acceptability of strategies to *key players* (segment D) is of major importance. It could be that these are major investors or particular agencies with a lot of power – for example, a major shareholder in a family firm or a government funding agency in a public-sector organisation. Often the most difficult issues relate to stakeholders in segment C. Although these might, in general, be relatively passive, a disastrous situation can arise when their level of interest is underrated and they reposition to segment D and frustrate the adoption

Figure 4.5 Stakeholder mapping: the power/interest matrix

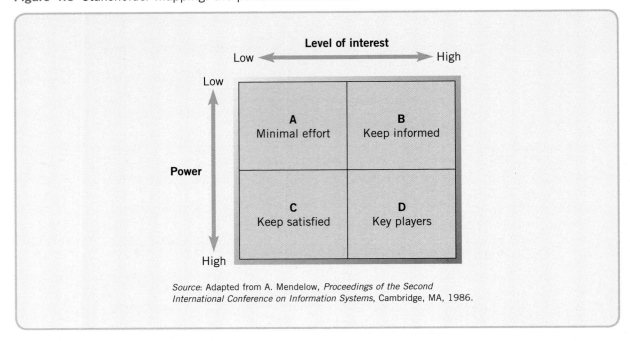

Source: Adapted from A. Mendelow, *Proceedings of the Second International Conference on Information Systems*, Cambridge, MA, 1986.

of a new strategy. Institutional shareholders such as pension funds or insurance firms can fall into this category. They may show little interest unless share prices start to dip, but may then demand to be heard by senior management. Managers might choose to address the expectations of stakeholders in segment B, for example community groups, through information provision. It may be important not to alienate such stakeholders because they can be crucially important 'allies' in influencing the attitudes of more powerful stakeholders: for example, through lobbying.

Stakeholder mapping can also help in understanding the following three issues:

● Who the key *blockers* and *facilitators* of a strategy are likely to be and the appropriate response.

● Whether *repositioning* of certain stakeholders is desirable and/or feasible: for example, to lessen the influence of a key player or, in certain instances, to ensure that there are more key players who will champion the strategy (this is often critical in the public-sector context).

● *Maintaining* the level of interest or power of some key stakeholders: for example, public 'endorsement' by powerful suppliers or customers may be critical to the success of a strategy. It may also be necessary to discourage some stakeholders from repositioning themselves. This is what is meant by *keep satisfied* in relation to stakeholders in segment C, and to a lesser extent *keep informed* for those in segment B.

All this can raise difficult ethical issues for managers in deciding the role they should play in the political activity surrounding stakeholder management: see Illustration 4.4 on EADS for an example of conflict among stakeholders. For example, should managers be simple, honest brokers balancing the conflicting expectations of all stakeholder groups? Or should they be answerable to one stakeholder – such as shareholders – and hence is their role to ensure the

ILLUSTRATION 4.4

Conflict at the European Aeronautic Defence and Space Company

Strains are emerging between stakeholders in this complex consortium, with political repercussions.

The European Aeronautic Defence and Space Company (EADS) was established in 2000 as a means to group some of Europe's most important aeronautics and related activities. In particular, EADS brought together Aérospatiale-Matra of France, DaimlerChrysler Aerospace AG (DASA) of Germany, and Construcciones Aeronáuticas SA (CASA) of Spain. By 2013, EADS included Airbus, the world's leading manufacturer of commercial aircraft; Airbus Military covering tanker, transport and mission aircraft; Eurocopter, the world's largest helicopter supplier; Astrium, the European leader in space programmes such as Ariane and Galileo; and Cassidian, a major provider of defence and security systems for missiles and fighter jets. With revenues of €50 bn (about £40 bn or $65 bn) and 120,000 employees, EADS was one of Europe's largest manufacturers, exporters and investors in R&D, besides spending €31 bn annually with suppliers, mostly in Europe.

The ownership of EADS is complex, with 50.66 per cent owned by a three-way international partnership. The partners are SOGEADE (22.36 per cent), two-thirds owned by the French state and one third owned by the French media company Lagardère; the German car manufacturer Daimler AG (22.36 per cent), representing the German government and some major German banks as well; and SEPI (5.44 per cent), a Spanish state holding company. The remainder of the stock is traded publicly, though the French state owns a further 0.06 per cent this stock. EADS had made substantial losses in 2009, but returned to profitability in the following two years.

During 2011–12, the chief executive, Frenchman Louis Gallois, was promoting a strategy of greater internationalisation. This internationalisation, he argued, required a reduction in French and German state ownership. State ownership restricted EADS's ability to make major acquisitions in the US and emerging markets. Overseas acquisitions could access valuable technologies and manufacturing bases, and help win orders in markets where a local presence was seen as critical. Gallois also believed that the ownership structure gave the 'controlling shareholders a feeling of being trapped and always creating the risk of inequalities between different categories of shareholders'.

Early 2012 saw furious arguments between German and French partners. The immediate cause was the decision to move EADS's overall headquarters from Munich to Toulouse, the location of the subsidiary Airbus headquarters and with more than 16,000 staff already. Although there were only 300 staff involved in the EADS headquarters move, the German deputy economics minister wrote a letter to EADS alleging an 'unacceptable' bias towards French management and production in France. He particularly complained that €500 m aid supplied by the German government for the development of the A350 aircraft had not led to the promised strengthening of Airbus's north German sites in Hamburg (with 13,000 employees) and Bremen (with more than 3,000 employees). He demanded that the company put more Germans in top posts at Airbus or risk losing German development aid and export-credit guarantees. German anxiety was increased by the fact that two thirds of EADS's revenues came from civil Airbus sales, while Germany was home to the Cassidian military division, whose revenues were falling because of government spending cuts. CEO Gallois responded that the German minister's letter was not in 'accordance with the governance of a listed company. We will choose the best industrial set-up in the company's interests – without external interference.'

Main sources: Financial Times, 19 June 2011, 2 March 2012, 8 March 2012.

Questions

1 With reference to the power/interest matrix (Figure 4.5), how would powerful stakeholders' level of interest vary with regard to the location of the EADS headquarters and internationalisation?

2 Given the ownership structure, is CEO Gallois right to assert the primacy of company interests and reject German ministerial 'interference'?

acceptability of their strategies to other stakeholders? Or are they, as many authors suggest, the real power themselves, constructing strategies to suit their own purposes and managing stakeholder expectations to ensure acceptance of these strategies?

4.4.3 Power[24]

In considering stakeholder expectations the previous section highlighted the importance of power and how it is shared unequally between various stakeholders. For the purposes of this discussion, **power is the ability of individuals or groups to persuade, induce or coerce others into following certain courses of action**. As Table 4.2 shows, there are different sources of power. It is not only derived from people's hierarchical position within an organisation or formal corporate governance arrangements. It could be a function of the resources or know-how they control or the networks they have built up, for example.

The relative importance of these sources of power will vary over time. Indeed changes in the business environment can significantly shift the power balance between organisations and their stakeholders. For example, consumers' knowledge of different companies' offerings through internet browsing has increased their power as they compare different offerings and reduce their traditional loyalty to a particular supplier. The distribution of power will also vary in relation to the strategy under consideration. For example, a corporate finance function will

Table 4.2 Sources and indicators of power

Sources of power	
Within organisations	**For external stakeholders**
• Hierarchy (formal power), e.g. autocratic decision making	• Control of strategic resources, e.g. materials, labour, money
• Influence (informal power), e.g. charismatic leadership	• Involvement in strategy implementation, e.g. distribution outlets, agents
• Control of strategic resources, e.g. strategic products	• Possession of knowledge or skills, e.g. subcontractors, partners
• Possession of knowledge and skills, e.g. computer specialists	• Through internal links, e.g. informal influence
• Control of the human environment, e.g. negotiating skills	
• Involvement in strategy implementation, e.g. by exercising discretion	
Indicators of power	
Within organisations	**For external stakeholders**
• Status	• Status
• Claim on resources	• Resource dependence
• Representation	• Negotiating arrangements
• Symbols	• Symbols

be more powerful in relation to developments requiring new capital or revenue commitments than in relation to ones which are largely self-financing or within the financial authority of separate divisions or subsidiaries.

Since there are a variety of different sources of power, it is useful to look for *indicators of power*, the visible signs that stakeholders have been able to exploit sources of power. These include: the *status* of the individual or group (such as job grade or reputation); the *claim on resources* (such as budget size); *representation* in powerful positions; and *symbols* of power (such as office size or use of titles and names). For external stakeholders, a key indicator is the organisation's *resource dependence*, in other words its dependence on particularly large shareholders, lenders, customers or suppliers. One way of assessing resource dependence is to consider the ease with which a supplier, financier or customer could switch or be switched at short notice.

An underlying theme in this chapter has been that strategists have to consider the overall strategic purpose of their organisations. However, a central question that arises is what stakeholder expectations they should respond to in so doing. The Key Debate at the end of this chapter provides three views on this in the context of publicly quoted large commercial organisations.

(4.5) SOCIAL RESPONSIBILITY AND ETHICS[25]

Underlying the discussion of corporate governance is an issue highlighted in the introduction to this chapter. Is the purpose of an organisation and its strategy for the benefit of a primary stakeholder such as the shareholders of a company, or is it there for the benefit of a wider group of stakeholders? In turn this raises the question of societal expectations placed on organisations, how these impact on an organisation's purposes and, in turn, on its strategy. This section considers, first, *corporate social responsibility*: the role businesses and other organisations might take in society. Second, it considers the *ethics* of the behaviour and actions of people in relation to the strategy of their organisations.

4.5.1 Corporate social responsibility

The sheer size and global reach of many companies means that they are bound to have significant influence on society. Further, the widely publicised corporate scandals and failures of the last two decades have fuelled a concern about the role they play. The regulatory environment and the corporate governance arrangements for an organisation determine its minimum obligations towards its stakeholders. However, such legal and regulatory frameworks set minimum obligations and stakeholders typically expect greater responsibility on the part of organisations. **Corporate social responsibility** (CSR) **is the commitment by organisations to behave ethically and contribute to economic development while improving the quality of life of the workforce and their families as well as the local community and society at large.**[26] CSR is therefore concerned with the ways in which an organisation exceeds its minimum legal obligations.

Different organisations take different stances on CSR. Table 4.3 outlines four basic types to illustrate these differences. They represent a progressively more inclusive 'list' of stakeholder interests and a greater breadth of criteria against which strategies and performance will be judged. The discussion that follows also explains what such stances typically involve

Table 4.3 **Corporate social responsibility stances**

	Laissez-faire	Enlightened self-interest	Forum for stakeholder interaction	Shaper of society
Rationale	Legal compliance: make a profit, pay taxes and provide jobs	Sound business sense	Sustainability or triple bottom line	Social and market change
Leadership	Peripheral	Supportive	Champion	Visionary
Management	Middle-management responsibility	Systems to ensure good practice	Board-level issue; organisation-wide monitoring	Individual responsibility throughout the organisation
Mode	Defensive to outside pressures	Reactive to outside pressures	Proactive	Defining
Stakeholder relationships	Unilateral	Interactive	Partnership	Multi-organisation alliances

in terms of the ways companies act.[27] Illustration 4.5 discusses how leading clothing retailer H&M pursues social responsibility in order to give it a more ethical profile than some of its rivals and pre-empt protests against the clothing industry's traditionally wasteful and exploitative practices.

The *laissez-faire* view (literally 'let do' in French) represents an extreme stance. In this view, organisations should be let alone to get on with things on their own account. Proponents argue that the only responsibility of business is to make a profit and provide for the interests of shareholders.[28] It is for government to protect society through legislation and regulation; organisations need do no more than meet these minimum obligations. Expecting companies to exercise social duties beyond this only confuses decision making and undermines the accountability of managers to their shareholders. In this view, society benefits anyway from the profits: after all, these can either be used for further investment in the business or be paid out to shareholders, who may be pensioners relying on the income or similar. This laissez-faire stance may be taken by executives who are persuaded of it ideologically or by smaller businesses that do not have the resources to do other than minimally comply with regulations.

Enlightened self-interest is guided by recognition of the potential long-term financial benefit to the shareholder of well-managed relationships with other stakeholders. Here the justification for social responsibility is that it makes good business sense. For most organisations a good reputation in the eyes of customers and suppliers is important to long-term financial success. Working constructively with suppliers or local communities can actually increase the 'value' available for all stakeholders to share: for example, helping improve the quality of marginal suppliers in the developing world is likely to create a stronger overall supply chain; supporting education in the local workforce will increase the availability of skilled labour. Indeed, there is mounting evidence that responsible strategies can also reward shareholders.[29] Thus, like any other form of investment or promotion expenditure, corporate philanthropy or welfare provision might be regarded as sensible expenditure.

Managers with this enlightened self-interest stance take the view that organisations have not only *responsibilities to* society, but also *relationships with* other stakeholders. So communication with stakeholder groups is likely to be more interactive than for laissez-faire-type organisations. They may well also set up systems and policies to ensure compliance with best practice (e.g. ISO 14000 certification, the protection of human rights in overseas operations, etc.) and begin to monitor their social responsibility performance. Top management may also play more of a part, at least insofar as they support the firm taking a more proactive social role.

A *forum for stakeholder interaction*[30] explicitly incorporates multiple stakeholder interests and expectations rather than just shareholders as influences on organisational purposes and strategies. Here the argument is that the performance of an organisation should be measured in a more pluralistic way than just through the financial bottom line. Such organisations adopt the principle of *sustainability* in strategy, one that ensures a better quality of life by attending to all three dimensions of environmental protection, social responsibility and economic welfare. Social responsibility here can be measured in terms of *the triple bottom line* – social and environmental benefits as well as profits (see section 11.2.1). Companies in this category might retain uneconomic units to preserve jobs, avoid manufacturing or selling 'anti-social' products and be prepared to bear reductions in profitability for the social good. Sustainability will typically have board-level champions in these kinds of organisations.

Shapers of society regard financial considerations as of secondary importance or a constraint. These are visionary organisations seeking to change society and social norms. Public-sector organisations and charities are typically committed to this kind of stance. There are also *social entrepreneurs* who found new organisations that earn revenues but pursue a specific social purpose (see Chapter 9). For example, Traidcraft UK is a public limited company with a chain of retail shops that fights developing world poverty by promoting 'fair trade'. For shapers of society, the social role is the *raison d'être* of the business, not profits. Financial viability is important only as providing the means for continuing the social mission.

Table 4.4 provides some questions against which an organisation's actions on CSR can be assessed.

4.5.2 The ethics of individuals and managers

Ethical issues have to be faced at the individual as well as corporate level and can pose difficult dilemmas for individuals and managers. For example, what is the responsibility of an individual who believes that the strategy of his or her organisation is unethical (e.g. its trading practices) or is not adequately representing the legitimate interests of one or more stakeholder groups? Should that person leave the company on the grounds of a mismatch of values; or is *whistle-blowing* appropriate, such as divulging information to outside bodies, for example regulatory bodies or the press?

Given that strategy development can be an intensely political process with implications for the personal careers of those concerned, managers can find difficulties establishing and maintaining a position of integrity. There is also potential conflict between what strategies are in managers' own best interests and what strategies are in the longer-term interests of their organisation and the shareholders. Some organisations set down explicit guidelines they expect their employees to follow. Texas Instruments posed these questions:[31]

Is the action legal? . . . If not, stop immediately.

Does it comply with our values? . . . If it does not, stop.

If you do it would you feel bad? . . . Ask your own conscience if you can live with it.

How would this look in the newspaper? . . . Ask if this goes public tomorrow would you do it today?

If you know it's wrong . . . don't do it.

If you are not sure . . . ask; and keep asking until you get an answer.

Table 4.4 Some questions of corporate social responsibility

Should organisations be responsible for . . .

INTERNAL ASPECTS

Exployee welfare
. . . providing medical care, assistance with housing finance, extended sick leave, assistance for dependants, etc.?

Working conditions
. . . job security, enhancing working surroundings, social and sporting clubs, above-minimum safety standards, training and development, etc.?

Job design
. . . designing jobs to the increased satisfaction of workers rather than just for economic efficiency? This would include issues of work/life balance?

Intellectual property
. . . respecting the private knowledge of individuals and not claiming corporate ownership?

EXTERNAL ASPECTS

Environmental issues
. . . reducing pollution to below legal standards if competitors are not doing so?
. . . energy conservation?

Products
. . . dangers arising from the careless use of products by consumers?

Markets and marketing
. . . deciding not to sell in some markets?
. . . advertising standards?

Suppliers
. . . 'fair' terms of trade?
. . . blacklisting suppliers?

Employment
. . . positive discrimination in favour of minorities?
. . . maintaining jobs?

Community activity
. . . sponsoring local events and supporting local good works?

Human rights
. . . respecting human rights in relation to: child labour, workers' and union rights, oppressive political regimes? Both directly and in the choice of markets, suppliers and partners?

ILLUSTRATION 4.5

H&M's sustainability strategy

Swedish clothing retailer H&M claims to be pursuing a strategy that delivers profits, environmental gains and worker benefits.

H&M is the world's second-largest clothing retailer, just behind Inditex, owner of Zara. It has 2,500 stores worldwide, operating in 44 countries. It sells about 550 million items of clothing per year. As such, it has traditionally been a leader in so-called 'fast-fashion', the retailing of cheap fashion items which are designed to be worn only a few times before disposal.

Fast-fashion is a voracious industry. There are now 30–50 trend-driven fashion seasons a year. Eighty billion garments are made annually worldwide, from virgin resources. There are 40 million garment workers in the world, predominantly making fast-fashion. A garment worker in Bangladesh, a major supplier, earns an average monthly wage of $40. A pair of underpants costs about one pence (or roughly a Euro cent) to make in a Third World sweat shop. Fast-fashion is a target of international campaign groups such as the 'Clean Clothes Campaign'.

During 2012, the Clean Clothes Campaign organised mass 'faint-ins' in prominent stores such as Gap, Zara and H&M across Europe, drawing attention to how under-nourished women workers frequently faint at work in Third World garment factories. A Clean Clothes spokesperson says: 'The human cost of brands like H&M or Zara paying poverty wages is seen when hundreds of workers pass out due to exhaustion and malnutrition . . . For decades, global fashion brands have made excuses about why they shouldn't pay a living wage. It's not a choice, it's a pressing necessity. Hiding behind . . . company codes of conduct is no longer acceptable.'

In 2012, H&M launched its new 'Conscious' range of clothing, making use of a large proportion of recycled materials and more environmentally-friendly virgin materials such as hemp. The company's website explained the motivation: 'Our vision is that all business operations shall be run in a way that is economically, socially and environmentally sustainable.' This was accompanied by a Sustainability Report with some impressive statistics: for example, 2.5 million shoes were made during 2011 using lower-impact water-based solvents and H&M was the biggest user of organic cotton in the world.

Guardian journalist Lucy Singh asked H&M's Head of Sustainability, Helena Helmersson, whether she could offer guarantees for the sustainability of the company's products across its ranges. Helmersson responded:

'I don't think guarantee is the right word. A lot of people ask for guarantees: "Can you guarantee labour conditions? Can you guarantee zero chemicals?" Of course we cannot when we're such a huge company operating in very challenging conditions. What I can say is that we do the very best we can with a lot of resources and a clear direction of what we're supposed to do. We're working really hard . . . Remember that H&M does not own any factories itself. We are to some extent dependent on the suppliers – it is impossible to be in full control.'

Between 2006 and 2012, H&M's share price has increased by more than a third, well ahead of the local Stockholm market index. Sales too have increased by a third and total operating profit after tax in this period has been nearly SEK98 billion (€11 billion). H&M's return on capital employed for year-end 2011 is 47.1 per cent.

Main sources: *Guardian*, 7 April 2012; *Ecouterre*, 21 September 2012; www.hm.com; H&M Concsious Actions and Sustainability Report, 2011.

Questions

1 Where would you place H&M in terms of the four stances on social responsibility in Table 4.2?

2 What are the kinds of triple-bottom-line measures that would be appropriate for a sustainable strategy in clothing retail (see also section 11.2.1)?

KEY DEBATE

Three views on the purpose of a business

Since there is no one categoric view of the overarching purpose of a business, stakeholders, including managers, have to decide.

Milton Friedman and profit maximisation

Milton Friedman, the renowned economist, wrote:

'In a free enterprise, private property system, a corporate executive is an employee of the owners of the business. He has direct responsibility to his employers. That responsibility is to conduct the business in accordance with their desires, which generally will be to make as much money as possible while conforming to the basic rules of society . . . What does it mean to say that the corporate executive has a "social responsibility"? . . . If the statement is not pure rhetoric, it must mean that he is to act in some way that is not in the interests of his employers . . . Insofar as his actions in accord with his "social responsibility" reduce returns to stockholders, he is spending their money. Insofar as his actions raise the price to customers, he is spending the customers' money. Insofar as his actions lower the wages of some employees he is spending their money.'

Charles Handy's stakeholder view

Charles Handy has a less respectful view of owners:

'There is, first, a clear and important need to meet the expectations of a company's theoretical owners: the shareholders. It would, however, be more accurate to call them investors, perhaps even gamblers. They have none of the pride or responsibility of ownership and are . . . only there for the money . . . But to turn shareholders' needs into a purpose is to be guilty of a logical confusion. To mistake a necessary condition for a sufficient one. We need to eat to live; food is a necessary condition of life. But if we lived mainly to eat, making food a sufficient or sole purpose of life, we would become gross. The purpose of a business, in other words, is not to make a profit. It is to make a profit so that the business can do something more or better. That "something" becomes the real justification for the business.'

The 'new capitalists' argument

In their book *The New Capitalists*, Davis, Lukommik and Pitt-Watson point out that major corporations are often owned by millions of savers – the 'new capitalists' – through pension and other investment funds. Each of these funds holds shares in many companies. Davis and colleagues then argue:

'Imagine that all your savings were invested in one company. The success of that company alone would be your only interest. You would want it to survive, prosper and grow, even if that did damage to the economic system as a whole. But your perspective would change if you had investments in lots of companies. [Then] it is to your disadvantage that any business should seek to behave socially irresponsibly towards other businesses, the customers, employees or society generally. By so doing they will damage the interests of other firms in which you have an interest. The new capitalist has an interest in all the firms in which he or she is investing behaving responsibly.'

Sources: M. Friedman, 'The social responsibility of business is to increase its profits', *New York Times Magazine*, 13 September 1970; C. Handy, 'What's a business for?', *Harvard Business Review*, vol. 80, no. 12 (2002), pp. 49–55; S. Davis, J. Lukommik and D. Pitt-Watson, *The New Capitalists*, Harvard Business School Press, 2006.

Questions

1 Which view would you be more likely to hold:

   a as a manager?

   b as a shareholder?

   c as a pensioner?

2 What are the implications of the different views for how managers go about developing organisational strategy?

Perhaps the biggest challenge for managers is to develop a high level of self-awareness of their own behaviour in relation to the issues raised above.[32] This can be difficult because it requires them to stand apart from often deep-rooted and taken-for-granted assumptions that are part of the culture of their organisation – a key theme of the next chapter.

SUMMARY

- An important managerial task is to decide how the organisation should express its strategic purpose through statements of *mission*, *vision*, *values* and *objectives*.

- The purpose of an organisation will be influenced by the expectations of its *stakeholders*.

- The influence of some key stakeholders will be represented formally within the *governance structure* of an organisation. This can be represented in terms of a *governance chain*, showing the links between ultimate beneficiaries and the managers of an organisation.

- There are two generic governance structure systems: the *shareholder model* and the *stakeholder model*, though there are variations of these internationally.

- Different stakeholders exercise different influence on organisational purpose and strategy, dependent on the extent of their power and interest. Managers can assess the influence of different stakeholder groups through *stakeholder analysis*.

- Organisations adopt different stances on *corporate social responsibility* depending on how they perceive their role in society. Individual managers may also be faced with ethical dilemmas relating to the purpose of their organisation or the actions it takes.

VIDEO ASSIGNMENTS

Visit **MyStrategyLab** and watch the case study for Chapter 4 (which features various companies).

1 Using the video interviews and section 4.5 of the text, discuss the importance of corporate social responsibility to the companies featured in the video.

2 How does corporate social responsibility relate to stakeholder expectations and governance in determining the purpose of an organisation? Use the companies featured in the video as examples.

WORK ASSIGNMENTS

✱ *Denotes more advanced work assignments.*
* *Refers to a case study in the Text and Cases edition.*

4.1 Write mission and vision statements for any of Manchester United FC*, Sustainability*, HomeCo* or an organisation of your choice and suggest what strategic objectives managers might set. Explain why you think these are appropriate.

4.2 For Drinking Partners (end chapter case) or Adnams* or an organisation of your choice, map out a governance chain that identifies the key players through to the beneficiaries of the organisation's good (or poor) performance. To what extent do you think managers are:

a knowledgeable about the expectations of beneficiaries;

b actively pursuing their interests;

c keeping them informed?

4.3 What are your own views of the strengths and weaknesses of the stakeholder and shareholder models of governance?

4.4✱ Identify organisations that correspond to the overall stances on corporate social responsibility described in Table 4.3.

4.5 Identify the key corporate social responsibility issues which are of major concern in the Brewing* or Advertising (Chapter 2 end case) industries or an industry or public service of your choice (refer to Table 4.4). Compare the approach of two or more organisations in that industry, and explain how this relates to their competitive standing.

4.6✱ Using the stakeholder mapping power/interests matrix, identify and map out the stakeholders for International AIDS Alliance*, Manchester United*, QR National (Anrizon)* or an organisation of your choice in relation to:

a current strategies;

b different future strategies of your choice.

What are the implications of your analysis for the strategy of the organisation?

Integrative assignment

4.7 Using specific examples suggest how changes in corporate governance and in expectations about corporate social responsibility may require organisations to deal differently with environmental opportunities and threats (Chapter 2) or develop new capabilities (Chapter 3).

RECOMMENDED KEY READINGS

- The case for the importance of clarity of strategic values and vision is especially strongly made by J. Collins and J. Porras, *Built to Last: Successful Habits of Visionary Companies*, Harper Business, 2002 (in particular see Chapter 11).

- A good review of important ideas in both corporate governance and corporate social responsibility is S. Benn and D. Bolton, *Key Concepts in Corporate Responsibility*, Sage, 2011. Specifically on corporate governance, a leading guide is B. Tricker, *Corporate Governance: Principles, Policies and Practices*, 2nd edn, Oxford University Press, 2012. For a comprehensive review of corporate social responsibility, see A. Crane, A. McWilliams, D. Matten and D. Siegel, *The Oxford Handbook of Corporate Social Responsibility*, Oxford University Press, 2009.

REFERENCES

1. Cynthia A. Montgomery, 'Putting leadership back into strategy', *Harvard Business Review* (January 2008), pp. 54–60.
2. See J. Collins and J. Porras, *Built to Last: Successful Habits of Visionary Companies*, Harper Business, 2002.
3. J. Collins and J. Porras, 'Building your company's vision', *Harvard Business Review* (September–October 1996), pp. 65–77.
4. See Sayan Chatterjee, 'Core objectives: clarity in designing strategy', *California Management Review*, vol. 47, no. 2 (2005), pp. 33–49. For some advantages of ambiguity, see J. Sillince, P. Jarzabkowski and D. Shaw, 'Shaping strategic action through the rhetorical construction and exploitation of ambiguity', *Organization Science*, vol. 22, no. 2 (2011), pp. 1–21.
5. For example, see B. Bartkus, M. Glassman and B. McAfee, 'Mission statements: are they smoke and mirrors?', *Business Horizons*, vol. 43, no. 6 (2000), pp. 23–8.
6. See P. Lencioni, 'Make your values mean something', *Harvard Business Review*, vol. 80, no. 7 (2002), pp. 113–17; and S. Kantabutra and G. Avery, 'The power of vision: statements that resonate', *Journal of Business Strategy*, vol. 31, no. 1 (2009), pp. 37–45.
7. See for instance M. Nordqvist and L. Melin, 'Entrepreneurial families and family firms', *Entrepreneurship and Regional Development*, vol. 22, no. 3–4 (2010), pp. 211–39.
8. In the United Kingdom and associated countries, this kind of corporation is called a public limited company (plc); in Francophone countries, it is the Société Anonyme (SA); in Germany, it is the Aktiengesellschaft (AG).
9. *The Economist*, 'The rise of state capitalism' (21 January 2012).
10. For a discussion, see R. Rumelt (2005), 'Theory, strategy and entrepreneurship', *Handbook of Entrepreneurship Research*, vol. 2 (2005), pp. 11–32.
11. Credit Suisse, *Asian Family Businesses Report 2011: Key Trends, Economic Contribution and Performance*, Singapore, 2011.
12. I. Le Bretton-Miller, D. Miller and R.H. Lester, 'Stewardship or agency? A social embeddedness reconciliation of conduct and performance in public family businesses', *Organization Science*, vol. 22, no. 3 (2011), pp. 704–21.
13. The Ownership Commission, *Plurality, stewardship and engagement*, London, 2012.
14. Useful general references on corporate governance are: R. Monks and N. Minow (eds), *Corporate Governance*, 4th edn, Blackwell, 2008. Also see Ruth Aguilera and Gregory Jackson, 'The cross-national diversity of corporate governance: dimensions and determinants', *Academy of Management Review*, vol. 28, no. 3 (2003), pp. 447–65.
15. This definition is adapted from S. Jacoby, 'Corporate governance and society', *Challenge*, vol. 48, no. 4 (2005), pp. 69–87.
16. A recent debate on principal–agent theory is: D. Miller and C. Sardais, 'Angel agents: agency theory reconsidered', *Academy of Management Perspectives*, vol. 25, no. 2 (2011), pp. 6–13; and V. Mehrotra, 'Angel agents: what we can (and cannot) learn from Pierre Lefaucheux's stewardship of Régie Renault', *Academy of Management Perspectives*, vol. 25, no. 2 (2011), pp. 14–20.
17. S. Letza, X. Sun and J. Kirkbride, 'Shareholding versus stakeholding: a critical review of corporate governance', *Corporate Governance*, vol. 12 no. 3 (2005), pp. 242–62. Within this broad classification, there are other models: see, for example, A. Murphy and K. Topyan, 'Corporate governance: a critical survey of key concepts, issues, and recent reforms in the US', *Employee Responsibility and Rights Journal*, vol. 17, no. 2 (2005), pp. 75–89.
18. M.N. Young, M.W. Peng, D. Ahlstrom, G.D. Bruton and Y. Jiang, 'Corporate governance in emerging economies: a review of the principal–principal perspective', *Journal of Management Studies*, vol. 45, no. 1 (2008), pp. 1467–86.
19. R. Greenwood, M. Raynard, F. Kodeih, E. Micelotta and M. Lounsbury, 'Institutional complexity and organisational responses', *Academy of Management Annals*, vol. 5, no. 1 (2011), pp. 317–71.
20. In the USA: the Sarbanes–Oxley Act (2002). In the UK: D. Higgs, 'Review of the role and effectiveness of non-executive directors', UK Department of Trade and Industry, 2003.
21. J. Sonnenfeld, 'What makes great boards great', *Harvard Business Review*, vol. 80, no. 9 (2002), pp. 106–13.

22. R.E. Freeman, *Strategic Management: A Stakeholder Approach*, Pitman, 1984. Also see L. Bidhan, A. Parmar and R.E. Freeman, 'Stakeholder theory: the state of the art', *Academy of Management Annals*, vol. 4, no. 1 (2010), pp. 403–45. Our approach to stakeholder mapping has been adapted from A. Mendelow, *Proceedings of the 2nd International Conference on Information Systems*, Cambridge, MA, 1991. See also Graham Kenny, 'From the stakeholder viewpoint: designing measurable objectives', *Journal of Business Strategy*, vol. 33, no. 6 (2012), pp. 40–6.

23. D. Walker, L. Bourne and A. Shelley, 'Influence, stakeholder mapping and visualization', *Construction Management and Economics* [serial online], vol. 26, no. 6 (2008), pp. 645–58.

24. D. Buchanan and R. Badham, *Power, Politics and Organisational Change: Winning the Turf Game*, Sage, 1999, provide a useful analysis of the relationship between power and strategy.

25. B. Kelley, *Ethics at Work*, Gower, 1999, covers many of the issues in this section and includes the Institute of Management guidelines on ethical management. Also see M.T. Brown, *Corporate Integrity: Rethinking Organisational Ethics and Leadership*, Cambridge University Press, 2005.

26. This definition is based on that by the World Business Council for Sustainable Development.

27. P. Mirvis and B. Googins, 'Stages of corporate citizenship', *California Management Review*, vol. 48, no. 2 (2006), pp. 104–26.

28. Often quoted as a summary of Milton Friedman's argument is M. Friedman: 'The social responsibility of business is to increase its profits', *New York Times Magazine* (13 September 1970). See also A. McWilliams and D. Seigel, 'Corporate social responsibility: a theory of the firm perspective', *Academy of Management Review*, vol. 26 (2001), pp. 117–27.

29. See M. Porter and M. Kramer, 'Creating shared value', *Harvard Business Review*, vol. 89, no. 1/2 (2011), pp. 62–77; and D. Vogel, 'Is there a market for virtue? The business case for corporate social responsibility', *California Management Review*, vol. 47, no. 4 (2005), pp. 19–45. For a sceptical view: A. Karnani, 'Doing well by doing good: the grand illusion', *California Management Review*, vol. 53, no. 2 (2011), pp. 69–86. For some evidence, see C. E. Hull and S. Rothenberg, 'Firm performance: the interactions of corporate social performance with innovation and industry differentiation', *Strategic Management Journal*, vol. 29 (2008), pp. 781–9.

30. H. Hummels, 'Organizing ethics: a stakeholder debate', *Journal of Business Ethics*, vol. 17, no. 13 (1998), pp. 1403–19.

31. We are grateful to Angela Sutherland of Glasgow Caledonian University for this example.

32. M.R. Banaji, M.H. Bazerman and D. Chugh, 'How (UN) ethical are you?', *Harvard Business Review*, vol. 81, no. 12 (2003), pp. 56–64.

Drinking partners: India's United Breweries Holdings Ltd

In 2012, United Breweries Holdings Ltd (UBHL) was one of India's most powerful and dynamic conglomerates. Under the leadership of its colourful chairman Vijay Mallya, it controlled India's largest brewery, India's largest spirits company, a leading domestic and international airline, a Formula One racing team, and substantial chemicals and fertiliser interests. But the UBHL empire was tottering under heavy debts and Vijay Mallya himself faced an arrest warrant for bouncing cheques. Partnership with the London-based Diageo drinks business offered one route to survival. But how far could anyone rely on a partner with Mallya's record?

King of the Good Times

Vijay Mallya had inherited control of UBHL at the age of 28, upon the death of his father in 1983. His father had himself taken over the original core business of United Breweries from its British management in the period around Indian Independence in 1947, and built from this a diverse and complex conglomerate of subsidiary companies. Vijay Mallya spent the early years of his leadership of UBHL by divesting non-core businesses and reorganising the tangle of subsidiaries into a clearer divisional structure based on coherent business areas. UBHL grew rapidly and by 2007 Vijay Mallya ranked 664 on the *Forbes* global list of billionaires, with an estimated fortune of $1.5 bn (about £950 m or €1.2 bn).

As it entered the second decade of the century, UBHL was selling about 60 per cent of India's spirits and 50 per cent of its beer. The group was organised into four main businesses, each with substantial external shareholders: for example, the Dutch brewer Heineken was a substantial minority shareholder in the brewing business. However, Mallya's effective control of each business was guaranteed by UBHL's position as the largest shareholder, if not the majority owner (see Figure 1). These arrangements maximised control while reducing capital obligations. Mallya's overall control of the parent UBHL was assured by dominance of the voting A class shares, while Indian and foreign institutional shareholders held the overwhelming majority of non-voting B class shares.

Though clearly a shrewd businessman, Mallya has his extravagant side. Playing on the name of his most prominent beer brand, Kingfisher, he often describes himself as 'King of the Good Times'. He likes to surround himself with beautiful models and actresses, and the annual Kingfisher Calendar is famed in India for its photographs of scantily-clad women. He owns several expensive yachts and a fleet of luxury vintage cars. In 2008, Mallya and a business partner bought a Formula One racing team, renamed Force India. A similar patriotic theme underpinned his acquisition of the sword of the great Indian leader, Tipu Sultan, captured by the British in the eighteenth century, and his generous assistance

Figure 1 United Breweries Holdings Ltd, principal businesses, 2011

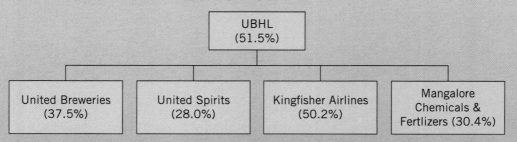

As of 2011, Vijay Mallya and associates controlled 51.5 per cent of UBHL. Shares in each of the principal businesses controlled directly by UBHL or by Mallya and associates are indicated in brackets

with the repatriation of some of the few surviving artefacts owned by Mahatma Gandhi, India's campaigner for Independence. Mallya's personal popularity was reflected in his election to the Upper House of India's federal parliament.

But it was Mallya's extravagance in the business realm that was pushing UBHL to the brink in 2012.

Internationalisation and diversification

The first of two fatally extravagant moves was Mallya's diversification into airlines. To celebrate his son's 18th birthday, Mallya launched Kingfisher Airlines in 2005, with 50.2 per cent of the ownership in his hands. It might have been a good opportunity: the Indian air market was growing and deregulated. Mallya gave the new airline a glitzy launch. Promoting its superior food and pretty female staff, Mallya declared that the Kingfisher Airline would have neither business class nor economy class, but its own 'K class' – a rather pricey compromise. In 2008, Kingfisher paid over the odds to buy India's pioneering low-cost carrier, Deccan Airlines. The merged airline boasted 100-plus aircraft, 300 daily flights, over 7,000 employees and a domestic market share of about 30 per cent. With Deccan's track-record, Kingfisher was able to launch international services as well, with an order for the new Airbus A380 superjumbo jet. Mallya, sporting long hair and a beard, did not discourage comparisons with another flamboyant airline boss, Sir Richard Branson of Virgin.

Unfortunately, domestic deregulation also brought a surfeit of competition to the Indian airline market. At the same time, fuel prices were rising and crowded airports were demanding higher landing fees. By 2011, all but one Indian airline was making losses. Kingfisher had never made a profit in its entire existence. By 2012, Kingfisher had been forced to ground all but 15 of its aircraft, airports and fuel suppliers had not been paid, and most of its employees, including pilots, had received no salary for seven months. Kingfisher's total debts and losses stood at about $4.5 bn. Although Kingfisher had by now been transferred formally outside the group and UBHL had been forced to dilute its ownership to about 30 per cent, the holding company still guaranteed $2.2 bn of the airline's debt. Canadian research firm Veritas warned that Kingfisher would drag down UBHL. The holding company was 'staring into a black hole. We believe that the ill-conceived foray into the airline business has already cost UBHL shareholders dearly, and that their ownership of India's premier liquor and beer assets has been sacrificed at the altar of egoistic ambitions.'

The second extravagant move was into international markets, with the 2007 acquisition of the leading Scottish whisky company Whyte & Mackay. UBHL's United Spirits business needed access to genuine Scotch whisky brands as its increasingly sophisticated Indian customers sought higher-quality spirits than those traditionally made in India. Rivals such as Diageo, with about one third of the world's whisky market and owner of the world's leading Johnnie Walker brand, were suspected of deliberately squeezing their supplies to United Spirits in order to build their own position in India. Acquisition of Whyte & Mackay gave United Spirits control over more than 140 venerable whisky brands, all genuine Scotch. United Spirits became the third-largest spirits producer in the world, behind Diageo and Pernod Ricard.

But Mallya had paid more for Whyte & Mackay than he could really afford: the United Spirits business was left with debts of $1.1 bn. In 2009, Whyte & Mackay was forced to cut about 15 per cent of its jobs. That year, UBHL entered talks with Diageo about selling a stake in the United Spirits business in order to secure a cash injection. The talks failed amid concerns about price, managerial control and a possible intervention by competition authorities. With the holding company stock price crashing to about 10 per cent of its former high (Figure 2), UBHL staggered on until the crisis of 2012.

Foreign rescue?

The year 2012 had not started well for UBHL. As well as continuing losses in Kingfisher, both United Spirits and United Breweries saw net profits fall by more than 80 per cent in the first three months. Mallya desperately needed partners in order to keep UBHL afloat. Diageo, the world's largest spirits producer, was again a prime candidate.

Price had been an issue in the 2009 discussions with Diageo, but Mallya was in a much weaker negotiating position now. There remained monopoly concerns, given the combined power of Diageo and UBHL in the whisky market, but these could probably be satisfied by some selective divestments. Moreover, Diageo was still interested, as rival Pernod Ricard was now making rapid progress in India, one of the largest spirits markets in the world. UBHL was not discouraging rumours that there were possibly three other candidates for a United Spirits stake. For Diageo, though, the deal-breaker could be managerial control.

Figure 2 UBHL stock price performance, 2007–12 (rupees)

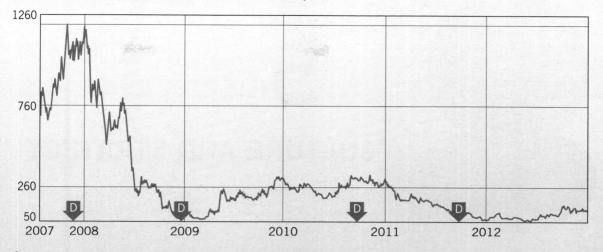

Source: www.moneycontrol.com, 28 December 2012 ('D' refers to dividend payments).

Diageo's chief worry as a large multinational was its exposure to the somewhat idiosyncratic Vijay Mallya. In 2011, Diageo itself had been fined $15 m by the American Securities and Exchange Commission for bribing government officials in India, Thailand and South Korea. The company had given a pledge to 'cease and desist' from such corrupt practices, and risked much larger penalties for any repeat offences. Even as a minority partner, Diageo would be liable for any corruption at United Spirits. However, Mallya was set upon maintaining control. He told the Indian *Business Standard* newspaper: 'One must also understand that running an alcohol beverages business in India across 28 cities is not an easy task for a relatively new player (like Diageo). They will require me to run their business effectively and control of the business is one aspect of that.'

In November 2012, Diageo and UBHL reached a deal. The terms were complex. Diageo would buy 19.3 per cent of United Spirits' existing shares from Mallya's personal and related holdings, while United Spirits would issue new equity, amounting to 10 per cent of the expanded capital base, to Diageo. Together, these steps would give Diageo an initial 27 per cent of the voting shares in United Spirits. Diageo would also launch an open offer to external shareholders in United Spirits, in order to take its total holding up to 53.4 per cent. The deal would cost Diageo up to $1.9 bn. The price valued United Spirits at 20 times annual earnings (before interest, tax, depreciation and amortisation), about a third more than usual for acquisitions in the international drinks business.

Mallya described the deal as a 'win–win'. Diageo would be able to use United Spirits' unparalleled Indian distribution channels for its high-profile brands, and UBHL would be able to ease its various debts. Mallya himself would be left in control of 13.5 per cent of United Spirits' expanded equity and was allowed to continue his position as United Spirits chairman. Mallya insisted to the media: 'I have not sold the family silver, or family jewels; I have only embellished them . . . If you have the impression that I have passed on control, and moved out, that is not the correct impression.'

Principal sources: *The Times*, 26 September 2012; *Business Standard*, 27 September 2012; *India Business Journal*, 6 November 2012; *Financial Times*, 9 November 2012; *Times of India*, 11 November 2012.

Questions

1 Consider the governance chain leading from the various shareholders of UBHL to the managers in the main businesses, with particular reference to United Spirits. Why might there be breakdowns in accountability and control in this chain?

2 Group the various key stakeholders discussed in this case (economic, social/political, community and technological). What risks do key stakeholder groups face (including Diageo)?

5

CULTURE AND STRATEGY

Learning outcomes

After reading this chapter you should be able to:

● Analyse how *history* influences the strategic position of an organisation.

● Analyse the influence of an *organisation's culture* on its strategy using the *cultural web*.

● Recognise the importance of strategists questioning the *taken-for-granted aspects of a culture*.

● Identify organisations which may be experiencing the symptoms of *strategic drift*.

Key terms

cultural web p. 155

legitimacy p. 150

organisational culture p. 147

organisational field p. 150

paradigm p. 153

path dependency p. 143

recipe p. 150

strategic drift p. 162

(5.1) INTRODUCTION

Chapters 2, 3 and 4 have considered the important influences of the environment, organisational capabilities and stakeholder expectations on the development of strategy. Vital as these are to understand, there is a danger that managers fail to take into account other significant issues. Many organisations have long histories. The large Japanese Mitsui Group was founded in the seventeenth century; Daimler was founded in the nineteenth century; managers in the UK retailer Sainsbury's still refer to the founding principles of the Sainsbury family in the nineteenth century. All these and many public-sector organisations – government departments, the police, universities, for example – are strongly influenced by their historical legacies that have become embedded in their cultures. The cultural heritage of an organisation may work to its advantage because it cannot be readily replicated by its competitors. Culture may, however, also be problematic since it can be a significant barrier to change. Either way, if an organisation's strategy is to be understood, so must the history and culture that influenced it. This is the focus of this chapter.

After summarising this chapter (see Figure 5.1), the next section, 5.2, examines the influence of the history of an organisation on its current and future strategy and goes on to consider how that history can be analysed. Section 5.3 then explains what is meant by culture and how cultural influences at the regional, national, institutional and organisational levels influence current and future strategy. It then suggests how a culture can be analysed and its influence on strategy understood. The chapter concludes in section 5.4 by explaining the phenomenon of *strategic drift* that highlights the importance of history and culture in relation to strategy development and identifies important challenges managers face in managing that development.

Figure 5.1 The influence of history and culture

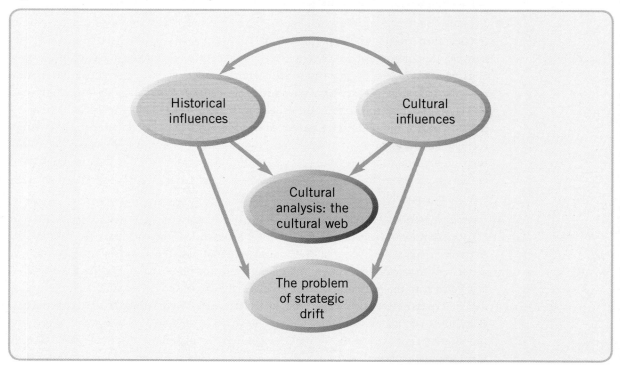

The theme of this chapter is, then, that an understanding of the history and culture of an organisation is important because they can be a major influence on its strategy. It should, however, be borne in mind that historical and cultural perspectives can also help an understanding of both the opportunities and constraints that organisations face. The business environment (Chapter 2) cannot be understood without considering how it has developed over time. The capabilities of an organisation (Chapter 3), especially those that provide organisations with competitive advantage, may have built up over time in ways unique to that organisation. In so doing such capabilities may become part of the culture of an organisation – the taken-for-granted way of doing things – and therefore difficult for other organisations to copy. However, they may also be difficult to change. The power and influence of different stakeholders (Chapter 4) are also likely to have historical origins. An understanding of an organisation's history and culture also informs the evaluation of the feasibility of a strategy (Chapter 11), helps explain how strategies develop (Chapter 12) and informs the challenges of strategic change (Chapter 14).

(5.2) WHY IS HISTORY IMPORTANT?

Taking history's influence on strategy development seriously can have at least four benefits:[1]

- *History and managers' experience*. Managers' own experience is an important influence on strategy development (see the discussion on the 'experience lens' in the Commentary at the end of this part of the book). Managers may have spent many years in an organisation or in an industry such that the experience on which they base their decisions may be heavily influenced by the past. It is helpful if managers can 'stand apart' from that history so as to understand the influence it has on them, the extent to which it constrains them and the opportunities it may offer them.

- *Learning from the past*. Understanding the current strategic position of an organisation in terms of the past can provide useful lessons. For example, have there been historical trends or cycles that may repeat themselves as is the case in the construction and paper industries? How have competitors responded to strategic moves in the past? A historical perspective may also help managers see what gave rise to events that were seen as surprises in the past and learn from how their organisation dealt with them. They might also ask 'what if' questions. Asking what might have happened had there been other influences in the environment, different responses to strategic moves from competitors or different leadership within their organisation all make the present more evidently a product of circumstances. The current strategic position may then be seen as less fixed and possibilities for change in the future more possible.

- *Innovation based on historic capabilities*. In the BMW museum in Munich there is a quote: 'Anyone who wants to design for the future has to leaf through the past.'[2] While the museum is about the history of BMW, it is also about how the lessons of the past can give rise to new ideas and innovation. Indeed the Innovation and Technology Division of BMW is sited next to the museum and the archives of BMW. Innovation may build on historic capabilities in at least two ways. First, as technologies change, firms with experience and skills built over time that are most appropriate to those changes tend to innovate more than those that do not.[3] Or it could be that there are new combinations of knowledge as capabilities built up in adjacent technologies are adapted in innovative ways to new technological opportunities. For example, successful firms that created the TV industry were previously radio manufacturers. They exhibited greater innovation as the industry developed than the non-radio producers by building on their historic capabilities in assembling small components and in mass distribution.[4] If managers seek to build future strategy on historic capabilities they do, however, need to ask if changes in markets, technologies and other aspects of the environment discussed in Chapter 2 are potentially consistent with those capabilities. They need to develop a sensitivity, not only to the historic capabilities that matter but also to the relationship of these to an evolving environment.

- *History as legitimisation*. History can be used as a resource to legitimise strategies or strategic change. For example, in the Swedish bank Handelsbanken, there were frequent stories about the successful turnaround strategy of a highly respected managing director, Jan Wallender, appointed in 1970 following a crisis in the bank.[5] Such stories served to emphasise the continuity of current strategy and structure with the success of that era. Past successes effecting strategic change in innovation or product development may also be used as evidence of the organisational potential in managing change and innovation or to encourage commitment to future changes. Managers may also deliberately draw on the past to legitimise the strategy of an organisation in its market, as has been the case with businesses as varied as bankers Rothschilds, US whisky distillers Jack Daniels, jeans manufacturer Levis Strauss and, of course, many eminent universities.

5.2.1 Path dependency

A useful way of thinking of the role and influence of history is through the concept of **path dependency where early events and decisions establish 'policy paths' that have lasting effects on subsequent events and decisions.**[6] This suggests that organisational decisions may be historically conditioned.

Examples often relate to technology. There are many instances where the technology we employ is better explained by path dependency than by the optimisation of such technology. A famous one is the system used for organising characters on typewriter keyboards in most English-speaking countries: QWERTY. This originated in the nineteenth century as a way of reducing the problem of the keys on mechanical typewriters getting tangled when sales people demonstrated the machine at maximum speed by typing the word 'typewriter'. There are more optimal layouts, but QWERTY has remained with us for over 150 years despite changes in typewriter technology and the eventual development of personal computers.[7] There are countless other examples ranging from technologies in nuclear power stations through to vehicle engines.

Path dependency is, however, not just about technology. It also relates to any form of behaviour that has its origins in the past and becomes entrenched such that 'lock-in' occurs. This could begin with a decision which, of itself, may or may not be especially significant and where consequential succeeding events are unforeseeable. For example, Hollywood was originally chosen by the few silent film makers of the early nineteenth century because what was then a quiet backwater had a reliable climate for filming. This initial decision led to more and more film makers joining those already there. Eventually the build-up of film-making services and skills and the availability of actors meant that Hollywood became *the* place to make films. So an initial, maybe fortuitous decision achieves 'positive feedback' (the attraction of many film makers and actors) and leads to the development of self-reinforcing mechanisms. Such self-reinforcing mechanisms could include the development of logistics, technology and training that make up systems of production, selling, marketing and recruiting,[8] externally reinforced by repeated usage of a product or service by networks of customers and suppliers. The result could be '*lock-in*' where the infrastructure of an industry comes to be based around a product or service such that there are costs of switching from the standard offering.

Similar patterns of path dependency and lock-in gave rise to the concentration of automobile production in Detroit (USA), Formula One constructors in mid-England and industry clusters more generally. A further example is that of accounting systems. Lock-in here has occurred at multiple levels involving networks comprising what accountants do, those with whom they interact within and outside their organisation, the skills, standards and systems in which they are trained and objects and technologies they generate or use. All these have developed over time and mutually reinforce each other, as Figure 5.2 shows. They also persist despite increasing numbers of experts, both in the accountancy profession and elsewhere,[9] who point to fundamental weaknesses in such systems, not least the failure of accounting systems to provide measures for many of the factors that account for the market value of firms.

Path dependency is, then, a way of thinking about how historical events and decisions, within and around an organisation, have an effect on that organisation for good or ill in at least three ways:

● *Building strategy around the path-dependent capabilities* that may have developed within an organisation. This is at the root of much of the argument put forward for the building of competitive advantage discussed in Chapter 3 and further developed in Chapter 6. Path dependency has been shown to explain organisational strategies.[10] Firms tend to enter

Figure 5.2 Path dependency and lock-in

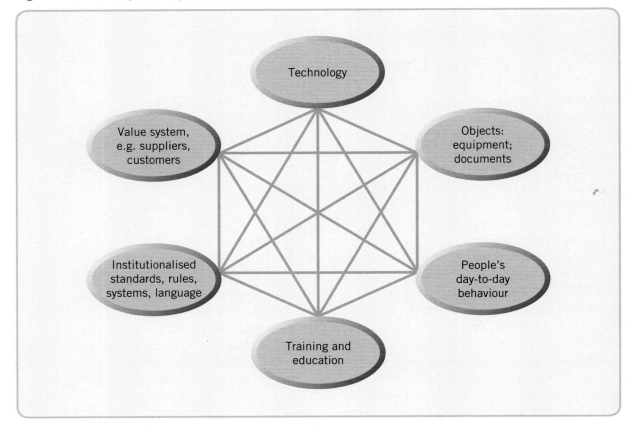

markets, focus on market segments and diversify in line with the previous path-dependent capabilities they have developed. In so doing they tend to focus on types of customers that they have serviced or capabilities on which their success has been based. This may be a basis for success but can also have negative influences as Illustration 5.1 shows. Path dependency has been described as like the 'furrows in a road' that become deeper and deeper as more and more traffic goes along. Once that happens the traffic has no option but to go along those furrows. Hence capabilities, once the bases of competitive advantage and success, become difficult to change leading to the phenomenon of strategic drift explained in section 5.4 later in the chapter.

- *Path creation* suggests that some managers, while acknowledging the relevance and potential benefits of history, may actively seek to amend and deviate from path-dependent ways of doing things. In so doing, they may be sensitive enough to history to recognise what they can and cannot change. Going too far may be risky (see the discussion on 'legitimacy' in section 5.3.2 below), but setting in motion changes that are accepted as appropriate and beneficial by others in the network may be a way of achieving advantage. Arguably this is what new players such as online providers or retailers such as Tesco and Marks & Spencer have done in the insurance market and banking. They have not tried to change basic principles of insurance and banking provision, but they have significantly changed the way in which insurance and banking are sold and distributed. In such circumstances managers need to see the past in relation to the future and ask what is relevant from the past that can help with the future and what the future demands that is not required from the past.

- *Management style* may also have its roots in history. This may be not only in terms of the values of the founder, which indeed may have a strong influence, but also in the interplay between past ways of doing things and the lessons learned from the organisation's evolving environment. Take Tesco as an example again. It became one of the most successful international retailers. In its early days it was a family firm run by founder Jack Cohen, renowned for his authoritative and confrontational style. This gave rise to internal conflicts within the firm, within the Cohen family and between suppliers and Tesco. As Tesco developed, the historic conflict evolved into productive challenge and contestation between managers that, arguably, substantially contributed to its success, especially from the 1990s to 2010.[11] Again, however, there is another side to these potential benefits. Just as capabilities that are path dependent and rooted in history may become entrenched, so might management style and this too may not be in line with the needs of a changing environment, giving rise to problems of change (see Chapter 14).

5.2.2 Historical analysis

How then might managers undertake an historical strategic analysis of their organisation? There are four ways this may be done:[12]

- *Chronological analysis.* At the most basic level this involves setting down a chronology of key events showing changes in the organisation's environment – especially its markets – how the organisation's strategy itself has changed and with what consequences – not least financial. Some firms have done this much more extensively by commissioning corporate histories. These may sometimes be little more than public relations exercises, but the better ones are serious exercises in documenting history[13] and can help sensitise managers to the sort of questions raised above.

ILLUSTRATION 5.1

History and strategy at Unilever[1]

The historical legacy of an organisation can be at the root of major strategic issues.

In 1927 Dutch companies Jurgens and Van den Bergh merged to form Margarine Unie. Then in 1929 British Lever Brothers merged with Margarine Unie to form Unilever. Inherited from the Dutch side was the desire to achieve consensus within the business. The Lever legacy was the pursuit of market leadership through product development and geographical expansion.[2]

The governance structure reflected the merger. In 1930 the boards of Unilever NV, the Dutch company, and Unilever Ltd, the British company, delegated corporate authority to a 'special committee' headed by the chairmen of NV and Ltd, and a third member, the chairman-in-waiting for either NV or Ltd. This was to have a long-lasting effect. As one former Unilever director put it, 'From the merger in 1929, our strategy has suffered from the need to manage the balance between the Dutch and English sides of the business.'

However, there was synergy. The Dutch, strong in Continental Europe, specialised in edible fats; the British, strong in the then Commonwealth countries, specialised in soap. Unilever sought to build on this to make itself too large and diversified to fail through product and geographical leadership, together with a respect for local market needs and the virtues of local initiative and control.

In terms of products, by the 1970s, Unilever had diversified into fishing, shipping, retailing, packaging and plastics, convenience foods, ice cream, tea, personal care products, speciality chemicals, animal feeds as well as the original oils, fats and detergents.

Unilever's decentralisation gave rise to long-standing superiority in many emerging markets, where adaptation in line with local needs was encouraged. This contrasted to the standardised approach of Procter & Gamble who, without the multicompany heritage, developed a more 'mass marketing' approach as early as 1931.

Autonomy also resulted in the power of local 'barons' who resisted Unilever's attempts to become more globally coordinated in the 1960s and 1970s. For example, 'coordinators', introduced in 1959 to create a greater uniformity for international brands, were seen as threatening the company's devolved power. The US business went to the lengths of anti-trust claims to resist more central control.

It was not until the 1990s that attempts to achieve a global strategy began to take shape. In response to investor concern the company decided to focus on seven business areas and scrap the special committee.

By the beginning of this century investors were still critical of a portfolio they believed lacked coherence and a management unwilling to deal with it. Indicative was the demise of the frozen food business Birds Eye, once a 'star' of the portfolio, whose failure to change to address changing market conditions showed how Unilever's 'steady-as-she-goes' approach resulted in a failure to act on long-evident problems.

In 2008 Unilever appointed its first ever chief executive from outside, Paul Polman, whose career had been with rivals Procter & Gamble and Nestlé. His appointment was applauded by the financial markets. He quickly announced a focus on emerging markets and on sustainability. In 2011 he restructured the company to decentralise operations but to have product categories under global heads reporting to him.

Sources
1. This illustration is based on the account of Unilever's history in *Strategic Transformation: Changing while Winning*, by M. Hensmans, G. Johnson and G. Yip, Palgrave, 2013.
2. Wilson, C. *The History of Unilever: A Study in Economic Growth and Social Change*, vol. 2, p. 38, Cassell, 1954.

Questions

1 What symptoms of path dependency are evident in the Unilever story?

2 Extend the examples of organisations given on page 145 that have deliberately employed their history to legitimise their strategies.

- *Cyclical influences.* Is there evidence of cyclical influences? These include economic cycles, but perhaps also cycles of industry activity, such as periods of high levels of mergers and acquisitions. Understanding when these cycles might occur and how industry and market forces can change during such cycles can inform decisions on whether to build strategy in line with those cycles or in a counter-cyclical fashion.

- *Key events and decisions.* History may be regarded as continuous but historical events can also be significant for an organisation at particular points in time. These could be particularly significant events, in terms of either industry change or an organisation's strategic decisions. Or they might be policies laid down by a founder or by powerful senior executives; or major successes or failures; or defining periods of time that managers have come to see as especially important; for example, the Wallander era at Handelsbanken. This could, of course, be for the good: it may help provide a clear overall direction strategically that contributes to the sort of vision discussed in the previous chapter. It could, on the other hand, be a major barrier to challenging existing strategies or changing strategic direction. A famous example is Henry Ford's maxim 'You can have any colour provided it's black', which set a trajectory for mass production and low variety in the car industry for decades.

- *Historical narratives.* How do people in an organisation talk about and explain its history? In trying to understand the foundations of the strategy of an organisation a new chief executive or an external consultant will typically spend a good deal of time talking with people to try and understand the meaning and gain insights from their personal accounts of history. What do they have to say about the way they see their organisation and its past, not least in terms of the origins of success? In turn, what are the implications for future strategy development? Does what people say suggest an organisation with the historic capabilities of relevance to current markets and customers; one capable of innovation and change or one so rooted in past ways of doing things that will be difficult to change?

History, then, is important in terms of how it influences current strategy for better or worse. It is not always easy, however, to trace the links to the organisation as it currently exists. It is here that understanding the organisation's culture becomes important. The current culture of an organisation is, to a great extent, the legacy of its history; history becomes 'encapsulated in culture'.[14] So understanding an organisation's culture is one way of understanding the historical influences, which, as we have seen, can be very powerful. The next section goes on to explain what culture is and how it can be analysed.

(5.3) WHAT IS CULTURE AND WHY IS IT IMPORTANT?

Edgar Schein defines *organisational culture* as the 'basic *assumptions and beliefs* that are shared by members of an organisation, that operate unconsciously and define in a basic taken-for-granted fashion an organisation's view of itself and its environment'.[15] Related to this are taken-for-granted *ways 'we do things around here'*[16] that accumulate over time. So **organisational culture is the taken-for-granted assumptions and behaviours that make sense of people's organisational context** and therefore contributes to how groups of people respond and behave in relation to issues they face. It therefore has important influences on the development and change of organisational strategy.

Figure 5.3 Cultural frames of reference

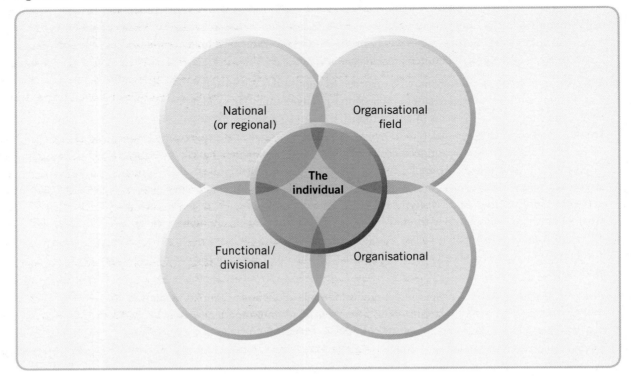

Different cultural contexts are likely to influence individuals, as Figure 5.3 shows. The sections that follow explain these different cultural frames of reference and then show how culture can be analysed and characterised as a means of understanding its influences on both current and future organisational purposes and strategies. The Key Debate at the end of the chapter then raises some questions about undertaking such analysis.

5.3.1 Geographically based cultures

Many writers, perhaps the most well known of whom is Geert Hofstede,[17] have shown how attitudes to work, authority, equality and other important factors differ from one country to another. Such differences have been shaped by powerful cultural forces concerned with history, religion and even climate over many centuries. Organisations that operate internationally need to understand and cope with such differences, which can manifest themselves in terms of different standards, values and expectations in the various countries in which they operate.[18] For example, Wal mart failed to develop its retail presence in Germany and China because it did not understand how local shopping behaviour differed from that in the USA. Indeed many Western firms that seek to build a presence in China have had to adjust to different cultural norms in terms of buyer and supplier behaviour as well as employee relations. Illustration 5.2 also shows how cultural differences underpin different conceptions of management between Chinese and Western managers.

Although they are not shown separately in Figure 5.3 (for reasons of simplification), it may also be important to understand *subnational* (usually regional) cultures. For example, attitudes

ILLUSTRATION 5.2

Project management: Chinese and UK perspectives

A study of how project management is viewed in China and the UK brought to the surface significant different perspectives on management.

Project management can be important in the implementation of strategy and since the 1980s has become increasingly recognised in China as a useful management tool. Researchers have, however, found different conceptions of project management between managers in China and managers in the UK. These findings, in turn, inform an understanding of some underlying differences of the wider conception of management itself.

Relationship with the company

Chinese managers saw their personal career development as strongly linked to the company's development: none of those studied had changed their company since the start of their career in the construction industry. UK managers, on the other hand, were more individualistic and most had changed companies several times.

Teamwork

Both Chinese and UK managers placed a high value on teamwork, relationships with clients and with subcontractors, but interpreted these differently. Chinese managers saw the team like a family where the team leader was like the father of the family and team members should support each other. So Chinese managers preferred to stay with their established teams and select new team members introduced to them by other members of the team. UK managers placed an emphasis on respect and trust but much more within the work context and with much less concern for how long people had worked in the team.

Relationship with clients

Chinese managers saw the client as: 'like your parents; you need to do whatever they instruct you . . . you need to do all you can to make them happy'. It was also important to build strong personal relationships with the client. UK managers saw the client as the provider of project funds, with a greater emphasis on contractual relationships: 'we deliver what the client wants, based on the contract'.

Relationship with subcontractors

For Chinese managers, subcontractors were like brothers and sisters of their project team family. They recognised that there could be competition with subcontractors but saw the answer to this as the building of long-term relationships. UK managers also saw subcontractors as members of the project team but with an emphasis on their specialised techniques and skills. Again they preferred to keep a more impersonal, contractual distance.

Conflict resolution

Both groups of managers acknowledged that conflict with clients or subcontractors could be a possibility. For Chinese managers negotiation was the basis of conflict resolution. Failure to resolve problems which might end with a claim against a subcontractor was regarded as a loss of 'face' and reputation. Conflicts needed to be resolved amicably. Though they also preferred to settle things amicably, UK managers again emphasised contractual conditions. Claims on clients or contractual penalties on subcontractors were normal project management practice.

Attitudes to uncertainty

Both Chinese and UK managers accepted uncertainty as inherent in project management. However, Chinese managers found this more stressful and problematic than UK managers, who, rather, enjoyed the challenges that arose: 'I am very lucky in my job in that I have numerous different challenges every day and it's full of change.'

Source: Ping Chen and David Partington, 'An interpretive comparison of Chinese and Western conceptions of relationships in construction project management work', *International Journal of Project Management*, vol. 22, no. 5 (2004), pp. 397–406.

Questions

1 In what other aspects of managing strategy might the differences identified here be important?
2 If you are seeking to operate in a country with a very different culture, how would you set about trying to understand that culture and its underlying assumptions?

to some aspects of employment and supplier relationships may differ at a regional level even in a relatively small and cohesive country like the UK, and quite markedly elsewhere in Europe (e.g. between northern and southern Italy). Such differences can affect the success of a strategy. For example, even within a country the integration of mergers between similar businesses can be problematic given regional differences of customer behaviour or employee attitudes and experience.[19]

5.3.2 **Organisational fields**[20]

The culture of an organisation is also shaped by 'work-based' groupings such as an industry (or sector), a profession or what is sometimes known as 'an organisational field'. An **organisational field is a community of organisations that interact more frequently with one another than with those outside the field and that have developed a shared meaning system.**[21] Such organisations may share a common technology, set of regulations or education and training. In turn this can mean that they tend to cohere around a **recipe:**[22] **a set of assumptions, norms and routines held in common within an organisational field about the appropriate purposes and strategies of field members;** in effect a 'shared wisdom'. For example, there are many organisations in the organisational field of 'justice', such as lawyers, police, courts, prisons and probation services. The roles of each are different and their detailed prescriptions as to how justice should be achieved differ. However, they are all committed to the principle that justice is a good thing which is worth striving for, they interact frequently on this issue, have developed shared ways of understanding and debating issues that arise and operate common routines or readily accommodate the routines of others in the field. Similar coherence around a recipe is common in other organisational fields: for example, professional services such as accountancy (see Illustration 5.3), medicine and industrial sectors such as engineering.

This links to the concept of path dependency discussed above. The different parties in an organisational field form a self-reinforcing network built on such assumptions and behaviours that, quite likely, will lead to behavioural lock-in. Indeed professions, or trade associations, often attempt to formalise an organisational field where the membership is exclusive and the behaviour of members is regulated. Such cultural influences can be advantageous in maintaining standards and consistency between individual providers. Managers can, however, become 'institutionalised' such that they do not see the opportunities or indeed threats from outside their organisational field and the recipes they inherit become difficult to change.

Institutionalisation in turn leads to the idea of legitimacy. **Legitimacy is concerned with meeting the expectations within an organisational field in terms of assumptions, behaviours and strategies.** Just as previous chapters have shown the important influence of environmental forces (Chapter 2), strategic capabilities (Chapter 3) and stakeholder expectations (Chapter 4), strategies can be shaped by the need for legitimacy in several ways. For example, this may occur through *regulation* (e.g. standards and codes of behaviour specified, perhaps by a professional body), *normative expectations* (what is socially expected), or simply that which is taken for granted as being appropriate (e.g. the *recipe*). Over time, there tends to develop a consensus within an organisational field about strategies that will be successful or acceptable – so strategies themselves become legitimised. By conforming to such norms, organisations may secure approval, support and public endorsement, thus increasing their legitimacy. Stepping outside that strategy may be risky because important stakeholders (such as customers or bankers) may not see such a move as legitimate. Therefore, organisations tend to mimic each other's strategies. There may be differences in strategies between organisations but within bounds of legitimacy.[23] This is shown in the discussion of strategy in Illustration 5.3. Of course,

ILLUSTRATION

ILLUSTRATION 5.3

Strategy debate in an accounting firm

The perceived legitimacy of a strategy may have different roots.

Edward Grey, the Managing Partner of QDG, one of the larger accountancy firms in the world, was discussing its global development with two of his senior partners. Global development had been the main issue at the firm's international committee in the USA the previous week. Like most accountancy firms, QDG was organised along national lines. Its origins were in auditing but it now offered tax and financial advice, corporate recovery and information systems services. International cooperation was based on personal contacts of partners across the world. However, large clients were beginning to demand a 'seamless global service'. At the meeting was Alan Clark, with 20 years' experience as a partner and high reputation in the accountancy profession, and Michael Jones, new to QDG and unlike the others not an accountant, who headed up the information systems arm of QDG, having been recruited from a consultancy firm.

Grey: 'Unless we move towards a more global form of business, QDG could lose its position as one of the leading accountancy firms in the world. Our competitors are moving this way, so we have to. The issue is how?'

Clark was sympathetic but cautionary. He pointed out that clients were entering growing economies such as China. 'Governments there will insist on international standards of practice, but they have difficulties. For example, in China historically there has been no real concept of profit, let alone how to measure it. If there is to be a market economy, the need for the services we provide is high. There are however major problems, not least, the enormous number of people required. It is not possible to churn out experienced accountants overnight. Our professional standards would be compromised. The firm cannot be driven by market opportunity at the expense of standards. There is another issue. Our business is based on personal relationships and trust; this must not be compromised in the name of "global integration".'

Michael Jones suggested that the problem was more challenging: 'All our competitors are going global. They will be pitching for the same clients, offering the same services and the same standard

of service. Where is the difference? To achieve any competitive advantage we need to do things differently and think beyond the obvious. For example, why not a two-tier partnership, where smaller countries are non-equity partners. That would allow us to make decisions more quickly, allow us to enforce standards and give formal authority to senior partners looking after our major international clients.'

Alan Clark had expected this: 'This is not an opportunity to make money; it's about the development of proper systems for the economies of previously closed countries. We need to cooperate with other firms to make sure that there are compatible standards. This cannot be helped by changing a partnership structure that has served well for a hundred years.'

Grey: 'The view at last week's meeting was certainly that there is a need for a more internationally coordinated firm, with a more effective client management system, less reliance on who knows whom and more on drawing on the best of our people when we need them.'

Clark: 'I could equally argue that we have an unparalleled network of personal relationships throughout the world which we have been building for decades. That what we have to do is strengthen this using modern technology and modern communications.'

Edward Grey reconciled himself to a lengthy discussion.

Source: Adapted from the case study in G. Johnson and R. Greenwood, 'Institutional theory and strategic management', in *Strategic Management: A Multiple-Perspective Approach*, edited by Mark Jenkins and V. Ambrosini, Palgrave, 2007.

Questions

1 What are the underlying assumptions of the arguments being advanced by the three partners?

2 What may be the origins of these assumptions?

3 How do the different views correspond to the discussions of strategic capabilities (Chapter 3) and competitive strategy (Chapter 6)?

some businesses that begin as fringe players may actually be the foundation of successful future strategies (e.g. internet providers of downloadable music), but *initially* this may not be seen – customers may remain loyal to established companies; investors and bankers may be reluctant to fund such ventures; and existing players in the market may dismiss what they see as aberrations.

Because recipes vary from one field to another, the transition of managers between sectors can prove difficult. For example, private-sector managers have been encouraged to join public services in an attempt to inject new ways of doing things into the public sector. Many have found difficulties in gaining acceptance of their ways of working and in adjusting their management style to the different traditions and expectations of their new organisation, for example in issues like consensus building as part of the decision-making process. Or, to take the example in Illustration 5.3, Michael Jones's different career background means he has some quite different views on strategy from his accountant colleagues.

5.3.3 Organisational culture

As the different definitions of culture provided at the beginning of this section suggest, culture can be conceived as consisting of different layers. The four proposed by Edgar Schein[24] are (see Figure 5.4):

- *Values* may be easy to identify in terms of those formally stated by an organisation since they are often explicit, perhaps written down (see section 4.2). The values driving a strategy may, however, be different from those in formal statements. For example, in the last decade, many banks espoused values of shareholder value creation, careful risk management and, of course, high levels of customer service. But they indulged in highly risky lending, resulting in the need for huge government financial support in 2009. It is therefore important to delve beneath espoused values to uncover underlying, perhaps taken-for-granted, values that can help explain the strategy actually being pursued by an organisation (see section 5.3.7 below).

- *Beliefs* are more specific. They can typically be discerned in how people talk about issues the organisation faces; for example, a belief that the company should not trade with particular countries or, as with Alan Clark in Illustration 5.3, a belief in the rightness of accountancy systems and standards.

With regard to both values and beliefs it is important to remember that, in relation to culture, the concern is with the collective rather than individuals' values and beliefs. Indeed it may be that individuals in organisations have values and beliefs that at times run counter to their organisation's, which can give rise to the sort of ethical tensions and problems discussed in section 4.4.2.

- *Behaviours* are the day-to-day way in which an organisation operates and that be seen by people both inside and often outside the organisation. This includes the work routines, how the organisation is structured and controlled and 'softer' issues around symbolic behaviours (see section 5.3.6 below). These behaviours may become the taken-for-granted 'ways we do things around here' that are potentially the bases for inimitable strategic capabilities (see section 3.3.3) but also significant barriers to achieving strategic change if that becomes necessary (see Chapter 14).

Figure 5.4 Culture in four layers

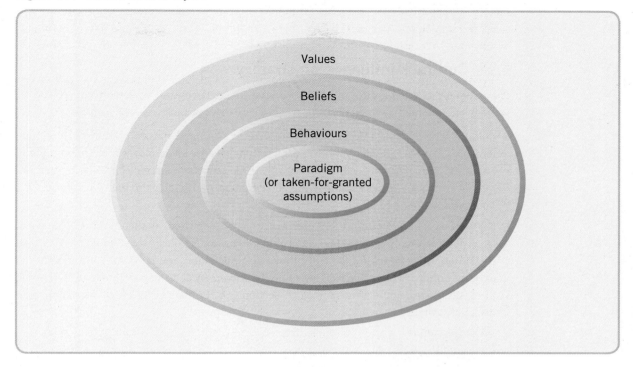

- *Taken-for-granted assumptions* are the core of an organisation's culture which, in this book, we refer to as the organisational *paradigm*. The **paradigm is the set of assumptions held in common and taken for granted in an organisation.** In effect these shared assumptions represent *collective experience* about fundamental aspects of the organisation that, in turn, guide people in that organisation about how to view and respond to different circumstances that they face. The paradigm can underpin successful strategies by providing a basis of common understanding in an organisation but, again, can be a major problem when major strategic change is needed (see Chapter 14). The importance of the paradigm is discussed further in section 5.3.6.

5.3.4 **Organisational subcultures**

In seeking to understand the relationship between culture and an organisation's strategies, it may be possible to identify some aspects of culture that pervade the whole organisation. However, there may also be important *subcultures*. These may relate to the structure of the organisation: for example, the differences between geographical divisions in a multinational company, or between functional groups such as finance, marketing and operations. Differences between divisions may be particularly evident in organisations that have grown through acquisition. Also different divisions may be pursuing different types of strategy that require or foster different cultures. Indeed, aligning strategic positioning and organisational culture is a critical feature of successful organisations. Differences between business functions can also relate to the different nature of work in different functions. For example, in a major oil company differences are likely between those functions engaged in 'upstream' exploration, where time horizons may be in decades, and those concerned with 'downstream' retailing, with much shorter market-driven time horizons. Arguably, this is one reason why Shell took the decision to sell its retail outlets and other downstream activities.

5.3.5 Culture's influence on strategy

The taken-for-granted nature of culture is what makes it centrally important in relation to strategy and the management of strategy. There are three primary reasons for this:

● *Cultural 'glue'*. There are benefits in the taken-for-granted nature of culture. Josephine Rydberg-Dumont, president of IKEA, argues that, because all employees cohere around the founding principles and values of the firm, it reduces the need for constant supervision. Moreover, since one such value is the benefit of constantly questioning the status quo, it 'fuels' innovation.

● *Captured by culture*. Organisations can, however, be 'captured' by their culture. Managers, faced with a changing business environment, are more likely to attempt to deal with the situation by searching for what they can understand and cope with in terms of the existing culture. The result is likely to be the incremental strategic change with the risk of eventual strategic drift explained in section 5.4. Culture is, in effect, an unintended driver of strategy.

● *Managing culture*. Because it is difficult to observe, identify and control that which is taken for granted, it is also difficult to manage. This is why having a way to analyse culture so as to make it more evident is important – the subject of the next section. (However, see the Key Debate at the end of the chapter.)

Mark Fields, President of Ford Motor Company in 2006, famously argued that 'culture eats strategy for breakfast', by which he meant to emphasise the dominant influence of culture on the strategy of the business. The likely effect of culture on strategy is shown in Figure 5.5.[25] Faced with a stimulus for action, such as declining performance, managers first try to improve the implementation of existing strategy (step 1). This might be through trying to lower cost, improve efficiency, tighten controls or improve accepted ways of doing things. If this is not effective, a change of strategy may occur, but a change in line with the existing culture (step 2). For example, managers may seek to extend the market for their business, but assume that it will be similar to their existing market, and therefore set about managing the new venture in much the same way as they have been used to. Alternatively, even where managers know intellectually that they need to change strategy, indeed know technologically how to do so, they find themselves constrained by path-dependent organisational routines and assumptions or political processes, as seems likely in the case of Kodak (see Illustration 5.5). This often happens, for example, when there are attempts to change highly bureaucratic organisations to be customer-orientated. Even if people accept the need to change a culture's emphasis on the importance of conforming to established rules, routines and reporting relationships, they do not readily do so. It is a fallacy to assume that reasoned argument necessarily changes deeply embedded assumptions rooted in collective experience built up over long periods of time. Readers need only think of their own experience in trying to persuade others to rethink their religious beliefs, or, indeed, allegiances to sports teams, to realise this. Changes in strategy which entail a fundamental change to an organisation's culture (step 3) are likely to be rare and triggered by dramatic evidence of the redundancy of that culture such as a financial crisis or major loss of market share.

Figure 5.5 Culture's influence on strategy development

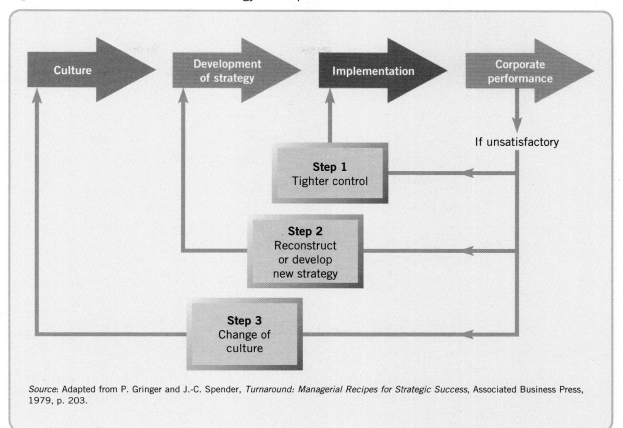

Source: Adapted from P. Gringer and J.-C. Spender, *Turnaround: Managerial Recipes for Strategic Success*, Associated Business Press, 1979, p. 203.

5.3.6 **Analysing culture: the cultural web**

In order to understand the existing culture and its effects it is important to be able to analyse an organisation's culture. The cultural web[26] is a means of doing this (see Figure 5.6). The **cultural web shows the behavioural, physical and symbolic manifestations of a culture** that inform and are informed by the taken-for-granted assumptions, or paradigm, of an organisa-tion. It is in effect the inner two ovals in Figure 5.4. The cultural web can be used to understand culture in any of the frames of reference discussed above but is most often used at the organ-isational and/or functional levels in Figure 5.3.[27] The elements of the cultural web are as follows:

● The *paradigm* is at the core of Figure 5.6. As previously defined it is the set of assumptions held in common and taken for granted in an organisation. The assumptions of the paradigm are, quite likely, very basic. For example, a common problem in technology and engineering firms is the propensity of people to focus on the technical excellence of products rather than customer-perceived needs. Or the paradigm of practitioners in the National Health Service in the UK is about curing illnesses. It is quite likely that, even if the rational view is to build a strategy around the engineering business's customer needs or the need for prevention (as distinct from curing) of illnesses, people in those organisations may still interpret issues and behave in line with its paradigm. So understanding what the paradigm is and how it informs debate on strategy matters. The problem is that, since it is unlikely to be talked

Figure 5.6 The cultural web of an organisation

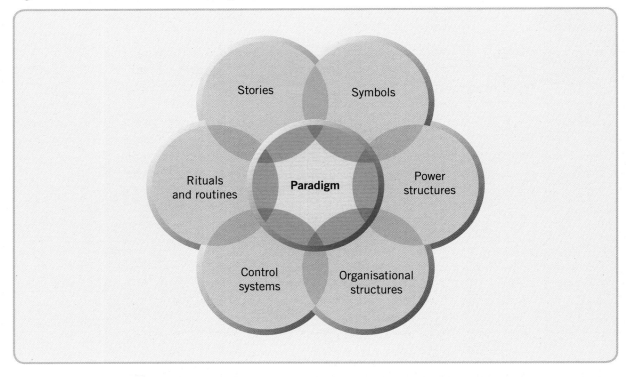

about, or even be something that people are conscious of, trying to identify it can be difficult, especially if you are part of that organisation. Outside observers may find it easier to identify simply by listening to what people say and emphasise. One way of 'insiders' getting to see the assumptions they take for granted is to focus initially on other aspects of the cultural web because these are to do with more visible manifestations of culture. Moreover these other aspects are likely to act to reinforce the assumptions of the paradigm.

- *Routines* are 'the way we do things around here' on a day-to-day basis. These may have a long history and may well be common across organisations. At their best, routines lubricate the working of the organisation, and may provide a basis for distinctive organisational capabilities. However, they can also represent a taken-for-grantedness about how things should happen which, again, can guide how people deal with situations and be difficult to change. For example, managers trying to achieve greater customer focus in engineering firms often report that customer-facing sales engineers routinely tend to tell customers what they need rather than listening to their needs.

- The *rituals*[28] of organisational life are particular activities or special events that emphasise, highlight or reinforce what is important in the culture. Examples include training pro-grammes, interview panels, promotion and assessment procedures, sales conferences and so on. An extreme example, of course, is the ritualistic training of army recruits to prepare them for the discipline required in conflict. However, rituals can also be informal activities such as drinks in the pub after work or gossiping around photocopying machines. A check-list of rituals is provided in Chapter 14 (see Table 14.2).

- The *stories* told by members of an organisation to each other, to outsiders, to new recru-its, and so on, may act to embed the present in its organisational history and also flag up important events and personalities. They typically have to do with successes, disasters, heroes, villains and mavericks (who deviate from the norm). They can be a way of letting people know what is conventionally important in an organisation.

- *Symbols* are objects, events, acts or people that convey, maintain or create meaning over and above their functional purpose. For example, offices and office layout, cars and job titles have a functional purpose, but are also typically signals about status and hierarchy. Particular people may come to represent especially important aspects of an organisation or historic turning points. The form of language used in an organisation can also be particularly revealing, especially with regard to customers or clients. For example, in a major teaching hospital in the UK, consultants described patients as 'clinical material'. While this might be amusing, it reveals something of the underlying assumptions of the paradigm that might play a significant role in influencing strategy. Although symbols are shown separately in the cultural web, it should be remembered that many elements of the web are symbolic. So, routines, control and reward systems and structures are not only functional but also symbolic.

- *Power* was defined in Chapter 4 as the ability of individuals or groups to persuade, induce or coerce others into following certain courses of action. So *power structures* are distributions of power to groups of people in an organisation. The most powerful individuals or groups are likely to be closely associated with the paradigm and long-established ways of doing things. In analysing power the guidance given in Chapter 4 (section 4.5.2) is useful.

- *Organisational structures* are the roles, responsibilities and reporting relationships in organisations. These are likely to reflect power structures and how they manifest themselves. Formal hierarchical, mechanistic structures may emphasise that strategy is the province of top managers and everyone else is 'working to orders'. Structures with less emphasis on formal reporting relationships might indicate more participative strategy making. Highly devolved structures (as discussed in Chapter 13) may signify that collaboration is less important than competition and so on.

- *Control systems* are the formal and informal ways of monitoring and supporting people within and around an organisation and tend to emphasise what is seen to be important in the organisation. They include measurements and reward systems. For example, public-service organisations have often been accused of being concerned more with stewardship of funds than with quality of service. This is reflected in their control systems, which are more about accounting for spending rather than with quality of service. Remuneration schemes are a significant control mechanism. Individually based bonus schemes related to volume are likely to signal a culture of individuality, internal competition and an emphasis on sales volume rather than teamwork and an emphasis on quality.

As the banking crisis of 2009 onwards developed, many familiar with the banking industry blamed the problems on 'the banking culture', which needed to change. Notably missing, however, were specifics as to what that culture was, so it was difficult to be clear about just what needed to change. Illustration 5.4 shows two cultural webs drawn up on the basis of interviews with longstanding employees of the retail side of Barclays Bank. They show some of the differences between the culture of Barclays prior to the 1990s and at the time of the crisis. In the past it was a paternalistic culture, in terms of both assumptions about customers and the way in which staff were treated, with an emphasis on avoiding risk. The branch manager,

ILLUSTRATION 5.4

Cultural webs of Barclays Retail

The cultural web can be used to identify the taken-for-granted
behaviours and assumptions of an organisation.

The cultural web of Barclays Retail pre-1990s

Stories
Do's and don't's
Privacy stories
Manager stories;
'stern but quite nice'
No gossip about
customers

Symbols
The branch itself
The manager as pillar
of the community
'Proper dress' prescribed
Oak panelled manager's office
Manual equipment

Rituals and routines
Branch cheque clearing
Handling cash
Managers see key
customers
Managers exercise
discretion on lending
Banking training
and exams

Core assumptions
We know what's best
for customers financially
Low risk
Branch centric
Paternal

Power structures
Local matters
The local manager (male)
Regional directorate as
'remote gods'

Control systems
Inspection (audits)
without notice
Discretionary lending
limits for managers

**Organisational
structures**
Strict hierarchy within
branch and from
branch to head office

often a 'pillar of the community', was a dominant influence on the service provided as well as
a symbol of what Barclays stood for. The branches themselves were where bank staff 'looked
after' customers and processed their cash and cheques and where the manager interviewed
important customers and made decisions, for example about loans and credit limits. Propriety
in matters financial was ensured by periodic unannounced audits by otherwise remote head
office staff. This culture changed with the centralisation of bank services and operations and
with the growing importance of investment banking on the profits of Barclays (together with
other banks). Retail banking had become secondary to investment banking; the branches

The cultural web of Barclays Retail in the 2000s

Stories
'Procedure is king'
Stories about retail;
not wider banking
If you want to 'get on'
work in a specialist
department

Symbols
Branch layout for financial
services (no grille;
open plan; sofas)
Office 'for use' not for manager
Cash dispensing mechanised
Standard uniform must be worn

Rituals and routines
Receive and give out money
Sell products
Automated centralised
cheque clearance
Area briefing meetings
for managers

Core assumptions
Do what customers want
Sell financial services
We don't make money
from retail banking

Power structures
Head office
(named people
recognised)
Central specialisms
Local manager has
no power

Control systems
No discretion
Highly systematised
Individual targets and
incentives
League tables for
branches

**Organisational
structures**
Local manager administers
several branches
All infrastructure
centralised

Questions

1 How might the webs help those seeking to address the problems of 'the banking culture'?
2 How do the various elements of the web interrelate?
3 Draw up a cultural web for an organisation of your choice.

had become vehicles for selling financial services; staff were incentivised to do so; the local branch manager was no more and local discretion was removed. Cash was increasingly automatically dispensed, cheques were cleared centrally and staff operated to standardised procedures. The layout of the branch itself de-emphasised financial security or the role of a branch manager; it was more open plan facilitating contact between staff and customers.

It was this sales culture, also common in other banks, which led to the huge fines imposed for the mis-selling of payment protection insurance policies by Barclays as well as other banks.

5.3.7 Undertaking cultural analysis

If an analysis of the culture of an organisation is to be undertaken, there are some important issues to bear in mind:

- *Questions to ask.* Figure 5.7 outlines some of the questions that might help build up an understanding of culture using the cultural web.

- *Statements of cultural values.* As section 4.2 and section 5.4.3 above explained, organisations may make public statements of their values, beliefs and purposes, for example in annual reports, mission or values statements and business plans. There is a danger that these are seen as useful descriptions of the organisational culture. But this is likely to be at best only partially true, and at worst misleading. This is not to suggest that there is any organised deception. It is simply that the statements of values and beliefs are often carefully considered and carefully crafted statements of the aspirations of a particular stakeholder (such as the CEO) rather than descriptions of the actual culture. For example, an outside observer of a police force might conclude from its public statements of purpose and priorities that it had a balanced approach to the various aspects of police work – catching criminals, crime prevention, community relations. However, a deeper probing might reveal that (in cultural terms) there is the 'real' police work (catching criminals) and the 'lesser work' (crime prevention, community relations).

- *Pulling it together.* The detailed 'map' produced by the cultural web can be a rich source of information about an organisation's culture, but it is useful to be able to characterise the culture that the information conveys. Sometimes this is possible by means of graphic descriptors. For example, managers who undertook a cultural analysis in the UK National Health Service (NHS) summed up their culture as 'The National Sickness Service'. Although this approach is rather crude and unscientific, it can be powerful in terms of organisational members seeing the organisation as it really is – which may not be immediately apparent from all of the detailed points in the cultural web. It can also help people to understand that culture may drive strategy; for example, a 'national sickness service' will prioritise strategies that are about developments in curing sick people above strategies of health promotion and prevention. So those favouring health promotion strategies need to understand that they are facing the need to change a culture.

If managers are to develop strategies that are different from those of the past, they need to be able to challenge, question and potentially change the organisational culture that underpins the current strategy. In this context, the cultural analysis suggested in this chapter can inform aspects of strategic management discussed in other parts of this book. These include the following:

- *Strategic capabilities.* As Chapter 3 makes clear, historically embedded capabilities are, very likely, part of the culture of the organisation. The cultural analysis of the organisation therefore provides a complementary basis of analysis to an examination of strategic capabilities (see Chapter 3). In effect, such an analysis of capabilities should end up digging into the culture of the organisation, especially in terms of its routines, control systems and the everyday way in which the organisation runs.

- *Strategy development.* An understanding of organisational culture sensitises managers to the way in which historical and cultural influences will likely affect future strategy for good or ill. It therefore relates to the discussion on strategy development in Chapter 12.

Figure 5.7 The cultural web: some useful questions

Stories
- What core beliefs do stories reflect?
- What stories are commonly told, e.g. to newcomers?
- How do these reflect core assumptions and beliefs?
- What norms do the mavericks deviate from?

Symbols
- What objects, events or people do people in the organisation particularly identify with?
- What are these related to in the history of the organisation?
- What aspects of strategy are highlighted in publicity?

Routines and rituals
- Which routines are emphasised?
- Which are embedded in history?
- What behaviour do routines encourage?
- What are the key rituals?
- What assumptions and core beliefs do they reflect?
- What do training programmes emphasise?
- How easy are rituals/routines to change?

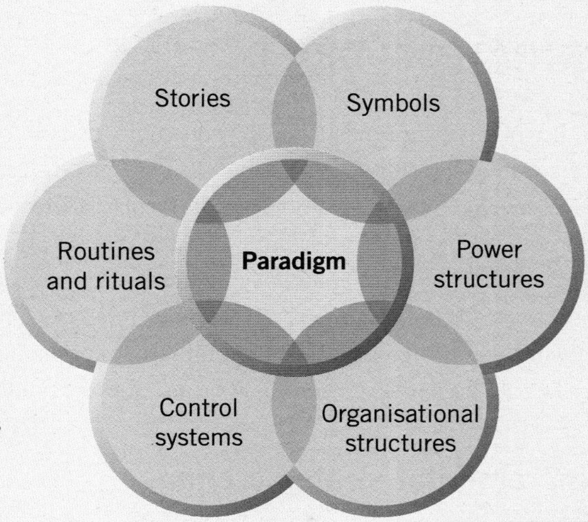

Power structures
- Where does power reside? Indicators include:
  (a) status
  (b) claim on resources
  (c) symbols of power
- Who 'makes things happen'?
- Who stops things happening?

Stories · Symbols · Routines and rituals · Paradigm · Power structures · Control systems · Organisational structures

Control systems
- What is most closely monitored/controlled?
- Is emphasis on reward or punishment?
- Are controls rooted in history or current strategies?
- Are there many/few controls?

Organisational structures
- What are the formal *and* informal structures?
- How rigid are the structures?
- Do structures encourage collaboration or competition?
- What types of power structure do they support?

Overall
- What do the answers to these questions suggest are the (few) fundamental assumptions that are the paradigm?
- How would you characterise the dominant culture?
- How easy is this to change?
- How and to what extent do aspects of the web inter relate and re-enforce each other?

- *Managing strategic change.* An analysis of the culture also provides a basis for the management of strategic change, since it provides a picture of the existing culture that can be set against a desired strategy so as to give insights as to what may constrain the development of that strategy or what needs to be changed in order to achieve it. This is discussed more extensively in Chapter 14 on managing strategic change.

- *Leadership and management style.* Chapter 14 also raises questions about leadership and management style. If one of the major requirements of a strategist is to be able to encourage the questioning of that which is taken for granted, it is likely to require a management style – indeed a culture – that allows and encourages such questioning. If the leadership style is such as to discourage such questioning, it is unlikely that the lessons of history will be learned and more likely that the dictates of history will be followed.

● *Culture and experience.* There have been repeated references in this section to the role culture plays as a vehicle by which meaning is created in organisations. This is discussed more fully in the Commentary on the experience lens and provides a useful way in which many aspects of strategy can be considered (see the Commentaries throughout the book).

(5.4) STRATEGIC DRIFT

The influence of an organisation's history and culture on its strategic direction is evident in the pattern of strategy development depicted in Figure 5.8. **Strategic drift**[29] **is the tendency for strategies to develop incrementally on the basis of historical and cultural influences, but fail to keep pace with a changing environment.** An example of strategic drift in Kodak is given in Illustration 5.5. The reasons and consequences of strategic drift are important to understand, not only because it is common, but also because it helps explain why organisations often seem to stagnate in their strategy development and their performance. Strategic drift also highlights some significant challenges for managers that, in turn, point to some important lessons.

5.4.1 Incremental strategic change

Strategies of organisations most often change gradually. There is a tendency for strategies to develop on the basis of what the organisation has done in the past – especially if that has been

Figure 5.8 Strategic drift

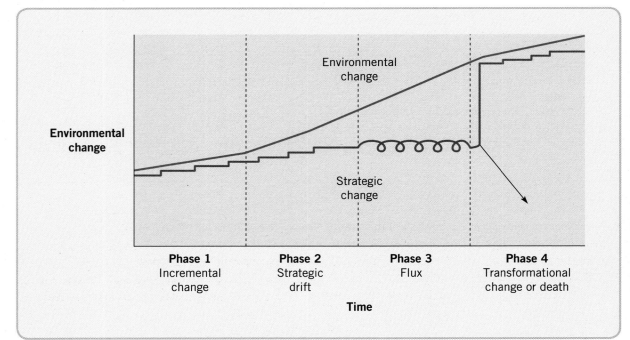

ILLUSTRATION 5.5

Kodak: the decline and fall of a market leader

Knowledge of technological and market changes may not be enough to avoid strategic drift.

In the twentieth century Kodak, the manufacturer of photographic film and cameras, was one of the world's most valuable brands. Based in Rochester in New York State, by 1976 Kodak had 90 per cent of film and 85 per cent share of camera sales in the USA, by 1996 turnover was $16 billion and in 1999 profits nearly $2.5 billion. Initially, known for its innovative technology and marketing, it had developed digital camera technology by 1975, but did not launch digital cameras until the late 1990s by when it was too late.

By 2011 its traditional photography business had been almost entirely eroded by, first, digital cameras and then by smart phones. Turnover was only $6 billion, it was loss making, the share price had plummeted and in 2012 it filed for bankruptcy protection. How did Kodak miss such a fundamental shift in the market?

According to Steve Sasson, the engineer who invented the first digital camera, the response to his invention in Kodak was dismissive because it was filmless photography. There were similar responses to early internal intelligence reports on digital technology: 'Larry Matteson, a former Kodak executive . . . recalls writing a report in 1979 detailing fairly accurately how different parts of the market would switch from film to digital, starting with government reconnaissance, then professional photography and finally the mass market, all by 2010.'[1] Another internal report in the early 1980s concluded that digital technology would take over the camera industry in about 10 years; 10 years in which Kodak could work out its response.

The Kodak response was to use digital to enhance the film business. For example, in 1996 Kodak launched a film system using digital technology to provide users with a preview of shots taken and indicate the number of prints required. It flopped.

It was executives in the film division who carried most weight and they were over-confident about Kodak's brand strength. They also misjudged the speed of the change in customer buying preferences. For example, they believed that people in fast-developing markets such as China would buy lots of film, but many moved from no camera at all to digital. The profit margin on digital was also tiny compared with film and there was a real fear of product cannibalisation. Rosabeth Moss Kanter of Harvard Business School also pointed to the Kodak culture: 'Working in a one company town did not help . . . Kodak's bosses in Rochester seldom heard much criticism . . .'. Moreover, 'executives suffered from a mentality of perfect products, rather than the hi-tech mindset of make it, launch it, fix it.'[1] They also moved slowly: 'Even when Kodak decided to diversify, it took years to make its first acquisition.'[1] Kodak's attempts to diversify by developing the thousands of chemicals its researchers had created for use in film for the drug market also failed.

In 1989, the Kodak board needed to choose a new CEO. The choice was between Kay R. Whitmore, a long-serving executive in the traditional film business, and Phil Samper, who was more associated with digital technology. The board chose Whitmore, who insisted that he would make sure Kodak stayed closer to its core businesses in film and photographic chemicals.[2]

As late as 2007, a Kodak marketing video announced that 'Kodak is back' and 'wasn't going to play grab ass anymore' with digital.[3]

Sources
1. *The Economist*, 'The last Kodak moment?', 14 January 2012.
2. *New York Times*, 9 December 1989.
3. Chunka Mui, 'How Kodak failed', *Forbes*, 18 January 2012.

Questions

1 Which of the reasons for strategic drift are evident in the Kodak story?

2 Drawing on the lessons from Part I of the book, how might Kodak's problems have been avoided?

successful.[30] This is discussed more fully in Chapter 12. This was the case for Kodak, which dominated the market for camera film throughout most of the twentieth century. To take another example, for many years UK retailer HMV had successfully developed its business by adapting to changing technology and tastes in the entertainment market. HMV had made huge profits as music lovers replaced their vinyl records with CDs; it introduced DVDs and computer games when they arrived on the market, and increased the space allocation to them as demand increased. This is shown in phase 1 of Figure 5.8. In most successful businesses there are usually long periods of relative *continuity* during which established strategy remains largely unchanged or changes very *incrementally*. There are three main reasons for this:

- *Alignment with environmental change*. It could be that the environment, particularly the market, is changing gradually and the organisation is keeping in line with those changes by such incremental change. It would make no sense for the strategy to change dramatically when the market is not doing so.

- *The success of the past*. There may be a natural unwillingness by managers to change a strategy significantly if it has been successful in the past. This will especially be so if that strategy is built on capabilities that have been shown to be the basis of competitive advantage (see Chapters 3 and 6) or of innovation (see Chapter 9). Managers quite understandably will argue that they should stick to what they know and do best.

- *Experimentation around a theme*. Managers may have learned how to build variations around their successful formula, in effect experimenting without moving too far from their capability base. (This is akin to what some writers have referred to as 'logical incrementalism'; see section 12.3.1.)

This poses challenges for managers, however. For how long and to what extent can they rely on incremental change being sufficient? When should they make more fundamental strategic changes? And how can they detect when this is necessary?

5.4.2 **The tendency towards strategic drift**

For many years HMV persisted in the conviction that there was a market for the sale of music and DVDs through specialist retail outlets. HMV continued to adjust its retail formats and extended product ranges in the search for a sustainable competitive position. Senior management in particular had difficulty, however, reconciling themselves to the need for more fundamental change to their business model given the shifts in the first decade of this century to the way in which people accessed music, films and games through the internet. A similar persistence with established strategy was evident in Kodak.

Given that an organisation's strategy may continue to change incrementally, there does not need to be sudden or dramatic environmental changes for the strategy to become less aligned with the environment. Phase 2 of Figure 5.8 shows environmental change accelerating, but it is not sudden. For HMV it was not as if changes in buyer behaviour or the growth in supermarket sales of CDs and DVDs happened overnight. These changes took place over years. The problem that gives rise to strategic drift is that, as with many organisations, HMV's strategy was not keeping pace with these changes. There are at least five reasons for this:

- *Steady as you go*. Chapter 2 has provided ways to analyse the environment and such analyses may yield insights. But how are managers to be sure of the direction and significance of such changes? Or changes may be seen as temporary. Managers may be understandably wary of changing what they are likely to see as a winning strategy, on the basis of what might only be a fad in the market, or a temporary downturn in demand. It may be easy to see major changes with hindsight, but it may not be so easy to see their significance as they are happening. Rebecca Henderson of MIT suggested how a Kodak executive might have responded to reports on the threat of digital technology (see Illustration 5.5): '. . . you are suggesting that we invest millions of dollars in a market that may, or may not exist but that is certainly smaller than our existing market, to develop a product that customers may or may not want using a business model that will almost certainly give us lower margins than our existing product lines . . . Tell me again just why we should make this investment?'[31]

- *Building on the familiar.* Managers may see changes in the environment about which they are uncertain or which they do not entirely understand. In these circumstances they may try to minimise the extent to which they are faced with such uncertainty by looking for answers that are familiar, which they understand and which have served them well in the past. This will lead to a bias towards continued incremental strategic change.

- *Core rigidities.* Capabilities that have been bases of competitive advantage can become difficult to change; in effect *core rigidities*.[32] This occurs because ways of doing things develop over time and become more and more embedded in organisational routines that reinforce, rely on each other and are difficult to unravel. Such routines may also become taken for granted. As the discussion in section 3.3.3 explains, this may be an advantage because it is difficult for competitors to imitate strategic capabilities based on routines that are interconnected and taken for granted. Taken-for-granted capabilities rarely get questioned, however, and therefore tend to persist beyond their usefulness.

- *Relationships become shackles.*[33] Success may have been built on excellent relationships with customers, suppliers and employees. Maintaining these may quite rightly be seen as fundamental to the long-term health of the organisation. Yet these relationships may make it difficult to make significant changes to strategy that could entail changing routes to market or the customer base, developing products requiring different suppliers or changing the skill base of the organisation with the risk of disrupting relationships with the workforce.

- *Lagged performance effects.* The effects of such drift may not be easy to see in terms of the performance of the organisation. Financial performance may continue to hold up in the early stages of strategic drift. Customers may be loyal and the organisation, by becoming more efficient, cutting costs or simply trying harder, may continue to exhibit high levels of performance. So there may not be internal signals of the need for change, or indeed pressure from external observers, to make major changes.

For all these reasons, as the consultants McKinsey point out, the tendency is for 'most companies to allocate the same resources to the same business units year after year'.[34]

However, over time, if strategic drift continues, there will be symptoms that become evident: a downturn in financial performance, a loss in market share to competitors or a decline in the share price. Indeed such a downturn may happen quite rapidly once external observers, not least competitors and financial analysts, have identified that such drift has occurred. Even the most successful companies may drift in this way. Indeed, there is a tendency – which Danny Miller has called the Icarus Paradox[35] – for businesses to become victims of the very success of their past. They become captured by the formula that has delivered that success.

5.4.3 **A period of flux**

The next phase (phase 3) may be a period of *flux* triggered by the downturn in performance. Strategies may change but in no very clear direction. There may also be management changes, often at the very top as the organisation comes under pressure from its stakeholders to make changes, not least shareholders in the case of a public company. There may be internal rivalry as to which strategy to follow, quite likely based on differences of opinion as to whether future strategy should be based on historic capabilities or whether those capabilities are becoming redundant. Indeed, there have been highly publicised boardroom rows when this has happened. All this may result in a further deterioration of confidence in the organisation: perhaps a further drop in performance or share price, a difficulty in recruiting high-quality management, or a further loss of customers' loyalty. By 2012 HMV had closed many of its stores and shoppers would find its product offering skewed towards video games and DVDs but also merchandise such as T-shirts and posters in an attempt to ramp up sales.

5.4.4 **Transformational change or death**

As things get worse it is likely that the outcome (phase 4) will be one of three possibilities. (a) The organisation may die; in the case of a commercial organisation it may go into receivership for example, as Kodak did in 2012 and HMV did in 2013. Some private companies can, however, experience a lingering death as their, often, owner managers persist in following the strategy of the past. (b) It may get taken over by another organisation. (c) Or it may go through a period of *transformational change*. Such change could take form in multiple changes related to the organisation's strategy; perhaps a change to its whole business model (see section 9.2.4) as well as changes in the top management of the organisation and perhaps the way the organisation is structured.

Transformational change does not take place frequently in organisations and usually follows a major downturn in performance. Often it is transformational changes that are heralded as the success stories of top executives; this is where they most visibly make a difference. The problem is that, from the point of view of market position, shareholder wealth and jobs, it may be rather late. Competitive position may have been lost, shareholder value has probably already been destroyed and, very likely, many jobs will have been lost too. The time when 'making a difference' really matters most is in phases 1 or 2 in Figure 5.8, before an organisation suffers performance decline. However, a study of 215 major UK firms over the 20-year period 1983–2003 identified only four that could be said to have *both* maintained consistently high levels of performance and effected major transformational change over that period.[36] The problem is that, very likely, strategic drift is not easy to see before performance suffers. So, to avoid the damaging effects of strategic drift, it is vital to take seriously the extent to which historical tendencies in strategy development tend to persist in the cultural fabric of organisations. There is also emerging evidence that firms that are able to enact change regularly before pressured to do so benefit in terms of financial performance.[37]

KEY DEBATE
Understanding organisational culture

If organisational culture is so important an influence on strategy, then understanding what it is and its influences are of key importance. But is this possible?

There are many tools and techniques for analysing organisational cultures. Denison Consulting,[1] based in Ann Arbour, Michigan, employs the Denison model to help clients diagnose their cultures.

Denison argues that there are four key cultural traits that affect performance measures such as profitability, sales growth, quality, and market value. Founder Dan Denison explained:[2]

'Generally speaking, an organisation's sense of *Mission* and its *Adaptability* can forecast its growth rate fairly well. A growth company sets its vision on external markets, and is sensitive to the changes in the market. Its actions are informed by the market and it clearly understands the significance of its existence in the market. If a corporation has strong *Involvement* and *Consistency*, and the company culture is very "internal," the company may not grow quickly, but performance indicators such as quality and efficiency are typically pretty good. Innovative companies always get high scores in aspects of *Adaptability* and *Involvement*. A company with a strong *Mission* and *Consistency* will have steady performance over a long time period.'

These traits are further broken down into 60 items, measured via a five-point Likert scale in a survey that managers can complete. The results produce a picture of the culture. Denison argues that the highest-performing firms are those that score high on all four of the key traits. It also suggests that survey results can be used to identify the weaknesses in an organisation's culture, track changes in the culture and benchmark against other companies.

However, Mats Alvesson[3] suggests that there is a tendency to simplify and trivialise what organisational culture means. Managers often fall victim to 'sins' that include:

Reifying culture: Seeing culture as something 'thing-like' that, for example, directly links to performance or can be readily managed. What really matters is the meaning shared by a collective and that is a more complex idea.

Essentialising culture: Describing culture in terms of a few essential traits. The danger is a 'too strongly ordered and superficial view on culture'. The need is for a more careful interpretation and a recognition of variations within a culture.

Consensualising culture: 'Shared meanings do not necessarily imply consensus and harmony . . . an organisation may be characterised by shared ideas and beliefs about the significance of self interest, fierce internal competition and a view of corporate life as fairly harsh and jungle-like.'

Totalising culture: Assuming that a culture can be captured 'once and for all' when 'it is the shared meanings on a specific topic that is of interest to pay attention to' such as core competences or the future of an industry.

Unifying culture: 'Equating cultural boundaries with formal or legal ones, as implied by terms such as corporate culture or national culture.'

Alvesson grants, however, that there are 'sometimes pragmatic reasons . . . for simplifications and the expression of something accessible – which often leads to some of the sins above . . . My point is, however, that the traps and temptations should be handled with great care and care taken that they are not "privileged".'

Sources
1. www.denisonconsulting.com.
2. Xuejun Yi, 'The yin and yang of corporate culture', *Harvard Business Review*, China, January 2008, pp. 70–82.
3. M. Alvesson, *Understanding Organisational Culture*, Sage, 2002, pp. 186–9.

Questions

1 Which of Alvesson's 'sins' apply to the Denison model?

2 To what extent do Alvesson's sins apply to the cultural web?

3 If, as Alvesson suggests, pragmatically some of the sins are difficult to avoid, how can managers avoid 'privileging' them?

4 Undertake a cultural analysis of an organisation. To what extent did you find yourself committing any of the 'sins'?

SUMMARY

- The *history and culture* of an organisation may contribute to the distinct and unique nature of an organisation's strategic capabilities.

- Historical, *path-dependent processes* may play a significant part in the success or failure of an organisation and need to be understood by managers. There are historical analyses that can be conducted to help uncover these influences.

- *Cultural and institutional influences* both inform and constrain the strategic development of organisations.

- *Organisational culture* is the basic taken-for-granted assumptions, beliefs and behaviours shared by members of an organisation.

- An understanding of the culture of an organisation and its relationship to organisational strategy can be gained by using the *cultural web*.

- Historic and cultural influences may give rise to *strategic drift* as strategy develops incrementally on the basis of such influences and fails to keep pace with a changing environment.

WORK ASSIGNMENTS

✱ *Denotes more advanced work assignments.*
* *Refers to a case study in the Text and Cases edition.*

5.1✱ In the context of section 5.2, undertake a historical analysis of the strategy development of an organisation of your choice and consider the question: 'Does history matter in managing strategy?'

5.2 Map out an organisational field (see section 5.4.2) within which an organisation of your choice operates. (As a basis for this you could, for example, use accountancy, an organisation operating in the public sector such as a university or Formula One*.)

5.3 Identify (a) an organisation where its publicly stated values correspond with your experience of it and (b) one where they do not. Explain why (a) and (b) might be so.

5.4 Use the questions in Figure 5.8 to plot a cultural web for Barclays Investment Bank, Adnams* or an organisation of your choice.

5.5 Identify four organisations that, in your view, are in the different phases of strategic drift (see the explanation of the phases in section 5.4). Justify your selection.

5.6✱ By using a number of the examples from above and taking into account the issues raised in the Key Debate, critically appraise the assertion that 'culture can only really be usefully analysed by the symptoms displayed in the way the organisation operates'. (You may wish to refer to Schein's book in the recommended key readings to assist you with this task.)

Integrative assignment

5.7✱ Choose an example of a major change in strategy of an organisation. Explain to what extent and how its strategic capabilities and its organisation culture changed. (Refer to Chapters 3, 5, 6, and 14.)

VIDEO ASSIGNMENTS

Visit *MyStrategyLab* and watch the case study for Chapter 5 (which features various companies).

1 Give examples from the video clips of what is meant by 'organisational culture'.

2 Use the video clips to explain how an organisation's culture can be a valuable asset in implementing a strategy.

RECOMMENDED KEY READINGS

- For a historical perspective on strategy see: Manuel Hensmans, Gerry Johnson and George Yip, *Strategic Transformation: Changing while Winning*, Palgrave Macmillan, 2013 (summarised in G. Johnson, G. Yip and M. Hensmans, 'Achieving successful strategic transformation', *MIT Sloan Management Review*, vol. 53, no. 3 (2012), pp. 25–32); and John T. Seaman Jr and George David Smith, 'Your company's history as a leadership tool', *Harvard Business Review* (December 2012), 1–10.

- For a summary and illustrated explanation of institutional theory see Gerry Johnson and Royston Greenwood, 'Institutional theory and strategy', in *Strategic Management: A Multiple-Perspective Approach*, edited by Mark Jenkins and V. Ambrosini, Palgrave, 2007.

- For a comprehensive and critical explanation of organisational culture see Mats Alvesson, *Understanding Organisational Culture*, Sage, 2002.

- For a more thorough explanation of the phenomenon of strategic drift and the cultural web see Gerry Johnson, 'Rethinking incrementalism', *Strategic Management Journal*, vol. 9 (1988), pp. 75–91, and 'Managing strategic change – strategy, culture and action', *Long Range Planning*, vol. 25, no. 1 (1992), pp. 28–36.

REFERENCES

1. See J.T. Seaman Jr and G.D. Smith, 'Your company's history as a leadership tool', *Harvard Business Review* (December 2012), pp. 1–10.

2. This quote by André Malroux and the story of the BMW museum was provided by the business historian Mary Rose.

3. See D. Holbrook, W. Cohen, D. Hounshell and S. Klepper, 'The nature, sources and consequences of firm differences in the early history of the semiconductor industry', *Strategic Management Journal*, vol. 21, no. 10–11 (2000), pp. 107–42.

4. S. Klepper and K.L. Simons, 'Dominance by birthright: entry of prior radio producers and competitive ramifications in the US television receiver industry', *Strategic Management Journal*, vol. 21, no. 10–11 (2000), pp. 987–1016.

5. O. Brunninge, 'Using history in organization: how managers make purposeful reference to history in strategy processes', *Journal of Organizational Change Management*, vol. 22, no. 1 (2009), pp. 8–26.

6. W.B. Arthur, 'Competing technologies, increasing returns and lock in by historical events', *Economic Journal*, vol. 99 (1989), pp. 116–31.

7. P.A. David, 'Clio and the economics of QWERTY', *American Economic Review*, vol. 75, no. 2 (1985), pp. 332–7, but also for a challenge to David's argument see S.J. Liebowitz, and S.E. Margolis, 'The fable of the keys'. *Journal of Law & Economics*, vol. 30, April 1990, pp. 1–26.

8. For discussions of path dependency in an organisational context see: Jorg Sydow, George Schraeyogg and Jochen Koch, 'Organisational path dependance: opening the black box', *Academy of Management Review*, vol. 34, no. 4 (2009), pp. 689–708. The same authors provide a case example of the German book club Bertelsmann AG in G. Schreyögg, J. Sydow and P. Holtman, 'How history matters in organisations: the case of path dependence.' *Management & Organizational History*, vol. 6, no. 1 (2011), pp. 81–100.

9. The world's biggest accounting firms have called for radical reform; 'Big four in call for real time accounts', *Financial Times* (8 November 2006), p. 1.

10. Holbrook et al. (reference 3 above).

11. See M. Hensmans, G. Johnson and G. Yip, *Strategic Transformation: Changing while Winning*, Palgrave Macmillan, 2013.

12. Also see D.J. Jeremy, 'Business history and strategy', in *The Handbook of Strategy and Management*, pp. 436–60, edited by A. Pettigrew, H. Thomas and R. Whittington, Sage, 2002.

13. For good examples of corporate histories see G. Jones, *Renewing Unilever: Transformation and Tradition*, Oxford University Press, 2005; R. Fitzgerald, *Rowntrees and the Marketing Revolution, 1862–1969*, Cambridge University Press, 1995; T.R. Gourvish, *British Railways 1948–73*, Cambridge University Press, 1986.

14. This quote is from S. Finkelstein, 'Why smart executives fail: four case histories of how people learn the wrong lessons from history', *Business History*, vol. 48, no. 2 (2006), pp. 153–70.

15. This definition of culture is taken from E. Schein, *Organisational Culture and Leadership*, 3rd edn, Jossey-Bass, 2004, p. 6.

16. This is how Terrence Deal and Alan Kennedy define organisational culture in *Corporate Cultures: the Rites and Rituals of Corporate Life*, Addison-Wesley, 1982.

17. See G. Hofstede, *Culture's Consequences*, Sage, 2nd edn, 2001. For critiques of Hofstede's work, see B. McSweeney, 'Hofstede's model of national cultural differences and their consequences: a triumph of faith – a failure of analysis', *Human Relations*, vol. 55, no. 1 (2002), pp. 89–118 and A.M. Soares, M. Farhangmeher and A.S. Shoham, 'Hofstede's dimensions of culture in international marketing studies', *Journal of Business Research*, vol. 60, no. 3 (2007), pp. 277–84.

18. On cross-cultural managerment also see R. Lewis, *When Cultures Collide: Managing Successfully across Cultures*, 2nd edn, Brealey, 2000, a practical guide for managers. It offers an insight into different national cultures, business conventions and leadership styles. Also S. Schneider and J.-L. Barsoux, *Managing across Cultures*, 2nd edn, Financial Times Prentice Hall, 2003.

19. For example, differences in regional cultures impacted on the integration of banking mergers in Nigeria, as shown by 'E. Gomes, D. Angwin and K. Melahi, HRM practices throughout the mergers and acquisition (M&A) process: a study of domestic deals in the Nigerian banking industry', *International Journal of Human Resource Management*, vol. 23, no. 14 (2012), pp. 2874–900.

20. A useful review of research on this topic is: T. Dacin, J. Goodstein and R. Scott, 'Institutional theory and institutional change: introduction to the special research forum', *Academy of Management Journal*, vol. 45, no. 1 (2002), pp. 45–57. For a more general review see G. Johnson and R. Greenwood, 'Institutional theory and strategy', in *Strategic Management: a Multiple-Perspective Approach*, edited by Mark Jenkins and V. Ambrosini, Palgrave, 2007.

21. This definition is taken from W. Scott, *Institutions and Organizations*, Sage, 1995.

22. The term 'recipe' was introduced to refer to industries by J.-C. Spender, *Industry Recipes: the Nature and Sources of Management Judgement*, Blackwell, 1989. We have broadened its use by applying it to *organisational fields*. The fundamental idea that behaviours are driven by a collective set of norms and values remains unchanged.

23. D. Deephouse, 'To be different or to be the same? It's a question (and theory) of strategic balance', *Strategic Management Journal*, vol. 20, no. 2 (1999), pp. 147–66.

24. E. Schein (see reference 15) and A. Brown, *Organisational Culture*, Financial Times Prentice Hall, 1998, are useful in understanding the relationship between organisational culture and strategy. For a useful critique of the concept of organisational culture see M. Alvesson, *Understanding Organizational Culture*, Sage, 2002.

25. Figure 5.4 is adapted from the original in P. Grinyer and J.-C. Spender, *Turnaround: Managerial Recipes for Strategic Success*, Associated British Press, 1979, p. 203.

26. A fuller explanation of the cultural web can be found in G. Johnson, *Strategic Change and the Management Process*, Blackwell, 1987, and G. Johnson, 'Managing strategic change: strategy, culture and action', *Long Range Planning*, vol. 25, no. 1 (1992), pp. 28–36.

27. A practical explanation of cultural web mapping is a 'white paper' by Gerry Johnson, 'Mapping and Re-mapping Organisational Culture: a Local Government Example', www.strategyexplorers.com.

28. See A.C.T. Smith and B. Stewart, 'Organizational rituals: features, functions and mechanisms', *International Journal of Management Reviews*, vol. 13, no. 2 (2011), pp. 113–33; and G. Islam and M.J. Zyphur 'Rituals in organizations: a review and expansion of current theory', *Group & Organization Management*, vol. 34 (2009), pp. 114–39.

29. For an explanation of strategic drift see G. Johnson, 'Rethinking incrementalism', *Strategic Management Journal*, vol. 9 (1988), pp. 75–91; and 'Managing strategic change – strategy, culture and action', *Long Range Planning*, vol. 25, no. 1 (1992), pp. 28–36. Also see E. Romanelli and M.T. Tushman, 'Organizational transformation as punctuated equilibrium: an empirical test', *Academy of Management Journal*, vol. 7, no. 5 (1994), pp. 1141–66. They explain the tendency of strategies to develop incrementally with periodic transformational change.

30. See D. Miller and P. Friesen, 'Momentum and revolution in organisational adaptation', *Academy of Management Journal*, vol. 23, no. 4 (1980), pp. 591–614.

31. John Naughton, 'The lessons we can learn from the rise and fall of Kodak', *Observer Discover*, 22 January 2012.

32. See D. Leonard-Barton, 'Core capabilities and core rigidities: a paradox in managing new product development', *Strategic Management Journal*, vol. 13 (1992), pp. 111–25.

33. This is a term used by Donald S. Sull in accounting for the decline of high-performing firms (see 'Why good companies go bad', *Harvard Business Review*, July/August (1999), pp. 42–52).

34. S. Hall, D. Lovallo and R. Musters, 'How to put your money where your strategy is', *McKinsey Quarterley* (March 2012).

35. In *The Icarus Paradox* (Harper-Collins, 1990) Danny Miller makes a convincing case that organisations' success leads to a number of potentially pathological tendencies, not least of which are the tendencies to inflate the durability of bases of success and to build future strategies relatively uncritically. Hence the idea of the Icarus paradox, building on the Greek mythological character, Icarus, who successfully built himself wings to fly but then flew too close to the sun such that they melted.

36. See G. Yip, T. Devinney and G. Johnson, 'Measuring long-term superior performance: the UK's long term superior performers 1984–2003', *Long Range Planning*, vol. 43, no. 3 (2009), pp. 390–413.

37. P. Klarner and S. Raisch, 'Move to the beat – rhythms of change and firm performance', *Academy of Management Journal*, vol. 56, no. 1 (2013), pp. 160–84.

Bonuses and 'gaming' at Barclays Bank

In 2012 Bob Diamond, the CEO of Barclays Bank, resigned in the wake of government, shareholder and media criticism of the bank's manipulation of the inter-bank lending rate, Libor. That criticism was often linked to a condemnation of the culture at Barclays, in particular the investment arm of the bank, which the UK Financial Services Authority called 'a culture of gaming' and BBC's *Panorama* programme dubbed a 'bonus culture'.

Quaker origins

What was so widely condemned as malpractice at Barclays seemed alien to a bank with its origins. The founding families were from the Quaker religious movement, with their emphasis on sobriety, pacifism and high ethical standards, and their descendants were still in important executive positions in the mid-twentieth century. As the *Financial Times* observed:

> 'In many ways the bank resembled a club and, as so often with British clubs, the thing worked surprisingly well despite its flaws . . . It was, in fact, the most innovative of the British clearing banks in the post-war period. In 1967 it installed the world's first auto-mated cash teller machine . . . Barclays also came up with the first plastic payment device, Barclaycard, still outstandingly successful.'

The success did not continue: 1986 brought 'Big Bang', the deregulation of financial markets in the UK. One effect was the entry of US investment banks, so increasing competition and doing away with the 'clubby' culture of the past. Barclays responded by attempting a rapid growth strategy with disastrous results; by the early 1990s it needed to raise additional funds through two rights issues.

The development of investment banking

Barclays began in 1809 and, as Overend, Gurney & Co. built a reputation for accepting bills from other banks to reinvest in businesses – an early form of investment banking. However, poor investments led to bankruptcy in

Bob Diamond

the 1890s contributing to the merger of several Quaker banks in 1896 to form Barclays. Barclays therefore inherited investment banking, risk aversion and a conservative approach to growth until the late 1980s.

The interest in investment banking received a huge impetus after Big Bang. Barclays embarked on acquisitions including a stock broker. The outcome was the formation of an investment bank – Barclays de Zoete Wedd (BZW). In common with other investment banks who got involved in equities trading, however, Barclays had great difficulty combining conventional and investment banking in a coherent model. As the *Financial Times* put it:

> 'The chief problem was culture. As Michael Lewis, author of Liar's Poker, a commentary on Wall Street in the 1980s, memorably put it, a commercial banker was someone who had a wife, a station wagon, 2.2 children and a dog that brought him his slippers when he returned home from work at 6 pm. An investment banker, by contrast, was a breed apart, a member of a master race of dealmakers. He possessed vast, almost unimaginable talent and ambition. If he had a

dog it snarled. He had two little red sports cars yet wanted four. To get them, he was, for a man in a suit, surprisingly willing to cause trouble.'

Investment banking was notorious for its hard work and 'hard play'. It was common for investment bankers to work through the night or to be seen to be doing so – stories had it that they would own two suit jackets so they could leave one on the back of the chair to pretend they were still in the office working. It was also a 'can-do' mentality which legitimated, for example, a day trip to Australia for a one-hour meeting. No expense was spared on flights, entertainment or accommodation provided a big deal was signed. There was also much visible excess with traders spending thousands of pounds a night at champagne bars.

The development of investment banking

In 1994 Martin Taylor, a former *Financial Times* journalist who had been chairman of Courtaulds Textiles, was appointed as chief executive of Barclays. His initial assessment was that BZW was underperforming in a highly competitive and overcrowded market. He decided to bring in new personnel and this included Bob Diamond, who had established a reputation as a trader in investment banking at CS First Boston in New York.

Martin Taylor's concerns continued. In 1997 he presented a paper to the board arguing that the various activities of BZW lacked scale in an increasingly global market and that Barclays should exit investment banking. The board did not accept the argument, believing that Barclays needed to further develop its investment banking. They did, however, succumb to investor pressure on the relatively low returns being generated from BZW and decided to dispose of its corporate finance business, leaving an emphasis on trading, Bob Diamond's area of expertise. Martin Taylor resigned in 1998.

Throughout the first decade of the new century, Bob Diamond's influence grew. A past employee of Barclays investment arm, interviewed in a BBC *Panorama* programme, claimed that Bob Diamond 'installed Wall Street values into Barclays; it was every man for himself . . . It was all about doing ever bigger deals' and being willing to take 'extreme risks' to make 'super profits' and generate huge bonuses for the traders involved. Diamond also grew the much criticised Structured Capital Markets 'tax planning' business, which many saw as Barclays 'tax avoidance' business. Employing only a hundred people by 2010 this business was generating £1 (1.2 euros;

$1.5) billion a year in profits. This was where the highest bonuses were paid.

Bob Diamond succeeded in growing the trading arm of the bank into a major profit contributor accounting for 58 per cent of Barclays overall pre-tax earnings by 2011. He also succeeded in achieving a powerful position on Wall Street for Barclays with what the *Financial Times* described as the 'opportunistic grab for Lehman Brothers' US business after its collapse in 2008'. His reward was to become chief executive of the whole bank early in 2011. Yet, there were already signs of future problems. There were investigations into the mis-selling of payment protection insurance by the retail banks and for the manipulation of the inter-bank lending rate, Libor, to generate unfair profits, in both of which Barclays was heavily involved. Traders at Barclays were under investigation for allegedly manipulating Californian electricity prices. There was widespread criticism of the bank's tax avoidance activities and public criticism of Bob Diamond's huge remuneration package, estimated by the BBC *Panorama* programme to be around £120 million between 2007 and 2012. While Barclays publicity still made reference to its Quaker heritage, its reputation was 'in tatters'. Bob Diamond resigned in 2012.

Bonuses and tribal bonding

Many attributed Barclays' problems to the 'bonus culture' so evident in the investment bank. The *Financial Times* quoted Philip Augar, who ran NatWest's global equities business between 1992 and 1995:

'The battleground between conventional bankers and investment bankers usually concerned pay and resources . . . the bonus round in an investment bank is the most important time of year. Get it wrong and the business unravels; pay too much and profitability is shot to ribbons. In a universal institution, the retail and commercial bankers often, maybe always, feel that too many of the investment profits are being paid to staff and inevitably resent the fact that investment bankers' bonuses are bigger than their own. For their part, the investment bankers always fear that the management wants to build the investment side on the cheap.'

Barclays was criticised for continuing to pay high bonuses to staff even after the financial crisis of 2008–9. BBC's *Panorama* calculated that in 2010–11 payments to shareholders had amounted to £1.4 billion while payment of bonuses for staff amounted to £6 billion. Martin Taylor, interviewed on the *Panorama* programme, argued that, in effect, shareholders were subsidising the payment of bonuses and that the bonus levels were unjustified.

However the *Guardian* newspaper argued that the roots of the problem were not just a matter of remuneration. It asked why people inside Barclays who knew what was happening with regard to Libor did nothing and suggested it was because of a culture 'of fierce tribal bonding':

'. . . it is clear that at least some people in finance are not primarily driven by money. But they are afraid, powerless, or both. Indeed, if you had to design a working environment that encouraged short-termist conformism and discouraged whistle blowing, then the finance sector would be your blueprint.

Take job security. In most big banks you can receive notice and find yourself being marched out of the building by security five minutes later. Some banks have annual "cullings", but even those who have avoided this have been going through redundancy rounds because of the harsh economic climate . . . If this creates a climate of fear, consider the average career pattern. Most people try to switch banks or roles every few years. Imagine when you know there is a huge problem in your bank – you also know it's time to move on to the next job.

Add to this the fact that people in finance are generally overpaid, so if they move to another industry they have to take a cut – which affects their ability to pay school fees and mortgages. That is assuming they can find a job – because (in 2012) the economy isn't exactly booming and skills that are highly valued in finance are next to worthless elsewhere.

Finally, there's the psychological dynamic, perhaps the strongest of all. Most high-flyers in investment banks describe their job not as work, but as a life. . . . Bankers work in teams, and the ethic there is: you are with us or you're against us. Speaking out makes you vulnerable. If you have a guilty secret hidden somewhere, they'll find it and expose you . . . If you go public about something in the bank you believe to be wrong, in one stroke you place yourself outside of that world. It's not just your job – it's your identity.'

The future

By 2012 and following the similarly questionable behaviour of UK banks such as RBS and Lloyds, as well as other European banks such as UBS and US banks such as J.P. Morgan, the whole business model of UK banks was being questioned. The Vickers Commission, established by the UK government to review the future of banking, was considering the separation of retail from investment banking. Early in 2013 there was a European Union directive that bankers' bonuses could be no more than one year's salary unless approved by shareholders. The new Barclays CEO Antony Jenkins also undertook a strategic review of the firm, examining the performance and reputation of 75 business units. In February 2013 this concluded that 39 business units were in good shape, 15 needed some attention, 17 needed serious attention to avoid closure or sale and 4 would definitely be sold or closed, 1 of which was its Structured Capital Markets business unit. Investment banking would remain with only modest proposed changes.

An internal memo from Jenkins to all Barclays staff also stated:

'Over a period of almost 20 years, banking became too aggressive, too focused on the short term, too disconnected from the needs of our customers and clients, and wider society. We were not immune at Barclays from these mistakes . . . Performance assessment will be based not just on what we deliver but on how we deliver it. We must never again be in a position of rewarding people for making the bank money in a way which is unethical or inconsistent with our values.'

Going forwards, Barclays staff would receive training on the central importance of five core values: respect, integrity, service, excellence and stewardship.

Sources: John Plender, 'How traders trumped Quakers', *Financial Times*, 6 July 2012.
Panorama: Inside Barclays: Banking on Bonuses, 11 February 2013. http://www.youtube.com/watch?v=FejXTeLAQOY.
Joris Luyendijk, 'Barclays emails reveal a climate of fear and fierce tribal bonding among traders', *Guardian*, 28 June 2012.
P. Jenkins, D. Schäfer and J. Thompson, 'Evangelism belies change at Barclays', *Financial Times*, 12 February 2013.

Questions

1 Undertake a cultural web analysis of Barclays Bank's investment arm.

2 How might your cultural web from 1 above and the cultural webs for Barclay's retail (Illustration 5.4) be of help to Antony Jenkins?

3 If you were Antony Jenkins, how might you draw on Barclay's history in order to redefine the company's strategy and culture?

COMMENTARY ON PART I
THE STRATEGY LENSES AND
THE STRATEGIC POSITION

The last five chapters have introduced a wide range of strategy concepts and frameworks. Some of these adopt an economic focus on market structures, for instance Chapter 2's five forces analysis. Others are more sociological, such as the highlighting of legitimacy in Chapters 4 and 5. Some concepts and frameworks emphasise opportunities for innovation, as in the strategy canvas of Chapter 2. Others stress conservatism in organisations, for example strategic drift and organisational culture in Chapter 5. Generally, the chapters assume objectivity in analysis, but issues such as the principal–agent problem in Chapter 4 warn of the scope for divergent political interests in organisations, while organisational culture can be a source of bias too. What should be clear from these chapters, therefore, is that there are many different ways of seeing strategy. The strategy lenses offer four basic approaches to exploring strategic issues, each emphasising their particular sets of concepts and frameworks, and each with distinct implications for practice.

The four strategy lenses are as follows:

- **The design lens views strategy development as a logical process of analysis and evaluation.** This is the most commonly held view about how strategy is developed and what managing strategy is about. It encourages objective analysis through the use of formal concepts and frameworks.

- **The experience lens views strategy development as the outcome of people's taken-for-granted assumptions and ways of doing things.** Given that strategies are chosen and implemented by people, then their experience is going to matter. Strategy through the experience lens puts people, culture and history centre stage in strategy development.

- **The variety lens* views strategy as the bubbling up of new ideas from the variety of people in and around organisations.** Top managers cannot know everything about their organisations and markets. According to the variety lens, therefore, strategy can emerge not just from the top, but also from the periphery and bottom of the organisation.

- **The discourse lens views language as important both for understanding and changing strategy and for managerial power and identity.** Managers are always using language to pursue their objectives. Through this lens, unpicking managers' discourse can uncover hidden meanings and political interests.

Exploring strategy through these four lenses is useful because they all raise different questions and suggest different insights. Think of everyday discussions you have. It is not unusual for people to say: 'But what if you looked at it this way instead?' Taking just one view can lead to a partial and perhaps biased understanding. Looking at an issue another way can give a much fuller picture, generating new and different insights. For example, is a proposed strategy the result of objective analysis or is it rather the reflection of the proposer's personal experience or political self-interest? The lenses can also prompt different options or solutions to strategic problems. For example, again, should organisations rely just on top managers to create new strategies, or rather expect future strategy to emerge from initiatives and experiments occurring at the bottom of the organisation? Thus taking a multi-perspective approach to strategy can help managers and students consider a wider range of issues and responses.

---

* In previous editions, the variety lens was known as the ideas lens.

The rest of this Commentary explains the four lenses in more detail. In particular, it will compare how each relates to the following three key dimensions of managing strategy:

- *Rationality*: the extent to which the development of strategy is rationally managed. The design lens assumes high rationality, but the other lenses question this.

- *Innovation*: the extent to which strategy is likely to develop innovative, change-oriented organisations, or alternatively consolidate past experience and existing power structures.

- *Legitimacy*: the extent to which strategy analysis and discourse fits with the expectations of key stakeholders, thereby reinforcing managers' power and identities in organisations.

This Commentary concludes with a short case on Nokia, illustrating how the four lenses can be used to explore a real company's strategy. There will be shorter Commentaries later in the book helping readers to reflect on the concepts and frameworks highlighted in Parts II and III. Meanwhile, this Commentary relates mostly to the material in the first five chapters of this book.

The design lens

The design lens evokes an image of the strategist as detached designer, drawing up precise blueprints distant from the messy realities of action. In terms of the three key dimensions, the design lens therefore puts a strong premium on rational analysis and decision-making (see Figure C.i).[1] Because of its overt commitment to optimising the performance of organisations, the design lens tends also to be highly legitimate, especially to owners and regulators. Rational analysis is what counts, not passion or intuition. However, this commitment to dry analysis can sometimes work against innovation.

The design lens is associated broadly with strategy theorists such as the former Lockheed Corporation strategic planner Igor Ansoff or the economics-trained Harvard Business School Professor Michael Porter.[2] It has its origins in traditional economists' expectations about perfect information and 'rational economic man', and is further informed by management science techniques for resource optimisation. The design lens is also how strategy is often explained in textbooks, by teachers and indeed by managers. The design lens makes the following three assumptions about how strategic decisions are made:

- *Systematic analysis is key*. Although there are many influences on an organisation's performance, careful analysis can identify those that are most significant. In this view, calculating

Figure C.i Design lens

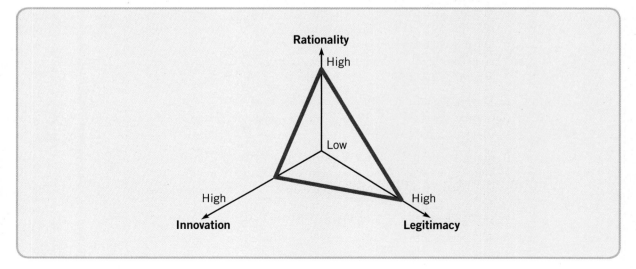

the attractiveness of an industry using Porter's five forces (Chapter 2), and identifying strategic capabilities using Valuable, Rare, Inimitable and Non-Substitutable criteria (Chapter 3), would be standard processes for estimating future performance.

- *Analysis precedes action.* In the design lens, strategy is generally seen as a linear process. Decisions about strategy are separate from and precede implementation. From this point of view, therefore, environmental analysis – for example, forecasting industry life cycles or projecting scenarios (Chapter 2) – is the crucial first step in strategy making.

- *Objectives should be clear.* Rational analysis and decision making need unambiguous criteria by which to evaluate options. Missions and visions (Chapter 4) should be set in advance as precisely as possible, with little scope for adjustment as new opportunities or constraints are discovered in action.

These design lens assumptions about how decisions should be made are in turn associated with two key views about the nature of organisations:

- *Organisations are hierarchies.* It is the responsibility of top management to plan the destiny of the organisation. The responsibility of the rest of the organisation is simply to implement the strategy decided at the top.

- *Organisations work mechanically.* This hierarchical approach implies a view of organisations as engineered systems or even machines. Pulling the right organisational levers should produce predictable results. Principal–agent problems can be controlled by the appropriate gearing of incentives (Chapter 4). Even organisational cultures (Chapter 5) can be designed from above.

Implications

The design lens has practical implications for both managers and students. From the design point of view, it is worth investing extensive time in formal analysis, especially economic forms of analysis. Formal strategic planning and financial calculations are crucial parts of the design lens approach. But even if strategic plans do not always produce the expected results, there are two further reasons for taking a design lens approach:

- *Dealing with complexity and uncertainty.* The design lens provides a means of talking about complex and uncertain issues in a rational, logical and structured way. Even if rational analysis can sometimes over-simplify or convey undue precision, it is usually better than just concluding that everything is all just too complicated for any kind of plan or calculation. Strategy is more than guesswork.

- *Meeting stakeholder expectations.* As well as the sheer analytical value of a design approach, adopting rational procedures is something that important stakeholders (see Chapter 4) such as banks, financial analysts, investors and employees typically expect. For these audiences, analysis is highly legitimate. Taking a design lens approach is therefore an important means of gaining the support and confidence of significant internal and external actors.

Employing the techniques of rational strategy analysis can also have implications for managerial power and personal identity. These side-effects will be discussed further with the discourse lens later.

In summary, the design lens is useful in highlighting the potential value of systematic analysis, step-by-step sequences and the careful engineering of organisational objectives and systems. However, the design lens does have its limits. In particular, a narrow design lens tends to underestimate the positive role of intuition and experience, the scope for unplanned and bottom-up initiatives, and the power effects of strategy analysis. Different lenses can provide useful insights into these other elements of strategy development.

Strategy as experience

The experience lens sees strategy as coming less from objective analysis on a clean sheet of paper and more from the prior experience of the organisation's managers. History and culture matter. Strategy is shaped by people's individual and collective taken-for-granted assumptions and ways of doing things. As indicated in Figure C.ii, the experience lens therefore places less emphasis than the design lens on rationality. It also sets low expectations in terms of innovation and change. Legitimacy is important, but this is defined in terms of personal experience or organisational routines and culture rather than simple appeal to analysis and 'the facts'.

The experience lens is based on a good deal of research about how strategies actually develop in the real world. As early as the 1950s, Nobel prize winner Herbert Simon was developing the Behavioral Theory of the Firm, based on how managers really behave.[3] The Behavioral Theory of the Firm underlines two kinds of problem for rational analysis in practice:

- *External constraints*: Behavioral theory points to real-world barriers to rationality: for example, it is practically impossible to obtain all the information required for comprehensive analysis; it is hard to forecast accurately in an uncertain future; and there are cost and time limits to undertaking complete analyses. In these conditions, managers often 'satisfice' when analysing strategic options: in other words, they settle for adequate solutions rather than the rational optimum.

- *Internal psychological limitations*: Behavioral theory underlines how managers suffer from 'bounded rationality', human limitations on the intellectual ability to process information and carry out analysis. They are also liable to 'cognitive bias': in other words, managers tend to be selective in the attention they give to issues and often automatically favour some types of solutions rather than others.

Cognitive bias is often based on managers' experience, both individual and collective:

- *Individual experience* can particularly shape managers' taken-for-granted assumptions about what is important and what kinds of actions work best. Influential sources of experience can be education and training. For example, accountants tend to see things differently to engineers; managers with MBAs are often accused of favouring excessively analytical approaches to solving problems. Other kinds of influential individual experience are personal careers.

Figure C.ii Experience lens

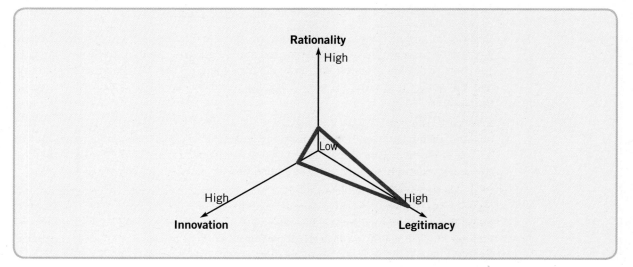

Thus a manager who had spent his or her career in the traditional television industry (for instance, the British BBC or the German ARD) might have found it difficult to recognise new internet media channels (for instance, YouTube) as true competitors. Differences in individual experience within an organisation can lead to debate and negotiation between managers with divergent views about what is important and what should be done. Stakeholder mapping (Chapter 4) of different managers' power and interest can be useful in resolving divergent views.

- *Collective experience* tends to form habitual patterns of thinking and acting, which can translate into standard responses to strategic issues. One kind of collective experience is encapsulated in organisational culture, as discussed in Chapter 5. Another kind of collective experience is reflected by national culture: so for instance Chinese and American managers may see the world differently (Chapter 5). A third kind of collective experience is embodied in industry 'recipes' (Chapter 5), based on years of regular interaction between existing competitors: for example, managers in the clothing industry come to believe over time that style is important to success, even though new ideas from outside the industry imply that new technologies may be the source of competitive advantage in the future. By contrast with individual experience, collective experience tends to suppress debate in management teams, and it becomes hard to challenge the consensus. A consequence can be 'strategic drift' (section 5.2), with everybody agreeing to continue as before, even in the face of environmental change.

Implications

The experience lens has significant implications for strategy. First there are two important warnings:

- *Analysis is typically biased to some extent*: all managers – and even students – bring their own particular experience to any set of strategic issues. It is very hard to analyse a situation as if from a clean sheet of paper. You should distrust claims to complete objectivity. Ask where people are coming from.

- *Watch out for undue conservatism*: experience is likely to lead to routinised responses, even to new problems. Tried-and-tested solutions become too legitimate; managers become powerful because of successes experienced in the past. 'Path dependency' and 'lock-in' are enduring risks (Chapter 5). Organisations can end up like old-fashioned generals, always fighting the last war.

On the other hand, the experience lens has some positive practical advice:

- *Analysis can cost more than it's worth*: because good information is hard and expensive to get, and because analysis can consume too much time, sometimes it is sensible simply to cut short information search and analysis. Depending on the availability of information and the ability to analyse it, beyond a certain point it might be sensible just to drop the analysis.

- *Experience may provide a good enough guide*: if analysis is not going to produce perfect answers, then relying on the rules-of-thumb and instincts of experienced managers may be at least as effective. Sometimes a quick response that is half right is better than an analytical response that is only slightly better but much slower.

- *Challenge the consensus*: while established rules-of-thumb can be effective, sometimes it is necessary to challenge the consensus in an organisation. As in Chapter 12, 'groupthink' is a risk. It is useful to encourage a diversity of views within an organisation, for instance via non-executive directors (Chapter 4), or by bringing in new leaders from outside the organisation (Chapter 11), or by encouraging more participation from all employees, for instance by 'jamming' (Chapter 15).

Strategy as variety

The extent to which the design and experience lenses help explain innovation is rather limited. The variety lens, on the other hand, emphasises innovation and change. However, as indicated in Figure C.iii, the variety lens puts low value on rational analysis and tends to give little weight to what is simply legitimate in an organisation. Viewed through the variety lens, strategies are seen as emerging from the different ideas that bubble up from the variety in and around organisations.

The variety lens builds on two theoretical perspectives from the natural sciences, both emphasising spontaneity. First there is *evolutionary theory*, in which natural phenomena evolve through a Darwinian process of variety, selection and retention.[4] Various genetic mutations emerge as more or less random experiments; some variations are selected for success by their environments; and these successful variations may be retained over the long term because of continuing good environmental fit. Second, there is *complexity theory*, where phenomena are characterised by complex, dynamic sets of interactions, from which surprisingly stable patterns of order may emerge.[5] An example is how hundreds of birds can move as a cohesive flock, without any bird apparently in command. In both evolutionary and complexity theories, variety in the form of many experiments or interactions leads to coherent and effective outcomes. These outcomes are generated spontaneously, with very little top-down direction.

Moving from nature to strategy, the variety lens de-emphasises the deliberate decision making of the design lens. Likewise, the emphasis on spontaneity contrasts with the conservatism of the experience lens. For human organisations, the three elements of evolutionary theory work as follows:

- *Variety*: organisations and their environments potentially offer a rich 'ecology' for the generation of different ideas and initiatives. There are many kinds of people and many kinds of circumstance. Sales people working closely with customers may be able to sense new opportunities at least as well as top managers at headquarters. Since people interact with their environment throughout the organisation, new ideas often come from low down in the hierarchy, not just from the top.[6] Complexity theorist Bill McKelvey refers to this as the 'distributed intelligence' of an organisation.[7] Variety can even come from apparent mistakes, just as genetic mutations come from imperfect genes. A famous example is Post-it notes, which originated from an 'imperfect' glue being applied to paper, but resulted in a semi-adhesive for which the researcher saw market potential.

Figure C.iii Variety lens

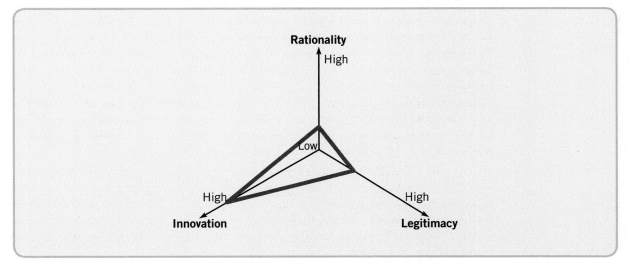

- *Selection*: in nature, selection is 'blind', determined by environmental fit rather than deliberate intervention. In organisations, selection can be nearly as blind, with strategies selected according to how well they match prevailing cultures or standard investment criteria. In this view, there is an 'internal ecology' within organisations, with ideas and initiatives winning out against competing ideas and initiatives according to their internal fit.[8] A good idea may fail simply because it does not meet existing selection rules, regardless of its overall merits: for example, a company may apply standard return on capital criteria that are outdated on the basis of the current real cost of capital (see Chapter 11 on strategy evaluation). On the other hand, as in complexity theory, ideas can gain rapid momentum as they attract 'positive feedback': the support of one important set of actors can attract the support of another, and the support of that set of actors attracts the support of still others, and so on in an escalating process. Thus selection mechanisms can be self-reinforcing, speeding the passage of both good and bad ideas.

- *Retention*: as well as processes of selection, there are processes of retention. Retention refers to the preservation and reproduction over time of selected variations.[9] Retention may happen as particular policies or preferences become embedded in the organisation. Retention may be achieved by instituting formal procedures: for example, job descriptions, accounting and control systems, management information systems, training and organisation structure. Often it is done through more informal processes of routinisation, in which simple repetition of certain routine behaviours leads to the eventual imprinting of such routines in the culture and capabilities of the organisation.

Implications

A key insight from the variety lens is that managers need to be wary of assuming they can wholly control the generation and adoption of new ideas. However, there are a number of things managers can do to foster initiatives and prevent the undue suppression of good ideas. At the same time, the variety lens points both managers and students to distinctive sources of innovation in organisations. We highlight three key implications:

- *Allow for emergence*: rather than being deliberately designed, strategies often emerge from the bottom and the periphery of organisations, accumulating coherence over time. As in Chapter 1, Henry Mintzberg's definition of strategy as an emergent 'pattern' rather than an explicit statement is widely relevant. Managers and students should not necessarily trust in the stated strategic vision and mission (Chapter 4), but rather look to what is actually happening, especially on the ground. The future of an organisation may well be emerging from somewhere far outside headquarters' formal initiatives.

- *Encourage interaction, experiment and change*: from a variety lens point of view, organisations can be too stable and ordered. To generate variety, managers should promote potentially disruptive interactions across internal and external organisational boundaries: cross-departmental initiatives are important internally and communication with customers, suppliers, partners and innovators should be extensive externally. Google encourages experiments by giving staff 20 per cent of their time to pursue their own projects. Complexity theorists prescribe regular change in order to stay at the dynamic 'edge of chaos', the delicate balancing point where organisations neither settle down into excessive stability nor topple over into destructive chaos.[10]

- *Attend to the rules*: if strategies tend get adopted according to their fit with established organisational cultures or investment criteria, then managers need to attend at least as much to setting the context for strategy as to individual strategic decisions. As above, managers should create a context conducive to interaction, experiment and change. But they should particularly attend to the selection and retention rules by which strategies are allowed to emerge. Drawing on complexity theory, Kathy Eisenhardt encourages the design of 'simple rules', clear guidelines for strategy selection and retention.[11] For example, the movie studio Miramax only selects movies that revolve round a central human condition (e.g. love), feature an appealing but flawed central character, and have a clear story-line. The Danish hearing aid company Oticon does not retain projects where any key team member chooses to switch from that project to another.

Strategy as discourse

In many ways management is about discourse. Managers spend 75 per cent of their time communicating: for example, gathering information, persuading others or following up decisions.[12] In particular, strategy has a high discursive component, involving both talk and text. Strategy is debated in meetings, written as formal plans, explained in annual reports and media releases, presented on PowerPoints, and communicated to employees.[13] The discourse lens recognises this discursive component as central to strategy. Here, as indicated in Figure C.iv, the legitimacy of discourse is particularly important. The importance of legitimacy, however, can work against both objective rationality and organisational innovation.

An important influence on the discourse lens is the work of the French philosopher Michel Foucault. Foucault stresses the subtle effects that language can have on understanding, power and personal identities. For example, he shows how changing scientific discourses in the seventeenth and eighteenth centuries redefined insanity as an illness rather than a natural foolishness.[14] The insane now had a new identity, medically ill, and became subject to a new power, the medical doctors with the task of curing them. Those taking a discourse lens are similarly sensitive to how strategy discourse can shape understanding, change personal identities and disseminate power.

These three effects of strategy discourse are explored as follows:

- *Shaping understanding*: the language of strategy has characteristics that make it convincing to others.[15] Its concepts and jargon have high legitimacy in many organisations. Here the discourse lens reveals the design lens in another light. The legitimacy of strategy discourse gives the analytic apparatus of the design lens a persuasiveness that often goes beyond the technical effectiveness of the analysis itself. Drawing on established techniques such as Porter' five forces (section 2.3.1) or fashionable concepts such as Blue Ocean strategy (section 2.4.3) can add to the authority of strategic recommendations. The ability to write

Figure C.iv Discourse lens

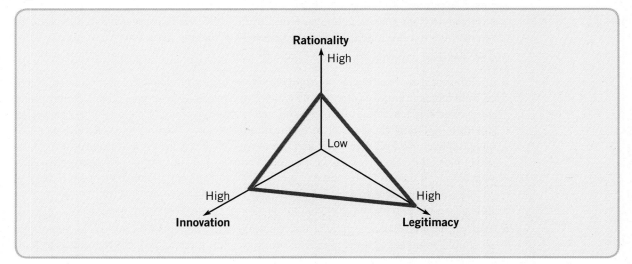

inspiring vision and mission statements (Chapter 4) can help motivate a whole organisation. The justification of strategic change by the radical rhetoric of hypercompetition (Chapter 2) or disruptive innovation (Chapter 8) may give legitimacy to radical actions that might otherwise be rejected as excessive. In other words, managers draw on the rhetoric of strategy and the apparent 'rightness' of strategy concepts to convince others they should comply.

- *Defining identities*: how managers talk about strategy also positions them in relation to others, either by their own deliberate choice or as a result of how they are perceived.[16] Discourse therefore influences the identity and legitimacy of managers as 'strategists'. The ability to use the rational analytical language of the design lens helps define managers as legitimate participants in the strategy process. Of course, sometimes other kinds of discursive identity may be appropriate. For example, in some contexts the language of the heroic leader (Chapter 14) or the innovative entrepreneur (Chapter 9) might offer more support for the decision-maker's identity than simple rational analyst. Whatever the precise identity, the assumptions built into strategy discourse are liable to affect behaviour. For example, lower-level managers and professionals who internalise the strategy discourse of competitiveness and performance as part of their identities come to prioritise those values in their everyday work, subordinating to some degree the administrative or professional values (such as equity or care) that might otherwise be important in their roles.

- *Instrument of power*: here strategy discourse is linked to power and control.[17] By understanding the concepts of strategy, or being seen to do so, top managers or strategy specialists are positioned as having the knowledge about how to deal with the really difficult problems the organisation faces. The possession of such knowledge gives them power over others who do not have it. Design lens discourse, with its commitment to demanding forms of technical analysis, can be particularly elitist and exclusive. Thus mastering the discursive language of the design lens offers a political advantage as well as an analytical one. At the same time, the internalisation of strategy discourse by employees renders them more compliant to the strategy: they see pursuing the strategy as a natural part of their role. In this sense discourse is associated with power when it attracts followers and is self-reproducing and self-reinforcing. Insofar as strategy discourse serves the interests of the powerful, it may suppress innovation and change and distort objective rational analysis from the point of view of the organisation as a whole.

Implications

The discourse lens suggests the importance of the appearance, as well as the reality, of rational argument. Through the discourse lens, strategies need to be legitimate, not simply correct. Strategy discourse, moreover, helps define who holds the identity of legitimate participant in strategic decision making and gives power to the decisions that are ultimately made. The fundamental lesson for managers and students is that the language of strategy matters.

The implications of the discourse lens have both instrumental and critical aspects:

- *Use strategy discourse skillfully*: the right discourse can add legitimacy to particular strategies or individuals in an organisation. This discourse needs to match particular contexts and circumstances. Justifying a strategy to a potential investor may call for a logical, highly quantitative financial case; explaining the same strategy to employees may involve emphasising implications for job security and career growth. For some organisations, the analytic discourse of the design lens will be a legitimate mode of justification; in other organisations, appeal to technical or professional values may be more effective. The instrumental value of the discourse lens lies in this: using the right language matters both for justifying and imposing strategies and for participating in strategy discussions in the first place.

- *Treat strategy discourse sceptically*: just as strategy discourse can be used instrumentally, so should managers and students be ready to take a critical perspective towards such discourse. Are concepts and frameworks being used as a smokescreen for some particular individuals or groups in an organisation to advance their sectional power and interests? Are strengths and weaknesses, threats and opportunities (section 3.4.4) being mystified or exaggerated? Are the grandiose ambitions of vision and mission statements just empty rhetoric (section 4.2)? Seeing strategy as discourse can prompt the healthy questioning of concepts, ideas and rhetorics that might otherwise be taken for granted. The discourse lens encourages managers and students to see through the surface language of strategy to uncover the deeper interests and motives behind it. Adopters of the discourse lens are naturally sceptical.

Conclusion

The core assumptions and the key implications of the four lenses of design, experience, variety and discourse are summarised in Table C.i. They are not offered here as an exhaustive list, but to crystalise the distinctive perspectives of each lens. Indeed, this Commentary as a whole is merely an introduction and you may usefully explore each of the lenses further yourself. After all, each of the lenses presented here actually includes several perspectives itself. For example, the variety lens builds on both evolutionary theory and complexity theory, each of which offers distinctive points of their own. So, within these lenses there are finer-grained insights to discover. The references at the end of this Commentary should help with deeper exploration of the lenses. In addition there are whole books written that provide multiple perspectives on strategy, from the four different ones that Richard Whittington offers, to the ten of Henry Mintzberg and his co-authors, or even the thirteen 'images' provided in the collection by Stephen Cummings and David Wilson.[18]

However, the overarching message that comes from all four lenses is this: in considering a topic like strategy, it is often valuable to take more than one perspective. The rational analysis of the design lens may not be enough. Use the experience lens to consider sources of

Table C.i A summary of the strategy lenses

	Strategy as:			
	Design	**Experience**	**Variety**	**Discourse**
Strategy develops through . . .	A logical process of analysis and evaluation	People's experience, assumptions and taken-for-granted ways of doing things	Ideas bubbling up from the variety of people in and around organisations	Managers seeking influence, power and legitimacy through the language they use
Assumptions about organisations	Mechanistic, hierarchical, rational systems	Cultures based on experience, legitimacy and past success	Complex, diverse and spontaneous systems	Arenas of power and influence shaped by discourse
Role of top management	Strategic decision-makers	Enactors of their experience	Creators of context	Manipulators of language
Key implications	Undertake careful and thorough analysis of strategic issues	Recognise that people's experience is central but also needs challenging	Look for ideas from the bottom and periphery of the organisation	See through strategy language to uncover hidden assumptions and interests

unconscious bias; take a variety lens approach to be sensitive to spontaneous initiatives from the bottom or periphery; stay sceptical by interpreting strategy talk through the discourse lens. It is because different perspectives are important that we shall return to the four lenses in the Commentaries at the ends of Parts II and III of this book. Throughout your course, we encourage you to approach the topics of strategy with eyes open to different points of view. To get into the habit, you might now want to consider the short Nokia case through the four strategy lenses.

REFERENCES

1. A useful review of the principles of rational decision making can be found in J.G. March, *A Primer on Decision Making: How Decisions Happen*, Simon & Schuster, 1994, Chapter 1, Limited liability, pp. 1–35.
2. An introduction to Ansoff's thought is Moussetis, 'Ansoff revisited', *Journal of Management History*, vol. 17, no. 1 (2011), pp. 102–25. R. Porter discusses his thinking in N. Argyres and A. McGahan, 'An interview with Michael Porter', *Academy of Management Executive*, vol. 16, no. 2, (2002), pp. 43–52.
3. An updated view of the Behavioral Theory of the Firm is in G. Gavetti, D. Levinthal and W. Ocasio, 'The Behavioral Theory of the Firm: assessment and prospects', *Academy of Management Annals*, vol. 6, no.1 (2012) pp. 1–40. A contrast with traditional economics is provided in M. Augier, 'The early evolution of the foundations for behavioral organization theory and strategy', *European Management Journal*, vol. 28, (2012), 84–102.
4. W.P. Barnett, and R. Burgelman, 'Evolutionary perspectives on strategy', *Strategic Management Journal*, vol. 17, S1 (2007), pp. 5–19.
5. P. Anderson, A. Meyer, K.M. Eisenhardt, K. Carley and A. Pettigrew, 'Introduction to the special issue: applications of complexity theory to organization science', *Organization Science*, vol. 10, no. 3 (1999), pp. 233–6.
6. See G. Johnson and A.S. Huff, 'Everyday innovation/everyday strategy', in G. Hamel, G.K. Prahalad, H. Thomas and D. O'Neal (eds), *Strategic Flexibility – Managing in a Turbulent Environment*, Wiley, 1998, pp. 13–27. Patrick Regnér also shows how new strategic directions can grow from the periphery of organisations in the face of opposition from the centre, see 'Strategy creation in the periphery: inductive versus deductive strategy making', *Journal of Management Studies*, vol. 40, no. 1 (2003), pp. 57–82.
7. Bill McKelvey, a complexity theorist, argues that the variety within this distributed intelligence is increased because individual managers seek to become better informed about their environment: see B. McKelvey, 'Simple rules for improving corporate IQ: basic lessons from complexity science', in P. Andriani and G. Passiante (eds), *Complexity, Theory and the Management of Networks*, Imperial College Press, 2004.
8. R. Burgelman and A. Grove, 'Let chaos reign, then rein in chaos – repeatedly: managing strategic dynamics for corporate longevity', *Strategic Management Journal*, vol. 28, no. 10 (2007), pp. 965–9.
9. B. McKelvey and H. Aldrich, 'Populations, natural selection, and applied organizational science', *Administrative Science Quarterly*, vol. 28, no. 1 (1983), pp. 101–28.
10. K.M. Eisenhardt and S. Brown, 'Competing on the edge: strategy as structured chaos', *Long Range Planning*, vol. 31, no. 5 (1998), pp. 786–9.
11. C B. Bingham, and K.M. Eisenhardt, 'Rational heuristics: the 'simple rules' that strategists learn from process experience.' *Strategic Management Journal*, vol. 32, no. 13 (2011) pp. 1437–64.
12. H. Mintzberg, *The Nature of Managerial Work*, Harper & Row, 1973.
13. See A. Spee and P. Jarzabkowski, 'Strategic planning as communicative process', *Organization Studies*, vol. 32, no. 9 (2011), pp. 1217–45. Also W. Küpers, S. Mantere and M. Statler, 'Strategy as storytelling: a phenomenological collaboration', *Journal of Management Inquiry*, vol. 22, no. 1 (2013), pp. 83–100.
14. M. Foucault, *Discipline and Punish*, Vintage, 1995.
15. D. Barry and M. Elmes, 'Strategy retold: toward a narrative view of strategic discourse', *Academy of Management Review*, vol. 22, no. 2 (1997).
16. S. Mantere and E. Vaara, 'On the problem of participation in strategy: a critical discursive perspective', *Organization Science*, vol. 19, no. 2 (2008), pp. 341–58.
17. C. Hardy and R. Thomas, 'Strategy, discourse and practice: the intensification of power', *Journal of Management Studies*, forthcoming (2013).
18. R. Whittington, *What is Strategy – and Does it Matter?*, Thompson, 2000; H. Mintzberg, B. Ahlstrand and J. Lampel, *Strategy Safari*, Prentice Hall, 1998; S. Cummings and D. Wilson, *Images of Strategy*, Sage, 2003.

Nokia through the lenses

In 2012, Nokia was in crisis. It had ceded leadership of the global mobile phone market to Samsung and its share price was less than 10 per cent of its peak just five years earlier. But the company's CEO Stephen Elop reminded employees and investors of the company's history. Nokia had been through crisis and transition before. Elop insisted it would do so again.

Nokia had started out in 1865 as a Finnish paper pulp mill. The company only began to take its modern form in 1966 when it had merged with the Finnish Rubber Works and the Finnish Cable Company to form a conglomerate with businesses ranging from rubber boots to aluminium parts. The Finnish Cable Works had established a small electronics department in 1960 in one corner of its main factory. This electronics department in turn spawned several businesses, including a mobile phone unit launched in 1979 through a joint venture with another Finnish company, Salora.

During the 1980s, Nokia became committed to an active diversification strategy, especially internationally. Businesses were acquired in the television and computer industries, and Salora itself was taken over in 1984. By 1987, an internal strategic planning document identified over 30 strategic business units in a Boston Consulting Group portfolio matrix (see Chapter 7), with mobile phone labelled one of several 'star' businesses ripe for investment.

But Nokia then hit a very rough patch. Its chairman and CEO committed suicide in 1988, and many of its industrial markets were hit hard by the collapse of the then Soviet Union. There was a period of losses and top management turmoil, from which finally emerged a new CEO, Jorma Ollila. Ollila had only arrived at Nokia in 1985, after an early career in the American investment bank Citibank. Since 1990, he had been head of the mobile phone business, then accounting for only 10 per cent of Nokia's total sales.

On appointment as CEO, Ollila had promised continuity. In fact, the company rapidly focused on mobile phones. By 1996, mobile phones accounted for 60 per cent of Nokia sales and two years later Nokia became the

Stephen Elop and Steve Ballmer

Source: Simon Dawson/Bloomberg via Getty Images

world's largest mobile phone company. Other businesses were divested, so that soon the only other substantial business was Nokia's telecommunications networks and infrastructure business (merged with Siemens in 2007).

Nokia's phone business flourished for more than a decade, until two cataclysmic events: first, Apple's launch of the iPhone in 2007 and then the 2009 launch of Google's Android operating system supported by companies such as HTC and Samsung. At the same time, Chinese manufacturers began to attack Nokia's position in low-cost phones, especially in developing markets. In 2010, Nokia responded to the growing pressure by appointing its first non-Finnish CEO, the Canadian Stephen Elop.

Elop joined from Microsoft, another company struggling in the phone market, though he himself had been responsible for Microsoft's Office products business. The new CEO launched a wide-ranging strategic review: 'The very first day I began, I sent out an email to all of the employees and I asked them:[17] what do you think I need to change? What do you think I need not or should not change? What are you afraid I'm going to miss?' A key issue that he and his management team struggled with during the first year was whether Nokia should continue with its own operating system. Operating systems are highly expensive to develop and sustain and need to be attractive to external software developers in order to secure a competitive range of apps. Within a few months, Elop and his team had decided to abandon Nokia's own operating system. There were two alternative operating systems available: Google's or Microsoft's. Elop inclined towards Microsoft. His reasoning was that Microsoft was the weaker of the two, and therefore needed Nokia more than Google did. Nokia also feared being just another Android phone manufacturer competing on the same basis as HTC or Samsung.

In February 2011, Elop released what would become his famous 'burning platform' memo to all employees. Nokia was compared to a man on a burning oil platform, who could only survive by leaping into the sea. Nokia had been too slow, and must now make a dramatic move. Elop told his employees: 'We poured gasoline on our own burning platform. I believe we have lacked accountability and leadership to align and direct the company through these disruptive times. We had a series of misses. We haven't been delivering innovation fast enough. We're not collaborating internally. Nokia, our platform is burning.' Several days later, he announced to the world that he was abandoning Nokia's own operating system in favour of Microsoft's, sealed by a public handshake with his old boss, Steve Ballmer, CEO of Microsoft. A senior Google executive commented on the Nokia–Microsoft alliance: 'two turkeys do not make an eagle'.

Nokia's first phones with the new operating system were not an immediate success and Nokia's losses deepened. By spring 2012, Stephen Elop was describing Nokia in terms of a famous Finnish long-distance runner, Lasse Virén, who had tripped during a race in 1972 but still won in the end: 'like Virén we are off the grass, on the track and running again'. But Nokia's share price was still only one fifth of what it had been at the time when the alliance had been announced. Many speculated that Nokia would not survive as an independent company at all. Indeed, in the summer of 2013, Nokia announced that its mobile phone business would be sold to Microsoft, with Stephen Elop returning to his original employer as well. Elop was now a leading candidate to succeed Steve Ballmer as CEO of Microsoft as a whole.

Key sources: J. Aspara, J.A. Lamberg, A. Laukia and H. Tikkanen, 'Strategic management of business model transformation: lessons from Nokia', *Management Decision*, vol. 49, no. 4 (2011), pp. 622–47; *Financial Times*, 9 February 2011, 11 April 2011 and 3 May 2012.

Questions

1 How could you use the design lens, the experience lens and the variety lens to account for the development of the mobile phone business within Nokia?

2 How could you use the design lens and the experience lens to explain Stephen Elop's adoption of the Microsoft operating system?

3 Comment on Stephen Elop's changing language from a discourse lens perspective.

PART II

STRATEGIC CHOICES

This part explains strategic choices in terms of:

- How organisations relate to competitors in terms of their competitive business strategies.

- How broad and diverse organisations should be in terms of their corporate portfolios.

- How far organisations should extend themselves internationally.

- How organisations are created and innovate.

- How organisations pursue strategies through organic development, acquisitions or strategic alliances.

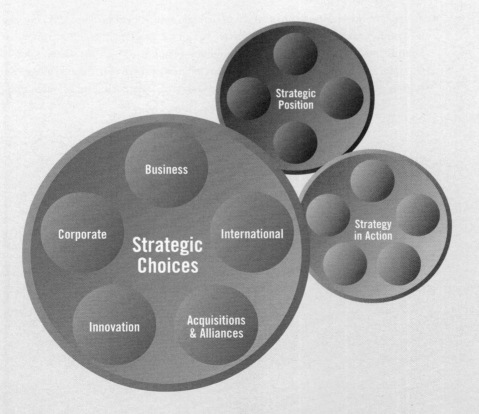

INTRODUCTION TO PART II

This part is concerned with the strategic choices, or options, potentially available to an organisation for responding to the positioning issues discussed in Part I of the book. There are three overarching choices to be made as shown in Figure II.2. These are:

- Choices as to *how an organisation at a business level positions itself in relation to competitors*. This is a matter of deciding how to compete in a market. For example, should the business compete on the basis of cost or differentiation? Or is competitive advantage possible through being more flexible and fleet-of-foot than competitors? Or is a more cooperative approach to competitors appropriate? These *business strategy* questions are addressed in Chapter 6.

- Choices of *strategic direction*: in other words, which products, industries and markets to pursue. Should the organisation be very focused on just a few products and markets? Or should it be much broader in scope, perhaps very diversified in terms of both products (or services) and markets? Should it create new products or should it enter new territories? These questions relate to corporate strategy, addressed in Chapter 7, international strategy in Chapter 8 and innovation and entrepreneurial strategy, as discussed in Chapter 9.

- Choices about *methods by which to pursue strategies.* For any of these choices, should they be pursued independently by organic development, by acquisitions or by strategic alliances with other organisations? This is the theme of Chapter 10.

The discussion in these chapters provides frameworks and rationales for a wide range of strategic choices. But some words of warning are important here:

- *Strategic choices relate back to analysis of strategic position.* Part I of the book has provided ways in which strategists can identify forces at work in the business environment (Chapter 2), identify and build on strategic capabilities (Chapter 3), meet stakeholder expectations (Chapter 4) and build on the benefits, as well as be aware of the constraints, of their organisation's historical and cultural context (Chapter 5). Exploring these issues will provide the

Figure II.2 Strategic choices

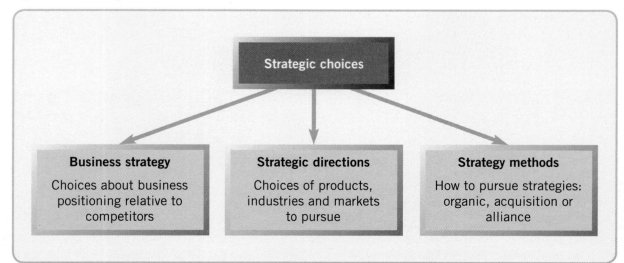

foundation for considering strategic options. However, the *Exploring Strategy* Model (Figure 1.2) implies that issues of position, choice and action overlap. Thus working through the choices of Part II is also likely to feed back into the initial analysis of strategic position. Similarly, the potential of some strategic choices will only be revealed in action, the theme of Part III.

- *Key strategic issues.* Choices have to be made in the context of an organisation's strategic position, of course. But here it is important that the analysis of strategic position distinguishes the *key strategic issues* from all the many positioning issues that are likely to arise. Analysis needs to avoid producing a very long list of observations without any clarity of what such key issues are. There is no single 'strategy tool' for this. Identifying key strategic issues is a matter of informed judgement and, because managers usually work in groups, of debate. The analytic tools provided can help, but are not a substitute for judgement.

6

BUSINESS STRATEGY

Learning outcomes

After reading this chapter you should be able to:

● Identify *strategic business units* (SBUs) in organisations.

● Assess business strategy in terms of the generic strategies of *cost leadership*, *differentiation* and *focus*.

● Identify business strategies suited to *hypercompetitive* conditions.

● Assess the benefits of *cooperation* in business strategy.

● Apply principles of *game theory* to business strategy.

MyStrategyLab

MyStrategyLab is designed to help you make the most of your studies. Visit **www.pearsoned.co.uk/mystrategylab** to discover a wide range of resources, including:

● A personalised **Study plan** that will help you understand core concepts

● **Audio and video clips** that put the spotlight on strategy in the real world

● **Online glossaries and flashcards** that provide helpful reminders when you're looking for some quick revision.

(6.1) INTRODUCTION

This chapter is about a fundamental strategic choice: what strategy should a business unit (or other organisational subunit) adopt in its market? Business strategy questions are fundamental both to standalone small businesses and to all the many business units that typically make up large diversified organisations. Thus a restaurant business has to decide a range of issues such as menus, décor and prices in the light of competition from other restaurants locally. Similarly, in a large diversified corporation such as Unilever or Nestlé, every business unit must decide how it should operate in its own particular market. For example, Unilever's ice-cream business has to decide how it will compete against Nestlé's ice-cream business on a range of dimensions including product features, pricing, branding and distribution channels. These kinds of *business* strategy issues are distinct from the question as to whether Unilever should own an ice-cream business in the first place: this is a matter of *corporate* strategy, the subject of Chapter 7.

Figure 6.1 shows the main themes that provide the structure for the rest of the chapter. Starting from a definition of *strategic business units* (SBUs), the chapter has two main themes:

- *Generic competitive strategies*, including *cost leadership, differentiation, focus* and *hybrid* strategies. An important theme here will be how far these strategies are sustainable over time and here *strategic lock-in* is often important.

- *Interactive strategies*, building on the notion of generic strategies to consider interaction with competitors, especially in *hypercompetitive environments*, and including both *cooperative strategies* and *game theory*.

Business strategy is not just relevant to the private business sector. Charities and public-sector organisations both cooperate and compete. Thus charities compete between each other for support from donors. Public-sector organisations also need to be 'competitive' against comparable organisations in order to satisfy their stakeholders, secure their funding and protect themselves from alternative suppliers from the private sector. Schools compete in terms of examination results, while hospitals compete in terms of waiting times, treatment survival

Figure 6.1 Business strategy

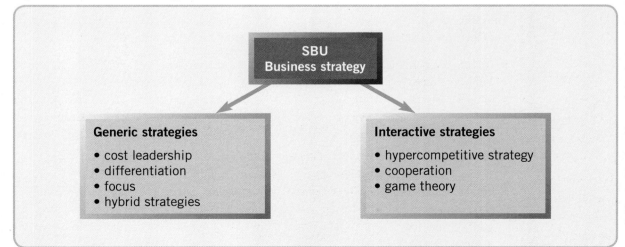

rates and so on. Although some of the detailed implications may vary between sectors, wherever comparison is possible with other similar organisations, basic principles of business strategy are likely to be relevant. Very few organisations can afford to be demonstrably inferior to peers, and almost all have to make choices on key competitive variables such as costs, prices and quality.

(6.2) IDENTIFYING STRATEGIC BUSINESS UNITS

The starting point for business strategy is identifying the relevant business unit. A **strategic business unit** (SBU) **supplies goods or services for a distinct domain of activity**. A small business focused on a single market, such as a restaurant or specialist retailer, would count as a strategic business unit. More commonly, though, SBUs refer to the distinct businesses within a large diversified corporation (sometimes these SBUs are called 'divisions' or 'profit centres'). For example, Nestlé has SBUs focused on Confectionery products, Beverage products and Dairy products, among others. Typically within a large diversified corporation, each SBU will have responsibility for its own business strategy and profit performance. In a large public-sector organisation, such as a local authority, individual schools might be considered as SBUs, with their domain of activity being education in a geographical area.

Thus the SBU concept has three effects within large organisations. First, SBUs decentralise initiative to smaller units within the corporation as a whole. In Nestlé, Beverages can pursue its business strategy without continuously seeking permission from central headquarters for minor adjustments (see also section 7.6 on the role of the centre). Second, SBUs allow large corporations to vary their business strategies according to the different needs of the various external markets they serve. Nestlé does not have to impose the same business strategy (e.g. a focus on supermarket distribution) across all its SBUs. Finally, the SBU concept encourages accountability. If managers determine the business strategy for their own SBU, then they can be held accountable for the success or failure of that strategy.

Identifying the right boundaries for SBUs is often complex.[1] Distinct markets can be defined at different levels of analysis: for example, Nestlé's Confectionery business could be further segmented by target market (the mass market KitKat, or the sophisticated Cailler brand), distribution channel (supermarket or small retailer) or geography (Europe or Asia). In many corporations, SBU boundaries change frequently as well: the computer company Dell is well known for reorganising its SBUs continuously, as market conditions change and units get too big. There are two basic criteria that can help in identifying appropriate SBUs:

- *Market-based criteria*. Different parts of an organisation might be regarded as the same SBU if they are targeting the same *customer types*, through the same sorts of *channels* and facing similar *competitors*. On the other hand, it would usually be sensible to distinguish a unit tailoring products or services to specific local needs from one that offers standardised products or services globally.

- *Capabilities-based criteria*. Parts of an organisation should only be regarded as the same SBU if they have similar strategic capabilities. Many traditional retailers or financial services companies operate their internet services as distinct SBUs. Even though they may be targeting very similar customers, the capabilities involved in the internet-based businesses are typically too different to the original physical stores or outlets to manage within the same unit.

6.3 GENERIC COMPETITIVE STRATEGIES

This section introduces the competitive element of business strategy, with cooperation addressed particularly in section 6.4. **Competitive strategy is concerned with how an SBU strategic achieves competitive advantage in its domain of activity.** Competitive strategy therefore involves issues such as costs, product features and branding. In turn, **competitive advantage is about how an SBU creates value for its users both greater than the costs of supplying them and superior to that of rival SBUs.** Competitive advantages should underpin competitive strategies. There are two important features of competitive advantage. To be *competitive* at all, the SBU must ensure that customers see sufficient value that they are prepared to pay more than the costs of supply. To have an *advantage*, the SBU must be able to create greater value than competitors. In the absence of a competitive advantage, an SBU's competitive strategy is always vulnerable to competitors with better products or offering lower prices.

Michael Porter[2] argues that there are two fundamental means of achieving competitive advantage. An SBU can have structurally lower costs than its competitors. Or it can have products or services that are 'differentiated' from competitors' products in ways that are so valued by customers that it can charge higher prices. In defining competitive strategies, Porter adds a further dimension based on the scope of customers that the business chooses to serve. Businesses can choose to focus on narrow customer segments, for example a particular demographic group such as the youth market. Alternatively they can adopt a broad scope, targeting customers across a range of characteristics such as age, wealth or geography.

Porter's distinctions between cost, differentiation and scope define a set of 'generic' strategies: in other words, basic types of strategy that hold across many kinds of business situations. These three generic strategies are illustrated in Figure 6.2. In the top left-hand corner is a strategy of *cost leadership*, as exemplified in the British women's clothing market by retailers such as Primark. Primark seeks to use large economies of scale and tight cost discipline to serve a wide

Figure 6.2 Three generic strategies

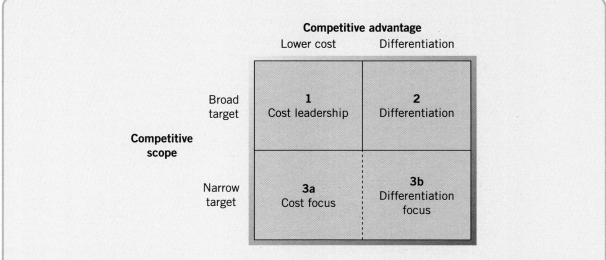

Source: Adapted with the permission of The Free Press, a Division of Simon & Schuster, Inc., from *Competitive Advantage: Creating and Sustaining Superior Performance* by Michael E. Porter. Copyright © 1985, 1998 by Michael E. Porter. All rights reserved.

range of women with reasonably fashionable clothing at a good price. Monsoon's shops pursue a strategy of *differentiation*, offering arty styles ('boho chic') to women across a range of ages at significantly higher prices. The third generic strategy is *focus*, involving a narrow competitive scope. Porter distinguishes between cost focus and differentiation focus, but for him narrow scope is such a distinctive fundamental principle that these two are merely variations on the same basic theme of narrowness. For example, Evans targets only women needing larger-sized clothing, achieving a higher price for its distinctive products (promoted by Beth Ditto) through a *differentiation focus* strategy. On the other hand, the clothing lines of the major supermarkets target shoppers who are simply looking for good-value standard clothing for their families, a *cost focus* strategy. The rest of this section discusses these three generic strategies in more detail.

6.3.1 Cost leadership

Cost-leadership strategy involves becoming the lowest-cost organisation in a domain of activity. There are four key *cost drivers* that can help deliver cost leadership, as follows:

- *Input costs* are often very important, for example labour or raw materials. Many companies seek competitive advantage through locating their labour-intensive operations in countries with low labour costs. Examples might be service call centres in India or manufacturing in China. Location close to raw material sources can also be advantageous, as for example the Brazilian steel producer CSN which benefits from its own local iron-ore facilities.

- *Economies of scale* refer to how increasing scale usually reduces the average costs of operation over a particular time period, perhaps a month or a year. Economies of scale are important wherever there are high fixed costs. Fixed costs are those costs necessary for a level of output: for example, a pharmaceutical manufacturer typically needs to do extensive R&D before it produces a single pill. Economies of scale come from spreading these fixed costs over high levels of output: the average cost due to an expensive R&D project halves when output increases from one million to two million units. Economies of scale in purchasing can also reduce input costs. The large airlines, for example, are able to negotiate steep discounts from aircraft manufacturers. For the cost-leader, it is important to reach the output level equivalent to the *minimum efficient scale*. Note, though, that *diseconomies of scale* are possible. Large volumes of output that require special overtime payments to workers or involve the neglect of equipment maintenance can soon become very expensive. As in Figure 6.3, therefore, the economies of scale curve is typically somewhat U-shaped, with the average cost per unit actually increasing beyond a certain point.

- *Experience*[3] can be a key source of cost efficiency. The *experience curve* implies that the cumulative experience gained by an organisation with each unit of output leads to reductions in unit costs (see Figure 6.3). For example, for many electronic components per unit costs can drop as much as 95 per cent every time the accumulated volume doubles. There is no time limit: simply the more experience an organisation has in an activity, the more efficient it gets at doing it. The efficiencies are basically of two sorts. First, there are gains in labour productivity as staff simply learn to do things more cheaply over time (this is the specific *learning curve* effect). Second, costs are saved through more efficient designs or equipment as experience shows what works best. The experience curve has three important implications for business strategy. First, entry timing into a market is important: early entrants into a market will have experience that late entrants do not yet have and so will gain a cost advantage. Second, it is important to gain and hold market share, as companies with higher market

Figure 6.3 Economies of scale and the experience curve

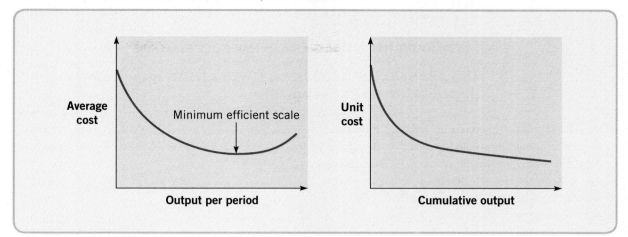

share have more 'cumulative experience' simply because of their greater volumes. Finally, although the gains from experience are typically greatest at the start, as indicated by the steep initial curve in Figure 6.3, improvements normally continue over time. Opportunities for cost reduction are theoretically endless. Figure 6.3 compares the experience curve and economies of scale in order to underline the contrast here. Unlike scale, where diseconomies appear beyond a certain point, the experience curve implies at worst a flattening of the rate of cost reduction. Cost savings due to accumulated experience are continuously available.

● *Product/process design* also influences cost. Efficiency can be 'designed in' at the outset. For example, engineers can choose to build a product from cheap standard components rather than expensive specialised components. Organisations can choose to interact with customers exclusively through cheap web-based methods, rather than via telephone or stores. Organisations can also tailor their offerings in order to meet the most important customer needs, saving money by ignoring others: this, arguably, is the strategy of Barnet, the 'easy-Council' (Illustration 6.1). In designing a product or service, it is important to recognise *whole-life costs*: in other words, the costs to the customer not just of purchase but of subsequent use and maintenance. In the photocopier market, for example, Canon eroded Xerox's advantage (which was built on service and a support network) by designing a copier that needed far less servicing.

Porter underlines two tough requirements for cost-based strategies. First of all, the principle of competitive advantage indicates that a business's cost structure needs to be *lowest* cost (i.e. lower than all competitors'). Having the second-lowest cost structure implies a competitive disadvantage against somebody. Competitors with higher costs than the cost-leader are always at risk of being undercut on price, especially in market downturns. For businesses competing on a cost basis, cost leadership is always more secure than being second or third in terms of costs.

Porter's second requirement is that low cost should not be pursued in total disregard for quality. To sell its products or services, the cost-leader has to be able to meet market standards. For example, low-cost Chinese car producers seeking to export into Western markets need to offer not only cars that are cheap, but cars that meet acceptable norms in terms of style, service network, reliability, resale value and other important characteristics. Cost-leaders have two options here:

ILLUSTRATION 6.1

easyCouncils: a not so easy low-cost strategy

The London Borough of Barnet has chosen a budget airline model for its services, on the lines of easyJet.

In 2008–9, with pressures on budgets increasing, Conservative-Party-controlled councils in the United Kingdom were looking to save costs by adopting the low-cost model pioneered by airlines such as Ryanair and easyJet. Barnet, a borough council in North London with a population of over 300,000, is one of the pioneers.

The Conservative borough council was led at the time by a former PwC management consultant, Mike Freer. In a context of falling central government subsidies, and wanting to save local taxes, the council was looking to cut costs by £15 m (~€16.5 m; ~$22.5 m) a year. In 2008, the council launched a consultation process on radical reform called 'Future Shape'. In 2009, it declared its intention to adopt a budget airline model, which council officials dubbed 'easyCouncil'.

Mike Freer gave some examples. Just as budget airlines allow passengers to pay extra for priority boarding, in future householders will be able to pay extra to jump the queue in order to get faster responses on planning applications for new buildings or house extensions. Similarly, as airline passengers can choose whether to have a meal or not (and pay accordingly), users of adult social care will be allowed to choose their own options. Freer explained to the *Guardian*:

'In the past we would do things for our residents rather than letting them choose for themselves. We would tell them they need one hour help shopping, or one hour cleaning, meals-on-wheels, and they would get it, like it or not. Instead, we will assess what level of personal care they need, place a value on it and give them the budget. If they say, "Frankly, I'd like a weekend in Eastbourne [a holiday resort]", they can have it.'

Opposition Labour leader Alison Moore warned in the *Guardian*:

'There is a real danger of problems in the local community and that vulnerable people will lose out. People who are dependent on care services may find that they aren't there at the same quality as before.'

None the less, the new low-cost strategy was launched in 2009. Unfortunately, the costs of retraining staff, building an in-house delivery team, hiring consultants and closing facilities were higher than originally projected. The council estimated it spent £1.5 m on delivering the first year of the reform programme. On the other hand, savings were slower to come through than expected, with a series of strikes by council workers resisting job cuts and the transfer of many employees to private-sector subcontractors. Savings in the first year were just £1.4 m, less than half of what had been projected. Alison Moore, leader of the Opposition, commented: 'Barnet claim that easy-Council is all about a relentless drive for efficiency, so it is absurd that in the first year, they've spent more money than they've saved.' By this time, Mike Freer had moved on to become a Member of Parliament. However, Lynne Hillan, the new council leader, said it was too soon to judge. Big savings would come soon: 'The programme took longer to establish than planned because we took the decision to develop an in-house team of officers. I've no doubt this will give us the most efficient process and the greatest long-term savings.'

Sources: Guardian, 27 August 2009; Guardian, 26 October 2010; The Economist, 22 September 2012.

Questions

1 What are the advantages and disadvantages of this approach to low-cost council services?

2 In what sense do borough councils 'compete'?

Figure 6.4 Costs, prices and profits for generic strategies

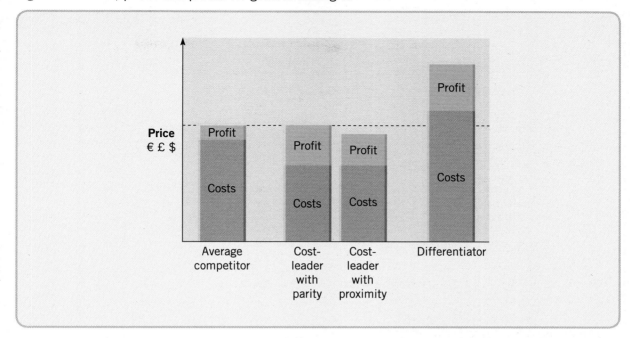

- *Parity* (in other words, equivalence) with competitors in product or service features valued by customers. Parity allows the cost-leader to charge the same prices as the average competitor in the marketplace, while translating its cost advantage wholly into extra profit (as in the second column of Figure 6.4). The Brazilian steel producer CSN, with its cheap iron-ore sources, is able to charge the average price for its steel, and take the cost difference in greater profit.

- *Proximity* (closeness) to competitors in terms of features. Where a competitor is sufficiently close to competitors in terms of product or service features, customers may only require small cuts in prices to compensate for the slightly lower quality. As in the third column in Figure 6.4, the proximate cost-leader still earns better profits than the average competitor because its lower price eats up only a part of its cost advantage. This proximate cost-leadership strategy might be the option chosen initially by Chinese car manufacturers in export markets, for example.

6.3.2 **Differentiation strategies**

For Porter, the principal alternative to cost leadership is differentiation.[4] **Differentiation involves uniqueness along some dimension that is sufficiently valued by customers to allow a price premium.** Relevant points of differentiation vary between markets. Within each market too, businesses may differentiate along different dimensions. Thus in clothing retail, competitors may differentiate by store size, locations or fashion. In cars, competitors may differentiate by safety, style or fuel efficiency. Where there are many alternative dimensions that are valued by customers, it is possible to have many different types of differentiation strategy in a market. Thus, even at the same top end of the car market, BMW and Mercedes differentiate in different ways, the first typically with a sportier image, the second with more conservative values.

Figure 6.5 Mapping differentiation in the US airline industry

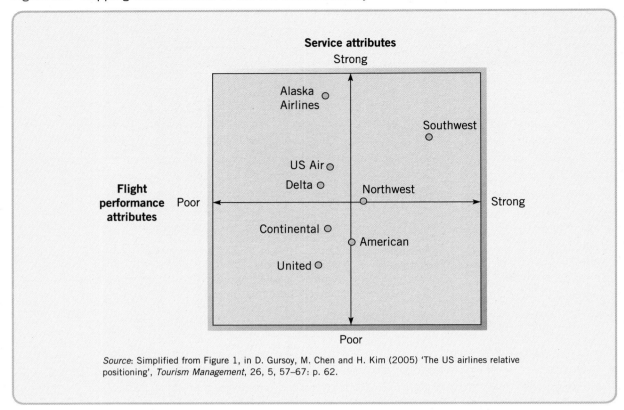

Source: Simplified from Figure 1, in D. Gursoy, M. Chen and H. Kim (2005) 'The US airlines relative positioning', *Tourism Management*, 26, 5, 57–67: p. 62.

The strategy canvas provides one means of mapping these various kinds of differentiation (see section 2.4.3).

Managers can identify potential for differentiation by using perceptual mapping of their products or services against those of competitors. For example, Figure 6.5 maps customer perceptions of American airline companies in the 2000s along two bundles of attributes: flight performance attributes such as delays, and service attributes such as baggage problems or boarding complaints. Most of the larger airlines are quite closely bunched together. For example, US Air and Delta are not significantly differentiated from each other in terms of on-time flights, and they are perceived similarly in terms of service elements such as boarding, ticketing and reservations. One airline that does stand out as a differentiator is Southwest, which does well in terms of both flight delays and service. In the period studied, Southwest was also the most profitable of these airlines. It seems that Southwest was able to differentiate on attributes that were highly valued by its customers.

However, the attributes on which to differentiate need to be chosen carefully. Differentiation strategies require clarity about two key factors:

● *The strategic customer*. It is vital to identify clearly the strategic customer on whose needs the differentiation is based. This is not always straightforward, as discussed in section 2.4.2. For example, for a newspaper business, the strategic customers could be readers (who pay a purchase price), advertisers (who pay for advertising), or both. Finding a distinctive means of prioritising customers can be a valuable source of differentiation.

- *Key competitors.* It is very easy for a differentiator to draw the boundaries for comparison too tightly, concentrating on a particular niche. Thus specialist Italian clothing company Benetton originally had a strong position with its specialist knitwear shops. However, it lost ground because it did not recognise early enough that general retailers such as Marks & Spencer could also compete in the same product space of colourful pullovers and similar products.

There is an important condition for a successful differentiation strategy. Differentiation allows higher prices, but usually comes at a cost. To create a point of valuable differentiation typically involves additional investments, for example in R&D, branding or staff quality. The differentiator can expect that its costs will be higher than those of the average competitor. But, as in the fourth column of Figure 6.4, the differentiator needs to ensure that the additional costs of differentiation do not exceed the gains in price. It is easy to pile on additional costs in ways that are not valued sufficiently by customers. The historic failures under British ownership of the luxury car companies Rolls-Royce and Bentley against top-end Mercedes cars are partly attributable to the expensive crafting of wood and leather interiors, the full cost of which even wealthy customers were not prepared to pay for. Just as cost-leaders should not neglect quality, so should differentiators attend closely to costs, especially in areas irrelevant to their sources of differentiation. As in Illustration 6.2, Volvo's differentiation strategy in the Indian bus market seems to have involved keeping an eye on costs as well.

6.3.3 Focus strategies

Porter distinguishes focus as the third generic strategy, based on competitive scope. A **focus strategy targets a narrow segment or domain of activity and tailors its products or services to the needs of that specific segment to the exclusion of others.** Focus strategies come in two variants, according to the underlying sources of competitive advantage, cost or differentiation. In air travel, Ryanair follows a *cost focus strategy*, targeting price-conscious holiday travellers with no need for connecting flights. In the domestic detergent market, the Belgian company Ecover follows a *differentiation focus* strategy, gaining a price premium over rivals on account of its ecological cleaning products.

The focuser achieves competitive advantage by dedicating itself to serving its target segments better than others which are trying to cover a wider range of segments. Serving a broad range of segments can bring disadvantages in terms of coordination, compromise or inflexibility. Focus strategies are able to seek out the weak spots of broad cost-leaders and differentiators:

- *Cost focusers* identify areas where broader cost-based strategies fail because of the added costs of trying to satisfy a wide range of needs. For instance, in the United Kingdom food retail market, Iceland Foods has a cost-focused strategy concentrated on frozen and chilled foods, reducing costs against generalist discount food retailers such as Aldi which have all the complexity of fresh foods and groceries as well as their own frozen and chilled food ranges.

- *Differentiation focusers* look for specific needs that broader differentiators do not serve so well. Focus on one particular need helps to build specialist knowledge and technology, increases commitment to service and can improve brand recognition and customer loyalty. For example, ARM Holdings dominates the world market for mobile phone chips, despite being only a fraction of the size of the leading microprocessor manufacturers, AMD and Intel, which also make chips for a wide range of computers.

ILLUSTRATION 6.2

Volvo's different Indian buses

Volvo has a strategy to sell buses at nearly four times the prevailing market price.

The Indian bus market has long been dominated by two home players, subsidiaries of major Indian conglomerates: Tata Motors and Ashok Leyland. The two companies made simple coaches on a design that had hardly changed for decades. On top of a basic truck chassis, the two companies bolted a rudimentary coach body. Engines were a meagre 110–120 horse-power, and roared heartily as they hauled their loads up the steep mountain roads of India. Mounted at the front, the heat from the over-strained engines would pervade the whole bus. Air conditioning was a matter of open windows, through which the dust and noise of the Indian roads would pour. Suspension was old-fashioned, guaranteeing a shaky ride on pot-holed roads. Bags were typically slung on the top of the bus, where they were easily soiled and at high risk of theft. But at least the buses were cheap, selling to local bus companies at around Rs 1.2 m (€15,000; $21,000).

In 1997, Swedish bus company Volvo decided to enter the market, with buses priced at Rs 4 m, nearly four times as much as local products. Akash Passey, Volvo's first Indian employee, commissioned a consultancy company to evaluate prospects. The consultancy company recommended that Volvo should not even try. Passey told the *Financial Times*: 'My response was simple – I took the report and went to the nearest dustbin and threw it in.' Passey entered the market in 2001 with the high-priced luxury buses.

Passey used the time to develop a distinctive strategy. His basic product had superior features. Volvo's standard engines were 240–250 hp and mounted at the back, ensuring a faster and quieter ride. Air conditioning was standard of course. The positioning of the engine and the specific bus design of the chassis meant a more roomy interior, plus storage for bags internally. But Passey realised this would not be enough. He commented to the *Financial Times*: 'You had to do a lot of things to break the way business is done normally.'

Volvo offered post-sale maintenance services, increasing life expectancy of buses from three to ten years, and allowing bus operating companies to dispense with their own expensive maintenance workshops. Free training was given to drivers, so they drove more safely and took more care of their buses. The company advertised the benefits of the buses direct to customers in cinemas, rather than simply promoting them to the bus operators. To kick-start the market, Volvo supplied about 20 subsidised trial units to selected operators. Volvo trainees rode these buses, alerting the company immediately when something went wrong so Volvo could immediately send its engineers. Faster, smoother and more reliable travel allowed the bus operators to increase their ticket prices for the luxury Volvo buses by 35 per cent.

Business people and the middle classes were delighted with the new Volvo services. Speedier, more comfortable journeys allowed them to arrive fresh for meetings and potentially to save the costs of overnight stays. Tata and Ashok Leyland both now produce their own luxury buses, with Mercedes and Isuzu following Volvo into the market. None the less, the phrase 'taking a Volvo' has become synonymous with choosing a luxury bus service in India, rather as 'hoover' came to refer to any kind of vacuum cleaner.

In 2008, Volvo opened a new state-of-the-art bus factory in Bangalore. It is Volvo's most efficient bus factory worldwide, producing a fully built bus in 20–25 days. Annual capacity is 1,000 buses per year.

Source: Adapted from J. Leahy, 'Volvo takes a lead in India', *Financial Times*, 31 August 2009.

Questions

1 Rank the elements of Passey's strategy for Volvo in order of importance. Could any have been dispensed with?

2 How sustainable is Volvo's luxury bus strategy?

Successful focus strategies depend on at least one of three key factors:

- *Distinct segment needs.* Focus strategies depend on the distinctiveness of segment needs. If segment distinctiveness erodes, it becomes harder to defend the segment against broader competitors. For example, when the boundaries blurred between smart phones used by general consumers and smart phones used by business people, it has become easier for Apple to attack the distinctive niche once dominated by BlackBerry's business phones.

- *Distinct segment value chains.* Focus strategies are strengthened if they have distinctive value chains that will be difficult or costly for rivals to construct. If the production processes and distribution channels are very similar, it is easy for a broad-based differentiator to push a specialised product through its own standardised value chain at a lower cost than a rival focuser. In detergents, Procter & Gamble cannot easily respond to Ecover because achieving the same ecological friendliness would involve transforming its purchasing and production processes.

- *Viable segment economics.* Segments can easily become too small to serve economically as demand or supply conditions change. For example, changing economies of scale and greater competition have eliminated from many smaller cities the traditional town-centre department stores, with their wider ranges of different kinds of goods from hardware to clothing.

6.3.4 'Stuck in the middle'?

Porter claims that managers face a crucial choice between the generic strategies of cost leadership, differentiation and focus. According to him, it is unwise to blur this choice. As earlier, the lowest-cost competitor can always undercut the second lowest-cost competitor. For a company seeking advantage through low costs, therefore, it makes no sense to add extra costs by half-hearted efforts at differentiation. For a differentiator, it is self-defeating to make economies that jeopardise the basis for differentiation. For a focuser, it is dangerous to move outside the original specialised segment, because products or services tailored to one set of customers are likely to have inappropriate costs or features for the new target customers. This was a problem for BlackBerry as it tried to move its secure business phones into the broader consumer market, for which the availability of apps was more important than the business need of email encryption. Porter's argument is that managers are generally best to choose which generic strategy they are pursuing and then stick rigorously to it. Otherwise there is a danger of being *stuck in the middle*, doing no strategy well.

Porter's warning about the danger of being stuck in the middle provides a useful discipline for managers. It is very easy for them to make incremental decisions that compromise the basic generic strategy. As profits accumulate, the successful cost-leader will be tempted to stop scrimping and saving. In hard times, a differentiator might easily cut back the R&D or advertising investments essential to its long-term differentiation advantage. Consistency with generic strategy provides a valuable check for managerial decision making.

However, Porter's argument for pure generic strategies is controversial.[5] For example, it has been suggested that the criticisms against combining generic strategie reflect a Western cultural preference for binary oppositions, as against an Eastern willingness to seek balance and synthesis. Thus Singapore Airlines has been able to combine strategies of service differentiation and low cost in a way that Western airlines have found difficult. Porter himself acknowledges there are circumstances in which the strategies can be combined:[6]

- *Organisational separation.* It is possible for a company to create separate SBUs, each pursuing different generic strategies and with different cost structures. The challenge, however, is to prevent negative spill-overs from one SBU to another. For example, a company mostly pursuing differentiated strategies is liable to have high head office costs that the low-cost SBUs will also have to bear. On the other hand, a cheap cost-leader might damage the brand value of a sister SBU seeking differentiation. Because of these kinds of trade offs, it can be very difficult to pursue different generic strategies within a single set of related businesses. Despite the success of Singapore Airlines, Europe's leading airline Lufthansa has struggled to combine its low-cost subsidiaries, Germanwings and BMI (now sold), with its traditional higher-service core business.

- *Technological or managerial innovation.* Sometimes technological innovations allow radical improvements in both cost and quality. Internet retailing reduces the costs of bookselling, at the same time as increasing differentiation by greater product range and, through online book reviews, better advice. Managerial innovations are capable of such simultaneous improvements too. The Japanese car manufacturers' introduction of Total Quality Management led to reductions in production line mistakes that both cut manufacturing costs and improved car reliability, a point of successful differentiation.

- *Competitive failures.* Where competitors are also stuck in the middle, there is less competitive pressure to remove competitive disadvantage. Equally, where a company dominates a particular market, competitive pressures for consistency with a single competitive strategy are reduced.

6.3.5 **The Strategy Clock**

The **Strategy Clock** provides another way of approaching the generic strategies (see Figure 6.6), one which gives more scope for *hybrid* strategies.[7] The Strategy Clock has two distinctive features. First, it is focused on prices to customers rather than costs to the organisation: because prices are more visible than costs, the Strategy Clock can be easier to use in comparing competitors. Second, the circular design of the clock allows for more continuous choices than Michael Porter's sharp contrast between cost leadership and differentiation: there is a full range of incremental adjustments that can be made between the 7 o'clock position at the bottom of the low-price strategy and the 2 o'clock position at the bottom of the differentiation strategy. Organisations often travel around the clock, as they adjust their pricing and benefits over time.

The Strategy Clock identifies three zones of feasible strategies, and one zone likely to lead to ultimate failure:

- *Differentiation (zone 1).* This zone contains a range of feasible strategies for building on high perceptions of product or service benefits among customers. Close to the 12 o'clock position is a strategy of *differentiation without price premium.* Differentiation without a price premium combines high perceived benefits and moderate prices, typically used to gain market share. If high benefits also entail relatively high costs, this moderate pricing strategy would only be sustainable in the short term. Once increased market share has been achieved, it might be logical to move to *differentiation with price premium* closer to a 1 or 2 o'clock position. Movement all the way towards the 2 o'clock position is likely to involve a focus strategy, in Michael Porter's terms. Such a *focused differentiation* strategy targets a

Figure 6.6 The Strategy Clock

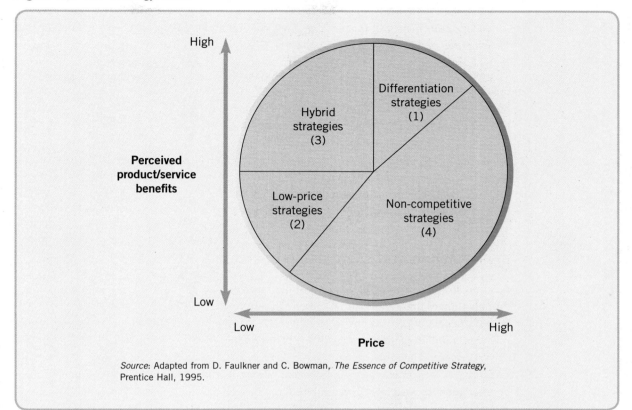

Source: Adapted from D. Faulkner and C. Bowman, *The Essence of Competitive Strategy*, Prentice Hall, 1995.

niche where the higher prices and reduced benefits are sustainable, for instance because of a lack of competition in a particular geographical area.

- *Low-price (zone 2).* This zone allows for different combinations of low prices and low perceived value. Close to the 9 o'clock position, a standard *low-price* strategy would gain market share, by combining low prices with reasonable value (at parity with competitors). To be sustainable, this strategy needs to be underpinned by some cost advantage, such as economies of scale gained through increased market share. Without such a cost advantage, cuts in benefits or increases in prices become necessary eventually. A variation on the standard low-price strategy is the *no-frills* strategy, close to the 7 o'clock position. No-frills strategies involve both low benefits and low prices, similar to low-cost airlines such as Ryanair (which even proposed to charge for use of its on-board toilets).

- *Hybrid strategy (zone 3).* A distinctive feature of the Strategy Clock is the space it allows between low-price and differentiation strategies.[8] Hybrid strategies involve both lower prices than differentiation strategies, and higher benefits than low-price strategies. Hybrid strategies are often used to make aggressive bids for increased market share. They can also be an effective way of entering a new market, for instance overseas. Even in the case of innovations with high benefits, it can make sense to price low initially in order to gain experience curve efficiencies or lock-in through network effects (see section 6.3.6). Some companies sustain hybrid strategies over long periods of time: for example, furniture store IKEA, which uses scale advantages to combine relatively low prices with differentiated Swedish design (see Chapter end case).

- *Non-competitive strategies (zone 4)*. The final set of strategies occupies a zone of unfeasible economics, with low benefits and high prices. Unless businesses have exceptional strategic lock-in, customers will quickly reject these combinations. Typically these strategies lead to failure.

The Strategy Clock's focus on price, and its scope for incremental adjustments in strategy, provide a more dynamic view on strategy than Porter's generic strategies. Instead of organisations being fairly fixed in terms of either a cost or a differentiation strategy, they can move around the clock. For example, an organisation might start with a *low-price* strategy to gain market share, later shift to a higher-priced *differentiation with premium* strategy in order to reap profits, and then move back to a *hybrid strategy* in order to defend itself from new entrants. However, Porter's generic strategies do remind managers that costs are critical. Unless an organisation has some secure cost advantage (such as economies of scale), a hybrid strategy of high perceived benefits and low prices is unlikely to be sustainable for long.

6.3.6 Lock-in and sustainable business strategies

Business strategies should ideally be sustainable over time. This may involve having competitive advantages that rivals cannot match. Thus, as in section 3.3, strategies are more likely to be sustained if underpinned by capabilities that combine all the VRIO characteristics of value, rarity, inimitability and non-substitutability. Another approach to sustaining business strategies is creating 'lock-in'.

Strategic lock-in is where users become dependent on a supplier and are unable to use another supplier without substantial switching costs.[9] Strategic lock-in is related to the concept of path dependency (see section 5.2.1) and essentially extends the principles of inimitability and non-substitutability. Under conditions of lock-in, imitators and substitutes are unable to attract customers. This is particularly valuable to differentiators. With customers securely locked in, it becomes possible to keep prices well above costs.

Lock-in can be achieved in two main ways:

- *Controlling complementary products or services*. Opportunities for lock-in to a particular product or service arise where other products or services are necessary for customers using it. This is often known as the 'razor and blade' strategy: once a customer has bought a particular kind of razor, he or she is obliged to buy compatible blades to use it. Apple originally applied a similar strategy when it used Digital Rights Management to ensure that music bought on its iTunes store could only be played on its own iPod players. To switch to a Sony player would mean losing access to all the iTunes music previously purchased.

- *Creating a proprietary industry standard*. Sometimes companies are so successful that they create an industry standard under their own control. Similar to the razor and blade effect, as customers invest in training and systems using that standard, it becomes more expensive to switch to another product or service. However, with industry standards, *network effects* also operate: as other members of the network also adopt the same standard, it becomes even more valuable to stay within it. Microsoft built this kind of proprietary standard with its Windows operating system, which holds more than 90 per cent of the market. For a business to switch to another operating system would mean retraining staff and translating files onto the new system, while perhaps creating communications problems with network members (such as customers or suppliers) who had stuck with Windows.

(6.4) **INTERACTIVE STRATEGIES**

Generic strategies need to be chosen, and adjusted, in the light of competitors' strategies. If everybody else is chasing after cost leadership, then a differentiation strategy might be sensible. Thus business strategy choices *interact* with those of competitors. This section starts by considering business strategy in the light of competitor moves, especially in hypercompetition. It then addresses the option of cooperation and closes with game theory, which helps managers choose between competition and more cooperative strategies.

6.4.1 **Interactive price and quality strategies**

Richard D'Aveni depicts competitor interactions in terms of movements against the variables of price (the vertical axis) and perceived quality (the horizontal axis), similar to the Strategy Clock: see Figure 6.7.[10] Although D'Aveni applies his analysis to the very fast-moving environments he terms 'hypercompetitive' (see section 2.3.1), similar reasoning applies wherever competitors' moves are interdependent.

Figure 6.7 shows different organisations competing by emphasising either low prices or high quality or some mixture of the two. Graph (i) starts with a 'first value line', describing various trade-offs in terms of price and perceived quality that are acceptable to customers. The cost-leading firm (here L) offers relatively poor perceived quality, but customers accept this because of the lower price. While the relative positions on the graph should not be taken exactly literally, in the car market this cost-leading position might describe some of Hyundai's products. The differentiator (D) has a higher price, but much better quality. This might be Mercedes. In between, there are a range of perfectly acceptable combinations, with the mid-point firm (M) offering a combination of reasonable prices and reasonable quality. This might be Ford. M's strategy is on the first value line and therefore entirely viable at this stage. On the other hand, firm U is uncompetitive, falling behind the value line. Its price is higher than M's, and its quality is worse. U's predicament is typical of the business that is 'stuck in the middle', in Porter's terms. U no longer offers acceptable value and must quickly move back onto the value line or fail.

In any market, competitors and their moves or counter-moves can be plotted against these two axes of price and perceived value. For example, in graph (i) of Figure 6.7, the differentiator (D) makes an aggressive move by substantially improving its perceived quality while holding its prices. This improvement in quality shifts customer expectations of quality right across the market. These changed expectations are reflected by the new, second value line (in green). With the second value line, even the cost-leader (L) may have to make some improvement to quality, or accept a small price cut. But the greatest threat is for the mid-point competitor, M. To catch up with the second value line, M must respond either by making a substantial improvement in quality while holding prices, or by slashing prices, or by some combination of the two.

However, mid-point competitor M also has the option of an aggressive counter-attack. Given the necessary capabilities, M might choose to push the value line still further outwards, wrong-footing differentiator D by creating a third value line that is even more demanding in terms of the price-perceived quality trade-off. The starting point in graph (ii) of Figure 6.7 is all three competitors L, M and D successfully reaching the second value line (uncompetitive U has disappeared). However, M's next move is to go beyond the second value line by making radical

Figure 6.7 Interactive price and quality strategies

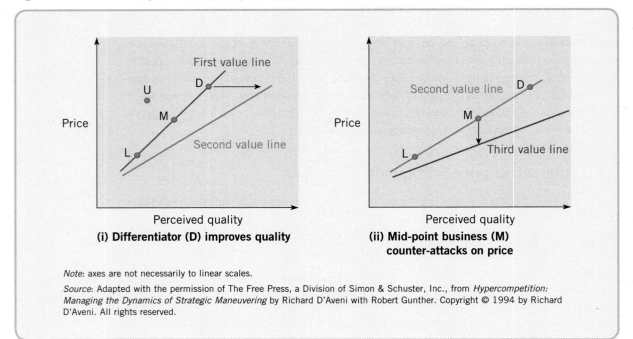

(i) Differentiator (D) improves quality

(ii) Mid-point business (M) counter-attacks on price

Note: axes are not necessarily to linear scales.

Source: Adapted with the permission of The Free Press, a Division of Simon & Schuster, Inc., from *Hypercompetition: Managing the Dynamics of Strategic Maneuvering* by Richard D'Aveni with Robert Gunther. Copyright © 1994 by Richard D'Aveni. All rights reserved.

cuts in price while sustaining its new level of perceived quality. Again, customer expectations are changed and a third value line (in red) is established. Now it is differentiator D that is at most risk of being left behind, and it faces hard choices about how to respond in terms of price and quality.

Plotting moves and counter-moves in these terms underlines the dynamic and interactive nature of business strategy. Economically viable positions along the value line are always in danger of being superseded as competitors move either downwards in terms of price or outwards in terms of perceived quality. The generic strategies of cost leadership and differentiation should not be seen as static positions, but as dynamic trajectories along the axes of price and quality. The movement towards more 'local' Starbucks stores demonstrates the need to be continually moving along the trajectory of differentiation (see Illustration 6.3).

A more detailed example of the sequence of decisions and possible options involved in competitive interaction is given in Figure 6.8.[11] This illustrates the situation of a business facing a low-price competitor, for example a high-cost Western manufacturer facing possible attack by cheap imports from Asia. There are three key decisions:

● *Threat assessment.* The first decision point is whether the threat is substantial or not. If there is a threat, the high-cost organisation should not automatically respond to a low-price competitor by trying to match prices: it is likely to lose a price war with its existing cost structure. The high-cost organisation needs a more sophisticated response.

● *Differentiation response.* If there are enough consumers prepared to pay for them, the high-cost organisation can seek out new points of differentiation. For example, a Western manufacturer may exploit its closeness to local markets by improving service levels. At the same time, unnecessary costs should be stripped out. If increased differentiation is not possible, then more radical cost solutions should be sought.

ILLUSTRATION 6.3

McCafés versus Starbucks

Starbucks coffee chain changes its strategy in response to McDonald's challenge.

Fast food chain McDonald's has launched a worldwide challenge to coffee giant Starbucks with its new concept, McCafés. The McCafé concept had emerged in Australia in the 1990s. McCafés typically operate within or next to regular McDonald's outlets. They use high-quality coffee machines and sell different blends of coffee according to the tastes of local markets. By 2012, there were 1,500 McCafé outlets in the USA, and 600 in Germany. McCafés are spreading rapidly across Europe, from Spain to the Ukraine (in the United Kingdom, McCafé products are still sold under the usual McDonald's brand).

Starbucks is the world's largest coffee chain, with nearly 20,000 stores across 60 countries from Canada to China. Founded in 1971, Starbucks was bought as a small Seattle coffee shop chain by Howard Schultz in 1988. The Starbucks' original concept was good coffee, brewed in an intimate atmosphere by skilled 'barristas'. Schultz expanded rapidly, with his first store outside North America opening in Tokyo in 1996. In 2001, Schultz retired as CEO and under the next two CEOs Starbucks continued its expansion. But in 2007, performance was beginning to flag. Schultz wrote a famous 'Valentine's Day memo' to the then CEO, complaining that growth had led to a 'commoditisation' of the Starbucks' concept. The introduction of automatic espresso machines to speed up service removed the distinctive coffee odour in the shops and deskilled the barristas. The next year, Schultz returned to the helm as CEO.

As he started back in his old job, Howard Schultz proclaimed:

'We are laser-focused on delivering the finest quality coffee and getting the customer experience right every time. We have. . . . been putting our feet into the shoes of our customers and are responding directly to their needs. Our customers are telling us they want value and quality and we will deliver that in a way that is meaningful to them and authentic to Starbucks.'

Schultz famously closed all the stores worldwide for an afternoon in order to retrain the barristas in the skills of brewing good coffee. Starbucks also improved its food offerings: in 2012, the company bought the bakery chain La Boulange for $100 m. So as to access its innovative, quality food products for transfer to Starbucks outlets, the standard Starbucks international store format was relaxed in order to allow more variety according to locality. Local artefacts, bolder colours, bigger community noticeboards and even second-hand furniture were used to create more individual stores. Starbucks stores offered free wi-fi to users.

McDonald's is aiming to match Starbucks' changes. Thus McDonald's too introduced free wi-fi. The quality and price of McDonald's coffees are highly competitive. Thus a McCafé frappé drink cost $3.99 for a 16 ounce drink in 2012 (against $4.20 for a Big Mac burger); Starbucks' equivalent frappuccino cost $5.45. The Canadian *Globe and Mail* reviewed the two companies' products in 2011. The comment on McCafé was: 'It tastes like a combination of damp forest and uncleaned coffee maker.' As for the Starbucks product, it was 'bitter; burnt toast. This is so bad, it's the antithesis of coffee.' Overall, the *Globe and Mail* rated McCafé as slightly superior.

Sources: Financial Times, 26 May 2009; smartmoney.com, 23 July 2012; the *Globe and Mail*, 8 November 2011.

Questions

1 Plot the moves of McDonald's and Starbucks on the axes of price and perceived quality, as in Figure 6.7.

2 What should be done by a company with a similar original position to Starbucks, but operating in a market where McCafé has not yet arrived (e.g. Costa Coffee in the United Kingdom)?

Figure 6.8 Responding to low-cost rivals

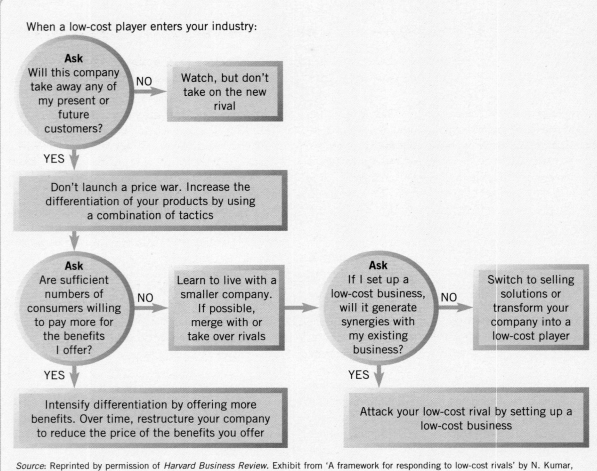

● *Cost response*. Merger with other high-cost organisations may help reduce costs and match prices through economies of scale. If a low-cost business is synergistic with (in other words, has benefits for) the existing business, this can be an effective platform for an aggressive cost-based counter-attack. If there is neither scope for further differentiation nor synergy between the existing business and a possible new low-cost business, then the existing business must sooner or later be abandoned. For a Western manufacturer, one option might be to outsource all production to low-cost operators, simply applying its design and branding expertise. Another option would be to abandon manufacturing in favour of becoming a 'solutions provider', aggregating manufactured components from different suppliers and adding value through whole-systems design, consultantcy or service.

Equivalent decisions would have to be made, of course, by a low-price competitor facing a differentiator. When Apple entered the phone market with its expensive touchscreen iPhone, established handset manufacturers had first to decide whether Apple was a serious long-term threat, and then choose how far they should either match the iPhone's features or increase the price differential between their products and Apple's expensive ones.

6.4.2 Interactive strategies in hypercompetition

According to Richard D'Aveni, the kinds of move and counter-move outlined in the preceding section are a constant feature of hypercompetitive environments. As in section 2.3.1, hypercompetition describes markets with continuous disequilibrium and change, for example popular music or consumer electronics. In these conditions, it may no longer be possible to plan for sustainable positions of competitive advantage. Indeed, planning for long-term sustainability may actually destroy competitive advantage by slowing down response. Managers have to be able to act faster than their competitors.

Successful competitive interaction in hypercompetition demands speed and initiative rather than defensiveness. Richard D'Aveni highlights four key principles:

- *Cannibalise bases of success*: sustaining old advantages distracts from developing new advantages. An organisation has to be willing to cannibalise the basis of its own success. Intel, traditionally a dominant supplier of microchips for computers, has had to jeopardise its traditional markets by pushing hard into the smart phone and tablet markets.

- *Series of small moves rather than big moves*: smaller moves create more flexibility and give a series of temporary advantages. At the same time, smaller moves make it harder for competitors to detect and counter the overall strategic direction. Apple, for example, tends to make incremental improvements to its products between the launches of major innovations, such as the iPhone in 2007 and the iPad in 2010.

- *Be unpredictable.* If competitors can see a pattern they can predict the next competitive moves and quickly learn how to imitate or outflank an organisation. So surprise, unpredictability, even apparent irrationality can be important. Managers must learn ways of appearing to be unpredictable to the external world while, internally, thinking strategies through. Apple likes to keep competitors guessing about its next major product move: many had been speculating that the company was about to enter the television market when it produced the iPad.

- *Mislead the competition.* Drawing on the lessons of game theory (see section 6.4.4), the organisation might signal particular moves, but then do something else (e.g. talk about alliances, and then make an acquisition). Or the organisation might disguise initial success in a market, until ready to respond to competitor retaliation.[12]

6.4.3 Cooperative strategy

So far the emphasis has been on competition and competitive advantage. However, the competitive moves and counter-moves in section 6.4.1 make it clear that sometimes competition can escalate in a way that is dangerous to all competitors. It can be in the self-interest of organisations to restrain competition. Moreover, advantage may not always be achieved just by competing. Collaboration between some organisations in a market may give them advantage over other competitors in the same market, or potential new entrants. Collaboration can be explicit in terms of formal agreements to cooperate, or tacit in terms of informal mutual understandings between organisations. In short, while organisations need to avoid illegal collusion, business strategy includes cooperative options as well as competitive ones.[13]

Figure 6.9 illustrates various kinds of benefits from cooperation between firms in terms of Michael Porter's five forces of buyers, suppliers, rivals, entrants and substitutes (section 2.3.1). Key benefits of cooperation are as follows:

Figure 6.9 Cooperating with rivals

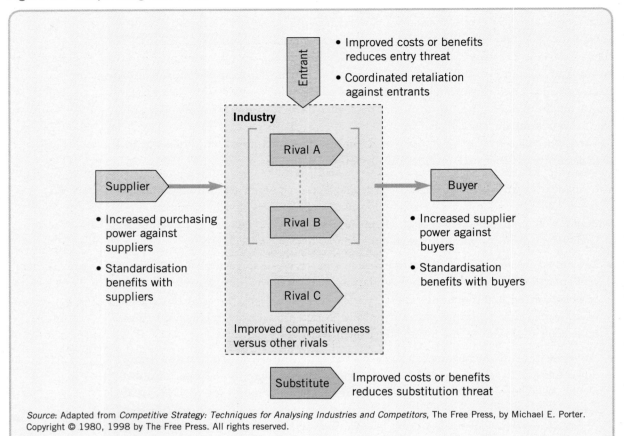

- *Suppliers.* In Figure 6.9, cooperation between rivals A and B in an industry will increase their purchasing power against suppliers. Sometimes this increased cooperation is used simply to squeeze supplier prices. However, cooperation between rivals A and B may enable them to standardise requirements, allowing suppliers to make cost reductions to all parties' benefit. For example, if two car manufacturers agreed on common component specifications, their suppliers could gain economies through production of the standardised part on a greater scale (this kind of *complementarity* is discussed in section 2.3).

- *Buyers.* Conversely, cooperation between rivals A and B will increase their power as suppliers vis-à-vis buyers. It will be harder for buyers to shop around. Such *collusion* between rivals can help maintain or raise prices, though it may well attract penalties from competition regulators. On the other hand, buyers may benefit if their inputs are standardised, again enabling reductions in costs that all can share. For example, if food manufacturers supplying a retailer agree on common pallet sizes for deliveries, the retailer can manage its warehouses much more efficiently.

- *Rivals.* If cooperative rivals A and B are getting benefits with regard to both buyers and suppliers, other competitors without such agreements – in Figure 6.9, rival C – will be at a competitive disadvantage. Rival C will be in danger of being squeezed out of the industry. This was the predicament of Three in Illustration 6.4.

ILLUSTRATION 6.4

Mobile payment systems: cooperating to pay

Cooperative agreements in mobile payment systems may leave some players out.

The opportunities in mobile payment systems ('mobile wallets') attracted a very wide range of competitors and approaches. In 2011, the value of mobile payments worldwide was $240 bn, a sum expected to triple in the following five years. Companies which could skim even a tiny percentage of this total through offering mobile payment services could earn fortunes. Moreover, they would have access to valuable data about which consumers bought what, where and when. It was hardly surprising that companies as diverse as Google, Apple, Facebook, PayPal, Visa, Barclays and Blackberry were crowding into the new market, each with its own particular systems. Indeed, the diversity of possible systems was creating confusion, with retailers and restaurants hesitating to adopt before seeing which system would finally come out on top.

One important initiative was 'Project Oscar', a joint venture launched by the United Kingdom's three leading mobile phone operators Vodafone, Telefónica's O2 and EverythingEverywhere, the merged businesses of DeutscheTelekom and France Telecom. Project Oscar involved giving customers SIM cards that would allow them to store debit and credit card details on their phones and pay for goods or transport either online via their mobile or by tapping the handset on a special reader at the till or ticket barrier, using Near Field Communication (NFC) technology. This contrasted with the Google system, for instance, which involved getting a whole new phone. The three partners in Project Oscar declared: 'If approved, the joint venture will benefit UK plc as a whole. It will promote competition by bringing together the necessary scale to offer a credible alternative to the established online payments and advertising platforms offered by large US-based internet players.'

But not everybody was happy at the prospect of the dominant phone operators collaborating in this way. The United Kingdom's fourth mobile phone operator, Three, complained: 'The JV (Project Oscar) will control and sell access to over 90 per cent of UK mobile subscribers and their data, thus allowing Deutsche Telekom, France Telecom, Vodafone and Telefónica to foreclose the market to third-parties and neatly do away with the inconvenience of competing with each other.' In April 2012, with the support of Google, Three successfully referred the joint venture to the European competition authorities.

The European Commission investigated, aware of a long history of illicit collusion between the various mobile phone operators in Europe. However, the Commission came down in favour of Project Oscar. It declared:

'As a result of its in-depth investigation, the Commission concluded that the joint venture will not likely lead to a significant impediment to effective competition in the EEA within the meaning of the Merger Regulation. The market investigation revealed that a number of alternatives already exist and much more are very likely to emerge in the near future to ensure adequate competitive pressure on the joint venture's mobile wallet platform. Some of these alternatives may rely on a secure access to the SIM card of the mobile handsets in order to store sensitive data like bank account numbers, etc. This access will be controlled by the mobile network operators, including in particular the three parents of the joint venture. However, other alternatives exist which do not store sensitive data on SIM cards and it is unlikely that the creation of the joint venture will allow the parent mobile network operators to block these alternative routes to market using technical or commercial means.'

Sources: Guardian, 7 March 2012; Financial Times, 8 March 2012 and 29 April 2012; Communications World, 5 September 2012.

Questions

1 In terms of Figure 6.9, what are the benefits to the Project Oscar partners of collaboration?

2 What options are available now to the excluded Three?

- *Entrants*. Similarly, potential entrants will likely lack the advantages of the combined rivals A and B. Moreover, A and B can coordinate their retaliation strategies against any new entrant, for example by cutting prices by the same proportions in order to protect their own relative positions while undermining the competitiveness of the new entrant.

- *Substitutes*. Finally, the improved costs or efficiencies that come from cooperation between rivals A and B reduce the incentives for buyers to look to substitutes. Steel companies have cooperated on research to reduce the weight of steel used in cars, in order to discourage car manufacturers from switching to lighter substitutes such as aluminium or plastics.

Further kinds of cooperation will be considered under alliance strategy in section 10.4.

6.4.4 Game theory

Game theory provides important insights into competitor interaction.[14] The 'game' refers to the kinds of interactive moves two players make in a game of chess. **Game theory encourages an organisation to consider competitors' likely moves and the implications of these moves for its own strategy.** Game theorists are alert to two kinds of interaction in particular. First, game theorists consider how a *competitor response* to a strategic move might change the original assumptions behind that move: for example, challenging a competitor in one area might lead to a counter-attack in another. Second, game theorists are sensitive to the *strategic signals*, or messages, their moves might convey to competitors, for example with regard to how fiercely they seem willing to defend their position in a particular market. In the light of possible attacks and counter-attacks, game theorists often advise a more cooperative approach than head-to-head competition.

Game theory is particularly relevant where competitors are *interdependent*. Interdependence exists where the outcome of choices made by one competitor is dependent on the choices made by other competitors. For example, the success of price cuts by a retailer depends on the responses of its rivals: if rivals do not match the price cuts, then the price-cutter gains market share; but if rivals follow the price cuts, nobody gains market share and all players suffer from the lower prices. Anticipating competitor counter-moves is clearly vital to deciding whether to go forward with the price-cutting strategy.

There are two important guiding principles that arise from interdependence:

- *Get in the mind of the competitors*. Strategists need to put themselves in the position of competitors, take a view about what competitors are likely to do and choose their own strategy in this light. They need to understand their competitors' game-plan to plan their own.

- *Think forwards and reason backwards*. Strategists should choose their competitive moves on the basis of understanding the likely responses of competitors. Think forwards to what competitors might do in the future, and then reason backwards to what would be sensible to do in the light of this now.

Game theory insights can be gained through two methods. On the one hand, *war gaming* is helpful where it is important to get stakeholders to deeply appreciate each others' positions through actually playing out their respective roles, and where there is uncertainty about the range of outcomes. Illustration 6.5 provides a public policy example from South Africa. On the other hand, *mathematical game theory* is useful where there is a clear but limited range of outcomes and the values associated with each outcome can be reasonably quantified.

ILLUSTRATION 6.5

War gaming in South Africa

Deloitte proposes war games to develop a strategic solution to a major pollution problem in South Africa.

Deloitte, one of the 'big four' professional service firms, has nearly 200,000 employees offering accountancy, tax, consulting and business advisory services in 150 countries around the world. In 2010, it also got into the war gaming business. In particular, it bought a small simulation company developed by the War Studies Group at King's College, University of London.

War gaming originated with the Prussian Army in the late nineteenth century and developed particularly during the Cold War in the twentieth century. War games place the players in the positions of different actors (e.g. enemies or allies), and ask them to play out a sequence of moves and counter-moves as if they were the actors themselves. Two famous principles help guide the play. The first is from Sun Tzu, the Chinese general who wrote the military treatise *The Art of War* about 500 years BC: 'To know your enemy, you must become your enemy.' The second principle is from the nineteenth-century German General Helmuth von Moltke: 'No plan ever survives the first collision with the enemy.' War games thus help players understand how the various players will act as action unfolds over time. Deloitte uses war gaming simulations to help clients plot strategies for new product introductions, pricing changes and new market entries, all situations where competitor reactions can be highly significant. But they can be used in complex public policy arenas too.

The problem of mine drainage around Johannesburg in South Africa is an example. Gold has been mined there since 1886, but the mining process ends up by mixing water, oxygen and heavy metals to create a diluted sulphuric acid. This acid is seeping out into water sources and is now polluting 10 per cent of the potable water supplied by the local water company. In an area that is short of water, this is potentially disastrous. Worse, the mines must be continuously pumped out in order to avoid flooding the vicinity, including local towns and an important bird sanctuary. The trouble is, many of the mines are no longer owned by their original developers, and current owners dispute their responsibilities, which are liable to be very expensive.

There are clearly many stakeholders involved. First there are the mining companies, whose mines are the source of the problem. There are the various local municipal authorities, threatened by both flooding and polluted water. There are no less than five national government departments involved, from Mining to Agriculture, each with its own interests to defend. Local farmers are very concerned about the threat to the water supply that is vital to their agriculture.

A war game helps players respond to various scenarios. What if there was major pollution? This would be a catastrophe for local communities, but it would also threaten the labour supply for the mining companies: this possible cost should be factored into the calculations of the mining companies as they contemplate the extent to which they would be prepared to pay for solutions. On the other hand, what if the mining companies were forced to solve the problem wholly at their expense? Would the mining companies then prefer simply to abandon the mines, or at least reduce investment in capacity, with knock-on effects on local employment? Putting players into the position of the various stakeholders helps everybody understand fully the interests involved and even, perhaps, to see possibilities for shared solutions.

Source: Based on Deloitte, 'War gaming may just be the answer to solving South Africa's own Chenobyl', 2011.

Questions

1 War games can be used to guide new product introductions, pricing changes and new market entries. Can you think of other business situations where they could be useful?

2 Are there any limits or dangers to comparing business strategy to war?

One of the most famous illustrations of mathematical game theory is the *prisoner's dilemma*. Game theorists identify many situations where organisations' strategic decisions are similar to the dilemma of two prisoners accused of serial crimes together and being interrogated in separate prison cells without the possibility of communicating with each other. The prisoners have to decide on the relative merits of: (i) loyally supporting each other by refusing to divulge any information to their interrogators; and (ii) seeking an advantage by betraying the other. If both stay silent, they might get away with most of their crimes and only suffer some lesser punishment, perhaps for just one or two offences. The interrogators, though, will tempt each of them to divulge full information by offering them their freedom if only they betray their fellow criminal. However, if both betray, then the judge is unlikely to be grateful for the confessions, and will punish them for all their crimes. The dilemma for each of the prisoners is how much to trust in their mutual loyalty: if they both refuse to divulge, they can both get away with the lesser punishment; on the other hand, if one is sure that the other will not betray, it makes even more sense to betray the loyal one as that allows the betrayer to go totally free. The two prisoners are clearly interdependent. But because they cannot communicate, they each have to get in the mind of the other, think forwards to what they might do, and then reason backwards in order to decide what their own strategy should be – stay silent or betray.

The prisoner's dilemma has its equivalence in business where there are two major players competing head-to-head against each other in a situation of tight interdependence. This is the position of Airbus and Boeing in the aircraft business, Sony and Microsoft in the games market, or British Airways and Virgin in transatlantic travel. It would be relevant to the strategic decisions of two such interdependent companies in a range of situations: for example, if one company was thinking about making a major investment in an innovative new product that the other company could match. For two such competitors to communicate directly about their strategies in these situations would likely be judged illegal by the competition authorities. They therefore have to get into each other's minds, think forwards and reason backwards. How will the other company act or react, and, in the light of that, what strategy is best?

The kind of situation two interdependent competitors could get into is represented in the prisoner's dilemma matrix of Figure 6.10. Suppose the two main aircraft manufacturers Airbus and Boeing were both under pricing pressure, perhaps because of falling demand. They each have to decide whether to announce radical price cuts or to hold their prices up. If both choose to hold their prices, neither gets an advantage over the other and they both get the returns represented in the top left-hand quadrant of Figure 6.10: for the sake of illustration, each might earn profits of €500 m. However, if one competitor pursues the radical price cuts on its own while the other does not, the pattern of returns might be quite different: the radical price-cutter attracts a significantly larger share of airline customers and earns €700 m profits through spreading fixed costs over greater sales, while the market-share-losing competitor earns only €100 m (as represented in the top-right and bottom-left quadrants). This situation might tempt one of the competitors to choose radical price cuts for two reasons: first, there is the prospect of higher profits; but, second, there is the risk of the other competitor cutting prices while leaving it behind. The problem is that if each reasons in the same way, the two competitors will *both* cut prices at once. They will thus set off a price war in which neither gains share and they both end up with the unsatisfactory return of just €300 m (the bottom-right quadrant).

The dilemma in Figure 6.10 is awkward because cooperation is simultaneously attractive and difficult to achieve. The most attractive strategy for Airbus and Boeing jointly is for them

Figure 6.10 Prisoner's dilemma game in aircraft manufacture

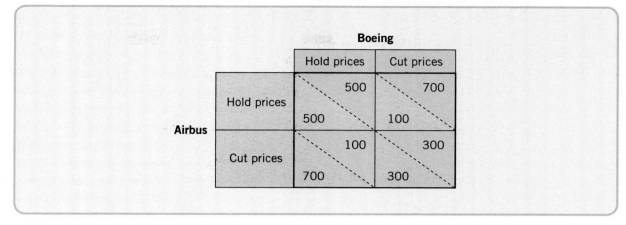

both to hold their prices, yet in practice they are likely to cut prices because they must expect the other to do so anyway. A distinctive feature of game theory is that it frequently highlights the value of a more cooperative approach to competitor interaction, rather than aggressive competition. The cooperation need not be in the form of an explicit agreement: cooperation can be tacit, supported by the recognition of mutual self-interest in not attacking each other head-to-head. Game theory therefore encourages managers to consider how a 'game' can be transformed from lose–lose competition to win–win cooperation. There are four principles that can help here:

- *Ensure repetition*. The prisoner's dilemma above assumes just one interaction. The thinking forwards is quite limited. In many circumstances, though, it is easier to achieve tacit co-operation if the two players know that they will be making similar interdependent decisions over time. Ensuring repetition makes cooperation much more likely. In a repetitive game, starting with a cooperative approach, and only making more aggressive moves in *response* to the aggression of the other player, has been shown generally to help players maintain a mutually satisfactory position of tacit cooperation. In this approach, both Airbus and Boeing would start by holding their prices; if one cut its prices, the other would simply cut its prices for one period, hoping that the first would move back to the higher price level; if the first company did move back to the higher prices, the second would follow. The idea is that in repeated interactions over time, players can learn from each other's moves and counter-moves the benefits of cooperation.

- *Signalling*. Another insight from game theory is that strategic moves are also signals to com-petitors. Strategists need to be aware of the messages that their moves convey and read the messages of their competitors' moves. If Airbus failed to punish a price cut of Boeing with its own price cut, then Boeing might decide that Airbus was not serious about the market and would continue its price-cutting strategy. Responding aggressively to an initial price cut may actually support long-term cooperation in a repeated game.

- *Deterrence*. As above, signalling can clearly be about deterring unwanted strategic moves by competitors. During the Cold War, game theorists attribute the lack of direct warfare between the USA and the Soviet Union to the fact that both possessed nuclear deterrents: if one country attacked the other, then the second country would retaliate with a nuclear

KEY DEBATE

To be different or the same?

Can differentiation strategies rebound, making an organisation seem dangerously eccentric rather than delivering competitive advantage?

This chapter has introduced the potential value of differentiation strategies, in which the organisation emphasises its uniqueness. This is consistent also with the argument of the resource-based view (Chapter 3) in favour of the distinctiveness and inimitability of an organisation's resources. But how far should an organisation push its uniqueness, especially if there is a danger of its beginning to be seen as simply eccentric?

McKinsey & Co. consultant Philipp Natterman makes a strong case for differentiation.[1] He tracks the relationship between profitability and differentiation (in terms of pricing and product features) over long periods in both the personal computer and mobile phone industries. He finds that as differentiation falls over time, so too do industry profit margins. Natterman blames management techniques such as benchmarking (Chapter 3), which tend to encourage convergence on industry 'best practices'. The trouble with best practices is that they easily become standard practices. There is no competitive advantage in following the herd.

However, 'institutional theorists' such as Paul DiMaggio and Walter Powell point to some advantages in herd-like behaviour.[2] They think of industries as 'organisational fields' in which all sorts of actors must interact – customers, suppliers, employees and regulators. The ability of these actors to interact effectively depends upon being legitimate in the eyes of other actors in the field. Over time, industries develop institutionalised norms of legitimate behaviour, which it makes sense for everybody to follow. It is easier for customers and suppliers to do business with organisations that are more or less the same as the others in the industry. It is reassuring to potential employees and industry regulators if organisations do not seem highly eccentric. Especially when there is high uncertainty about what drives performance – for example, in knowledge-based industries – it can be a lot better to be legitimate than different. To the extent that customers, suppliers, employees and regulators value conformity, then it is valuable in itself. Being a 'misfit' can be costly.

This institutionalist appreciation of conformity makes sense of a lot of strategic behaviour. For example, merger waves in some industries seem to be driven by bandwagons, in which organisations become panicked into making acquisitions simply for fear of being left behind. Likewise, many management initiatives, such as business process re-engineering, e-business or outsourcing, are the product of fads and fashions as much as hard objective analysis. The insight from institutionalist theory, however, is that following the fashion is not necessarily a bad thing.

Thus institutional theory and the resource-based view appear to have opposing perspectives on the value of differentiation. David Deephouse has investigated this apparent trade-off between differentiation and conformity in the American banking industry and found a curvilinear relationship between differentiation and financial performance.[3] Strong conformity led to inferior performance; moderate differentiation was associated with improved performance; extreme differentiation appeared to damage performance.

Deephouse concludes in favour of 'balance' between differentiation and conformity. He also suggests that the value of differentiation depends on the extent to which key actors in the industry – customers, suppliers, employees, and so on – have converged on institutionalised norms of appropriate strategy. It seems that strategies can be too differentiated, but that how much 'too differentiated' is depends on the kind of industry that one is in.

Notes
1. P.M. Natterman, 'Best practice does not equal best strategy', *McKinsey Quarterly*, no. 2 (2000), pp. 22–31.
2. P. DiMaggio and W. Powell, 'The iron cage revisited: institutional isomorphism and collective rationality in organizational fields', *American Sociological Review*, vol. 48 (1983), pp. 147–60.
3. D. Deephouse, 'To be different or to be the same? It's a question (and theory) of strategic balance', *Strategic Management Journal*, vol. 20 (1999), pp. 147–66.

Questions

1 To what extent do (a) universities and (b) car manufacturers compete by being different or the same?

2 Considering the nature of their industries, and key players within them, why might these organisations adopt these approaches to conformity or differentiation?

attack. This was known as 'mutually assured destruction' (MAD), but it worked. In a similar vein, interdependent competitors have to demonstrate that the costs of an unwanted move will be very high. Two effective forms of deterrent would be maintaining extra capacity that could be used to flood the market, or holding a minor position in a competitor's key market that could easily be expanded. Even if these investments in deterrence are expensive, they may be worthwhile if they encourage cooperation.

- *Commitment.* It is important also to signal commitment. When the Roman invader Julius Caesar burnt his ships on the shores of England, the message was to his adversaries as much as his own invading army. The Britons knew that Caesar would fight to the death: they had strong incentives to negotiate a peace with him. Caesar's signal of commitment was credible because it was costly and irreversible. Similarly, if a company invests heavily in developing its brand in a market, or building up a portfolio of patents, then competitors will know that it is highly committed: they will therefore be cautious about attacking it head-on. Again, additional investments have a signalling value that can help cooperation long-term.

SUMMARY

- Business strategy is concerned with seeking competitive advantage in markets at the *business* rather than *corporate* level.

- Business strategy needs to be considered and defined in terms of *strategic business units* (SBUs).

- Porter's framework and the Strategy Clock define various *generic strategies*, including *cost-leadership*, *differentiation*, *focus* and *hybrid* strategies.

- Managers need to consider how business strategies can be sustained through strategic capabilities and/or the ability to achieve a '*lock-in*' position with buyers.

- In *hypercompetitive* conditions sustainable competitive advantage is difficult to achieve. Competitors need to be able to cannibalise, make small moves, be unpredictable and mislead their rivals.

- *Cooperative strategies* may offer alternatives to competitive strategies or may run in parallel.

- Game theory encourages managers to get in the mind of competitors and think forwards and reason backwards.

VIDEO ASSIGNMENTS

Visit MyStrategyLab and watch the CISCO case study for Chapter 6.

1 Explain the concept of generic strategy using either Porter's framework or the Strategy Clock drawing on examples from the IT sector.

2 Using section 6.4, explain how 'hypercompetition strategies' and 'cooperative strategies' are used by CISCO to enhance its competitive advantage.

WORK ASSIGNMENTS

✱ Denotes more advanced work assignments.
* Refers to a case study in the Text and Case edition.

6.1 What are the advantages and what are the disadvantages of applying principles of business strategy to public-sector or charity organisations? Illustrate your argument by reference to a public-sector organisation of your choice.

6.2 Using either Porter's generic strategies or the Strategy Clock, identify examples of organisations following strategies of differentiation, low cost or low price, and stuck-in-the-middle or hybrid. How successful are these strategies?

6.3✱ You have been appointed personal assistant to the chief executive of a major manufacturing firm, who has asked you to explain what is meant by 'differentiation' and why it is important. Write a brief report addressing these questions.

6.4✱ Choose an industry or sector which is becoming more and more competitive (e.g. financial services or fashion retailing). How might the principles of hypercompetitive strategies apply to that industry or sector?

6.5✱ Drawing on section 6.4 (on cooperative strategies) write a report for the chief executive of a business in a competitive market (e.g. pharmaceuticals* or Formula One*) explaining when and in what ways cooperation rather than direct competition might make sense.

Integrative assignment

6.6✱ Applying game theory ideas from section 6.4.4 to issues of international strategy (Chapter 8), how might a domestic player discourage an overseas player from entering into its home market?

RECOMMENDED KEY READINGS

- The foundations of the discussions of generic competitive strategies are to be found in the writings of Michael Porter, which include *Competitive Strategy* (1980) and *Competitive Advantage* (1985), both published by Free Press. Both are recommended for readers who wish to understand the background to discussions in section 6.3 on competitive strategy and competitive advantage.

- Hypercompetition, and the strategies associated with it, are explained in Richard D'Aveni, *Hypercompetitive*

Rivalries: Competing in Highly Dynamic Environments, Free Press, 1995.

- There is much written on game theory but a good deal of it can be rather inaccessible to the lay reader. Exceptions are R. McCain, *Game Theory: a Non-technical Introduction to the Analysis of Strategy*, South Western, 2003; and A. Dixit and B. Nalebuff, *The Art of Strategy: a Game Theorist's Guide to Success in Business and Life*, Norton, 2008.

REFERENCES

1. For a detailed discussion as to how organisational structures might 'address' an organisation's mix of SBUs, see M. Goold and A. Campbell, *Designing Effective Organizations: How to Create Structured Networks*, Jossey-Bass, 2002. Also K. Eisenhardt and S. Brown, 'Patching', *Harvard Business Review*, vol. 77, no. 3 (1999), p. 72.

2. This section draws heavily on M. Porter, *Competitive Advantage*, Free Press, 1985. For a more recent discussion of the generic strategies concept, see J. Parnell, 'Generic strategies after two decades: a reconceptualisation of competitive strategy', *Management Decision*, vol. 48, no. 8 (2006), pp. 1139–54.

3. P. Conley, *Experience Curves as a Planning Tool*, available as a pamphlet from the Boston Consulting Group. See also A.C. Hax and N.S. Majluf, in R.G. Dyson (ed.), *Strategic Planning: Models and Analytical Techniques*, Wiley, 1990.

4. B. Sharp and J. Dawes, 'What is differentiation and how does it work?', *Journal of Marketing Management*, vol. 17, nos 7/8 (2001), pp. 739–59, reviews the relationship between differentiation and profitability.

5. See, for example, D. Miller, 'The generic strategy trap', *Journal of Business Strategy*, vol. 13, no. 1 (1992), pp. 37–42; and S. Thornhill and R. White, 'Strategic purity: a multi-industry evaluation of pure vs hybrid business strategies', *Strategic Management Journal*, vol. 28, no. 5 (2007), pp. 553–61; Heracleous L. and Wirtz J., 'Singapore Airlines' balancing act', *Harvard Business Review*, July–August (2010), pp. 145–151.

6. C. Markides and C. Charitou, 'Competing with dual business models: a contingency approach', *Academy of Management Executive*, vol. 18, no. 3 (2004), pp. 22–36.

7. See D. Faulkner and C. Bowman, *The Essence of Competitive Strategy*, Prentice Hall, 1995.

8. For empirical support for the benefits of a hybrid strategy, see E. Pertusa-Ortega, J. Molina-Azorín and E. Claver-Cortés, 'Competitive strategies and firm performance: a comparative analysis of pure, hybrid and "stuck-in-the-middle" strategies in Spanish firms', *British Journal of Management*, vol. 20, no. 4 (2008), pp. 508–23.

9. W.B. Arthur, 'Increasing returns and the new world of business', *Harvard Business Review*, July–August (1996), pp. 100–9. See also the concept of system lock-in in A. Hax and D. Wilde, 'The Delta Model – discovering new sources of profitability in a networked economy', *European Management Journal*, vol. 19, no. 4 (2001), pp. 379–91.

10. R. D'Aveni, *Hypercompetition: Managing the Dynamics of Strategic Maneuvering*, Free Press, 1994.

11. This analysis is based on N. Kumar, 'Strategies to fight low cost rivals', *Harvard Business Review*, vol. 84, no. 12 (2006), pp. 104–13.

12. For other examples of misleading signals, see G. Stalk Jr, 'Curveball: strategies to fool the competition', *Harvard Business Review*, September (2006), pp. 115–22.

13. Useful books on collaborative strategies are Y. Doz and G. Hamel, *Alliance Advantage: The Art of Creating Value through Partnering*, Harvard Business School Press, 1998; *Creating Collaborative Advantage*, ed. Chris Huxham, Sage, 1996; and D. Faulkner, *Strategic Alliances: Cooperating to Compete*, McGraw-Hill, 1995.

14. For readings on game theory, see B. Nalebuff and A. Brandenburger, *Co-opetition*, Profile Books, 1997; R. McCain, *Game Theory: A Non-technical Introduction to the Analysis of Strategy*, South Western, 2003; and, for a summary, S. Regan, 'Game theory perspective', in M. Jenkins and V. Ambrosini (eds), *Advanced Strategic Management: a Multi-Perspective Approach*, 2nd edn, Palgrave Macmillan, 2007, pp. 83–101. A recent practical example is in H. Lindstädt and J. Müller, 'Making game theory work for managers', *McKinsey Quarterly*, December (2009).

The IKEA approach

Kevan Scholes*

'In times when many nations and people face economic challenges our vision of creating a better everyday life for the many people is more relevant than ever. To make it possible to furnish functionally, individually and sustainably – even when the economy is tight.'

This was Mikael Ohlsson, IKEA's Chief Executive, speaking in 2012[1] while reporting a sales increase of 6.9 per cent (to €25.2 billion), profits of €3 billion and share gains in most markets. At the same time average prices had fallen by 2.6 per cent. IKEA had become the world's largest home furnishings company with 287 stores in 26 countries and employing 131,000 people.

The home furnishings market[2]

By the late 2000s home furnishings was a huge market worldwide with retail sales in excess of $US600 bn in items such as furniture, household textiles and floor coverings. More than 50 per cent of these sales were in furniture stores. Table 1 compares the geographical spread of the market and IKEA sales by region.

Table 1 **The geographical spread of the market and of IKEA sales by region**

	Europe	Americas	Asia/Pacific
% of global market	52	29	19
% of IKEA sales	79	14	7

IKEA's competitors

The home furnishings market was highly fragmented with competition occurring locally rather than globally. In each region that IKEA had stores it would typically face competitors of several types:

- Multinational furniture retailers (like IKEA) all of whom were considerably smaller than IKEA. These included the Danish company Jysk (turnover ~ €2.5 bn).
- Companies specialising in just part of the furniture product range and operating in several countries – such as Alno from Germany in kitchens.
- Multi-branch retail furniture outlets whose sales were mainly in one country such as DFS in the UK. The US market was dominated by such players (e.g. Bed, Bath & Beyond Inc. with revenues of some $US9 bn).
- Non-specialist companies who carried furniture as part of a wider product range. In the UK the largest operator was the Home Retail Group whose subsidiary Argos offered some 33,000 general merchandise products through its network of 340 stores and online sales. Despite this more generalist offering Argos was number one in UK furniture retailing. General DIY companies such as Kingfisher (through B&Q in the UK and Castorama in France) were attempting to capture more of the bottom end of the furniture market.
- Small and/or specialised retailers and/or manufacturers. These accounted for some 90 per cent of the market in Europe.

IKEA's approach

IKEA had been founded by Ingvar Kamprad in 1943 in the small Swedish town of Älmhult. But it did not open its first major furniture store until 1958. The company's success had been achieved through the now legendary IKEA business model – revolutionary in the furnishing industry of its early years (see Table 2). The guiding business philosophy of Kampard was that of improving the everyday life of people by making products more affordable. This was achieved by massive (20 per cent +) reductions in sales prices vs competitors which, in turn, required aggressive reductions in IKEA's costs.

* This case was prepared by Kevan Scholes, Emeritus Professor of Strategic Management at Sheffield Business School. It is intended as a basis for class discussion and not as an illustration of good or bad management practice. © Kevan Scholes 2013. Not to be reproduced or quoted without permission.

Table 2 IKEA's 'upside-down' business model

Element of the business model	Traditional furniture retailer	IKEA
Design	Traditional	Modern (Swedish)
Target households	Older, established	Families with children
Style of shop	Small specialist shops	All furnishing items in big stores
Location	City centre	Out-of-town
Product focus	Individual items	'Room sets'
Marketing	Advertising	Catalogue (free)
Price	High	Low
Product assembly	Ready assembled	Flat pack – self-assembly
Sourcing	Local	Global
Brand	Manufacturers'	IKEA
Financial focus	Gross margin	Sales revenue
Overheads	Often high	Frugal – no perks

Reasons for success

In his book *The IKEA Edge*[3] published in 2011, Anders Dahlvig reflected on the reasons for IKEA's success before, during and after his period as CEO (1999–2009). He felt that the success of IKEA was built on a clear and detailed understanding of the furnishing market and IKEA's success criteria:

'IKEA's success has grown from stability and consistency regarding the big picture but with lots of action and innovation in the detail (evolution rather than revolution)'[4] . . . (IKEA's five success criteria were): 1. Design, function, and quality at low prices; 2. Unique (Scandinavian) design; 3. Inspiration, ideas and complete solutions; 4. Everything in one place; 5. "A day out", the shopping experience . . . You may well say that they are similar to those of most companies. The difference, in my opinion, is that IKEA is much better at delivering on these customer needs than are other retailers . . . Most competitors focus on one or at most two of these customer needs. High-street shops focus on design and inspiration. Out-of-town low-cost retailers focus on price. Department stores focus on choice. The real strength of IKEA lies in the combination of all five.[5]

IKEA's competitive strategy

Dahlvig explained IKEA's approach to competition:

'You can choose to adapt your company's product range to the markets you are operating in, or you can choose to shift the market's preference towards your own range and style. IKEA has chosen the latter. By doing this, the company can maintain a unique and distinct profile.

This is, however, a more difficult path to follow.'[6] '. . . A significant understanding of the customer's situation at home is the basis for IKEA's product development and the creation of the main media through which the product is presented to the public.'[7] '. . . For most competitors, having the lowest price seems to mean being 5 to 10 per cent cheaper than the competition on comparable products. At IKEA, this means being a minimum 20 per cent cheaper and often up to 50 per cent cheaper than the competition.'[8]

Global expansion

By 1999 IKEA was operating 158 stores in 29 countries with a turnover the equivalent of €7.6 bn. Despite IKEA's strong global position Dahlvig felt there was much opportunity and need for improvement:

'So far growth has come from going "wide but thin". We have stores in 29 countries but with limited market share in most markets. Now we enter a new phase where the focus will be to go "deep" and concentrate on our existing markets . . . We shall focus on continued strong volume growth, 10 per cent pa for 10 years.'[9]

He explained his reasoning:

'Why make the change? First of all, we were impelled by the changing character of the competition. For many years, the competition had been very fragmented and local in nature. However, many of the very big retail companies were shifting strategy. From being local, they were looking to a global expansion, not least in the emerging markets like China, Russia and Eastern Europe. They were also broadening their product range, moving away from food or traditional DIY products towards more home furnishing. These were big companies with much more muscle than IKEA's traditional competitors. They had both financial resources and operational retailing competence on a par with IKEA. One way to dissuade them from entering into the home furnishing arena was to aggressively reduce prices and increase the company's presence with more stores in all local markets in the countries where IKEA was operating. Market leadership in each market was the objective. Another reason for the shift in strategy was cost efficiency. Growing sales in existing stores is the most cost-efficient way to grow the company.'[10]

Managing the value chain

Dahlvig explained that IKEA's strategy crucially requires the 'design' and control of IKEA's wider value chain in detail:

'The secret is the control and coordination of the whole value chain from raw material, production, and range development, to distribution into stores. Most other companies working in the retail sector have control either of the retail end (stores and distribution) or the product design and production end. IKEA's vertical integration makes it a complex company compared to most, since it owns both production, range development, distribution, and stores.'[11]
... This included backward integration by extending the activities of Swedwood (IKEA's manufacturing arm) beyond furniture factories, into control over the raw materials, saw mills, board suppliers, and component factories.'[12]

'(The challenge) ... is how to combine strong specialist functions within "one" company view and approach ... differentiation through controlling the whole value chain is key to success. There are some very important factors that have helped keep the company together: a strong vision, the business idea, company values, a common store concept, a common product range, and a common distribution and buying organisation.'[13]

'The one disappointment (in my 10 years) was that the cost level did not decrease as much as planned. We'd needed productivity gains of 10 per cent pa or more, and we managed only around a 4 to 6 per cent. Better than planned margins compensated for this, and thus the profit level was in line with the plan. Nevertheless, a low price company must be a low cost company.'[14]

China and India

IKEA first opened in China in 1998 and it had eight stores by 2012. The Chinese market was extremely challenging for a company that had built global success through standardisation.[15] The main problems were that in developing markets IKEA products were expensive relative to local competitors and the consumer shopping expectations were centred on small, local shops and personal service. So inevitably there had to be some flexibility in approach by IKEA. For example, it presented an image as exclusive Western European interior design specialists – popular with younger, affluent, city dwellers. The shops were smaller than usual for IKEA and typically nearer city centres. Because DIY was not well developed in China IKEA offered home delivery and assembly services. Catalogues were only available *in store*. Crucially stores were allowed to source almost 50 per cent locally (against the company average of about 25 per cent) in order to keep prices competitive.

This experience would be useful when IKEA entered India. It was announced in 2012 that IKEA was to invest €1.5 bn in opening 25 stores over 15 to 20 years.[16]

New leaders but same formula?

Michael Ohlsson succeeded Dahlvig as CEO in 2009 – having already worked for IKEA for 30 years. The company commented: 'Mikael Ohlsson has strong implementation skills and is a great ambassador of the IKEA Culture. He is well suited to continue the change process that Anders Dahlvig has initiated.'[17]

Indeed, despite extremely challenging economic conditions the company's success continued, exceeding €25 bn sales by 2012. In September 2012 IKEA announced that Ohlsson would retire in 2013 and be succeeded by another internal appointee – Peter Agnefjäll (18 years at IKEA). Agnefjäll told Reuters that 'under his leadership, the company will increase the number of store openings between 20 and 25 every year, from 2014 to 2015.'[18]

So perhaps the IKEA approach still had a bright future?

Sources
1. 'Welcome inside 2011' from IKEA website: www.ikea.com.
2. Data in this section come from the IKEA website 2012 and from the DataMonitor report on Global Home Furnishings Retail Industry Profile (reference code: 0199-2243, publication date: April 2008).
3. Anders Dahlvig, *The Ikea Edge*, McGraw-Hill, 2011.
4. Reference 3, p. 65.

5. Reference 3, p. 62.
6. Reference 3, p. 63.
7. Reference 3, p. 63.
8. Reference 3, p. 74.
9. Reference 3, p. 120.
10. Reference 3, p. 123.
11. Reference 3, p. 75.
12. Reference 3, p. 83.
13. Reference 3, p. 95.
14. Reference 3, p. 124.
15. U. Johansson and A. Thelander, 'A standardised approach to the world? IKEA in China', *International Journal of Quality and Service Sciences*, vol. 1, no. 2 (2009), pp. 199–219.
16. Reuters, 23 June 2012.
17. IKEA press release, 24 April 2009.
18. Reported by www.valuewalk.com, 18 September 2012.

Questions

1 Identify where (in its value network) and how IKEA has achieved cost leadership.

2 Identify how IKEA has achieved differentiation from its competitors.

3 Explain how IKEA tries to ensure that its 'Hybrid' strategy remains sustainable and does not become 'stuck-in-the-middle'.

4 What are the lessons from China about IKEA's approach?

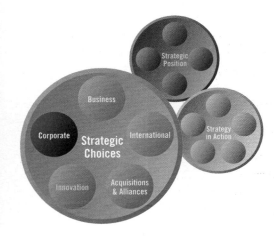

7

CORPORATE STRATEGY AND DIVERSIFICATION

Learning objectives

After reading this chapter, you should be able to:

● Identify alternative strategy options, including *market penetration*, *product development*, *market development* and *diversification*.

● Distinguish between different diversification strategies (*related* and *conglomerate* diversification) and evaluate *diversification drivers*.

● Assess the relative benefits of *vertical integration* and *outsourcing*.

● Analyse the ways in which a *corporate parent* can add or destroy value for its portfolio of business units.

● Analyse *portfolios* of business units and judge which to invest in and which to divest.

MyStrategyLab

MyStrategyLab is designed to help you make the most of your studies. Visit **www.pearsoned.co.uk/mystrategylab** to discover a wide range of resources, including:

● A personalised **Study plan** that will help you understand core concepts

● **Audio and video clips** that put the spotlight on strategy in the real world

● **Online glossaries and flashcards** that provide helpful reminders when you're looking for some quick revision.

(7.1) **INTRODUCTION**

Chapter 6 was concerned with *competitive strategy* – the ways in which a single business unit (SBU) or organisational unit can compete in a given market space, for instance through cost leadership or differentiation. However, organisations may choose to enter many new product and market areas (see Figure PII.1 in Part II introduction). Tata Group, one of India's largest companies, began as a trading organisation and soon moved into hotels and textiles. Since that time Tata has diversified further into steel, motors, consultancy, technologies, tea, chemicals, power, communications. As organisations add new units and capabilities, their strategies may no longer be solely concerned with *competitive strategy* in one market space at the business level, but with choices concerning different businesses or markets. These related choices include which business unit(s) to buy, the direction(s) an organisation might pursue and how resources may be allocated efficiently across multiple business activities. These choices, indicated in Figure 7.1, inform decisions about how broad an organisation should be. This 'scope' of an organisation is central to *corporate strategy* and the focus of this chapter.

Scope is concerned with how far an organisation should be diversified in terms of products and markets. As the opening example shows an organisation may increase its scope by engaging in market spaces or products different to its current ones. Section 7.2 introduces a classic product market framework which uses these categories for identifying different growth directions for an organisation. This indicates different *diversification* strategies open to an organisation, according to the novelty of products or markets. Underpinning diversification choices are a range of drivers, which are discussed in Section 7.3, including increasing market power, reducing risk and exploiting superior internal processes. The performance implications of diversification are, then, reviewed in Section 7.4.

Another way of increasing the scope of an organisation is *vertical integration*, discussed in Section 7.5. It allows an organisation to act as an internal supplier or a customer to itself (as

Figure 7.1 Strategic directions and corporate-level strategy

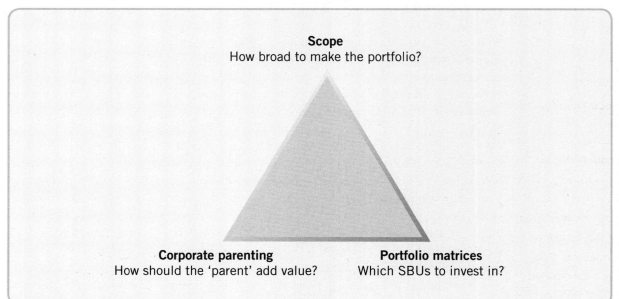

Scope
How broad to make the portfolio?

Corporate parenting
How should the 'parent' add value?

Portfolio matrices
Which SBUs to invest in?

for example an oil company supplies its petrol to its own petrol stations). The organisation may decide to *outsource* certain activities – to 'dis-integrate' by subcontracting an internal activity to an external supplier – as this may improve organisational efficiency. The scope of the organisation may therefore be adjusted through growth or contraction.

If an organisation has decided to operate in different areas of activity, head office executives, the 'corporate level', need to manage these to add value to the group. Section 7.6 discusses the value-adding effect of head office, termed **parenting advantage**, to the individual business units that make up the organisation's portfolio. How, then, do corporate-level activities, decisions and resources add value to the actual businesses? As will be seen in the Key Debate at the end of this chapter, there is considerable scepticism about the value-adding role of corporate-level strategy.

In order to decide which industries and businesses organisations should invest in or dispose of, the corporate centre needs to assess whether the *portfolio* of businesses is worth more under its management than the individual businesses would be worth standing alone. Section 7.7 reviews portfolio matrices, which are useful techniques to help structure corporate-level choices about businesses in which to invest and those to divest.

This chapter is not just about large commercial businesses. Even small businesses may consist of a number of business units. For example, a local building company may be undertaking contract work for local government, work for industrial buyers and for local homeowners. Not only are these different market segments, but the mode of operation and capabilities required for competitive success in each also likely to be different. Moreover, the owner of that business has to take decisions about the extent of investment and activity in each segment. Public-sector organisations such as local government or health services also provide different services, which correspond to business units in commercial organisations. Corporate-level strategy is also highly relevant to the appropriate drawing of organisational boundaries in the public sector. Privatisation and outsourcing decisions can be considered as responses to the failure of public-sector organisations to add sufficient value by their parenting.

(7.2) STRATEGY DIRECTIONS

The Ansoff product/market growth matrix[1] is a corporate strategy framework for generating four basic directions for organisational growth: see Figure 7.2 for an adapted version. Typically an organisation starts in the zone around point A, the top left-hand corner of Figure 7.2. According to Ansoff, the organisation may choose between *penetrating* still further within its existing sphere (staying in zone A) or increasing its diversity along the two axes of increasing novelty of markets or increasing novelty of products. This process of increasing the diversity of the range of products and/or markets served by an organisation is known as 'diversification'. **Diversification involves increasing the range of products or markets served by an organisation.** Related diversification **involves expanding into products or services with relationships to the existing business.** Thus on Ansoff's axes the organisation has two related diversification strategies available: moving to zone B, *developing new products* for its existing markets or moving to zone C by bringing its existing products into *new markets*. In each case, the further along the two axes, the more diversified is the strategy. Alternatively, the organisation can move in both directions at once, following a *conglomerate diversification* strategy with altogether new markets and new products (zone D). Thus **conglomerate (unrelated) diversification involves diversifying into products or services with no relationships to existing businesses.**

Figure 7.2 Corporate strategy directions

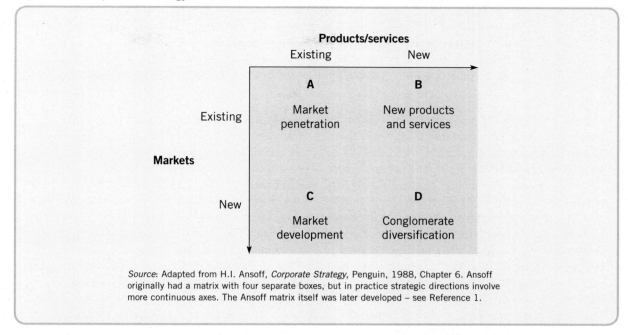

Source: Adapted from H.I. Ansoff, *Corporate Strategy*, Penguin, 1988, Chapter 6. Ansoff originally had a matrix with four separate boxes, but in practice strategic directions involve more continuous axes. The Ansoff matrix itself was later developed – see Reference 1.

Ansoff's axes can be used effectively in brainstorming strategic options, checking that options in all four zones have been properly considered. Illustration 7.1 traces the evolution of a social enterprise raising questions about how businesses might think about Ansoff's matrix in choosing their strategic direction. The next section will consider each of Ansoff's four main directions in some detail. Section 7.5 will examine the additional option of *vertical integration*.

7.2.1 **Market penetration**

For a simple, undiversified business, the most obvious strategic option is often increased penetration of its existing market, with its existing products. **Market penetration implies increasing share of current markets with the current product range.** This strategy builds on established strategic capabilities and does not require the organisation to venture into uncharted territory. The organisation's scope is exactly the same. Moreover, greater market share implies increased power vis-à-vis buyers and suppliers (in terms of Porter's five forces), greater economies of scale and experience curve benefits.

However, organisations seeking greater market penetration may face two constraints:

● *Retaliation from competitors.* In terms of the five forces (section 2.3.1), increasing market penetration is likely to exacerbate industry rivalry as other competitors in the market defend their share. Increased rivalry might involve price wars or expensive marketing battles, which may cost more than any market-share gains are actually worth. The dangers of provoking fierce retaliation are greater in low-growth markets, as any gains in volume will be much more at the expense of other players. Where retaliation is a danger, organisations seeking market penetration need strategic capabilities that give a clear competitive advantage. In low-growth or declining markets, it can be more effective simply to acquire competitors. Some companies have grown quickly in this way. For example, in the steel industry the Indian

ILLUSTRATION 7.1

Baking change into the community

How Greyston's diversification transforms a depressed community.

Probably best known for producing the brownies in the famous Ben and Jerry's ice creams, the Greyston Bakery is part of the Greyston Foundation – a $15 m (£9 m; €11.25 m) integrated network of for-profit and not-for-profit entities. The Foundation provides a wide array of services to benefit its local depressed community.

A Zen Buddhist meditation group started the bakery in 1982. They located in the poor neighbourhood of Yonkers, New York, where they perceived a need to create jobs for people in the community who were 'hard to employ' – the homeless, those with spotted employment histories, prison records and past substance-abuse problems. Radically they used an 'open hiring' practice that continues today, in which anybody who applies for a job has an opportunity to work, on a first-come, first-hired basis. Employees have to show up for work on time, perform the job, and have an appropriate attitude for three months and are then automatically made permanent employees. As SVP David Rome says, 'we judge people based on their performance in the operation, not on their background'. There is high initial turnover but the average tenure is about three years. Greyston considers it a success when an employee moves on to a new job using his or her new skills. According to CEO Julius Walls, 'The company provides opportunities and resources to its employees so they can be successful not only in the workplace but in their personal lives. We don't hire people to bake brownies; we bake brownies to hire people.'

As the bakery expanded it realised that providing jobs to the community was not enough. In 1991, working with governmental agencies, Greyston Family Inn was opened to provide permanent housing for homeless people. Currently there are three buildings, providing 50 housing units. A child daycare centre was also started with after-school care as one of the most pressing needs in the community for working parents to fill the gap left by public schools. In 1992 Greyston Health Services was formed, to help poor people with HIV/AIDS, and in 1997 Issan House opened with 35 permanent housing units for those with HIV/AIDS, mental illness or chemical dependency. Other ventures included Greyston Garden Project, five community-run gardens on neglected properties and a technology education centre. In 2011, a local retail bakery/café was opened and, in 2012, with the help of the Foundation's real-estate division, a new bakery was constructed, for $10 m in a public–private partnership project with the city, on a long dormant brownfield (contaminated) site.

The Foundation is an umbrella for all Greyston organisations, providing centralised management, fundraising, real-estate development, and planning services. It now comprises four interrelated organisations: bakery, healthcare services, child and family programmes, and real-estate development. The Foundation's social mission of supporting low-income people to forge a path to self-sufficiency and community transformation is blended with business collaboration to enable continual growth.

In 2012, Greyston Bakery celebrated its 30th anniversary, and received a fantastic present from New York State: to become a Benefit Corporation, allowing Greyston to demonstrate higher standards of corporate purpose, accountability and transparency. As Foundation CEO Steven Brown says, 'Really, we were a benefit corporation long before the term was coined. You're in business for a much larger community that has a stake in what you are doing. The extent that we can create value and opportunity is the path out of distress for many of these communities. It's not easy, but we're growing.'

Sources: www.greyston.org; http://www.pegasuscom.com/levpoints/ greystonint.html; http://www.huffingtonpost.com/jesse-seaver/ businesses-non-profit-social-enterprise; http://www.youtube.com/ watch?v=2WLzV7JfVSc.

Questions

1 What were the motivation(s) for Greyston Bakery's diversifications?

2 Referring to the Ansoff matrix, how would you classify these diversifications?

company LNM (Mittal) moved rapidly in the 2000s to become the largest steel producer in the world by acquiring struggling steel companies around the world. Acquisitions may reduce rivalry, by taking out independent players and controlling them under one umbrella.

- *Legal constraints.* Greater market penetration can raise concerns from official competition regulators concerning excessive market power. Most countries have regulators with the powers to restrain powerful companies or prevent mergers and acquisitions that would create such excessive power. In the United Kingdom, the Competition Commission can investigate any merger or acquisition that would account for more than 25 per cent of the national market, and either halt the deal or propose measures that would reduce market power. The European Commission has an overview of the whole European market and can similarly intervene. For example, when the German T-Mobile and French Orange companies proposed to merge their UK mobile phone operations in 2010, the European Commission insisted that the merged companies should divest a quarter of their combined share of the key mobile phone 1800 MHz spectrum.[2]

Market penetration may also not be an option where economic constraints are severe, for instance during a market downturn or public-sector funding crisis. Here organisations will need to consider the strategic option of *retrenchment*: withdrawal from marginal activities in order to concentrate on the most valuable segments and products within their existing business. However, where growth is still sought after, the Ansoff axes suggest further directions, as follows.

7.2.2 Product development

Product development is where organisations deliver modified or new products (or services) to existing markets. This can involve varying degrees of diversification along the horizontal axis of Figure 7.2. For Apple, developing its products from the original iPod, through iPhone to iPad involved little diversification: although the technologies differed, Apple was targeting the same customers and using very similar production processes and distribution channels. Despite the potential for benefits from relatedness, product development can be an expensive and high-risk activity for at least two reasons:

- *New strategic capabilities.* Product development strategies typically involve mastering new processes or technologies that are unfamiliar to the organisation. For example, the digital revolution is forcing universities to reconsider the way learning materials are acquired and provided to students and the nature of the student/academic interface. High-quality content available free online and virtual engagement with students now raise the question of how universities should consider redeploying their resources in the future. Success is likely to depend on a willingness to acquire new technological capabilities, to engage in organisational restructuring and new marketing capabilities to manage customer perceptions. Thus product development typically involves heavy investments and can have high risk of project failures.

- *Project management risk.* Even within fairly familiar domains, product development projects are typically subject to the risk of delays and increased costs due to project complexity and changing project specifications over time. An extreme example is Boeing's Dreamliner 787 aircraft: making innovative use of carbon-fibre composites, the Dreamliner had a history of delays even before launch in 2010, and required $2.5 bn (~ £1.75 bn) write-offs due to cancelled orders. Since then subsequent delamination of the aft fuselage and most recently batteries catching fire in 2013 resulted in fleets being grounded.

Strategies for product development are considered further in Chapter 9.

7.2.3 **Market development**

Product development can be risky and expensive. Market development can be more attractive by being potentially cheaper and quicker to execute. **Market development involves offering existing products to new markets.** Again, the degree of diversification varies along Figure 7.2's downward axis. Typically, of course, market development entails some product development as well, if only in terms of packaging or service. Nonetheless, market development remains a form of related diversification given its origins in similar products. Market development takes two basic forms:

- *New users.* Here an example would be aluminium, whose original users, packaging and cutlery manufacturers are now supplemented by users in aerospace and automobiles.
- *New geographies.* The prime example of this is internationalisation, but the spread of a small retailer into new towns would also be a case.

In all cases, it is essential that market development strategies be based on products or services that meet the *critical success factors* of the new market (see section 2.4.3). Strategies based on simply off loading traditional products or services in new markets are likely to fail. Moreover, market development faces similar problems to product development. In terms of strategic capabilities, market developers often lack the right marketing skills and brands to make progress in a market with unfamiliar customers. On the management side, the challenge is coordinating between different users and geographies, which might all have different needs. *International market development strategy is considered in Chapter 8.*

7.2.4 **Conglomerate diversification**

Conglomerate (or unrelated) diversification takes the organisation beyond both its existing markets and its existing products (i.e. zone D in Figure 7.2). In this sense, it radically increases the organisation's scope. Conglomerate diversification strategies can create value as businesses may benefit from being part of a larger group. This may allow consumers to have greater confidence in the business unit's products and services than before and larger size may also reduce the costs of finance. However, conglomerate strategies are often not trusted by many observers because there are no obvious ways in which the businesses can work together to generate additional value, over and above the businesses remaining on their own. In addition, there is often an additional bureaucratic cost of the managers at headquarters who control them. For this reason, conglomerate companies' share prices can suffer from what is called the 'conglomerate discount' – in other words, a lower valuation than the combined individual constituent businesses would have on their own. In 2012, the shares in French conglomerate Vivendi, with wide interests in mobile telephony and media, were trading down 25 per cent on the previous year and its break-up value was estimated as at least twice the value of the shares. At a shareholder meeting in Corsica in June, senior management stoked speculation when they said 'discussions about whether it should split up its businesses or sell off some assets were "not taboo"'.

However, it is important to recognise that the distinction between related and conglomerate (unrelated) diversification is often a matter of degree. Relationships that might have seemed valuable in related diversification may not turn out to be as valuable as expected. Thus the large accounting firms have often struggled in translating their skills and client contacts developed in auditing into effective consulting practices. Similarly, relationships may change in importance over time, as the nature of technologies or customers change: see, for example, the decision by Zodiac to divest itself of its iconic boat business (Illustration 7.2).

ILLUSTRATION 7.2

Zodiac deflates: from boats to aerospace

For 117 years the Zodiac Group has diversified and then re-centred through de-diversification.

The Zodiac Group is probably best known for its Zodiac inflatable boats, used by Jacques Cousteau and seen in harbours around the world. But by 2012, Zodiac was a world leader in aerospace equipment. How had this transformation come about?

The Zodiac company was founded in 1896 by Maurice Mallet after his first hot-air balloon ascent. Zodiac manufactured only dirigible airships for 40 years until 1937, when the German Zeppelin *Hindenburg* crashed near New York, abruptly halting the airship market. With its traditional activity extinguished, Zodiac decided to leverage its technical expertise and moved to inflatable boats. This proved to be very successful with over one million Zodiac rubber inflatables sold worldwide by 2004.

However, increasing competition from Italian manufacturers led Zodiac to diversify. In 1978, it acquired Aerazur, a company specialising in parachutes, life vests and inflatable life rafts. These products had strong market and technical synergies with rubber boats and their main customers were aircraft manufacturers. Zodiac confirmed this move to a new market in 1987 by taking over Air Cruisers, a manufacturer of inflatable escape slides for aeroplanes. As a consequence, Zodiac became a key supplier to Boeing, McDonnell Douglas and Airbus. This position was strengthened through takeovers of leading manufacturers of aeroplane seats: Sicma Aero Seats (France) and Weber Aircraft (USA) and MAG Aerospace, the world leader for aircraft vacuum waste systems. In 1999, Zodiac took over Intertechnique, a leading player in active components for aircraft (fuel circulation, hydraulics, oxygen and life support, electrical power, flight-deck controls and displays, systems monitoring, etc.). By combining these competences with its traditional expertise in inflatable products, Zodiac launched a new business unit: airbags for the automobile industry.

In parallel to these diversifications, Zodiac strengthened its position in inflatable boats by the takeover of several competitors: Bombard-L'Angevinière in 1980, Sevylor in 1981, Hurricane and Metzeler in 1987. The company also developed a swimming-pool business from its first product line, back in 1981, based on inflatable structure technology. Through takeovers Zodiac now produced rigid above-ground pools, modular in-ground pools, pool cleaners and water purification systems, inflatable beach gear and air mattresses.

However, by 2007, aircraft products accounted for 80 per cent of group turnover. For some airline equipment Zodiac held a 40 per cent market share globally and produced electrical power systems for the Airbus A380 and Boeing 787. Zodiac had even reached Mars: NASA Mars probes *Spirit* and *Opportunity* were equipped with Zodiac equipment.

In 2007 the marine and leisure businesses, which accounted for 19 per cent of turnover, were sold, with Chief Executive Jean-Louis Gérondeau saying 'this would reinforce Zodiac's acquisition capabilities, in the aerospace sector'. It was also a response to pressure from financial analysts, who considered Zodiac too diversified. The sale funded three further acquisitions of aircraft cabin equipment companies, Driessen, Adder and TIA in 2008, and Zodiac renamed itself Zodiac Aerospace. Although subject to a takeover bid from Safran, a French aeronautics group, in 2012, Zodiac rebuffed the bid and announced higher than expected profits of €319 m due to buoyant aerospace demand and two recent acquisitions (Heath Tecna Aircraft (interiors); Contour Aerospace (seats)). Re-pivoted, Zodiac is now a world leader in aerospace equipment and installed systems for commercial aircraft and helicopters.

Source: Based on an illustration by Frédéric Fréry, ESCP Europe Business School.

Questions

1 Explain the ways in which relatedness informed Zodiac's diversification strategy over time.

2 What are the advantages and potential dangers of its decision to focus on the aircraft products market?

(7.3) DIVERSIFICATION DRIVERS

Diversification might be chosen for a variety of reasons, some more value-creating than others.[3] Growth in organisational size is rarely a good enough reason for diversification on its own: growth must be profitable. Indeed, growth can often be merely a form of 'empire building', especially in the public sector. Diversification decisions need to be approached sceptically.

Four potentially value-creating drivers for diversification are as follows.

- *Exploiting economies of scope.* **Economies of scope refer to efficiency gains through applying the organisation's existing resources or competences to new markets or services.**[4] If an organisation has under-utilised resources or competences that it cannot effectively close or sell to other potential users, it is efficient to use these resources or competences by diversification into a new activity. In other words, there are economies to be gained by extending the scope of the organisation's activities. For example, many universities have large resources in terms of halls of residence, which they must have for their students but which are under-utilised out of term-time. These halls of residence are more efficiently used if the universities expand the scope of their activities into conferencing and tourism during holiday periods. Economies of scope may apply to both *tangible* resources, such as halls of residence, and *intangible* resources and competences, such as brands or staff skills.

- *Stretching corporate management competences ('dominant logics').* This is a special case of economies of scope, and refers to the potential for applying the skills of talented corporate-level managers (referred to as 'corporate parenting skills' in section 7.6) to new businesses. The **dominant logic is the set of corporate-level managerial competences applied across the portfolio of businesses.**[5] Corporate-level managers may have competences that can be applied even to businesses not sharing resources at the operating-unit level. Thus the French luxury-goods conglomerate LVMH includes a wide range of businesses – from champagne, through fashion, jewellery and perfumes, to financial media – that share very few operational resources or business-level competences. However, LVMH creates value for these specialised companies by applying corporate-level competences in developing classic brands and nurturing highly creative people that are relevant to all its individual businesses. See also the discussion of dominant logic at Berkshire Hathaway in Illustration 7.4 later.

- *Exploiting superior internal processes.* Internal processes within a diversified corporation can often be more efficient than external processes in the open market. This is especially the case where external capital and labour markets do not yet work well, as in many developing economies. In these circumstances, well-managed conglomerates can make sense, even if their constituent businesses do not have operating relationships with each other. For example, China has many conglomerates because it is able to mobilise internal investment, develop managers and exploit networks in a way that standalone Chinese companies, relying on imperfect markets, cannot. For example, China's largest privately owned conglomerate, the Fosun Group, owns steel mills, pharmaceutical companies and China's largest retailer, Yuyuan Tourist Mart.[6]

- *Increasing market power.*[7] Being diversified in many businesses can increase power vis-à-vis competitors in at least two ways. First, having the same wide portfolio of products as a competitor increases the potential for *mutual forbearance*. The ability to retaliate across the whole range of the portfolio acts to discourage the competitor from making any aggressive moves at all. Two similarly diversified competitors are thus likely to forbear from competing aggressively with each other. Second, having a diversified range of businesses increases the power to *cross-subsidise* one business from the profits of the others. On the one hand, the ability to cross-subsidise can support aggressive bids to drive competitors out of a particular market. On the other hand, knowing this power to cross-subsidise a particular business, competitors without equivalent power will be reluctant to attack that business.

Where diversification creates value, it is described as 'synergistic'.[8] **Synergy refers to the benefits gained where activities or assets complement each other so that their combined effect is greater than the sum of the parts** (the famous $2 + 2 = 5$ equation). Thus a film company and a music publisher would be synergistic if they were worth more together than separately – if the music publisher had the sole rights to music used in the film company productions for instance. However, synergies are often harder to identify and more costly to extract in practice than managers like to admit.[9]

Indeed, some drivers for diversification involve negative synergies, in other words value destruction. Three potentially value-destroying diversification drivers are:

- *Responding to market decline* is one common but doubtful driver for diversification. Rather than let the managers of a declining business invest spare funds in a new business, conventional finance theory suggests it is usually best to let shareholders find new growth investment opportunities for themselves. For example, Kodak (see Illustration 5.5 in Chapter 5), the US photo film corporation, spent billions of dollars on diversification acquisitions such as chemicals, desktop radiotherapy, photocopiers, telecommunications and inkjet printers in order to compensate for market decline in its main product. Many of these initiatives failed and the decline of the core business continued until Kodak went bankrupt. Shareholders might have preferred Kodak simply to hand back the large surpluses generated for decades beforehand rather than spending on costly acquisitions. If shareholders had wanted to invest in the chemicals, telecommunications or printers, they could have invested in the original dominant companies themselves.

- *Spreading risk* across a range of markets is another common justification for diversification. Again, conventional finance theory is very sceptical about risk-spreading by diversification. Shareholders can easily spread their risk by taking small stakes in dozens of very different companies themselves. Diversification strategies, on the other hand, are likely to involve a limited range of fairly related markets. While managers might like the security of having more than one market, shareholders typically do not need each of the companies they invest in to be diversified as well – they would prefer managers to concentrate on managing their core business as well as they can. However, conventional finance theory does not apply to private businesses, where the owners have a large proportion of their assets tied up in their company: here it can make sense to diversify risk across a number of distinct activities, so that if one part is in trouble, the whole business is not pulled down.

- *Managerial ambition* can sometimes drive inappropriate diversification. It is argued that the managers of British banks such as Royal Bank of Scotland (at one point the fifth-largest bank in the world) and HBOS (Britain's largest housing-lender) promoted strategies of excessive growth and diversification into new markets during the first decade of the twenty-first century. Such growth and diversification gave the managers short-term benefits in terms of managerial bonuses and prestige. But going beyond their areas of true expertise soon brought financial disaster, leading to the nationalisation of RBS and the takeover of HBOS by rival bank Lloyds.

(7.4) DIVERSIFICATION AND PERFORMANCE

Because most large corporations today are diversified, but also because diversification can sometimes be in management's self-interest, many scholars and policy-makers have been concerned to establish whether diversified companies really perform better than undiversified companies. After all, it would be deeply troubling if large corporations were diversifying simply to spread risk for managers, to save managerial jobs in declining businesses or to generate short-term growth, as in the case of RBS and HBOS.

Research studies of diversification have particularly focused on the relative benefits of related diversification and conglomerate or unrelated diversification. Researchers generally find that related or limited diversifiers outperform both firms that remain specialised and those that have unrelated or extensively diversified strategies.[10] In other words, the diversification–performance relationship tends to follow an inverted (or upside-down) U-shape, as in Figure 7.3. The implication is that some diversification is good – but not too much.

However, these performance studies produce statistical averages. Some related diversification strategies fail – as in the case of some accounting firms' ventures in consulting – while some conglomerates succeed – as in the case of LVMH. The case against unrelated diversification is not solid, and effective dominant logics or particular national contexts can play in its favour. For instance, conglomerate diversification may be particularly effective in developing economies as a form of protection against institutional weaknesses such as poor law enforcement, lack of quality labour, capricious political contexts. The conclusion from the performance studies is that, although on average related diversification pays better than unrelated, any diversification strategy needs rigorous questioning on its particular merits.

Figure 7.3 Diversity and performance

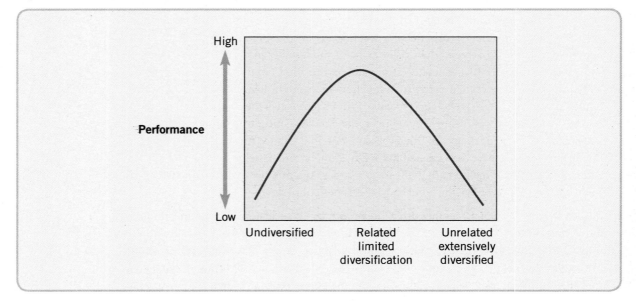

(7.5) VERTICAL INTEGRATION

As well as diversification, another direction for corporate strategy can be vertical integration. **Vertical integration describes entering activities where the organisation is its own supplier or customer.** Thus it involves operating at another stage of the value network (see section 3.4.2). This section considers both vertical integration and vertical dis-integration, particularly in the form of outsourcing.

7.5.1 Forward and backward integration

Vertical integration can go in either of two directions:

- **Backward integration** refers to development into activities concerned with the inputs into the company's current business (i.e. they are further back in the value network). For example, the acquisition by a car manufacturer of a component supplier would be a backward integration move.

- **Forward integration** refers to development into activities concerned with the outputs of a company's current business (i.e. are further forward in the value network). For a car manufacturer, forward integration would be into car retail, repairs and servicing.

Thus vertical integration is like diversification in increasing corporate scope. The difference is that it brings together activities up and down the same value network, while diversification typically involves more or less different value networks. However, because realising synergies involves bringing together different value networks, diversification (especially related diversification) is sometimes also described as *horizontal integration*. For example, a company diversified in cars, trucks and buses could find benefits in integrating aspects of the various design or component-sourcing processes. The relationship between horizontal integration and vertical integration is depicted in Figure 7.4.

Vertical integration is often favoured because it seems to 'capture' more of the profits in a value network. The car manufacturer gains the retailer's profits as well. However, it is important to be aware of two dangers. First, vertical integration involves investment. Expensive investments in activities that are less profitable than the original core business will be unattractive to shareholders because they are reducing their *average* or overall rate of return on investment. Second, even if there is a degree of relatedness through the value network, vertical integration is likely to involve quite different strategic capabilities. Thus car manufacturers who forwardly integrate into car service and repair have found that managing networks of small service outlets is very different to managing large manufacturing plants. Growing appreciation of both the risks of diluting overall returns on investment and the distinct capabilities involved at different stages of the value network has led many companies in recent years to vertically *dis*-integrate.

7.5.2 To integrate or to outsource?

Where a part of vertically integrated operations is not adding value to the overall business, it may be replaced through outsourcing or subcontracting. **Outsourcing is the process by which activities previously carried out internally are subcontracted to external suppliers.** Outsourcing

Figure 7.4 Diversification and integration options: car manufacturer example

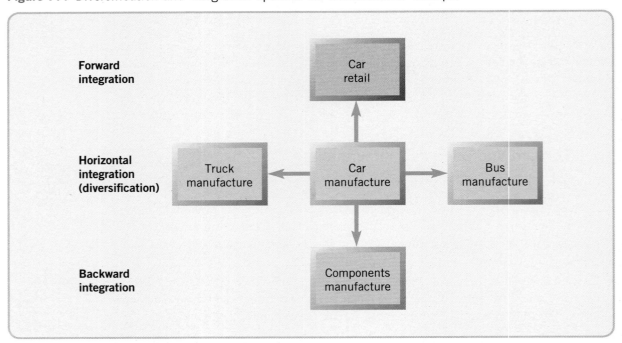

can refer to the subcontracting of components in manufacturing, but is now particularly common for services such as information technology, customer call centres and human resource management (see Illustration 7.3). The argument for outsourcing to specialist suppliers is often based on strategic capabilities. Specialists in a particular activity are likely to have superior capabilities than an organisation for which that particular activity is not a central part of its business. A specialist IT contractor is usually better at IT than the IT department of a steel company.

However, Nobel prize-winning economist Oliver Williamson has argued that the decision to integrate or outsource involves more than just relative capabilities. His *transaction cost framework* helps analyse the relative costs and benefits of managing ('transacting') activities internally or externally (see also the Key Debate at the end of this chapter).[11] In assessing whether to integrate or outsource an activity, he warns against underestimating the long-term costs of *opportunism* by external subcontractors (or indeed any other organisation in a market relationship). Subcontractors are liable over time to take advantage of their position, either to reduce its standards or to extract higher prices. Market relationships tend to fail in controlling subcontractor opportunism where:

- there are *few alternatives* to the subcontractor and it is hard to shop around;
- the product or service is *complex and changing*, and therefore impossible to specify fully in a legally binding contract;
- investments have been made in *specific assets*, which the subcontractors know will have little value if they withhold their product or service.

Both capabilities and transaction cost reasoning have influenced the outsourcing decisions of the Royal Bank of Scotland, see Illustration 7.3.

ILLUSTRATION 7.3

'Out of sight – out of mind'? Outsourcing at Royal Bank of Scotland

In 2012, Royal Bank of Scotland (RBS) experienced a major crisis when its customers could not withdraw cash. Was this the consequence of outsourcing?

In June 2012 RBS encountered severe problems when 10 million retail and business customers suddenly found they could not access their cash. This was highly damaging to the bank's reputation and could result in significant customer loss. The problem was faulty updating of CA-7 – critical software that controls the batch processing systems dealing with retail banking transactions. Generally regarded as 'a very common and reliable product, it processes accounts overnight via thousands of pieces of work' such as ATM transactions, bank-to-bank salary payments, and so on, and finishes by updating the account master copy with the definitive balance. Described as a huge game of Jenga (the tower game played with interlaced wood blocks), all transactions are related, so everything needs to be processed in order. Thus Tuesday's batch must run before Wednesday's to avoid, for example, penalising someone who has a large sum of money leave their account on Wednesday that might put them in debt but which would be covered by money arriving on Tuesday. In updating CA-7, files were deleted or corrupted so the master copy was wrong for three nights – meaning millions of transactions were not processed. RBS branches had to extend their opening hours to reassure customers about their accounts.

Unions argued the disaster was due to 'offshoring' UK IT jobs to India. 'RBS has 40 years' experience running this system and banks as a rule don't drop the ball like this', remarked one bank employee. However, the general banking crisis had pressured UK banks to reduce their costs. RBS, which had suffered badly from the banking crisis, let thousands of UK staff go and transferred their roles to Chennai, India. As one former employee complained, 'we were having to pass 10–20+ years worth of mainframe knowledge onto people who'd never heard of a mainframe outside of a museum . . .'.

Offshore outsourcing was once heralded as the saviour of UK IT departments, cutting costs without compromising quality. Thousands of IT jobs were axed in the name of 'efficiency', many outsourced to India with much lower wages than the UK. Indeed in February 2012 RBS advertised it was urgently seeking computer graduates with several years' experience of using CA-7.

However, India's staff attrition rates in 2012 were at an all-time high with people changing jobs very quickly for just a few extra rupees, leaving insufficient time for adequate cultural awareness training. Quality at call centres suffered. At the same time the UK was in recession with a devaluing pound greatly reducing wage disparity between India and the UK.

RBS's overseas problems were not uncommon with other banks experiencing loss of private data and in some instances criminal activity. Spanish-owned Santander UK – a bank created from Abbey National, Alliance & Leicester and Bradford & Bingley – also found that outsourced IT systems for these banks could not be trusted and so became the first of the major UK financial institutions to bring back its call centres and software from India to the UK, so that it could take care of its customer base. Ana Botin, Santander UK's Chief Executive, said the move was 'the most important factor in terms of satisfaction with the bank'. This 'inshoring' of strategic assets raises the question of whether strategic assets can afford to be 'out of sight and out of mind'.

Sources: http://www.guardian.co.uk/technology/2012/jun/25/how-natwest-it-meltdown; http://www.hrzone.co.uk/topic/business-life-style/shoring-new-shoring-call-centres-come-back-uk/112654.

Questions

1 In terms of transaction and capability costs, why might outsourcing be attractive to companies?

2 What might be the risks of 'insourcing'?

This transaction cost framework suggests that the costs of opportunism can outweigh the benefits of subcontracting to organisations with superior strategic capabilities. For example, mining companies in isolated parts of the Australian outback typically own and operate housing for their workers. The isolation creates specific assets (the housing is worth nothing if the mine closes down) and a lack of alternatives (the nearest town might be a hundred miles away). Consequently, there would be large risks to both partners if the mine subcontracted housing to an independent company specialising in worker accommodation, however strong its capabilities. Transaction cost economics therefore offers the following advice: if there are few alternative suppliers, if activities are complex and likely to change, and if there are significant investments in specific assets, then it is likely to be better to vertically integrate rather than outsource.

In sum, the decision to integrate or subcontract rests on the balance between two distinct factors:

- *Relative strategic capabilities*. Does the subcontractor have the potential to do the work significantly better?
- *Risk of opportunism*. Is the subcontractor likely to take advantage of the relationship over time?

(7.6) VALUE CREATION AND THE CORPORATE PARENT

Sometimes corporate parents are not adding value to their constituent businesses. Where there is no added value, it is usually best to divest the relevant businesses from the corporate portfolio. Thus in 2012 Rupert Murdoch of News Corporation announced the separation of the troubled newspaper and book publishing assets from the more valuable film and TV business – the latter contributed 90 per cent of group profits. The group could no longer add value to the former businesses, which were mired in public scandals, and these were also causing significant damage to the group's reputation as a whole. In the public sector too, units such as schools or hospitals are increasingly being given freedom from parenting authorities, because independence is seen as more effective. Some theorists even challenge the notion of corporate-level strategy altogether, the subject of the Key Debate at the end of this chapter. This section examines how corporate parents can both add and destroy value, and considers three different parenting approaches that can be effective.

7.6.1 Value-adding and value-destroying activities of corporate parents[12]

Corporate parents need to demonstrate that they create more value than they cost. This applies to both commercial and public-sector organisations. For public-sector organisations, privatisation or outsourcing is likely to be the consequence of failure to demonstrate value. Companies whose shares are traded freely on the stock markets face a further challenge. They must demonstrate they create more value than any other rival corporate parent could create. Failure to do so is likely to lead to a hostile takeover or break-up. Rival companies that think they can create more value out of the business units can bid for the company's shares, on the expectation of either running the businesses better or selling them off to other potential parents. If the rival's bid is more attractive and credible than what the current parent can promise, shareholders will back it at the expense of incumbent management.

In this sense, competition takes place between different corporate parents for the right to own and control businesses. In this 'market for corporate control', corporate parents must show that they have *parenting advantage*, on the same principle that business units must demonstrate competitive advantage. They must demonstrate that they are the best possible parents for the businesses they control. Parents therefore must have a very clear approach to how they create value. In practice, however, many of their activities can be value-destroying as well as value-creating.

Value-adding activities[13]

There are five main types of activity by which a corporate parent can add value:

- *Envisioning.* The corporate parent can provide a clear overall vision or *strategic intent* for its business units.[14] This vision should guide and motivate the business unit managers in order to maximise corporation-wide performance through commitment to a common purpose. The vision should also provide stakeholders with a *clear external image* about what the organisation as a whole is about: this can reassure shareholders about the rationale for having a diversified strategy in the first place. Finally, a clear vision provides a *discipline* on the corporate parent to stop its wandering into inappropriate activities or taking on unnecessary costs.

- *Facilitating synergies.* The corporate parent can facilitate cooperation and sharing across the business units, so improving the *synergies* from being within the same corporate organisation. This can be achieved through incentives, rewards, and remuneration schemes.

- *Coaching.* The corporate parent can help business unit managers develop strategic capabilities, by coaching them to improve their skills and confidence. Corporate-wide management courses are one effective means of achieving these objectives, as bringing managers across the business to learn strategy skills also allows them to build relationships between each other and perceive opportunities for cooperation.

- *Providing central services and resources.* The centre is obviously a provider of capital for *investment*. The centre can also provide central services such as treasury, tax and human resource advice, which if centralised can have *sufficient scale* to be efficient and to build up *relevant expertise*. Centralised services often have greater *leverage*: for example, combining the purchases of separate business units increases their bargaining power for shared inputs such as energy. This leverage can be helpful in *brokering* with external bodies, such as government regulators, or other companies in negotiating alliances. Finally, the centre can have an important role in managing expertise within the corporate whole, for instance by *transferring managers* across the business units or by creating shared *knowledge management* systems via corporate intranets.

- *Intervening.* Finally, the corporate parent can also intervene within its business units in order to ensure appropriate performance. The corporate parent should be able to closely *monitor* business unit performance and *improve performance* either by replacing weak managers or by assisting them in turning around their businesses. The parent can also *challenge and develop* the strategic ambitions of business units, so that satisfactorily performing businesses are encouraged to perform even better.

Value-destroying activities

However, there are also three broad ways in which the corporate parent can inadvertently destroy value:

● *Adding management costs.* Most simply, the staff and facilities of the corporate centre are expensive. The corporate centre typically has the best-paid managers and the most luxurious offices. It is the actual businesses that have to generate the revenues that pay for them. If their costs are greater than the value they create, then the corporate centre's managers are net value-destroying.

● *Adding bureaucratic complexity.* As well as these direct financial costs, there is the 'bureaucratic fog' created by an additional layer of management and the need to coordinate with sister businesses. These typically slow down managers' responses to issues and lead to compromises between the interests of individual businesses.

● *Obscuring financial performance.* One danger in a large diversified company is that the under-performance of weak businesses can be obscured. Weak businesses might be cross-subsidised by the stronger ones. Internally, the possibility of hiding weak performance diminishes the incentives for business unit managers to strive as hard as they can for their businesses: they have a parental safety-net. Externally, shareholders and financial analysts cannot easily judge the performance of individual units within the corporate whole. Diversified companies' share prices are often marked down, because shareholders prefer the 'pure plays' of standalone units, where weak performance cannot be hidden.[15]

These dangers suggest clear paths for corporate parents that wish to avoid value destruction. They should keep a close eye on centre costs, both financial and bureaucratic, ensuring that they are no more than required by their corporate strategy. They should also do all they can to promote financial transparency, so that business units remain under pressure to perform and shareholders are confident that there are no hidden disasters.

Overall, there are many ways in which corporate parents can add value. It is, of course, difficult to pursue them all and some are hard to mix with others. For example, a corporate parent that does a great deal of top-down intervening is less likely to be seen by its managers as a helpful coach and facilitator. Business unit managers will concentrate on maximising their own individual performance rather than looking out for ways to cooperate with other business unit managers for the greater good of the whole. For this reason, corporate parenting roles tend to fall into three main types, each coherent within itself but distinct from the others.[16] These three types of corporate parenting role are summarised in Figure 7.5.

7.6.2 The portfolio manager

The **portfolio manager** **operates as an active investor in a way that shareholders in the stock market are either too dispersed or too inexpert to be able to do.** In effect, the portfolio manager is acting as an agent on behalf of financial markets and shareholders with a view to extracting more value from the various businesses than they could achieve themselves. Its role is to identify and acquire under-valued assets or businesses and improve them. The portfolio manager might do this, for example, by acquiring another corporation, divesting low-performing businesses within it and intervening to improve the performance of those with potential. Such corporations may not be much concerned about the relatedness (see section 7.2) of the business units in their portfolio, typically adopting a conglomerate strategy. Their role is not to get closely involved in the routine management of the businesses, only to act over short periods of time to improve performance. In terms of the value-creating activities identified earlier, the portfolio manager concentrates on intervening and the provision (or withdrawal) of investment.

Figure 7.5 Portfolio managers, synergy managers and parental developers

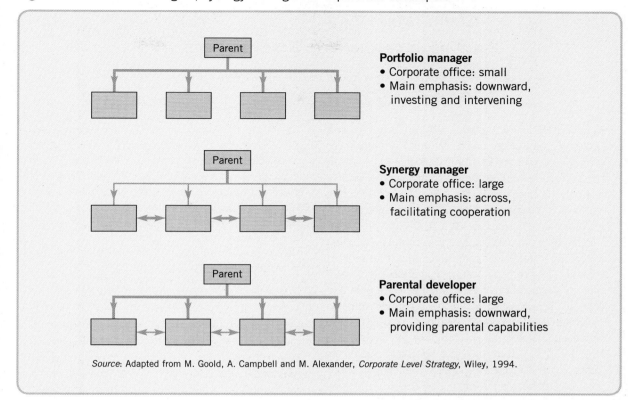

Source: Adapted from M. Goold, A. Campbell and M. Alexander, *Corporate Level Strategy*, Wiley, 1994.

Portfolio managers seek to keep the cost of the centre low, for example by having a small corporate staff with few central services, leaving the business units alone so that their chief executives have a high degree of autonomy. They set clear financial targets for those chief executives, offering high rewards if they achieve them and likely loss of position if they do not. Such corporate parents can, of course, manage quite a large number of such businesses because they are not directly managing the everyday strategies of those businesses. Rather they are acting from above, setting financial targets, making central evaluations about the well-being and future prospects of such businesses, and investing, intervening or divesting accordingly.

Some argue that the days of the portfolio manager are gone. Improving financial markets mean that the scope for finding and investing cheaply in under-performing companies is much reduced. However, some portfolio managers remain and are successful. Private equity firms such as Apax Partners or Blackstone operate a portfolio management style, typically investing in, improving and then divesting companies in loosely knit portfolios. For example, in 2012, Blackstone owned companies in power generation, water treatment, camera manufacture, banking, railway operation and seed development totalling more than 990,000 employees around the world. Illustration 7.4 includes a description of the portfolio parenting approach of Warren Buffett at Berkshire Hathaway.

7.6.3 **The synergy manager**

Obtaining synergy is often seen as the prime rationale for the corporate parent.[17] The **synergy manager is a corporate parent seeking to enhance value for business units by managing synergies**

ILLUSTRATION 7.4

Eating its own cooking: Berkshire Hathaway's parenting

A portfolio manager seeks to manage a highly diverse set of business units for shareholders.

Berkshire Hathaway's plain-speaking Chairman and CEO is Warren Buffett, one of the world's richest men. With annual sales of $162 bn (£97 bn; €121 bn) in 2012, Buffet founded this conglomerate with a small textile business in the early 1960s. Berkshire Hathaway's businesses now are highly diverse with large insurance businesses (GEICO, General Re, NRG), manufacturers of carpets, building products, clothing and footwear, retail companies and private jet service, NetJets. The company also has significant long-term minority stakes in businesses such as Coca-Cola and General Electric. Aged 83 in 2013, Buffett remains highly active with major acquisitions in 2009 (BNSF, the second largest railway company in the USA for $34 bn), 2011 (Lubrizol, the speciality chemicals company for $9 bn cash), 2013 (Heinz, purchased with 3G Capital Management, for $23.3 bn). Since the mid-1960s, Berkshire has averaged 19.7 per cent growth in book value per year.

Berkshire Hathaway annual reports explain how Buffet and Deputy Chairman Charlie Munger run the business:

'Charlie Munger and I think of our shareholders as owner-partners, and of ourselves as managing partners. (Because of the size of our shareholdings we are also, for better or worse, controlling partners.) We do not view the company itself as the ultimate owner of our business assets but instead view the company as a conduit through which our share-holders own the assets . . . In line with Berkshire's owner-orientation, most of our directors have a major portion of their net worth invested in the company. We eat our own cooking.'

Berkshire has a clear 'dominant logic':

'Charlie and I avoid businesses whose futures we can't evaluate, no matter how exciting their products may be. In the past, it required no brilliance for people to foresee the fabulous growth that awaited such industries as autos (in 1910), aircraft (in 1930) and television sets (in 1950). But the future then also included competitive dynamics that would decimate almost all of the companies entering those industries. Even the survivors tended to come away bleeding. Just because Charlie and I can clearly see dramatic growth ahead for an industry does not mean we can judge what its profit margins and returns on capital will be as a host of competitors battle for supremacy. At Berkshire we will stick with businesses whose profit picture for decades to come seems reasonably predictable. Even then, we will make plenty of mistakes.'

Buffett also explains how they manage their subsidiary businesses:

'We subcontract all of the heavy lifting to the managers of our subsidiaries. In fact, we delegate almost to the point of abdication: though Berkshire has about 257,000 employees, only 21 of these are at headquarters. Charlie and I mainly attend to capital allocation and the care of our key managers. Most are happiest when they are left alone to run their businesses, and that is just how we leave them. That puts them in charge of all operating decisions and of dispatching the excess cash they generate to headquarters. By sending it to us, they don't get diverted by the various enticements that would come their way were they responsible for deploying the cash their businesses throw off. Furthermore, Charlie and I are exposed to a much wider range of possibilities for investing these funds than any of our managers could find.'

Even after Heinz and other acquisitions Berkshire Hathaway still had a huge cash pile in 2013. The billionaire investor had his 'elephant gun loaded for a $15 bn acquisition' – a deal he was 'salivating' to do.

Questions

1 In what ways does Berkshire Hathaway fit the archetypal portfolio manager (see section 7.6.2)?

2 With $20 bn to invest, suggest industries and businesses Warren Buffett is likely never to invest in.

across business units. Synergies are likely to be particularly rich when new activities are closely related to the core business. In terms of value-creating activities, the focus is threefold: envisioning to build a common purpose; facilitating cooperation across businesses; and providing central services and resources. For example, at Apple, Steve Jobs' vision of his personal computers being the digital hub of the new digital lifestyle guided managers across the iMac computer, iPod, iPhone and iPad businesses to ensure seamless connections between the fast-developing offerings. The result is enhanced value through better customer experience. A metals company diversified into both steel and aluminium might centralise its energy procurement, gaining synergy benefits through increased bargaining power over suppliers.

However, achieving such synergistic benefits involves at least three challenges:

- *Excessive costs*. The benefits in sharing and cooperation need to outweigh the costs of undertaking such integration, both direct financial costs and opportunity costs. Managing synergistic relationships tends to involve expensive investments in management time.

- *Overcoming self-interest*. Managers in the business units have to want to cooperate. Especially where managers are rewarded largely according to the performance of their own particular business unit, they are likely to be unwilling to sacrifice their time and resources for the common good.

- *Illusory synergies*. It is easy to overestimate the value of skills or resources to other businesses. This is particularly common when the corporate centre needs to justify a new venture or the acquisition of a new company. Claimed synergies often prove illusory when managers actually have to put them into practice.

The failure of many companies to extract expected synergies from their businesses has led to growing scepticism about the notion of synergy. Synergistic benefits are not as easy to achieve as would appear. For example, in 2012 Hewlett Packard was forced to write down the value of its acquisition of Autonomy, a British software company, by €3.8 bn (£3 bn, $5 bn), as it failed to achieve anticipated integration benefits (the internal politics at HP associated with this decision are described in Illustration 12.4 in Chapter 12). Hewlett Packard blamed the former management team of Autonomy for fraudulent misrepresentation during the due diligence process. Nevertheless synergy continues to be a common theme in corporate-level strategy, as Illustration 7.2 on Zodiac exemplifies.

7.6.4 **The parental developer**[18]

The **parental developer seeks to employ its own central capabilities to add value to its businesses**. This is not so much about how the parent can develop benefits *across* business units or transfer capabilities between business units, as in the case of managing synergy. Rather parental developers focus on the resources or capabilities they have as parents which they can transfer *downwards* to enhance the potential of business units. For example, a parent could have a valuable brand or specialist skills in financial management or product development. If such parenting capabilities exist, corporate managers then need to identify a '*parenting opportunity*': a business which is not fulfilling its potential but which could be improved by applying the parenting capability, such as branding or product development. Such parenting opportunities are therefore more common in the case of related rather than unrelated diversified strategies and are likely to involve exchanges of managers and other resources across the businesses. Key value-creating activities for the parent will be the provision of central services and resources.

For example, a consumer products company might offer substantial guidance on branding and distribution from the centre; a technology company might run a large central R&D laboratory. There are two crucial challenges to managing a parental developer:

- *Parental focus.* Corporate parents need to be rigorous and focused in identifying their unique value-adding capabilities. They should always be asking what others can do better than them, and focus their energy and time on activities where they really do add value. Other central services should typically be outsourced to specialist companies that can do it better.

- *The 'crown jewel' problem.* Some diversified companies have business units in their portfolios which are performing well but to which the parent adds little value. These can become 'crown jewels', to which corporate parents become excessively attached. The logic of the parental development approach is: if the centre cannot add value, it is just a cost and therefore destroying value. Parental developers should divest businesses[19] they do not add value to, even profitable ones. Funds raised by selling a profitable business can be reinvested in businesses where the parent can add value.

(7.7) PORTFOLIO MATRICES

Section 7.6 discussed rationales for corporate parents of multi-business organisations. This section introduces models by which managers can determine financial investment and divestment within their portfolios of business.[20] Each model gives more or less attention to at least one of three criteria:

- the *balance* of the portfolio (e.g. in relation to its markets and the needs of the corporation);

- the *attractiveness* of the business units in terms of how strong they are individually and how profitable their markets or industries are likely to be; and

- the *'fit'* that the business units have with each other in terms of potential synergies or the extent to which the corporate parent will be good at looking after them.

7.7.1 The BCG (or growth/share) matrix[21]

One of the most common and longstanding ways of conceiving of the balance of a portfolio of businesses is the Boston Consulting Group (BCG) matrix (see Figure 7.6). The **BCG matrix uses market share and market growth criteria for determining the attractiveness and balance of a business portfolio.** High market share and high growth are, of course, attractive. However, the BCG matrix also warns that high growth demands heavy investment, for instance to expand capacity or develop brands. There needs to be a balance within the portfolio, so that there are some low-growth businesses that are making sufficient surplus to fund the investment needs of higher-growth businesses.

The growth/share axes of the BCG matrix define four sorts of business:

- A *star* is a business unit within a portfolio that has a high market share in a growing market. The business unit may be spending heavily to keep up with growth, but high market share should yield sufficient profits to make it more or less self-sufficient in terms of investment needs.

- A *question mark* (or problem child) is a business unit within a portfolio that is in a growing market, but does not yet have high market share. Developing question marks into stars, with high market share, takes heavy investment. Many question marks fail to develop, so the BCG advises corporate parents to nurture several at a time. It is important to make sure

Figure 7.6 The growth share (or BCG) matrix

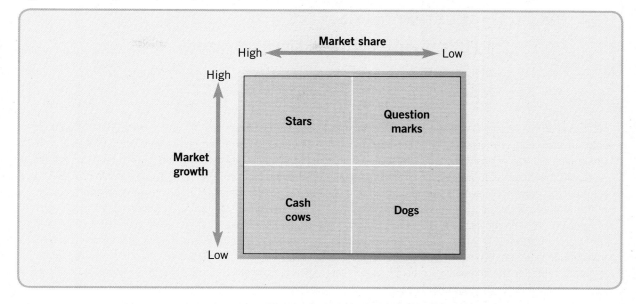

that some question marks develop into stars, as existing stars eventually become cash cows and cash cows may decline into dogs.

- A *cash cow* is a business unit within a portfolio that has a high market share in a mature market. However, because growth is low, investments needs are less, while high market share means that the business unit should be profitable. The cash cow should then be a cash provider, helping to fund investments in question marks.

- *Dogs* are business units within a portfolio that have low share in static or declining markets and are thus the worst of all combinations. They may be a cash drain and use up a dispro-portionate amount of managerial time and company resources. The BCG usually recom-mends divestment or closure.

The BCG matrix has several advantages. It provides a good way of visualising the different needs and potential of all the diverse businesses within the corporate portfolio. It warns corpor-ate parents of the financial demands of what might otherwise look like a desirable portfolio of high-growth businesses. It also reminds corporate parents that stars are likely eventually to wane. Finally, it provides a useful discipline to business unit managers, underlining the fact that the corporate parent ultimately owns the surplus resources they generate and can allocate them according to what is best for the corporate whole. Cash cows should not hoard their profits.

However, there are at least four potential problems with the BCG matrix:

- *Definitional vagueness.* It can be hard to decide what high and low growth or share mean in particular situations. Managers are often keen to define themselves as 'high-share' by defining their market in a particularly narrow way (e.g. by ignoring relevant international markets).

- *Capital market assumptions.* The notion that a corporate parent needs a balanced portfolio to finance investment from internal sources (cash cows) assumes that capital cannot be raised in external markets, for instance by issuing shares or raising loans. The notion of a balanced portfolio may be more relevant in countries where capital markets are under-developed or in private companies that wish to minimise dependence on external shareholders or banks.

ILLUSTRATION 7.5

ITC's diverse portfolio: smelling sweeter

Originally the Imperial Tobacco Company of India, ITC now has a portfolio stretching from cigarettes to fragrances.

ITC is one of India's largest consumer goods companies, with an increasingly diversified product portfolio. Its Chairman, Y.C. Deveshwar, describes its strategy thus: 'It is ITC's endeavour to continuously explore opportunities for growth by synergising and blending its multiple core competences to create new epicentres of growth. The employees of ITC are inspired by the vision of growing ITC into one of India's premier institutions and are willing to go the extra mile to generate value for the economy, in the process creating growing value for the shareholders.'

Founded in 1910 as the Imperial Tobacco Company of India, with brands such as Wills, Gold Cut and John Players, ITC now holds about two thirds of the market for cigarettes in India, with Philip Morris and BAT distant seconds with about 13 per cent each. However, cigarettes in India are highly discouraged by the Indian government, and increasingly heavily taxed.

ITC has a long diversification history. The company's original activities in the growth of leaf tobacco developed into a range of agricultural businesses, including edible oils, fruit pulp, spices and frozen foods. In the 1920s, ITC set up a packaging and printing business originally to supply its cigarette business. By 2012, this was India's largest packaging solutions provider. In 1975, ITC entered the hotel business, becoming the country's second largest operator with over 100 hotels by 2009, ranging from de luxe to economy. In 1979, the company also entered the paperboard industry, and three decades later was the country's largest producer.

The early twenty-first century saw many new diversification initiatives, especially in the booming Fast-Moving Consumer Goods (FMCG) sector. Initially it started in the food business, with Kitchens-of-India ready-to-eat gourmet foods, the *Aashirvaad* wheat-flour business, Sunfeast biscuits and Bingo snacks. ITC's own agri-businesses were an important source of supply for these initiatives. By 2008 *Aashirvaad* reached over 50 per cent Indian market share, and Sunfeast and Bingo had 12 and 11 per cent respectively. At the same time, ITC took advantage of the strong brand values

of its Wills cigarettes to launch Wills Lifestyle, a range of upmarket clothing stores, with its own designs. In 2009, Wills Lifestyle was recognised as India's 'Most Admired Fashion Brand of the Year'. In 2005, ITC launched its personal care business, again using its cigarette brand names: for example 'Essenza Di Wills' (fragrances) and 'Fiama Di Wills' (hair and skin care).

In 2012 Australia announced that cigarette manufacturers have to sell their produce in drab green packages with graphic pictorial warnings. Market research done by the Public Health Foundation of India and Hriday, a health awareness NGO, showed more than 80 per cent of people felt plain packaging would help reduce the attractiveness and appeal of tobacco products. India's Health Ministry officials warned such initiatives may be used in the future. With the cigarette industry facing systemic risk globally and manufacturer share prices being adversely affected, should ITC be concerned about its product portfolio?

ITC segmental sales and profits (Rs in Crores)

Segment	2011 sales	2011 profits	2009 sales	2009 profits
Cigarettes	22,250	6,907	15,115	4,184
Other FMCG	5,537	(195)	3,010	(483)
Hotels	996	279	1,014	316
Agribusiness	3,507	643	2,284	256
Paperboard, paper and packaging	2,579	936	1,719	509

5 Rs in Crores: ~ US $1,000,000; ~ €700,000. Profits are before interest and tax. Figures in brackets are losses.

Sources: ITC annual reports; M. Balaji, *ITC: Adding Shareholder Value through Diversifications*, IBSCDC, 2006; B. Gopal and S. Kora, *Indian Conglomerate ITC*, IBS Research Centre, 2009; *Business Standard*, 6 November 2012.

Questions

1 How well does ITC's portfolio fit in terms of the BCG matrix?

2 Identify and evaluate the various synergies in ITC's business.

- *Unkind to animals.* Both cash cows and dogs receive ungenerous treatment, the first being simply milked, the second terminated or cast out of the corporate home. This treatment can cause *motivation problems*, as managers in these units see little point in working hard for the sake of other businesses. There is also the danger of the *self-fulfilling prophecy.* Cash cows will become dogs even more quickly than the model expects if they are simply milked and denied adequate investment.

- *Ignores commercial linkages.* The matrix assumes there are *no commercial ties to other business units* in the portfolio. For instance, a business unit in the portfolio may depend upon keeping a dog alive. These commercial links are less important in conglomerate strategies, where divestments or closures are unlikely to have knock-on effects on other parts of the portfolio.

7.7.2 The directional policy (GE–McKinsey) matrix

Another way to consider a portfolio of businesses is by means of the *directional policy matrix*[22] which categorises business units into those with good prospects and those with less good prospects. The matrix was originally developed by McKinsey & Co. consultants in order to help the American conglomerate General Electric manage its portfolio of business units. Specifically, the directional policy matrix positions business units according to (i) how attractive the relevant market is in which they are operating, and (ii) the competitive strength of the SBU in that market. Attractiveness can be identified by PESTEL or five forces analyses; business unit strength can be defined by competitor analysis (for instance, the strategy canvas); see section 2.4.3. Some analysts also choose to show graphically how large the market is for a given business unit's activity, and even the market share of that business unit, as shown in Figure 7.7.

Figure 7.7 Directional policy (GE–McKinsey) matrix

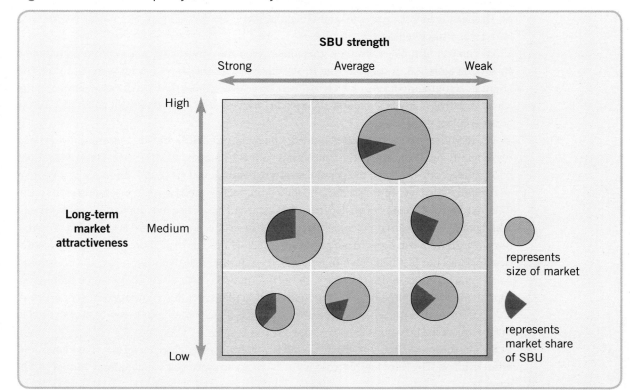

Figure 7.8 Strategy guidelines based on the directional policy matrix

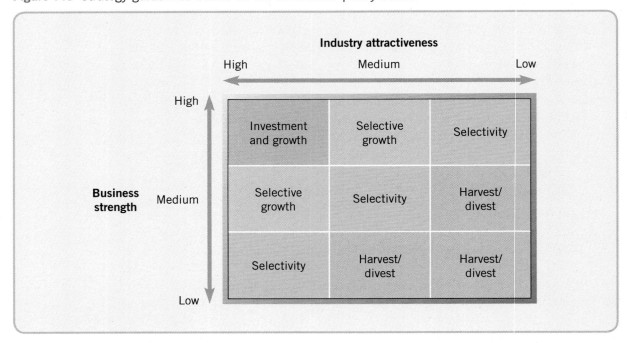

For example, managers in a firm with the portfolio shown in Figure 7.7 will be concerned that they have relatively low shares in the largest and most attractive market, whereas their greatest strength is in a market with only medium attractiveness and smaller markets with little long-term attractiveness.

The matrix also offers strategy guidelines given the positioning of the business units, as shown in Figure 7.8. It suggests that the businesses with the highest growth potential and the greatest strength are those in which to invest for growth. Those that are the weakest and in the least attractive markets should be divested or 'harvested' (i.e. used to yield as much cash as possible before divesting).

The directional policy matrix is more complex than the BCG matrix. However, it can have two advantages. First, unlike the simpler four-box BCG matrix, the nine cells of the directional policy matrix acknowledge the possibility of a difficult middle ground. Here managers have to be carefully selective. In this sense, the directional policy matrix is less mechanistic than the BCG matrix, encouraging open debate on less clear-cut cases. Second, the two axes of the directional policy matrix are not based on single measures (i.e. market share and market growth). Business strength can derive from many other factors than market share, and industry attractiveness does not just boil down to industry growth rates. On the other hand, the directional policy matrix shares some problems with the BCG matrix, particularly about vague definitions, capital market assumptions, motivation and self-fulfilling prophecy and ignoring commercial linkages. Overall, however, the value of the matrix is to help managers invest in the businesses that are most likely to pay off.

So far the discussion has been about the logic of portfolios in terms of balance and attractiveness. The third logic is to do with 'fit' with the particular capabilities of the corporate parent.

7.7.3 The parenting matrix

The *parenting matrix* (or Ashridge Portfolio Display) developed by consultants Michael Goold and Andrew Campbell introduces parental fit as an important criterion for including businesses in the portfolio.[23]

Businesses may be attractive in terms of the BCG or directional policy matrices, but if the parent cannot add value, then the parent ought to be cautious about acquiring or retaining them.

There are two key dimensions of fit in the parenting matrix (see Figure 7.9):

● 'Feel'. This is a measure of the fit between each business unit's critical success factors (see section 2.4.3) and the capabilities (in terms of competences and resources) of the corporate parent. In other words, does the corporate parent have the necessary 'feel', or understanding, for the businesses it will parent?

● 'Benefit'. This measures the fit between the parenting opportunities, or needs, of business units and the capabilities of the parent. Parenting opportunities are about the upside, areas in which good parenting can benefit the business (for instance, by bringing marketing

Figure 7.9 The parenting matrix: the Ashridge Portfolio Display

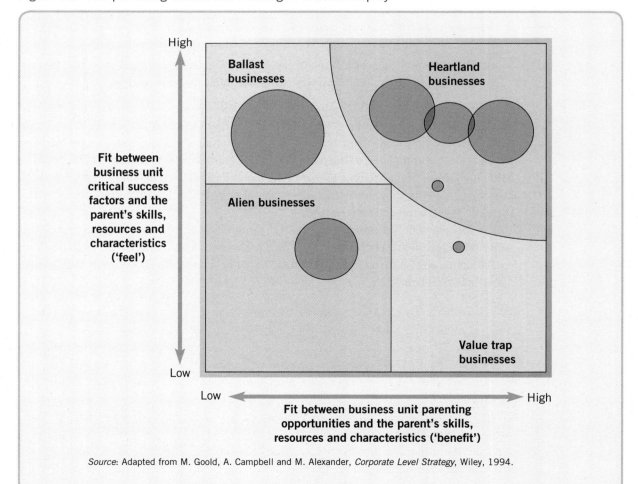

Source: Adapted from M. Goold, A. Campbell and M. Alexander, *Corporate Level Strategy*, Wiley, 1994.

expertise). For the benefit to be realised, of course, the parent must have the right capabilities to match the parenting opportunities.

The power of using these two dimensions of fit is as follows. It is easy to see that a corporate parent should avoid running businesses that it has no feel for. What is less clear is that parenting should be avoided if there is no benefit. This challenges the corporate parenting of even businesses for which the parent has high feel. Businesses for which a corporate parent has high feel but can add little benefit should either be run with a very light touch or be divested.

Figure 7.9 shows four kinds of business along these two dimensions of feel and benefit:

- *Heartland* business units are ones which the parent understands well and can continue to add value to. They should be at the core of future strategy.

- *Ballast* business units are ones the parent understands well but can do little for. They would probably be at least as successful as independent companies. If not divested, they should be spared as much corporate bureaucracy as possible.

- *Value trap* business units are dangerous. They appear attractive because there are opportunities to add value (for instance, marketing could be improved). But they are deceptively attractive, because the parent's lack of feel will result in more harm than good (i.e. the parent lacks the right marketing skills). The parent will need to acquire new capabilities if it is to be able to move value trap businesses into the heartland. It might be easier to divest to another corporate parent that could add value, and will pay well for the chance.

- *Alien* business units are clear misfits. They offer little opportunity to add value and the parent does not understand them anyway. Exit is definitely the best strategy.

This approach to considering corporate portfolios places the emphasis firmly on how the parent benefits the business units. This is the question that observers are asking of the Virgin Group in the end of chapter case. It requires careful analysis of both parenting capabilities and business unit parenting needs. The parenting matrix can therefore assist hard decisions where either high feel or high parenting opportunities tempt the corporate parent to acquire or retain businesses. Parents should concentrate on actual or potential heartland businesses, where there is both high feel and high benefit.

The concept of fit has equal relevance in the public sector. The implication is that public-sector managers should control directly only those services and activities for which they have special managerial expertise. Other services should be outsourced or set up as independent agencies (see section 7.5).

KEY DEBATE
Why have corporate-level strategies anyway?

Do we really need diversified corporations?

The notion of corporate strategy assumes that corporations should own and control businesses in a range of markets or products. But 'transaction cost' economist Oliver Williamson believes that diversified corporations should only exist in the presence of 'market failures' (see also section 7.5.2). If markets worked well, there would be no need for business units to be coordinated through managerial structures. Business units could be independent, coordinating where necessary by simple transactions in the marketplace. The 'invisible hand' of the market could replace the 'visible hand' of managers at corporate headquarters. There would be no 'corporate strategy'.

Market failures favouring the diversified corporation occur for two reasons:

- *'Bounded rationality'*: people cannot know everything that is going on in the market, so perfectly rational market transactions are impossible. Information, for instance on quality and costs, can sometimes be better inside the corporate fold.

- *'Opportunism'*: independent businesses trading between each other may behave opportunistically, for example by cheating on delivery or quality promises. Cheating can sometimes be policed and punished more easily within a corporate hierarchy.

According to Williamson, activities should only be brought into the corporation when the 'transaction costs' of coping with bounded rationality (gaining information) and opportunism (guarding against cheats) are lower inside the corporate hierarchy than they would be if simply relying on transactions in the marketplace.

This comparison of the transaction costs of markets and hierarchies has powerful implications for trends in product diversification:

- Improving capital markets may reduce the relative information advantages of conglomerates in managing a set of unrelated businesses. As markets get better at capturing information there will be less need for conglomerates.

- Improving protection of intellectual property rights may increase the incentives for corporations to license out their technologies to companies, rather than trying to do everything themselves. If the prospect of collecting royalties improves, there is less advantage for corporations keeping everything in-house.

Thus, fewer market failures also mean narrower product scope.

Williamson's 'transaction cost' view puts a heavy burden on corporations to justify themselves. Two justifications are possible. First, knowledge is hard to trade in the market. Buyers can only know the value of new knowledge once they have already bought it. Because they can trust each other, colleagues in different businesses within the same corporation are better at transferring knowledge than independent companies are in the open market. Second, corporations are not just about minimising the costs of information and cheating, but also about maximising the value of the combined resources. Bringing creative people together enhances knowledge exchange, innovation and motivation. Corporations create value as well as minimise cost.

Forty years of empirical research has failed to find unequivocal evidence of the under-performance of diversification although in sophisticated markets the prevailing view is that performance is an inverted 'U'-shape. Nevertheless successful conglomerates such as Berkshire Hathaway and 3M persist in developed markets and elsewhere, such as India and China, diversified businesses are common. The persistence of diversified firms as well as transaction cost economics suggests there is truth in the theory but this may not be whole picture.

Sources: O.E. Williamson, 'Strategy research: governance and competence perspectives', *Strategic Management Journal*, vol. 12 (1998), pp. 75–94; B. Kogut and U. Zander, 'What firms do? Coordination, identity and learning', *Organisation Science*, vol. 7, no. 5 (1996), pp. 502–19; Y.M. Zhou, 'Synergy, coordination costs, and diversification choices', *Strategic Management Journal*, vol. 32, no. 6 (2011), pp. 624–39.

Questions

1 Consider a diversified corporation such as Virgin (end of chapter case): what kinds of hard-to-trade knowledge might be transferred between product and country subsidiaries? Is this likely to be of increasing or decreasing importance?

2 Why might diversified corporations be more common in developing economies than the developed world?

SUMMARY

- Many corporations comprise several, sometimes many, business units. Corporate strategy involves the decisions and activities above the level of business units. It is concerned with the scope of the organisation.

- Organisational *scope* is often considered in terms of *related* and *unrelated* diversification.

- Corporate parents may seek to add value by adopting different parenting roles: the *portfolio manager*, the *synergy manager* or the *parental developer*.

- There are several portfolio models to help corporate parents manage their businesses, of which the most common are: the *BCG matrix*, the *directional policy matrix* and the *parenting matrix*.

- *Divestment* and *outsourcing* should be considered as well as diversification, particularly in the light of relative strategic capabilities and the transaction costs of *opportunism*.

WORK ASSIGNMENTS

✱ *Denotes more advanced work assignments.*
* *Refers to a case study in the Text and Cases edition.*

7.1 Using the Ansoff axes (Figure 7.2), identify and explain corporate strategic directions for any one of these case organisations: CRH*, Marks & Spencer*, SABMiller*.

7.2 Go to the website of any large multi-business organisation (e.g. Google, SABMiller*, Siemens, Tata Group, Virgin Group) and assess the degree to which its corporate-level strategy is characterised by (a) related or unrelated diversification and (b) a coherent 'dominant logic' (see section 7.3).

7.3 For any large multi-business corporation (as in 7.2), Marks & Spencer* or the Virgin Group, explain how the corporate parent should best create value for its component businesses (as portfolio manager, synergy manager or parental developer: see section 7.6). Would all the businesses fit equally well?

7.4✱ For any large multi-business corporation (as in 7.2), SABMiller* or the Virgin Group (end of chapter case), plot the business units on a portfolio matrix (e.g. the BCG matrix: section 7.7.1). Justify any assumptions about the relative positions of businesses on the relevant axes of the matrix. What managerial conclusions do you draw from this analysis?

Integrative assignment

7.5 Take a case of a recent merger or acquisition (see Chapter 10), and assess the extent to which it involved related or unrelated diversification (if either) and how far it was consistent with the company's existing dominant logic. Using share price information (see www.bigcharts.com or similar), assess shareholders' reaction to the merger or acquisition. How do you explain this reaction?

VIDEO ASSIGNMENTS

Visit *MyStrategyLab* and watch the SWAST case study for Chapter 7.

1 Using Figure 7.2 as a starting point, explain how the South Western Ambulance Trust has developed the strategic direction of its activities?

2 What changes in corporate-level strategy has SWAST had to introduce in order to combat the increasing threats in its environment? What further changes do you anticipate in the near future?

RECOMMENDED KEY READINGS

● An accessible discussion of corporate strategy is provided by A. Campbell and R. Park, *The Growth Gamble: When Leaders Should Bet on Big New Businesses*, Nicholas Brealey, 2005.

● M. Goold and K. Luchs, 'Why diversify: four decades of management thinking', in D. Faulkner and A. Campbell (eds), *The Oxford Handbook of Strategy*, vol. 2, Oxford University Press, pp. 18–42, 2003, provides an authoritative overview of the diversification option over time.

● L. Capron and W. Mitchell, *Build, Borrow or Buy: solving the growth dilemma*, Harvard Business Press, 2012, provides a good review of the arguments for and against different modes of growth.

● A good review of the current state of corporate portfolio management research is provided by M. Nippa, U. Pidua and H. Rubner, 'Corporate portfolio management: appraising four decades of academic research', *Academy of Management Perspectives*, November 2011, pp. 50–66.

REFERENCES

1. This figure is an extension of the product/market matrix: see I. Ansoff, *Corporate Strategy*, 1988, Chapter 6. The Ansoff matrix was later developed into the one shown below.

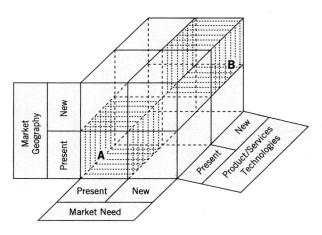

2. For the European Commission competition authority, http://ec.europa.eu/comm/competition; for the UK Competition Commission, see http://www.competition-commission.org.uk/.

3. For discussions of the challenge of sustained growth and diversification, see A. Campbell and R. Parks, *The Growth Gamble*, Nicholas Brealy, 2005; and D. Laurie, Y. Doz and C. Sheer, 'Creating new growth platforms', *Harvard Business Review*, vol. 84, no. 5 (2006), pp. 80–90.

4. On economies of scope, see D.J. Teece, 'Towards an economic theory of the multi-product firm', *Journal of Economic Behavior and Organization*, vol. 3 (1982), pp. 39–63.

5. See C.K. Prahalad and R. Bettis, 'The dominant logic: a new link between diversity and performance', *Strategic Management Journal*, vol. 6, no. 1 (1986), pp. 485–501; R. Bettis and C.K. Prahalad, 'The dominant logic: retrospective and extension', *Strategic Management Journal*, vol. 16, no. 1 (1995), pp. 5–15.

6. See C. Markides, 'Corporate strategy: the role of the centre', in A. Pettigrew, H. Thomas and R. Whittington (eds), *Handbook of Strategy and Management*, Sage, 2002. For a discussion of recent Chinese diversification patterns, see A. Delios, N. Zhou and W.W. Xu, 'Ownership structure and the diversification and performance of publicly-listed companies in China', *Business Horizons*, vol. 51, no. 6 (2008), pp. 802–21.

7. These benefits are often discussed in terms of 'multimarket' or 'multipoint' competition: see J. Anand, L. Mesquita and R. Vassolo, 'The dynamics of multimarket competition in exploration and exploitation activities', *Academy of Management Journal*, vol. 52, no. 4 (2009), pp. 802–21.

8. M. Goold and A. Campbell, 'Desperately seeking synergy', *Harvard Business Review*, vol. 76, no. 2 (1998), pp. 131–45. See also Y.M. Zhou, 'Synergy, coordination costs, and

diversification choices', *Strategic Management Journal*, vol. 32, no. 6 (2011), pp. 624–39.

9. A. Pehrson, 'Business relatedness and performance: a study of managerial perceptions', *Strategic Management Journal*, vol. 27, no. 3 (2006), pp. 265–82. See also F. Neffke and M. Henning, 'Skill relatedness and firm diversification', *Strategic Management Journal*, vol. 34, no. 3 (2013), pp. 297–316.

10. L.E. Palich, L.B. Cardinal and C. Miller, 'Curvilinearity in the diversification-performance linkage: an examination of over three decades of research', *Strategic Management Journal*, vol. 21 (2000), pp. 155–74. The inverted-U relationship is the research consensus, but studies often disagree, particularly finding variations over time and across countries. For recent context-sensitive studies, see M. Mayer and R. Whittington, 'Diversification in context: a cross national and cross temporal extension', *Strategic Management Journal*, vol. 24 (2003), pp. 773–81; and A. Chakrabarti, K. Singh and I. Mahmood, 'Diversification and performance: evidence from East Asian firms', *Strategic Management Journal*, vol. 28 (2007), pp. 101–20. There are also variations by type of diversification – see M. Geoffrey, G.M. Kistruck, I. Qureshi and P.W. Beamish, 'Geographic and product diversification in charitable organizations', *Journal of Management*, vol. 39, no. 2 (2011), pp. 496–530.

11. For a discussion and cases on the relative guidance of transaction cost and capabilities thinking, see R. McIvor, 'How the transaction cost and resource-based theories of the firm inform outsourcing evaluation', *Journal of Operations Management*, vol. 27, no. 1 (2009), pp. 45–63. See also T. Holcomb and M. Hitt, 'Toward a model of strategic outsourcing', *Journal of Operations Management*, vol. 25, no. 2 (2007), pp. 464–81.

12. For a good discussion of corporate parenting roles, see Markides in reference 6 above. A recent empirical study of corporate headquarters is D. Collis, D. Young and M. Goold, 'The size, structure and performance of corporate headquarters', *Strategic Management Journal*, vol. 28, no. 4 (2007), pp. 383–406.

13. M. Goold, A. Campbell and M. Alexander, *Corporate Level Strategy*, Wiley, 1994, is concerned with both the value-adding and value-destroying capacity of corporate parents.

14. For a discussion of the role of clarity of mission, see A. Campbell, M. Devine and D. Young, *A Sense of Mission*, Hutchinson Business, 1990.

15. E. Zuckerman, 'Focusing the corporate product: securities analysts and de-diversification', *Administrative Science Quarterly*, vol. 45, no. 3 (2000), pp. 591–619.

16. The first two rationales discussed here are based on M. Porter, 'From competitive advantage to corporate strategy', *Harvard Business Review*, vol. 65, no. 3 (1987), pp. 43–59.

17. See A. Campbell and K. Luchs, *Strategic Synergy*, Butterworth–Heinemann, 1992.

18. The logic of parental development is explained extensively in Goold, Campbell and Alexander (see reference 13 above). For more on the dynamics of organisational structure see J. Joseph and W. Ocasio, 'Architecture, attention, and adaptation in the multi-business firm: General Electric from 1951 to 2001', *Strategic Management Journal*, vol. 33, no. 6 (2013), pp. 633–60.

19. J. Xia, and S., Li, 'The divestiture of acquired subunits: a resource dependence approach', *Strategic Management Journal*, vol. 34, no. 2 (2013), pp. 131–48.

20. A good review of the current state of corporate portfolio management research is provided by M. Nippa, U. Pidua and H. Rubner, 'Corporate portfolio management: appraising four decades of academic research', *Academy of Management Perspectives*, vol. 25, no. 4 (2011), pp. 50–66.

21. For a more extensive discussion of the use of the growth share matrix see A.C. Hax and N.S. Majluf in R.G. Dyson (ed.), *Strategic Planning: Models and Analytical Techniques*, Wiley, 1990; and D. Faulkner, 'Portfolio matrices', in V. Ambrosini (ed.), *Exploring Techniques of Analysis and Evaluation in Strategic Management*, Prentice Hall, 1998; for source explanations of the BCG matrix see B.D. Henderson, *Henderson on Corporate Strategy*, Abt Books, 1979.

22. A. Hax and N. Majluf, 'The use of the industry attractiveness business strength matrix in strategic planning', in R. Dyson (ed.), *Strategic Planning: Models and Analytical Techniques*, Wiley, 1990.

23. The discussion in this section draws on M. Goold, A. Campbell and M. Alexander, *Corporate Level Strategy*, Wiley, 1994, which provides an excellent basis for understanding issues of parenting.

Strategic development at Virgin 2013

John Treciokas

Introduction

The Virgin Group is a highly diversified organisation with one of the best-known brands in the UK. Sir Richard Branson, Virgin's charismatic founder, who is one of the UK's richest and highly regarded entrepreneurs, leads the group. However, there are signs that Richard Branson may be stepping back from Virgin's businesses to concentrate on environmental and charity activities. This is causing concern about Virgin's future, as its strategy and business model are not widely understood. Investors are now questioning the extent to which the success of Virgin is due to Branson's entrepreneurial flair rather than the group's structure and business model.

The Virgin Group has grown over the years to become one of the largest private companies in the UK. It has more than 200 branded companies worldwide, employing around 50,000 employees in 34 countries with revenues in excess of £13 billion (approx. US $21 billion) in 2011. Richard Branson has always been integral to the growth of the company from its foundation to the present day. His flamboyant style and flair for publicity generate interest and awareness, which has enabled Virgin to create a brand image, that the group believes, adds value to any business that bears the Virgin name.

The Virgin Group is unusual in many ways, with a unique structure and distinctive image. However, questions are being raised about its sustainability. Does the parent company add value to the wide array of businesses in the group? Does the portfolio itself make strategic sense? It is also suspected the group struggles with profitability. Will the Virgin Group survive should Richard Branson depart?

Virgin's origins and style

The Virgin Group's beginnings can be traced to Richard Branson selling mail-order records in 1970 when he was just 20 years old. This allowed him to easily undercut high street retailers and the business experienced rapid growth. In 1971 Richard Branson opened an Oxford

Richard Branson

Source: Steve Bell/Rex Features.

Street store, which he named 'Virgin Records', to reflect his youth and naivety in business. Further expansion followed as he moved into record publishing with an instant hit album 'Tubular Bells', by unknown musician Mike Oldfield, in 1973. Virgin Records courted controversy by signing the Sex Pistols, a 'punk rock group' whose rude and anti-establishment behaviour brought plenty of public exposure. Risk-taking, optimism, irreverence and attracting publicity epitomised Branson's philosophy from the outset.

This philosophy was very visible when, in 1984, Richard Branson was inspired by an American lawyer to create a low-cost transatlantic airline – Virgin Atlantic. These routes were dominated by British Airways, and so began a long rivalry. When Virgin Atlantic managed to procure landing slots at Heathrow airport in 1991, this rivalry intensified leading to a 'dirty tricks' campaign by British Airways against Virgin Atlantic. The ensuing court battle, which Virgin won, was bitter and fought very publically in the media which often represented Virgin as the underdog fighting an oppressor.

Meanwhile Virgin Atlantic had huge financing needs with initial cash for operations coming from Virgin Records and its subsequent sale to EMI for £500 m. The group then needed an initial public offering of 35 per cent ownership of many Virgin businesses on the London and NASDAQ stock markets. This situation did not last long, however, as Branson's personality was not compatible with the accountability required of a chairman of a public corporation. In 1988 he bought out the external shareholders and returned the group to private ownership.

Virgin growth

Again a private company, the group grew rapidly, through a mixture of acquisitions, joint ventures and new start-ups (Appendix 1, below, lists a selection of new businesses).

Many of the new business initiatives seem to have been pure opportunism or on the whim of Richard Branson. For instance, in explaining why Virgin Records America was established in 1987, he commented: 'We were flying there a lot so it made sense to expand there too.' Since the early 1990s when the group was primarily involved in travel/holidays and music, it expanded into a wide range of businesses. For instance, the development of digital technologies allowed Virgin to grow its retail interests into online sales of music as well as many other products including cars, financial products and wine. The beginning of cellular communications and deregulation of the telecommunications sector in the UK led to the setting up of Virgin Mobile. Deregulation of the railways in the UK provided Virgin with the opportunity to form Virgin Rail, operating a passenger rail service on the West Coast of England, and deregulation in Australia and Nigeria allowed Virgin to set up other low-cost airlines. Branson was also drawn to markets where he perceived undue conservatism, a lack of innovation and an under-served customer. For instance, Virgin entered into health clubs (Virgin Active), biofuels (Virgin Fuels), drinks (Virgin drinks), clothing, cosmetics, comics,

weddings (Virgin Bride) and, in 2012, even a passenger service into suborbital space (Virgin Galactic). Commenting on this latest venture, Richard Branson said, 'Virgin is an adventurous company because I am an adventurer as well as an entrepreneur.' In the same year Virgin Money purchased Northern Rock, a medium-sized UK mortgage provider, from the government (which had nationalised the troubled company in the financial crisis of 2007). The move gave Virgin a much bigger stake in financial services – a growth area. The first new Virgin Money Store opened in July and by the end of the year 75 Northern Rock branches were rebranded to Virgin Money. Virgin paid £747 m for Northern Rock although commentators remarked it was an excellent deal for Virgin at the taxpayers' expense.

Since 2007 Richard Branson has become increasingly interested in environmental issues, launching the 'Virgin Earth Challenge' – to remove large amounts of carbon dioxide from the atmosphere; a 'People & Planet' initiative – to ensure all Virgin companies contribute to a sustainable society; Virgin Unite – to work with partners to improve social and environmental issues; and a Virgin Green Fund to invest in companies in the renewable energy and resource efficiency sectors. It seems that Branson is turning his attention to non-profit and corporate social responsibility issues.

Corporate rationale

In 2013 Virgin had the appearance of a very untraditional multi-business organisation. The group does not provide an organisational structure chart but a discernible grouping of business has become evident within five broad categories (see Figure 1). A cursory inspection of Figure 1 shows that these categories are very broad indeed, for

Figure 1

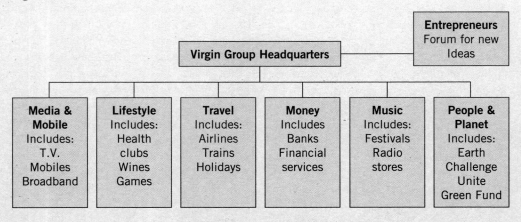

instance 'Lifestyle' includes health clubs, books, games and balloon flights!

The operating companies themselves are all separate entities, financed on a standalone basis. Indeed most of the companies are new start-ups and Branson's approach is for each to succeed within the first year or exit the market. The key rationale to whether Virgin backs a new venture is 'does an opportunity exist for restructuring a market and creating competitive advantage?' The group puts itself in the customer's shoes to see what it could make better. It also considers whether there could be beneficial interaction with other Virgin businesses.

Each business is 'ring-fenced', so that lenders to one company have no rights over the assets of another and financial results are not consolidated. Branson's view is that consolidating income and assets of the companies is misleading and irrelevant for a private company.

Virgin has a mix of privately owned and public listed companies as well as a mix of start-up small businesses and very large corporate ventures. Each may have very different strategic reasoning – some may be an attempt to keep Virgin in the public eye, some are 'anti-establishment' and others about offering customers a better and more fun alternative. The businesses might also be a method of training and developing managers. The larger start-ups are serious strategic moves into new industries.

Each company has no direct lines of reporting or control in a group with minimal management layers and no bureaucracy. This mirrors Richard Branson's disrespect for hierarchy and his preference for informality and individual responsibility from employees. Companies are linked through a complex network of parent subsidiary relations involving 'holding companies' with the ultimate holding company being registered in the British Virgin Islands – a tax haven. The group believes that the separation of businesses enables the group to retain a spirit of entrepreneurialism, which depends on the enthusiasm and commitment of its employees. The group states on its own website that Virgin is a 'leading branded venture capital organisation' and its companies are part of a family rather than a hierarchy. 'There is a tiny board and no massive global HQ, but it works for us!'

The managers of each business are given significant autonomy once the business is up and running. This embodies Branson's ethos of shaping and building businesses around people. Managers are trusted, have high levels of responsibility and have financial incentives that could turn them into millionaires – indeed one of Branson's proudest claims is the creation of many millionaire managers.

One commonality across all the businesses is the Virgin brand, which the group says is about being the consumer's champion for value for money, good quality, brilliant customer service, innovation, anti-establishment and fun. These attributes are the way in which the group differentiates its products and services. In a number of instances observers have commented that Virgin's ventures are driven more by fun than commercial logic. For instance, painting the Union Jack on Virgin Atlantic aircraft when British Airways removed theirs, or positioning an airship with the slogan 'BA can't get it up' over the London Eye, a giant Ferris wheel in central London, which BA was struggling to erect.

In addition to the brand, Richard Branson sees Virgin as adding value in three main ways. These are its public relations and marketing skills; its experience with 'greenfield' start-ups and Virgin's understanding of the opportunities presented by 'institutionalised' markets. Virgin sees an 'institutionalised 'market as one dominated by a few competitors who are not giving good value to customers because they have become inefficient, complacent or preoccupied with rivals. In addition, one might add that the group has an extensive network of contacts and partners.

There is a belief that any type of business could work if Virgin was able to leverage its distinctive capabilities to the new opportunity. There is also a shrewd sense of risk versus reward. As the company says, 'Virgin frequently creates partnerships with others and excels in combining skills, knowledge and operational expertise from a range of industries to build exciting and successful companies'. Virgin invites entrepreneurs to submit their business ideas for consideration and possible Virgin involvement. An example of this was the Virgin Group's move into clothing and cosmetics with an initial outlay of only £1,000 while its partner, Victory Corporation, invested £20 million.

Recent developments

Not all of Virgin's companies are successful and not all meet the standards of customer service that Virgin would like to see. Both Virgin Media and Virgin Rail have had many customer complaints and in the summer of 2012 Virgin Rail seemed to have lost its franchise on the West Coast railway line. Virgin managed to get this decision quashed as serious technical errors were made by the UK's Department of Transport. The company released a statement on 29 October 2012 stating the following:

'This will help ensure we deliver the best result for the passenger and taxpayer, as well as getting the best out of the private sector and the key role it plays in a successful UK rail system.'

Critics have suggested that Rail is a weakness in Virgin's portfolio and it will be interesting to see how committed Branson is to this business.

In February 2013 Liberty Global agreed to purchase Virgin Media for approximately £15 billion. Branson's own share of this was 2 per cent. Virgin will continue earning around £10 million a year for its 30-year brand-licensing agreement. To what extent Liberty will continue to use the Virgin brand and operational expertise is difficult to establish at this stage.

Much of Virgin's brand appeal is linked to Richard Branson himself, his antics, values and personality. His appeal to the British public is his sense of fair play and irreverence. In particular he has created an image of a 'cheeky entrepreneur' who has battled the mighty 'monopoly' of British Airways. But critics suggest that the Virgin brand may now be over-extended, have limited appeal internationally and the UK consumer may be beginning to tire of Richard Branson's stunts. The other lesser-known image of Richard Branson is one of a ruthless, crafty businessman always trying to get one over on his rivals.

It is difficult to discover the overall financial position of Virgin as it is made up of so many individual companies (many private and offshore) and there are no consolidated accounts. Investments in operating companies are also often transferred between group companies. Branson has argued that he pursues growth, not profits, and builds companies for the long term. The group emphasises maximising return to Virgin group equity through high financial leverage and the use of equity partners. None the less, Virgin Atlantic in 2011 posted an £80.2 m loss; Virgin America has yet to post an annual profit and in its first five years of trading made a loss of approximately $500 m. Virgin Media made a profit of £93 m in 2011, but its cumulative profit and loss account stands at a negative £3,259 m. Virgin Trains in the UK made a profit of £41 m in 2011.

In interviews Richard Branson does not mention his departure but states that the company has been carefully groomed to continue without him, and that the brand is now global and sufficiently well known such that his publicity stunts are no longer required. Richard Branson may now be allowing other people to guide the Virgin Group, but observers are divided about the nature of the group's business model with some seeing it as a private equity organisation (though many of the businesses are start-ups), or a branded venture capital organisation (but the group incubates its own businesses). Others suggest it might be a conglomerate but the group rarely makes acquisitions. Recent appointments at the very top of Virgin are former finance experts who are not renowned for the informal, collaborative and personal style epitomised by Richard Branson. If Sir Richard Branson steps aside, what will the future hold for the Virgin group – will it survive?

References and sources
T. Bower, *Branson*, Harper Perennial, 2008.
R. Branson, *Like A Virgin*, Virgin Books 2012.
The Economist, 'Virgin rebirth', 12 September 2008.
S. Goff, Retail Banking Correspondent, 8 January 2010.
J. Treanor, http://www.guardian.co.uk/profile/jilltreanor, city editor, *Guardian*, 1 January 2012.
Virgin Group's Corporate and Sustainable Development Report 2010.
http://www.businessweek.com, November 2007.
http://www.economist.com/blogs/schumpeter/2013/02/libertys-takeover-virgin-media.
http://www.ft.com/cms/s/0/a04c8138-f1f7-11e1-bba3-00144feabdc0.html#axzz2LHmLSkgB.
http://www.guardian.co.uk/media/2013/feb/06/virgin-media-takeover-john-malone-liberty-global.
http://www.redmayne.co.uk/research/securitydetails/financials.htm?tkr=VMED.
http://www.reuters.com, 16 December 2009.
http://www.virgin.com.

Questions

1 What directions of strategic development have been followed by Virgin over the period of the case (use Figure 7.2 as a guide)?

2 What is the corporate rationale for Virgin as a group of companies?

3 How does the Virgin Group as a corporate parent add value to its businesses? To what extent are these parenting skills relevant to the various businesses in the group?

4 What should the future corporate strategy be?

Appendix 1 Strategic developments of the Virgin Group 1970–2012

1970	Branson founds the Virgin business selling records
1971	First Virgin record shop opened
1977	Virgin record label is launched
1984	Virgin Atlantic, a long-haul airline is founded
1985	Virgin Holidays is founded
1986	Virgin Group PLC formed
1987	Virgin Records America is launched
1988–90	Virgin Megastores are opened in prime city locations in Europe, USA and finally Japan in a joint venture with Marui
	Branson takes Virgin Group PLC private for £248 m
1991	Virgin Publishing formed through merging Virgin Books and WH Allen PLC
	Virgin Games formed
1992	Virgin Records sold for £510 m
1993	Virgin Games floated as Virgin Interactive Entertainment PLC with Hasbro and Blockbuster taking minority stakes
	Virgin Radio commences broadcasting
1994	Virgin Retail acquires Our Price chain of shops
	Virgin Vodka and Virgin Cola are launched as joint venture with Cott Corp.
	Virgin City Jet service launched London to Dublin
1995	Virgin Direct launches a financial investment product in joint venture with Norwich Union
1996	Virgin Express Airline, a low-cost short-haul airline starts up
	Virgin Net an internet service provider is launched
1997	Virgin Trains is founded to run West Coast rail franchise in the UK
	Virgin Cosmetics launches with four flagship stores
	Virgin One telephone bank account launched in collaboration with Royal Bank of Scotland
	Virgin Bride retail chain formed
1999	Virgin Mobile is launched in joint venture with Deutsche Telekom
	Virgin Health starts a network of health clubs
	Virgin Cinemas is sold for £215 m
	49 per cent of Virgin Atlantic sold to Singapore Airlines for $500 m
2000	Virgin Mobile launches US wireless phone service (JV with Sprint)
	Virgin Mobile launches Australian wireless phone (JV with Cable and Wireless)
	Virgin Blue launched (low-cost airline – Australia)
	Virgin Cars launched to sell online
2001	50 per cent of Virgin Blue sold
2002	Virgin Bikes launched
2004	Virgin Digital launched to sell online music
2005	Virgin mobile launched in Canada
2006	Virgin acquires the Holmes Place chain of health clubs
	Virgin Media is launched in partnership with NTL-Telewest
	Virgin Mobile and Virgin Money launched in South Africa
	Virgin Fuel launched
	Virgin Cars closed
2007	Virgin Health Bank launched
	Virgin America (airline) launched
	Virgin Earth Challenge and World Citizen initiatives are launched
2008	Virgin Mobile launches in India in a joint venture with Tata Teleservices
2009	Virgin Green Fund launched
2010	Virgin Hotels launches
	Virgin Racing launched (Formula One)
	Virgin Gaming launched
	Virgin Produced launched (film and TV production company)
	Virgin Money US withdraws from the market
	Virgin Money acquires Church House Trust to acquire UK banking licence
2011	Virgin Cosmetics and Virgin Money (USA) are closed
	Virgin launches Virgin Oceanic, a deep-sea exploration submarine
	Virgin Active acquires Esporta for £80 m
	Virgin Unite (charitable foundation) launches Branson's Centre for Entrepreneurship
2012	Virgin Galactic completes hot-fire rocket tests and develops a revolutionary satellite launch vehicle

Source: Based on www.virgin.com.

8

INTERNATIONAL STRATEGY

Learning outcomes

After reading this chapter, you should be able to:

- Assess the *internationalisation potential* of different markets.

- Identify sources of competitive advantage in international strategy, through both exploitation of *local factors* and *global sourcing*.

- Understand the difference between *global integration* and *local responsiveness* and four main types of international strategy.

- *Rank markets* for entry or expansion, taking into account attractiveness, cultural and other forms of distance and competitor retaliation threats.

- Assess the relative merits of different *market entry modes*, including joint ventures, licensing and foreign direct investment.

MyStrategyLab

MyStrategyLab is designed to help you make the most of your studies. Visit **www.pearsoned.co.uk/mystrategylab** to discover a wide range of resources, including:

- A personalised **Study plan** that will help you understand core concepts
- **Audio and video clips** that put the spotlight on strategy in the real world
- **Online glossaries and flashcards** that provide helpful reminders when you're looking for some quick revision.

(8.1) INTRODUCTION

The last chapter introduced market development as a strategy, in relation to the Ansoff axes. This chapter focuses on a specific but important kind of market development, operating in different geographical markets. This is a challenge for many kinds of organisations nowadays. There are of course the large traditional multinationals such as Nestlé, Toyota and McDonald's. But recent years have seen the rise of emerging-country multinationals from Brazil, Russia, India and China. New small firms are also increasingly 'born global', building international relationships right from the start. Public-sector organisations too are having to make choices about collaboration, outsourcing and even competition with overseas organisations. European Union legislation requires public-service organisations to accept tenders from non-national suppliers.

Figure 8.1 identifies the five main themes of this chapter, with international strategy as the core. The themes are as follows:

- *Internationalisation drivers.* Drivers include market demand, the potential for cost advantages, government pressures and inducements and the need to respond to competitor moves. Given the risks and costs of international strategy, managers need to know that the drivers are strong to justify adopting an international strategy in the first place.

- *Geographical and firm-specific advantages.* In international competition, advantages might come from firm-specific and geographical advantages. Firm-specific advantages are the unique strategic capabilities proprietary to an organisation as discussed in Chapter 3.

Figure 8.1 International strategy: five main themes

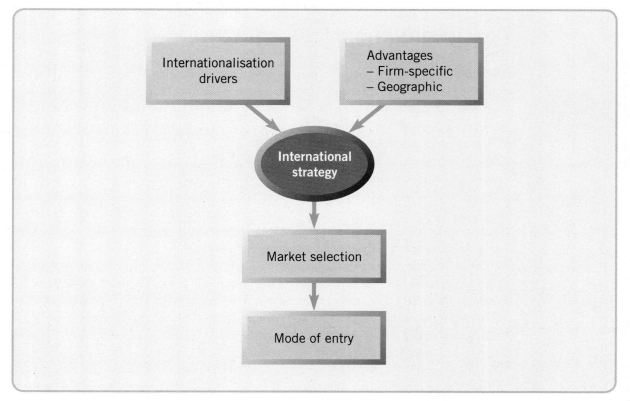

Geographical advantages might come both from the geographic location of the original business and from the international configuration of their value network. **Managers need to appraise these potential sources of competitive advantage carefully: if there are no competitive advantages, international strategy is liable to fail.**

- *International strategy.* If drivers and advantages are sufficiently strong to merit an international strategy, then a range of strategic approaches are opened up, from the simplest export strategies to the most complex global strategies.

- *Market selection.* Having adopted the broad approach to international strategy, the question next is which country markets to prioritise and which to steer clear of. The issues here range from the economic to the cultural and political.

- *Entry mode.* Finally, once target countries are selected, managers have to determine how they should enter each particular market. Again, export is a simple place to start, but there are licensing, franchising, joint venture and wholly owned subsidiary alternatives to consider as well.

The chapter takes a cautious view on international strategy. Despite the fashionable talk of increasing 'globalisation', there are many challenges and many pressures for localisation as well.[1] The chapter will therefore also consider the financial performance implications of growing internationalisation and the Key Debate at the end of this chapter considers the controversy around global, local and regional strategies.

The chapter distinguishes between international strategy and global strategy. **International strategy refers to a range of options for operating outside an organisation's country of origin.** Global strategy is only one kind of international strategy. **Global strategy involves high coordination of extensive activities dispersed geographically in many countries around the world.** This chapter keeps open alternative options to full global strategy.

8.2 INTERNATIONALISATION DRIVERS

There are many general pressures increasing internationalisation. Barriers to international trade, investment and migration are all now much lower than they were a couple of decades ago. Better international legal frameworks mean that it is less risky to deal with unfamiliar partners. Improvements in communications – from cheaper air travel to the internet – make movement and the spread of ideas much easier around the world. Not least, the success of new economic powerhouses such as the so-called BRICs – Brazil, Russia, India and China – is generating new opportunities and challenges for business internationally.[2]

However, not all these internationalisation trends are one-way. Nor do they hold for all industries. For example, migration is now becoming more difficult between some countries. Trade barriers still exist for some products, especially those relating to defence technologies. Many countries protect their leading companies from takeover by overseas rivals. Markets vary widely in the extent to which consumer needs are standardising – compare computer operating systems to the highly variable national tastes in chocolate. Some so-called multinationals are in fact concentrated in very particular markets, for example North America and Western Europe, or have a quite limited set of international links, for example in supply or outsourcing arrangements with just one or two countries overseas. In short, managers need to beware of 'global boloney', by which economic integration into a single homogenised and competitive world is wildly exaggerated (see the Key Debate at the end of this chapter). As in the Chinese retail market (Illustration 8.1), international drivers are usually a lot more

ILLUSTRATION 8.1

Chinese retail: global or local?

In China Carrefour and Walmart have found that internationalisation is not a simple process.

China is a magnet for ambitious Western supermarket chains. With an annual growth rate of 13 per cent a year, the Chinese market is expected to grow to $1.5 (€1.2) trillion in 2015 and 520 million people are expected to join the Chinese upper middle class by 2025.

Two leading Western companies in the Chinese retail market are French supermarket chain Carrefour and the world's largest retailer, the American Walmart. The two companies have had very different strategies. French supermarket chain Carrefour was the first to enter the Chinese market in a substantial fashion, entering in 1995, after six years' experience in neighbouring Taiwan. Although Walmart and Carrefour have expanded rapidly and are among the top 10 retailers in China (Carrefour has around 200 stores and Walmart more than 370), they are far from reaching saturation and are still tiny compared to their respective home countries, where they each have about 4,500 stores. Both chains have encountered challenges including problems adapting to local taste and local competition.

Carrefour is following a decentralised strategy: except in Shanghai, where it has several stores, Carrefour allows its local store managers, scattered across the many different regions of China, to make their own purchasing and supply decisions. In contrast, Walmart's initial approach had been based on its standard centralised purchasing and distribution strategy, supplying as much as it can from its new, state-of-the-art distribution centre in Shenzen. Walmart has, however, moved away from its headquarters-driven approach to give more sway to local store managers and has experimented with a smaller-scale local store format. One early discovery for Walmart was that Chinese consumers prefer frequent shopping trips in contrast to Walmart's home-based experience where customers drive to out-of-town stores and fill their cars with large multi-packs.

Another discovery for Western retailers is the amount of regional variation in this vast and multi-

ethnic country and the need to give their Chinese stores a local flavour. In the north of China, soya sauces are important; in central China, chilli pepper sauces are required; in the south, it is oyster sauces that matter. For fruit, northerners must have dates; southerners want lychees. In the north, the cold means more demand for red meat and, because customers are wearing layers of clothing, wider store aisles. Northerners do not have much access to hot water, so they wash their hair less frequently, meaning that small sachets of shampoo sell better than large bottles.

The growth of companies such as Carrefour and Walmart demonstrates that there is a substantial market for the Western retail model. Carrefour, for example, was a pioneer of 'private label' goods in China, while Walmart brings logistical expertise. But progress has been slow as home-grown companies have imitated and proven they often are more flexible and experimental with new store formats. Walmart turned to profit only in 2008 and has decided to slow down its expansion in China and Carrefour's 2–3 per cent margins are significantly below the nearly 5 per cent margins it enjoys in France. In 2011 local authorities accused Walmart of mislabelling ordinary pork as organic and closed down 13 stores for two weeks and Carrefour has repeatedly been obliged to deny that it was considering leaving China.

Sources: Financial Times, Wall Street Journal and Euromonitor (various).

Questions

1 What are the pros and cons of the different China strategies pursued by Carrefour and Walmart?

2 What might be the dangers for a large Western retailer in staying out of the Chinese market?

Figure 8.2 Drivers of internationalisation

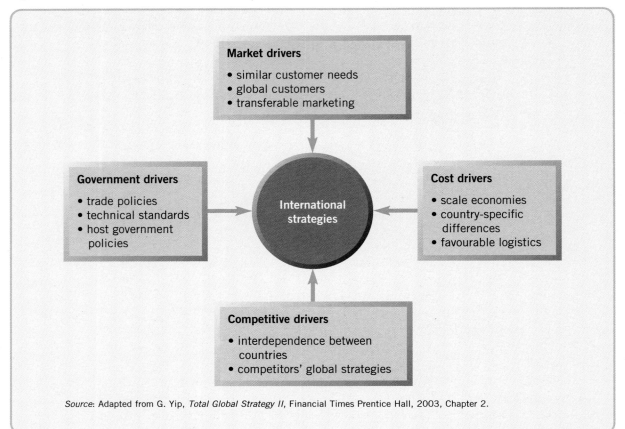

Source: Adapted from G. Yip, *Total Global Strategy II*, Financial Times Prentice Hall, 2003, Chapter 2.

complicated than that: Chinese markets not only are very different from Western ones, but vary widely within China itself.

Given internationalisation's complexity, international strategy should be underpinned by a careful assessment of trends in each particular market. George Yip provides a framework for analysing 'drivers of globalisation'. In the terms of this chapter, these globalisation drivers can be thought of as 'internationalisation drivers' more generally. In this book, therefore, **Yip's globalisation framework sees international strategy potential as determined by market drivers, cost drivers, government drivers and competitive drivers** (see Figure 8.2).[3] In more detail, the four drivers are as follows:

● *Market drivers*. A critical facilitator of internationalisation is standardisation of market characteristics. There are three components underlying this driver. First, the presence of *similar customer needs and tastes*: for example, the fact that in most societies consumers have similar needs for easy credit has promoted the worldwide spread of a handful of credit card companies such as Visa. Second is the presence of *global customers*: for example, car component companies have become more international as their customers, such as Toyota or Ford, have internationalised, and required standardised components for all their factories around the world. Finally, *transferable marketing* promotes market globalisation: brands such as Coca-Cola are still successfully marketed in very similar ways across the world.

- *Cost drivers.* Costs can be reduced by operating internationally. Again, there are three main elements to cost drivers. First, increasing volume beyond what a national market might support can give *scale economies*, both on the production side and in purchasing of supplies. Companies from smaller countries such as the Netherlands, Switzerland and Taiwan tend therefore to become proportionately much more international than companies from the USA, which have a vast market at home. Scale economies are particularly important in industries with high product development costs, as in the aircraft industry, where initial costs need to be spread over the large volumes of international markets. Second, internationalisation is promoted where it is possible to take advantage of variations in *country-specific differences*. Thus it makes sense to locate the manufacture of clothing in Africa or Bangladesh where labour is still considerably cheaper, but to keep design activities in cities such as New York, Paris, Milan or London, where fashion expertise is concentrated. The third element is *favourable logistics*, or the costs of moving products or services across borders relative to their final value. From this point of view, microchips are easy to source internationally, while bulky materials such as assembled furniture are harder.

- *Government drivers.* There are three main factors here that facilitate internationalisation. First, *reduction of barriers to trade and investment* has accelerated internationalisation. During the last couple of decades national governments have reduced restrictions on both flow of goods and capital. The World Trade Organization has been instrumental in reducing trade barriers globally.[4] Similarly, the emergence of regional economic integration partnerships like the European Union, the North American Free Trade Agreement and the Association of Southeast Asian Nations Economic Community has promoted this development. No government, however, allows complete economic openness and it typically varies widely from industry to industry, with agriculture and high-tech industries related to defence likely to be particularly sensitive. *The liberalisation and adoption of free markets* in many countries around the globe have also encouraged international trade and investments. This of course includes the collapse of the Soviet Union and liberalisation of Eastern Europe, China's free market reforms and market-based reforms in numerous Asian and South American economies. A third important government factor is *technology standardisation*. Compatible technical standards make it easier for companies to access different markets as they can enter many markets with the same product or service without adapting to local idiosyncratic standards.

- *Competitive drivers.* These relate specifically to globalisation as an integrated worldwide strategy rather than simpler international strategies. These have two elements. First, *interdependence* between country operations increases the pressure for global coordination. For example, a business with a plant in Mexico serving both the US and the Japanese markets has to coordinate carefully between the three locations: surging sales in one country, or a collapse in another, will have significant knock-on effects on the other countries. The second element relates directly to competitor strategy. The presence of *globalised competitors* increases the pressure to adopt a global strategy in response because competitors may use one country's profits to cross-subsidise their operations in another. A company with a loosely coordinated international strategy is vulnerable to globalised competitors, because it is unable to support country subsidiaries under attack from targeted, subsidised competition. The danger is of piecemeal withdrawal from countries under attack, and the gradual undermining of any overall economies of scale that the international player may have started with.[5]

The key insight from Yip's drivers framework is that the internationalisation potential of industries is variable. There are many different factors that can support it as indicated above, but others can inhibit it. For example, customer needs and tastes for many food products inhibit internationalisation of them and local governments often impose tariff barriers, ownership restrictions and local content requirements on foreign entrants. An important step in determining an internationalisation strategy is a realistic assessment of the true scope for internationalisation in the particular industry. In the Chinese retail case (Illustration 8.1), it may be that the Western entry both includes market and competitive drivers.

8.3 GEOGRAPHIC SOURCES OF ADVANTAGE

As for any strategy, internationalisation needs to be based on strategic capabilities providing a sustainable competitive advantage. This competitive advantage has usually to be substantial. After all, a competitor entering a market from overseas typically starts with considerable *dis*advantages relative to existing home competitors, which will usually have superior market knowledge, established relationships with local customers, strong supply chains and the like. A foreign entrant must have significant competitive advantages for it to overcome these inherent advantages of local competitors. Tesco's failure in the USA is an example of this. After seven years and investments of about £1 bn (€1.2 bn) in its US Fresh & Easy business Tesco was forced to withdraw. Unlike in the UK, Tesco had no significant competitive advantage over the strong US domestic retailers. Internationalisation thus requires building on the sources of sustainable competitive advantage that we have discussed earlier in Chapters 3 and 6 including the organisation's unique strengths in resources and capabilities. While these *firm- or organisation-specific advantages* are important, competitive advantage in an international context also depends on *country-specific or geographic advantages*.[6]

As is clear from the earlier discussion of cost drivers in international strategy, the geographical location of activities is a crucial source of potential advantage and one of the distinguishing features of international strategy relative to other diversification strategies. As Bruce Kogut at Columbia University has explained, an organisation can improve the configuration of its *value chain and system*[7] by taking advantage of country-specific differences (see section 3.4.2). There are two principal opportunities available: the exploitation of particular *locational advantages*, often in the company's home country, and sourcing advantages overseas via an *international value system*.

8.3.1 Locational advantage: Porter's Diamond[8]

Countries and regions within them, and organisations originating in those, often benefit from competitive advantages grounded in specific local conditions. They become associated with specific types of enduring competitive advantage: for example, the Swiss in private banking, the northern Italians in leather and fur fashion goods, and the Taiwanese in laptop computers. Michael Porter has proposed a four-pointed 'diamond' to explain why some locations tend to produce firms with sustained competitive advantages in some industries more than others (see Figure 8.3). Specifically, **Porter's Diamond suggests that locational advantages may stem from local factor conditions; local demand conditions; local related and supporting industries; and from local firm strategy structure and rivalry.** These four interacting determinants of locational advantage work as follows:

Figure 8.3 Porter's Diamond – the determinants of national advantages

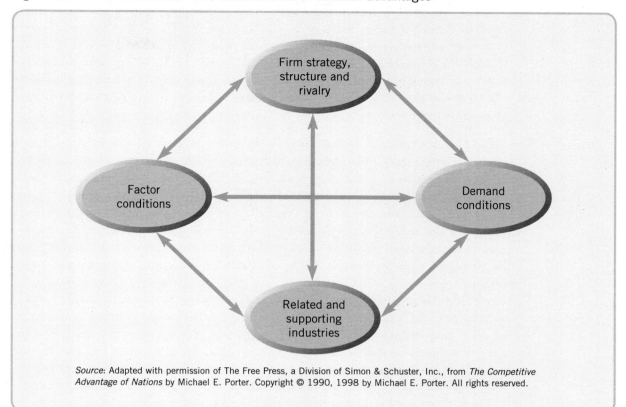

- *Factor conditions.* These refer to the 'factors of production' that go into making a product or service (i.e. raw materials, land and labour). Factor condition advantages at a national level can translate into general competitive advantages for national firms in international markets. For example, the linguistic ability of the Swiss has traditionally provided a significant advantage to their banking industry. Cheap energy has traditionally provided an advantage for the North American aluminium industry.

- *Home demand conditions.* The nature of the domestic customers can become a source of competitive advantage. Dealing with sophisticated and demanding customers at home helps train a company to be effective overseas. For example, America's long distances have led to competitive strength in very large truck engines. Sophisticated local customers in France and Italy have helped keep their local fashion industries at the leading edge for many decades.

- *Related and supporting industries.* Local 'clusters' of related and mutually supporting industries can be an important source of competitive advantage. These are often regionally based, making personal interaction easier. In northern Italy, for example, the leather footwear industry, the leatherworking machinery industry and the design services which underpin them group together in the same regional cluster to each other's mutual benefit. Silicon Valley forms a cluster of hardware, software, research and venture capital organisations which together create a virtuous circle of high-technology enterprise.

- *Firm strategy, industry structure and rivalry.* The characteristic strategies, industry structures and rivalries in different countries can also be bases of advantage. German companies' strategy of investing in technical excellence gives them a characteristic advantage in engineering industries and creates large pools of expertise. A competitive local industry structure is also helpful: if too dominant in their home territory, local organisations can become complacent and lose advantage overseas. Some domestic rivalry can actually be an advantage, therefore. For example, the long-run success of the Japanese car companies is partly based on government policy sustaining several national players (unlike in the United Kingdom, where they were all merged into one) and the Swiss pharmaceuticals industry became strong in part because each company had to compete with several strong local rivals.

Porter's Diamond model underlines the environmental conditions and structural attributes of nations and their regions that contribute to their competitive advantage. It has been used by governments aiming to increase the competitive advantage of their local industries. The argument that rivalry can be positive has led to a major policy shift in many countries towards encouraging local competition rather than protecting home-based industries. Governments can also foster local industries by raising safety or environmental standards (i.e. creating sophisticated demand conditions) or encouraging cooperation between suppliers and buyers on a domestic level (i.e. building clusters of related and supporting industries in particular regions).

For individual organisations, however, the value of Porter's Diamond is to identify the extent to which they can build on home-based advantages to create competitive advantage in relation to others internationally. To compete with local actors, organisations must carefully exploit the distinct environmental conditions and structural attributes illustrated in Figure 8.3. For example, Dutch brewing companies – such as Heineken – had an advantage in early internationalisation due to the combination of sophisticated consumers and limited room to grow at home. Volvo Trucks, the Swedish truck and construction equipment manufacturer, has achieved global success by building on a local network of sophisticated engineering partners and suppliers and a local demand orientated towards reliability and safety. Before embarking on an internationalisation strategy, managers should seek out sources of general locational advantage to underpin their company's individual sources of advantage.

8.3.2 The international value system

The sources of geographic advantage need, however, not be purely domestic. In addition, as companies continue to internationalise, the country of origin becomes relatively less important for competitive advantage.[9] For companies with most of their sales abroad, like the telecom giant Ericsson with 95 per cent of sales outside Sweden, the configuration of the local environments where they operate is at least as important as their domestic environment. This implies that for international companies, advantage also needs to be drawn from the international configuration of their *value system* (see section 3.4.2). Here the different skills, resources and costs of countries around the world can be systematically exploited in order to locate each element of the value chain in that country or region where it can be conducted most effectively and efficiently. This may be achieved through both foreign direct investments and joint ventures but also through **global sourcing: purchasing services and components from the most appropriate suppliers around the world, regardless of their location.** For example, in the UK for many years the National Health Service has been sourcing medical personnel from overseas to offset a shortfall in domestic skills and capacity. Smaller organisations can also build on the broader system of suppliers, channels and customers as demonstrated in Illustration 8.2.

ILLUSTRATION 8.2

The international 'Joint Effort Enterprise'

For Blue Skies international strategy is something more than profit alone.

Blue Skies specialises in producing fresh-cut fruit and juice products from a network of factories in Africa and South America. It supplies over 12 major European retailers, including Waitrose in the UK, Albert Heijn in the Netherlands and Monoprix in France. The company has factories in Ghana, Egypt, South Africa and Brazil. Its biggest factory is in Ghana and employs over 1,500 people and sources fruit from over 100 small to medium-sized farms. Blue Skies believes in value adding at source whereby the raw materials are processed within the country of origin rather than shipped overseas and processed elsewhere. By doing this, as much as 70 per cent of the value of the finished product stays within the country of origin, compared to as little as 15 per cent if it is processed outside.

Blue Skies works within a framework it has developed called the 'Joint Effort Enterprise' (JEE). While it is their model for a sustainable business, it is not a model which has been introduced to respond to the growing hype around 'sustainability'. Instead it is a set of principles from the foundation of the business in 1998 to ensure that the organisation would endure. The JEE is principally made up of three strands: a diverse society, a culture of respect and a drive for profit. The latter must not, however, come at the expense of all the other strands. Blue Skies believes that this model ensures that it retains the best people and conserves the resources they rely on, so that they can produce the best quality products and therefore generate the income that keeps the organisation going. Its approach is 'based on fairness in business, respect for each other and above all, trust'. In addition, Blue Skies raised over £400,000 (€480,000) in partnership with two European retailers and completed over 10 projects in Ghana and South Africa including the construction of schools, latrines and community centres. The Blue Skies JEE approach has also been awarded a Queens Award for Enterprise in the Sustainable Development Category in both 2008 and 2011.

During the last few years Blue Skies has encountered several international challenges: a world recession, rising energy prices, exchange rate volatility, shortage of raw materials, etc. It realises that these are challenges that an international operation across three continents must be ready and willing to respond to. Accordingly, it has undertaken a number of initiatives:

- Developing products for local and dollar-based markets to reduce exposure to exchange rate losses and supply chain disruption.
- Expanding its supply base around the world to ensure year-round supply of fruit.
- Helping its suppliers achieve agricultural standards such as LEAF (Linking Environment and Farming) to ensure sustainability of supply.
- Growing the Blue Skies Foundation to strengthen its relationship with staff, farmers and their communities.
- Developing plans to generate renewable energy to reduce electricity costs and greenhouse gas emissions.
- Opening a European-based contingency factory to ensure consistency of supply during supply chain disruption.

Source: Prepared by Edwina Goodwin, Leicester Business School, De Montfort University.

Questions

1 What internationalisation drivers (Figure 8.2) do you think were most important for Blue Skies' decision to enter its specific markets?

2 How does Blue Skies strategy fit into a broader international value system including suppliers, channels and customers (see also Figure 3.5)?

3 To what extent is JEE key to Blue Skies' international strategy and competitive advantage or rather a social entrepreneurship effort?

Different locational advantages can be identified:

- *Cost advantages* include labour costs, transportation and communications costs and taxation and investment incentives. Labour costs are important. American and European firms, for example, have moved much of their software programming tasks to India where a computer programmer costs an American firm about one quarter of what it would pay for a worker with comparable skills in the USA. As wages in India have risen, some IT firms have started to move work to even more low-cost locations such as Thailand and Vietnam.

- *Unique local capabilities* may allow an organisation to enhance its competitive advantage. Gradually value-creating and innovative activity becomes geographically dispersed across multiple centres of excellence within multinational organisations.[10] For example, leading European pharmaceuticals company GSK has R&D laboratories in Boston and the Research Triangle in North Carolina in order to establish research collaborations with the prominent universities and hospitals in those areas. Internationalisation, therefore, is increasingly not only about exploiting an organisation's existing capabilities in new national markets, but about developing strategic capabilities by drawing on capabilities found elsewhere in the world.

- *National market characteristics* can enable organisations to develop differentiated product offerings aimed at different market segments. American guitar-maker Gibson, for example, complements its US-made products with often similar, lower-cost alternatives produced in South Korea under the Epiphone brand. However, because of the American music tradition, Gibson's high-end guitars benefit from the reputation of still being 'made in the USA'.

(8.4) INTERNATIONAL STRATEGIES

Given their organisation-specific advantages and the ability to obtain sources of international competitive advantage through geographic home-based factors or international value systems, organisations still face difficult questions about what kind of international strategy to pursue. The fundamental issue in formulating an international strategy is to balance pressures for *global integration* versus those for *local responsiveness*.[11] Pressures for global integration encourage organisations to coordinate their activities across diverse countries to gain efficient operations. The internationalisation drivers discussed above (section 8.2) indicate forces that organisations can build on to achieve lower costs and higher quality in operations and activities on a global scale. However, there are conflicting pressures that also encourage organisations to become locally responsive and meet the specific needs in each individual country (see section 8.5.1 below). Values and attitudes, cultures, laws, institutions and economics differ across countries, which imply differences in customer preferences, product and service standards, regulations and human resources that all need to be addressed. These two opposing pressures – global integration vs local responsiveness – put contradictory demands on an organisation's international strategy. High pressure for global integration implies an increased need to concentrate and coordinate operations globally. In contrast, high pressure for local responsiveness implies a greater need to disperse operations and adapt to local demand.

This key problem is sometimes referred to as the **global–local dilemma**: the **extent to which products and services may be standardised across national boundaries or need to be adapted to meet the requirements of specific national markets.** For some products and services – such as televisions – markets appear similar across the world, offering huge potential scale economies if design, production and delivery can be centralised. For other products and

Figure 8.4 Four international strategies

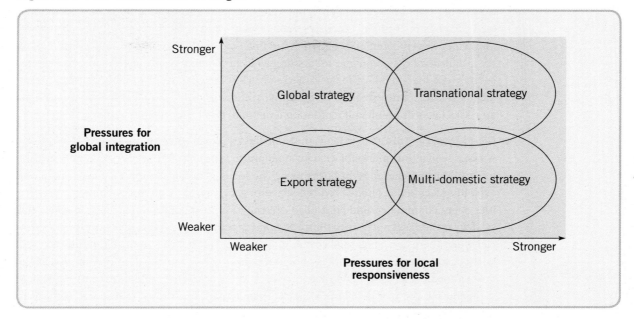

services – such as television programming – tastes still seem highly national-specific, drawing companies to decentralise operations and control as near as possible to the local market.

This dilemma between global integration and local responsiveness suggests several possible international strategies, ranging from emphasising one of the dimensions to complex responses that try to combine both. Organisations need to assess to what degree there are potential advantages of cost and quality of global integration and balance those pressures against the need to adapt products and/or services to local conditions. This section introduces four different kinds of international strategy, based on strategic choices about this balance (see Figure 8.4). The four basic international strategies are:[12]

- *Export strategy*. This strategy leverages home country capabilities, innovations and products in different foreign countries. It is advantageous when both pressures for global integration and local responsiveness are low, as shown in Figure 8.4. Companies that have distinctive capabilities together with strong reputation and brand names often follow this strategy with success. Google, for example, centralises its R&D and the core architecture underlying its internet services at its headquarters in California in the USA and exploits it internationally with minor adaptations except for local languages and alphabets. The downside of this approach is the limits of a home country centralised view of the business with risks of skilled local competitors getting ahead. Google, for example, meets strong local rivals in Baidu in China and Naver in Korea with superior mastery of the language and understanding of consumer behaviour.

- *Multi-domestic strategy*. This is a strategy that maximises local responsiveness. It is based on different product or service offerings and operations in each country depending on local market conditions and customer preferences. Each country is treated differently with a considerable autonomy for each country manager to best meet the needs of the local markets and customers in that particular country. As in the export strategy, this strategy is similarly loosely coordinated internationally. The organisation becomes a collection of relatively independent units with value chain activities adapted to specific local conditions. This multi-domestic approach is particularly appropriate when there are strong benefits to adapting to local needs and when there are limited efficiency gains from integration. It is common in food and consumer product industries where local idiosyncratic preferences are significant. Marketing-driven companies often pursue this type of strategy. For example, Frito-Lay, a US branded-snacks company, tailors its global products to local tastes and even creates entirely new snack products for local markets.[13] The disadvantages of a multi-domestic strategy include manufacturing inefficiencies, a proliferation of costly product and service variations and risks towards brand and reputation if national practices become too diverse.

- *Global strategy.* This is a strategy that maximises global integration. In this strategy the world is seen as one marketplace with standardised products and services that fully exploits integration and efficiency in operations. The focus is on capturing scale economies and exploiting location economies worldwide with geographically dispersed value chain activities being coordinated and controlled centrally from headquarters. In these respects this strategy is the exact opposite to the multi-domestic strategy. A global strategy is most beneficial when there are substantial cost or quality efficiency benefits from standardisation and when customer needs are relatively homogeneous across countries. It is a common strategy for commodities or commodity-like products. Mexican Cemex, one of the largest cement companies in the world, follows a global strategy with centralised and shared services in information technology, R&D, human resources and financial services across countries and regions.[14] Non-commodity companies can also follow a global strategy, like Sweden's furniture retailer IKEA. Based on a strong home base they standardise products and marketing with limited local adaptation to gain maximum global integration efficiency. The drawback of the global strategy is reduced flexibility due to standardisation that limits possibilities to adapting activities and products to local conditions.[15] This has, for example, led IKEA to make minor modifications of some furniture offerings to suit local tastes.

- *Transnational strategy.* This is the most complex strategy that tries to maximise both responsiveness and integration. Its aim is to unite the key advantages of the multi-domestic and global strategies while minimising their disadvantages. In addition, it maximises learning and knowledge exchange between dispersed units. In this strategy products and services and operational activities are, subject to minimum efficiency standards, adapted to local conditions in each country. In contrast to the multi-domestic strategy, however, this strategy also leverages learning and innovation across units in different countries. The value chain configuration includes an intricate combination of centralised manufacturing to increase efficiency combined with distributed assembly and local adaptations. Coordination is neither centralised at home nor dispersed in foreign countries, but encourages knowledge flows from wherever ideas and innovations come from. The major advantage of this strategy is its capacity to support efficiency and effectiveness while at the same time being able to serve local needs and leverage learning across units. General Electric has been celebrated as having a transnational strategy that emphasises seeking and exchanging ideas irrespective where they come from. The company swaps ideas regarding efficiency, customer responsiveness and innovation across different parts of the value chain and diverse countries worldwide.[16] However, while it is argued that transnational strategies are becoming increasingly necessary, many firms find it difficult to implement given its complexity and the fundamental trade-off between integration and responsiveness. ABB, the Swiss–Swedish engineering giant, was once identified as the archetypal transnational company, but later ran into serious problems.[17]

In practice, these four international strategies are not absolutely distinct as indicated by the overlapping ovals in Figure 8.4. They are rather illustrative examples of alternative international strategies. Global integration and local responsiveness are matters of degree rather than sharp distinctions. Moreover, choices between them will be influenced by changes in the internationalisation drivers introduced earlier. It is rare that companies adopt a pure form of international strategy; instead they often blend approaches and are located somewhere between the four strategies. As exemplified above, IKEA has a global strategy, but also makes some minor local adaptations, which may take it towards more of a transnational strategy.

Often regions (e.g. Europe or North America) play a larger role in international strategy than individual countries or global expansion. Thus many multinationals compromise between local and global logics by opting for *regional strategies*.[18] The aim of this strategy is to attain some of the economic efficiency and location advantages of more global strategies while simultaneously reaching local adaptation advantages. Regions are treated as relatively homogenous markets with value chain activities concentrated within them. Sales data suggest that many multinational companies follow this type of strategy focused on one or two regions including the triad of the European Union, the North American Free Trade Agreement and/or Japan/Asia.[19] For example, over 85 per cent of all cars sold within each region of Europe, North America and Japan are built in that same region. This regional approach to international strategy emphasises that distances and differences between nations are still relatively large (see section 8.5.1 below), which makes global integration difficult (see also the Key Debate at the end of this chapter).

These differences can, however, be exploited in arbitrage for value creation. *Arbitrage* implies that multinationals take advantage of price differences between two or more markets by purchasing goods cheaply in one market and selling them at a higher price in another. For example, Walmart is known for sourcing much of what the company sells in the USA from China. Not only price differences, but differences in labour costs, in knowledge, capital and taxes can be exploited by operating in diverse countries. Google is known for exploiting tax differences between countries in its international operations, for example the relatively low Irish corporation tax. The potential for arbitrage in multinationals is substantial and it has been suggested as a third significant international strategy dimension, besides integration and responsiveness.[20] Finally, different international strategies require diverse organising requirements for success, which is discussed in Chapter 13 (section 13.2.4).

(8.5) MARKET SELECTION AND ENTRY

Having decided on an international strategy built on significant sources of competitive advantage and supported by strong internationalisation drivers, managers need next to decide which countries to enter. Not all countries are equally attractive. To an extent, however, countries can initially be compared using standard environmental analysis techniques, for example along the dimensions identified in the PESTEL framework (see section 2.2.1) or according to the industry five forces (section 2.3). However, there are specific determinants of market attractiveness that need to be considered in internationalisation strategy: the intrinsic characteristics of the market. A key point here is how initial estimates of country attractiveness can be modified by various measures of *distance*. The section concludes by considering different *entry modes* into national markets.

8.5.1 **Market characteristics**

At least four elements of the PESTEL framework are particularly important in comparing countries for entry:

- *Political.* Political environments vary widely between countries and can alter rapidly. Russia since the fall of communism has seen frequent swings for and against private foreign enterprise. Governments can of course create significant opportunities for organisations. For example, the British government has traditionally promoted the financial services industry in the City of London by offering tax advantages to high-earning financiers from abroad and providing a 'light-touch' regulatory environment. It is important, however, to determine the level of *political risk* before entering a country. Toyota, for example, found itself the subject of an unexpected consumer boycott in China because of political tensions over a territorial dispute between China and Japan. There is also a risk that governments simply take over companies. In 2012 the Argentinian government nationalised the Spanish oil company Repsol's 57 per cent stake in Argentina's largest oil extractor and refinery.

- *Economic.* Key comparators in deciding entry are levels of gross domestic product and disposable income which help in estimating the potential size of the market. Fast-growth economies obviously provide opportunities, and in developing economies such as China and India growth is translating into an even faster creation of a high-consumption middle class. At the same time entirely new high-growth markets are opening up in Africa including Nigeria and Ghana.

- *Social.* Social factors will clearly be important, for example the availability of a well-trained workforce or the size of demographic market segments – old or young – relevant to the strategy. Cultural variations also need to be considered, for instance in defining tastes in the marketplace.

- *Legal.* Countries vary widely in their legal regime, determining the extent to which businesses can enforce contracts, protect intellectual property or avoid corruption. Similarly, policing will be important for the security of employees, a factor that in the past has deterred business in some African countries.

A common procedure is to rank country markets against each other on criteria such as these and then to choose the countries for entry that offer the highest relative scores. However, Pankaj Ghemawat from Spain's IESE Business School has pointed out that what matters is not just the attractiveness of different countries relative to each other, but also the compatibility of the countries with the internationalising firm itself.[21] Thus Ghemawat underlines the importance of *match* between country and firm. For firms coming from any particular country, some countries are more 'distant' – or mismatched – than others. For example, a Spanish company might be 'closer' to a South American market than an East Asian market and might therefore prefer that market even if it ranked lower on standard criteria of attractiveness. As well as a relative ranking of countries, therefore, each company has to add its assessment of countries in terms of closeness of match.

Ghemawat's 'CAGE framework' measures the match between countries and companies according to four dimensions of distance, reflected by the letters of the acronym. Thus the **CAGE framework** **emphasises the importance of cultural, administrative, geographical and economic distance**, as follows:

- *Cultural distance.* The distance dimension here relates to differences in language, ethnicity, religion and social norms. Cultural distance is not just a matter of similarity in consumer

ILLUSTRATION 8.3

Nordic Industrial Park: bridging distance across international markets

When a resource-constrained firm enters a high-distance market, it helps greatly if it can utilise a low-distance entry point.

The lure of the Chinese market has led several Western companies to venture into a context that is unfamiliar and bewildering, especially for small and medium-sized enterprises (SMEs) lacking the deep pockets of large multinationals. It is useful for SMEs to have a 'bridge' into a high-distance market. One way to accomplish this to use a foreign-owned industrial park (i.e. a space designated for industrial use).

Consider the case of the Nordic Industrial Park (NIP) which provides a physical space for offices and light-manufacturing facilities, and a range of value-added services to set up a business in China. These include legal services (e.g. registering the company and drafting contracts), human resource management (e.g. recruitment, payroll and expat relocation), accounting (e.g. financial reporting), and information and communication technology (e.g. internet access).

NIP was co-founded by Ove Nodland, a Norwegian who first went to China in 1994 to manage a state-owned enterprise that had attracted Norwegian investment. Next, Nodland helped set up a rare-earth magnet venture for another Norwegian concern in Ningbo, a port city in Zhejiang province just south of Shanghai (the commercial centre of China) and renowned for its entrepreneurialism. Nodland knew that even though rules might be set in Beijing (the national capital and political centre of China), they were implemented by local officials – and so they mattered greatly. He invested considerable energies in building close relationships with the city's mayor and other officials, and took care to ensure that the company complied with local regulations and aligned itself with local governmental priorities. Nodland's local guanxi (network connections) grew rapidly. However, the magnet company's target market was the IT industry, and when the dot-com bubble burst, demand collapsed. Nodland was now saddled with a facility to do business in Ningbo, but with little scope to achieve the intended scale of success.

After some thought, Nodland came up with an alternative use for his facility and connections. He reckoned that he was well placed to help European SMEs enter China. He chose to focus on what he knew best: firms from the Nordic region (Denmark, Finland, Iceland, Norway and Sweden) setting up a base in Ningbo. Thus was born the concept of NIP in 2002. It became operational within two years.

From the perspective of a European SME entering NIP, there are multiple benefits:

- *Process:* Lower start-up costs. NIP leverages its knowledge of the Chinese business environment by hand-holding clients through the complexities associated with starting and running a business in China, thereby allowing firms to focus their time and energies on core business activities.
- *Physical environment:* A familiar ambience. NIP's architecture and design mimics Scandinavian features that set it apart from standard Chinese buildings. Not only does this give expat managers a sense of the familiar, it is also a symbolic reminder to Chinese employees that they are part of a Western organisation.
- *People:* A like-minded community. By virtue of being part of the largest concentration of Nordic companies in China, expat managers have the opportunity to share experiences with and pick up 'tricks of the trade' from other managers with a similar cultural background through hallway conversations and lunchtime meetings.

Of course, entering a facility like NIP comes at a cost, but offers benefits in terms of 'reducing distance'.

Source: Prepared by Shameen Prashantham, Nottingham University Business School China.

Questions

1 Consider NIP's services in light of the CAGE framework and analyse how they may help reduce distance.

2 What might be the drawbacks in being located in an industrial park?

Figure 8.5 International cross-cultural comparison

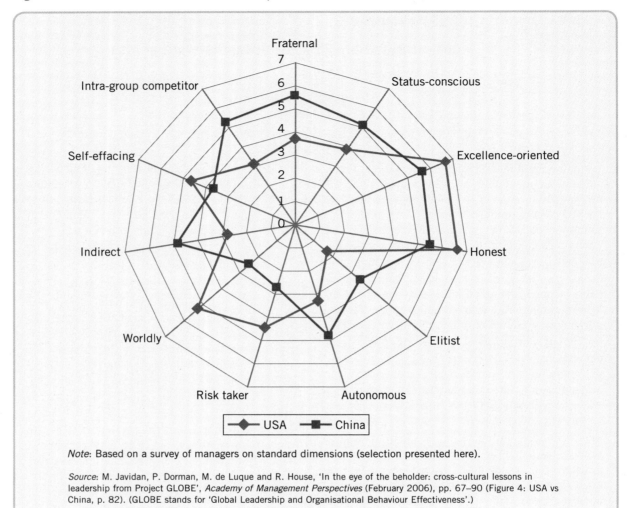

Note: Based on a survey of managers on standard dimensions (selection presented here).

Source: M. Javidan, P. Dorman, M. de Luque and R. House, 'In the eye of the beholder: cross-cultural lessons in leadership from Project GLOBE', *Academy of Management Perspectives* (February 2006), pp. 67–90 (Figure 4: USA vs China, p. 82). (GLOBE stands for 'Global Leadership and Organisational Behaviour Effectiveness'.)

tastes, but extends to important compatibilities in terms of managerial behaviours. Here, for example, US firms might be closer to Canada than to Mexico, which Spanish firms might find relatively compatible. Figure 8.5 draws on the GLOBE survey of 17,000 managers from 62 different societal cultures around the world to contrast specifically the orientations of American and Chinese managers on some key cultural dimensions. According to this GLOBE survey, American managers appear to be typically more risk-taking, while Chinese managers are more autonomous. One way to shrink distance is through cooperation with local partners, which is demonstrated in Illustration 8.3.

● *Administrative and political distance.* Here distance is in terms of incompatible administrative, political or legal traditions. Colonial ties can diminish difference, so that the shared heritage of France and its former West African colonies creates certain understandings that go beyond linguistic advantages. See also, for example, the experience of the Brazilian Vale company in Mozambique, where shared Portuguese heritage made a difference (Illustration 8.4). Institutional weaknesses – for example, slow or corrupt administration – can open up

ILLUSTRATION 8.4

Vale – a Brazilian giant in different cultures

Rapid overseas expansion brings this Brazilian multinational some contrasting experiences.

Until the late 1990s, Brazil's Vale mining company was a state-owned sleeping giant. Vale, the world's largest iron-ore producer and the second-largest miner overall by volume and market value, was privatised in 1997. Since then the company has transformed itself into a dynamic conglomerate and expanded globally. As the former CEO Roger Agnelli commented in 2010: 'Vale used to be fundamentally an iron-ore company. We used to operate essentially in Brazil. Now we are in 36 countries.' Although Vale has been described as 'one of the world's most powerful and aggressive mining companies' its international experiences have been mixed as shown in the examples below and consequently the new CEO Murilo Ferreira has somewhat slowed down Vale's global expansion.

Vale's $17.6 bn (€13.2 bn or £10.5 bn) takeover in 2006 of Inco, the world's largest nickel producer, was its first major overseas acquisition. Canada's largest national newspaper, the *Globe and Mail*, described Vale's arrival as 'The great Canadian mining disaster.' Many Canadians resented this takeover by what they regarded as a business from a developing country. Of 29 senior Canadian managers in early 2007, three years later 23 had departed, mostly voluntarily. At one tense meeting a Brazilian manager riposted: 'How come, if you're so smart, you didn't take *us* over?' The clash resulted in a strike that lasted almost a year. While the conflict was finally resolved it was seen as a sign of potential confrontations when companies from emerging economies such as Brazil, China and India expand into new, unfamiliar territories.

The booming demand from China has been a gift and Vale's export of iron ore there account for about 30 per cent of revenues. Compared to main rivals Australian miners BHP and Rio Tinto, Vale, however, has a considerable disadvantage: distance. Vale's solution has been to develop giant iron-ore vessels. A fleet of 100 of the so-called 'Valemaxes' would reduce shipping costs to China by 20 per cent and carbon emission by 35 per cent. The giant ships have, however, ignited controversy among Chinese authorities, especially when one developed a crack in a ballast tank. The struggling Chinese shipbuilding community has been particularly critical as it claims that the mega-carriers would drive freight rates down. All this has resulted in a ban on the Valemaxes to dock at China's ports, forcing Vale to unload in Malaysia and the Philippines instead.

A contrast so far has been Vale's experience in Mozambique. Like many Brazilian companies, Vale has been attracted to the two African countries of Angola and Mozambique because of the shared cultural and linguistic heritage of Portuguese colonialism. About half the 3 million black African slaves sent to Brazil between 1700 and 1850 came from Angola and in the 1820s, settlers in Angola and Mozambique applied to join the newly independent Brazil in a federation. Vale first invested $1.7 bn (€1.3 bn) in Moatize, considered by investors to be one of the world's largest untapped coal reserves. Because of its success Vale has decided to expand Moatize's capacity from 11 million to 26 million tonnes per year with an additional investment of $6 bn (€4.5 bn) including the expansion of railway linkages and infrastructure. Vale's CEO, Murilo Ferreira, confirms Africa's significance for the company's strategy: 'It's a new frontier . . . Africa is very important. We want to grow there.'

Sources: *Financial Times*, 25 February 2010; *Financial Times*, 9 February 2010; *Financial Times*, 11 February 2010; *Financial Times*, 12 April 2012; *Financial Times*, 1 October 2012; mining-technology.com, 24 November 2011; miningweekly.com, 18 May 2012.

Questions

1 Suggest three reasons for Vale's different reception in Canada and Mozambique.

2 What can Vale do to mitigate the problems the company encounters when expanding globally?

distance between countries. So too can political differences: Chinese companies are increasingly able to operate in parts of the world that American companies are finding harder, for example parts of the Middle East and Africa.

- *Geographical distance.* This is not just a matter of the kilometres separating one country from another, but involves other geographical characteristics of the country such as size, sea-access and the quality of communications infrastructure. Transport infrastructure can shrink or exaggerate physical distance. France is much closer to large parts of Continental Europe than to the United Kingdom, because of the barrier presented by the English Channel and the latter relatively poor road and rail infrastructure. The possibility for individual companies to reduce geographic distances is illustrated by the development of mega-ship carriers by the Brazilian mining company Vale in Illustration 8.4.

- *Economic.* The final element of the CAGE framework refers particularly to wealth distances. There are of course huge disparities in wealth internationally: around the world, there are 4 billion people beneath the poverty income threshold of less than \$2 a day.[22] Multinationals from rich countries are typically weak at serving such very poor consumers. However, these rich-country multinationals are losing out on large markets if they only concentrate on the wealthy elites overseas. University of Michigan academic C.K. Prahalad pointed out that the aggregated wealth of those at the 'base of the pyramid' in terms of income distribution is very substantial: simple mathematics means that those 4 billion below the poverty threshold represent a market of more than \$2,000 bn per year. If rich-country multinationals can develop new capabilities to serve these numerically huge markets, they can bridge the economic distance, and thereby both significantly extend their presence in booming economies such as China and India and bring to these poor consumers the benefits that are claimed for Western goods. See Illustration 8.5 for examples of innovative base of the pyramid strategies.

8.5.2 Competitive characteristics

Assessing the relative attractiveness of markets by PESTEL and CAGE analyses is only the first step. The second element relates to competition. Here, of course, Michael Porter's five forces framework can help (see section 2.3). For example, country markets with many existing competitors, powerful buyers (perhaps large retail chains such as in much of North America and Northern Europe) and low barriers to further new entrants from overseas would typically be unattractive. However, an additional consideration is the likelihood of retaliation from other competitors.

In the five forces framework, retaliation potential relates to rivalry and entry, but managers can extend this by using insights directly from 'game theory' (see section 6.4.4). Here the likelihood and ferocity of potential competitor reactions are added to the simple calculation of relative country market attractiveness. As in Figure 8.6, country markets can be assessed according to three criteria:[23]

- *Market attractiveness* to the new entrant, based on PESTEL, CAGE and five forces analyses, for example. In Figure 8.6, countries A and B are the most attractive to the entrant.

- *Defender's reactiveness*, likely to be influenced by the market's attractiveness to the defender but also by the extent to which the defender is working with a globally integrated, rather than multi-domestic, strategy. A defender will be more reactive if the markets are important to it and it has the managerial capabilities to coordinate its response. Here, the defender is highly reactive in countries A and D.

ILLUSTRATION 8.5

Base of the pyramid strategies

Base of the pyramid strategy means more than just low prices. Base of the pyramid involves designing new products, forming partnership, reshaping distribution channels and introducing novel financing solutions.

Product design

A key problem in the developing world is the poor quality of piped water. Unilever Hindustan, India's largest consumer goods company, owned by Anglo-Dutch Unilever, developed a water filter that makes water as safe as boiling. It is marketed and sold through the wide Unilever distribution network. The filter has attracted over three million households, mainly in India's mega- or middle-sized cities. However, at $35 (€26) it is still unattainable for millions of Indians who live on less than a dollar a day. In an effort to reach rural customers Unilever has therefore started to market a light-version (lower capacity) of the filter. The success of the product on the Indian market has led Unilever Hindustan to introduce the water filter in other markets in Asia, Eastern Europe and South Africa.

Partnerships

First Energy Oorja started as a partnership between the Indian Institute of Science Bangalore and British Petroleum (BP) Emerging Consumer Market (ECM) division to develop a stove using the 'power of innovation and a strong understanding of consumer energy needs'. It was later acquired by The Alchemists Ark (TAA), a privately held business consulting firm. The First Energy Oorja stoves are low-smoke, low-cost stoves, which work on pellets – an organic biofuel made of processed agricultural waste. First Energy Oorja works in close partnership with both local non-governmental organisations and dealer networks in rural markets to distribute and market the stove. This distribution model ensures that the product reaches remote Indian locations.

Distribution channels

Bayer CropScience, a global firm that develops and manufactures crop protection products, initiated a Green World venture in Kenya. It introduced small packs of pesticides and trained a network of small, rural agrodealers to guide and educate small farmers on product handling and use. It also provided further support and marketing via radio. Bayer CropScience carefully selected dealers based on their reputation in the community and sales volumes. Today about 25 per cent of its horticultural retail revenues in Kenya now come from Green World stores.

Financial solutions

Cemex, a global cement corporation from Mexico, has been an innovative pioneer in designing a microfinancing system, 'Patrimonio Hoy' (Property Now), for the poor in Mexico and later in the rest of Latin America. In the past, building houses for this group had often proved lengthy and risky because without savings or access to credit, low-income families could only buy small amounts of building material at a time. Patrimonio Hoy is a solution to this. It is a combination of savings and credit schemes in which Cemex provides collateral-free financing to customers via a membership system based on small monthly fees. Customers demonstrate their savings discipline by regular monthly payments and Cemex develops trust in them by delivering building raw materials early on credit. The programme is a success and Cemex reports that it has reached 265 million families so far.

Sources: Swiss Agency for Development and Cooperation, 2011; Institute for Financial and Management Research, 2012; A. Karamchandani, M. Kubzansky and N. Lalwani, 'Is the bottom of the pyramid really for you?', *Harvard Business Review*, March 2011; *Business Today*, December 2011.

Questions

1 Can you imagine any risks or dangers that Western companies might face in pursuing base of the pyramid strategies?

2 Is there anything that Western companies might learn from base of the pyramid strategies in emerging markets that might be valuable in their home markets?

Figure 8.6 International competitor retaliation

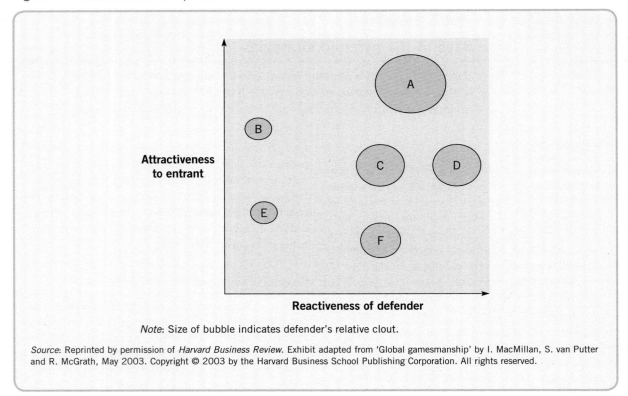

Note: Size of bubble indicates defender's relative clout.

Source: Reprinted by permission of *Harvard Business Review*. Exhibit adapted from 'Global gamesmanship' by I. MacMillan, S. van Putter and R. McGrath, May 2003. Copyright © 2003 by the Harvard Business School Publishing Corporation. All rights reserved.

● *Defender's clout*, that is the power that the defender is able to muster in order to fight back. Clout is typically a function of share in the particular market, but might be influenced by connections to other powerful local players, such as retailers or government. In Figure 8.6, clout is represented by the size of the bubbles, with the defender having most clout in countries A, C, D and F.

Choice of country to enter can be significantly modified by adding reactiveness and clout to calculations of attractiveness. Relying only on attractiveness, the top-ranked country to enter in Figure 8.6 is country A. Unfortunately, it is also one in which the defender is highly reactive, and the one in which it has most clout. Country B becomes a better international move than A. In turn, country C is a better prospect than country D, because, even though they are equally attractive, the defender is less reactive. One surprising result of taking defender reactiveness and clout into account is the re-evaluation of country E: although ranked fifth on simple attractiveness, it might rank second overall if competitor retaliation is allowed for.

This sort of analysis is particularly fruitful for considering the international moves of two interdependent competitors, such as Unilever and Procter & Gamble or British Airways and Singapore Airlines. In these cases the analysis is relevant to any aggressive strategic move, for instance the expansion of existing operations in a country as well as initial entry. Especially in the case of globally integrated competitors, moreover, the overall clout of the defender must be taken into account. The defender may choose to retaliate in other markets than the targeted one, counter-attacking wherever it has the clout to do damage to the aggressor. Naturally, too, this kind of analysis can be applied to interactions between diversified competitors as well as international ones: each bubble could represent different products or services.

8.5.3 **Entry modes**

Once a particular national market has been selected for entry, an organisation needs to choose how to enter that market. Entry modes differ in the degree of resource commitment to a particular market and the extent to which an organisation is operationally involved in a particular location. In order of increasing resource commitment, the four key entry mode types are: *exporting*; contractual arrangement through *licensing and franchising* to local partners, as McDonald's does to restaurant operators; *joint ventures*, in other words the establishment of jointly owned businesses; and *wholly owned subsidiaries*, through either the acquisition of established companies or 'greenfield' investments, the development of facilities from scratch.

The *staged international expansion* model emphasises the role of experience in determining entry mode. Internationalisation typically brings organisations into unfamiliar territory, requiring managers to learn new ways of doing business.[24] The staged international expansion model proposes a sequential process whereby companies gradually increase their commitment to newly entered markets, as they build market knowledge and capabilities. Thus firms might enter initially by licensing or exporting, thereby acquiring some local knowledge while minimising local investments. As they gain knowledge and confidence, firms can then increase their exposure, perhaps first by a joint venture and finally by creating a wholly owned subsidiary. For example, the leading Danish wind turbine manufacturer Vestas first entered the US market through exports. Subsequently Vestas established manufacturing and R&D facilities in Eastern Colorado to strengthen its competitive position versus domestic players and now supplies 90 per cent of components required for the assembly of a final turbine within the USA.

However, the gradualism of staged international expansion is now challenged by two phenomena:

- '*Born-global firms*', in other words new small firms that internationalise rapidly at early stages in their development.[25] New technologies now help small firms link up to international sources of expertise, supply and customers worldwide. For such firms, waiting till they have enough international experience is not an option: international strategy is a condition of existence. For example, companies like Twitter and Instagram internationalised quickly from being small start-ups. Other types of companies may also internationalise fast. Blue Skies in Illustration 8.2 with operations across three continents is an example of a small company that started out as a mini-multinational.

- *Emerging-country multinationals* also often move quickly through entry modes. Prominent examples are the Chinese white-goods multinational Haier, the Indian pharmaceuticals company Ranbaxy Laboratories and Mexico's Cemex cement company mentioned above.[26] Such companies typically develop *unique capabilities* in their home market that then need to be rolled out quickly worldwide before competitors catch up. For example, Haier became skilled at very efficient production of simple white goods, providing a cost advantage that is transferable outside its Chinese manufacturing base. Haier now has factories in Italy and the USA, as well as the Philippines, Malaysia, Indonesia, Egypt, Nigeria and elsewhere round the world. The rapid internationalisation made by emerging multinationals from China has largely been based on acquisitions. These are often high-profile acquisitions as illustrated by the Chinese conglomerate Wanda buying the second-biggest movie theatre chain in the USA, AMC (see the end Case example).[27]

Where the demands and pace of international competition rule out more gradualist staged expansion, two fundamental principles can help guide choice of market entry mode:

- *The breadth of competitive advantage* in the target market. This determines whether entry into the market can be done relying upon the company's own capabilities, or whether it must draw on the capabilities of local partners, for instance to access distribution channels or to manufacture locally.

- *Tradability*, in other words the ability to rely on trading relationships, rather than the firm's own presence. Tradability is determined by two factors: ease of transport from home country to target country, and the quality of legal protection in the target country. Legal protection refers for example to the ability to enforce contracts, to safeguard performance standards or to protect intellectual property such as patented technologies. Tradability is low where it is unsafe to trade through market-based contracts with local partners.

Other case-specific factors are liable to enter the calculation of appropriate entry mode as well, not least the availability of suitable local partners. None the less, the two principles of competitive advantage and tradability do suggest the following broad guidelines for entry mode (Figure 8.7):

- *Export* is the baseline option, and is suitable where the product or services are easily transported from country to country and where the home-based competitive advantages are sufficiently broad to minimise reliance on local companies.

- *License or franchise* the product or service where competitive advantages are too narrow to go it alone, but the legal environment is such that licensees and franchisees can be relied on not to abuse their contracts, under-perform on standards or steal the intellectual property.

- *Joint ventures* work where competitive advantages are narrow, but local licensees or franchisees cannot be trusted with intellectual property or long-term performance. A joint venture involving shared ownership gives the foreign company more direct control and ensures that the local partner has an interest in maximising the value of the common enterprise rather than solely its own standalone interests.

Figure 8.7 Modes of international market entry

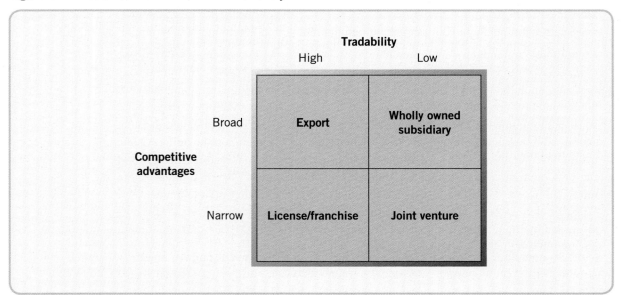

- *Wholly owned subsidiary* is an attractive route where competitive advantages are sufficiently broad not to depend on local partners, but where nevertheless transport difficulties rule out simple export. Such wholly owned subsidiaries can be via new greenfield investments (as for example many Japanese car companies have entered European markets) or via acquisition, where the integration of a local firm completes the breadth of competitive advantage required.

(8.6) INTERNATIONALISATION AND PERFORMANCE

Just as for product and service diversity discussed in section 7.4 the relationship between internationalisation and performance has been extensively researched.[28] Some of the main findings from such research are these:

- *An inverted U-curve.* While the potential performance benefits of internationalisation are substantial, in that it allows firms to realise economies of scale and scope and benefit from the locational advantages available in countries around the globe, the combination of diverse locations and diverse business units also gives rise to high levels of organisational complexity. At some point, the costs of organisational complexity may exceed the benefits of internationalisations. Accordingly, theory and the balance of evidence suggest an inverted U-shaped relationship between internationalisation and performance (similar to the findings on product/service diversification shown in section 7.4), with moderate levels of internationalisation leading to the best results. However, Yip's research on large British companies suggests that managers may be getting better at internationalisation, with substantially internationalised firms actually seeing performance improving to the point where international sales are above about 40 per cent of total sales.[29] Experience and commitment to internationalisation may be able to deliver strong performance for highly internationalised firms.

- *Service-sector disadvantages.* A number of studies have suggested that, in contrast to firms in the manufacturing sector, internationalisation may not lead to improved performance for service-sector firms. There are three possible reasons for such an effect. First, the operations of foreign service firms in some sectors (such as accountants or banks) remain tightly regulated and restricted in many countries; second, due to the intangible nature of services, they are often more sensitive to cultural differences and require greater adaptation than manufactured products which may lead to higher initial learning costs; third, the services typically require a significant local presence and reduce the scope for the exploitation of economies of scale in production compared to manufacturing firms.[30]

- *Internationalisation and product diversity.* An important question to consider is the interaction between internationalisation and product/service diversification. Compared to single-business firms it has been suggested that product-diversified firms are likely to do better from international expansion because they have already developed the necessary skills and structures for managing internal diversity.[31] At the other end of the spectrum there is general consensus that firms that are highly diversified in terms of both product and international markets are likely to face excessive costs of coordination and control leading to poor performance. As many firms have not yet reached levels of internationalisation where negative effects outweigh possible gains and because of current scepticism with regard to the benefits of high levels of product diversification, many companies currently opt for reducing their product diversity while building their international scope. Unilever, for example, has been combining a strategy of growing internationalisation with de-diversification.

(8.7) ROLES IN AN INTERNATIONAL PORTFOLIO

Just as for product diversification, international strategies imply different relationships between subsidiary operations and the corporate centre. The complexity of the strategies followed by organisations such as General Electric or Unilever can result in highly differentiated networks of subsidiaries with a range of distinct strategic roles. Subsidiaries may play different roles according to the level of local resources and capabilities available to them and the strategic importance of their local environment (see Figure 8.8):[32]

- *Strategic leaders* are subsidiaries that not only hold valuable resources and capabilities, but are also located in countries that are crucial for competitive success because of, for example, the size of the local market or the accessibility of key technologies. Japanese and European subsidiaries in the USA often play this role. Increasingly, subsidiaries are seen as playing important strategic roles with entrepreneurial potential for the whole multinational organisation.[33] Subsidiaries and subunits are either assigned strategic roles or take autonomous strategic initiatives. Hewlett Packard, for example, is known to have used both approaches.[34]

- *Contributors* are subsidiaries located in countries of lesser strategic significance, but with sufficiently valuable internal capabilities to nevertheless play key roles in a multinational organisation's competitive success. The Australian subsidiary of the Swedish telecommunications firm Ericsson played such a role in developing specialised systems for the firm's mobile phone business.

Figure 8.8 Subsidiary roles in multinational firms

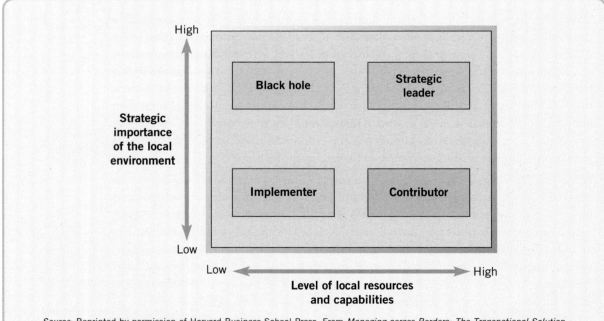

- *Implementers*, though not contributing substantially to the enhancement of a firm's competitive advantage, are important in the sense that they help generate vital financial resources. In this sense, they are similar to the 'cash cows' of the Boston Consulting Group matrix. The danger is that they turn into the equivalent of 'dogs'.

- *Black holes* are subsidiaries located in countries that are crucial for competitive success but with low-level resources or capabilities. This is a position many subsidiaries of American and European firms found themselves in over long periods in Japan. They have some of the characteristics of 'question marks' in the Boston Consulting Group matrix, requiring heavy investment (like an astrophysicist's black hole, sucking matter in). Possibilities for overcoming this unattractive position include the development of alliances and the selective and targeted development of key resources and capabilities.

These various subsidiary roles relate to how these subsidiaries are generally controlled and managed, and this is discussed in Chapter 13.

SUMMARY

- Internationalisation potential in any particular market is determined by Yip's four drivers of internationalisation: market, cost, government and competitors' strategies.

- *Sources of advantage* in international strategy can be drawn from both national sources of advantage, as captured in Porter's Diamond, and global sourcing through the international value system.

- There are *four main types of international strategy*, varying according to extent of coordination and geographical configuration: *export strategy*, *multi-domestic strategy*, *global strategy* and *transnational strategy*.

- *Market selection* for international entry or expansion should be based on attractiveness, multidimensional measures of distance and expectations of competitor retaliation.

- *Modes of entry* into new markets include *export*, *licensing* and *franchising*, *joint ventures* and *overseas wholly owned subsidiaries*.

- Internationalisation has an uncertain relationship to financial performance, with an inverted U-curve warning against over-internationalisation.

- Subsidiaries in an international firm can be managed by portfolio methods just like businesses in a diversified firm.

VIDEO ASSIGNMENTS

Visit *MyStrategyLab* and watch the CISCO case study for Chapter 8.

1 Using the concepts in section 8.5, analyse and recommend the appropriate market selection and entry mode for CISCO – refer to both the markets and the mode of entry/development.

2 Using Yip's model (Figure 8.2) and insights from the video, explain and discuss the drivers of internationalisation in the IT industries.

KEY DEBATE

Global, local or regional?

Debate rages over whether companies are really becoming more global, or whether local or indeed regional pressures remain strong.

Ted Levitt, Harvard Business School professor and former non-executive director of the international advertising firm Saatchi & Saatchi, has provocatively made the case for deep commitment to global strategies in all kinds of markets. He argues that modern communications technologies are creating homogeneous market needs, while manufacturing technologies are increasing the benefits of scale. Given the cost advantages of scale, and the diminishing importance of consumer differences, companies that commit to truly global strategies will be able to use low prices to sweep out all competitors still focused on local needs. He argues: 'The global company will seek to standardise its offering everywhere . . . Companies that do not adapt to the new global realities will become victims of those that do.' He cites Coca-Cola, Rolex, Sony and McDonald's as exemplars of the trend. Companies should not hanker over detailed differences left over from the past, but recognise the big picture of coming globalisation.

Levitt's sweeping argument brought a spirited response from American academics Gerry Wind and Susan Douglas, warning of 'the Myth of Globalisation'. They challenge both the trend to homogenisation and the growing role of scale economies. Even apparently global companies adapt to country needs: for example, Coca-Cola sells local products in Japan alongside its classic Coke, and its Dasani bottled water is a success in the USA, but a failure in Europe. As to scale, new flexible automation technologies may even be reducing economic order sizes, allowing short production runs adapted to local needs. Wind and Douglas warn that blind confidence in the inevitability of globalisation will surely lead to business disappointment.

Between the two poles of global and local there is a more recent third position: regional. Pankaj Ghemawat points out that most international trade is intra-regional. European countries trade predominantly with each other. The trend towards intra-regional trade is actually growing, from about 40 per cent of all trade 40 years ago to 55 per cent at the beginning of the twenty-first century. Alan Rugman calculates that in the early years of the twenty-first century over 300 of the world's largest corporations still have more than half their sales in their home region. An apparently global company like McDonald's is effectively bi-regional, with 80 per cent of its sales concentrated in North America and Europe, and the multinational General Electric has 60 per cent of its sales in North America.

Ted Levitt might be impatient with these empirical details. The essential issue for him is: where are things going in the future? Certainly there are still local differences in taste, but are these declining overall? And are sales really the appropriate proxy for globalisation as the regional advocates suggest? According to this reasoning a US firm that acquires raw materials in one region and country, produces parts in another, offshores its accounting to a third and its R&D in yet another would not be considered global if its majority of sales were in the North American Free Trade Agreement (NAFTA).

Sources: T. Levitt, 'The globalisation of markets', *Harvard Business Review*, May–June (1983), pp. 92–102; S.P. Douglas and Y. Wind 'The myth of globalization', *Columbia Journal of World Business*, vol. 22, no. 4 (1987), pp. 19–29; P. Ghemawat, 'Regional strategies for global leadership', *Harvard Business Review*, December (2005), pp. 98–108; A. Rugman, *The Regional Multinationals – MNEs and 'global' strategic management*, Cambridge University Press, 2005. A. Rugman and A. Verbeke, 'A new perspective on the regional and global strategies of multinational service firms', *Management International Review*, vol. 48. no. 4 (2008), pp. 397–411.

Questions

1 Make a list of products and services which are getting more 'global' over time; then make a list of products and services which are still very 'local'.

2 How many countries in the world have you visited in your lifetime? How many countries had your parents visited by the same age?

WORK ASSIGNMENTS

* *Denotes more advanced work assignments.*
* *Refers to a case study in the Text and Case edition.*

8.1 Using Figure 8.2 (Yip's internationalisation drivers), compare two markets you are familiar with and analyse how strong each of the drivers is for increased international strategy.

8.2 Visit the websites of the following companies and try to plot their international strategies in one of the four international strategy types of Figure 8.4 (each company primarily fits one strategy): Nestlé, ABB, Louis Vuitton and Lenovo.

8.3 Using the CAGE framework (section 8.5.1), assess the relative 'distance' of the USA, China, India and France for a British company (or a company from a country of your choice).

8.4 Using the diverse modes of international market entry of Figure 8.7 classify the entry mode of H&M*, Tesco* or SABMiller* or any other multinational corporation with which you are familiar.

8.5 Critically evaluate t he suggestion that globalisation is mostly beneficial for companies.

8.6 Take any part of the public or not-for-profit sector (e.g. education, health) and explain how far internationalisation has affected its management and consider how far it may do so in the future.

Integrative assignment

8.7 As in 8.2, use the four international strategies of Figure 8.4. to classify the international strategy of H&M*, Tesco* or any other multinational corporation with which you are familiar. Drawing on section 13.2.4, how does this corporation's organisational structure fit (or not fit) this strategy?

RECOMMENDED KEY READINGS

- A useful collection of academic articles on international business is in A. Rugman and T. Brewer (eds), *The Oxford Handbook of International Business*, Oxford University Press, 2003. For a collection of seminal contributions in research on multinational corporations see J.H. Dunning, *The theory of transnational corporations*, vol. 1, Routledge, 1993.

- An invigorating perspective on international strategy is provided by G.S. Yip and G.T. Hult, *Total Global Strategy*, Pearson, 2012. A comprehensive general textbook is S. Segal-Horn and D. Faulkner, *Understanding Global Strategy*, Southwestern, 2010.

- A critical evaluation of the emphasis on globalisation and global integration contrasted with a regional focus

can be found in A.M. Rugman, *The Regional Multinational – MNEs and 'global' strategic management*, Cambridge University Press, 2005; A.M. Rugman, *The End of Globalisation*, Random House, 2000; and P. Ghemawat, *Redefining Global Strategy*, Harvard Business School Press, 2007.

- An eye-opening introduction to the detailed workings – and inefficiencies – of today's global economy today is P. Rivoli, *The Travels of a T-Shirt in the Global Economy: an Economist Examines the Markets, Power and Politics of World Trade*, Wiley, 2006. A more optimistic view is in T. Friedman, *The World Is Flat: the Globalised World in the Twenty-First Century*, Penguin, 2006.

REFERENCES

1. For another cautious view, see M. Alexander and H. Korine, 'Why you shouldn't go global', *Harvard Business Review* (December 2008), pp. 70–7.
2. T. Friedman, *The World Is Flat: the Globalized World in the Twenty-First Century*, Penguin, 2006; and P. Rivoli, *The*

Travels of a T-Shirt in the Global Economy: an Economist Examines the Markets, Power and Politics of World Trade, Wiley, 2006.
3. G.S. Yip and G.T. Hult, *Total Global Strategy*, Pearson, 2012.

4. Useful industry-specific data on trends in openness to trade and investment can be found at the World Trade Organization's site, www.wto.org.

5. G. Hamel and C.K. Prahalad, 'Do you really have a global strategy?', *Harvard Business Review*, vol. 63, no. 4 (1985), pp. 139–48.

6. For a discussion of firm-specific advantages ('FSAs') and country-specific advantages ('CSAs') see A.M. Rugman, *The Regional Multinational – MNEs and 'global' strategic management*, Cambridge University Press, 2005, A. Rugman and A. Verbeke, 'Location, competitiveness and the multinational enterprise', in A.M. Rugman (ed.), *Oxford handbook of international business*, pp. 150–177, Oxford University Press, 2008; and A. Verbeke, *International business strategy*, Cambridge University Press, 2009.

7. B. Kogut, 'Designing global strategies: comparative and competitive value added changes', *Sloan Management Review*, vol. 27 (1985), pp. 15–28.

8. M. Porter, *The Competitive Advantage of Nations*, Macmillan, 1990; and M. Porter, *On Competition*, Harvard Business Press, 2008.

9. See reference 7 above.

10. J.A. Cantwell, 'The globalization of technology: what remains of the product life cycle model?', *Cambridge Journal of Economics*, vol. 19, no. 1 (1995), pp. 155–74; and A. Rugman and A. Verbeke 'Location, competitiveness and the multinational enterprise', in A.M. Rugman (ed.), *Oxford Handbook of International Business*, pp. 150–77, Oxford University Press, 2008.

11. The integration–responsiveness framework builds on the original works by C.A. Bartlett, 'Building and managing the transnational: the new organizational challenge', in M.E. Porter (ed.), *Competition in Global Industries*, Harvard Business School Press, pp. 367–401, 1986; and C.K. Prahalad and Y. Doz, *The Multinational Mission: Balancing local demands and global vision*, Free Press, 1987.

12. The typology builds on the basic framework of C.A. Bartlett and S. Ghoshal, *Managing across Borders: the Transnational Solution*, The Harvard Business School Press, 1989 (2nd updated edn, 1998); and S. Ghoshal and N. Nohria, 'Horses for courses: organizational forms for multinational corporations', *Sloan Management Review*, vol. 34 (1993), pp. 23–35. The typology was later confirmed in a large-scale empirical investigation by A.W. Harzing, 'An empirical analysis and extension of the Bartlett and Ghoshal typology of multinational companies', *Journal of International Business*, vol. 32, no. 1 (2000), pp. 101–20. For a similar typology see M. Porter, 'Changing patterns of international competition', *California Management Review*, vol. 28, no. 2 (1987), pp. 9–39. For a critical evaluation see T.M. Devinney, D.F. Midgley and S. Venaik, 'The optimal performance of the global firm: formalizing and extending the integration-responsiveness rramework', *Organization Science*, vol. 11, no. 6 (2000), pp. 674–95.

13. For a discussion of companies that build on the multi-domestic route see A. Rugman and R. Hodgetts, 'The end of global strategy', *European Management Journal*, vol. 19, no. 4 (2001), pp. 333–43.

14. For a detailed account of Cemex strategy see P. Ghemawat, *Redefining Global Strategy*, Harvard Business School Press, 2007.

15. For a discussion of the limits of global strategy see A. Rugman and R. Hodgetts in reference 13 above.

16. For a more in-depth discussion of how General Electric (GE) tries to combine a global and multi-domestic ('glocal-ization') strategy with innovation in emerging markets see J.R.I. Immelt, V. Govindarajan and C. Trimble, 'How GE is disrupting itself', *Harvard Business Review*, October (2009), pp. 57–65.

17. For an analysis of the transnational strategy and ABB as an example, see C.A. Bartlett and S. Ghoshal, *Managing across Borders: the Transnational Solution*, 2nd edn, Harvard Business School Press, 1998, pp. 259–72; and S. Ghoshal and C. Bartlett, *The Individualized Corporation*, Harper Business, 1997.

18. For criticism of the integration–responsiveness framework and its shortcoming in taking regions into account and a detailed discussion of regional strategy see A.M. Rugman, *The Regional Multinational – MNEs and 'global' strategic management*, pp. 48–53 and 201–12, Cambridge University Press, 2005. Further analysis of regional strategies can be found in P. Ghemawat, 'Regional strategies for global leadership', *Harvard Business Review*, December (2005), pp. 98–108.

19. For an in-depth examination of the regional sales data see A. Rugman and A. Verbeke, 'A perspective on regional and global strategies of multinational enterprises', *Journal of International Business*, vol. 35 (2004), pp. 3–18; and A.M. Rugman, *The End of Globalization*, Random House, 2000; A.M. Rugman and S. Girod, 'Retail multinationals and globalization: the evidence is regional', *European Management Journal*, vol. 21, no. 1 (2003), pp. 24–37; and A.M. Rugman, reference 18 above.

20. P. Ghemawat, 'Reconceptualizing international strategy and organization', *Strategic Organization*, vol. 6, no. 2 (2008), pp. 195–206.

21. P. Ghemawat, 'Distance still matters', *Harvard Business Review*, September (2001), pp. 137–47; and P. Ghemawat, *Redefining Global Strategy*, Harvard Business School Press, 2007.

22. C.K. Prahalad and A. Hammond, 'Serving the world's poor, profitably', *Harvard Business Review*, September (2002), pp. 48–55; Economist Intelligence Unit, 'From subsistence to sustainable: a bottom-up perspective on the role of business in poverty alleviation', 24 April 2009.

23. This framework is introduced in I. MacMillan, A. van Putten and R. McGrath, 'global Gamesmanship', *Harvard Business Review*, vol. 81, no. 5 (2003), pp. 62–71.

24. For detailed discussions about the role of learning and experience in market entry see: M.F. Guillén, 'Experience, imitation, and the sequence of foreign entry: wholly owned and joint-venture manufacturing by South Korean firms and business groups in China, 1987–1995', *Journal of*

International Business Studies, vol. 83 (2003), pp. 185–98; and M.K. Erramilli, 'The experience factor in foreign market entry modes by service firms', *Journal of International Business Studies*, vol. 22, no. 3 (1991), pp. 479–501.

25. G. Knights and T. Cavusil, 'A taxonomy of born-global firms', *Management International Review*, vol. 45, no. 3 (2005), pp. 15–35.

26. For analyses of emerging-country multinationals, see T. Khanna and K. Palepu, 'Emerging giants: building world-class companies in developing countries', *Harvard Business Review* (October 2006), pp. 60–9; P. Gammeltoft, H. Barnard and A. Madhok, 'Emerging multinationals, emerging theory: macro- and micro-level perspectives', *Journal of International Management*, vol. 16, no. 1 (2010), pp. 95–101; and the special issue on 'The internationalization of Chinese and Indian firms – trends, motivations and strategy', *Industrial and Corporate Change*, vol. 18, no. 2 (2009).

27. For a detailed analysis of the unique aspects of Chinese multinationals see M.W. Peng, 'The global strategy of emerging multinationals from China', *Global Strategy Journal*, vol. 2, no. 2 (2012), pp. 97–107.

28. A useful review of the international dimension is M. Hitt and R.E. Hoskisson, 'International diversification: effects on innovation and firm performance in product-diversified firms', *Academy of Management Journal*, vol. 40, no. 4 (1997), pp. 767–98. For a meta-analytic review of previous studies of multinationality–performance relationships and what the effects depend on, see A.H. Kirca, K. Roth, G.T.M. Hult and S.T. Cavusgil, 'The role of context in the multinationality-performance relationships: a meta-analytic review', *Global Strategy Journal*, vol. 2, no. 2 (2012), pp. 108–21.

29. For detailed results on British companies, see G. Yip, A. Rugman and A. Kudina, 'International success of British companies', *Long Range Planning*, vol. 39, no. 1 (2006), pp. 241–64.

30. See N. Capar and M. Kotabe, 'The relationship between international diversification and performance in service firms', *Journal of International Business Studies*, vol. 34 (2003), pp. 345–55; and F.J. Contractor, S.K. Kundu and C. Hsu, 'A three-stage theory of international expansion: the link between multinationality and performance in the service sector', *Journal of International Business Studies*, vol. 34 (2003), pp. 5–18.

31. See S.C. Chang and C.-F. Wang, 'The effect of product diversification strategies on the relationship between international diversification and firm performance', *Journal of World Business*, vol. 42, no. 1 (2007), pp. 61–79; and C.H. Oh and F.J. Contractor, 'The role of territorial coverage and product diversification in the multinationality-performance relationship', *Global Strategy Journal*, vol. 2, no. 2 (2012), pp. 122–36.

32. See C.A. Bartlett and S. Ghoshal, 'Tap your subsidiaries for global reach', *Harvard Business Review*, November–December (1986), pp. 87–94; C.A. Bartlett and S. Ghoshal, *Managing across Borders: the Transnational Solution*, Harvard Business School Press, 1989, pp. 105–11; and A.M. Rugman and A. Verbeke, 'Extending the theory of the multinational enterprise: internalization and strategic management perspectives', *Journal of International Business Studies*, vol. 34 (2003), pp. 125–37.

33. For a discussion about the strategic role of subsidiaries see J. Birkinshaw and A.J. Morrison, 'Configurations of strategy and structure in multinational subsidiaries', *Journal of International Business Studies*, vol. 26, no. 4 (1996), pp. 729–94; and A. Rugman and A. Verbeke, 'Subsidiary-specific advantages in multinational enterprises', *Strategic Management Journal*, vol. 22, no. 3 (2001), pp. 237–50.

34. For an analysis of subsidiary and subunit initiatives in multinational corporations, see J. Birkinshaw, *Entrepreneurship and the Global Firm*, Sage, 2000.

China comes to Hollywood: Wanda's acquisition of AMC

Introduction

Chinese acquisitions of US assets and businesses have reached record levels during the last few years, reaching investments of about $35 bn (€26 bn or £21 bn) in 2011. Despite this Wanda's $2.6 bn acquisition of US second-largest cinema chain AMC sent shock wave's through the USA and especially Hollywood. It creates the world's largest cinema company by revenues and Wanda will control about 10 per cent of the global cinema market. It was the biggest Chinese acquisition of a US company ever and marked a new era as Chinese investment reached into the heart of US entertainment and culture. Although Chinese acquisitions in the USA have proven to be controversial before, this one may prove to be even more challenging and it was speculated that a Hollywood ending was far from certain. According to one analyst the deal strengthens Wanda's global status as movie theatre owner:

Gerry Lopez, CEO of AMC Entertainment Holdings, left, shakes hands with Zhang Lin, Vice President of Wanda during a signing ceremony in Beijing, China, Monday, 21 May 2012.

> 'Wanda has been the largest theatre owner in the second largest film market in the world. Now the deal makes it also the owner of the second largest theatre chain in the largest film market.'

Wanda Cinema Line Corp. is China's largest operator by cinema screens with over 730 screens. Its cinema operations generated $282 m in box office revenue in 2011 at 86 movie theatres cinemas all around China. The plan is to expand to about 2,000 screens by 2015. A month before the deal Mr Wang Jianlin, the Chairman of Wanda, had said that he would announce 'a merger that surprises the world' and when the acquisition was announced he likened the deal to 'airing a huge advertisement on the international stage'. According to Mr Wang the AMC acquisition is a significant step in turning Wanda into a multinational company within 10 years and a truly international business group that will last for a 'century'.

The deal means that Wanda takes a 100 per cent stake in AMC and bears all its debts and the company will also invest $500 m in AMC theatre refurbishments and advertising. AMC is the second-biggest cinema chain operator in North America, which is the world's biggest

film market with ticket sales of over $10 bn. AMC has more than 5,000 screens in 346 cinema theatres in this market and is the world's largest operator of IMAX and 3D screens including 120 and 2,170 screens respectively.

Although the announced acquisition was huge it is relatively small compared with the rest of the Dalian Wanda real-estate conglomerate. Dalian Wanda Group Corp. Ltd includes assets of over $35 bn, annual revenue of about $17 bn and 55,000 employees. Wanda, which means 'a thousand roads lead here', consists of five-star hotels, tourist resorts, theme parks and shopping malls. The 'Wanda Plaza' complexes that combine malls with housing and hotels have been a huge success in China and can be found in more than 60 Chinese cities.

Mr Wang Jianlin, the Founder, Chairman and President of Dalian Wanda, is the sixth-richest man in China. He joined the army as a teenager and stayed in the military for 17 years. In 1988 he founded Dalian Wanda and rode the wave of China's phenomenal growth by investing in property. His military background and ties to local officials helped him as large commercial land sales are handled by local governments. As he was willing to take on whatever property the local government was ready to give, he became popular with officials. Soon Wanda was the first property company to work in several cities.

A landmark deal

AMC was considered a 'trophy' acquisition in the American entertainment industry and it was described as a landmark deal by analysts and investors. As announced by the Chairman and President, Mr Wang:

> 'This acquisition will help make Wanda a truly global cinema owner, with theatres and technology that enhance the movie-going experience for audiences in the world's two largest movie markets.'

Mr Wang considered the deal to be a springboard to expand Wanda's global cinema presence further with the goal to reach 20 per cent of the world movie theatre market by 2020. He also said that Wanda is considering more acquisitions abroad in entertainment, hotels and retail and said it might try to buy into a global hotel brand or hotel management company as he explained that Wanda wants to be a big company 'not just in China, but in the world'.

At the announcement of the deal AMC's Gerry Lopez, Chief Executive Officer and President, explained:

> 'As the film and exhibition business continues its global expansion, the time has never been more opportune to welcome the enthusiastic support of our new owners. Wanda and AMC are both dedicated to providing our customers with a premier entertainment experience and state-of-the-art amenities and share corporate cultures focused on strategic growth and innovation. With Wanda as its partner, AMC will continue to seek out new ways to expand and invest in the movie-going experience.'

To further expand on its home market Wanda will benefit from the know-how of AMC, which operates on a market five times Chinese annual box office sales. AMC has an established worldwide network of cinema theatres and this will give Wanda a reputable brand. There is also a trend for more foreign movies in China and the transaction may allow Wanda to secure more Hollywood movies for distribution in China. In February 2012 China agreed to open up its cinemas to more American films and through the acquisition Wanda gains more clout in negotiating with major Hollywood studios that are eager to expand into the rapidly growing Chinese market. Wanda is also a contestant in the race for a licence to distribute

foreign films in China, which is now in the hands of two state-owned companies. However, it is uncertain to what degree the acquisition will please the authorities and increase Wanda's chance of winning the licence. There are also opportunities for Wanda in the USA apart from the cinemas themselves, as AMC is considered to be a platform for the development of commercial property, hotels and shopping malls in the USA.

Wanda and the Chinese entertainment industry

Wanda has a history of investing in culture and entertainment and this aligns with China's overall ambition to invest in the sector. When the deal was announced the Chairman and President of Wanda, Mr Wang, accordingly declared:

> 'Wanda has a deep commitment to investing in the entertainment business and is already the largest in this sector in China, with more than US$1.6 billion invested in cultural and entertainment activities since 2005. We share with AMC a passion for the growth of the worldwide movie industry. We look forward to partnering with AMC's management team and employees to build on the many strengths of the company.'

Wanda's press release on the transaction continued:

> 'The Wanda Group began to massively invest in cultural industries in 2005. It has entered five industries, including central cultural district, big stage show, film production and projection, entertainment chain and Chinese calligraphy and painting collection. Wanda has invested more than $1.6 billion in cultural industries and become the nation's largest enterprise investor in cultural industries.'

Wanda's acquisition is part of a more general effort to develop China's own home-grown culture and entertainment industry. Cinema is an increasingly popular recreational activity in China and the film market is booming. China has seen an increase of 30 per cent in box office sales during the last couple of years, reaching $2.1 bn in 2011, and passed Japan as the biggest market for Hollywood films outside the USA in 2012. The country is investing heavily in film, animation and is in the midst of a multiplex building boom to provide entertainment to the expanding middle class. It is adding an average of 8 movie screens a day to its current 9,200 screens. The goal is to build about 25,000 cinema screens nationwide in the next five years. By 2040, the government aims to have 40,000 screens (about the size in the USA in 2012). There are also efforts to build film production companies. In brief, cinema operation is a growing business as people are willing to spend on entertainment as their income increases.

Managing the US entry

Wanda's acquisition of AMC was the largest overseas cultural investment of a Chinese private enterprise ever and raised some concerns in the USA. AMC is a US household name, 'once epitomised as the all-American movie-watching experience'. It is thus a significant expansion of Chinese influence in the American film industry and some were anxious about this effect as many American movies are censored or even banned in China. Mr Wang is after all a Communist Party member, who sits on China's top advisory council. Wanda's acquisition of AMC thus increases concerns that Chinese-style censorship of politically controversial movies may become commonplace also in the USA. As reported by *USA Today*: 'Beijing is investing heavily in projecting its "soft power", or cultural influence, by boosting Chinese state media's presence abroad, including the USA, where the Chinese government has also run advertisements in New York's Times Square.'

Chinese investments in the USA had raised concerns earlier and the US government has rejected investments in the past in the telecommunications and energy industry due to national security concerns. However, cinema is unlikely to be considered a strategic industry for the USA. The acquisition, however, requires regulatory approval both in the USA and China.

Mr Wang also assured that Wanda has 'no plans to promote Chinese films in the United States' and that AMC CEO Lopez 'will decide what movies will be shown' in AMC theatres. It was also made clear that AMC would continue to be operated from its headquarters in Kansas City. Mr Wang said Wanda will retain AMC senior management and would not interfere with everyday operations and programming decisions, which should remain with the US management. He continued to say that the most important part of the deal was securing that more than 40 senior AMC managers would stay after the takeover and he further explained: 'The crucial thing is to keep the enthusiasm of the current management and the workers . . . You have to put the human factors first. The only thing that changed is the boss.'

Sources: *AMC* press release, 20 May 2012, Chinadaily.com, 23 May 2012, *Dalian Wanda* press release, 21 May 2012, *Financial Times*, 22 May 2012, 23 May 2012, 26 May 2012, 28 May 2012, LAtimes.com, 20 May 2012, *New York Times*, 20 May 2012, *Reuters*, 21 May 2012, *The Washington Post*, 21 May 2012, *Wall Street Journal*, 21 May 2012.

Questions

1 Considering Yip's globalisation framework (Figure 8.2), what drivers of internationalisation do you think were most important when Wanda entered the US market through its AMC acquisition?

2 What national sources of competitive advantage might Wanda draw from its Chinese base? What disadvantages derive from its Chinese base?

3 In the light of the CAGE framework, what challenges may Wanda meet as it enters the US market?

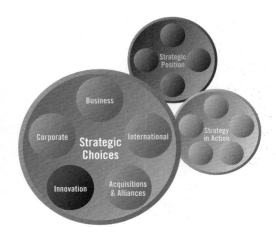

9

INNOVATION AND ENTREPRENEURSHIP

Learning outcomes

After reading this chapter you should be able to:

- Identify and respond to key *innovation dilemmas*, such as the relative emphases to place on technologies or markets, product or process innovations, open versus closed innovation, and the underlying business model.

- Anticipate and to some extent influence the *diffusion* (or spread) of innovations.

- Decide when being a *first-mover* or a *follower* is most appropriate in innovation, and how an incumbent organisation should respond to innovative challengers.

- Anticipate both key issues facing entrepreneurs as they go through the *stages of growth*, from start-up to exit, and the choices involved in *entrepreneurial strategies*.

- Evaluate opportunities and choices facing *social entrepreneurs* as they create new ventures to address social problems.

Key terms

business model p. 301

diffusion p. 305

disruptive innovation p. 310

entrepreneurial life cycle p. 312

first-mover advantage p. 308

innovation p. 296

open innovation p. 300

platform leadership p. 301

S-curve p. 306

social entrepreneurs p. 317

tipping point p. 307

MyStrategyLab

MyStrategyLab is designed to help you make the most of your studies. Visit **www.pearsoned.co.uk/mystrategylab** to discover a wide range of resources, including:

- A personalised **Study plan** that will help you understand core concepts
- **Audio and video clips** that put the spotlight on strategy in the real world
- **Online glossaries and flashcards** that provide helpful reminders when you're looking for some quick revision.

(9.1) INTRODUCTION

This chapter is about creating the new – both new products and services and new business models and organisations. Creating value for firms and customers, such innovation and entrepreneurship are fundamental to today's economy. But they also pose hard choices. For example, should a company look always to be a pioneer in new technologies, or rather be a fast follower, as Samsung typically is? How should a company react to radical innovations that threaten to destroy its existing revenues, as the Kodak film business had to with the rise of electronic cameras? How should entrepreneurs handle takeover bids from powerful rich companies: in 2012, photo-sharing site Instagram's founders persuaded Facebook to buy the company for $1 billion (£750 m; €700 m) after just two years of business. The chapter focuses particularly on the choices involved in innovation and entrepreneurship.

Entrepreneurship is a fundamental organisational process. All businesses start with an act of entrepreneurship, but large established firms also practice entrepreneurship in the form of 'corporate entrepreneurship' (section 10.2), while many people pursue 'social entrepreneurship' for the public good. Innovation is a key aspect of business-level strategy as introduced in Chapter 6, with implications for cost, price and sustained competitive advantage. As such, it too is relevant in both public and private spheres. Promoting greater innovation and entrepreneurship is crucial to the improvement of public services.

The two main themes that link innovation and entrepreneurship are *timing* and *relationships* (see Figure 9.1). Timing decisions include when to be first-mover or fast second in innovation; when, and if, an innovation will reach its tipping point, the point where demand takes off; and, for an entrepreneurial new venture, when founders should finally exit their enterprise. The other theme is relationships. Creating innovations or new organisations is very rarely done alone. Successful innovation and entrepreneurship are typically done through relationships. These relationships come in many forms: sometimes relationships between organisations and

Figure 9.1 The innovation–entrepreneurship framework

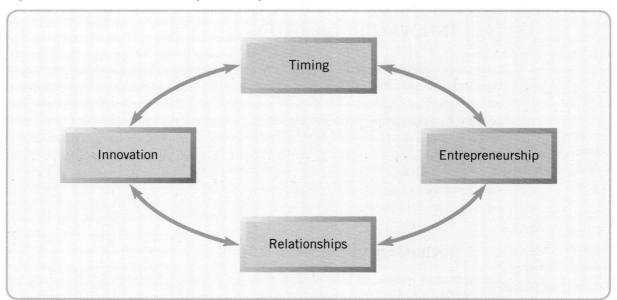

their customers; sometimes relationships between big business and small start-ups; sometimes between business and 'social entrepreneurs'.

Within Figure 9.1's broad framework, this chapter will examine first innovation, then entrepreneurship:

- Section 9.2 starts with four fundamental *innovation dilemmas*: technology push as against market pull; product innovation rather than process innovation; open versus closed innovation; and, finally, technological as opposed to broader business model innovation. None of these are absolute 'either–or' dilemmas, but managers and entrepreneurs must choose where to concentrate their limited resources.

- Section 9.3 considers issues surrounding the *diffusion*, or spread, of innovations in the marketplace. Diffusion processes often follow *S-curve patterns*, raising further typical issues for decision, particularly with regard to tipping points and tripping points.

- Section 9.4 completes the discussion of innovation by considering choices with regard to timing. This includes *first-mover* advantages and disadvantages, the advantages of being '*fast second*' into a market, and the issue of how established *incumbents* should respond to innovative challengers.

- Section 9.5 addresses *entrepreneurship*. The section discusses typical choices facing entrepreneurs as their ventures progress through the uncertain *stages of growth*, from start-up to exit. The section also considers *entrepreneurial strategies*. Finally, it examines the kinds of *relationships* that entrepreneurs may have to form, particularly with larger firms practising 'open innovation'.

- Finally Section 9.6 introduces *social entrepreneurship*, by which individuals and small groups can launch innovative and flexible new initiatives that larger public agencies are often unable to pursue. Again, social entrepreneurs face choices with regard to relationships, particularly with big business.

The Key Debate at the end of this chapter brings entrepreneurship and innovation together again by considering the issue of whether small or large firms are better at innovation.

(9.2) INNOVATION DILEMMAS

Innovation raises fundamental strategic dilemmas for strategists. Innovation is more complex than just invention. *Invention* involves the conversion of new knowledge into a new product, process or service. **Innovation involves the conversion of new knowledge into a new product, process or service *and* the putting of this new product, process or service into actual use.**[1] The strategic dilemmas stem from this more extended process. Strategists have to make choices with regard to four fundamental issues: how far to follow technological opportunity as against market demand; how much to invest in product innovation rather than process innovation; how far to open themselves up to innovative ideas from outside; and finally whether to focus on technological innovation rather than extending innovation to their whole business model.[2]

9.2.1 Technology push or market pull

People often see innovation as driven by technology. In the pure version of this *technology push* view, it is the new knowledge created by technologists or scientists that pushes the innovation process. Research and development laboratories produce new products, processes or services and then hand them over to the rest of the organisation to manufacture, market and distribute. According to this push perspective, managers should listen primarily to their scientists and technologists, let them follow their hunches and support them with ample resources. Generous R&D budgets are crucial to making innovation happen. For example, leading pharmaceutical company Pfizer spent $750 m on research on a drug for Alzheimer's disease, before abandoning the effort in 2012.

An alternative approach to innovation is *market pull*. Market pull reflects a view of innovation that goes beyond invention and sees the importance of actual use. In many sectors users, not producers, are common sources of important innovations. In designing their innovation strategies, therefore, organisations should listen in the first place to users rather than their own scientists and technologists. There are two prominent but contrasting approaches to market pull:

- *Lead users*: according to MIT professor Eric Von Hippel, in many markets it is lead users who are the principal source of innovation.[3] In medical surgery, top surgeons often adapt existing surgical instruments in order to carry out new types of operation. In extreme sports such as snowboarding or windsurfing, it is leading sportspeople who make the improvements necessary for greater performance. In this view, then, it is the pull of market experts that is responsible for innovation. Managers need to build close relationships with lead users such as the best surgeons or sporting champions. Marketing and sales functions identify the lead users of a field and then scientists and technologists translate their inventive ideas into commercial products, processes or services that the wider market can use. For example, the Danish toy company Lego runs a special 'Ambassador Program' to keep close to 150 specialised user groups around the world; specialist users in design and architecture were responsible for originating the Lego Jewellery and Lego Architecture ranges.

- *Frugal innovation*: at the other end of the user continuum is the pull exerted by ordinary consumers, particularly the poor in emerging markets.[4] Rather than the expensive research-intensive model of the traditional technology push approach, frugality is the guiding principle here. Frugal innovation involves sensitivity to poor people's real needs. Responding not only to these users' lack of money, but also to the tough conditions in which they live, frugal innovation typically emphasises low cost, simplicity, robustness and easy maintenance. The Tata Nano car is a famous example, a simple car produced for the Indian market for only $2,000. Muruganatham's cheap sanitary towels are another example, this time emphasising opportunities to create employment for the economically disadvantaged too (see Illustration 9.1).

The lead user and frugal innovation approaches are opposite ends of a spectrum, one elitist, the other basic. Many organisations will choose somewhere in between. But fundamentally both approaches share a key insight: innovations do not just come from scientific research, but can be pulled by users in the external market.

There are merits to both the technology push and market pull views. Relying heavily on existing users can make companies too conservative and vulnerable to disruptive technologies that uncover needs unforeseen by existing markets (see section 9.4.3). On the other hand, history is littered with examples of companies that have blindly pursued technological excellence without regard to real market needs. Technology push and market pull are best seen as extreme views, therefore helping to focus attention on a fundamental choice: relatively how much to rely on science and technology as sources of innovation, rather than what people

ILLUSTRATION 9.1

Frugal sanitary towels

Arunachalam Muruganantham aims to transform the lives of Indian women with a fundamental innovation.

High school drop-out and welder Arunachalam Muruganantham has developed a low-cost sanitary towel the hard way. In India, only 12 per cent of women can afford to use sanitary towels for their monthly periods, the rest making do with old rags and even husks or sand. As Muruganantham's wife explained to him, if she bought the expensive sanitary towels on the market, the family would have to do without milk. But the cost for many women is infections and even cervical cancer.

Muruganantham determined to find a cheap way of supplying Indian women with proper sanitary towels. In Indian society, however, the issue was taboo. The local hospital was unhelpful, and even Muruganantham's wife and sisters refused to talk about the problem. A survey of college girls failed. Muruganantham's prototypes were scorned by his wife. At his wits' end, Muruganantham experimented on himself, carrying a bladder inflated with goat's blood while wearing one of his own sanitary towels and women's undergarments. His tests while walking and cycling around the village created a local scandal. His wife moved out.

Muruganantham characterised the issue as a 'triple A problem – Affordability, Availability and Awareness'. But after four years of research, he finally built a machine for producing sanitary towels at less than half the price of those offered by rivals such as Procter & Gamble and Johnson & Johnson. The machines are cheap and hand-operated, enabling small-scale local production by units employing six to ten women each. Muruganantham believes that the small businesses using his machines could create up to one million jobs: 'The model of mass-production is outdated. Now it is about production by the mass of people.'

Muruganantham sells the machines to local entrepreneurs, charities and self-help groups, who produce the sanitary towels without fancy marketing. Often the women who make the towels are the best marketers, passing on the benefits by word-of-mouth. Resident women dealers are appointed for particular streets or villages, and they inform local women about the dangers of traditional methods at the same time as offering their products. Towels are often sold singly rather than in bulk packets, and are even sold through barter. Muruganantham explains the marketing: 'It's done silently and even the male members of their families don't know.'

By 2012, Muruganantham had machines operating in 23 states within India and was declaring his ambition to make India a 100 per cent sanitary towel using nation. He was also contemplating launch in Africa and spin-off projects such as nappies for babies and incontinence pads for elderly people. Muruganantham was confident about the sustainability of his model: 'We compete very comfortably with the big giants (such as Procter & Gamble). That's why they call me the corporate bomber.' His wife has moved back in with him.

Sources: BBC World Service, 6 August 2012; *Economic Times*, 18 January 2012; *The Hindu*, 9 February 2012.

Questions

1 Identify the various features of Muruganantham's approach that make his sanitary towel business a typical or not so typical 'frugal innovation'.

2 Could a large company such as Procter & Gamble imitate this strategy?

are actually doing in the marketplace. The key is to manage the balance actively. For a stagnant organisation looking for radical innovation, it might be worth redeploying effort from whichever model currently predominates: for the technology push organisation to use more market pull or for the market pull organisation to invest more in fundamental research.

9.2.2 Product or process innovation

Just as managers must manage the balance between technology and market pull, so must they determine the relative emphasis to place on product or process innovation. *Product innovation* relates to the final product (or service) to be sold, especially with regard to its features; *process innovation* relates to the way in which this product is produced and distributed, especially with regard to improvements in cost or reliability. Some firms specialise more in product innovation, others more in process innovation. For example, in computers, Apple has generally concentrated its efforts on designing attractive product features (for instance, the iPad tablet), while Dell has innovated in terms of efficient processes, for instance direct sales, modularity and build-to-order.

The relative importance of product innovation and process innovation typically changes as industries evolve over time.[5] Usually the first stages of an industry are dominated by product innovation based on new features. Thus the early history of the automobile was dominated by competition as to whether cars should be fuelled by steam, electricity or petrol, have their engines at the front or at the rear, and have three wheels or four.[6] Industries eventually coalesce around a *dominant design*, the standard configuration of basic features: after Henry Ford's 1908 Model T, cars generally became petrol-driven, with their engines at the front and four wheels. Once such a dominant design is established, innovation switches to process innovation, as competition shifts to producing the dominant design as efficiently as possible. Henry Ford's great process innovation was the moving assembly line, introduced in 1913. Finally, the cycle is liable to start again, as some significant innovation challenges the dominant design: in the case of cars recently, the emergence of electric power.[4]

Figure 9.2 provides a general model of the relationship between product and process innovation over time. The model has several strategic implications:

- *New developing industries* typically favour product innovation, as competition is still around defining the basic features of the product or service.

- *Maturing industries* typically favour process innovation, as competition shifts towards efficient production of a dominant design of product or service.

- *Small new entrants* typically have the greatest opportunity when dominant designs are either not yet established or beginning to collapse. Thus, in the early stages of the automobile industry, before Ford's Model T, there were more than a hundred mostly small competitors, each with its own combination of product features. The recent challenge to the petrol-based dominant design has provided opportunities to small companies such as the Californian start-up Tesla Motors, which had produced more than 2,000 electric-powered Roadsters by the beginning of 2012.

- *Large incumbent firms* typically have the advantage during periods of dominant design stability, when scale economies and the ability to roll out process innovations matter most. With the success of the Model T and the assembly line, by the 1930s there were just four large American automobile manufacturers, namely Ford, General Motors, Chrysler and American Motors, all producing very similar kinds of cars.

Figure 9.2 Product and process innovation

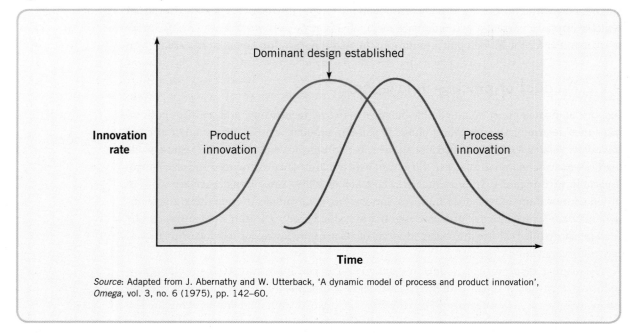

Source: Adapted from J. Abernathy and W. Utterback, 'A dynamic model of process and product innovation', *Omega*, vol. 3, no. 6 (1975), pp. 142–60.

This sequence of product to process innovation is not always a neat one. In practice, product and process innovation are often pursued in tandem.[7] For example, each new generation of microprocessor also requires simultaneous process innovation in order to manufacture the new microprocessor with increasing precision. However, the model does help managers confront the issue of where to focus, whether more on product features or more on process efficiency. It also points to whether competitive advantage is likely to be with small new entrants or large incumbent firms. Other things being equal, small start-ups should time their entry for periods of instability in dominant design and focus on product rather than process innovation.

9.2.3 **Open or closed innovation**

The traditional approach to innovation has been to rely on the organisation's own internal resources – its laboratories and marketing departments. Innovation in this approach is secretive, anxious to protect intellectual property and avoid competitors free-riding on ideas. This 'closed' model of innovation contrasts with the newer 'open model' of innovation.[8] **Open innovation involves the deliberate import and export of knowledge by an organisation in order to accelerate and enhance its innovation**. The motivating idea of open innovation is that exchanging ideas openly is likely to produce better products more quickly than the internal, closed approach. Speedier and superior products are what are needed to keep ahead of the competition, not obsessive secrecy.

Open innovation is being widely adopted. For example, technology giant IBM has established a network of 10 'collaboratories' with other companies and universities, in countries ranging from Switzerland to Saudi Arabia. Last.fm, the online music service, hosts special 'hack days', when it invites its users for a day of free food, drink and work on developing new applications together. *Crowdsourcing* is an increasingly popular form of open innovation and means that a company or organisation broadcasts a specific problem to a crowd of individuals or teams often in tournaments with prizes awarded to the best solution.[9] Companies such as Procter & Gamble, Eli Lilly and Dow Chemicals use the network company InnoCentive to set innovation 'challenges' (or problems) in open competition over the internet: by 2012, 1,215 challenges had been solved by a community of 260,000 'solvers', winning prizes of up to $1 m.

Open innovation typically requires careful support of collaborators. In particular, dominant firms may need to exercise platform leadership. **Platform leadership refers to how large firms consciously nurture independent companies through successive waves of innovation around their basic technological 'platform'.**[10] Video games console companies such as Microsoft and Sony have to manage relationships with a host of large and small video games publishers in order to ensure that their consoles are supported by an attractive set of games, making full use of the latest technological possibilities. Intel, whose microprocessors are used by a host of computer and mobile phone companies, regularly publishes 'roadmaps' outlining several years ahead the new products it expects to release, allowing customers to plan their own new product development processes (see Illustration 9.2 for Fujitsu's cloud computing roadmap).

The balance between open and closed innovation depends on three key factors:

- *Competitive rivalry*. In highly rivalrous industries, partners are liable to behave opportunistically and steal innovations. Closed innovation is better where such rivalrous behaviours can be anticipated.

- *One-shot innovation*. Opportunistic behaviour is more likely where innovation involves a major shift in technology, likely to put winners substantially ahead and losers permanently behind. Open innovation works best where innovation is more continuous, so encouraging more reciprocal behaviour over time.

- *Tight-linked innovation*. Where technologies are complex and tightly interlinked, open innovation risks introducing damagingly inconsistent elements, with knock-on effects throughout the product range. Apple, with its smoothly integrated range of products from computers to phones, has therefore tended to prefer closed innovation in order to protect the quality of the user experience.

9.2.4 **Technological or business model innovation**

Many successful innovations do not rely simply upon new science or technology, but involve reorganising into new combinations all the elements of a business. Here innovators are creating whole new *business models*, bringing customers, producers and suppliers together in new ways, with or without new technologies.[11] A **business model describes how an organisation manages incomes and costs through the structural arrangement of its activities.** For the ultra-cheap airline Ryanair, business model innovation involved the generation of revenues via direct sales through the internet, thereby cutting out intermediary travel agents, while also using cheap secondary airports. Internet sales and cheaper airports were much more important than technological innovation. The internet technology itself was not Ryanair's creation and it had the same aeroplanes as most of its competitors. Thus it can be as effective to innovate in terms of business model as in technology.

Opportunities for business model innovation can be analysed in terms of the value chain, value net or activity systems frameworks introduced in sections 3.4.2 and 3.4.3. These frameworks point managers and entrepreneurs to two basic areas for potential innovation:

- *The product*. A new business model may redefine what the product or service is and how it is produced. In terms of the value chain specifically, this concerns technology development,

ILLUSTRATION 9.2

The disruptive cloud

Japanese computer giant Fujitsu plots a roadmap to navigate the transition to cloud computing.

Fujitsu is the world's third-largest information technology services company, after IBM and Hewlett Packard. It offers a range of products and services in the areas of computing, telecommunications and microelectronics. In 2010, it launched a new cloud computing business to take advantage of the transition from the traditional model of in-house business computing. David Gentle, Director of Foresight at Fujitsu's Cloud and Strategic Service Offerings business, describes the transition as a disruptive innovation: 'It's a bit like a salmon that is swimming upstream and then has to make a leap to get to the next smooth stretch of water.'

Cloud computing relies on the internet to deliver computer services from external suppliers direct to users. Dropbox and Apple's iCloud are consumer cloud services. For business, the cloud comes in three main forms: 'Software as a Service' (SaaS), such as Microsoft Office via the internet; 'Infrastructure as a Service' (IaaS), such as Amazon's EC2 virtual computer capacity; and 'Platform as a Service' (PaaS), which provides a computing platform with operating system, web server and database, such as Google's App Engine.

Fujitsu describes the transition from the traditional model to the Cloud Computing Era in a technology 'roadmap' titled 'The Cloud Paradigm Shift'. The roadmap describes the traditional client–server model, where the computing power is supplied by in-house servers, as offering a trajectory of steadily improving *technology* efficiency. This culminates in the so-called Private Cloud, cloud services provided by the business itself. The shift to the 'Public Cloud' (with full adoption of SaaS, IaaS and PaaS) brings a leap in value. By tapping into the shared resources of external suppliers, a business gains access to huge economies of scale and the innovations possible by specialist suppliers. The new trajectory increases value by improving *business* efficiency.

The shift is disruptive, though. Purchasers in IT functions will no longer need such large investments in physical servers and staff. As traditional server products and related services decline, Fujitsu is transitioning its business to meet the demands of the new market. David Gentle explains the function of the roadmap in this context: 'This roadmap is the first slide in any conversation with customers, partners and staff internally. It shows the future, as well as anchoring on the past. It helps get everyone on the same page.'

procurement, inbound logistics, operations and procurement. For example, when Nucor pioneered electric-arc mini-mill technology in the steel industry, it was able to use scrap metal as its raw material rather than pure iron, employ non-unionised labour and outsource a lot of its product development to its equipment supplier Voest Alpine.

- *The selling.* A new business model may change the way in which the organisation generates its revenues, with implications for selling and distribution. In terms of the value chain, this concerns outbound logistics, marketing, sales and service. Nucor, for example, sold its cheap but low-quality steel at standard prices on the internet, in contrast to the traditional steel producers' reliance on elaborate negotiations with individual customers on prices and specifications.

The business model concept emphasises the fundamental features of how business activities are organised. In terms of business models, mature industries therefore often have a lot of standardisation. For example, most accounting firms are organised in similar ways: their business model involves earning the majority of income from audit and relying on a high ratio

Fujitsu's Cloud Roadmap

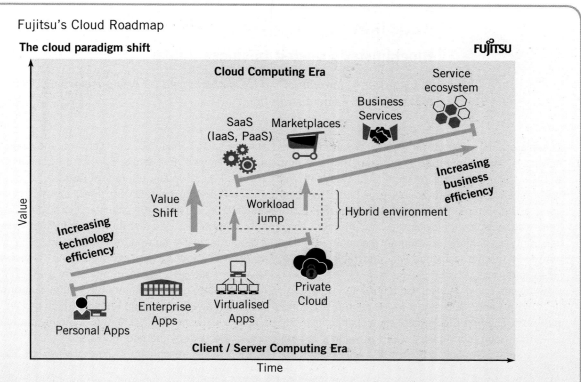

Source: *Making the Transition to Cloud*, Fujitsu Services Ltd. (Gentle, David 2011). With permission from Fujitsu Limited UK.

Questions

1 Why might some groups be apprehensive about the Cloud Computing Era?

2 What are the advantages of a visual roadmap of this kind? What are the limitations to this visual approach?

---

of junior staff to partners. Business strategy within an industry characterised by standardised business models is mostly about differentiation. Thus accounting firms might differentiate themselves within the same model by emphasising particular kinds of sectoral expertise or international networks.

However, the fundamental nature of business models means that business model innovation tends to imply radical change. Business model innovation is not just a matter of technology, but involves a wide range of the firm's activities. Thus the business model concept helps managers and entrepreneurs consider science and technology as just one part of the whole package that contributes to innovation. Innovation can be drawn from all parts of the value chain, not just technology development. Indeed, radical technological innovation often requires business model innovation too. For example, in order to promote adoption of its innovative electric cars in France, Toyota formed a partnership with electricity supplier EDF and local authorities to create networks of subsidised public charging points. Illustration 9.3 describes the radical repercussions of business model innovation in the movie rental business.

ILLUSTRATION 9.3

Blockbuster's busted business model

Blockbuster's store rental model is challenged by new business models for movie and game distribution.

There are a lot of ways for people to see a movie nowadays. They can go to the cinema. They can buy a DVD from specialist retailers such as HMV or large supermarkets such as Tesco or Lidl. They can order a DVD online and receive it through the post. They can download movies via the internet. They can rent via a kiosk or vending machine. Or they can do it the old-fashioned way and rent it from a video store.

Blockbuster, of course, is famous for its stores: in 2010 it had 7,000 stores in 18 countries around the world. The first Blockbuster store opened in 1985 in Texas. Soon Blockbuster was the world's largest movie rental company, and in 1994 was bought by media conglomerate Viacom for $7.6 bn (€3 bn). Ten years later, as Blockbuster's growth stalled, Viacom spun it off as an independent company again, now valued at $7.5 bn.

Blockbuster's business model had been an attractive one. Two decades ago, in a period of limited television channels, movie rental had given customers unheard-of choice of viewing. Blockbuster used its huge buying power to obtain the latest releases from the film studios at little cost. Blockbuster would give 40 per cent of the rental income to the studios and supply them with information on usage for market research purposes. Studios typically would hold back from releasing the movie to other rental companies or to retailers for an initial period, making Blockbuster the essential outlet for the latest hits. Blockbuster was able to leverage this business model into rapid growth, using a mixture of its own stores, franchising and acquisitions. It also extended the model to the rental of video games.

However, the market is now much more complex. For a start, television channels began to proliferate. In the USA, Netflix emerged in 1997, originally using a rental-by-mail model. By 2009, Netflix had mailed its two-billionth DVD. In the United Kingdom, DVD mail-rental company Lovefilm was founded in 2002, and by 2010 had 50 per cent of the national market, as well as a strong position in Scandinavia. The mail-rental model offers customers a far greater choice (Lovefilm has 70,000 titles, against the few hundred in a typical Blockbuster store) and needs only a few centralised distribution centres, as against a labour-intensive network of retail stores. Moreover, as internet capacity has improved, both Netflix and Lovefilm have also begun to stream movies straight to customers' computers. Another rental model was pioneered by 2003 start-up Redbox, which had established a network of 22,000 DVD vending machines across the USA by the end of 2009.

Blockbuster responded in several ways. In 2004, it launched its own online rental service, with customers able to return their DVDs simply through a local store. In 2009, Blockbuster launched vending machines in the USA. The company closed more than 1,800 stores. It withdrew from some national markets altogether, for example Spain, Portugal, Ecuador and Peru. But, after continued heavy losses, Blockbuster filed for bankruptcy in 2010. The next year, the company was bought for $233 m by the satellite TV company Dish networks. Store closures continued, and the whole retail management team were dismissed.

Sources: Financial Times, 24 February 2010; The Times, 28 December 2009; The Express on Sunday, 28 February 2010.

Questions

1 Compare the pros and cons of the various business models for movie consumption.

2 What potential competitive advantages did Blockbuster have as a company as the new business models emerged in the last decade or so?

(9.3) INNOVATION DIFFUSION

So far, this chapter has been concerned with sources and types of innovation, for example technology push or market pull. This section moves to the diffusion of innovations after they have been introduced.[12] **Diffusion is the process by which innovations spread among users.** Since innovation is typically expensive, its commercial attractiveness can hinge on the pace – extent and speed – at which the market adopts new products and services. This pace of diffusion is something managers can influence from both the supply and demand sides, and which they can also model using the S-curve.

9.3.1 The pace of diffusion

The pace of diffusion can vary widely according to the nature of the products concerned. It took 38 years for the television to reach 150 million units sold; it took just 7 years for Apple's iPod to reach the same number. The pace of diffusion is influenced by a combination of supply-side and demand-side factors, over which managers have considerable control. On the *supply side*, pace is determined by product features such as:

- *Degree of improvement* in performance above current products (from a customer's perspective) that provides incentive to change. For example, 3G mobile phones did not provide sufficient performance improvement to prompt rapid switch in many markets. Managers need to make sure innovation benefits sufficiently exceed costs.

- *Compatibility* with other factors, for example digital TV becomes more attractive as the broadcasting networks change their programmes to that format. Managers and entrepreneurs therefore need to ensure appropriate complementary products and services are in place.

- *Complexity*, either in the product itself or in the marketing methods being used to commercialise the product: unduly complex pricing structures, as with many financial service products such as pensions, discourage consumer adoption. Simple pricing structures typically accelerate adoptions.

- *Experimentation* – the ability to test products before commitment to a final decision – either directly or through the availability of information about the experience of other customers. Free initial trial periods are often used to encourage diffusion.

- *Relationship management*, in other words how easy it is to get information, place orders and receive support. Google's 2010 launch of its first phone, the Android Nexus One, was hampered because the company was not used to providing the access to help staff that mobile phone customers generally expect. Managers and entrepreneurs need to put in place an appropriate relationship management process to assist new users.

On the *demand side*, simple affordability is of course key. Beyond this, there are three further factors that tend to drive the pace of diffusion:

- *Market awareness*. Many potentially successful products have failed through lack of consumer awareness – particularly when the promotional effort of the innovator has been confined to 'push' promotion to its intermediaries (e.g. distributors).

- *Network effects* refer to the way that demand growth for some products accelerates as more people adopt the product or service. Once a critical mass of users have adopted, it becomes of much greater benefit, or even necessary, for others to adopt it too. With nearly one billion users, Facebook is practically the obligatory social network for most readers of this book. Likewise, people use Microsoft PowerPoint because almost all their collaborators are likely to use it too (see also section 6.3.6).

● *Customer propensity to adopt*: the distribution of potential customers from early-adopter groups (keen to adopt first) through to laggards (typically indifferent to innovations). Innovations are often targeted initially at early-adopter groups – typically the young and the wealthy – in order to build the critical mass that will encourage more laggardly groups – the poorer and older – to join the bandwagon. Clothing fashion trends typically start with the wealthy and then are diffused to the wider population. Managers and entrepreneurs therefore need to target innovations initially at likely early-adopters.

9.3.2 The diffusion S-curve

The pace of diffusion is typically not steady. Successful innovations often diffuse according to a broad *S-curve* pattern.[13] The shape of the **S-curve reflects a process of initial slow adoption of innovation, followed by a rapid acceleration in diffusion, leading to a plateau representing the limit to demand** (Figure 9.3). The height of the S-curve shows the extent of diffusion; the shape of the S-curve shows the speed.

Diffusion rarely follows exactly this pattern, but none the less the S-curve can help managers and entrepreneurs anticipate forthcoming issues. In particular, the S-curve points to four likely decision points:

● *Timing of the 'tipping point'*. Demand for a new product or service may initially be slow but then reaches a tipping point when it explodes onto a rapid upwards path of growth.[14]

Figure 9.3 The diffusion S-curve

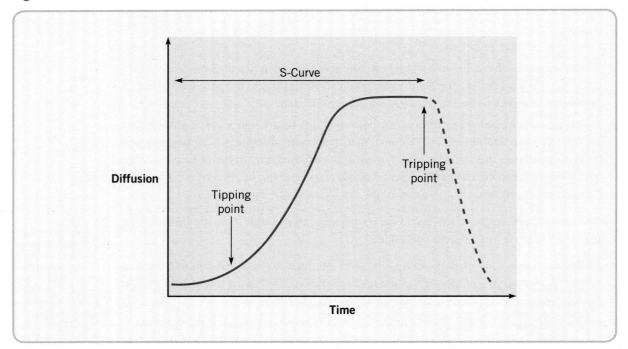

A **tipping point is where demand for a product or service suddenly takes off, with explosive growth.** Tipping points are particularly explosive where there are strong *network effects*: in other words, where the value of a product or service is increased the more people in a network use them. Being aware of a possible tipping point ahead can help managers plan investment in capacity and distribution. Companies can easily underestimate demand. In the mid-1980s, American companies predicted that by 2000 there would be 900,000 mobile phones worldwide. That year came, and 900,000 phones were sold every 19 hours. The Finnish company Nokia was able to seize worldwide leadership. Failing to anticipate a tipping point leads to missed sales and easy opportunities for competitors.

- *Timing of the plateau.* The S-curve also alerts managers to a likely eventual slowdown in demand growth. Again, it is tempting to extrapolate existing growth rates forwards, especially when they are highly satisfactory. But heavy investment immediately before growth turns down is likely to leave firms with over-capacity and carrying extra costs in a period of industry shake-out.

- *Extent of diffusion.* The S-curve does not necessarily lead to one hundred per cent diffusion among potential users. Most innovations fail to displace previous-generation products and services altogether. For example, in music, traditional turntables and LP discs are still preferred over CD and MP3 players by many disc jockeys and music connoisseurs. A critical issue for managers then is to estimate the final ceiling on diffusion, being careful not to assume that tipping point growth will necessarily take over the whole market.

- *Timing of the 'tripping point'.* The tripping point is the opposite of the tipping point, referring to when demand suddenly collapses.[15] Of course, decline is usually more gradual. However, the presence of network effects can lead to relatively few customer defections setting off a market landslide. Such landslides are very hard to reverse. This is what happened to social networking site MySpace, as American and European users defected to Facebook. The tripping point concept warns managers all the time that a small dip in quarterly sales could presage a rapid collapse.

To summarise, the S-curve is a useful concept to help managers and entrepreneurs avoid simply extrapolating next year's sales from last year's sales. However, the tripping point also underlines the fact that innovations do not follow an inevitable process, and their diffusion patterns can be interrupted or reversed at any point. Most innovations, of course, do not even reach a tipping point, let alone a tripping point. As marketing guru Geoffrey Moore has pointed out, there is often a deep 'chasm' to cross between specialised early-adopters of a product and the mainstream market.[16] The Segway Human Transporter, launched in 2001 as the environmentally-friendly technology that would replace the car, sold 6,000 units in its first two years, despite launch production capacity of nearly 500,000 a year.

(9.4) INNOVATORS AND FOLLOWERS

A key choice for managers is whether to lead or to follow in innovation. The S-curve concept seems to promote leadership in innovation. First-movers get the easy sales of early fast growth and can establish a dominant position. There are plenty of examples of first-movers who have built enduring positions on the basis of innovation leadership: Coca-Cola in drinks and Hoover in vacuum cleaners are powerful century-old examples. On the other hand, many first-movers fail. Even the powerful Microsoft failed with its tablet computer launched in 2001. Nine years later, Apple swept the market with its iPad tablet computer.

9.4.1 First-mover advantages and disadvantages

A **first-mover advantage exists where an organisation is better off than its competitors as a result of being first to market with a new product, process or service.** Fundamentally, the first-mover is a monopolist, theoretically able to charge customers high prices without fear of immediate undercutting by competitors. In practice, however, innovators often prefer to sacrifice profit margins for sales growth and, besides, monopoly is usually temporary. There are five potentially more robust first-mover advantages:[17]

- *Experience curve benefits* accrue to first-movers, as their rapid accumulation of experience with the innovation gives them greater expertise than late entrants still relatively unfamiliar with the new product, process or service (see section 6.3.1).
- *Scale benefits* are typically enjoyed by first-movers, as they establish earlier than competitors the volumes necessary for mass production and bulk purchasing, for example.
- *Pre-emption of scarce resources* is an opportunity for first-movers, as late-movers will not have the same access to key raw materials, skilled labour or components, and will have to pay dearly for them.
- *Reputation* can be enhanced by being first, especially since consumers have little 'mind-space' to recognise new brands once a dominant brand has been established in the market.
- *Buyer switching costs* can be exploited by first-movers, by locking in their customers with privileged or sticky relationships that later challengers can only break with difficulty. Switching costs can be increased by establishing and exploiting a *technological standard* (see section 6.3.6).

Experience curve benefits, economies of scale and the pre-emption of scarce resources all confer cost advantages on first-movers. It is possible for them to retaliate against challengers with a price war. Superior reputation and customer lock-in provide a marketing advantage, allowing first-movers to charge high prices, which can then be reinvested in order to consolidate their position against late-entry competitors.

But the experience of Microsoft with its tablet computer shows that first-mover advantages are not necessarily overwhelming. Late-movers have two principal potential advantages:[18]

- *Free-riding*. Late-movers can imitate technological and other innovation at less expense than originally incurred by the pioneers. Research suggests that the costs of imitation are only 65 per cent of the cost of innovation.
- *Learning*. Late-movers can observe what worked well and what did not work well for innovators. They may not make so many mistakes and be able to get it right first time.

9.4.2 First or second?

Given the potential advantages of late-movers, managers and entrepreneurs face a hard choice between striving to be first or coming in later. London Business School's Costas Markides and Paul Geroski argue that the most appropriate response to innovation, especially radical innovation, is often not to be a first-mover, but to be a '*fast second*'.[19] A fast second strategy involves being one of the first to imitate the original innovator. Thus fast second companies may not literally be the second company into the market, but they dominate the second generation of competitors. For example, the French Bookeen company pioneered the e-book market in the early 2000s, but was followed by Sony's eReader in 2006 and Amazon's Kindle in 2007.

There are three contextual factors to consider in choosing between innovating and imitating:

- *Capacity for profit capture*. David Teece of the University of California Berkeley emphasises the importance of innovators being able to capture for themselves the profits of their innovations.[20] This depends on the ease with which followers can imitate. The likelihood of imitation depends on two primary factors. First, imitation is likely if the innovation is in itself *easy to replicate*: for example, if there is little tacit knowledge involved or if it is embedded in a product that is sold in the external marketplace (unlike many process technologies) and is therefore easy to 'reverse-engineer' (see section 3.3). Second, imitation is facilitated if *intellectual property rights* are weak, for example where patents are hard to define or defend.[21] In 2012, Apple successfully sued Samsung for breaches of its iPhone patents, but the $1 bn fine was less than half of what Apple had originally sought from the courts and was a fraction of the Korean technology giant's $18 bn annual profits.

- *Complementary assets*. Possession of the assets or resources necessary to scale up the production and marketing of the innovation is often critical.[22] Many small European biotech start-up companies face this constraint in the pharmaceuticals industry, where marketing and distribution channels in the USA, the world's largest market, are essential complementary assets, but are dominated by the big established pharmaceutical companies. Small European start-ups can find themselves obliged either to sell out to a larger company with the complementary marketing and distribution assets, or to license their innovation to them on disadvantageous terms. For organisations wishing to remain independent and to exploit their innovations themselves, there is little point in investing heavily to be first-mover in the absence of the necessary complementary assets.

- *Fast-moving arenas*. Where markets or technologies are moving very fast, and especially where both are highly dynamic, first-movers are unlikely to establish a durable advantage. The American electronics company Magnavox was the first to launch an electronic video game console in 1972, the Odyssey. But both the market and the technologies were evolving quickly. Magnavox only survived into the second generation of video game consoles, finally exiting in 1984. The eighth generation is now firmly dominated by Microsoft (entered in 2001), Sony (entered in 1994) and Nintendo (entered in 1983). In slower-moving markets and technologies, such as Coca-Cola's drinks arena, durable first-mover advantages are more probable. Managers and entrepreneurs need, therefore, to assess future market and technological dynamism in calculating the likely value of first-mover advantage.

9.4.3 The incumbent's response

For established companies in a market, innovation is often not so much an opportunity as a threat. Kodak's dominance of the photographic film market was made nearly worthless by the sudden rise of digital photography (Illustration 5.5). Likewise, Blockbuster's network of video stores became redundant with the rise of internet film downloads (see Illustration 9.3).

As Harvard Business School's Clay Christensen has shown, the problem for incumbents can be twofold.[23] First, managers can become too attached to existing assets and skills: understandably, as these are what their careers have been built on. Second, relationships between incumbent organisations and their customers can become too close. Existing customers typically prefer incremental improvements to current technologies, and are unable to imagine completely new technologies. Incumbents are reluctant to 'cannibalise' their existing business by introducing something radically different. After all, as in Figure 9.4, incumbents usually have some scope for improving their existing technology, along the steady upwards trajectory described as Technology 1. Innovations on this trajectory are termed 'sustaining innovations', because they at least allow the existing technology to meet existing customer expectations.

The challenge for incumbents, however, is disruptive innovation. A **disruptive innovation creates substantial growth by offering a new performance trajectory that, even if initially inferior to the performance of existing technologies, has the potential to become markedly superior.** This superior performance can produce spectacular growth, either by creating new sets of customers or by undercutting the cost base of rival existing business models. Such disruptive innovation involves the shift from Technology 1 in Figure 9.4 to Technology 2. Disruptive innovations are hard for incumbents to respond to because poor performance in the early days is likely to upset existing customer relationships and because they typically involve changing their whole business model. Thus, in the music industry, the major record companies were long content to keep on selling traditional CDs through retailers, marketing

Figure 9.4 Disruptive innovation

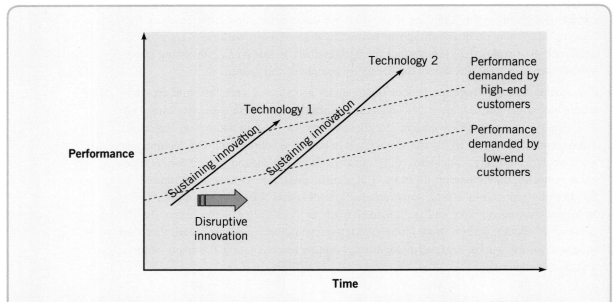

them through promotions and radio-plugging. They responded to online music simply by prosecuting operators such as Napster for breach of copyright and highlighting the relatively poor sound quality of peer-to-peer file sharing. In 2011, the number of online music downloads overtook the number of CD sales in the USA, and control of distribution had passed to services such as Apple's iTunes. Incumbents can follow two policies to help keep them responsive to potentially disruptive innovations:

● *Develop a portfolio of real options.* Companies that are most challenged by disruptive innovations tend to be those built upon a single business model and with one main product or service. Columbia's Rita McGrath and Wharton's Ian MacMillan recommend that companies build portfolios of *real options* in order to maintain organisational dynamism.[24] Real options are limited investments that keep opportunities open for the future (for a more technical discussion, see section 11.3.2). Establishing an R&D team in a speculative new technology or acquiring a small start-up in a nascent market would both be examples of real options, each giving the potential to scale up fast should the opportunity turn out to be substantial. McGrath and MacMillan's portfolio identifies three different kinds of options (Figure 9.5). Options where the market is broadly known, but the technologies are still uncertain, are *positioning options*: a company might want several of these, to ensure some position in an important market, by one technology or another. On the other hand, a company might have a strong technology, but be very uncertain about appropriate markets, in which case it would want to bet on several *scouting options* to explore which markets are actually best. Finally, a company would want some *stepping stone* options, very unlikely in

Figure 9.5 Portfolio of innovation options

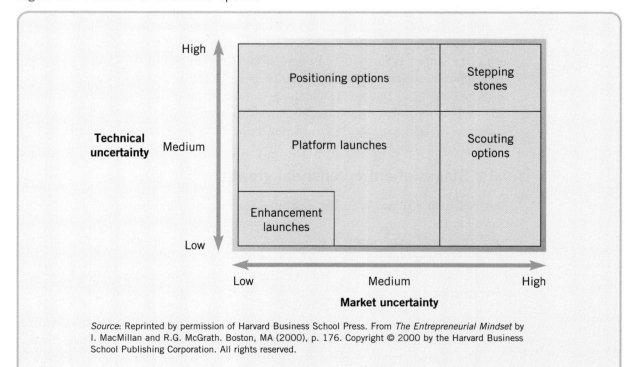

themselves to work, but possibly leading to something more promising in the future. Even if they do not turn a profit, stepping stones should provide valuable learning opportunities. An important principle for options is: 'Fail fast, fail cheap, try again.'

● *Develop new venture units.* New ventures, especially when undertaken from a real options perspective, may need protection from the usual systems and disciplines of a core business. It would make no sense to hold the managers of a real option strictly accountable for sales growth and profit margin: their primary objective is preparation and learning. For this reason, large incumbent organisations often establish relatively autonomous 'new venture units', sometimes called new venture divisions, which can nurture new ideas or acquire fledgling businesses with a longer-term view.[25] For example, in 2011, BMW launched a new venture unit called Project i, based in New York and backed by $100 m, in order to acquire innovative new ideas from outside: one of its first investments has been in start-up company Parkatmyhouse, which links people seeking to rent a parking space or garage with those who have one to spare. The risks of such autonomous venture units are twofold.[26] First, the new units may be denied resources that the core business could easily supply, such as branding or management information systems. Second, innovation becomes isolated from the core business: for the core organisation, innovation is something that somebody else does.

Whether by developing real options, internal venture units or equivalent means, it is clear that established incumbents need to be able to support a spirit corporate entrepreneurship (see section 7.2).

(9.5) ENTREPRENEURSHIP AND RELATIONSHIPS

Given the difficulties of large incumbent firms in fostering innovation, many would conclude that the best approach is to start up a new venture from scratch. Independent entrepreneurs such as the Samwer brothers, the creators of Rocket Internet, and Larry Page and Sergey Brin of Google are exemplars of this entrepreneurial approach to innovation (see Case examples for Chapters 3 and 12).[27] This section introduces some key issues for entrepreneurial innovators, and then points to a more complex set of relationships with large firms, raising further choices for entrepreneurs. It concludes by considering the opportunities of social entrepreneurship.

9.5.1 Stages of entrepreneurial growth

Entrepreneurial ventures are often seen as going through four stages of a life cycle: see Figure 9.6. The entrepreneurial life cycle **progresses through start-up, growth, maturity and exit.**[28] Of course, most ventures do not make it through all the stages – the estimated failure rate of new businesses in their first year is more than one fifth, with two thirds going out of business within six years.[29] However, each of these four stages raises key questions for entrepreneurs:

● *Start-up.* There are many challenges at this stage, but one key question with implications for both survival and growth are sources of capital. Loans from family and friends are common sources of funds, but these are typically limited and, given the new-business failure rate, likely to lead to embarrassment. Bank loans and credit cards can provide funding too,

Figure 9.6 Stages of entrepreneurial growth and typical challenges

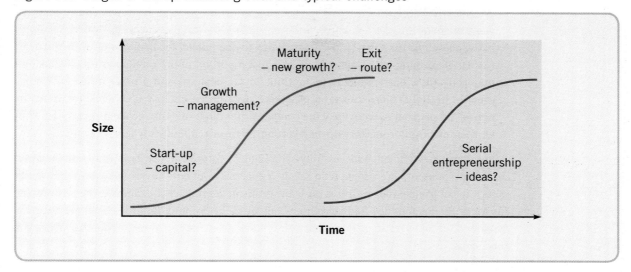

and there is often government funding, especially for new technologies or economically disadvantaged social groups or geographical areas. *Venture capitalists* are specialised investors in new ventures, especially when there is some track record. Venture capitalists usually insist on a seat on the venture's board of directors and may instal their preferred managers. Venture capitalist backing has been shown to significantly increase the chances of a venture's success, but venture capitalists typically accept only about one 1 in 400 propositions put to them.[30]

- *Growth.* A key challenge for growth ventures is management. Entrepreneurs have to be ready to move from doing to managing. Typically this transition occurs as the venture grows beyond about 20 employees. Many entrepreneurs make poor managers: if they had wanted to be managers, they would probably be working in a large corporation in the first place. The choice entrepreneurs have to make is whether to rely on their own managerial skills or to bring in professional managers. In 2010, Twitter's co-founder Evan Williams handed over as chief executive to Dick Costolo, himself a former entrepreneur but also with experience as a manager in technology giant Google.

- *Maturity.* The challenge for entrepreneurs at this stage is retaining their enthusiasm and commitment and generating new growth. This is a period when entrepreneurship changes to *intrapreneurship*, the generation of new ventures from inside the organisation. An important option is usually *diversification* into new business areas, a topic dealt with in Chapter 7. Amazon.com in the USA has moved from book-selling to automotive parts, groceries and clothing. When generating new ventures at this stage, it is critical to recall the odds on success. Research suggests that many small high-tech firms fail to manage the transition to a second generation of technology, and that it is often better at this point simply to look for exit.[31]

- *Exit.* Exit refers to departure from the venture, either by the founding entrepreneurs or by the original investors, or both. At the point of exit, entrepreneurs and venture capitalists will seek to release capital as a reward for their input and risk-taking. Entrepreneurs may consider three prime routes to exit. A simple *trade sale* of the venture to another company is a common route. Thus in 2012 the founders of photo-sharing site Instagram sold their company to Facebook for $300 m cash and $700 m worth of Facebook shares just two years after starting the company. Another exit route for highly successful enterprises is an *initial public offering* (IPO), the sale of shares to the public, for instance on the American NASDAQ exchange. IPOs usually involve just a portion of the total shares available, and may thus allow entrepreneurs to continue in the business and provide funds for further growth. In 2012, Mark Zuckerberg raised $16 bn in Facebook's IPO, while retaining for himself 28 per cent ownership of the company. It is often said that good entrepreneurs plan for their exit right from start-up, and certainly venture capitalists will insist on this.

Entrepreneurs who have successfully exited a first venture often become *serial entrepreneurs*. Serial entrepreneurs are people who set up a succession of enterprises, investing the capital raised on exit from earlier ventures into new growing ventures. For example, serial entrepreneur Mark Pincus founded and sold three companies before founding the social games giant Zynga in 2007. For serial entrepreneurs, the challenge often is no longer so much funding but good ideas.

9.5.2 Entrepreneurial strategies

Entrepreneurs usually start with one main business, though over time they will often experiment with other ventures and the original business itself may evolve quite radically. Given the importance of a single main business, issues of business strategy (Chapter 6) predominate over issues of corporate strategy (Chapter 7) for most entrepreneurs, at least early on. Thus entrepreneurs will typically have to choose between the generic business strategies of differentiation, cost and focus, for example (section 6.3).

For an entrepreneurial (or small) business, however, business strategy issues are not exactly the same as for more established or larger businesses.[32] There are two characteristics of entrepreneurial businesses that can be particularly influential for strategy choice:

- *Resource scarcity*: start-up enterprises usually face very considerable resource constraints, in terms of finances and managerial capacity especially. Entrepreneurial businesses therefore need to be highly selective in their strategic moves, careful not to waste scarce resources on too many initiatives. They should be extra cautious about competing head-to-head with wealthier players, where there is a risk of wars of attrition.

- *Relative invisibility*: as new and small players, entrepreneurial businesses are typically less visible to larger, established businesses. Lower visibility means that entrepreneurial businesses face less risk of prompt incumbent retaliation for any aggressive strategic moves. Entrepreneurial businesses may therefore have more time to press forward their attack before meeting any counter-attack.

This combination of resource disadvantage and invisibility advantage influences business strategy choices differently according to the kind of market the entrepreneur is operating in:

- *New markets*: entrepreneurial firms in new markets, where products and customer segments are not yet settled, generally do best by exploring potential opportunities fast. Speed of entry is important given the difficulties of competing against larger players in the same product or segment. Even if enjoying a first-mover advantage, it can be better to abandon a market position that is beginning to attract more powerful competitors, and to explore new opportunities instead. In fast-growing markets, large businesses are typically better able to assemble the resources necessary to take advantage of increasing scale. For entrepreneurial firms, therefore, timing is vital: picking the right moments to enter and then to retreat are the crucial decisions.

● *Established markets*: in more established markets, where large firms are already present, entrepreneurial firms are more successful if they can find niches that are still not occupied. These niches are often better supplied by low-cost adaptations of existing products rather than by radical innovations, which are liable to be too risky and expensive for a small-scale enterprise. The key is generally not to attack large incumbents directly and to rely on their inattention to small-scale moves to delay any competitive imitation on their part.

The above strategies are cautious ones, dictated by resource constraints and fear of large-firm retaliation or imitation. These are not the heroic entrepreneurial strategies that capture the headlines, but the strategies that are adopted by the typical new business. For every revolutionary entrepreneur that has created new markets and beaten off well-resourced challengers, there are countless forgotten failures. In this respect, Google and Facebook are exceptions, not the rule. Given the high risks of entrepreneurship, it is important not to generalise from a handful of spectacular successes (see Illustration 9.4 for a failure example).

9.5.3 Entrepreneurial relationships

For many, entrepreneurship is about independence, working for oneself. This pride in independence is reinforced by a common stereotype of entrepreneurs as heroic individuals, starting their businesses at night in a university laboratory, or in the spare room at home or in a local lock-up garage. William Hewlett and David Packard, founders of the famous computing and printer company HP, and Steve Jobs of Apple, are oft-quoted examples of the garage stereotype. But digging beneath the stereotype soon reveals a more complex story, in which relationships with large companies can be important right from the start. Often entrepreneurs have worked for large companies beforehand, and continue to use relationships afterwards.[33] While Hewlett came fairly directly out of Stanford University's laboratories, Packard worked at General Electric and Litton Industries. The HP company used Litton Industries' foundries early on, and later used relationships at General Electric to recruit experienced managers. Steve Jobs worked for William Hewlett for a summer job aged 12, and later was the 40th employee at video games company Atari.

Thus entrepreneurship often involves managing relationships with other companies, especially big companies. Three concepts are particularly influential here:

● *Corporate venturing.* As in section 9.4.3, many large corporations have developed corporate venture units that invest externally in new ventures as safeguards against disruptive innovations and potential drivers of future growth.[34] Entrepreneurs gain by accessing not just capital but also knowledge of large-company thinking in their domain and contacts with other members of the large company's network. It is crucial that both entrepreneurs and corporate venture capitalists continuously monitor the expectations behind the investment: is the investment more profit-driven in terms of expecting good financial returns or is it more strategic, in the sense of being about technological or market development? Shifting expectations on the part of the corporate venture capitalist can lead to the disruption of longer-term plans by the entrepreneurial new venture. Companies such as Ericsson and Diageo have even closed down their venture units entirely.

ILLUSTRATION 9.4

Nearly billionaires

Adam Goldberg and Wayne Ting had the same idea as Facebook's Mark Zuckerberg – and first.

In 2003, Golderg and Ting were engineering students at the prestigious Columbia University, New York. Goldberg was president of his class and hearing lots of complains about lack of community spirit. Over the summer, he designed a social network for his fellow engineers. Unlike other existing social networks such as MySpace and Friendster, this was the first network which overlaid a virtual community on a real community. Mark Zuckerberg would try the same idea at Harvard the next year.

Three quarters of Columbia's engineering students signed up to the Columbia network over the summer. Goldberg improved the network and relaunched it as CU Community in January 2004, open to all the university's students. Most Columbia students signed up within a month. CU Community was sophisticated for its time. When Facebook launched in February 2004, it only allowed members to 'friend' and 'poke' each other. CU Community also allowed blogging, sharing and cross-profile commenting. Goldberg did not worry about Facebook: 'It was totally different. It had an emphasis on directory functionality, less emphasis on sharing. I didn't think there was much competition. We were the Columbia community, they were Harvard.'

Then in March Facebook launched in other elite American universities such as Yale, Stanford and Columbia. Goldberg, now joined by Wayne Ting, transformed CU Community into Campus Network and launched in elite American universities as well. But Facebook outpaced the new Campus Network. By summer 2004, Facebook had already overtaken Goldberg and Ting's network even at Columbia.

Goldberg and Ting now plunged into the competition full-time. They suspended their studies, and moved to Montreal, hiring three other software developers to help them. But resources were tight. Campus Network refused funds from venture capitalists and turned down some large advertisers, including MTV. The two entrepreneurs slept in the office on air mattresses, hiding them away as the three employees turned up for work so they would not know they were homeless.

None the less, Campus Network developed a sophisticated product, with fully customisable pages, multiple designs and backgrounds. Facebook was simpler. The feel of Campus Network was a bit like Dungeon and Dragons, unlike the clean aesthetics of early Facebook. Ting commented on the logic behind the early development of Campus Network: 'Why would you go to a site that only had poking and a photo [like Facebook then] when you can share photos, share music and share your thoughts on a blog?' Looking back, though, he observed: 'A good website should have functionalities that 70 or 80 per cent of users want to use. We had functions that only 10 per cent wanted – nobody blogged, nobody even blogs today.'

Campus Network reached 250,000 users by 2005, but at the same point Facebook had reached one million. Goldberg and Ting decided to wind down the network and returned to Columbia as students in the autumn of 2005. The venture had cost them personally something between $100,000 and $200,000, as well as more than a year of their lives. Ting reflected in 2012, when an MBA student at Harvard Business School: 'There are still moments when you feel a deep sense of regret . . . Could we have succeeded? I think that's a really painful question . . . There are fleeting moments like that. But I'm much prouder that we took a risk and we learnt from it.'

Sources: Slate, 29 September 2010; BBC, 21 December 2010.

Questions

1 What do you learn from the experience of Goldberg and Ting which could be useful to launching a new enterprise?

2 Are there any unmet needs in your community, at college or elsewhere, that could be turned into a business opportunity?

- *Spin-offs (or spin-outs).* These in a sense go in the opposite direction to corporate venturing, involving the generation of small innovative units *from* larger organisations.[35] Companies such as Fairchild Semiconductor are famous for generating many successful spin-offs, including Intel, AMD and LSI Logic. Spin-off relationships can be mutually supportive, with the larger parent organisation offering the new venture seed capital and access to its marketing or technological resources. The spin-off gains the flexibility of being independent, while the parent retains a stake in any future success. Sometimes parents will seek to buy out the spin-off entrepreneurs, and reintegrate the venture into the original organisation.[36] For entrepreneurial spin-off companies, therefore, there are potential benefits to managing a constructive relationship with their original parent.

- *Ecosystems.* Following the 'open innovation' approach (section 9.2.3), high-technology companies such as Cisco, IBM and Intel often foster 'ecosystems' of smaller companies. These ecosystems are communities of connected suppliers, agents, distributors, franchisees, technology entrepreneurs and makers of complementary products.[37] Thus Apple has created an ecosystem of apps around its iPhone. The superiority of Apple's app offering gives it a competitive advantage over Nokia or BlackBerry, for example. Moreover, Apple app writers get the benefit of a large and often lucrative market. Small entrepreneurial firms wishing to participate in such ecosystems have to be skilled in managing relationships with powerful technological leaders.

9.5.4 Social entrepreneurship

Entrepreneurship is not just a matter for the private sector. The public sector has seen increasing calls for a more entrepreneurial approach to service creation and delivery. Recently too the notion of social entrepreneurship has become common. **Social entrepreneurs are individuals and groups who create independent organisations to mobilise ideas and resources to address social problems, typically earning revenues but on a not-for-profit basis.**[38] Independence and revenues generated in the market give social entrepreneurs the flexibility and dynamism to pursue social problems that pure public-sector organisations are often too bureaucratic, or too politically constrained, to tackle. Social entrepreneurs have pursued a wide range of initiatives, including small loans ('micro-credit') to peasants by the Grameen Bank in Bangladesh, employment creation by the Mondragon cooperative in the Basque region of Spain, and fair trade by Traidcraft in the United Kingdom. This wide range of initiatives raises at least three key choices for social entrepreneurs:

- *Social mission.* For social entrepreneurs, the social mission is primary. The social mission can embrace two elements: end objectives and operational processes. For example, the Grameen Bank has the end objective of reducing rural poverty, especially for women. The process is empowering poor people's own business initiatives by providing micro-credit at a scale and to people that conventional banks would ignore.

- *Organisational form.* Many social enterprises take on cooperative forms, involving their employees and other stakeholders on a democratic basis and thus building commitment and channels for ideas. This form of organisation raises the issue of which stakeholders to include, and which to exclude. Cooperatives can also be slow to take hard decisions. Social enterprises therefore sometimes take more hierarchical charity or company forms of organisation. Cafédirect, the fair-trade beverages company, even became a publicly listed company, paying its first dividend to shareholders in 2006.

ILLUSTRATION 9.5

Sociable rats in search of a model

Rats have proved they can detect landmines in Africa. The problem now is how to make the rats pay.

There are 70 countries around the world affected by landmines left behind from earlier wars. In 2008, these landmines caused 5,200 casualties worldwide. Large areas of land are too dangerous to use for agriculture. But traditional mine-detecting equipment or mine-detecting dogs are very expensive.

Belgian Bart Weetjens had an idea: use rats. Rats have a very sensitive sense of smell, well able to detect the TNT in landmines. As Weetjens told the *Boston Globe*: 'Rats are organised, sensitive, sociable and smart.' In 1998, Weetjens established APOPO as a social enterprise dedicated to developing the potential for rats in de-mining. In 2003, Weetjens began field testing African giant pouched rats in Mozambique, a country with three million landmines. The following year, APOPO's first 11 rats passed their offical test on a real minefield and were ready for action.

The rats work on a Pavlovian basis: for each detected mine, they get a banana or some peanuts. Rats are cheap to train: $4,000 (€2,800) per rat, compared to $40,000 for dogs. They are easier to house and transport than dogs, and also less susceptible to tropical diseases. Because they are lighter than dogs, they do not trip off landmines themselves. Finally, rats are more sociable than dogs: they will work with anyone who rewards them, while dogs are inflexible, only working with those to whom they have formed an attachment. A single rat can inspect 1,000 square feet in about 30 minutes, something that would take a human a whole day working with an electronic mine detector.

Initial funding for APOPO's development phase had come from the University of Antwerp and the Belgian Directorate for International Co-operation. By 2008, more than half of its funding was coming from various government grants, over a third from philanthropic foundations and corporate gifts, some 6 per cent from technical and research institutes and about 5 per cent from APOPO's own fund-raising. Principal among these fund-raising initiatives is the 'Hero Rat'

scheme. For €5 ($7) a month, supporters can adopt a rat, each with a name and picture on APOPO's website.

The problem for APOPO is securing its viability. Because grants are typically just to cover costs, APOPO has never made the kinds of profits necessary to build financial reserves. Now that the rats are a proven concept, research funding is harder to get. As yet, there is no secure business model.

In 2010, financial adviser Alvin Hall visited APOPO on behalf of the BBC. He advised Weetjens to increase the minimum donation for adopting a 'Hero Rat'. He also proposed the creation of an endowment fund, allowing large donations to give APOPO some permanent capital. Hall also encouraged APOPO to think about diversification ventures.

One promising avenue for diversification is tuberculosis (TB) detection. APOPO is running trials in Tanzania using the rats to detect TB in the saliva of sick patients. TB is responsible for 1.7 million deaths each year, mainly in poor countries. Apparently these sensitive rats can process as many saliva samples in a few minutes as a human lab technician can in a whole day. The rats have even detected TB in samples that had been missed by conventional tests. APOPO's 2010 mission statement reflects this widening role: 'to become the centre of excellence in detection rat technologies, to enhance the impact of life-saving actions'.

Sources: www.apopo.org; *Boston Globe*, 23 November 2008; www.bbc.co.uk, 5 March 2010.

Questions

1 What are the advantages and disadvantages of a social enterprise approach in this kind of domain?

2 What would be your advice to Bart Weetjens as he searches for a secure long-term business model?

KEY DEBATE

Are large firms better innovators than small firms?

The famous Austrian economist Joseph Schumpeter proposed that large firms are proportionately more innovative than small firms. This proposition is a controversial one. If true, it would discourage laboratory scientists and engineers from leaving their large-firm employers to set up their own ventures. It would encourage large firms like Google and Cisco to keep on buying up small innovative firms and absorbing them into their own corporate strategies. It would make government policy-makers more tolerant of huge, domineering firms like Microsoft who claim that their large scale is important to continued innovation in computer software.

Schumpeter's proposition for the advantages of large firms in innovation has several points in its favour:

● Large firms have greater and more diverse resources, helping them to bring together all the various necessary elements for innovation.

● Large firms may have a greater propensity for innovation risk, knowing that they can absorb the costs of innovation failure.

● Large firms have better incentives to innovate, because they are more likely to be able to capitalise on innovation, having all the required complementary assets (distribution channels and so on) to roll it out fast and under their control.

On the other hand, there are good reasons why small firms might be more innovative:

● Small firms are typically more cohesive, so that knowledge is more easily shared.

● Small firms are typically more flexible and less bureaucratic, so that they can innovate faster and more boldly.

● Small firms are more motivated to innovate simply to survive, while large firms can simply defend and exploit their dominance of existing markets.

There has been plenty of research on whether small or large firms are proportionately more innovative. Some researchers have focused on the input side, for example measuring whether large firms are more research intensive in terms of R&D expenditure as a percentage of sales. Other researchers have focused on the output side, for example counting whether large firms have proportionately greater numbers of patents for innovations. There is no final consensus on the overall patterns of innovation. However, recent research findings suggest that in general:

● Large firms are relatively less research intensive in high-technology industries, for example electronics and software.

● Large firms are relatively more innovative in service industries than in manufacturing industries.

It seems that the research so far cannot provide any firm rules about whether large or small firms are better innovators in general. However, research scientists, acquisitive large firms and government policy-makers need to consider carefully the specifics of particular industries.

Sources: C. Camisón-Zornosa, R. Lapiedra-Alcani, M. Segarra-Ciprés and M. Boronat-Navarro, 'A meta-analysis of innovation and organisational size', *Organisation Studies*, vol. 25, no. 3 (2004), pp. 331–61.

C-Y. Lee and T. Sung, 'Schumpeter's legacy: a new perspective on the relationship between firm size and R&D', *Research Policy*, vol. 34 (2005), pp. 914–31.

Question

1 What kinds of managerial action might you consider if you were trying to increase the innovativeness of a large firm in a high-technology manufacturing industry?

● *Business model*. Social enterprises typically rely to a large extent on revenues earned in the marketplace, not just government subsidy or charitable donations. Housing associations collect rents, micro-credit organisations charge interest and fair-trade organisations sell produce. Social entrepreneurs are no different to other entrepreneurs, therefore, in having to design an efficient and effective business model. This business model might involve innovative changes in the value chain. Thus fair-trade organisations have often become much more closely involved with their suppliers than commercial organisations, for example advising farmers on agriculture and providing education and infrastructure support to their communities. Illustration 9.5 shows how mine-clearing venture APOPO is struggling to find a viable business model.

Social entrepreneurs, just like other entrepreneurs, often have to forge relationships with large commercial companies. Harvard Business School's Rosabeth Moss Kanter points out that the benefits to large companies can go beyond a feel good factor and attractive publicity.[39] She shows that involvement in social enterprise can help develop new technologies and services, access new pools of potential employees, and create relationships with government and other agencies that can eventually turn into new markets. Kanter concludes that large companies should develop clear strategies with regard to social entrepreneurship, not treat it as ad hoc charity.

SUMMARY

● Strategists face four fundamental dilemmas in innovation: the relative emphasis to put on *technology push* or *market pull*; whether to focus on *product* or *process innovation*; how much to rely on '*open innovation*'; and finally how far to concentrate on technological innovation as opposed to broader *business model innovation*.

● Innovations often diffuse into the marketplace according to *an S-curve model* in which slow start-up is followed by accelerating growth (the tipping point) and finally a flattening of demand. Managers should watch out for 'tripping points'.

● Managers have a choice between being first into the marketplace and entering later. Innovators can capture *first-mover advantages*. However, '*fast second*' *strategies* are often more attractive.

● Established incumbents' businesses should beware *disruptive innovations*. Incumbents can stave off inertia by developing portfolios of real options and by organising autonomous *new venture units*.

● Entrepreneurs face characteristic dilemmas as their businesses go through the *entrepreneurial life cycle* of start-up, growth, maturity and exit. Entrepreneurial strategies are particularly influenced by *resource scarcity* and *relative invisibility*. Entrepreneurs have to choose how they relate to large firms, particularly as they may become involved in their *ecosystems* or strategies for open innovation.

● *Social entrepreneurship* offers a flexible way of addressing social problems, but raises issues about appropriate missions, organisational forms and business models.

VIDEO ASSIGNMENTS

Visit **MyStrategyLab** and watch the Alyssa Smith case study for Chapter 9.

1 Using the video extracts and section 9.5.1, what can we learn about the characteristics needed to be a successful entrepreneur and the challenges that entrepreneurs typically face as they move through the 'entrepreneurial life cycle'?

2 Using Alyssa Smith's experience as a starting point, explain why it is important for entrepreneurs to develop key relationships as part of their approach to business.

WORK ASSIGNMENTS

✱ *Denotes more advanced work assignments.*
* *Refers to a case study in the Text and Cases edition.*

9.1✱ For a new product or service that you have recently experienced and enjoyed, investigate the strategy of the company responsible. With reference to the dilemmas of section 9.2, explain whether the innovation was more technology push or market pull, product or process driven, or technological or more broadly business model based.

9.2 Go to a web traffic site (such as alexa.com) and compare over time trends in terms of 'page views' or 'reach' for older sites (such as Amazon.com) and newer sites (such as instagram.com, or any that has more recently emerged). With reference to section 9.3, how do you explain these trends and how would you project them forward?

9.3✱ With regard to a new product or service that you have recently experienced and enjoyed (as in 9.1), investigate the strategic responses of 'incumbents' to this innovation. To what extent is the innovation disruptive for them (see section 9.4.3)?

9.4 With reference to the entrepreneurial life cycle, identify the position of Rovio (chapter Case example), Feed Henry*, Hotel du Vin* or Flight Centre*. What managerial issues might this case company anticipate in the coming years?

9.5 Use the internet to identify a social entrepreneurial venture that interests you (via www.skollfoundation.org, for example), and, with regard to section 9.5.3, identify its social mission, its organisational form and its business model.

Integrative assignment

9.6 Consider a for-profit or social entrepreneurial idea that you or your friends or colleagues might have. Drawing on section 15.4.4, outline the elements of a strategic plan for this possible venture. What more information do you need to get?

RECOMMENDED KEY READINGS

- A. Osterwald and Y. Pigneur, *Business Model Generation*, Wiley, 2010, is an engaging, practical handbook relevant to both innovation and entrepreneurship.

- P. Trott, *Innovation Management and New Product Development*, 5th edn, Financial Times Prentice Hall, 2011, provides a comprehensive overview of innovation

strategy issues. P.A. Wickham, *Strategic Entrepreneurship*, 5th edn, Prentice Hall, 2013, is a standard European text with regard to entrepreneurial strategy.

- Social entrepreneurship is discussed usefully in R. Ridley-Duff and M. Bull, *Understanding Social Enterprise: Theory and Practice*, Sage, 2011.

REFERENCES

1. This definition adapts, in order to include the public sector, the definition in P. Trott, *Innovation Management and New Product Development*, 5th edn, Financial Times Prentice Hall, 2011.

2. A good discussion of the academic theories that underpin these dilemmas is in R. Rothwell, 'Successful industrial innovation: critical factors for the 1990s', *R&D Management*, vol. 22, no. 3 (1992), pp. 221–39.

3. E. von Hippel, *Democratizing Innovation*, MIT Press, 2005; Y.M. Antorini, A. Muniz and T. Askildsen, 'Collaborating with customer communities: lessons from the Lego Group', *MIT Sloan Management Review*, vol. 53, no. 3 (2012), pp. 73–9.

4. D. Nocera, 'Can we progress from solipsistic science to frugal innovation?', *Daedalus*, vol. 143, no. 3 (2012), pp. 45–52; and M. Sarkar, 'Moving forward by going in reverse: emerging trends in global innovation and knowledge strategies', *Global Strategy Journal*, vol. 1 (2011), pp. 237–42.

5. J. Abernathy and W. Utterback, 'A dynamic model of process and product innovation', *Omega*, vol. 3, no. 6 (1975), pp. 142–60.

6. P. Anderson and M.L. Tushman, 'Technological discontinuities and dominant designs: a cyclical model of technological change', *Administrative Science Quarterly*, vol. 35 (1990), pp. 604–33.

7. J. Tang, 'Competition and innovation behaviour', *Research Policy*, vol. 35 (2006), pp. 68–82.

8. H. Chesbrough and M. Appleyard, 'Open innovation and strategy', *California Management Review*, vol. 50, no. 1 (2007), pp. 57–73; O. Gasman, E. Enkel and H. Chesbrough, 'The future of open innovation', *R&D Management*, vol. 38, no. 1 (2010), pp. 1–9.

9. L.B. Jeppesen and K. Lakhani, 'Marginality and problem solving: effectiveness in broadcast search', *Organization Science*, vol. 21, no. 5 (2010), 1016–33.

10. A. Gawer and M. Cusumano, *Platform Leadership: How Intel, Microsoft and Cisco Drive Industry Innovation*, Harvard Business School Press, 2002.

11. See the special issue on business models in *Long Range Planning*, 2010, especially D.J. Teece, 'Business models, business strategy and innovation', *Long Range Planning*, vol. 43, nos 3/4 (2010), pp. 172–94; H. Chesbrough, 'Business model innovation: it's not just about technology

anymore', *Strategy & Leadership*, vol. 35, no. 6 (2007), pp. 12–17; R. Amit and C. Zott, 'Creating value through business model innovation', *MIT Sloan Management Review*, vol. 53, no. 3 (2012), pp. 41–9.

12. Innovation diffusion is discussed in the classic E. Rogers, *Diffusion of Innovations*, Free Press, 1995; C. Kim and R. Maubourgne, 'Knowing a winning idea when you see one', *Harvard Business Review*, vol. 78, no. 5 (2000), pp. 129–38; and J. Cummings and J. Doh, 'Identifying who matters: mapping key players in multiple environments', *California Management Review*, vol. 42, no. 2 (2000), pp. 83–104 (see especially pp. 91–7).

13. J. Nichols and S. Roslow, 'The S-curve: an aid to strategic marketing', *The Journal of Consumer Marketing*, vol. 3, no. 2 (1986), pp. 53–64; and F. Suarez and G. Lanzolla, 'The half-truth of first-mover advantage', *Harvard Business Review*, vol. 83, no. 4 (2005), pp. 121–7. This S-curve refers to innovation diffusion. However, the S-curve effect sometimes also refers to the diminishing performance increases available from a maturing technology: A. Sood and G. Tellis, 'Technological evolution and radical innovation', *Journal of Marketing*, vol. 69, no. 3 (2005), pp. 152–68.

14. M. Gladwell, *The Tipping Point*, Abacus, 2000. Tipping points are also important in public policy and can help anticipate emerging problems, for example crime waves and epidemics.

15. S. Brown, 'The tripping point', *Marketing Research*, vol. 17, no. 1 (2005), pp. 8–13.

16. G. Moore, *Crossing the Chasm: marketing and selling high-tech products to mainstream customers*, 2nd edn, Harper Perennial, 2002.

17. C. Markides and P. Geroski, *Fast Second: How Smart Companies Bypass Radical Innovation to Enter and Dominate New Markets*, Jossey-Bass, 2005; Lieberman, M. and D. Montgomery, 'First-mover (dis)advantages: retrospective and link with the resource-based view', *Strategic Management Journal*, vol. 19, no. 12 (1998), pp. 1111–25; and P.F. Suarez and G. Lanzolla, 'The half-truth of first-mover advantage', *Harvard Business Review*, vol. 83, no. 4 (2005), pp. 121–7.

18. F. Suarez and G. Lanzolla, 'The half-truth of first-mover advantage', *Harvard Business Review*, vol. 83, no. 4 (2005), pp. 121–7. See also S. Min, U. Manohar and

W. Robinson, 'Market pioneer and early follower survival risks: a contingency analysis of really new versus incrementally new product-markets', *Journal of Marketing*, vol. 70, no. 1 (2006), pp. 15–33.

19. C. Markides and P. Geroski, *Fast Second: How Smart Companies Bypass Radical Innovation to Enter and Dominate New Markets*, Jossey-Bass, 2005. See also the discussion of B. Buisson and P. Silberzahn, 'Blue Ocean or fast-second innovation?', *International Journal of Innovation Management*, vol. 14, no. 3 (2010), pp. 359–78.

20. David Teece, the academic authority in this area, refers to the capacity to capture profits as 'the appropriability regime': see D. Teece, *Managing Intellectual Capital*, Oxford University Press, 2000.

21. The key book on intellectual property strategy is A. Poltorak and P.J. Lerner, *Essentials of Intellectual Property: Law, Economics and Strategy*, Wiley, 2009.

22. D. Teece, *Managing Intellectual Capital*, Oxford University Press, 2000.

23. See J. Bower and C. Christensen, 'Disruptive technologies: catching the wave', *Harvard Business Review*, vol. 73, no. 1 (1995), pp. 43–53; and C. Christensen and M.E. Raynor, *The Innovator's Solution*, Harvard Business School Press, 2003.

24. R.G. McGrath and I. MacMillan, *The Entrepreneurial Mindset*, Harvard Business School Press, 2000.

25. C. Christensen and M.E. Raynor, *The Innovator's Solution*, Harvard Business School Press, 2003.

26. V. Govindarajan and C. Trimble, 'Organizational DNA for strategic innovation', *California Management Review*, vol. 43, no. 3 (2005), pp. 47–75.

27. Excellent textbooks on strategic entrepreneurship include J.A. Timmons, *New Venture Creation: Entrepreneurship in the 21st Century*, 6th edn, Irwin, 2004; and P.A. Wickham, *Strategic Entrepreneurship*, 5th edn, Pearson, 2013.

28. D. Flynn and A. Forman, 'Life cycles of new venture organizations: different factors affecting performance', *Journal of Developmental Entrepreneurship*, vol. 6, no. 1 (2001), pp. 41–58.

29. D. Flynn and A. Forman, 'Life cycles of new venture organizations: different factors affecting performance', *Journal of Developmental Entrepreneurship*, vol. 6, no. 1 (2001), pp. 41–58.

30. D. Flynn and A. Forman, 'Life cycles of new venture organizations: different factors affecting performance', *Journal of Developmental Entrepreneurship*, vol. 6, no. 1 (2001), pp. 41–58.

31. For a detailed account of Cisco's policy of taking over high-technology firms, see D. Mayer and M. Kenney, 'Economic action does not take place in a vacuum: understanding Cisco's acquisition and development strategy', *Industry and Innovation*, vol. 11, no. 4 (2004), pp. 293–325.

32. R. Katila, E. Chen and H. Piezunka, 'All the right moves: how entrepreneurial firms compete effectively', *Strategic Entrepreneurship Journal*, vol. 6, no. 2 (2012), pp. 116–132; and M. Chen and D. Hambrick, 'Speed, stealth and selective attack: how small firms differ from large firms in competitive behavior', *Academy of Management Journal*, vol. 35, no. 3 (1995), pp. 453–82.

33. P. Audia and C. Rider, 'A garage and an idea: what more does an entrepreneur need?', *California Management Review*, vol. 40, no. 1 (2005), pp. 6–28.

34. H. Chesbrough, 'Making sense of corporate venture capital', *Harvard Business Review*, vol. 80, no. 3 (2002), pp. 4–11; A. Campbell, J. Birkinshaw, A. Morrison and R. van Basten Batenburg, 'The future of corporate venturing', *MIT Sloan Management Review*, vol. 45, no. 1 (2003), pp. 33–41. See also the discussion of corporate entrepreneurship in Chapter 10.

35. S. Klepper, 'Spinoffs: a review and synthesis', *European Management Review*, vol. 6 (2009), pp. 159–71.

36. A. Parhankangas and P. Arenius, 'From a corporate venture to an independent company: a base for a taxonomy for corporate spin-off firms', *Research Policy*, vol. 32 (2003), pp. 463–81.

37. B. Iyer, C.-H. Lee and N. Venkatraman, 'Managing in a "Small World Ecosystem"', *California Management Review*, 48, 3 (2006), pp. 28–47.

38. A. Nicholls (ed.) *Social Entrepreneurship: New Paradigms of Sustainable Social Change*, Oxford University Press (2006); J. Austin, H. Stevenson and J. Wei-Skillern. 'Social and commercial entrepreneurship: same, different, or both?' *Entrepreneurship Theory and Practice*, vol. 30, no. 1 (2006), pp. 1–22.

39. R. Moss Kanter, 'From spare change to real change', *Harvard Business Review*, May–June (1999).

Rovio Entertainment: Disney of the smart phone age?

Daryl Chapman, Metropolia Business School

Richard Whittington, Saïd Business School

Introduction

Rovio Entertainment Ltd is most famous for its Angry Birds smart-phone game, in which colourful birds are catapulted at egg-stealing pigs. The company is based in Finland, and its management team consist of Mikael Hed, Chief Executive Officer, Niklas Hed, Head of Research and Development, and Peter Vesterbacka, Chief Marketing Officer and self-proclaimed 'Mighty Eagle'. Angry Birds became a top-selling app on Apple's App Store in 2010, the start of a stream of business ventures including broadcast media, merchandising, publishing, retail stores and playgrounds. With about 500 employees at the end of 2012, Peter Vesterbacka told *Wired Magazine* that Rovio could follow the world's largest entertainment company: 'We definitely look to Disney as a model.'

The team

Rovio was founded in 2003 by Niklas Hed and two classmates at Helsinki University of Technology after they won a game-development competition sponsored by Nokia and Hewlett Packard. The company initially did well in work-for-hire jobs, developing games for Electronic Arts, Nokia and Real Networks. Niklas's cousin Mikael Hed, with an MBA from Tulane University in the USA, soon joined. Mikel's father, Kaj Hed, had been a successful software entrepreneur, selling an earlier business for $150 m (£100 m, €110 m). Kaj Hed invested one million euros and became company chairman: Kaj still owns 70 per cent of the equity. Peter Vesterbacka only joined full time in 2010, as Angry Birds began to take off. However, Vesterbacka, a business developer from Hewlett Packard active in the Finnish start-up scene for many years, had been encouraging Rovio and helping from the sidelines since 2003.

Although Rovio had been successful at creating games and selling them to established third-party companies, the company's ambition was to create a major game success of its own. Niklas Hed thought it would take about 15 tries to create a world-beater, but Angry Birds turned out to be Rovio's 52nd attempt. Meanwhile, there were clashes over strategy. In 2005 Mikael Hed left the company after a row with his father, Kaj, whom he accused of being over-controlling. By 2008, Rovio had had to slash employment from 50 to just 12. But in 2009, Mikael came back, making peace with his father and sensing an opportunity with the new Apple iPhone and its App Store. The combination of the striking Angry Bird characters with the success of the Apple iPhone finally created a winning formula.

Rovio used Chillingo, a well-connected British games publisher, to negotiate a deal with Apple and push Angry Birds into world markets. In February 2010, Chillingo persuaded Apple to feature Angry Birds as the game of the week on the Apple App Store's front page: Angry Birds shot to No. 1 in the United Kingdom; five months later, it was top of the US charts as well. Chillingo was bought by Electronic Arts during 2010, and Rovio declared that it would no longer use any publishing intermediaries. In October, 2010, Rovio launched the free Android Angry Birds, winning two million downloads in three days. By 2011, Angry Birds and its various branded spin-offs had earned €50 m, on the back of a game which originally cost only €100,000 to develop. In March 2011 Mikael Hed was cautiously excited, telling *Wired Magazine*: 'I know how fragile the gaming industry is; I'm super-paranoid. But I feel at the moment that we are walking. We should be running.'

The New Disney?

Like Disney with Mickey Mouse, Rovio saw the potential of transferring its powerful brand to other products. Partnering with the American toy manufacturer Commonwealth Toy & Novelty, Rovio was able to place Angry Birds soft toys and T-shirts in US shops as early as 2010. Rovio soon had more than 400 partners, including Coca-Cola, Intel and Kraft. The number of Angry Bird products reached 20,000, including board games, fridge magnets and key chains. *Fast Company* magazine estimated in 2012 that total sales of Angry

Birds merchandise might approach $650 million or so. Rovio receives royalties on sales of its licensed products ranging from 5 to 20 per cent.

Rovio also partnered with Samsung to include a motion-controlled Angry Birds game on its smart televisions. Samsung was aiming to sell 25 million of these TVs in 2012. In November 2012, the company launched the Rovio Channel, letting users of the Samsung TV sets download games as well as the new Angry Birds Toons show and a comic-book series. The Rovio channel builds on the success of the Angry Birds YouTube channel, which has attracted more than 750 million views. The Rovio Channel is also due to launch on Mac, PC, iOS and Android devices, but Rovio prioritised TV as a medium that millions of families use together every day. An Angry Birds 3D movie is planned for release in 2016.

Meanwhile, Rovio has launched its first Angry Birds playground in Finland, in partnership with the Finnish adventure playground designer Lappset, the American entertainment designer BDR Design and the Italian roller coaster manufacturer, Antonia Zamperla. In one sense, the playgrounds strategy mimics Disney's theme parks, but the playgrounds are much smaller. Rovio wants to create a more 'distributed' means of physical interaction with families and children than the occasional visit to Disneyland: the Angry Birds playgrounds are local and can be visited every day. The plan is to roll these playgrounds out internationally, with its first opening in the United Kingdom in the summer of 2012. There are already unlicensed Angry Birds playgrounds in China.

Indeed, export markets have always been important to Rovio, coming from a small northern European country as it does. The company has offices in Shanghai, Stockholm, Tokyo, Seoul, South Korea and Santa Monica, California. The USA is Rovio's largest market, followed closely by China. Rovio launched in China in 2011 and opened three retail stores in Beijing and Shanghai during 2012, with 200 more planned within the next year. Official licensed playgrounds are opening in China too. Peter Vesterbacka told *Fast Company*: 'Over time, China will be our biggest market. It's important for us to be very local. We want to be more Chinese than the Chinese companies.'

Rovio has not neglected its original core gaming business. With 63 levels when first released, Angry Birds now has more than 360. All sorts of variations have been launched, including Angry Birds Star Wars developed in conjunction with Lucasfilm. During 2012, Rovio repeated its success with the launch of Bad Piggies, featuring pigs stranded on a desert island looking for

Table 1 Top paid iPhone apps, February 2013 (with developer names, countries and foundation dates)

1. Clear Vision 2 (FDG Entertainment, Germany, 2002)
2. WhatsApp Messenger (Whats App Inc., United States, 2009)
3. Minecraft – Pocket Edition (Mojang AB, Sweden, 2009)
4. Angry Birds Star Wars (Rovio, Finland, 2003)
5. Wood Camera (Bright Mango, United States, 2012)
6. Sleep Cycle alarm clock (Maciek Drejak Labs, Sweden, 2008)
7. Plague Inc (Ndemic Creations, United Kingdom, 2012)
8. Arms Cartel Global (Pixel Addicts, United States, 2001)
9. Fruit Ninja (Halfbrick Studios, Australia, 2001)
10. Bloons TD 5 (Ninja Kiwi, New Zealand, 2007)

Source: AppData, 2013, plus internet search.

eggs: it too reached Number 1 on Apple's App Store. Amazing Alex was also launched in 2012 to create a human character for Rovio, but proved relatively less successful.

A mix of success and failure is to be expected in games. The app market is extremely dynamic, with new games and apps emerging all the time (see Table 1 for top paid apps in early 2013). Disney Mobile had five games at Number 1 on the Apple App Store during 2012. On the other hand, the one-man British developer Ndemic could score a hit with its star Plague Inc. game, at a development cost of just $5,000. Peter Parmentier, Chief Executive of Electronic Arts Mobile (responsible for Tetris, the Sims and Fifa), told the *Guardian* newspaper: 'The marketplace in mobile is arguably the most competitive in the industry. There are more and more apps launching every day, which creates a challenging environment for developers and consumers alike. While I think we will always see that one breakaway hit that takes on a life of its own, we find that consumers seek high quality entertainment and recognisable brands in such a crowded environment.'

Growth plans

Rovio's growth requires investment. In early 2011, the company raised $42 m from three venture capital funds, ceding 21 per cent of the ownership in return (Niklas Hed, Mikael Hed and Peter Vesterbacka between them were left with 8 per cent). One of the venture capitalists was Niklas Zennström, co-founder of Skype, who also joined Rovio's board. The extra capital helped Rovio make two strategic and talent acquisitions that year: first Kombo Animation Studio, then Futuremark Games Studio. During 2012, Rovio had talked of an initial public offering for 2013 with the aim of raising

Table 2 Selected leading games companies

	Key businesses	2011 revenues	2011 employees
Activision (US/French)	Computer, social and mobile games	$4.76 bn	7,738
Disney (US)	Film, TV, parks, merchandising, online media, etc.	$42.28 bn	166,000
Electronic Arts (US)	Computer, social and mobile games	$4.44 bn	9,925
Zynga (US)	Social and gambling games (internet and mobile)	$1.14 bn	2,846

$1 bn for further investment. However, in early 2013, Peter Vesterbacka appeared to crush all such talk of an IPO: 'For us right now, we are running a very successful operation, we are growing very, very fast and we are insanely profitable so we can fund our own growth.'

Rovio's growth is building on a new business model for games. The original games model had involved purchasing a disc in a box for €20 or so. Rovio distributes its games over the internet either for about €1 to €4 each via Apple's App Store or, supported by advertising, for free on Android. Where Rovio differs from most other new mobile app companies is its emphasis on brand licensing for other physical products, such as soft toys, drinks and similar items. Revenues from the App Store, advertising and licensed physical products are very roughly equal, but physical products are pulling ahead. Total revenues are estimated at about €150 m for 2012. At the centre of the business are Rovio's brands, especially the Angry Birds themselves. The company believes that the brands will be valuable so long as fans are kept happy with a continuous stream of engaging new games and free upgrades. Rovio concentrates its efforts on game development and brand management: production of physical products is licensed out to partner companies. Although the early physical retail stores are being run by Rovio itself, the virtual store and logistics support are operated by partners that specialise in e-commerce and shipping.

Growth on the back of strong brands is, of course, something that Disney has long been good at (see Table 2 for a comparison with Disney and some competitors). Rovio sees itself as more than a games company, just as Disney saw itself as more than a cartoons company. The target is for more than half its revenues to come from physical products. Mikael Hed explained his ambitions for Rovio to *Fast Company* by drawing two arcs: the first, a narrow curve with a pronounced fall-off from its peak; the second, a much broader curve triple the height of the first. 'A lot of our competitors have an equally myopic view. They've found this hill,' he said, drawing an arrow to the crest of the first arc, 'and say, here's the maximum amount of money you can make with a mobile game. But what we're building' – pointing to the other arc – 'is about the lifetime value of a fan. That picture is much more interesting.'

During 2012, Rovio turned down a $2 bn acquisition offer from Zynga, the US games company famous for Farmville. The Angry Birds company seems determined to aim its catapult directly at US entertainments giant Disney.

Key sources: Wired Magazine, 7 March 2011; Guardian, Media Network, 15 November 2012; Fast Company, 26 November 2012; The Next Web, 21 December 2012.

Questions

1 What are the advantages and disadvantages of Rovio's business model?

2 What strategy might Zynga have pursued with Rovio if it had succeeded in its acquisition?

10

MERGERS, ACQUISITIONS AND ALLIANCES

Learning outcomes

After reading this chapter you should be able to:

● Identity key strategic motives for *mergers and acquisitions* and *strategic alliances.*

● Identity key issues in the successful management of *mergers and acquisitions* and *strategic alliances.*

● Identity the appropriate choices between *organic* development, *mergers and acquisitions* and *strategic alliances.*

● Identity *key success factors* of different growth options.

MyStrategyLab

MyStrategyLab is designed to help you make the most of your studies. Visit **www.pearsoned.co.uk/mystrategylab** to discover a wide range of resources, including:

- A personalised **Study plan** that will help you understand core concepts
- **Audio and video clips** that put the spotlight on strategy in the real world
- **Online glossaries and flashcards** that provide helpful reminders when you're looking for some quick revision.

(10.1) INTRODUCTION

Mergers, acquisitions and alliances are all common methods for achieving growth strategies and often in the news. For example, in 2012 the largest express carrier and parcel distribution company in the world, UPS, acquired Dutch rival TNT Express for $6.77 bn (€5.2 bn) in a friendly all-cash deal. This acquisition furthered UPS's ambitions to improve its competitive position in European markets and created a global leader in the logistics industry with more than $60 bn (€45 bn) of revenues. In the same year, Tingyi Corporation of Tianjin, China, and PepsiCo Inc., announced the creation of a strategic beverage alliance to manufacture, sell and distribute PepsiCo's carbonated soft drinks in China, which may become the world's largest beverage market.

This chapter therefore addresses mergers, acquisitions and alliances as key methods for pursuing strategic options. It will consider them alongside the principal alternative of 'organic' development, in other words the pursuit of a strategy relying on a company's own resources. Figure 10.1 shows how the main strategic options considered in the previous three chapters – diversification, internationalisation and innovation – can all be achieved through mergers and acquisitions, alliances and organic development. Of course, these three methods can also be used for many other strategies as well, for example consolidating markets or building scale advantages.

The chapter starts with organic development. Organic development is the default option: relying on the organisation's internal resources is the natural first option to consider. The chapter then introduces the two principal external options: first mergers and acquisitions (often abbreviated as M&A) and then strategic alliances. The final section compares the two external options against the internal option of organic development. Given the frequent failures of acquisitions and alliances, the fundamental issue is when to acquire, when to ally or when is it better to 'do it yourself'? The final section also considers key success factors in M&A and alliances. The problematic success record of acquisitions in particular is the subject of the Key Debate at the end of this chapter.

Figure 10.1 Three strategy methods

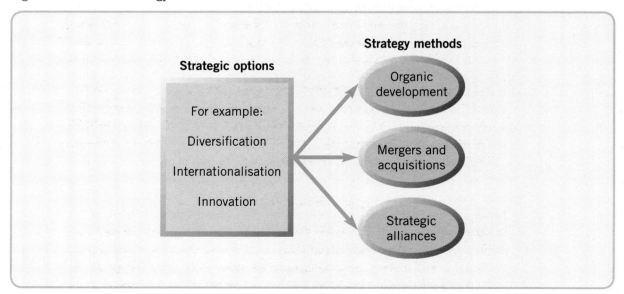

(10.2) ORGANIC DEVELOPMENT

The default method for pursuing a strategy is to 'do it yourself', relying on internal capabilities. Thus **organic development is where a strategy is pursued by building on and developing an organisation's own capabilities**. For example, Amazon's entry into the e-books market with its Kindle product was principally organic, relying on its own subsidiary Lab126 and drawing on its expertise in book retailing, internet retail and software. For Amazon, this do-it-yourself (DIY) diversification method was preferable to allying with an existing e-book producer such as Sony or buying a relevant hi-tech start-up such as the French pioneer Bookeen as it could work within its own ecosystem for greater synergy gain (see section 7.3).

There are five principal advantages to relying on organic development:

- *Knowledge and learning.* Using the organisation's existing capabilities to pursue a new strategy can enhance organisational knowledge and learning. Direct involvement in a new market or technology is likely to promote the acquisition and internalisation of deeper knowledge than a hands-off strategic alliance, for example.

- *Spreading investment over time.* Acquisitions typically require an immediate upfront payment for the target company. Organic development allows the spreading of investment over the whole time span of the strategy's development. This reduction of upfront commitment may make it easier to reverse or adjust a strategy if conditions change.

- *No availability constraints.* Organic development has the advantage of not being dependent on the availability of suitable acquisition targets or potential alliance partners. There are few acquisition opportunities for foreign companies wanting to enter the Japanese market, for example. Organic developers also do not have to wait until the perfectly matched acquisition target comes onto the market.

- *Strategic independence.* The independence provided by organic development means that an organisation does not need to make the same compromises as might be necessary if it made an alliance with a partner organisation. For example, partnership with a foreign collaborator is likely to involve constraints on marketing activity in external markets and may limit future strategic choices.

- *Culture management.* Organic development allows new activities to be created in the existing cultural environment, which reduces the risk of culture clash.

The reliance of organic development on internal capabilities can be slow, expensive and risky. It is not easy to use existing capabilities as the platform for major leaps in terms of innovation, diversification or internationalisation, for example. However, organic development can be very successful and, as in the example of Amazon's Kindle, be sufficiently radical to merit the term 'corporate entrepreneurship'. **Corporate entrepreneurship refers to radical change in the organisation's business, driven principally by the organisation's own capabilities.**[1] Bringing together the words 'entrepreneurship' and 'corporate' underlines the potential for significant change or novelty not only by external entrepreneurship (see also corporate venture units in section 9.5.2), but also by reliance on internal capabilities from within the corporate organisation. Thus for Amazon, the Kindle was a radical entrepreneurial step, taking it from retailing into the design of innovative consumer electronic products.

The concept of corporate entrepreneurship is valuable because it encourages an entrepreneurial attitude inside the firm. There are many examples of corporate entrepreneurship, such as the creation of low-cost airline Ryanair from inside the aircraft leasing company Guinness Peat. Often, however, organisations have to go beyond their own internal capabilities and look externally for methods to pursue their strategies. The main themes of this chapter, therefore, are first mergers and acquisitions and second strategic alliances.

(10.3) MERGERS AND ACQUISITIONS

Mergers and acquisitions (M&A) frequently grab the headlines, as they involve large sums of money and very public competitions for shareholder support. They can also provide a speedy means of achieving major strategic objectives. However, they can also lead to spectacular failures too. A famous case is that of the Royal Bank of Scotland, whose 2007 takeover of the Dutch ABN AMRO, for \$98.5 bn (€71 bn), ended in commercial disaster and the bank's nationalisation by the British government.

10.3.1 Types of mergers and acquisitions

Mergers and acquisitions are typically about the combination of two or more organisations. In an acquisition (or takeover) this generally means an acquirer *taking control* of another company through share purchase. Thus **'acquisition' is achieved by purchasing a majority of shares in a target company**. Most acquisitions are *friendly*, where the target's management recommend accepting the acquirer's deal to its shareholders. This is good for acquirers as the target management are more likely to work with them to complete the deal and remain to integrate both companies. Sometimes acquisitions are *hostile*, where target management refuse the acquirer's offer. The acquirer therefore appeals directly to the target's shareholders for ownership of their shares. These deals can be very acrimonious with target company management obstructing efforts to obtain key information and not helping integrate the two organisations post-deal. Acquirers are generally larger than target companies although occasionally there may be 'reverse' takeovers, where acquirers are smaller than targets.

A **merger** is different in character to an acquisition as it is **the combination of two previously separate organisations in order to form a new company**. For example, in 2012 Random House and Penguin, two big publishers, announced a merger to form Penguin Random House to reduce costs and increase their negotiating power with distributors such as Amazon. Merger partners are often of similar size, with expectations of broadly equal status, unlike an acquisition where the acquirer generally dominates. In practice, the terms 'merger' and 'acquisition' are often used interchangeably, hence the common shorthand M&A.

Mergers and acquisitions can also happen in the public and non-profit sectors: for example, the Finnish government created the new Aalto University in 2010 by merging the Helsinki School of Economics, the Helsinki University of Art and Design and the Helsinki University of Technology. Publicly owned institutions frequently build up highly distinctive cultures or systems of their own, as if they were in fact independent organisations. Where there are major cultural or systems differences between organisations, the scale and depth of the managerial issues approximate to those that would be involved in a change of ownership. 'Merger' is therefore often used in such cases because that better reflects the scale of the task involved than simply 'reorganisation'.

10.3.2 **Timing of mergers and acquisitions**

Since records began in the late nineteenth century, mergers and acquisitions have shown a cyclical quality, involving high peaks and deep troughs. Thus 2007 was a record year for global mergers and acquisitions, with transactions taking place worth around $4.14 trn (€2.9 trn), four times the amount of the previous trough in 2002. As the worldwide recession took hold, the value of global M&A in 2011 fell to $2.56 trn (€1.8 trn).[2] These cycles are broadly linked to changes in the global economy but are also influenced by new regulations, the availability of finance, stock market performance, technological disturbances and the supply of available target firms. They may also be driven by over-optimism on the part of managers, shareholders and bankers during upturns, and by exaggerated loss of confidence during downturns. This cyclical pattern suggests that there are better times than others for making an acquisition. At the top of a cycle, target companies are likely to be very highly priced, which may reduce the chances of success for an acquirer. The £5 bn merger between house builders Taylor Woodrow and George Wimpey in 2007 saw the value of the share price crash by nearly 90 per cent in the following year when the recession started. These cycles should warn managers that M&A may have a strong fashion or bandwagon element. Especially in an upturn, managers should ask very carefully whether acquisitions are really justified as prices may be high.

Global activity in mergers has traditionally been dominated by North America and Western Europe, whereas it has been much less common in other economies, for example Japan. Many national governance systems put barriers in the way of acquisitions, especially hostile acquisitions (see section 4.3.2). However, companies from fast-developing economies such as China and India have become very active in large-scale acquisitions in order to access Western markets or technology, or to secure material resources needed for growth. For example, Sinopec's (China Petrochemical Corp) acquisition, in 2012, of US oil and natural gas producer Devon Energy Corp for €1.69 bn (£1.46 bn; $2.2 bn), was the Chinese group's 11th deal in a year. The Indian company Tata has also made many acquisitions including buying UK companies Tetley Tea, British Salt, the car companies Jaguar and Land Rover and the Anglo-Dutch steel company Corus (see Illustration 10.2 later).

10.3.3 **Motives for mergers and acquisitions**

Motives for M&A can be strategic, financial and managerial[3] (see Illustration 10.1).

Strategic motives for M&A

Strategic motives for M&A involve improving the competitive advantage of the organisation. These motives are often related to the reasons for diversification in general (see section 7.3). Strategic motives can be categorised in three main ways:[4]

- *Extension*. M&A can be used to extend the reach of a firm in terms of geography, products or markets. Acquisitions can be speedy ways of extending international reach. Thus in 2010 the Chinese Geely car company bought the Swedish Volvo car company in order to build its global presence. Acquisitions can also be an effective way of extending into new markets, as in diversification (see Chapter 7).

- *Consolidation*. M&A can be used to consolidate the competitors in an industry. Bringing together two competitors can have at least three beneficial effects. In the first place, it

ILLUSTRATION 10.1

Who bought whom?

Movie giant Disney's acquisition of Marvel proves analysts wrong, but problems may lie ahead.

Summer means one thing in Hollywood: big, blockbuster movies. But in 2012 a single superhero film 'ka-powed' all others with $1.5 bn (€1.12 bn, £0.9 bn) global ticket sales, becoming the third-highest grossing title of all time. *The Avengers*, from Disney's Marvel unit, stormed the box office, bringing *Iron Man*, *The Incredible Hulk* and *Thor* together. Its success largely overturned analysts' criticisms of Disney's 2009 $4 bn purchase of Marvel, as overpayment.

On paper, the acquisition looked a perfect fit. Disney was rethinking its entire approach to film making in response to a contracting home entertainment market and falling DVD sales as every studio in Hollywood was under pressure to cut costs. Ready to move to a franchise-led strategy, producing films and brands that could generate sequels and spin-offs, Disney acquired Pixar in 2006, and then Marvel, a brand that could deliver movies with stories that appealed to teenage boys – a demographic Disney found elusive.

The acquisition was not only about movies. Disney planned to use Marvel's vast library of superhero characters throughout its business from theme parks to television shows and consumer products, adding Incredible Hulk underpants and Iron Man lunch boxes to Disney's staple inventory of Mickey Mouse merchandise. In addition the deal retained Marvel's CEO, Isaac 'Ike' Perlmutter. His hard-driving approach to gain a 'big bang for each buck' appealed to Disney; 'Marvel could make a great looking movie for a fraction of the price of a Jerry Bruckheimer (*Pirates of the Caribbean* producer) movie.'

However, the deal also added dramatic tension to the family-oriented company based in Burbank, California – largely, it appears, because of Ike's management style. As Marvel's largest shareholder before Disney, he took much of his $1.5 bn payment in Disney shares, giving him a seat at the decision-making table. Since then he has become a force within Disney. He is a skilled cost-cutter and has been described as obsessive about saving money. 'He used to do this thing in our office that people would laugh at. If there was some used paper lying around he would rip it into eight pieces and would have a new memo pad.'

But Ike's strong opinions and cost-cutting capabilities often put him at odds with colleagues. His interest in merchandising and toy licensing has shaken things up throughout Disney's Consumer Products Division (DCP) – one of Disney's smaller divisions but accounting for 10 per cent of all group profits (2011). The head of DCP had repeated conflicts with Ike over the direction of the division and left in 2012 along with the heads of communications, publishing, HR, Disney stores, and the toys business. Three female executives hired a lawyer to seek individual financial settlements and another filed an internal complaint alleging Ike threatened her. DCP has now been reorganised around Disney's big TV and film franchises rather than individual product categories.

The box office and commercial successes Marvel has produced for Disney have won Ike admirers inside and outside the group. With sequels to *Thor*, *Captain America* and *The Avengers* in the works, analysts are speaking about the upside of the deal. But some former Disney employees warn of culture collisions ahead. 'You would think that Disney, with all its heritage and culture, would prevail, but the common question in the hallways [at DCP] was: remind me who bought who here?'

Sources: Financial Times, 1 and 4 September 2009, 7 September 2011, 13 July and 8 August 2012.

Questions

1 Why did Disney acquire Marvel?
2 Critically assess how well these companies fit together in (i) strategic and (ii) organisational terms.

increases market power by reducing competition: this might enable the newly consolidated company to raise prices for customers. Second, the combination of two competitors can increase efficiency through reducing surplus capacity or sharing resources, for instance head office facilities or distribution channels. Finally, the greater scale of the combined operations may increase production efficiency or increase bargaining power with suppliers, forcing them to reduce their prices.

- *Capabilities*. The third broad strategic motive for M&A is to increase a company's capabilities. High-tech companies such as Cisco and Microsoft regard acquisitions of entrepreneurial technology companies as a part of their R&D effort. Instead of researching a new technology from scratch, they allow entrepreneurial start-ups to prove the idea, and then take over these companies in order to incorporate the technological capability within their own portfolio (see section 9.5.2). Capabilities-driven acquisitions are often useful where industries are converging (see section 2.3.1). For example, Google and Apple have made substantial acquisitions in order to gain a foothold in the new high-growth mobile advertising market. Google's €576 m (£500 m; $750 m) acquisition of AdMob and Apple's €212 m (£183 m; $275 m) acquisition of Quattro Wireless in 2010, aimed at achieving a notable presence in the new competitive space where there is convergence between telephony and advertising industries.

Financial motives for M&A

Financial motives concern the optimal use of financial resources, rather than directly improving the actual business. There are three main financial motives:

- *Financial efficiency*. It may be efficient to bring together a company with a strong balance sheet (i.e. it has plenty of cash) with another company that has a weak balance sheet (i.e. it has high debt). The company with a weak balance sheet can save on interest payments by using the stronger company's assets to pay off its debt, and it can also get investment funds from the stronger company that it could not have accessed otherwise. The company with the strong balance sheet may be able to drive a good bargain in acquiring the weaker company. Also, a company with a booming share price can purchase other companies very efficiently by offering to pay the target company's shareholders with its own shares (equity), rather than paying with cash upfront.

- *Tax efficiency*. Sometimes there may be tax advantages from bringing together different companies. For example, profits or tax losses may be transferrable within the organisation in order to benefit from different tax regimes between industries or countries. Naturally, there are legal restrictions on this strategy.

- *Asset stripping or unbundling*. Some companies are effective at spotting other companies whose underlying assets are worth more than the price of the company as a whole. This makes it possible to buy such companies and then rapidly sell off ('unbundle') different business units to various buyers for a total price substantially in excess of what was originally paid for the whole. Although this is often dismissed as merely opportunistic profiteering ('asset stripping'), if the business units find better corporate parents through this unbundling process, there can be a real gain in economic effectiveness.

Managerial motives for M&A

As for diversification (see section 7.3), acquisitions may sometimes serve managers' interests rather than shareholders' interests. 'Managerial' motives are so called, therefore, because they are self-serving rather than efficiency-driven. M&A may serve managerial self-interest for two types of reason:

- *Personal ambition.* There are three ways that acquisitions can satisfy the personal ambition of senior managers, regardless of the real value being created. First, senior managers' personal financial incentives may be tied to short-term growth targets or share price targets that are more easily achieved by large and spectacular acquisitions than the more gradualist and lower-profile alternative of organic growth. Second, large acquisitions attract media attention, with opportunities to boost personal reputations through flattering media interviews and appearances. Here there is the so-called 'managerial hubris' (vanity) effect: managers who have been successful in earlier acquisitions become over-confident and embark on more and more acquisitions, each riskier and more expensive than the one before.[5] Finally, acquisitions provide opportunities to give friends and colleagues greater responsibility, helping to cement personal loyalty by developing individuals' careers.

- *Bandwagon effects.* As noted earlier, acquisitions are highly cyclical. In an upswing, there are three kinds of pressure on senior managers to join the acquisition bandwagon. First, when many other firms are making acquisitions, financial analysts and the business media may criticise more cautious managers for undue conservatism. Second, shareholders will fear that their company is being left behind, as they see opportunities for their business being snatched by rivals. Lastly, managers will worry that if their company is not acquiring, it will become the target of a hostile bid itself. For managers wanting a quiet life during a 'merger boom', the easiest strategy may be simply to join in. But the danger is making an acquisition the company does not really need and it can be one reason for paying too much.

In sum, there are bad reasons as well as good reasons for acquisitions and mergers. The average performance of acquisitions is unimpressive, with evidence suggesting that half of acquisitions fail (see Key Debate at the end of the chapter). However, alternative growth methods also exhibit similar levels of performance. Nevertheless it is worth asking sceptical questions of any M&A strategy. The converse can be true of course: there can be bad reasons for resisting a hostile takeover. Senior managers may resist being acquired because they fear losing their jobs, even if the price offered represents a good deal for their shareholders.

10.3.4 M&A processes

Acquisitions take time. First there is the search to identify an acquisition target with the best possible fit. This process may take years but under some circumstances can be completed very rapidly indeed. Then there is the process of negotiating the deal: to agree on terms and conditions and the right price. Finally managers will need to decide on the extent to which the new and old businesses will need to be integrated – and this will have significant implications for the amount of time required to create value. In other words, acquisition should be seen as a process over time. Each step in this process imposes different tasks on managers (see Figure 10.2). This section will consider three key steps: target choice, negotiation and integration.

Target choice in M&A

There are two main criteria to apply, strategic fit and organisational fit:[6]

- *Strategic fit*: this refers to the extent to which the target firm strengthens or complements the acquiring firm's strategy. Strategic fit relates to the original strategic motives for the

Figure 10.2 The acquisition process

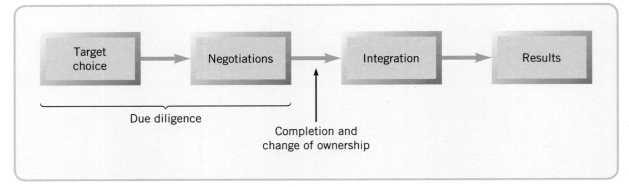

acquisition: extension, consolidation and capabilities. Managers need to assess strategic fit very carefully. The danger is that potential synergies (see section 7.3) in M&A are often exaggerated in order to justify high acquisition prices. Also, negative synergies ('contagion') between the companies involved are easily neglected.[7] An example of negative synergy was when the Bank of America bought the aggressive investment bank Merrill Lynch for $47 bn (~ €33 bn) in 2008. Under its new owner, Merrill Lynch lost business because it was no longer allowed to advise on deals targeting the extensive list of corporations that were already lending clients of Bank of America. Consequently Merrill Lynch was a less valuable business with its new parent than when free to chase any deal it wanted.

● *Organisational fit*: this refers to the match between the management practices, cultural practices and staff characteristics between the target and the acquiring firms. Large mismatches between the two are likely to cause significant integration problems. The acquisition of Marvel by Disney raised many questions of organisational fit (see Illustration 10.1). International acquisitions can be particularly liable to organisational misfits, because of cultural and language differences between countries,[8] although the extent to which there is actual cultural clash will be determined by the extent of integration intended. A comparison of the two companies' cultural webs (section 5.3.6) might be helpful to highlight potential misfit.

Together, strategic and organisational fit determine the potential for the acquirer to add value, the parenting issue raised in section 7.6. Where there is poor organisational fit, attempts by the acquirer to integrate the target are likely to destroy value regardless of how well the target fits strategically. For instance, the merger between French and American telecoms equipment manufacturers Alcatel and Lucent resulted in significant culture clashes for several years post-deal with losses running into billions of dollars and the departure of the two top executives.

The two criteria of strategic and organisational fit are important components of 'due diligence' – a structured investigation of target companies that generally takes place before a deal is closed. In 2012 Hewlett Packard was forced to write down the value of its acquisition of Autonomy, a British software company, by €3.8 bn (£3 bn, $5 bn), alleging the former management team had fraudulently misrepresented the company during due diligence (see end of chapter Key Debate). Strategic and organisational fit can be used to create a screen according to which potential acquisition targets can be ruled in or ruled out. Note that, because the set of firms that meet the criteria *and* that are actually available for purchase is likely to be small, it is very tempting for managers to relax the criteria too far in order to build a large enough pool of possible acquisitions. Strict strategic and organisational fit criteria are particularly liable to be forgotten after the failure of an initial acquisition bid. Once having committed publicly to an acquisition strategy, senior managers are susceptible to making ill-considered bids for other targets 'on the rebound'.

Negotiation in M&A

The negotiation process in M&A is critical to the outcome of friendly deals. If top managements cannot agree because the price is not right, the terms and conditions are unacceptable, or they cannot get on with each other, the deal will not take place. In terms of price, offer the target too little and the bid will be unsuccessful: senior managers will lose credibility and the company will have wasted a lot of management time. Pay too much, though, and the acquisition is unlikely ever to make a profit net of the original acquisition price.

Ways in which the price is established by the acquirer are through the use of various valuation methods, including financial analysis techniques such as payback period, discounted cash flow, asset valuation and shareholder value analysis (see Chapter 11).[9] For acquisition of publicly quoted companies, there is the additional guide of the market value of the target company's shares. However, acquirers typically do not simply pay the current market value of the target, but have to pay a so-called *premium for control*. This premium is the additional amount that the acquirer has to pay to win control compared to the ordinary valuation of the target's shares as an independent company. Depending on the state of the financial markets, this premium might involve paying at least 30 per cent more for shares in a friendly takeover than normal. Especially where the target resists the initial bid, or other potential acquirers join in with their own bids, it is very easy for bid prices to escalate well beyond the true economic value of the target.

It is therefore very important for the acquirer to be disciplined regarding the price that it will pay. Acquisitions are liable to the *winner's curse* – in order to win acceptance of the bid, the acquirer may pay so much that the original cost can never be earned back.[10] This winner's curse effect operated when the Royal Bank of Scotland's consortium competed with Barclays Bank to acquire the Dutch bank ABN AMRO: the Royal Bank of Scotland won, but the excessive price of €70 bn ($98 bn) soon drove the victor into financial collapse and government ownership. The negative effects of paying too much can be worsened if the acquirer tries to justify the price by cutting back essential investments in order to improve immediate profits. In what is called the *vicious circle of overvaluation*, over-paying firms can easily undermine the original rationale of the acquisition by imposing savings on exactly the assets (e.g. brand marketing, product R&D or key staff) that made up the strategic value of the target company in the first place.

Integration in M&A

The ability to extract value from an acquisition will depend critically on the approach to integrating the new business with the old. Integration is frequently challenging because of problems of organisational fit. For example, there might be strong cultural differences between the two organisations (see section 5.3) or they might have incompatible financial or information technology systems (see section 13.3). Poor integration can cause acquisitions to fail (see Illustration 10.2 for difficulties and successes experienced by Indian conglomerate Tata in its integration of British car company Jaguar Land Rover). Getting the right approach to integration of merged or acquired companies is crucial.

ILLUSTRATION 10.2

Staying power

Hailed a triumph in 2012, Tata's acquisition of Jaguar and Land Rover (JLR) was perceived as extravagant in 2008, saying more about Indian imperial ambitions than commercial logic. How was success achieved?

The largest privately owned Indian company, Tata Group, has interests in steel, hotels, telecommunications and consulting. It has pursued internationalisation with acquisitions including Corus, the Anglo-Dutch steel company, and, in 2008, JLR. At €1.7 bn (£1.4 bn, $2.2 bn) the acquisition from struggling Ford Motors gave Tata two well-known brands and enlarged its global footprint. But critics asked how could a company known for commercial vehicles and cheap cars (the Nano), do better than a gargantuan of the global auto world, which had pumped billions into the brands, when there were no obvious synergies?

Unfortunately the deal coincided with the global financial crisis. Petrol prices spiked, bank collapses spooked consumers, credit markets froze and demand for luxury cars was hit hard. JLR sales plunged 32 per cent in 10 months and lost €807 m in the year. Tata's debt nearly doubled to €12.9 bn hitting its share price and credit rating. With 16,000 employees at five UK sites, there was alarm that some might close and production be sent overseas. As one banker remarked, 'if they carry on operating JLR as it is, it will fail'. Tata pleaded with the British government for assistance, but support for JLR was refused.

Chairman Ratan Tata was quick to reassure with a personal visit to JLR. He recalled his father had bought a classic Jaguar half a century ago and talked about reviving the revered British Daimler brand and returning Jaguar to racing. Further, 600 more skilled staff were hired to help develop environmentally-friendly cars.

JLR still faced challenges. It had relied on Ford Credit to finance its operations and sales and now needed to switch financing to other providers. All its information technology was based on Ford systems and CEO David Smith commented: 'the IT is an absolute hydra'. To improve efficiencies and save the marques, 2,200 jobs were slashed and tough cuts were made to operation costs.

However, Tata did not insist on tight integration into the group. A three-man strategy board, comprising Ratan Tata, the Head of Tata Automotive and David Smith, Overseas JLR. But the JLR executive committee, directly responsible for company operations, had no Tata representatives. Smith commented: 'Tata wants us to be autonomous – I've got all the executive authority I need . . . We can make decisions quickly – very different from life at Ford. Relationships with Tata are based on individual relationships'. Ratan Tata also commanded respect: 'The designers love him, because he's an architect and not only quite capable of telling them what he thinks; he can say it in the right language too' (Smith). JLR has also used Tata Motors' expertise in cost control and Tata Consultancy Division's skills in information technology.

In 2012 JRL introduced new models including the hot-selling Range Rover Evoque – an all-aluminium-bodied car originally started by Ford, boasting improved fuel consumption and better performance. Second-quarter pre-tax profits were up 77 per cent and sales were up 27 per cent on the previous year helped by strong demand in India and China; 1,000 jobs have been added in the UK and new manufacturing capacity is being built abroad. The 'staying power' of Tata has been rewarded.

Sources: Management Today, 1 May 2009; *Financial Times*, 4 August 2008; *The Hindu*, 2 September 2012; *Financial Times*, 7 November 2012.

Questions

1 Using Haspeslagh and Jemison's matrix, assess Tata's integration approach to JLR.

2 How do you explain Tata's success at JLR?

INSEAD's Philippe Haspeslagh and David Jemison[11] argue that the most suitable approach to integration depends on two key criteria:

- *The extent of strategic interdependence.* This is the need for the transfer or sharing of capabilities (e.g. technology) or resources (e.g. manufacturing facilities). The presumption is that significant transfer or sharing through tight integration will enable the 'creation' of value from the acquisition. Of course, some acquisitions 'capture' value purely through the ownership of assets and so there is less need for integration. These unrelated or conglomerate diversifications (see section 7.2) may only be integrated in terms of their financial systems.

- *The need for organisational autonomy.* Where an acquired firm has a very distinct culture, or is geographically distant, or is dominated by prima donna professionals or star performers, integration may be problematic. For this reason some acquisitions need high levels of organisational autonomy. But in some circumstances it is the distinctiveness of the acquired organisation that is valuable to the acquirer.[12] In this case it is best to learn gradually from the distinct culture, rather than risk spoiling it by hurried or overly tight integration.

As in Figure 10.3, therefore, these two criteria drive four integration approaches[13] which have important implications for the length of integration period and choice of top management for the acquired company:[14]

- *Absorption* is preferred where a high level of strategic interdependence is necessary and there is little need for organisational autonomy. Absorption requires rapid adjustment of the acquired company's old strategies and structures to the needs of the new owner, and corresponding changes to the acquired company's culture and systems. In this type of acquisition it is usual to appoint a new top manager in order to manage the organisation differently.[15]

- *Preservation* is appropriate where the acquired company is well run but not very compatible with the acquirer. The high need for autonomy and low need for integration may be found

Figure 10.3 Acquisition integration matrix

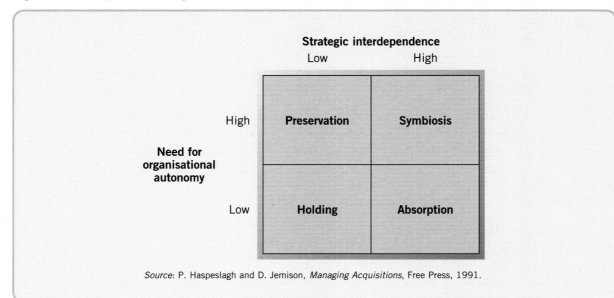

Source: P. Haspeslagh and D. Jemison, *Managing Acquisitions*, Free Press, 1991.

in conglomerate deals. The preservation style depends on allowing old strategies, cultures and systems to continue in the acquired company much as before. Changes from the acquirer are generally confined to the essential minimum such as adjusting financial reporting procedures for control. In this situation it is advisable to retain the incumbent top manager.

- *Symbiosis* is indicated where there is strong need for strategic interdependence, but also a requirement for high autonomy – perhaps in a professional services organisation dependent on the creativity of its staff. Symbiosis implies that both acquired firm and acquiring firm learn the best qualities from the other. This learning process takes time and it is often the case that it is best to retain the incumbent top manager in the early stages to stabilise the acquisition before bringing in a new top manager to make far-reaching changes. This is the most complex of the integration approaches.

- *Holding* is a residual category where there is little to be gained by integration. These acquisitions may occur when the acquired company is in poor financial health and rapid remedial action is required.[16] The acquirer will not integrate the company into its own business to avoid contamination but will impose stringent short-term targets and strategies in order to solve its problems. In these cases it is normal to retain the incumbent top managers as they can act more rapidly than a new appointment. These businesses may often be for sale.

Especially for the more active absorption and symbiosis forms of integration, the ultimate success of the acquisition will depend upon how well the integration process is managed. Here methods of managing strategic change explained in Chapter 14 will be relevant. However, because acquisitions often involve the loss of jobs, sudden career changes, management relocations and the cancellation of projects, it is argued that organisational justice is particularly important for successful integration.[17] *Organisational justice* refers to the perceived fairness of managerial actions, in terms of distribution, procedure and information. Thus:

- *Distributive justice* refers to the distribution of rewards and posts: for example, it will be seen as unfair in a merger between equals if the large majority of senior management posts go to one of the partners, and not the other.

- *Procedural justice* refers to the procedures by which decisions are made: for example, if integration decisions are made through appropriate committees or task forces with representation from both sides, then the perception of fair procedures is likely to be high.

- *Informational justice* is about how information is used and communicated in the integration: if decisions are explained well to all those involved, they are more likely to be accepted positively.

Kraft offended principles of both procedural and informational justice when it assured investors and employees before its 2010 takeover of Cadbury that it would keep open the Somerdale chocolate factory near Bristol, with its 400 workers. Within a month of completing the takeover, Kraft announced that production would be transferred to Poland, causing political controversy and a loss of trust among acquired employees.

10.3.5 M&A strategy over time

M&A strategies evolve over time as deals are rarely one-off events for an organisation:

- *Serial acquirers* are companies that make multiple acquisitions, often in parallel. Working on simultaneous acquisitions is very demanding of managerial time and skills. However, repeating the acquisition process does provide an opportunity for acquiring companies to accumulate experience about how to do M&A better. Cisco Systems is well known as a successful serial acquirer. By end of 2012 it had made 157 acquisitions since its first deal in 1993, accounting for at least 50 per cent of revenue. Carrying out lots of M&A means that serial acquirers often develop specialist teams for managing the acquisition process, from target selection through due diligence and negotiation to post-acquisition integration. The amount of work in selecting and evaluating targets is significant. In order to make just 50 software acquisitions, IBM had to assess around 500 different potential acquisition targets, choosing not to proceed in the vast majority of cases. And for those 50 acquisitions, IBM also had to establish 50 different integration teams, with 10 or more teams each working in parallel at any one time.[18]

- *Divesture (or divestment)* is the process of selling a business that no longer fits the corporate strategy.[19] This is obviously a central part of 'asset-stripping' strategy (see section 10.3.2), but ought to be on the agenda of every diversified corporation. The key determinant of divesture is whether the corporate parent has 'parenting advantage': in other words, the corporate parent can add more value to the business unit than other potential owners of the business (see section 7.4). A corporate parent that does not have parenting advantage should divest the business for the best price it can obtain. Corporate parents are often reluctant to divest businesses, seeing it as an admission of failure. However, a dynamic perspective on M&A would encourage managers to view divestures positively. Funds raised by the sale of an ill-fitting business can be used either to invest in retained businesses or to buy other businesses that fit the corporate strategy better. Obtaining a good price for the divested unit can recoup any losses it may have originally made. Sometimes, however, a less positive reason for divesture is pressure from competition authorities, which may force the sale of businesses to reduce companies' market power. For example, in 2012 Vivendi's Universal Music Group sold businesses amounting to 10 per cent of revenue in order to gain European regulators' approval for its €1.9 bn acquisition of EMI's recorded music business.

Acquisitions, therefore, are an important method for pursuing strategies. However, they are not easy to carry out and they are sometimes adopted for misguided reasons. It is important to consider the alternative of strategic alliances.

(10.4) STRATEGIC ALLIANCES

M&A bring together companies through complete changes in ownership. However, companies also often work together in strategic alliances that involve collaboration with only partial changes in ownership, or no ownership changes at all as the parent companies remain distinct. Thus a strategic alliance **is where two or more organisations share resources and activities to pursue a common strategy**. This is a popular method among companies for pursuing strategy. Accenture has estimated that the average large corporation is managing around 30 alliances at any one time.[20]

Alliance strategy challenges the traditional organisation-centred approach to strategy in at least two ways. First, practitioners of alliance strategy need to think about strategy in terms of the collective success of their networks as well as their individual organisations' self-interest.[21] Collective strategy **is about how the whole network of alliances, of which an organisation is a member, competes against rival networks of alliances.** Thus for Microsoft, competitive success for its Xbox games console relies heavily on the collective strength of its network of independent games developers such as Bungie Studios (makers of Halo), Crystal Dynamics (Tomb Raider), Rockstar North (Grand Auto Theft Auto V) and Crytek Studios (Crysis 3). Part of Microsoft's strategy must include developing a stronger ecosystem of games developers than its rivals such as Sony and Nintendo. Collective strategy also challenges the individualistic approach to strategy by highlighting the importance of effective collaboration. Thus success involves collaborating as well as competing. **Collaborative advantage is about managing alliances better than competitors.**[22] For Microsoft to maximise the value of the Xbox, it is not enough for it to have a stronger network than rivals such as Sony and Nintendo, but it must be better at working with its network in order to ensure that its members keep on producing the best games. The more effectively it collaborates, the more successful it will be. Illustration 10.3 describes Apple's approach to collective strategy and collaboration for the iPad.

10.4.1 Types of strategic alliance

In terms of ownership, there are two main kinds of strategic alliance:

- *Equity alliances* involve the creation of a new entity that is owned separately by the partners involved. The most common form of equity alliance is the *joint venture*, where two organisations remain independent but set up a new organisation jointly owned by the parents. For example, Virgin Mobile India Limited is a cellular telephone service provider company which is a joint venture formed in 2008 between Tata Tele service, part of Tata Group, India, and Richard Branson's Virgin Service Group. The joint venture company uses Tata's network to offer its services under the brand name Virgin Mobile. A *consortium alliance* involves several partners setting up a venture together. For example, IBM, Hewlett Packard, Toshiba and Samsung are partners in the Sematech research consortium, working together on the latest semiconductor technologies.

- *Non-equity alliances* are typically looser, without the commitment implied by ownership. Non-equity alliances are often based on contracts. One common form of contractual alliance is franchising, where one organisation (the franchisor) gives another organisation (the franchisee) the right to sell the franchisor's products or services in a particular location in return for a fee or royalty. Kall-Kwik printing, 7-Eleven convenience stores, McDonald's restaurants and Subway are examples of franchising. Licensing is a similar kind of contractual alliance, allowing partners to use intellectual property such as patents or brands in return for a fee. Long-term subcontracting agreements are another form of loose non-equity alliance, common in automobile supply. For example, the Canadian subcontractor Magna has long-term contracts to assemble the bodies and frames for car companies such as Ford, Honda and Mercedes.

The public and voluntary sectors often get involved in both equity and non-equity strategic alliances. Governments have increasingly encouraged the public sector to contract out the building and maintenance of capital projects such as hospitals and schools under long-term contracts. Individual public organisations often band together to form purchasing consortia as well. A good example of this is university libraries, which typically negotiate collectively for the purchase of journals and books from publishers. Voluntary organisations pool their resources in alliance too. For example, relief organisations in areas suffering from natural or human-made disasters typically have to cooperate in order to deliver the full range of services in difficult circumstances. Although public- and voluntary-sector organisations might often be seen as more naturally cooperative than private-sector organisations, many of the issues that follow apply to all three kinds of organisation.

ILLUSTRATION 10.3

Apple's iPad advantage

Gaining competitive advantage through collaboration?

With much fanfare, a new version of Apple's iPad was launched on 16 March 2012. Apple had dominated the tablet market with its iPad for two years. iPad's light-weight touchscreen and new operating system, iOS, designed from the ground up for portable performance, had won may admirers. But among the first customers on 16 March were buyers who just could not wait to tear the gadget apart, to better understand iPad's success.

Market research firm iSuppli's 'teardown' analysis revealed the €622 (£497, $829), 4G 64GB model cost $409 to make, just 49 per cent of its retail price. iSuppli identified Broadcom and Qualcomm as suppliers of Bluetooth and Wi-Fi chips, STMicroelectronics the gyroscope, Cirrus Logic the audio chip, three Taiwanese companies the touchscreen components and Sony the camera CMOS sensor. Samsung, a rival manufacturer of its own tablet, provided a significant portion of the iPad: the expensive display, battery and processor chip.

Apple was therefore at the heart of a network. However, it had always protected its intellectual property. No hardware was licensed, ensuring control of production and maintenance of its premium pricing policy. It was impossible for any independent company to manufacture cheap iPads, in the way for instance Taiwanese manufacturers produced cheap IBM/Microsoft-compatible personal computers in the 1980s.

iPad's success attracted a swarm of companies into the accessory market, with US company Griffin and Logitech from Switzerland supplying attractive add-ons including ultrathin keyboards, cases and touchscreen stylus. Apple licensed them the necessary technology for this and benefited from attractive complementary products and royalties. But the relationship was arm's-length, with no advanced information about new products.

Originally controlling access to iOS, Apple opened up access for the iPad, allowing third-party apps development and stimulating the new App Stores industry. The attractiveness of iOS and strong consumer demand encouraged software developers to produce for Apple first.

Consumers liked the ease of use and vast ecosystem of Apple's iPad but challenges were mounting. Amazon's low-cost 'content consumption device', Kindle, offered a vast library of movies but lacked Apple's beauty and had few apps. Google's low-priced Nexus 10, manufactured by Samsung, aimed to profit from business services use rather than hardware. Its improved screen resolution and Android operating system challenged iPad's technology and it shared many characteristics of other ecosystems with streaming apps and a consistent user experience. Samsung's own tablet, Galaxy Tab, had similar advantages along with compelling design and openness to non-Apple standards. Microsoft aimed to profit from its hardware, Surface, but was not particularly innovative, lacking a comparable software ecosystem and its tie to Windows could be a hindrance.

In September 2012 Apple briefly surpassed Exxon Mobile as the world's largest company by capitalisation. However, problems were surfacing with declining growth rate in iPad sales in a growing market and Apple shares falling 30 per cent in six months. In addition Apple was also embroiled in lawsuits against Samsung over its Galaxy Tablet design. Samsung was also counter-suing. In November 2012 Apple dropped Samsung as its provider of batteries in preference for Chinese manufacturers.

Sources: G. Linden, K. Kraemer and J. Dedrick, 'Who captures value in a global innovation network?', *Communications of the ACM*, vol. 52, no. 3 (2009), pp. 140–5; 'Tablet wars', *Telegraph*, 6 November 2012; F. MacMahon, 'Tablet wars', 4 December 2012, *BroadcastEngineering.com*; A. Hesseldahl, 'Apple's new ipad costs at least $316 to build, IHS iSuppli teardown shows', 16 March 2012, http://allthingsd.com.

Questions

1 What are the pros and cons of Apple's tight control of licensing?

2 What role has 'ecosystem' played in Apple's competitive advantage?

Figure 10.4 Strategic alliance motives

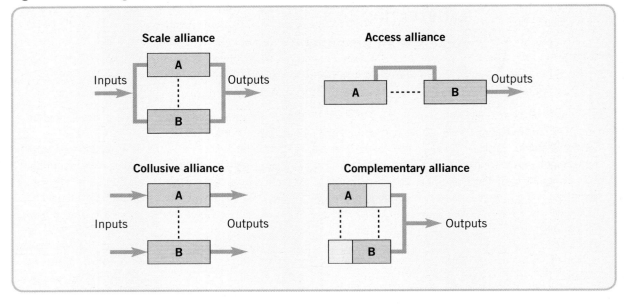

10.4.2 **Motives for alliances**

Strategic alliances allow an organisation to rapidly extend its strategic advantage and generally require less commitment than other forms of expansion. A key motivator is sharing resources or activities, although there may be less obvious reasons as well. Four broad rationales for alliances can be identified, as summarised in Figure 10.4:

● *Scale alliances*. Here organisations combine in order to achieve necessary scale. The capabilities of each partner may be quite similar (as indicated by the similarity of the A and B organisations in Figure 10.4), but together they can achieve advantages that they could not easily manage on their own. Thus combining together can provide economies of scale in the production of outputs (products or services). Combining might also provide economies of scale in terms of inputs, for example by reducing purchasing costs of raw materials or services. Thus health management organisations often combine together to negotiate better prices with pharmaceutical companies. Finally, combining allows the partners to share risk as well. Instead of organisations stretching themselves to find enough resources on their own, partnering can help each partner avoid committing so many resources of their own that failure would jeopardise the existence of the whole organisation.

● *Access alliances*. Organisations frequently ally in order to access the capabilities of another organisation that are required in order to produce or sell its products and services. For example, in countries such as China and India, a Western company (in Figure 10.4, organisation A) might need to partner with a local distributor (organisation B) in order to access effectively the national market for its products and services. Here organisation B is critical to organisation A's ability to sell. Access alliances can work in the opposite direction. Thus organisation B might seek a licensing alliance in order to access inputs from organisation A, for example technologies or brands. Here organisation A is critical to organisation B's ability to produce or market its products and services. Access can be about tangible resources such as distribution channels or products as well as intangible resources such as knowledge and social/political connections.

- *Complementary alliances*. These can be seen as a form of access alliance, but involve organisations at similar points in the value network combining their distinctive resources so that they bolster each partner's particular gaps or weaknesses. Figure 10.4 shows an alliance where the strengths of organisation A (indicated by the darker shading) match the weaknesses of organisation B (indicated by the lighter shading); conversely, the strengths of organisation B match the weaknesses of organisation A. By partnering, the two organisations can bring together complementary strengths in order to overcome their individual weaknesses. An example of this is the General Motors–Toyota NUMMI alliance: here the complementarity lies in General Motors getting access to the Japanese car company's manufacturing expertise, while Toyota obtains the American car company's local marketing knowledge.

- *Collusive alliances*. Occasionally organisations secretly collude together in order to increase their market power. By combining together into cartels, they reduce competition in the marketplace, enabling them to extract higher prices from their customers or lower prices from suppliers. Such collusive cartels among for-profit businesses are generally illegal, so there is no public agreement between them (hence the absence of brackets joining the two collusive organisations in Figure 10.4) and regulators will act to discourage this activity. For instance, mobile phone operators are often accused of collusive behaviour. In 2012 Thailand's three largest mobile phone operators bid 41.63 bn baht (€1.0 bn, $1.3 bn) for a 3G licence, just 2.8 per cent higher than the minimum price, giving rise to criticism that they had colluded. In not-for-profit sectors collusive alliances do take place and they may also be justified politically in sensitive for-profit industries such as defence or aerospace due to national interests and where the costs of development are far greater than an individual firm can sustain.

It can be seen that strategic alliances, like M&A, have mixed motives. Cooperation is often a good thing, but it is important to be aware of collusive motivations. These are likely to work against the interests of other competitors, customers and suppliers.

10.4.3 Strategic alliance processes

Like acquisitions and mergers, strategic alliances need to be understood as processes unfolding over time. Many alliances are relatively short lived although there are examples of some which last for very long periods indeed. For example, General Electric (USA) and SNECMA (France) have been partners since 1974 in a continuous alliance for the development and production of small aero-engines – this arrangement has been recently extended to 2040. The needs and capabilities of the partners in a long standing alliance such as this are bound to change over time. However, the absence of full ownership means that emerging differences cannot simply be reconciled by managerial authority; they have to be negotiated between independent partners. This lack of control by one side or the other means the managerial processes in alliances are particularly demanding. The management challenges, moreover, will change over time.

The fact that neither partner is in control, while alliances must typically be managed over time, highlights the importance of two themes in the various stages of the alliance process:

- *Co-evolution*. Rather than thinking of strategic alliances as fixed at a particular point of time, they are better seen as co-evolutionary processes.[23] The concept of co-evolution underlines the way in which partners, strategies, capabilities and environments are constantly changing. As they change, they need realignment so that they can evolve in harmony. A co-evolutionary perspective on alliances therefore places the emphasis on flexibility and change. At completion, an alliance is unlikely to be the same as envisaged at the start.

● *Trust.* Given the probable co-evolutionary nature of alliances, and the lack of control of one partner over the other, trust becomes highly important to the success of alliances over time.[24] All future possibilities cannot be specified in the initial alliance contract. Each partner will have made investments that are vulnerable to the selfish behaviour of the other. This implies the need for partners to behave in a trustworthy fashion through the whole lifetime of the alliance. Trust in a relationship is something that has to be continuously earned. Trust is often particularly fragile in alliances between the public and private sectors, where the profit motive is suspect on one side, and sudden shifts in political agendas are feared on the other.

The International HIV/AIDS Alliance shows the importance co-evolution and trust: see Illustration 10.5.

The themes of trust and co-evolution surface in various ways at different stages in the life span of a strategic alliance. Figure 10.5 provides a simple stage model of strategic alliance evolution. The amount of committed resources changes at each stage, but issues of trust and co-evolution recur throughout:

● *Courtship.* First there is the initial process of courting potential partners, where the main resource commitment is managerial time. This courtship process should not be rushed, as the willingness of both partners is required. Similar criteria apply to alliances at this stage as to acquisitions. Each partner has to see a strategic fit, according to the rationales in section 10.3.2. Equally, each partner has to see an organisational fit. Organisational fit can be considered as for acquisitions (section 10.3.4). However, because alliances do not entail the same degree of control as acquisitions, mutual trust between partners will need to be particularly strong right from the outset.

Figure 10.5 Alliance evolution

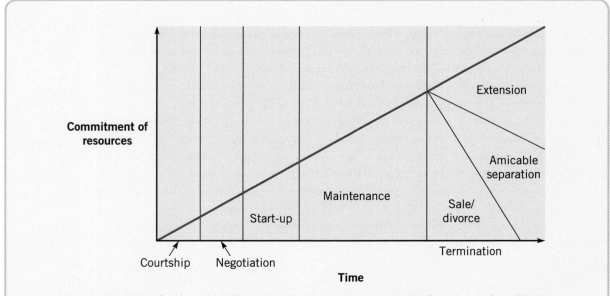

Source: Adapted from E. Murray and J. Mahon, 'Strategic alliances: gateway to the New Europe', *Long Range Planning*, vol. 26 (1993), p. 109.

ILLUSTRATION 10.4

International HIV/AIDS Alliance: trust and co-evolution

An international non-governmental organisation committed to support HIV communities.

Thirty-four million people live with HIV globally and in 2011 the HIV epidemic resulted in 1.7 m deaths. Millions are denied their human rights, resulting in ill-health, isolation, abuse and financial insecurity. Most AIDS deaths can be prevented with access to antiretroviral therapy (ART).

The International HIV/AIDS Alliance ('the Alliance') was formed in 1993 to address this enormous problem. The emphasis has been on developing the capacity for local responses to HIV, rather than direct service provision. The Alliance delivers much of its work – technical expertise and financial support to community-based responses and projects – through nationally based independent not-for-profit Linking Organisations (LOs) that vary in capacity, size and scope. By end 2012 the Alliance was a global partnership of 41 LOs, 7 Technical Support Hubs and an International Secretariat (Secretariat), reaching 4.4 million people. The seven regional Technical Support Hubs, each hosted by a LO, consist of small teams of support providers and regional experts who work with LOs, community-based organisations, governments and other sectors to strengthen their leadership, technical capacity and responsiveness to HIV.

The Alliance is governed by a board of trustees, which has to approve the Alliance's strategy and keep it within mission. The trustees also appoint the Alliance's executive director. The Secretariat is based in Brighton, UK, with offices in Washington, DC, Delhi, Brussels and Geneva. Initially the Alliance acted as a technical support and funding agency, building the capacity of community organisations and dispensing funds from donors to community-based organisations with a technical, project-driven approach. Later strategic activities such as enhancing quality, disseminating best practice, accrediting organisations and working to make more resources available became more important. As LOs developed, the Secretariat role became increasingly one of providing technical support, promoting learning across the Secretariat, LOs and Hubs, policy and advocacy.

The Secretariat also monitored and evaluated programming, and policy, and raised funds largely from government donor agencies. All LOs sign a Charter and Linking Agreement which describes the Alliance's purpose, how it works, its values and commitments and how these will be honoured. An accreditation system evaluates, improves and accredits the LOs as robust organisations operating under certain standards. As Awo Ablo, the Alliance Director of External Relations, pointed out, however, it is important to understand the historic relationship between the LOs and the Secretariat: 'The principle of equality between the LOs and the secretariat is in the DNA of the Alliance. So, the secretariat does not sit above the LOs.' In this sense the Alliance thinks of itself as a 'family' where joint agreement is important.

However, the Alliance's structure is evolving. Ten years ago, Secretariat technical experts flew out to provide support to LOs. This became expensive, and such support increasingly became available as some LOs developed expertise and could act as technical providers to other LOs. These larger LOs have also attracted direct donor support. The Secretariat increasingly acts as an architect of cooperation, binding civil society organisations together to deliver the AIDS mission.

By 2012 funds for fighting AIDS were diminishing and disappearing altogether from countries where donors argue that their economies are rich enough to support themselves. This posed the question: what role should the whole Alliance and Secretariat play in future?

Note: For further information on International HIV/AIDS Alliance strategy development, see the case study in the Text and Cases edition.

Source: http://www.aidsalliance.org.

Questions

1 What role does trust play in the Alliance?
2 What evidence is there that this Alliance has evolved and continues to evolve?

● *Negotiation.* Partners need, of course, to negotiate carefully their mutual roles at the outset. In equity alliances, the partners also have to negotiate the proportion of ownership each will have in the final joint venture, the profit share and managerial responsibilities. There is likely to be a significant commitment of managerial time at this stage, as it is important to get initial contracts clear and correct and it is worth spending time working out how disputes during the life of the alliance will be resolved. In the case of the Areva–Siemens joint venture (Illustration 10.5), Siemens regretted the low share that it originally agreed. Although the negotiation of ownership proportions in a joint venture is similar to the valuation process in acquisitions, strategic alliance contracts generally involve a great deal more. Key behaviours required of each partner need to be specified upfront. However, a ruthless negotiation style can also damage trust going forward. Moreover, co-evolution implies the need to anticipate change. In an acquired unit, it is possible to make adjustments simply by managerial authority. In alliances, initial contracts may be considered binding even when starting conditions have changed. It is wise to include an option for renegotiating initial terms right at the outset.

● *Start-up.* This involves considerable investment of material and human resources and trust is very important. First, the initial operation of the alliance puts the original alliance agreements to the test. Informal adjustments to working realities are likely to be required. Also, people from outside the original negotiation team are typically now obliged to work together on a day-to-day basis. They may not have the same understanding of the alliance as those who initiated it. Without the mutual trust to make adjustments and smooth misunderstandings, the alliance is liable to break up. This early period in an alliance's evolution is the one with the highest rate of failure.

● *Maintenance.* This refers to the ongoing operation of the strategic alliance, with increasing resources likely to be committed. The lesson of co-evolution is that alliance maintenance is not a simple matter of stability. Alliances have to be actively managed to allow for changing external circumstances. The internal dynamics of the partnership are likely to evolve as well as the partners build experience. Here again trust is extremely important. Gary Hamel has warned that alliances often become 'competitions for competence.'[25] Because partners are interacting closely, they can begin to learn each other's particular competences. This learning can develop into a competition for competence, with the partner that learns the fastest becoming the more powerful. The more powerful partner may consequently be able to renegotiate the terms in its favour or even break up the alliance and go it alone. If on the other hand the partners wish to maintain their strategic alliance, trustworthy behaviour that does not threaten the other partner's competence is essential to maintaining the cooperative relationships necessary for the day-to-day working of the alliance.

● *Termination.* Often an alliance will have had an agreed time span or purpose right from the start, so termination is a matter of completion rather than failure. Here separation is amicable. Sometimes the alliance has been so successful that the partners will wish to extend the alliance by agreeing a new alliance between themselves, committing still more resources. Sometimes too the alliance will have been more of a success for one party than the other, with one partner wishing to buy the other's share in order to commit fully, while the other partner decides to sell out. The sale of one party's interest need not be a sign of failure as their strategic agenda may have changed since alliance formation. However, sometimes it can end in bitter divorce, as when Areva threatened to take Siemens to court (see Illustration 10.5). Termination needs to be managed carefully, therefore. Co-evolution

ILLUSTRATION 10.5

Nuclear fission: Areva and Siemens break up

Co-evolution is not easy, as two leading French and German companies discover.

In 2001, Siemens, the German industrial conglomerate, and Areva, the French nuclear industry giant, merged their nuclear reactor businesses into a new joint venture called Areva NP. The joint venture was 34 per cent owned by Siemens, 66 per cent owned by Areva. As the German government had promised to exit nuclear power altogether for environmental reasons, Siemens no longer saw nuclear power as central to its strategy. The joint venture agreement gave the French a right-to-buy option for the Siemens minority stake.

In 2009, the new Siemens CEO, Peter Löscher, sent Areva's CEO Ann Lauvergeon a short email announcing that the Germans would be exercising their right to sell their stake to the French. The email took Madame Lauvergeon completely by surprise: 'It made me think of those men who abandon their wives by leaving a note on the kitchen table.' What had gone wrong in the eight years? Areva NP had been a success. It was the global leader in a market for nuclear reactors that was booming again. Rising oil prices and alarm over global warming made nuclear power increasingly attractive. By 2009, after many years of minimal construction, 51 plants were being built around the world, with 171 more planned. Areva NP was active not only in Europe but in the USA and China.

The recovery of the nuclear industry was in fact one source of the problem: with a new CEO, Siemens wanted back in. Siemens was frustrated by its lack of control as a minority shareholder, and by the slow decision making in Areva NP generally. Moreover, it wanted to get a larger slice of the business than just the nuclear reactors – the big profits were elsewhere in the value chain, in fuel and recycling. Areva, the French parent company, already had a significant presence through the whole value chain.

During 2007, Siemens looked either to increase its stake in Areva NP to 50:50 or to take a direct stake in the French parent, Areva. But, with more than 80 per cent owned by the French government, Areva was not easily for sale. Moreover, Nicolas Sarkozy, then a senior French government minister and soon French President, told German Chancellor Angela Merkel that France could not tolerate a role for Siemens while the German government refused to back nuclear power in its own country. Siemens had to enrol Merkel's support to prevent Areva from exercising its right-to-buy option and forcing Siemens to sell.

In late 2008, Siemens began talks with the Russian nuclear power giant Rosatom. Rosatom had a presence through the whole value chain, including the highly profitable fuel business. With memories of the Soviet nuclear disaster at Chernobyl still live, Rosatom needed Siemens' high reputation for quality. In March 2009, Siemens and Rosatom announced a joint venture with the ambition of displacing Areva NP as world leader.

Ending the Areva NP joint venture was not simple, however. Siemens' strength was in hardware, but Areva owned the software that made it work. Areva was obliged to buy Siemens' stake (~€4 bn; ~$5.6 bn), but lacked the funds to do so. Also, the original joint venture agreement had included an 11-year non-compete clause in case of breakdown. As far as Areva was concerned, Siemens' new joint venture put it in breach of the contract, and so not entitled to the full value of its stake. And the two companies were still working together on various nuclear power stations. Indeed, Areva and Siemens were being jointly sued for €2 bn for cost and time over-runs on a project in Finland. In 2009 Areva took sole control of the joint venture but disputes continued. In 2012 the European Commission ruled the non-compete clause was excessive, anti-competitive and unduly onerous on Siemens – it had to be reduced to three years post joint venture. It was a messy divorce.

Sources: L'Expansion, 1 April 2009; Financial Times, 28 April 2009; http://www.europa.eu/rapid/press-release_IP-12-618_en.htm.

Questions

1 Why did co-evolution break down in the Areva NP joint venture?

2 Why was the termination of this joint venture messy?

implies that mutual trust is likely to be valuable after the completion of any particular partnership. Partners may be engaged in several different joint projects at the same time. For example, Cisco and IBM are partners on multiple simultaneous projects in wireless communications, IT security, data centres and data storage. The partners may need to come together again for new projects in the future. Thus Nokia, Ericsson and Siemens have had mobile telephone technology joint projects since the mid-1990s. Maintaining mutual trust in the termination stage is vital if partners are to co-evolve through generations of multiple projects.

(10.5) COMPARING ACQUISITIONS, ALLIANCES AND ORGANIC DEVELOPMENT

It will be clear so far that all three methods of M&A, strategic alliances and organic development have their own advantages and disadvantages. There are also some similarities. This section first considers criteria for choosing between the three methods, and then draws together some key success factors for M&A and alliances.

10.5.1 Buy, ally or DIY?

Acquisitions and strategic alliances have high failure rates. As in the Key Debate at the end of this chapter, acquisitions are thought to fail about half the time. Acquisitions can go wrong because of excessive initial valuations, exaggerated expectations of strategic fit, underestimated problems of organisational fit and all the other issues pointed to in this chapter. But strategic alliances too have roughly 50 per cent failure rates.[26] Alliances also suffer from miscalculations in terms of strategic and organisational fit, but, given the lack of control on either side, have their own particular issues of trust and co-evolution as well. With these high failure rates, acquisitions and alliances need to be considered cautiously alongside the default option of organic development (Do-It-Yourself).

The best approach will differ according to circumstances. Figure 10.6 presents a 'buy, ally or DIY' matrix summarising four key factors that can help in choosing between acquisitions, alliances and organic development:[27]

- *Urgency.* Acquisitions are a rapid method for pursuing a strategy. It would probably take decades for Tata to build up on its own two international luxury car brands equivalent to Jaguar and Land Rover (Illustration 10.2). Tata's purchase of the two brands gave an immediate kick-start to its strategy. Alliances too may accelerate strategy delivery by accessing additional resources or skills, though usually less quickly than a simple acquisition. Typically organic development (DIY) is slowest: everything has to be made from scratch.

- *Uncertainty.* It is often better to choose the alliance route where there is high uncertainty in terms of the markets or technologies involved. On the upside, if the markets or technologies turn out to be a success, it might be possible to turn the alliance into a full acquisition, especially if a buy option has been included in the initial alliance contract. If the venture turns out a failure, then at least the loss is shared with the alliance partner. Acquisitions may also be resold if they fail but often at a much lower price than the original purchase. On the other hand, a failed organic development might have to be written off entirely,

Figure 10.6 Buy, ally or DIY matrix

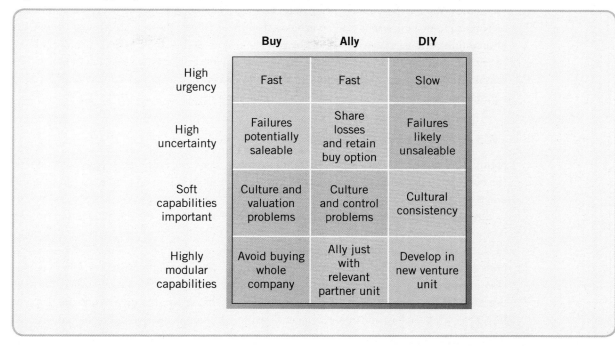

with no sale value, because the business unit involved has never been on the market beforehand.

- *Type of capabilities.* Acquisitions work best when the desired capabilities (resources or competences) are 'hard', for example physical investments in manufacturing facilities. Hard resources such as factories are easier to put a value on in the bidding process than 'soft' resources such as people or brands. Hard resources are also typically easier to control post-acquisition than people and skills. As with the Disney takeover of Marvel (see Illustration 10.1), acquisitions pose the risk of significant cultural problems. Sometimes too the acquiring company's own image can tarnish the brand image of the target company. Acquisition of soft resources and competences should be approached with great caution. Indeed, the DIY organic method is typically the most effective with sensitive soft capabilities such as people. Internal ventures are likely to be culturally consistent at least. Even alliances can involve culture clashes between people from the two sides, and it is harder to control an alliance partner than an acquired unit.

- *Modularity of capabilities.* If the sought-after capabilities are highly modular, in other words they are distributed in clearly distinct sections or divisions of the proposed partners, then an alliance tends to make sense. A joint venture linking just the relevant sections of each partner can be formed, leaving each to run the rest of its businesses independently. There is no need to buy the whole of the other organisation. An acquisition can be problematic if it means buying the whole company, not just the modules that the acquirer is interested in. The DIY organic method can also be effective under conditions of modularity, as the new business can be developed under the umbrella of a distinct 'new venture division' (see section 9.5.2), rather than embroiling the whole organisation.

Of course, the choice between the three options of buy, ally and DIY is not unconstrained. Frequently there are no suitable acquisition targets or alliance partners available. One problem for voluntary organisations and charities is that the changes of ownership involved in M&A are much harder to achieve than in the private sector, so that their options are likely to be restricted to alliances or organic development in any case. The key message of Figure 10.6 remains none the less: it is important to weigh up the available options systematically and to avoid favouring one or the other without careful analysis.

10.5.2 **Key success factors**

Figure 10.6 indicates that, despite high failure rates, M&A and strategic alliances can still be the best option in certain circumstances. The question then is how to manage M&A and alliances as effectively as possible.

Strategic fit is critical in both M&A and alliances. The target or the partner should suit the desired strategy. As in section 10.3.4, it is very easy to overestimate synergies – and neglect negative synergies – in alliances as well as M&A. However, organisational fit is vital as well, in both cases. In particular, cultural differences are hard to manage, especially where people resources are important. Because of the lack of control, organisational fit issues are liable to be even harder to manage in alliances than in acquisitions, where the ownership rights of the buyer at least provide some managerial authority. Valuation likewise is a crucial issue in both M&A and equity alliances. Acquisitions are liable to the 'winner's curse' (section 10.3.4) of excessive valuation, particularly where there have been bid battles between competitors. But even alliance partners need to assess their relative contributions accurately in order to ensure that they do not commit too many resources with too little return and too little control.

M&A and alliances each raise some very distinct issues to manage. At the start of the process, alliances rely on courtship between willing partners, whereas that need not be the same for M&A. Mergers do require mutual willingness of course, but, if negotiations go poorly, there often remains the option of the *hostile takeover* bid. The process of a hostile bid is principally about persuading shareholders rather than talking with the target's managers. In M&A, a crucial issue is the right approach to *integration*: absorption, preservation, symbiosis, holding. In strategic alliances, the option to fully integrate the two partners into a single whole does not exist. Rather the task is the continued maintenance of a partnership between independent organisations that must *co-evolve*. Finally, *divesture* of acquired units and the *termination* of alliances tend to differ. Divestures are typically one-off transactions with purchasers, with limited consequences for future relationships. On the other hand, the way in which alliances are terminated may have repercussions for important future relationships, as new projects and simultaneous projects often involve the same partners. In sum, it can be seen that the necessity for courtship, co-evolution and sensitive termination frequently makes the strategic alliance process a much more delicate one than simple acquisition.

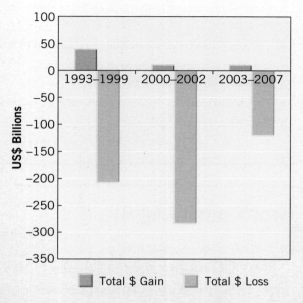

KEY DEBATE

Merger madness?

Mergers and acquisitions involve huge sums of money, but how wisely is it being spent?

This chapter has introduced the importance of mergers and acquisitions as a method of development, but also pointed to some challenges. In some cases there have been some spectacular failures. In 2011 Hewlett Packard ('HP') purchased Autonomy, a British software firm specialising in 'unstructured' data analysis, for €8.3 bn (£6.7 bn; $11.1 bn). On 24 November 2012, HP startled analysts who had been expecting an announcement of $2.2 bn net profits for the group that it had made an $8.8 bn loss. HP blamed the Autonomy acquisition for this situation, saying that HP had had to write down its value by €6.6 bn, and ascribing €3.8 bn of this to 'serious accounting improprieties, disclosure failure and outright misrepresentation'. The shares of HP which stood at €22.1 just prior to the deal announcement, now stood at €8.7, their lowest level for 10 years.

Harvard Business School professor Michael Porter has been a prominent sceptic of mergers and acquisitions, noting that half of all acquired companies are sold off again within a few years. The figure shows the aggregate dollar return (i.e. the change in stock price associated with the acquisition announcement) of acquiring companies in the USA between 1993 and 2007. In 2000, acquiring firms' shareholders lost, in all, more than $275 bn. In the whole period of 1993 to 2007, acquiring firms' shareholders lost more than $550 bn.

One interpretation of these large losses is that mergers and acquisitions represent a reckless waste of money by managers who are careless of investors' interests. Indeed there is evidence that CEOs suffer the consequences, over half being replaced within a relatively short time period. It might be appropriate therefore to make mergers and acquisitions more difficult by legislating to help target companies resist or refuse hostile bids. If the law restricted hostile bids, wasteful acquisitions could be cut.

There are drawbacks to restricting mergers and acquisitions, however. Even if acquiring companies often fail to make money for their shareholders, they can improve the profitability of the system as a whole in at least two ways:

- The threat of being taken over if they do not satisfy their shareholders helps keep managers focused on performance. The financial press reports just such threats regularly.

- Mergers and acquisitions can be an effective way of restructuring stagnant firms and industries. The absence of hostile takeovers in Japan is often blamed for the slow restructuring of Japanese industry since the early 1990s.

Sources: M. Porter, 'From competitive advantage to corporate strategy', *Harvard Business Review*, May–June (1987), pp. 43–60; S.B. Moeller, F.P. Schlingemann and R.M. Stulz, 'Wealth destruction on a massive scale?', *Journal of Finance*, vol. 60, no. 2 (2005), pp. 757–82; K.M. Lehn and M. Zhao, 'CEO turnover after acquisitions: are bad bidders fired?', *Journal of Finance*, vol. LXI, no. 4 (2006), pp. 1759–810; 'Jump in hostile takeover bids', *Financial Times*, 3 June 2012. G. Alexandridis, C.F. Mavrovitis and N.G. Travlos, 'How have M&As changed? Evidence from the sixth merger wave'. *The European Journal of Finance*, vol. 18, no. 8 (2012), pp. 663–88.

Questions

1 For a recent large merger or acquisition, track the share prices of the companies involved (using www.bigcharts.com, for instance), for several weeks both before and after the announcement. What do the share price movements suggest about the merits of the deal?

2 Identify a hostile takeover threat from press reports. What action did the company's management do to resist the takeover?

SUMMARY

- There are three broad methods for pursuing a growth strategy: *mergers and acquisitions, strategic alliances* and *organic development*.

- Organic development can be either continuous or radical. Radical organic development is termed *corporate entrepreneurship*.

- Acquisitions can be *hostile* or *friendly*. Motives for mergers and acquisitions can be *strategic, financial* or *managerial*.

- The acquisition process includes *target choice, valuation* and *integration*.

- Strategic alliances can be *equity* or *non-equity*. Key motives for strategic alliances include *scale, access, complementarity* and *collusion*.

- The strategic alliance process relies on *co-evolution* and *trust*.

- The choice between acquisition, alliance and organic methods is influenced by four key factors: *urgency, uncertainty, type of capabilities* and *modularity of capabilities*.

WORK ASSIGNMENTS

✱ *Denotes more advanced work assignments.*
* *Refers to a case study in the Text and Cases edition.*

10.1 Write a short (about 10 lines) statement to a chief executive who has asked you to advise whether or not the company should develop through M&A. Write a similar statement to a chief executive of a hospital who is considering possible mergers with other hospitals.

10.2✱ For a recently announced acquisition, track the share prices (using www.bigcharts.com, for example) of both the acquiring firm and the target firm in the period surrounding the bid. What do you conclude from the behaviour of the share prices about how investors regard the bid? Which company's investors are likely to benefit more?

10.3✱ For a recently announced acquisition, or for the acquisitions of Eidos by Square Enix in the end of chapter case, or Jaguar Land Rover by Tata (Illustration 10.2), explain which post-acquisition integration approach might be most appropriate in these situations and why other integration approaches may be less effective.

10.4✱ With reference to either Disney's acquisition of Marvel (Illustration 10.1), SABMiller's* acquisitions, the acquisition of Cadbury* by Kraft, or end of chapter case 'Final Fantasy', explain why, when the objectives are the mutual creation of value, acquirers chose to make acquisitions rather than alliances.

10.5 Which development approach is a family-owned company likely to prefer? Explain your reasoning.

Integrative assignment

10.6✱ With so many M&A failing, explain why managers continue to transact these deals. In particular consider alternative methods for strategic realignment that may be available to an organisation as well as the possible consequences of a company not using M&A. Now interpret your answer in terms of all the stakeholders who may be affected by an M&A transaction. What conclusions can you draw?

VIDEO ASSIGNMENTS

Visit **MyStrategyLab** and watch the Love Da Pop case study for Chapter 10.

1 What are the main benefits that 'Love Da Pop' might expect to gain from working with Corn Poppers? Are there any risks for Love Da Pop?

2 What does it take for strategic alliances, such as that between Love Da Pop and Corn Poppers, to work effectively and be sustained over a long period?

RECOMMENDED KEY READINGS

- A comprehensive book on mergers and acquisitions is: S. Sudarsanam. *Creating value from mergers and acquisitions: the challenges*, 2nd edn, FT Prentice Hall, 2010. For some alternative perspectives, see the collection by D.N. Angwin (ed.), *Mergers and Acquisitions*, Blackwell, 2007.

- A useful book on strategic alliances is J. Child, D. Faulkner and S. Tallman, *Cooperative Strategy: Managing Alliances, Networks and Joint Ventures*, 2nd edn, Oxford University Press, 2005.

- A book which contrasts the benefits of different modes of expansion is L. Capron and W. Mitchell, *Build, Buy, Borrow: Solving the growth dilemma*, Harvard Business Review Press, 2012.

REFERENCES

1. P. Sharma and J. Chrisman, 'Towards a reconciliation of the definitional issues in the field of corporate entrepreneurship', *Entrepreneurial Theory and Practice*, Spring (1998), pp. 11–27; D. Garvin and L. Levesque, 'Meeting the challenge of corporate entrepreneurship', *Harvard Business Review*, October (2006), pp. 102–12.

2. *Financial Times*, 29 February 2012. It is worth noting that the number of deals only fell to 41,000, which suggests that M&A are an important and constant way in which businesses adjust to changing contexts.

3. D.N. Angwin, 'Motive archetypes in mergers and acquisitions (M&A): the implications of a configurational approach to performance', *Advances in Mergers and Acquisitions*, vol. 6 (2007), pp. 77–105. A useful conceptual model of motives and mitigating variables is J. Haleblian, C.E. Devers, G. McNamara, M.A. Carpenter and R.B. Davison, 'Taking stock of what we know about mergers and acquisitions: a review and research agenda', *Journal of Management*, vol. 35 (2009), pp. 469–502.

4. This adapts J. Bower, 'Not all M&As are alike – and that matters', *Harvard Business Review*, March (2001), pp. 93–101.

5. M. Hayward and D. Hambrick, 'Explaining the premiums paid for large acquisitions: evidence of CEO hubris', *Administrative Science Quarterly*, vol. 42 (1997), pp. 103–27; J.-Y. Kim, J. Haleblian and S. Finkelstein, 'When firms are desperate to grow via acquisition: the effect of growth patterns and acquisition experience on acquisition premiums', *Administrative Science Quarterly*, vol. 56, no. 1 (2011), pp. 26–60.

6. This builds on D. Jemison and S. Sitkin, 'Corporate acquisitions: a process perspective', *Academy of Management Review*, vol. 11, no. 1 (1986), pp. 145–63.

7. J.M. Shaver, 'A paradox of synergy: contagion and capacity effects in mergers and acquisitions', *Academy of Management Review*, vol. 31, no. 4 (2006), pp. 962–78.

8. See J. Child, D. Faulkner and R. Pitkethly, *The Management of International Acquisitions*, Oxford University Press, 2001.

9. A useful discussion of valuation methods in acquisitions is in Chapter 9 of D. Sadlter, D. Smith and A. Campbell, *Smarter Acquisitions*, Prentice Hall, 2008.

10. N. Varaiya and K. Ferris, 'Overpaying in corporate takeovers: the winner's curse', *Financial Analysts Journal*, vol. 43, no. 3 (1987), pp. 64–70.

11. P. Haspeslagh and D. Jemison, *Managing Acquisitions: Creating Value through Corporate Renewal*, Free Press, 1991; P. Puranam, H. Singh and S. Chaudhuri, 'Integrating acquired capabilities: when structural integration is (un)necessary', *Organization Science*, vol. 20, no. 2 (2009), pp. 313–28.

12. G. Stahl and A. Voigt, 'Do cultural differences matter in mergers and acquisitions? A tentative model and examination', *Organization Science*, vol. 19, no. 1 (2008), pp. 160–78.

13. See D.N. Angwin, 'Typologies in M&A research', in D. Faulkner, S. Teerikangas, and R. Joseph (eds), *Oxford Handbook of Mergers and Acquisitions*, Oxford University Press, 2012, pp. 40–70 for a review.

14. D.N. Angwin, 'Typologies in M&A research', in D. Faulkner, S. Teerikangas and R. Joseph (eds), *Oxford Handbook of Mergers and Acquisitions*, Oxford University Press, 2012, pp. 40–70; D.N. Angwin and M. Meadows, 'The choice of insider or outsider top executives in acquired companies', *Long Range Planning*, vol. 37 (2009), pp. 239–57.

15. D.N. Angwin, and M. Meadows (2009) 'The choice of insider or outsider top executives in acquired companies', *Long Range Planning*, vol. 37 (2009), pp. 239–57.

16. D.N. Angwin and M. Meadows, 'Acquiring poorly performing companies during recession', *Journal of General Management*, vol. 38, no. 1 (2012), pp. 1–22.

17. K. Ellis, T. Reus and B. Lamont, 'The effects of procedural and informational justice in the integration of related acquisitions', *Strategic Management Journal*, vol. 30 (2009), pp. 137–61.

18. R. Uhlaner and A. West, 'Running a winning M&A shop', *McKinsey Quarterly*, March (2008), pp. 106–12.

19. L. Dranikoff, T. Koller and A. Schneider, 'Divesture: strategy's missing link', *Harvard Business Review*, May (2002), pp. 75–83; and M. Brauer, 'What have we acquired and what should we acquire in divesture research? A review and research agenda', *Journal of Management*, vol. 32, no. 6 (2006), pp. 751–85; H. Berry, 'When do firms divest foreign operations?' *Organization Science*, vol. 24, no. 1 (2013), pp. 246–61; J. Xia and S. Li, 'The divestiture of acquired subunits: a resource dependence approach', *Strategic Management Journal*, vol. 34, no. 2 (2013), pp. 131–48.

20. Andersen Consulting, *Dispelling the Myths of Strategic Alliances*, 1999.

21. R. Bresser, 'Matching collective and competitive strategies', *Strategic Management Journal*, vol. 9, no. 4 (1988), pp. 375–85.

22. J. Dyer, *Collaborative Advantage*, Oxford University Press, 2000.

23. A. Inkpen and S. Curral, 'The coevolution of trust, control, and learning in joint ventures', *Organization Science*, vol. 15, no. 5 (2004), pp. 586–99; R. ul-Huq, *Alliances and Co-evolution in the Banking Sector*, Palgrave, 2005.

24. A. Arino and J. de la Torre, 'Relational quality: managing trust in corporate alliances', *California Management Review*, vol. 44, no. 1 (2001), pp. 109–31.

25. G. Hamel, *Alliance Advantage: the Art of Creating Value through Partnering*, Harvard Business School Press, 1998.

26. Andersen Consulting, *Dispelling the Myths of Strategic Alliances*, 1999.

27. This draws on J. Dyer, P. Kale and H. Singh, 'When to ally and when to acquire?', *Harvard Business Review*, vol. 82, nos 7/8 (2004), pp. 108–15; and X. Yin and M. Shanley, 'Industry determinants of the merger versus alliance decision', *Academy of Management Review*, vol. 31, no. 2 (2008), pp. 473–91.

'*Final Fantasy*?' Acquisitions and alliances in electronic games

After several difficult years Japanese games maker Square Enix posted revenues in 2012 of ¥127.9 billion ($1.6 bn; £993 m; €1.23 bn), an increase of 2.1 per cent over the prior year, with net profits of ¥6.1 billion – a marked improvement on the previous year's loss of ¥12 billion. Famous for its role-playing games such as the *Final Fantasy* series, this turnaround in fortunes followed several years of radical strategic initiatives including strategic alliances with the strategy games developers Double Helix and Gas Powered Games in the USA and Wargaming.net in the United Kingdom. Most radically in 2009, it had also acquired the British Eidos Group, famous for the Lara Croft games. Square Enix President Yoichi Wada commented at the time: 'Our goal is to become one of the top ten players in the world's media and entertainment industry. Since the games market is global, both our contact with our customers and our game development must become global too.'

Source: iStockphoto.

The Japanese games industry

Square Enix's strategic moves in 2009 came at a challenging time for the Japanese games industry. The Japanese had enjoyed two decades of domination built on the worldwide success of Japanese consoles such as the Sony PlayStation. But the growing success of Microsoft's Xbox gave an opportunity to American games developers to return to the console market. Indeed, American games developers found that their development skills were more transferable in the new cross-over markets, where games needed to be developed for PCs, consoles and mobile phones alike. Moreover, the Americans had the advantage of proximity to Hollywood, bringing in new creative talent and offering opportunities for film tie-ins. At the same time, Japan's ageing population was shrinking the market for traditional electronic games.

Square Enix's Yōichi Wada recognised the predicament of the Japanese industry vis-à-vis the Americans:

'In the last five to ten years, the Japanese games industry has become a closed environment, with no new people coming in, no new ideas, almost xenophobic . . . The lag with the US is very clear. The US games industry was not good in the past but it has now attracted people from the computer industry and from Hollywood, which has led to strong growth.'[1]

At the same time, the basic economics of the games industry is changing, with rising costs due to growing technological sophistication. A typical modern game can cost from $3,000,000 to over $20,000,000 to develop.[2] Games generally take from one to three years to develop. Yet only 1 in 20 games is estimated ever to make a profit. In other words, the risks are very high and the necessary scale to compete is rising.

Square Enix's strategy

Square Enix itself was a merger in 2003 between Square (founded in 1983 and famous for *Final Fantasy* role-playing game) and Enix (founded in 1975 with its role-playing *Dragon Quest* series). Yōichi Wada, President of Square, became the president of the new merged company.

Square Enix's strategy is based on 'polymorphic content'. Its various franchises (*Final Fantasy*, *Dragon Quest* and so on) are developed for all hardware or media, such as consoles, mobile phones, online, PCs rather than any single gaming platform. There are also spin-offs including

TV series, films, comics and novels. In 2005, Square Enix bought the Japanese arcade-game company Taito Corporation, famous for its *Space Invaders* game. *Space Invaders* versions have appeared on PlayStation, Xbox and Wii consoles, as well as PCs.

By 2008, Yōichi Wada was presiding over a company that was increasingly diversified, with sales of ¥136 bn (about €1 bn) and just over 3,000 employees. However, it was still overwhelmingly Japanese (85 per cent of sales at home) and lacked scale by comparison with competitors such as Electronic Arts and Activision. On the plus side, Square Enix reportedly had a 'war-chest' available for acquisitions of about Y40 bn (about €300 m).[3] During the summer of 2008, Square Enix made a friendly bid for the Japanese game developer Tecmo, whose fighting games *Ninja Garden* and *Dead or Alive* were popular in North America and Europe. Tecmo rejected the bid. Wada began to look overseas.

Lara Croft falls

Eidos is a British games company best known for the action-adventure games series *Tomb Raider*, starring the extraordinary Lara Croft. However, during 2008, disappointing sales for *Tomb Raider: Underworld* drove its share price down from £5 (~€5.5; ~$7.5) to around 30 pence. Eidos's founder and Chief Executive, Jane Cavanagh, was forced to resign. The company declared losses of £136 m, on sales of £119 m (down from £179 m two years earlier). In April 2009, Square Enix bought the company for £84 m, a premium of 129 per cent over Eidos's current market value. Given the declining success of the *Tomb Raider* franchise, many speculated that Square Enix had overpaid for its first overseas acquisition.

The acquisition of Eidos did offer Square Enix global reach, however. About one third of Eidos's sales were in the USA and 40 per cent in Europe, excluding the United Kingdom. Eidos also brought Square Enix its first studios outside Japan, with studios in the United Kingdom, Denmark, Hungary, the USA, Canada and China. Yōichi Wada commented: 'It is significant that we have opened a window for creative talents worldwide.'

Wada chose to keep Phil Rogers, the new Eidos Chief Executive, and the rest of his management team in place. Wada described a new group structure, in which Square Enix, the arcade business Taito and Eidos would each be standalone divisions: 'Our aim is to implement a hybrid management structure which avoids the extremes of being either too global or too local.'[4] He

continued: 'The Group's management and administration departments will be integrated, while our product and service delivery will be established locally in each territory to maximise our business opportunities through better understanding of local customers' tastes and commercial practices.' Wada also recognised the new strength that Eidos brought in action-adventure games, by contrast with Square Enix's traditional core of role-playing games. He declared his commitment both to sharing technologies across the businesses and to sustaining particular strengths: 'While promoting shared technology and expertise among our studios, we will also develop products which reflect the unique identity of each studio, regardless of locality.' Wada also commented on the nature of the skilled games developers he was acquiring: 'It is always difficult to manage creatives anywhere in the world. We want to cherish the Eidos studio culture but change it where it is necessary.'[5]

One thing that Square Enix was quick to do was to end the Eidos distribution agreement with Warner Bros for its products in the USA. Square Enix regarded itself as strong enough to do that itself.

Strategic alliances

At the same time as acquiring Eidos, Square Enix cemented three significant strategic alliances. In the United Kingdom, Square Enix tied up with the strategy game developer Wargaming.net (famous for the *Massive Assault* series) in order to produce the World War II game *Order of War*. This would enter the market at the end of 2009 as Square Enix's first global product release. In the USA, Square Enix formed partnerships with Gas Powered Games (producer of the *Supreme Commander* strategy game) and with Double Helix (producer of the *Front Mission* strategy series). Together with the Eidos acquisition, these partnerships significantly extended Square Enix's range beyond its traditional core in role-playing games. They also extended the company's geographical reach. Yōichi Wada commented: 'We see great opportunities in North American and European markets, both of which are expected to be maintaining sustainable growth over these coming years. Therefore it is crucial that we create alliances with proven developers such as Gas Powered Games in order to serve these significant markets better by providing products and services in tune with customer tastes.'[6]

All three of these new partners were relatively small (around 100 employees each), privately owned and had their origins as start-ups during the 1990s. The founders' motivations are explained by Chris Taylor at Gas Powered Games:

> 'I had that dream really from the day I first walked into my first full time job as a games programmer. I wanted to be the guy running the company . . . We've created our own original IPs (intellectual properties) consistently. Some are great, some are not so great, but the fact is you have to keep throwing darts at the board. You have to keep trying to make great stuff, and you can't do that if you're inside of a large megalithic corporation to the same degree . . .'[7]

Chris Taylor described how Square Enix, traditionally a role-playing company, and Gas Powered Games, more a strategy game developer, were working together on their first venture, *Supreme Commander 2*:

> 'One of the things that we took as a cue from Square Enix was the way they embrace character and story. We were all into that, so that was easy. When we asked them, "How should we develop our game to work with their philosophy?", they said, "Don't do that because we want you to do what you do. You make games for the Western market, and we're interested in making games for the Western market." So if we changed, we would be missing the point. Which was terrific, because that meant we could do what we loved to do, make great RTS (real-time strategy) games . . . and if we tried to change them in any way, we'd be moving away from the goal.'[8]

A games enthusiast's view

Through alliances and mergers, Square Enix had transformed its profile. From its base in Japanese-style role-playing games, it was developing a significant presence in strategy and action adventure. It had studios across the world. Its various games titles were big across Asia, Europe and America. Games enthusiast Randy commented:

> 'Square Enix publishing a western-developed game? Is the far-reaching JRPG (Japanese role-playing game) developer dumping the androgynous boy-heroes and shovel-wide swords for WWII fatigues and M1 Carbines? No, not entirely. But they *are* bringing Wargaming.net into the fold to do it for them. First, Square Enix buys out the house that Lara Croft built, and now they're into real-time strategy war games. *Nothing in this life makes sense anymore.*'[9]

Looking forwards

Following the alliances and mergers, Square Enix's financial performance began to suffer, particularly in the increasingly competitive console market. However, in 2012 the digital division was performing well with *Final Fantasy XIII-2*, *Deus Ex: Human Revolution* and the Mobage simulation game *Sengoku Ixa* – with two million registered users – spurring the division to revenues of ¥71.9 billion, up 11.9 per cent year-on-year, and operating profit of ¥12.6 billion, up 11.7 per cent. Square Enix reported it had 'internal reserves' for investments that could 'enhance the company's value'. This could include 'capital investments and M&A to expand and develop new businesses'. Such deals would be a part of a broader strategy to meet the demands of an increasingly digital, networked, multi-device world market.

References
1. M. Palmer, 'Square Enix views Eidos as a jump to next level', *Financial Times*, 28 April 2009.
2. 'Cost of making games set to soar', www.bbcnews.co.uk, 17 November 2005.
3. 'Square Enix needs to show growth scenario to market', *Nikkei*, 9 October 2007.
4. Joint interview with Yoichi Wada and Phil Rogers, www.square-enix.com, 26 May 2009.
5. M. Palmer, 'Square Enix views Eidos as a jump to next level', *Financial Times*, 28 April 2009.
6. 'Square Enix and Gas Powered Games announce strategic partnership', *Newswire Association*, 12 November 2008.
7. P. Elliott, 'Foot on the gas', *gamesindustry.biz*, 19 August 2008.
8. X. de Matos, 'Interview: Chris Taylor on Supreme Commander 2', *joystiq.com*, 9 June 2009.
9. Randy, 'Square Enix tries hand at WWI RTS with Order of War', *Gaming Nexus*, 17 April 2009. Italics in original.

Questions

1. Explain why Square Enix chose alliances in some cases and acquisitions in others.

2. How should Square Enix manage its Eidos acquisition in order to maximise value creation, and how might that management approach change over time?

3. What are the strengths and weaknesses of the alliance strategy, and what problems might Square Enix anticipate over time?

4. What methods of expansion would you recommend to the management of Square Enix now they appear to have the resources and intention to grow?

COMMENTARY ON PART II

The central concern of Part II has been the strategic choices available to organisations, including business strategy, diversification, internationalisation, innovation, acquisitions and alliances. Although the chapters provide various rationales and evidence for these strategic choices, this book recognises that the decisions between them are often not wholly objective and rational. Indeed, the four contrasting 'strategy lenses' (introduced in the Commentary at the end of Part I) each propose very different expectations about strategic decisions. This Commentary applies the same four lenses to the issues raised in Part II, focused on strategic choices. The four lenses raise questions about how to generate the options for strategic choice, assumptions about other organisations, and what is likely to matter in the success of various options.

Design lens

The design lens places high value on extensive information search and analysis for generating strategic options. Logical, optimal choices are important. The design lens therefore recommends you to:

- *Consider all options*: strategy choices should be made between a large initial range, with techniques such as the Ansoff growth matrix (section 7.2) used to generate options.
- *Ensure fit between choice and purpose*: preferred options should be checked carefully for consistency with the purpose, goals and objectives of the organisation (Chapter 4).
- *Maximise returns*: the optimal choice is one that maximises the returns on investment, whether that is investment of capital or effort (Chapter 11).

Experience lens

In this view, strategy develops incrementally based on the past history and culture of the organisation and its members. So the set of strategic options to choose from is unlikely to be comprehensive and cultural factors can generate behaviours different from might be expected on a simplistically rational point of view. You should therefore:

- *Challenge standard responses*: for example, just because a particular diversification option (Chapter 7) or international entry mode (Chapter 8) has always worked before, does not mean that the same should be done again.
- *Respect cultural differences*: in integrating acquisitions (Chapter 10), cooperating with alliance partners (Chapter 10) or going international (Chapter 8), the experience lens suggests it is very important to take account of the other organisation's history and culture, as well as more objective factors.
- *Adjust competitor analysis*: if experience shapes strategy, simple analyses of competitor interaction, as sometimes in game theory (Chapter 6), may need to be adjusted in order to avoid exaggerating the likely speed of competitors' moves or making excessive assumptions about the rationality of their responses.

STRATEGIC CHOICES

This Commentary therefore reconsiders some of the issues of Part II in the light of the four strategy lenses. Note that:

- There is no suggestion here that any one of these lenses is better than the others. It is usually beneficial to explore strategic options using more than one lens, in order to get more than one point of view.
- For a deeper understanding of this Commentary, you might want to review the Part I Commentary, following Chapter 5, which provides a fuller introduction of the four lenses, plus an illustrative case.

Variety lens

The emphasis here is on the variety and spontaneity of strategic options and their possible origins in the organisational periphery. The variety lens is orientated towards innovation. Thus the variety lens encourages you to:

- *Look beyond top management*: from a variety lens point of view, the strategies generated by top management are liable to be limited, so you should look more broadly for ideas about strategic options, for instance by using 'open innovation' or 'market pull' approaches (section 9.2).
- *Learn from acquisitions and partners*: if the top has no monopoly of wisdom, exploring acquired units or alliance partners (Chapter 10) for underappreciated initiatives or capabilities might uncover new strategic options going far beyond what was planned in the original acquisition or alliance.
- *Expect surprises*: in an environment liable to spontaneous innovation, you should be sensitive to the potential for sudden 'disruptive innovations' and consider holding a strong portfolio of 'real options' (section 9.4).

Discourse lens

According to this lens, the strategic options that rise to the surface will typically be shaped by the legitimate discourse of the organisation and the underlying self-interest of various managers. The discourse lens recognises the power of language. So you should:

- *Watch your language*: attend to discursive framing of your strategic options, recognising the emotional resonance of labels such as 'star' and 'dog', or 'heartland' and 'alien', in portfolio analyses for instance (Chapter 7) and the different meanings such labels might have in various national cultures (Chapter 9).
- *Distrust others' language*: strategic options that draw heavily on apparently legitimate or fashionable discourses such as synergy (Chapter 7), innovation and entrepreneurship (Chapter 9) or partnership and ecosystems (Chapter 10) should be probed particularly critically for shaky reasoning or self-interested motives.
- *Look out for managerial interests*: the discourse with which strategic options are framed may hide managerial self-interest, especially in regard to strategies such as unrelated diversification (Chapter 7) or aggressive acquisitions (Chapter 10) that often perform badly for shareholders.

PART III

STRATEGY IN ACTION

This part explains:

- Criteria and techniques that can be used to evaluate organisational performance and strategic options.

- How strategies develop in organisations; in particular, the processes that may give rise to intended strategies or to emergent strategies.

- The way in which organisational structures and systems of control are important in organising for strategic success.

- The leadership and management of strategic change.

- Who strategists are and what they do in practice.

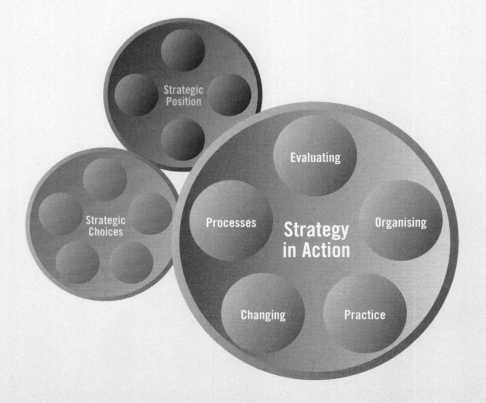

INTRODUCTION TO PART III

The first two parts of the book have been concerned with how a strategist can think through the strategic position of an organisation and the strategic choices available to it. In this part of the book the focus moves to strategy in action. It is concerned with how a strategy actually takes shape in an organisation and what strategists actually do.

The next chapter explains ways in which managers can assess the performance of the strategic options introduced in Part II and then evaluate alternatives. It stresses both economic and non-economic performance measures and then introduces three criteria to apply in making further choices. *Suitability* asks whether a strategy addresses the key issues relating to the opportunities and constraints an organisation faces. *Acceptability* asks whether a strategy meets the expectations of stakeholders. And *feasibility* invites an explicit consideration of whether a strategy could work in practice. In each case tools and techniques of evaluation are provided, explained and illustrated.

Chapter 12 examines two broadly different explanations *of how strategies actually develop* in organisations. Do strategies come about in organisations through a sequence of first analysis and then implementation? In other words, do strategies develop on the basis of deliberate intent? Or is strategy more emergent, for example on the basis of people's experience or as a result of responses to competitive action? And what are the implications of these different explanations for managing strategy?

Chapter 13 considers the relationship between strategy and how an organisation functions in terms of people working with each other within different *structures and systems*. These structures and systems may be formally established by management or may be more informal relationships, but they will all affect the organisation's ability to deliver its strategy. The chapter considers how successful organising requires these various elements to work together in order to create mutually reinforcing *configurations* of structures and systems that are matched to an organisation's strategies.

The development of a new strategy may also require significant change for an organisation and this is the theme of Chapter 14. The *leadership of strategic change* is examined, first by acknowledging that managing change is not the same in all organisations; in other words, change context matters. The chapter then examines different approaches to managing change, including styles of managing change and the variety of levers employed to manage strategic change. The chapter concludes by revisiting the importance of context to consider how different levers might be employed in different change contexts.

This part of the book then concludes by discussing *what strategists themselves actually do*. It examines three issues in the practice of strategy. The first is: who gets included in strategy-making activities? Participants in strategy making can be managers at all levels, with consultants and planners too. Second, what are the activities that strategists actually do? These range from selling strategic issues to strategy communications. Lastly, there are the kinds of methodologies that strategists use, including strategy workshops, projects, hypothesis testing and business plans.

11

EVALUATING STRATEGIES

Learning outcomes

After reading this chapter you should be able to:

- Assess the performance outcomes of different strategies in terms of direct *economic* outcomes and overall organisational *effectiveness*.

- Assess performance and the need for new strategies using *gap analysis*.

- Employ three *success criteria* for evaluating strategic options:
  - *Suitability*: whether a strategy addresses the key issues relating to the *opportunities and constraints* an organisation faces.
  - *Acceptability*: whether a strategy meets the *expectations* of stakeholders.
  - *Feasibility*: whether a strategy could *work in practice*.

- Use for each of these a range of different *techniques for evaluating strategic options*, both financial and non-financial.

MyStrategyLab is designed to help you make the most of your studies. Visit **www.pearsoned.co.uk/mystrategylab** to discover a wide range of resources, including:

- A personalised **Study plan** that will help you understand core concepts
- **Audio and video clips** that put the spotlight on strategy in the real world
- **Online glossaries and flashcards** that provide helpful reminders when you're looking for some quick revision.

Key terms

acceptability p. 379

feasibility p. 390

gap analysis p. 369

returns p. 382

risk p. 379

suitability p. 372

(11.1) INTRODUCTION

In 2012, mobile phone company BlackBerry installed a new Chief Executive, Thorsten Heins. He replaced the company's co-founders Mike Lazaradis and Jim Balsillie, whose recent performance had been much criticised. The company had missed its own financial targets, its share-price had dropped 75 per cent in the last 12 months and there had been delays in the launch of new products. Thorsten Heins' own assessment was not entirely gloomy, highlighting a 35 per cent growth in the BlackBerry subscriber base over the previous year. However, he clearly needed to do something to improve performance. Among the options Heins had to evaluate was whether to return BlackBerry's main focus to the business market from which BlackBerry had originally come, and whether to abandon the company's own operating system in favour of the much more popular Android operating system. For Heins, there were two key questions therefore: what level of performance did he need to achieve, and what criteria should he use to evaluate his options?

This chapter is about assessing organisational performance and evaluating different strategic options. It follows the focus in Part II on various strategic options, such as differentiation, diversification, internationalisation, innovation and acquisitions. Now it is time to consider how to judge these strategies. Managers have to assess how well their existing strategies are performing and evaluate alternatives. This chapter focuses on systematic criteria and techniques from a rational 'Design' perspective, in the terms of the Strategy Lenses. Chapter 12 considers the place of these systematic criteria and techniques within the complex processes of strategy development as a whole.

The chapter begins by addressing organisational performance. Here we consider a range of organisational performance measures, both *economic* measures and broader measures of organisational *effectiveness*. We address the question of performance *comparators*: in other words, what should an organisation's performance be compared to? We also introduce *gap analysis* as a tool for assessing departures from desired levels of performance. Gap analysis can be used as well to identify the scale of the strategic initiatives which may be needed in order to close the gap between actual and desired levels of performance. The chapter goes on to propose three criteria for evaluating possible strategic initiatives, summarised by the acronym **SAF**e: *Suitability*, *Acceptability* and *Feasibility*, with the small 'e' in the acronym standing for evaluation.

Figure 11.1 organises the key elements of this chapter in a logical flow. Here managers first assess performance; next they identify the extent of any gap between desired and actual or projected performance; finally they assess the strategic options for filling any such gap. The adopted options themselves eventually feed back into performance in the future.

Figure 11.1 Evaluating strategies

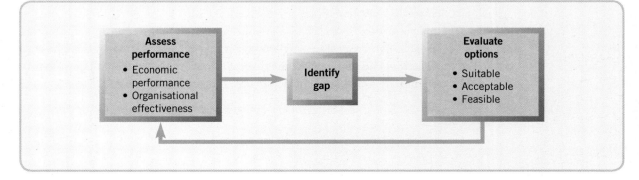

(11.2) ORGANISATIONAL PERFORMANCE

There are many ways by which to measure organisational performance, with none having clear superiority. This section introduces a range of criteria, both direct economic measures and broader effectiveness measures. It goes on to consider the various comparisons against which performance may be assessed. It finally discusses gap analysis.

11.2.1 Performance measures

We can distinguish between two basic approaches to performance: direct economic performance and overall organisational effectiveness:[1]

- *Economic* performance refers to direct measures of success in terms of economic outcomes. These economic outcomes have three main dimensions. First, there is performance in *product markets*: for example, sales growth or market share. Second, there are accounting measures of *profitability*, such as profit margin or return on capital employed (see section 11.3.2 below). Finally, economic performance may be reflected in *financial market* measures such as movements in share price. These economic measures may seem objective, but they can be conflicting and need careful interpretation. Sales growth, for example, may be achieved by cutting prices, thereby reducing profit margins. To return to the introductory BlackBerry example, on the share price measure, the company was doing badly, but the product-market measure of subscriber growth was more positive. This potential for economic performance measures to point in different directions suggests that economic performance is best evaluated by more than one measure. It is also why many organisations are now looking to more comprehensive measures of effectiveness as well.

- *Effectiveness* refers to a broader set of performance criteria than just economic, for example measures reflecting internal operational efficiency or measures relevant to stakeholders such as employees and external communities. One important broad measure of effectiveness is the *balanced scorecard*, which considers four perspectives on performance simultaneously.[2] Thus the balanced scorecard considers the customer perspective, using measures such as customer satisfaction or product quality; the internal business perspective, for instance productivity measures or project management measures; the innovation and learning perspective, measuring new product introductions or employee skills, for example; and finally the financial perspective, focused typically on profitability or share price performance. Another similarly broad measure of performance is the *triple bottom line*, which pays explicit attention to corporate social responsibility and the environment. Thus the triple bottom line has three dimensions: economic measures of performance such as sales, profits and share price; social measures, such as employee training, health and safety and contributions to the local community; and finally environmental measures such as pollution, recycling and wastage targets. Both the balanced scorecard and the triple bottom line share a view that overall effectiveness depends not only on economic performance, but on a range of factors that support the long-term prosperity of the organisation.

11.2.2 **Performance comparisons**

When considering performance, it is important to be clear about what you are measuring *against*: in other words, performance relative to what? There are three main comparisons to consider:

- *Organisastional targets*: a key set of performance criteria are management's own targets, whether expressed in terms of overall vision and mission or more specific objectives, for instance economic outcomes such as sales growth or profitability. Investors are particularly sensitive to performance against financial criteria such as earnings targets. Failure to meet expectations set by these targets often leads to the dismissal of the organisation's chief executive or chief financial officer.[3] Returning to the example at the start of this chapter, it was partly the failure to meet their own financial targets that cost Lazaradis and Balsillie their jobs as joint CEOs at BlackBerry. Similarly, Aviva's CEO lost his job for missed targets (Illustration 13.2). Performance against organisational targets can be approached via gap analysis, as in section 11.2.3 below.

- *Trends over time*: investors and other stakeholders are clearly concerned about whether performance is improving or declining over time. Improvement may suggest good strategy and increasing momentum into the future. Decline may suggest poor strategy and the need for change. However, it is important to take a relevant time period for comparing trends: except in very fast-changing markets, it is typically useful to examine trends over several years in order to smooth out short-run cyclical effects, for example. Note too that performance trends are rarely sustained. It has been shown that only about 5 per cent of firms are able to sustain superior performance for as long as 10 years.[4] From this perspective, one predictor of future declines in performance is an extended period of good performance in preceding years.

- *Comparator organisations*: the final comparison is performance relative to other comparable organisations, as in benchmarking (section 3.4.1). Comparators are typically competitors, but where there are no competitors, or where it is useful to encourage new approaches, comparators can be other organisations doing equivalent things (e.g. a utility company might compare its efficiency in billing and customer service with an insurance company). For established companies, it is often possible to compare with competitors' performance using accounting measures such as profitability or sales growth. Again, the trend over an extended time period is generally useful. Similarly, it is possible for quoted companies to compare their share price performance against that of specific competitors, or against an index of competitors in the same industry, or against the overall index for the stock market in which they are quoted (this is the stock market in which they are competing for investor support). A sustained decline in relative share price typically implies falling confidence in future performance. Note that comparison against individual star performers can often be misleading. Because financial returns are typically related to risk, high performers may simply have undertaken risky strategies, which it might be unwise to imitate.[5] The results of firms that have undertaken similar strategies but finally gone bankrupt or been taken over are unavailable for comparison.

11.2.3 **Gap analysis**

Gap analysis **compares achieved or projected performance with desired performance.**[6] It is particularly useful for identifying performance shortfalls ('gaps') and, when involving projections,

Figure 11.2 Gap analysis

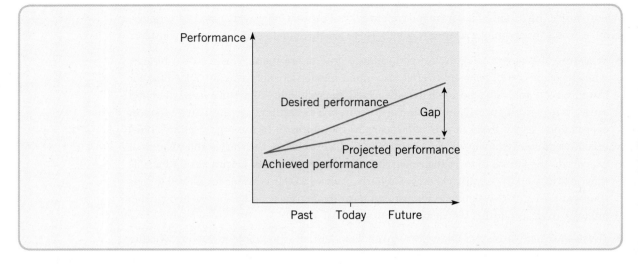

can help in anticipating future problems. The size of the gap provides a guide to the extent to which strategy needs to be changed. Figure 11.2 shows a gap analysis where the vertical axis is some measure of performance (e.g. sales growth or profitability) and the horizontal axis shows time, both up to 'today' and into the future. The upper line represents the organisation's desired performance, perhaps a set of targets or the standard set by competitor organisations. The lower line represents both achieved performance to today and projected performance based on a continuation of the existing strategy into the future (this is necessarily an estimate). In Figure 11.2, there is already a gap between achieved and desired performance: performance is clearly unsatisfactory.

However, the gap in Figure 11.2 is projected to become even bigger on the basis of the existing strategy. Assuming ongoing commitment to the desired level of performance, the organisation clearly needs to adjust its existing strategy in order to close the gap. We shall introduce a number of ways for evaluating strategic options in these and equivalent circumstances later in the chapter.

11.2.4 Complexities of performance analysis

Before considering strategy evaluation, we should underline the complex nature of performance analysis. We have already indicated how some measures might be contradictory in the short term at least: for example, sales growth can be obtained by reducing profit margins. Multidimensional measures of effectiveness such as the balanced scorecard or the triple bottom line are particularly subject to trade-offs: it is easy to see how cutting back on costly environmental protection policies might improve short-term profits.

However, there are three further sources of possible complexity. First, organisations are liable to manipulate outcomes in order to meet key performance indicators.[7] For example, organisations can defer non-urgent expenditures or book sales-orders early in order to meet short-term earnings targets. Second, organisations can legitimately manage performance

ILLUSTRATION 11.1

Poor performance?

In 2012, the CEO of Aviva, a large insurance company, lost his job. How fair were the accusations of sustained poor performance at the company?

Aviva is the United Kingdom's largest insurance company, and the sixth largest in the world. Its chief executive between 2007 and 2012 was Andrew Moss, formerly the company's Chief Financial Officer. Under his leadership, the company had expanded strongly in continental Europe, so that the region accounted for about 37 per cent of its insurance business by 2012.

Many observers were disappointed by the results, however. On becoming CEO, Moss had declared a target of doubling earnings per share by the end of 2012, from 48.5 pence in 2007 to 97 pence. In 2011, earnings per share were just 5.8 pence. Moss had begun a process of disposing of less successful businesses. None the less, between 2007 and 2012, Aviva's shares steadily underperformed the key indexes of which it was a member, trailing the FTSE 100 index by 52 per cent and the FTSE 350 Insurance Industry index by 47 per cent over the whole period. Comparisons were often made with the Prudential, the United Kingdom's third-largest insurance company, against which Aviva had launched an unsuccessful acquisition bid in 2006. In the period since that bid, the Prudential had invested heavily in its Asian business, which accounted for more than 40 per cent of its customers by 2012. The table compares the two companies' sales and operating profits between 2007 and 2011. The figure compares share price performance for the five years to 2012.

£ bn	2007	2008	2009	2010	2011
Aviva sales	50.2	51.4	45.1	47.1	40.6
Prudential sales	18.1	18.8	20.0	24.2	25.3
Aviva operating profit	2.2	2.3	2.0	2.6	2.3
Prudential operating profit	1.2	1.3	1.6	1.9	2.1

Moss's departure was put down not only to objective measures of performance, but also to an alienating style of interaction with investors and analysts. One financial analyst commented: 'He was accused of being complacent, arrogant and out of touch. But in terms of strategy, what more could he really have done?' Aviva's Chairman, Lord Sharman, defended his own record and that of his CEO, blaming results on the financial crisis since 2008 and disproportionate exposure to Europe's struggling economies: 'I'm not prepared to accept responsibility for the banking crisis or for the European debt crisis. Both have had very significant impacts on the company.' Was Moss paying the price for failings that were outside his control, and that with a bit more personal charm he could have smoothed over?

Main sources: Financial Times, 30 April and 8 May 2012.

Questions

1 What mistakes did Moss make?
2 Should Andrew Moss and Lord Sharman be held responsible for their strategic bet on European markets rather than Asian markets?

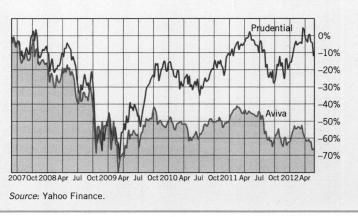

Source: Yahoo Finance.

perceptions and expectations: they are not wholly objective and fixed. For example, CEOs frequently communicate with key investors, financial analysts and the media so as to ensure favourable interpretations of strategies and results.[8] Finally, what matters in terms of performance often changes over time. For example, measures of corporate social responsibility such as the triple bottom line have become more important in recent times and, since the financial crisis starting 2008, banks have had to attend more to measures of capital adequacy to prove they are secure against bad debts.

(11.3) SUITABILITY

The previous section identified gap analysis as a means for considering the extent of new initiatives required to meet desired performance targets. The rest of this chapter discusses means for evaluating possible new initiatives using the SAFe evaluation criteria of suitability, acceptability and feasibility: see Table 11.1. This section deals with suitability.

Suitability is concerned with assessing which proposed strategies address the *key opportunities and threats* an organisation faces through an understanding of the strategic position of an organisation: it is therefore concerned with the overall *rationale* of a strategy. A suitability analysis is therefore likely to draw extensively from the concepts and frameworks introduced in Parts I and II of this book. However, at the most basic level, a suitability analysis involves assessing the extent to which a proposed strategy:

- exploits the *opportunities* in the environment and avoids the *threats*;
- capitalises on the organisation's *strengths* and avoids or remedies the *weaknesses*.

The concepts and frameworks already discussed in Chapters 2 to 5 can be especially helpful in understanding suitability. Some examples are shown in Table 11.2: other frameworks and

Table 11.1 **The SAFe criteria and techniques of evaluation**

Suitability	• Does a proposed strategy address the *key opportunities and threats* an organisation faces?
Acceptability	• Does a proposed strategy meet the *expectations of stakeholders*? • Is the level of risk acceptable? • Is the likely return acceptable? • Will stakeholder reactions be positive?
Feasibility	• Would a proposed strategy work in *practice*? • Can the strategy be financed? • Do people and their skills exist or can they be obtained? • Can the required resources be obtained and integrated?

Table 11.2 **Suitability of strategic options in relation to strategic position**

Concept	Chapter/ section	Helps with understanding	Suitable strategies address (examples)
PESTEL	Chapter 2.2	Key environmental drivers Changes in industry structure	Industry cycles Industry convergence Major environmental changes
Scenarios	Chapter 2.2	Extent of uncertainty/risk Extent to which strategic options are mutually exclusive	Need for contingency plans or 'low-cost probes'
Five forces	Chapter 2.3	Industry attractiveness Competitive forces	Reducing competitive intensity Development of barriers to new entrants
Strategic groups	Chapter 2.4	Attractiveness of groups Mobility barriers Strategic spaces	Need to reposition to a more attractive group or to an available strategic space
Strategic capabilities	Chapter 3.2	Industry threshold standards Bases of competitive advantage	Eliminating weaknesses Exploiting strengths
Value chain	Chapter 3.4	Opportunities for vertical integration or outsourcing	Extent of vertical integration or possible outsourcing
Cultural web	Chapter 5.3	The links between organisational culture and the current strategy	The strategic options most aligned with the prevailing culture

techniques from Part I could be used in equivalent ways. However, the various techniques will raise many issues. It is therefore important that the really key strategic issues are identified from among all these. A major skill of a strategist is to be able to work out what really matters. Strategy is about priorities; long lists should be avoided.

The discussions about possible strategic choices in Part II were concerned with not only understanding what choices might be available to organisations, but also providing reasons why each might be considered. So the examples in those sections also illustrate why strategies might be regarded as *suitable*. Table 11.3 summarises these points from earlier sections (particularly Chapters 7 and 10) and provides examples of reasons why strategies might be regarded as suitable. There are, however, also a number of screening techniques that can be used to assess the suitability of proposed strategies by reviewing their relative merits against key opportunities and constraints.

11.3.1 **Ranking**

Here possible strategies are assessed against key factors relating to the strategic position of the organisation and a score (or ranking) established for each option. Illustration 11.2 gives an example. One of the advantages of this approach is that it forces a debate about the implications and impacts of specific key factors on specific strategic proposals. Ranking therefore helps overcome the unconscious biases of each individual manager.

Table 11.3 **Some examples of suitability**

Strategic option	Why this option might be suitable in terms of:	
	Environment	**Capability**
Directions		
Retrenchment	Withdraw from declining markets Maintain market share	Identify and focus on established strengths
Market penetration	Gain market share for advantage	Exploit superior resources and capabilities
New products and services	Exploit knowledge of customer needs	Exploit R&D
Market development	Current markets saturated New opportunities for: geographical spread, entering new segments or new uses	Exploit current products and capabilities
Diversification	Current markets saturated or declining; new opportunities for expansion beyond core businesses	Exploit strategic capabilities in new arenas
Methods		
Organic diversification	Partners or acquisitions not available or not suitable	Building on own capabilities Learning and competence development
Merger/acquisition	Speed Supply/demand	Acquire capabilities Scale and scope economies
Alliance	Speed Industry norm Required for market entry	Complementary capabilities Learning from partners

More sophisticated approaches to ranking can assign weightings to factors in recognition that some will be of more importance in the evaluation than others. It should, however, be remembered that assigning numbers, of itself, is not a basis of evaluation; any scoring or weighting is only a reflection of the quality of the analysis and debate that goes into the scoring.

A similar approach can be adopted in relation to examining proposed strategies in terms of the responses of competitors. Section 6.4.4 on game theory emphasised that the viability of a strategy should take into account how competitors might react to a particular strategy. Ranking can be used for this purpose. Each proposed strategy is considered in terms of how competitors might respond. In effect the key factors are the key competitors' potential responses. Suitability is assessed in terms of which proposed strategy would be most likely to be minimise or blunt adverse competitor responses.

ILLUSTRATION 11.2

Ranking options for SRR Consulting

Ranking can usefully provide an initial view of the suitability of strategic options by comparing them against the key strategic factors from the SWOT analysis (section 3.4.4).

Simon and Ruth were both IT specialists who returned to their companies after completing their MBAs. Raj, a friend of theirs, had been an IT consultant who did the same MBA course a year later. His MBA project looked at the feasibility of setting up an IT consultancy partnership with Simon and Ruth. SRR was established in 2011. Their strategy was initially to build on 'outsourcing' the IT needs of the organisations they worked for. Raj had worked on IT assignments for business start-ups for a consultancy: 'It was not big business for them and they were delighted to have me operate as an associate; in effect outsourcing that work.' Simon worked for a medium-sized local engineering business and Ruth for a retailer with a small chain of local shops. As Simon explained: 'Neither of our employers really needed IT specialists full-time: an outsourced facility made good economic sense.'

Ruth continued: 'Our first year went well. We provided a good service to our previous employers together with developing business with some other contacts. We are both the owners and the consultants of SRR and our overheads are pretty low so we have made a reasonable living. Our problem now is, where from here? We are keen to grow the business, not just because we would like a higher income, but because with our rather limited client base we are vulnerable. We have built on our IT expertise and the sectors we know, but we have reached something of a ceiling with regard to our personal contacts. We can see a number of possible options. There is an opportunity on the management development aspects of IT; how can IT be used to aid better management? Most of our clients don't understand this. Our problem is

that we are not trainers so we would need to develop those skills or hire someone who has them. Another option is to actively go out and develop new contacts. The problems here are that it means branching out into sectors unfamiliar to us and that will take our time – which won't be fee earning – so it would reduce our income at least in the short term. Linked to this is the possibility of going for much bigger clients. This might get us bigger fees, perhaps, but it would quite possibly mean competition with some big competitors. In the last year our business has also been very local. We could stick with the same sectors we know but broaden the geographic area. The problem there, of course, is we are not known. Finally we have been approached by another IT consultancy about the possibility of a merger. They operate in complementary sectors and do have training capabilities, but it is bigger than us and I don't know if we are ready to lose our own identity yet.'

Simon, Ruth and Raj had begun a ranking exercise to look at these options as shown below.

Questions

1 Are there other options or factors that you think Simon, Ruth and Raj should consider?

2 How could you improve the ranking analysis?

3 Consider the most favoured options in terms of acceptability and feasibility criteria.

Ranking exercise

	Key strategic factors								
Strategic options	Fit with technical competences	Fit with sector know-how	Builds on our known reputation	Increases non-fee-earning management time	Reached our 'contact ceiling'	Builds on client need	Higher fee income	Increased competition	Ranking
1 Develop new contacts	✓	✗	✓	✗	✓	?	?	?	3–2 (B)
2 Develop bigger clients	✗	?	✗	✗	✗	✗	✗	✗	3–3 (C)
3 Geographic market development	✗	✗	✗	✗	✗	✗	✗	✗	5–3 (B)
4 Develop IT training	✗	✗	✗	✗	✗	✗	✗	✗	6–2 (A)
5 Merger	✗	✗	?	✗	✗	?	?	✗	5–0 (A)

✓ = favourable; ✗ = unfavourable; ? = uncertain or irrelevant.
A = most suitable; B = possible; C = unsuitable.

11.3.2 Screening through scenarios

Here strategic options are considered against a range of future scenarios (see section 2.2). This is especially useful where a high degree of uncertainty exists. Suitable options are ones that make sense in terms of the various scenarios. As a result of such analysis it may be that several strategic options need to be 'kept open', perhaps in the form of contingency plans. Or it could be that an option being considered is found to be suitable in different scenarios. Indeed a criterion of strategy evaluation for the energy company Shell is that a chosen strategy needs to be suitable in terms of a range of different crude oil prices.

One of the other advantages of screening through scenarios is that, as managers screen the possible strategies in terms of the different scenarios, they come to see which would be most suitable in different environmental contexts. This can then sensitise managers to the need for changes in strategy, or changes in strategic emphasis, given changes in the environment.

11.3.3 Screening for bases of competitive advantage

One of the key issues in evaluating a strategy is whether it is likely to draw on the organisation's bases of competitive advantage. Quite possibly the factors relating to this may already have been built into the ranking exercises explained above. However, if they have not, then it may be sensible to consider this question specifically.

As in Chapter 3, the likely bases of competitive advantage reside in the strategic capabilities of an organisation. Screening for bases of competitive advantage therefore requires an analysis of how the proposed strategy is underpinned by strategic capabilities that satisfy the VRIO criteria:

- *Value*: does the strategy provide value to customers? One test of this is whether the strategy would command a premium price in the marketplace. Alternatively, the strategic capabilities should support a cost advantage.

- *Rarity*: does the strategy draw on assets that are sufficiently rare to prevent rapid copying by competitors?

- *Inimitability*: if the required assets are not rare, is the strategy sufficiently complex or non-transparent to be difficult for competitors to imitate (or substitute)?

- *Organisational support*: if the strategy is hard to imitate, does the organisation have in place the organisational means actually to implement the strategy (see also the discussion of feasibility in section 11.5)?

The various strategic options can be compared systematically against these four VRIO criteria in a simple matrix, with the options as horizontal rows and the individual VRIO criteria as columns.

11.3.4 Decision trees

Decision trees can also be used to assess strategic options against a list of key factors. Here options are 'eliminated' and preferred options emerge by progressively introducing requirements which must be met (such as growth, investment or diversity). Illustration 11.3 provides an example. The end point of the decision tree is a number of discrete development opportunities. The elimination process is achieved by identifying a few key elements or criteria which possible strategies need to achieve. In Illustration 11.3 these are growth, investment and diversification. As the illustration shows, choosing growth as an important requirement of a future strategy ranks options 1–4 more highly than 5–8. At the second step, the need for low

ILLUSTRATION 11.3

A strategic decision tree for a law firm

Decision trees evaluate future options by progressively eliminating others as additional criteria are introduced to the evaluation.

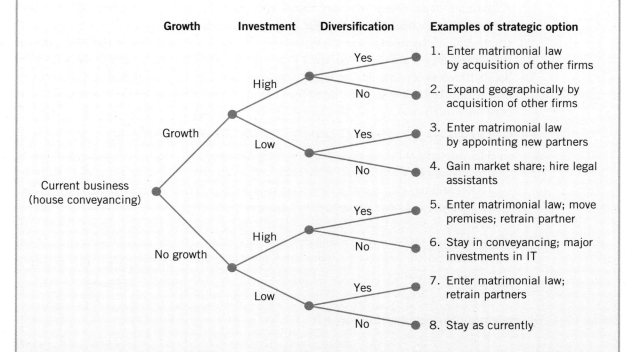

| Growth | Investment | Diversification | Examples of strategic option |

1. Enter matrimonial law by acquisition of other firms
2. Expand geographically by acquisition of other firms
3. Enter matrimonial law by appointing new partners
4. Gain market share; hire legal assistants
5. Enter matrimonial law; move premises; retrain partner
6. Stay in conveyancing; major investments in IT
7. Enter matrimonial law; retrain partners
8. Stay as currently

A law firm had most of its work related to house conveyancing (the legal aspects of buying property) where profits had been significantly squeezed. Therefore, it wanted to consider a range of new strategies for the future. Using a strategic decision tree it was able to eliminate certain options by identifying a few key criteria which future developments would incorporate, such as growth, investment (in premises, IT systems or acquisitions), and diversification (e.g. into matrimonial law which, in turn, often brings house conveyancing work as families 'reshape').

Analysis of the decision tree reveals that if the partners of the firm wish growth to be an important aspect of future strategies, options 1–4 are ranked more highly than options 5–8. At the second step, the need for low-investment strategies would rank options 3 and 4 above 1 and 2, and so on.

The partners were aware that this technique has limitations in that the choice at each branch of the tree can tend to be simplistic. Answering 'yes' or 'no'

to diversification does not allow for the wide variety of alternatives which might exist between these two extremes, for example *adapting the 'style' of the conveyancing service* (this could be an important variant of options 6 or 8). Nevertheless, as a starting point for evaluation, the decision tree provided a useful framework.

Questions

1 Try reversing the sequence of the three parameters (to diversification, investment and growth) and redraw the decision tree. Do the same eight options still emerge?

2 Add a fourth parameter to the decision tree. This new parameter is development by *internal methods* or by *acquisition*. List your 16 options in the right-hand column.

investment strategies would rank options 3 and 4 above 1 and 2; and so on. The danger here is that the choice at each branch on the tree can tend to be simplistic. For example, as the illustration points out, answering 'yes' or 'no' to diversification does not allow for the wide variety of options which might exist within this strategy.

11.3.5 Life-cycle analysis

A *life-cycle analysis* assesses whether a strategy is likely to be appropriate given the stage of the industry life cycle (section 2.3.2). Table 11.4 shows a matrix with two dimensions. The industry situation is described in five stages, from development to decline. The competitive position has three categories ranging from weak to strong. The purpose of the matrix is to establish the appropriateness of particular strategies in relation to these two dimensions. The consultancy firm Arthur D. Little suggests a number of criteria for establishing where an organisation is positioned on the matrix and what types of strategy are most likely to be suitable:

● *Strong competitive position*: generally strong competitors should consider aggressive strategies throughout the life cycle. Early on, that implies rapid growth, for instance reinforcing cost advantages though experience curve effects, or extending advantages by broadening scope. Later on, strong competitors may take advantage of their relative strength to drive out weaker competitors by aggressive pricing or innovation, plus acquisitions where appropriate. In maturity, harvesting any weaker activities in the portfolio – through closure or perhaps sale – becomes important. Investment in innovation and differentiation may be less important. In the final stage, strong competitors might aim to be the last remaining player, leaving them the chance to exploit market power through high prices.

Table 11.4 The industry life-cycle/portfolio matrix

Competitive position	Stages of industry life cycle				
	Development	**Growth**	**Shake-out**	**Mature**	**Decline**
Strong	Fast grow	Attain cost leadership Differentiate Broaden scope	Reinforce cost and differentiation advantages Drive out weaker competitors by innovation or price wars Acquire weaker competitors	Consolidate industry through acquisitions Harvest weaker activities Cut unnecessary costs (e.g. differentiation or innovation)	Drive out remaining competitors Exploit market power Cut unnecessary costs
Middling	Fast grow Differentiate Focus	Catch up Differentiate Focus Find niche	Harvest weaker activities Seek alliances or mergers	Retrench Turnaround Seek alliances or mergers Exit by sale	Seek alliances or mergers Exit by sale or closure
Weak	Find niche Catch up	Turnaround Retrench Seek alliances, mergers or acquirers	Seek alliances, mergers or acquirers Exit	Seek alliances, mergers or acquirers Exit	Seek alliances, mergers or acquirers Exit

Source: Adapted from Arthur D. Little.

- *Middling competitive position*: early in the life cycle, middling competitors should generally be considering urgent steps either to strengthen their overall position (perhaps by mergers or alliances) or to find a relatively protected niche. Later on, competitors still with a middling position should take seriously the option of selling the business to a stronger rival, one with 'parenting advantage' for example (see Chapter 6).

- *Weak competitive position*: for those competitors with a weak competitive position, the options facing middling competitors are accelerated. If weak competitors cannot rapidly transform their position or find a protected niche, they should promptly consider closure or sale to a stronger competitor.

While this matrix is of use in providing general guidance for evaluating possible strategies over the life cycle, it does not, of itself, provide directive answers. Each organisation must make decisions on its own merits according to its precise individual circumstances. Organisations should beware too that the life-cycle stages are not irreversible. As in Chapter 3, industries can 'de-mature', so that investments in innovation and differentiation, for example, can again become highly important.

11.4 ACCEPTABILITY

Acceptability is concerned with **whether the expected performance outcomes of a proposed strategy meet the expectations of stakeholders**. These can be of three types, the '3 Rs': *Risk, Returns* and *Reaction of stakeholders*. It is sensible to use more than one approach in assessing the acceptability of a strategy.

11.4.1 Risk

The first R is the *risk* an organisation faces in pursuing a strategy. **Risk concerns the extent to which strategic outcomes are unpredictable, especially with regard to possible negative outcomes.** It is important to be sensitive to the downside. Risk can be high for organisations with major long-term programmes of innovation, or where high levels of uncertainty exist about key issues in the environment, or where there are high levels of public concern about new developments – such as genetically modified crops.[9] A key issue is to establish the acceptable level of risk for the organisation. Is the organisation prepared to 'bet the company' on a single strategic initiative, risking total destruction, or does it prefer a more cautious approach of maintaining several less unpredictable and lower-stakes initiatives? Formal *risk assessments* are often incorporated into business plans as well as the investment appraisals of major projects. Chosen strategies should be within the limits of acceptable risk for the organisation. Young entrepreneurs may have a higher tolerance for risk than established family businesses, for example. Importantly, risks other than ones with immediate financial impact should be included, such as risk to corporate reputation or brand image. Developing a good understanding of an organisation's strategic position (Part I of this book) is at the core of good risk assessment. However, the following tools can also be helpful in a risk assessment.

Sensitivity analysis[10]

Sometimes referred to as *what-if* analysis, sensitivity analysis allows each of the important assumptions underlying a particular strategy to be questioned and challenged. In particular, it tests how sensitive the predicted performance outcome (e.g. profit) is to each of these assumptions. For example, the key assumptions underlying a strategy might be that market demand will grow by 5 per cent a year, or that a new product will achieve a given sales level, or that certain expensive machines will operate at 90 per cent loading. Sensitivity analysis asks what would be the effect on performance (e.g. profitability) of variations on these assumptions. For example, if market demand grew at only 1 per cent, or by as much as 10 per cent, would either of these extremes alter the decision to pursue that strategy? This can help develop a clearer picture of the risks of making particular strategic decisions and the degree of confidence managers might have in a given decision. Illustration 11.4 shows how sensitivity analysis can be used.

Financial risk[11]

Financial risk refers to the possibility that the organisation may not be able to meet the key financial obligations necessary for survival. Managers need to ensure that strategies meet acceptable levels of financial risk. Two key measures are important here.

First, there is the level of *gearing*, the amount of debt the company has relative to its equity. Strategies that increase the gearing (or 'leverage') of a company also raise the level of financial

ILLUSTRATION 11.4

Sensitivity analysis

Sensitivity analysis is a useful technique for assessing the extent to which the success of a preferred strategy is dependent on the key assumptions which underlie that strategy.

In 2012 the Dunsmore Chemical Company was a single-product company trading in a mature and relatively stable market. It was intended to use this established situation as a 'cash cow' to generate funds for a new venture with a related product. Estimates had shown that the company would need to generate some £4 m (€4.4 m; $6 m) cash between 2013 and 2018 for this new venture to be possible.

Although the expected performance of the company was for a cash flow of £9.5 m over that period (the *base case*), management were concerned to assess the likely impact of three key factors:

- Possible increases in *production costs* (labour, overheads and materials), which might be as much as 3 per cent p.a. in real terms.
- *Capacity-fill*, which might be reduced by as much as 25 per cent due to ageing plant and uncertain labour relations.
- *Price levels*, which might be affected by the threatened entry of a new major competitor. This

(a) Sensitivity of cash flow to changes in real production costs.

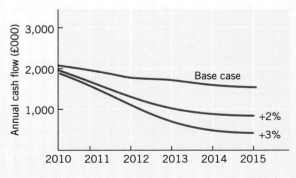

could squeeze prices by as much as 3 per cent p.a. in real terms.

It was decided to use sensitivity analysis to assess the possible impact of each of these factors on the company's ability to generate £4 m. The results are shown in the graphs.

risk. This is because interest payments on debt are mandatory and inflexible: if performance dips and the interest cannot be paid, the company risks bankruptcy.

A second kind of financial risk measure relates to an organisation's *liquidity*. Liquidity refers to the amount of liquid assets (typically cash) that is available to pay immediate bills. Many businesses fail not because they are inherently unprofitable, but because of a lack of liquid assets, whether their own or obtained through short-term loans. For example, a small manufacturer with a rapid growth strategy may be tempted to take on lots of orders, but then find that it has to pay its suppliers for the raw materials before it actually receives the payments for the goods it has produced. Again, a company that cannot pay its bills risks bankruptcy.

Break-even analysis

Break-even analysis[12] is a simple and widely used approach which allows variations in assumptions about key variables in a strategy to be examined. It demonstrates at what point in terms of revenue the business will recover its fixed and variable costs and therefore break even. It can therefore be used to assess the risks associated with different price and cost structures of strategies as shown in Illustration 11.5.

(b) Sensitivity of cash flow to changes in plant utilisation.

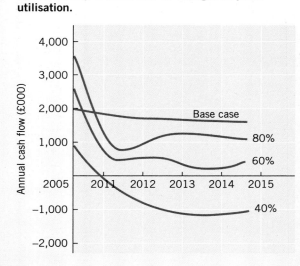

(c) Sensitivity of cash flow to reductions in real price.

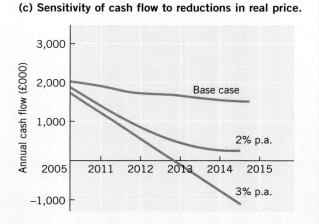

From this analysis, management concluded that their target of £4 m would be achieved with *capacity utilisation* as low as 60 per cent, which was certainly going to be achieved. Increased *production costs* of 3 per cent p.a. would still allow the company to achieve the £4 m target over the period. In contrast, *price squeezes* of 3 per cent p.a. would result in a shortfall of £2 m.

Management concluded from this analysis that the key factor which should affect their thinking on this matter was the likely impact of new competition and the extent to which they could protect price levels if such competition emerged. They therefore developed an aggressive marketing strategy to deter potential entrants.

Questions

What should the company do if its marketing campaigns fail to stop real price erosion:

1   Push to achieve more sales volume/ capacity fill?

2   Reduce unit costs of production?

3   Something else?

ILLUSTRATION 11.5

Using break-even analysis to examine strategic options

Break-even analysis can be a simple way of quantifying some of the key factors which would determine the success or failure of a strategy.

A manufacturing company was considering the launch of a new consumer durable product into a market segment where most products were sold to wholesalers which supplied the retail trade. The total market was worth about €4.8 m (or $6.6 m) (at manufacturers' prices) – about 630,000 units. The market leader had about 30 per cent market share in a competitive market where retailers were increasing their buying power. The company wished to evaluate the relative merits of a high-price/high-quality product sold to wholesalers (strategy A) or an own-brand product sold directly to retailers (strategy B).

The table summarises the market and cost structure for the market leader and these alternative strategies.

The table shows that the company would require about 22 per cent and 13 per cent market share respectively for strategies A and B to break even.

Questions

1. Which option would you choose? Why?

2. What would be the main risks attached to that option and how would you attempt to minimise these risks?

3. Create another option (strategy C) and explain the kind of break-even profile which would be needed to make it more attractive than either strategy A or strategy B.

Market and cost structure (€)	Market leader	Strategy A	Strategy B
Price to retailer	10.00	12.00	8.00
Price to wholesaler	7.00	8.40	–
Total variable costs (TVC)	3.50	4.00	3.10
Contribution to profit per unit sold (= Price sold – TVC)	3.50	4.40	4.90
Fixed costs (FC)	500,000	500,000	500,000
Break-even point: no. of units to sell (= FC/Contribution to profit)	142,857	136,363	81,633
Total market size (units)	630,000	630,000	630,000
Break-even point: market share (= Break-even point units/Mkt size)	22.6%	21.6%	13.0%
Actual market share	30.0%	–	–

11.4.2 Returns

The second R is **returns**. These are **a measure of the financial effectiveness of a strategy**. In the private sector, shareholders expect a financial return on their investment. In the public sector, funders (typically government departments) are likely to measure returns in terms of the 'value for money' of services delivered. Measures of return are a common way of assessing proposed new ventures or major projects within businesses. An assessment of the financial effectiveness of any specific strategy should be a key criterion of acceptability.

Financial analysis[13]

There are three common approaches to financial return (see Figure 11.3):

Figure 11.3 Assessing profitability

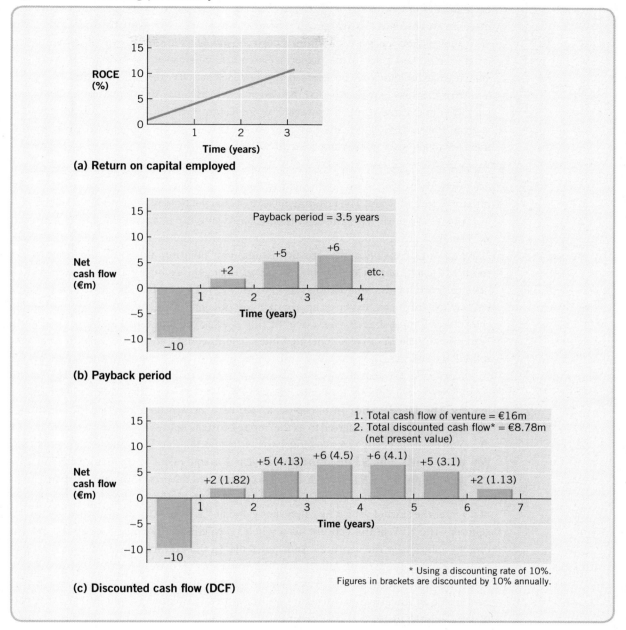

(a) Return on capital employed

(b) Payback period

(c) Discounted cash flow (DCF)

* Using a discounting rate of 10%.
Figures in brackets are discounted by 10% annually.

- *Return on capital employed (ROCE)* calculates profitability in relation to capital for a specific time period after a new strategy is in place: as for example in Figure 11.3(a), a ROCE of 10 per cent by year 3. The ROCE (typically profit before interest and tax – PBIT – divided by capital employed) is a measure of the earning power of the capital resources used in implementing a particular strategic option. Its weakness is that it does not focus on cash flow or the timing of cash flows (see the explanation of DCF below).

- The *payback period* assesses the length of time it takes before the cumulative cash flows for a strategic option become positive. In the example in Figure 11.3(b) the payback period is three-and-half years. This measure has the virtue of simplicity and is most often used where the difficulty of forecasting is high and therefore risk is high. In such circumstances this measure can be used to select projects or strategies that have the quickest payback. Thus acceptable payback periods vary from industry to industry. A venture capitalist investing in a high-technology start-up may expect a fast return, whereas public infrastructure projects such as road building may be assessed over payback periods exceeding 50 years. One problem with the basic payback period method is that it assumes that forecast cash flows are equally valuable in the future, however risky or distant: €100 predicted in three years' time is given the same weight as €100 next year. Organisations therefore often use 'discount' methods to allow for greater uncertainty in the more distant future.

● *Discounted cash flow (DCF)* is a widely used investment appraisal technique using common cash-flow forecasting techniques which 'discounts' (gives less value to) earnings the further into the future they are. The resulting measure is the net present value (or NPV) of the project, one of the most widely used criteria for assessing the financial viability of a project. In principle, given limited resources, the project with the best NPV should be selected. However, a DCF is only as valid as the assumptions built into it, so it is important to test sensitivity to different evaluations and scenarios. Taking the example of DCF in Figure 11.3(c), once the cash inflows and outflows have been assessed for each of the years of a strategic option they are discounted by an appropriate cost of capital. This cost of capital is the 'hurdle' that projects must exceed. The discount rate reflects the fact that cash generated early is more valuable than cash generated later. The discount rate is also set at a level that reflects the riskiness of the strategy under consideration (i.e. a higher rate for greater risk). In the example, the cost of capital or discounting rate of 10 per cent (after tax) reflects the rate of return required by those providing finance for the venture – shareholders and/or lenders. The 10 per cent cost of capital shown here *includes* an allowance for inflation of about 3–4 per cent. It is referred to as the 'money cost of capital'. By contrast, the 'real' cost of capital is 6–7 per cent *after* allowing for or *excluding* inflation. The projected after-tax cash flow of £2 m (€2.2 m; $3 m) at the start of year 2 is equivalent to receiving £1.82 m now – £2 m multiplied by 0.91 or 1 ÷ 1.10; £1.82 m is called the *present value* of receiving £2 m at the start of year 2 at a cost of capital of 10 per cent. Similarly, the after-tax cash flow of £5 m at the start of year 3 has a present value of £4.13 m – £5 m multiplied by 1/1.10 squared. The NPV of the venture, as a whole, is calculated by adding up all the annual present values over the venture's anticipated life. In the example, this is seven years. The NPV works out at £8.78 m. Allowing for the time value of money, the £8.78 m is the extra value that the strategic initiative will generate during its entire lifetime. However, it would be sensible to undertake a sensitivity analysis, for example by assuming different levels of sales volume increases, or different costs of capital in order to establish what resulting NPV measures would be and at what point the NPV falls below zero. For example, in Figure 11.3(c) a cost of capital or discounting rate of about 32 per cent would produce a zero NPV. Such sensitivity testing is, then, a way in which DCF can be used to assess risk. The Key Debate at the end of the chapter discusses how the use of DCF is regarded differently in different countries.

With regard to these three approaches to assessing returns, it is important to remember that there are no absolute standards as to what constitutes good or poor return. It will differ between industries and countries and between different stakeholders. So it is important to establish what return is seen as acceptable by which stakeholders. Views also differ as to which measures give the best assessment of return, as will be seen below. Three further problems of financial analysis are as follows:

- *The problem of uncertainty.* Be wary of the apparent thoroughness of the various approaches to financial analysis. Most were developed for the purposes of investment appraisal. Therefore, they focus on discrete projects where the additional cash inflows and outflows can be predicted with relative certainty: for example, a retailer opening a new store has a good idea about likely turnover based on previous experience of similar stores in similar areas. Such assumptions are not necessarily valid in many strategic contexts because the outcomes are much less certain. It is as strategy implementation proceeds (with the associated cash-flow consequences) that outcomes become clearer (see the discussion of 'real options' below).

- *The problem of specificity.* Financial appraisals tend to focus on direct *tangible* costs and benefits rather than the strategy more broadly. However, it is often not easy to identify such costs and benefits, or the cash flows specific to a proposed strategy, since it may not be possible to isolate them from other ongoing business activities. Moreover such costs and benefits may have spill-over effects. For example, a new product may look unprofitable as a single project. But it may make strategic sense by enhancing the market acceptability of other products in a company's portfolio.

- *Assumptions.* Financial analysis is only as good as the assumptions built into the analysis. If assumptions about sales levels or costs are misguided, for example, then the value of the analysis is reduced, even misleading. This is one reason why sensitivity testing based on variations of assumptions is important.

Shareholder value analysis

Shareholder value analysis[14] (SVA) is a form of financial analysis that poses very directly the question: which proposed strategies would most increase shareholder value? There are several measures of shareholder value, but two are common:

- *Total shareholder return (TSR)* makes use of share price and dividend measures. In any financial year, the TSR is equal to the increase in the price of a share, plus the dividends received per share in that year. This is then divided by the share price at the start of the financial year. A simple example is given as Table 11.5(a). The TSR measure is attractive because it captures both aspects of shareholder value: capital gains (or losses) in the share price as well as income in the form of dividends. However, because this measure relies on the availability of a share price, it is inapplicable to privately held companies and can be only roughly applied to individual business units within a publicly quoted company. It is also potentially limited as a measure of strategic success because share prices may rise and fall for many reasons outside the responsibility of the company's managers.

- *Economic value added (EVA) or economic profit* relies on accounting data. It introduces the notion of 'cost of capital': the cost of equity capital is the required dividend and capital gain; the cost of debt capital is the interest rate. Meeting the cost of capital is normally essential to securing financial support. If the operating profit (after tax) is greater than the cost of the capital required to produce that profit, then EVA is positive. An example is given as Table 11.5(b). An important feature of EVA is that the cost of capital allows for risk: the higher the risk, the higher the cost of capital. Especially for risky strategies, it is quite possible to be apparently profitable while not actually meeting the cost of capital. EVA does not rely on share prices, so it can be applied to individual business units and projects within

Table 11.5 **Measures of shareholder value**

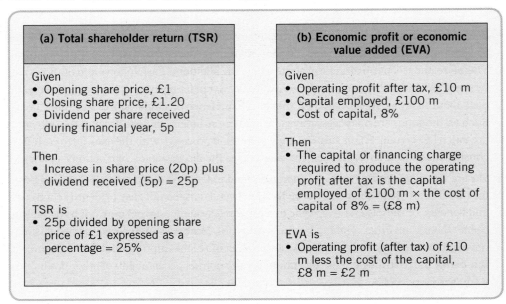

(a) Total shareholder return (TSR)	(b) Economic profit or economic value added (EVA)
Given • Opening share price, £1 • Closing share price, £1.20 • Dividend per share received during financial year, 5p Then • Increase in share price (20p) plus dividend received (5p) = 25p TSR is • 25p divided by opening share price of £1 expressed as a percentage = 25%	Given • Operating profit after tax, £10 m • Capital employed, £100 m • Cost of capital, 8% Then • The capital or financing charge required to produce the operating profit after tax is the capital employed of £100 m × the cost of capital of 8% = (£8 m) EVA is • Operating profit (after tax) of £10 m less the cost of the capital, £8 m = £2 m

a company, with the cost of capital being adjusted according to the risk profile of each individual venture.

Although shareholder value analysis has helped address some of the shortcomings of traditional financial analyses, it has been criticised for over-emphasising short-term shareholder returns, and neglecting other stakeholders – customers, employees and communities – that are important to long-run organisational survival.[15] Nevertheless, the idea of valuing a strategy may give greater realism and clarity to otherwise vague claims for strategic benefits. But firms that employ SVA are advised to do so with an eye both to the long term and to the value of the firm as a whole.[16]

Cost–benefit[17]

Profit measures may be too narrow an interpretation of return, particularly where wider benefits than organisational profit are important. This is usually so for major public infrastructure projects for example, such as the siting of an airport or a sewer construction project (see Illustration 11.6). The *cost–benefit* concept suggests that a money value should be put on all the costs and benefits of a strategy, including tangible and intangible returns to people and organisations other than the one 'sponsoring' the project or strategy.

Although in practice monetary valuation is often difficult, it can be done and, despite the difficulties, cost–benefit analysis is useful provided its limitations are understood. Its major benefit is in forcing managers to be explicit about the various factors that influence strategic choice. So, even if people disagree on the value that should be assigned to particular costs or benefits, at least they can argue their case on common ground and compare the merits of the various arguments.

Real options[18]

Many of the previous approaches value strategic initiatives on a standalone basis. There are, however, situations where the strategic benefits and opportunities only become clear as

ILLUSTRATION 11.6

Sewerage construction project

Investment in items of infrastructure – such as sewers – often requires a careful consideration of the wider costs and benefits of the project.

The UK's privatised water companies were monopolies supplying water and disposing of sewage. One of their priorities was investment in new sewerage systems to meet the increasing standards required by law. They frequently used cost–benefit analysis to assess projects. The figures below are from an actual analysis.

Cost/benefit	£m*	£m*
Multiplier/linkage benefits		0.9
Flood prevention		2.5
Reduced traffic disruption		7.2
Amenity benefits		4.6
Investment benefit		23.6
Encouragement of visitors		4.0
Total benefits		42.8
Costs		
Construction cost	18.2	
Less: Unskilled labour cost	(4.7)	
Opportunity cost of construction	(13.5)	
Present value of net benefits (NPV)	29.3	

* (£1 m is about €1.1 m or $1.5 m)

Note: Figures discounted at a *real* discount rate of 5% over 40 years.

Benefits

Benefits result mainly from reduced use of rivers as overflow sewers. There are also economic benefits resulting from construction. The following benefits are quantified in the table:

- The multiplier benefit to the local economy of increased spending by those employed on the project.
- The linkage benefit to the local economy of purchases from local firms, including the multiplier effect of such spending.
- Reduced risk of flooding from overflows or old sewers collapsing – flood probabilities can be quantified using historical records, and the cost of flood damage by detailed assessment of the property vulnerable to damage.
- Reduced traffic disruption from flooding and road closures for repairs to old sewers – statistics on the costs of delays to users, traffic flows on roads affected and past closure frequency can be used to quantify savings.
- Increased amenity value of rivers (e.g. for boating and fishing) can be measured by surveys asking visitors what the value is to them or by looking at the effect on demand of charges imposed elsewhere.
- Increased rental values and take-up of space can be measured by consultation with developers and observed effects elsewhere.
- Increased visitor numbers to riverside facilities resulting from reduced pollution.

Construction cost

This is net of the cost of unskilled labour. Use of unskilled labour is not a burden on the economy, and its cost must be deducted to arrive at opportunity cost.

Net benefits

Once the difficult task of quantifying costs and benefits is complete, standard discounting techniques can be used to calculate net present value and internal rate of return, and analysis can then proceed as for conventional projects.

Source: G. Owen, formerly of Sheffield Business School.

Questions

1 What do you feel about the appropriateness of the listed benefits?

2 How easy or difficult is it to assign money values to these benefits?

implementation proceeds. For example, a diversification strategy may develop in several steps: it may take many years for the success of the initial diversification move to become clear and for possible follow-up opportunities to emerge. In these circumstances the traditional DCF approach discussed above will tend to undervalue an initial strategic move because it does not take into account the value of options that could be opened up by the initiative going forward.[19] In pharmaceuticals, for example, many research projects fail to produce new drugs with the intended benefit. There could, however, be other outcomes of value to a failed project: the research could create valuable new knowledge or provide a 'platform' from which other products or process improvements spring. So a strategy should be seen as a *series* of 'real' options (i.e. opportunities at points in time as the strategy takes shape) which should be evaluated as such. Illustration 11.7 provides an example. A real options approach to evaluation therefore typically increases the expected value of a project because it adds the expected value of possible future options created by that project going forward. There are four main benefits of this approach:

- *Bringing strategic and financial evaluation closer together*. Arguably it provides a clearer understanding of both strategic and financial return and risk of a strategy by examining each step (option) separately.

- *Valuing emerging options*. In taking such an approach, it allows a value to be placed on new options made available by the initial strategic decision. The value of the first step is increased by the opportunities that it opens up.

- *Coping with uncertainty*. Advocates of a real options approach argue it provides an alternative to profitability analyses that require managers to make assumptions about future conditions that may well not be realistic. As such it can be linked into ways of analysing uncertain futures such as scenario analysis (section 2.2). Applying a real options approach encourages managers to defer irreversible decisions as far as possible because the passage of time will clarify expected returns – even to the extent that apparently unfavourable strategies might prove viable at a later date.

- *Offsetting conservatism*. One problem with financial analyses such as DCF is that high hurdle or discount rates set to reflect risk and uncertainty mean that ambitious but uncertain projects (and strategies) tend not to receive support. The real options approach, on the other hand, tends to value higher, more ambitious strategies. There have, therefore, been calls to employ real options together with more traditional financial evaluation such as DCF. In effect DCF provides the cautionary view and real options the more optimistic view.

Note that a real options approach is more useful where a strategy can be structured in the form of options – for example, where there are stages, as in pharmaceutical development – such that each stage gives the possibility of abandoning or deferring going forward. It would not give the same advantages of flexibility to a project where major capital outlay was required at the beginning.

11.4.3 Reaction of stakeholders

The third R is the likely *reaction* of stakeholders to a proposed strategy. Section 4.4 showed how *stakeholder mapping* can be used to understand the political context and consider the political agenda in an organisation. It also showed how stakeholder mapping can be used to consider the likely reactions of stakeholders to new strategies and thus evaluate the

ILLUSTRATION 11.7

Real options evaluation for developing premium beers in India

A real options approach can be used to evaluate proposed projects with multiple options.

A brewer of premium beers had been exporting its products to India for many years. It was considering an investment in brewing capacity in India. Although it was envisaged that, initially, this would take the form of brewing standard products locally and distributing through existing distributors, there were other ideas being discussed, though these were all contingent on the building of the brewery. Management took a real options approach to evaluating the project as set out in the figure below.

The evaluation of the proposal to build the brewery considered three options: to invest now, at a later date, or not invest at all. However, the building of the brewery opened other options. One of these was to cease operating through existing third-party distributors and open up its own distribution network. Again, there were alternatives here. Should it invest in this immediately after the brewery was built, at a later date or not invest in it at all and continue through the current distributors? The investment in the brewery, especially if better distribution systems were to be developed, in turn opened up other options. Currently being discussed, for example, was whether there existed a market opportunity to develop and produce beers tailored more specifically to the Indian market. Again, should there be investment in this soon after the building of the brewery, at a later date, or not at all? It was also recognised that other options might emerge if the project went forward.

The board used a real options approach, not least because it needed to factor in the potential added value of the options opened up by the brewery.

The board would employ DCF to evaluate the brewery project. However, it would also evaluate the other options assuming the brewery was built. In each of these evaluation exercises DCF would also be used, adjusting the cost of capital to the perceived risk of the options. This would give an indication of NPV for each of those options. The possible positive NPVs of the subsequent options could then be taken into account in assessing the attractiveness of the initial brewery project.

The board also recognised that, if it invested in the brewery so as to further develop its presence in India, greater clarity on both costs and market opportunities would emerge as the project progressed. So it would make sense to revisit the evaluation of the other options at later stages as such information became available.

Question

1 What are the advantages of the real options approach to this evaluation over other approaches (a) to building the brewery; and (b) to other ideas being considered?

A real options approach to a brewery development

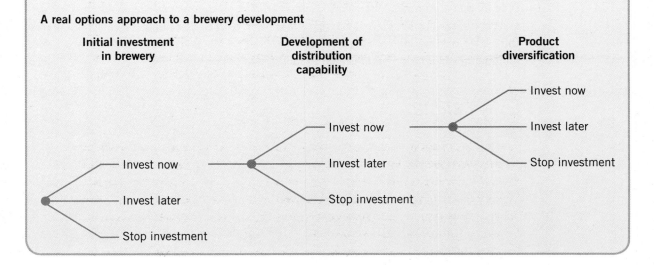

acceptability of a strategy. There are many situations where stakeholder reactions could be crucial. For example:

- *Owners'* (e.g. shareholders, family owners, the state) financial expectations have to be taken into account and the extent to which these are met will influence the acceptability of a strategy. A proposed strategy might also call for the financial restructuring of a business, for example an issue of new shares, which could be unacceptable, for example to a powerful group of shareholders, since it dilutes their voting power.

- *Bankers* and other providers of interest-bearing loans are concerned about the *risk* attached to their loans and the competence with which this is managed. It is likely they will manage this risk through taking securities against it. None the less a good track record in managing that risk could be regarded (in itself) as a reason for bankers to invest further with some companies and not others. The extent to which a proposed strategy could affect the capital structure of the company could also be important. For example, would it increase the gearing ratio (of debt to equity), which determines how sensitive the solvency of the company is to changes in its profit position? Interest cover is a similar measure that relates interest payments to profit. They will also be concerned with the *liquidity* of the company, because a deteriorating liquidity position may require correction through additional loans and an increased risk profile. So the question needs to be asked: how will the proposed strategy affect liquidity?

- *Regulators* are important stakeholders in industries such as telecommunications, financial services, pharmaceuticals and power. They may have what amounts to decision-making powers over aspects of an organisation's strategy, such as price or geographic expansion.

- *Employees and unions* may resist strategic moves such as relocation, outsourcing or divestment if they see them as likely to result in job losses.

- *The local community* will be concerned about jobs but also with the *social cost* of an organisation's strategies, such as pollution or reputation loss – an issue of growing concern. Matters of business ethics and social responsibility were discussed in section 4.4.

- *Customers* may also object to a strategy. Their sanction is to cease buying from the company, perhaps switching to a competitor. For example, a new business model, such as marketing online, might run the risk of a backlash from existing retail channels, which could jeopardise the success of the strategy.

Overall, there is a need to be conscious of the impact on the various stakeholders of the strategic options being considered. Managers also need to understand how the capability to meet the varied expectations of stakeholders could enable the success of some strategies while limiting the ability of an organisation to succeed with other strategies.

(11.5) FEASIBILITY

Feasibility is **concerned with whether a strategy could work in practice**: in other words, whether an organisation has the capabilities to deliver a strategy. An assessment of feasibility is likely to involve two key questions: (i) do the resources and competences currently exist to implement a strategy effectively? And (ii) if not, can they be obtained? These questions can be applied to any resource area that has a bearing on the viability of a proposed strategy. Here the focus is on three areas, however: finance, people (and their skills) and the importance of resource integration.

11.5.1 **Financial feasibility**

A central issue in considering a proposed strategy is the funding required for it. It is therefore important to forecast the *cash-flow*[20] implications of the strategy. The need is to identify the cash required for a strategy, the cash generated by following the strategy and the timing of any new funding requirements. This then informs consideration of the likely sources for obtaining funds.

Managers need to be familiar with different sources of funds as well as the advantages and drawbacks of these. This is well explained in standard financial texts.[21] This is a matter not only of the feasibility of a strategy, but also its acceptability to different stakeholders, not least those providing the funds. So the discussion in section 11.3.3 is relevant here too. Decisions on which funding sources to use will also be influenced by the current financial situation of the organisation such as ownership (e.g. whether the business is privately held or publicly quoted) and by the overall corporate goals and strategic priorities of the organisation. For example, there will be different financial needs if a business is seeking rapid growth by acquisition compared with if it is seeking to consolidate its past performance.

A useful way of considering funding is in terms of which financial strategies might be needed for different 'phases' of the life cycle of a business (as opposed to an industry life cycle): see Table 11.6. In turn this raises the question as to whether such sources of finance are available and, if not, whether the proposed strategy is both feasible and acceptable.

- *Start-up businesses*[22] are high-risk businesses. They are at the beginning of their life cycle and are not yet established in their markets; moreover, they are likely to require substantial investment. A standalone business in this situation might, for example, seek to finance such growth from specialists in this kind of investment, such as venture capitalists who, themselves, seek to offset risk by having a portfolio of such investments. Schemes for private investors (so-called 'business angels') have also become popular. Providers of such funds are, however, likely to be demanding, given the high business risk. Thus venture capitalists or business angels typically require a high proportion of the equity ownership in exchange for even quite small injections of funds.
- *Growth businesses* may remain in a volatile and highly competitive market position. The degree of business risk may therefore remain high, as will the cost of capital in such

Table 11.6 **Financial strategy and the business life cycle**

Life-cycle phase	Funding requirement	Cost of capital	Business risk	Likely funding source(s)	Dividends
Start-up	High	High	High	Personal debt Equity (angel and venture capital)	Zero
Growth	High	Medium	High	Debentures and equity (growth investors)	Nominal
Maturity	Low/medium	Low	Low	Debt, equity and retained earnings	High
Exit/decline	Low	Medium/high	Medium	Debt, retained earnings	High

circumstances. However, if a business in this phase has begun to establish itself in its markets, perhaps as a market leader in a growing market, then the cost of capital may be lower. In either case, since the main attractions to investors here are the product or business concept and the prospect of future earnings, equity capital is likely to be appropriate, perhaps by public flotation.

- *Mature businesses* are those operating in mature markets and the likelihood is that funding requirements will decline. If such a business has achieved a strong competitive position with a high market share, it should be generating regular and substantial surpluses. Here the business risk is lower and the opportunity for retained earnings is high. In these circumstances, if funding is required, it may make sense to raise this through debt capital as well as equity, since reliable returns can be used to service such debt. Provided increased debt (*gearing* or *leverage*) does not lead to an unacceptable level of risk, this cheaper debt funding will in fact increase the residual profits achieved by a company in these circumstances.

- *Declining businesses* are likely to find it difficult to attract equity finance. However, borrowing may be possible if secured against residual assets in the business. At this stage, it is likely that the emphasis in the business will be on cost cutting, and it could well be that the cash flows from such businesses are quite strong. Risk is medium, especially if decline looks to be gradual. However, there is the chance of sudden shake-out with battles for survival.

This life-cycle framework does not, however, always hold. For example, a company seeking to develop *new and innovative businesses* on a regular basis might, in effect, be acting as its own venture capitalist, accepting high risk at the business level and seeking to offset such risk by 'cash cows' in its portfolio (see section 7.7). Or some companies may need to sell off businesses as they mature to raise capital for further investment in new ventures. Public-sector managers know about the need to balance the financial risk of services too. They need a steady core to their service where budgets are certain to be met, hence reducing the financial risk of the more speculative aspects of their service.

11.5.2 **People and skills**

Chapter 3 showed how organisations that achieve sustainable competitive advantage may do so on the basis of competences that are embedded in the skills, knowledge and experience of people in that organisation. Indeed, ultimately the success of a strategy will likely depend on how it is delivered by people in the organisation. These could be managers but they could also be more junior people in the organisation who are none the less critical to a strategy, for example as the front-line contact with customers. Three questions arise: do people in the organisation currently have the competences to deliver a proposed strategy? Are the systems to support those people fit for the strategy? If not, can the competences be obtained or developed?

The first step here is the same as suggested in section 11.3.3 for the screening for competitive advantage. The need is to identify the key strategic capabilities underpinning a proposed strategy, but specifically in terms of the people and skills required. The second step is to determine if these exist in the organisation. It could be, of course, that the proposed strategy is built on the argument that they do. If so, how realistic is this? Or it could be that the assumption is that these can be obtained or developed. Again, is this realistic?

Many of the issues of feasibility in relation to the structures and systems to support such competence development and people are addressed in Chapter 13 on organising and Chapter 14 on managing strategic change. Other critical questions that need to be considered include:[23]

- *Work organisation.* Will changes in work content and priority-setting significantly alter the orientation of people's jobs? Will managers need to think differently about the tasks that need to be done? What are the critical criteria for effectiveness needed? Are these different from current requirements?

- *Rewards.* How will people need to be incentivised? Will people's career aspirations be affected? How will any significant shifts in power, influence and credibility need to be rewarded and recognised?

- *Relationships.* Will interactions between key people need to change? What are the consequences for the levels of trust, task competence and values-congruence? Will conflict and political rivalry be likely?

- *Training and development.* Are current training and mentoring systems appropriate? It may be necessary to take into account the balance between the need to ensure the successful delivery of strategy in the short term and the required future development of people's capabilities.

- *Recruitment and promotion.* Given these issues, will new people need to be recruited into the organisation, or can talent be promoted and supported from below?

11.5.3 Integrating resources

The success of a strategy is likely to depend on the management of many resource areas; not only people and finance, but also physical resources, such as buildings, information, technology and the resources provided by suppliers and partners. It is possible, but not likely, that a proposed strategy builds only on existing resources. It is more likely that additional resources will be required. The feasibility of a strategy therefore needs to be considered in terms of the ability to obtain and integrate such resources – both inside the organisation and in the wider value network. Serious problems can result from the failure to think through resourcing needs across the business. Thus the public-sector expansion strategy of the contracting firm G4S was derailed in 2012 when it found it could not supply 10,000 security staff for the London Olympics just two weeks before the start of the Games: errors included over-optimistic initial estimates of what was needed, poor recruitment and training of staff, accommodation problems, faulty management information, and inadequate internal and external communications. As a result, G4S lost contracts with UK prisons, two directors had to resign and profits were down by one third for the year.

(11.6) EVALUATION CRITERIA: FOUR QUALIFICATIONS

There are four qualifications that need to be made to this chapter's discussion of evaluation criteria:

- *Conflicting conclusions and management judgement.* Conflicting conclusions can arise from the application of the criteria of suitability, acceptability and feasibility. A proposed strategy might look eminently suitable but not be acceptable to major stakeholders, for example. It is therefore important to remember that the criteria discussed here are useful in helping think through strategic options but are not a replacement for management judgement. Managers faced with a strategy they see as suitable, but which key stakeholders object to,

KEY DEBATE

What is the best approach to strategic investment decisions?

There are differences around the world in the bases and types of analyses used for strategic investment decisions (SIDs). Chris Carr has particularly highlighted the difference between the bases of SIDs in the USA and UK where shareholder models of governance prevail and countries where stakeholder models prevail such as Japan and, traditionally, Germany (see section 4.3.2). The differences highlighted are these:

- In the USA and UK there is an emphasis on financial bases of appraisal. This goes hand in hand with the widespread use of DCF as a financial basis of evaluation. In a set of studies carried out over a 10-year period, 100 per cent of managers in firms questioned in the USA reported using the DCF approach. The comparable figure in the UK was 50 per cent of firms. The widespread use of DCF also went hand in hand with expected internal rates of return for proposed projects. This focus on financial analysis was argued to be associated with the need to meet the expectations of the financial markets and, in particular, the pressures for short-term results due to the relatively arm's-length relationships with institutional investors in the USA and UK.

- In Japan and Germany there was an emphasis on broader bases of strategic appraisal and the importance of achieving long-term viable and secure market positioning. Here, the popularity of DCF was markedly less: in Germany (28 per cent) and Japan (18 per cent). Other methods of analysis such as *payback* and *return on capital employed* [ROCE] were more widely applied and rates of return expectations were lower, more flexible or, as in Japan, not much emphasised. All this may be because of firms' closer relationships with financial institutions (e.g. banks) or the higher incidence of family ownership (as in Germany) encouraging a longer-term perspective, reducing the threat of acquisition pressure and for short-term results.

Perhaps because of the emphasis on a broader strategic approach, there was also less of a concern with more sophisticated methods of financial appraisal.

The evidence of explanations lying in the governance systems seems to be borne out in Germany where changes are occurring. Here family ownership of firms remains common. In these firms, there appears to have been little change in the SID analysis over time. The preference is for measures of payback and ROCE at lower levels of target return and longer time frames: 5/7 years as opposed to 2/3 years in the USA and UK. But in the publicly owned corporations in Germany there has been a shift towards the US/UK approach.

Barwise, Marsh and Wensley have argued that there really should be no conflict between a financial and a strategic orientation: that good financial analysis complements rather than contradicts good strategy analysis, providing that, built into any financial analysis, there are assumptions about markets and bases of sustainable competitive advantage. So the role of financial analysis should be to highlight rather than mask such key issues.

Sources: C. Carr, 'Are German, Japanese and Anglo-Saxon strategic decision styles still divergent in the context of globalisation?', *Journal of Management Studies*, vol. 42, no. 6 (2005), pp. 1155–88; P. Barwise, P. Marsh and R. Wensley, 'Must finance and strategy clash?', *Harvard Business Review*, September–October (1989), pp. 85–90.

Questions

1 What are the arguments for the evaluation of strategic options being based on an emphasis:
(a) on financial bases of evaluation;
(b) broader strategic bases of evaluation?

2 What kinds of decisions are better suited to financial evaluation and what kind might require broader strategic forms of evaluation?

have to rely on their own judgement on the best course of action, but this should be better informed through the analysis and evaluation they have undertaken.

- *Consistency between the different elements of a strategy*. It should be clear from the chapters in Part II that there are several elements of a strategy, so an important question is whether the component parts work together as a 'package'. So *competitive strategy* (such as low cost or differentiation), strategy *direction* (such as product development or diversification) and *method*s of pursuing strategies (such as organic development, acquisition or alliances) need to be considered as a whole and be consistent. There are dangers if they are not. For example, suppose an organisation wishes to develop a differentiation strategy by building on its capabilities developed over many years to develop new products or services within a market it knows well. There may be dangers in looking to develop those new products through acquiring other businesses which might have very different capabilities that are incompatible with the strengths of the business.

- *The implementation and development of strategies* may throw up issues that might make organisations reconsider whether particular strategic options are, in fact, feasible or uncover factors that change views on the suitability or acceptability of a strategy. This may lead to a reshaping, or even abandoning, of strategic options. It therefore needs to be recognised that, in practice, strategy evaluation may take place through implementation, or at least partial implementation. This is another reason why experimentation, low-cost probes and real options evaluation may make sense.

- *Strategy development in practice*. More generally, it should not be assumed that the careful and systematic evaluation of strategy is necessarily the norm in organisations. Strategies may develop in other ways. This is the subject of Chapter 12 which follows. The final chapter (15) also explains what managers actually do in managing strategic issues.

SUMMARY

- Performance can be assessed in terms of both *economic* performance and overall organisational *effectiveness*.

- *Gap analysis* indicates the extent to which achieved or projected performance diverges from desired performance and the scale of the strategic initiatives required to close the gap.

- Strategies can be evaluated according to the three SAFe criteria of *suitability* in view of organisational opportunities and threats, *acceptability* to key stakeholders and *feasibility* in terms of capacity for implementation.

VIDEO ASSIGNMENTS

Visit *MyStrategyLab* and watch the SWAST case study for Chapter 11.

1 Using the video extracts, explain and discuss the measures of effectiveness that the South Western Ambulance Trust employs to monitor its organisational performance.

2 How can new technology help SWAST to improve its operational performance?

WORK ASSIGNMENTS

✱ *Denotes more advanced work assignments.*
* *Denotes case study in the Text and Case edition.*

11.1 Identify a quoted company (perhaps a company that you are interested in working for) and assess its share price performance over time relative to relevant national stock market indices (e.g. S&P 500 for the USA, CAC 40 for France or FTSE 100 for UK) and close competitors. (Sites such as Yahoo Finance or MSN.Money provide relevant data for free.)

11.2 Undertake a ranking analysis of the choices available to easySolution, Aids Alliance* or an organisation of your choice similar to that shown in Illustration 11.2.

11.3 Using the criteria of suitability, acceptability and feasibility undertake an evaluation of the strategic options that might exist for easySolution, AIDS Alliance*, Mexican NTOs*, HomeCo* or an organisation of your choice.

11.4 Undertake a risk assessment to inform the evaluation of strategic options for an organisation of your choice.

11.5 Write an executive report on how sources of funding need to be related to the nature of an industry and the types of strategies that an organisation is pursuing.

11.6✱ Using examples from your answer to previous assignments, make a critical appraisal of the statement that 'Strategic choice is, in the end, a highly subjective matter. It is dangerous to believe that, in reality, analytical techniques will ever change this situation.' Refer to the Commentary at the end of Part II of the book.

Integrative assignment

11.7 Explain how the SAFe criteria might differ between public- and private-sector organisations. Show how this relates to both the nature of the business environment (Chapter 2) and the expectations of stakeholders (Chapter 4).

RECOMMENDED KEY READINGS

- Readers may wish to consult one or more standard texts on finance. For example: G. Arnold, *Corporate Financial Management*, 5th edn, Financial Times Prentice Hall, 2012; P. Atrill, *Financial Management for Decision Makers*, 6th edn, Financial Times Prentice Hall, 2011.

- A classic paper that considers the relationship between financial approaches to evaluation and 'strategic' approaches is P. Barwise, P. Marsh and R. Wensley, 'Must finance and strategy clash?', *Harvard Business Review*, September–October (1989), pp. 85–90.

REFERENCES

1. This distinction between economic and effectiveness measures follows the distinction between performance and effectiveness in P. Richard, T. Devinney, G. Yip and G. Johnson, 'Measuring organizational performance: towards methodological best practice', *Journal of Management*, vol. 35 (2009), pp. 718–747.

2. R. Kaplan and D. Norton, 'Using the Balanced Scorecard as a strategic management system', *Harvard Business Review*, January–February (1996), pp. 75–85.

3. R. Mergenthaler, S. Rajgopal and S. Srinivasan, 'CEO and CFO career penalties to missing quarterly analysts forecasts', *Harvard Business School Working Paper*, no. 14 (2009).

4. R. Wiggins and T. Ruefli, 'Temporal dynamics and the incidence and persistence of superior economic performance', *Organization Science*, vol. 13, no. 1 (2002), pp. 82–105.

5. J. Denrell, 'Selection bias and the perils of benchmarking', *Harvard Business Review*, vol. 83, no. 4 (2005), pp. 114–19.

6. K. Cohen and R. Cyert, 'Strategy: formulation, implementation, and monitoring', *Journal of Business*, vol. 46, no. 3 (1973), pp. 349–67.

7. X. Zhang, K. Bartol and K. Smith, 'CEOs on the edge: earnings manipulation and stock-based incentive misalignment', *Academy of Management Journal*, vol. 51, no. 2 (2008), pp. 241–58.

8. B. Lev, 'How to win investors over', *Harvard Business Review*, November (2011), pp. 53–62.

9. M. Frigo and R. Anderson, 'Strategic risk management', *Journal of Corporate Accounting and Finance*, vol. 22, no. 3 (2011), pp. 81–8.

10. For those readers interested in the details of sensitivity analysis see A. Satelli, K. Chan and M. Scott (eds), *Sensitivity Analysis*, Wiley, 2000.

11. See C. Walsh, *Master the Management Metrics That Drive and Control Your Business*, 4th edn, Financial Times Prentice Hall, 2005.

12. Break-even analysis is covered in most standard accountancy texts. See, for example, G. Arnold, *Corporate Financial Management*, 4th edn, Financial Times Prentice Hall, 2009.

13. Most standard finance and accounting texts explain in more detail the financial analyses summarised here. For example, see G. Arnold (reference 12 above), Chapter 4.

14. The main proponent of shareholder value analysis is A. Rappaport, *Creating Shareholder Value: the New Standard for Business Performance*, 2nd edn, Free Press, 1998. See also R. Mill's chapter, 'Understanding and using shareholder value analysis', Chapter 15 in V. Ambrosini with G. Johnson and K. Scholes (eds), *Exploring Techniques of Analysis and Evaluation in Strategic Management*, Prentice Hall, 1998.

15. M.E. Raynor, 'End shareholder value tyranny: put the corporation first', *Strategy & Leadership*, vol. 37 no. 1 (2009), pp. 4–11.

16. This point is made clear in a research study reported by P. Haspeslagh, T. Noda and F. Boulos, 'It's not just about the numbers', *Harvard Business Review*, July–August (2001), pp. 65–73.

17. A 'classic' explanation of cost–benefit analysis is J.L. King, 'Cost–benefit analysis for decision-making', *Journal of Systems Management*, vol. 31, no. 5 (1980), pp. 24–39. A detailed example in the water industry can be found in: N. Poew, 'Water companies' service performance and environmental trade-off', *Journal of Environmental Planning and Management*, vol. 45, no. 3 (2002), pp. 363–79.

18. Real options evaluation can get lost in the mathematics, so readers wishing to gain more detail of how real options analysis works can consult one of the following: T. Copeland, 'The real options approach to capital allocation', *Strategic Finance*, vol. 83, no. 4 (2001), pp. 33–7; and P. Boer, *The Real Options Solution: Finding Total Value in a High Risk World*, Wiley, 2002. Also see M.M. Kayali, 'Real options as a tool for making strategic investment decisions', *Journal of American Academy of Business*, vol. 8, no. 1 (2006), pp. 282–7; C. Krychowski and B.V. Quelin, 'Real options and strategic investment decisions: can they be of use to scholars?', *Academy of Management Perspectives*, vol. 24, no. 2 (2010), pp. 65–78.

19. T. Luehrman, 'Strategy as a portfolio of real options', *Harvard Business Review*, vol. 76, no. 5 (1998), pp. 89–99.

20. See G. Arnold on funds flow analysis (reference 12 above), Chapter 3, p. 108.

21. See P. Atrill, *Financial Management for Decision Makers*, 4th edn, Financial Times Prentice Hall, 2006, Chapters 6 and 7; G. Arnold (reference 12 above), Part IV.

22. J. Nofsinger and W. Wang, 'Determinants of start-up firm external financing worldwide', *Journal of Banking and Finance*, vol. 35, no. 9 (2011), 2282–94.

23. These issues are based on those identified by C. Marsh, P. Sparrow, M. Hird, S. Balain and A. Hesketh, 'Integrated organization design: the new strategic priority for HR directors', in P.R. Sparrow, A. Hesketh, C. Cooper, and M. Hird (eds), *Leading HR*, Palgrave Macmillan, 2009.

EasySolution

The business idea

One thing always annoyed Camilla Oxley as she worked on her biochemistry doctorate at the University of Oxford. Each day she wasted about 20 minutes manually preparing the 'buffer solutions' in which she would carry out her experiments. She calculated that this repetitive and tedious task would consume about 500 hours across her whole time as a doctoral student.

Buffer solutions, though, were absolutely critical to her research work – and that carried out by about 150,000 laboratory research groups in the United Kingdom and USA alone. Buffer solutions involve creating varying mixes of liquid chemicals which must have an exact pH (acid–alkali balance) at a particular temperature. The mixes must be absolutely accurate for the reliability of the experiment. A bad mix could lead to the discarding of chemicals worth up to £100 (~€110; ~$150) or so per litre. Because of the tedium of daily preparation, researchers have been known to create large stocks of buffer solutions which deteriorated over time and so jeopardised the reliability of many weeks of experimental work.

Camilla believed that the tedious process of buffer solution preparation should be automated in a machine. After all, computers were helping to automate other parts of the experimental process. The average number of experiments carried out per day by researchers had trebled in recent years. Manual buffer solution preparation was becoming a bottle-neck.

Camilla mentioned her automation idea to fellow biochemistry doctoral student Jochen Klingelhoefer. Jochen had a background in electrical engineering and technical consulting and was also involved in Oxford University's entrepreneurial community. He knew that the university's business idea competition, Idea Idol, was coming up in March 2009. Camilla and he teamed together to prepare a two-minute 'elevator pitch' for a machine for the automated preparation of buffer solutions, called EasySolution. Against more than a hundred initial competitors, EasySolution emerged as winners of Idea Idol 2009.

Camilla Oxley preparing a buffer solution

After success at Idea Idol, everything began to snowball for EasySolution. The prize was worth £7,500, plus £2,000 worth of free advice from a local law firm. EasySolution's success had also attracted the attention of two Saïd Business School MBA students: Ville Lehtonen, with an MSc in computer sciences and experience in product management, business-to-business sales and private equity; and Andrew Hunt, a graduate in classical languages and with a prizewinning background in marketing. With Ville as Chief Executive Officer, Jochen as Chief Technology Officer, Andrew as Director for Business Development and Camilla as Chief Science Officer, the four formed an equally owned new company, LabMinds Ltd, in order to take EasySolution to market.

The business plan

The four started work on a business plan for the new company, eventually to be presented to a group of 'business angels' (early-stage investors) in September 2009. A survey of 200 potential users in the University of Oxford, plus discussions with product development companies, helped to refine the original product idea.

Table 1 **Product prices and costs**

	Sale	Maintenance
Revenue	£9,990	£1,500
Production cost	−£3,000	–
Delivery	−£750	–
Service	–	−£300
Replacement	–	−£120
VAT (15%)	−£814	−£141
Commission (20%)	−£1,085	−£188
Gross profit	£4,341	£751
Profit margin	43.5%	50.1%

EasySolution was now defined as a machine that could make exact mixes of solutions with precise pH values at particular temperatures, according to commands delivered via internet, intranet or touch screen. Creation of solutions would take one minute, and exact contents, time of creation and name of creator would be recorded in a log entry accessible to the laboratory manager. The proposed price of a machine was £9,990 (about €11,000), just below the level at which complex purchasing procedures are typically triggered in university laboratories. There would also be a maintenance charge of 15 per cent for the machine, in line with rates paid for comparable laboratory devices (see Table 1). The only similar machines were typically much larger: for example, the American scientific products giant Millipore manufactured systems capable of producing solutions of 100 litres upwards, against the 1 litre or so for EasySolution. The only substitute was the purchase of standard buffer solutions from large scientific supplies companies, but these were typically expensive (£20 upwards) and required ordering well in advance.

The business plan proposed development of the core EasySolution machine in five key phases (see Table 2). The first phase would be devoted to a feasibility study

funded by the founding team themselves, friends and family and hopefully grants from various government schemes supporting new businesses. The feasibility study, development and prototyping would be carried out by specialist companies DC Allen and Design Technology International Ltd. Development work would continue into phase 2, before production and launch of the core EasySolution product in phase 3. Phase 4 represents the continued growth of the company, leading towards eventual exit. Exit was expected to be in the form of either sale to an established large pharmaceutical or scientific equipment company or an initial public offering (IPO) to investors at large. The business plan pointed to the success of earlier start-ups in the specialised scientific products market, such as Harvard Bioscience and PerkinElmer, in achieving exit valuations based on net profit multiples of between 14 and 17.

Table 3 summarises the financial forecasts presented to investors. As above, the first year would be mostly concerned with development and investment. Sales were only expected to take off in year 2 (phase 3), with 350 units sold. By year 3, machine sales were expected to reach £15 m, with significant additional revenues from maintenance worth £1.65 m. Production and maintenance were to be outsourced to specialised companies. After production, delivery and maintenance costs, LabMinds expected a gross profit of more than £7 m in year 3.

Net profits in Table 3 came after significant operating (OPEX) and capital (CAPEX) expenditures. Operating expenditures planned in the first year included modest salaries for the management team, office charges, travel and marketing. In the second year, OPEX was expected to rise significantly, with the hiring of a finance director, an office manager, a software team and the building of a professional sales team for the USA as well as

Table 2 **LabMinds' proposed development stages**

Phase 1 (Month 1)	Development company DC Allen runs a feasibility study to identify not only the best way to create the whole system (based on the product specification by LabMinds), but also the easiest ways to get around core patents. The two core patents (likely described in product description) will be filed in this phase. Financing need: roughly £30,000
Phase 2 (Months 2–7)	Proof of principles created on a level where the system can be demonstrated to potential customers to support pre-sales efforts. The official goal is to be able to create any solution at any temperature and pH combination, and being able to prove the sterility of the machine. Financing need: roughly £150,000
Phase 3 (Months 8–19)	Prepare production. All the certifications necessary (nature of the product and the target market requires a rather wide range) will be acquired during this period. In parallel everything is being set up for mass production and the aesthetic aspects of the product are being finished. Financing need: roughly £500,000
Phase 4 (Unknown)	Day-to-day operations with sales and marketing clearly being in their element now. Financing need: roughly £1,000,000 mainly to fuel the marketing and sales efforts
Phase 5	Exit

Table 3 LabMinds' revenue, profit and investment forecasts

(000s)	Year 1	Year 2	Year 3
Unit sales	0	350	1500
Sales revenue		£3,496	£14,985
Maint revenue		£263	£1,650
Gross profit		£1,653	£7,345
OPEX	–£211	–£1,166	–£2,000
CAPEX	–£432	–£271	–£500
Net profit	–£643	£216	£4,845
Investment	£650	£1,000	
Government	£270	£126	
Debt financing	£25	£200	
Founding capital	£10		

the United Kingdom. Capital expenditures were more front-loaded. Plans in the first year included more than £400,000 for payment to the product development companies DC Allen and Design Technology International Ltd, and a further £21,000 to create a family of patents intended to protect LabMinds' intellectual property. The business plan predicted continuing capital expenditures on product development and patents for the second year, though at a lower rate. CAPEX was expected to rise again in year 3 with the development of further complementary machines.

Funding for the early years was expected to come from various sources. The founders themselves would put in an initial £15,000 and would raise convertible loans for a further £25,000 (a convertible loan gives the lender the option of converting the debt to equity). Various government support schemes were expected to contribute significantly, and a consultant was to be retained to assist in making grant applications. The most important source of funds, however, would be business angels and similar investors, with two rounds of invest-

ment in the first year and a third substantial one (£1 m) in the second. The investors in the first two rounds were expected to acquire about 40–50 per cent of the equity, and the investor in the third and largest round would receive just under 10 per cent of the equity. By the end of the second year, other employees and advisors were expected to hold a further 10 per cent or so of the equity. The business plan envisaged that at this point the original four founders would still own 25–35 per cent of a company valued at around £10 m.

Investors were being offered access to a potentially huge market. The LabMinds' team estimated the potential total market for EasySolution machines at about £1.0 bn annually in the United Kingdom and the USA alone. Annual maintenance revenues for this market could reach £150 m. But laboratories were not the only potential market. The business plan also pointed out that the basic technology could find other applications, for example in coffee-making or the preparation of cocktails for bars. LabMinds had a lot of upside.

Questions

1 Imagine that you are a potential investor hearing a short pitch from the EasySolution team based on the 2009 business plan. Using the SAFe framework, what questions would you raise with the team under:

   a Suitability?

   b Acceptability?

   c Feasibility?

2 If you were interested in investing in EasySolutions, which round of investment would you prefer to participate in? Why?

12

STRATEGY DEVELOPMENT PROCESSES

Learning outcomes

After reading this chapter you should be able to:

● Understand what is meant by *deliberate* and *emergent* strategy development.

● Identify deliberate processes of strategy development in organisations including: the role *of strategic leadership, strategic planning systems* and *externally imposed strategy*.

● Identify processes that give rise to emergent strategy development such as: *logical incrementalism, political processes, strategy as continuity* and *organisational systems*.

● Consider the implications and some of the challenges of managing strategy development in organisations.

Key terms

deliberate strategy p. 404

emergent strategy p. 410

learning organisation p. 411

logical incrementalism p. 411

strategic planning p. 405

(12.1) INTRODUCTION

We are familiar with successful strategies: Google's dominance of the internet; Ryanair becoming one of the most profitable airlines in the world; Apple's development of the iPhone and iPad; Zara's internationalisation in the fashion market. We also know about failed strategies: Kodak in photography, the Royal Bank of Scotland in banking; Saab's attempted internationalisation in automobiles. Much of Parts I and II of this book help us understand this. They addressed how strategists might understand the strategic position of their organisation and what strategic choices are sensible. However, none of this directly addresses the question that is the theme of this chapter: *how do strategies actually develop?* (Chapter 15 then examines in more detail which people get involved in these processes and what they actually do in developing strategies.)

Figure 12.1 summarises the structure of this chapter. It is organised around two views of strategy development: strategy as deliberate and strategy as emergent.[1] The *deliberate strategy* development view is that strategies come about as the result of the considered intentions of top management. It is a view in line with the *design view* of strategy development explained in the commentary sections of this book. The second view is that of *emergent strategy* development; that strategies do not develop on the basis of a grand plan but tend to emerge in organisations over time. The discussion in the Commentaries of the *experience* and *variety* lenses relates to this explanation. As the chapter will show, however, these two explanations of how strategies develop are not mutually exclusive. As Figure 12.1 shows, they are both likely to influence the eventual strategy that actually comes about – the *realised strategy*.

The next section (12.2) of the chapter discusses deliberate strategy development. First, there is an explanation of how strategies may be the outcome of *leadership*, *'command'* or *vision* of individuals. This is followed by a discussion of what formal *planning systems* in organisations might look like and the role they play. The section concludes by explaining how strategies

Figure 12.1 Deliberate and emergent strategy development

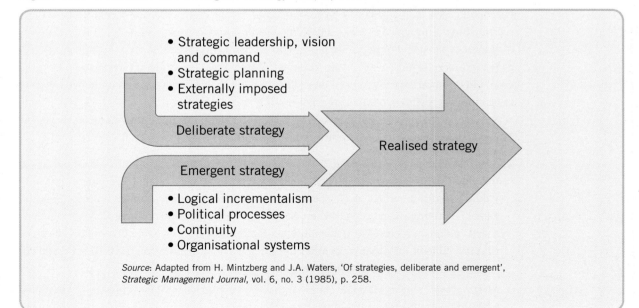

Source: Adapted from H. Mintzberg and J.A. Waters, 'Of strategies, deliberate and emergent', *Strategic Management Journal*, vol. 6, no. 3 (1985), p. 258.

might be deliberately *imposed* on organisations from the outside. Section 12.3 of the chapter then switches to explanations of how strategies might emerge in organisations. The section offers four explanations of how this might occur: *logical incrementalism*, the influence of *political processes* in organisations, strategy as *continuity* and finally how strategies could be the *outcome of organisational systems*. The final section of the chapter (12.4) raises *implications for managing strategy development* including:

- How different approaches to strategy development may be more or less well suited to *different contexts*.

- Some of the challenges that arise from managing the *processes of deliberate and emergent strategy*.

(12.2) DELIBERATE STRATEGY DEVELOPMENT

Deliberate strategy involves intentional formulation or planning. Such intentionality may take different forms. It could be the intentionality of a *strategic leader*, for example a CEO or the founder of a firm. It could be through a process of *strategic planning* involving many managers. Or it might be experienced as the *external imposition* of strategy formulated elsewhere.

12.2.1 The role of the strategic leader

An organisation's strategy may be influenced by strategic leaders: individuals (or perhaps a small group of individuals) whose personality, position or reputation makes them central to the strategy development process. This could be because he or she is the owner or founder of the organisation. This is often the case in small businesses and family businesses, but may also persist when a business becomes very large.[2] Such is the case with Richard Branson at Virgin or Ratan Tata of the Tata Corporation. Or it could be that an individual chief executive has played a central role in directing the strategy of an organisation, as with Mark Zuckerberg at Facebook or Michael O'Leary at Ryanair. Research has shown that founder CEOs and CEOs recruited to a firm typically make different contributions to strategic success, at least in terms of market expansion. Founders are more successful at achieving rapid growth in nascent, fast-growing markets, most likely by applying what they have learnt from their previous experience. CEOs that are recruited need more time to build their knowledge and influence but tend to be more successful in complex market conditions.[3]

Strategy, then, may be – or may be seen to be – the deliberate intention of a strategic leader. This may manifest itself in different ways:

- *Strategic leadership as command.* The strategy of an organisation might be dictated by an individual. This is, perhaps, most evident in owner-managed small firms, where that individual is in direct control of all aspects of the business. Canadian scholars Danny Miller and Isabel Le Breton-Miller[4] suggest there are advantages and disadvantages here. On the plus side it can mean speed of strategy adaptation and 'sharp, innovative, unorthodox strategies that are difficult for other companies to imitate'. The downside can, however, be 'hubris, excessive risk taking, quirky, irrelevant strategies'.

- *Strategic leadership as vision.* It could be that a strategic leader determines or is associated with an overall vision, mission, or strategic intent (see section 4.2) that motivates others, helps create the shared beliefs within which people can work together effectively and guides the more detailed strategy developed by others in an organisation. James Collins and Jerry Porras's study[5] of US firms with long-term high performance concluded that this is a centrally important role of the strategic leader. For example, Ingvar Kamprad, IKEA's founder's, vision, 'To create a better everyday life for the many', has motivated and guided subsequent generations of IKEA managers and staff.

- *Strategic leadership as decision making.* Whichever strategy development processes exist, there could be many different views on future strategy within an organisation and, perhaps, much but incomplete evidence to support those views. One of the key roles of leaders is to have the ability to weigh such different views, interpret data, have the confidence to take timely decisions to invest in key resources or markets and the authority to get others to buy into those decisions.

- *Strategic leadership as the embodiment of strategy.* A founder or chief executive of an organisation may represent its strategy. This may be unintentional but can also be deliberate: for example, Richard Branson no longer runs Virgin on a day-to-day basis, but he is seen as the embodiment of the Virgin strategy (see the Chapter 7 Case example) and is frequently the public face of the company.

Illustration 12.1 provides examples of how strategic leaders have influenced different aspects of strategy in their organisations.

12.2.2 Strategic planning systems

A second way in which intended strategies develop is through formalised **strategic planning**: **systematic analysis and exploration to develop an organisation's** strategy. In a study of strategic planning systems of major oil companies, Rob Grant[6] of Bocconi University noted the following stages in the planning cycle:

- *Initial guidelines.* The cycle's starting point is usually a set of guidelines or assumptions about the external environment (e.g. price levels and supply and demand conditions) and the overall priorities, guidelines and expectations of the corporate centre.

- *Business-level planning.* In the light of these guidelines, business units or divisions draw up strategic plans to present to the corporate centre. Corporate centre executives then discuss those plans with the business managers usually in face-to-face meetings. On the basis of these discussions the businesses revise their plans for further discussion.

- *Corporate-level planning.* The corporate plan results from the aggregation of the business plans. This coordination may be undertaken by a corporate planning department that, in effect, has a coordination role. The corporate board then has to approve the corporate plan.

- *Financial and strategic targets* are then likely to be extracted to provide a basis for performance monitoring of businesses and key strategic priorities on the basis of the plan.

Illustration 12.2 is a schematic representation of how strategic planning takes form in a large multinational drinks company.

Grant found that some of the companies he studied were much more formal and systematised than others (e.g. the French Elf Aquitaine and Italian ENI), with greater reliance on written reports and formal presentations, more fixed planning cycles, less flexibility and more specific

ILLUSTRATION 12.1

The influence of strategic leaders

Founders and chief executives may have a profound effect on an organisation's strategy.

On governance and purpose

In an interview Paul Polman, the Chief Executive of Unilever, said:[1]

'I don't think our fiduciary duty is to put share-holders first. I say the opposite. What we firmly believe is that if we focus our company on improving the lives of the world's citizens and come up with genuine sustainable solutions, we are more in synch with consumers and society and ultimately this will result in good shareholder returns. Why would you invest in a company which is out of synch with the needs of society, that does not take its social compliance in its supply chain seriously, that does not think about the costs of externalities, or of its negative impacts on society? . . . Historically, too many CEOs have just responded to shareholders instead of actively seeking out the right shareholders . . . Most CEOs go to visit their existing shareholders; we go to visit the ones we don't yet have.'

Polman reduced the holding of Unilever shares by hedge funds from 15 per cent in 2009 to less than 5 per cent by 2012.

On the focus of the strategy[2]

'It took ten years for Amazon.com to post a profit, but during that time, founder and CEO Jeff Bezos insisted that his customer-centric strategies were sound, and that they would build long-term strength and success for the company.'

Jeff Bezos claimed:

'If there's one reason we have done better than of our peers in the Internet space over the last six years, it is because we have focused like a laser on customer experience, and that really does matter, I think, in any business. It certainly matters online, where word of mouth is so very, very powerful.'

On envisioning the future[2]

Quotes from one of history's most famous fast food retailing leaders reveal what Ray Kroc was thinking as he built McDonald's:

'That night (in 1954) in my motel room I did a lot of heavy thinking about what I'd seen during the day. Visions of McDonald's restaurants dotting crossroads all over the country paraded through my brain.'

'The McDonald brothers were simply not on my wavelength at all. I was obsessed with the idea of making McDonald's the biggest and the best. They were content with what they had; they didn't want to be bothered with more risks and more demands.'

On the portfolio of a business

When Mike Jackson arrived as Chief Executive of car dealers AutoNation, the auto industry was selling as many as 17 million units a year, but its high fixed costs made him face what would happen if the economic environment changed. At his first management meeting he therefore announced his desire to find a business model that would let AutoNation break even if the auto industry sold only 10 million units: 'Everybody looked at me like I had six heads', he recalls. 'Eventually we came to the conclusion that amongst other things it would take a credit crisis to get volumes that low, because in our business nothing moves without credit. So we got out of the finance and leasing business.'[3]

Sources
1. Jo Confino; Guardian Professional Network, 24 April 2012.
2. Barbara Farfan, About.com Guide, 8 May 2012.
3. D. Carey, M. Patsalos-Fox and M. Useem, 'Leadership lessons for hard times', *McKinsey Quarterly*, July 2009.

Questions

1 Can you provide other examples of founders' or chief executives' influence on strategy?

2 What else would you emphasise as an important contribution CEOs make to strategy development?

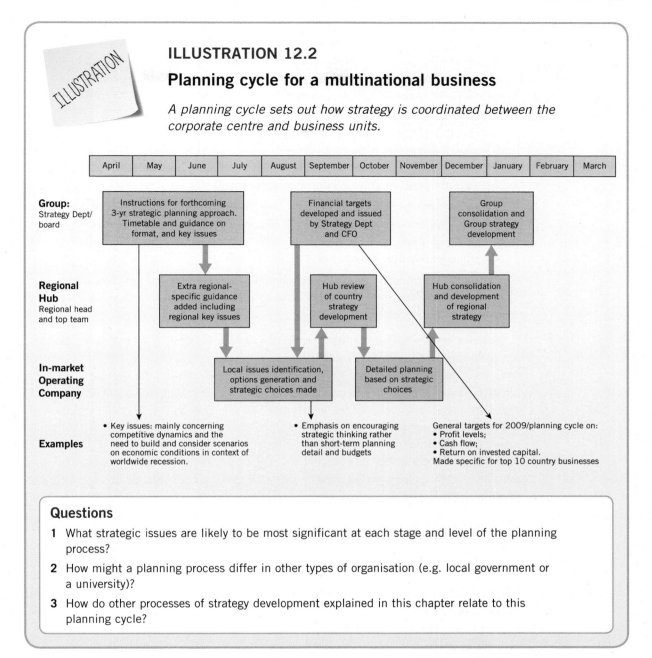

ILLUSTRATION 12.2

Planning cycle for a multinational business

A planning cycle sets out how strategy is coordinated between the corporate centre and business units.

April	May	June	July	August	September	October	November	December	January	February	March

Group:
Strategy Dept/
board

> Instructions for forthcoming 3-yr strategic planning approach. Timetable and guidance on format, and key issues

> Financial targets developed and issued by Strategy Dept and CFO

> Group consolidation and Group strategy development

Regional Hub
Regional head and top team

> Extra regional-specific guidance added including regional key issues

> Hub review of country strategy development

> Hub consolidation and development of regional strategy

In-market Operating Company

> Local issues identification, options generation and strategic choices made

> Detailed planning based on strategic choices

Examples

- Key issues: mainly concerning competitive dynamics and the need to build and consider scenarios on economic conditions in context of worldwide recession.

- Emphasis on encouraging strategic thinking rather than short-term planning detail and budgets

General targets for 2009/planning cycle on:
- Profit levels;
- Cash flow;
- Return on invested capital.
Made specific for top 10 country businesses

Questions

1 What strategic issues are likely to be most significant at each stage and level of the planning process?

2 How might a planning process differ in other types of organisation (e.g. local government or a university)?

3 How do other processes of strategy development explained in this chapter relate to this planning cycle?

objectives and targets relating to the formal plans. Where there was more informality or flexibility (e.g. BP, Texaco and Exxon), companies placed greater emphasis on more general financial targets. Central corporate planning departments also played different roles. In some organisations they acted primarily as coordinators of business plans. In others they were more like internal consultants, helping business unit managers to formulate their plans.

Strategic planning may play several roles. Typically four are emphasised:

- *Formulating* strategy by providing means by which managers can understand strategic issues, for example by establishing overall *objectives*, encouraging the use of *analytic tools* such as those explained in this book and by *encouraging a longer-term view* of strategy than might otherwise occur. Planning horizons and associated objectives and bases of analysis vary, of course. In a fast-moving consumer goods company 3- to 5-year plans may be appropriate. In companies which have to take very long-term views on capital investment, such as those in the oil industry, planning horizons can be as long as 15 years (in Exxon) or 20 years (in Shell).

- *Learning*: Rita McGrath and Ian MacMillan argue that managers can benefit from planning if they see it as a means of learning rather than a means of 'getting the right answers'. They emphasise 'discovery-driven' planning which emphasises the need for *questioning and challenging* received wisdom and the taken for granted.

- *Integraton*: Strategic planning systems may have the explicit purpose of *coordinating* business-level strategies within an overall corporate strategy. Paula Jarzabkowski and Julia Balogun[7] also show, however, that they can provide a valuable forum for negotiation and compromise and, thus, the reconciliation of different views on future strategy.

- *Communicating* intended strategy throughout an organisation and *providing clarity on the purpose and objectives* of a strategy *or strategic milestones* against which performance and progress can be reviewed.

However, it should be recognised that planning systems may also play other roles. If people are encouraged to be involved in planning processes it can help to create *ownership* of the strategy. Saku Mantere[8] at Helsinki University has also shown that it may provide a forum for *middle managers to influence* strategic issues beyond their operational responsibilities (he calls these 'strategy champions'). Strategic planning can also provide a *sense of security* and logic, not least among senior management who believe they *should* be proactively determining the future strategy and exercising control over the destiny of their organisation.

Henry Mintzberg has, however, challenged the extent to which planning provides such benefits.[9] Arguably there are five main dangers in the way in which formal systems of strategic planning have been employed:

- *Confusing managing strategy with planning.* Managers may see themselves as managing strategy when what they are doing is going through the processes of planning. Strategy is, of course, not the same as 'the plan': strategy is the long-term direction that the organisation follows – the realised strategy in Figure 12.1 – not just a written document. Linked to this may be a confusion between *budgetary processes* and strategic planning processes.[10] The two may come to be seen as the same so that strategic planning gets reduced to the production of financial forecasts rather than thinking through of the sort of issues discussed in this book. Of course it may be important to build the output of strategic planning into the budgetary process, but they are not the same.

- *Detachment from reality.* The managers responsible for the implementation of strategies, usually line managers, may be so busy with the day-to-day operations of the business that they cede responsibility for strategic issues to specialists or consultants. However, these rarely have power in the organisation to make things happen. The result can be that strategic planning becomes removed from the reality of operations and the experience and knowledge of operating managers. If formal planning systems are to be useful, those responsible for them need to draw on such experience and involve people throughout the organisation. In the absence of such involvement there is the danger that the resulting strategy is not owned widely in the organisation.

- *Paralysis by analysis.* Ann Langley[11] of HEC Montreal showed that planning can get bogged down in the interminable exchange of analytically based reports between different parties who do not agree or do not prioritise the same issues. Strategic planning can also become over-detailed in its approach, concentrating on extensive analysis that, while technically sound, misses the major strategic issues facing the organisation. It is not unusual to find companies with huge amounts of information on their markets, but with little clarity about the strategic importance of that information. The result can be *information overload* with no clear outcome.

- *Over-complex planning processes.* There is a danger that the process of strategic planning may be so cumbersome that it takes too long or, because individuals or groups contribute to only part of it, they do not understand the whole picture. The result can be that the realised strategy at one level, for example the business level, does not correspond to the intended strategy at the corporate level. This is particularly problematic in large multi-business firms.

- *Dampening of innovation.* Highly formalised and rigid systems of planning, especially if linked to very tight and detailed mechanisms of control, can contribute to an inflexible, hierarchical organisation with a resultant stifling of ideas and dampening of innovative capacity. This is a reason why new venture units are sometimes set up in larger firms, which do not have to follow their formalised planning systems (see section 9.4.3).

Strategic planning has continuously been ranked first or second in the survey of the use of management tools used in organisations conducted by Bain,[12] the management consultancy. However, the evidence of the extent to which the pursuit of such systemised planning results in organisations performing better than others is equivocal[13] – not least because it is difficult to isolate formal planning as the dominant or determining effect on performance. However, there is some evidence that planning may be beneficial if it is designed to work in conjunction with bottom-up emergent processes of strategy development,[14] a process that may be thought of as the 'planned emergence' of strategy. It may also be especially beneficial in dynamic environments, where decentralised authority for strategic decisions is required (see Chapter 13) but where there is a need for coordination of strategies arising from such decentralisation.[15]

While strategic planning remains common, there has been a decline in formal corporate planning departments[16] and a shift to business unit managers taking responsibility for strategy development and planning (see Chapter 15). Strategic planning has also become less a vehicle for top-down development of intended strategy and more of a vehicle for the coordination of strategy emerging from below.

12.2.3 **Externally imposed strategy**

Managers may face what they see as the imposition of strategy by powerful external stakeholders. Strategies being imposed in such ways may have been determined elsewhere, perhaps through systematic strategic planning, or they may have developed in a more emergent fashion (see section 12.3 below). However, to the managers of the organisation having it imposed on them, it is experienced as a top-down deliberate strategy.

For example, government may dictate a particular strategic direction as in the public sector, or where it exercises extensive regulatory powers in an industry. In the UK public sector direct intervention has been employed for schools or hospitals deemed to be under-performing badly, with specialist managers being sent in to turn round the ailing organisations and impose a new strategic direction. Government may also choose to deregulate or privatise a sector or organisation currently in the public sector. For example, in Scandinavia, and in Sweden in particular, schools, healthcare and public transport have been deregulated and private-sector companies are now actively engaged in their management. Businesses in the private sector may also be subject to such imposed strategic direction, or significant constraints on their choices. A multinational corporation seeking to develop businesses in some parts of the world may be subject to governmental requirements to do this in certain ways, perhaps through joint ventures or local alliances. An operating business within a multidivisional organisation may also regard the overall corporate strategic direction of its parent as akin to imposed strategy. Venture capitalists may also impose strategies on the businesses they acquire.[17]

(12.3) EMERGENT STRATEGY DEVELOPMENT

Although strategy development is often described as though it is the deliberate intention of top management, an alternative explanation is that of **emergent strategy**: that **strategies emerge on the basis of a series of decisions, which a pattern becomes clear over time**. This explains an organisation's strategy, not as a 'grand plan', but as a developing 'pattern in a stream of decisions'[18] where top managers draw together emerging themes of strategy from lower down in the organisation, rather than direct strategy from the top. The pattern that emerges may subsequently be more formally described, for example in annual reports and strategic plans, and be seen as the deliberate strategy of the organisation. It will not, however, have been the plan that developed the strategy; it will be the emerging strategy that informed the plan.

There are different explanations of emergent strategy[19] and this section summarises the main ones. They are: logical incrementalism, strategy as the outcome of political processes, as continuity and, finally, as the outcome of organisational systems and routines. All four emphasise that strategy development is not necessarily the province of top management alone, but may be more devolved within organisations. Figure 12.2 shows how the different explanations can be thought of in terms of a continuum according to how deliberately managed the processes are.

Figure 12.2 A continuum of emergent strategy development processes

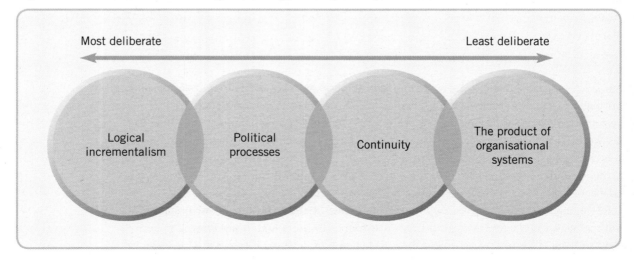

12.3.1 **Logical incrementalism**

The first explanation of how strategies may emerge is that of *logical incrementalism*. This explanation, in effect, bridges deliberate and emergent processes in that it explains how management may deliberately cultivate a bottom-up, experimental basis for strategies to emerge. Logical incrementalism was a term coined by James Quinn in his study of how strategies developed in multinational businesses. It is **the development of strategy by experimentation and learning** 'from partial commitments rather than through global formulations of total strategies'.[20] There are three main characteristics of strategy development in this way:

- *Environmental uncertainty.* Managers realise that they cannot do away with the uncertainty of their environment by relying on analyses of historical data or predicting how it will change. Rather, they try to be sensitive to environmental signals by encouraging constant environmental scanning throughout the organisation.

- *General goals.* There may be a reluctance to specify precise objectives too early, as this might stifle ideas and prevent innovation and experimentation. So more general rather than specific goals may be preferred, with managers trying to move towards them incrementally.

- *Experimentation.*[21] Managers seek to develop a strong, secure, but flexible, core business. They then build on the experience gained in that business to inform decisions both about its development and experimentation with 'side-bet' ventures. Commitment to strategic options may therefore be tentative in the early stages of strategy development. Such experiments are not the sole responsibility of top management. They emerge from what Quinn describes as '*subsystems*' in the organisation – groups of people involved in, for example, product development, product positioning, diversification, external relations and so on.

Quinn argued that, despite its emergent nature, logical incrementalism can be 'a conscious, purposeful, proactive, executive practice' to improve information available for decisions and build people's psychological identification with the development of strategy. Logical incrementalism therefore suggests that strategy development can be deliberate, whilst relying on organisational subsystems to sense what is happening in the environment and to try out ideas through experimentataion. It is a view of strategy development similar to the descriptions that managers themselves often give of how strategies come about in their organisations as Illustration 12.3 shows.

Arguably, developing strategies in such a way has considerable benefits. Continual testing and gradual strategy implementation provide improved quality of information for decision making and enable the better sequencing of the elements of major decisions. Since change will be gradual, the possibility of creating and developing a commitment to change throughout the organisation is increased. Because the different parts, or 'subsystems', of the organisation are in a continual state of interplay, the managers of each can learn from each other about the feasibility of a course of action. Such processes also take account of the political nature of organisational life, since smaller changes are less likely to face the same degree of resistance as major changes. Moreover, the formulation of strategy in this way means that the implications of the strategy are continually being tested out. This continual readjustment makes sense if the environment is considered as a continually changing influence on the organisation.

Given logical incrementalism's emphasis on learning, it is a view of strategy development which corresponds to the 'learning organisation'[22] – an organisation **that is capable of continual regeneration from the variety of knowledge, experience and skills within a culture that**

ILLUSTRATION 12.3

An incrementalist view of strategic management

Managers often see strategy as developing through continual adaptation to keep in line with the changing environment.

- 'You know there is a simple analogy you can make. To move forward when you walk, you create an imbalance, you lean forward and you don't know what is going to happen. Fortunately, you put a foot ahead of you and you recover your balance. Well, that's what we're doing all the time, so it is never comfortable.'[1]

- 'I begin wide-ranging discussions with people inside and outside the corporation. From these a pattern eventually emerges. It's like fitting together a jigsaw puzzle. At first the vague outline of an approach appears like the sail of a ship in a puzzle. Then suddenly the rest of the puzzle becomes quite clear. You wonder why you didn't see it all along.'[2]

- 'We haven't stood still in the past and I can't see with our present set-up that we shall stand still in the future; but what I really mean is that it is a path of evolution rather than revolution. Some companies get a successful formula and stick to that rigidly because that is what they know — for example, [Company X] did not really adapt to change, so they had to take what was a revolution. We hopefully have changed gradually and that's what I think we should do. We are always looking for fresh openings without going off at a tangent.'[3]

- 'In our business you cannot know the future; it's changing so fast. That's why I employ some of the best brains in the industry. Their job is to keep at the forefront of what's happening and, through what they are working on, to help create that future. I don't give them a strategic plan to work to; my job is to discern a strategy from what they tell me and what they are doing. Of course, they don't always agree — why would they, they can't *know* the future either — which means there's a good deal of debate, a good deal of trial and error and a good deal of judgement involved.'[4]

- 'The analogy of a chess game is useful in this context. The objective of chess is clear: to gain victory by capturing your opponent's king. Most players begin with a strategic move; that assumes a countermove by the opponent. If the countermove materialises, then the next move follows automatically, based on a previous winning strategy. However, the beauty of chess is the unpredictability of one's opponent's moves. To attempt to predict the outcome of chess is impossible, and therefore players limit themselves to working on possibilities and probabilities of moves that are not too far ahead.'[5]

Sources
1. Quotes from interviews conducted by A. Bailey as part of a research project sponsored by the Economic and Social Research Council (Grant No.: R000235100).
2. Extract from J.B. Quinn, *Strategies for Change*, Irwin, 1980.
3. Extracts from G. Johnson, *Strategic Change and the Management Process*, Blackwell, 1987.
4. CEO of a hi-tech business in an interview with a co-author.
5. From a manager on a MBA course.

Questions

1 With reference to these explanations of strategy development, what are the main advantages of developing strategies incrementally? Are there disadvantages or dangers?

2 Is incremental strategy development bound to result in strategic drift (see section 5.4)? How might this be avoided?

encourages questioning and challenge. Proponents of the learning organisation argue that formal structures and systems of organisations typically stifle organisational knowledge and creativity. They argue that the aim of top management should be to facilitate rather than direct strategy development by building pluralistic organisations, where ideas bubble up from below, conflicting ideas and views are surfaced and become the basis of debate; where knowledge is readily shared and experimentation is the norm such that ideas are tried out in action. The emphasis is not so much on hierarchies as on different interest groups that need to co-operate and learn from each other. In many respects there are similarities here to implications of the variety lens discussed in the Commentaries.

12.3.2 Strategy as the outcome of political processes

A second explanation of how strategies may emerge is that they are the outcome of the bargaining and power politics that go on between executives or between coalitions within an organisation and its major stakeholders. Managers may well have different views on issues and how they should be addressed; they are therefore likely to seek to position themselves such that their views prevail. They may also seek to pursue strategies or control resources to enhance their political status. The **political view of strategy development**[23] is, then, that **strategies develop as the outcome of bargaining and negotiation among powerful interest groups** (or stakeholders). This is the world of boardroom battles often portrayed in film and TV dramas.

A political perspective on strategic management suggests that the rational and analytic processes often associated with developing strategy (see section 12.2.2 above and the design lens in the Commentary) may not be as objective and dispassionate as they appear. Objectives may reflect the ambitions of powerful people. Information used in strategic debate is not always politically neutral. A manager or coalition may exercise power over another because they control important sources of information. Powerful individuals and groups may also strongly influence which issues get prioritised. In such circumstances it is bargaining and negotiation that give rise to strategy rather than careful analysis and deliberate intent. Indeed strategic planning processes, themselves, may provide an arena within which managers form coalitions to gain influence.

None of this should be surprising. In approaching strategic problems, people are likely to be differently influenced by at least:

- *Personal experience* from their roles within the organisation.

- *Competition for resources and influence* between the different subsystems in the organisation and people within them who are likely to be interested in preserving or enhancing their positions.[24]

- *The relative influence of stakeholders* on different parts of the organisation. For example, a finance department may be especially sensitive to the influence of financial institutions whilst a sales or marketing department will be strongly influenced by customers.

- *Different access to information* given their roles and functional affiliations.

In such circumstances there are two reasons to expect strategy development to build gradually on the current strategy. First, if different views prevail and different parties exercise their political muscle, compromise may be inevitable. Second, it is quite possible that it is from the pursuit of the current strategy that power has been gained by those wielding it. Indeed it may be very threatening to their power if significant changes in strategy were to occur. It is likely

ILLUSTRATION 12.4

Boardroom battles at Hewlett Packard

Political processes in organisations can influence the development of strategy.

By 2012 Hewlett Packard's (HP's) turnover exceeded $120 billion but profits were declining and it was losing share in its markets. For over a decade the difficulties in arriving at a coherent strategy were exacerbated by the infighting within the board.

In 2002 the then CEO, Carly Fiorina, publicly criticised Walter Hewlett, board member and son of the founder, for his opposition to the Compaq acquisition. According to Fortune, the HP board then was leaking confidential information to the press, accusing each other of lying and even refusing to be in the same room with one another.

Then under Mark Hurd's five years as CEO the emphasis was on cost cutting. Though the share price increased significantly, this disguised a demoralised workforce and a lack of innovation, not helped by Hurd's autocratic leadership style. In 2010 Mark Hurd departed. The exit was fractious with a fellow director, Hurd supporter Joel Hyatt, openly criticising the investigation headed by two other directors that led to it.

The next CEO was an outsider, Leo Apotheker, who had been sacked as CEO of SAP in 2010 – a surprise appointment not least because SAP was much smaller than HP. Initially, however, he improved employee morale, undoing Hurd's salary cuts and making known his wish to return to innovative ways.

The decision was taken to reshuffle the board. Board members lobbied, both for themselves but also against other board members, not least Hyatt. Chairman Ray Lane asked that Hyatt and another of Hurd's supporters stand down, but 'as a matter of balance' asked the two who had led the Hurd investigation to stand down too.

In May 2011 Apotheker issued a profits warning internally, with a plea to 'watch every penny'. The email was leaked and, made public, contradicted the positive messages given to investors. It became apparent that 'Apotheker seemed not to trust (some) longstanding HP executives . . . they returned the sentiment'.

Apotheker believed that HP should focus on business-to-business sales for PCs and printers, move into higher-margin areas, spin off its PC division and invest significantly in its software business. There was also the launch of a tablet computer in 2011 but it was 'ungainly, slow . . . with a subpar battery' and flopped.

Apotheker also wanted to acquire the British data company, Autonomy. CFO Cathie Lesjak and Apotheker discussed the matter privately, but she then argued to the board that it was overpriced and 'not in the best interests of the company . . . Lesjak was considered a voice of sobriety and here she was on the verge of insubordination, directly resisting a key element of her boss's strategy'.

In August the Autonomy deal, the possible spin-off and the decision to end the tablet initiative were announced to investors. Shares plunged, many PC customers ceased dealing with HP and investors objected to a major acquisition.

In mid-September Apotheker learnt of his dismissal in the press before he was told personally by Lane that he had lost board support. Lane then argued that the failures were Apotheker's not the current board's, since it had not selected him.

Meg Whitman was then appointed CEO. Her strategy seemed to be 'better . . . execution of what (HP) were doing to give time to sort out a long term strategy'. The share price dropped still further.

Source: Based on quotes from Fortune Global Forum, 8 May 2012 James Bandler, Doris Burke; http://tech.fortune.cnn.com/2012÷05/08/500-hp-apotheker/.

Questions

1 Identify other examples of political activity at the top of organisations that affected strategy.

2 What bases of political influence might executives draw on in disagreements between themselves?

that a search for a compromise solution accommodating different power bases will end up with a strategy which is an adaptation of what has gone before. Illustration 12.4 shows how political influence at board level has affected strategy development at Hewlett Packard.

There are, however, more positive ways of seeing political processes. The conflict and tensions that manifest themselves in political activity, arising as they do from different expectations or interests, can be the source of new ideas[25] (see the discussion on the variety lens in the Commentaries) or challenges to old ways of doing things. New ideas may be supported or opposed by different 'champions' who will battle over what is the best idea or the best way forward. Arguably, if such conflict and tensions did not exist, neither would innovation. Further, as section 14.4.6 shows, the exercise of power may be important in the management of strategic change.

12.3.3 Strategy as continuity

A third explanation of how strategies may emerge is as the product of established ways of doing things or of prior decisions which inform or constrain strategy development. In many ways this is to be expected. It would be strange and, arguably, dysfunctional for an organisation to change its strategy fundamentally very often, especially if it has been successful. So one way of explaining emergent strategy is that managers seek to maintain a continuity of strategy. There are, however, also explanations that suggest that such continuity may be less deliberate; that it could be the outcome of path dependency or of organisational culture:

- *Emergent strategy as managed continuity*. The strategy of an organisation may develop on the basis of a series of strategic moves each of which makes sense in terms of previous moves. Figure 12.3 illustrates this. A business may start with a new product idea. Its initial success may give rise to product development and product extensions building on this initial success. Investment in resources to support and develop the growing business might follow. There may then be launches of the product into new markets. Over time the company may then become more acquisitive, perhaps seeking to diversify into related products. In this way each strategic move is informed by the rationale of the previous strategic move, such that over time the overall strategic approach of the organisation becomes more and more established. It is common to find management justifying successive strategic moves in this way.

- *Path-dependent strategy development*. There is, however, a less deliberate explanation of such continuity. Path dependency was explained in section 5.2. Path dependency is where early events and decisions establish 'policy paths' that have lasting effects on subsequent events and decisions.[26] It therefore explains strategic decisions as historically conditioned. It also adds a degree of potential perversity to the pattern of continuity. The same decision sequence shown in the sort of incremental progression explained in Figure 12.3 may hold even if the opening move (in this case a product launch) is not especially successful. For example, a company may develop a product based on technology to which it is wedded and on the basis of which there is some initial success in the market. However, even if the initial success does not continue, further product development and product extensions may take place, perhaps because the company has invested large amounts of capital in the technology. Mixed success with these new products may then encourage managers to acquire another company in a related area in an attempt to strengthen the initial product range. Experience with this acquisition gives managers confidence to make further acquisitions in more diversified product areas. Thus the business ends up as a widely diversified company

Figure 12.3 Strategic direction from prior decisions

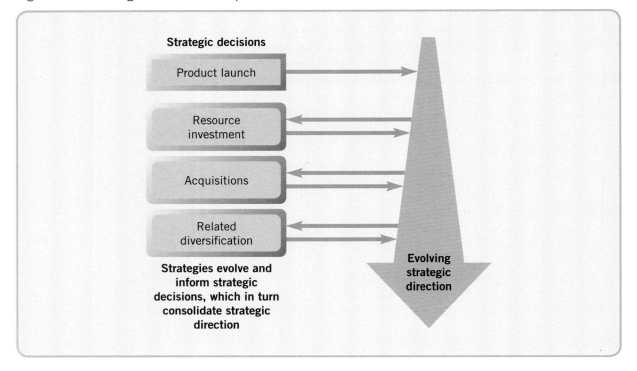

when it originally sought only to launch a single new product. In effect the company pursues a strategy in which it reinforces sub-optimal prior strategic decisions: they 'dig the hole deeper'.

- *Organisation culture and strategy development.* The influence of culture on strategy was also explained in section 5.4. Here the emphasis is on strategy development as the outcome of the taken-for-granted assumptions, routines and behaviours in organisations. This taken-for-grantedness works to define, or at least guide, how people view their organisation and its environment. It also tends to constrain what is seen as appropriate behaviour and activity. It is very likely, then, that decisions about future strategy will be within the bounds of the culture and that a pattern of continuity will be the outcome, subsequently post-rationalised by managers. Examples of this are given in Chapter 5 together with the potential problems that can arise. Not least among these is that such culturally bounded strategy development can lead to strategic drift (see section 5.4).

12.3.4 **Strategy as the product of organisational systems**

A fourth explanation of how strategies may emerge is on the basis of an organisation's systems. Rather than seeing strategy development as about foresight and anticipation taking form in directive plans from the top of the organisation, strategy development can be seen as the outcome of managers at much lower levels making sense of and dealing with problems and opportunities by applying established ways of doing things. There are echoes here of logical incrementalism, but there is less emphasis on deliberate experimentation. Rather the emphasis is on the influence of the systems and routines with which managers are familiar and which guide and constrain their decisions. Two useful explanations have developed as to how this occurs: the resource allocation process[27] (RAP) explanation of strategy development and the attention-based view[28] (ABV) of strategy development. Both support the argument advanced by Harvard's Joe Bower and Clark Gilbert that: 'The cumulative impact of the allocation of resources by managers at any level has more real-world effect on strategy than any plans developed at headquarters.'[29]

A classic example of how the resource allocation process can influence strategy is Robert Burgelman's study[30] of how Intel became a microprocessor company in the 1980s. This is explained in Illustration 12.5. There are two main insights that this explanation of strategy development offers, shown graphically in Figure 12.4:

- *Organisational systems as a basis for making sense of issues.* Managers are likely to make sense of issues they face on the basis of the systems and routines with which they are familiar and which directly affect them. For example, a finance director will be primarily concerned with the financial systems of the organisation or an operations director with operations. Managers within a business unit will be primarily concerned with the systems relating to that business; managers at the corporate level with systems at that level. Reward systems for company directors based on year-on-year earnings growth can encourage a focus on short-term rather than long-term strategies. Overhead allocation routines can exaggerate the profitability of some products or services and therefore encourage their perceived significance and development at the expense of others. Targets set by government for those managing public services can result in a focus on some issues at the expense of others.

Figure 12.4 Strategy development as the product of structures, systems and routines

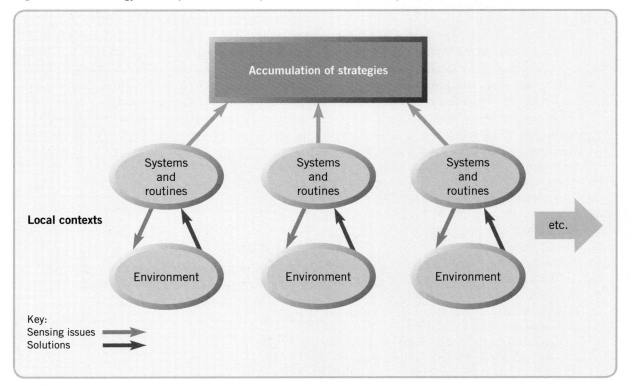

ILLUSTRATION 12.5

The development of the microprocessor business at Intel

Resource allocation systems rather than management's intention may drive strategy development.

Between 1968 and 1985 Intel specialised in integrated circuit memory products. By the early 1980s it had two main product areas. DRAM (Dynamic Random Access Memory) had been the basis of the firm's growth and top management remained committed to R&D investment in it. However, given increased competition, DRAMs had lost market share. EPROM (Erasable Programmable Read Only Memory) had become Intel's most profitable product. There was also the emerging business in microprocessors. Microprocessors, however, involved different processes, with an emphasis on chip design rather than manufacturing processes as in the other product areas.

By the end of the 1980s, however, it was the microprocessor business that emerged as the basis of Intel's future growth and identity. This did not happen because of top management's planned direction. They remained committed to the memory business. However, in a company in which there had been an ethos of top-down financial rigour, a resource allocation rule had been created by the first finance director designed to maintain Intel as a technological leading-edge company. It stipulated that manufacturing capacity was allocated in proportion to the profit margins achieved in the different product sectors.

The emphasis within the DRAM group was on finding sophisticated technical solutions to DRAM's problems; it was, however, innovation in markets where innovation was no longer commerically viable. DRAM managers none the less continued to fight to have manufacturing capacity assigned purely to DRAM, proposing that capacity be allocated on the basis of manufacturing cost. Senior management refused, however, to change the basis of resource allocation.

By the early 1980s DRAMs amounted to only 5 per cent of Intel's revenue, down from 90 per cent. Since DRAM profits were also declining and microprocessor profits were increasing, over time DRAM lost manufacturing capacity within Intel to the microprocessor area. Once this decision was made to keep the resource allocation rule, the strategic freedom left to corporate managers to recover the founding businesses to which they were very attached diminished as market share fell beyond what could be deemed worthwhile recovering. DRAM managers had to compete internally with the technological prowess of the other product areas where morale and excitement were at high levels and innovation was happening in an increasingly dynamic market. And as microprocessors became more and more profitable, the business received increased funding, with manufacturing capacity and investment increasingly allocated away from memory towards them, providing it with the basis for future growth. Eventually corporate managers realised that Intel would never be a player in the 64K DRAM memory game, despite having been the creator of the business. In 1985, top management came to realise they had to withdraw from the DRAM market.

Lingering resistance to the exit continued. Manufacturing personnel ignored implications of exiting from DRAM by trying to show they could compete in the marketplace externally, by explaining failure in terms of the strong dollar against the Japanese yen and battling with poor morale. Eventually Andy Grove, CEO from 1987, took the executive decision to withdraw from EPROM too, leaving no doubt that microprocessors now represented Intel's future strategic direction. The subsequent exit from EPROM was rapidly executed. Staff associated with EPROM left and set up their own business.

Source: Based on the case study on Intel by Jill Shepherd (Segal Graduate School of Business, Simon Fraser University, Canada) in 8th edition of *Exploring Corporate Strategy*, Pearson, 2008.

Questions

1 What other examples can you think of where resource allocation processes strongly influence strategy development?

2 What role should top management play in relation to resource allocation processes in organisations?

Vertical reporting relationships in hierarchies will focus managers' attention on issues within their part of the organisation as distinct from cooperating on wider issues across the wider organisation. Managers in a business unit, close to a market, may pay attention to routines and systems to do with competitors and customers whereas senior corporate executives may be concerned with balancing resource allocation across businesses, with systems relating to financial markets and with government regulation. This is one reason why middle-management concerns about changes in markets may go unheeded.[31]

Whereas top-down explanations of strategy development assume that managers' focus of attention will readily cohere around clearly identified overarching 'strategic issues', this explanation emphasises that (i) it may not be analysis of an organisation's overall strategic position so much as local systems that surface issues that get attended to; and (ii) such issues are likely to be locally defined.

● *Organisational systems provide bases of solutions to strategic issues.* Systems and routines also provide solutions that managers can draw on when faced with problems. However, responses may differ depending on the context the managers are in and the associated systems and routines. A common example is the way in which different responses emerge as a result of a downturn in company performance. Marketing managers, seeing this as a downturn in the market, may originate solutions which are to do with sales promotion and advertising to generate more sales, research and development managers may see it as a need for product innovation and accountants may see it as a need for tighter controls and cost cutting. Each is drawing on the context in which they find themselves and the associated systems and routines for dealing with such problems.

Again it should be emphasised that this explanation of strategy development does not exclude other explanations. For example, it helps explain why strategy development is likely to be a political process (section 12.3.2) since it recognises that there will be different perceptions of strategic issues and different views on solutions. The explanation does, however, de-emphasise top-down strategic planning and suggests it is an accumulation of local decisions strongly influenced by local context that accounts for strategy development. It may be, however, that such local decisions are then post-rationalised into an apparently coherent strategy in the form of a strategic plan. There is also evidence that the sponsors of successful exploratory and innovatory local initiatives tend to employ rational justification and draw on formal authority in support of such initiatives.[32]

(12.4) IMPLICATIONS FOR MANAGING STRATEGY DEVELOPMENT

It should be clear from the different explanations of strategy development processes that they are not discrete or mutually exclusive: multiple processes are likely to be evident.[33] For example, planning systems exist in most large organisations, but there will also undoubtedly be political activity; indeed the planning system itself may be used for negotiating purposes. There will also be a history of prior strategic decisions and established systems and procedures which will affect future decisions. As was explained at the beginning of the chapter, then, the strategy of an organisation is likely to develop in both deliberate and emergent ways.

It is also likely that processes of strategy development will be seen differently by different people. For example, senior executives tend to see strategy development in terms of deliberate,

Figure 12.5 Strategy development in different contexts

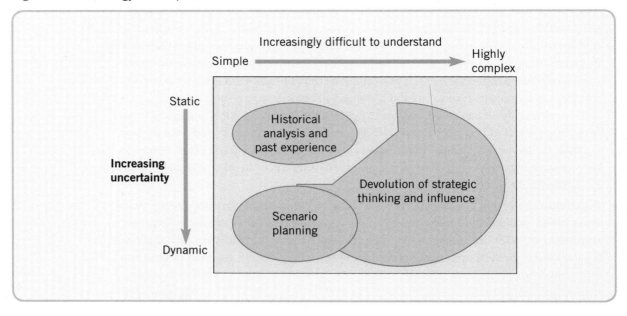

rational, analytic planned processes, whereas middle managers see strategy development more as the result of cultural and political processes. Managers in public-sector organisations tend to see strategy as externally imposed more than managers in commercial businesses, largely because their organisations are answerable to government bodies.[34] People who work in family businesses tend to see more evidence of the influence of powerful individuals, who may be the owners of the businesses. The chapter's Key Debate shows very different accounts of the strategy development for a highly successful strategy.

12.4.1 **Strategy development in different contexts**

Whilst there is no one right way in which strategies are developed, it is helpful if managers recognise the potential benefits and pitfalls of different processes of strategy development. Organisations differ in their size, form and complexity. They also face different environments, so different processes for managing strategy may make sense in different circumstances. Figure 12.5 provides a way of considering this by showing how organisations may seek to cope with conditions which are more or less stable or dynamic and simple or complex:[35]

● In *simple/static* conditions, the environment is relatively straightforward to understand and is not undergoing significant change. The organisation itself is also not overly complex; for example, it may be operating in a single market or with a narrow portfolio. Raw materials suppliers and some mass-manufacturing companies are examples. In such circumstances, if environmental change does occur, it may be predictable, so it could make sense to analyse the environment extensively on an historical basis as a means of trying to forecast likely future conditions. In situations of relatively low complexity, it may also be possible to identify some predictors of environmental influences. For example, in public services, demographic data such as birth rates might be used as lead indicators to determine the required provision of schooling, healthcare or social services. So in simple/static conditions systematic strategic planning is possible, perhaps with central planners taking the lead. It is also likely that past experience and prior decisions will be a significant influence since little is changing. The potential problem is, of course, that conditions change; for example, the environment becomes more dynamic and the established processes are not suited to such conditions.

● In *dynamic* conditions, managers need to consider the environment of the future, not just of the past. The degree of uncertainty therefore increases. They may employ structured ways of making sense of the future, such as *scenario planning*, discussed in section 2.2.2, or they may rely more on encouraging active sensing of environmental changes lower down in the organisation where people are operating closer to the changes that are taking place, for example in the market or in technology. Organisations seek to do this in various ways. For example, through strategy workshops and more open strategy making involving much wider participation in strategy development (see sections 15.2.5 and 15.4.1) or by seeking to create organisational conditions that encourage individuals and groups to be sensitive to signals from the changing environment, forward thinking and challenging, approximating to *logical inrementalism* and *organisational learning* (section 12.3.1).

● Organisations in *complex* situations face an environment difficult to comprehend. For example, a multinational firm, or a major public service such as a local government authority with many services, is complex because of its diversity. In such circumstances such organisations may seek structural solutions; for example, they may subdivide their organisation into units where managers have particular expertise and have responsibility for strategic decision making within those units (see section 13.2.2). Such organisations may, of course, also face dynamic conditions and therefore a combination of complexity and uncertainty. With more and more sophisticated technology, there is an increasing move towards this condition of greatest uncertainty. In such circumstances it is simply not feasible for top management to understand all the influences on future strategy so there will be an even greater need to devolve strategy thinking and influence within the organisation.

Considering the ways in which strategy may be developed in different contexts in turn has a number of implications:

● *The top management role in strategy development.* Do top managers see themselves as the detailed planners of strategy throughout the organisation; as the ones who set broad strategic direction and cultivate managers below them who can develop more detailed strategies; or as developing their own capabilities to detect and build upon strategies and strategic ideas as they emerge from within the rest of the organisation?

● *Different strategy development roles at different organisational levels.* A study of corporate parents' relationship to their business units or subsidiaries[36] found that there were distinct differences in the strategy development approaches and roles at these different levels. The business units/subsidiaries were playing the experimental role. Highly reliant on informal contacts with their markets, managers' decisions were made largely on the basis of their experience. The executives at the centre were more concerned with the search for order throughout the business and therefore on planning, building on existing resources and refining existing strategy. While this study was industry specific – the telecommunications industry – it does make the point that managers at different levels will likely play different roles. So the building of productive dialogue between the different levels may be very important.

● *The roles of strategic planning.* Strategic planning has different roles to play. The simpler the conditions faced by the organisation, the more it may be possible for planning to direct the strategy. The more the strategy development is devolved, however, the more there is likely to be the problem of the coordination of an overall strategy for an organisation. In such circumstances strategic planning may also play a role but as a coordinating and communication mechanism. This may be useful because it may be important that there is a formal explanation of the strategy for the stakeholders of the organisation. The danger, however, is that planning does little more than pull together 'received wisdom' such that it merely post-rationalises where the organisation has come from. If strategic planning systems are to

KEY DEBATE

Honda and the US motorcycle market in the 1960s

There are different explanations of how successful strategies develop.

In 1984, Richard Pascale published a paper which described the success Honda had experienced with the launch of its motorcycles in the US market in the 1960s. It was a paper that has generated discussion about strategy development processes ever since. First he gave explanations provided by the Boston Consulting Group (BCG):

'The success of the Japanese manufacturers originated with the growth of their domestic market during the 1950s. This resulted in a highly competitive cost position which the Japanese used as a springboard for penetration of world markets with small motorcycles in the early 1960s . . . The basic philosophy of the Japanese manufacturers is that high volumes per model provide the potential for high productivity as a result of using capital intensive and highly automated techniques. Their market strategies are therefore directed towards developing these high model volumes, hence the careful attention that we have observed them giving to growth and market share.'

Thus the BCG's account is a rational one based upon the deliberate intention of building up a cost advantage based on volume.

Pascale's second version of events was based on interviews with the Japanese executives who launched the motorcycles in the USA:

'In truth, we had no strategy other than the idea of seeing if we could sell something in the United States. It was a new frontier, a new challenge, and it fitted the "success against all odds" culture that Mr Honda had cultivated. We did not discuss profits or deadlines for breakeven . . . We knew our products . . . were good but not far superior. Mr Honda was especially confident of the 250cc and 305cc machines. The shape of the handlebar on these larger machines looked like the eyebrow of Buddha, which he felt was a strong selling point . . . We configured our start-up inventory with 25 per cent of each of our four products – the 50cc Supercub and the 125cc, 250cc and 305cc machines. In dollar value terms, of course, the inventory was heavily weighted towards the larger bikes . . . We were entirely in the dark the first year. Following Mr Honda's and our own instincts, we had not attempted to move the 50cc Supercubs . . . They seemed wholly unsuitable for the US market where everything was bigger and more luxurious . . . We used the Honda 50s be useful it is, then, important that they encourage the challenge of received wisdom and ways of doing things.

- *Strategic inflection points.* Robert Burgelman and Andy Grove[37] argue that all organisations face what they call 'strategic inflection points' where there are shifts in fundamental industry dynamics which management need to recognise and act upon. In such circumstances it may well be that the symptoms are recognised by managers close to such changes who may then press for changes in strategy. The problem may be that other, perhaps top, management may be busily working to maximise their competitive advantage and returns in the prevailing industry structure. The result could be a build-up of 'dissonance' within the organisation. Burgelman and Grove argue that top managers need to learn when to take such dissonance seriously. This relates to the challenge of organisational ambidexterity which is discussed more fully in section 14.5.4.

---

ourselves to ride around Los Angeles on errands. They attracted a lot of attention. But we still hesitated to push the 50cc bikes out of fear they might harm our image in a heavily macho market. But when the larger bikes started breaking, we had no choice. And surprisingly, the retailers who wanted to sell them weren't motorcycle dealers, they were sporting goods stores.'

Two very different accounts, yet they describe the same market success. Since the publication of the paper, many writers on strategy have hotly debated what these accounts actually represent. For example, Henry Mintzberg observed: 'the conception of a novel strategy is a creative process (of synthesis), to which there are no formal techniques (analysis)'. He argued any formal planning was in the implementation of the strategy: 'strategy had to be conceived informally before it could be programmed formally'. He went on to add, 'While we run around being "rational", they use their common sense . . . they came to America prepared to *learn*.'

Michael Goold, the author of the original BCG report, defended it on the grounds that:

'its purpose was to discern what lay behind and accounted for Honda's success in a way that would help others to think through what strategies would be likely to work. It tries to discern patterns in Honda's strategic decisions and actions and to use these patterns in identifying what works well and badly.'

Richard Rumelt concluded that:

'the "design school" is right about the reality of forces like scaled economies, accumulated experience and accumulative development of core competences over time . . . but my own experience is that coherent strategy based upon analyses and understandings of these forces is much more often imputed than actually observed'.

And Pascale himself concluded that the serendipitous nature of Honda's strategy showed the importance of learning; that the real lessons in developing strategies were the importance of an organisation's agility and that this resides in its culture, rather than its analyses.

Sources: This case example is based on R.T. Pascale, 'Perspectives on strategy: the real story behind Honda's success', *California Management Review*, vol. 26, no. 3 (Spring 1984), pp. 47–72; and H. Mintzberg, R.T. Pascale, M. Goold and R.P. Rumelt, 'The Honda effect revisited', *California Management Review*, vol. 38, no. 4 (1996), pp. 78–116.

Questions

1 Are the different accounts mutually exclusive?

2 Which of the different explanations of strategy development explained in the chapter do you discern in the Honda story?

3 Do you think Honda would have been more or less successful if it had adopted a more formalised strategic planning approach to the launch?

12.4.2 **Managing deliberate and emergent strategy**

This chapter began by drawing the distinction between deliberate and emergent strategy and has shown that in most organisations there are processes at work that are characteristic of both. There are some issues that arise from a recognition of this:

- *Unrealised strategy.* There will, very likely, be aspects of a deliberate strategy that do not come to be realised in practice. There are several reasons for this: the environment changes and managers decide that the strategy, as planned, should not be put into effect; the plans prove to be unworkable or unacceptable in practice; or the emergent strategy comes to dominate. There is, however, a danger. Managers may espouse a deliberate strategy, perhaps the result of a strategic planning process, but the organisation may be following a different strategy in reality. We experience this as customers of organisations that have stated strategies quite different from what we experience – government agencies that are there purportedly to serve our interests but act as bureaucratic officialdom, companies that claim they offer excellent customer service but operate call centres that frustrate customers and fail to solve problems, universities that claim excellence of teaching but are more concerned with their staff's research, or vice versa. It should not, however, be assumed that top managers are always close enough to customers to understand the extent of difference between what is intended as the strategy and what is actually happening. Managers need to take steps to check if the deliberate strategy is actually being realised.

- *Managing emergent strategy.* The processes of strategy development that give rise to emergent strategy may be rooted in organisational routines and culture, but they are not unmanageable. Indeed, this is as much about managing strategy as is strategic planning. Resource allocation processes can be changed; political processes can be analysed and managed (see section 4.5.2 on stakeholder analysis); challenge to the norms and routines of organisational culture can be encouraged. A clear mission or vision can help direct the bottom-up strategy development and strategic planning systems can help coordinate the outcomes of such processes.

- *The challenge of strategic drift.* A major strategic challenge facing managers was identified in section 5.4 as the risk of strategic drift: the tendency for strategies to develop incrementally on the basis of historical and cultural influences, but fail to keep pace with a changing environment. The explanations of emergent strategy in section 12.3 of this chapter suggest that such a pattern may be a natural outcome of the influence of prior decisions, organisational culture and political processes. This further highlights that strategy development processes in organisations need to encourage people to have the capacity and willingness to challenge and change their core assumptions and ways of doing things.

SUMMARY

This chapter has dealt with different ways in which strategy development occurs in organisations. The main lessons of the chapter are:

- It is important to distinguish between *deliberate* strategy – the desired strategic direction deliberately planned by managers – and *emergent strategy*, which may develop in a less deliberate way from the behaviours and activities inherent within an organisation.

- Most often the process of strategy development is described in terms of a deliberately formulated intended strategy as a result of *planning systems* carried out objectively and dispassionately. There are benefits and disbenefits of formal strategic planning systems. However, there is evidence to show that such formal systems are not an adequate explanation of strategy development as it occurs in practice.

- Deliberate strategy may also come about on the basis of central *command, the vision of strategic leaders* or the *imposition of strategies* by external stakeholders.

- Strategies may emerge from within organisations. This may be explained in terms of:

  - How organisations may proactively try to cope through processes of *logical incrementalism and organisational learning.*

  - The outcome of the bargaining associated with *political activity* resulting in a negotiated strategy.

  - Strategy development on the basis of *continuity* rooted in *prior decisions, path dependency* and the taken-for-granted elements of *organisational culture* that favour certain strategies.

  - Strategies developing because *organisational systems* favour some strategy projects over others.

- In managing strategy development processes, managers face challenges including:

  - Recognising that different processes of strategy development may be needed *in different contexts.*

  - Managing the processes that may give rise to *emergent strategy* as well as *deliberate strategy.*

VIDEO ASSIGNMENTS

VIDEO ASSIGNMENTS

Visit *MyStrategyLab* and watch the Pearson case study for Chapter 12.

1 Describe the strategic planning process in Pearson. How does it correspond to that shown in Illustration 12.2?

2 What does Mark Anderson see as the main benefits of the planning process at Pearson? Are there any benefits from taking on strategic initiatives from outside the planning process?

WORK ASSIGNMENTS

* *Denotes more advanced work assignments.*
* *Refers to a case study in the Text and Cases edition.*

12.1   Read the annual report of a company with which you are familiar as a customer (e.g. a retailer or transport company). Identify the main characteristics of the intended deliberate strategy as explained in the annual report, and the characteristics of the realised strategy as you perceive it as a customer.

12.2   Using the different explanations in sections 12.2 and 12.3, characterise how strategies have developed in different organisations (e.g. Google, Adnams* and Ocean Park*).

12.3*   Planning systems exist in many different organisations. What role should planning play in a public-sector organisation such as local government, a not-for-profit organisation such as AIDS Alliance* and a multinational corporation such as SABMiller*?

12.4*   Incremental patterns of strategy development are common in organisations, and managers see advantages in this. However, there are also risks of strategic drift. Using the different explanations in sections 12.2 and 12.3, suggest how such drift might be avoided.

12.5   Suggest why different approaches to strategy development might be appropriate in different organisations such as a university, a fashion retailer, a diversified multinational corporation and a high-technology company.

Integrative assignment

12.6*   Assume you were asked to advise a chief executive of a long-established, historically successful multinational business with highly experienced managers that is experiencing declining profits and falling market share. What might you expect to be the causes of the problems? What processes of strategy development would you propose to address them?

RECOMMENDED KEY READINGS

- A much quoted paper that describes different patterns of strategy development is H. Mintzberg and J.A. Waters, 'Of strategies, deliberate and emergent', *Strategic Management Journal*, vol. 6, no. 3 (1985), pp. 257–72.

- The changing role of strategic planning in the oil industry is explained by Rob Grant; see 'Strategic planning in a turbulent environment: evidence from the oil majors', *Strategic Management Journal*, vol. 24 (2003), pp. 491–517.

- S. Elbanna provides a useful explanation of differences between deliberate, intended strategy development and explanations of emergent and incremental strategy development in 'Strategic decision making: process perspectives', *International Journal of Management Reviews*, vol. 8, no. 1 (2006), pp. 1–20.

- A fascinating case study of the effects of resource allocation routines on the developing strategy of Intel is provided by Robert Burgelman in 'Fading memories: a process theory of strategic business exit in dynamic environments', *Administrative Science Quarterly*, vol. 39 (1994), pp. 34–56.

REFERENCES

1. See H. Mintzberg and J.A. Waters, 'Of strategies, deliberate and emergent', *Strategic Management Journal*, vol. 6, no. 3 (1985), pp. 257–72.

2. T. Nelson, 'The persistence of founder influence: management, ownership, and performance effects at initial public offering', *Strategic Management Journal*, vol. 24 (2003), pp. 707–24.

3. D. Souder, Z. Simsek and S.G. Johnson, 'The differing effects of agent and founder CEOs on the firm's market expansion', *Strategic Management Journal*, vol. 33, no. 1 (2012), pp. 23–42.

4. The role of a command style in small businesses is discussed in D. Miller and I. Le Breton-Miller, 'Management insights from great and struggling family businesses', *Long Range Planning*, vol. 38 (2005), pp. 517–30. The quotes here are from p. 519.

5. J. Collins and J. Porras, *Built to last*, Harper Business, 1994.

6. R. Grant, 'Strategic planning in a turbulent environment: evidence from the oil majors', *Strategic Management Journal*, vol. 24 (2003), pp. 491–517.

7. See P. Jarzabkowski and J. Balogun, 'The practice and process of delivering integration through strategic planning', *Journal of Management Studies*, vol. 46, no. 8 (2009), pp. 1255–88. P. Spee and P. Jarzabkowski, 'Strategic planning as communicative process', vol. 32, no. 9 (2011), pp. 1217–45, also explain how clarity on strategy may emerge as different parties involved iterate versions of the plan.

8. Saku Mantere, 'Strategic practices as enablers and disablers of championing activity', *Strategic Organization*, vol. 3, no. 2 (2005), pp. 157–84.

9. Many of these dangers are drawn from H. Mintzberg, *The Rise and Fall of Strategic Planning*, Prentice Hall, 1994.

10. The confusion of strategic planning and budgeting is identified as a significant 'bad strategy' practice by Richard Rumelt in *Good Strategy/Bad Strategy: The difference and why it matters*, Profile Books, 2011.

11. Ann Langley, 'Between "Paralysis by Analysis" and "Extinction by Instinct"', *Sloan Management Review*, Spring (1995), pp. 63–76.

12. See http://www.bain.com/publications/business-insights/management-tools-and-trends-2011.aspx#. Also, see evidence from other surveys such as G.P. Hodgkinson, R. Whittington, G. Johnson and M. Schwarz, 'The role of strategy workshops in strategy development processes: formality, communication, co-ordination and inclusion', *Long Range Planning*, vol. 39 (2006), pp. 479–96; also R. Whittington and Cailluet, 'The crafts of strategy', *Long Range Planning*, vol. 41 (2008), pp. 241–7.

13. Studies on the relationship between formal planning and financial performance are largely inconclusive. Some studies have shown benefits in particular contexts. For example, it is argued there are benefits to entrepreneurs setting up new ventures; see F. Delmar and S. Shane, 'Does business planning facilitate the development of new ventures?', *Strategic Management Journal*, vol. 24 (2003), pp. 1165–85. And other studies actually show the benefits of strategic analysis and strategic thinking, rather than the benefits of formal planning systems; e.g. see C.C. Miller and L.B. Cardinal, 'Strategic planning and firm performance: a synthesis of more than two decades of research', *Academy of Management Journal*, vol. 37, no. 6 (1994), pp. 1649–65.

14. P.J. Brews and M.R. Hunt, 'Learning to plan and planning to learn: resolving the planning school/learning school debate', *Strategic Management Journal*, vol. 20 (1999), pp. 889–913.

15. T.J. Andersen, 'Integrating decentralized strategy making and strategic planning processes in dynamic environments', *Journal of Management Studies*, vol. 41, no. 8 (2004), pp. 1271–99. Also M. Ketokivi and X. Castaner, 'Strategic planning as an integrative device', *Administrative Science Quarterly*, vol. 49 (2004), pp. 337–65.

16. See R. Grant, reference 6 above.

17. See B. King, 'Strategizing at leading venture capital firms: of planning, opportunism and deliberate emergence', *Long Range Planning*, vol. 41 (2008), pp. 345–66.

18. See H. Mintzberg and J.A. Waters reference 1 above.

19. See S. Elbanna, 'Strategic decision making: process perspectives', *International Journal of Management Reviews*, vol. 8, no. 1 (2006), pp. 1–20.

20. See J.B. Quinn, *Strategies for Change*, Irwin, 1980, p. 58.

21. For a more extensive discussion of experimentation see O. Sorenson, 'Strategy as quasi-experimentation', *Strategic Organization*, vol. 1 (2003), p. 337.

22. The concept of the learning organisation is explained in P. Senge, *The Fifth Discipline: the Art and Practice of the Learning Organization*, Doubleday/Century, 1990. Also M. Crossan, H.W. Lane and R.E. White, 'An organizational learning framework: from intuition to institution', *Academy of Management Review*, vol. 24, no. 3 (1999), pp. 522–37.

23. See V.K. Narayanan and L. Fahey, 'The micro-politics of strategy formulation', *The Academy of Management Review*, vol. 7, no. 1 (1982), pp. 109–40.

24. For an example of how different political coalitions can influence strategy see S. Maitlis and T. Lawrence, 'Orchestral manoeuvres in the dark: understanding failure in organizational strategizing', *Journal of Management Studies*, vol. 40, no. 1 (2003), pp. 109–40.

25. See P. Regnér, 'Strategy creation in the periphery: inductive versus deductive strategy making', *Journal of Management Studies*, vol. 40, no. 1 (2003), pp. 57–82.

26. W.B. Arthur, 'Competing technologies, increasing returns and lock in by historical events', *Economic Journal*, vol. 99 (1989), pp. 116–31.

27. The RAP explanation is sometimes known as the Bower–Burgelman explanation of strategy development after two

US professors – Joe Bower and Robert Burgelman. Their original studies are J.L. Bower, *Managing the Resource Allocation Process: a Study of Corporate Planning and Investment*, Irwin, 1972; and R.A. Burgelman, 'A model of the interaction of strategic behavior, corporate context and the concept of strategy', *Academy of Management Review*, vol. 81, no. 1 (1983), pp. 61–70; and 'A process model of internal corporate venturing in the diversified major firm', *Administrative Science Quarterly*, vol. 28 (1983), pp. 223–44. Also see J.L. Bower and C.G. Gilbert, 'A revised model of the resource allocation process', in *From Resource Allocation to Strategy*, eds J.L. Bower and C.G. Gilbert, pp. 439–55, Oxford University Press, 2005.

28. W. Ocasio, 'Towards an attention-based view of the firm', *Strategic Management Journal*, vol. 18 (Summer Special Issue, 1997), pp. 187–206.

29. J.L. Bower and C.G. Gilbert, 'How managers' everyday decisions create or destroy your company's strategy', *Harvard Business Review*, February (2007), p. 2.

30. The Intel case is also written up by Robert Burgelman, see *Strategy as Destiny: How Strategy Making Shapes a Company's Future*, Free Press, 2002. Also see R. Burgelman, 'Fading memories: a process theory of strategic business exit in dynamic environments', *Administrative Science Quarterly*, vol. 39 (1994), pp. 34–56.

31. J.S. McMullen, D.A. Shepherd and H. Patzelt, 'Managerial (in)attention to competitive threats', *Journal of Management Studies*, vol. 46, no. 2 (2009), pp. 157–80.

32. C. Lechner and S.W. Floyd, 'Group influence activities and the performance of strategic initiatives', *Strategic Management Journal*, vol. 33, no. 5 (2012), pp. 478–96.

33. Insights into the importance of multiple processes of strategy development can be found in S.L. Hart, 'An integrative framework for strategy-making processes', *Academy of Management Review*, vol. 17, no. 2 (1992), pp. 327–51.

34. For a discussion of the differences between strategy development in the public and private sectors, see N. Collier, F. Fishwick and G. Johnson, 'The processes of strategy development in the public sector', in *Exploring Public Sector Strategy*, eds G. Johnson and K. Scholes, Pearson Education, 2001.

35. R. Duncan's research, on which this classification is based, can be found in 'Characteristics of organisational environments and perceived environmental uncertainty', *Administrative Science Quarterly*, vol. 17, no. 3 (1972), pp. 313–27.

36. See P. Regner, 25 above.

37. R.A. Burgelman and A.S. Grove, 'Let chaos reign, then rein in chaos – repeatedly: managing strategic dynamics for corporate longevity', *Strategic Management Journal*, vol. 28 (2007), pp. 965–79.

Google: who drives the strategy?

Phyl Johnson

From an idea to a verb in less than 15 years: 'to Google – to search the Internet.'

If you want the answer to a question what do you do? You Google it. It is one of the few companies whose product's name has become so synonymous with its offering that it has become a commonly used verb. By 2012 Google had a market capitalisation of $249.19 bn (£149.51 bn; €186.89 bn). With a network of over 1 million computers worldwide, it was the dominant player in internet search (66 per cent of searches were through Google, way ahead of Microsoft's 'Bing' (15 per cent) and former giant Yahoo (14 per cent)). The vast majority of Google's revenue came from search-related advertising. It was, however, under serious threat on several fronts. Well-publicised poor financial results in 2012 left some commentators asking if Google was reaching the limits of its growth.[1] And there were those who questioned if its idiosyncratic management style could continue given its size and increasingly diversified portfolio.

About Google

Google started life as the brainchild of Larry Page and Sergey Brin when they were students at Stanford University in the USA. When Page and Brin launched their own search engine product, it gained followers and users quickly, attracted financial backing and enabled them to launch their IPO to the US stock market in 2004 raising a whopping $1.67 bn.

From the beginning Google was different. Instead of using investment banks as dictators of the initial share price for the IPO, they launched a kind of open IPO auction with buyers deciding on the fair price for a share. Page sent an open letter to shareholders explaining that Google was not a conventional company and did not intend to become one; it was about breaking the mould.

This continued as Google set up a two-tier board of directors, a model which, though common in some European countries (e.g. the Netherlands), is rare in the USA. The advantage for Page and Brin was the additional distance it placed between *them* and their shareholders and the increased managerial freedom it offered to them to run their company their way.

Page and Brin also recruited successful CEO Eric Schmidt from Novell Inc. and, between the three of them, shared power at the top. Schmidt dealt with administration and Google's investors and had the most traditional CEO role. Page was centrally concerned with the social structure of Google while Brin took a lead in the area of ethics.

How it was

It could be difficult to work out who was responsible for what inside Googleplex (Google's HQ) in Mountain View, California. There was a famously unstructured style of operating; in 2009 Eric Schmidt claimed that their strategy was based on trial and error:

> 'Google is unusual because it's really organised from the bottom up . . . It often feels at Google people are pretty much doing what they think best and they tolerate having us around . . . We don't really have a five-year plan . . . We really focus on what's new, what's exciting and how can you win quickly with your new idea.'[2]

With regard to product development, their approach was to launch a part-finished (*beta*) product, let Google fanatics find it, toy with it, error-check and de-bug it – an imaginative use of end users but also a significant release of control. Control of workflow, quality and to a large extent the nature of projects underway at any one time were down to employees and not management. Google was a famously light-managed organisation. It had a 1:20 ratio of employees to managers – half the number of managers than in the average American organisation (1:10) and considerably fewer than some European countries (France 1:7.5).

CFO Patrick Pichette tells of being in a meeting room with an influential businessman and being kicked out by a group of young engineers who wanted the *room* for their meeting. For him the lesson was that at Google the leadership is 'an overhead' whereas the engineers 'write the code, they make the real stuff that makes Google happen'.[3]

Engineers worked in small autonomous teams and the work they produced was quality assured using peer review rather than classical supervision or clear strategic guidelines. So there was the potential for these small work teams with their freedom for self-initiated project work to create a situation of project proliferation. Moreover, engineers at Google were allowed to allocate 20 per cent of their work time to personal projects that interest them as a means to stimulate innovation and the creation of new knowledge as well as potential products. However, some commentators suggested that many engineers spent more like 30 per cent of their time on such projects.

Google was proud of its laissez-faire approach to management and product development:

'Google is run by its culture and not by me ... It's much easier to have an employee base in which everybody is doing exactly what they want every day. They're much easier to manage because they never have any problems. They're always excited, they're always working on whatever they care about ... But it's a very different model than the traditional, hierarchical model where there's the CEO statement and this is the strategy and this is what you will do, and it's very, very measured. We put up with a certain amount of chaos from that.'

Eric Schmidt: CEO[4]

There were, however, some areas of rigidity built into the system. One was that of recruitment. With such a highly rated employment brand, Google could afford to be choosy. Close to 100 talented applicants chased each job. The pay was competitive but not way ahead of the competition. However, perks, including free meals, a swimming pool and massages, all helped attract employees. So too did the 20 per cent of free time engineers could spend on their own interests. In return Google had rigid recruitment criteria and processes. Engineers had to have either a Masters or Doctorate from a leading university and pass a series of assessment tests and interviews. The criteria for these were derived in a highly scientific manner. In effect Google recruited against a psychometric profile of *googleness* and could therefore hire and hopefully retain a fairly predictable employee population: much easier to manage.

Peer review is also a stringent form of performance management. Among professionals, reputation is key and if someone is being reviewed by peers the pattern is towards higher-quality work. The way peer reviews were carried out, in common with many other processes within Google, was formulaic. For example, work teams were kept small and limited to a maximum of six; projects worked on were limited in number; deadlines were short (no longer than six weeks); and as ever in Google there was measurement. As Eric Schmidt commented:

'We're very analytical. We measure everything, and we systematised every aspect of what's happening in the company. For example, we introduced a spreadsheet product this week. I've already received hourly updates on the number of people who came in to apply to use the spreadsheet, the number of people using it, the size of the spreadsheet.'[5]

What it became

In October 2012 Google saw 10 per cent of the value of the corporation ($24 bn) wiped in just two days. In the USA its stock was crashing so fast it had to be suspended. Why? Because the amount advertisers were prepared to pay click-by-click fell by 15 per cent and Google's earnings in the third quarter showed profits 20 per cent down on 2011. To make matters worse these data were released to the market by accident before they should have been and with a crucial explanation from Larry Page missing.

The meteoric rise of Facebook (also selling advertising space) and the wave of internet users switching to tablets and handheld devices (where advertising is harder to see and therefore has a lower price) hit Google hard. With the lion's share of its revenue coming from advertising, the criticism of being a one-trick-pony was being levelled at Google.

So Google needed to change. In the words of Sergey Brin: 'We want to let a 1000 flowers bloom, but now we need to make a bouquet.'[6] Google was being talked about as leaner and meaner. There was a rumour that the famous 20 per cent free engineer time was at risk. But Google remained committed to its 70–20–10 formula where 70 per cent of effort is spent on search, 20 per cent on products that are not quite there yet and 10 per cent on brand-new stuff.

The most significant change inside was that Larry Page took the role of sole CEO in 2011. Brin moved to spend four days of his week working on projects and Schmidt moved to an advisory role as Chairman. Page's stance was to require the organisation to be more effective and focused. He closed down projects, called an end to email wars between different factions and required decision making to be speeded up. He took action to halt the talent drain of the 12,000 engineer population to Facebook by offering a 10 per cent pay rise along with a sizable bonus.

Google had also made over 100 acquisitions, some as large as Motorola and YouTube, others smaller but helping Google develop new service offerings. In 2011 alone there were 79 acquisitions or significant investments in other businesses. In the first quarter of 2012, however, it had made none: Page appeared to have put a hold on the acquisition stream.

Page's CEO role also released Brin back into innovative development. He was responsible for top-secret projects called Google X, focused on robotics and artificial intelligence, in a separate location. Google was attempting to diversify. It had Google+ to rival Facebook and was developing its Motorola acquisition to rival the smart-phone dominance of Apple. By 2012 Google's driverless car had also clocked up 300,000 driverless hours on US roads, all incident free. None the less, observers were reporting that, nervous of the unexciting performance of some recently launched Google products, Larry Page was placing less emphasis on experimentation and more on operational efficiency.[7] Perhaps a different approach to strategy was needed from that outlined by Eric Schmidt in 2009: by 2012 Mountain View had business strategists who worked on 'global, cross-functional projects at the heart of what we do'.

Sources: Primary source B. Girard, *The Google Way: How one company is revolutionising management as we know it*. No Starch Press, 2009.

1. H. Peterson, H. Gye, Louise Boyle and P. Campbell, 'Could Google disappear? Analysts warn of Google's demise if the search engine fails to improve mobile advertising'. *Daily Mail*, 20 October 2012.
2. Interview by Nicholas Carlson of Google CEO Eric Schmidt: 'We Don't Really Have A Five-Year Plan', *Washington Post Leadership series*, 20 May 2009.
3. M. Ahmed, 'Its going Gangbusters at Goggleplex, where the code writers run the company and the chiefs are up the wall', *The Times*, 3 January 2011.
4. As reference 2 above.
5. B. Girard, *The Google Way: How one company is revolutionising management as we know it*. No Starch Press, 2009, p. 97.
6. M. Ahmed, 'Leaner, meaner, but dreams are still there to be chased', *The Times*, 24 November 2011.
7. See http://www.youtube.com/watch?v=tk5P-KvnLgE. And to get a feel for the Mountain View Googleplex: http://www.youtube.com/watch?v=4CSHuRirYOw.

Questions

1 Explain how Google's strategy has been developed over the years.

2 What are the strengths and weaknesses of its approach?

3 In what ways should Google's approach to strategy development change in the future?

13

ORGANISING FOR SUCCESS

Learning outcomes

After reading this chapter you should be able to:

● Analyse main organisational *structural types* in terms of their strengths and weaknesses.

● Identify key issues in designing organisational *control systems* (such as planning and performance targeting systems).

● Recognise how the three strands of strategy, structure and systems should reinforce each other in *organisational configurations* and the managerial dilemmas involved.

MyStrategyLab

MyStrategyLab is designed to help you make the most of your studies. Visit **www.pearsoned.co.uk/mystrategylab** to discover a wide range of resources, including:

• A personalised **Study plan** that will help you understand core concepts

• **Audio and video clips** that put the spotlight on strategy in the real world

• **Online glossaries and flashcards** that provide helpful reminders when you're looking for some quick revision.

(13.1) INTRODUCTION

Strategies only happen because people do what is required. If the American multinational retailer Walmart wants to achieve its strategy, it needs to get its 2.2 million employees pointing in the right direction – just as a sports team has to ensure that all its members will play the right kind of game. Thus strategies require organising and this involves both structures and systems. If the organisation does not support the strategy, then even the cleverest strategy will fail because of poor implementation.

This chapter examines organising for successful strategy implementation. It focuses particularly on two key elements of organisational 'design': organisational structures and organisational systems. **Structures give people formally defined roles, responsibilities and lines of reporting.** These structures can be seen as the skeletons of organisations, providing the basic frameworks on which everything is built. **Systems support and control people as they carry out structurally defined roles and responsibilities.** Systems can be seen as the muscles of organisations, giving them movement and coherence.

Figure 13.1 expresses the interdependency between strategy, structure and systems. In the ideal organisational design, all three should support each other in a circular process of mutual reinforcement. This chapter captures the importance of mutual reinforcement between elements with the concept of *configuration*, explained in section 13.4. However, the chapter will also underline how difficult it sometimes can be to configure the organisation in order to support strategy. In particular, the Key Debate at the end of the chapter questions the extent to which formal organisational structures can be simply reshaped to align with strategy. Sometimes the organisational elements of structure and systems can get out of synchrony with the strategy, fatally undermining it or even redefining its direction. Figure 13.1 captures the potential for structures and systems to shape strategy by showing them as feeding *into* strategy, as well as flowing *from* it.

Figure 13.1 Organisational configurations: strategy, structure and systems

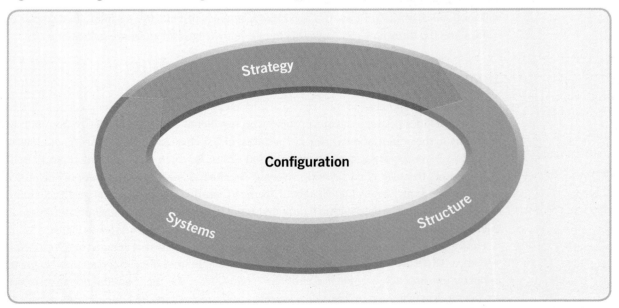

This chapter addresses the following topics therefore:

● *Structures*, defining the formal roles, responsibilities and lines of reporting in organisations. The chapter considers the main types of structures, including functional, divisional, matrix, project and transnational structures.

● *Systems*, supporting and controlling people within and around an organisation. These systems include direct mechanisms such as performance targeting and planning, and more indirect ones such as cultural and market systems.

● *Configurations*, the mutually supporting elements that make up an organisation's design. As well as strategy, structure and systems, these elements can include staff, style, skills and superordinate goals, as encapsulated in the *McKinsey 7-S framework*.

(13.2) STRUCTURAL TYPES

Managers often describe their organisation by drawing an organisation chart, mapping out its formal structure. These structural charts define the levels and roles in an organisation. They are important to managers because they describe who is responsible for what. They can have major implications for organisational priorities and interactions in the marketplace: as at Qwikster, getting the structure wrong can be very damaging (see Illustration 13.1).

This section reviews five basic structural types: functional, divisional, matrix, transnational and project.[1] Broadly, the first two of these tend to emphasise one structural dimension over another, either functional specialisms or business divisions. The three that follow tend to mix structural dimensions more evenly, for instance trying to give product and geographical units equal weight. However, none of these structures is a universal solution to the challenges of organising. Rather, the right structure depends on the particular kinds of challenges each organisation faces. Researchers propose a wide number of important challenges (sometimes called 'contingencies') shaping organisational structure, including organisational size, extent of diversification and type of technology.[2] This implies that the first step in organisational design is deciding what the key challenges facing the organisation actually are. Section 13.2.6 will particularly focus on how the five structural types fit both the traditional challenge of control and the three new challenges of change, knowledge and internationalisation.

13.2.1 The functional structure

Even a small entrepreneurial start-up, once it involves more than one person, needs to divide up responsibilities between different people. The **functional structure divides responsibilities according to the organisation's primary specialist roles such as production, research and sales**. Figure 13.2 represents a typical organisation chart for such a functional organisation. This kind of structure is particularly relevant to small or start-up organisations, or larger organisations that have retained narrow, rather than diverse, product ranges. Functional structures may also be used within a multidivisional structure (see below), where the divisions themselves may split themselves up according to functional departments (as in Figure 13.2).

Figure 13.2 also summarises the potential advantages and disadvantages of a functional structure. There are advantages in that it gives senior managers direct hands-on involvement in operations and allows greater operational control from the top. The functional structure provides a clear definition of roles and tasks, increasing accountability. Functional departments

ILLUSTRATION 13.1

Structural fault: Qwikster's quick demise

Netflix's introduction of the new Qwikster structure is a multi-billion-dollar failure.

In 2011, Netflix, the USA's largest online DVD rental and internet streaming company, faced a dilemma. Internet streaming of movies was clearly a growth business, one which competitors such as Amazon were beginning to enter. On the other hand, DVD rental by mail was facing long-term decline. In September 2011, Reed Hastings, CEO and joint founder of the company, responded to the dilemma with a structural solution. He proposed to split his business into two separate parts: henceforth streaming would be done exclusively under the Netflix label, while DVD rental would be done exclusively in a new organisational unit called Qwikster. In a blog post, Hastings explained his motivation: 'For the past five years, my greatest fear at Netflix has been that we wouldn't make the leap from success in DVDs to success in streaming. Most companies that are great at something – like AOL dialup or Borders bookstores – do not become great at new things people want (streaming for us) because they are afraid to hurt their initial business. Eventually these companies realise their error of not focusing enough on the new thing, and then the company fights desperately and hopelessly to recover. Companies rarely die from moving too fast, and they frequently die from moving too slowly.'

There were other reasons for the proposed split. The DVD business requires large warehouse and logistics operations, while streaming requires large internet resources. For DVDs, competitors include Blockbuster and Redbox, whereas streaming rivals include Amazon, iTunes and cable TV companies. As a standalone unit, managers in the streaming business could promote their alternative model without worrying about protecting the DVD business, still the larger part of Netflix's profits overall.

For customers, though, the split was less attractive. In future, customers would have to deal with two sites to get what they had previously got through one site. The DVD site offered many more movies, and tended to have more recent releases. Movie viewing recom-

mendations for one site would not transfer to the other site. DVD renters would no longer receive the distinctive Netflix DVD envelopes which had strong brand loyalty.

The customer response was hostile. In the month following Qwikster's launch Netflix lost hundreds of thousands of subscribers. The Netflix share price fell more than 60 per cent, wiping out more than $3 bn in value. CEO Reed Hastings joked in a Facebook message that he feared poisoning by some of his investors: 'I think I might need a food taster. I can hardly blame them.'

On 10 October 2011, three weeks after the original Qwikster announcement, Hastings blogged that the new unit would not go ahead after all, and that all business would continue under the Netflix label. Hastings explained: 'There is a difference between moving quickly – which Netflix has done very well for years – and moving too fast, which is what we did in this case.' Despite his reversal of the structural change, repercussions were still being felt a year later: Netflix's market share of DVD rentals in 2012 had dropped from 35 per cent to 27 per cent, and rival Redbox had taken market leadership.

Sources: *Wall Street Journal*, 11 October 2011; *Strategy+Business*, 2 April 2012; *PC Magazine*, 17 September 2012.

Questions

1 How do the pros and cons of the Qwikster structure fit with those associated with the divisional structure (see section 13.2.2)?

2 In the light of the planning, cultural, market and targeting systems discussed in section 13.3, what else would Netflix have needed to do to manage the separation of the streaming business and the rental business?

Figure 13.2 A functional structure

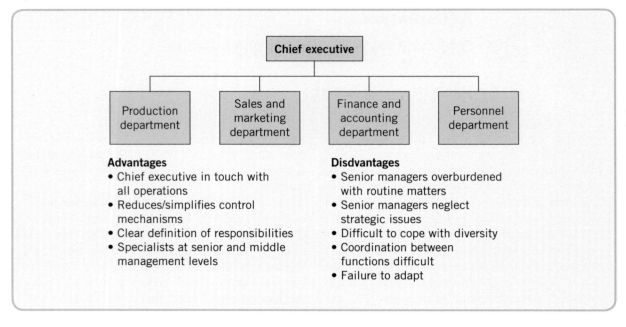

also provide concentrations of expertise, thus fostering knowledge development in areas of functional specialism.

However, there are disadvantages, particularly as organisations become larger or more diverse. Perhaps the major concern in a fast-moving world is that senior managers focus too much on their functional responsibilities, becoming overburdened with routine operations and too concerned with narrow functional interests. As a result, they find it hard either to take a strategic view of the organisation as a whole or to coordinate separate functions quickly. Thus functional organisations can be inflexible, poor at adapting to change. Separate functional departments tend also to be inward-looking – so-called 'functional silos' – making it difficult to integrate the knowledge of different functional specialists. Finally, because they are centralised around particular functions, functional structures are not good at coping with product or geographical diversity. For example, a central marketing department may try to impose a uniform approach to advertising regardless of the diverse needs of the organisation's various business units around the world.

13.2.2 The divisional structure

A **divisional structure is built up of separate divisions on the basis of products, services or geographical areas** (see Figure 13.3). Divisionalisation often comes about as an attempt to overcome the problems that functional structures have in dealing with the diversity mentioned above.[3] Each division can respond to the specific requirements of its product/market strategy, using its own set of functional departments. A similar situation exists in many public services, where the organisation is structured around *service departments* such as recreation, social services and education.

There are several potential advantages to divisional structures. As self-standing business units, it is possible to control divisions from a distance by monitoring business performance

Figure 13.3 A multidivisional structure

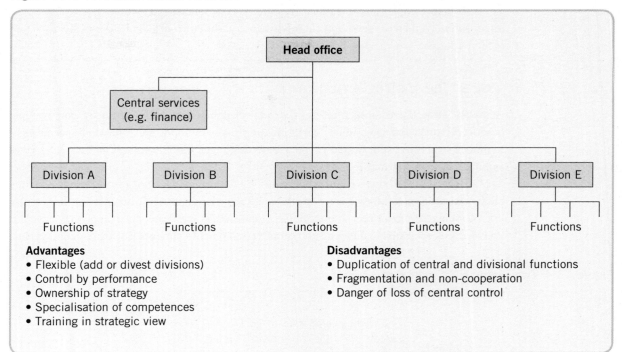

Advantages
- Flexible (add or divest divisions)
- Control by performance
- Ownership of strategy
- Specialisation of competences
- Training in strategic view

Disadvantages
- Duplication of central and divisional functions
- Fragmentation and non-cooperation
- Danger of loss of central control

(see section 13.3.3). Having divisions also provides flexibility because organisations can add, close or merge divisions as circumstances change. Divisional managers have greater personal ownership for their own divisional strategies. Geographical divisions – for example, a European division or a North American division – offer a means of managing internationally (see section 13.2.4). There can be benefits of specialisation within a division, allowing competences to develop with a clearer focus on a particular product group, technology or customer group. Management responsibility for a whole divisional business is good training in taking a strategic view for managers expecting to go on to a main board position.

However, divisional structures can also have disadvantages of three main types. First, divisions can become so self-sufficient that they are *de facto* independent businesses, but duplicating the functions and costs of the corporate centre of the company. In such cases of *de facto* independence, it may make more sense to split the company into independent businesses, and de-mergers of this type are now common. Second, divisionalisation tends to get in the way of cooperation and knowledge-sharing between business units: divisions can quite literally divide. Expertise is fragmented and divisional performance targets provide poor incentives to collaborate with other divisions. Finally, divisions may become too autonomous, especially where joint ventures and partnership dilute ownership. Here, divisions pursue their own strategies almost regardless of the needs of the corporate parent. In these cases, divisional companies become *holding companies*, where the corporate centre effectively 'holds' the various businesses in a largely financial sense, exercising little control and adding little value. Figure 13.3 summarises these potential advantages and disadvantages of a multidivisional structure.

Large and complex divisional companies often have a second tier of *subdivisions* within their main divisions. Treating smaller strategic business units as subdivisions within a large division reduces the number of units that the corporate centre has to deal with directly. Subdivisions can also help complex organisations respond to contradictory pressures. For example, an organisation could have geographical subdivisions within a set of global product divisions (see section 13.2.4).

13.2.3 The matrix structure

A **matrix structure combines different structural dimensions simultaneously, for example product divisions and geographical territories or product divisions and functional specialisms.**[4] In matrix structures, staff typically report to two managers rather than one. Figure 13.4 gives examples of such a structure.

Matrix structures have several advantages. They promote *knowledge-sharing* because they allow separate areas of knowledge to be integrated across organisational boundaries. Particularly in professional service organisations, matrix organisations can be helpful in applying particular knowledge specialisms to different market or geographical segments. For example, to serve a

Figure 13.4 Two examples of matrix structures

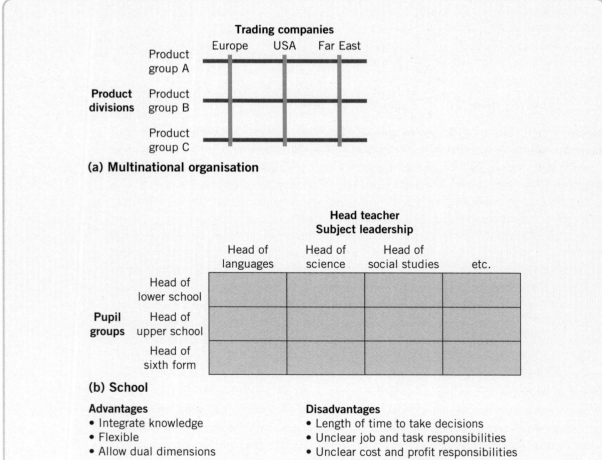

(a) **Multinational organisation**

(b) **School**

Advantages	Disadvantages
• Integrate knowledge	• Length of time to take decisions
• Flexible	• Unclear job and task responsibilities
• Allow dual dimensions	• Unclear cost and profit responsibilities
	• High degrees of conflict

particular client, a consulting firm may draw on people from groups with particular knowledge specialisms (e.g. strategy or organisation design) and others grouped according to particular markets (industry sectors or geographical regions). Figure 13.4 shows how a school might combine the separate knowledge of subject specialists to create programmes of study tailored differently to various age groups. Matrix organisations are *flexible*, because they allow different dimensions of the organisation to be mixed together. They are particularly attractive to organisations operating globally, because of the possible mix between local and global dimensions. For example, a global company may prefer geographically defined divisions as the operating units for local marketing (because of their specialist local knowledge of customers). But at the same time it may still want global product units responsible for the worldwide coordination of product development and manufacturing, taking advantage of economies of scale and specialisation. However, because a matrix structure replaces single lines of authority with multiple cross-matrix relationships, this often brings problems. In particular, it will typically take *longer to reach decisions* because of bargaining between the managers of different dimensions. There may also be *conflict* because staff find themselves responsible to managers from two structural dimensions. In short, matrix organisations are hard to control.

As with any structure, but particularly with the matrix structure, the critical issue in practice is the way it actually works (i.e. behaviours and relationships). The key ingredient in a successful matrix structure can be senior managers good at sustaining collaborative relationships (across the matrix) and coping with the messiness and ambiguity which that can bring. It is for this reason that Chris Bartlett and Sumantra Ghoshal describe the matrix as involving a 'frame of mind' as much as a formal structure.[5]

13.2.4 Multinational/transnational structures

Operating internationally adds an extra dimension to the structural challenge. As in Figure 13.5, there are essentially four structural designs available for multinationals. Three are simple extensions of the principles of the divisional structure (section 13.2.2), so are dealt with briefly. The fourth, the transnational structure, is more complex and will be explained at more length.

The three simpler multinational structures are as follows:

- *International divisions.* An international division is a standalone division added alongside the structure of the main home-based business. This is often the kind of structure adopted by corporations with large domestic markets (such as in the USA or China), where an initial entry into overseas markets is relatively small-scale and does not require structural change to the original, much bigger, home businesses. For example, a Chinese car, truck and motorbike manufacturer might have separate divisions for each of its product areas in its home market of China, but run its overseas businesses in a separate 'international division' combining all three product areas together. The international division is typically run from headquarters, but not integrated with the domestic business. As in Figure 13.5, the international division is centralised, but not highly coordinated with other parts of the business.

- *Local subsidiaries.* These subsidiaries typically have most of the functions required to operate on their own in their particular local market, for example design, production and marketing. They are thus a form of geographic divisional structure. They have high local responsiveness and are loosely coordinated. A local subsidiary structure is very common in professional services such as law, accounting and advertising, where there are few economies of scale and responsiveness to local regulations, relationships or tastes is very important. This structure

ILLUSTRATION 13.2

Reckitt's new strategy and structure

Incoming Chief Executive Rakesh Kapoor launches a new strategy with a structure to match.

Reckitt Benckiser is a £9 bn ($14 bn; €10.5 bn) revenue multinational and a major player in household, health, personal care and pharmaceutical products. Key brands include Finish dishwasher tablets, Air Wick air fresheners and Durex condoms. However, growth was slow in its core markets of Europe and North America, while rivals such as Unilever and Procter & Gamble were growing faster in the so-called emerging markets of China, India, Russia and similar. Reckitt Benckiser had only 38 per cent of revenues in emerging markets, with just 2 per cent from China.

The new Chief Executive Rakesh Kapoor declared a new strategy of emerging market growth. By 2016, he was aiming at 45 per cent of revenue in emerging markets. The share of marketing expenditure devoted to emerging markets would rise in the same period from 44 per cent to 55 per cent. Emerging market capital expenditure would go from 50 per cent to 80 per cent.

The new strategy would be supported by a new structure. In 2012 the company's annual report explained: 'A new organisation structure will drive strategy. To deliver accelerated growth we are going to substantially increase our focus on six of the world's highest growth geographic clusters of consumers. These are built around the emerging markets of Brazil, Russia, India, China (BRIC), as well as Africa and the Middle East . . . We have created two new Area organisations to manage these high-growth emerging market clusters, instead of just one.' Thus the existing Emerging Markets business would be split into two divisions: LAPAC (Latin America and Asia), and RUMEA (Russia, Middle East and Africa). Meanwhile, the two largest business units, Europe and North America, would be merged into a single geographical division (ENA), with its headquarters based in Amsterdam. The Annual Report explained: 'We are seeing increasingly homogenous consumer, trade and competitive environments in developed mar-

kets . . . The Europe regions and North America will report into one Area lead (manager) to drive increased speed to market and to get scale efficiencies to drive higher growth.' The elimination of the North American headquarters would also save £30 m a year.

Reckitt Benckiser's new geographical structure contrasted with its rivals' structural approaches. For example, Unilever had eight regional 'clusters': Europe, North America, Latin America, North Asia, South East Asia & Australasia, South Asia, Africa, and North Africa, Middle East and Russia. Procter & Gamble, on the other hand, emphasised two global business units: Beauty & Grooming and Household Care.

There were some doubts about Reckitt Benckiser's structural change. Would Amsterdam be able to run the North American business, source of 25 per cent of profits, from across the Atlantic? Would it be able to match Procter & Gamble in North America, especially given the Cincinnati headquarters of its two global business units? Can North America and Europe really be treated as one? After all, Americans are happy to use washing-up liquid to clean their hands. And was Reckitt Benckiser right to merge the two main markets into one large unit when rival Unilever was split into smaller, more focused units? Yet investors liked the new strategy and structure: the share price rose 3 per cent on announcement.

Sources: Financial Times, 8 February 2012; Reuters, 8 February 2012; Reckitt Benckiser Annual Report, 2012.

Questions

1 In what ways would the new structure support the new strategy?

2 Assess the relative advantages of Unilever's smaller regional units and Procter & Gamble's two global business units in these consumer markets (refer to section 13.2.4).

Figure 13.5 Multinational structures

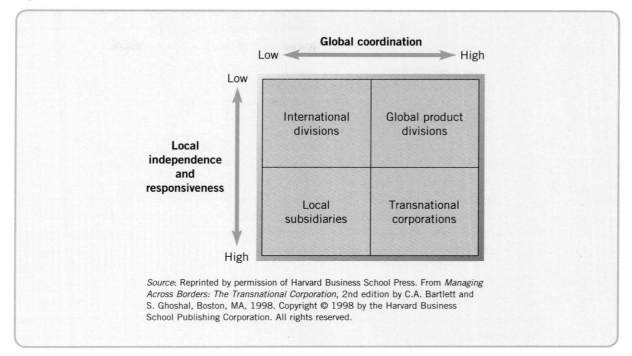

fits the multi-domestic strategy introduced in Chapter 8. A variant of local subsidiaries are geographical regional units, for instance Latin America and Asia, as at Reckitt Benckiser (Illustration 13.2).

- *Global product divisions.* This kind of structure is often used where economies of scale are very important. Organising the design, production and marketing on the basis of global divisions rather than local subsidiaries typically maximises cost efficiency. It also helps direct central resources to targeted markets and facilitates cross-subsidisation of unprofitable geographical markets. To return to the Chinese car, truck and motorbike manufacturer, there would be just three divisions, each responsible for its particular product area across the whole world, China included. There would be very little scope for adaptation to local tastes or regulations in particular markets. In global product divisions, local responsiveness would typically be very low. This structure fits the global strategy introduced in Chapter 8.

The international division, local subsidiary and global product division structures all have their particular advantages, whether it is managing relative size, maximising local responsiveness or achieving economies of scale. The fourth structure, however, tries to integrate the advantages of the local subsidiary structure with those of the global product divisional structure.

In terms of Figure 13.5, **the transnational structure combines local responsiveness with high global coordination.**[6] According to Bartlett and Ghoshal, transnational structures are similar to matrices but distinguish themselves by their focus on knowledge-sharing, specialisation and network management, as follows:

- *Knowledge-sharing.* While each national or regional business has a good deal of autonomy, in the transnational they should see themselves as sources of ideas and capabilities for the whole corporation. Thus a good idea that has been developed locally is offered for adoption by other national or regional units around the world.

- *Specialisation.* National (or regional) units specialise in areas of expertise in order to achieve greater scale economies on behalf of the whole corporation. Thus a national unit that has particular competences in manufacturing a particular product, for example, may be given responsibility for manufacturing that product on behalf of other units across the world.

- *Network management.* The corporate centre has the role of managing this global network of specialisms and knowledge. It does so first by establishing the specialist role of each business unit, then sustaining the systems and relationships required to make the network of business units operate in an integrated and effective manner.

The success of a transnational corporation is dependent on the ability *simultaneously* to achieve global competences, local responsiveness and organisation-wide innovation and learning. Theoretically the transnational combines the best of local decentralisation with the best of global centralisation. However, the transnational can be very demanding of managers in terms of willingness to work not just at their national business units but for the good of the transnational as a whole. Diffuse responsibilities also make for similar complexities and control problems to those of the matrix organisation.[7]

13.2.5 Project-based structures[8]

Many organisations rely heavily on project teams with a finite life span. A **project-based structure is one where teams are created, undertake the work (e.g. internal or external contracts) and are then dissolved**.[9] This can be particularly appropriate for organisations that deliver large and expensive goods or services (civil engineering, information systems, films) or those delivering time-limited events (conferences, sporting events or consulting engagements). The organisation structure is a constantly changing collection of project teams created, steered and glued together loosely by a small corporate group. Many organisations use such teams in a more ad hoc way to complement the 'main' structure. For example, *task forces* are set up to make progress on new elements of strategy or to provide momentum where the regular structure of the organisation is not effective.

The project-based structure can be highly flexible, with projects being set up and dissolved as required. Because project teams should have clear tasks to achieve within a defined period, accountability and control are good. As project team members will typically be drawn from different departments within the firm, projects can be effective at knowledge exchange. Projects can also draw on members internationally and, because project life spans are typically short, project teams may be more willing to work temporarily around the world. There are disadvantages, however. Organisations are prone to proliferate projects in an ill-coordinated fashion. The constant breaking up of project teams can also hinder the accumulation of knowledge over time or within specialisms.

Overall, project-based structures have been growing in importance because of their inherent flexibility. Such flexibility can be vital in a fast-moving world where individual knowledge and competences need to be redeployed and integrated quickly and in novel ways.

13.2.6 Choosing structures

From the discussion so far, it should be clear that functional, divisional, matrix, transnational and project structures each have their own advantages and disadvantages. Organisational designers, therefore, have to choose structures according to the particular strategic challenges (or 'contingencies') they face. Here the various structures are considered in the light of four general challenges that have become particularly important for many contemporary organisations in recent years:

- The need for *control* over strategy implementation in a world where organisations are increasingly large, complex and under scrutiny. One extreme of complexity is the American retailer Walmart, with its 2.2 million employees and 15 brands, operating in Asia, Europe and the Americas. Control is also important because investors, regulators and pressure groups typically watch closely to see that organisations actually deliver on the strategic promises they make.

- The *speed of change* and the increased levels of *uncertainty* in the business environment, as discussed in Chapter 2. As a result, organisations need to have flexible designs and be skilled at reorganising.

- The growing importance of *knowledge creation* and *knowledge-sharing* as a fundamental ingredient of strategic success, as discussed in Chapter 3. Organisational designs should both support critical mass in terms of expertise and encourage people to share their knowledge.

- The rise of *internationalisation*, as discussed in Chapter 8. Organising for an international context has many challenges: communicating across wider geography, coordinating more diversity and building relationships across diverse cultures are some examples. Swiss multinational Nestlé has 450 factories around the world, being present in 86 countries in all. Internationalisation also brings greater recognition of different kinds of organising around the world.

Table 13.1 summarises how the five basic structures – functional, multidivisional, matrix, transnational and project – meet these challenges of control, change, knowledge and internationalisation faced by many contemporary organisations. No structure scores high across all four challenges. Organisational designers therefore face trade-offs and choices. If they seek control, but are less concerned for flexibility in response to change or global reach, then they might prefer a functional structure. If they want to foster knowledge and flexibility on a global scale, then they might consider a matrix or transnational structure. In other words, structural choice depends on the particular strategic challenges the organisation faces. The difficult trade-offs involved are illustrated by the controversy around Netflix's Qwikster restructuring (Illustration 13.1). In reality, few organisations adopt a structure that is just like one of the pure structural types discussed above. Structures often blend different types into hybrid structures (see section 13.4.1 below), tailor-made to the particular mix of challenges facing the organisation.

While Table 13.1 considers general challenges for contemporary organisations, Goold and Campbell provide *nine design tests* against which to check specific tailor-made structural solutions.[10] The first four tests stress fit with the key objectives and constraints of the organisation:

- *The Market-Advantage Test*. This test of fit with market strategy is fundamental, following Alfred Chandler's classic principle that 'structure follows strategy': that is first define the strategy, then fit the structure.[11] For example, if integrated services are important to market advantage, then they should probably not be split between different structural units.

- *The Parenting Advantage Test*. The structural design should fit the 'parenting' role of the corporate centre (see Chapter 7). For example, if the corporate centre aims to add value as a synergy manager, then it should design a structure that places important integrative specialisms, such as marketing or research, at the centre.

Table 13.1 **Comparison of structures**

Challenge	Functional	Multidivisional	Matrix	Transnational	Project
Control	***	**	*	**	**
Change	*	**	***	***	***
Knowledge	**	*	***	***	**
Internationalisation	*	**	***	***	**

* Stars indicate typical capacities to cope with each challenge, with three stars indicating high, two indicating medium and one indicating poor.

- *The People Test*. The structural design must fit the people available. It is dangerous to switch completely from a functional structure to a multidivisional structure if, as is likely, the organisation lacks managers with competence in running decentralised business units.

- *The Feasibility Test*. This is a catch-all category, indicating that the structure must fit legal, stakeholder, trade union or similar constraints. For example, after scandals involving biased research, investment banks are now required by financial regulators to separate their research departments from their deal-making departments.

Goold and Campbell then propose five more tests based on good general organisational design principles, as follows:

- *The Specialised Cultures Test*. This test reflects the value of bringing together specialists so that they can develop their expertise in close collaboration with each other. A structure scores poorly if it breaks up important specialist cultures.

- *The Difficult Links Test*. This test asks whether a proposed structure will set up links between parts of the organisations that are important but bound to be strained. For example, extreme decentralisation to profit-accountable business units is likely to strain relationships with a central research and development department. Unless compensating mechanisms are put in place, this kind of structure is likely to fail.

- *The Redundant Hierarchy Test*. Any structural design should be checked in case it has too many layers of management, causing undue blockages and expense. Delayering in response to redundant hierarchies has been an important structural trend in recent years.

- *The Accountability Test*. This test stresses the importance of clear lines of accountability, ensuring the control and commitment of managers throughout the structure. Because of their dual lines of reporting, matrix structures are often accused of lacking clear accountability.

- *The Flexibility Test*. While not all organisations will face the same general rise in environmental velocity as referred to with regard to Table 13.1, a final important test is whether the design will be sufficiently flexible to accommodate possible changes in the future. Here Kathleen Eisenhardt argues for structural 'modularity' (i.e. standardisation) in order to allow easy 'patching' (i.e. transfer) of one part of the organisation to another part of the organisation, as market needs change.[13] For example, if strategic business units are similar in structural size and internal management systems throughout a large organisation, it becomes easy to transfer them from one division to another according to changing business needs.

Goold and Campbell's nine tests provide a rigorous screen for effective structures. But even if the structural design passes these tests, the structure still needs to be matched to the other key element of an organisation's configuration, its systems. Systems too will have to reinforce strategy and structure.

(13.3) SYSTEMS

Structure is a key ingredient of organising for success. But structures can only work if they are supported by formal and informal organisational systems, the 'muscles' of the organisation.[14] Systems help ensure control over strategy implementation. Small organisations may be able to rely on *direct supervision*, where a single manager or entrepreneur monitors activity in person. But larger or more complex organisations typically need more elaborate structures and systems if they are to be effective over time. The limited success of the Occupy Wall Street movement in 2011 and 2012 demonstrates the roles of structures and systems (see Illustration 13.3).

Systems as means of control can be subdivided in two ways. First, systems tend to emphasise either control over inputs or control over outputs. Input control systems concern themselves with the *resources* consumed in the strategy, especially financial resources and human commitment. Output control systems focus on ensuring satisfactory *results*, for example the meeting of targets or achieving market competitiveness. The second subdivision is between direct and indirect controls. Direct controls involve *close supervision* or monitoring. Indirect controls are more *hands-off*, setting up the conditions whereby desired behaviours are achieved semi-automatically. How the four systems we shall consider emphasise input or output controls and direct or indirect control is summarised in Table 13.2.

Organisations normally use a blend of these control systems, but some will dominate over others according to the strategic challenges. As for structures, these challenges include change, knowledge and internationalisation and different systems cope with some of these better than others. As we shall see, direct measures tend to require that the controllers have high levels of knowledge of what the controlled are supposed to do. In many knowledge-intensive organisations, especially those generating innovation and change, controllers rarely have a good understanding of what their expert employees are doing, nor can they easily define what they are potentially capable of doing. In these conditions, it is usually better to rely on indirect controls such as performance targeting: at least they can know when a unit has made its revenue or profitability targets. Direct control works better in simple and stable businesses, where input requirements are stable and well understood, or where key outcomes are unambiguous. Utility businesses supplying power or water might respond well to direct forms of control.

Table 13.2 **Types of control systems**

	Input	Output
Direct	Planning systems	Performance targeting
Indirect	Cultural systems	Internal markets

ILLUSTRATION 13.3

Occupy Wall Street: How anarchists do structure and systems

The Occupy Wall Street movement has a distinctive management approach, but may lack staying power.

During 2011, young people in New York were angry about debt, the financial system and lack of jobs. Inspired by the Arab Spring and the Madrid protests of the 'Indignados', various community and anarchist groups attempted to mobilise the discontent. Occupy Wall Street (OWS) sprang up at an informal anarchist rally in a New York park on 2 August 2011. Called the 'General Assembly', the rally followed typical anarchist egalitarian or 'horizontal' principles. The General Assembly was a place for debate rather than formal speeches. By the end of the day the anarchists' General Assembly had gathered about 50 participants, eclipsing a more formally organised protest rally at the other end of the park. The anarchists committed to decision by consensus and rejected the idea of leaders. The General Assembly's first big decision was to occupy Wall Street, or at least the adjacent Zuccotti Park, on 17 September.

The first day's Wall Street–Zuccotti Park occupation drew about 700 people. Numbers fluctuated thereafter, but peaked one day in October with 30,000 participants. The OWS slogan in favour of 'the 99 per cent' of ordinary people struck a world-wide chord. Similar occupations sprang up across North America, in London, Sydney and Tokyo, all declaring loose affiliations with OWS but with no formal links. Organising Zuccotti Park was hard enough.

OWS stuck to the horizontal principles of the anarchist General Assembly, but numbers attending fluctuated, and tensions arose between so-called occasional 'tourists' and the hard-core who maintained the occupation more continuously. Sometimes General Assembly meetings had more than a thousand participants. Decision making was slow or ineffective. No central political programme could be agreed, and formal affiliation with the local trade union movement was resisted. Although a series of committees emerged ('legal', 'facilitation' and so on), it took weeks to organise sanitation and laundry in Zuccotti Park. One point of dissension was drumming, a symbol of the OWS movement: the General Assembly finally decided that drumming should be limited to certain hours, but many drummers refused to follow the policy and drummed all night.

In November, the police finally evicted OWS from Zuccotti Park, with 200 arrests. OWS continued to organise sporadic protests over the winter, but momentum was fading. Although some kind of hierarchy had emerged, with designated 'organisers' (not leaders), fragmentation was increasing. By December, there were 101 different working groups, dedicated to issues from OWS communications to Yoga, and with no coordinated meeting schedules. In April 2012, the General Assembly was reported near collapse amongst dissension and exhaustion. None the less, a small anniversary demonstration of several hundred was organised for 17 September 2012, in cooperation with local trade unions.

Looking back on the year, one of the earliest OWS participants told the *Financial Times*: 'We had the manpower . . . The biggest problem Occupy had was message control. When it comes down to it, if you want to have an effective movement you need to move as one and for that you need organisational infrastructure. It got to the point where we were having more meetings about meetings and conversations about conversations than about how we can successfully organise and make our issues heard.'

Sources: Business Week, 26 October 2011; *Financial Times*, 27 October 2011, 17 September 2012.

Questions

1 What advantages did the horizontal anarchist approach to structure and systems have?

2 Which structures and systems appeared deficient for Occupy Wall Street?

13.3.1 Planning systems

Planning systems **plan and control the allocation of resources and monitor their utilisation.** The focus is on the direct control of inputs. These might be simple financial inputs (as in budgeting), human inputs (as in planning for managerial succession) or long-term investments (as particularly in strategic planning). This section concentrates on strategic oversight from the corporate centre, developing the discussion in Chapter 12.

Goold and Campbell's[15] typology of three *strategy styles* helps to identify the advantages and disadvantages of planning systems against other methods of corporate central oversight. The three strategy styles differ widely along two dimensions: the *dominant source of planning influence*, either top-down (from the corporate centre to the business units) or bottom-up (from the business units to the centre); and the *degree of performance accountability* for the business units, either tight or reasonably relaxed. As in Figure 13.6, the three strategy styles align themselves on these two dimensions thus:

- The *strategic planning* style is the archetypal planning system, hence its name. In the Goold and Campbell sense, the strategic planning style combines both a strong planning influence on strategic direction from the corporate centre with relatively relaxed performance accountability for the business units. The logic is that if the centre sets the strategic direction, business unit managers should not be held strictly accountable for disappointing results that might be due to an inappropriate plan in the first place. In the strategic planning style, the centre focuses on inputs in terms of allocating resources necessary to achieve the strategic plan, while exercising a high degree of direct control over how the plan is executed by the businesses.

- The *financial control* style involves very little central planning. The business units each set their own strategic plans, probably after some negotiation with the corporate centre, and

Figure 13.6 Strategy styles

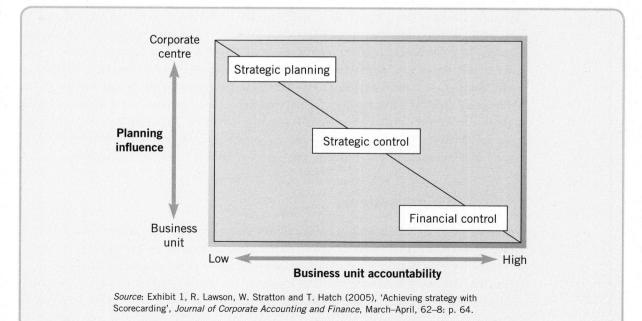

Source: Exhibit 1, R. Lawson, W. Stratton and T. Hatch (2005), 'Achieving strategy with Scorecarding', *Journal of Corporate Accounting and Finance*, March–April, 62–8: p. 64.

are then held strictly accountable for the results against these plans. This style differs from the strategic planning style in that control is against financial outputs, similar to a performance targeting system (see section 13.3.3). If the businesses devised the plans, then they should take full responsibility for success or failure. Business unit managers in the financial control style have a lot of autonomy and typically receive high bonus payments for success. But failure may easily lead to dismissal. The financial planning style fits with the portfolio manager or restructurer roles of the corporate centre referred to in Chapter 7.

● The *strategic control* style is in the middle, with a more consensual development of the strategic plan between the corporate centre and the business units and moderate levels of business unit accountability. Under the strategic control style, the centre will typically act as coach to its business unit managers, helping them to see and seize opportunities in a supportive manner. This style often relies on strong cultural systems to foster trust and mutual understanding (see section 13.3.3). Consequently, the strategic control style is often associated with the synergy manager or parental developer roles of the corporate centre discussed in Chapter 7.

Thus the three strategy styles vary with regard to their reliance on, and application of, planning systems. The direct control of inputs characteristic of the strategic planning style is only appropriate in certain circumstances. In particular, it makes sense where there are large, risky and long-range investments to be allocated: for example, an oil company typically has to take the decision to invest in the 10-year development of an oilfield at the corporate centre, rather than risk delegating it to business units whose resources and time horizons may be limited. On the other hand, the financial control style is suitable where investments are small, relatively frequent and well understood, as typically in a mature, non-capital-intensive business. The strategic control style is suitable where there are opportunities for collaborating across businesses and there is a need to nurture new ones.

The strategic planning style (not the practice of strategic planning in general) has become less common in the private sector in recent years. The style is seen as too rigid to adapt to changing circumstances and too top-down to reflect real business circumstances on the ground. However, it is important to recognise the internal consistency of all three styles, including strategic planning. Each achieves logical combinations of accountability and strategic influence. Problems occur when organisations construct systems of planning and accountability that depart substantially from the diagonal line in Figure 13.6. Too far below the line (the 'south-west' corner) implies an excessively relaxed combination of weak direction from the centre and low accountability for the businesses. Too far above the diagonal line (the 'north-east' corner) implies a harsh combination of strong direction from the centre and strict accountability in the businesses. In the 'north-east' corner, business managers are held accountable even for mistakes that may have their origins in the centre's own plans.

13.3.2 Cultural systems

Organisations typically have distinctive cultures which express basic assumptions and beliefs held by organisation members and define taken-for-granted ways of doing things (see Chapter 5). Despite their taken-for-granted, semi-conscious nature, organisational cultures can seem a tempting means of managerial control. Managers may therefore try to influence organisational culture through various deliberate mechanisms in order to achieve the kinds of employee behaviour required by their strategy.[16] Such **cultural systems aim to standardise norms of behaviour within an organisation in line with particular objectives**. Cultural systems exercise an *indirect* form of control, because of not requiring direct supervision: it becomes a matter of willing conformity or *self*-control by employees. Control is exerted on the *input* of employees, as the culture defines the norms of appropriate effort and initiative that employees will put into their jobs.

Three key cultural systems are:

- *Recruitment*. Here cultural conformity may be attempted by the selection of appropriate staff in the first place. Employers look to find people who will 'fit'. Thus some employers may favour recruiting people who have already shown themselves to be 'team-players' through sport or other activities.

- *Socialisation*. Here employee behaviours are shaped by social processes once they are at work. It often starts with the integration of new staff through training, induction and mentoring programmes. It typically continues with further training throughout a career. Symbols can also play a role in socialisation, for example the symbolic example of leaders' behaviours or the influence of office décor, dress codes or language.

- *Reward*. Appropriate behaviour can be encouraged through pay, promotion or symbolic processes (e.g. public praise). The desire to achieve the same rewards as successful people in the organisation will typically encourage imitative behaviour.

It is important to recognise that organisations' cultures are not fully under formal management control. Sometimes aspects of organisational culture may persistently contradict managerial intentions, as with peer-group pressure not to respond to organisational strategies. Cynicism and 'going through the motions' are common in some organisations. Sometimes the culture of an organisation may even drive its strategy (see Chapter 5). On the other hand, some cultures can bring about desired results, even without deliberate management intervention. For example, workers often form spontaneous and informal 'communities of practice', in which expert practitioners inside or even outside the organisation share their knowledge to generate innovative solutions to problems on their own initiative.[17] Examples of these informal communities of practice range from the Xerox photocopying engineers who would exchange information about problems and solutions over breakfast gatherings at the start of the day, to the programmer networks which support the development of Linux 'freeware' internationally over the internet.

13.3.3 Performance targeting systems

Performance targets focus on the *outputs* of an organisation (or part of an organisation), such as product quality, revenues or profits. These targets are often known as *key performance indicators* (KPIs). The performance of an organisation is judged, either internally or externally, on its ability to meet these targets. However, within specified boundaries, the organisation remains free on how targets should be achieved. This approach can be particularly appropriate in certain situations:

- *Within large businesses*, corporate centres may choose performance targets to control their business units without getting involved in the details of how they achieve them (as in the financial control style in section 13.3.1). These targets are often cascaded down the organisation as specific targets for subunits, functions and even individuals.

- In *regulated markets*, such as privatised utilities in the UK and elsewhere, government-appointed regulators increasingly exercise control through agreed key performance indicators (KPIs), such as service or quality levels, as a means of ensuring 'competitive' performance.[18]

- In *the public services*, where control of resource inputs was the dominant approach historically, governments are attempting to move control processes towards outputs (such as quality of service) and, more importantly, towards outcomes (e.g. patient mortality rates in healthcare).

Many managers find it difficult to develop a useful set of targets. There are at least three potential problems with targets:[19]

- *Inappropriate measures* of performance are quite common. For example, managers often prefer indicators that are easily measured or choose measures based on inadequate understanding of real needs on the ground. The result is a focus on the required measures rather than the factors that might be essential to long-term success. In the private sector, focus on short-term profit measures is common, at the expense of investment in the long-run prosperity of the business. To take a public-sector case, inappropriate 'national indicators' appeared to be a problem with child protection services in Illustration 13.4.

- *Inappropriate target levels* are a common problem. Managers are liable to give their superiors pessimistic forecasts so that targets are set at undemanding levels, which can then be easily met. On the other hand, superiors may over-compensate for their managers' pessimism, and end up setting excessively demanding targets. Unrealistically ambitious targets can either demotivate employees who see no hope of achieving them regardless of their effort, or encourage risky or dishonest behaviours in order to achieve the otherwise impossible.

- *Excessive internal competition* can be a result of targets focused on individual or subunit performance. Although an organisation by definition should be more than the sum of its parts, if individuals or subunits are being rewarded on their performance in isolation, they will have little incentive to collaborate with the other parts of the organisation. The struggle to meet individualistic targets will reduce the exchange of information and the sharing of resources. This kind of individualistic behaviour played a part in the fraud at UBS (Illustration 13.5).

These acknowledged difficulties with targets have led to the development of two techniques designed to encourage a more balanced approach to target-setting. The most fundamental has been the development of the balanced scorecard approach.[20] *Balanced scorecards* set performance targets according to a range of perspectives, not only financial. Thus balanced scorecards typically combine four specific perspectives: the *financial perspective*, which might include profit margins or cash flow; the *customer perspective*, which sets targets important to customers, such as delivery times or service levels; the *internal perspective*, with targets relating to operational effectiveness such as the development of IT systems or reductions in waste levels; and finally the future-orientated *innovation and learning perspective*, which targets activities that will be important to the long-run performance of the organisation, for example investment in training or research. Attending to targets relevant to all four perspectives helps ensure that managers do not focus on one set of targets (e.g. financial) at the expense of others, while also keeping an eye to the future through innovation and learning.

A second more balanced approach to target-setting is strategy mapping, developing the balanced scorecard idea. *Strategy maps* link different performance targets into a mutually supportive causal chain supporting strategic objectives. Figure 13.7 shows an extract of a strategy map for a delivery company based on the four perspectives of finance, customers, internal processes, and innovation and learning. In this map, investments in well-trained and

ILLUSTRATION 13.4

Structure, systems and saving children's lives

Changing structures and systems is not a quick fix in protecting children from parental abuse and neglect.

England and Wales have a problem: the homicide of children by their own parents. In the period 1998 to 2008, an average of about 40 children were killed by their parents annually. In 2008, about 200,000 children were living in households with a known high risk of domestic abuse and violence.

The death of 9-year-old Victoria Climbié in 2000 at the hands of her great aunt and boyfriend prompted a major reform of child protection services in England and Wales. Victoria Climbié's death had come after nine months of regular warning signs to the local social, police and medical services. The lack of coordination in picking up signs of abuse between these agencies was seen as a major weakness. One result was the merger of local education and children's social services into *unified children's services department*s. Another was to create '*common assessment frameworks*' (CAFs), a way for all agencies (from police to doctors) to record their dealing with a particular child on a standardised form accessible to all. A system of *national indicators* for measuring child protection was also introduced, measuring clear quantifiable variables such as numbers of case review meetings and re-registrations on the child protection register.

The homicide rate drifted down after the implementation of the reforms between 2003 and 2005, but then started to climb back towards the average, with 43 homicides in 2007–8. The 2007 death by neglect and abuse of 17-month-old 'Baby P' – in the same local authority area as Victoria Climbié and again after months of warning signs to police, medical and social work services – prompted a further review of services. The review found that under 10 per cent of local authorities had adopted the national indicators for child protection: local authorities complained that the targets were focused excessively on proper process and time-scales, rather than meaningful outcomes. None the less, the review basically confirmed the new structure and systems, while urging more effective implementation through better training of social workers, revised indicators, more resources, centralised computer support and improved communications between agencies.

On the ground, however, there was considerable dissatisfaction with the post-Climbié reforms. Some 81 per cent of professionals in one poll claimed that the merger between educational and social services was not working (www.publicservice.co.uk). Most of the merged departments were headed by former directors of education, with little understanding of the social work for which they were responsible. Social workers complained about excessive form filling in order to demonstrate correct procedures. A boy told the review: 'It seems like they have to do all this form filling – their bosses' bosses make them do it – but it makes them forget about us.' An academic commentator estimated that social workers were now spending 80 per cent of their time in front of computers rather than with clients. The common assessment framework (CAF) form is eight pages long. One school head reported to the *Guardian* newspaper: 'You can no longer pick up the phone to the agencies for advice or referral without hearing "Where is the CAF?".'

Speaking to the *Guardian*, Maggie Atkinson, Director for Learning and Children in the town of Gateshead, urged patience: 'Bringing services together into one department creates a different culture, not immediately, but over a period of time. This change in culture is only really beginning to be embedded in local services and to put it into reverse would be a wasted opportunity. It doesn't matter whether the director comes from education or social services. What you need to do the job is broad shoulders, effective management and a very strong team around you.'

Sources: L. Lightfoot, 'A marriage on the rocks', *Guardian*, 17 March 2009; 'The Protection of Children in England: a Progress Report', *Every Child Matters*, March 2009.

Questions

1 List the advantages and disadvantages of the new structure and systems for children's services.

2 What kinds of actions and initiatives might be appropriate in terms of the cultural systems of children's services?

Figure 13.7 A strategy map

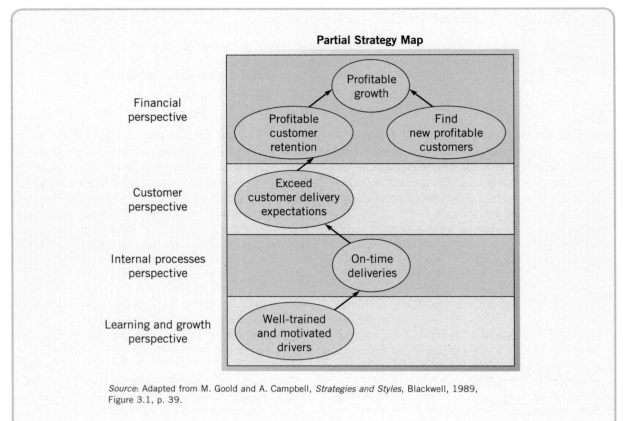

Source: Adapted from M. Goold and A. Campbell, *Strategies and Styles*, Blackwell, 1989, Figure 3.1, p. 39.

motivated drivers under the heading of 'innovation and learning' lead to on-time deliveries under the heading of 'internal processes', and thence to satisfied customers and finally to profitable growth. The causal chain between the various targets underlines the need for balance between them: each depends on the others for achievement. Thus strategy maps help in reducing the problem of partial measures referred to above; the problems of inappropriate target levels and internal competition are not so easily resolved.

13.3.4 Market systems

Market disciplines (or *internal markets*) can be brought inside organisations to control activities internally.[21] **Market systems typically involve some formalised system of 'contracting' for resources or inputs from other parts of an organisation and for supplying outputs to other parts of an organisation.** Control focuses on outputs, for example revenues earned in successful competition for internal contracts. The control is indirect: rather than accepting detailed performance targets determined externally, units have simply to earn their keep in competitive internal markets.

Internal markets can be used in a variety of ways. There might be *competitive bidding*, perhaps through the creation of an internal investment bank at the corporate centre to support new initiatives. Also, a customer–supplier relationship may be established between a central

ILLUSTRATION 13.5

Rogue banker or rogue bank?

In 2012, Kweku Adoboli was convicted for a fraud involving $2.3 bn. But were his actions a product of deep-rooted systems failures at accident-prone UBS?

In 2003, Kweku Adoboli graduated from the University of Nottingham with a degree in Computer Science and Management. Seven years later, he was earning £60,000 ($92,000; €70,000) in salary and £250,000 in bonuses at the London offices of UBS, Switzerland's largest bank. In 2012, he was facing the prospect of seven years in jail, after committing one of the largest frauds in British history.

Adoboli had worked himself up at UBS from so-called back-office jobs (recording and checking trades) to a position as associate director on the elite Delta One desk at UBS. In banking, Delta One desks trade using the bank's own capital, and typically engage in high-risk and innovative deals. As early as 2008, Adoboli had started to create fictitious deals to hide some of his trading losses, taking advantage of his knowledge of back-office systems. The concealment was successful and Adoboli gained a reputation as a star trader, with lavish bonuses to match. It was only in September 2011, as one of UBS's accountants finally began to probe, that Adoboli owned up to his fraud. At that point, UBS had over $10 bn at risk through his various trades.

UBS was the creation of a merger between two large Swiss banks in 1998, Union Bank of Switzerland and Swiss Bank Corporation. In 2000, the new bank merged with the leading American stockbroker Paine Webber, launching an aggressive strategy of growth. By 2006, UBS had risen from seventh-largest investment bank in terms of fees, to being one of the top four.

But this growth strategy had an underside. As the financial crisis loomed during 2007, the bank deliberately sold assets to its customers in order to reduce its own liabilities: it would later receive a $150 m fine in the USA for this mis-selling. The bank had also taken aggressive positions in the fatally flawed sub-prime mortgage market during the good years, leaving it exposed to losses of $38 bn. The Swiss government had to rescue the bank in 2008,

firing the then chief executive, with a further 11,000 job losses following. In 2009, the bank had to pay a fine of $781 m to the US government for its role in helping American citizens in tax evasion: one scheme had involved bank employees smuggling diamonds out of the country in toothpaste tubes. UBS faced another large fine ($160 m) in 2011, due to the rigging of the municipal bonds derivatives market.

In this context, some observers did not think that Adoboli's fraud was an aberration. The bank had been focused on headlong growth, paying rich rewards to those who seemed to deliver it. Top management had not attended to the true merger of the three main component companies. It was commented that Adoboli's Delta One desk had just five staff, working in close proximity to each other, and presumably very aware of what each of their colleagues was doing. A former UBS investment banker told the *New York Times*: 'The problem isn't the culture. The problem is that there wasn't a culture. There are silos. Everyone is separate. People cut their own deals, and it's every man for himself. A lot of people made a lot of money that way, and it fuelled jealousies and efforts to get even better deals. People thought of themselves first, and then maybe the bank, if they thought about it at all.'

Sources: New York Times, 24 September 2011; Financial Times, 19 September 2012.

Questions

1 In this account, what elements of UBS's systems appear to have been deficient, with regard to Adoboli and more generally?

2 What roles might the merger and growth strategy have played in the various failures at UBS?

service department, such as training or IT, and the operating units. Typically these internal markets are subject to considerable regulation. For example, the corporate centre might set rules for *transfer prices* between internal business units to prevent exploitative contract pricing, or insist on *service-level agreements* to ensure appropriate service by an essential internal supplier, such as IT, for the various units that depend on it.

Internal markets work well where complexity or rapid change makes detailed direct or input controls impractical. But market systems can create problems as well. First, they can increase bargaining between units, consuming important management time. Second, they may create a new bureaucracy monitoring all of the internal transfers of resources between units. Third, an overzealous use of market mechanisms can lead to dysfunctional competition and legalistic contracting, destroying cultures of collaboration and relationships. These have all been complaints made against the internal markets and semi-autonomous Foundation Trust Hospitals introduced in the UK's National Health Service. On the other hand, their proponents claim that these market processes free a traditionally over-centralised health service to innovate and respond to local needs, while market disciplines maintain overall control.

(13.4) CONFIGURATIONS

The introduction of this chapter introduced the concept of configurations. **Configurations are the set of organisational design elements that interlink together in order to support the intended strategy.** The introductory Figure 13.1 focused on the mutually supporting elements of strategy, structure and systems. This section begins by extending these three elements with the McKinsey 7-S framework and finishes by considering likely tensions or dilemmas amongst the elements of organisational design and some methods for managing them.

13.4.1 The McKinsey 7-S framework

The McKinsey & Co consulting company has developed a framework for assessing the degree to which the various elements of an organisation's design fit together in a mutually supporting manner. The *McKinsey 7-S framework* highlights the importance of fit between strategy, structure, systems, staff, style, skills and superordinate goals.[22] Together these seven elements can serve as a checklist in any organisational design exercise: see Figure 13.8.

This chapter has already addressed strategy, structure and systems. This section will comment on the remaining four elements of the 7-S framework, as follows:

● *Style* here refers to the leadership style of top managers in an organisation. Leadership styles may be collaborative, participative, directive or coercive, for instance (see Chapter 14). Managers' behavioural style can influence the culture of the whole organisation (see Chapter 5). The style should fit other aspects of the 7-S framework: for example, a highly directive or coercive style is not likely to fit a matrix organisation structure.

● *Staff* is about the kinds of people in the organisation and how they are developed. This relates to systems of recruitment, socialisation and reward (section 13.3.2). A key criterion for the feasibility of any strategy is: does the organisation have the people to match (see section 11.4.2)? A common constraint on structural change is the availability of the right people to head new departments and divisions (the 'People Test': see section 13.2.6).

Figure 13.8 The McKinsey 7 Ss

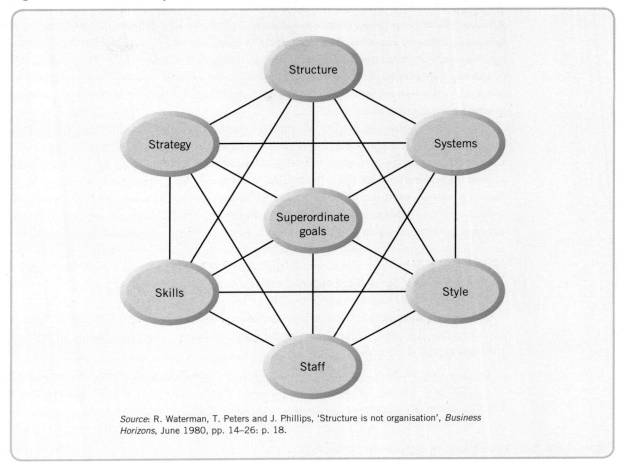

Source: R. Waterman, T. Peters and J. Phillips, 'Structure is not organisation', *Business Horizons*, June 1980, pp. 14–26: p. 18.

● *Skills* relates to staff, but in the 7-S framework refers more broadly to capabilities in general (see Chapter 3). The concept of capabilities here raises not only staff skills but also issues to do with how these skills are embedded in and captured by the organisation as a whole. For example, how do the organisation's training schemes, information technology and reward systems transform the talents of individuals into the organisational capabilities required by the strategy?

● *Superordinate goals* refers to the overarching goals or purpose of the organisation as a whole, in other words the mission, vision and objectives that form the organisational purpose (see Chapter 4). Superordinate goals are placed at the centre of the 7-S framework: all other elements should support these.

The McKinsey 7-S framework highlights at least three aspects of organising. First, organising involves a lot more than just getting the organisational structure right; there are many other elements to attend to. Second, the 7-S framework emphasises fit between all these elements: everything from structure to skills needs to be connected together. Third, if managers change one element of the 7-S, the concept of fit suggests they are likely to have to change all the other elements as well in order to keep them all appropriately aligned to each other. Changing one element in isolation is liable to make things worse until overall fit is restored.

13.4.2 Configuration dilemmas

Although the concept of configurations and the 7-S framework emphasise the importance of mutual fit between elements, in practice this is often hard to achieve. Managing typically involves trade-offs and tensions between different desirable states. Seeking perfect solutions on one element of the configuration may very well oblige compromises on another element. Given that many of these tensions are very hard to escape, this section briefly considers various ways in which they can at least be managed.

Figure 13.9 summarises five key dilemmas in organising. First, formal hierarchies are often necessary to ensure control and action, but they can sit uneasily with the informal networks that foster knowledge exchange and innovation. Second, vertical accountability promotes maximum performance by subordinates, but it can easily lead managers to maximise their own self-interest, at the expense of horizontal relationships. Third, empowering employees lower down the organisation gives scope for potentially valuable initiatives and experiments, but over the long term can lead to incoherence. Fourth, while centralisation might be needed for standardisation of products and processes, this can be at the cost of the initiative and flexibility fostered by decentralisation. Finally, adopting best practice on a particular element of the organisation, for instance financial controls, may actually be damaging if it does not fit with the needs of the organisation as a whole.

Managers should recognise that any organisational design is likely to face dilemmas of these kinds and that it is hard to optimise on all dimensions. However, they may be able to manage these dilemmas in three ways:

- By *subdividing* the organisation, so that the one part of the organisation is organised optimally according to one side of these dilemmas, while the rest responds to the other. Thus, for example, IBM created its revolutionary personal computer in a specialised new-venture

Figure 13.9 Some dilemmas in organising for success

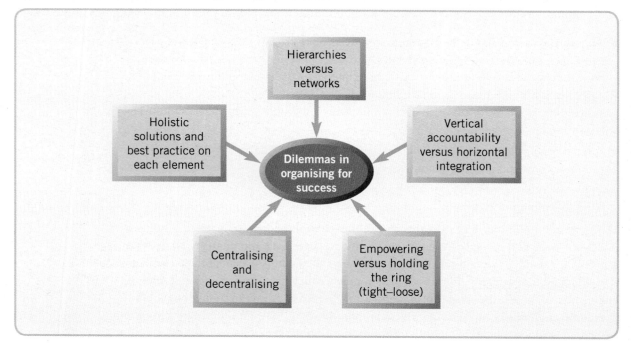

KEY DEBATE

Does structure follow strategy?

A key message of this chapter is that strategy and structure should fit together. But which determines which?

Alfred Chandler, Professor of Business History at Harvard Business School, proposed one of the fundamental rules of strategic management: 'unless structure follows strategy, inefficiency results'.[1] This logical sequence fits the 'design lens' for strategy, but does assume that structure is very much subordinate to strategy: structure can easily be fixed once the big strategic decisions are made. But some authors warn that this dangerously underestimates structure's role. Sometimes strategy follows structure.

Chandler's rule is based on the historical experience of companies like General Motors, Exxon and DuPont. DuPont, for example, was originally an explosives company. During the First World War, however, the company anticipated the peace by deliberately diversifying out of explosives into new civil markets such as plastics and paints. Yet the end of the war plunged DuPont into crisis. All its new businesses were loss-making; only explosives still made money. The problem was not the diversification strategy, but the structure that DuPont used to manage the new civil businesses. DuPont had retained its old functional structure, so that responsibilities for the production and marketing of all the new businesses were still centralised on single functional heads. They could not cope with the increased diversity. The solution was not to abandon the diversification strategy; rather it was to adopt a new structure with decentralised divisions for each of the separate businesses. DuPont thrives today with a variant of this multidivisional structure.

Hall and Saias accept the importance of strategy for structure but warn that the causality can go the other way.[2] An organisation's existing structure very much determines the kinds of strategic opportunities that its management will see and want to grasp. For instance, it is easy for a company with a decentralised multidivisional structure to make acquisitions and divestments: all it has to do is add or subtract divisions, with few ramifications for the rest of the business. On the other hand, it can be very hard for the top managers of a decentralised multidivisional organisation to see

opportunities for innovation and knowledge-sharing within the operations of the divisions: they are too far away from the real business. In other words, structures can shape strategies.

Amburgey and Dacin tested the relative impact of strategy and structure on each other by analysing the strategic and structural changes of more than 200 American corporations over nearly 30 years.[3] They found that moves towards decentralised structures were often followed by moves towards increasingly diversified strategies: here, structure was determining strategy. Overall, however, increased diversification was twice as likely to be followed by structural decentralisation as the other way round. In other words, structure does follow strategy, but only most of the time.

Henry Mintzberg concludes that 'structure follows strategy as the left foot follows the right'.[4] In other words, strategy and structure are related reciprocally rather than just one way. Mintzberg warns that a simple 'design' approach to strategy and structure can be misleading. Structure is not always easy to fix after the big strategic decisions have been made. Strategists should check to see that their existing structures are not constraining the kinds of strategies that they consider.

References

1. A. Chandler, *Strategy and Structure: Chapters in the History of American Enterprise*, MIT Press, 1962, p. 314.
2. D.J. Hall and M.A. Saias, 'Strategy follows structure!', *Strategic Management Journal*, vol. 1, no. 2 (1980), pp. 149–63.
3. T. Amburgey and T. Dacin, 'As the left foot follows the right? The dynamics of strategic and structural change', *Academy of Management Journal*, vol. 37, no. 6 (1994), pp. 1427–52.
4. H. Mintzberg, 'The Design School: reconsidering the basic premises of strategic management', *Strategic Management Journal*, vol. 11 (1990), pp. 171–95.

Question

Hall and Saias (1980) suggest that organisational structures can influence the kinds of strategies that management teams will pursue. What kinds of organisations might be particularly susceptible to structural constraints on their strategies?

division, kept separate from the traditional mainframe activities which were dominated by principles of hierarchy and vertical accountability highly antagonistic to radical innovation.[23]

- By *combining* different organising principles at the same time. Thus organisation design expert Jay Galbraith argues for the potential of 'hybrid structures': for instance, a 'front–back' structure combines centralised functional specialisms in manufacturing and research at the 'back', while customer-facing units at the front are organised in a more decentralised way around particular market segments, such as industry or geography.[24]

- By *reorganising* frequently so that no one side of the dilemma can become too entrenched. Given this pace of reorganising, many organisations are like pendulums, constantly swinging between centralisation and devolution, for example, without resting long on one side or the other.[25]

A final dilemma arising from the interconnectedness of configurations is which element drives the others. The extent to which strategic elements drive structural elements is the subject of the Key Debate.

SUMMARY

- Successful organising means responding to the key challenges facing the organisation. This chapter has stressed *control*, *change*, *knowledge* and *internationalisation*.

- There are many *structural types* (e.g. functional, divisional, matrix, transnational and project). Each structural type has its own strengths and weaknesses and responds differently to the challenges of control, change, knowledge and internationalisation.

- There is a range of different organisational *systems* to facilitate and control strategy. These systems can focus on either *inputs* or *outputs* and be *direct* or *indirect*.

- The separate organisational elements, summarised in the *McKinsey 7-S framework*, should come together to form a coherent *reinforcing configuration*. But these reinforcing cycles also raise tough dilemmas that can be managed by *subdividing*, *combining* and *reorganising*.

VIDEO ASSIGNMENTS

Visit **MyStrategyLab** and watch the Wilmington and Metapraxis case study for Chapter 13.

1 Using the video extracts and section 13.2 of the text, which of the basic organisation structural types best describes the structure of Wilmington? What are the advantages and disadvantages of this structure?

2 David Hammond at Metapraxis talks about the increase in 'empowerment' at the company. Discuss the advantages and disadvantages of this change.

WORK ASSIGNMENTS

✽ *Denotes more advanced work assignments.*
* *Refers to a case study in the Text and Cases edition.*

13.1   Go to the website of a large organisation you are familiar with and find its organisational chart (not all organisations provide these). Why is the organisation structured like this?

13.2   Referring to section 13.2.2 on the divisional structure, consider the advantages and disadvantages of creating divisions along different lines – such as product, geography or technology – with respect to a large organisation you are familiar with or a case organisation such as International HIV/AIDS Alliance*, Academies/Free Schools* or Unilever*.

13.3✽   Referring to Figure 13.7, write a short executive brief explaining how strategy maps could be a useful management system to monitor and control the performance of organisational units. Be sure to analyse both advantages and disadvantages of this approach.

13.4   As a middle manager with responsibility for a small business unit, which 'strategy style' (section 13.3.5) would you prefer to work within? In what sort of circumstances or corporate organisation would this style not work so well for you?

Integrative assignment

13.5   Take a recent merger or acquisition (see Chapter 10), ideally one involving two organisations of roughly equal size, and analyse how the deal has changed the acquiring or merged company's organisational structure. What do you conclude from the extent or lack of structural change for the new company going forward?

RECOMMENDED KEY READINGS

● The best single coverage of this chapter's issues is in R. Daft, *Understanding the Theory and Design of Organisations*, South-Western, 2009.

● For a collection of relevant articles, see the special issue 'Learning to design organisations', R. Dunbar and W. Starbuck (eds), *Organisation Science*, vol. 17, no. 2 (2006).

● M. Goold and A. Campbell, *Designing Effective Organisations*, Jossey-Bass, 2002, provides a practical guide to organisational design issues.

REFERENCES

1. Good reviews of recent tendencies in organisation structure are J.R. Galbraith, 'The future of organization design', *Journal of Organization Design*, vol. 1, no. 1 (2012), pp. 3–6; and N. Argyres and T. Zenger, 'Dynamics in organization structure', in A. Grandori (ed.), *Handbook of Economic Organization*, Edward Elgar, 2013.

2. For an introduction to the view that organisations should fit their structures to key challenges ('contingencies') see B. Luo and L. Donaldson, 'Misfits in organization design: information processing as a compensatory mechanism',

Journal of Organization Design, vol. 2, no. 1 (2013), pp. 2–10. See also R. Whittington, 'Organisational structure', in *The Oxford Handbook of Strategy*, Volume II, Oxford University Press, 2003, Chapter 28.

3. This view of divisionalisation as a response to diversity was originally put forward by A.D. Chandler, *Strategy and Structure*, MIT Press, 1962. See R. Whittington and M. Mayer, *The European Corporation: Strategy, Structure and Social Science*, Oxford University Press, 2000, for a summary of Chandler's argument in contemporary Europe.

4. For a review of current experience with matrix structures, see S. Thomas and L. D'Annunzio, 'Challenges and strategies of matrix organisations: top-level and mid-level managers' perspectives', *Human Resource Planning*, vol. 28, no. 1 (2005), pp. 39–48; and J. Galbraith, *Designing Matrix Structures that Actually Work*, Jossey-Bass, 2009.

5. See C. Bartlett and S. Ghoshal, 'Matrix management: not a structure, more a frame of mind', *Harvard Business Review*, vol. 68, no. 4 (1990), pp. 138–45.

6. C. Bartlett and S. Ghoshal, *Managing Across Borders*, 2nd edn, Harvard Business School Press, 2008.

7. Recent research finds that transnational structures generally perform better than either centralised or decentralised structures: see J.-N. Garbe and N. Richter, 'Causal analysis of the internationalization and performance relationship based on neural networks', *Journal of International Management*, vol. 15, no. 4 (2009), pp. 413–31.

8. The classic article on project-based organisations is by R. DeFillippi and M. Arthur, 'Paradox in project-based enterprise: the case of film-making', *California Management Review*, vol. 40, no. 2 (1998), pp. 125–45. For some difficulties, see M. Bresnen, A. Goussevskaia and J. Swann, 'Organizational routines, situated learning and processes of change in project-based organisations', *Project Management Journal*, vol. 36, no. 3 (2005), pp. 27–42.

9. For a discussion of more permanent team structures, see Thomas Mullern, 'Integrating the team-based structure in the business process: the case of Saab Training Systems', in A. Pettigrew and E. Fenton (eds), *The Innovating Organisation*, Sage, 2000.

10. M. Goold and A. Campbell, *Designing Effective Organisations*, Jossey-Bass, 2002. See also M. Goold and A. Campbell, 'Do you have a well-designed organisation?', *Harvard Business Review*, vol. 80, no. 3 (2002), pp. 117–224.

11. A.D. Chandler, *Strategy and Structure: Chapters in the History of American Enterprise*, MIT Press, 1962.

12. This practice of 'patching' parts of the organisation onto each other according to changing market needs is described in K. Eisenhardt and S. Brown, 'Patching: restitching business portfolios in dynamic markets', *Harvard Business Review*, vol. 75, no. 3 (1999), pp. 72–80.

13. The point has been argued by E. Fenton and A. Pettigrew, 'Theoretical perspectives on new forms of organising', in A. Pettigrew and E. Fenton (eds), *The Innovating Organisation*, Sage, 2000, Chapter 1.

14. M. Goold and A. Campbell, *Strategies and Styles*, Blackwell, 1987.

15. C. Casey, 'Come, join our family: discipline and integration in corporate organizational culture', *Human Relations*, vol. 52, no. 2 (1999), pp. 155–179; for an account of the socialisation of graduate trainees, see A.D. Brown and C. Coupland, 'Sounds of silence: graduate trainees, hegemony and resistance', *Organization Studies*, vol. 26, no. 7 (2005), pp. 1049–70.

16. E.C. Wenger and W.M. Snyder, 'Communities of practice: the organized frontier', *Harvard Business Review*, vol. 78, no. 1 (2000), pp. 139–46.

17. A. Maté, J. Trujillo and J. Mylopoulos, 'Conceptualizing and specifying key performance indicators in business strategy models', *Conceptual Modelling* (2012), pp. 282–91.

18. The value of goals and performance targets have been debated vigorously: see L. Ordonez, M. Schweitzer, A Galinksy and M. Bazerman, 'Goals gone wild: the systematic side effects of overprescribing goal setting', *Academy of Management Perspectives*, vol. 23, no. 1 (2009), pp. 6–16; and E. Locke and G. Latham, 'Has goal setting gone wild?', *Academy of Management Perspectives*, vol. 23, no. 1 (2009), pp. 17–23.

19. See R. Kaplan and D. Norton, 'Having trouble with your strategy? Then map it', *Harvard Business Review*, vol. 78, no. 5 (2000), pp. 167–76; and R. Kaplan and D. Norton, *Alignment: How to Apply the Balanced Scorecard to Strategy*, Harvard Business School Press, 2006.

20. See Gary Hamel, 'Bringing Silicon Valley inside', *Harvard Business Review*, vol. 77, no. 5 (1999), pp. 70–84. For a discussion of internal market challenges, see A. Vining, 'Internal market failure', *Journal of Management Studies*, vol. 40, no. 2 (2003), pp. 431–57.

21. R. Waterman, T. Peters and J. Phillips, 'Structure is not organization', *Business Horizons*, June (1980), pp. 14–26.

22. R.A. Burgelman, 'Managing the new venture division: implications for strategic management', *Strategic Management Journal*, vol. 6, no. 1 (1985), pp. 39–54.

23. J. Galbraith, 'Organising to deliver solutions', *Organizational Dynamics*, vol. 31, no. 2 (2002), pp. 194–207.

24. R. Whittington and M. Mayer, *Organising for Success: A Report on Knowledge*, CIPD, 2002.

25. For an analysis of this process at a leading pharmaceutical firm, see S. Karim and W. Mitchell, 'Innovating through acquisition and internal development: a quarter-century of boundary evolution at Johnson & Johnson', *Long Range Planning*, vol. 37, no. 6 (2004), pp. 525–38.

CASE EXAMPLE

One Sony?

Kazuo Hirai's April 2012 appointment as Chief Executive Officer of Sony Corporation would probably have surprised his younger self. After all, Hirai had started out as Japanese translator to the American hip-hop band the Beastie Boys. He had then become a video games designer and later led Sony's PlayStation business in the USA. However, by the time he finally became CEO at the age of 51, Sony was in deep trouble. One of Hirai's first moves was to change Sony's organisational structure. The aim was to create a more integrated business – 'One Sony'.

Business background

Sony's businesses spanned professional electronics such as semiconductors and medical devices, consumer electronics from televisions and mobile phones to computers and the PlayStation, together with 'content' businesses such as movies and music. As such, Sony was pitching against companies like the American success-story Apple and the Korean high-technology giant Samsung. Despite a proud history associated with such brands as the Sony Walkman audio devices or Sony Trinitron televisions, Sony was being left far behind. By 2012, Sony's stock price was less than half it had been five years before, while Apple and Samsung were two or three times as valuable (see Figure 1).

Sony's relative decline has not been for want of trying. In 2003, the company had suffered the so-called 'Sony shock', when both earnings and stock price had plunged simultaneously following a weak response to cheaper Asian electronics firms. The company reduced costs by cutting its workforce by nearly 20 per cent. In 2005, Sony had taken the then-revolutionary step of appointing its first foreigner as CEO, Howard Stringer, a Welsh-American with a background in the music and movie business. Stringer had announced that he would break down the company's vertical management system, which he described as a set of separate 'silos' with little coherence. He sought to integrate the company's hardware

Figure 1 **Sony's stock price performance relative to Apple and Samsung, 2008–12**

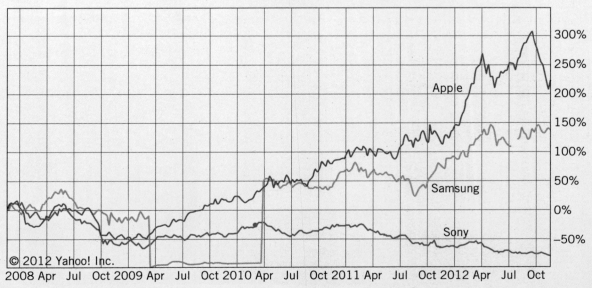

Source: Yahoo Finance. For comparison of price changes, all prices standardised to zero in 2008.

business, based in Japan, with its various content businesses, led by music and movies in the USA. Stringer's slogan had been 'Sony United'. But Stringer had been neither an engineer nor a Japanese speaker. It was reported that many of his diktats to the Japanese hardware businesses were largely ignored.

The financial results for 2011–12 confirmed Stringer's failure. Without a striking new product to compare with the original Walkman or Trinitron and still heavily reliant on an expensive Japanese manufacturing base, Sony's sales were down nearly 10 per cent while profits were negative. The 69-year-old Stringer became Company Chairman. Hirai, Sony's youngest ever CEO and the second non-engineer in a row, set to work.

New strategy and new structure

Hirai insisted that the new Sony would be focused predominantly on five key strategic initiatives. First of all was a strengthening of the core business, by which he meant digital imaging, games and mobile devices, including phones, tablets and laptops. Second, Hirai committed himself to returning the television business back to profitability, after eight years of consistent losses. Third, Sony would develop faster in emerging markets such as India and South America. The fourth

initiative was to accelerate innovation, particularly by integrating product areas. Finally, Sony was preparing to realign its business portfolio, with divestments expected of non-core businesses (e.g. the legacy chemicals business).

Hirai supported these strategic initiatives with a new organisational structure, designed to support his concept of 'One Sony'. The old structure had been based on two big groups centred on Japan and predominantly in hardware: the Professional, Device and Solutions Group, responsible for about half of all sales; and the Consumer Products and Services Group, responsible for another fifth of sales. Alongside these two major groups were several standalone businesses mostly based abroad, including Music, Pictures (movies) and the Sony–Ericsson joint venture in mobile phones (see Figure 2).

The new structure broke up the big groups, creating 12 standalone businesses in all (see Figure 3). The ending of the Sony–Ericsson joint venture in late 2011 allowed the mobile phone business to be brought closer to the VAIO and mobile computing business. Sony's medical-related businesses, previously dispersed across multiple units but now targeted for rapid growth, were folded into a dedicated medical business unit led by an executive at corporate level. The device and semiconductor businesses, including image sensors, became a single

Figure 2 Sony's organisational structure, 2011

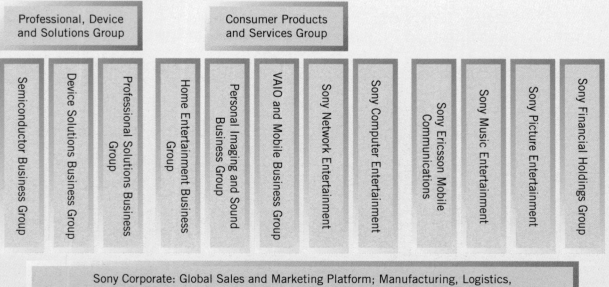

Source: Adapted from www.sony.net

Figure 3 Sony's organisational structure, 2012

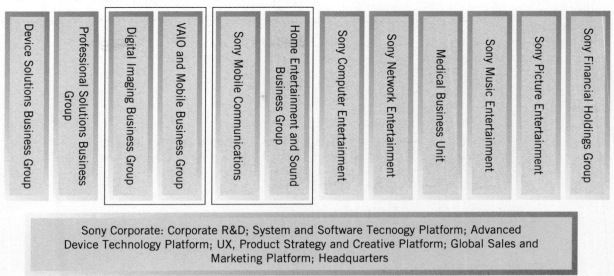

Device Solutions Business Group | Professional Solutions Business Group | Digital Imaging Business Group | VAIO and Mobile Business Group | Sony Mobile Communications | Home Entertainment and Sound Business Group | Sony Computer Entertainment | Sony Network Entertainment | Medical Business Unit | Sony Music Entertainment | Sony Picture Entertainment | Sony Financial Holdings Group

Sony Corporate: Corporate R&D; System and Software Tecnoogy Platform; Advanced Device Technology Platform; UX, Product Strategy and Creative Platform; Global Sales and Marketing Platform; Headquarters

Source: Adapted from www.sony.net

business group, Device Solutions. Sony Network Entertainment was strengthened, with all Sony's online offerings now included.

Hirai completed his structural changes by reinforcing headquarters resources and oversight, with several new senior management appointments. The aim was to leverage the company's broad portfolio by creating exclusive content for Sony's own devices. A single corporate-level executive was made responsible for User Experience ('UX'), Product Strategy and the Creative Platform, charged with strengthening horizontal integration and enhancing the experience across Sony's entire product and network service line-up. The same executive would oversee the mobile businesses, including smart phones, tablets and PCs (indicated by the box around the two relevant business groups). Digital Imaging and the Professional Solutions likewise came under the oversight of a single corporate-level executive. Hirai himself was to take direct responsibility for the Home Entertainment Business Group, including the troubled television business, pledging to give it the majority of his time in the coming months.

At an investors' meeting in April 2012, Hirai went beyond strategic and structural changes:

'The other thing is . . . the One Sony/One Management concept. That is really important, because I made sure that as I built my new management team, that everybody in the team is 100 per cent fully-committed and also aligned as to what needs to get done and

how we're going to get that done. And so we have a lot of discussions internally amongst the management team. Once we make that decision, then everybody moves in the same direction and we execute with speed. And I think that is another area that is quite different from some of the restructurings or the changes that we have made perhaps in the past.'

Results did not come quickly, however. In November 2012, the *Wall Street Journal* observed of Sony's new organisational chart: 'Far from providing clarity of purpose, the diagram should leave investors tearing their hair out. While new Chief Executive Kazuo Hirai shuffles the deckchairs on board the one-time electronics titan, Sony's stock is plunging into deep waters.'

Main sources: *Wall Street Journal*, 2 February 2012; Nikkei Report, 2 March 2012; Sony Corporation press release, Tokyo, 27 March 2012; CQ FD Disclosure, Sony Corporate Strategy Meeting Conference Call for Overseas Investors – Final, 12 April 2012; *Wall Street Journal*, 15 November 2012.

Suggested video clip: Networkworld: New Sony CEO has big plans for company turnaround. https://www.youtube.com/watch?v=jBxWZS4-rR8.

Questions

1 Assess the pros and cons of Hirai's structural changes.

2 What other initiatives beyond structural change might be necessary in order to create 'One Sony'?

14

LEADING STRATEGIC CHANGE

Learning outcomes

After reading this chapter you should be able to:

● Identify and assess different styles of leading strategic change.

● Analyse how *organisational context* might affect the design of strategic change.

● Undertake a *forcefield analysis* to identify forces blocking and facilitating change.

● Assess the value of different *levers* for strategic change.

● Identify *types* of required strategic change.

● Identify the approaches, pitfalls and problems of leading different types of strategic change.

Key terms

collaboration p. 469

direction p. 471

forcefield analysis p. 475

leadership 466

organisational ambidexterity p. 487

participation p. 469

situational leadership p. 468

turnaround strategy p. 484

14.1 INTRODUCTION

The global insurance business, Aviva, had been underperforming for years when Mark Wilson was appointed as Chief Executive in November 2012. Following the departure of the previous Chief Executive (see Illustration 11.1) there had been a review of the company's strategy which concluded that it needed to focus more on business segments in which it could succeed and make higher returns. Mark Wilson's priority was to implement that strategy and make the strategic changes necessary to improve performance. Managing strategy is not just about making strategic decisions; it is about leading strategic change, which is the focus of this chapter.

The theme of strategic change runs through much of this part of the text. Chapter 11 posed questions about the feasibility of strategies; could changes of strategy work in practice? Chapter 12 provided different explanations of how strategies develop. Chapter 13 addressed issues to do with organising to deliver strategies. However, central to strategic change are the leadership tasks of convincing people of the new strategy and enabling and ensuring that what they do delivers the strategy. While this leadership role is most often associated with chief executives it may, in fact, occur at different levels in organisations: other senior managers and middle managers too may take leadership roles in change.

Figure 14.1 provides a structure for the chapter. The chapter opens (section 14.2) by explaining different *roles of leaders of strategic change*, the different *styles of change leadership* and how these might be suited to different circumstances. Section 14.3 then reviews important issues that need to be considered in *diagnosing the context* leaders face when embarking on strategic change and, again, how their styles of change need to align with that context. Section 14.4 then considers what change leaders might do to effect strategic change, first by identifying *forces blocking or facilitating change*, then by considering the *levers for change* they might use. Section 14.6 draws all this together by considering what overall lessons can be drawn about leading different *types of strategic change programmes* and the common reasons for the *failure of strategic change programmes*.

In doing this the chapter builds on three key premises:

- *Strategy matters*. What has been written in Parts I and II of the text should be seen as essential in identifying the need for and direction of strategic change. So it is important to be clear about:
  - Why strategic change is needed (discussed in Chapters 2 to 5).
  - The bases of the strategy in terms of strategic purpose, perhaps encapsulated in a statement of vision or mission (section 4.2) and bases of competitive advantage (Chapter 6).
  - What the strategy is in terms of strategy directions and methods (Chapters 7 to 10).
- *Context matters*. The approach taken to managing strategic change needs to be *context-dependent*. There is, therefore, no 'one right way' of leading strategic change. Managers need to consider how to balance different approaches according to the circumstances they face.
- *Inertia* and *resistance* to change are likely. A major problem in leading change is the tendency of people to hold on to existing ways of doing things. Much of Chapter 5 and the discussion of the experience lens in the Commentary at the end of Part I explain why this is so.

Figure 14.1 Key elements in leading strategic change

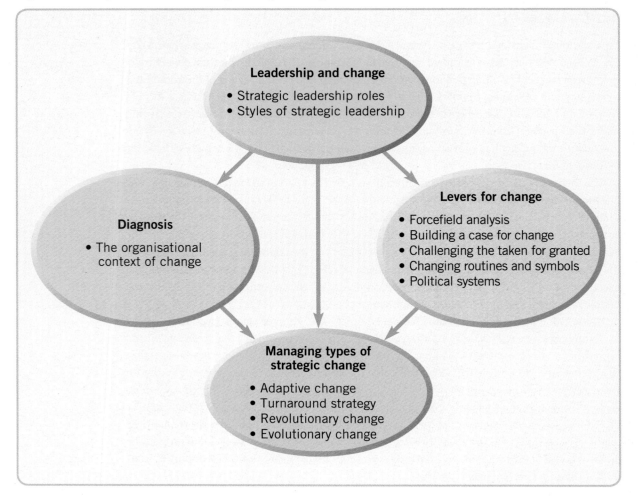

14.2 LEADERSHIP AND STRATEGIC CHANGE

Leadership is **the process of influencing an organisation (or group within an organisation) in its efforts towards achieving an aim or goal.**[1] Without effective leadership the risk is that people in an organisation are unclear about its purpose or lack motivation to deliver the strategy to achieve it. Harvard's John Kotter argues that 'good management' is about bringing order and consistency to operational aspects of organisations, such as quality and profitability of products and services. Leadership, 'by contrast is about coping with change'.[2] Strategic change is therefore central to leadership.

14.2.1 Strategic leadership roles

While leading strategic change is often associated with top management, and chief executives in particular, in fact it involves managers at different levels in an organisation.

Top managers

There are three key roles that are argued to be especially significant for top management, especially a CEO, in leading strategic change:

- *Envisioning future strategy.*[3] Effective strategic leaders at the top of an organisation need to ensure there exists a clear and compelling vision of the future and communicate clearly a strategy to achieve it both internally and to external stakeholders. In the absence of their doing so, those who attempt to lead change elsewhere in an organisation, for example middle managers, are likely to construct such a vision themselves. This may be well intentioned but can lead to confusion. This is an issue picked up in the Key Debate at the end of the chapter.

- *Aligning* the organisation to deliver that strategy. This involves ensuring that people in the organisation are committed to the strategy, motivated to make the changes needed and empowered to deliver those changes. In doing so, there is a need for leaders to build and foster relationships of trust and respect across the organisation. It can, however, also be necessary to change the management of the organisation to ensure such commitment, which is a reason that top teams often change as a precursor to or during strategic change.

- *Embodying change.* A strategic leader will be seen by others, not least those within the organisation, but also other stakeholders and outside observers, as intimately associated with a future strategy and a strategic change programme. A strategic leader is, then, symbolically highly significant in the change process and needs to be a role model for future strategy (see section 14.4.5 below on symbolic levers for change).

Middle managers

A top-down approach to managing strategy and strategic change sees middle managers as implementers of top management strategic plans. Here their role is to ensure that resources are allocated and controlled appropriately and to monitor the performance and behaviour of staff. However, middle managers have multiple roles in relation to the management of strategy (see section 15.2.3).[4] In the context of managing strategic change there are four roles to emphasise:

- *Advisers* to more senior management on requirements for change within an organisation. This is because they are often the closest to indications of market or technological changes that might signal the need for change. They are also well placed to be able to identify likely blockages to change. Middle managers may also provide a useful variety of experience and views that can stimulate thinking on strategy.[5]

- *'Sense making'* of strategy. Top management may set a strategic direction, but how it is explained and made sense of in specific contexts (e.g. a region of a multinational or a functional department) may, intentionally or not, be left to middle managers. If misinterpretation of that intended strategy is to be avoided, it is therefore vital that middle managers understand and feel an ownership of it. They are therefore a crucial *relevance bridge* between top management and members of the organisation at lower levels.[6]

- *Reinterpretation and adjustment* of strategic responses as events unfold (e.g. in terms of relationships with customers, suppliers, the workforce and so on); this is a vital role for which middle managers are uniquely qualified because they are in day-to-day contact with such aspects of the organisation and its environment.

- *Local leadership of change*: middle managers therefore have the roles of aligning and embodying change, as do top management, but at a local level.

The Key Debate at the end of the chapter takes this into account and considers strategic change in relation to a top-down perspective, but also in relation to roles played by middle managers and to a more 'bottom-up' view of change.

14.2.2 **Leadership styles**

Leaders are often categorised in two ways:

- *Transformational* (or *charismatic*) *leaders*, whose emphasis is on building a vision for the organisation, an organisational identity around collective values and beliefs to support that vision and energising people to achieve it. There is evidence that suggests that this approach to leadership has beneficial impact on people's motivation and job performance[7] and wider business performance when the people who work for them see the organisation facing uncertainty.[8]

- *Transactional leaders*, who focus more on 'hard' levers of change such as designing systems and controlling the organisation's activities. The emphasis here, then, is more likely to be on changes of structures, setting targets to be achieved, financial incentives, careful project management and the monitoring of organisational and individual performance.

One view would be that these styles are a matter of personal attributes. If so then what matters is that in situations of change, people with appropriate styles to the context of that change are appointed to lead it. Another view is that **successful strategic leaders adjust their leadership style to the context they face**.[9] This has become known as 'situational leadership'. Here this is explained, first by reviewing styles of strategic leadership more specifically, then by considering how these may need to differ by context.

Table 14.1 summarises four styles of leading strategic change:[10]

Table 14.1 **Styles of leading change**

Style	Description	Advantages	Disadvantages
Persuasion	Gain support for change by generating understanding and commitment through e.g. small-group briefings and delegation of responsibility for change.	Develops support for change and a wide base of understanding.	Time consuming. Fact-based argument and logic may not convince others of need for change. Or may gain notional support without active change.
Collaboration	Widespread involvement of employees on decisions about both what and how to change.	Spreads not only support but ownership of change by increasing levels of involvement.	Time consuming. Little control over decisions made.
Participation	Change leaders retain overall coordination and authority but delegate elements of the change process.	Spreads ownership and support of change, but within a controlled framework. Easier to shape decisions.	Can be perceived as manipulation.
Direction	Change leaders make most decisions about what to change and how. Use of authority to direct change.	Less time consuming. Provides a clear change direction and focus.	Potentially less support and commitment, so changes may be resisted.

Source: Adapted from J. Balogun and V. Hope Hailey, *Exploring strategic change*, 3rd edn, Prentice Hall, 2008.

- **Persuasion** of the need for and means of strategic change. Four phases of this style of change leadership have been advocated:[11]

  - Convince employees that change is imperative and why the new direction is the right one. Again this emphasises the necessity for clarity of future vision and strategy.

  - Since change is likely to be interpreted differently throughout the organisation, frame the changes in ways relevant to the different groups and functions that have to enact the change and gather feedback on how this is understood and communicated within those groups.

  - Ensure ongoing communication of the progress of change.

  - Reinforce behavioural guidelines in line with the change and reward the achievement of change goals.

  However, there are problems here. The assumption that reasoned argument in a top-down fashion will overcome perhaps years of embedded assumptions about what 'really matters' may be optimistic. There may be apparent acceptance of change without its actually being delivered. Such an approach to change can also take a long time and be costly, for example in terms of training and management time.

- **Collaboration**[12] **in the change process is the involvement of those affected by strategic change in setting the change agenda**; for example, in the identification of strategic issues, the strategic decision-making process, the setting of priorities, the planning of strategic change or the drawing up of action plans. Such involvement can foster a more positive attitude to change. People may also see the constraints the organisation faces as less significant and feel increased ownership of, and commitment to, a decision or change process. It may therefore be a way of building readiness and capability for change. However, there are potential problems here too. People may come up with change solutions that are not in line with, or do not achieve the expectations of, top management or key stakeholders. For example, there is the risk that solutions will be limited to those in line with the existing culture or that the agenda for change will be negotiated and may therefore be a compromise. A strategic change leader who takes this approach may, therefore, need to retain the ability to intervene in the process, though this runs the risk of demotivating employees who have been involved in the change process.

- **Participation** retains the coordination of and authority over processes of change by a strategic leader who delegates *elements* of the change process while retaining overall responsibility for that change, monitoring its progress and ensuring it occurs. Particular stages of change, such as ideas generation, data collection, detailed planning, the development of rationales for change or the identification of critical success factors, may be delegated to project teams or task forces. Such teams may not take full responsibility for the change process, but become involved in it and see their work building towards it. An advantage is that it involves members of the organisation, not only in originating ideas, but also in the *partial implementation* of solutions, helping build commitment to the change. For example, it has been shown that transformational leaders can effectively motivate employees by facilitating their interaction with beneficiaries (e.g. customers) as a way of showing how a strategic vision has meaning to those beneficiaries.[13] It may also be that the retention of the agenda and means of change by the strategic leader reduces the possibility of a negotiated compromise and means that more radical change can be achieved. The potential problem is that employees may see this approach as manipulation and consequently become disenchanted and demotivated.

ILLUSTRATION 14.1

Styles of leading change

Successful top executives highlight lessons for leading change.

Vision is central

'Good business leaders create a vision, articulate the vision, passionately own the vision, and relentlessly drive it to completion.'

Jack Welch, Chairman and CEO of
General Electric 1981–2001

Don't noodle

Terry Lundgren, CEO of Macy's and Bloomingdales departmental stores:

'I have always been a pretty good listener, and I am quick to admit that I do not have all the answers. So I am going to listen. But shortly after I listen, the second piece is to pull the trigger. I have all the input, and here is what we are going to do. People need closure on a decision. If you listen and then noodle on it, people get confused, and that's not effective leadership'.[1]

Coach but don't coddle

Allan G. Laffley, Chairman, President and CEO of Procter & Gamble till 2010:

'My approach to leadership is to raise aspiration and then achieve great execution . . . communicate priorities clearly, simply and frequently . . . to a large degree our division leaders must define their own future. I play the role of coach; but coaching doesn't mean coddling. I expect our managers to make choices . . . to help managers make these strategic choices leaders must sometimes challenge deeply held assumptions . . . Being a role model is vital . . . I know that I must be ready for moments of truth that alert the organisation to my commitment.'[2]

Clarity from the top and learning by doing

Carlos Ghosn led successful change following his appointment as CEO of Nissan and Renault. In a speech at INSEAD Business School early in the change pro-gramme (September 2002), Ghosn said:

'If people don't know the priority, don't understand the strategy, don't know where they are going, don't know what is the critical objective, you are heading for trouble. Confusion is the first sign of trouble. It's (the leader's) duty to clarify the environment, to make sure there is maximum light in the company . . . The biggest challenge is self confidence . . . (I had) to help Nissan people believe they could do a great job in this industry.'[3]

Developing antennae in the public sector

In 2010 Canadian Moya Greene took over as CEO of the Royal Mail, the UK's publically owned postal service which faced major decline in revenue from its traditional focus on letter mail and union opposition to privatisation. By 2012 there were signs that this decline had been halted and relationships with the unions much improved. She highlighted a key lesson from leading change in the public sector:

'My public sector experience helped me understand how easily sound policies can be derailed by small symbolic things. It may not matter that the policy change you are advocating is the product of fantastic analytics or years of brilliant stakeholder manage-ment; the tiniest spark can become a flash fire – something that takes hold and transforms perceptions. If you work in the public sector, you learn the value of developing antennae for popular perceptions and keeping them finely tuned.'[4]

Sources
1. Interview by Matthew Boyle, in *Fortune*, 12 December 2005, vol. 152, no. 12, pp. 126–7.
2. *Leadership Excellence*, November 2006, vol. 23, no. 11, pp. 9–10.
3. Reported in 'Redesigning Nissan (A): Carlos Ghosn takes charge', K. Hughes, J.-L. Barsoux and J-F Manzoni, INSEAD, 2003.
4. 'Leading in the 21st Century: an interview with Moya Greene', McKinsey & Co., September 2012.

Questions

1 How would you describe the styles of leadership illustrated here in terms of those explained in section 14.2.1?

2 Compare the different accounts. Are there commonalities and what are the differences?

3 Only some stakeholders are specifically mentioned in the examples. Does this mean that the style should be the same towards all stakeholders of the organisation? If not, how would they differ?

- **Direction** **involves the use of personal authority to establish clarity on both future strategy and how change will occur.** It is top-down management of strategic change where change 'solutions' and the means of change are 'sold' to others who are tasked with implementing them. The need here is for both clarity of strategic vision and the specifics of a change programme in terms of critical success factors and priorities. The approach may be needed if there is a need for fast change or control over the change agenda (e.g. to meet the expectations of dominant external stakeholders). The danger is that it can result in explicit resistance to change or people going along with the rhetoric of change while passively resisting it. It is also worth noting that even where top management people see themselves adopting participative styles, their subordinates may perceive this as directive and, indeed, may welcome such direction if they see major change is needed. In its most extreme form direction may take the form of coercion, the imposition of future strategy by the explicit use of power, but this is unlikely to be successful unless, for example, the organisation is facing a crisis.

It is important to point out that change leadership styles are not mutually exclusive. For example, change may be initiated with clear direction accompanied by the 'hard levers' of change associated with transactional leadership but be followed through with more the collaborative or participatory approaches more associated with transformational leadership. Moreover different styles may be needed in different parts of an organisation facing different circumstances or at different times as situations change. In short, required change leadership styles are likely to need to differ according to context. Illustration 14.1 provides examples of different strategic leadership styles.

(14.3) DIAGNOSING THE CHANGE CONTEXT

Leading change in a small entrepreneurial business, where a motivated team is driving change, is different from trying to do so in a major corporation, or a long-established public-sector organisation, with long established routines and systems and perhaps a great deal of resistance to change. If it is to be effective, the approach to leading change will be different depending on the *organisational context* in which it occurs.[14] It is therefore useful to consider the appropriateness of different styles of leading change to different contexts.

Julia Balogun and Veronica Hope Hailey's 'change kaleidoscope' (summarised in Figure 14.2), provides a framework by which to identify contextual features to take into account in designing change programmes. Here are some examples of the contextual features shown in Figure 14.2 and how some might require different styles of leading change:

- The *time* available for change could differ dramatically. A business may face immediate decline in turnover or profits from rapid changes in its markets. This is a quite different context for change compared with a business where the management may see the need for change as years away and have time to plan it carefully. Persuasion or collaboration may be most appropriate where incremental change is possible, but where change has to happen fast, *timing* may demand a more directive style.

- The *scope* of change might differ in terms of either the *breadth* of change across an organisation or the *depth* of culture change required. For example, the scope of change required in a global business with multiple brands and perhaps a long cultural heritage is likely to mean that the contribution of people throughout the organisation to a change programme will

Figure 14.2 The change kaleidoscope

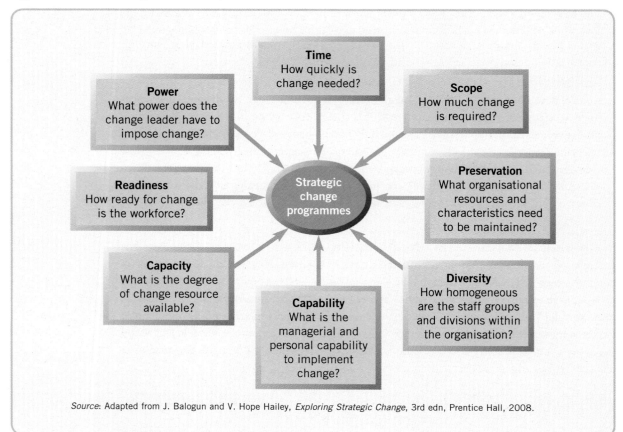

Source: Adapted from J. Balogun and V. Hope Hailey, *Exploring Strategic Change*, 3rd edn, Prentice Hall, 2008.

be necessary. In a successful small business where the breadth and depth of change will be much less, a more directive style may be possible.

- *Preservation* of some aspects of an organisation may be needed: in particular capabilities on which changes need to be based. Suppose, for example, that a computer software business needs to become more formally organised because of its successful growth. This could upset technical experts who have been used to a great deal of independence and ready access to senior management. Preserving their expertise and motivation could be vitally important, so involving them through collaboration or participation may well be important.

- A *diversity* of experience, views and opinions within an organisation may help the change process, but will require the involvement of people in that process. However, if an organisation has followed a strategy for many decades, such continuity may have led to a very homogeneous way of seeing the world, which could hamper change. So means of challenging taken-for-granted assumptions and routines will be needed.

- *Capacity* for change in terms of available resources will also be significant: change can be costly, not only in financial terms, but also in terms of management time. It is likely to be the responsibility of top management (or perhaps owners) to provide such resources.

- Who has the *power* to effect change? Often it is assumed that the chief executive has such power, but in the face of resistance from below, or perhaps resistance from external stakeholders, this may not be the case. It may also be that the chief executive supposes that others in the organisation have the power to effect change when they do not, or do not see themselves as having it. In organisations with *hierarchical power structures* a directive style may be common and it may be difficult to break away from it, not least because people expect it. On the other hand, in *'flatter'* power structures, a more networked or learning organisation described elsewhere in this text (see section 12.3.1), it is likely that collaboration and participation will be common, indeed desirable.

- Is there a *capability* of managing change in the organisation? There may be managers who have experience of leading change in the past, or a workforce that has seen the benefits of past changes, while people in another organisation may have little experience of change.

- What is the *readiness* for change? Is there a felt need for change across the organisation, widespread resistance, or pockets or levels of resistance in some parts of the organisation and readiness in others? Again different styles of leading change may be required in these different circumstances.

Illustration 14.2 gives an example of the contextual issues faced in trying to manage change in the UK Ministry of Defence (MOD).

Research on leadership has shown that leadership styles need to differ according, in particular, to the ability and willingness of employees to change. Bearing in mind these two contextual features, Figure 14.3 suggests that, where there is high readiness but low capability for change, then *persuasion*, involving education, training and coaching, may be appropriate. Where both readiness and capability are high, then *collaboration* may be possible and top management may be able to delegate much of the change agenda. Where capability is high but readiness is low, involving people in the change process while retaining overall central control (*participation*) may make sense. Where there is both low readiness and capability for change *direction* may be the most appropriate style if change is urgent or, it time is available to build capability and readiness, *participation* may be appropriate.

This consideration of context also raises an important overarching question: *is one-off change possible* or does it need to occur in stages? For example, in a study of attempts to manage change in hospitals[15] it was found that their governance and organisational structures prevented any clear authority to manage change. This, combined with the resource constraints

Figure 14.3 Styles of change leadership according to organisational capability and readiness

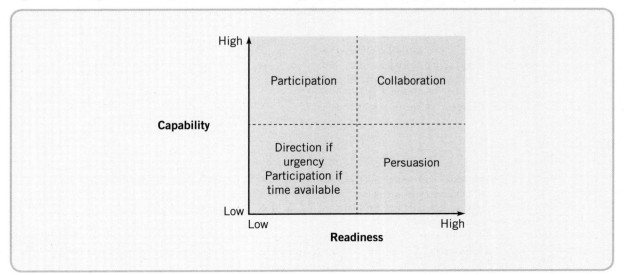

ILLUSTRATION 14.2

Challenges of change in the UK Ministry of Defence

Understanding the challenge of managing strategic change requires an understanding of the context of change.

The UK Ministry of Defence (MOD) was spared the worst of government cuts imposed in 2010, but still took a 7–8 per cent cut in budget. This was followed by a fuller strategic review in 2011 which proposed transformational change. The top eight recommendations were about structure and systems, but the underlying message was the need to address people and behavioural dimensions in the MOD. However, the MOD had been through numerous initiatives for change but with limited success. Why?

Scope

In 2012 the MOD comprised a workforce of about 270,000 (but reducing) which included 85,000 civilian personnel. It also relied on a further 300,000 in its supply chain. The MOD is the sum of numerous moving parts, so it is important for it to move in a coherent manner. However, change in one part of the system often runs into resistance and difficulty, or has unforeseen implications for other parts of the system.

Time

Military staff move locations frequently. Someone with 35 years of service may have moved 20 times. So three years is viewed as a feasible cycle time within a 'just do it' culture. Those who wish to make an impact do so by initiating change but moving on before initiatives are completed. However, follow-up is unlikely because 'you don't make your name by implementing another officer's change initiative'.

Preservation

A key element to be retained is the 'can do' culture of the military. However, politicians do not recognise that, with the staff cuts of serving personnel and civil servants, they cannot expect the MOD to carry out the full spectrum of capabilities previously delivered, let alone manage major changes.

Diversity

While views and expectations may differ significantly between the front-line commanders, civil servants and outsourced private-sector operators, the different groupings are themselves highly homogeneous in their views, processes and behaviours.

Capability and capacity

There is a lack of change management skills, with little investment in training in leading change. With the significant reduction in staff numbers many important roles needed to deliver change were being lost and not filled. Moreover the MOD was not clear about the skills and knowledge that it was losing as part of its downsizing. An MOD response to the need for changes in behaviours was the introduction in 2012 of the mantra 'Be – Think – Do': 'Be a leader. Think Defence. Do it better.'

Readiness

Much past and current change fundamentally affects the roles and responsibilities of front-line command staff and is heavily resisted. Change fatigue is also rife as a result of the numerous change initiatives, few of which run long enough to take effect.

Power

In typical military fashion some senior posts have had the word 'Transformation' included in their title and this is thought to get the job done. Such personnel may say the right things but action on the ground and leading by example are in short supply.

Source
By Professor Derrick Neal of the Defence Academy at Shrivenham, drawing on published studies and his own experience working with the MOD. The views expressed in this illustration are those of the author and are not necessarily the views held by Cranfield University or the MOD.

Questions

1 In your view, what are the main barriers to change facing the MOD?

2 Given the change kaleidoscope analysis, what three key questions about achieving strategic change would you pose to the MOD?

3 What approach to change should be adopted to improve the MOD's ability to manage change?

under which they laboured, meant that major one-off change initiatives were not likely to succeed. In such circumstances, it may be that the context needs to be changed before the strategic change itself can occur. Perhaps new managers with experience of leading change need to be introduced to enhance the capability and readiness to embark on a more significant strategic change programme. Or it may need to be recognised that change has to be managed in stages. The researchers in the hospital study reported above found that change tended to take place by one initiative making limited progress, then stalling, followed by a later one making further advances.

(14.4) LEVERS FOR STRATEGIC CHANGE

Most successful change initiatives rely on multiple means (or levers) for leading change.[16] This section considers what these are and how they might be identified. Some levers for change have already been discussed elsewhere in the text. The importance of clarity of a strategic vision was discussed in section 5.2 together with the importance of other goals and objectives and the effects of changes in organisational structure and control systems of organisations were addressed in Chapter 13. All these are important, but there are other levers too.

14.4.1 Forcefield analysis

A forcefield analysis can be helpful in providing **a view of forces at work in an organisation that act to prevent or facilitate change**. It allows some key questions to be asked:

- What aspects of the current situation would block change, and how can these be overcome?
- What aspects of the current situation might aid change in the desired direction, and how might these be reinforced?
- What needs to be introduced or developed to aid change?

Illustration 14.3 shows how a forcefield analysis was used by managers considering the intention to devolve strategic decisions within the European division of a global manufacturer.

A forcefield analysis can be informed by the change kaleidoscope but also by other concepts and frameworks in the text:

- *Mapping activity systems* (section 3.4.3) can provide insights into aspects of an organisation that have underpinned its past success. These may be a basis upon which future change might be built, or they may be ways of doing things that have ceased to be advantageous but are difficult to change.
- *Stakeholder mapping* (section 4.5.2) can provide insight into the power of different stakeholders to promote change or to resist change.
- *The culture web* (section 5.3.6). Strategic change often goes hand-in-hand with a perceived need to change the culture of the organisation. The culture web is a means of diagnosing organisational culture and therefore an understanding of the symbolic, routinised as well as structural and systemic factors that may be taken for granted and can act for or against change. It can also be used to envisage what the culture of an organisation would need to look like to deliver future strategy.
- *The 7-S framework* (section 13.4.1) can highlight aspects of the infrastructure of an organisation that may act to promote or block change.

ILLUSTRATION 14.3

A forcefield analysis for devolving strategy

A forcefield analysis can be used to identify aspects of the organisation that might aid change, blockages to change and what needs to be developed to aid change.

A Japanese multinational manufacturer had always been centralised in terms of strategic direction and, in particular, new product development. It had been hugely successful in Japan and had also developed a global footprint, largely through acquisitions of local manufacturers related to its core business. These acquired businesses operated largely independently of each other as manufacturing units reporting to Japan. Regionally based sales offices were responsible for selling the range of company products and identifying customer needs and, again, reported through to Japan.

In 2012 top management in Japan took the decision to devolve strategic decisions to geographic regional divisions. The decision was based on the desire to grow non-Japanese markets given the changing competitive landscape, especially the growing power of European customers in the world market, but also the need to understand and respond to local markets better. The view was that competitive strategy

and innovation needed to originate and develop nearer to regionally based customers rather than centrally in Japan.

Managers in Europe were charged with developing a plan to implement this devolution of strategy. They undertook a forcefield analysis to identify the key issues to be addressed, a summary of which is shown here.

It was market forces and a head office decision that were the main 'pushing forces' for change. But local managers also recognised that their career prospects could be enhanced. The 'resisting forces' were not only a function of the existing organisational structure, but also the lack of any pan-European infrastructure and the lack of European managers with strategic, as distinct from operational, expertise. The forcefield underlined the importance of establishing such an infrastructure and highlighted the need for IT systems to share information and ideas. It also raised the strategic importance of management development at the strategic level.

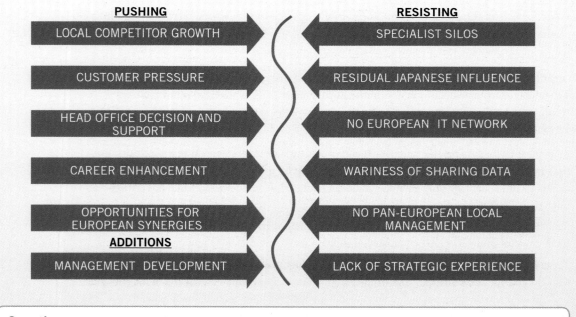

Questions

1 What might the problems be in devolving strategy to a European division?
2 Undertake a forcefield analysis for an organisation of your choice.

As well as helping to identify the current forces acting for and against change, each of these frameworks can also be used to help think through what else might be needed as additional forces to promote change.

14.4.2 A compelling case for change

Whichever style of management is adopted a convincing case for change has to be presented. McKinsey & Co, the consultants,[17] argue that too often the case for change is made in terms of top management's perception of what is important: for example, meeting expectations of shareholders or beating competition. When most managers and employees are asked, however, there are many more factors that motivate them: for example, the impact on society, on customers, on the local working team, or on employees' personal well-being. A compelling case for change needs to speak to these different bases of motivation, not just to top management perceptions of why change is needed. It may, of course, be difficult for top management to understand and relate to these different needs: so it may make sense to involve employees, themselves, in the creation of stories of change that, in effect, 'translate' corporate imperatives of change into local motivating messages. It is also important that the case for change does not just focus on the understanding of why change is needed, but the action required to deliver it.

14.4.3 Challenging the taken for granted

A major challenge in achieving strategic change can be the need to change often long standing mindsets or taken-for-granted assumptions – the paradigm (see section 5.3.6). There are different views on how this might be achieved.

One view is that sufficient evidence, perhaps in the form of careful strategic analysis, will itself serve to challenge and therefore change the paradigm. However, where long standing assumptions have persisted, they can be very resistant to change: people find ways of questioning, reconfiguring and reinterpreting such analysis to bring it in line with the existing paradigm. It may take much persistence to overcome this. Others argue that encouraging people to question and challenge each other's assumptions and received wisdom by making them explicit is valuable.[18] Scenario planning (see section 2.2.2) is similarly advocated as a way of overcoming individual biases and cultural assumptions by getting people to see possible different futures and the implications for their organisations. There is also research that shows that successful firms able to enact significant strategic changes while also maintaining high levels of performance have questioning and 'contestation' embedded within their cultures (see Illustration 14.5).[19]

14.4.4 Changing operational processes and routines

In the end, strategies are delivered through day-to-day processes and routines of the operations of the organisation. These might be formalised and codified or they might be less formal 'ways we do things around here' which can persist over time and guide people's behaviour. As has been seen in the discussion in Chapter 3, it may be that such routines can be the basis of an organisation's competitive advantage since they may be unique to the organisation and difficult to imitate. However, they can also be serious blockages to change. The relationship between strategic change and day-to-day processes and routines is therefore important to consider in at least three respects:

- *Planning operational change*. The planning of the implementation of an intended strategy requires the identification of the key changes in the routines required to deliver that strategy. In effect, strategic change needs to be considered in terms of the re-engineering of organisational processes.

- *Challenging operational assumptions*. Changing organisational processes and routines may also have the effect of challenging the often taken-for-granted assumptions under pinning them. In turn this may have the effect of getting people to question and challenge deep-rooted beliefs and assumptions in the organisation. Richard Pascale argues: 'It is easier to act your way into a better way of thinking than to think your way into a better way of acting';[20] in other words, it is easier to change behaviour and by so doing change taken-for-granted assumptions than to try to change taken-for-granted assumptions as a way of changing behaviour. If this is so, the style of change employed (see section 14.2.2 above) needs to take this into account: it suggests that attempting to persuade people to change may be less powerful than involving people in the activities of changing. Illustration 14.4 is an example of a change initiative that adopted this approach.

- *Bottom-up changes to routines*. Even when changes in routines are not planned from the top, people do change them and this may result in wider strategic change. This may occur through trial and error learning as people experiment with different routines associated with doing their jobs.[21] Or it could occur as people learn from and adapt the routines in other organisations.[22] Or it may occur more proactively by managers deliberately and persistently '*bending* the rules of the game' till they achieve enough support from different stakeholders such that new routines supporting a shift in strategy become acceptable.[23]

The overall lesson is that changes in routines may appear to be mundane, but they can have significant impact.

14.4.5 Symbolic changes[24]

Change levers are not always of an overt, formal nature: they may also be symbolic in nature. Symbols may be everyday things which are nevertheless especially meaningful in the context of a particular situation or organisation. (In this sense the organisational processes and routines discussed above are also symbolic in nature.) Changing symbols can help reshape beliefs and expectations because meaning becomes apparent in the day-to-day experiences people have of organisations, such as the symbols that surround them (e.g. office layout and décor), the type of language and technology used and organisational rituals. Consider some examples:

- Many *rituals*[25] of organisations are concerned with effecting or consolidating change. Table 14.2 identifies and gives examples of such rituals and suggests what role they might play in change processes. New rituals can be introduced or old rituals done away with as ways of signalling or reinforcing change.

- Changes in *physical aspects* of the work environment are powerful symbols of change. Typical here is a change of location for the head office, relocation of personnel, changes in dress or uniforms, and alterations to offices or office space.

- The *behaviour of managers*, particularly strategic leaders, is perhaps the most powerful symbol in relation to change. So, having made pronouncements about the need for change, it is vital that the visible behaviour of change agents be in line with such change.

ILLUSTRATION 14.4

Change levels to transform a business school

A strategy for change emphasising action rather than consensus seeking.

Critics argue that business schools have become too remote from the concerns of practising managers, instead privileging academic research, leading to an unsustainable situation primarily rewarding such research without generating funding for it. When George Yip was hired as Dean of Rotterdam School of Management (RSM), Erasmus University, the university gave him the objectives of increasing revenue by improving contacts with and relevance to business, while maintaining academic reputation. He explained his approach:

'A conventional approach to change emphasises the need to change attitudes first. But, as an outsider and foreigner, I doubted I could achieve change rapidly through persuasion in a national culture that emphasised consensus building through long discussions. I also had limited time, with a four-year contract. So at the outset I avoided saying that I would make major changes; that would create opposition immediately. Rather, I emphasised action before consensus building.

For example, only 1 per cent of articles published by faculty were in managerial journals such as *Harvard Business Review*. I set a target of 5 per cent, brought in editors of managerial journals to help train the faculty and instituted a cash bonus of up to €15,000 for a publication in a top managerial journal. Eventually I also persuaded the director of research that top managerial journals should have equal status with top academic journals in counting towards faculty members' release from teaching. Whenever someone published in such a journal I also sent a congratulatory email copying all faculty and staff; but not when someone published in an academic journal.

I also abandoned the tradition that the Dean chaired all defences of doctoral dissertations. I knew this would offend many faculty but I made clear my priority was engaging with external stakeholders, particularly corporate executives.

Academics were reluctant to engage with executives. So I revamped Advisory Board meetings.

As board members were top executives, I brought into each meeting one or two senior academics to present their research, emphasising that they would have to make it relevant to the audience. I also initiated an annual conference that combined panels of executives and faculty and created other events at which faculty would talk with practitioners.

In terms of personnel, I replaced those likely to generate the most opposition and appointed a supportive Vice Dean from among the existing department chairs, replacing the incumbent. I also created a new position of Director of External Relations and, together with the Director of Marketing, placed them on the Management Committee, the top body. There were objections from some, but I made sure I had the backing of the university leaders.

I delayed a formal discussion of the new strategy until my third year. By then attitudes were more favourable. As one professor told me, my most significant achievement as Dean was not the money raised or the rise in revenues, but the mindset change of faculty to recognise the need to connect to the world of business. I retired in July 2011 and the new Vice Dean became my successor. At the beginning of 2013 he was continuing and enhancing the new strategy.'

Source: Interview with George Yip.

Questions

1 What change levers explained in section 14.4 are evident in George Yip's approach?

2 Suggest routines, symbols and rituals that he might have changed to increase the focus of academics on the needs of managers.

3 Do you agree with Richard Pascale (and George Yip) that 'It is easier to act your way into a better way of thinking than to think your way into a better way of acting'? What are the potential dangers?

Table 14.2 **Organisational rituals and change**

Types of ritual	Role	Examples in change initiatives
Rites of passage	Signify a change of status or role	Induction to new roles Training programmes
Rites of enhancement	Recognise effort benefiting organisation	Awards ceremonies Promotions
Rites of renewal	Reassure that something is being done Focus attention on issues	Appointment of consultant Project teams and workshops
Rites of integration	Encourage shared commitment Reassert rightness of norms	Celebrations of achievement or new ways of doing things
Rites of conflict reduction	Reduce conflict and aggression	Negotiating committees
Rites of challenge	'Throwing down the gauntlet'	New CEO setting challenging goals

- The *language* used by change agents is also important.[26] Either consciously or unconsciously language and metaphor may be employed to galvanise change. Of course, there is also the danger that strategic leaders do not realise the significance of their language and, while espousing change, use language that signals adherence to the status quo, or personal reluctance to change.

However, there is an important qualification to the idea that the manipulation of symbols can be a useful lever for managing change. The significance and meaning of symbols are dependent on how they are interpreted. Since they may not be interpreted as intended, their impact is difficult to predict.

14.4.6 **Power and political systems**

Section 4.5 explained the importance of understanding the political context in and around an organisation. There is also a need to consider strategic change within this political context and as a political process. Illustration 14.4 also gives examples of political processes. To effect change powerful support may be required from individuals or groups or a reconfiguration of *power structures* may be necessary, especially if transformational change is required. Table 14.3 shows some of the mechanisms associated with managing change from a political perspective:[27]

- *Controlling or acquiring resources*, being identified with important resource areas or areas of expertise. Such resources might include for example funds, information, key organisational processes or key people. In particular the ability to withdraw or allocate such resources can be a powerful tool in overcoming resistance, persuading others to accept change or build readiness for change.

- *Association with powerful stakeholder groups* (or *elites*), or their supporters, can help build a power base or help overcome resistance to change. Or a manager facing resistance to change may seek out and win over someone highly respected from within the very group

Table 14.3 **Political mechanisms in organisations**

Activity areas	Mechanisms			Problems
	Resources	**Elites**	**Building alliances**	
Building the power base	Control of resources Acquisition of/identification with expertise Acquisition of additional resources	Sponsorship by an elite Association with an elite	Identification of change supporters Alliance building Team building	Time required for building Perceived duality of ideals Perceived as threat by existing elites
Overcoming resistance	Withdrawal of resources Use of 'counter-intelligence'	Breakdown or division of elites Association with change leader Association with respected outsider	Foster momentum for change Sponsorship/reward of change leaders	Striking from too low a power base Potentially destructive: need for rapid rebuilding
Achieving compliance	Giving resources	Removal of resistant elites Need for visible 'change hero'	Partial implementation and collaboration Implantation of 'disciples' Support for 'young Turks'	Converting the body of the organisation Slipping back

resistant to change. It may also be necessary to *remove individuals or groups* resistant to change. Who these are can vary – from powerful individuals in senior positions to whole layers of resistance, perhaps executives in a threatened function or service.

- *Building alliances* and *networks* of contacts and sympathisers may be important in overcoming the resistance of more powerful groups. Attempting to convert the whole organisation to an acceptance of change is difficult. There may, however, be parts of the organisation, or individuals, more sympathetic to change than others with whom support for change can be built. Marginalisation of those resistant to change may also be possible. However, the danger is that powerful groups in the organisation may regard the building of support coalitions, or acts of marginalisation, as a threat to their own power, leading to further resistance to change. An analysis of power and interest using the stakeholder mapping (section 4.5.1) can, therefore, be useful to identify bases of alliance and likely resistance.

Cynthia Hardy[28] also points out that change leaders may gain power through 'meaning power' by which she means the ability to use symbols, rituals and language to legitimise change, make change appear desirable, inevitable or help build excitement or optimism about change (see section 14.4.5).

However, the political aspects of change management are also potentially hazardous. Table 14.3 also summarises some of the problems. In overcoming resistance, the major problem may simply be the lack of power to undertake such activity. Trying to break down the status quo may become so destructive and take so long that the organisation cannot recover from it. If the process needs to take place, its replacement by some new set of beliefs and the implementation of a new strategy is vital and needs to be speedy. Further, as already identified, in implementing change, gaining the commitment of a few senior executives at the top of an organisation is one thing; it is quite another to convert the body of the organisation to an acceptance of significant change.

14.4.7 Change tactics

There are also more specific tactics of change which might be employed to facilitate the change process.

Timing

The importance of timing is often neglected in thinking about strategic change. But choosing the right time tactically to promote change is vital. For example:

- *Building on actual or perceived crisis* is especially useful the greater the degree of change needed. If there is a higher perceived risk in maintaining the status quo than in changing it, people are more likely to change. Change leaders may take advantages of performance downturns, competitive threats or threatened takeover as catalysts for strategic change.[29]

- *Windows of opportunity* in change processes may exist. The arrival of a new chief executive, the introduction of a new, highly successful product, or the arrival of a major competitive threat on the scene may provide opportunities to make more significant changes than might normally be possible. Since change will be regarded nervously, it may also be important to choose the time for promoting such change to avoid unnecessary fear and nervousness. For example, if there is a need for the removal of executives, this may be best done before rather than during the change programme. In such a way, the change programme can be seen as a potential improvement for the future rather than as the cause of such losses.

- *The symbolic signalling of time frames* may be important. In particular, conflicting messages about the timing of change should be avoided. For example, if rapid change is required, the maintenance of procedures or focus on issues that signal long time horizons may be counter-productive.

Visible short-term wins

A strategic change programme will require many detailed actions and tasks. It is important that some are seen to be successful quickly. Identifying some 'low-hanging fruit' – changes that may not be big but can be made easily and yield a quick payoff – can be useful. This could take the form, for example, of a retail chain introducing a new product range and demonstrating its success in the market or the breaking down of a long-established routine and the demonstration of a better way of doing things. In themselves, these may not be especially significant aspects of a new strategy, but they may be visible indicators of a new approach associated with that strategy. The demonstration of such wins can therefore galvanise commitment to the wider strategy.

One reason given for the inability to change is that resources are not available to do so. This may be overcome if it is possible to identify '*hot spots*' on which to focus resources and effort. For example, William Bratton, famously responsible for the Zero Tolerance policy of the New York Police Department, began by focusing resource and effort on narcotics-related crimes. Though associated with 50–70 per cent of all crimes he found they only had 5 per cent of the resources allocated by NYPD to tackle them. Success in this field led to the roll-out of his policies into other areas and to gaining the resources to do so.

(14.5) LEADING TYPES OF STRATEGIC CHANGE

This section brings together the main themes of the chapter by considering the different approaches change leaders might take given different types of strategic change. It concludes by summarising evidence as to why change programmes fail and the lessons that can be learnt from that.

Julia Balogun and Veronica Hope Hailey[30] identify four generic types of strategic change. The axes in Figure 14.4 are concerned with (i) the extent of change and (ii) the nature and urgency of change. In terms of the *extent* of change, the question is whether change can occur in line with the current business model and within the current culture as a *realignment* of strategy. Or is the change required more significant in terms of the current business model or culture, in effect more *transformational* change? Many of the tools of analysis in Part I of the text can help identify the extent of change required. For example, does the change require a substantial reconfiguration of the value chain (section 3.4.2), significant changes in the activities underpinning strategic capabilities (section 3.4.3) or major cultural change (section 5.4.6)? Care does, however, need to be taken in considering the significance of new strategies on the extent of change required. For example, a business may launch new products without requiring fundamental changes in the business model or culture of the organisation. On the other hand, some changes in strategy, even if they do not take the form of dramatic product changes, may require culture change. For example, the shift from a production focus for a manufacturer to a customer-led, service ethos may not entail major product changes, but may require significant culture change.

The other axis in Figure 14.4, the nature of change, is concerned with the speed at which change needs to happen. Arguably, it is beneficial for change in an organisation to be *incremental* since this allows time to build on the skills, routines and beliefs of those in the organisation.

Figure 14.4 Types of change

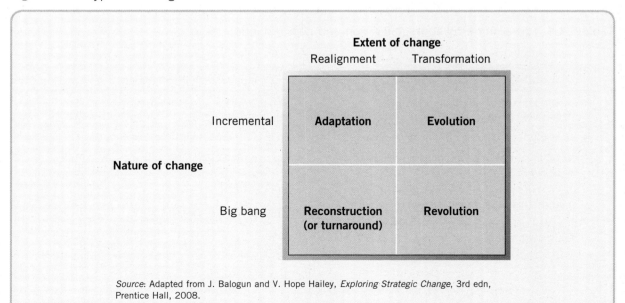

Source: Adapted from J. Balogun and V. Hope Hailey, *Exploring Strategic Change*, 3rd edn, Prentice Hall, 2008.

However, if an organisation faces crisis or needs to change direction fast a '*big bang*' approach to change might be needed on occasion.

14.5.1 Adaptation

As explained in section 5.4.1 and section 12.3, strategy development is often *incremental* in nature. It builds on rather than fundamentally changes prior strategy. It is what Figure 14.4 refers to as *adaptation*. Change is gradual, building on or amending what the organisation has been doing in the past and in line with the current business model and organisational culture. This might include changes in product design or methods of production, launches of new products or related diversification. This is the most common form of change in organisations. Though less common, the leadership of change is more often associated with the other more fundamental types of change identified in Figure 14.4.

14.5.2 Reconstruction: turnaround strategy

Reconstruction is change that may be rapid and involve a good deal of upheaval in an organisation, but which does not fundamentally change the culture or the business model. There could be a need for major structural changes or a major cost-cutting programme to deal with a decline in financial performance or difficult market conditions, in the absence of which a business could face closure, enter terminal decline or be taken over. This is commonly referred to as a **turnaround strategy, where the emphasis is on speed of change and rapid cost reduction and/or revenue generation**. The need is to prioritise the things that give quick and significant improvements. Typically it is a situation where a directive approach to change (see section 14.2.2) is required. Some of the main elements of turnaround strategies are as follows:[31]

● *Crisis stabilisation.* The aim is to regain control over the deteriorating position. This requires a short-term focus on cost reduction and/or revenue increase, typically involving some of the steps identified in Table 14.4. There is nothing novel about these steps: many of

Table 14.4 Turnaround: revenue generation and cost reduction steps

Increasing revenue	Reducing costs
● Ensure marketing mix tailored to key market segments	● Reduce labour costs and reduce costs of senior management
● Review pricing strategy to maximise revenue	● Focus on productivity improvement
● Focus organisational activities on needs of target market sector customers	● Reduce marketing costs not focused on target market
● Exploit additional opportunities for revenue creation related to target market	● Tighten financial controls
● Invest funds from reduction of costs in new growth areas	● Tight control on cash expenses
	● Establish competitive bidding for suppliers; defer creditor payments; speed up debtor payments
	● Reduce inventory
	● Eliminate non-profitable products/services

them are good management practice. The differences are the speed at which they are carried out and the focus of managerial attention on them. The most successful turnaround strategies also focus on reducing direct operational costs and on productivity gains. Less effective approaches pay less attention to these and more on the reduction of overheads.

However, too often turnarounds are seen as no more than cost-cutting exercises when a wider alignment between causes of decline and solutions may be important. For example, where the business decline is principally a result of changes in the external environment it may be folly to expect that cost cutting alone can lead to renewed growth. Other elements of turnaround strategies are therefore important:

- *Management changes.* Changes in management may be required, especially at the top. This usually includes the introduction of a new chairman or chief executive, as well as changes to the board, especially in marketing, sales and finance, for three main reasons. First, because the old management may well be the ones that were in charge when the problems developed and be seen as the cause of them by key stakeholders. Second, because it may be necessary to bring in management with experience of turnaround management. Third, because, if new management come from outside the organisation, they may bring different approaches to the way the organisation has operated in the past.

- *Gaining stakeholder support.* Poor quality of information may have been provided to key stakeholders. In a turnaround situation it is vital that key stakeholders, perhaps the bank or key shareholder groups, and employees are kept clearly informed of the situation and improvements as they are being made. It is also likely that a clear assessment of the power of different stakeholder groups (see section 4.5.1) will become vitally important in managing turnaround.

- *Clarifying the target market(s) and core products.* Central to turnaround success is ensuring clarity on the target market or market segments most likely to generate cash and grow profits. A successful turnaround strategy involves getting closer to customers and improving the flow of marketing information, especially to senior levels of management, so as to focus revenue-generating activities on key market segments. Of course, a reason for the poor performance of the organisation could be that it had this wrong in the first place. Clarifying the target market also provides the opportunity to discontinue or outsource products and services that are not targeted on those markets, eating up management time for little return or not making sufficient financial contribution.

- *Financial restructuring.* The financial structure of the organisation may need to be changed. This typically involves changing the existing capital structure, raising additional finance or renegotiating agreements with creditors, especially banks.

All of this requires the ability of management to prioritise those things that give quick and significant improvements.

14.5.3 Revolution

Revolution is change that requires rapid and major strategic as well as culture change. This could be in circumstances where the strategy has been so bounded by the existing culture that, even when environmental or competitive pressures might require fundamental change, the organisation has failed to respond. This might have occurred over many years (see the discussion of strategic drift in section 5.4) and resulted in circumstances where pressures for change are extreme – for example, a takeover threatens the continued existence of a firm.

Revolutionary change therefore differs from turnaround (or reconstruction) in two ways that make managing change especially challenging. First, the need is not only for fast change but, very likely, also for cultural change. Second, it may be that the need for change is not as evident to people in the organisation as in a turnaround situation, or that they have reasons to deny the need for change. This situation may have come about as a result of many years of relative decline in a market, with people wedded to products or processes no longer valued by customers – the problem of strategic drift. Or it could be that the problems of the organisation are visible and understood by its members, but that people cannot see a way forward. Leading change in such circumstances is likely to involve:

- *Clear strategic direction.* The need for the articulation of a clear strategic direction and decisive action in line with that direction is critical. This may of course include some of the decisions outlined above for turnaround: for example, portfolio changes and greater market focus. This is the type of change where individual CEOs who are seen to provide such direction are often credited with making a major difference. They may well also become the symbol of such change within an organisation and externally.

- *Top management changes.* The replacement of the CEO, senior executives or, perhaps, changes in board membership is common. Existing top management may be embedded within the past culture and their network of colleagues, customers or suppliers. New top managers do not have these established networks, nor are they embedded in the existing culture, so it is more likely that they will bring a fresh perspective and initiate or be ready to adopt new ideas and initiatives.[32] The introduction of new top management also signals the significance of change internally and externally. For similar reasons consultants may also be used not only to provide an analysis of the need for change, but also to signal how meaningful the change process is.

- *Multiple styles of change management.* While a *directive style* of change management is likely to be evident, this may need to be accompanied by other styles. It may be supported by determined efforts to *persuade* people about the need for change and the use of *participation* to involve people in aspects of change in which they have specific expertise or to overcome their resistance to change.

- *Culture change.* It may be possible to work with elements of the existing culture rather than attempt wholesale culture change. This involves identifying those aspects of culture that can be built upon and developed and those that have to be changed – in effect a forcefield approach (see section 14.4.1).

- *Monitoring change.* Revolutionary change is likely to require the setting and monitoring of unambiguous targets that people have to achieve. Often these will be linked to overall financial targets and in turn to improved returns to shareholders.

14.5.4 Evolution

Evolution is change in strategy that results in transformation, but incrementally. Arguably this is the most challenging type of strategic change since it involves building on and exploiting existing strategic capabilities while also developing new strategic capabilities. As Chapter 5 explains, however, in successful organisations many will see no pressing need for change and there will be a tendency to stick to historic bases of success, so the exploration for new ways of doing things may be limited. Managers and scholars alike have sought to identify ways in which the effective evolution of strategy might occur: how an organisation can change its business model and culture incrementally *and* keep pace with a changing environment, thus avoiding strategic drift. This section considers two ways in which this might be achieved.

Organisational ambidexterity

Ambidexterity is the ability to use both hands with equal facility. In organisational terms the word has been borrowed to mean both the exploitation of existing capabilities and the search for new capabilities. It is, of course, appropriate and necessary that an organisation should seek to *exploit* the capabilities it has built up over time in order to achieve and sustain competitive advantage. In so doing the tendency is towards *incremental* change since strategy will be built on established ways of doing things. If transformational change is to be achieved, however, there needs to be *exploration* for new capabilities and innovation. This is in line with the lesson from section 3.2.2 that organisations need the ability to renew and re-create their capabilities; they need to develop dynamic capabilities.

The conclusion is that there may be a need for **both the exploitation of existing capabilities and the exploration for new capabilities** – 'organisational ambidexterity'. However, this is likely to be problematic because the different processes associated with exploitation and exploration pose contradictions such as being both focused and flexible, efficient yet innovative, looking forward and backward and operating in multiple time frames.[33] There are, however, suggestions as to how this might be possible, some of which are shown in Illustration 14.5:

- *Structural ambidexterity*. Organisations may maintain the main core of the business devoted to exploitation with tighter control and careful planning but create separate units or temporary, perhaps project-based, teams for exploration[34] (see section 13.2.5). These exploratory units will be smaller in size, less tightly controlled[35] with much more emphasis on learning and processes to encourage new ideas.

- *Diversity rather than conformity*. Contradictory behaviours may be beneficial, so there may be benefits from diversity of views in line with the concept of *organisational learning* (see section 12.3.1). Such diversity might be on the basis of managers with different experience or different views on future strategy, which can give rise to useful debate. Such contesting of strategy may come to be 'normal' at senior levels in an organisation.[36] Stanford Univerity's Robert Burgelman[37] also argues that, close to the market and therefore perhaps at junior levels in an organisation, there will be those who are dissatisfied with the prevailing strategy or think it is inadequate in the face of changing industry circumstances and that senior executives need to channel this 'dissonance' into a 'searing intellectual debate' until a clearer strategic pattern emerges.

- *The role of leadership*. In turn this has implications for leadership roles in organisations. Leaders need to encourage and value different views and potentially contradictory behaviours rather than demanding uniformity.[38] This may mean running with new ideas and experiments to establish just what makes sense and what does not. However, they also need to have the authority, legitimacy and recognition to stop such experiments when it becomes clear that they are not worthwhile pursuing and make decisions about the direction that is to be followed, which, once taken, are followed by everyone in the organisation – including those who have previously dissented.

ILLUSTRATION 14.5

Traditions of successful evolutionary strategic transformation

An historical study identifies management bases of evolutionary transformational strategic change.

Very few companies have demonstrated the ability to both make transformational strategic changes while maintaining high levels of profitability. Such change usually follows a major downturn or crisis. A research study identified and traced the management processes over four decades in three UK firms that had achieved such transformations. The researchers identified 'traditions' that gave rise to such transformation, traditions that developed over time. They were not introduced by any one executive or written into documents or plans; they became part of the 'DNA' of the businesses. One of the companies was the retailer, Tesco.

A tradition of alternative coalitions

The companies had created parallel coalitions of senior executives. The first group, typically the more senior, focused on reinforcing current capabilities, current strengths and current successes. The second group, usually younger but still senior, actively looked to develop new strategies and new capabilities. This parallel system came to be an accepted part of how the company operated. It was encouraged and eventually institutionalised.

For instance, the original Tesco model was to 'pile it high and sell it cheap', which founder Jack Cohen perpetuated through a personal command and control management style. None the less, an alternative coalition around Ian MacLaurin and his team of operations-orientated managers developed in the 1960s that began to pursue more modern retail practices, introducing Tesco to a corporate model of management control. This alternative coalition took charge in the 1980s and 1990s and, in turn, there developed a new alternative coalition around Terry Leahy who developed the next stage of Tesco's strategy built around multiple segmented retail offerings. Leahy himself then took over in the 1990s through to 2011.

A tradition of constructive contestation

The development of alternative coalitions frequently originated in the context of significant conflict. At Tesco such conflict could be traced to boardroom battles between family members in the Cohen era and then between the two coalitions of managers in the 1960s and 1970s. Over time,

however, such conflicts became less intense and more respectful, evolving into 'constructive contestation'. This was not just a matter of senior executives advocating different points of view. Such contestation became culturally embedded; for example, if managers wanted to progress in the firm it was expected that they would 'fight their corner' in meetings with senior executives.

The tradition of exploiting 'happy accidents'

The two traditions of alternative coalitions and constructive contestation meant that new ideas continually surfaced. In turn this meant that the companies were well positioned to turn problems into opportunities. The researchers called these 'happy accidents' unanticipated circumstances or events which the alternative coalition used to develop new strategies. For example, economic downturn in the early 1990s hit Tesco, with its less established and younger customer portfolio. Puzzled why the business was not maintaining its recent levels of success, the CEO of that time, David Malpas, spent a day visiting competitors' stores in the company of the up-and-coming Terry Leahy. This exposed him to Leahy's views that Tesco had lost sight of its customers and needed to rethink its customer proposition. In turn this led to Leahy's elevation, the launch of multiple retail formats, a significantly reduced size of headquarters staff, streamlined management layers and international expansion.

Sources: M. Hensmans, G. Johnson and G. Yip, *Strategic Transformation: Changing while Winning*, Palgrave, 2013; also G. Johnson, G. Yip and M. Hensmans, 'Achieving successful strategic transformation', *MIT Sloan Management Review*, vol. 53, no. 3 (2012), pp. 25–32.

Questions

1 How do the 'traditions' relate to the explanations of evolutionary strategic change explained in section 14.5.4 and, in particular, the concept of organisational ambidexterity?

2 If the 'traditions' took decades to develop, is it possible for executives to manage their introduction into organisations? How?

- *Tight and loose systems.* All this suggests that there needs to be a balance between 'tight' systems of strategy development that can exploit existing capabilities – perhaps employing the disciplines of strategic planning – and 'looser' systems that encourage new ideas and experimentation. This might, in turn, be linked to the idea that there needs to be some over-all common 'glue', perhaps in the form of a clear *strategic intent* in terms of mission and values such that different units in the organisation may be allowed to express how such mission is achieved in their different ways.

Stages of evolution

A second way of conceiving of strategic change as evolution is in terms of the movement from one strategy to a changed strategy but over perhaps many years, perhaps guided from the top of an organisation. Here the principles that might guide change leaders are these:

- *Stages of transition.* Identifying interim stages in the change process is important. For example, in terms of the change context (see section 14.3) there may be insufficient readiness or an insufficient capacity to make major changes initially. It will therefore be important to establish these conditions before other major moves are taken.

- *Irreversible changes.* It may be possible to identify changes that, while not necessarily having immediate major impact, will have long-term and irreversible impacts. For example, a law firm or accountancy firm that wishes to achieve an evolutionary approach to strategic change might change the criteria for appointment of partners to achieve evolutionary change. The time horizons for the effects of such changes to take effect would be many years but, once made, the effects would be difficult to reverse.

- *Sustained top management commitment* will be required. The danger is that the momentum for change falters because people do not perceive consistent commitment to it from the top.

- *Winning hearts and minds.* Culture change is likely to be required in any transformational change. This may be more problematic than for revolutionary change because people may simply not recognise that there are problems with regard to the status quo. The likely need is for multiple levers for change to be used consistently: *persuasion* and *participation* as styles of managing change to allow people to see the need for change and contribute to what that change should be; the signalling of the meaning of change in ways that people throughout the organisation understand both rationally and emotionally; and levers that signal and achieve improved economic performance.

14.5.5 **Why change programmes fail**

Research into why change programmes fail can also provide lessons on the pitfalls to avoid. This section summarises seven of the main failings.[39]

- *Death by planning.* The emphasis is put on planning the change programme rather than delivering it. There is a continuous stream of proposals and reports, each one requiring agreement among managers affected by the changes. Subcommittees, project teams and working groups may be set up to examine problems and achieve buy-in. The result can be 'analysis paralysis' and a discourse about change rather than the delivery of change. This may also be linked to the politicisation of the change programme where meetings about change become forums for debate and political game-playing.

- *Loss of focus.* Change is often not a one-off process; it might require an ongoing series of initiatives, maybe over years. However, the risk is that these initiatives are seen by employees as 'change rituals' signifying very little. There is also the risk that the original intention of the change programme becomes eroded by other events taking place: for example, a redundancy programme.

- *Reinterpretation.* The attempted change becomes reinterpreted according to the old culture. For example, an engineering company's intended strategy of achieving differentiation by building on what customers valued was interpreted by the engineers within the firm as providing high levels of technical specification as determined by them, not by the customers.

- *Disconnectedness.* People affected by change may not see the change programme connecting to their reality. Senior executives, as proponents of the change, might not be seen to be credible in terms of understanding the realities of change on the ground. Or perhaps new systems and initiatives introduced are seen as out of line with the intentions of the intended change.

- *Behavioural compliance.* There is the danger that people appear to comply with the changes being pursued in the change programme without actually 'buying into' them. Change leaders may think they see change occurring, when all they see is superficial compliance.

- *Misreading scrutiny and resistance.* Change leaders are likely to face either resistance to the change or critical scrutiny of it. Often their response is to see such behaviour as negative and destructive. It can, on the other hand, be seen as ways in which 'change recipients' in the organisation are engaging with the changes in terms of its significance for them. Even if resistance occurs, this is a way of keeping the agenda for change on the table. Moreover, resistance that is explicit is more capable of being addressed than that which is passive or covert. So those managing the change programme need to see scrutiny and resistance as a basis for engaging others in the change programme.

- *Broken agreements and violation of trust.* The need for a clear message about the need for and direction of change has been emphasised in this chapter. However, if senior management fail to provide honest assessments of the situation or provide undertakings to employees on which they subsequently renege, then they will lose the trust and respect of employees and, very likely, ensure heightened resistance to change.

Many of the problems and challenges of managing strategic change are reflected in the Key Debate for this chapter.

KEY DEBATE

Strategic change from top to bottom

Strategic change has traditionally been seen as the responsibility of top management: but is this the most useful way of conceiving of strategic change?

John Kotter, one of the world's foremost authorities on leadership and change, argues that problems of strategic change arise because top executives fail to take the necessary steps to lead such changes. For Kotter these steps include:

- Establishing a sense of urgency on the basis of market threats or opportunities.
- Forming a powerful coalition of stakeholders for change.
- Creating and communicating a clear vision and strategy to direct the change and ensuring that the behaviour of the guiding coalition is in line with the vision.
- Removing obstacles to change, changing systems that undermine the vision and encouraging non-traditional ideas and activities.
- Creating short-term wins.
- Consolidating improvements but also continuing the process of change.

However, Julia Balogun studied a top management change initiative from the point of view of how middle managers interpreted it. She found that, while top managers believed they were being clear about the intended strategy, change actually took place by middle managers making sense of change initiatives in terms of their own *mental models* in relation to their *local responsibilities and conditions*, through discussion with their peers and on the basis of rumour. Top managers were inevitably too far removed from these dynamics and could not be expected to understand them in detail or manage them in specific ways. She argues that 'Senior managers can initiate and influence direction of change but not direct change.' They can:

- Monitor how people respond to change initiatives.
- Engage as much as possible with how people make sense of change and work with their reality, responding to their issues and interpretations.
- Live the changes they want others to adopt, especially avoiding inconsistencies between their actions, words and deeds.
- Focus on creating the understanding of higher-level principles rather than the details.

Hari Tsoukas and Robert Chia go further. They argue that change is an inherent property of organisations. Hierarchy and management control dampen that inherent change:

'Change programmes trigger ongoing change: they provide the discursive resources for making certain things possible, although what exactly will happen remains uncertain when a change programme is initiated. It must first be experienced before the possibilities it opens up are appreciated and taken up (if they are taken up). Change programmes are . . . locally adapted, improvised and elaborated . . . If this is accepted what is, then, the meaning of "planned change"? . . . Change has been taken to mean that which occurs as a consequence of deliberate managerial action. In the view put forward here such a definition is limited. Although managers certainly aim at achieving established ways of thinking and acting through implementing particular plans, nonetheless, change in organisations occurs without necessarily intentional managerial action as a result of individuals trying to accommodate new experience and realise new possibilities. In the view suggested here, an excessive preoccupation with planned change risks failing to recognise the always already changing texture of organisations.' (pp. 578–9)

Sources
J. Kotter, 'Leading change: why transformation efforts fail', *Harvard Business Review*, March–April (1995), pp. 59–67.
J. Balogun and G. Johnson, 'Organisational restructuring and middle manager sensemaking', *Academy of Management Journal*, vol. 47, no. 4 (2004), pp. 523–49.
J. Balogun, 'Managing change: steering a course between intended strategies and unanticipated outcomes', *Long Range Planning*, vol. 39 (2006), pp. 29–49.
H. Tsoukas and R. Chia, 'On organisational becoming: rethinking organisational change', *Organisation Science*, vol. 13, no. 5 (2002), pp. 567–82.

Questions

1 What are the problems associated with top-down or bottom-up views of change management?

2 If you were a senior executive, which approach would you take and in what circumstances?

3 Are the different views irreconcilable?

(You will find the perspectives on the management of strategy in the Commentaries useful background reading.)

SUMMARY

A recurrent theme in this chapter has been that approaches, styles and means of change need to be tailored to the context of that change. Bearing in mind this general point, this chapter has emphasised the following:

- *Situational leadership* suggests that strategic leaders need to adopt different *styles* of managing strategic change according to different contexts and in relation to the involvement and interest of different groups.

- The *change kaleidoscope* is a way of understanding how approaches to leading change relate to organisational context. The features of the kaleidoscope include the *resources and skills that need to be preserved*, the degree of *homogeneity or diversity* in the organisation, the *power* to make change happen and the *capacity, capability and readiness* for change.

- *Forcefield analysis* is a useful means of identifying blockages to change and potential levers for change.

- *Levers for managing strategic change* need to be considered in terms of the context of change. These levers include building a *compelling case for change*, *challenging the taken for granted*, the need to change *operational processes*, *routines* and *symbols*, the importance of *political processes*, and other change *tactics*.

- There are different *types of strategic change* which can be thought of in terms of the *extent* of culture change required and its *nature* – whether it can be achieved through incremental change or requires urgent action (the 'big bang' approach).

- *Different approaches to leading change* are likely to be required for the different types of change.

VIDEO ASSIGNMENTS

Visit *MyStrategyLab* and watch the Wilmington case study for Chapter 14.

1 How would you describe Charles Brady's style of leading change? Why might this style be particularly suited to a company like Wilmington?

2 Charles Brady claims that there have been significant changes in the company. In terms of section 14.5, what type of change does he describe? What might the advantages and disadvantages of this be?

WORK ASSIGNMENTS

✱ *Denotes more advanced work assignments.*
* *Refers to a case study in the Text and Cases edition.*

14.1 Compare and contrast the different styles of leading change you have read about in the press or in this text (e.g. Sergio Marchionne at Fiat and Chrysler, George Yip at Rotterdam School of Management, John Howie at Babcock Rail* and Steve Jobs at Apple*).

14.2 Drawing on section 14.2.2, assess the key contextual dimensions of an organisation (such as Barclays in Chapter 5) and consider how they should influence the design of a programme of strategic change.

14.3 Use a forcefield analysis to identify blockages and facilitators of change for an organisation (such as one for which you have considered the need for a change in strategic direction in a previous assignment). Identify what aspects of the changes suggested by this analysis can be managed as part of a change programme and how.

14.4✱ In the context of leading strategic change in a large corporation or public-sector organisation, to what extent, and why, do you agree with Richard Pascale's argument that it is easier to act ourselves into a better way of thinking than it is to think ourselves into a better way of acting? (References 20 to 28 will be useful here.)

14.5✱ There are a number of books by renowned senior executives who have led major changes in their organisation. Read one of these and note the levers and mechanisms for change they employed, using the approaches outlined in this chapter as a checklist. How effective do you think these were in the context that the change leader faced, and could other mechanisms have been used?

Integrative assignment

14.6✱ What would be the key issues for the corporate parent of a diversified organisation with a multi-domestic international strategy (see Chapter 8) wishing to change to a more related portfolio? Consider this in terms of (a) the strategic capabilities that the parent might require (Chapters 3 and 7), (b) the implications for organising and controlling its subsidiaries (Chapter 13), (c) the likely blockages to such change and (d) how these might be overcome (Chapter 14).

RECOMMENDED KEY READINGS

- For a succinct summary of research on effective leadership, including the leadership of change, see G. Yukl, 'Effective leadership behaviour: what we know and what questions need more attention,' *Academy of Management Perspectives*, vol. 26, no. 4 (2012), pp. 66–85.

- J. Balogun and V. Hope Hailey, *Exploring Strategic Change*, Prentice Hall, 3rd edn, 2008, builds on and extends many of the ideas in this chapter. In particular, it emphasises the importance of tailoring change programmes to organisational context and discusses more fully many of the change levers reviewed in this chapter.

- For an understanding of different approaches to leading change: M. Beer and N. Nohria, 'Cracking the code of change', *Harvard Business Review*, vol. 78, no. 3 (May–June 2000), pp. 133–41.

- For an understanding and for examples of organisational ambidexterity: C.A. O'Reilly and M.L. Tushman, 'Organisational ambidexterity in action: how managers explore and exploit' *California Management Review*, vol. 53, no. 4 (2011), pp. 5–22; and G. Johnson, G. Yip and M. Hensmans, 'Achieving successful strategic transformation', *MIT Sloan Management Review*, vol. 53, no. 3 (2012), pp. 25–32.

- The study of change programmes by L.C. Harris and E. Ogbonna, 'The unintended consequences of culture interventions: a study of unexpected outcomes', *British Journal of Management*, vol. 13, no. 1 (2002), pp. 31–49, provides a valuable insight into the problems of managing change in organisations.

REFERENCES

1. This definition of leadership is based on that offered by R.M. Stodgill, 'Leadership, membership and organization', *Psychological Bulletin*, vol. 47 (1950), pp. 1–14.

2. J. Kotter, 'What leaders really do', *Harvard Business Review* (December 2001), pp. 85–96.

3. See D. Ulrich, N. Smallwood and K. Sweetman, *Leadership Code: the Five Things Great Leaders Do*, Harvard Business School Press, 1999.

4. See S. Floyd and W. Wooldridge, *The Strategic Middle Manager: How to Create and Sustain Competitive Advantage*, Jossey-Bass, 1996.

5. See E. Mollick, 'People and process, suits and innovators: the role of individuals in firm performance', *Strategic Management Journal*, vol. 33, no. 9 (2012), pp. 1001–15.

6. See for example J. Balogun and G. Johnson: 'Organizational restructuring and middle manager sensemaking', *Academy of Management Journal* (August 2004), pp. 523–49; J. Balogun, 'Managing change: steering a course between intended strategies and unanticipated outcomes', *Long Range Planning*, vol. 39 (2006), pp. 29–49; J. Sillence and F. Mueller, 'Switching strategic perspective: the reframing of accounts of responsibility', *Organization Studies*, vol. 28, no. 2 (2007), pp. 155–76.

7. See T.A. Judge and R.F. Piccolo, 'Transformational and transactional leadership: a meta analytic test of their relative validity', *Journal of Applied Psychology*, vol. 89 (2004), pp. 755–68.

8. For this evidence see D.A. Waldman, G.G. Ramirez, R.J. House and P. Puranam, 'Does leadership matter? CEO leadership attributes and profitability under conditions of perceived environmental uncertainty', *Academy of Management Journal*, vol. 44, no. 1 (2001), pp. 134–43.

9. The discussion on different approaches of strategic leaders and evidence for the effectiveness of the adoption of different approaches can be found in D. Goleman, 'Leadership that gets results', *Harvard Business Review*, vol. 78, no. 2 (March–April 2000), pp. 78–90; and C.M. Farkas and S. Wetlaufer, 'The ways chief executive officers lead', *Harvard Business Review*, vol. 74, no. 3 (May–June 1996), pp. 110–12.

10. Different authors explain change styles in different ways. This section is based on the typologies used by J. Balogun and V. Hope Hailey, *Exploring Strategic Change*, 3rd edn, Prentice Hall, 2008, section 2.4, pp. 31–6; and D. Dunphy and D. Stace, 'The strategic management of corporate change', *Human Relations*, vol. 46, no. 8 (1993), pp. 905–20. For an alternative framework see R. Caldwell, 'Models of change agency: a fourfold classification', *British Journal of Management*, vol. 14, no. 2 (2003), pp. 131–42.

11. For example, D.A. Garvin and M.A. Roberto, 'Change through persuasion', *Harvard Business Review* (February 2005), pp. 104–12.

12. For a fuller explanation of collaboration see H. Ibarra and M.T. Hansen, 'Are you a collaborative leader?', *Harvard Business Review* (July–August 2011), pp. 69–74.

13. A.M. Grant, 'Leading with meaning: beneficiary contact, prosocial impact and the performance effects of transformational leadership', *Academy of Management Journal*, vol. 55, no. 2 (2012), pp. 458–76.

14. For an interesting example of how different contexts affect receptivity to change, see J. Newton, J. Graham, K. McLoughlin and A. Moore, 'Receptivity to change in a general medical practice', *British Journal of Management*, vol. 14, no. 2 (2003), pp. 143–53. And for a discussion of the problems of importing change programmes from the private sector to the public sector, see F. Ostroff, 'Change management in government', *Harvard Business Review*, vol. 84, no. 5 (May 2006), pp. 141–7.

15. See J.-L. Denis, L. Lamothe and A. Langley, 'The dynamics of collective change leadership and strategic change in pluralistic organizations', *Academy of Management Journal*, vol. 44, no. 4 (2001), pp. 809–37.

16. For a review of research that makes this point see D. Buchanan, L. Fitzgerald, D. Ketley, R. Gallop, J.L. Jones, S.S. Lamont, A. Neath and E. Whitby, 'No going back: a review of the literature on sustaining organizational change', *International Journal of Management Reviews*, vol. 7, no. 3 (2005), pp. 189–205.

17. See C. Aiken and S. Keller, 'The irrational side of change management', *McKinsey Quarterly*, no. 2 (2009), pp. 101–9.

18. For an example of this approach see J.M. Mezias, P. Grinyer and W.D. Guth, 'Changing collective cognition: a process model for strategic change', *Long Range Planning*, vol. 34, no. 1 (2001), pp. 71–95. Also for a systematic approach to strategy making and change based on such surfacing, see F. Ackermann and C. Eden with I. Brown, *The Practice of Making Strategy*, Sage, 2005.

19. See M. Hensmans, G. Johnson and G. Yip, *Strategic Transformation: Changing While Winning*, Palgrave, 2013; also G. Johnson, G. Yip and M. Hensmans, 'Achieving successful strategic transformation', *MIT Sloan Management Review*, vol. 53, no. 3 (2012), pp. 25–32.

20. This quote is on page 135 of R. Pascale, M. Millemann and L. Gioja, 'Changing the way we change', *Harvard Business Review*, vol. 75, no. 6 (November–December 1997), pp. 126–39.

21. See C. Rerup and M.S. Feldman, 'Routines as a source of change in organizational schemata: the role of trial and error learning', *Academy of Management Journal*, vol. 54, no. 3 (2011), pp. 577–610.

22. See H. Bresman, 'Changing routines: a process model of vicarious group learning in pharmaceutical R&D'. *Academy of Management Journal*, vol. 56, no. 1 (2013), pp. 35–61.

23. See G. Johnson, S. Smith and B. Codling, 'Institutional change and strategic agency: an empirical analysis of managers' experimentation with routines in strategic decision-making', in *The Cambridge Handbook of Strategy as Practice*, eds D. Golsorkhi, L. Rouleau, D. Seidl and E. Vaara, Cambridge University Press, 2010.

24. For a fuller discussion of this theme, see J.M. Higgins and C. McCallaster, 'If you want strategic change don't forget your cultural artefacts', *Journal of Change Management*, vol. 4, no. 1 (2004), pp. 63–73.

25. For a discussion of the role of rituals in change, see D. Sims, S. Fineman and Y. Gabriel, *Organizing and Organizations: an Introduction*, Sage, 1993; and H.M. Trice and J.M. Beyer, 'Using six organisational rites to change culture', in R.H. Kilman, M.J. Saxton, R. Serpa and associates (eds), *Gaining Control of the Corporate Culture*, Jossey-Bass, 1985.

26. See C. Hardy, I. Palmer and N. Phillips, 'Discourse as a strategic resource', *Human Relations*, vol. 53, no. 9 (2000), p. 1231.

27. Table 14.3 is based on observations of the role of political activities in organisations by, in particular, H. Mintzberg, *Power in and around Organizations*, Prentice Hall, 1983; and J. Pfeffer, *Power in Organizations*, Pitman, 1981. However, perhaps the most interesting book on political management remains Niccolo Machiavelli's sixteenth-century work, *The Prince* (available in Penguin Books, 2003).

28. C. Hardy, 'Understanding power; bringing about strategic change', *British Journal of Management*, vol. 7, special issue (1996), pp. 3–16.

29. M. Hensmans, G. Johnson and G. Yip (see reference 19) refer to 'happy accidents' that executives may use to build a momentum for change.

30. This part of the chapter draws on Chapter 3 of *Exploring Strategic Change* by J. Balogun and V. Hope Hailey, 3rd edn, Prentice Hall, 2008.

31. Turnaround strategy is extensively explained in D. Lovett and S. Slatter, *Corporate Turnaround*, Penguin Books, 1999; and P. Grinyer, D. Mayes and P. McKiernan, 'The sharpbenders: achieving a sustained improvement in performance', *Long Range Planning*, vol. 23, no. 1 (1990), pp. 116–25. Also see V.L. Barker and I.M. Duhaime, 'Strategic change in the turnaround process: theory and empirical evidence', *Strategic Management Journal*, vol. 18, no. 1 (1997), pp. 13–38.

32. See J. Battilana and T. Casciaro, 'Change agents, networks and institutions: a contingency theory of organizational change', *Academy of Management Journal*, vol. 35, no. 2 (2012), pp. 381–398.

33. See W.K. Smith and M. Tushman, 'Senior teams and managing contradictions: on the team dynamics of managing exploitation and exploration'. *Organization Science*, vol. 16, no. 5 (2005), pp. 522–36.

34. M.L. Tushman, and C.A. O'Reilly, 'Ambidextrous organizations: managing evolutionary and revolutionary change', *California Management Review*, vol. 38, no. 4 (1996), pp. 8–30.

35. R. Duncan, 'Characteristics of organisational environments and perceived environmental uncertainty', *Administrative Science Quarterly*, vol. 17, no. 3 (1972), pp. 313–27.

36. See Hensmans, Johnson and Yip (reference 19 above).

37. Robert Burgelman and Andrew Grove, 'Strategic dissonance', *California Management Review*, vol. 38, no. 2 (1996), pp. 8–28.

38. R.A. Burgelman and A.S. Grove, 'Let chaos reign, then rein in chaos – repeatedly: managing strategic dynamics for corporate longevity'. *Strategic Management Journal*, vol. 28 (2007), pp. 965–79: also C.A. O'Reilly and M.L. Tushman, 'Organizational ambidexterity in action: how managers explore and exploit', *California Management Review*, vol. 53, no. 4 (2011), pp. 5–22.

39. The observations and examples here are largely based on L.C. Harris and E. Ogbonna, 'The unintended consequences of culture interventions: a study of unexpected outcomes', *British Journal of Management*, vol. 13, no. 1 (2002), pp. 31–49; J.D. Ford, L.W. Ford and A.D. Amelio, 'Resistance to change: the rest of the story, *Academy of Management Review*, vol. 23 (2008), pp. 362–77; and D.A. Garvin and M.A. Roberto (reference 11 above).

Sergio Marchionne: leading change in Fiat and Chrysler

With dual Canadian and Italian citizenship, Sergio Marchionne speaks fluent English and Italian. With a first degree in philosophy, an MBA and a law degree, he first worked in accountancy, then in management positions in the printing, entertainment and chemicals industries before being elected to the board of Fiat S.p.A. in May 2003. Though he had no direct management experience in the automobile industry, he was then appointed Fiat's CEO in 2004. Since that time he has overseen turnaround programmes at Fiat, Europe's second-largest car manufacturer, then Chrysler, the third largest in the USA.

Source: Getty Images/Alessia Pierdomencio

Sergio Marchionne

'Whether in his office, on a public platform or even an award ceremony, Sergio Marchionne adopts an informal relaxed image, typically in a sweater rather than the traditional managerial suit. His relaxed manner does not, however, disguise distinct views on his role as a business leader: he wrote: "My job as CEO is not to make decisions about the business but to set stretch objectives and help our managers work out how to reach them." '[1]

In his assessment of those he selects to lead businesses he emphasises, among other qualities, the need for decisiveness, creativity, but also the ability to rethink assumptions and to lead change. He also believes in giving such leaders responsibility and the latitude to explore new ideas, accepting that means there will be 'hits and misses; you have to let them miss.'[2]

Turnaround at Fiat

When he took over as CEO at Fiat in 2004 he was the fifth CEO since 2001. The company was unprofitable, the products had a reputation for poor quality, its most recent new car launch had been unsuccessful and relationships with the unions were poor.

He spent his first 50 days touring the business, listening to people and analysing the situation. He found that senior executives were unused to taking responsibility for decisions; everything was referred upwards to the CEO. It was also common for executives to communicate to each other via their secretaries and spend their time fire fighting or avoiding problems. The company was dominated by engineers and it was engineering that provided the traditional career progression to senior management positions. The development of new models was also in their hands; they would then pass a new car to sales and marketing, complete with sales targets and price. As well as being inefficient, not surprisingly this gave rise to tensions between departments.

Following initial measures to reduce Fiat's debt level, Marchionne turned his attention to the leadership of the business. He decided that at the most senior levels, the habit of upward referral to the CEO was so ingrained it could not be changed: so many senior executives were 'let go'. In addition 2,000 other managers and staff were retired early. On the other hand, as he toured the company, he had identified young talented managers, often in areas such as marketing that were not the traditional routes to the top, or in geographic areas such as Latin America that were less influenced by head office and where managers tended to behave more autonomously and take personal initiative. He drew on this 'talent spotting' to make 20 leadership appointments as well as other promotions.

Marchionne prioritised taking a personal interest in high potential talent and regarded his personal engagement with them as more valuable than more formal assessment. He also believed that such personal engagement helped develop a top team with strongly held common values. His expectation of this new top cadre of leaders was that they should be given the responsibility of achieving the turnaround. He recognised that this was demanding:

> 'As I give people more responsibility, I also hold them more accountable. A leader who fails to meet an objective should suffer some consequences, but I don't believe that failing to meet an objective is the end of the world . . . (but) if you want to grow leaders, you can't let explanations and excuses become a way of life. That's a characteristic of the old Fiat we've left far behind.'[3]

Marchionne brought this team together to come up with a business plan around a stretch target, announced in July 2004, to make 2 billion euros in 2007. He recognised that this imposed target was highly ambitious, indeed some thought it unrealistic, but believed its virtue was that it forced managers to think differently and challenge old ways of doing things. To achieve greater integration and speed things up, Marchionne also took out several layers of management, eliminated a proliferation of committees and replaced them with a Group Executive Council that brought together executives from disparate operations such as tractors and trucks. To run Fiat Auto he also established a 24-person team with the aim of getting all parts of the company to talk to one another. To further encourage the sharing of ideas, he also began to move executives from one part of the business to another and required his top managers to accept multiple responsibilities for different parts of the business.

Marchionne saw one of his own major roles as the challenging of assumptions. He cites the example of questions he asked about why it took Fiat four years to develop a new model. The questions helped identify processes that could be removed, which meant that the new Cinquecento was developed and launched in just 18 months in 2006. 'You start removing a few bottlenecks in this way, and pretty soon people catch on and begin ripping their own processes apart.'[4] Such challenging of assumptions and processes was also aided by recruiting managers from outside the car industry and by benchmarking, not just against other car makers but also companies like Apple.

Not all of the moves were at top management level. Attention was also paid to the workforce, many of whom worked in the manufacturing units that Marchionne had seen to be inefficient and dispiriting:

> 'The easy thing for me to do would have been to shut down two plants and start reaggregating assets elsewhere. But had I done that, we would have had a very disgruntled workforce . . . We've opened kindergartens and grocery stores next to the plant to make it easier for people to balance their work and domestic obligations. We've redecorated all the dressing rooms and bathrooms . . . We're doing it because we recognise that the commitment we make as leaders to our workforce goes beyond what's negotiated in our labour contracts.'[5]

By 2006 Fiat was profitable.

Turnaround at Chrysler

By 2009 Chrysler was near to bankruptcy, it had no market value, investment had been slashed and potentially 300,000 jobs were on the line. With the support of the US and Canadian governments and trade unions the Fiat Group formed a strategic alliance with Chrysler with a 20 per cent stake. Marchionne was appointed CEO. His vision was that Fiat and Chrysler together could create a leading global player in the automobile sector given potential synergies in terms of purchasing power, distribution capabilities and product portfolios – Chrysler's jeeps, mini-vans and light trucks and Fiat's small cars and fuel-efficient engines.

When Marchionne took over at Chrysler in 2009, not only did he inherit a $6 billion high-interest government loan, he also found a fearful workforce and, like most of Detroit's car manufacturers, a company riddled with bureaucracy. One of his first acts was to point out, in a memo to Chrysler employees, the parallels with Fiat: 'Five years ago, I stepped into a very similar situation at Fiat. It was perceived by many as a failing, lethargic automaker that produced low-quality cars and was stymied by endless bureaucracies.'[6]

Like Fiat, Chrysler was highly hierarchical with managers reluctant to take decisions: 'This place was run by a chairman's office . . . the top floor (known as the Tower). It's empty now . . . Nothing happens there. I'm on the floor here with all the engineers.'[7]

Again Marchionne changed the management. He identified 26 young leaders from two or three levels below top management who had hitherto been stifled by the hierarchy. These reported directly to him in a flattened out organisation. The reorganisation also involved managers leaving who failed to match up to Marchionne's expectations.

Again Marchionne emphasised cost control; for example, the 2009 plan identified savings of $2.9 billion by 2014 by sharing parts and engines with Fiat. But there was also an emphasis on product development. Here he drew on the experience of his new executive team to focus on improvements to the product range, such as Ralph Gilles, in charge of product design:

> 'Everyone knew what was wrong with the cars. You ask any employee in the company, they could list ten things that they would do better. And when you're given the chance to do those ten things better, you end up with a product that exceeds the sum of its parts.'[8]

Another key component of the recovery was to deal with the product quality problem. Chrysler had been organised such that each brand had its own quality department. These separate departments were merged and new ways to measure quality introduced to provide greater oversight over all the brands. This attention to product and quality improvement went hand-in-hand with plant modernisation. The result was an upgrading of 16 models in 18 months.

When the Jefferson North assembly plant in Detroit was revamped the workforce was kept occupied with its most thorough cleaning since it opened in 1991. They welcomed Marchionne when he visited to review progress, but were even more delighted when President Obama later toured the plant and called it 'this magnificent factory'. Industrial relations were not, however, always so positive. The efforts to reduce costs meant cutting jobs, closing plants, holding down wages and terminating established union agreements. Union activists staged protests at presentations made by Marchionne.

By 2011 Chrysler announced an operating profit of $2 billion (compared with a net loss of $652 million in 2010) and repaid all government loans.

New challenges

In July 2011, Fiat's stake in Chrysler was increased to 53.5 per cent and in September 2011, Marchionne became Chairman of Chrysler. However, he faced new challenges.

By 2012 Chrysler was prospering. Capital spending was planned to rise to $4 billion from $3.1 billion in 2011 and profits were holding up. Fiat, however, was struggling to cope with five years of industry-wide decline in recessionary Europe with Italy performing particularly badly. Fiat's cars were still ranked second worst in terms of product quality in the USA,[9] it was making losses, sales forecasts and investment in Europe were being reduced and Italian plants were operating at 50 per cent capacity.[10]

Marchionne was trying to promote European industry-wide efforts to cut production capacity and, after one closure in 2011, was threatening to close a second Italian factory. He was also calling for government intervention to make it easier to close unprofitable factories and lay off workers. There seemed little support for industry-wide rationalisation from Volkswagen, BMW and Daimler who, while also suffering profit downturns, did not have Fiat's level of excess factory capacity in Europe. One industry observer suggested that, under Sergio Marchionne, the next few years at Fiat and Chrysler would be a 'white knuckle ride'.[11]

Sources
1. Sergio Marchionne, 'Fiat's extreme makeover', *Harvard Business Review*, December (2008), p. 46.
2. Lecture by Sergio Marchionne, 'Leading From Hell and Back', at Ross School of Business, Michigan University, 13 January 2012.
3. *Harvard Business Review*, December 2008, p. 46.
4. *Harvard Business Review*, December 2008, p. 47.
5. *Harvard Business Review*, December 2008, p. 48.
6. Peter Gumbe, 'Chrysler's Sergio Marchionne: the turnaround artista', *Time Magazine*, 18 June 2009.
7. Resurrecting Chrysler, *60 minutes*, CBS; interview with Steve Kroft, 25 March 2012, http://www.youtube.com/watch?v=h3ppoyWNN7s.
8. Resurrecting Chrysler, *60 minutes*, CBS (see 7 above).
9. J.D. Power and Associates (2012) US Initial Quality Study.
10. Tommaso Ebhardt, 'Marchionne seen missing Fiat sales target by $19 billion', *Business Week*, 29 October 2012.
11. Tommaso Ebhardt (see 10 above).

Questions

1 In relation to section 14.5, what was the type of change pursued at Fiat and Chrysler? Was this appropriate to the change context?

2 How would you describe the change style of Sergio Marchionne? Was this appropriate to the change context?

3 What levers for change were employed by Sergio Marchionne? What others might have been used and why?

4 Assess the effectiveness of the change programmes at Fiat and Chrysler.

15

THE PRACTICE OF STRATEGY

Learning outcomes

After reading this chapter you should be able to:

● Assess who to involve in strategising, with regard particularly to *top managers*, *strategy consultants*, *strategic planners* and *middle managers*.

● Evaluate different approaches to strategising activity, including *analysis*, *issue-selling*, *decision making* and *communicating*.

● Recognise key elements in various common strategy methodologies, including *strategy workshops*, *projects*, *hypothesis testing* and writing *business cases* and *strategic plans*.

MyStrategyLab

MyStrategyLab is designed to help you make the most of your studies. Visit **www.pearsoned.co.uk/mystrategylab** to discover a wide range of resources, including:

● A personalised **Study plan** that will help you understand core concepts

● **Audio and video clips** that put the spotlight on strategy in the real world

● **Online glossaries and flashcards** that provide helpful reminders when you're looking for some quick revision.

(15.1) INTRODUCTION

In 2012, 37-year-old Marissa Mayer moved from a senior position at Google to become Chief Executive of Yahoo, the struggling web-portal giant. She promised a 'deep-dive' review of Yahoo's situation before developing a new strategy to save the company from its longstanding decline. In between, Marissa Mayer was also due to give birth to her first child.

If you were appointed to a leadership position in an organisation, or took on the role of strategic planner or strategy consultant, what would you *do* to review and develop strategy? Who would you involve and how would you organise them? This final chapter focuses on the practice of making strategy. Whereas Chapter 12 introduced the overall organisational process of strategy development, this chapter is about what people do *inside* the process. The aim is to examine the practicalities of strategy making for top managers, strategic planning specialists, strategy consultants or managers lower down the organisation.

The chapter has three sections as shown in Figure 15.1:

- *The strategists*. The chapter starts by looking at the various people involved in making strategy. It does not assume that strategy is made just by top management. As pointed out in Chapter 12, strategy often involves people from all over the organisation, and even people from outside. The Key Debate at the end of the chapter addresses the controversial involvement of external strategy consultants. Readers can ask themselves how they fit into this set of strategists, now or in the future.

- *Strategising activities*. The chapter continues by considering the kinds of work and activity that strategists carry out in their strategy making. This includes not just the strategy analysis that has been central to a large part of this text, but also the selling of strategic issues, the realities of strategic decision making and the critical task of communicating strategic decisions throughout the organisation.

Figure 15.1 The pyramid of strategy practice

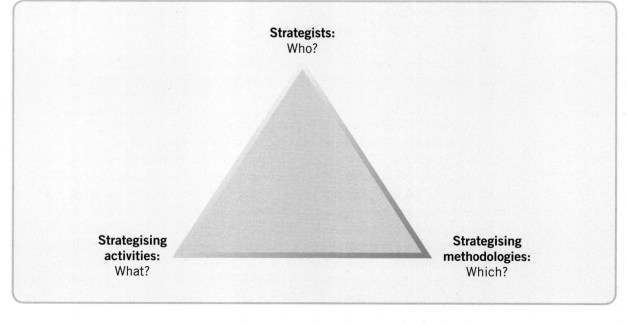

● *Strategising methodologies.* The final section covers some of the standard methodologies that managers use to carry out their strategising activities. This includes strategy workshops for formulating or communicating strategy; strategy projects and strategy consulting teams; hypothesis testing to guide strategy work; and the creation of strategic plans and business cases.

Figure 15.1 integrates these three sections in a *pyramid of practice.*[1] The pyramid highlights three questions that run through this chapter: *who* to include in strategy making; *what* to do in carrying out strategising activity; and *which* strategising methodologies to use in this strategising activity. Placing strategists at the top of the pyramid emphasises the role of managerial discretion and skill in strategy making. It is the strategists who drive both the strategising activity and the strategy methodologies that are at the base of the pyramid. Strategists' choices and skill with regard to activity and methodologies can make a real difference to final outcomes. The rest of the chapter seeks to guide practising strategists through the key choices they may have to make in action.

(15.2) THE STRATEGISTS

This section introduces the different types of people potentially involved in strategy. It starts at the top management level, but also addresses strategic planners, consultants and middle managers. One key issue is who *should* be involved in strategy making.

15.2.1 Top managers and directors

The conventional view is that strategy is the business of top management. This view suggests that top management are clearly separated from operational responsibilities, so that they can focus on overall strategy.[2] If top managers are directly involved in operations such as sales or service delivery, they are liable to get distracted from long-term issues by day-to-day responsibilities and to represent the interests of their departments or business units rather than the interests of their organisation as a whole. In the private sector at least, top managers' job titles underline this strategic responsibility: company directors set direction, managers manage.

In most organisations, it is the board of directors (or their equivalents) who holds ultimate responsibility for strategy (see Chapter 4). However, different roles are played by different board members, whether *chief executive officer*, the *top management team* or *non-executive directors*:

● The *chief executive officer* is often seen as the 'chief strategist', ultimately responsible for all strategic decisions. Chief executives of large companies typically spend about one third of their time on strategy.[3] Michael Porter stresses the value of a clear strategic leader, somebody capable of setting a disciplined approach to what fits and what does not fit the overall strategy.[4] In this view, the chief executive officer (or managing director or equivalent top individual) owns the strategy and is accountable for its success or failure. The clarity of this individual responsibility can no doubt focus attention. However, there are at least two dangers. First, centralising responsibility on the chief executive officer can lead to excessive personalisation. Organisations respond to setbacks simply by changing their chief executive officer, rather than examining deeply the internal sources of failure. Second, successful chief executives can become over-confident, seeing themselves as corporate heroes and launching strategic initiatives of ever-increasing ambition. The over-confidence of heroic leaders often leads to spectacular failures. Jim Collins' research on 'great' American companies that outperformed their rivals over the long term found that their chief executive officers were typically modest, steady and long-serving.[5]

- The *top management team*, often an organisation's executive directors, also share responsibility for strategy. They can bring additional experience and insight to the chief executive officer. In theory, they should be able to challenge the chief executive officer and increase strategic debate. In practice, the top management team are often constrained in at least three ways. First, except in the largest companies, top managers often carry operational responsibilities that either distract them or bias their strategic thinking: for example, in a business the marketing director will have ongoing concerns about marketing, the production director about production, and so on. In the public sector the top management team will also, very likely, be heads of operating departments. Second, top managers are also frequently appointed by the chief executive officer; consequently, they may lack the independence for real challenge. Finally, top management teams, especially where their members have similar backgrounds and face strong leadership, often suffer from '*groupthink*', the tendency to build strong consensus among team members and avoid internal questioning or conflict.[6] Top management teams can minimise groupthink by fostering diversity in membership (e.g. differences in age, career tracks and gender), by ensuring openness to outside views, for example those of non-executive directors, and by promoting internal debate and questioning. Research indicates that organisations with cultures of internal 'contestation' are more able to meet the challenge of strategic change over the long run (see Illustration 14.5).[7]

- *Non-executive directors* have no executive management responsibility within the organisation, and so in theory should be able to offer an external and objective view on strategy. Although this varies according to national corporate governance systems (see section 4.3.2), in a public company the chairman of the board is typically non-executive. The chairman will normally be consulted closely by the chief executive officer on strategy, as he or she will have a key role in liaising with investors. However, the ability of the chairman and other non-executives to contribute substantially to strategy can be limited. Non-executives are typically part-time appointments. The predominant role for non-executive directors in strategy, therefore, is consultative, reviewing and challenging strategy proposals that come from the top management executive team. A key role for them also is to ensure that the organisation has a rigorous system in place for the making and renewing of strategy. It is therefore important that non-executives are authoritative and experienced individuals, that they have independence from the top management executive team and that they are fully briefed before board meetings.

15.2.2 Strategic planners

Strategic planners, sometimes known as strategy directors, strategy analysts or similar, **are those with a formal responsibility for coordinating the strategy process** (see Chapter 12). Although small companies very rarely have full-time strategic planners, they are common in large companies and increasingly widespread in the public and not-for-profit sectors. As in Illustration 15.1, organisations frequently advertise for strategic planning jobs. Here, the personal specifications give a clear picture of the types of role a typical strategic planner might be expected to play. In a large corporation a strategic planner would be not only working on a three-year strategic plan, but investigating acquisition targets, monitoring competitors and

ILLUSTRATION 15.1

Wanted: Team member for strategy unit

The following job advertisement is adapted from several recent advertisements appearing in the Financial Times (exec-appointments. com). It gives an insight into the kind of work strategic planners do and the skills and background required.

Strategy Analyst sought for a fast-paced role in a multinational media business.

Reporting to the company's Chief Strategy Officer, the Strategy Analyst will be involved in driving the company's overall growth strategy across the business in Europe. The person appointed will be expected to carry out in-depth analyses of current and potential business strategies, business unit performance, customer markets and segments, and potential acquisition targets or joint venture partners in different territories. The person will probably have a Business Administration, Accounting or similar qualification.

Key responsibilities:

- collection of business and competitor intelligence
- evaluation of business unit performance, actual and potential
- evaluation of new market opportunities and initiatives
- evaluation of possible acquisition targets and joint venture partners
- contribution to strategic planning at the corporate-level
- assistance to business units in preparing their own strategic plans

Essential competences:

- good team player able to work in multicultural environments
- confidence with senior management
- comfortable with complex or ambiguous data and situations
- good project management and work priorisation skills

- excellent strategic and market analysis skills
- financial modelling skills, including DCF
- excellent Excel and PowerPoint skills
- good presentation, communication and influence skills
- prepared for frequent travel

Desirable experience:

The person appointed will be familiar with a multinational corporate environment and be comfortable working in different country contexts. Top-flight academic qualifications and relevant professional qualifications are also highly desirable.

Team:

The person appointed will join an existing team of four junior and senior Strategy Analysts based in the corporate head-office in central London. Previous post-holders have progressed to challenging roles elsewhere in the business within two to three years of appointment.

Questions

1 What would be the attractions of this job for you? What would be the disadvantages?

2 What relevant skills and experience do you already have, and what skills and experience would you still need to acquire before you were able to apply for this job?

helping business unit managers with their own plans. Thus the role is not just about analysis in the back office. Strategic planning also involves communications, teamwork and influencing skills.

Although the job in Illustration 15.1 is being advertised externally, strategic planners are often drawn from inside their own organisations. Internal strategic planners are likely to have an advantage in the important non-analytical parts of the job. As internal recruits, they bring to the planning role an understanding of the business, networks with key people in the organisation and credibility with internal audiences. Moreover, an internal appointment to a strategic planning role can serve as a developmental stage for managers on track for top management roles. Participating in strategy provides promising managers with exposure to senior management and gives them a view of the organisation as a whole.

Strategic planners do not take strategic decisions themselves. However, they typically have at least three important tasks:[8]

- *Information and analysis.* Strategic planners have the time, skills and resources to provide information and analysis for key decision-makers. This might be in response to some 'trigger' event – such as a possible merger – or as part of the regular planning cycle. A background of good information and analysis can leave an organisation much better prepared to respond quickly and confidently even to unexpected events. Strategic planners can also package this information and analysis in formats that ensure clear communication of strategic decisions.

- *Managers of the strategy process.* Strategic planners can assist and guide other managers through their strategic planning cycles (see Illustration 12.2 in Chapter 12). This can involve acting as a bridge between the corporate centre and the businesses by clarifying corporate expectations and guidelines. It could also involve helping business-level managers develop strategy by providing templates, analytical techniques and strategy training. This bridging role is important in achieving alignment of corporate-level and business-level strategies. Researchers[9] point out that this alignment is often lacking; many organisations do not link financial budgets to strategic priorities, or employee performance metrics to strategy implementation.

- *Special projects.* Strategic planners can be a useful resource to support top management on special projects, such as acquisitions or organisational change. Here strategy planners will typically work on project teams with middle managers from within the organisation and often with external consultants. Project management skills are likely to be important.

In addition to these tasks, strategic planners typically work closely with the CEO, discussing and helping refine his or her strategic thinking. Indeed, many strategic planners have their offices physically located close to the CEO. Although strategic planners may have relatively few resources – perhaps a small team of support staff – and little formal power, their closeness to the CEO typically makes them well-informed and influential. Managers throughout an organisation are likely to use them to sound out ideas.

15.2.3 Middle managers

As in section 15.2.1, a good deal of conventional management theory excludes middle managers from strategy making. Middle managers are seen as lacking an appropriately objective and long-term perspective, being too involved in operations. In this view, middle managers' role is limited to strategy implementation. This is, of course, a vital role.

However, there is a strong case for involving middle managers in strategy making itself. First, in fast-moving and competitive environments, organisations often need to decentralise strategic responsibilities to increase speed of response: it takes too long to refer everything to the top. Second, in knowledge-intensive sectors (such as design, consulting or finance, but many others too) the key source of competitive advantage is typically the knowledge of people actually involved in the operations of the business. Middle managers at operational level can understand and influence these knowledge-based sources of competitive advantage much more effectively than remote top managers. Many knowledge-intensive firms (e.g. lawyers or accountants) are organised as partnerships, where a significant proportion of staff have a right to consultation on strategic decisions in their formal role as partners, even if they are not themselves members of the top management group.

Against this background, there are at least four strategy roles middle managers can play:[10]

- *Information source.* Middle managers' knowledge and experience of the realities of the organisation and its market is likely to be greater than that of many top managers. So middle managers are a potential source of information about changes in the strategic position of the organisation.

- '*Sense making*' of strategy. Top management may set strategy, but it is often middle managers who have to explain it in the business units.[11] Middle managers are therefore a crucial *relevance bridge* between top management and members of the organisation at lower levels, in effect translating strategy into a message that is locally relevant. If misinterpretation of that intended strategy is to be avoided, it is therefore vital that middle managers understand and feel an ownership of it.

- *Reinterpretation and adjustment* of strategic responses as events unfold. A strategy may be set at a certain point of time, but circumstances may change or conditions in particular units may differ from assumptions held by top management. Middle managers are necessarily involved in strategy adaptation because of their day-to-day responsibilities in strategy implementation.

- *Champions of ideas.* Given their closeness to markets and operations, middle managers may not only provide information but champion new ideas that can be the foundation of new strategies.

Middle managers may increase their influence on strategy when they have:

- *Key organisational positions.*[12] Middle managers responsible for larger departments, business units or strategically important parts of the organisation have influence because they are likely to have critical knowledge. Also, managers with outward-facing roles (e.g. in marketing) tend to have greater strategic influence than managers with inward-facing roles (such as quality or operations).

- *Access to organisational networks.* Middle managers may not have hierarchical power, but can increase their influence by using their internal organisational networks. Drawing together information from network members can help provide an integrated perspective on what is happening in the organisation as a whole, something that otherwise can be difficult to get when occupying a specialised position in the middle of an organisation. Mobilising networks to raise issues and support proposals can also give more influence than any middle managers can achieve on their own. Strategically influential middle managers are therefore typically good networkers.

- *Access to the organisation's 'strategic conversation'.* Strategy making does not just happen in isolated, formal episodes, but is part of an ongoing strategic conversation among respected managers.[13] To participate in these strategic conversations middle managers should: maximise opportunities to mix formally and informally with top managers; become at ease with the particular language used to discuss strategy in their organisation; familiarise themselves carefully with the key strategic issues; and develop their own personal contribution to these strategic issues.

In the public sector elected politicians have traditionally been responsible for policy and public officials supposed to do the implementation. However, three trends are challenging this division of roles.[14] First, the rising importance of *specialised expertise* has shifted influence to public officials who may have made their careers in particular areas, while politicians are typically generalists. Second, public-sector reform in many countries has led to increased *externalisation of functions* to quasi-independent 'agencies' or 'QUANGOs' (quasi-autonomous non-governmental organisations) which, within certain constraints, can make decisions on their own. Third, the same reform processes have changed *internal structures* within public organisations, with decentralisation of units and more 'executive' responsibility granted to public officials. In short, strategy is increasingly part of the work of public officials too. The Wychavon case at the end of this chapter exemplifies some of these issues.

15.2.4 **Strategy consultants**

External consultants are often used in the development of strategy. Leading consultancy firms that focus on strategy include Bain, the Boston Consulting Group and McKinsey & Co. Most of the large general consultancy firms also have operations that provide services in strategy development and analysis. There are also smaller 'boutique' consultancy firms and individual consultants who specialise in strategy.

Consultants may play different roles in strategy development in organisations:[15]

- *Analysing, prioritising and generating options.* Strategic issues may have been identified by executives, but there may be so many of them, or disagreement about them, that the organisation faces a lack of clarity on how to go forward. Consultants may analyse such issues afresh and bring an external perspective to help prioritise them or generate options for executives to consider. This may, of course, involve challenging executives' preconceptions about their views of strategic issues.

- *Transferring knowledge.* Consultants are carriers of knowledge between their clients. Strategy ideas developed for one client can be offered to the next client.

- *Promoting strategic decisions.* Consultants do not take decisions themselves, but their analysis and ideas may substantially influence client decision-makers. A number of major consultancies have been criticised in the past for undue influence on the decisions made by their client organisation, leading to major problems. For example, General Electric blamed McKinsey & Co.'s advice that the economic crisis of 2008 onwards was only temporary for its decision to delay cost cutting and rationalisation until long after many of its competitors.

- *Implementing strategic change.* Consultants play a significant role in project planning, coaching and training often associated with strategic change. This is an area that has seen considerable growth, not least because consultants were criticised for leaving organisations with consultancy reports recommending strategies, but taking little responsibility for actually making these happen.

The value of strategy consultants is often controversial (see the Key Debate at the end of this chapter). But consultants are often blamed for failures when it is the client's poor management of the consulting process that is ultimately at fault. Many organisations select their consultants unsystematically, give poor initial project briefs and fail to learn from projects at the end. There are three key measures that client organisations can undertake to improve outcomes in strategy consulting:[16]

- *Professionalise purchasing of consulting services*. Instead of hiring consulting firms on the basis of personal relationships with key executives, as is often the case, professionalised purchasing can help ensure clear project briefs, a wide search for consulting suppliers, appropriate pricing, complementarity between different consulting projects and proper review at project-end. The German engineering company Siemens has professionalised its consultancy purchasing, for example establishing a shortlist of just 10 preferred management consulting suppliers.

- *Develop supervisory skills* in order to manage portfolios of consulting projects. The German railway company Deutsche Bahn and automobile giant Daimler both have central project offices that control and coordinate all consulting projects throughout their companies. As well as being involved in the initial purchasing decision, these offices can impose systematic governance structures on projects, with clear responsibilities and reporting processes, as well as review and formal assessment at project-end.

- *Partner effectively* with consultants to improve both effectiveness in carrying out the project and knowledge transfer at the end of it. Where possible, project teams should include a mix of consultants and managers from the client organisation, who can provide inside information, guide on internal politics and, sometimes, enhance credibility and receptiveness. As partners in the project, client managers retain knowledge and experience when the consultants have gone and can help in the implementation of recommendations.

15.2.5 Who to involve in strategy development?

This chapter has introduced a wide range of people who could potentially be involved in strategy: as well as the chief executive and the top management team, non-executive directors, strategic planners, strategic consultants and middle managers.

The general trend in recent years has been to include more people in the strategy process, moving towards more 'open strategy'.[17] Openness comes in two dimensions. First, there is openness in terms of including more participants from different constituencies inside and even outside the organisation (e.g. middle managers and other staff internally, and key suppliers or partners externally). Second, openness can come in the form of greater transparency about the strategy process itself, in other words what is revealed to both internal audiences such as staff and external audiences such as investors, partners and regulators. Openness is typically a matter of degree and rarely complete. There are pros and cons to greater openness. On the one hand, strategy can improve strategy formulation by accessing more ideas, and improve implementation by increasing key audiences' understanding and commitment. On the other hand, openness to too many participants can slow down the strategy process and risks the leaking of commercially sensitive information to competitors. The transparency of the process will be dealt with later in this chapter under the heading of Communicating (section 15.3.4). This section deals with who to actually include in making strategy.

There is no general rule about inclusion or exclusion in strategy making, but there are criteria that can guide managers. Research by McKinsey & Co. indicates that the people

ILLUSTRATION 15.2

The Barclays Jam

Barclays Bank used workgroups and 'jamming' to involve all its employees in its new strategy.

In October 2011, Ashok Vaswani became CEO of Barclays' UK Retail and Business Bank. With 35,000 employees and 1,600 branches, Barclays is one of the leading retail banks in the country. Like other UK banks, it had been hit both by recession and by accusations of mis-selling of financial products to consumers. However, the global head of retail banking had declared an ambition to make Barclays the 'Go To' bank for consumers, and Ashok set out at once to make this happen.

Ashok launched two initiatives to involve employees in the strategy. He immediately convened six workgroups of graduate trainees and young managers from around the country to address key issues for the implementation of the strategy. With about eight to ten members each, these workgroups were tasked to work on strategic issues such as customers, communications, colleagues and community. Working in their spare time, and mostly communicating virtually, these workgroups produced a flood of ideas, some of them taken up even before the final report-out. The formal reporting took place at a senior management retreat in December, from which a new strategic concept emerged: STAIRS, in other words Speed, Transparency, Access, Information and Results.

Ashok's second initiative was the 'Great Barclays Jam', launched in March 2012 in order to involve all employees in the new STAIRS concept. Barclays called on IBM's jamming technology, an online collaboration platform designed to facilitate communications and debate among large groups of people. The launch of the Jam was preceded by an intensive communications campaign. Ashok first ran a series of leadership days for 400 of the company's senior managers. A 'teaser film', voiced by a well-known British TV personality, was produced, promising employees the chance to discuss the company's future. Over 8,000 employees were invited to more than 70 information events held at 16 cinemas across the country, where they saw another specially produced film.

Further presentations were held in branches and call centres to reach remaining employees.

With this build-up, the Great Barclays Jam finally took place in March over three days. The Jam gave every employee the chance to debate the practical meaning of the STAIRS strategic concept and to contribute ideas on how to deliver it. During the Jam, there were live Question and Answer sessions with key executives, including Ashok Vaswani and Bob Diamond, the Barclays Group CEO at the time. Volunteers from across all areas of the business facilitated the discussion, based on the 30th floor of the Barclays head office, easily accessible by the Group's top managers one floor above. The volunteers signposted the most popular threads, highlighted top jammers and alerted participants to senior manager contributions.

The Great Barclays Jam attracted 19,000 registered participants, producing 20,000 comments over the three days. Participants were equally divided between managerial and non-managerial employees and reflected the bank's age distribution. Participation remained high throughout all three days. In all, the Jam produced 650 distinct ideas for business improvement. Ashok Vaswani instituted six new 'Business Councils' focused on various parts of the business with the specific task to implement STAIRS and take forward the most promising ideas from the Jam.

Sources: Interviews with Ashok Vaswani, Julian Davis and Tim Kiy at Barclays, and Richard Mound at IBM.

Questions

1 What do you think were the direct and indirect benefits of Ashok Vaswani's initiatives to involve Barclays' employees in the strategy?

2 If you were a smaller company, without the information technology resources of Barclays and IBM, how might you be able to get employee input into strategy development?

Figure 15.2 Who to include in strategy making?

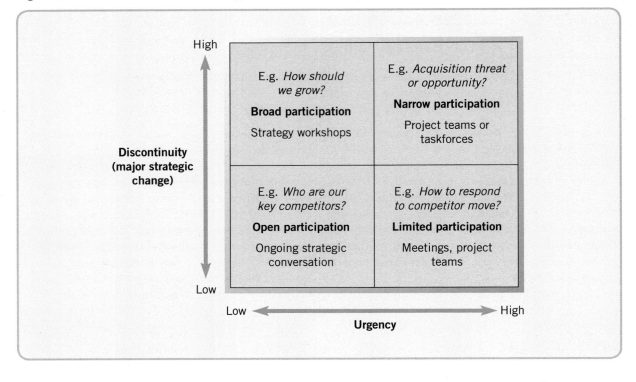

involved should vary according to the nature of the issue (see Figure 15.2).[18] For example, issues that are urgent and could involve major changes to strategy (such as an acquisition opportunity) are best approached by small special project teams, consisting of senior managers and perhaps planners and consultants. Issues which may be important but are not urgent (such as deciding on key competitors) can benefit from more prolonged and open strategic conversations, both formal and informal. Urgent issues that do not involve major change (such as responding to competitor threats) require only limited participation. Issues that may involve major changes but require idea generation over time (such as the search for global opportunities) might benefit from more open participation, though this might be organised more formally through a series of planned events, such as conferences bringing together large groups of managers in particular geographical regions.

Illustration 15.2 shows one approach to achieving inclusion at Barclay's Bank. The Wychavon end of chapter case provides a public-sector example.

15.3 STRATEGISING

Whereas the previous section introduced the key strategists, this section concentrates on what these people do – in other words, the activities of *strategising*. The section starts with strategy analysis, then issue-selling, decision making and communications about the chosen strategy. In practice, of course, these activities rarely follow this logical sequence, or they may not happen at all. As Chapter 12 made clear, strategies do not always come about in such ways and strategic decisions are often made without formal analysis and evaluation. So the section ends with a reminder about the often 'messy' nature of strategy development.

15.3.1 **Strategy analysis**

A good deal of this text is concerned with strategy analysis, and indeed analysis can be an important input into strategy making. However, managers often use a limited set of analytical tools and do not always follow textbook procedures. SWOT (strengths, weaknesses, opportunities and threats) analysis is by far the most widely used tool, but in practice managers often deviate from the technical ideal even with this simple tool.[19] For example, SWOT analyses tend to produce unmanageably long lists of factors (strengths, weaknesses, opportunities and threats), often well over 50 or so. These factors are rarely probed or refined, little substantive analysis is done to investigate them and they are often not followed up systematically in subsequent strategic discussions. (See the discussion on SWOT in section 3.4.4.)

However, criticism of managers for their analytical limitations may sometimes be misplaced. There are both *cost* and *purpose* issues to consider. First of all, analysis is costly in terms of both resources and time. There are of course the costs of gathering information, particularly if using consultants. But with regard to time there is also the risk of '*paralysis by analysis*', where managers spend too long perfecting their analyses and not enough time taking decisions and acting upon them.[20] Managers have to judge how much analysis they really need. Second, with regard to purpose, analysis is not always simply about providing the necessary information for good strategic decisions anyway. Ann Langley has shown that the purposes of analysis can be quite different.[21] Setting up a project to analyse an issue thoroughly may even be a deliberate form of *procrastination*, aimed at putting off a decision. Analysis can also be *symbolic*, for example to rationalise a decision after it has already effectively been made. Managers may be asked to analyse an issue in order to get their *buy-in* to decisions that they might otherwise resist. Analyses can also be *political*, to forward the agenda of a particular manager or part of the organisation.

The different purposes of strategy analysis have two key implications for managers:

- *Design the analysis according to the real purpose*. The range and quality of people involved, the time and budget allowed, and the subsequent communication of analysis results should all depend on underlying purpose, whether informational, political or symbolic. For example, prestigious strategy consulting firms are often useful for political and symbolic analyses. Involving a wide group of middle managers in the analysis may help with subsequent buy-in.

- *Invest appropriately in technical quality*. For many projects, improving the quality of the technical analysis will make a valuable addition to subsequent strategic decisions. On other occasions, insisting on technical perfection can be counter-productive. For example, a SWOT analysis that raises lots of issues may be a useful means of allowing managers to vent their own personal frustrations, before getting on with the real strategy work. It may sometimes be better to leave these issues on the table, rather than probing, challenging or even deleting them in a way that could unnecessarily alienate these managers for the following stages.

15.3.2 **Strategic issue-selling**

Organisations typically face many strategic issues at any point in time. But in complex organisations these issues may not be appreciated by those involved in developing strategy. Some issues will be filtered out by the organisational hierarchy; others will be sidelined by more urgent pressures. Moreover, senior managers will rarely have sufficient time and resources to deal with all the issues that do actually reach them, so strategic issues compete for attention. What gets top management attention are not necessarily the most important issues.[22] Issues need to be 'sold'.

Strategic issue-selling is the process of gaining the attention and support of top management and other important stakeholders for strategic issues. Managers need to consider at least four aspects in seeking attention and support for their issues:

● *Issue packaging*. Care should be taken with how issues are packaged or framed. Clearly the strategic importance of the issue needs to be underlined, particularly by linking it to *critical strategic goals* or *performance metrics* for the organisation. Generally clarity and succinctness win over complexity and length. It also usually helps if the issue is packaged with *potential solutions*. An issue can easily be put aside as too difficult to address if no ways forward are offered at the same time.

● *Formal and informal channels*. Managers need to balance formal and informal channels of influence. Figure 15.3 indicates some *formal channels* for selling issues in a multidivisional organisation (based on the American conglomerate General Electric). Here formal channels are split between corporate, line and staff. On the corporate side, they include the annual business reviews that the CEO carries out with each divisional head, plus the annual

Figure 15.3 Formal channels for issue-selling

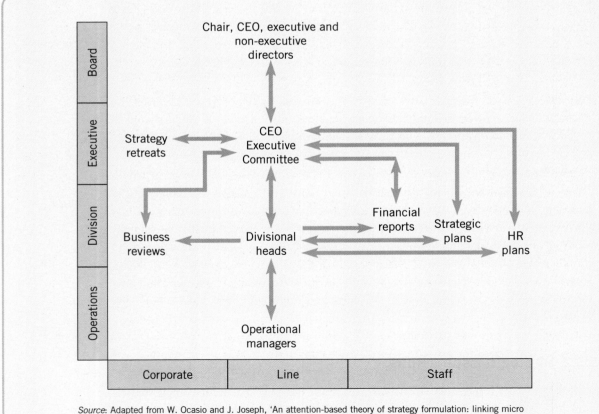

Source: Adapted from W. Ocasio and J. Joseph, 'An attention-based theory of strategy formulation: linking micro and macro perspectives in strategy processes', *Advances in Strategic Management*, vol. 22 (2005), pp. 39–62.

strategy retreats (or workshops) of the top executive team. The line channel involves the regular line interaction of operational managers, divisional heads and the CEO and other executive directors. Finally, there are the various reporting systems to staff functions, including finance, human resources and strategic planning. However, formal channels are rarely enough to sell strategic issues. *Informal channels* can be very important and often decisive in some organisations. Informal channels might include ad hoc conversations with influential managers in corridors, on journeys or over meals or drinks. Illustration 15.3 shows how informal channels can be important for consultants.

- *Sell alone or in coalitions.* Managers should consider whether to press their issue on their own or to assemble a *coalition of supporters*, preferably influential ones. A coalition adds credibility and weight to the issue. The ability to gather a coalition of supporters can be a good test of the issue's validity: if other managers are not persuaded, then the CEO is unlikely to be persuaded either. But notice that enlisting supporters may involve compromises or reciprocal support of other issues, so blurring the clarity of the case being put forward.

- *Timing.* Managers should also time their issue-selling carefully. For example, a short-term performance crisis, or the period before the handover to a new top management team, is not a good time to press long-term strategic issues.

15.3.3 Strategic decision making

Strategic decision making is not always rational. Nobel prize-winner Daniel Kahneman and colleagues have developed an approach called 'behavioural economics', which seeks to improve decision making by taking into account real-life human behaviour.[23] Kahneman points out that even senior managers bring 'cognitive biases' to their decisions: their mental processes are liable to neglect, distort or exaggerate certain issues. The trouble with cognitive biases is that, by definition, it is very hard for people to recognise what they are suffering from. However, Kahneman suggests that designing good decision-making processes can help remedy the ill-effects of these biases. He highlights five common decision-making biases, along with ways to reduce them:

- *Confirmation bias* is the tendency to seek out data that confirm a favoured course of action, and to neglect information that might disconfirm it. One way to counter this confirmation bias is to insist that alternative options are always considered in decision processes. Then the discussion shifts from whether or not to take a favoured action, to how much better it really is compared to the alternatives.

- *Anchoring bias* is the common error of being tied ('anchored') to one piece of information in making a decision. Anchors are often things that might have been valid in the past, but may not hold true in the future. For example, managers may rely on past sales trends, and neglect the possibility that these trends might change. Sometimes managers will make an initial estimate of a cost or revenue, and allow that value to become entrenched in their decision making, forgetting that it was only an estimate in the first place. One way of countering anchoring biases is to introduce different analytical methods into the process (for instance, a discounted cash flow as well as a pay back period analysis). A different analysis may surface unacknowledged assumptions or force out new data or insights.

- *Saliency bias* refers to when a particular analogy becomes unduly influential ('salient'). For example, managers may say a particular project is just like a successful project in the past,

ILLUSTRATION 15.3

Dinner with the consultants

Consultants operate through both formal and informal channels to influence strategic thinking.

Locco* was a major European automotive component manufacturer. In the mid-1990s, it began to experience declining profits. The CEO therefore invited consultants to undertake a strategic review of the firm. This consultancy team included a partner, a senior consultant and a junior consultant. Their recommendations led to changes in Locco's product and market strategy.

Like all other consultancy assignments the consultants undertook extensive analysis of industry data and company data. However, in addition to this more formal work, there was more informal engagement between the consultants and the management, including three dinners held during the period of the project.

At home with the CEO

At the beginning of the assignment the CEO invited the partner and senior consultant to meet senior managers at his home for dinner 'to get together in a more informal way . . . to get to know each other better . . . and . . . learn more about the history of our company', but also to establish trust between the managers and the consultants.

Others saw it differently. For example, the marketing and sales manager viewed it as an attempt by the CEO to influence the outcome of the project: '(he) likes to do this. While dining in his home you can hardly oppose his views.' The consulting partner was somewhat wary, fearing a hidden agenda but none the less seeing it as an opportunity to 'break the ice' as well as gaining political insight and understanding of the management dynamics.

Over dinner discussion was largely between the CEO and the consultants with the CEO setting out some concerns about the project, not least the danger of cost cutting leading to a loss of jobs. As they mingled over after-dinner drinks other sensitive issues were raised by other managers.

At the castle

In the third week of the project the consultant invited the CEO to a restaurant in a converted castle. He saw this as an opportunity to get to know the CEO better, to gain his agreement to the consultants' approach to the project, but also to gain a clearer understanding of the politics among the senior management and establish more insight into the CEO's perceived problems of Locco.

Over the meal the consultant established that there were two management 'camps' with different views of strategy. The consultant also took the opportunity to influence and gain the CEO's approval for the agenda for the next management meeting.

At the pizzeria

Some weeks later the senior consultant invited middle managers whom he saw as 'good implementers' for pizza and beer at an Italian restaurant to 'exchange information and get opinions on some of our analyses, see how some of the middle managers react . . .'. Some of those who attended were sceptical about the meeting but went along. Senior managers were not invited.

At the dinner the consultant discussed his initial analysis, particularly on strategic competences. He also raised some issues to do with the political dynamics within the senior management team. The consultant regarded the dinner as a success both in terms of establishing a rapport but also in establishing that 'some (of the managers) know exactly why the company has a problem . . . they already have some ideas for solutions . . . but their voices are not heard'. The managers who attended were, on the whole, also positive about the dinner, many regarding it as 'good fun' though others who were not there felt threatened by their absence.

* A pseudonym used by the researchers.

Adapted from A. Sturdy, M. Schwarz and A. Spicer, 'Guess who's coming to dinner? Structures and uses of liminality in strategic management consultancy', *Human Relations*, vol. 59, no. 7 (2006), pp. 929–60.

Questions

1 Why are informal settings such as dinners useful?

2 Could the consultants have influenced the agenda in more formal ways? How?

3 If you had been one of the managers at the Italian restaurant, what would your views of the meeting been?

minimising differences: on the analogy with past experience, they simply expect success to be repeated. It is important here to ask for other analogies, or to seek out possible differences between the successful case and the one being considered. A form of this saliency bias is the so-called 'halo effect', where a manager or organisation that has been successful in one domain is simply assumed to be successful in another: the manager or organisation is treated like a saint (with a 'halo') and assumed to do no wrong. Again, it is important here to check for differences. Just because a manager has been successful in managing a series of acquisitions does not mean he or she will be equally so in managing a joint venture.

- *Affect bias* occurs when managers become too emotionally attached to a particular option (too 'affectionate'). In cases of issue-selling, this is often called *champion's bias*: the likelihood that people will exaggerate their case in favour of their particular proposal. If the proposal comes from a team, it might be worth checking with members individually for signs of discomfort: it may be possible to obtain a more balanced view from the less enthusiastic team members. Having just the lead 'champion' present the proposal on his or her own maximises the danger of hearing the most positive side of the argument.

- *Risk bias* is where managers hold distorted views of risk. Managers are often over-optimistic in assessing their ability to deliver on projects. Here Kahneman recommends that instead of relying on the organisation's own assessment of its capabilities (an 'inside view'), decision-makers also look at the record of *other* organisations undertaking similar projects (an 'outside view'). It is easier to acknowledge the failures of other organisations than to undertake a sceptical review of one's own internal capabilities. On the other hand, managers can sometimes be biased towards pessimism, so-called 'risk aversion'. Their fear of failure may be greater than their appetite for success. Risk aversion can be reduced by reviewing incentives: the rewards of success can be either clarified or increased.

Thus Kahneman's behavioural view leads to concrete methodologies to reduce biases in strategic decision making. Overall, he encourages hurried managers to 'think slow' – to take the time to ask for additional views, analysis and data. Of course, managers should recognise the danger of paralysis by analysis (section 15.3.1): in fast-moving environments, the informed intuition of experienced managers may be more effective than thorough but time-consuming analyses.[24] However, Kahneman believes that the costs of error generally outweigh the costs of missed opportunities. It is important too not to exaggerate the importance of decision making in strategy. As explained in Chapter 12, many strategies are emergent rather than consciously decided anyway.

These insights from behavioural economics underline the potential benefits of constructive *conflict* in decision making.[25] Conflict can expose champion's biases. It can challenge optimistic self-assessments of managerial competence. Conflict is fostered by having diverse managerial teams, with members prepared to be devil's advocates, challenging assumptions or easy consensus. But productive conflict needs careful management. Table 15.1 uses the idea of 'games with rules' to summarise ways in which this might be done (see also the discussion on 'organisational ambidexterity' in section 14.3).

15.3.4 Communicating the strategy

Deciding strategy is only one step: strategic decisions need to be communicated. The rise of more open approaches to strategy has put a greater premium on transparency (section 15.2.5). Managers have to consider which stakeholders to inform (see Chapter 4) and how they should

Table 15.1 **Managing conflict**

Rulebook	• Establish clear behavioural boundaries. • Encourage dissenting voices. • Keep debate professional, not emotional.
Referees	• Ensure the leader is (a) open to differing views, (b) enforces the rules.
Playing field	• Ensure each side of the debate has a chance to win. • Be clear on the basis of resolution (e.g. decision from the top or consensus).
Gaps to exploit	• Does each group have a specific objective to champion?
Relationships	• Ensure individuals (a) deliver on their commitments, (b) behave with integrity. • Ensure leaders throughout the organisation further test perspectives up and down the hierarchy.
Energy levels	• Ensure sufficient tension to promote useful debate, but monitor this. • Do leaders understand what people really care about?
Outcomes	• Ensure leader gives bad news without damaging relationships. • Ensure dignity in losing and risk-taking rewarded.

Source: Reprinted by permission of *Harvard Business Review*. Exhibit from 'How to pick a good fight' by S.A. Joni and D. Beyer, December 2009, pp. 48–57. Copyright © 2009 by the Harvard Business School Publishing Corporation. All rights reserved.

tailor their messages to each. Shareholders, key customers and employees are likely to be particularly central, all with different needs. For every new strategy, there should be a communications strategy to match. It is also important to remember that communication is a two-way process. Harvard's Michael Beer and Russell A. Eisenstat[26] argue that effective communication needs to involve *both* advocacy of a strategy by senior management *and* inquiry about the concerns of influential internal and external stakeholders. In the absence of the former, there is lack of clarity, confusion and frustration. In the absence of the latter, concerns will surface in any case, but in ways that actively or passively undermine the new strategy.

As a minimum, effective employee communications are needed to ensure that the strategy is understood. In the absence of this there are two likely consequences:

● *Strategic intent will be reinterpreted.* As the Key Debate in Chapter 12 shows, it is inevitable that people in the organisation will interpret intended strategy in terms of their local context and operational responsibilities.[27] The more such reinterpretation occurs, the more unlikely it is the intended strategy will be implemented.

● *Established routines will continue.* Old habits die hard, so top management may underestimate the need to make very clear what behaviours are expected to deliver a strategy. Of course, effective communication is only one way in which change can be managed; the wider lessons of managing strategic change in this regard need to be taken into account (see Chapter 14).

In shaping a communications strategy for employees, four elements need to be considered in particular:[28]

● *Focus.* Communications should be focused on the key issues that the strategy addresses and the key components of the strategy. If top management cannot show they are clear on these, then it cannot be expected that others will be. If possible it also helps to avoid unnecessary detail or complex language. CEO Jack Welch's famous statement that General Electric should be 'either Number One or Number Two' in all its markets is remembered because of this clear focus on the importance of being a dominant player wherever the company competed.

- *Media.* Choosing appropriate media to convey the new strategy is important. Mass media such as emails, voicemails, company newsletters, videos, intranets and senior manager blogs can ensure that all staff receive the same message promptly, helping to avoid damaging uncertainty and rumour-mongering. However, face-to-face communications are important too in order to demonstrate the personal commitment of managers and allow for interaction with concerned staff. So, for example, senior managers may undertake *roadshows*, carrying their message directly to various groups of employees with conferences or workshops at different sites. They may also institute *cascades*, whereby each level of managers is tasked to convey the strategy message directly to the staff reporting to them, who in turn are required to convey the message to their staff, and so on through the organisation. Of course, if this is to be effective, it is essential that the key issues and components of the strategy are clear. Such roadshows and cascades may, of course, also raise new issues and should therefore be part of a two-way communication process.

- *Employee engagement.* If a two-way process of communication is to be achieved, it needs to involve multiple levels of management. Indeed, it is often helpful to engage employees more widely in the communication strategy, so that they can see what it means for them personally and how their role will change. Interchanges through roadshows and cascades can help, but some organisations use imaginative means to create more active engagement. For example, one British public-sector organisation invited all its staff to a day's conference introducing its new strategy, at which employees were invited to pin a photograph of themselves on a 'pledge wall', together with a hand-written promise to change at least one aspect of their work to fit the new strategy.[29]

- *Impact.* Communications should be impactful, with powerful and memorable words and visuals. A strong 'story-line' can help by encapsulating the journey ahead and imagined new futures for the organisation and its customers. One struggling medical centre in New Mexico communicated its new strategy, and inspired its staff, with a story-line representing the organisation as 'The Raiders of the Lost Art', adapting the film title to convey a simultaneous sense of courage in adversity and recovery of old values.[30]

15.3.5 The messiness of everyday strategising

There is a danger of seeing strategising as part of a neat, linear process driven by management rationality. Chapter 12 made it clear that this is not always so; there are multiple processes at work that contribute to the development of strategy. Formal analysis and meetings may take place, but these go hand-in-hand with more everyday practices. Senior executives do meet over lunch or coffee and discuss strategic issues. Managers spend most of their time in face-to-face meetings or telephone and email discussions with other managers. As sections 12.3.2 and 12.3.4 explained, in such settings, strategic issues and solutions may arise on the basis of organisational politics or simple chance. In such circumstances, managers need political acumen and the ability to build coherent strategic narratives from the often fragmented discussions that take place.[31]

(15.4) STRATEGY METHODOLOGIES

Strategists have a range of standard methodologies to organise and guide their strategising activity. The methodologies introduced here are not analytical concepts or techniques such as in most of the rest of the text, but widely used approaches to managing aspects of strategy work such as issue-selling or decision making. These could include strategy workshops (or 'away-days') and strategy projects. Projects may be driven by hypothesis-testing techniques. Finally, strategising output typically has to fit the format of a business case or strategic plan. This section introduces key issues in each of these methodologies.

15.4.1 Strategy workshops

Strategies are often made through series of managerial meetings. These meetings frequently take the specific form of **strategy workshops** (sometimes called strategy away-days or retreats).[32] Such workshops usually **involve groups of executives working intensively for one or two days, often away from the office, on organisational strategy.** Such executives are typically senior managers in the organisation, although workshops can also be a valuable mechanism for involving a wider group of managers. Workshops are used typically to formulate or reconsider strategy, but also to review the progress of current strategy, address strategy implementation issues and to communicate strategic decisions to a larger audience. Workshops can be either ad hoc or part of the regular strategic planning process, and they may be standalone or designed as a series of events. As well as facilitating strategy making, workshops can have additional roles in team-building and the personal development of individual participant. Illustration 15.4 shows how they can contribute to strategy development as well as how they can go wrong.

Strategy workshops can be a valuable part of an organisation's strategy-making activity. Research suggests, however, that their form can influence the nature of participants' debate of strategy and its likely success. Workshop design matters. Above all, whatever the purpose of the workshop is, clarity of that purpose is strongly correlated with perceived success. Given this, if the purpose is to *question existing strategy or develop new strategy* successful workshops are likely to involve:

- *Strategy concepts and tools* capable of promoting the questioning of the current strategy.
- *A specialist facilitator to* guide participants in the use of such tools and concepts, free managers to concentrate on the discussion, help keep the discussion focused on the strategic issues and ensure participants contribute equally to discussion.
- *The visible support of the workshop sponsor* (perhaps the CEO) for the questioning and the facilitator. In the absence of this the workshop is unlikely to succeed.
- *The diminishing of everyday functional and hierarchical roles.* This may be aided by a distinctive off-site location to signal how different from everyday routine the workshop is, help detach participants from day-to-day operational issues and symbolically affirm the occasion is not subject to the usual norms of executive team discussion. Ice-breaking and other apparently playful exercises – sometimes called 'serious play' – at the beginning of a workshop can help generate creativity and a willingness to challenge orthodoxies.[33]

On the other hand, workshops with the purpose of *reviewing the progress of current strategy* are likely to be successful if they have a more operational agenda and if participants maintain functional and hierarchical roles.

ILLUSTRATION 15.4

A tale of two workshops

How strategy workshops are designed is a significant influence on their success.

Given the growth of the business the directors of Hotelco* decided to hold two two-day workshops to rethink the organisational structure needed for the company's future strategic direction. Both workshops were facilitated by an external consultant.

Workshop 1

The first workshop was held in a luxury rural hotel in the south of England far away from Hotelco's modest offices. This was not just to 'get away from the office', but also because: 'It freed up the mind . . . It was a great experience.'

Together with one of the directors, the facilitator had organised the agenda. The 'command style' of the CEO was replaced by a participative approach orchestrated by the facilitator: 'He made it a more level playing field.' He had interviewed staff about the core values of the business and provided a report to the directors as a basis for the discussion: 'Does everyone know what Hotelco stands for?'

The directors became genuinely engaged with the discussion: 'It focused our minds. It made us all understand the things we were good at and . . . the things we were weak at and what we needed to do.' They regarded the workshop as a success, concluding that a change was needed from an authoritarian, command management style to a more structured and devolved approach to management, with responsibility being passed to middle levels, so freeing up the top team to focus more on strategy.

This outcome was not, however, carried forward. On their return to the office, the directors came to the conclusion that what was agreed during the workshop was unrealistic, that they were 'carried away with the process'. The result was significant back-tracking but without a clear consensus on a revised structure for the business.

Workshop 2

The second two-day workshop, two months later, was for the top team and their seven direct reports and used the same facilitator. It took place in one of the group's own hotels. Again the workshop began with a discussion of the interviews on Hotelco's values. One of the directors then made a presentation raising the idea of an operational board. However, in discussion it emerged that the directors were not uniformly committed to this – especially the CEO. Eventually, as the facilitator explained: 'I had to sit the four directors in another room and say: look, until you sort this out, you're just going to create problems . . . The four directors got into a heated argument and forgot about the other seven.'

This was not, however, how the directors saw it. Their view was that the facilitator was seeking to impose a solution rather than facilitate discussion.

With the directors in one room and the direct reports in another, the comments of each group were transmitted between rooms by the facilitator. It was a situation that satisfied no one. In the afternoon the CEO intervened, replacing the idea of a seven-person 'operational board' with an intermediary level of three 'divisional directors'.

No one was content with the workshop. One of the seven who was not to be a divisional director commented: 'I didn't know where I sat any more. I felt my job had been devalued.' A director also recognised: 'We left these people feeling really deflated.'

* Hotelco is a pseudonym for a small UK hotel group.

Questions

1 Evaluate the design of the two workshops in terms of the guidelines in section 15.4.1.

2 If you were a facilitator, how would you have organised the workshops differently?

3 What benefits (or disadvantages) might such workshops have in comparison with other approaches to strategy development for such an organisation?

Workshops are, however, prone to at least two problems. First, when reduced to a routine part of the strategic planning cycle, and involving the usual group of senior managers every year, workshops may not be able to produce new ideas that significantly challenge the status quo. On the other hand, workshops that are too radically separated from the ordinary routines of the organisation can become detached from subsequent action: it can be difficult to translate radical ideas and group enthusiasm back into the workplace.

In designing workshops that will be closely connected to subsequent action, managers should consider:

- *Identifying agreed actions* to be taken. Time should be set aside at the end of the workshop for a review of workshop outputs and agreement on necessary actions to follow up. However, this, of itself, may well not make a sufficiently powerful bridge to operational realities.

- *Establishing project groups.* Workshops can build on the cohesion built around particular issues by commissioning groups of managers to work together on specific tasks arising from the workshop and report on progress to senior management.

- *Nesting of workshops.* Especially if a workshop has expected participants to question current strategy and develop radical new ideas, it may be useful to have a series of workshops, each of which gradually becomes more and more grounded in operational realities.

- *Making visible commitment by the top management.* The chief executive or other senior manager needs to signal commitment to the outcomes of the workshop not only by their statements but by their actual behaviours.

15.4.2 **Strategy projects**

Both strategy making and strategy implementation are often organised in the form of projects or task forces.[34] **Strategy projects involve teams of people assigned to work on particular strategic issues over a defined period of time.** Projects can be instituted in order to explore problems or opportunities as part of the strategy development process. Or they might be instituted to implement agreed elements of a strategy, for example an organisational restructuring or the negotiation of a joint venture. Translating a strategic plan or workshop outcomes into a set of projects is a good means of ensuring that intentions are translated into action. They can also include a wider group of managers in strategy activity.

Strategy projects should be managed like any other project. In particular they need:

- *A clear brief or mandate.* The project's objectives should be agreed and carefully managed. These objectives are the measure of the project's success. 'Scope creep', by which additional objectives are added as the project goes on, is a common danger.

- *Top management commitment.* The continuing commitment of top management, especially the top management 'client' or 'sponsor', needs to be maintained. Top management agendas are frequently shifting, so communications should be regular.

- *Milestones and reviews.* The project should have from the outset clear milestones with an agreed schedule of intermediate achievements. These allow project review and adjustment where necessary, as well as a measure of ongoing success.

- *Appropriate resources.* The key resource is usually people. The right mix of skills needs to be in place, including project management skills, and effort should be invested in 'team-building' at the outset. Strategy projects are often part-time commitments for managers, who have to continue with their 'day jobs'. Attention needs to be paid to managing the balance between managers' ordinary responsibilities and project duties: the first can easily derail the second.

Projects can easily proliferate and compete. Senior management should have careful oversight of the whole portfolio of projects in an organisation, and be ready to merge and end projects according to changing circumstances. Otherwise a proliferation of projects can easily end up with so-called 'initiative fatigue'.

15.4.3 **Hypothesis testing**

Strategy project teams are typically under pressure to deliver solutions to complex problems under tight time constraints. **Hypothesis testing is a methodology used particularly in strategy projects for setting priorities in investigating issues and options** and is widely used by strategy consulting firms and members of strategy project teams.

Hypothesis testing in strategy is adapted from the hypothesis-testing procedures of science.[35] It starts with a proposition about how things are (*the descriptive hypothesis*), and then seeks to test it with real-world data. For example, a descriptive hypothesis in strategy could be that being large-scale in a particular industry is essential to profitability. To test it, a strategy project team would begin by gathering data on the size of organisations in the industry and correlate these with the organisations' profitabilities. Confirmation of this initial descriptive hypothesis (i.e. small organisations are relatively unprofitable) would then lead to several *prescriptive hypotheses* about what a particular organisation should do. For a small-scale organisation in the industry, prescriptive hypotheses would centre on how to increase scale: one prescriptive hypothesis in this case would be that acquisitions were a good means to achieve the necessary scale; another would be that alliances were the right way. These prescriptive hypotheses might then become the subjects of further data testing.

This kind of hypothesis testing is ultimately about setting practical priorities in strategy work. Hypothesis testing in business therefore differs from strict scientific procedure (see Illustration 15.5). The aim finally is to concentrate attention on a very limited set of promising hypotheses, not on the full set of all possibilities. Data are gathered in order to support favoured hypotheses, whereas in science the objective is formally to try to refute hypotheses. Business hypothesis testing aims to find a robust and satisfactory solution within time and resource constraints, not to find some ultimate scientific truth. Selecting the right hypotheses can be helped by applying quick and dirty testing (QDT). Quick and dirty testing relies on the project team's existing experience and easily accessed data in order to speedily reject unpromising hypotheses, before too much time is wasted on them.

15.4.4 **Business cases and strategic plans**

Strategising activities, such as workshops or projects, are typically orientated towards creating an output in the form of a *business case* or *strategic plan*. Keeping this end goal in mind provides a structure for the strategising work: what needs to be produced shapes the strategising activities. A business case usually **provides the data and argument in support of a particular strategy proposal, for example investment in new equipment. A strategic plan provides the data and argument in support of a strategy for the whole organisation.** It is therefore likely to be more comprehensive, taking an overall view of the organisation's direction over a substantial period

ILLUSTRATION 15.5

Hypothesis testing at a bank

This outline of a consulting engagement for a large, diversified bank shows how the hypothesis-testing process can shape a strategy project.

1 Defining the problem/question

The consultants' first step is to define the problem. As usual, the strategic problem has to do with the existence of a gap between what the client wants (here a certain level of profitability for a particular product) and what it has (declining profitability). In short, the consultants' problem is that the bank's profitability for this product is below target levels.

2 Develop a set of competing descriptive hypotheses about problem causes

The consultants gather some preliminary data and draw on their own experience to generate some possible descriptive hypotheses about the causes of the problem. Thus they know that some large national competitors are already exiting from this type of product; that profitability varies dramatically across competitors involved in this product; and that some specialised new entrants have taken significant market share. Three possible hypotheses emerge: that the industry structure is basically unattractive; that the bank lacks the right strategic capabilities; that the bank is targeting the wrong customer segments. The consultants use quick and dirty testing to reject the first two hypotheses: after all, some competitors are making profits and the bank has strong capabilities from long presence in this product area. Accordingly, the starting descriptive hypothesis is that the bank is targeting unprofitable customer segments.

3 Testing the starting descriptive hypothesis

The consultants next design a study to collect the data needed to support the descriptive hypothesis. They carry out a market segmentation analysis by customer group by doing interviews with customers across different geographies and income levels. They analyse the kinds of service different segments require and the fees they might pay. The consultants find that their data support their starting hypothesis: the bank's branches are concentrated in locations which prosperous customers willing to pay higher fees for this product do not use. (Had they not been able to confirm their hypothesis, the consultants would have returned to the other two competing hypotheses, step 2.)

4 Develop prescriptive hypotheses

The consultants then develop prescriptive hypotheses about actions necessary to attract more profitable customer segments. One prescriptive hypothesis is that a better portfolio of branch locations will enhance profitability. The consultants carry out data gathering and analysis to support this hypothesis, for example comparing the profitability of branches in different kinds of locations. They find that the few branches that happen to be in the right locations do have higher profitability with this product.

5 Make recommendations to the client

The consultants prepare a set of preliminary recommendations based on the descriptive hypothesis and validated prescriptive hypotheses: one of these is that the branch locations need changing. These recommendations are checked for acceptability and feasibility with key managers within the bank and adjusted according to feedback. Then the consultants make their formal presentation of final recommendations.

Source: Jeanne Liedtka, Darden School of Management, University of Virginia.

Questions

1 Select an important strategic issue facing an organisation that you are familiar with (or an organisation that is publicly in trouble or a case study organisation). Try generating a few descriptive hypotheses that address this issue. Use quick and dirty testing to select an initial descriptive hypothesis.

2 What data should you gather to confirm this descriptive hypothesis and how would you collect them? Should the descriptive hypothesis be confirmed, what possible prescriptive hypotheses follow?

of time. Many organisations have a standard template for making business cases or proposing a strategic plan, and where these exist, it is wise to work with that format. Where there is no standard template, it is worth investigating recent successful business cases or plans within the organisation, and borrowing features from them.

A project team intending to make a business case should aim to meet the following criteria:[36]

- *Focus on strategic needs.* The team should identify the organisation's overall strategy and relate its case closely to that, not just to any particular departmental needs. A business case should not look as if it is just an HR department or IT department project, for example. The focus should be on a few key issues, with clear priority normally given to those that are both strategically important and relatively easy to address.

- *Supported by key data.* The team will need to assemble appropriate data, with financial data demonstrating appropriate returns on any investment typically essential. However, qualitative data should not be neglected – for example, striking quotations from interviews with employees or key customers, or recent mini-cases of successes or failures in the organisation or at competitors. Some strategic benefits simply cannot be quantified, but are not the less important for that: information on competitor moves can be persuasive here. The team should provide background information on the rigour and extent of the research behind the data.

- *Provide a clear rationale.* Analysis and data are not enough; make it clear *why* the proposals are being made. The reasons for the choice of recommendations therefore need to be explicit. Many specific evaluation techniques that can be useful in a business case are explained in Chapter 11.

- *Demonstrate solutions and actions.* As suggested earlier, issues attached to solutions tend to get the most attention. The team should show how what is proposed will be acted on, and who will be responsible. Possible barriers should be clearly identified. Also recognise alternative scenarios, especially downside risk. Implementation feasibility is critical.

- *Provide clear progress measures.* When seeking significant investments over time, it is reassuring to offer clear measures to allow regular progress monitoring. Proposing review mechanisms also adds credibility to the business case.

Strategic plans are similar to business cases in terms of focus, data, actions and progress measures. Strategic plans are, however, more comprehensive, and they may be used for entrepreneurial start-ups, business units within a large organisation, or for an organisation as a whole. Again formats vary. However, a typical strategic plan has the following elements, which together should set a strategy team's working agenda:[37]

- *Mission, goals and objectives statement.* This is the point of the whole strategy, and the critical starting place. While it is the starting place, in practice a strategy team might iterate back to this in the light of other elements of the strategic plan. It is worth checking back with earlier statements that the organisation may have made to ensure consistency. Section 4.2 provides more guidance on mission, goals and objectives.

- *Environmental analysis.* This should cover the key issues identified in terms of the whole of the environment, both macro trends and more focused issues to do with customers, suppliers and competitors. The team should not stop at the analysis, but draw clear strategic implications. (See Chapter 2.)

- *Capability analysis.* This should include a clear identification of the key strengths and weaknesses of the organisation and its products relative to its competitors and include a clear statement of competitive advantage. (See Chapter 3.)

KEY DEBATE

What good are strategy consultants?

Strategy consultants are frequent participants in strategy making, and typically bring good analytical and project management skills. Why are they so controversial then?

There is no shortage of books criticising strategy consultants. Titles such as *Con Tricks*, *Dangerous Company* and *Rip Off!* provide the flavour. And there have been some spectacular failures. As in section 15.2.4, McKinsey & Co. took some of the blame for General Electric's slow response to the economic crisis of 2008 onwards.

The accusations made against strategy consultants are at least threefold. First, they rely too much on inexperienced young staff fresh out of business school, who, typically, have the slimmest understanding of how client organisations and their markets really work. Second, they are accused of handing over strategy recommendations, and then walking away from implementation. Third, they are perceived as expensive, overpaid individually and always trying to sell on unnecessary extra projects. Clients end up paying for more advice than they really need, much of it unrealistic and unimplementable.

These accusations may be unfair. Most large strategy consulting firms are now organised on industry lines, so building up expertise in particular areas, and they increasingly recruit experienced managers from these industries. Most consultants also prefer to work in joint client–advisor teams, so that clients are involved in generating the recommendations that they will have to implement. Some consultancies, such as Bain, make a point of getting closely involved in implementation too. Finally, consultants are in a competitive market and their clients are typically sophisticated buyers, not easily fooled into buying advice they do not need: the fact that strategy consulting business increased in Europe from €3 bn (~$4.2 bn) in 1996 to €12 bn in 2010 suggests there is plenty of real demand.

There is empirical support in favour of consultants too. Researchers Bergh and Gibbons find that finan-

cial markets generally greet news of the appointment of consultants with a rise in the stock price, indicating confidence in improved future performance. Besides, there are plenty of great corporate managers that have originated in strategy consulting: for example, Lou Gerstner, who turned around IBM, Sheryl Sandberg, COO of Facebook, and Meg Whitman, leader of first eBay and then Hewlett Packard, all started at McKinsey & Co.

There are clues to managing strategy consultants in the criticisms, however: for example, make sure to hire consultants with relevant experience; connect analysis to implementation; and keep a close eye on expenditure. James O'Shea and Charles Madigan close their book with a provocative quotation from Machiavelli's *The Prince*: 'Here is an infallible rule: a prince who is not himself wise cannot be wisely advised . . . Good advice depends on the shrewdness of the prince who seeks it, and not the shrewdness of the prince on good advice.'

Sources: The European Federation of Management Consultancy Associations (www.feaco.org); J. O'Shea and C. Madigan, *Dangerous Company: Consulting Powerhouses and the Businesss they Save and Ruin*, Penguin, 1998; C.D. McKenna, *The World's Newest Profession: Management Consulting in the Twentieth Century*, Cambridge University Press, 2006; D. Bergh and P. Gibbons, 'The stock market reaction to the hiring of consultants', *Journal of Management Studies*, vol. 48, no. 3 (2011), pp. 544–67.

Questions

1 What measures can a strategy consultant take to reassure a potential client of his or her effectiveness?

2 Are there any reasons to suspect that some people might want to exaggerate criticisms of strategy consultants' conduct?

- *Proposed strategy*. This should be clearly related to the environmental and organisational analyses and support the mission, goals and objectives. It should also make clear options that have been considered and why the proposed strategy is preferred. Particularly useful here are Chapters 6 to 11.

- *Resources*. The team will need to provide a detailed analysis of the resources required, with options for acquiring them. Critical resources are financial, so the plan should include income statements, cash flows and balance sheets over the period of the plan. Other important resources might be human, particularly managers or people with particular skills. A clear and realistic timetable for implementation is also needed.

- *Key changes*. What does the plan envisage, are the key changes required in structures, systems and culture and how are these to be managed? Chapters 13 and 14 are most relevant here.

SUMMARY

- The practice of strategy involves critical choices about *who to involve* in strategy, *what to do* in strategising activity, and *which strategising methodologies* to use in order to guide this activity.

- *Chief executive officers*, *senior managers*, *non-executive directors*, *strategic planners*, *strategy consultants* and *middle managers* are all involved in strategising. Their degree of appropriate involvement should depend on the nature of the strategic issues.

- Strategising activity can involve *analysing*, *issue-selling*, *decision making* and *communicating*. Managers should not expect these activities to be fully rational or logical and can valuably appeal to the non-rational characteristics of the people they work with.

- Practical methodologies to guide strategising activity include *strategy workshops*, *strategy projects*, *hypothesis testing* and *creating business cases and strategic plans*.

VIDEO ASSIGNMENTS

Visit *MyStrategyLab* and watch the Pearson case study for Chapter 15.

1 Explain what Mark Anderson does as a strategic planner.

2 What does Mark Anderson see as the main skills required by a strategist?

WORK ASSIGNMENTS

✱ *Denotes more advanced work assignments.*

* *Refers to a case study in the Text and Cases edition.*

15.1 Go to the careers or recruitment web page of one of the big strategy consultants (such as www.bain.com, www.bcg.com, www.mckinsey.com). What does this tell you about the nature of strategy consulting work? Would you like this work?

15.2 Go to the website of a large organisation (private or public sector) and assess the way it communicates its strategy to its audiences. With reference to section 15.3.4, how focused is the communication; how impactful is it; and how likely is it to engage employees?

15.3 If you had to design a strategy workshop, suggest who the participants in the workshop should be and what roles they should play in (a) the case where an organisation has to re-examine its fundamental strategy in the face of increased competitive threat; (b) the case where an organisation needs to gain commitment to a long-term, comprehensive programme of strategic change.

15.4✱ For any case study in the text, imagine yourself in the position of a strategy consultant and propose an initial descriptive hypothesis (section 15.4.3) and define the kinds of data that you would need to test it. What kinds of people would you want in your strategy project team (see sections 15.2.5 and 15.4.2)?

15.5✱ Go to a business plan archive (such as the University of Maryland's www.businessplanarchive.org or use a Google search). Select a business plan of interest to you and, in the light of section 15.4.4, assess its good points and its bad points.

Integrative assignment

15.6✱ For an organisation with which you are familiar, or one of the case organisations, write a strategic plan (for simplicity, you might choose to focus on an undiversified business or a business unit within a larger corporation). Where data are missing, make reasonable assumptions or propose ways of filling the gaps. Comment on whether and how you would provide different versions of this strategic plan for (a) investors; (b) employees.

RECOMMENDED KEY READINGS

- For a textbook overview of practice issues in strategy, see S. Paroutis, L. Heracleous and D. Angwin, *Practicing Strategy: Text and cases*, Sage, 2013, pp. 74–94.

- For an overview of research on the practice of strategy, see E. Vaara and R. Whittington, 'Strategy as practice:

taking practices seriously', *Academy of Management Annals*, vol. 6 (2012), pp. 285–336.

- A practical guide to strategising methodologies is provided by E. Rasiel and P.N. Friga, *The McKinsey Mind*, McGram-Hill, 2001, which has much more general relevance than that particular consulting firm.

REFERENCES

1. A theoretical basis for this pyramid can be found in R. Whittington, 'Completing the practice turn in strategy research', *Organization Studies*, vol. 27, no. 5 (2006), pp. 613–34; and P. Jarzabkowski, J. Balogun and D. Seidl, 'Strategizing: the challenges of a practice perspective', *Human Relations*, vol. 60, no. 1 (2007), pp. 5–27.

2. The classic statement is A. Chandler, *Strategy and Structure: Chapters in the History of American Enterprise*, MIT Press, 1962.

3. S. Kaplan and E. Beinhocker, 'The real value of strategic planning', *MIT Sloan Management Review*, Winter 2003, pp. 71–6.

4. M.E. Porter, 'What is strategy?', *Harvard Business Review* (November–December 1996), pp. 61–78.

5. J. Collins, *Good to Great*, Random House, 2001.

6. I. Janis, *Victims of Groupthink: a Psychological Study of Foreign-Policy Decisions and Fiascoes*, Houghton Mifflin, 1972; R.S. Baron, 'So right it's wrong: groupthink and the ubiquitous nature of polarized group decision making', in Mark P. Zanna (ed.), *Advances in Experimental Social Psychology*, vol. 37, pp. 219–53, Elsevier Academic Press, 2005.

7. M. Hensmans, G. Johnson and G. Yip, *Strategic Transformation: Changing While Winning*, Palgrave Macmillan, 2012.

8. E. Beinhocker and S. Kaplan, 'Tired of strategic planning?', *McKinsey Quarterly*, special edition on Risk and Resilience (2002), pp. 49–57; S. Kaplan and E. Beinhocker, 'The real value of strategic planning', *MIT Sloan Management Review* (Winter 2003), pp. 71–6; D. Angwin, S. Paroutis and S. Mitson, 'Connecting up strategy; are senior strategy directors a missing link?', *California Management Review*, vol. 51, no. 3 (2009), pp. 74–94.

9. R.S. Kaplan and D.P. Norton, 'The office of strategy management', *Harvard Business Review* (October 2005), pp. 72–80.

10. S. Floyd and W. Wooldridge, *The Strategic Middle Manager: How to Create and Sustain Competitive Advantage*, Jossey-Bass, 1996.

11. See for example J. Balogun and G. Johnson: 'Organizational restructuring and middle manager sensemaking', *Academy of Management Journal* (August 2004), pp. 523–49.

12. A. Watson and B. Wooldridge, 'Business unit manager influence on corporate-level strategy formulation', *Journal of Managerial Issues*, vol. 18, no. 2 (2005), pp. 147–61; S. Floyd and B. Wooldridge, 'Middle management's strategic influence and organizational performance', *Journal of Management Studies*, vol. 34, no. 3 (1997), pp. 465–85.

13. F. Westley, 'Middle managers and strategy: microdynamics of inclusion', *Strategic Management Journal*, vol. 11 (1990), pp. 337–51; S. Mantere and Vaara, E., 'On the problem of participation in strategy', *Organization Science*, vol. 19, no. 2 (2008), pp. 341–258.

14. See L.S. Oakes, B. Townley and D.J. Cooper, 'Business planning as pedagogy: language and control in a changing institutional field', *Administrative Science Quarterly*, vol. 43, no. 2 (1997), pp. 257–92; and G. Mulgan, *The Art of Public Strategy*, Oxford University Press, 2009.

15. For theoretical discussion of advisers in strategy, see L. Arendt, R. Priem and H. Ndofor, 'A CEO-adviser model of strategic decision-making', *Journal of Management*, vol. 31, no. 5 (2005), pp. 680–99.

16. S. Appelbaum, 'Critical success factors in the client-consulting relationship', *Journal of the American Academy of Business* (March 2004), pp. 184–91; M. Mohe, 'Generic strategies for managing consultants: insights from client companies in Germany', *Journal of Change Management*, vol. 5, no. 3 (2005), pp. 357–65.

17. R. Whittington, B. Basak-Yakis and L. Cailluet, 'Opening strategy: evolution of a precarious profession', *British Journal of Management*, vol. 22, no. 3 (2011), pp. 531–544; D. Stieger, K. Matzler, S. Chatterje and F. Ladstaetter-Fussenegger, 'Democratising strategy', *California Management Review*, vol. 54, no. 2 (2012), pp. 44–68.

18. E. Beinhocker and S. Kaplan (reference 8), Figure 2, p. 56.

19. P. Jarzabkowski, M. Giulietti and B. Oliveira, 'Building a strategy toolkit: lessons from business', AIM Executive briefing, 2009. See also T. Hill and R. Westbrook, 'SWOT analysis: it's time for a product recall', *Long Range Planning*, vol. 30, no. 1 (1997), pp. 46–52.

20. A. Langley, 'Between paralysis by analysis and extinction by instinct', *Sloan Management Review*, vol. 36, no. 3 (1995), pp. 63–76.

21. A. Langley, 'In search of rationality: the purposes behind the use of formal analysis in organisations', *Administrative Science Quarterly*, vol. 34 (1989), pp. 598–631.

22. This draws on the attention-based view of the firm: see J. Joseph and W. Ocasio, 'Architecture, attention and adaptation in the multibusiness firm: General Electric from 1951 to 2001', *Strategic Management Journal*, vol. 33, no. 6 (2012), pp. 633–660.

23. D. Kahneman, D. Lovallo and O. Siboney, 'Before you make that big decision', *Harvard Business Review* (June 2011), pp. 41–60; and D. Kahneman, *Thinking, Fast and Slow*, Allen & Unwin, 2012. A good set of papers on 'behavioural strategy' is in the *Strategic Management Journal* special issue 'the Psychological Foundations of Strategic Management', vol. 32, no. 13 (2011), eds T.C. Powell, D. Lovallo and C. Fox. These ideas are also associated with the experience lens, introduced in the Commentary to Part I.

24. K.M. Eisenhardt, J. Kahwajy and L.J. Bourgeois, 'Conflict and strategic choice: how top teams disagree', *California Management Review*, vol. 39, no. 2 (1997), pp. 42–62.

25. R.A. Burgelman and A.S. Grove, 'Let chaos reign, then rein in chaos – repeatedly: managing strategic dynamics for corporate longevity', *Strategic Management Journal*, vol. 28 (2007), pp. 965–79.

26. M. Beer and R.A. Eisenstat, 'How to have an honest conversation', *Harvard Business Review*, vol. 82, no. 2 (2004), pp. 82–9.

27. See Balogun and Johnson above (reference 11).

28. This builds on M. Thatcher, 'Breathing life into business strategy', *Strategic Communication Management*, vol. 10, no. 2 (2006), pp. 14–18; and R.H. Lengel and R.L. Daft, 'The selection of communication media as an executive skill', *Academy of Management Executive*, vol. 2, no. 3 (1988), pp. 225–32. For an academic account, see P. Spee and P. Jarzabkowski, 'Strategic planning as communicative process', *Organization Studies*, vol. 32, no. 9 (2011), pp. 1217–45.

29. R. Whittington, E. Molloy, M. Mayer and A. Smith, 'Practices of strategizing/organizing: broadening strategy work and skills', *Long Range Planning*, vol. 39 (2006), pp. 615–29.

30. G. Adamson, J. Pine, T. van Steenhoven and J. Kroupa, 'How story-telling can drive strategic change', *Strategy and Leadership*, vol. 34, no. 1 (2006), pp. 36–41.

31. J.D. Ford, 'Organizational change as shifting conversations', *Journal of Strategic Change*, vol, 12, no. 6 (1999), pp. 480–500.

32. This section builds on the case study research of G. Johnson, S. Prashantham, S. Floyd and N. Bourque, 'The ritualization of strategy workshops', *Organization Studies*, vol. 31, no. 12 (2010), pp. 1589–1618. See also B. Frisch and L. Chandler, 'Off-sites that work', *Harvard Business*

Review, vol. 84, no. 6 (2006), pp. 117–26. Strategy meetings in general have been discussed by P. Jarzabkowski and D. Seidl, 'The role of meetings in the social practice of strategy', *Organization Studies*, vol. 29 (2008), pp. 69–95; and I. Clarke, W. Kwon and R. Wodak, 'A context-sensitive approach to analyzing talk in strategy meetings', *British Journal of Management*, vol. 23 (2012), pp. 455–73.

33. L. Heracleous and C. Jacobs, 'The serious business of play', *MIT Quarterly* (Fall 2005), pp. 19–20.

34. P. Morris and A. Jamieson, 'Moving from corporate strategy to project strategy', *Project Management Journal*, vol. 36, no. 4 (2005), pp. 5–18; J. Kenny, 'Effective project management for strategic innovation and change in an organizational context', *Project Management Journal*, vol. 34, no. 1 (2003), pp. 43–53.

35. This section draws on E. Rasiel and P.N. Friga, *The McKinsey Mind*, McGraw-Hill, 2001; H. Courtney, *20/20 Foresight: Crafting Strategy in an Uncertain World*, McKinsey & Co., 2001.

36. J. Walker, 'Is your business case compelling?', *Human Resource Planning*, vol. 25, no. 1 (2002), pp. 12–15; M. Pratt, 'Seven steps to a business case', *Computer World*, 10 October 2005, pp. 35–6.

37. Useful books on writing a business plan include: C. Barrow, P. Barrow and R. Brown, *The Business Plan Workbook*, Kogan Page, 2008; and A.R. DeThomas and S.A. Derammelaan, *Writing a Convincing Business Plan*, Barron's Business Library, 2008.

Setting Wychavon's new strategy

The quiet, rural district of Wychavon is home to a surprisingly dynamic council. But the district council would need all the goodwill and capabilities it could find as it started setting its new 2012–16 strategy. With the economic crisis biting ever deeper, the council faced severe budget cuts. The council would draw on a wide range of inputs both from outside the organisation and from its middle managers, not always in expected ways.

The Wychavon context

Wychavon District Council is one of six districts within the English county council area of Worcestershire, situated between Birmingham and Wales. Wychavon is a relatively prosperous district of over 100,000 residents. Since 2001, it has been under Conservative Party control. In the May 2011 council elections it returned 38 Conservative councillors, five Liberal Democrats, one Labour and one Independent. Twelve of the elected councillors had been unopposed.

The district council's responsibilities include housing, district planning, benefits administration, environmental health, street cleaning, parks, leisure facilities, events and other local activities. The council had just over 400 employees in 2011, and a total expenditure of £12.1 m (€15 m). Services such as schools, libraries and transport are the responsibility of Worcestershire County Council.

Since 2007, the Leader of the Council – the senior political role – has been Paul Middlebrough. Paul had first been elected councillor in 2002, has a background in finance and works as a consultant in the education sector. Since 2004, Jack Hegarty has performed the 'Managing Director' senior council officer role: with over 25 years experience in local government, his leadership qualities have been recognised by awards from *The Times* newspaper in both 2007 and 2008. Fiona Narburgh is Head of Strategy and Communications, leading strategy at Wychavon for 10 years. These three describe themselves as part of 'Team Wychavon'.

Sometimes described as 'Wychavon plc', the district council is widely seen as well managed. In 2007, it was

designated 'Council of the Year' in England. In 2011, it had the eighth-lowest council tax nationally and was recognised as the fourth highest-ranked council in the *Sunday Times* list of 100 best places to work in the public and non-profit sectors. Leader Paul Middlebrough distinguishes Wychavon from the traditional English municipal council: 'Our style is more entrepreneurial than municipal.'

Wychavon's 2008–13 strategy

In the past, strategy had not been a strong feature of Wychavon's management. Long strategy documents had been produced, but little read. Shifts in government legislation and opportunities in terms of council property development meant that a good deal of activity was unplanned. Jack Hegarty commented: 'Rather than us being proactive, things just happened.'

However, in 2008 Wychavon undertook a major strategic review. After extensive internal and external consultation, the council identified five 'Priorities': *Safer*, referring to reduced fear of crime; *Greener*, referring to environmental improvements; *Healthier*, referring to reduced disease and health inequality; *Stronger*, referring to better economic prospects, housing and community relations; and finally *Successful*, referring to the council's own performance as an excellent and value-for-money deliverer of local services. The five priorities were summarised on a 'one-pager', distributed widely on a single sheet of paper and on posters around the district council offices and the local community.

The council shared the new strategy with council employees through staff forums, briefings and the council in-house magazine. As Head of Strategy and Communications, Fiona Narburgh commented on the importance of communicating the strategy: 'we're really keen on making sure people know about and buy into strategy'. Staff personal appraisals were tied to delivery of relevant strategy priorities. In 2010–11, the council reported that it had met or exceeded 31 of its 45 specific targets under the five priorities, with significant underperformance on only four. Over 90 per cent of employees reported knowing the council's strategy. Managing Director Jack Hegarty commented: 'our strong performance is all down to the engagement of our people; we simply couldn't deliver the great deal residents expect from us without the motivated team we now have'.

The 2012–16 strategy

By 2011, Wychavon was facing an increasingly challenging environment. The United Kingdom economy was firmly in recession. The new national government under Conservative Prime Minister David Cameron was introducing severe cuts: Wychavon was due to save £1.8 m on its budget over two years, a 15 per cent reduction. One third of the councillors elected in the May 2011 local elections had never served before.

Some councillors wondered what the purpose of a strategy was in these conditions. Was local government now just a matter of cuts? But Managing Director Jack Hegarty believed that these were exactly the tough conditions that demanded a strategic approach to priorities. He feared that the cuts could easily become 'an excuse for mediocrity', with excellence compromised across the board. Wychavon launched a new strategy-making process in 2011, managed by Fiona Narburgh.

The strategy process had several important inputs. Of course, councillors had insight into residents' needs, but they could not know everything about their areas. Wychavon drew on statistical and qualitative data too. Strategy Director Fiona Narburgh observed: 'evidence de-politicises the strategy'. At the end of 2009, the council had carried out a 'SIMALTO' exercise, using an external research company to interview 260 residents about their views on spending choices given different levels of budget cuts: one surprise was that residents generally chose to *increase* spending on youth facilities even while freezing or cutting all other council budget areas. The annual Worcestershire Viewpoint survey – covering the whole county – had also identified youth activities as important for residents, as well as employment and affordable housing. A survey of Wychavon councillors focused on the five 2008–13 priorities, revealing that they rated 'Successful' as the most important priority, 'Safer' as the least important. One final additional input was a 'peer review' undertaken with Elmbridge Borough Council, a similar council in the south of England: the Elmbridge contribution raised issues regarding Wychavon's approach to waste and recycling and strengthening the district council's rela-

tionships with parish councils, the smallest unit of local government in the English system.

The new 2012–16 strategic plan process started in July 2011 with what was described as an 'Away-Day at Home' – a strategy retreat carried out in the council's own offices. As well as councillors, the senior management team and the middle managers, Wychavon invited several outsiders: an external facilitator, a former chief executive of another local district, a local Member of Parliament, a local doctor, a prominent accountant, a nuclear energy expert, an academic expert on local government and a lawyer widely involved in public-sector work. Several of the district councillors were also county councillors, so the Worcestershire County perspective was also represented. Paul Middlebrough and Jack Hegarty presented a SWOT analysis of the district council, highlighting as strengths its risk-taking culture and strong motivation (among other things), and as one of its weaknesses the district's political homogeneity. Strategy Director Fiona Narburgh then presented various kinds of residents' data, ranging from hard facts on housing needs to opinions on the importance of 'value for money' in council services. She also raised the importance of councillor engagement with local residents. Away-day participants were then invited to form small discussion groups and to report back on the top three issues for Wychavon to a final plenary session. The day's activities helped the new group of councillors bind together and gave them a good overview of the district's situation.

The July 'Away-Day at Home' fed into a stream of work leading to a second strategy session one morning in October. This involved a smaller group, with senior Conservative councillors, senior managers, two middle management representatives and an external facilitator. The October session was intended to produce a more focused set of priorities than before, and the senior management team had narrowed the various options down to three overlapping possibilities focused on the economy, environment, communities and the council's own performance. However, the session was not entirely smooth. At one point in the discussion, local economy issues nearly swamped everything else. The meeting finally returned to the kind of balanced position aimed for at the start, with three priorities: *Strong economy*, referring to jobs, skills and housing; *Strong environment*, referring to energy, the natural environment and recycling; and *Strong communities*, referring to such things as youth activities and councillor engagement with residents. Health and crime were less prominent than before and the 2008–13 emphasis on a

Figure 1 Wychavon's 2012–16 strategy 'one-pager'

Source: Wychavon District Council.

'Successful Council' was incorporated into a new overarching statement of purpose: 'To be a progressive council delivering great value services and helping to create a strong economy, environment and community.'

The October strategy session produced a strong response from the middle manager group. They were keen to keep the strategy realistic. At their own November meeting, the middle managers proposed their own set of 'promises' (i.e. specific targets) with regard to each of the three priorities. The senior management team believed it was too early to go into such detail. After some debate, it was decided to convert the middle managers' proposed promises into questions, which the district sent out to local partners – the county council, housing associations, the police force, the college and business organisations – inviting them to indicate their preferences. The local partners broadly endorsed the three priorities, especially 'Strong economy', and guided Wychavon in terms of detailed promises.

The district considered launching another consultation meeting with partners in order to consider their input further, but decided against. As Fiona Narburgh commented: 'There's a conflict between consulting and deciding. There comes a time when it's time to stop consulting and start deciding.' It was time now to finalise the strategy. In January 2012, the executive board considered a draft strategy document. The draft was then presented at the staff briefing and team meetings. A 'promises workshop' was held with councillors, the senior management team and middle managers in order to rank the most important promises. In February, the full council approved the final set of three priorities, each with three goals, and supported by 19 specific promises (see Figure 1). The 'one-pager' was backed by a 60-page set of detailed 'delivery plans', specifying responsibilities for senior councillors and council managers in terms of promises, timetables and key performance indicators. In April, the new 2012–16 strategy went public, distributed to all residents through the council's *Wychavon* magazine.

The new strategy represented a significant shift. Priorities were more focused than before, with some now relatively downplayed. The synchronisation of the budget process with the strategy process ensured that aspirations were backed by resources: for example, the 'Strong economy' priority was backed by the commitment of £750,000 new money over three years, against a background of declining overall spend. Council leader Paul Middlebrough was pleased with the strategy process overall, while seeing scope for developing still further next time: 'Should we involve the public more? Is a more inclusive strategy a better strategy? We think it is. Certainly we do a lot to be inclusive internally. But is it better to be more inclusive externally, with the general public? It's not easy. It's a matter of finding the right groups to engage.'

Source: Interviews with Jack Hegarty, Cherrie Mansfield, Paul Middlebrough and Fiona Narburgh.

Questions

1 What was effective about Wychavon's 2012–16 strategy process and what was less effective?

2 What would you do differently in designing Wychavon's next strategy process?

COMMENTARY ON PART III

This part of *Exploring Strategy* has considered strategy in action. Although this is the last part, this does not imply that action necessarily follows logically from the analysis of strategic position and choices. Chapter 1 introduced the overall model for this text, made up of three overlapping circles of position, choices and action. The point of the model is that strategy should not be seen as simply a linear process: the issues raised in different parts of this text interact and inform each other. While for purposes of clarity this text presents strategy implementation following strategy formulation in a logical sequence, in practice this is by no means always so.

In this Commentary the strategy lenses are used to explore more deeply this key issue of how formulation and implementation fit together. What are the practical implications of the various lenses for how to put strategy into action?

Design lens

The design lens builds on the notion that thinking precedes organisational action, so that strategy is, indeed, a linear process. Rational analysis and design are seen as powerful motivators of strategic action. In this view therefore, managers should:

- *Make the business case*: the most important factor in persuading managerial colleagues and other internal and external stakeholders is logical analysis and evidence, for example rigorous evaluation criteria (Chapter 11) and business plans (Chapter 15).
- *Exercise tight change management*: strategies are best implemented through systematic use of the levers for change (Chapter 14) and strict project management (Chapter 15), leaving little scope for improvisation.
- *Reinforce coherent action*: strategies will be most effectively implemented if organisational structures and systems are configured so that they are mutually supporting (Chapter 13).

Experience lens

The experience lens is sceptical about the place of rationality in securing strategy implementation. Managerial biases and organisational conservatism mean that strategy is heavily influenced by the past. The experience lens suggests it is important to:

- *Challenge biases*: strategy evaluation and strategic plans (Chapters 11 and 12) are likely to be shaped by the experience of those who do them, so it is important to challenge what may be taken for granted.
- *Pick your teams carefully*: if strategies are shaped by the people involved in making them, then it really matters who is in your strategy development teams and projects (Chapter 15).
- *Recognise the challenge of change*: given the weight of past experience on organisations, the issues of leadership and change (Chapter 14) are likely to be among the most important and difficult in this whole text.

STRATEGY IN ACTION

Note that:

- There is no suggestion here that any one of these lenses is better the others. The point is to avoid using just one. Each lens gives you extra ways to explore strategic issues.

- For a deeper understanding of this Commentary, you might want to review the Part I Commentary, following Chapter 5, which provides a fuller introduction of the four lenses, plus an illustrative case. The Commentary at the end of Part II is also relevant.

Variety lens

According to the variety lens, strategies can bubble up from the periphery and are then often selected and retained according to semi-conscious organisational processes. Innovation does not come simply from top management command. The variety lens therefore encourages you to:

- *Favour inclusiveness*: in deciding who to include in strategy development (Chapter 12 and section 15.2), innovative strategies are more likely to come – and be implemented – if you include as many people as possible from outside the usual organisational elite.

- *Check the rules*: the variety lens points to the power of taken-for-granted procedures, so it is wise to review standard strategy evaluation criteria and organisational systems for hidden biases in strategy selection and retention (section 11.3 and section 13.3).

- *Be ready to go 'off-plan'*: given the role of surprise and spontaneity, flexibility is important and it may be necessary to abandon at least certain aspects of the original strategic plan (Chapter 12).

Discourse lens

Through this lens, language is highly influential on how strategies are interpreted and implemented. Discourse can both smooth and inhibit putting strategy into action. It is important to recognise that:

- *Words matter*: the symbolic power of language can make the difference between success and failure, for example in leading transformational change (section 14.4) or justifying performance (section 11.2).

- *Organisations are political*: discourses can be used to promote sectional interests, so it is important to be sensitive to, and sometimes challenge, the language of issue-selling (section 15.3) and alliance and network building (section 14.4) for example.

- *Language is an entry ticket*: for managers and consultants who seek to enter into the organisation's strategy conversation (section 15.2), it is vital to be able to speak the organisational language of strategy fluently and confidently.

CASE
STUDIES

CO-EDITED BY STEVE PYLE

GUIDE TO USING THE CASE STUDIES

The main text of this book includes 57 short illustrations, 15 key debates and 15 case examples which have been chosen to develop and illustrate specific issues in the text and/or provide practical examples of how business and public sector organisations are managing strategic issues. The case collection which follows allows the reader to extend this linking of theory and practice further by analysing the strategic issues of specific organisations in much greater depth and proposing 'solutions' to some of the problems or difficulties identified. There are also 40 classic cases on the Companion Website. These are a selection of cases from past editions of the book which remain relevant for teaching.

The case studies are intended to serve as a basis for class discussion and not as an illustration of either good or bad management practice. They have been chosen (or specifically written) to provide readers with a core of cases which, together, cover the main issues in the text. As such, they provide a useful backbone to a programme of study but could sensibly be supplemented by other material. We have provided a mixture of longer and shorter cases to increase the flexibility for teachers. Combined with the illustrations and the short case examples at the end of each chapter (in both versions of the book), this increases the reader's and tutor's choice. For example, we offer a number of options for exploring the issues in Chapter 2 on the environment. Thus the case example, Global Forces and the Advertising Industry, at the end of Chapter 2, provides a short case to test students' core understanding of the main environmental issues. In the case collection, the brewing industry case offers a concise focus on three companies in the same business environment, while the pharmaceutical industry case (or the Vodafone and the global communications industry case) have the materials for a more comprehensive analysis. However, if the purpose is simply to illustrate the use of 'five forces' analysis, Illustration 2.3 on the steel industry would suffice. Similarly, if the focus is scenario planning then the shale gas case is suitable.

Some cases are written entirely from published sources but most have been prepared in cooperation with, and approval of, the management of the organisation concerned. We would nonetheless also encourage readers and tutors to take every opportunity to explore live strategic issues in both their own organisation and others.

The following brief points of guidance should prove useful in selecting and using the case studies provided:

- The summary table that follows indicates the main focus of each of the chosen case studies, together with important subsidiary foci (where appropriate). In general, the sequence of cases is intended to mirror the chapter sequence. However, this should not be taken too literally because, of course, many of these cases cover a variety of issues. The 'classification' provided is therefore for guidance only. We expect readers to seek their own lessons from cases, and tutors to use cases in whichever way and sequence best fits the purpose of their programmes.

- In the Commentary at the end of Part I of the book we introduce the concept of 'strategy lenses'. Where there are cases that lend themselves to exploration through different lenses, this is indicated as a secondary focus for those cases.

- Where cases have been chosen to illustrate the issues of strategic choice and strategy in action covered later in the book, it will normally be a prerequisite that some type of analysis of the strategic position is undertaken, using the case material. So care needs to be taken to balance the time taken on such strategic analysis in order to allow the time required to analyse the main issues for which the case has been chosen.

- Where the text and cases are being used as the framework for a strategy programme (as we hope they will), it is important that students undertake additional reading from other sources and that their 'practical' work is supplemented by other material as mentioned above. Frequently, company websites can be used to provide additional information, especially the latest financial figures.

- The cases do not have questions attached (although suggested questions are provided in the instructor's manual), in order to allow programme leaders to use the case in the most appropriate way for their own purposes. However, the cases are written in such a way as to suggest the key issues they raise.

GUIDE TO THE MAIN FOCUS OF CASES IN THE BOOK

Key: ●● = major focus, ● = important subsidiary focus

PAGE	CASES	Introduction to strategy	Strategy lenses	The environment	Strategic capability	Strategic purpose	Culture and strategy	Business-level strategy	Directions and corporate-level strategy	International strategy	Innovation and entrepreneurship	Mergers, acquisitions and alliances	Strategy evaluation	Strategy development	Organising for success	Managing strategic change	The practice of management	Public sector/not-for-profit management	Small-business strategy
544	**The LEGO Group**: adopting a strategic approach	●●																	
549	**The global pharmaceutical industry** – in the land of shrinking giants			●●						●									
559	**Vodafone**: developing communications strategy in the UK market			●●				●											
567	**Global forces and the Western European brewing industry**			●●						●									
571	A source of cheap energy or a source of problems – the potential benefits and costs of **shale gas**			●●														●	
575	**H&M** in fast fashion: continued success?				●●		●			●	●								
583	**The Formula One constructors**: capabilities for success				●●			●		●									
591	Integration of a Corporate Social Responsibility programme in **Coloplast**					●●				●									
595	**Manchester United FC**: still successful despite new threats	●				●●													
600	**Pierre Fabre**: culture and the challenges of internationalisation	●			●		●●			●							●		
606	**Adnams** – a living company	●				●	●●	●									●		●
612	**Ryanair**: the low-fares airline – future directions?			●	●			●●		●									
624	**Marks & Spencer**: is this as good as it gets?							●●	●								●		
629	**Hotel du Vin**: strategic entrepreneurship and innovative continuity in the boutique hotel sector							●●			●								●●
634	Going for growth: **Teva's** global strategy								●	●●		●●							
639	**CRH plc**: dimensions of successful corporate strategy								●●	●		●							
647	**SABMiller**: from strength to strength								●●	●									
657	The internationalisation of **Tesco** – new frontiers and new problems									●●			●						
662	**Gridsum** and the **Microsoft** partner ecosystem: engaging in China and beyond?									●●		●							●

PAGE NUMBER IN THE BOOK	CASES	Introduction to strategy	Strategy lenses	The environment	Strategic capability	Strategic purpose	Culture and strategy	Business-level strategy	Directions and corporate-level strategy	International strategy	Innovation and entrepreneurship	Mergers, acquisitions and alliances	Strategy evaluation	Strategy development	Organising for success	Managing strategic change	The practice of management	Public sector/not-for-profit management	Small-business strategy
666	**Severstal** and the global steel industry			●						●●		●	●						
671	**FeedHenry** – innovating in the cloud							●			●●	●							●
676	**Flight Centre Limited**	●						●			●●				●●	●			
680	Strategic leadership and innovation at **Apple, Inc.** '						●			●	●●					●			
686	'Where's Irene and just exactly is she up to?' The acquisition of **Cadbury PLC by Kraft Foods**, 2010					●						●●							
695	**Gazprom and NIS**: the oil and gas industry in Serbia					●	●					●●							
700	**International HIV/AIDS Alliance (B)**: a strategy for 2020					●						●	●●		●			●●	
707	The **Mexican narco-trafficking problem**							●					●●					●	
715	Dancing with the mouse: a strategic metamorphosis at **Ocean Park**, Hong Kong					●									●●			●	
721	**GMB**: strategic leadership in a trade union	●													●●	●		●●	
727	**Academies and Free Schools**					●										●●		●●	
731	Paul Polman and the revitalisation of **Unilever**						●	●								●●			
738	**LEAX**: managing growth in a volatile world				●										●	●●			●
742	Changing tracks at **Babcock Rail**					●									●	●●			
749	In the boardroom **at HomeCo**					●		●						●				●●	●
755	**QR National – Aurizon**					●		●										●●	

Key: ●● = major focus, ● = important subsidiary focus

GUIDE TO THE CLASSIC CASES ON THE COMPANION WEBSITE*

CASES	Introduction to strategy	The environment	Strategic capability	Strategic purpose	Culture and strategy	Business-level strategy	Directions and corporate-level strategy	International strategy	Innovation and entrepreneurship	Mergers, acquisitions and alliances	Strategy evaluation	Strategy development processes	Organising for success	Leading strategic change	The practice of management	Public sector/not-for-profit management	Small-business strategy
Ministry of Sound: rapid growth but a questionable future	●●																●
Electrolux	●●																
Airline industry post-9/11: reshaping strategies and planning for the future in the wake of global shock		●●															
European tour operators: confronting competition in the tourism industry		●●						●									
Amazon.com 2007 to early 2009			●●			●											
Inside **Dyson** – a distinctive company?			●●														
Sheffield Theatres: strategy formulation for a wide audience of public and commercial stakeholders				●●												●●	
(RED)				●●													
Iona				●●												●●	
Hermes Fund Management, Total and Premier Oil: the responsibility and accountability of business				●●													
Marks & Spencer (A): can new initiatives and new management reverse a decline?					●●												
Cultural turnaround at **Club Med**					●●												
Cordia LLP: service reform in the public sector					●●												
Thorntons: a variety of strategies in the manufacture and retail of chocolates						●●											
Madonna: the reigning queen of pop						●●											
Marks & Spencer (C): where next for the icon of British retailing?						●	●●										
News Corporation: corporate logic and corporate management in a worldwide media business							●●										
Lenovo computers: East meets West								●●									
Coopers Creek: developments in domestic and international collaboration for a New Zealand winery			●					●●									●●
Skype: innovator and entrepreneurs									●●								

* Classic cases are available at **www.pearsoned.co.uk/mystrategylab**

CASES	Introduction to strategy	The environment	Strategic capability	Strategic purpose	Culture and strategy	Business-level strategy	Directions and corporate-level strategy	International strategy	Innovation and entrepreneurship	Mergers, acquisitions and alliances	Strategy evaluation	Strategy development processes	Organising for success	Leading strategic change	The practice of management	Public sector/not-for-profit management	Small-business strategy
Sustaining the Magic of Bang & Olnfsen					●	●		●				●		●			
Eden Project (A): inspiration, innovation and entrepreneurship to create a new 'wonder of the world'									●								
Eden Project (B): latest developments in a successful tourist attraction									●								
Police mergers: are mergers the best way forward in tackling major crime?										●						●	
Alliance Boots: a major merger in the pharmaceutical distribution and retailing sector										●							
TNK-BP: from Russia without love – a joint venture that almost fell apart					●					●							
Final Fantasy captures Lara Croft										●							
International HIV/AIDS Alliance (A)			●							●	●		●			●	
Doman Synthetic Fibres plc (B)			●								●						
Ericsson: innovation from the periphery – the development of mobile telephone systems												●					
Direct & Care: strategy development in the multi-stakeholder context of public sector services												●				●	
Hurricane Katrina: human-made disaster?													●				
Arts Council: changes in structure and responsibilities in funding the arts in the UK													●			●	
BBC: structural changes to deliver a better service													●			●	
Managing change at **Faslane**														●			
Marks & Spencer (B): turnaround at the high street legend														●			
Forestry Commission: from forestry management to service provider: the challenge of managing change				●										●			
UNHCR: managing change in a global not-for-profit organisation		●											●		●		
Ray Ozzie: software strategist															●		
NHS Direct: managing in difficult times																●	

CASE STUDY

The LEGO Group: adopting a strategic approach

Anders Bille Jensen

The LEGO Group had historically been a successful, family-led, innovative and high-growth company in the global toy industry. However, the company hit some hard times in the 1990s and early 2000s. Following a successful turnaround the company is now on a growth trajectory, requiring ongoing efforts involving many aspects of strategic management.

• • •

Playing is part of everybody's childhood. It is fun, educational and important for the development of our individual physical, intellectual and social skills and competences. There are many ways to play, and companies in the global toy industry compete fiercely and must constantly change to gain and maintain the interest of children and their parents.

It was therefore a pleasure for Jørgen Vig Knudstorp,[1] CEO of the LEGO Group, when he announced the results for 2012:

'We are again able to present a result which exceeds our imagination.'

Sales amounted to DKK23.4 billion (£2.64bn; $4.04bn; €3.14bn),[2] an increase of 25%, and net profits were DKK5.6 billion, up by 35% (see Table 1). In addition, the LEGO Group improved its market share to 8.6%, ranking it third in the global toy market. Sustaining and managing growth remains a key strategic challenge for the 80-year-old LEGO Group.

The LEGO brick – a major factor in the expansion of the LEGO Group

The company was founded in 1932 in the village of Billund, Denmark, by Ole Kirk Christiansen. Wooden toys quickly became the best-selling item, and the company took the name 'LEGO' – a conjunction of the Danish words 'LEg GOdt' ('play well'). In 1949 the company started producing early versions of the well-known LEGO plastic bricks. In 1958 the current interlocking principle with studs and tubes was invented and patented. The tightly

Source: Dorling Kindersley

gripping pieces made it possible to build more stable and bigger constructions than before. The public was reluctant to accept them at first, preferring more traditional wooden toys than plastic (then a new material). However, the LEGO bricks gained in popularity and the basic bricks were supplemented with figures and technical features, such as small electronic engines, which extended the playing opportunities. The first LEGOLAND theme park was established in 1968 in Billund. Internationally, the LEGO Group began to grow and the number of employees increased from just 65 in 1950 to 1000 in 1970. Even during the economically difficult environment of the 1970s and 1980s, the LEGO Group continued to be successful by

Table 1 **Key financial figures, 2003–12**

Financial highlights

in Mn DKK	2012	2011	2010	2009	2008	2007	2006	2005	2004	2003
Consolidated income statement										
Revenue	23,405	18,731	16,014	11,661	9,526	8,027	7,798	7,027	6,295	6,770
Expenses	(15,453)	(13,065)	(10,899)	(8,659)	(7,522)	(6,556)	(6,393)	(6,605)	(6,394)	(7,919)
Operating profit	7,952	5,666	4,973	2,902	2,100	1,471	1,405	423	(99)	(1,148)
Financial income and expenses	(430)	(124)	(84)	(15)	(248)	(35)	(44)	(51)	(75)	88
Restructuring costs, impairment[1]						(22)	(80)	(43)	(813)	(455)
Profit before tax	7,522	5,542	4,889	2,887	1,852	1,414	1,281	329	(987)	(1,515)
Net profit for the year	5,613	4,160	3,718	2,204	1,352	1,028	1,290	214	(1,800)	(888)
Consolidated balance sheet										
Total assets	16,352	12,904	10,972	7,788	6,496	6,009	6,907	7,058	5,160	8,785
Net assets, discontinuing activities[2]									1,367	
Equity	9,864	6,975	5,473	3,291	2,066	1,679	1,191	563	404	2,344
Liabilities	6,488	5,929	5,499	4,497	4,430	4,330	5,716	6,495	5,160	6,441
Cash flow statement										
Cash flows from operating activities	6,220	3,828	3,744	2,712	1,954	1,033	1,157	587	720	989
Investments[3]	1,787	1,580	1,200	1,258	443	399	316	237	285	653
Cash flows from financing activities	(4,535)	(2,519)	(3,477)	(906)	(1,682)	(467)	597	(656)	(70)	(205)
Total cash flows	(88)	(233)	(671)	558	128	592	1,925	1,570	443	(541)
Employees										
Employees, continuing activities	10,400	9,374	8,365	7,286	5,388	4,199	4,908	5,302	5,603	6,535
Employees, discontinuing activities[4]								1,322	1,029	1,160
Financial ratios (%)										
Gross margin	71.1	70.5	72.4	70.3	66.8	65.0	64.9	58.0	57.9	54.3
Operating margin	34.0	30.2	31.1	24.9	22.0	18.1	17.0	5.4	(14.5)	(23.7)
Net profit margin	24.0	22.2	23.2	18.9	14.2	12.8	16.5	3.0	(28.6)	(13.1)
Return on equity (ROE)	66.7	66.8	84.8	82.3	72.2	71.6	147.1	44.2	(131.0)	(28.1)
Return on invested capital 1	40.2	133.4	161.2	139.5	101.8	69.7	63.6	16.2	(2.0)	(13.5)
Equity ratio[4]	60.3	54.1	49.9	42.3	31.8	27.9	17.2	8.0	5.9	26.7

All figures in million DKK

Source: Excerpts from highlights in the annual reports 2012 and 2007. Figures have not been reported completely consistently and may not be fully comparable due to omission of specific items and changes in accounting practices

1 Restructuring and impairment costs related to actions taken during the crisis years
2 Including investments in property, plant, equipment and intangible assets
3 LEGOLAND Park employees
4 Excluding a subordinate loan provided by the owners

introducing innovative products (e.g. LEGO TECHNIC, and new play themes like LEGO Castle, LEGO Space and LEGO Cowboys). It also took its first steps into new markets, notably the USA, South America and Asia. In 1985 the company employed 5000 people (3000 in Billund). Successful development continued into the early 1990s.

A family-run company

This development was driven by the family from the early years until the late 1990s. When Ole, the founder, died in 1958 the company was taken over by his son, Godtfred. As a junior Vice President, Godtfred had been one of the main driving forces behind the growth of the company for some years. Third-generation Kjeld was the first to hold a graduate degree from a business school. After gaining experience in the Swiss subsidiary, Kjeld took over as CEO in 1978 while Godtfred continued serving on the board and remained passionate about the development of the company and its products until his death in 1995. Under Kjeld's leadership the LEGO brand had become established as a unique and iconic brand. Success had been built on a combination of effective leadership, innovative products and international growth. In 1996 the company received the IMD 'Distinguished Family Business Award'.

A difficult time

In the mid-1990s Kjeld was planning for the future. Growth in electronic toys and changes in playing habits were a concern. Would kids stop playing with traditional toys? There were, however, also a lot of opportunities which could be based on the existing strong position of the group. Kjeld was also keen on combining initiatives with a new, decentralised management structure, which could take the LEGO Group into the future.

In 1995, major new 10-year objectives were set, plans were made, resources allocated and initiatives were launched. The overall objectives were to become the best-known brand among families with children, to grow sales by 100–200% over a 10-year period, and to establish three or four LEGOLAND parks. The brand would be expanded by entering into alliances with partners in related areas such as films, clothing and games. A new and more decentralised management style was also introduced to strengthen the management of the organisation and make it less dependent on Kjeld. Over the next few years, a number of senior and long-serving managers left, as they disagreed with the new management style and/or with the new strategy. Conversely, new managers and specialists were hired to support the new strategy.

The whole expansion plan proved to be too ambitious and resulted in significant problems for the company. Profitability declined and eventually turned into losses; debt increased to a level that threatened the autonomy of the company. The company was facing a crisis.

Kjeld realised that the LEGO Group was facing problems which were unfamiliar to the company and its current management. He stepped back and an external chief operating officer (COO) was hired. The performance and results of the company continued to fluctuate, showing no consistent development. Kjeld stepped in again at the beginning of 2004 and the COO left the company. At that time, however, outsiders began to question who was running the business: the family, the new managers, or – worst case – the banks? Late that year, Kjeld handed over the CEO position to Jørgen Vig Knudstorp ('Jørgen'), then a 35-year-old executive Vice President. His relatively young age and his background caused some discussion in the press. However, he had a good track record. Jørgen holds a BA in Economics and a PhD from the University of Aarhus (Denmark). He worked at McKinsey & Co. as a Management Consultant (1998–2001) before joining the LEGO Group as Director, Strategic Development. He was promoted to become Senior Vice President, Corporate Affairs.[3]

Would he be able to handle the task or would he fail?

Back on track and creating the basic recipe of growth

The LEGO Group became profitable again in 2005 and began a growth journey which has been going on since then. Profitability has also increased significantly (see

Table 1). The development has been based on a number of interacting and mutually supporting initiatives.

Focus on the core business and improvement of the capital structure

As a privately owned business the LEGO Group must be able to finance its own activities and service its debt. During the crisis the LEGOLAND parks were (partly) divested, which reduced the debt burden. In addition to these structural initiatives an important element has been the rebirth of the traditional business. The combined effect of debt reduction, growth and improving profitability has resulted in a strong financial position which is clearly seen from the equity ratio,[4] which – after paying out dividends – has been doubled since 2008.

Focus on sales and distribution

As with many other manufacturing companies, the LEGO Group is dependent on retailers. Having attractive brands and products (for end customers) is crucial for leveraging bargaining power towards distribution partners. This dimension is increasingly important as retailers are expanding and consolidating on a global scale. Such partners are big companies such as Toys R Us with turnover in the region of $14 billion, and Wal-mart with sales in the region of $450 billion. Good relations are also important in order to align expectations, obtain market information and fine-tune sales in both the short and the long run. The LEGO Group actively involves major retailers in the planning of the future product portfolio. As a recent development, direct sales through online channels and brand retail stores have increased to 10% of sales.

Focus on cost, quality and supply chain

The toy market is highly seasonal with peak sales in the second half of the year (Christmas), which makes production planning a challenge. Many toy manufacturers spend the first half of the year building up stocks of finished goods which are then sold and distributed in the latter half of the year. This is a challenge, as the specific composition of the sales is difficult to predict. During the crisis years, the LEGO Group tried to outsource production of the bricks in order to save costs. This soon proved to be a mistake, as quick market feedback, flexibility and fast adjustments in the supply chain were lost as external sourcing partners could not cope. Simultaneously maintaining quality and having an ability to respond to short-term changes in demand are key success factors.

Focus on innovation

To stay ahead of the competition and align with changes in children's playing habits, differences between markets and segments (e.g. boy/girl, geographies and cultures) and technological innovation, a continuous flow of new products is needed. Such products are both classic LEGO products but also launches based on current themes such as new movies. This strategy has paid off as up to 60% of annual sales are from product innovations, most recently 'Ninjago' and 'LEGO Friends', in addition to product renewals within the 'LEGO StarWars' and 'LEGO City' assortment. Approximately 160 employees are dedicated to development. The LEGO Group has been very successful in including users through open innovation processes. LEGO users – of all ages and all over the world – are encouraged to add new models based on their own ideas. These proposals are then evaluated by the management and ranked in user panels. The most successful ones are included in the assortment. A new line of products, LEGO Architecture, was initiated by a user interested in constructing famous buildings in LEGO. Further, the LEGO Group won 4 out of 12 awards at the Toy Fair 2013. The combined innovation effort is important to ensure interest from users, high levels of turnover in retail outlets and staying ahead of competitors.

Focus on the brand and brick quality

Over the years, the LEGO Group has focused on brand building and product quality to compensate for the expiration of patents. At the core of this strategy has been an accumulated knowledge about plastics and production technologies. The results are superior gripping power of the bricks and leadership in non-poisonous plastics which imitators have not yet been able to achieve. Direct imitation and compatible bricks are therefore more a threat to the brand (as consumers may take inferior imitations for LEGO products), rather than direct sales threats.

Not everything, however, has been successful. Entering the digital scene has been a challenge. A major initiative – an online multi-player game – called 'LEGO Universe', in which players could build, create and play together via the internet, was launched in 2010 after several postponements. It was not very successful and had to be withdrawn again. Other games, however, have sold in millions. It remains a priority for LEGO to provide offerings that facilitate children's options of moving between the digital world and the physical construction bricks when playing.

The LEGO Group's overall development, so far, has been successful. In a stagnant toy market – some geographical regions are even declining – the Group has been able to grow sales from DKK 7 billion in 2005 to more than DKK 23 billion in 2012.[5] Product lines include pre-school, traditional bricks, play themes, licensed products, robots, games and educational products. As a result the LEGO Group has an estimated 8.6% share of the global toy market (up from 4.8% in 2008), ranking it as number three in the market.

Future challenges

Jørgen does not perceive the current, successful position as a final destination, but rather as a starting point for taking on new initiatives to ensure continuous improvements and sustained growth. As the LEGO group is a highly focused company, there are no other product ranges to compensate for any failures. Keeping up performance and growth remains a priority. Just a few years ago many decisions were strongly influenced by financial necessity. Today the LEGO Group has a strong financial position, strong growth and more options than it has had for years. The context of the decisions has changed dramatically, but they are still very important for the future development of the company. Jørgen is thinking about what should guide his strategic decisions. One lesson from the last decade stands out: the LEGO Group has developed a new understanding of its roots, its successes and its failures. The company has decided to stay close to construction toys and develop in this area, applying the 'obviously LEGO, but never seen before' principle, reflecting newness but also a natural recognition and fit with the LEGO brand. This understanding can only be helpful to a certain extent – multiple markets, products and organisational entities require a more fine-grained and systematic approach.

As Jørgen adds:

> 'The LEGO brick will continue to be our foundation. In some markets we don't have a huge presence yet, and there our goal is to increase market share by raising awareness and attracting new audiences to our products. Whereas in other markets, for example Germany, we already have a high market share so to increase that we need to cater for new target groups with new products.'

Taking the reflections a step further, some of the LEGO Group's potential strategic challenges are as follows.

Geographical scope and market presence

Balancing existing and new/high-growth markets remains a challenge despite the recent growth taking place in a broad range of markets. LEGO's big markets are well established, but to a certain degree are mature and stagnant markets. Still, doubling the market share in the USA would mean significant growth. The Asian region accounts for approximately 10% of the total sales, and market shares range from 3 to 25%. Asia and South America require ongoing investments in local organisations and facilities, as these are markets where the LEGO Group has only limited knowledge. Taking the uncertainty in the global market into consideration, are the speed of growth and the balance of markets optimal?

Handling the growth

Further expansion of production in existing and new facilities spread over the world requires significant funds. With a healthy cash flow and a good equity ratio, the financial situation is currently not a major concern. However, maintaining a high and successful level of innovation, building capacity and hiring more than 1000 new employees (in 2013 alone) require significant organisational resources and add to the complexity of the group, for example in maintaining quality levels, financial controls and compliance with local laws. Can the organisation cope with this growth? Where – and how – should it be strengthened?

Girls – pursuing the growth opportunity

Historically, LEGO has had a higher appeal to boys than girls. Over two decades the company has tried several times to adapt its products and communications to girls. After four years of preparation a breakthrough was achieved in 2012. LEGO Friends® (a product range specifically aimed at girls) has resulted in significant sales and demand above capacity. Apparently there is a large female market. How should this success be followed up?

Navigating in the competitive arena

The success of the LEGO Group has not gone unnoticed by its competitors. Recently Mattel and Mega Brands have decided to form a partnership. For girls they have created a 'playing universe' which combines the Barbie doll with bricks from Mega Bloks. For boys the combination is to apply the Hot Wheels brand from Mattel with bricks from Mega Brands. Hasbro has launched Kre-O to build on its Transformers universe. Bricks from both Mega Brands and Hasbro are compatible with LEGO bricks. In addition there are other players in the market, as well as substitutes in the form of video games. Should this affect the strategic agenda of the LEGO Group? To what extent should the company pursue its own agenda and/or respond to competitors' initiatives?

Playing in the digital and new media age

The LEGO Group has not been successful in this area, despite multiple attempts and allocating huge resources. During the last two decades it has witnessed companies in these sectors growing into big companies, including game producers Bandai-Namco and Tomy-Takara from Japan (with combined sales of $6.5 billion). Why is it that the LEGO Group did not succeed with LEGO Universe? Should the LEGO Group take any new major initiatives in this area or remain satisfied with its current development?

Education and play

Although the idea of educational toys is not new, a separate business unit has been established for educational products. This business unit has grown significantly and sales in 2012 exceeded DKK1 billion, but sales are unevenly distributed in different geographic regions (with market leadership in some markets). How does this affect the positioning of the LEGO brand in various markets?

As the LEGO Group grows, the challenges are changing and include both short- and longer-term issues and issues related to each other. Obviously, these decisions will have different implications in terms of the resources and capabilities they require. Additionally, such decisions determine which markets and which competitors the LEGO Group will face. Further, it has to be remembered that the LEGO Group is not a public company and has to finance its growth from its own capacity to generate funds. On the other hand this protects the company from broader investor pressure and possible takeover attempts.

Imagine you are in Jørgen's position and have to prepare the strategic agenda. What do you think about these issues? What information would you need? What resources can you get – how and when? Who would you involve in the strategy process? What tools would you use? How much can you plan in advance and what type of activities need a more action-orientated approach?

Notes and references

1. Jørgen Vig Knudstorp was appointed in 2004 and was the first CEO from outside the family.
2. DKK1 = £0.114 = $0.175 = €0.134.
3. See http://www.imd.org/about/foundationboard/knudstorp.cfm for further details.
4. Equity ratio is defined as equity/total assets. In general, a high equity ratio indicates a strong capital structure of the company, especially if combined with a strong cash flow.
5. By comparison, Mattel, the world's largest toy company, has annual sales of approximately DKK 40 billion ($7.1 billion) and Hasbro of DKK 23 billion ($4.1 billion). In Asia a big player is the Japanese-based Bandai-Namco company.

CASE STUDY

The global pharmaceutical industry – in the land of shrinking giants

Sarah Holland

• • •

A CEO's dilemma

On 1 October 2012, Pascal Soriot started work as CEO of AstraZeneca. His new role was described as 'one of the toughest turnaround jobs in the world'.[1] AstraZeneca was a top five global pharmaceutical company with $37 billion (£24.4bn; €28.8bn)[2] in annual revenues, but had experienced painful setbacks: a string of products that failed in late-stage clinical trials or hit hurdles when submitted for marketing approval. In one of his first tasks as CEO, Soriot announced that for the nine months to September 2012, revenues fell 17% compared to 2011, with pre-tax profit dropping 23%. Barely a month earlier, Soriot had been running the pharma business at Roche, noted for its success in innovation. Faced now with a barren pipeline of new products and looming patent expiries on medicines worth $10 billion in the USA alone, it was clear that Soriot needed to act swiftly, but how?

Industry evolution

As described in Box 1, the pharmaceutical industry is characterised by a highly risky and lengthy research and development (R&D) process, intense competition for *intellectual property*, stringent government regulation and powerful purchaser pressures. How has this unusual picture come about?

The origins of the modern pharmaceutical industry date from the late nineteenth century, when dyestuffs were found to have antiseptic properties. Penicillin was a major discovery, and R&D became firmly established within the sector. The market developed some unusual characteristics. Decision making was in the hands of medical practitioners, whereas patients (the final consumers) and payers (governments or insurance companies) had little knowledge or influence. Consequently, medical practitioners were insensitive to price but susceptible to the efforts of sales representatives.

Two important developments occurred in the 1970s. Firstly, the tragedy of thalidomide (an anti-emetic for morning sickness that caused birth defects) led to much tighter regulatory controls on clinical trials. Secondly, legislation was enacted to set a fixed period on patent protection – typically 20 years. On patent expiry, rivals could launch generic medicines with exactly the same active ingredients as the original brand at a lower price.

The dramatic impact of generic competitors is illustrated by Merck's top-selling asthma and allergy drug Singulair, which lost 90% of US sales just four weeks after patent expiry in 2012. Generics had a major impact on the industry, driving innovation and a race to market, since the time during which R&D costs could be recouped was drastically curtailed.

The pharmaceutical industry is unusual, since in many countries it is subject to a 'monopsony' – there is effectively only one powerful purchaser, the government. Since the 1980s, governments have focused on pharmaceuticals as a politically easy target in efforts to control rising healthcare expenditure. Many have introduced price or reimbursement controls. The industry has lacked the public or political support to resist these changes.

Business environment

Ageing populations create pressure on healthcare systems, since over-65s consume four times as much healthcare per head as younger people. Combined with an epidemic of chronic disease linked to obesity, this created an unsustainable situation. Universal coverage systems, as in the UK, were slow to introduce the latest treatments, despite a doubling of healthcare spending from 1990 to 2011. The insurance-funded system in the USA could afford the latest innovations, but nearly 49 million Americans, over 15% of the population, lacked any health insurance.[3]

BOX 1 The drug development process

The pharmaceutical industry has long new-product lead times, with the period from discovery to marketing authorisation typically taking almost 12 years (Figure 1). New product development can be divided into distinct research and development phases. The research phase produces a *new chemical entity* (NCE) with the desired characteristics to be an effective drug. Development encompasses all of the formulation, toxicology and clinical trial work necessary to meet stringent regulatory requirements for marketing approval.

During all of these phases 'attrition' occurs, as promising agents fail particular hurdles, so most R&D projects never result in a marketed drug. Late-stage failures are particularly costly and not uncommon – in May 2012 Roche announced the failure of dalcetrapib, after an estimated investment of $800 million. Of those that reach the market, 80% fail to recoup their R&D investment. The cost of developing a new drug is estimated at over $1 billion. When the costs of all the projects that do not reach fruition are considered, it becomes clear that pharmaceutical R&D is a very high-stakes game.

Given the enormous risks and considerable investment involved, it is not surprising that pharmaceutical companies compete fiercely to establish and retain *intellectual property* rights. Only by securing a patent that can be defended against imitators can the value of all this R&D be recouped.

The industry is subjected to rigorous regulatory scrutiny. Government agencies such as the *Food and Drug Administration* (FDA) in the USA thoroughly examine all of the data to support the purity, stability, safety, efficacy and tolerability of a new agent. The time taken is governed by legislation and typically averages 12 months. Obtaining marketing approval is no longer the end of the road in many countries, as further hurdles must be overcome in demonstrating the value of the new drug to justify price and/or reimbursement to cost-conscious payers.

Figure 1 **Creating new pharmaceuticals: it takes 10–15 years on average for an experimental drug to travel from the lab to patients.**

	Discovery/ preclinical testing		Clinical trials				FDA	Phase IV
			Phase I	Phase II	Phase III			
Years	6.5		1.5	2	3.5		1.5	
Test population	Laboratory and animal studies	File IND at FDA	20 to 100 healthy volunteers	100 to 500 patient volunteers	1,000 to 5,000 patient volunteers	File NDA/BLA at FDA	Review process/ approval	Additional post-marketing testing required by FDA
Purpose	Assess safety, biological activity and formulations		Determine safety and dosage	Evaluate effectiveness, look for side effects	Confirm effectiveness, monitor adverse reactions from long-term use			
Success rate	5,000 compounds evaluated		5 enter trials				1 approved	

Source: PhRMA, Medicines in Development – Biotechnology – 2006 Report, p. 51

In response to these pressures, payers used a variety of methods to control pharmaceutical spending (see Table 1). Some put the emphasis on the manufacturer and distributor, others on the prescriber and patient. Controls were designed to reward genuine advances – price and/or reimbursement levels were based on perceived innovation and superior effectiveness.

In countries with supply-side controls, negotiating price or reimbursement could take up to a year. In those with demand-side controls, market penetration was delayed

Table 1 **Methods used to control pharmaceutical spending**

Controls on suppliers	Mixed effect	Controls to influence demand
Negotiated prices Average pricing Reference pricing Positive and negative lists Constraints on wholesalers and pharmacists Imposed price cuts Pay for performance	Partial reimbursement at price negotiated with manufacturer Generic substitution	Patient co-payments Treatment guidelines Indicative or fixed budgets Incentives to prescribe or dispense generics or parallel imports Transfer from prescription-only to OTC e-prescribing tools

while negotiating with bodies such as the *National Institute for Clinical Excellence* (NICE) in the UK. NICE typified a general trend towards *evidence-based medicine*, where payers expected objective evidence of effectiveness to justify funding new therapies. The impact of NICE decisions reverberated beyond the UK, as countries collaborated internationally on value assessments. Where new drugs were approved for funding, this was increasingly in the context of formal patient selection and treatment guidelines, so their use was carefully controlled and individual prescribers had limited decision-making power.

Switching to generics is one way to cut drug expenditure. Countries experimented with 'e-prescribing' where physicians were presented with recommended options. Payers were increasingly effective in establishing generic drugs as first-line treatment for chronic diseases such as osteoporosis, asthma and depression, with patented drugs only used if generics failed. In volume terms, generic drugs were growing and patented drugs were in decline – so sales growth for patented drugs relied on securing ever higher prices for innovation.

The industry adopted a number of strategic responses to these challenges. *Pharmacoeconomic evaluations* were conducted to demonstrate the added value offered by a new drug from improved efficacy, safety, tolerability or ease of use. For example, a study of the cost of diabetes – the fastest-growing chronic disease in the world – found that 60% was driven by hospitalisations, which could often be avoided by correct outpatient use of medicines. Companies introduced *disease management initiatives*, which focused on the goals of the healthcare system for a specific disease. Firms then offered a broad-based service to improve disease outcomes, positioning products as part of the solution. A later innovation was the 'pay for performance' deal; for example, UK reimbursement of the cancer drug Velcade was linked to disease response. Payers valued 'real-world evidence': that is how drugs performed in real populations rather than the artificial populations studied in trials.

One challenge in demonstrating real-world drug performance was that counterfeit products were a real and growing problem, putting patient safety and lives at risk. In

one case, vials of the cancer medicine Avastin were found to contain no active ingredients. Seizures at EU borders increased from just over 500,000 articles in 2005 to over 4 million by 2007. The illicit trade exploded and global sales were estimated at over $100 billion by 2010. Drug manufacturers and distributors were forced to invest in countermeasures, such as traceability and authentication technologies.

Government price controls created another challenge for the industry in the form of 'parallel trade'. The principle of free movement of goods across the Single European Market meant that distributors were free to source drugs in low-price markets and ship them to high-price markets, pocketing the difference. EU parallel trade in pharmaceuticals was estimated at €5.1 billion by 2010, with the highest penetration in Denmark where it accounted for 24.3% of pharmacy sales.[4]

Industry sectors

Prescription-only or *ethical* drugs contribute about 85% of the $955 billion global pharmaceutical market by value and 50% by volume. Ethical products divide into conventional pharmaceuticals and more complex *biopharmaceutical* agents and vaccines (see Box 2). The other 15% of the market comprises *over-the-counter* (OTC) medicines, which may be purchased without prescription. Both ethical and OTC medicines may be patented or *generic*.

The typical cost structure of ethical pharmaceutical companies comprises manufacturing of goods (25%), research and development (16–24%), administration (10%), and sales and marketing (25%). The key strategic capabilities of these companies are R&D and sales and marketing. Pressure on margins created an incentive to restructure manufacturing, rationalising and relocating production sites and outsourcing to *contract manufacturing organisations* (CMOs).

Manufacturing and distribution efficiency is key for generics manufacturers, whose operating margins are typically half those of ethical companies. In the 1990s, US generics prices collapsed, accompanied by a shakeout to determine cost leadership. The speed and aggression of

BOX 2 Biologics – the future or the past?

Biopharmaceuticals or 'biologics' are large molecules that behave like natural substances, such as proteins and monoclonal antibodies. The discovery and design of biologics entails optimising specificity and affinity, and making the molecules as close to human substances as possible to avoid provoking an immune response. Biologics are produced through large-scale fermentation in very costly plants. They are given by injection and used to treat specialist conditions such as cancer and rheumatoid arthritis. Biologics are much more specific in their action than small molecules; this avoids unexpected 'off target' side effects, and increases the success rate from Phase 1 to launch from 7% to 12%.[5] Because of their benefits and use in high unmet need diseases, biologics generally secure higher prices than small molecules.

Initially associated with biotechs, biologics became mainstream, contributing $157 billion in 2011, and are expected to provide seven of the top 10 brands by 2016. Companies that invested early benefited from this rapid growth. Others noted this success and many acquired biologics capabilities. In his first press conference as CEO in October 2012, Pascal Soriot said he had been looking at AstraZeneca's biologics portfolio 'very closely' and saw a number of products that could have 'nice potential'.

In addition to lower attrition and superior pricing, biologics are at far less risk from generic threat. The sophisticated capabilities required to develop and manufacture a complex *biosimilar* product take substantial investment. Furthermore, regulators were slow to clarify requirements for approval. However, top generics companies clearly saw the potential. Sandoz led the way with human growth hormone and erythropoietin in the EU. The lure of stealing sales from blockbuster biologics attracted non-traditional players into the field, such as Celltrion and Samsung from South Korea. Even so, serious biosimilar competition was not expected before 2015 and due to the investment involved was likely to drive more gradual price erosion than small-molecule generics.

---

generic attacks on branded products increased sharply. Economies of scale, including finance to support complex patent disputes, proved decisive and the sector consolidated. Given the number of *blockbusters* facing patent expiry and markets with still untapped potential (e.g. Italy, Spain, France and Japan), not surprisingly growth in generics outstripped the overall market. In sharp contrast to stagnating branded medicines, the global market for generics was projected to increase from $242 billion in 2011 to over $400 billion by 2016.

A new type of industry player appeared in the 1980s – small biotechnology start-ups backed by venture capital to exploit the opportunities created by molecular biology and genetic engineering. Initially, *biotechs* were associated with biologics (see Box 2). Biotechs now pursue a huge variety of core capabilities, creating a global, extraordinarily diverse and innovative sector. Because of the long product development cycle, most biotechs take years to reach profitability, if at all, and revenues are concentrated in a tiny subgroup of highly profitable firms. The global credit squeeze had a dramatic effect on the sector from 2008: biotech IPOs became very rare, and access to venture and debt funding dried up. To conserve cash, companies restructured to cut jobs and programmes, and made deals with cash-rich pharma companies. Seeing little return on decades of investment, venture capital focused on new areas and new funding halved. Creative business models were needed to keep biotechs afloat. Companies sought support from charitable foundations, venture philanthropists and governments. The corporate venture funds of *big pharma* companies became an important source of start-up funding.

Over-the-counter (OTC) medicines are bought by consumers without a prescription. The global OTC market was estimated at $127 billion in 2010 with the top 10 manufacturers accounting for more than half of volume. Consumer brand loyalty provides defence against generic competition and prolongs the product life cycle. Consistently outperforming the ethical sector globally, OTC sales were boosted by innovation, promotion of self-medication and expansion of distribution channels. Sales accelerated in emerging markets, providing global players with a rare source of growth and a quick way to gain presence in these key markets. Consumer marketing skills were key, especially with new competition from companies such as Danone and Nestlé who were capitalising on growing consumer interest in personal well-being by making health claims for so-called *nutraceuticals*.

Another important category of medicine is vaccines, which has re-emerged as a key revenue generator. Prophylactic vaccines often provide lifelong protection

BOX 3 US dominance under threat?

A number of factors have contributed to industry globalisation. Chief is the international convergence of medical science and practice under the influence of modern communications technology and increased travel and information exchange. Well-funded US universities and hospitals generally lead their fields, while US scientific congresses provide the most prestigious platforms for new discoveries.

Leading corporations have globalised, and are present in all significant markets. Production sites have a global mandate and are selected by worldwide screening. R&D is sourced from the best place worldwide, which often means the USA. Strong US market growth gave US companies a springboard in achieving global ambitions, and in 2011 they occupied five of the top 10 slots (see Table 2 below).

Biotechnology companies are 'born global' – from their inception they draw upon a global pool of collaborators and investors, rather than growing from small domestic beginnings. Once again the USA dominates – publicly traded biotechs employ over four times more people in the USA than in the EU, with a similar ratio for R&D spend. US biotechs still secure the majority of venture capital investment.

In the longer term, US pre-eminence in biomedical research may be under threat from Asia. Global companies opened more R&D sites in Asia, while closing them in the USA and EU. The Chinese government declared its intention to become a leader in the field and poured money into new universities and science parks. The number of Chinese graduates in natural sciences overtook those from the USA in 2004, and continues on a sharp growth trajectory. Routine chemistry and toxicology were already often outsourced to China, but as US returnees sought more innovative projects this began to extend up the value chain. India accounted for about 30% of global generics, but had similar ambitions to become a major source of R&D and was an important location for cost-effective clinical trials.

against serious diseases, preventing at least 3 million deaths annually worldwide and saving an estimated $7–$20 healthcare dollars for every dollar spent on vaccines. This nearly $30 billion market is highly concentrated – just five global players account for nearly 80% of market share. Their vaccine sales more than doubled between 2006 and 2011 as they launched high-priced vaccines for new applications such as human papilloma virus (HPV). Entry barriers are high, with specialised skills required in manufacturing, conducting large and complex clinical trials and managing surveillance programmes. Vaccines have higher development success rates and lower risk of generic entry than conventional medicines, and offer blockbuster sales potential. Novartis, AstraZeneca and Pfizer all entered the sector through acquisitions in 2006–9.

Key markets

The majority of global pharmaceutical sales originate in the USA, Japan, the EU, China and Brazil, with 10 key countries contributing over 80% of the global market. Pharmaceutical market growth is strongly aligned with GDP growth. The USA is by far the largest market by volume and value – $347 billion in 2011, over a third of global sales. Historically the fastest-growing key market, US growth collapsed in 2010, the consequence of patent expires, fewer new products and reduced consumer demand. Nevertheless, the USA remained

critical to success – for *new chemical entities* (NCEs) launched during 2006–10, nearly 60% of sales were from the USA, compared with less than 25% from the EU (see Box 3).

Following regulatory changes in 1997, *direct-to-consumer* (DTC) advertising transformed the US marketplace and fuelled growth. However, companies' costs for providing healthcare benefits to employees were increasing, exceeding $12,000 on average in 2012, with employees contributing a further $8500 per head.[6] *Managed care organisations* (MCOs) asked consumers for increasing co-payment and implemented other cost-control measures. Medicare reforms extended drug coverage for the elderly, but gave the government new pricing leverage as the largest direct purchaser of medicines. These pressures constrained expected annual growth to no more than 1–4% from 2012 to 2016. Uncertainty remained around the impact of the Patient Protection and Affordable Care Act (March 2010), which had the potential to extend healthcare coverage to all Americans.

Japan has the second-largest market for pharmaceuticals, with sales of $111 billion in 2011. The Japanese operating environment was historically very different from those of the USA and EU. This divergence occurred at all levels, from medical practice, regulatory requirements and the lack of generics, to distribution and the accepted approach to sales and marketing. Not surprisingly, domestic companies dominate the market. Economic recession caused tax revenues to fall, while the cost of treating the world's most rapidly ageing population rose. This resulted in changes to healthcare funding, regular price cuts and the introduction of stringent price controls, limiting annual market growth to an average below 4% from 2007 to 2011, with contraction predicted from 2012 to 2017.

The European pharmaceutical market, which contributed 28% of global sales in 2011, was highly fragmented and driven by governments' forever-changing cost containment plans, resulting in a lack of predictability for companies' operational planning. The UK market fell from fifth position to tenth between 2006 and 2011, illustrating the strong impact of NICE decisions on reimbursement and access. European market growth was expected to fall to between 0% and 3% from 2012 to 2016. Securing cash flow was another key issue in the struggling economies of Southern Europe – at the end of 2011, the industry was owed €12.5 billion by just four EU countries.[7]

For industry players to maintain growth they had to either capture a disproportionate share of established markets, or focus on accessing those still in their growth phase. In contrast to the stagnant developed markets, the regions of Africa, Australasia and Latin America were predicted to grow at 10–13% per year between 2012 and 2016. Thanks to their growth, these regions constituted an ever larger share of the global market, making up nearly a quarter by 2011. With its growing GDP and huge population, China alone was expected to contribute nearly 30% of global market growth in 2016 and to become the third-largest market globally. One of the few bright spots in AstraZeneca's Q3 2012 results was 23% growth in China and Russia.

IMS Health identified a diverse group of 17 'pharmerging' markets (e.g. Brazil, Russia, India, China, Mexico and Indonesia). In addition to the high-net-worth individuals who could afford the most innovative treatments, their middle-class populations were growing more rapidly than at any time in history. The key challenge was to adapt to these countries' varied needs and environments, and to recognise the distinct opportunities offered by large cities. Some companies built their strategy on premium-priced generics, offering the reassurance of a known brand and a reliable manufacturer, so-called *branded generics*. However, this approach was highly vulnerable to local generic competition and reference pricing reforms. Other companies expanded access to innovative medicines through tiered pricing. For example, Gilead's Access Programme provided its HIV medicines at steep discounts in 132 countries.

Innovation

Pharmaceutical companies' key contribution to medical progress is the ability to turn fundamental research findings into proven innovative treatments that are widely available and accessible.[8] Companies with consistently high levels of R&D spending and productivity became industry leaders. For this reason, stock market valuations place importance on the R&D *pipeline* (i.e. the products in development) as well as on the marketed products. When Pascal Soriot took over at AstraZeneca, the company was trading at the lowest multiple among big pharmaceutical companies.

The holy grail of pharmaceutical R&D used to be the *blockbuster*. Blockbuster drugs were genuine advances that achieved rapid, deep market penetration. Because of their superlative market performance, blockbusters determined the fortunes of individual companies. Glaxo went from being a small player to a top global company on the strength of a single drug – Zantac for stomach ulcers. A blockbuster was typically a long-term therapy for a common disease that offered a step change in efficacy or tolerability, marketed globally with annual sales exceeding $1 billion.

While blockbusters made immense contributions to company fortunes, they were few and far between. Andrew Witty, the CEO of GlaxoSmithKline, likened the hunt to 'finding a needle in a haystack right when you need it'. Focusing on blockbusters exposed an already high-stakes industry to even greater levels of risk. This was dramatically brought home in September 2004 when the cardiovascular safety risks of Vioxx emerged, and Merck withdrew the brand from the market. Merck lost $2.5 billion in sales, a quarter of its stock market value, and faced the prospect of numerous liability suits. Blockbusters exacerbate the impact of patent expiries, creating the so-called 'patent cliff'. The top 10 companies were projected to lose over $100 billion in sales from 2013 to 2018 due to generic erosion, with nearly $20 billion to be borne by Pfizer alone. Witty argued that the industry must move from being 'blockbuster dependent' to 'blockbuster capable' – that is, able to develop and commercialise blockbusters, but also efficient at developing and commercialising a steady stream of drugs in the $50–$500 million range.

Unfortunately, R&D productivity was in decline and development times were lengthening. The number of trials and the number of patients required for each new drug application increased enormously. The average cost to develop a new drug exceeded $1 billion and had grown at double the rate of inflation for 20 years. Despite increasing R&D spend from 11% of annual sales to 20% or more, the industry was struggling to replace the value lost through patent expiries. Attrition increased as companies put higher hurdles in place to address payer needs for meaningful clinical benefit and the demands of safety-conscious regulators. Employing thousands of in-house scientists to develop drug candidates from scratch had turned into a billion-dollar gamble that simply was not delivering. Bernard Munos of InnoThink argued that by 2014 there would be 'an implosion of the old model'.[9] Pfizer alone announced $1.5 billion in R&D cuts in 2011.

Companies endeavoured to become both creative and efficient. They narrowed their areas of therapeutic focus, and invested in alliances with academic institutions, seeking depth of expertise. Strategic outsourcing to *contract research organisations* (CROs) reduced fixed costs and leveraged lower cost geographies. Lilly created a special unit to conduct small clinical tests to quickly and cheaply shake out molecules that were not going to make it. Recognising that biopharmaceuticals had a lower attrition rate, companies acquired biologics capabilities. Some reorganised their R&D to create smaller and more nimble units – GlaxoSmithKline's research centres competed for funding like internal biotechs. All sought external innovation through licensing deals and acquisitions, although with few real jewels available the cost of deals spiralled.

To better manage some of the tremendous risks involved, companies moved towards a more network-based approach to innovation. For diseases that were just too tough to tackle alone, 'pre-competitive' collaboration allowed costs and insights to be shared. Companies, foundations and regulators working on Alzheimer's disease pooled data and resources to create a shared understanding of the disease and how best to monitor it. Where large, long-term studies were needed to gain approval, companies began to pool assets, moving only the best forward. In diabetes, AstraZeneca and BMS paired up to develop drugs together, sharing cost, risk and reward, as did Lilly and Boehringer Ingelheim in 2011.

In making the move from Roche to AstraZeneca, some commentators believed Pascal Soriot was moving from a company driven by science to one driven by process. He declared his intent: 'my priority is to restore the Company to growth and scientific leadership . . . our core is innovation. It's clear and will remain so.'

Sales and marketing

In the blockbuster era, sales and marketing capability was important to competitive advantage. A company that developed a strong global franchise with its customers could maximise return on its products and was in a good position to attract the best in-licensing candidates.

The traditional focus of drug marketing was the personal *detail* in which a sales representative ('rep') discussed the merits of a drug in a face-to-face meeting with a doctor and provided free samples. Promotion was subject to industry self-regulation. For example, in the UK, reps had to pass an examination testing medical knowledge. In some countries, government regulatory agencies checked that promotional claims were consistent with the data.

There were important differences in the marketing of 'primary care' and 'specialist' products. Office-based practitioners generally prescribed primary care products, whereas treatment with specialist products was typically initiated in hospitals. Sales volume, marketing spend and skills required differed for the two segments. Product-led muscle marketing was key in the primary care sector, while specialist products involved more cost-effective targeted relationship marketing.

The term 'high compression marketing' was coined to describe global launches of primary care brands. This involved near-simultaneous worldwide launches, global branding, and heavy investment in promotion. The aim was to create a rapid take-off curve that maximised return by creating higher peak year sales earlier in the product life cycle. A typical example was the launch of Celebrex in 1999, which netted $1 billion sales in the first nine months. In the USA an important marketing tool was *direct-to-consumer* (DTC) advertising, in which spending peaked at $5.4 billion in 2006. DTC was costly because of the vast target audience and expensive television advertising, but profitable. Well-informed patients asked for drugs by brand name, creating a powerful 'pull' strategy.

Sales-force size was historically a key competitive attribute. However, as blockbusters dried up, sales-force productivity declined sharply. Over 500,000 sales reps were made redundant between 2006 and 2008, while use of contract sales forces and digital channels increased. The primary care marketing model became more complex and multi-layered, with slimmed down resources focused on demonstrating value to key gatekeepers.

As pipelines shifted to high unmet need diseases treated by specialists, the era of lavish launches and massive sales forces was over. Selling became a more complex process with multiple stakeholders interested in cost-effectiveness as well as clinical arguments, requiring new skills. In a watershed moment in 2011, Vertex challenged much larger Merck in the hepatitis C market, pitting its protease inhibitor Incivek head to head against Merck's Victrelis. Vertex emerged the clear victor, signalling that size was no longer a critical advantage. In fact, the fastest-growing companies were expected to be speciality players such as Gilead, Celgene, Vertex and Biogen Idec.

Sales and marketing could still provide sustainable competitive advantage. A few companies built strategies around specific customer groups, aiming to satisfy their needs on multiple dimensions. In other words, they developed a franchise. The broad-based approach of Baxter in renal dialysis and Novo Nordisk in diabetes care, utilising a web of alliances to address multiple customer needs, made them formidable competitors. These companies did not rely on R&D innovation and were thus less vulnerable to generic competition.

Corporate social responsibility

During the twentieth century, average life expectancy in developed countries increased by over 20 years. Much of this improvement can be attributed to pharmaceutical innovation. Few other industries have done as much for the well-being of humankind. Furthermore, at a global level the industry has the highest ratio of R&D to net sales, funds nearly a fifth of all industrial R&D investment, and makes a significant contribution to skilled employment.[10] So how did an industry that has delivered these benefits acquire such a tarnished image and become an easy target for government intervention?

Pharmaceuticals have characteristics of 'public goods' – that is, expensive to produce but inexpensive to reproduce. The manufacturing cost of drugs is often tiny compared with the cost of R&D that led to the discovery. Setting prices that attempt to recoup R&D therefore looks like corporate greed in comparison with the very low prices that can be charged for generics.

Some companies damaged the industry's overall reputation. In July 2012, GSK paid $3 billion in the largest healthcare fraud settlement in US history. The drug giant pleaded guilty to promoting two drugs for unapproved uses. The Deputy US Attorney General declared the settlement 'unprecedented in both size and scope'. Even more seriously, companies were accused of putting profits before patient safety. After the withdrawal of Vioxx, Merck was accused of ignoring problems during product development, and publishing misleading scientific results. As a consequence, the FDA was empowered to demand Risk Evaluation and Mitigation Strategies (REMS) – costly additional programmes to monitor and ensure drug safety after product approval. By the end of 2008, one-third of new drug approvals involved REMS.

The industry also faced condemnation of its response to the enormous unmet need in developing countries. Although effective drugs and vaccines existed for many diseases affecting millions, often their cost was beyond the means of the people who needed them. It was argued that companies could reallocate R&D efforts in favour of tropical diseases, sell low-priced essential drugs and provide technology transfer. In response, most global players donated medicines for neglected diseases, and a few went further, for example making molecules and patents freely available to researchers.

Industry mergers and acquisitions

The pharmaceutical market remains relatively fragmented, with very large numbers of domestic and regional players. However, it has consolidated at the global level, with the top 10 companies holding 43% of the market in 2011. Even so, total market capitalisation of the top 10 players was actually lower in 2012 than in 2001. Table 2 shows how the industry response to slowing revenues and declining productivity was a wave of mergers and acquisitions. Mergers resulted in the formation of Novartis, Sanofi, AstraZeneca and GlaxoSmithKline, while Pfizer acquired Warner-Lambert, Pharmacia and Wyeth. Even Merck, which had doggedly followed an organic growth strategy, announced a merger with Schering-Plough in March 2009. A striking development was the appearance of Teva (see case study – text and cases edition only) on the leader board – a company that built its success on generics.

Table 2 Leading global pharmaceutical companies, 2008 and 2011

2008		2011			
Company	Total sales ($bn)	Company	Total sales ($bn)	Share of global market	Sales growth (2010 to 2011)
Pfizer[1, 3] (US)	43.4	Pfizer[6] (US)	56.4	6.6%	−0.7%
GlaxoSmithKline[2] (UK)	36.5	Novartis (CH)	51.6	6.0%	10.0%
Novartis (CH)	36.2	Merck & Co.[5] (US)	40.1	4.7%	6.9%
Sanofi-Aventis[4] (Fr)	35.6	Sanofi (Fr)	39.5	4.6%	2.6%
AstraZeneca (UK)	32.5	AstraZeneca (UK)	37.0	4.3%	3.1%
Roche (CH)	30.3	Roche (CH)	34.9	4.1%	5.8%
Johnson & Johnson (US)	29.4	GlaxoSmithKline (UK)	34.5	4.0%	1.5%
Merck & Co. (US)	26.2	Johnson & Johnson (US)	27.7	3.2%	0%
Abbott (US)	19.5	Abbott (US)	25.9	3.0%	6.6%
Lilly (US)	19.1	Teva (Israel)	23.9	2.8%	−2.4%

Notes

Ref.	Created	Originating companies	
1	2000	Warner-Lambert (US)	Pfizer (US)
2	2000	Glaxo Wellcome (UK)	SmithKline Beecham (UK)
3	2003	Pfizer (US)	Pharmacia (US)
4	2004	Sanofi (France)	Aventis (France)
5	2009	Merck (US)	Schering-Plough (US)
6	2009	Pfizer (US)	Wyeth (US)

One rationale for M&A was to combine a company with a strong pipeline but weak sales and marketing with its converse. The acquisition of Warner-Lambert gave Pfizer full marketing rights to Lipitor, which Pfizer then built into the world's best-selling drug. Another motive was to acquire global commercial reach. The acquisition of Nycomed in May 2011 transformed Takeda from a Japanese player with limited geographic reach to a global company. Mergers were also motivated by falling revenue and the attraction of eliminating duplicated costs. Within a month of merging with Wyeth in October 2009, Pfizer announced a 35% reduction in R&D square footage with six site closures.

Turning necessity into opportunity, companies seized the chance to access growth segments. In February 2011, Sanofi acquired Genzyme, the leading player in rare disease, one of pharma's few growth segments. Sanofi also acquired Medley, the third-largest pharmaceutical company in Brazil, in 2009, and merged with the Chinese company BMP Sunstone in 2011. Other industry acquisitions have increased presence in vaccines, biologics, consumer health and generics.

As the *initial public offering* (IPO) market for biotechs dwindled, venture capitalists turned to M&A as the best way to recover the cash they had invested, and the number of biotech acquisitions rose sharply. Biotechs with exciting assets could command remarkable prices, as desperate big pharmas, Japanese companies seeking to globalise and newly rich speciality players all entered the fray. Public biotechs became targets too: Gilead paid $11 billion for Pharmasset in November 2011. Gilead was the world leader in combination therapies for HIV and saw the opportunity to repeat this success in hepatitis C.

Where next?

At the start of 2013, global pharmaceutical companies were pursuing a wider variety of strategies than in 2001, with greater emphasis on diversification. Six of the top 10 had acquired vaccine businesses, and the same number had made belated moves into biopharmaceuticals. Seven were well positioned to benefit from the growth in generics – but was this the right focus for a high-margin, innovation-based industry? Seven companies retained animal health businesses, while some players emphasised consumer health. Most had expanded their presence in emerging markets.

An intriguing response to environmental change was pioneered by Roche, which positioned itself as operating a 'personalised healthcare' business model. Roche was the global leader in diagnostics and its strategy was to offer value through targeting treatments to patients that would benefit most. This concept appealed to regulators and payers, who endorsed the linkage of high-priced cancer drugs such as Zelboraf for melanoma with diagnostic tests to identify suitable patients. Investing in discovery and development of tests added further to cost and complexity, but offered the chance to reduce attrition, build unique competences and secure rapid market uptake. Most of the early Roche portfolio was being developed with *companion diagnostics*. Others such as Pfizer followed, and four of the top 10 acquired diagnostics businesses.

A related but more embryonic field was healthcare information technology. Other sectors were able to analyse huge data sets to generate and exploit highly personalised consumer insights, but the pharmaceutical industry was slow to harness the power of 'big data'. Electronic health records offered an opportunity to detect patterns and gain new insights. However, there were huge challenges: even simple tests were not standardised between hospitals, and there were low adoption rates and poor interoperability of medical records systems. Nevertheless, visionary players were starting to tackle these problems, with Google and IBM viewing healthcare as a key growth opportunity. Information technology enabled and empowered patients to participate in healthcare innovation. In a groundbreaking example, *Nature Biotechnology* reported on a clinical trial set up and conducted by patients themselves.[11]

Summary

The industry is facing its toughest outlook yet with both big pharma and biotech sectors starting to shrink. The industry has made a tremendous contribution to human well-being, yet is vilified in the media and targeted by governments in their efforts to curb spiralling healthcare costs. R&D costs have risen sharply, but productivity is down and the product life cycle shortened. Product approval, pricing/reimbursement and promotion are subject to increasingly onerous regulation, yet free trade allows wholesalers to extract a large chunk from the value chain. Exciting opportunities remain – large emerging markets, ageing populations, scientific advances, personalised healthcare, more educated consumers, information technology and, of course, unmet medical need. However, the blockbuster paradigm has failed and industry consolidation has driven the need to cut costs to survive. Speciality players seem better placed to succeed in the new networked environment than the old giants. The industry more than ever needs to get a handle on the slippery business of scientific creativity and provide its critics with evidence of its value by offering a true step change in outcomes for patients.

Notes and references
1. http://www.businessinsider.com/pascal-soriot-joins-astrazeneca-2012-8#ixzz295p7YOA4
2. $1 = £0.65 = €0.77.
3. *Income, Poverty, and Health Insurance Coverage in the United States: 2011*, US Census Bureau, September 2012.
4. *The Pharmaceutical Industry in Facts & Figures 2012*, EFPIA.

5. *Nature Reviews Drug Discovery*, **8**, 609–10 (2009).
6. www.insurancejournal.com/news/national/2012/05/15/247598.htm
7. *EFPIA Annual Report 2011*.
8. 'The truth about drug innovation: Thirty-five summary case histories on private sector contributions to pharmaceutical science', Manhattan Institute for Policy Research, June 2008, http://www.manhattan-institute.org/html/mpr_06.htm
9. *Nature*, **471**, 17–18 (2011), doi:10.1038/471017a.
10. *The 2011 EU Industrial R&D Investment Scoreboard*, Joint Research Centre, Directorate General Research & Innovation, European Commission.
11. 'Accelerated clinical discovery using self-reported patient data collected online and a patient-matching algorithm', *Nature Biotechnology*, **29**, 411–14 (2011).

APPENDIX: GLOSSARY

big pharma A group term for large globalised pharmaceutical companies.

biologic, or biopharmaceutical Large molecules that behave like natural substances, such as therapeutic proteins and monoclonal antibodies.

biosimilar Molecules designed to mimic the therapeutic effects of an original biologic agent – similar in molecular structure but not identical.

biotech Shorthand for biotechnology; biotech companies typically discover and develop products, which may be diagnostics, therapeutics or vaccines. However, some biotechs simply provide services to other companies.

blockbuster A drug that is marketed globally and has annual sales exceeding $1 billion.

branded generics Original brands that have lost patent protection and are priced similarly to identical generic medicines, but offer the reassurance that they are produced by an established manufacturer.

companion diagnostic A diagnostic product to be used alongside a drug, to identify patients that are either best suited, or not suited, to receive the therapy.

contract manufacturing organisation (CMO) A service organisation that undertakes manufacturing activities on behalf of a pharma or biotech company, thus avoiding the need for capital investment in manufacturing plants.

contract research organisation (CRO) A service organisation that undertakes laboratory or clinical research activities on behalf of a pharma or biotech company; this has evolved from a project-based model to more strategic relationships.

detail/detailing Detailing refers to a sales call in which a pharmaceutical sales representative ('rep') discusses the merits of a drug in a face-to-face meeting with a doctor and may provide free samples.

direct-to-consumer (DTC) DTC advertising involves communication of promotional messages directly to consumers via print, radio, television and the internet.

disease management initiatives These involve understanding the goals of the healthcare system in addressing a specific disease. The firm then aligns itself with the healthcare providers, to offer an integrated service that improves eventual disease outcomes, positioning its products as one part of the solution.

ethical Ethical medicines can only be obtained with a prescription from a qualified medical practitioner.

evidence-based medicine Basing medical decisions, and decisions to fund therapy, on objective evidence of effectiveness.

Food and Drug Administration (FDA) The FDA is responsible for approving drugs for marketing in the USA and regulating the US pharmaceutical market.

generic medicine A medicine that contains exactly the same active ingredients as the original brand, but is typically launched at less than 60% of the price. Generics manufacturers cannot use the original manufacturer's brand name. Drugs are known by both a brand and a 'generic' name: for example, Viagra is a Pfizer brand name; the generic name is 'sildenafil'. Generic names refer to the active ingredients and are independent of manufacturer.

initial public offering (IPO) Launch of a company on the stock market.

intellectual property Proprietary knowledge that can be defended against imitation using patent law.

managed care organisation (MCO) MCOs operate within the US healthcare market and act as an interface between patients and healthcare providers such as hospitals. MCOs provide defined healthcare benefits for client populations in return for regular premiums, which may be paid by individuals or their employers.

market exclusivity Period during which a first-in-class drug is the only product of its type on the market and faces no class competition.

National Institute for Clinical Effectiveness (NICE) A government-funded organisation in the UK that aims to provide evidence-based guidelines on the optimal and most cost-effective use of drugs and other medical interventions.

new chemical entity (NCE) A completely new molecule launched as a medical treatment for the first time.

nutraceutical A nutrition (food) product for which health benefits are claimed.

over-the-counter (OTC) medicines OTC medicines can be purchased by consumers without a prescription.

patient co-payments Payments where the patient pays some of the drug cost.

pharmacoeconomic evaluation A demonstration of the added value offered by a new drug from improved efficacy, safety, tolerability or ease of use.

pipeline Drugs that are in development but have not yet reached the market.

CASE STUDY

Vodafone: developing communications strategy in the UK market

Roger Strang

In 2012, Vodafone, the world's second-largest mobile telephone operator by revenue, was under increasing pressure to develop a strategy to ensure leadership in the rapidly growing market for high-speed internet services in its UK home market. The challenge for Vodaphone was that the development of new technologies for voice, data and video transmission was blurring the boundaries among traditional industries and forcing reconsideration of what services were required to be a leader in the communications industry of the future.

●　●　●

This growth in demand for internet services had attracted the interest not only of Vodafone's traditional competitors in the mobile telephone industry, but from other communications companies such as BT (the largest provider of fixed-line telephones), Virgin Media (the largest cable TV operator in the UK) and Sky Broadcasting, which was the UK's largest provider of satellite-based television. Other new competitors included a spin-off from the largest UK retailer of mobile handsets, TalkTalk, and traditional suppliers such as Apple, Nokia and Google which had been investing heavily in digital content as well as hardware and software.

In addition to changes in competition, Vodafone and other operators faced rapid changes in technology with the growth of IP (Internet Protocol) allowing voice, data and video to be digitised for high-speed distribution over multiple networks, the emergence of new broadcasting technologies such as Wi-MAX (extended Wi-Fi), and the continued upgrading of speeds over fixed and mobile networks. The rapid adoption of smartphones and tablet computers also increased demand for mobile internet services. The UK had switched to digital television, and operators were offering services such as 'on-demand' viewing and digital video recording, which were challenging traditional business models.

There had also been significant regulatory changes in the UK communications industry, which had been a global leader in opening up communications markets to competition across the full range of services. These changes included privatising the national telephone company, BT,

Source: Alamy Images/Rob Wilkinson

and forcing it to allow access to its network at competitive rates; allowing 'virtual' mobile operators', or MVNOs, which could lease network capacity without the capital cost of building their own; and supporting competition in television and internet services. Ofcom ('Office of Communications') was the UK regulator charged with ensuring competition and delivery of basic services. Consumers had benefited greatly from these technological and regulatory changes, with real costs of communication falling by 40% between 2003 and 2011 and rapid growth in the number of competitors as well as the range and quality of hardware and services provided.

In the light of these technical and regulatory changes, many of the competitors in the market were building their strategies around a perceived consumer need for 'converged' services. This meant providing multiple services ranging up to the 'quad play' (fixed-line telephony, mobile telephony, television and broadband internet) offered initially by Virgin Media and more recently by other providers.

In 2012, most of the companies offered at least three of these services (a 'triple play') which varied depending on the nature of their networks and their willingness to invest or form partnerships. Vodafone was unique among major operators in focusing largely on mobile services, and this was a concern to both shareholders and managers within the company. Management's challenge was to decide whether they should add fixed-line-based services and, if so, whether the services should be provided by their own networks (built or acquired) or through partnerships.

The UK market

In early 2012 the UK was slowly recovering from the global financial crisis, with GDP growth less than 1% for the year, rising to 3% by 2015. This crisis had begun to have a devastating impact in 2008 and the UK government, like those in most developed countries, invested heavily to save the large banks, protect depositors and stimulate economic activity. The Conservative-led coalition government had implemented an austerity programme to reduce the level of public borrowing but, as in much of Europe, the economic recovery had been slow and there was widespread concern that the country would be hit by a further recession.

The longer-term outlook was more positive. Immigration and increasing birth rates meant that the population (62 million) was expected to grow by 4% over the next five years. There was hope that the public spending constraints to reduce the debt would be offset by growing private sector activity. The 2012 Olympics were held later in the year in London and this stimulated some growth in investment and tourism. The UK was also partially insulated from the economic challenges of countries in the Eurozone, so had more freedom to adopt growth policies.

Fixed-line telephone

The UK fixed-line telephone market was declining, although at a slower rate than in other European countries. Ofcom reported that the number of lines had dropped from 34.9 million in 2003 to 33 million in 2011 (see Table 1). Call minutes on fixed lines had decreased by 15% from 167 billion to 138 billion over the same period. By 2012 only 48% of UK voice minutes originated from fixed-line phones, down from 55% in 2009. Trends in revenue from voice and other services are given in Table 2. Ofcom research found that 15% of UK households were 'mobile only' in early 2012, compared to the EU average of 26%.

As in most countries, the UK fixed-line network had been developed by the government, which subsequently privatised the service as British Telecom or BT. In order to encourage competition, the regulator required BT to offer other operators wholesale service through its network at competitive terms. This eventually forced BT to set up a separate division, 'Openreach', to provide network voice and internet services to other operators as well as to other

Table 1 UK connections and trends

	(millions)		
	2009	2010	2011
Fixed lines (total)	33.5	33.4	33.2
Fixed broadband	17.8	19.1	20.4
Mobile active subscriptions	80.3	81.2	81.6
Mobile broadband	4.1	4.8	5.1

Source: Ofcom, *Media Report 2012*, © Ofcom copyright 2012

Table 2 UK communications industry: revenues and trends

	(£bn)		
	2009	2010	2011
FIXED LINE			
Voice	9.7	9.4	8.9
Data (residential internet)	3.3	3.4	3.4
Corporate data services	3.3	3.3	3.6
Total	16.3	16.1	15.9
MOBILE			
Voice	10.9	10.6	10.6
Messaging	2.6	2.6	2.5
Data	1.5	1.7	2.0
Total	15.0	14.9	15.1
TELEVISION			
Subscriptions	4.6	4.8	5.2
Advertising	3.1	3.5	3.6
Licence fee	2.7	2.7	2.7
Other (sponsorships, shopping, etc.)	0.7	0.7	0.8
Total	11.1	11.7	12.3

Sources: Ofcom, *Media Report 2012*, © Ofcom copyright 2012

divisions of BT. Ofcom went further and in 2002 introduced a process called Local Loop Unbundling (LLU), which required BT to allow other operators to install their own equipment in BT local exchanges to provide voice and internet services to their own customers. This meant that operators could provide these services without the cost of building and maintaining connections to every household.

After further price cuts and operating changes were imposed on BT in 2004 and 2005, LLU became an attractive option for other operators, which rapidly expanded their services. Operators using LLU have significant upfront costs for buying and installing network equipment, but after that they have low monthly line rental charges which were set by Ofcom. Growth was further encouraged in 2008 when BT announced a £2.5bn (€2.95bn; $3.79bn)[1] network upgrade using fibre optic cable to provide 'superfast' broadband. By late 2011, Fibre To The Cabinet (FTTC) had reached almost one-third of UK households. In that year other operators added 400,000 LLU lines for a total of 7.9 million connections compared with 6 million for BT (up 600,000).

The low incremental costs of providing voice services meant that many operators were able to provide bundles of fixed-line voice and broadband, including 'free' broadband with voice services. By the end of 2011 BT exchanges reaching 89% of the population had been unbundled and most UK consumers had a choice of fixed-line voice provider. The result was that in 2011, BT's share of fixed-line voice minutes fell to 36% with strong competition from Virgin Media, TalkTalk and Sky as well as some mobile operators. There was also limited but growing competition from voice calls using the internet from suppliers such as Vonage and Skype.

Mobile telephone

Ofcom reported that at the end of 2011 there were 81.6 million active mobile subscriptions in the UK, up only 400,000 from the previous year (Table 1). With a population of 62 million, this gave a penetration rate of over 130%, similar to those of other developed markets in Europe. Mobile revenues in 2011 were estimated at £15.1 billion, up 1% from 2010 as increasing demand for data offset decreases in voice demand and lower pricing. The year 2011 saw the first-ever year-to-year reduction in voice minutes, which Ofcom research suggested could be due to greater use of emails, messaging and social networks, all of which were growing rapidly. Average monthly revenue per subscriber (ARPU) was £15.40, continuing a slow but steady decline due to increasing price competition.

The slow growth and price competition had put pressure on operators' margins in what was the most competitive market in the developed world. All operators also faced the capital cost of building the next generation (4G) network

beginning in late 2012. In 2010 the third- and fourth-largest operators, Orange (France Télécom) and T-Mobile (Deutsche Telekom), merged to become the market leader with almost 40% share of traffic. In response, the second- and third-largest operators, O$_2$ (Telefonica) and Vodafone, concluded a network-sharing agreement to reduce their operating costs by jointly managing their network infrastructure. The smallest operator, '3', had entered the market with a network-sharing agreement with T-Mobile and this agreement became part of the merger.

In addition to the four major network operators there were more than 70 mobile virtual network operators (MVNOs) which leased network services and resold them under their own brand, thus avoiding the capital costs of setting up a network. MVNOs were an inexpensive way for fixed-line operators (e.g. Virgin, BT and TalkTalk) to provide mobile services or to capitalise on well-known brands (e.g. Tesco) or to reach special market segments (e.g. the Chinese population in the UK). The number and market share of MVNOs continued to grow, reaching an estimated 13% of subscribers at the end of 2011.

The large wireless operators purchase handsets under global contracts with the major suppliers and use discounting of handsets to attract new subscribers. Samsung had 26% of the UK handset market and had moved ahead of Nokia (23%) and Apple (10%), with new competitors from China growing at the low end of the market. In recent years operators have been able to negotiate with suppliers to introduce their own branded handsets. Mobile handset sales in the UK declined in 2009 for the first time as UK wireless operators followed their low-cost competitors in offering SIM-card-only plans, which allow consumers to use their current handsets and pay a significantly lower monthly tariff.

Although overall handset sales were down slightly in 2011, sales of smartphones (iPhone, BlackBerry and their competitors with enhanced computing capability and internet access) were up from 32% to 39% of the market. Apple had entered the UK market with its revolutionary iPhone in late 2007 under an exclusive arrangement with O$_2$. The iPhone was very successful in the UK with over 2 million sold in the first year. The exclusive arrangement ended in late 2009 when Orange began selling the iPhone and Vodafone in 2010. By early 2012 Samsung and other manufacturers using the Android operating system from Google had matched many of the iPhone features, but the iPhone still commanded a price premium.

Smartphone users generated several times more revenue through their demand for a range of data services. In 2011 many users were concerned about managing their data use, so opted for prepaid contracts and used Wi-Fi connections where possible, usually at home but also at the increasing number of public 'hotspots' around the UK. Wi-Fi was also important for the small but rapidly growing number of tablet users in the UK (over 1 million by the end of 2011).

Average annual churn (customer switching) rates in the mobile market had been over 20% annually, helped by the introduction of number portability in 2007 and competitive tactics such as subsidising handsets for new subscribers. Some operators, notably O₂, had tried to reduce churn by providing a superior customer experience, but the biggest impact came from switching most post-paid customers to longer contracts. By 2011 most contracts were 24 months compared with 12 months in 2007. Overall, post-paid contracts grew to 49% of subscribers in early 2012. Contract users were preferred by operators since they were more loyal, their usage rates were four times higher and, despite continuing price declines, they paid an estimated 10% more per minute than prepaid.

Television

Television in the UK is dominated by the five 'public service broadcast' channels BBC 1, BBC 2, ITV 1, Channel 4 and Five. The BBC channels, together with their additional channels and radio services, are supported by an annual licence fee paid by all UK residents with a TV set in their homes. ITV and the other two channels also provide additional 'portfolio' channels and are supported by advertising. Television services are also provided by what Ofcom defines as 'multichannel operators' led by BSkyB, UKTV, Viacom and Virgin, which are largely supported by a mix of subscription and advertising. All together Ofcom reports that there were 515 channels available at the end of 2011 compared with 490 channels in 2009. As noted in Table 2, subscription revenue continued to increase in 2011 but advertising revenue only increased slightly due to the economic recession and the growth in online advertising.

In 2011 BBC1 continued to be the market leader, but all the public service providers had lost share of viewers for their primary channels. However, the gain in viewers for its portfolio of channels (generally with more specialised content, e.g. BBC4) increased its overall audience share. The BBC's iPlayer, which allows on-demand viewing by storing 30 days of programming, also strengthened its position. Virgin and Sky had also introduced digital recorders, and in 2011 over 60% of UK households reported 'catch-up' viewing via DVRs or the internet.

Overall, the TV operators spent £5.5 billion for content in 2011, a slight increase over 2010. The largest portion was £1.7 billion for sports and films, up 12% from 2010. Sport was one of the few forms of content that many viewers wanted to watch in real time, and the cost of broadcast rights to English Premier League football had escalated each time the contract was up for bid. In the current contract Sky broadcast the most games, together with ESPN. Bidding for a new contract later in 2012 was intense,

with BT looking to use sport (as Sky had done) to draw subscribers to its network. EU regulators were concerned that there was a trend to major sports leagues not being available on free-to-air television and were discussing regulatory changes to force that facility. The difficulty was that the leagues themselves had become very dependent on the broadcast rights income.

In early 2011 there were estimated to be 26 million UK homes with TV, a slight increase over the previous year. The switch to digital terrestrial TV (DTTV – signals which require a special aerial and either a set-top box or a specially equipped TV) was completed. Using this DTTV platform, the Freeview package of more than 50 TV and 20 radio channels was available to virtually all UK households, encouraging more viewing of specialist channels. By the end of 2011, 5% of UK households had 'Smart TVs' (internet equipped) and growth was expected to be rapid.

In 2011 there were 12 million households with DTTV only, almost 10 million homes equipped to receive satellite TV and 4 million homes with cable connections. Most of the households receiving satellite signals were Sky subscribers (8 million) and most of the cable homes were customers of Virgin Media. Cable was potentially available to 49% of the 24 million UK households, satellite service was available to virtually all homes, and IPTV (Internet Protocol TV or TV broadcast using the internet) was available to 79% of households. Network operators were increasingly using IPTV for their own TV services, and several were combining with the main TV channels to launch an IPTV service, YouView, later in 2012.

Broadband internet

In early 2012 Ofcom estimated that 80% of UK households had broadband internet access, up from 77% a year earlier (the vast majority of households had some form of internet access). Table 1 shows more than 20 million fixed lines and over 5 million mobile connections (cards or 'dongles' providing internet access via cellular networks to laptops). As noted above, the rapid growth of broadband in the UK has been helped by local loop unbundling. The economics of this has encouraged consolidation among the 700 internet service providers and by 2011 the four largest providers had 85% of all connections (see Table 3).

Table 3 Fixed broadband % market share 2011

BT Retail	29
Virgin	20
TalkTalk	18
Sky	18
Orange	3
O₂	3
Other	8

Sources: Ofcom, *Media Report 2012*, Ofcom copyright 2012

Many homes and small businesses were still served by fixed lines using ADSL technology, which worked with the existing copper wire telephone networks but was limited in the speeds that could be delivered, particularly for users distant from exchanges and in the evenings when usage increased. This led to a 'speed gap' between claimed speed and actual speed, which frustrated consumers and contributed to churn rates of 1% a month. In 2011 Ofcom contrasted the average claimed speed of 17 Mbps (megabits per second) with the actual average speed of just under 8 Mbps, compared with 10 Mbps and 4 Mbps respectively in 2007. Ofcom also noted that data use increases with increased speed, with the average fixed-line user going from 17 GB/month in 2011 to 23 GB/month in early 2012.

The growing use of the internet for video and other high-volume applications encouraged operators to invest in higher-speed technology and infrastructure. The BT fibre optic network promised speeds of up to 40 Mbps, with up to 100 Mbps if it was connected with fibre to the home (FTTH). Household fibre connection costs were decreasing but in 2012 were still estimated at £400 per household. The speed and reliability champion was Virgin, which had the advantage of its coaxial cable TV network. It had announced plans to double speeds on its network to 100 Mbps by 2013 and had tested up to 200 Mbps. Ofcom estimated that there were 1.4 million superfast (over 24 Mbps) broadband connections in early 2012, triple the number a year earlier, and that superfast service was available to over 60% of UK households.

All major mobile operators provided mobile broadband access through 3G cards for laptops, primarily for business users. This market had become increasingly competitive with many packages available for less than £20 per month. Demand for these connections slowed dramatically from 2010 as use of smartphones grew. Most of these subscribers (75%) also had a fixed-line broadband subscription so saw the mobile service as complementary.

This was not necessarily the case with smartphone and tablet users (not included in the 5.1 million connections) who also wanted higher-capacity services, so the speed gap was an issue for mobile users as well. Ofcom found that even with the latest 3G technology the actual speed was only 2 Mbps, depending on location, network capacity, load and other factors. Ofcom estimated the new 4G technology would significantly increase that to 6–8 Mbps (operators claimed much higher), which was expected to be adequate for streaming video but certainly still much slower than the new 'superfast' fixed lines. As noted earlier, mobile users took advantage of the higher speed and lower costs available over Wi-Fi in 'hotspots'. There were over 15,000 hotspots in the UK in early 2012. The largest operator of these was Sky, which had acquired the market leader, followed by BT Openzone.

Bundled services

In 2012 most major operators were providing multiple communications services or bundles, defined as any combination of two or more services (e.g. fixed-line voice and internet). Ofcom reported that 57% of UK households purchased some form of bundled services in early 2012, up 4% from the previous year. Of these, 60% bought 'double play' (usually fixed voice and broadband from a single supplier), while 40% bought 'triple play' (usually by adding in TV) and 1% purchased all four services.

Virgin had been the most active in promoting multiple services and noted in its annual report that the more services consumers purchased, the more loyal they were likely to be. The average churn for its cable customers buying a single service was 35% a year, compared with 19% for dual, 12% for triple and only 5% for quad. The challenge of marketing multiple services was illustrated by the fact that only 20% of Virgin's cable customers also purchased Virgin Mobile – although this was triple its overall market share. Sky and BT were also active in promoting a full range of services.

Competitor strategies

The largest wireless operator in 2012 was **Everything Everywhere (EE)**, the joint venture formed by Orange and T-Mobile with annual revenues of £7 billion. Their strategy was to keep their original brands for 3G services and launch 4G services under their parent brand of Everything Everywhere.

Regulatory decisions on 4G services were made in 2012 to allow companies to launch in mid-2013, but EE had decided to begin building its 4G infrastructure in the hope that it could launch before the end of 2012. As the brand implied, EE offered a full range of communication services and claimed to be 'The most advanced digital communications company in the UK.' Orange had moved aggressively into the fixed voice and broadband market via LLU and had 3% share of the fixed broadband market. It was investing in its own fibre optic network to be able to deliver superfast broadband to 50% of UK households, and it was targeting heavy TV users.

Under the agreement between O_2 and Vodafone, the joint venture would operate existing mobile services while each company would develop its 4G services on top of the shared network. The new services were planned to launch in summer 2013.

O_2 targeted higher-end consumers and had an above-market share of smartphone users (41%), based on being the launch operator for iPhone, and a lower customer churn rate based on its investment in customer service. O_2 also provided fixed-line voice and broadband internet through the acquisition of an internet services provider,

'Be', in 2007, and continuing investment in LLU. O_2 had a fixed-line broadband share of 3% in 2011 and was investing in expanding its network of hotspots. O_2 UK is a subsidiary of Telefonica, originally the Spanish national telecommunications operator but by 2012 a major multinational company with over 300 million subscribers to its wireless, fixed-line, internet and pay-TV services. Telefonica sees itself as 'one of the world's leading integrated operators in the telecommunications sector'.

BT offered a full range of services with its long-term UK strapline of 'Bringing It All Together'. In 2012 its corporate strategy was built around three core elements:

1 Customer service delivery (improving the customer experience)
2 Cost transformation (improving productivity and procurement)
3 Investing for the future (higher-value services in converging markets and international services).

Total company revenue in FY 2012 was £19.3bn (down 4%) with EBITDA of £6.1bn (up 4%) and Free Cash Flow of £2.5bn (up 18%). UK retail and wholesale accounted for almost 50% of company revenue.

BT was the dominant player in providing both fixed-line voice and broadband services in the UK. Its core was its national fixed-line network which reached 99% of UK households and which was being upgraded to fibre at an expected cost of £2.5 billion. BT also offered mobile services through its own MVNO which was hosted by Vodafone. BT Vision was a pay-TV service delivered over BT's network which offered all the Freeview channels plus Sky Sports and ESPN as well as pay-per-view programmes. There was also an extensive library of on-demand programming and material for personal video recorders. Despite its late start against Sky and Virgin, BT Vision had 4% of the pay-TV market in early 2012. BT also targeted business customers who needed both high-capacity fixed lines for data and mobile access to allow employees to work anywhere.

BSkyB or Sky was a publicly traded UK company in 2012 but was 39% owned by News Corporation, the global media group. Its goal was to be the overall market leader: 'We want to be first choice for entertainment and communications.' Revenues in FY 2012 were £6.8bn (up 3%), 'allocated profit' (after one-time items) £1.2bn (up 14%) and 'adjusted free cash flow' (after capital expenditures) £0.9bn (up 3%). By early 2012 Sky reported 10.3 million television subscribers, 3.9 million telephone subscribers and 4 million for broadband.

In 1988 Sky began its core pay-TV services over satellite, eventually including a package of 25 of its own channels covering sports, news, entertainment, gambling and special interests, which it offers along with many others. In 2006,

in partnership with BT, it began offering fixed-line voice (Sky Talk) and broadband (Sky Broadband) and later began work on a fibre optic network. By 2012 over half of the TV subscriptions included a digital video recorder to allow subscribers to 'control their viewing'. Sky had acquired 'The Cloud' in 2010, and by 2012 claimed its subscribers could access 11,000 hotspots throughout the UK.

Sky relied on attracting viewers by securing rights to sports, first-run movies and popular TV series but had been under pressure from Ofcom to wholesale more of its channels to other operators. Sky aggressively promoted multiple product purchases among its subscribers and in its 2012 annual report noted that 3.4 million subscribers purchased the triple play of TV, broadband and home telephony, an increase of 21% over the previous year.

TalkTalk had been demerged from the leading retailer Carphone Warehouse in 2010 with a strong base of internet (it had acquired AOL UK and Tiscali) and fixed voice customers. By 2012 it was positioned as 'The best value for money broadband and voice provider in the UK market.' Revenues for FY 2011 (ending March 2012) were £1.8bn (up 6%) with net profits of £0.122bn (up 13%) and free cash flow of £0.156bn (up 32%).

TalkTalk had invested in LLU and had unbundled over 2000 exchanges, reaching 86% of the UK population by early 2012. It had also invested £600 million to build its own fibre network to offer superfast broadband and had a total of 3.6 million customers on its network in early 2012. A key part of its strategy in 2012 was 'delivering value for money quad play services' so it had begun to offer mobile services through an MVNO and announced an IPTV network to be launched by the end of 2012. The TV network would offer Freeview plus Sky Sports and Movies as well as an on-demand library and a personal video recorder.

Virgin Media was formed in 2007 when the cable company NTL:Telewest rebranded following its 2006 acquisition of the UK's largest MVNO, Virgin Mobile. It was quick to capitalise on its range of services and in 2008 noted in its annual report that it provided 'the first "quad-play" offering of television, broadband, fixed line telephone and mobile telephone services in the UK'. At the end of 2011, 84% of the subscribers purchased multiple services, with 16% buying the four services and 64% buying the triple play (excluding mobile). Revenues in 2011 were £4.0bn (up 3%) with operating income of £0.540bn (up 5%) and operating cash flow of £1.597bn (up 5%). Virgin Media also recorded the first positive net income in its history of £76 million as write-offs from the acquisition were reduced.

The core of Virgin's business was its network which incorporated fibre to its own cabinets and then a combination of coaxial cable and copper lines to individual households. This gave it the fastest and most consistent broadband capability in the UK, a position it supported with ongoing investment which would double speeds (to a minimum of 30 Mbps by 2013). In 2012, Virgin's cable network passed 13 million UK households of which 3.8 million were TV subscribers, 4 million broadband and 4.2 million telephone (only the broadband numbers had increased significantly over the previous year). An additional 248,000 subscribers were served by LLU lines operated by Cable & Wireless and sold under the Virgin National brand.

Virgin Mobile had 3 million subscribers and was expanding its number of Wi-Fi hotspots. Virgin's TV service offered more than 175 channels, including Freeview and Sky Sports and Movies. In December 2010 it began partnering with TiVo to introduce an integrated set-top box to manage TV, internet and video recording and had sold 438,000 by the end of the first year.

Vodafone strategy

Vodafone began as Racal Telecom, a division of Racal Electronics, and completed the first UK mobile call in 1985. It adopted the name Vodafone Group plc when it became an independent public company in 1991. Beginning in the mid-1990s, Vodafone began an aggressive strategy of global growth through acquisitions, and by early 2012 the company operated in 30 countries (with partner networks in 40 more) and had 404 million customers. The company described itself as 'the world's leading telecommunications company', noting that it had operations throughout Europe, the Middle East, Africa, Asia, the Americas and Australasia. The group has focused primarily on mobile telephones but in 2007 began to acquire or lease fixed-line capacity in a number of European countries.

Vodafone's global growth in emerging markets had been enthusiastically led by CEO Arun Sarin, but in 2008 he was succeeded by Vittorio Colao who came in with a strong reputation as a cost cutter. In late 2010 he announced a new corporate strategy to 'develop from a strong Vodafone to a more valuable Vodafone' by focusing on four key growth areas:

1. Data services. Customer appetite for the mobile internet and related services will be the single biggest driver of our business going forward.
2. Emerging markets. Our businesses in Africa and India are growing strongly as mobile communications are having a transformational impact on people's lives.
3. Enterprise and total communications. Businesses account for a large part of our activity and growth in this sector will be driven by employees becoming more mobile, devices more secure and the convergence of fixed and wireless communications.

Table 4 Operating results, Vodafone Corporate and UK

(fiscal year ending 31 March (£m))

	2012	2011	2010
Corporate			
Revenue	46,417	45,884	44,472
Gross profit	14,871	15,070	15,033
Net profit after tax	7,003	7,870	8,618
Net cash flow operations	12,775	11,995	13,064
UK			
Revenue	5,397	5,271	4,931
EBITDA	1,294	1,233	1,141

Source: Vodafone Annual Report 2012

4. New services. Machine-to-machine, mobile commerce, and operator billing, among many others, offer exciting new avenues for growth.

Source: Vodafone Annual Report, 2012

Vodafone Group and Vodafone UK operating results are given in Table 4. Despite the investment in emerging markets such as India and Africa, overall revenue growth was slow with organic growth at around 1–2% annually. Cash flow was strong but corporate profits were affected by substantial write-downs of acquisitions in several markets in Europe and elsewhere as growth slowed and pricing became more competitive.

Despite slow growth in mature markets, Vodafone executives saw a growth opportunity in mobile data services. The 2012 Annual Report noted that worldwide mobile data revenue was expected to grow by $142 billion over the next five years while mobile voice revenues were expected to decline by $27 billion over the same period. Over one-third of all Vodafone customers worldwide used mobile data in early 2012 and data revenues were growing at over 20% annually. Vodafone reported investing £6 billion a year to provide a high-quality data experience and claimed download speeds of 5.6 Mbps and uplink speeds of 1.8 Mbps in its major markets. In the UK, for example, Vodafone had added 1,300 base stations in FY 2012 for a total of 14,600 to improve capacity and service quality.

Vodafone UK faced a number of challenges in 2012. It had lost the leadership in the UK mobile telephone market to O_2 and with the merger of Orange and T-Mobile it had dropped to third. In early 2012 it had 19 million customers and 26% of the UK mobile market by revenue. The average churn rate in 2011 had dropped to 18% but was still higher than those of O_2 and EE. Vodafone had been the last major operator to market the iPhone and so had a lower share of smartphone users than O_2. Vodafone had targeted high-value consumers and did have an above-average share of contract customers and above-average ARPU, but again this was similar to O_2. Vodafone had also been the first to launch 3G services in the UK but was now expected to be 6–9 months behind EE in introducing 4G.

Vodafone also targeted businesses and reported a 37% share of the UK enterprise market. It found that integrated services ('total communications') were important to business customers and had a partnership with BT to provide fixed-line services to companies and jointly provide corporate services. Vodafone also used BT fixed lines to carry mobile services across the country to relieve pressure on its network. In return Vodafone hosted the BT mobile network. Vodafone was also the leader in marketing 'dongles' for laptop internet connections but, as noted above, sales had levelled off with the growth of smartphones. The company had also pioneered special services for business travellers but these had subsequently been matched by competitors.

Vodafone did offer fixed voice and broadband using wholesale services from BT, but its prices were high and it had few subscribers. The priority was to partner with leading internet companies to provide products and services that integrate the mobile and PC environments and thus 'enable consumers to use their mobiles to replicate fixed-line activities'. The company sought to be more competitive against fixed-line competitors by offering fixed-line prices when customers call from within or near their home (Vodafone at Home).

Vodafone UK was headed by Gary Laurence, who had been appointed CEO in September 2008 as the fifth CEO in five years. He had previously been CEO of Vodafone Netherlands and before that held a number of marketing positions in Vodafone Corporate. He had joined the company in 2000 when the internet service provider he headed, Vizzavi, was acquired by Vodafone. As he reviewed the situation, he could see three major options:

1 to continue the current course of focusing on mobile voice and data;
2 to look for a partner to provide a stronger fixed broadband offering; or
3 to invest in its own fixed voice and broadband network through LLU directly or through an acquisition.

Vodafone UK was consistently profitable and a leader in mobile internet in the UK, so the mobile focus strategy had proven to be effective. It was also not clear, despite strong marketing efforts, that consumers really wanted to buy all their services from one supplier. Vodafone was also investing in upgrading its network to provide the fastest mobile connection speeds in the UK and was already working with its suppliers on technologies for the next generation of wireless (4G). The company was hoping to offer transmission speeds of up to 20 Mbps. This would be adequate for most current applications, including video viewing, but would it be sufficient for new applications and would it appeal to consumers used to higher speeds and greater reliability from faster fixed networks?

A partnership would allow Vodafone to gain access to a network with less capital investment than building or acquiring a network. A logical partner would be BT with whom Vodafone already had a relationship in which it leased fixed-line services and in turn hosted BT's MVNO. Vodafone also had a joint venture with O_2 to manage its mobile network, so perhaps this could be extended to the fixed-line network. In any partnership there would be questions of control, branding and the ability to secure a competitive advantage using a shared network.

Building or acquiring its own network would involve considerable capital expense but it would allow Vodafone to integrate horizontally to provide a full range of voice and data services under its control and with its established brand. The building costs could be reduced by unbundling exchanges on a regional basis where Vodafone was strongest. Although there had been consolidation among internet service providers, there were some smaller operators that could be acquired. Based on recent acquisitions, the cost would be £150 to £200 per subscriber.

Notes and references
1. £1 = $1.53 = €1.17.

CASE STUDY

Global forces and the Western European brewing industry

Richard Whittington

This case is centred on the Western European brewing industry and examines how brewers have responded to increasing competitive pressure by consolidation through acquisitions, alliances and internationalisation. By 2013, the question is: how much further can these strategies go?

• • •

In the second decade of the twenty-first century, European brewers faced a surprising paradox. The traditional centre of the beer industry worldwide and home to some of the world's largest brewers, Europe, was turning off beer. Western European beer consumption had fallen by nearly 10% between 2006 and 2011, while burgeoning in emerging markets worldwide (see Table 1). In 2011, Europe's largest market, Germany, ranked only fifth in the world with 5% of world consumption, behind China (24%), the USA (13%), Brazil (7%) and Russia (5%). China and Brazil are expected to grow at 5.5% a year between 2011 and 2016.

Table 2 details the long-term trends in Western European beer consumption. Decline in traditional key markets is due to several factors. Governments are campaigning strongly against drinking and driving, affecting the propensity to drink beer in restaurants, pubs and bars. There is increasing awareness of the effects of alcohol on health and fitness. Particularly in the United Kingdom, there is growing hostility to so-called 'binge drinking': excessive alcohol consumption

in pubs and clubs. Wines have also become increasingly popular in Northern European markets. However, beer consumption per capita varies widely between countries, being four times higher in Germany than in Italy, for example. Some traditionally low-consumption West European markets have been showing good growth.

The drive against drinking and driving and binge drinking has helped shift sales from the 'on-trade' (beer consumed on the premises, as in pubs or restaurants) to the 'off-trade' (retail). The Western European off-trade increased from 46% of volume in 2006 to 59% in 2011. The off-trade is increasingly dominated by large supermarket chains such as Tesco and Carrefour, which often use cut-price offers on beer in order to lure people into their shops. More than one-fifth of beer volume is now sold through supermarkets. German retailers such as Aldi and Lidl have had considerable success with their own 'private-label' (rather than brewery-branded) beers.

Pubs have suffered – in the United Kingdom, an estimated 18 pubs closed per week during 2012. However,

Table 1 **World beer consumption, 2006–11 (million litres)**

Geographies	2006	2007	2008	2009	2010	2011
World	169,102.9	178,909.6	182,741.5	183,463.7	185,969.2	189,430.6
Asia Pacific	50,945.8	56,211.6	58,646.5	61,197.3	64,113.6	66,973.0
Australasia	2,138.2	2,164.3	2,197.3	2,200.0	2,097.3	2,026.2
Eastern Europe	23,634.5	26,124.5	26,212.8	24,655.9	23,907.8	23,666.1
Latin America	26,146.2	27,612.9	28,436.5	28,834.7	29,683.6	30,747.2
Middle East and Africa	9,928.1	10,362.0	11,091.2	11,683.7	12,382.4	13,121.6
North America	26,523.9	26,901.5	27,210.5	26,795.6	26,260.8	25,848.5
Western Europe	29,786.2	29,532.9	28,946.7	28,096.5	27,523.8	27,048.0

Source: Euromonitor, 2012

Table 2 European beer consumption by country and year (hundreds of litres)

Country	1980	2000	2007	2011
Austria	7,651	8,762	9,100	9,105
Belgium	12,945	10,064	9,137	8,574
Denmark	6,698	5,452	4,840	3,654
Finland	2,738	4,024	4,073	4,732
France	23,745	21,420	18,781	20,000
Germany[1]	89,820	103,105	91,000	87,655
Greece	N/A	4,288	4,600	4,005
Ireland	4,174	5,594	5,193	4,721
Italy	9,539	16,289	17,766	17,715
Netherlands	12,213	13,129	12,910	11,974
Norway[2]	7,651	2,327	2,670	2,426
Portugal	3,534	6,453	6,200	5,320
Spain	20,065	29,151	35,658	35,196
Sweden	3,935	5,011	4,900	4,806
Switzerland[2]	4,433	4,194	4,489	4,626
UK	65,490	57,007	51,300	44,843

Notes

1 1980 excludes GDR; figures adjusted

2 Non-EU countries

Source: based on information from www.Brewersofeurope.org

although on-trade volumes are falling in Europe, the sales values are generally rising, as brewers introduce higher-priced premium products such as non-alcoholic beers, craft beers and fruit-flavoured beers. On the other hand, a good deal of this increasing demand for premium products is being satisfied by the import of apparently exotic beers from overseas (see Table 3). Imports are further encouraged by international supermarket chains.

Table 3 Imports of beer by country

Country	Imports 2002 (% of consumption)	Imports 2011 (% of consumption)
Austria	5.1	7.4
Belgium	4.7	12.8
Denmark	2.6	10.5
Finland	2.3	10.1
France	23.0	42.9
Germany	3.1	8.5
Greece	4.1	14.2
Ireland	N/A	42.5
Italy	27.2	36.0
Netherlands	3.2	20.3
Norway	5.4	3.3
Portugal	1.1	1.7
Spain	11.7	7.4
Sweden	N/A	24.1
Switzerland	15.4	23.3
United Kingdom	10.9	21.2

Note: Import figures do not include beers brewed under licence in the home country; also countries vary in measuring per cent of consumption.

Source: based on information from www.Brewersofeurope.org

Brewers' main purchasing costs are packaging (accounting for around half of non-labour costs), raw materials (such as barley) and energy. The European packaging industry is highly concentrated, dominated by international companies such as Crown (in cans) and Owens-Illinois (in glass bottles). In the United Kingdom, for example, there are just three can makers: Ball Packaging Europe, Crown Bevcan and REXAM.

Acquisition, licensing and strategic alliances have all occurred as the leading brewers battle to control the market. There are global pressures for consolidation due to over-capacity within the industry, the need to contain costs and benefits of leveraging strong brands. For example, the world's largest brewer, A-B InBev, originates from the 2004 merger of Belgian brewer Interbrew with AmBev, the Brazilian brewery group, and the 2008 acquisition of the American brewer Anheuser-Busch. In 2002, South African Breweries acquired the Miller Group (USA) and Pilsner Urquell in the Czech Republic, becoming SABMiller. SABMiller in turn bought Dutch specialist Grolsch in 2007, formed a joint venture with Molson Coors in the USA in 2008, and bought the Australian brewery Fosters in 2011. Players in the fast-growing Chinese and Latin American markets are being snapped up by the large international brewers too: Dutch Heineken bought Mexico's second-largest brewery, FEMSA, in 2010 and the Asia Pacific Brewery of Singapore in 2012.

Table 4 lists the world's top 10 brewing companies, which accounted for more than 60% of world beer volumes in 2011. However, there are still many specialist, regional and micro breweries. Germany, with its pub-brewing tradition (the Brauhaus), still had 1,341 separate breweries in 2011, owned by 1,315 separate brewing companies. None the less, market concentration has increased in Western Europe: in 2000 the top two players (Heineken and Interbrew) had 19.3% of the market, while in 2011 the top two players (Heineken and Carlsberg) held 27.4% of the market, with A-B InBev accounting for a further 9.8%.

Concentration in the industry has led to concerns about anti-competitive practices. The European Commission fined Heineken and Kronenbourg in 2004 for price-fixing in France, and Heineken, Grolsch and Bavaria in 2007 for a price-fixing cartel in the Dutch market. In the United Kingdom, half of pubs are still tied to major brewers for their supply and it is alleged that these so-called 'beer ties' add around 6–7% to pub beer prices: in 2009 the UK competition regulator officially rejected a complaint of anti-competitive practices, but encouraged brewers to allow its tied pubs to feature independent beers. In 2013, the US Department of Justice forced A-B InBev to sell the American assets of its Mexican acquisition Modelo, which would have taken the world's largest brewer from 40% to 46% of the American market (Molson Coors controlled another 30%).

Table 4 The world's top 10 brewery companies by volume, 2000 and 2011

2000		2011	
Company	Share global volume (%)	Company	Share global volume (%)
Anheuser-Busch (US)	8.8	A-B InBev (Belgium)	18.2
AmBev (Brazil)	4.6	SABMiller (UK)	9.8
Heineken (The Netherlands)	4.3	Heineken (The Netherlands)	8.8
Interbrew (Belgium)	4.0	Carlsberg (Denmark)	5.5
Miller (US)	3.6	China Resources (China)	5.4
SAB (South Africa)	3.3	Tsingtao (China)	3.6
Modelo (Mexico)	2.7	Modelo (Mexico)	3.0
Coors (US)	2.0	Beijing Yanjing (China)	2.9
Asahi (Japan)	2.0	Molson Coors (US)	2.7
Kirin (J apan)	1.9	Kirin (Japan)	2.6

Source: Euromonitor International, 2012

Three brewing companies

The European market contains many very different kinds of competitor: this section introduces the world's largest brewer and two outliers.

Anheuser-Busch InBev (Belgium)

A-B InBev has roots going back to 1366, but has transformed itself in the last decade with a series of spectacular mergers. First, InBev was created in 2004 from the merger of Belgian InterBrew and Brazilian AmBev. As well as making it the second-largest brewing company in the world, this merger gave it a significant position in the Latin American soft drinks market. Then in 2008 InBev acquired the leading American brewer Anheuser-Busch for $52bn (£36.4bn),[1] making the company indisputably the world leader. The company has 40% share of the US market, and in 2013 took over Mexico's leading brewer, Modelo, famous for its global Corona brand. The company now has over 200 beer brands, led by such well-known international beers as Beck's, Budweiser and Stella Artois. A-B InBev has the number one position in 19 national markets globally. However, in 2009 the company sold its Central and Eastern European beer operations to help raise funds to pay for the Anheuser-Busch acquisition. It also sold its minority stake in the second-largest Chinese brewery Tsingtao, though it has since acquired majority control of several Chinese regional breweries.

The company is frank about its strategy: to transform itself from the biggest brewing company in the world to the best. It aims to do this by building strong global brands and increasing efficiency. Efficiency gains will come from more central coordination of purchasing, including media and IT; from the optimisation of its inherited network of breweries; and from the sharing of best practice across sites internationally. A-B InBev is increasingly emphasising internally generated growth and improved margins from its existing business. Its declared intention is to be 'The Best Beer Company in a Better World'.

Greene King (United Kingdom)

Established in 1799, Greene King is now the largest domestic British brewer, owner of famous brands such as Abbot, IPA and Old Speckled Hen. It has expanded through a series of acquisitions including Ruddles (1995), Morland (1999) and Hardys and Hansons (2006). Acquisition is typically followed by the closure of the acquired brewery, the termination of minor brands and the transfer of major brand production to its main brewery in Bury St Edmunds. This strategy has led to critics calling the company 'Greedy King'. IPA is the UK's top cask ale, with over 20% of the on-trade market, and Old Speckled Hen is the top premium UK ale with more than one-eighth of the multiple retailer market. Greene King is unusual amongst contemporary breweries in operating many of its own pubs, having added to its original chain several acquisitions (notably Laurels with 432 pubs and Belhaven with 271). In 2007, it also bought the Loch Fyne restaurant chain and the company has invested in offering good casual eating in its pubs as well. Greene King now operates nearly 2000 pubs across the United Kingdom, with a particularly dominant position in its home region of East Anglia. Greene King explains its success formula in brewing thus: 'The Brewing Company's continued out-performance is driven by a consistent, focused strategy: most importantly, we brew high quality beer from an efficient, single-site brewery; [and] we have a focused brand portfolio, minimising the complexity and cost of a multibrand strategy.'[2]

Tsingtao (China)

Tsingtao Brewery was founded in 1903 by German settlers in China. After state ownership under communism, Tsingtao was privatised in the early 1990s and listed on the Hong Kong Stock Exchange in 1993. In 2009, the Japanese Asahi Breweries held 19.9% of the shares, purchased from A-B InBev (which also sold the remainder of its original stake – 7% – to a Chinese private investor).

Tsingtao has 14% market share of its home market but has long had an export orientation, accounting for more than 50% of China's beer exports. Tsingtao Beer was introduced to the USA in 1972 and is the Chinese brand-leader in the US market. A bottle of Tsingtao appeared in the 1982 science fiction film *Blade Runner*. Tsingtao set up its European office in 1992 and its beer is now sold in 62 countries. Tsingtao's priority for now is adjacent Asian markets, with a new brewery announced in Thailand in 2012. However, it has described its ambition thus: 'To promote the continuous growth of the sales volume and income to step forward (sic) the target of becoming an international great company'.[3]

Key sources
Ernst & Young, *The Contribution Made by Beer to the European Economy*, 2009.
Euromonitor, *Strategies for Growth in an Increasingly Consolidated Global Beer Market*, 2012.
Euromonitor International, *Global Alcoholic Drinks: Beer – Opportunities in Niche Categories*, 2011.

Notes and references
1. $1 = £0.65.
2. http://www.greenekingreports.com/home/
3. https://www.tsingtaobeer.com/

CASE STUDY

A source of cheap energy or a source of problems – the potential benefits and costs of shale gas

Steve Pyle and Bob Dover

The exploitation of shale gas reserves is transforming the energy sector in the USA but is causing widespread concern on environmental grounds. This case examines the development of the industry and explores these environmental concerns. Prospects for shale gas in Europe are much less certain and this case allows students to explore alternative scenarios for the industry.

• • •

In May 2012 temperatures rose to 94°F (34°C) in New York State. There was insufficient electrical power to cope with the demand for air conditioning. The generating and distribution companies took the decision to switch off the power in the suburbs. The rationale was that it was less risky to upset consumers in the suburbs than to trap thousands in subways and airports. Finally, the consequences of decades of under-investment in power generation hit New York in ways familiar to the developing world . . . the lights went out!

Resolving the energy supply issue is a worldwide challenge. In California, the richest state in the USA, despite the increasing population and the boom in local industries, no new power stations have been built since 1985. In Germany, reaction to the Fukushima meltdown disaster in Japan caused the German government to accelerate the closure of Germany's nuclear power plants and effectively ended the domestic nuclear industry. Yet energy demand is likely to keep on growing while supplies of fossil fuels are finite. If energy prices keep on rising, this will have major consequences for industry and society. For example, futurologists suggest that some industries, for example, automobiles and airlines, will have to change fundamentally if virtual communications replace physical communications.

However, one development holds out some hope. Every year, the President of the USA gives his 'State of the Union' address. Here is what Barack Obama said in January 2012:

> 'We have a supply of natural gas that can last America nearly 100 years and my administration will take every possible action to safely develop this energy. The

Anti-fracking campaigners in the UK.

development of natural gas will create jobs and power trucks and factories in ways that are cleaner and cheaper, proving that we don't have to choose between our environment and our economy.'

He was reflecting on developments that had already started to occur. In the previous five years, shale gas production in the USA had increased by 500%, and accounted for 30% of US total gas output compared to just 4% in 2005. US corporations have already invested intensively in shale gas production, and the US wholesale gas price halved in the first half of 2012. Could the potential of widespread exploitation of shale gas reserves change the outlook for energy over the next century? Will Europe and the rest of the world follow the USA in large-scale development of shale gas and oil?

Sources of energy in the twenty-first century

Oil reserves are finite and most oil and gas reserves are located in politically unstable regions such as the Middle East, Nigeria and Venezuela. Oil companies continue to seek new sources of oil, for example in the South China Sea and off the coast of the Falkland Islands (where sovereignty is being disputed because of the potential sources of oil and gas). Less accessible deposits, in the form of tar sands, shale oil and deep sea wells, start to become financially justifiable when the oil price exceeds $95 per barrel (£62; €73).[1] The cost of extraction and transport for these sources of oil is relatively large – up to four to five times higher – but the increasing demand for energy has opened up these sources to development.

Alternative renewable sources of energy, driven both by economic realities and by the Kyoto protocols on climate change, have also been seen as an answer to the progressive exhaustion of fossil fuels. However, only two countries use renewable energy for 100% of their power requirements – Iceland (geothermal energy) and New Zealand (hydroelectric energy) – and both need to import oil for transportation needs. Alternative non-fossil sources of power continue to attract investment. Onshore and offshore wind turbines are being built, although operating experience has raised concerns about maintainability and reliability. Tidal barrage schemes are well proven in the limited areas where combinations of strong currents and high tidal ranges are present. Wave power shows promise and solar power has been commercially exploited for years, mainly at a domestic rather than an industrial level. Even in Northern Europe, governments have discovered that, with incentives, consumers will invest in solar panels. However, this still accounts for a very small percentage of consumption.

Finally, nuclear power retains its place as a method of generating electrical power at the lowest cost of the non-fossil-fuel alternatives, but there is the major problem of decommissioning and end-of-life storage of highly radioactive spent fuel. Nuclear power also requires massive capital expenditure and constancy of political support – both are in short supply.

Shale gas and oil – realising the potential in the USA

Shale gas is nothing new but it took the development of two technologies working in parallel to make its extraction feasible and economically viable. First, there was the development of steerable drilling rigs. Instead of the need to position a rig and drill vertically down until the drill bit strikes oil, it is now possible to drill down and then steer the drill rig to continue to drill horizontally, along and within a layer of gas- or oil-bearing shale rock. This means that a number of wells can be drilled from the same above-ground platform.

The second technology is the development of hydraulic fracturing ('fracking') where liquids are pumped under very high pressure, sufficient to crack open the shale rock, to release the gas and oil trapped inside and bring it to the surface (see Figure 1). These reserves of trapped energy can now be released and the reserves seem to be enormous. It is estimated that fracking is now used in 90% of US oil and gas rigs.

By 2012 the US market for energy had taken up the opportunities for cheap energy with enthusiasm. In power generation, every coal-fired electricity generator with access to shale gas had changed over, or was in the process of changing over, to gas firing. This has reduced the prices of both gas and coal. Supporters of shale gas also argue that gas fields typically give rise to lower CO_2 emissions than coal and do not require costly treatment to remove mercury compounds. It is estimated that, at current production rates, the USA has over a century's supply of gas, half of it stored in shale and other 'unconventional' formations.

A 2011 US study by IHS Global Insight asserts that the shale gas revolution is having deep, sustained economic benefits by creating jobs, reducing consumer costs, and stimulating growth in the USA.

Shale gas and oil outside the USA

The shale gas revolution has certainly had a major impact on the US energy sector, but does it have the same potential in the rest of the world? The USA has a lot of shale gas deposits and the seams are thicker than are found in most other regions. There is a long tradition of onshore drilling and the USA has the infrastructure to support the shale gas industry. Moreover, large areas of the USA are not densely populated and the drilling operations are less intrusive. The US government has given a lot of support to the industry and provided big tax incentives. The circumstances that have enabled the exploitation of shale gas are most prevalent in North America, but there is still a lot of potential elsewhere if the problems can be overcome.

The shale gas revolution may spread to China, Australia, Argentina and Europe – all of which have extensive shale deposits. It has been estimated that global gas production could increase by 50% between 2010 and 2035, with the less accessible sources (primarily shale gas) supplying two-thirds of the growth.[2]

However, many of the factors behind the US gas boom (including liberal regulation of pipelines, a well-aimed subsidy and abundant drilling rigs) do not exist elsewhere. The rapidity of US growth is therefore unlikely to be matched. Moreover, environmental opposition is greater

Figure 1 **The hydraulic fracturing process ('fracking')**

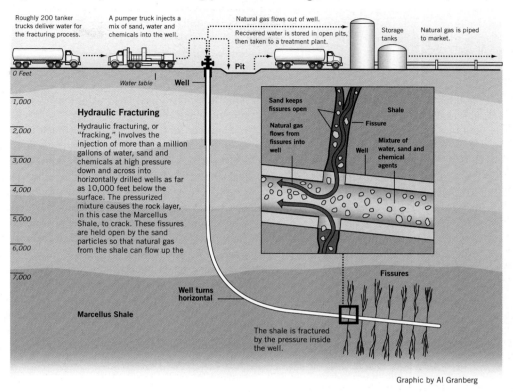

Graphic by Al Granberg

Source: http://uk.images.search.yahoo.com/r/_ylt=A0PDodt91QBShgcAbVxWBQx.;_ylu=X3oDMTBtdXBkbHJyBHNlYwNm
cC1hdHRyaWIEc2xrA3J1cmw-/SIG=1266evjc2/EXP=1375815165/**http%3a//www.frackfreesomerset.org/what-is-fracking/

outside the USA and is particularly strong in Europe. Despite the potential of shale gas and oil, there are very real doubts that they will be commercially successful or politically acceptable in Europe.

Environmental concerns

Despite the high levels of shale deposits, there would need to be high initial investment to exploit these deposits on an economic scale. Environmental concerns have slowed down the exploitation of these deposits and threaten any large-scale expansion. France and Bulgaria have banned fracking altogether. 'Greens' in the USA and Australia are also rallying against the industry.

The anti-frackers argue that producing shale gas uses a lot of energy and water, and can cause pollution in several ways. Fracking fluids are complex mixtures of chemicals but the main component is water, and lots of it. Depending on depth and geology, 5 million gallons per well could be needed, and double this figure is possible. The supply of water itself can be a major problem in some environments.

The second ingredient is a so-called 'proppant' to 'prop open' the fissures and fractures. This has to be an incom-

pressible solid (e.g. sand, quartz or tungsten), and small quantities of acids, surfactants and friction reducers are also used. Concerns about these toxic materials have been raised. A report by the Tyndall Centre at the University of Manchester said: 'It poses significant potential risks to human health and the environment through ground and surface water contamination.'[3]

Local opposition is often vociferous. When shale gas exploration was proposed in Wales a campaign strongly opposed the exploratory drilling. Louise Evans, who lives near the proposed site, said: 'The more I find out about fracking, the more I don't want it in the Vale or even the UK. It's in its infancy in the UK and people don't know about it – yet.'[3] The worry is that fracking fluids regurgitated up well-shafts might percolate into the water supply. A graver fear is that large amounts of methane, a powerful greenhouse gas, could be emitted during the entire process of exploration and production. Some also fear that fracking might induce earthquakes – it was linked to 50 tiny tremors in northern England in 2011, resulting in the UK government placing a temporary moratorium on fracking while the risks were considered. However, in December 2012 the moratorium was lifted as the government claimed that tough new environmental controls would ensure safety.

Not everyone agrees. Andy Atkins of Friends of the Earth says: 'Giving the green light to fracking for shale gas will send shock waves across the UK. Communities will be disturbed by this reckless decision which threatens to contaminate our air and water.'[4]

Elsewhere, opponents point out that drilling operations involve issues as diverse as the impact of heavy road vehicle traffic, polluting air emissions and damaging water quality.

The impact of shale oil and gas development on global warming is also a cause for concern, especially as there seems to be an excessive amount of 'flaring' (burning off excess gas at the well-head) associated with the process. Robert Howarth from Cornell University has said: 'We have used the best available data [and] the conclusion is that shale gas may indeed be quite damaging to global warming, quite likely as bad or worse than coal.'[5] However, others argue that these worries are exaggerated. A report from the American Petroleum Institute (2010) states that 'There are zero confirmed cases of groundwater contamination connected to the fracking operation in one million wells hydraulically fractured over the last 60 years.'

There are many reports worldwide of methane gas contamination of groundwater in the neighbourhood of drilling operations. However, the industry would claim that this can happen for a number of reasons not directly attributable to fracking, such as poor drilling practice when the well passes though an area of methane, abandoned wells, vibrations during drilling, or even natural ground movements. Advocates argue that the risks from shale gas can be managed. Properly concreted well-shafts do not leak; regurgitants can be collected and made safe; preventing gas venting and flaring would limit methane emissions to acceptable levels; and the risk of tremors can be contained by careful monitoring. The IEA estimates that such safety measures would add only 7% to the cost of the average shale gas well.

The impact of shale oil and gas

The economic and social effects of the discovery and exploitation of shale oil and gas are likely to be profound but are uncertain. Optimists, especially in the USA, see this as a watershed development ushering in an era of cheaper energy, reduced reliance on politically volatile regions and a major impetus for growth and regeneration. Sceptics, especially in Europe, see it as at best a short-term fix to the fundamental problem of over-reliance on fossil fuels.

There is no doubt that shale oil and gas have already had a significant impact in the USA – the country is now moving towards self-sufficiency in energy. If shale gas can be successfully and economically converted into liquid fuels on a large scale, the impact could indeed be revolutionary.

However, in Europe the view is much less upbeat. The economic and environmental costs of exploiting shale gas are seen as a significant barrier to cheaper energy – indeed it may be that shale gas will not be economically viable since the shale gas layers are thinner and more expensive to mine in Europe than in the USA. The environmental lobby is certain to make a stand against widespread shale gas drilling operations, which will delay operations and add to cost. Money spent on developing shale gas may divert resources from investment in renewable energy (which may be the only long-term solution to energy shortages) and could prove to be a false dawn.

France is very cautious about the prospects for shale gas. In September 2012, President François Hollande announced that his government had rejected seven proposals to use hydraulic drilling to explore shale gas: 'In the current form, no one can say that gas and shale exploration through hydraulic drilling, the only technique known today, is not exempt from posing great health and environment risks.'[6]

Germany too is very reluctant to embrace this technology. Germany's environment minister has said he does not want to make it easy for companies to 'frack' for shale gas: 'The message is we want to limit fracking, we don't want to facilitate it, and anyway I don't see in the foreseeable future that fracking will be employed anywhere within Germany.'[7]

A really interesting interactive graphic can be found at: http://www.ft.com/cms/s/2/96c7fde6-64f4-11df-aa4d-00144feab49a.html#axzz2bBUADUWQ.

Notes and references
1. $1 = £0.65 = €0.77.
2. *The Economist*, 2 June 2012.
3. www.walesonline.co.uk
4. *Independent*, 13 December 2012.
5. http://www.bbc.co.uk/news/
6. RFI France, 15 September 2012.
7. www.guardian.co.uk, 11 February 2013.

CASE STUDY

H&M in fast fashion: continued success?

Patrick Regnér and H. Emre Yildiz

The case examines the role of strategic capabilities in building competitive advantage and the key issues to consider while evaluating the sustainability of competitiveness. H&M has enjoyed a leading position in the global fashion and apparel market thanks to its unique concept, business model and ability to combine elegant designs with affordable prices. That position, however, has been challenged by key competitors and H&M needs to consider this and evaluate the sustainability of competitive advantage in its strategic capabilities. The case explores the areas and functions in which H&M has enjoyed advantage vis-à-vis its competitors and how, if at all, this advantage can be sustained in the long term.

• • •

Introduction

The apparel retailer H&M had made an incredible journey from a single store established by the founder Erling Persson in Sweden in 1947 to a pioneering 'fast-fashion' business with 2,206 stores in 43 countries and 94,000 employees worldwide. 'Fast fashion' refers to a quick response to new trends and fashion items that are made available in stores immediately thereafter. By the time Persson's 34-year-old grandson Karl-Johan Persson took over as CEO in 2009, H&M had become the global leader in the 'fast-fashion' segment with a distinctive business approach that challenged most competitors. The business model, commonly referred to as 'cheap-and-chic', emphasised high fashion at prices significantly below those of competitors, with the fundamental principle being 'Fashion and quality at the best price'.

The new CEO aimed to sustain H&M's remarkable annual growth rate of 20% as he stated in the 2011 annual report: 'In 2010 we stepped up our investments in order to strengthen the brand further and secure future expansion.'

H&M opened another 218 stores in that year with the most spectacular opening being on the Champs-Élysées in Paris. The following year yet another 230 new stores were opened, including 35 in China. However, Zara, the prime retail brand of Spain's Inditex, opened 120 new outlets in China during that same year and later during the year Inditex overtook H&M to become the world's biggest fashion retailer by market capitalisation. For the first time H&M was seriously challenged by Zara's rapid expansion, not least because of its fast growth in emerging markets. The increased competition and the fact that margins had started to erode due to increased cotton prices and rising production costs in Asia put the H&M high-fashion/low-price formula and aggressive expansion under scrutiny. Investors had come to trust H&M's model that relied on a set of unique resources and capabilities, but Zara's success questioned the sustainability of the formula.

The increased competition for consumer spending in the fast-fashion business was further intensified by the poor economic situation. With 70% of shareholder voting rights controlled by the company's founding Persson family, H&M's chief executive Karl-Johan Persson tried to calm investors and emphasised the long-term view:

'We have great respect for the economic climate. In this situation it is extra important to have a long-term perspective and to always make sure we give the best combination of fashion and quality for money in every market.'[1]

'. . . we are investing for the future and we always have the customers in focus. Despite increased purchasing costs, we have continued to strengthen our customer offering – for example, by not raising our prices to customers.'[2]

H&M relentlessly continued to emphasise the long-term view in its expansion strategy. For 2013 H&M planned a net addition of 300 new stores, with China, the USA and the UK expected to be the largest growth markets. H&M also planned to enter new markets, including South America (Chile and Mexico), Bulgaria, Latvia, Indonesia and Thailand. Despite these continuous aggressive expansion plans, analysts had some doubts:

This case was prepared by Patrick Regnér and H. Emre Yildiz, Stockholm School of Economics. It is intended as a basis for class discussion and not as an illustration of good or bad practice. © P. Regnér and H.E. Yildiz. Not to be reproduced or quoted without permission.

'There are fears that the product is not good enough, brand appeal is fading or that prices have been undercut by an even cheaper competitor. These are big questions.'
Adam Cochrane, analyst at UBS[3]

The apparel industry

The total market size of the global textiles, apparel and luxury goods market was worth $3049.5 billion (£2018.8bn; €2388.4bn)[4] in 2011, which corresponds to a compound annual growth rate of just 3.7% for the period 2007–11.[5] This slow growth increases competition, which is further intensified due to a large number of small players; however, there are a number of large international incumbents including Inditex (Zara), Gap and H&M, with Zara being H&M's most significant competitor (see Table 1). A somewhat smaller but new and vibrant player is the Japanese company UNIQLO, which has started to expand aggressively. Moreover, fashion, by its very nature, is unpredictable and fickle – trends are prone to sharp and unpredictable changes, which makes competition uncertain. The end consumers have an enormous selection of garments to choose from and will quickly adopt new trends. In the 'fast-fashion' category they are also extremely cost-conscious and will look for bargains.

Some of the players in the industry are able to act as both manufacturers and retailers. Examples of this are the Gap Corporation and Inditex: both manufacture their own products and sell them in their own stores. There are a multitude of suppliers for retailers to choose from. As international trade liberalises, the number of suppliers globally increases and competition among manufacturers in low-wage regions intensifies. Switching from one supplier to another is not a major issue, although it entails the risk that choosing low-cost suppliers may involve a more extended supply chain that may not be able to cope with sudden changes in demand in an industry which is susceptible to changes in fashion. There is also a risk that low-cost suppliers may not be up to quality standards.

Entry to the retail industry does not require a large capital outlay; setting up a single independent retail store is within the means of many entrepreneurs and there are plenty of suppliers to choose from. However, on a global scale, a few large corporations account for a major share of total industry revenues. Their size and economies of scale bring about the ability to build brands in multiple retail outlets, and considerably greater buying power when negotiating with suppliers (see Table 2).

The spirit of Hennes and Mauritz (H&M)

H&M is an abbreviation of 'Hennes' (the name of the first women's apparel store opened by Erling Persson in 1947) and 'Mauritz' (a later acquisition of a men's clothing store). The company has undergone a tremendous transformation from having just one store and a domestic focus to becoming one of the world's largest fashion retailers. As argued by one of the few journalists that has access to the company: 'The story of H&M does not really concern clothing, but from the beginning one man's vision – or rather unbreakable stubbornness, devotion to a goal and knowledge of human nature.'[6]

Not unlike IKEA in furniture, the H&M philosophy is to make fashion affordable for everyone: 'Fashion and quality at the best price'. The roots of the H&M 'spirit' can be traced back to the 1940s, when Erling Persson started to conduct what he called 'the primitive trade of buying and selling'[6] with the essence of 'tradesman-ship'. This was also maintained at the core of the company's culture when his son Stefan Persson took over as CEO in the 1980s. Even after Karl-Johan Persson took over in 2009 the leadership style and organisational culture still relied on Erling Persson's basic values and beliefs, based on his strong business acumen including thrift, no-nonsense decision making and delegation of responsibility. These are fundamental ingredients of 'the spirit of H&M', which remained the shared and tacit understanding of how to do business in H&M. It is underlined by seven codified core values: '(1) Keep it simple, (2) Straightforward and open-minded, (3) Constant improvement, (4) Entrepreneurial spirit, (5) Cost conscious, (6) Team work and (7) Belief in people.'[7]

Another aspect of the H&M spirit is the extraordinary focus on employee involvement. This participatory management philosophy is one of the reasons why H&M is seen as a company where experimentation, trial-and-error learning, fast decision making and willingness to take initiatives and try new ideas define the basic pillars of organisational culture. Another key ingredient in the culture of H&M is the active encouragement of this spirit at all organisational levels.[8] Trying new things is also encouraged among purchasing managers, but while trying something new and making mistakes is OK it is important that the same mistake is not repeated.

Experimentation is also present at the store level where interior decoration, lighting, colours, clothes displays and even locations are swiftly changed depending on sales and customer preferences. However, the range within which new ideas can be tried is clearly bounded by H&M's core ideas and values. In a memo to its employees, H&M specifies this as follows: 'Our employees all contribute to making H&M what it is today. We have a strong corporate culture – the spirit of H&M – that is based on simplicity, a down-to-earth approach, entrepreneurship, team spirit, straight lines, common sense and a belief in individuals and their ability to use their initiative.'[9]

Swedish national values also play a role – including a humble, informal and non-hierarchical management style combined with the 'democratisation of fashion'. Creative

Table 1 H&M and its multinational competitors

	Positioning and segments	Business model	Key figures	Financials
H&M	H&M is a retailer of fashion apparel, cosmetics, accessories and shoes for women, men, teenagers and children. The *Collection of Style* (COS) offers customers a combination of timelessness and distinctive trends, for both women and men. The *Monki* stores provide innovative collections and an inspiring fashion experience characterised by playfulness and colourful graphic design. *Weekday* sells its own brands but also commissions design collaborations with independent fashion labels. The *Cheap Monday* stores combine influences from street fashion and subcultures with a catwalk vibe. The latest addition is the luxury store concept '*& Other Stories*'.	The business is operated from leased store premises, through internet and catalogue sales and some franchise stores. H&M does not own any factories. Production is outsourced to independent suppliers. H&M's growth target is to increase the number of stores by 10–15% per year, and at the same time increase sales in comparable units. This growth is entirely self-financed. The collections are created by 140 in-house designers.	At the end of 2010, H&M had 2,206 stores which included 50 franchise stores, 35 *COS* stores, 48 *Monki* stores, 18 *Weekday* stores and one *Cheap Monday* store. The group outsources product manufacturing to 700 independent suppliers through its 16 local production offices in Asia and Europe. The company employs more than 94,000 people.	The company recorded revenue of $16,137 million in the fiscal year ending November 2011, an increase of 1.4% compared to fiscal year 2010. Its net income was $2,321 million in fiscal year 2011, compared to a net income of $2,880 million in the preceding year.
Inditex (Zara)	The flagship brand of the company is *Zara*. Zara also operates *Kiddy's Class* stores, which specialise in junior fashion. The *Pull and Bear* format offers casual clothing. It caters primarily to young males and females and offers a range that starts from sophisticated urban fashions to casual wear. *Bershka* stores are large and spacious. They are intended to be meeting points for street fashion, music and art. *Massimo Dutti* stores are located in prime retail locations and offer basic, contemporary styles in next-generation fabrics including high-quality garments. *Stradivarius* is aimed at young fashion-conscious customers, offering international fashion with the latest designs. *Oysho* offers fashion trends in women's lingerie and undergarments.	With an in-house design and a tightly controlled factory and distribution network, the company has the ability to take a design from drawing board to store shelf in just two weeks. That enables *Zara* to launch new items every week, which keeps customers coming back again and again to check out the latest styles. The company also has a policy of zero advertising and instead invests its revenues in opening up new stores.	*Zara* is present in 74 countries, with a network of 1,608 stores located in major cities throughout the world. *Pull and Bear* has opened 626 shops in the main streets and shopping centres of 44 countries. *Massimo Dutti* operates 630 stores in 60 countries. The *Bershka* sales format has 651 stores in 44 countries. There are currently 515 *Stradivarius* stores in 37 countries. There are currently 392 *Oysho* stores in 23 countries.	The company recorded revenue of $17,159 million in the fiscal year ending January 2011, an increase of 13.0% compared to fiscal year 2010. Its net income was $2372 million in fiscal year 2011, compared to a net income of $1828 million in the preceding year.
Gap	Under the *Gap* brand, the company offers an extensive range of apparel at moderate price points. *Banana Republic* was acquired by the company in 1983. This brand offers sophisticated, fashionable collections at higher price points than the Gap brand. The Old Navy brand was launched in 1994 to address the market for value-priced family apparel. The brand *Athleta* offers customers performance-driven women's sports and active apparel and footwear for a variety of activities.	The company operates through two segments: stores and direct sales. The stores segment includes the results of the retail stores for each of the company's brands: Gap, Banana Republic, Old Navy and Athleta. The direct segment includes the results of the online business for each of the company's web-based brands.	The company sources private-label merchandise from approximately 590 vendors and non-private-label merchandise from approximately 430 vendors. These vendors are spread across 50 nations. The company operates over 3200 stores worldwide, and has around 132,000 employees.	The company recorded revenue of $14,664 million in the fiscal year ending January 2011, an increase of 3.3% compared to fiscal year 2010. Its net income was $1,204 million in fiscal year 2011, compared to a net income of $1,102 million in the preceding year.
UNIQLO	The company is a retail chain operator specialising in in-house designed casual clothing for men and women. The company operates stores under the name of *UNIQLO*. The company is the leading clothing retail chain in Japan in terms of both sales and profits. UNIQLO is a member of Fast Retailing Group, which also operates other chain stores under the franchise names *Theory* (fashionable basic clothes that suit a contemporary lifestyle), *Comptoir des Cotonniers* (the brand nurtures a sense of natural authenticity and flattering femininity), *Princesse tam.tam* (corsetry, lounge wear and swimwear brand), and *G.U.* (an entirely new business model for a company offering extremely low-priced clothing in the Japanese market).	*UNIQLO* has established a SPA (Speciality store retailer of Private label Apparel) business model encompassing all stages of the business – from design and production to final sale. By continuously refining this SPA model, *UNIQLO* differentiates itself from the competition by developing unique products. The company quickly makes adjustments to production to reflect the latest sales environment and minimise store-operation costs, such as personnel costs and rent. This is how *UNIQLO* provides such high-quality clothing at such reasonable prices.	*UNIQLO* Japan operated a network of 848 stores at the end of June 2012. UNIQLO International had a total of 275 stores as of May 2012. Of that total, 135 stores are located in China, 16 in Hong Kong, 75 in South Korea, 17 in Taiwan, 6 in Singapore, 5 in Malaysia, 4 in Thailand, 10 in the United Kingdom, 2 in France, 2 in Russia and 3 in the USA. *UNIQLO* has around 70 partner factories, and roughly 75% of *UNIQLO* products are made in China.	The company recorded revenue of $7835 million as of the end of August 2011, an increase of 0.6% compared to fiscal year 2010. Its net income was $688 million in fiscal year 2011, compared to a net income of $787 million in the preceding year.

Source: company websites

Table 2 **Comparative financial data**

	H&M[1]	Inditex (Zara)[1]	Gap[2]	Uniqlo[3]
Key figures (thousand US dollars)				
Operating revenue (turnover)	16,137,877	17,159,719	14,664,000	7,835,853
Income before tax	3,072,386	3,180,253	1,982,000	1,294,111
Net income	2,321,088	2,372,369	1,204,000	688,928
Cash flow	2,799,654	3,298,037	1,860,000	n.a.
Total assets	8,830,140	13,460,382	7,065,000	3,081,094
Shareholders' funds	6,470,467	8,748,196	4,080,000	994,934
Current ratio	2.70	1.94	1.87	1.07
Profit margin (%)	19.04	18.53	13.52	16.52
Return on shareholders' funds (%)	47.48	36.35	48.58	130.07
Return on capital employed (%)	46.11	32.51	n.a.	117.81
Solvency ratio (%)	73.28	64.99	57.75	32.29
Price/earnings ratio	19.76	19.86	n.a.	n.a.
Number of employees	64,874	100,138	n.a.	4,150
Profitability ratios				
Return on shareholders' funds (%)	47.48	36.35	48.58	130.07
Return on capital employed (%)	46.11	32.51	n.a.	117.81
Return on total assets (%)	34.79	23.63	28.05	42.00
Profit margin (%)	19.04	18.53	13.52	16.52
Gross margin (%)	60.47	57.48	44.55	49.14
EBITDA margin (%)	21.49	23.71	17.89	n.a.
EBIT margin (%)	18.53	18.31	13.42	17.70
Cash flow/turnover (%)	17.35	19.22	12.68	n.a.
Structure ratios				
Current ratio	2.70	1.94	1.87	1.07
Liquidity ratio	1.77	1.49	1.10	0.72
Shareholders' liquidity ratio	33.24	8.35	4.58	9.48
Solvency ratio (%)	73.28	64.99	57.75	32.29
Gearing (%)	3.01	12.02	21.89	10.55

Notes:
1 As of 30 November 2011 and for 12 months
2 As of 29 January 2011 and for 12 months
3 As of 31 August 2011 and for 12 months

Sources: Mint Global, Bureau van Dijk

advisor Margareta van den Bosch comments: 'We're a very democratic society [in Sweden] . . . We keep what we do simple and we think it's wrong that fashion should be the preserve of the rich.'[10]

Despite this humility, results are central, something which is emphasised by Erling Persson's early focus on '*takten*' or 'the pace', which still remains a fundamental practice at all organisational levels. It is a straightforward and persuasive weekly list that includes sales and other key figures compared to the previous day, month and year. On this list each manager can clearly see exactly how much has been sold of each individual product. The buyers use this information to reallocate production or shipments, reducing potential over-stocking problems. This itemised report also allows buyers to maintain a high level of turnover, keeping the apparel on the sales floor up to date. All employees are also made aware of these results; and if sales are up from the previous day, the sales figures are applauded during store morning meetings.

Limited attention to titles and work descriptions is also a characteristic of H&M: 'At H&M we do not have any work descriptions. It provides considerable freedom, but it also makes it more difficult to blame someone else and claim that something is not part of your duties. Some love it, but others leave after a few weeks.'[11]

In line with this emphasis on informality, independent decision making is celebrated and decentralisation is encouraged within the limits of the organisational culture. However, central functions like buying and logistics also have a considerable influence and the organisation is in a sense 'a peculiar mix of strong centralisation and delegation'. The flat and simple organisational structure has also been more challenging to preserve due to H&M's tremendous growth. The company has a matrix country/function organisation, with each executive management team member for a function being responsible for the results of work within their function in each country.

Store operations and management

The company always positions its stores in the very best locations, whether in a city or a small-town shopping centre. This has been a firm principle of H&M's since the first shop opened in 1947, and the principle is still strictly adhered to. The store is the most important communication channel H&M has with its customers and it must be inviting and inspiring, strengthening the brand and offering local customers the best possible shopping experience.

Instead of claiming full ownership of the property, H&M opts for renting store premises, which increases flexibility and adaptability. By renting space, the company is able to adapt more quickly to the changing demand patterns and location attraction in its key markets.

The window display – where the customer meets H&M – is perhaps the most important part of the store. Guidelines for store design and display windows are created centrally based on a large 'test store' in Stockholm. Every two or three years a completely new interiors programme is created. Although centrally guided, every store is unique as it showcases different items in the window display, although they may come from the same collection. Displays, both in windows and inside stores, are changed frequently. This way, consumers are continually attracted to visit the stores to keep up with the latest collections.

In line with H&M values, decision making is decentralised and store managers have considerable autonomy. The shop manager runs the business like an entrepreneur and is authorised to take independent decisions within the overall guidelines, essentially like running one's own business. This increases employee loyalty and commitment to the organisation and is a great motivator.

Marketing and social media

H&M's strong brand image is associated with value and stylish collections. In addition to 200 in-house designer collaborations with famous designers, there is a unique approach that has been employed by H&M over the years. This includes the collections designed by Stella McCartney in 2005, by avant-garde Dutch designers Viktor & Rolf in 2006, by Madonna in 2007, by the Italian designer Roberto Cavalli and Kylie Minogue in 2007, by Sonia Rykiel in 2009, by Versace in 2011 and by Italian fashion label Marni in 2012.

Highlighting the brand's high level of awareness, H&M was ranked 21st among the top 100 most valuable global brands according to Interbrand in 2011, with a brand value of $16.5 billion. In comparison, Zara ranked 44th with US$8 billion, and Gap came in at number 84 with US$4 billion. This huge difference can partly be attributed to H&M's long-term advertising campaigns with high-profile celebrities. In order to enhance the value of its brand name, H&M spends around 5% of its revenues on advertising.

In addition to conventional channels, H&M has also established a strong social media presence. The company aims to become part of its customers' daily lives through its pages on Facebook, Twitter, Instagram, Google+ and YouTube as well as the Chinese social networks Youku and Sina Weibo. Each network is updated on a regular basis. Through social media, millions of H&M followers share ideas and opinions and get quick answers to their queries. New fashion videos and reports are uploaded onto YouTube weekly and have already had more than 15 million hits. Through the H&M apps customers can explore the latest collections and campaigns, find out what's new at H&M and locate stores. At its launch in August 2010, the iPhone app was the most downloaded application in almost all of H&M's markets.

Design

Design is centralised at the Stockholm headquarters and includes a team of almost 200 designers and about 100 pattern makers. The centralisation of design allows for minimal time-to-market and the design team has direct contact with the production offices around the globe. This allows for a rapid-response manufacturing process to capitalise on design trends immediately. The design team works intensively with new trends, materials and colours from what is popularly known as the 'White Room' and is supported by the 50 production offices around the world.

Much effort is put into researching and predicting emerging market trends. H&M designers hold customer surveys, dialogue sessions and focus groups, and pick up trends from employees in the global stores and then add their own particular features. They need to have an up-to-the-minute fashion feedback focus and be conscious of the very latest trends. According to Ann-Sofie Johansson, head of H&M design department: 'We try to look out for trendsetters, what's popping, vintage looks, what's happening at music festivals. The Internet is getting more important as are catwalk shows, but these are more of a confirmation of what we know is out there.'

She and her team pick up inspiration in several ways – notes from travels, fashion classics offered by Paris, Milan, New York, London and Tokyo, textile fairs, street fashion and exhibitions: 'Celebrity inspiration is also important, as well as what bloggers are saying and old-fashioned sources such as music, magazines, movies and costume dramas.'[12]

However, H&M always adds its own touch to the design, creating collections that strike a good balance between the latest trends and the basics. Margareta Van den Bosch, creative adviser and former head designer, says: 'We get inspiration from everywhere, but the most important thing is to make it your own way. Quality means carefully testing everything before it hits the shops, from jeans to lipstick. But it also means H&M is a fashion house in its own right, with its own trends. We do not copy.'[13]

Apart from size adjustments, for example in the Asian market, no special changes are made to the collection to adapt to the needs in specific countries. H&M argues that: 'It is important that H&M keeps its own personality in each country, and fashion has become more global, more international.'[14] Similar trends are appearing the world over. Of course, this is also driven by economies of scale in buying and manufacturing.

Buying, local production offices and Corporate Social Responsibility (CSR)

H&M does not own any factories. Instead, manufacturing is primarily outsourced to low-cost countries with approximately 70% of production in the Far East and South Asia and the remainder in Africa, Europe and the Middle East. With the focus on economies of scale, including low-wage and high-volume production, the company maintains low input costs and often has the latest trends in its stores within a month of the initial design.[15] H&M also constantly redefines its production and distribution in response to changing market and production conditions to ensure that they continuously improve the efficiency of the production flow. This way, H&M has been able to reduce lead times by 15–20% in recent years.[16] In 2011 H&M worked with 747 suppliers of which 150 were considered long-term strategic partners. Buying is centralised in Stockholm and has always had a central role in H&M. Managers within this function have often been the best paid in the entire organisation.

To reduce lead times, the 50 production offices are in direct contact with suppliers and report back to central procurement in Stockholm. They mediate between the large network of independent suppliers and the central purchasing office to identify the right suppliers to place orders with, in order to optimise time and cost decisions and ensure that these decisions follow H&M's CSR policies. Each supplier owns or subcontracts multiple factories; globally, 1,652 factories were approved for making goods for H&M. H&M conducted a total of 2,024 annual audits of suppliers, of which 78% were unannounced. CSR has increased in importance for H&M. Being a high-profile and visible player in the textile and apparel industry, the company is under constant scrutiny in terms of working conditions and wage levels in the overseas suppliers they work with. Being fully cognisant of this, H&M pays particular attention to CSR and takes several actions throughout its value chain to keep its brand name away from the usual criticisms aimed at the

textile industry. H&M also produces a special collection (the Conscious Collection) using sustainable materials. The company has formulated seven commitments called 'H&M Conscious Actions'. These include adopting ethical practices, improving working conditions and using natural resources responsibly. Other projects include community investments.[17]

Logistics: distribution, warehousing and IT

Buyers and production offices are closely integrated throughout the value chain with distribution centres, warehouses and the stores around the globe. To reduce poor buying decisions and to increase flexibility in allowing stores to restock quickly during the season with best-selling products, H&M makes sure not to place orders too early. H&M puts more emphasis on economies of scale in its supply chain set-up compared to Zara, which focuses on flexibility and speed:

> 'Lead-times vary from two to three weeks up to six months. The different lead-times reflect differences in the nature of the goods. The trick is to know the right time to order each item. A short lead-time is not always the best, since the right lead-time is a matter of bringing price and quality into balance.'[18]

H&M controls virtually all logistics internally except for external contractors handling transportation. The integrated logistics function is a key business process for H&M that supports cost-efficient supply of goods and generates economies of scale: 'H&M can offer the best price by avoiding middlemen, buying the right product from the right market, being cost-conscious at every stage and having efficient distribution.'[19]

This integrated direct distribution channel ensures that H&M stores receive new shipments daily, giving the company further control over supply and demand shifts. Store-keeping of merchandise is minimised and individual stores do not have backup stocks; they are replenished as required from a central warehouse. They also shift merchandise around internally, depending on demand. For example, if a particular fashion proves exceptionally popular to men in a particular region, but not in another, they can shift inventory from the first region to the second. The distribution set-up also enables H&M to respond to market segment changes within a country.

To support the swift and efficient flow of goods, H&M logistics depend on effective information sharing and the latest IT systems that are continuously being developed. These systems not only allow for more optimal decisions regarding demand and supply, but also provide information for understanding customer needs and the placement of products.

Taking H&M's mix of supply chain management, logistics and IT into consideration, the company is considered a world leader in these areas:

'Its centralised logistics and warehouse system, close coordination of the procurement staff with the production offices, intelligent use of ICT [information and communication technologies] tools, purchasing flexibility and overall a central governing model, has incredibly reduced the lead time and improved logistics to have lightning-fast turnaround speed of just 20 days, making it a truly unique supply chain innovator.'[20]

Human Resource Management (HRM)

Key to the recipe of H&M's success is its ability to establish a strong corporate culture with well-defined values, and to make sure its employees understand and internalise these values in their job. One important element to ensure that this culture is alive is to integrate it into HRM's recruitment process and training.

Internal promotion and job rotation are two central ingredients in H&M's HRM policies, and experience, loyalty and continuity are highly regarded. These two aspects are central to keep on cultivating and disseminating the H&M spirit and culture throughout the organisation. The steady growth in H&M provides ample opportunities for employees to take on new challenges in another store, department, role or country. Aligning corporate and individual goals with development and growth strategies is essential for H&M:

'The key words for continual growth are responsibility and commitment. We have committed employees and we are prepared to delegate responsibility at every level. I tell employees, if you do not grow, neither will H&M.'

Head of HRM, Pär Darj[21]

A participative culture is thus central to the spirit of H&M and the leadership philosophy emphasises straightforward and direct relationships with employees. The HRM policies emphasise the core value – 'We believe in people' – and the open-door policy, granting all employees the right and possibility to discuss any work-related issue directly with the management.

Consequently, H&M values personal qualities much more than formal qualifications; great school grades and all the university credits in the world are no guarantee of a job or a fast-track career. More than anything, H&M looks for people with the right personality – people can gather skills as they go along, but personality and attitude can not be taught. H&M is a fast company with a high tempo and needs employees who are self-driven, who like responsibility and decision making and who are capable of leading. A love of fashion combined with a focus on sales is perceived as a major advantage.

Internationalisation and expansion

While H&M's skill in providing fashionable and elegant clothes at fashionable prices and catering for the dynamic tastes and preferences of customers can broadly be identified as the main drivers of its success, perhaps its unique advantage lies in its ability to replicate the same business concept and 'spirit' across time and space. Since the 1990s, international expansion has been aggressive and the company has moved into Eastern European markets, the Middle East, Asian markets and Russia. By 2005 H&M had expanded into more than 20 countries with more than 1,000 stores.

Continuous growth by replicating the same business model and store concept thus defines the core of the company's expansion strategy. Prior to moving to a new country or city, H&M first conducts a thorough evaluation of market potential. This is done according to factors like demographic structure, purchasing power, economic growth, infrastructure and political risk.

H&M's strategy is to recruit local people wherever it opens a new store. H&M looks for those who have the 'right' personality and potential to understand and adopt the core values of the organisation. Another element is to use formal training programmes as well as on-the-job training to socialise employees into this culture and make sure that they understand and act according to the core values of the company. These socialisation mechanisms are the means by which H&M successfully adopts a 'mental franchising' model, in which the ownership of each and every store remains in the hands of H&M whereas the shop managers often run their shop as if it were their own.

All of these initiatives are essential ingredients of H&M's constant growth strategy, in which the ambition is to create and re-create the basic and fundamental values and the overall H&M spirit. To this end, the company keeps formal rules and procedures to a minimum and instead prefers to equip its employees with tacit skills via experiential learning in the field. This way, H&M makes sure that those who work in new outlets are exposed to and infused with the original spirit. Combining this with the values of initiative taking and entrepreneurship, H&M has been able to stay ahead of its competitors by moving fast and reaching large markets based on applying a simple business model universally and making subtle modifications and adaptations at the local level.

H&M's growth to become one of the largest global fashion retailers is an incredible success story – from one store in 1947 to 2,500 in 2012. In 2013 H&M was planning to open another 300 stores and also plans to open a much anticipated new luxury-label format of stores called '& Other Stories'. It also plans to develop online sales in the USA and open its largest store in the world on Fifth Avenue, New York. However, fashion retailing history is full of companies that have confidently expanded into new international markets, but later have been forced to retreat and drastically curtail their growth – from Marks & Spencer to C&A and Benetton. The question for H&M and its third-generation leader Karl-Johan Persson is to what extent will H&M's resources, capabilities, practices and knowledge be enough to keep up with the competition, including new and vigorous entrants? Will these entrants be able to replicate H&M's success?

Notes and references

1. As quoted in *Financial Times*, 29 September 2011: 'H&M continue aggressive expansion' by Clare MacCarthy.
2. As quoted in *Financial Times*, 29 March 2012: 'H&M to launch new line of stores' by Michael Stothard.
3. As quoted in *Financial Times*, 26 January 2012: 'H&M defend strategy as margins fall' by Michael Stothard.
4. $1 = £0.65 = €0.77.
5. Marketline (2012) Industry Profile: Global Textiles, Apparel & Luxury Goods. Ref. Code: 0199-1016.
6. Pettersson, B. (2001) *Handelsmännen*, Månpocket: Stockholm, p. 21.
7. H&M website: http://about.hm.com/AboutSection/en/About/Facts-About-HM/About-HM/Business-Concept-and-Growth.html
8. Pettersson, B. (2001) *Handelsmännen*, Månpocket: Stockholm, p. 91.
9. http://about.hm.com/content/dam/hm/about/documents/en/Corporate%20Governance/Remuneration/Presentation%20HM%20Incentive%20Program%202010_en.pdf
10. As quoted by *Daily Mail/Mail online*: 'H&M: Meet the brains behind fashion's megabrand' by Jo Craven: http://www.dailymail.co.uk/home/you/article-1249693/H-M-Meet-brains-fashions-megabrand.html#ixzz27Tr5wTLk
11. Jan Jacobsen, as quoted in Pettersson, B. (2001) *Handelsmännen*, Månpocket: Stockholm, pp. 261–2.
12. As quoted by *The Star online*: 'High street label H&M serves up inspiring fashion at affordable prices' by Patsy Kam: http://thestar.com.my/lifestyle/story.asp?file=/2012/9/20/lifearts/12000618&sec=lifearts
13. As quoted by Chinadaily.com, 'H&M: from the inside' by Nishita Mehta-Jasani.
14. Margareta Van den Bosch, creative advisor, as quoted by Chinadaily.com, 'H&M: from the inside' by Nishita Mehta-Jasani.
15. Capell, 2002, *Business Week*.
16. The European e-business market watch: http://ec.europa.eu/enterprise/archives/e-business-watch/studies/case_studies/documents/Case%20Studies%202004/CS_SR01_Textile_2-HM.pdf
17. http://about.hm.com/content/hm/AboutSection/en/About/Sustainability/Commitments/Communities.html
18. Kihlén, T. *On Logistics in the Strategy of the Firm*, Linköping University, Sweden.
19. Annual Report 2011.
20. Pal, R. (2011) 'Identifying organizational distinctive competence by business mapping in a global textile context', *Journal of Textile and Apparel Technology and Management*, 7(4), pp. 1–23.
21. Annual Report 2008.

Recommended videos

http://www.youtube.com/watch?v=CHYogtRrrUY – interview with CEO Karl-Johan Persson by Bloomberg on strategy, costs and internet sales (note: the correct name for the interviewed current H&M CEO is Karl-Johan Persson).

http://www.youtube.com/hm – official YouTube channel of H&M where video clips on new campaigns and promotions are shared.

CASE STUDY

The Formula 1 constructors: capabilities for success

Mark Jenkins

This case describes four periods of dominance by particular firms in a highly competitive technological context. Formula 1 (F1) motorsport is the pinnacle of automotive technology. Highly specialised constructors design and build single-seat racing cars (and sometimes engines) to compete for annual championships which bring huge financial and reputational rewards. The case study examines four contrasting companies in different competitive time periods in terms of how they both created and lost the basis for sustained competitive advantage.

● ● ●

'For the most part, it's just commerce, but between two and four on a Sunday afternoon, it's still a sport.'

Frank Williams, Managing Director, Williams F1[1]

In 1945 the Fédération Internationale de l'Automobile (FIA) established Formula A as the premier level of motorsport. In the years that followed Formula A became referred to as Formula 1 (F1) and a drivers' world championship was introduced in 1950. By the mid-1960s F1 had moved from being a basis for car manufacturers to promote and test their products, to a highly specialist business where purpose-built cars were developed through leading-edge technology. Having enjoyed exponential growth during the 1990s, F1 had become a TV sporting event which enjoyed the third highest audience in the world, surpassed only by the Olympics and World Cup Soccer.

There have been between 10 and 14 racing car constructors competing in F1 at any one time. In 2012 the top three teams were Red Bull Racing, Ferrari and McLaren Racing, all medium-sized businesses turning over between $300 million (€235m; £200m) and $400 million (€313m; £265m)[2] per annum. For the first three years of its entry into F1 in 2002 Toyota was estimated to have committed $1 billion in capital and running costs, of which only one-fifth came from sponsorship. The top teams would typically have their own testing and development equipment, which would include wind-tunnels and other facilities. The larger teams employ around 500 people, a quarter of whom travel around the world attending Grand Prix every two to three weeks throughout the F1 season (March to November). Labour costs account for around 25% of the budget. All the teams would have highly qualified technical staff which would include race engineers (who work with the driver to

Source: Corbis/Michael Kim

set up the car), designers, aerodynamicists, composite experts (to work with specialised carbon-composite materials) and systems specialists.

In addition to sponsorship, revenue is provided by prize money generated by winning championship points. The prize money is a way of dividing up the royalties earned from media coverage and other revenues negotiated, on behalf of the teams by the commercial rights holder, Formula One Management (FOM). In 2010 around 15% of Ferrari's budget was estimated to come from prize money.

The Formula 1 constructors provide a unique context to consider the competitive advantage of different multi-million-pound organisations over time. The pace of change and the basis of advantage are constantly changing, shown by the fact that since the start of the world championships, only two constructors have won the championship consecutively for four years or longer (McLaren, 1988–91; Ferrari, 1999–2004) and only Ferrari (1975–7), Williams (1992–4) and Red Bull Racing (2010–12) have won for three consecutive years.

The remainder of the case considers the four most recent of these periods of competitive dominance in chronological order. For a complete list of driver and team championship winners see the following links: http://www.formula1.com/teams_and_drivers/hall_of_fame/ and http://en.wikipedia.org/wiki/List_of_Formula_One_World_Drivers%27_Champions.

McLaren and Honda domination in the late 1980s

The period from 1988 to 1991 was unusual in the hyper-competitive world of F1, where the pace of change is rarely matched in any other competitive environment. This period was notable because of the dominance of one constructor. In 1988 the McLaren team won 15 of the 16 races. Such dominance had not been seen before and will almost certainly never be seen again.

Founded by New Zealander and F1 driver Bruce McLaren in 1966, the McLaren team had their first victory in the Belgian Grand Prix of 1968. Tragically, McLaren himself was killed two years later in a testing accident. Lawyer and family friend Teddy Mayer took over as team leader and in 1974 secured a long-term sponsorship from Philip Morris to promote the Marlboro brand of cigarettes. This partnership was to last until 1996, one of the most enduring relationships between a constructor and a 'flagship' sponsor. In September 1980, Ron Dennis became joint team principal with Mayer, a position which he took over solely in 1982, when Mayer was 'encouraged' by Philip Morris to take a less active role in the management of McLaren.

Dennis had been a mechanic for the highly successful Cooper team in 1966, but left to set up his own Formula Two team (a smaller, less expensive form of motor sport) in 1971. By the end of the 1970s he had built up a reputation for professionalism and immaculate presentation. His 'Project Four' company brought in designer John Barnard who had some radical ideas about using carbon fibre, rather than metal, as the basis for a racing car chassis. These ideas were to provide the basis for the MP4 car. Both Dennis and Barnard were perfectionists, with Dennis's obsession with immaculate presentation and attention to detail complemented by Barnard's uncompromising quest for technical excellence.

In 1986 John Barnard left to join the struggling Ferrari team. The partnership between Dennis and Barnard had been stormy, but a huge amount had been achieved through the energy of these two individuals, Dennis providing the managerial and commercial acumen and Barnard highly innovative design skills. To replace Barnard, Brabham designer Gordon Murray was brought into the team, perhaps best known for developing the innovative 'fan car' for Brabham in 1978. Murray, like Barnard, was at the leading edge of F1 car design.

A further factor in McLaren's success had been its relationship with engine suppliers. In the mid-1980s turbo charging became the key technology and in 1983 McLaren used a Porsche turbo engine which was funded by the electronics company TAG. However, the emerging force in engine development was Honda, which had re-entered F1 in 1983 in partnership with Williams. Importantly, the engines were supported by a significant commitment from Honda in both people and resources. Honda used the relationship as an opportunity to develop some of its most talented engineers and to transfer F1 design and development capabilities to its production car programme. In the mid-1980s the Williams/Honda partnership was very successful, but following Frank Williams' road accident in 1986, Honda began to have doubts about the future of the Williams team and agreed to supply both McLaren and Lotus for the 1987 season.

Halfway through 1987 McLaren announced that it had recruited two of the top drivers in F1 to the team for the 1988 season: Alain Prost and Ayrton Senna. This was unusual, as most teams tended to have a clear hierarchy, with a lead driver being supported by a 'number two' who was regarded as less skilful and/or less experienced than the lead driver; this hierarchy reduced the competitive tensions between the two drivers and their respective engineering teams. However, McLaren appeared to feel that it would be able to deal with the potential problems which might result from having two major drivers.

Prost and Senna were real contrasts. Senna was fast, determined and ruthless. Prost was also fast, but a great tactician and adept at team politics, making sure that the whole team were behind him. It was rumoured that a key reason for Honda moving to McLaren was that it now had Alain Prost.

In 1988 the Honda-powered MP4 car was without question the fastest and most reliable car on the circuit. This meant that effectively the only real competition for Prost and Senna was each other. This competition between two highly committed and talented drivers resulted in one of the most enduring and bitter feuds the sport has ever known. In 1990 the acrimony with Senna culminated in Prost moving to Ferrari.

Ron Dennis and his professional management style became synonymous with the success of McLaren, indicating that the era of the 'one-man band' Formula One constructor was past. His record since taking over in 1982 has been impressive. Eddie Jordan, principal of the Jordan team, held him in high regard: 'He's won that many Grand Prix, he's won that many championships, he's been on pole that many times and he's got the best drivers. Everyone hates him; but they only hate him because he's the best.'[3]

Dennis's negotiating and marketing abilities were legendary throughout Formula 1. McLaren also created its own marketing consultancy operation where the smaller teams engaged it to find sponsors. In 1991 *Management Week* had Ron Dennis on the front cover with the question: 'Is Ron Dennis Britain's best manager?' Dennis likens the management of McLaren to that of a game of chess: '. . . you've got to get all the elements right, the overall package, the budget, the designer, the engine, the drivers, and the organisation.'[4]

Dennis is renowned for being hyper-competitive and once chastised a driver who was delighted with finishing second with the comment, 'Just remember, second place is the first of the losers.'[5]

Dennis's ambitions went beyond F1 and in 1988 he had begun a project to build a road-going car, the McLaren F1. In many ways this mirrored the development of Ferrari who had made the progression from producing dedicated racing cars to also developing road-going cars. The McLaren F1 was launched in 1994 and with a price tag of £634,000 and a top speed of 231 mph (370 kph) became the most expensive and fastest road-going car in the world.

The McLaren–Honda combination had dominated F1 from 1988 through to 1991, and it was difficult to see what more could be achieved. In September 1992 Honda confirmed that that it was pulling out of F1. It had been hugely successful and achieved all of its objectives; it was now time to stand back and find some new challenges. Dennis had been told about Honda's thinking in late 1991, but it appeared that he had not taken it seriously enough and the team had no real engine alternatives. This meant they lost valuable winter development time as they tried to find a new engine supplier. In 1993 they competed with 'off the shelf' Ford engines available to any team who had the cash to buy them. Senna's skills still gave McLaren five victories, despite having a less than competitive car. However, at the end of 1993 Senna left the McLaren team to move to Williams, whom he saw as having the superior car and engine combination. Former world champion and adviser to Ferrari, Niki Lauda, saw this as the terminal blow: 'Senna was a leader. He told them exactly what was wrong with the car. Hakkinen [Senna's replacement] is not in a position to do that, so the reaction time is much longer. Senna motivated the designers.'[6]

The mid-1990s were a particularly difficult period for McLaren. Having tried Peugeot engines in 1994, it moved to Mercedes in 1995. Mercedes had been considering a major commitment to F1 and in 1995 it concluded a deal which involved taking equity stakes in McLaren (40%) and also in specialist engine builder Ilmor Engineering based near Northampton (which they subsequently purchased) who were to build the Mercedes engines used in F1.

Williams and the technological revolution: the mid-1990s

During the period 1992–4 Williams cars won 27 out of 48 races, they secured the F1 constructors' title in all three years, and the world championship for drivers was won in a Williams in 1992 (Nigel Mansell) and 1993 (Alain Prost).

Like many of the founders of F1 teams, Frank Williams began as a driver, perhaps not of the same standing as Bruce McLaren or Jack Brabham, but none the less someone who lived and breathed motor racing. His desire to remain in the sport led him to develop a business buying and selling racing cars and spare parts and in 1968 Frank Williams (Racing Cars) Ltd was formed. A series of triumphs, tragedies and near-bankruptcies led up to the establishment of Williams Grand Prix Engineering in 1977 when Frank Williams teamed up with technical director Patrick Head. Frank Williams' approach and style owed a lot to the difficult years in the 1970s when he survived on his wits and very little else, including operating from a public telephone box near the workshop when the phones were disconnected as he had not paid the bill. His style could be described as autocratic, entrepreneurial and certainly frugal, despite the multi-million-pound funding he managed to extract from the likes of Canon, R.J. Reynolds and Rothmans. Williams saw his role as providing the resources for the best car to be built. His longstanding relationship with Head was pivotal to the team and brought together a blend of entrepreneurial energy and technical excellence needed to succeed in F1.

The first car from this new alliance was the FW06, designed by Patrick Head and with financial support from Saudi Airlines. The team enjoyed success in 1980 and 1981 by winning the constructors' championship in both years and with Alan Jones winning the drivers' title in 1980. Jones was a forthright Australian who knew what he wanted and was not afraid to voice his opinions. His approach to working with the team was very influential and coloured Frank Williams' view of drivers: 'I took a very masculine attitude towards drivers and assumed that they should behave – or should be treated – like Alan.'[7]

Further success occurred in 1986 and 1987 with Nelson Piquet winning the drivers' title in 1987 and Williams the constructors' title in both years. This was despite the road accident in 1986 which left Frank Williams quadriplegic and confined to a wheelchair. However, 1988 was Williams' worst season: with Honda having switched to supplying McLaren, Williams was forced to use uncompetitive Judd V10 engines. Williams did not win a single race, McLaren won 15 of the 16 Grand Prix of 1988 and a disillusioned Nigel Mansell left and went to Ferrari. Frank Williams had to search frantically for a new engine deal, which he found in 1990 with Renault. This relationship became a far-reaching and durable one, with Renault putting human and financial resources into the project with Williams. Williams also sought to develop the relationship further and extended its activities with Renault by running its team for the British Touring Car Championship, and also provided engineering input and the Williams name for a special edition of the Renault Clio.

In 1990 a lack of driver talent meant that the team were able to win only two races. In 1991 Nigel Mansell was persuaded to return from retirement by Frank Williams and narrowly missed taking the 1991 title, but in 1992 the team dominated the circuits, effectively winning the championship by the middle of the season. Nigel Mansell went into the record books by winning the first five consecutive races of the season. However, deterioration in the relationship between Williams and Mansell led to the driver's retirement from F1 at the end of the year.

In a sport where personnel change teams frequently, the stable relationship between Williams and Head provided enviable continuity compared with the rest of the field. Head's designs had often been functional rather than innovative, but he had always been able to take a good idea and develop it further. These included ground effect (originally developed by Lotus), carbon-composite monocoque (McLaren), semi-automatic gearbox (Ferrari) and active suspension (Lotus). The car development process was always a top priority at Williams, and Head was supported by many junior designers who then went on to be highly influential in F1, such as Neil Oatley (McLaren), Adrian Newey (McLaren and Red Bull), Frank Dernie (Ligier, Lotus, Arrows and Toyota) and Ross Brawn (Benetton, Ferrari, Brawn and Mercedes).

This focus on developing the car and engine combination sometimes meant that the driver took second place in the Williams philosophy, despite the fact that a good test driver, who could help the technicians define and solve problems, was essential to the development process. There had been a number of high-profile disputes with drivers which had, in part, been attributable to the 'masculine' approach of Frank Williams to dealing with drivers. In 1992 Nigel Mansell left when he felt his 'number one' driver position was threatened by the recruitment of Alain Prost for 1993 (although Prost himself left the following year for the same reason regarding the hiring of Ayrton Senna). A similar situation arose when the 1996 world champion, Damon Hill, was not retained for the 1997 season and was replaced by Heinz-Harald Frentzen. In an interview with the Sunday Times Patrick Head set out the reasons for the decision not to hold onto Hill: 'We are an engineering company and that is what we focus on. Ferrari are probably the only team where you can say the driver is of paramount importance and that is because [Michael] Schumacher is three-quarters of a second a lap quicker than anyone else.'[8]

This emphasis on the driver being only part of the equation was not lost on Paul Stewart who was concentrating on developing the Stewart Grand Prix entry to F1 in 1996: 'If you look at the Williams team, they rely on a solid framework, their organisation, their engine, their car design is all amalgamated into something that gives a platform for everyone to work on. They don't believe putting millions into a driver is going to make all the difference.'[9]

Williams' emphatic dominance in the 1992 season was due to a number of factors: the development of the powerful and reliable Renault engine was perfectly complemented by the FW15 chassis, which incorporated Patrick Head's development of some of the innovations of the early 1990s, namely semi-automatic gearboxes, drive-by-wire technology and Williams' own active suspension system. As summarised by a senior manager at Williams F1: 'I think we actually were better able to exploit the technology that was available and led that technology revolution. We were better able to exploit it to the full, before the others caught up . . . it wasn't just one thing but a combination of 10 things, each one giving you another 200–300th of a second; if you add them up you a get a couple of seconds of advantage.'[10]

However, in 1993 the Benetton team made a great deal of progress with both gearbox and suspension innovations largely attributed to the development skills of their new driver, Michael Schumacher. Williams' technical lead coupled with the tactical racing skills of Alain Prost, supported by promoted test driver Damon Hill (due to Mansell's sudden exit), secured the 1993 world championship and constructors' championship for Williams F1.

The year 1994 was disastrous, although Williams won the constructors' championship for the third successive year (this was always its declared primary objective, with the drivers' championship very much a secondary aim). Frank Williams had, for some time, regarded Brazilian Ayrton Senna as the best driver around and now, with the obvious performance advantage of the FW15 chassis and the Renault V10 engine, Senna was keen to move to Williams, which he did, partnered by Damon Hill for the 1994 season. Tragically at the San Marino Grand Prix on 1 May 1994 Senna was killed in an accident, an event which devastated not only the Williams team but the sport as a whole.

In 1995 the Benetton team had eclipsed the Williams domination. Benetton had developed a car using many of the technological innovations used by Williams (with the help of ex-Williams designer, Ross Brawn). In addition Renault's ambitions to match Honda's previous domination of the sport as an engine supplier from 1986 to 1991 led it to end exclusive supply to Williams and also to provide Benetton with its engines. The year 1995 was when

Benetton and Michael Schumacher broke the three-year domination of the Williams team. However, in 1996 Schumacher moved to the then uncompetitive Ferrari team for £27 million, putting him in third place in the Forbes chart of sports top earners. This left the way clear for Williams to dominate the season, with Benetton failing to fill the gap left by Schumacher.

Ferrari: the return to glory, 1999–2004

In the 1980s, legendary F1 team Ferrari were struggling, winning only six races in the period from 1984 to 1988. A key problem was that new developments in aerodynamics and the use of composite materials had emerged from the UK's 'motorsport valley'. Ferrari had traditionally focused on the engine as its competitive advantage, which made perfect sense given that, unlike most of the competition, who outsourced their engines from suppliers such as Cosworth and Renault, Ferrari designed and manufactured its own engines. However, it appeared that these new technologies were effectively substituting superior engine power with enhanced grip due to aerodynamic downforce and improved chassis rigidity.

In 1986 British designer John Barnard was recruited to the top technical role, but was not prepared to move to Italy. Surprisingly, Enzo Ferrari allowed him to establish a design and development facility near Guildford in Surrey that became known as the Ferrari 'GTO' or Guildford Technical Office. It seemed that rather than being a unique and distinctively Italian F1 team, Ferrari was now prepared to imitate the British constructors whom Enzo had previously referred to as '*garagistes*' or '*assemblatori*'. The concept of the GTO was that it would concentrate on the design of the following year's car, whereas in Maranello Ferrari would focus on building and racing the current car. However, the fact that Barnard was defining the technical direction of Ferrari meant that he became increasingly involved in activities at both sites.

Enzo Ferrari's death in 1988 created a vacuum which was filled by executives from Fiat S.P.A. It was written into the contract between Ferrari and Fiat that on Enzo's death Fiat's stake would be increased from 40% to 90%; this led to attempts to run Ferrari as a formal subsidiary of the Fiat Group. Barnard became frustrated with the politics of the situation and left to join Benetton in 1989. In 1992 Fiat appointed Luca di Montezemolo as CEO with a mandate to take Ferrari back to the top. Montezemolo had been highly successful as team manager for Ferrari during the mid-1970s and had subsequently taken on a range of high-profile management roles, including running Italy's hosting of the Soccer World Cup in 1990. One of his first actions was to reappoint John Barnard as technical director and re-establish GTO. 'If you want to make pasta, then you

have to be in Parma. I want to make a sophisticated F1 project, so I want to be involved in England.'[11]

With an Englishman heading up design, he followed this up with the appointment of a Frenchman, Jean Todt, to handle the overall management of the team. Both appointments were clear signals to all involved in Ferrari that things were going to change. Todt had no prior experience in F1 but had been in motorsport management for many years and had led a successful rally and sports car programme at Peugeot.

But the physical separation between design and development in Guildford and the racing operation in Maranello was not a sustainable arrangement, and Barnard and Ferrari again parted company in 1996. At the end of 1996 Ferrari recruited double world champion Michael Schumacher from the Benetton team and followed this by recruiting two further individuals from Benetton: Rory Byrne, who had overall responsibility for designing the car, and Ross Brawn, who managed the entire technical operation. With Barnard and his UK operation gone, Byrne and Brawn faced the task of building up a new design department in Maranello of around 50 people. One of the most important tasks for the new team was to take advantage of the fact that Ferrari made its own engines, by integrating the design of the engine, chassis and aerodynamics as early in the process as possible. Ferrari's historic emphasis on the engine was replaced by a focus on integration, summarised by Ross Brawn: 'It's not an engine, it's not an aero-package, it's not a chassis. It's a Ferrari.'[12]

At this time Ferrari also entered into a long-term partnership with Shell to provide both financial and technical support to the team, a departure for Ferrari, which had previously worked with Italian petroleum giant Agip. In these kinds of arrangements Ferrari led a trend away from selling space on cars to long-term commercial and technological arrangements, with coordinated marketing strategies for commercial partners to maximise the benefits of their investments.

This rejuvenated team provided the basis for Michael Schumacher's dominance of F1. In 1999 they won their first constructors' championship for 12 years. In 2000 Ferrari secured both championships and it was at this point that it felt it had truly returned to the glory of the mid-1970s, its having been 21 years since its last drivers' world championship. In 2002 Schumacher and Ferrari were so dominant that a series of regulation changes were introduced to try to make the racing more competitive.

Schumacher's talent as a driver and a motivator of the team (he learnt Japanese to converse with an engine technician recruited from Honda) was critical, but another key aspect in Ferrari's advantage for 2002 had been its relationship with Bridgestone tyres (other leading teams used Michelin tyres) which designed and developed its compounds specifically for Michael Schumacher in a Ferrari. Despite stronger competition from Williams, McLaren and Renault, in 2003 Ferrari won both drivers' and constructors' titles and repeated the feat again in 2004, giving it a record-breaking sixth consecutive constructors' title and Michael Schumacher a seventh world championship, breaking Juan Fangio's record which had stood since 1957.

In 2005 and 2006 the competition became much stronger and, despite being competitive, Ferrari lost the drivers' and constructors' titles to the Renault F1 team (formerly Benetton). Renault benefited from the rising talent of Fernando Alonso, who proved himself a match for Schumacher in both driving and team motivation. In 2005 changes in the regulations meant that tyres were required to last for the whole race, which often benefited the Michelin technology used by Renault and left Ferrari struggling towards the end of the race on its Bridgestone tyres. In 2006 a more drastic change to the regulations meant that the constructors had to shift from 3.5 litre V10 engines to smaller V8s, with engine design to be frozen for three years from 2007. In many ways an engine change should have benefited Ferrari, but it struggled to get the performance in the early part of the season. Towards the end of the 2006 season Michael Schumacher announced his intention to retire at the end of the year, Jean Todt was promoted to CEO, highly experienced engine director Paolo Martinelli moved to a job with Fiat, and Ross Brawn announced he was taking a sabbatical in 2007.

Red Bull Racing: a new formula for success

On Monday 15 November 2004 the Ford Motor Company announced that it was selling the Jaguar Racing F1 team to the Red Bull beverage company for a 'nominal sum', and in exchange Red Bull agreed to underwrite the team for at least three years, securing around 350 jobs at their facility in Milton Keynes. Eight years later at the 2012 US Grand Prix in Austin, Texas, Sebastian Vettel's second place was enough to secure a third consecutive constructors' championship for Red Bull Racing, making it only the fourth constructor in the history of Formula 1 to have achieved such a feat.

The man behind the purchase of Jaguar Racing was Dietrich Mateschitz, an Austrian entrepreneur who had founded Red Bull GmbH in 1987 and effectively created a new category in beverages – energy drinks. In 2013 the *New York Times* reported that the US energy drink market was worth around $10 billion with Red Bull holding around 40% of this rapidly growing sector. Mateschitz had focused on building the Red Bull brand by association with a wide range of sports, including more extreme sports such as mountain biking, BMX biking, air racing, skydiving – and motor racing.

Red Bull's first involvement with Formula 1 came in 1995 when it acquired a majority stake in the struggling Sauber Team, for which it received title sponsorship in a period when the television audience of F1 was doubling to over 150 million people. In 2001 Red Bull launched the Red Bull Junior team under the guidance of former sports car racer Dr Helmut Marko. Red Bull Juniors support and develop young drivers in a range of different formulae with the intention of bringing new talent into Formula 1. In addition to financial support, the programme provides structured driving and fitness training. In 2004 the scheme had 15 drivers under contract, including a 16-year-old German, Sebastian Vettel, whom Red Bull had first supported driving karts when he was 12 years old. Markko made the following comment about him in 2004: '. . . his main difference to the other drivers is his head. When it comes to qualifying on one lap he can get his act together and do the job. He is also physically the fittest. He is competing in Formula BMW for the second year and we expect him to win.'[13]

In 2001 Dietrich Mateschitz disagreed with Sauber over the choice of drivers for 2002, Mateschitz wanting Red Bull Junior driver Enrique Bernoldi, with Peter Sauber favouring an unknown Finnish driver, Kimi Raikkonen, who went on to be world champion with Ferrari. Mateschitz sold his stake in Sauber to Crédit Suisse and considered acquiring the Arrows team in 2002 in order to secure a drive for Bernoldi. That fell through and Arrows went into liquidation. In 2004, keen to find a drive for the Red Bull Junior driver Christian Klien, Mateschitz entered into discussions with Jaguar Racing and discovered that Ford was considering the sale of the team; he made the purchase in November 2004.

Initially he intended the incumbent management team, Tony Purnell and Dave Pitchforth, to run the team, but a dispute over drivers for 2005 led to their leaving the company and being replaced by Christian Horner as team principal for the start of 2005. At only 31 years old, Horner was a surprising appointment, particularly in terms of his age and his lack of F1 experience prior to his appointment. As a racing driver, Horner, along with his father Garry, had established his own racing team, Arden, in 1997 to contest the FIA Formula 3000 championship. In 1999 he stepped out of the cockpit and concentrated entirely on managing the team. Markko already knew Horner as they had both run teams in F3000, and so had already observed Horner's management style as a competitor.

Mateschitz wanted Red Bull Racing to display some of the non-conformist values he felt were central to the Red Bull brand. At the first European race of 2005 the Red Bull Energy Station made its first appearance – an immense three-storey hospitality centre which needed 25 people to assemble it and 11 trucks to transport it. This redefined standards in the F1 paddock. In contrast to those of all the other teams, the Red Bull facility was open access to everyone within the paddock; it belted out loud music and served drinks and snacks for all. It was particularly popular with the F1 media who could now use the facility to unwind or catch up on the gossip of the day. Red Bull also produced the *Red Bulletin*, available free within the paddock, a rather irreverent publication that featured many of the Red Bull sportsmen and women.

But even if Red Bull liked to be non-conformist and youthful, most of all it wanted to win. Horner recognised that a key component in bringing success to Red Bull Racing was the recruitment of a leading F1 designer. He set his sights very high, and in 2005 attempted to recruit McLaren chief designer Adrian Newey, one of the elite designers in F1 whose salary was greater than those of many of the drivers. This was a high-risk strategy: back in May 2001 Jaguar Racing team principal and close friend of Newey, Bobby Rahal, had signed a five-year deal with Newey to secure his services as technical director; however, two days later Newey changed his mind and signed a further contract with McLaren up to the end of July 2005. Rahal subsequently ended up leaving the team at the end of 2001. Horner enlisted the help of Red Bull driver David Coulthard, who had worked with Newey at both Williams and McLaren, a meeting was set up and Newey was invited to Austria to meet Mateschitz. In a magazine interview Horner describes how the deal was finalised:

'Adrian, we'd love to have you. Do you want to come? He stated a figure that caught my attention because it was about 70% higher than I'd warned Dietrich we might have to pay. I called Dietrich, he went quiet for a few seconds, then he said, "Let's go for it." That's the great thing about Red Bull. It's his company, it belongs just to him and one other person in Thailand. No board meetings, no shareholders' approvals, just an instant decision.'[14]

The decision to bring Newey into the team was undoubtedly an expensive one, but it also marked a turn in fortunes for the team, which Horner attributes to the influence of their new technical director:

'Adrian forced a change of culture on us, because the way he works is completely different. We weren't prepared for the amount of detail he gets involved in. For starters, he still uses a drawing board [most design F1 work is undertaken using computer aided design, and the designs are worked up on computers]. I had to do a deal with Martin Whitmarsh to get McLaren to release his beloved board which had followed him there from Williams and is now in his office at Red Bull Racing. In F1 nowadays a technical director is usually a technical manager, someone who chairs meetings and agrees philosophy and strategic direction, but isn't involved in the actual architecture of the car. Adrian draws the surfaces of the car himself and then passes that over to the aerodynamicists and designers. He stimulates and encourages them, they feed off him, and he feeds off them.'

Although Horner is technically the man in charge, he and Newey run the team together: 'Adrian very much has an input into driver choice, he's involved in all the major decisions. Dietrich will have the final say on the big things – choice of driver, engine, strategic investment – but Adrian and I run the business day to day.'[15]

In 2007 Red Bull Racing started using Renault engines, the first team outside the Renault works team to be supplied with Renault engines for some time, Renault having won the constructors' trophy in 2005 and 2006. Newey had previously worked with Renault when designing the world-championship-winning Williams FW14B. When the team won their first constructors' championship and drivers' championship with Sebastian Vettel in 2010, it seemed that all the investment had finally paid off.

By the start of 2012 Red Bull Racing had grown to 550 employees, and the team had enjoyed two world championship drivers' and constructors' championships. It was to prove to be a good year for the Milton Keynes team, which achieved both constructors' and drivers' world championships yet again, putting them into a very elite club of four teams who had won the constructors' trophy three or more times in a row.

The changing face of Formula 1

In 2009 the World Motorsport Council, the decision-making body of the FIA, adopted a proposal put forward by the Environmentally Sustainable Motorsport Commission (ESMC) that future motorsport should be efficiency based rather than capacity based. In other words, rather than defining motorsport categories by the size of engines used, it would now be based on measures such as the amount of fuel used or the amount of CO_2 generated. This led to radical new F1 regulations for the 2014 season, the most significant being restrictions on the size of the fuel tank and the flow of fuel to the engine. In 2012 an F1 car used around 160 kg of fuel in a race; in 2014 cars are limited to 100 kg.[16] In addition, the engine specification will move from a 2.4 litre normally aspirated V8 to a 1.6 litre V6 turbo-charged engine. The Kinetic Energy Recovery Systems (KERS) that were brought in from 2009 and provided an additional 60 kW of power would be replaced by an Energy Recovery System (ERS) producing double the power of KERS. All of these changes meant that the most successful cars will be those that can make the most efficient use of the fuel available. At the end of 2012 only three engine suppliers remained committed to providing F1 power plants for 2014 – Renault, Ferrari and Mercedes. For Red Bull Racing's Christian Horner this could mean a change in the established order: 'What we need to be careful of is that we don't make the engine and power plant a key performance differentiator between teams. If you end up on the wrong or the right power plant in 2014, that could prove crucial.'[17]

In addition to a focus on fuel efficiency, efforts were also continuing to reduce the costs involved in competing in Formula 1. Regulations were introduced in 2009 attempting to reduce costs to the level of the early 1990s through a ban on testing, wind-tunnel usage and temporary shutdown of factories. In 1992 Frank Williams' team employed 190 people (they won the world championship that year), whereas in 2008 they employed 540, so they are looking at a 65% reduction in infrastructure from 2008 levels. All of this suggests that the F1 teams need to find new and more cost-effective ways of creating competitive advantage.

Looking at the F1 constructors raises some important questions around the challenge of sustaining successful performance in a highly competitive context. How are these teams able to sustain success after they have dominated the championships? What are the different ways in which this can be achieved in different organisations? And how does the basis for success shift over time? These four examples illustrate some of the challenges which organisations face in attempting both to create and to sustain competitive advantage.

Notes and references
1. Roebuck, N. 'Frank Williams: the enthusiast turned realist', *Independent*, 12 July 1992.
2. $1 = £0.65 = €0.77.
3. Jacques, M. and Robson, D. 'McLaren lose the key', *Independent*, 9 July 1994, p. 18.
4. Ibid., p. 19.
5. Henry, A. (1998) *McLaren: The Epic Years*. Yeovil, Somerset: Haynes Publishing, p. 179.
6. Jacques, M. and Robson, D. 'McLaren lose the key', *Independent*, 9 July 1994, p. 19.
7. Sir Frank Williams, quoted in *Autocar & Motor*, 9 March 1994, p. 78.
8. Patrick Head, quoted in *The Sunday Times*, 8 September 1996, p. 14.
9. Quote from an interview with the author.
10. Quote from an interview with the author.
11. Interview in *Autosport*, 10 September 1992, p. 30.
12. Jenkins, M., Pasternak, K. and West, R. (2008) *Performance at the Limit: Business Lessons from Formula 1 Motor Racing*, 2nd edn, Cambridge: Cambridge University Press, p. 48.
13. Cutler, M. (2004) 'The future is bullish for Red Bull's youngsters', *BusinessF1*, 2, 4, April, pp. 343–6.
14. Taylor, S. (2012) 'Lunch with Christian Horner'. *Motorsport*, 88, 1, pp. 67–72.
15. Ibid.
16. 'The Rev Revolution', *F1 Racing*, 203, January 2013, pp. 96–8.
17. 'Horner's Blueprint for Formula 1', *Autosport online*, 19 October 2012.

CASE STUDY

Integration of a Corporate Social Responsibility programme in Coloplast

Christina Berg Johansen

The notion of 'strategic Corporate Social Responsibility' is gaining ground, and corporate leaders are looking to reap the commercial benefits of CSR, while simultaneously improving the societies they are part of. In Denmark, medical devices company Coloplast has a vision to help users in emerging markets, while building valuable business insight, through its CSR programme 'Access to Healthcare'. However, this proved more difficult than the initial lofty vision promised.

● ● ●

In 2007, the Danish medical devices company Coloplast celebrated its 50th anniversary with great pride. In 1957 a nurse and a plastics engineer founded Coloplast, which over the years became a world leader in the business of ostomy bags[1] and appliances, with related business areas such as continence care, advanced wound care and surgical urology. By 2007, Coloplast had grown to 7000 employees, its revenue growth was 20% compared to an average 8% in the years before, and revenue was DKK8.047 million (£0.91m; $1.38m; €1.08m).[2] Furthermore, it looked like Coloplast was successfully managing the transition to 'offshoring' its production to big plants in China and Hungary.

Coloplast wanted to celebrate its 50 years by 'giving something back' to society and its stakeholders: the nurses, doctors and patients using its products. The result was the launch of 'Access to Healthcare – Coloplast Donation Programme': a Corporate Social Responsibility (CSR) programme designed to improve conditions for end-users in emerging and poor markets. 'Access to Healthcare' would spend at least DKK50 million over the following 10 years by donating to social and educational projects within Coloplast's areas of expertise. This would improve local treatment and help underprivileged end-users enjoy better lives.

However, over the next four years, Access to Healthcare dwindled into near-oblivion, completed few projects, showed meagre results and was not even able to spend its allocated DKK5 million per year. Not until 2012 did Access to Healthcare find its feet and relevance, as an effect of reconceptualising and restructuring the programme. What happened in between?

Foundation: idealistic visions

In September 2007, Access to Healthcare was an expense the company could afford. Its fundamental idea was philanthropic, and it had no business case or return on investment projections. It was a highly independent project in the organisation, conceptualised by a narrow group of managers comprising the CEO, the ethics manager and a trusted marketing project manager.

In designing the programme, the CEO was inspired by different corporate philanthropic foundations, particularly the World Diabetes Foundation, an independent operation of Danish pharmaceutical giant Novo Nordisk. Coloplast designed a 'mini-version' of a foundation, granting project assessment and donation rights to a mainly external board. On the board were three externals, representing a global stoma nurses' association, a global doctors' association and the expertise from the World Diabetes Foundation through its managing director. The internal representatives were the CEO and the senior vice president of Coloplast's Asia Pacific region. The idea behind the board was to ensure Access to Healthcare's independence from day-to-day business and to leave funding decisions to the involved stakeholders (nurses and doctors), whose primary focus was the needs of patients rather than the need to sell products.

From the outset, the Access to Healthcare manager and other managers discussed the programme's overarching objectives. Some managers saw Access to Healthcare's social objectives as a moral obligation to help poor end-users. Others tried to incorporate business aspects, such as the provision of new knowledge about customers in emerging markets and the Asia Pacific region, and relationship marketing support to subsidiaries in those markets.

Access to Healthcare did not have a clear strategy. The programme formally rested on the practice of donations to project applicants in the shape of NGOs[3] and interest groups, and on the pursuit of social meaning over business value. This could also be observed in the programme's original strategy draft, which stated that Access to Healthcare should be a 'commitment to the UN Global Compact and the Millennium Development Goals' and would 'extend [Coloplast's] listening and responding abilities to include our stakeholders all over the world.'[4] Simultaneously, the draft stated that Access to Healthcare was valuable for business, because it could: 'secure access and knowledge to growth in the long run'.

This support of business growth was, however, mainly a statement of interest, since no organisational strategies or processes linked the programme with other parts of the business and the draft was never developed into tangible strategic plans. The strategic guideline was that if you as a company behave ethically with three overarching stakeholder groups – customers, employees and society – you will be paid back plentifully. As expressed by the CEO: 'The idea was that if we balanced the offering to these three stakeholder groups optimally, then there would also be the maximum long-term payback to the shareholders.'

Disruption: times of corporate crisis

In early August 2008, Coloplast released an announcement reducing organic growth as well as EBIT margin expectations. The expected gains from moving production to Hungary had not materialised, and there were serious management issues in the Global Operations Division. These were dealt with through managerial restructuring, and some weeks later another change was announced: the CEO was resigning and a new and leaner top management were to take over. The Chief Commercial Officer Lars Rasmussen became the new CEO and his previous position was cut. Chief Financial Officer (CFO) Lene Skole stayed in place. This new leadership aimed to raise profitability and create a stronger and more coherent Coloplast strategy. Within a few months, the new management had eliminated several hundred jobs, initiated cost-cutting in all departments and was launching a new strategic tool: the short-term business priority strategy named 'The Agenda'. Through 8–10 changing priorities, The Agenda targeted either sales generation or cost-efficiency. Corporate practices not included on The Agenda

became at best peripheral, at worst officially questioned. The new CEO Lars Rasmussen repeatedly stated at organisation-wide Agenda presentations: 'If you do not see your work represented on The Agenda, you should consider if you are doing the right things.'

Practices such as CSR and Access to Healthcare were not on The Agenda, neither were emerging market strategies, whose share in Coloplast profits was much lower than those of European markets and therefore not an immediate priority. Raising profitability was the vital concern in Coloplast, and more developmental, long-term opportunities were marginalised, if not abandoned.

Access to Healthcare had lost its main protector, the previous CEO, and was generally ignored and left to its independent board and programme manager, who kept working to create projects that could be approved by the board. The programme needed to keep a low profile, and therefore did not make any official announcements of Access to Healthcare funds to relevant NGOs. The programme manager later reflected:

> '[It was] terrible! I mean, you could sit on your chair and say, "well, I'm just waiting for something to happen". That is not me. So I had to find solutions of course. So I was really struggling. . . . I mean, I could only get support from a few of my very old network friends.'

To create better strategic conditions for the now marginalised programme, the programme manager found a department to host Access to Healthcare: People & Communications. But there were no natural anchor points for Access to Healthcare in that department, and management there were busy with more immediate priorities such as media relations and supporting the internal turnaround. Instead the programme manager turned to her own internal network for help. These were headquarters-based managers who were responsible for the Rest of World region, and they helped facilitate contact between Access to Healthcare and local country managers. However, they too were marginalised in the restructuring process, and were pressed for resources for anything beyond simple sales efforts. Based on dialogues between country managers and headquarters, a series of project ideas were born, targeting nurses and doctors with education and awareness-building, for example nurses' education in China, and diabetic wound care training for doctors in India. Projects were often conceived by the local Coloplast office, and then formulated in collaboration with the official applicant organisations such as the International Ostomy Association, the International Spinal Cord Society, the China Nursing Association, and local wound care doctors' associations. The role of Coloplast was, however, not visible in the official application, since this had to be submitted as an independent NGO project description.

The social nature of Access to Healthcare was changing, and although the programme was formally still doing philanthropy with healthcare NGOs in poor markets, it had taken a pragmatic turn by engaging with managers in Coloplast's emerging markets. These were bound by strict sales-focused budgets, and saw Access to Healthcare as a means to strengthen their marketing efforts. By offering educational opportunities to influential doctors' and nurses' organisations, they were able to build important relationships in their own markets – similar to what Coloplast's marketing projects had done in core markets.

Getting from project idea to application to final contract and project commencement was, however, an ambiguous and lengthy process. In some cases it lasted more than 18 months, involving several rounds of assessment by the board, adjusted applications, budget changes, and uncertainty around contract signing. Two years after its launch, Access to Healthcare had only six projects either approved or in the pipeline, varying in size from US$22,000 to $241,000 and in duration from two-day workshops to three-year educational programmes. The annual budget of DKK5m was not spent. There were no results to communicate, since projects had hardly started. The programme manager felt misunderstood and resigned, and the programme came close to termination. CFO Lene Skole, who was now the top person responsible for Access to Healthcare, decided, together with the head of People & Communications, to give the programme a second chance – not least because it was initially a public commitment with positive branding potential.

Reorientation: legitimising the business perspective

In November 2009, Access to Healthcare got its second programme manager, also from the marketing department. He began his work in Access to Healthcare by networking across headquarters and visiting emerging market offices, and built strong agreement that Access to Healthcare could and should support business there. In early 2011 this resulted in the termination of the external board and the last remains of the 'foundation' approach. The new programme manager was working to find a new corporate 'fit' for the programme, and struggled to 'describe that fine line between when it is enough of a marketing program . . . to be of interest to Coloplast, without compromising the promise to the user'. There were still only a few projects, as it was hard for even the more engaged emerging market managers to find time for the complicated Access to Healthcare project development.

Meanwhile, a last round of cost trimming was being rolled out in headquarters. The option to eliminate Access to Healthcare was, once again, seriously considered.

Against the programme were its relatively high costs and little business value. In its favour were the future prospects of emerging markets, and the role it could play in these. By late 2010, Coloplast was ready to expand its strategic vision in order to boost growth – revenue was growing and the EBIT margin had increased from 12% in 2007–08 to 21% in 2009–10. In 2011, emerging markets such as China reappeared on The Agenda because of their high growth rates. Since Access to Healthcare had several projects in China, positive attention was turned towards it.

Business integration: building healthcare policy

Top management decided to keep Access to Healthcare and leverage its special aims and abilities as a 'non-commercial' programme. The programme manager was dismissed and Access to Healthcare was handed over to the third programme manager since its inception: the senior public affairs manager in charge of emerging market geographies.

The new programme manager related Access to Healthcare to the evolving growth strategy in Coloplast, which was based on an ambition to be among the big global corporations in the med-tech industry globally. As part of this strategy, the Chinese market was promoted to the status of a sales region in the company, providing it with more resources for market development. Also, in regions such as Latin America, Coloplast was looking to have an impact on national and regional healthcare policy to increase reimbursement opportunities for its products. These were the types of strategic activity that Access to Healthcare projects could support, and the new programme manager relaunched Access to Healthcare as a 'partnership programme' in this way. Subsidiaries were made responsible for reaching out to local interest groups and powerful healthcare professionals and building projects with them. Marketing objectives were dropped, and the programme's potential as a market development tool was buttressed, as the new programme manager explained: 'We are trying to think a little more holistically . . . in terms of how do you create a system of care in these places, . . . making sure that these projects are also addressing the policymaking community in these countries.'

The programme focused on powerful local organisations and political units. This decisively placed the individual and poor end-users outside most projects' scope – the aim was not to help individuals directly, but to change the healthcare systems to Coloplast's (and their) later benefit.

The integration of Access to Healthcare in the company was enthusiastically described by the head of the People & Communications department in an internal newsletter in December 2011: 'Mark [the new programme manager] and I visited Lene [the CFO] with a revitalised concept for Access to Healthcare. Now with energy, simplicity, genuine commitment from the markets and easy to understand Access to Healthcare is back now.'

Managers from Coloplast's emerging markets were queuing up to create Access to Healthcare projects. The new programme manager decided to spend considerable time with regional and country managers to help them assess realistic projects with clear advocacy and policy effects. It did not come naturally to these managers to work with non-commercial targets and measures, though they were keen on strengthening this side of their business. So the programme manager focused on making the actual impacts of the Access to Healthcare project clearer. He hired an external consultancy to help build tools and guidelines for Coloplast managers interested in Access to Healthcare projects, and visited local country offices for more in-depth development. He encouraged local managers to select external partners for their policy impact and reach of healthcare professionals, and the new application system required the roles of both partners and Coloplast to be clearly described.

By late 2012, seven new projects had been contracted, spread across China, Brazil, Argentina, India and South Africa. In 2012, Access to Healthcare for the first time managed to use all its funds for projects.

So is Access to Healthcare now a successful CSR programme? The implementation and results from the new projects over the next few years will tell. One major challenge is the lack of time and skills in local Coloplast offices for working well with partners, and pursuing non-commercial goals that are still not part of the core strategy. On the other hand, Access to Healthcare is now a recognised political tool that connects with the general public affairs work in Coloplast, and may be able to play a strong role in building emerging markets. Whether that makes for a successful CSR programme, or is actually something completely different from CSR, is a discussion that Coloplast has now had for five years and which has yet to come to a conclusion.

Notes

1. An ostomy pouching system (also called a bag) is a medical device that provides a means for the collection of waste from a surgically diverted biological system.
2. DKK1 = £0.114 = $0.175 = €0.134.
3. NGO stands for Non-Government Organisations. They are not-for-profit organisations which are separate from local or national governments.
4. This and all subsequent quotations are taken from the author's own interviews.

CASE STUDY

Manchester United FC: still successful despite new threats

Steve Pyle

This case describes the continuing success of Manchester United in English professional football despite the club's debts and the controversies concerning its ownership. Football in Europe is entering an era of financial 'fair play' – will Manchester United continue to thrive or be overtaken by richer clubs? The case involves a number of issues, including ownership structures, football finances, governance and the expectations of different stakeholders.

● ● ●

Introduction

Manchester United is the most celebrated football club in the UK, although in 2012 its supremacy was challenged by both Manchester City (who won the English Premier League in 2012) and Chelsea (who won the Premier League in 2010 and the European Champions League in 2012). Both of these clubs have mega-rich owners who, unlike Manchester United, have invested heavily without plunging the club into massive debt.

Within Europe, Manchester United (MUFC) was the third biggest club behind only Real Madrid and Barcelona in terms of turnover, while Chelsea was sixth and Manchester City 12th in 2010–11. Both Chelsea and Manchester City have ambitious owners and are likely to gain more success and higher revenues in the future. Although MUFC remains successful, 2011–12 was somewhat less impressive, having finished second to Manchester City in the Premier League and suffering an early exit in the European Champions League. None the less, Manchester United remains a top team, despite their precarious financial position. In the year to June 2011 MUFC increased revenues to a record level of £331.4 million (€392.8m; $502.6m)[1] and increased profits before interest and taxation to £100.7 million. Fortunately, 2012–13 was a more successful year in both the Premier and European Champions Leagues, and revenues and profits were higher in the second half of 2012. Debt remains at very high levels despite launching a share issue on the US stock exchange in August 2012.

Football finances in Europe are coming under much greater scrutiny, as UEFA has launched a 'financial fair

Source: Rex Features/McPix Ltd

play' policy aimed at limiting excessive expenditure and unsustainable debt levels among European clubs. Can Manchester United continue to outperform its rivals or will its two decades of dominance come to an end? Will MUFC's unpopular ownership by the Glazer family remain in place or will the club return to plc status? Will the club be taken over by yet another ambitious billionaire attracted by 'the beautiful game' or will the real fans get a look in?

Manchester United FC – a proud history

Manchester United's business success and global brand is rooted in the club's history. The club achieved limited success in the first 70 years of its existence, but in the 1950s manager Matt Busby built a brilliant young team that were devastated in 1958 by the Munich air disaster in which many of the best players died. The club recovered and attracted many thousands of admirers who started to follow the club. Manchester United continued to develop young and exciting teams and won the English league in 1965 and 1967. Manchester United became the first English club to win the European Cup in 1968. It also became the best-supported club in the country, and its fame began to spread overseas. After the English Premier League was introduced in 1992–3, Manchester United began to dominate the English game, winning the league championship 12 times in the first 20 years.

For many years the club had been run as a private limited company with majority control in the hands of the Edwards family. In 1989 the club was valued at £10m, but over the next 30 years the valuation of the club rocketed as the value of an iconic football brand was realised and the commercialisation of football became greater. When live televised matches became the norm after the 1980s, it was realised that big football clubs could be very valuable assets. How could such a club be in financial difficulty?

Manchester United becomes a public limited company

Martin Edwards, Chairman of the club in 1980, was concerned by the strategic problems of raising funds for ground improvements and improving playing success by attracting top players. In 1991 the club was floated on the London Stock Exchange with a valuation of £40m. As a public limited company (plc) the club was able to raise further capital by share issues in 1994 and 1997. At the time of the flotation in 1991, very few football clubs had the ownership structure of a plc and it was a controversial move. The manager Alex Ferguson said: 'When the plc started there were grave doubts about it – I had them myself – but I think the supporters came round.'[2]

What brought the supporters round was the success of the team and the increased financial revenues the club was attracting. In May 1997 Peter Kenyon was recruited for his marketing and branding expertise. Later, as chief executive, he helped to build the club's global business interests. MUFC's sales of replica kits and club-related gifts continued to expand and its merchandising success became the benchmark for the industry. Increasingly, Manchester United became a well-known brand across the world. In 2003 Peter Kenyon was lured away by a huge financial package from rivals Chelsea who were financed by Russian billionaire Roman Abramovich. Kenyon's position was successfully filled by his deputy, David Gill, whose financial expertise had been instrumental in the success of the plc.

Clean sheets or balance sheets?

A public limited company has a different set of purposes and priorities compared to other forms of ownership structures common among football clubs. Shareholders demand profits and, although some shares were held by supporters, the vast majority were owned by financial institutions that were looking for a return on their investment. MUFC as a plc was at the forefront of the revolution that was changing football from a traditional working-class sport into a multinational business. Clubs were now receiving huge sums from the media (Sky TV had massively increased the value of football on TV) and clubs were getting a lot more income from sponsors. Some genuine football supporters began to feel alienated by the club's values and global aspirations – should a football club be striving for profits? The range of stakeholders that needed to be satisfied had become considerably wider, as is evident from the club's 1999 annual report: 'We have to ensure that shareholders, loyal supporters, customers and key commercial partners alike benefit from our performance.'[3]

In the 14 years when MUFC was a plc (1991–2005), the club dominated English football (winning the Premier League title eight times and the FA Cup four times) and the profits were rolling in. Everyone seemed to be benefiting from the success, but there was an undercurrent of dissatisfaction among some supporters and resentment from other clubs.

The Glazer takeover – a return to private ownership

One of the disadvantages of plc status is the risk of a takeover. Manchester United was a cash-rich club and the potential to exploit the brand attracted predatory interest. In the early 2000s Malcolm Glazer (a multi-millionaire with diverse business interests in the USA) began to build a shareholding stake in MUFC. Glazer had no real knowledge of football but had successfully acquired Tampa Bay Buccaneers – an American football team – and thought he could replicate that success. Glazer saw the potential of a strong brand and believed that he might be able to market it successfully in the USA and globally.

A group called 'Shareholders United' rallied support among small shareholders (mostly supporters of the club) and tried to block the takeover, but to no avail. Throughout the takeover battle many fans bitterly opposed the acquisition, and initially this opposition was shared by the Board of Directors. David Gill, the CEO, cautioned against the acquisition, saying: 'The Board continues to believe that Glazer's business plan assumptions are aggressive and could be damaging.'[4]

One group of disillusioned fans even founded a new independent football club, called FC United of Manchester, and this small club has survived in minor league football – but it is no real threat. As Glazer kept increasing the price he offered, the Board was forced to accept that at £3 per share this represented a fair valuation and, although the plc Board never actually recommended the offer, it no longer actively opposed it and Glazer was able to make the necessary deals. Glazer steadily built his stake – financial institutions will almost always sell at the right price. By May 2005 Glazer had increased his stake to the critical 75% level. He was therefore able to de-list the club from the stock exchange and soon afterwards he bought out all the remaining shares. When the final takeover was complete the valuation of MUFC was estimated at £800m. However, the Glazer family were not rich enough to finance the deal themselves and had to borrow heavily to gain control, much of this debt (about £275m) being secured against the football club's own assets. Moreover, a significant part of this finance was obtained at high rates of interest from US hedge funds. After being debt-free for almost 15 years as a plc, MUFC had become a privately owned company with total debts estimated at £660m, incurring annual interest payments of about £60m.

The Glazer years

Immediately after the takeover, the Glazer family began to pursue policies to dampen hostility. They pledged funds for transfers and offered new contracts to Sir Alex Ferguson and David Gill to ensure continuity. They assured fans that they were not after a quick profit. Malcolm Glazer was an old man and appointed his sons (Joel, Ave and Bryan) to the Board to oversee the business.

During the takeover, fans were worried that ticket prices would soar in order to pay the increased costs of the borrowing undertaken by the Glazers. This fear may be misplaced. Ticket prices have gone up but they are still cheaper than at many premiership clubs – notably Chelsea and Arsenal. The stadium is full for almost every match and there is a long waiting list for season tickets.

Manchester United continued to invest heavily in the stadium and its facilities – the developments completed in 2006 took ground capacity up to 75,691, making it by far the largest club ground in England. Average attendances (and match day revenues) are higher than those of key rivals: in 2011–12 Manchester United had an average league attendance of 75,387 compared to its next biggest rival Arsenal, whose average attendance was 60,000. Indeed, in Europe only Barcelona and Borussia Dortmund command higher average attendances. The Manchester United Superstore is still by far the most lucrative club shop in the country, and sponsorships together with commercial income (most importantly broadcasting fees) ensure that the revenues continue to rise. This has enabled the club to service the interest payments on the debts.

Refinancing

Clearly, the financial position of the club needed attention, with debts of £716.5 million outstanding in January 2010. Later that year a bond issue generated £504 million, which enabled MUFC to pay off most of the debt held by international banks. The annual interest payable on these bonds – which are due to mature on 1 February 2017 – is approximately £45 million per annum, but this was considerably less than was previously paid out. Despite restructuring, the club's debt prompted protests from fans – supporters started wearing green and gold scarves, the club's original colours. Banners stating 'Love United Hate Glazer' appeared around the ground.

The Manchester United Supporters' Trust (who had opposed the Glazers from the start) held meetings with a group of wealthy fans, dubbed the 'Red Knights', with plans to buy out the Glazers' controlling interest. The group stated that they would pay a 'sensible' amount for the club and baulked at the Glazers' valuation of the club, which was significantly higher than they were willing to pay. No exact figures have been published, but it seems the Red Knights were unwilling to pay more than £1.2bn whereas the Glazers valued the club at over £1.6bn. It soon became apparent that the Glazers were not going to sell out.

In July 2012, the club decided to list shares on the New York Stock Exchange, thereby diluting the Glazers' ownership but without losing control. Shares were set to go on sale at $16 but the price was cut to $14 on the day of the launch following negative comments from analysts. The shares traded poorly at first but have recovered to trade at $19 in February 2013. Manchester United was valued by Forbes at $2.3 billion in 2012, making it the most valuable football club in the world.

On the playing side, success has continued despite the massive investments made by Chelsea, Arsenal, Liverpool and particularly Manchester City. Manchester United completed a hat trick of league titles in 2009 and won again in 2011. They also reached the European Champions League final in both 2008 and 2009, beating Chelsea in 2008 and losing to Barcelona in 2009. However, 2011–12 was less successful, being its first season without a major trophy since 2005, and it failed to qualify for the knockout stages of the European Champions League for the first time since 2006. The 2012–13 season showed signs of improvement, with better performance in both the English Premier League and the European Champions League. The club has continued to sign top players but has tended to look for younger (and cheaper) players, such as Javier Hernandez (in 2010) and Phil Jones (in 2011). None the less, in 2012 there was the bold move to sign Robin Van Persie for £24m from Arsenal, signalling that Manchester United can still compete for the best. From the perspective of 2012, the fortunes of the club looked good, but how long could it last?

Alternative ownership structures

There are alternatives to the debt-financed pattern of ownership that is now common in the English Premier League. In Germany all professional clubs are required to have at least 51% ownership by the members. In Spain the two richest clubs (Real Madrid and Barcelona) are owned and operated by the members. Never the less, this does not stop these clubs taking on debt – the seemingly irresistible drive to be successful demands that spending often exceeds income. The membership ownership model does exist in England but only at relatively lower levels of the football pyramid, for example AFC Wimbledon in the fourth tier.

A further possibility would be for clubs to be supported by large firms that use the clubs as part of a promotion strategy and support the local clubs in the communities where they are located; for example, Philips support PSV Eindhoven and Bayer support Bayer Leverkusen. It is also possible for local government bodies to support clubs financially and in other ways (provision of stadia) but this is not common at senior levels of football.

Some clubs are lucky enough to have rich benefactors who provide funding. Chelsea are backed by the billionaire support of Roman Abramovich and are secure as long as Abramovich retains his financial support.

The latest clubs to receive massive financial support from mega-rich owners include Manchester City, which is fully owned by Sheikh Mansour (part of the UAE's ruling family) with an estimated individual net worth of at least £17 billion. Since taking over, he has cleared Manchester City's £305 million debt. Similarly, Qatar Investment Authority acquired Paris Saint-Germain in 2012. PSG president Nasser Al-Khelaifi announced that he expected to invest €100m to build a strong team.

However, a sudden influx of wealth can backfire if the rich owners then lose interest or switch their funds to other sports clubs. Malaga FC was taken over by Sheikh Abdullah Al-Thani, a member of the Qatari royal family, who spent heavily in 2010–11 – only for the funding to dry up in 2012. A transfer ban was imposed by the Spanish League after non-payment of outstanding fees, and key players have been sold. A lack of continuing interest and support from the owners has left the club in deep financial trouble.

It was problems like this and the spiralling debt at many top clubs that persuaded UEFA and its president Michel Platini to develop a 'Financial Fair Play' policy. Platini expressed the concerns of many when he said:

> 'The goal is not to win titles but to make money to pay off debts. Look at Chelsea and Manchester United. FIFA and UEFA owe it to themselves to fight this. I am very concerned by clubs being bought by foreigners. I don't see why Americans come to invest in these clubs if not to turn them into 'products'. It's a never ending gold rush.'[5]

The 'Financial Fair Play' regulations

Many clubs, like MUFC, have reported repeated financial losses; moreover, the wider economic situation has created difficult market conditions for clubs in Europe. Many clubs have experienced liquidity shortfalls, leading to delayed payments to other clubs, employees and social/tax authorities. With Platini as a driving force, UEFA decided to take action and set about tackling these problems. UEFA's Executive Committee unanimously approved a 'financial fair play' concept for the game's well-being in September 2009 and published their policy in 2010,[6] the principal objectives being to:

- introduce more discipline and rationality in football club finances
- decrease pressure on salaries and transfer fees and limit inflationary effects
- encourage clubs to compete with(in) their revenues
- encourage long-term investments in the youth sector and infrastructure
- protect the long-term viability of European club football
- ensure clubs settle their liabilities on a timely basis.

One important aspect of the policy is an obligation for clubs to balance their books or 'break even'. Clubs cannot repeatedly spend more than their generated revenues, and will be obliged to meet all their transfer and employee payment commitments. Higher-risk clubs that fail to meet key indicators will be required to provide budgets detailing their strategic plans. UEFA has a range of sanctions including warnings, fines, deduction of points and disqualification from tournaments. A Financial Control Panel has been set up to monitor and ensure that clubs adhere to the Financial Fair Play requirements. The measures will be implemented over a three-year period and enforced from 2014–15 onwards.

There are, however, concerns that these regulations will not stop billionaire owners pumping funds into clubs and circumventing the regulations. If benefactors put money into the club in the form of excessive sponsorship, it would show up as football-related income. This would circumvent the ban on cash injections under Financial Fair Play and would allow the club to balance its books and facilitate more spending.

Some wonder whether Manchester City is already doing this. Since being bought by Sheikh Mansour in August 2008, £800m has been pumped into the club. Manchester City has managed to nearly triple its income, from £56.9m in 2007–8 to £153.2m in 2010–11. Gate receipts and media income have all risen sharply, but by far the biggest factor has been commercial income, which has gone from £23.4m in 2009 to £64.7m in 2010/11. The biggest driver of that growth has been sponsorship. Not all of City's sponsors are suspect. However, it is striking that among its portfolio of new commercial partners it counts four companies that are either owned or controlled by the UAE's government – Mansour's family, in other words. Etihad's new 10-year £400m sponsorship deal with City is so astonishingly rich that in August UEFA announced that it would investigate the deal. This loophole will have to be closed, as Arsenal manager Arsene Wenger noted: 'It raises the real question about the credibility of Financial Fair Play. If Financial Fair Play is to have a chance, the sponsorship has to be at market price.'[7]

None the less, the Financial Fair Play regulations do seem to be having some effect. In 2012 total transfer spending was significantly reduced in England and across Europe. Moreover, even the big spenders (notably Chelsea and Manchester City) were keen to offload several highly paid players before spending on new players.

Future prospects

Manchester United has supported the Financial Fair Play regulations, since it is less constrained by them than its closest rivals – MUFC has much higher football revenues than Manchester City, Chelsea, Liverpool or Arsenal. Moreover, as the 2012 season was coming to an end, success on the football field seemed to have been restored. The Glazer family could look back on what looks like being a successful gamble – they could sell the club at a huge profit. Nevertheless, the position could soon change. Without playing success, revenues would plummet – MUFC has to keep qualifying for the European Champions League. The debt level remains high, and without regular profits the interest payments would become a major burden.

Postscript

In May 2013, after this case study had been completed, Sir Alex Ferguson announced his retirement. He was replaced by the new manager, David Moyes (recruited from Everton FC) for the 2013–14 season. In addition, the Chief Executive, David Gill, also announced that he was to step down at the end of June 2013 to be replaced by Ed Woodward (Executive Vice Chairman). MUFC now face an even bigger challenge to continue their success under new leadership.

Notes and references
1. £1 = $1.53 = €1.17.
2. MUFC website, www.manutd.com, 22 November 2004.
3. MUFC plc annual report 1999.
4. MUFC Board statement as quoted by www.joinmust.co.uk on 26 July 2005.
5. *Times online*, www.timesonline.co.uk, 7 June 2008.
6. ©UEFA.com 1998–2012. All rights reserved.
7. www.espn.go.com/sports/soccer/news/_/id/7355528/soccer-financial-fair-play-end-football-reckless-spending, 4 January 2012.

CASE STUDY

Pierre Fabre: culture and the challenges of internationalisation

Ludovic Cailluet

The Pierre Fabre Group is France's second-largest independent pharmaceutical group. Founded and managed by a pharmacist since 1962, it retains a strong corporate culture. Its international development has been rapid, especially so in the two last decades. Growth has been based on its dermo-cosmetics brands. In entering markets outside Europe, the group faces new obstacles that question both its business model (based on distribution through pharmacists) and its corporate culture.

● ● ●

Pierre Fabre, a pharmacist born in 1926, founded the company bearing his name in the 1950s. The venture has become a respected multinational pharmaceutical group specialising in skin-care and cosmetic products with major brands such as Avène, Klorane and Ducray. While thriving internationally, the company has remained firmly rooted to its culture, values and place of origin. In 2012, with over 10,000 employees, the Pierre Fabre Group remains the second-largest independent pharmaceutical company in France. Its growth rests on three divisions: pharmacy (oncology, central nervous system, cardiovascular system, immunology and dermatology), family medication (Over The Counter pharmaceuticals), and dermo-cosmetics. In 2011, Pierre Fabre had a turnover of €1.92 billion (£1.62bn; $2.46bn)[1] of which 50% came from overseas operations. About 45% of the Pierre Fabre Laboratories employees live and work in south-west France. Over the years, the group has also established several major plants elsewhere in France and abroad, with 53 subsidiaries and sales offices. The heart of the enterprise and its headquarters remain in Castres, a quiet town of 42,000 inhabitants in south-west France.

Sustained growth has raised several management issues within the company. The Group has had to adapt its managerial practices to suit its size, its strong international flavour and its diversification. In doing so, the central dilemma faced by the Pierre Fabre Group has been how to bring about this transformation while maintaining its core values and culture, which are key to its success and identity

Source: Getty

and vital to the Group's cohesion. As the company grows in geographically and culturally distant lands, it has become increasingly difficult to preserve and transmit this unique heritage.

In 2005, M. Pierre Fabre transferred shares to the company's workforce via an employee stock purchase plan. In 2012, 91% of the employees entitled to join are shareholders. Aided by bonuses, they control 6.7% of the shares. The six largest European subsidiaries were offered the same deal in 2008 and their staff subscribed at the same rate. Between 1999 and 2008 Pierre Fabre has donated 65% of its shares to the non-profit Pierre Fabre Foundation while announcing a restructuring of the Group's management. PFP, an intermediary holding company, was created with an entirely new board of external directors. The strategy of

This case was prepared by Ludovic Cailluet, University of the Littoral Opale Coast, based on a research project conducted in 2003–6 by Ludovic Cailluet, Eric Jolivet of Toulouse University and Matthias Kipping of Pompeu Fabra University in collaboration with Ombline de Saint-Exupéry. It is intended as a basis for class discussion and not as an illustration of good or bad practice.

the group has since been constrained by PFP's constitution, which states: 'The obligation to ensure the company's continued independence, the diversity of its activities and its regional implantation.'[2]

Development of the Group

Pierre Fabre grew up in Castres in a family of textile traders. In 1944, he entered the Toulouse University School of Pharmacy, graduated in 1949 and in 1950 borrowed family money to acquire a pharmacy in Castres.

Having exhausted all the avenues for growth in his pharmacy, Pierre Fabre moved towards the manufacture of drugs by setting up a semi-industrial laboratory in 1955. The turning point came with the introduction in 1956 of *Cyclo3®*, a veinotonic. He conducted new development activity supported by a personal and professional network of colleagues, primarily from Toulouse University. He added natural extracts of a plant (*Ruscus aculeatus*) which grew abundantly in the region. While its beneficial effects were long known, Pierre Fabre was the first to turn it into a convenient form, improving its efficiency and safety. Unlike many pharmacist–entrepreneurs of the 1950s, Pierre Fabre invested all his profits in the development of the business.

Keeping an eye on the market: the 'Pierre Fabre way'

The entry into dermo-cosmetics by the acquisition of the Klorane laboratories in 1965 was the result of shrewd analysis in a period when the dermo-cosmetic category was almost non-existent. Klorane, a small company, was known for its range of skin treatment soap and shampoos. Pierre Fabre acquired the business and relocated it to Castres. He then reinvented the Klorane brand, segmenting the product range while introducing a new line for babies using vegetable compounds. The innovation extended to the business side, with direct marketing targeted at young mothers. By 1967, some 20,000 sample sachets per month were being dispatched to maternity wards. The Group acquired various brands such as Ducray in the subsequent decade, completely revamped them and employed selective distribution.

Right from the beginning, all products were distributed exclusively in pharmacies, which in France are independent shops owned by graduates in pharmacy supported by a limited number of wholesale operators (*répartiteurs*). This was done with the help of dedicated marketing teams and sales representatives who constituted (along with the research division) the backbone of the enterprise.

The company based its success from its early days on the 'magic triangle' of competence linking client/patient,

prescriber (physician, dermatologist or paediatrician) and pharmacist. It has used the medical legitimacy of its products to justify premium pricing.

Intuition and creativity

M. Pierre Fabre has a creative mind that often prefers to follow instinct rather than any deliberate strategy based purely on financial considerations. He has also followed his personal preferences and turned these into business opportunities. He was, for instance, interested in the curative properties of thermal spring waters and plant extraction. From that vision, the company has built two successful brands: Galénic and Avène. Galénic was created in 1978 to care for the emerging segment of skin-care products – between pure cosmetics and dermatological creams. It became quickly the 'Clarins of the pharmacies', a cosmetics line adapted to sensitive skin and sold through beauty consultants inside pharmacies. The initial growth of Galénic was also fuelled by its Elancyl line, a slimming programme sold as a system including a massage glove and soap, which was an immediate international best-seller.

Avène, created first as a Galénic product line, is a range of skin-care specialities, especially suited for very sensitive skin. It was developed after the acquisition of a spa north of Montpellier. Using the unique properties of the Avène spring water, it became the leading franchise of the Group and was made an autonomous brand in 1990. In terms of sales, in less than 20 years Avène has established its dominant position within the pharmacy sector in Europe and is a serious competitor for L'Oréal in Asia.

The medical reputation of the dermo-cosmetics brands of Pierre Fabre (Aderma, Ducray, Galénic, Pierre Fabre Dermatologie, René Furterer) has been based on a unique integrated system to procure plant ingredients, through long-term partnerships with farmers, for the manufacturing of cosmetics.

Innovation and research

Given the size of the enterprise, the research output of the Pierre Fabre Laboratories has been remarkable. While the amount spent on R&D (€161 million) seems modest when compared with the big pharmaceutical companies, it still represents a sizeable 20% of the drug division's turnover for 2011. The discovery and development of Navelbine was a major breakthrough for its research division. It was a scientific and technological *tour de force* made possible by working closely with public research laboratories (CNRS) which helped discover the drug. It was subsequently developed by the Laboratoires Pierre Fabre and was a major commercial success for the company's oncology division.

Since the end of the 1960s, a clear link has also been forged between pharmaceutical research and dermo-cosmetics development. This helped to raise the quality of the formulations in both areas. The Pierre Fabre Laboratories began to be widely known for their expertise in the development of Galénic formulations with enhanced benefits for patients. A great source of pride for the Group was certification by the US Food and Drug Administration (FDA) of two of its drug factories. Very rarely achieved in Europe, the FDA label has allowed the laboratories to offer production service to many other pharmaceutical companies, yielding additional revenues.

The company has always spent a lot on taking care of physicians and pharmacists, visiting them and offering training and services with regular invitations to visit the headquarters and factories of the company in Castres where they receive lavish treatment. The company has funded scientific congresses and medical studies, especially in cosmetics and dermatology, to establish itself as a respected player within the medical community.

Regional anchorage and aesthetics

From the beginning, M. Pierre Fabre was very attached to his regional roots. In the late 1960s, he chose to set up his enterprise close to his home instead of going to some regional city such as Montpellier or Toulouse. Although these cities offered substantial advantages in terms of infrastructure and were steeped in rich medical and academic traditions, the entrepreneur chose family and personal ties, including political ones, over logistic considerations. The fact of being 'local' was seen as an advantage, a badge of honour and the guarantee of excellent access to regional decision-makers. Recruitment remained strongly parochial, biased towards the local workforce. Pierre Fabre believed this reinforced the feeling of 'belonging', of cohesion, and promoted a sense of 'social peace'. Consequently, employment remained very stable, with a large number of spouses and children also working for the Group.

Nevertheless, the enterprise quickly learnt to recruit a diverse range of managers and executives. Until very recently, almost all were French, but the Group has set internationalisation of its managers as one of the objectives to be attained in the near future.

The fact that the Group's headquarters were located at Castres sometimes made it difficult for recruitment of executives: 'There is no question that the location (at Castres) is a handicap . . . Some do not wish to leave Paris . . . they cannot adapt themselves to the life of a small town where everybody knows what is going on .'

Gradually, this inconvenience turned into an attraction for many executives looking for a more sedate lifestyle. The efforts of the human resource department also did much in this regard:

> 'There exist completely different cultures . . . There are those who come from the Tarn area, to whom Pierre Fabre is everything . . . And then there are those from outside, who have come from Paris or elsewhere, who have known other companies before, they do not at all have the same emotional bond with Pierre Fabre, but what is interesting is to have both kinds . . . This enterprise . . . has never been shy of mixing teams, of intermingling persons of all ages for example.'

Pierre Fabre's commitment to the region did not end with the hiring of local personnel. The company bought and restored several family estates in and around Castres. They include the mansion 'Le Carla', where the founder's office is now situated, and others house the corporate headquarters and the Pierre Fabre Foundation. A visit to the building and the immaculately kept park leaves a lasting impression. In the words of one executive: 'At Carla, it feels as though we have been received at [Pierre Fabre's] house, I meet the spouses of many employees who miss not having been to Carla . . . I have often invited people to Carla just to give them an opportunity to be there.'

The combination of local roots and a serious pharmaceutical company provides sales forces with a very specific and rich narrative. The fact that the company uses natural active components extracted from plants completes a strong story for clients, partners and distributors. This is particularly true outside France in places where the name of Pierre Fabre is unknown. It is becoming important in a context of popular interest in sustainable development and green issues.

Being a Pierre Fabre manager

The success of such an enterprise owes much to its employees. The first characteristic most often cited by the managers themselves is the attention and care given to the individual: 'Here we are not just a number.'

The integration process is very well crafted, with attention given to spouses in the case of relocation. There are examples of managers who have been able to retain their jobs, sometimes on a part-time basis, while they were fighting against cancer. This quality is visible at the top of the hierarchy and percolates down to the grass roots of the organisation. A study conducted in 2008 on the individual values of Pierre Fabre employees concluded that a strong sense of community was one of the characteristics of the company. This is often not the case in an industry regularly shaken by cuts in the workforce following mergers and acquisitions.

At the same time, belonging to a 'family' also entails greater commitment and greater sacrifice. The company expects a high degree of availability, which for managers can include holidays and weekends: 'There is a culture of perpetual availability for the evenings, for dinners with clients, etc. This includes everybody, irrespective of seniority or posting.'

Attention to detail and autonomy

From the beginning, the enterprise retained its rigour regarding production, quality control and detail. This mentality also pervades its managerial style. At the same time, most managers recognise that they have great autonomy when it comes to making important decisions. They are encouraged to be 'intrapreneurs' to a certain extent.

All managers are required to be an 'expert' in their domain. Their grasp of the subject is constantly tested and stress is laid on prompt and rigorous implementation. Preparing for a meeting is extremely important. However, having figures and details at one's fingertips is not enough; force of conviction and attitude are also highly valued. The annual 'senior staff meetings' and the 'marketing seminars' are intense periods when the product chiefs and group leaders defend their projects in front of executives, often including the founder of the company.

Managers who have known other companies in the pharmaceutical sector, especially the larger, international ones, have been struck by the rapidity of the decision-making process at Pierre Fabre:

'I have been with the real heavy-weights; surrounded by financiers and cut-off from the ground-realities . . . my aim [in coming here] was to get back to the vibrant atmosphere of a smaller enterprise. When one asks for funds . . . one does not have to go through the entire process of going to the "board", the assessments, the processing delays . . . Here, things move much more quickly in terms of decision-making and action.'

The challenges of going international

Since the 1980s it has become clear to the company that its over-reliance on the French market may become a liability. The domestic market accounted for 80% of sales in 1982. Though still essential, the company realised that it was not going to grow at the same pace it once had. In fact the government's fight to reduce budget deficits has brought cuts in reimbursement for many of Pierre Fabre's prescription drugs since the 1990s. Even in cosmetics, the French market has become mature with slow or limited growth likely in the future. As a consequence, Pierre Fabre has turned to international markets since the mid-1980s, and in 2011 international sales represented 52% of the total revenues of the Group (Figure 1).

Figure 1 Pierre Fabre Group turnover (€000 at 2010 prices), 1961–2010

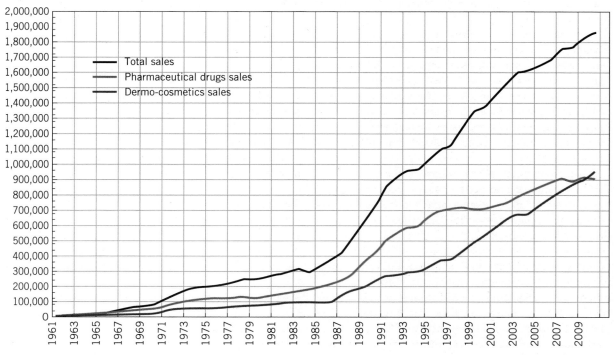

Source: reconstructed from Pierre Fabre archives

Pierre Fabre has invested in its international development through direct subsidiaries and joint ventures and, where the turnover does not justify such measures, through distribution contracts with partner companies. This has not been realised without challenges, mostly linked with organisational learning, cultural and marketing issues.

Not surprisingly, there are many differences in the economic and institutional forms of pharmacy between Europe, the USA and Asia. Despite having common roots, even across Europe there are many differences. In twentieth-century Europe, differences were based on different government regulations. Regulation of the pharmacy profession is very often built on 'soft law' by the professional bodies. In France, the Ordre National des Pharmaciens (National Order of Pharmacists) created a code of conduct and is a compulsory participant in any national negotiation on the profession. The various associations set professional standards and enforce them, having disciplinary power over a pharmacist guilty of severe wrongdoing. As a consequence, changes in the practices of the trade have to be accepted by the professional associations. Similar regulations applied in Austria and Belgium where the profession was very conservative, and it was almost impossible for a pharmacist to sell anything other than prescription drugs. Pharmacists contravening this rule were at risk of losing their licence. This made it difficult for companies distributing cosmetics through pharmacies to break through.

Early European successes

Pierre Fabre's first subsidiary (Arzneimittel Fabre GmbH) was created in 1969, a joint venture with Boehringer Mannheim (BM) in Germany. In 1972 Pierre Fabre created another joint venture with a local Spanish pharmaceutical company in Barcelona (Laboratorios Reig-Joffré), a company already distributing its products. Spanish law at that time banned the importation of drugs; Pierre Fabre had to find a local manufacturer to market its bestseller Cyclo 3 in Spain, a country whose economic and social development was gathering pace. After Spain signed a tax treaty with France in 1970, Pierre Fabre acquired a minority shareholding (majority shareholding by foreigners was not permitted in Spain until 1977) in the Sociedad Anonima de Farmacologia General (Safargen).

In Spain, Pierre Fabre was very successful because of the similarities of the system with France, which permitted economies of scale and scope and a fast learning curve for the company. As in France, there were large numbers of pharmacists and dermatologists in Spain. Regulation was very close to the French model for cosmetics and as a consequence the company had few issues adapting its ranges of products and their advertising. The same happened in Italy with a subsidiary created in 1973, in Portugal in 1977 and in Greece in 1986.

Mass versus selective distribution

In much of Western Europe the dermo-cosmetics concept worked well, with the existence of the so-called triangle of competence relying on the pharmacist, the brands and the prescribers around the patient/client. However, it was not possible to re-create such a selective distribution system in the UK and the USA. In these countries, independent pharmacists were rare. The distribution of prescription drugs was controlled by groups, and sensitive skin cosmetics were sold on a similar basis to mass products. (The mass market is a non-selective channel that Pierre Fabre had always refused to enter in Europe until forced by legal decisions against exclusive pharmacy distribution in 1988.) In the USA the distributor's role is only to create a physical contact between the client and the product offered by a manufacturer. This type of relationship was completely foreign to Pierre Fabre's managers in the 1980s and the very opposite to their company values of building long-term relationships with intermediaries such as the pharmacists. In the USA, however, Pierre Fabre had no alternative and the result was a complete failure.

Realising that its brands and company culture did not fit with the institutions of the US drugstore, Pierre Fabre Inc. made a strategic change in the 1990s. Starting almost from zero, the company decided to re-enter the market through the medical profession. Pierre Fabre Inc. first built a network of clinical researchers by attracting opinion leaders in the field of dermatology. In a second phase it acquired a small cosmetics company (Physician's Formula Cosmetics, PHFC), providing a credible presence and access to the community of American dermatologists. As 'Doctor's brands' became very successful in the early 2000s in the USA the acquisition became all the more relevant. The change in the US strategy of Pierre Fabre was completed by the development of a sales network that promotes dispensing products to the dermatologists.

Despite these efforts towards the medical community, sales remained relatively modest, as access to the distribution system was still very difficult for dermo-cosmetics products. As a consequence, although arch-rivals in Europe, Pierre Fabre and L'Oréal entered into a surprising partnership in 2003. To try to educate the American market and create a commercial space adapted to their skin treatment products necessitating advice, the two French companies decided to go back to the drugstores. For a brand like Avène or La Roche Posay (L'Oréal) designed for very sensitive skins, the credibility comes from the dermatologist's prescription; however, sales need the channel of the drugstore beyond the dispensing market to achieve volume.

Creating space in the drugstore

The Pierre Fabre–L'Oréal joint venture (DSC US Services) was set up to overcome the barrier of a limited market – a category had to be created to fill the gap between the mass-market offer (e.g. Oil of Olay, Neutrogena) and the selective brands sold in department stores (e.g. Clinique, Lancôme). DSC attempted to promote dermo-cosmetics in the US drugstore chains. Sales representatives met drugstore chain executives to persuade them to create a dedicated space within their stores to distribute dermo-cosmetics. In these spaces, beauty consultants would be available for clients to advise them about sensitive skin products. Brooks, the American subsidiary of Canadian drugstore company Jean Coutu, was the first US chain to create such spaces. It recruited beauty consultants who were trained by DSC US Services on skin, dermatology and dermo-cosmetics.

While it had based its international development in many countries on local partners resembling itself, usually pharmacists turned industrialists or distributors and family-controlled firms, Pierre Fabre had difficulties in finding similar partners in the UK and USA. However, in Canada, the Group found an exemplary partner in the drugstore chain Jean Coutu. Mr Jean Coutu, a pharmacist

born in 1927, had founded his group of companies in 1969 in Quebec and had met Pierre Fabre for the first time in 1975. Jean Coutu had expanded through a franchise system into a major corporation with 19,000 employees in 2010. Through the Jean Coutu pharmacies, Pierre Fabre has been able to establish a dermo-cosmetics commercial space in almost every drugstore in Quebec and Ontario, the most populated provinces in Canada. The dermatology brands Avène and Aderma have had notable successes in Canada, despite the cultural and commercial differences. In the Jean Coutu case, the drugstores are very different from the French or Spanish pharmacies, with mass-market products alongside selective brands. Nevertheless, as in many other countries, the pharmacist has been replaced in the 'triangle' by beauty consultants or aestheticians who have been trained in Canada by employees of Pierre Fabre Dermocosmétique Ltd (Canada).

Postscript
Pierre Fabre died on 20 July 2013 in his house near Castres at the age of 87. He had been Chairman of the company since 1962. A life-long bachelor without children, he left his company shares to the Foundation. It will be interesting to see if the unique culture and business model of the Pierre Fabre Group will live on after his death.

Notes and references
1. €1 = £0.85 = $1.31.
2. All quotations are taken from the author's interviews with Pierre Fabre employees.

CASE STUDY

Adnams – a living company

Julie Verity and Kim Turnbull James

This is a case about the long-term survival and evolution of a UK-based SME, one that has an iconic brand and a strong local position. It covers all aspects of the company, providing an opportunity to discuss competitive strategy, corporate governance, core competences, customer and brand value, culture, innovation, leadership and strategy process and decision making. Adnams is a unique company and this can make for interesting and probing discussions about the nature of strategy and strategy making.

• • •

Adnams is a mid-sized brewery business based in Southwold in Suffolk, UK, with a turnover in 2012 of about £50m ($75.8m; €59.2m).[1] Adnams also owns and operates hotels and pubs mostly in and around Suffolk and Norfolk. Roughly 420 people work at Adnams and there are 1,200 shareholders. Andy Wood joined the company in 1994 with responsibility for developing customer service and supply chain operations. He joined the Board in 2000 with the additional responsibilities of sales, marketing and the wine business; he became Managing Director in 2006 and Chief Executive in 2010.

Andy Wood describes himself as a guardian of Adnams who is privileged to share in its history and development. He does not believe in 'white charger leadership': 'Instead, I want to celebrate others and push them to the front.'

At the time of writing, he was also aware of significant challenges:

'There is a lot going on – a lot of the business is moving on-line and we need to spread the net as a defence mechanism. We will always be a manufacturer . . . but we are stretching the brand into long drinks and food and leisure; becoming more of a broad church. The competition are demanding this, we can't compete with the macro- or micro-brewers.'

This case was prepared by Julie Verity and Kim Turnbull James and was made possible because of funding from the Cranfield/Thurnham legacy. It is intended as a basis for class discussion and not as an illustration of good or bad practice. Thanks to people at Adnams who generously gave their time for interviews. © Julie Verity and Kim Turnbull James 2013. Not to be reproduced or quoted without permission.

Suffolk connections

'If you took the brewery out of Southwold you would rip its heart out.'[2]

Southwold and beer have lived together for the past 650 years. Beer was sold from the site of the current Swan Hotel in Southwold from 1345 using hops grown locally to brew the beer. The Sole Bay Brewery was moved a short distance away from The Swan in 1660 and has stood on the same site in Southwold for 450 years. In 1872, both the brewery and the hotel were bought by the Adnams family and one of the Adnams brothers established the enterprise officially as Adnams & Company Ltd in 1890. The business grew as a brewery with associated inns, located mainly in Suffolk and Norfolk. As one employee explained: 'People ask me where I work, and when I tell them – Adnams – they say: "that's in Southwold". This happens all the time – people automatically make links between the name and the place.'[3]

Southwold is a seaside town located in an area of natural beauty which is rich in wildlife. The town itself has great charm. The landscape lends much to the image and flavour of Adnams products and hence the business. The business and its brand are closely linked to its Soutwold roots and the Suffolk environment.

One example is Adnams Hotels. The Swan and The Crown are a long-established part of the portfolio, commanding prime positions in the heart of Southwold, close to the beach and the sea front with its rows of Victorian, brightly painted beach huts. A famous landmark in Southwold is the landlocked lighthouse. Sixteen of the Swan Hotel's rooms are named 'The Lighthouse Rooms', because they look out on the lighthouse.

Another example is in the visual identity of the Adnams brand. Simon Loftus, then chairman and part owner, launched a new corporate identity in 1999. He took this further in 2003 with the launch of an iconic advertising campaign called 'Beer from the Coast'. In the same year the annual report included the following pictures and commentary:

'September saw the launch of our "Beer from the Coast" marketing campaign . . . Illustrations depicting coastal scenes were produced by a local artist . . . The Daily Telegraph named our posters "Ad of the Week" with the following comment: "You can almost smell the sea looking at these posters. They combine head and heart appeal; the product message is that Adnams is a brewer, based on the coast; the intangible message is that Adnams is the ultimate local brewer offering a beer drinking pleasure that the big brewers can never match." We couldn't have put it better ourselves.'[4]

Andy Wood commented in 2010:

'I think there are more and more consumers who are looking for products with provenance; with a sense of place that they can relate to. There are a growing number of people who are more aware of what they are eating and drinking. Their health and well-being is important to them and local food and drink, plus knowing and trusting it is genuine, this is all part of what the Adnams brand has at its heart.'

Family connections

The Loftus family bought a stake in Adnams in 1902. This means that the two families, Adnams and Loftus, have jointly given about 250 years of service and stewardship to the company. Generations of these families have lived locally, invested locally, joined the fabric of the local society and employed thousands of local people. During the 1960s, these families were under pressure to sell out at a time of consolidation in the brewing industry and growing market demand, but they chose to retain the company's independence and local identity. Long-term commitment to Adnams is no less today, and while the company is listed with traded shares, the families retain a controlling stake.

Further family connections can be found among shareholders. Adnams' shares are relatively illiquid: shareholders form long-term connections with Adnams. Andy Wood added: 'Our shares trade at a high multiple. One reason for this being our status – we are listed on the baby market[5] – it is a good way for families to transfer capital from one generation to another, because of the tax exemption.'

Customer connections

Adnams tries hard to keep close and tight connections with customers. The wine business is an early example, which Simon Loftus took control of when he first started working for the company. It was his idea to shorten the distance between suppliers, Adnams and its customers, bringing the consumer and grower into contact with each other by telling the growers' stories. This was a first among wine merchants, setting Adnams apart from the pack. The senior wine buyer at Adnams said:

'Simon turned a sleepy Suffolk wine merchant into one of England's premier wine merchants; not in terms of volume, but in terms of profile. We are front-edge. We buy wines from people who are interested in something different and, therefore, are interesting. We do this rather than buy wines that are perfectly good but middle-of-the-road. It is important for Adnams to have an opinion. If we sell wines that are populist, we have no difference. So, we are looking for the superlatives on the landscape and we price them very competitively.'

The marketing activity at Adnams has evolved to suit the rural nature of Suffolk, where as the head of marketing explained: 'Putting up a billboard will not work. The media opportunities to touch customers here are rare; we have to be much more targeted and direct.'

Having worked previously for one of the UK's largest multiple grocers, the constraints of the location were starkly evident to her. Learning to adapt to the demands of the situation, however, had resulted in fun, creative and cost-effective ways to engage customers. One idea was to take the brand to customers. For example, 120,000 people visit the annual Suffolk Show. There is also a Norfolk Show and other festivals in and around East Anglia which attract local people and holidaymakers. To these, Adnams sends the Mobile Beach Hut or the Mobile Boat Bar from which customers can sample their products directly. Adnams also formed partnerships with the local football club (Ipswich Town) and the nearest racecourse (Newmarket) to host events.

However, Adnams is not just a local company but increasingly has a national market and is expanding its overseas opportunities. Andy Wood commented:

'I think we were the first real beer brand to go onto Twitter and we have many thousands of followers. We use blogs regularly to get our message out there. Last week we had 59 mentions on the web, through our tracking software, we know that these were re-used or read by 38,000 people. We think social media, allied to our authenticity is favouring us: we can make links in many more ways than we could before.'

Renewal

Early in the 2000s Adnams committed to updating its assets. Today the Southwold brewery is one of the most modern, energy- and water-efficient brew streams in the UK: 90% of the waste heat from the process of brewing is captured and recycled, lowering energy use dramatically. Traditionally, it took eight pints of water to make one pint of beer, but this has been reduced to 3.2 pints with the latest technology. Quality was also up, with less than 0.1% (down from about 1%) of barrels returned because of spoilt beer. The cost of this renewal was £4m. Production capacity was increased by adding new fermentation tanks, but, extraordinarily, the exterior of the building retains its original Victorian façade.

A further £6m was spent building a new distribution centre which became another Adnams' success story. *Management Today*, for example, wrote:

'The firm's bottles are the lightest – and thus the greenest – on the market. And to top it all, the new £6m distribution centre opened in October 2006 has been called the greenest warehouse in the country. Thanks to natural construction materials and a reed-covered-roof, it doesn't need heating and air-conditioning systems to maintain an even temperature and should save £500,000 on energy bills over the next 10 years. It was also a low carbon build, as the hemp-and-lime block walls lock 150 tonnes of carbon into the structure.'

The new distribution centre cost 20% more to build than would the usual 'distribution shed'. Initial costing put the excess at much higher than this, but the huge rise in market prices for steel at the time reduced the differential. For this small/medium-sized company whose annual turnover is about £50m and whose profits range between £3m and £4m, this extra upfront outlay could have appeared extravagant. Andy Wood explained:

'We wanted to do something of which we could be proud. Second, we all thought fossil-based fuels were going to get more expensive and that polluters would have to pay for their pollution. We needed to be better at keeping our energy consumption low for both reasons. Third, we have a framework for decision making. We look at return on capital employed, internal capability and capacity and our value base.[6] If these things align we go ahead. So, in this case, spending more up-front would make our ROCE harder to meet, but the sustainable argument made it the right thing to do. Our shareholders tell us this is right and they stick with us through thick and thin.'

The investment in the distribution centre paid off. It was 10 times the size of the old refrigerated store and, despite this extra capacity and escalating utility prices, running costs by 2010 were less than those of five years earlier. Water is collected from the roof and used for the toilets and showers. The office space is open plan, airy and purposely designed and provides a great place for customer service, HR, IT services and logistics teams to work together.

Sustainability is one of Adnams' values, but it has not been adopted just because it became trendy to be environmentally conscious, and the meaning of sustainability to Adnams is not limited to being 'green'. For example, in 1981 Adnams bought a farm in order to recycle the brewery waste in an environmentally efficient way. The farm produced prize-winning beef and pork. Adnams' management argue that it is the longevity of the *enterprise* that its people value as well as having pride in what they do. The leaders at Adnams think about themselves as stewards who look after the company for a while and who want to leave it in better shape for survival than when they took over. Andy said: 'We are trying to build a model for tomorrow. In the new world this will be a good way to generate wealth – one that is not rapacious.'

The company also sought to reduce carbon emissions by 30%. To achieve this, an anaerobic digester plant was opened in 2010 on the Adnams Bio Energy site. The digester is fed by food and brewing waste and the biogas produced is used as fuel for Adnams' trucks that deliver wines and ales. Dual-fuel trucks (biogas and diesel) are more expensive to buy than straight diesel vehicles, but the operations director estimated that when the whole fleet was converted the annual diesel bill could reduce to £60,000 rather than the predicted cost of £350,000.

Innovation

UK consumers' attitudes about alcohol and drinking habits are volatile. The market environment generally is hard to read. Competitor moves, regulatory changes, even the weather all play a part in its up-and-down nature. Some longer-term trends are:

- Decline in the number of, and sales from, traditional 'wet-led pubs' (i.e. those where drink rather than food is the main focus), which accelerated after 1 July 2007 when smoking was banned inside public buildings in the UK
- Consolidation among the large corporate breweries and proliferation of very small micro-breweries
- Increased consumption of alcohol at home
- Supermarkets taking an increasing share of wine, spirits and beer sales
- Increasing awareness of health-related issues, and the dangers of alcohol misuse.

Adnams needed to innovate to keep pace with this challenging market. For example, as the 2011 *Good Pub Guide* said: 'Adnams stands out, with its interesting and seasonally changing range of splendid ales (good wines too), now very widely available.'

According to Fergus, the master brewer, renewal of the brewery and flexibility of the new brew stream also facilitated change: 'The brew house does let us do a lot that we couldn't with the old kit because the old brew stream was only designed to do an English style of brewing. Now we can respond to the market and have also led the market with new beers.'

Andy Wood believes and encourages innovative behaviour everywhere: 'Innovation is about the mindset of *all* our people.'

An illustration is given by the Head of Hotels about Mary, who looks after breakfast service in The Swan:

'I told her about a hotel in London where the boiled eggs at breakfast were served with hand-knitted, individual bobble hats – to keep them warm. Five days later, Mary brought in a prototype for our restaurant. She had made it herself, in her own time, with her own materials and so we started serving eggs with bobble hats. Now she has to keep knitting, because our customers like them so much they ask if they can have one to take home.'

Andy had done a lot to encourage this behaviour; it had not always been like this. Long-timers at Adnams would explain that it was patriarchal and top-down: a caring organisation, but also a closed one.[7] Over the last two decades it had changed. As one employee explained:

'It has become a more open structure and if you want to, if you had the drive and capability, you could work your way up. Before, it was all about dead-men's shoes. It is quite dramatically different in the way it has modernised itself and involved new people, but at the same time, it remains completely anchored in Southwold.'

Portfolio

Beer is at the heart of Adnams' ecosystem, but the business is more complex than this suggests. Beer brands are sold through three channels: (1) direct through the 70 Adnams' licensed pubs, direct through Adnams' shops and hotels and to independent free-trade pubs in East Anglia and London, (2) to large pub-owning companies and wholesalers for distribution throughout the UK, and (3) to supermarkets and other off-trade outlets. Wine is sold direct through the tied estate and Adnams' hotels, through shops and by mail order.

Adnams' distribution centre stocks 3,000 lines, supplying the tied estate with all it needs from spirits, mixers and bottled mineral water to cordials and peanuts. All logistics are in-house. The company has its own fleet of trucks and draymen, a customer service centre and warehouse team. While Adnams owns and manages the two Southwold hotels, the other four in the portfolio are managed by Adnams but remain on the balance sheets of their original owners.[8] The hotels are showcases for Adnams' products and skills, as well as commercial, profitable businesses.

In 2012 there were 12 'Cellar & Kitchen' shops selling Adnams' brands and classic cookware. Diversification into retail started in 2006–7 which management admit, with hindsight, was a terrible time to expand any business. But, given the longer-term pressures in Adnams' traditional markets, becoming more diverse made sense to Andy Wood, even if it did start as an experiment:

'Our shareholders don't want us to dilute their holding. We need to find ways to grow without access to large amounts of capital. We have always had a small retail offer in Southwold. We have the supply chain and some products. We have some experience about how to package the offer. Expanding our retail proposition gives us the opportunity to reach new consumers – close to 50%

of all purchases from our shops are made by women – this compares with beer which is predominately sold to men. We tried it in Holkham, a shop in the middle of nowhere, and it did really well. Interestingly, and what we probably didn't anticipate, is that we sell a lot of beer from the shops as well.'

Stores were set up in the more affluent parts of East Anglia – towns that, like Southwold, tended to have high proportions of second-home ownership. By mid-2012, the stores were generating sales of around £11m – more than a fifth of Adnams' total turnover. The next step was already in execution, the addition of selected Adnams' branded foods: olive oil, balsamic vinegar, tomato ketchup and marmalade spiked with Adnams ale.

In 2010 Adnams was diversifying again, this time into spirits. A change in UK tax rules made it possible for brewers to distil alcohol for the first time and Adnams committed early, building a distiller in the brewery yard. The marketing manager was excited:

'Customers are looking for quality and to escape the mass market. It is about purity and a hand-crafted product. We have the space, the raw materials, distribution channels and customers. We know that with the Adnams name on a product we sell more than if it doesn't have the brand. So it makes sense – a lot of sense. We are going to distil vodka, gin, and oaked vodka and in time, we will sell a whisky.'

By 2012, out of Adnams' 420 employees there were only a dozen in the brewing team and only four of them actually do the brewing. Although Andy described the business as a brewery, it has evolved into a much more complex operation than this. The brand is about provenance – the food and drink are associated with their place of origin and all its qualities; the hotels are in lovely locations where customers can retreat and be looked after; the pubs are all individual and idiosyncratic to their locale. While beer is at Adnams' heart, Andy's view is: 'We help people relax; we are in the relaxation business.'

Internal connections

People are proud to work at Adnams. Karen Hester started working at Adnams in 1990 as a part-time cleaner. By 1994 she was a transport clerk and in 1996 she became Transport Manager. Karen was promoted again in 2000 into Andy Wood's old job as Head of Logistics and in 2003 added the customer services team to her remit. During this time, she led the relocation and rebuilding of the distribution centre. In 2006, after a successful move to the new site, Karen became Operations Director when she added the brewery to her team. IT and HR were added in 2008, when Andy thought these services were becoming isolated. In the

same year, she was nominated for and won the prestigious East of England Business Woman of the Year Award. In 2010, Karen took on oversight of the tenanted pubs. Karen insists she can do every one of her teams' jobs – and probably has done at some point in her career at Adnams. She is a director, but she gladly helps pick orders at Christmas when the staff are at their busiest.

Staff turnover at Adnams is low and people have a sense of belonging. For example, three weeks after a new team leader was appointed, he said:

'The really good thing about the people here is that when you ask them to do something it gets done; problems are solved between us. I was worried when I started because there was no clocking-on, but there was no need because everyone is here at 6.30, the lights are on and people are working. We should finish at 4 pm, but it could be 4.30 pm, 5 pm: we finish when the work is done and no one claims overtime. But on the days when we have done all the work, we ask Fergus if we can finish early. We do what needs to be done because here, you feel you are one of the cornerstones of the business.'

Karen believes that communication is what makes organisations succeed and, when there is a lack of it, to fail. For the redesign of the distribution centre, she insisted on one open-plan office where teams sit in 'pods' but where there are no dividing walls between teams. Every morning at 9 am she meets with all her managers for what she describes as: 'a quick chat about what happened yesterday, what needs putting right today and what will be done by tomorrow'. Everyone knows, at high level, what everyone else is doing.

Once a month Karen has a 'snack and chat' with her brewery staff – because they are not part of her open-plan office. This happens at 10 am in the Swan Hotel where a room is reserved, egg and bacon rolls and coffee arrive, and: 'We sit and talk. I tell them what is going on and they tell me what is happening in their world and we have a chat about what is bubbling – it is an hour for airing thoughts.'

Three or four times a year she visits her draymen and takes all 10 for a meal and a chat. The months she does not visit, her manager does. Her customer service team sit in the distribution centre and mostly chat to customers about their orders and deliveries. Very few customers use email or fax (though this is an option), as Karen said: 'Our customers like talking to us and we like listening. We can improve our service to them if we know more about them.'

If there is a problem that needs resolving, Karen has cake and a chat with all those involved:

'We change a lot. People don't really like it, but the best way to make it happen is to be inclusive. An example is when we decided to distribute the wine from here. This was a big change . . . I explained that if we didn't do this

I would have to make two of the warehouse staff – two of them – redundant. I told them to go away and think about it and to let me know which two wanted to go. They decided we should implement the changes and save the jobs. In the process we actually created six new jobs for the local community. I always think about how I would make a change happen, but I always invite the people involved to tell me how to do it better and if they have great ideas, we do it their way.'

Tenants among the tied estate are not employees of Adnams[9] but that does not mean their ideas are not welcomed. In the past, the most significant part of the relationship between tenants and the company was the rent level set for the pub. The process was less than transparent to the tenants. There were many stories among tenants about the unfairness of this process, which prompted one of them to write to Andy with a proposal of how to do it differently:

'I wrote to him proposing what I thought was a better way to set rents for us landlords. My point was that it didn't have to be so complex or difficult. So, Andy invited me to talk with him . . . and it has grown from there . . . This is different from the past when there was an attitude among the senior leaders that we were here just to sell their beer and if it all goes wrong, there will always be someone else who would come and rent a pub. Now, Andy and Karen provide a support network that you can choose to opt into.'

Going forward

There is a feeling of stability at Adnams despite its mid-size, its increasingly competitive landscape and the challenge of being a family business that is opening itself up to more outside influences. Andy Wood stresses the skills of leaders and followers in equal measure that mean Adnams can constantly adapt and survive:

'We need a framework – we need to steer . . . but at the same time we need our people to bring their own intelligence to the business and for us to reinforce the great behaviours that they already display in their work – excellent customer service for instance, and having ideas of how to improve their work. So it is learning new disciplines, being clear in where you are going but still allowing that culture where you respect the individual and what they know.'

Figure 1

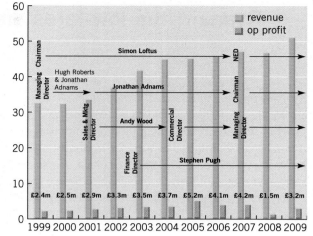

Revenue and operating profit, 1999–2009, and leadership

Respect and pride are two words that are heard often in Adnams' conversations and literature. As one employee said: 'Lots of companies talk about this stuff, but you don't expect it to be like that when you work there. That is what took me some time getting used to – here they mean it – it really is authentic!'

Figure 1 summarises the revenue, operating profit and leadership during 1999–2009.

Notes and references
1. £1 = $1.53 = €1.17.
2. Adnams' employee.
3. Adnams' employee.
4. Adnams' Annual Report 2003.
5. Adnams trade on the Plus Market Index (formerly known as Ofex) and have A and B shares. Both share types are known to be illiquid, but of the two A is the least liquid.
6. For the Adnams Values see http://adnams.co.uk/about/our-values
7. Adnams was one of the first companies to set up a profit-sharing scheme for employees – in 1960. This was followed by an employees' trust in 1977 and the employee share ownership scheme in 1992, which means that longer-serving employees can hold Adnams' shares and often own part of the company.
8. Adnams manages these hotels. A manager and chef respond directly to Adnams and the hotels are rebranded Adnams. There is no equity ownership or financial risk; it is the brand that is extended and ultimately at risk.
9. Landlords pay a rent for an Adnams pub and manage it as their own business. They have to sell Adnams' 'wet' products, but can develop the business in other ways (by selling food, for example) and retain the profits from these sales.

CASE STUDY

Ryanair: the low-fares airline – future directions?

Eleanor O'Higgins

Ryanair, the first and largest budget airline in Europe, has enjoyed remarkable growth and success. However, are Ryanair's strategic business model and its implementation robust enough to withstand the challenges it faces in its environment, notably economic recession and uncertainty about fuel prices? The case illustrates how to analyse and deploy internal resources and capabilities to add perceived value to customers, thereby delivering sustainable strategic advantage. It also explores the difficulties that hamper achieving and retaining such advantage. The reader is invited to devise and evaluate strategic options for Ryanair, including elements of corporate strategy in relation to its attempts to take over Aer Lingus, the Irish national carrier.

● ● ●

'The worst sort of business is one that grows rapidly, requires significant capital to engender the growth, and then earns little or no money. Think airlines. Here a durable competitive advantage has proven elusive ever since the days of the Wright Brothers. Indeed, if a far-sighted capitalist had been present at Kitty Hawk, he would have done his successors a huge favour by shooting Orville down.'

Warren Buffett, annual letter to
Berkshire Hathaway shareholders, February 2008

While the words of Warren Buffett were generally true, as airlines had seen no economic profit over a 40-year period to 2012, there were exceptions. Most noteworthy was Ryanair, the Irish budget airline, which had been consistently reporting earnings in excess of 20%. With 76 million passengers in 2012, Ryanair nominated itself as the world's favourite airline, since it carried more international passengers than any other airline.

The question was whether Ryanair could continue to defy industry trends that had caused so much distress to its competitors. In January 2010, CEO Michael O'Leary had observed: 'The environment is, from Ryanair's perspective, great, because it is awful. We're doing remarkably well because this is the time when the lowest-cost producer wins.'

Would this still continue to be the case?

Overview of Ryanair

As of July 2012, Ryanair ran more than 1,500 flights per day from 51 bases on 1,500 routes across 28 European

Source: Press Association Images

countries, connecting over 165 destinations. It operated a fleet of 294 new Boeing 737-800 aircraft with firm orders for 11 new aircraft to be delivered over the next year.

Ryanair was founded in 1985 by the Ryan family to provide scheduled passenger services between Ireland and the UK, as an alternative to the then state monopoly airline, Aer Lingus. Initially, Ryanair was a full-service carrier, with two classes of seating, leasing three different types of aircraft. Despite growth in passenger volumes, by the end of 1990 the company had disposed of five chief executives and accumulated losses of IR£20 million.[1] Its fight to survive in the early 1990s saw the airline transformed to become Europe's first low-fares, no-frills carrier, built on the model of Southwest Airlines, the successful US airline. A new management team led by Michael O'Leary was appointed. Ryanair floated on the Dublin Stock Exchange in 1997 and is now quoted on the Dublin and London Stock Exchanges and on the NASDAQ-100.

Table 1 **Ryanair consolidated income statement (€m)**

	Year ended 31 March		
	2012	**2011**	**2010**
Operating revenues			
Scheduled revenues	3,504.0	2,827.9	2,324.5
Ancillary revenues	886.2	801.6	663.6
Total operating revenues – continuing operations	**4,390.2**	**3,629.5**	**2,988.1**
Operating expenses			
Staff costs	(415.0)	(376.1)	(335.0)
Depreciation	(309.2)	(277.7)	(235.4)
Fuel and oil	(1,593.6)	(1,227.0)	(893.9)
Maintenance, materials and repairs	(104.0)	(93.9)	(86.0)
Aircraft rentals	(90.7)	(97.2)	(95.5)
Route charges	(460.5)	(410.6)	(336.3)
Airport and handling charges	(554.0)	(491.8)	(459.1)
Marketing, distribution and other costs	(180.0)	(154.6)	(144.8)
Icelandic volcanic ash-related cost	–	(12.4)	–
Total operating expenses	**(3,707.0)**	**(3,141.3)**	**(2,586.0)**
Operating profit – continuing operations	**683.2**	**488.2**	**402.1**
Other income/(expense)			
Finance income	44.3	27.2	23.5
Finance expense	(109.2)	(93.9)	(72.1)
Foreign exchange gain/(loss)	4.3	(0.6)	(1.0)
Loss on impairment of available-for-sale financial asset	–	–	(13.5)
Gain on disposal of property, plant and equipment	10.4	–	2.0
Total other expenses	**(50.2)**	**(67.3)**	**(61.1)**
Profit before tax	**633.0**	**420.9**	**341.0**
Tax expense on profit on ordinary activities	(72.6)	(46.3)	(35.7)
Profit for the year – all attributable to equity holders of parent	**560.4**	**374.6**	**305.3**
Basic earnings per ordinary share (euro cents)	38.03	25.21	20.68
Diluted earnings per ordinary share (euro cents)	37.94	25.14	20.60
Number of ordinary shares (millions)	1,473.7	1,485.7	1,476.4
Number of diluted shares (millions)	1,477.0	1,490.1	1,481.7

Source: Ryanair Annual Report, 2012

After its makeover into a budget airline, Ryanair never looked back, as it added new bases, routes and aircraft. Despite the up-and-down cycles of the airline industry over the decades, Ryanair continued its upwards trajectory, being among the world's most profitable airlines and leaving almost all others behind.[2]

Twenty years later

In July 2012, some 20 years after its transformation, as other airlines struggled, Ryanair's results were typical for the company. Full-year profits had increased 25% to a record €503 million (£424m; $645m).[3] Revenue increased 19% to €4325 million (£3647m; $544m) and average fares rose 16%, with a 5% increase in traffic to 76 million passengers. Unit costs rose by 13% due to a 30% increase in fuel costs and a 6% increase in sector length. Ancillary revenue outpaced traffic growth, rising by 11% to €886 million (£747m; $1136m) or 21% of total revenue. Ryanair's financial data are given in Tables 1, 2 and 3.

Michael O'Leary called the outcome a 'commendable result', especially considering the higher fuel costs and a deep recession in Europe. However, his positivity was tinged with concerns over what lay ahead. Despite an expected 5% traffic increase to 79 million passengers, he warned that profits could fall by as much as 20%, into the €400 to €440 million range, due to further fuel price rises and other costs, recession, austerity, currency concerns and lower fares at new and growing bases in Hungary, Poland, provincial UK, and Spain.

Ancillary revenues

Ryanair provides various ancillary services, including in-flight beverages, food and merchandise, console entertainment sales and internet-related services. It distributes accommodation, travel insurance and car rentals through its website. Delivering these services through the internet enables Ryanair to increase sales while reducing unit costs. Ancillary revenue initiatives were constantly being

Table 2 **Ryanair consolidated balance sheet (€m)**

	Year ended 31 March		
	2012	**2011**	**2010**
Non-current assets			
Property, plant and equipment	4,925.2	4,933.7	4,314.2
Intangible assets	46.8	46.8	46.8
Available-for-sale financial assets	149.7	114.0	116.2
Derivative financial instruments	3.3	23.9	22.8
Total non-current assets	**5,125.0**	**5,118.4**	**4,500.0**
Current assets			
Inventories	2.8	2.7	2.5
Other assets	64.9	99.4	80.6
Current tax	9.3	0.5	–
Trade receivables	51.5	50.6	44.3
Derivative financial instruments	231.9	383.8	122.6
Restricted cash	35.1	42.9	67.8
Financial assets: cash > 3 months	772.2	869.4	1,267.7
Cash and cash equivalents	2,708.3	2,028.3	1,477.9
Total current assets	**3,876.0**	**3,477.6**	**3,063.4**
Total assets	**9,001.0**	**8,596.0**	**7,563.4**
Current liabilities			
Trade payables	181.2	150.8	154.0
Accrued expenses and other liabilities	1,237.2	1,224.3	1,088.2
Current maturities of debt	368.4	336.7	265.5
Current tax	–	–	0.9
Derivative financial instruments	28.2	125.4	41.0
Total current liabilities	**1,815.0**	**1,837.2**	**1,549.6**
Non-current liabilities			
Provisions	103.2	89.6	102.9
Derivative financial instruments	53.6	8.3	35.4
Deferred tax	319.4	267.7	199.6
Other creditors	146.3	126.6	136.6
Non-current maturities of debt	3,256.8	3,312.7	2,690.7
Total non-current liabilities	**3,879.3**	**3,804.9**	**3,165.2**
Shareholders' equity			
Issued share capital	9.3	9.5	9.4
Share premium account	666.4	659.3	631.9
Capital redemption reserve	0.7	0.5	0.5
Retained earnings	2,400.1	1,967.6	2,083.5
Other reserves	230.2	317.0	123.3
Total shareholders' equity	**3,306.7**	**2,953.9**	**2,848.6**
Total liabilities and shareholders' equity	**9,001.0**	**8,596.0**	**7,563.4**

Source: Ryanair Annual Report, 2012

introduced to raise extra revenue. It was the first airline to charge for check-in luggage and in-flight food and beverages. Virtually all budget airlines have followed suit, as they have with other Ryanair initiatives. It has continued to find ways of charging passengers for services once considered inclusive. Passengers are charged extra for checking in at the airport rather than online (which also incurs a charge). While avoiding pre-assigned seats, an extra charge procures 'priority boarding' purchased in advance for £10/€10 per flight, an initiative followed by many traditional carriers, such as British Airways, charging passengers to book seats online.

In the fiscal year 2012, Ryanair's ancillary revenues per passenger rose from €11.12 in the 2011 fiscal year to €11.69. Revenues from non-flight scheduled operations, including excess baggage charges, debit and credit card transactions, sales of rail and bus tickets, accommodation, travel insurance and car rental, increased 12.4% from €574.2 million to €645.6 million, while revenues from in-flight sales increased 6.4% from €100.7 million in the

Table 3 **Ryanair selected operating data**

	Year ended 31 March			
	2012	**2011**	**2010**	**2009**
Operating data				
Average yield per revenue passenger mile (RPM) (€)	0.059	0.053	0.052	0.060
Average yield per available seat mile (ASM) (€)	0.048	0.045	0.043	0.050
Average fuel cost per US gallon (€)	2.075	1.756	1.515	2.351
Cost per ASM (CASM) (€)	0.051	0.049	0.047	0.058
Operating margin	14%	14%	13%	5%
Break-even load factor	70%	72%	73%	79%
Average booked passenger fare (€)	45.36	39.24	34.95	40.02
Ancillary revenue per booked passenger (€)	11.69	11.12	9.98	10.21
Break-even load factor	70%	72%	73%	79%
Other data				
Revenue passengers booked	75,814,551	72,062,659	66,503,999	58,565,663
Revenue passenger miles	58,584,451,085	53,256,894,035	44,841,072,500	39,202,293,374
Available seat miles	71,139,686,423	63,358,255,401	53,469,635,740	47,102,503,388
Booked passenger load factor	82%	83%	82%	81%
Average length of passenger haul (miles)	771	727	661	654
Sectors flown	489,759	463,460	427,900	380,915
Number of airports served at period end	159	158	153	143
Average daily flight hour utilisation (hours)	8.47	8.36	8.89	9.59
Personnel at period end	8,388	8,560	7,168	6,616
Personnel per aircraft at period end	30	31	31	36
Booked passengers per personnel at period end	9,038	8,418	9,253	8,852

Source: Ryanair Annual Report, 2012

2011 fiscal year to €107.2 million. Revenues from internet-related services, primarily commissions received from products sold on Ryanair.com or linked websites, increased 5.3% from €126.7 million in the 2011 fiscal year to €133.4 million in the 2012 fiscal year. The rate of increase in revenues from all ancillary revenue categories exceeded the increase in overall passengers booked; they accounted for 20.2% of Ryanair's total operating revenues in 2012, compared to 22.1% in 2011.

Investor perspectives

Ryanair shares reached a high of €6.30 in April 2007 and plummeted to €1.97 in October 2008, as global equity markets tumbled. By mid-2009, the shares were trading in the €3.20 to €3.40 range, with an expected medium-term target of €4.20, based on expected earnings and a P/E ratio of 13. In February 2013, its shares traded at about €5.75 with a P/E ratio of 14.9, up from €4.75 three months earlier.

After its flotation in 1996, Ryanair's policy was not to pay dividends on its shares. It retained earnings to fund its business operations, the acquisition of additional aircraft required for new markets, expansion of existing services, and routine fleet replacements. However, thanks to a healthy balance sheet and the suspension of its aircraft buying programme when negotiations with Boeing broke down, the no-dividend policy changed. In June 2010, Ryanair announced a special dividend of €0.34 per share,

returning almost €500 million to shareholders. A second special dividend of €0.34 per share, totalling approximately €489 million, was paid in November 2012. With the second special dividend Ryanair has returned €1.53 billion in dividends and share buybacks to shareholders over a five-year period. This was almost three times the total amount the company had raised from its initial €559 million flotation and four secondary offers in 1998, 2000, 2001 and 2002.

Ryanair's operational approach

Ryanair has stuck closely to the low-cost/low-fares model. Ever-decreasing costs was the mantra, as it constantly adapted its model to the European arena and changing conditions. In this respect, Ryanair differed in its application of the Southwest Airlines prototype, and its main European rival easyJet, as these two were not as frill-cutting. One observer described the difference between easyJet and Ryanair as: 'EasyJet is classy cheap, rather than just plain cheap.'[4]

The Ryanair fleet

Ryanair continued its fleet commonality policy, using only Boeing 737 planes, to keep staff training and aircraft maintenance costs as low as possible. Over the years, it purchased new, more environmentally-friendly aircraft, reducing the average age of its 294 aircraft to less than four years – among the youngest fleets in Europe. The newer aircraft produced 50% less emissions, 45% less fuel burn and 45% lower noise emissions per seat. Winglet modification provided better performance and a 2% reduction in fuel consumption, a saving which the company believed could be improved. Despite larger seat capacity, new aircraft did not require more crew. While Ryanair's fleet size has continued to rise alongside its purchases, it has disposed of its older, less efficient planes.

In 2009, Ryanair sought to repeat its 2002 coup when it placed aircraft orders at the bottom of the market. However, talks with Boeing for the purchase of 100 aircraft between 2013 and 2015 broke down. Thus, after the final delivery of 11 aircraft in 2013 to complete its existing Boeing contract, Ryanair had no further aircraft on order in 2012. Notwithstanding previous strict adherence to Boeing 737 planes, in an attempt to extract greater discounts from Boeing, Ryanair sought to open negotiations with other manufacturers, such as Airbus, the European aircraft manufacturer. The latter rebuffed the Ryanair invitation, declaring this sales campaign would be too expensive and time-consuming. Even so, Ryanair hinted that it had an interest in Airbus's new generation of fuel-efficient aircraft, and that it had the economies of scale to run a mixed fleet between Boeing and Airbus models. More recently, in June 2011, the company signed a Memorandum of Understanding with COMAC, a Chinese aircraft manufacturer, to cooperate and work together in relation to the development of a 174–200-seat commercial aircraft.

Since 2009, in response to high fuel prices and lower winter yields, Ryanair has adopted a policy of grounding a portion of its fleet during the winter months (from November to March). In the winter of 2011–12, Ryanair grounded approximately 80 aircraft, and in May 2012 announced that it intended to ground approximately 80 aircraft during 2012–13.

Staff costs and productivity

Ryanair refuses to recognise trade unions and negotiates with Employee Representative Committees (ERCs). Its 2012 employee count of 8388 was slightly down on 8,560 in 2011, mainly due to 230 fewer cabin staff, with fewer aircraft in operation and staff laid off during winter. Therefore, staff costs decreased 1.7% on a per-ASM basis, while in absolute terms these costs increased 10.3% from €376.1 million in 2011 to €415.0 million in the 2012 fiscal year. The increase in absolute terms was primarily attributable to a 10.5% increase in total hours flown and a company-wide pay increase of 2% granted in April 2011.

Ryanair's employees earn productivity-based incentive payments, consisting of 47% and 37% of total pay for cabin crew and pilots respectively. By tailoring rosters, the carrier maximised productivity and time off for crew members, while none the less complying with EU regulations which impose a ceiling on pilot flying hours to prevent dangerous fatigue. Its passenger-per-employee ratio of approximately 8,500 was the highest in the industry.

Generally, on-board crew have to pay for their initial training and uniforms. Ryanair has licensed approved organisations in Sweden and Holland to operate pilot training courses, using Ryanair's syllabus, to grant Boeing 737-type ratings. Based on their performance, trainee pilots may be offered a position operating on Ryanair aircraft.

Passenger service

Ryanair pioneered cost-cutting/yield-enhancing measures for passenger check-in and luggage handling. One was priority boarding and web-based check-in. Charging for check-in bags encouraged passengers to travel with less or no check-in luggage, thus saving on costs and enhancing speed. Before checked-in bags were charged, 80% of passengers travelled with checked-in luggage; two years later this had fallen to 30%. From October 2009, Ryanair adopted a 100% web check-in policy, enabling a reduction in staff numbers calculated to save €50 million per year. Ryanair claims that 'passengers love web check-in. Never again will they have to arrive early at an airport to waste time in a useless check-in queue. As more passengers travel with carry-on luggage only, they will never again waste valuable time at arrival baggage carousels either. These measures allow Ryanair to save our passengers valuable time, as well as lots of money.'[5]

A logical next step announced by Ryanair was a move to 100% carry-on luggage. Passengers would bring additional bags to the boarding gate, to be placed in the hold and returned to them as they deplane on arrival. This would allow more efficient airport terminals to be developed without check-in desks, baggage halls or computerised baggage systems. However, the idea never took off, probably for security reasons, as it would have required passengers to carry hold baggage through security to the aircraft.

Airport charges and route policy

Consistent with the budget model, Ryanair's routes were point-to-point only. It reduced airport charges by avoiding congested main airports, choosing secondary and regional destinations, eager to increase passenger throughput. Usually these airports are significantly further than the main airports from the city centres they serve, 'from nowhere to nowhere' in the words of Sir Stelios Haji-Ioannou, founder of easyJet, Ryanair's biggest competitor.[6] For example, Ryanair uses Frankfurt Hahn (123 kilometres from Frankfurt), Torp (100 km from Oslo) and Charleroi (60 km from Brussels). In December 2003, the Advertising Standards Authority rebuked Ryanair, upholding a complaint of misleading advertising for attaching 'Lyon' to its advertisements for flights to St Etienne, 62 kilometres from Lyon.

Ryanair constantly denounced charges and conditions imposed by most governments at airports in the form of Air Passenger Duties (APDs). In 2009, the Irish government introduced a €10 Air Travel Tax on all passengers departing from Irish airports on routes longer than 300 kilometres but subsequently reduced it to €3 in 2011. The UK government had been gradually raising its APDs over a five-year period from £5 to £13 in April 2012. The German government introduced an air passenger tax of €8 in 2011, subsequently reduced to €7.50 in 2012. In Austria, the government introduced an ecological air travel levy of €8 in 2011.

Ryanair's special ire is reserved for Dublin and Stansted Airports, bemoaning a 40% price increase at Dublin Airport, largely to pay for a second terminal costing €1.2 billion and derided by Ryanair as a white elephant. The airline was:

> 'Deeply concerned by continued understaffing of security at Stansted which led to repeated passenger and flight delays . . . management of Stansted security is inept, and BAA has again proven that it is incapable of providing adequate or appropriate security services at Stansted. This shambles again highlights that BAA is an inefficient, incompetent airport monopoly.'[7]

When BAA appealed against its break-up, ordered by the UK Competition Commission in 2009, Ryanair secured the right to intervene in the appeal in support of the Commission, and applauded the loss of the appeal by BAA. In August 2012, BAA finally accepted the sell-off of Stansted and abandoned further appeals against the 2009 orders of the Competition Commission, having already complied with the orders to sell Edinburgh and Gatwick Airports.

In summer 2012, Ryanair disclosed that it was interested in taking a 25% interest in Stansted, as part of a consortium which wanted it as an anchor tenant. Ryanair's ownership would allow it to introduce a low-cost, quick-turnaround model at Stansted, and reduce the landing fees. However, commentators observed that other competing airlines might be deterred from using Stansted Airport if Ryanair had control, given its already dominant position. In fact, Ryanair later pulled out as it became clear that BAA would not sell to a consortium which included it.

Marketing strategy

Ryanair has promoted its website heavily through newspaper, radio and television advertising. Internet bookings accounted for 99% of all reservations. Ryanair minimises its marketing and advertising costs, relying on free publicity, by its own admission, 'through controversial and topical advertising, press conferences and publicity stunts'.

Other marketing activities include distribution of advertising and promotional material and cooperative advertising campaigns with other travel-related entities and local tourist boards.

Ryanair's high profile has inspired both outrage and admiration among politicians, competitors, customers and observers. It has made controversial news: it annoyed the Queen of Spain by using her picture without permission in marketing material, it announced plans to charge passengers for using toilets on its flights, and it engaged in high-profile battles with the European Commission. Ryanair has made news for its achievements too, winning international awards such as Best Managed Airline and receiving a 2009 'FT-ArcelorMittal Boldness in Business' Award. This Award announcement said that Ryanair had: 'changed the airline business outside North America – driving the way the industry operates through its pricing, the destinations it flies to and the passenger numbers it carries'.[8]

The Aer Lingus saga

During 2007, in a surprise bid, Ryanair acquired a 25.2% stake in Aer Lingus, a week after the flotation of the Irish national carrier. It subsequently increased its holding to 29.8%, at a total aggregate cost of €407.2 million. By July 2009, the investment had been written down to €79.7 million. At the time of the initial bid Ryanair declared its intention to retain the Aer Lingus brand and:

> 'up-grade their dated long-haul product, and reduce their short-haul fares by 2.5% per year for a minimum of 4 years . . . one strong Irish airline group will be rewarding for consumers and will enable both to vigorously compete with the mega carriers in Europe . . . there are significant opportunities, by combining the purchasing power of Ryanair and Aer Lingus, to substantially reduce its operating costs, increase efficiencies, and pass these savings on in the form of lower fares to Aer Lingus' consumers'.[9]

However, according to a *Financial Times* commentator: 'Ryanair's bid for Aer Lingus was a "folie de grandeur".'[10] Even Michael O'Leary admitted it was: 'A stupid investment. At the time, it was the right strategy to go for one combined airline but it has now proven to be a disaster.'[11]

Aer Lingus rejected Ryanair's approach, stating that it had acted in 'a hostile, anticompetitive manner designed to eliminate a rival at a derisory price'. A combined Ryanair–Aer Lingus operation would account for 80% of all flights between Ireland and other European countries.

The bid was opposed by a loose alliance representing almost 47% of Aer Lingus shares. This included the Irish government, which retained a 25.4% holding, and two investment funds operated on behalf of Aer Lingus pilots and accounting for about 4% of shares. A critical 12.6% shareholding was controlled by the Aer Lingus Employee Share Ownership Trust (ESOT), which had the right to appoint two directors and a stake in future profits. Its members rejected the Ryanair offer by a 97% majority vote.

Faced with shareholder opposition and a blocking decision by the European Commission on competition grounds, Ryanair abandoned this bid but returned in December 2008 with an offer of €1.40 per share, a premium of approximately 25% over the closing price. In July 2010, the European General Court upheld the European Commission's decision to block the takeover of Aer Lingus by Ryanair. However, it did not go as far as forcing Ryanair to sell its stake in Aer Lingus, an action that Aer Lingus wanted the Court to impose.

Despite the European judgment, later in 2010 the UK Office of Fair Trading (OFT) announced that it would conduct a preliminary competition investigation into Ryanair's 29.8% holding in Aer Lingus. Unlike the European Commission, the OFT has the power to force Ryanair to divest its stake in Aer Lingus. Opposing the investigation, Ryanair argued that the UK OFT had no jurisdiction in the matter, and a four-month time limit after the European ruling for the case to be brought had elapsed. A failed appeal by Ryanair to the UK Competition Appeals Tribunal to suspend the OFT investigation in August 2012 was further appealed to the UK Court of Appeal by the airline.

Meanwhile, in June 2012, Ryanair made its third offer to purchase all the ordinary shares of Aer Lingus, at €1.30 per share, a premium of 38.3% over the then closing price. It gave a number of reasons for the timing and nature of its offer:

- Continued consolidation of European airlines, citing the takeover by the International Airlines Group (IAG, the parent company of British Airways) of BMI, whereby the Number 1 airline at Heathrow was allowed to acquire the Number 2.
- Additional capacity available at Dublin Airport and traffic decline from 23.3 million passengers annually in 2007 to 18.7 million in 2011, resulting in Dublin Airport operating at approximately 50% capacity.
- Under the terms of a bailout to Ireland provided by the European Commission, the European Central Bank and the International Monetary Fund, the Irish government was obliged to sell its stake in a number of state assets, including Aer Lingus.
- Etihad, an Abu-Dhabi-based airline, had acquired a 3% stake in Aer Lingus and had expressed an interest in buying the Irish government's 25% stake in Aer Lingus.
- The Employee Share Ownership Trust had been disbanded since December 2010 and the shares distributed to the individual members; Ryanair believed that its new offer was now capable of reaching over 50% acceptance, with or without the Irish government's acceptance.

Notwithstanding Ryanair's reference to it as a 'small and uncompetitive airline', Aer Lingus had made an €84 million profit in 2011, recording higher revenues, passenger numbers and yield per passenger, on both short- and long-haul flights. It had gross cash of €895m on its balance sheet.

Ryanair declared itself willing to offer the European Commission appropriate remedies to allay competition concerns, so that the efficiencies and synergies arising from the combination should convince the Commission to approve the proposed merger. Again Ryanair offered to keep Aer Lingus as a separate company, to maintain its brand, to grow its traffic from 9.5 million to over 14.5 million passengers over a five-year period post-acquisition by increasing Aer Lingus' short-haul traffic at certain major European airports where it currently operated and Ryanair did not, and to increase Aer Lingus' transatlantic traffic from Ireland. Was the latter reminiscent of Ryanair's 2007 announcement to offer €10 transatlantic flights, an idea which appeared to have been shelved in 2009? However, in August 2012, the European Commission announced a second-phase investigation into the bid, to be completed in early 2013, because its preliminary investigation raised 'potential competition concerns'.

It is noteworthy that, in 2011, Ryanair and Aer Lingus together accounted for 80% of traffic at Dublin Airport, 84% at Cork Airport and 64% at Shannon Airport. To placate the various competition authorities, Ryanair approached at least six airlines (Air France-KLM, easyJet, Etihad, FlyBe, IAG and Virgin) to operate competing services on some of the Aer Lingus routes. Notwithstanding a plan to engage FlyBe to take over 46 of Aer Lingus' short-haul routes, in February 2013 the EU Commission blocked the takeover bid on the basis that it would penalise passengers travelling in and out of Ireland with respect to choice and fares. Ryanair declared that it would appeal against the decision.

The *Financial Times* declared Ryanair's bid 'a waste of time and effort for both bidder and target', and voiced suspicions that it was 'a ploy to trump a UK inquiry into whether it should have to dispose of its 29.8% Aer Lingus stake'.[12]

An issue in the takeover was the entry of Etihad into the picture. While Ryanair was content for Etihad to purchase the government stake, and to remain a minority shareholder, it was mooted that Etihad was interested in buying Ryanair's existing 29.8% stake. However, there was no possibility of Etihad assuming a white knight position to rescue Aer Lingus from Ryanair's clutches, since rules barring foreign companies from owning a majority stake in a European airline would prevent Etihad from taking on the whole of Ryanair and the government's holdings with its own existing 3% stake. Moreover, Irish company law requires an investor with 30% of issued shares to make an offer for the whole group.

Risks and challenges

Apart from its foray into Aer Lingus, Ryanair faced various challenges in 2012, some specific to itself and some general to the aviation industry.

Fuel costs

Perhaps the greatest concern in input costs was fuel. Jet fuel prices are subject to wide fluctuations, increases in demand and disruptions in supply, factors which Ryanair can neither predict nor control. In such volatile circumstances, hedging is the only answer. As international prices for jet fuel are denominated in US dollars, Ryanair's fuel costs are also subject to exchange rate risks, exacerbated by a severe Eurozone crisis in 2012, when the value of the euro fell from $1.45 to $1.25. Ryanair's declaration of 'no fuel surcharges ever' and its reliance on low fares limit its capacity to pass on increased fuel costs. Oil prices increased substantially in 2011 and 2012 and remain at elevated levels. While Ryanair has hedged fuel contracts and currency, the volatility of oil prices and currency fluctuations make long forward hedging problematic.

Risks associated with the euro

Headquartered in Ireland, Ryanair's reporting currency is the euro. With its extensive route system within Eurozone countries, the company would be very adversely affected by a break-up of the euro, or if a number of countries, including Ireland, were forced to leave the Eurozone. A break-up of the euro or the exit of one or more members from it would jeopardise the value of Ryanair's euro-denominated assets. As with fuel costs, other operating inputs purchased abroad in non-euro currencies could become more expensive, further undermining profitability. With so much of Ryanair's business conducted in the UK, the collapse of the euro against sterling could be especially difficult.

Sharp economic downturn

The global recession commencing in 2008 created unfavourable economic conditions, high unemployment rates, constrained credit markets and reduced spending by leisure and business passengers. The continuing European recession had repercussions for Ryanair and other Europe-based airlines. Although it succeeded in achieving higher yields in 2012, continued recession limited the scope for raising fares to offset higher input costs. It could restrict the

company's passenger volume growth in a highly competitive environment where other budget carriers, charter and traditional airlines competed on its routes. In addition, in Europe, road transport and high-speed rail put further competitive pressure on airlines.

Ryanair's growth plans entailed investment in new aircraft and routes. If growth in passenger traffic did not keep pace with its planned fleet expansion, overcapacity could result. Related pressures were additional marketing costs and reduced yields from lower fares to promote new additional routes. In its drive for growth, Ryanair was likely to encounter increased competition, putting further downward pressure on yields, as airlines struggled to fill vacant seats to cover fixed costs.

Access to suitable airports, airport charges and government taxes

Ryanair's growth is dependent on access to a sufficient number of suitable take-off and landing slots at costs consistent with its budget strategy. In many cases, there is competition for these slots, along with the threat that airports will raise charges. Ryanair constantly rails against airport charges at Dublin and Stansted, redeploying aircraft to airports with lower charges. Recently it cancelled routes from Madrid and Barcelona following an increase of over 100% in charges at these airports. Indirectly, Ryanair is also vulnerable to extra taxes and charges, such as tourist taxes imposed by governments, discussed above.

Passenger compensation

From 17 February 2005, an EU regulation provided for standardised and immediate assistance for air passengers at EU airports for long delays, cancellations and denied boarding. Passengers affected by cancellations must be offered a refund or re-routing, and free assistance while waiting for their re-routed flight, specifically meals, refreshments, and hotel accommodation where an overnight stay is necessary. Financial compensation is payable, unless the airline can prove unavoidable exceptional circumstances, like political instability, weather conditions, security and safety risks or strikes. Until April 2010, the new regulation was largely ignored and had no material impact on Ryanair, despite the emergence of online 'advisors' to help passengers make claims against airlines when their flights had been cancelled or delayed.

However, the compensation issue was highlighted dramatically with the eruption of Iceland's Eyjafjallajökull volcano. Its volcanic ash forced the closure of much European airspace for six days in April 2010, with further disruptions in May. The losses to Europe's airlines from flight cancellations and compensation were estimated at €2.5 billion. The closures caused the cancellation of 9,490 Ryanair flights for 1.5 million passengers. Many airlines demanded government aid to make up for lost revenue and the cost of feeding and lodging stranded passengers. They contended that flawed computer models used by member states were partly to blame for grounding planes even after it was safe to resume services. The EU Commission noted that fiscal conditions prevented cash-constrained governments from offering aid to airlines, even if the rules could be bent to allow such aid. Ryanair argued strongly against offering aid to airlines, as did easyJet, on the grounds that it could be used as a back door to prop up ailing airlines, especially national carriers.

Initially Ryanair declared that it would not compensate passengers for food and accommodation expenses incurred from flight cancellations, although it would offer refunds. It argued that it was ludicrous that passengers could claim unlimited sums to cover their expenses, irrespective of the cost of their ticket, and that the compensation regulations were discriminatory, as competitor ferry, coach and train operators were obliged to reimburse passengers only to a maximum of the ticket price paid. It claimed that such a situation was not sustainable. However, several days into the crisis, Michael O'Leary said that Ryanair would reimburse 'reasonable costs' to passengers caught up in the chaos in April. Asked if Ryanair would make it difficult for passengers to make claims, O'Leary responded 'Perish the thought.'[13] In fact, in 2012, the company estimated that the non-recoverable fixed costs associated with the cancellations, as well as the reimbursement claims for the initial 20 days of closure of European aerospace, would amount to approximately €29 million.

Later in 2010, Ryanair was obliged to cancel flights to and from Spain during wildcat strikes by Spanish air traffic controllers in August, and again in December when severe weather forced the closure of some airports for several days. This meant lost revenue and more compensation.

Industrial relations

Following pay freezes in 2009 and 2010, Ryanair granted a 2% company-wide pay increase in 2011. It was criticised constantly for refusing union recognition and allegedly providing poor working conditions, as the British Airline Pilots Association (BALPA) tried to organise Ryanair pilots in the UK, maintaining the right to ballot Ryanair pilots to join the union. In July 2006, the Irish High Court ruled that Ryanair had bullied pilots to accept new contracts, where pilots would have to pay €15,000 for retraining on new aircraft if they subsequently left the airline, or if the company was forced to negotiate with unions during the following five years. Meanwhile, Ryanair was contesting the claims of some pilots for victimisation under the new contracts. By 2009, only 11 of the 64 pilots who had lodged the claim remained with the company and still had claims.

Ryanair was ordered to pay 'well in excess' of €1 million in legal costs after a court refused the airline access to the names and addresses of pilots who posted critical comments about the company, on a site hosted by the British and Irish pilots' unions. It claimed anonymous pilots were using a website to intimidate and harass foreign-based pilots to dissuade them from working for the company.

The company maintains its right to treat its crew operating from bases in other higher-paying countries as if they were on Irish territory, and therefore subject to Irish labour laws, which are less exacting than those pertaining in other European jurisdictions. Up to 2013, Ryanair was able to resist challenges to this approach.

Ryanair has conceded that winter lay-offs due to grounding of aircraft could have an unsettling effect on staff, disrupting full-time permanent employment. Notwithstanding the adversarial incidents in its industrial relations history, Ryanair appears to have no problems recruiting staff, including pilots.

Environmental concerns

Aviation fuel has been exempt from carbon taxes, but in 2012 the EU established an Emissions Trading Scheme encompassing the aviation industry, creating a new cost for airlines. Under the legislation, airlines are granted initial CO_2 allowances based on historical performance and an efficiency benchmark. Any shortage of allowances would have to be purchased in the open market and/or at government auctions. For Ryanair the cost of these allowances to cover the shortage that could arise in 2012 were estimated to be in the region of €10 to €15 million. Despite its young, fuel-efficient, minimal-pollution aircraft, the company estimates that the related cost could increase significantly over the coming years, depending on carbon credit prices and future decisions on growth. Therefore, it has contended that any environmental taxation scheme should be to the benefit of more efficient carriers, and that airlines with low load factors, generating high fuel consumption and emissions per passenger, and those offering connecting rather then point-to-point flights, should be penalised. Indeed, independent research by Brighter Planet ranks Ryanair first in the world among airlines on CO_2 efficiency.[14]

Sundry legal actions

Ryanair has been in litigation with the EU about alleged receipt of state aid at certain airports. An EU ruling in 2004 held that it had received illegal state aid from publicly owned Charleroi Airport, its Brussels base. Ryanair was ordered to repay €4 million. On appeal, in 2008 the original EU decision was overturned, and Ryanair was refunded. Never the less, the EU launched further investigations into allegations of illegal aid purportedly subsidising Ryanair at as many as 18 publicly owned airports, such as Paris Beauvais in France and Lübeck and Frankfurt Hahn in Germany. Competitors launched other legal challenges against Ryanair. Furthermore, Ryanair vigorously opposed French government attempts to protect Air France–KLM by forcing easyJet and Ryanair to move their French-based staff from British employment contracts to more expensive French ones.

Frequently, Ryanair took the initiative on alleged illegal aid to rivals. It filed a complaint with the EU Commission accusing Air France–KLM of attempting to block competition after the French airline filed a case, alleging that Marseille was acting illegally by offering discount airlines cut-price fees at its second, no-frills terminal. In addition, Ryanair called on the Commission to investigate allegations that Air France had received almost €1 billion in illegal state aid, benefiting unfairly from up to 50% discounted landing and passenger charges on flights within France. Adverse rulings on these airport cases could curtail Ryanair's growth if it was prevented from making advantageous deals with publicly owned airports and confined to the fewer privately owned airports across Europe.

On another front, Ryanair was being sued by three airport authorities over alleged delays in paying airport charges. After it called for the presiding judge, Mr Justice Peter Kelly, to withdraw on grounds of bias against Ryanair in previous proceedings, the judge did indeed withdraw, not because he admitted Ryanair's charges but to avoid delay in the case. He stood by his previous comments that: 'Ryanair told untruths to and about the court and . . . that the airline and the truth made uncomfortable bedfellows'.[15]

Customer services and perceptions

'The customer is usually wrong. The only time you hear from a customer is when they're complaining because they want to break our rules. Why can't I get a refund for my non-refundable ticket? B***** off.'[16]

So proclaimed Michael O'Leary.

Ryanair's Skytrax two-star rating is the worst for budget airlines in Europe. There have been suggestions that Ryanair's 'obsessive' focus on the bottom line may have dented its public image. There was growing criticism of extra charges continually being imposed by Ryanair on passengers, many on unavoidable services, like check-in. In some instances, these extra charges made Ryanair allegedly more expensive than BA.[17]

Ryanair dropped its plan to charge passengers for using on-board toilets, but was pressing ahead with proposals to remove two of the three lavatories on each plane and replace them with seats. Michael O'Leary asserted that this move would lower air fares by about 5% for all passengers, cutting £2 from a typical £40 ticket.

Ryanair features on many consumer complaint websites. In a blog entitled '20 reasons never to fly Ryanair', extra charges for booking fees, overweight baggage and low baggage weight limits, premium-rate helplines, and the fact that 'you are always being flogged stuff', were enumerated.[18] When the *Irish Times* put customers' gripes on its *Pricewatch* blog to Ryanair's head of communications, he dismissed them as 'subjective and inaccurate rubbish' and even implied that *Pricewatch* had made them up to 'further some class of anti-Ryanair agenda'.[19] Among the complaints were: 'Customers want to be treated like a human being, to get to their desired destination (not 50/60 miles away) . . . I'm sick of that miserable booking charge/service charge/admin charge system.'

So, why are so many people willing to put up with an airline that, in the words of *The Economist*, 'has become a byword for appalling customer service, misleading advertising claims and jeering rudeness'?[20] Ryanair has responded, declaring that, in effect, customers vote with their feet by choosing it for the four tenets of customer service – low fares, a good on-time record, few cancellations and few lost bags. 'If you want anything more – go away', admonishes Michael O'Leary.[21] The *Financial Times* aerospace correspondent observed that Ryanair still offered relative value compared to rail alternatives, at least on a journey from London to Scotland, even when Ryanair's extras are included.

Unexpected disasters

In the airline industry, there is always the possibility that accidents and catastrophic events may occur, due to natural or human-made causes. Among these are accidents and safety-related incidents, terrorist hijackings, outbreaks of contagious disease such as epidemics like swine flu, and weather and natural phenomena that interfere with flights, such as the ash cloud occurrence in 2010. All these incidents can undermine passenger confidence and bookings.

In August 2012, Ryanair faced an investigation by the Spanish Ministry of Public Works after emergency landings of three Ryanair aircraft at Valencia Airport after the aeroplanes had run out of fuel. The aircraft had been diverted to Valencia when they were prevented from landing at Madrid, due to an electrical storm. The Ryanair flights, with others, were put in a holding pattern, but only the Ryanair flights had to instigate emergency procedures because they were running low on fuel. This incident raised questions about Ryanair's fuel policy – to take on the minimum possible to save money. A newspaper cited internal memos sent to pilots reminding them of Ryanair's policy against carrying more than the recommended amounts of fuel. However, Ryanair insisted that fuel levels never fell below the permitted minima during the Valencia incidents, and that all of the company's aircraft operate with required fuel levels. If irregularities were to be found at Ryanair, it could face the loss of its operating licence for three years, with additional fines of up to €4.5 million.

Ryanair maintains various insurances: aviation third-party liability, passenger liability, employer liability, directors and officers' liability, aircraft loss or damage, and other business insurance, consistent with industry standards. Ryanair believes its insurance coverage is adequate, although not comprehensive. This insurance does not cover claims for losses incurred when, due to unforeseen events, airspace is closed and aircraft are grounded such as the closures associated with the ash cloud. It is almost impossible to insure against what may be unlimited liabilities. For instance, EU legislation provides for unlimited liability of an air carrier in the event of death or injuries suffered by passengers.

Other risks and challenges

As listed in its own report, Ryanair faced other risks, some specific and some generic to the industry:

- Prices and availability of new aircraft
- Instability in credit and capital markets which could impair efforts to obtain financing for new aircraft
- Potential impairments from Ryanair's 29.8% stake in Aer Lingus, especially if its latest takeover bid were to fail
- Dependence on key personnel, especially Michael O'Leary
- Dependence on external service providers
- Dependence on its internet website should it break down, even though there are robust backup procedures in place
- A potential rise in Irish Corporation Tax, since Ireland may be under pressure to raise its tax regime as part of its EU/IMF bailout conditions.

Ryanair's competitive space

Rising oil prices and EU-wide recession have accelerated the rate of change in the competitive landscape. The Association of European Airlines forecast a loss of €1.5 billion for European carriers in 2012. A number of EU airlines closed in 2012, including Malev (Hungary), Spanair (Catalonia), OLT (Poland), Air Finland and Cimber Sterling (Denmark). IAG, which purchased BMI from Lufthansa earlier in 2012, announced that BmiBaby would close in 2012 if sale negotiations were unsuccessful. Among many European airlines reporting losses were SAS, Air Berlin, Air France–KLM, IAG (BA and Iberia) and Virgin. Ryanair responded tactically to these developments by opening a new base in Budapest and expanding bases in Spain, Scandinavia and the UK. More European failures were expected as higher oil prices and recession continued to expose airlines already operating at the margins or making substantial losses. Furthermore, the predicaments of carriers such as British Airways were compounded by huge pension fund deficits.

Some industry analysts considered that the economic recession could offer an opportunity for budget carriers, as passengers who continued to travel were expected to trade down. By 2012, budget airlines accounted for over 37% of scheduled intra-European traffic. Ryanair was the clear market leader, with easyJet another dominant force. The two were often compared, since both operated mainly out of the UK and served similar markets. However, it was debatable whether easyJet, through its use of primary airports, would be better than Ryanair in capturing the traffic trading down from network carriers.

Other budget carriers, of diverse size and growth ambitions, trajectories and regional emphases, varied in levels of passenger services and the use of main or secondary airports. A comparison with the US budget airline market indicates that penetration in Europe was less than in the USA, which suggests scope for growth in the sector in Europe.

Leading Ryanair into the future

'It is good to have someone like Michael O'Leary around. He scares people to death.'

This praise of Ryanair's CEO came from fellow Irishman, Willie Walsh, CEO of BA.[22] O'Leary has been described as: 'At turns, arrogant and rude, then charming, affable and humorous, has terrorised rivals and regulators for more than a decade. So far, they have waited in vain for him to trip up or his enthusiasm to wane.'[23]

In fact, Michael O'Leary had been pronouncing his intention to depart from the airline 'in two years' time' since 2005. He declared that he would sever all links with the airline, refusing to 'move upstairs' as chairman.

In 2012, Michael O'Leary held 3.5% of Ryanair's share capital, worth €203 million. His pay topped €1.272 million after he received a bonus of €504,000 – a 24% increase on the fiscal 2011 bonus of €440,000, on top of basic pay of €768,000 which had increased by 29% from €595,000.

Although O'Leary consistently praised the contributions and achievements of his management team, Ryanair was inextricably identified with him. He was credited with single-handedly transforming European air transport. In 2001, O'Leary received the European Businessman of the Year Award from *Fortune* magazine; in 2004, the *Financial Times* named him as one of 25 European 'business stars' who have made a difference, describing him as personifying 'the brash new Irish business elite' and possessing 'a head for numbers, a shrewd marketing brain and a ruthless competitive streak'.[24] Present and former staff have lauded O'Leary's leadership style:

'Michael's genius is his ability to motivate and energise people . . . There is an incredible energy in that place.

People work incredibly hard and get a lot out of it. They operate a very lean operation . . . It is without peer.'

Tim Jeans, a former sales and
marketing director of Ryanair[25]

O'Leary's publicity-seeking antics are legendary. These included his 'declaration of war' on easyJet when, wearing an army uniform, he drove a tank to easyJet's headquarters at Luton Airport. When Ryanair opened its hub at Milan Bergamo, he flew there on a jet bearing the slogan 'Arrividerci Alitalia'. He has dressed as St Patrick and as the Pope to promote ticket offers. Another provocative idea enunciated by O'Leary was the recommendation that co-pilots could be eliminated on flights, so aircraft could fly with just one pilot, since 'the computer does most of the flying now' and 'a flight attendant could do the job of a co-pilot, if needed'.[26]

A self-confessed 'loudmouth' whose outspokenness has made him a figure of public debate, he is called everything from 'arrogant pig' to 'messiah'.[27] His avowed enemies include trade unions, politicians who impose airport taxes (calling former UK Prime Minister Gordon Brown a 'twit' and a 'Scottish miser'[28]), environmentalists, bloggers who rant about poor service, travel agents, reporters who expect free seats, regulators and the EU Commission, and airport owners like BAA, whom he once called 'overcharging rapists'.[29] An EU Commissioner, Philippe Busquin, denounced Michael O'Leary as 'irritating' and insisted he is not the only Commissioner who is 'allergic to the mere mention of the name of Ryanair's arrogant chief'.[30] This history is not something that would endear him to the EU Commission in his quest to gain approval for Ryanair's bid for Aer Lingus.

An *Irish Times* columnist suggested that 'maybe it's time for Ryanair to jettison O'Leary', asserting that he has become a caricature of himself, fulfilling all 15 warning signs of an executive about to fail.[31] Professor Sydney Finklestein identified these signs under five headings – ignoring change, the wrong vision, getting too close, arrogant attitudes, and old formulae. However, having demonstrated the extent to which O'Leary meets the failure criteria, the columnist concluded: 'So, is it time for Ryanair to dump Mr O'Leary? It depends whether you prefer the track record of one of the most successful businessmen in modern aviation, or the theories of a US academic from an Ivy League school.'

So, how do these comments and his hands-on management style fit with Michael O'Leary's declaration to part company with Ryanair? Would he really go, and, if so, what would happen to Ryanair and its ambitions? No one really knows the answer to these questions, but it would certainly lie in O'Leary's propensity to surprise his admirers and detractors alike.

Notes and references
1. IR£ is the Irish pound, the official currency of Ireland until 1999 when GB£1 was approximately IR£1.12.
2. Chevreux Credit Agricole Group (2012) *European Airlines Chasing Real Profits*.
3. €1 = £0.85 = $1.31.
4. Guthrie, J. (2009) 'Sir Stelios beknighted as suits prove bolder risk takers'. *Financial Times*, 30 July, p. 16.
5. Ryanair Annual Report 2009.
6. Lyall, S. (2009) 'No apologies from the boss of a no-frills airline'. *The New York Times*, 1 August (The Saturday Profile).
7. Ryanair 2007 half-yearly results.
8. The FT ArcelorMittal Boldness in Business Awards 2009. *Financial Times* supplement, 20 March, p. 25.
9. Statement from Ryanair's half-yearly results presentation, 6 November 2006.
10. LEX (2009) 'Ryanair'. *Financial Times*, 3 June, p. 16.
11. Noonan, L. (2009) 'O'Leary admits stake in Aer Lingus was stupid disaster'. *Irish Independent*, 6 March.
12. LEX (2012) 'Ryanair/Aer Lingus'. *Financial Times*, 30 August, p. 14.
13. Guardian newspaper blog, http://www.guardian.co.uk/world/blog/2010/apr/22/iceland-volcano-compensation (accessed 19 May 2010).
14. King, M. and Hough, I. (2011) *Air Travel: Carbon and Energy Efficiency*. Shelburne, VT, and San Francisco, CA: Brighter Planet.
15. Carolan, M. (2010) 'Judge pulls out of Ryanair case without altering previous findings or comments'. *Irish Times*, 22 June.
16. Gillette, F. (2010) 'Ryanair's O'Leary mulls one-euro toilets, standing passengers'. Bloomberg.com, 2 September.
17. Waite, R. and Swinford, S. (2009) 'Ryanair more expensive than BA on some flights'. *Sunday Times*, 9 August.
18. Money Central (2009) 'WBLG: Twenty reasons never to fly Ryanair'. *Times Online*, 20 March.
19. Pope, C. (2009) 'Pricewatch Daily'. *Irish Times*, 14 August, p. 11.
20. Lyall, S. (2009) 'No apologies from the boss of a no-frills airline'. *The New York Times*, 1 August (The Saturday Profile).
21. Ibid.
22. Done, K. (2008) 'O'Leary shows it is not yet the end for budget air travel'. *Financial Times*, 2 August, p. 11.
23. The FT ArcelorMittal Boldness in Business Awards 2009. *Financial Times* supplement, 20 March, p. 21.
24. Groom, B. (2004) 'Leaders of the new Europe: Business stars chart a course for the profits of the future'. *Financial Times*, 20 April.
25. Bowley, G. (2003) 'How low can you go?' *Financial Times Magazine*, Issue No. 9, 21 June.
26. Clark, P. (2010) 'Ryanair's latest no-frills idea: sack the boss'. *Financial Times*, 14 September.
27. Bowley, G. (2003) 'How low can you go?' *Financial Times Magazine*, Issue No. 9, 21 June.
28. Lyall, S. (2009) 'No apologies from the boss of a no-frills airline'. *The New York Times*, 1 August (The Saturday Profile).
29. Ibid.
30. Creaton, S. (2004) 'Turbulent times for Ryanair's high-flier'. *Irish Times*, 31 January.
31. McManus, J. (2003) 'Maybe it's time for Ryanair to jettison O'Leary'. *Irish Times*, 11 August.

CASE STUDY

Marks & Spencer: is this as good as it gets?

Phyl Johnson

At the start of 2013 Marks & Spencer, the UK-based international retailer with one of the longest histories and strongest pedigrees on the high street, had delivered below-expectation results. It had disappointed investors, but was ambitiously investing and winning international retail awards for its pioneering, socially responsible business model. What's the story?

• • •

In its heyday, Marks & Spencer (M&S) had been the undisputed leader of British retail. However, in 2012 a constant critique seemed to be 'business as usual' for M&S – high expectations from investors, a requirement for 'more–more–more' driven perhaps by a desire to return to former glories. Big initiatives underway, a lot of change-orientated energy and yet, according to retail commentators, not much major was really changing. M&S was working hard and more than surviving in the difficult retail climate. This case explores change in M&S and explores the question: 'Is what M&S is delivering going to be as good as it is possible to get?'

Who are M&S?

In 2013, UK-based retailer M&S had 21 million visitors to its stores each week. It offered clothing in womenswear, menswear and kidswear, holding 11% of the UK clothing market as well as home products (furnishing and furniture) and food retail. It operated and stocked over 107,000 square feet of retail space in its 703 stores in the UK. Outside the UK, M&S operated a further 387 stores spread across 43 territories. Being a multi-channel retailer, it also operated over the phone and online. It operated its business according to an environmentally driven business model called 'Plan A'.

In the 1990s, this firm outperformed the stock market by a significant margin. By 2000 it became a rather average stock, sustained until late 2008 when the retail market crashed. The firm recovered but has remained a below-market performer (see Table 1).

Folklore and ancient tales

Michael Marks began his penny market stalls in the late 1880s and soon partnered with Tom Spencer, a cashier of Marks's supplier. From this beginning Marks & Spencer grew steadily. Simon Marks took over the running of M&S from his father, turning the penny bazaars into stores, establishing a simple pricing policy and introducing the 'St Michael' logo as a sign of quality. There was a feeling of camaraderie and a close-knit familial atmosphere within the stores, with staff employed whom the managers believed would 'fit in' and become part of the family. Staff were also treated better and paid more than in other companies. The family nature of this firm dominated top

Table 1 **Financial summary 2005–12**

Year	Group revenue (£ million)	Group profit (£ million)	Market share, general merchandise	Earnings per share	Visitors per week in UK stores (million people)
2005–6	7,797	855	10.4%	19.4p	19.8
2006–7	8,588	1,044	11.1%	31.4p	21
2007–8	9,022	1,089	11%	40.4p	21.8
2008–9	9,062	768.9	10.7%	28p	21.6
2009–10	9,536	843.9	11.2%	33p	21
2010–11	9,740	824.9	11.7%	34.8p	20.7
2011–12	9,934	810.0	11.7%	34.9p	20.3

Source: derived by the author from M&S annual accounts

management as well: until the late 1970s, the board was made up of family members only.

Throughout the 1980s and 1990s in particular, M&S was hugely successful in terms of its delivery of high quality and a highly reliable brand to its customers, this in turn earning outstanding reward in profit and market share. Successive chief executives were renowned for their attention to detail in regard to supplier control, merchandise and store layout, and it seemed to work. This stock was the darling of investors, significantly outperforming the market year after year. Historically, M&S was run using a tried, tested and trusted recipe (a way of doing business) and this unchanging M&S formula won and won big.

Confident and comfortable at the top of the tree, M&S was able to luxuriate in doing business in the way it chose with little or no competition. Other retailers competing in the same multi-offering space as M&S were Littlewoods, who are no longer on the UK high street, and British Home Stores (BHS). Direct womenswear competition came from names now long gone, such as Richard Shops, Etam and Chelsea Girl as well as those remaining like Principles, Top Shop and Dorothy Perkins. At this time there was no Next, H&M, Primark, Zara or supermarket clothing. M&S traded with a particular power-brand of leader: strong-willed, autocratic, big-personality people. One of the most famous of these power brokers was Sir Richard Greenbury, joint Chair and CEO from 1988 to 1999, who was famous for having strong opinions and being committed to the recipe of the past.

During Greenbury's tenure M&S had the best of times, days of glory during which it held more than twice the market share of any other retailer. The reputation for good-quality clothing was built on basics, the essentials which every customer needed and which would outlast current fashions and trends seen in other high street retailers. All assistants carried tape measures to assure a good fit and, as product remained in the store year round, exchanges and refunds were not problematic. As such, as late as the 1990s M&S had no fitting rooms, took no credit cards, rarely held

sales and ignored the loyalty card schemes sweeping British retailing. Until the late 1990s its customers worked around these inconveniences and helped the firm to record its record-breaking year of trading in 1997–8 when pre-tax profit topped the £1 billion mark ($1.52bn; €1.19bn). That was a financial result it took M&S 10 long years and three CEOs to repeat.

M&S also had the worst of times under Greenbury. By 1998 it was clear that the M&S recipe was no longer working. Share prices plummeted and this serious jolt led to many years of turbulence that a future CEO (Sir Stuart Rose) later referred to as lost years. M&S was forced to wake up to its contemporary marketplace on several fronts at once. First, its allegiance to British suppliers simply became too costly and it was slow to follow its rivals' lead into sourcing cheaper goods from low-cost countries. Second, its customers had been departing to competitors and in M&S womenswear it found itself squeezed by Next, Oasis and Gap from the upper end and by George at Asda and Matalan from the lower end. Third, its home-bred bureaucracy and strongly embedded way of doing business meant that change, however badly needed, would come slowly. M&S had lost touch with the marketplace and the results showed a 23% decline in profit in the first-half profits in 1998 that snowballed to a 50% reduction by the year end and a startling tumble of more than 80% between 1998 and 2001.

Sir Richard Greenbury departed and it took M&S four erratic years to find a true successor. During those four years, M&S worked its way through Peter Salsbury (tenure of one year, including a profit warning), Luc Vandevelde (CEO, who took the Chair role and proclaimed, prematurely, that he had turned M&S around) and Roger Holmes (innovator of the store-within-a-store segmentation of M&S). Eventually, in 2004, M&S appointed Sir Stuart Rose.

The man who would be king

In 2004, Rose inherited a changed M&S. Solid work had been accomplished by Vandevelde and Holmes. Their major contributions to the story of M&S were the launch of the Simply Food stores in train and petrol stations, the first foray into corporate social responsibility, and the Per Una sub-brand. Along with retail fashion entrepreneur George Davies (formerly of Next and George at Asda), they launched the womenswear sub-brand Per Una that still remained in-store in 2013 and has sustained years of success under its colourfully woven belt.

However, a constant criticism levelled at M&S, which it openly admitted to, was the failure to attract the high-spending 35–50-year-old female demographic. During the early phase of his six-year CEO tenure, Rose fought off a high-profile takeover bid. A downturn in results had left M&S vulnerable to the takeover attempts of Sir Philip Green, a larger-than-life character in UK retailing and owner of the influential Arcadia Group that held the high street chains Top Shop, Dorothy Perkins, Miss Selfridge and Wallis. Through the summer of 2004 Green's repeated takeover attempts were fought off by the M&S board that hired Rose. The clincher for many investors to reject the takeover bid was Stuart Rose's commitment to beat Sir Philip's 400p share price. Rose offered a commitment to 450p, the investors backed him and in late December 2005 he delivered; the share price hit a six-year high at 504p.

Sir Stuart's tenure was a busy period. He and M&S had highs and lows. He avoided the 'T' word (turnaround) to keep expectations low whilst proclaiming a narrative of radical change. Some later argued he delivered only 'business as usual' and no form of radical change at all. One thing was certain, though: he was very, very busy.

He launched an 11-point strategic plan and spent millions to revamp tired stores, livened up employee attitudes and injected interest into stale clothing ranges. He often spoke with an air of caution to the institutional investors, sending a message of change but requesting patience for the results to show the benefits.

Looking back at his six-year CEO tenure, there were three or four particularly high impact changes he made. First, he oversaw the launch of M&S Direct and worked along with the powerhouse of online retail, Amazon, to make the most of this sales channel. Second, he put M&S on TV. Marketing director Steven Sharp turned out a series of glossy TV advertising campaigns. He used well-known actors and actresses to star in his commercials or offer voice-overs. The brand 'Your M&S' was central to these extremely successful campaigns. Third, he focused on the womenswear problems by hiring Kate Bostock, a former director of the successful George clothing line at Asda. Fourth, he pioneered the 'Plan A' corporate responsibility initiative in 2007 that in 2012 won M&S the worldwide 'responsible retailer of the year' award. He launched 180 commitments across varied initiatives aimed at addressing social inequality and enabling sustainable lifestyles in the context of the planet's finite resources. By 2012, 11 million garments had been donated to the charity Oxfam, 1.7 billion fewer carrier bags had been used, 147 million hangers had been collected, and £11.4 million had been spent on community projects in Bangladesh, with multiple carbon-neutral products and an overall 30% reduction in waste.

'Plan A' was a big success for Sir Stuart. Financial results, however, were mixed. Up until 2007 increases in like-for-like sales delivered the outcomes investors were looking for. Commentators talked of a turnaround. Sub-brands like Per Una and Autograph were successful in womenswear, and Kate Bostock was promoted to become overall head of retail (with the exception of food) and take a place on the board of directors.

The UK's swift slide into recession in 2008 had a significant impact on sales, and by September of that year M&S saw its worst quarterly sales since 2005, with a 6% fall in like-for-like sales with food falling marginally less than clothing and homeware. Rose announced a curtailment of capital expenditure, seeing not only his famed refurbishment programme grind to a halt but a scaling back of investment across the board. This was in direct contradiction to his promise less than a year earlier. These measures were all designed to ensure the board would not have to recommend a cut in dividend. However, by 2009 that is precisely what happened and investors saw a 20.9% dividend cut.

Mixed results appeared in 2009, with the drop in overall sales slowing down and with M&S Food giving a boost when figures showed it to be the most improved food retailer in the UK in terms of customer loyalty over the past decade. Sitting second only to Asda in the 2009 data, M&S had overtaken Waitrose, its direct premium rival. Inspection of the figures revealed that M&S overtook Tesco and Sainsbury's in terms of loyalty as far back as 2002 in the Vandevelde era, leading some critics to question the extent of Rose's own impact on M&S Food.

The biggest issue for the leadership of M&S in 2009 was the worsening relationship between its board and its investors. In the first half of the year, Rose and his Marketing Director (Stephen Sharp) were both forced to give up a £1 million package of bonuses in shares in order to appease shareholders. The non-executive director Louise Patten, who had signed off on the bonuses, came under fire at the annual general meeting with a motion to block her reappointment. Rose had already been forced to sell his stake in the business of another of his non-executive directors (Martha Lane-Fox), with this level of involvement being considered inappropriate. But the primary issue that occupied investors was Rose's position as joint Chair and CEO. He survived a much publicised shareholder revolt at the July AGM but the size of the vote (over 40% voting against Rose's reappointment as Chair) was seen as a clear signal of the need for investors to be reassured about the future.

Finally, in July 2009, Rose ended the uncertainty by announcing his intention to stand down as CEO in 2010 but not as Chair until 2011. Old stories of too much power in one pair of hands echoed around Sir Stuart, and big expectations of change at M&S lingered even after his six years of what was referred to as a 'tumultuous'[1] effort. On the day he left, 4 January 2011, the share price sat below the 400p Philip Green had offered seven years previously.

Back to the future

Marc Bolland became the new CEO of M&S on 1 May 2010. He was a retailer with a track record suited to the market. During his tenure at UK supermarket Morrisons he saw an extra half-million customers in the stores and almost doubled net profits.

On appointment, the realisation may just have occurred to Bolland that the job at M&S could be bigger than anticipated. The arch-critic of Sir Stuart, Tony Shiret (then of Crédit Suisse) argued that M&S was not the transformed offering that it projected itself to be. Throughout 2009 he repeatedly commented in the press that M&S was still failing to be a hit with the mid-age range demographic and that two-thirds of its customers were still 55 years plus – not that much had changed. The general view was that, except for cost savings, M&S had made little financial progress since Rose took over in 2004. Should change be more far-reaching?

In an extremely challenging retail climate Bolland had a fight on his hands. The retail climate through 2010, 2011, 2012 and 2013 was tough and there was ferocious discounting on the high street. Many big names left the UK high street (Woolworths, Comet, C&A, Littlewoods, Borders) and others went into receivership – HMV, Republic (owner of Diesel) and FCUK. Even the charmed and one-time Per Una partner George Davies failed with his 'GivE' womenswear stores. Rose had spent more than £2bn on M&S stores and yet they were still reported to be shabby,[2] there were many marginal high street locations, a significant lagging behind on the acquisition of retail space, a supply chain that needed modernising, and that elusive womenswear market to sort out.

In particular, the position of distribution centres was problematic for M&S. In May of 2013 there was much criticism in the press highlighting the stock tracking as 20 years out of date. H&M claimed to be capable of getting designs from the drawing board to stores in a fortnight. M&S took longer than that time to ship its product coming into UK ports to its stores. Although M&S had managed to open a new 900,000 sq ft warehouse in the UK in spring 2013, it needed to get its two others on stream almost immediately. The reality was at least a three-year wait for site two. Site three is yet to be secured.

As many incoming leaders had done before him, Marc Bolland took a little time to appraise the landscape before announcing his vision for the future and the changes he wanted to see. He had a lot of stores to fill with a lot of stock: 16.2 million square feet in the UK. John Lewis, M&S's closest rival in the UK, had only 5 million.

The strategic plan

- £900 million investment funded from existing cash flows
- Phase one, 2010–13: focus on core market and space growth
- Phase two, 2013–15: accelerate the extension from the multi-channel platform
- Aim to be the UK's leading multi-channel store
- From £800m to £1bn of group profit by 2014
- Move from a UK retailer that exports to an international retailer using franchises, joint ventures and wholly owned models
- Better in-store navigation around the sub-brands
- Introduce 'Conran'-designed furniture range
- Upgrade and streamline stores
- Grow the food offering, looking at wines, flowers and distinctive international brands.

One key challenge, however, was to clarify exactly what M&S was to its customers and potential customer base. One commentator suggested that: 'To its older customers, M&S is a clothing store that also has a food department, but to many younger shoppers, M&S is a food store with a sideline in clothing.'[3]

M&S had too much retail space to fill for shoppers to be this unclear. Even within womenswear, M&S's offering was confused. Primark does cheap, Zara does trendy, Debenhams does 'Designers at Debenhams', and M&S does what: knickers? One thing that shoppers did know was that M&S was not turning stock round fast enough. Zara refreshed its stock four times a week and got a design into store within 15 days. At M&S the corresponding figures were three to four weeks and eight weeks respectively.[4] What was M&S's true brand identity?

Perhaps as a direct result of this issue of brand identity, at the end of 2012 and the start of 2013 M&S's corporate brand was in the doldrums again. Early in 2012 there had been much talked about operational failures when in womenswear it simply ran out of key stock lines. There had been a brief flutter of takeover rumours in the autumn of 2012, provoked by a 6.8% drop in the quarterly sales figures, the worst results in three years with a horrific 28% fall in the sales figures in womenswear rumoured.[5] This sat against the backdrop of full shops in the Zara chain, excellent figures from online retailer Asos, and UK high street department store John Lewis seeing its sales leaping by

15%. The year 2013 began with a fall of 3.8% in seasonal sales compared with the previous year, in sharp contrast to Debenhams' 2.9% increase.

Heads rolled as Marc Bolland took what he referred to as the 'necessary steps'[6] to improve the performance of fashion and homeware, and former favourite and head of retail Kate Bostock was relieved of her position, only to announce a move to rival Asos in October 2012. Her role in womenswear was taken by Belinda Earl, former CEO of UK department store Debenhams and more recently of high-end womenswear retailer Jaeger. Stephanie Chen also joined the womenswear team, bringing her pedigree of House of Fraser, Bibba and Designers at Debenhams with her. M&S watchers had high hopes for the end to what some customers referred to as a 'clothes piled up like a bring-and-buy sale'[7] feel to M&S.

Much of the business press featured stories on the out-of-fashion retailer, all pointing to the brand and sub-brand confusion as a major contributor. In almost every article the journalists and city analysts called for better navigation from M&S: navigation around its stores and navigation into what they saw as a gloomy future.

However, M&S does have a great resilience to downturns. It remains a profitable business, it brings in profit margins of 8%, it has an operating cash flow of over £1bn a year, and its balance sheet is considered to be in good shape.[8] It had lasted 128 years and had its own museum to record its long history. Maybe it was the investors who needed to think about radical change, changing their own mind sets perhaps to recognise that 'Is this is as good as it gets for M&S?'

Notes and references
1. Andrea Felsted (2012) 'Former M&S top man keeps himself busy', *Financial Times*, 16 September.
2. Patience Wheatcroft (2012) 'Don't write it off. Marks still have Andrea Felsted. M&S finds itself going out of fashion', *Financial Times*, 13 July.
3. Andrea Felsted (2012) 'M&S finds itself going out of fashion', *Financial Times*, 13 July.
4. Laura Craik (2012) 'How M&S lost the plot', *The Times*, 10 November.
5. Rupert Neate (2012) 'Belinda Earl: from Saturday girl to M&S style director', *Guardian*, 20 July.
6. Zoe Wood (2012) 'Kate Bostock to join M&S's online rival Asos', *Guardian*, 9 October.
7. Rupert Neate, op. cit.
8. Sarah Gordon (2012) 'M&S death rumours greatly exaggerated', *Financial Times*, 26 September.

CASE STUDY

Hotel du Vin: strategic entrepreneurship and innovative continuity in the boutique hotel sector

Michelle Lowe, Neil Wrigley and Katherine Cudworth

The Hotel du Vin chain is a pioneering, award-winning boutique hotel group operating in the UK. It was established in 1994 by Robin Hutson and Gerard Basset under the 'Alternative Hotel Group' company name. The chain experienced steady but consistently successful growth throughout the 1990s and 2000s until the group, six hotels strong, was sold in 2004. This case study explores six dimensions of strategic entrepreneurship that defined the development of this iconic British firm.

● ● ●

Creating the brand: origins of the Hotel du Vin chain

Beginning in 1994 with a 13-bed hotel in Winchester, the co-founders of Hotel du Vin (HduV), Robin Hutson and Gerard Basset – previously Managing Director and Head Sommelier, respectively, at the UK's premier country house hotel, Chewton Glen – attempted to fill a gap which they had identified in the UK hotel market for quality-driven, affordable provincial hotels. Building the brand initially around a quality and affordable in-house bistro, extensive cellar and a central theme of wine, the HduV in Winchester achieved remarkable initial success – a 90% occupancy rate within the first few months of its opening and critical acclaim from the UK media.

Three years later the proto-chain expanded with a second and larger opening of a 34-bed hotel in Tunbridge Wells. By raising a further investment of £5 million ($7.65m; €5.85m)[1] from both initial and new investors, including Anita and Gordon Roddick of The Body Shop, the chain expanded to four hotels by 2001 with openings in Bristol (1999) and Birmingham (2001). By the autumn of 2004 the group had added two further hotels, in Brighton and Harrogate, taking its portfolio to six sites. Additionally, it had acquired, and was in the advanced stage of developing, a former brewery in Henley-on-Thames, and had purchased the rights to develop a highly attractive 41-bed site in Cambridge. It had also begun discussions relating to four other potential hotel sites.

Hotel du Vin & Bistro, Winchester, Hampshire.

Source: Alamy/Jeremy Hoare

This case was prepared by Michelle Lowe, School of Management, Neil Wrigley, School of Geography, and Katherine Cudworth, University of Southampton. It is intended as a basis for class discussion and not as an illustration of good or bad practice.

Achieving a turnover exceeding £18 million per annum and an occupancy rate close to 80% by 2004, HduV had an enviable reputation for quality and enjoyed a high public profile – AA 'Hotel of the Year' (2002) and the *Guardian*'s and the *Observer*'s 'Best UK Hotel' (2003). At this point the co-founders and their financial backers accepted an acquisition bid from the British-based property company Marylebone Warwick Balfour (MWB) Group Holdings for £66.4 million. Significantly, £10 million of this related to the valuation of the HduV brand.

The innovative nature of its initial development and expansion

HduV was an iconic pioneer of the UK boutique hotel market. Like other major players which developed in the sector in the mid-1990s, such as Malmaison and Firmdale Hotels, HduV sought a blend of quality design and service which was able to respond to changing consumer cultures, such as a growing willingness to pay for quality at affordable prices, the growth of gastro-dining, and early forms of what in the 2000s became known as 'restaurants with rooms'.

A career-long hotelier, Hutson honed his skills in a series of hands-on roles that saw him rise to the post of Managing Director of Chewton Glen (a luxury country house hotel). After eight years in the role he began to question his long-term prospects in hotel management when it had become clear that there was no opportunity for equity investment and progression from a salaried position. The catalyst for the initial business plan was a lunchtime visit by Hutson and Basset to the Lansdowne Pub in Primrose Hill, London, an early frontrunner among London's gastro-pubs. Taking further inspiration from successful hotels and restaurants in London, such as Conran, 190 Queens Gate and Blakes, the co-founders formulated an innovative model for the provincial hotel market which focused on a wine-orientated bistro experience with an affordable luxury hotel element. That business plan began with an initial formulation 'on the back of a cigarette-packet' – a level of informality that continued with the arrangements for financing the first HduV hotel. That financing saw Hutson seek investment from a wide network of friends and family, and via contacts made through his role at Chewton Glen, but significantly it included two important venture capital investors, Ashley Levett and Charlie Vincent. These 'business angels' brought not only financing to the project but a necessary level of expertise, given the co-founders limited financial experience.

Press reviews of Hotel du Vin

'Hotel du Vin have the whole of Britain to clean up. They get it right, while just about all the others get it wrong.'
Times Magazine, 5 February 2000

'Where many hotels fall down is in maintaining consistency of their product. Not so for Hotel du Vin . . . Hotel du Vin demonstrates the wow factor. It shows the innovation that everyone in the industry should aspire to.'
The Sunday Times, 29 July 2001

The tying together of hospitality and wine, based on the core competences of the directors of HduV, meant that the company was able to leverage a key competitive advantage from the context of a rapidly growing UK wine market. Business partner and co-founder Gerard Basset, a former World Champion holder of 'Sommelier of the Year', provided the core capability for the HduV wine branding and was commended by Hutson for his knowledge, which brought 'credibility' to the business concept. Consumers in the UK were spending an increasing amount on wine by the late 1990s, with wine's share of the market for alcoholic drinks increasing by almost a third to 28% between 1997 and 1999. Significantly, this gave the co-founders the opportunity to introduce brand-building events such as wine classes and tastings. They had recognised that many of the hotels operating in the market at that time tended to neglect food and beverage as a source of revenue and relied more heavily on room occupancy. In contrast, the forefronting of the wine elements of the brand at HduV allowed the development of multiple ancillary income streams. As HduV Finance Director Peter Chittick commented, these multiple ancillary income streams allowed the hotel group to avoid what he calls 'black spaces' and developed a model that worked: 'Lunch, dinner, hotel, week, weekend, weekday – 365 days a year.'

Building the brand and appreciating its property element

As the company developed, the role of property in the HduV brand became more and more clear and emerged as one of the key cornerstones of the hotel group's identity and value proposition. As highlighted by Chittick in *Business South Magazine* in June 2003: 'The HduV brand is all about beautiful buildings, fabulous food and wine, a relaxed, informal atmosphere and sensible prices.'

Hutson clearly drove this dimension of the brand, hand-selecting quirky buildings and previously overlooked sites. Together with his wife Judy, he sympathetically and carefully restored those buildings, ensuring each had their own idiosyncratic interiors, mixing classic and contemporary design which anticipated the 'shabby chic' design trend of the 2000s and which emphasised and complemented each building's history. The distinctive and historical buildings, including a 1715 Georgian house, a Grade II listed 1765 Georgian mansion, an eighteenth-century sugar refinery, a nineteenth-century eye hospital and a former brewery, were what Hutson aptly described as 'distressed assets, in the middle of good towns' and increasingly came to embody the property-backed nature of the HduV brand. When recounting how he identified 'good towns' and suitable new hotel sites, Hutson lists particular indicators that he would intuitively look for (types of cars parked at the railway station, or the presence of 'brass plaques') to judge the number of professionals. He had a feel for these indicators, and of the 'growing buzz' of the towns. He used intensive on-the-ground research, or what he has described as 'wearing out his shoe leather'. The key to each new HduV site was his intrinsic ability to sense pent-up demand for sophisticated but relaxed cosmopolitan-style hotels.

In addition, he realised the value of being the first mover in the boutique hotel chain sector to enter such towns. In this way, HduV became the first boutique hotel chain to move into Tunbridge Wells, Bristol, Birmingham, Harrogate Cambridge and Henley, firmly placing HduV 'ahead of the curve'. In the case of Birmingham, which broke his normal model of provincial towns, Hutson relied on his sense of the renewal and rediscovery of that city and the architectural attraction of the revitalised 'Merchant City' in which the hotel was located.

The challenge posed by the need to balance innovative entrepreneurship and brand management

As the acknowledged creative force behind the growing chain, Hutson admits that the transition from innovative entrepreneur to manager was not a straightforward one, particularly in regards to his quest for idiosyncratic design. He told *Locum Destination Review* in 2002:

> 'With four executive directors and another four non-executives, I'm having to learn to be a bit more democratic these days . . . I'm probably a control freak, but someone has to look after the detail and that's the way it works . . . it's so much part of us, I couldn't possibly do just a cookie-cutter chain.'

Despite the firm's growing success, Hutson and his co-directors were resistant to the notion of rapidly expanding the chain. Indeed, privately they had acknowledged a limit of developing only eight to ten hotels in the chain early on in the venture. As HduV began to reach that target and its 10-year milestone, the co-founders began to voice concern that the company was becoming too large and unyielding for them to control, to the detriment of the service offer. Hutson recalls how the firm began to become less flexible and started to lose the cohesiveness vital to effective knowledge sharing between management and employees:

> 'I'd got to the stage where I didn't know all the staff members' names and, you know, things were going on in the hotels that I'd lost control of . . . Gerard would talk about this as well . . . we'd recognise things that were not as good as they should be and not . . . not as we intended them, and just very difficult to influence and turn around really.'[2]

In order to tackle the management issue of maintaining and controlling the HduV brand, Hutson employed a strategy of 'incubation', which he felt helped 'keep the culture going' as HduV grew. Each new hotel that opened was run by a manager who had previous experience of running the Winchester HduV. In this way managers were initiated in Winchester and the directors had the opportunity to oversee their proficiency before promoting them to the responsibility of running a newly opened part of the chain. As Mike Warren, Brand Director at HduV, notes: '[It] was a direct transfer of the knowledge, skills – bang! Open [the new HduV] and do what we do in Winchester.'[3]

However, due to the continuing expansion of the group, this strategy of incubation and 'bringing up staff through the ranks', in order to imbue workers with an implicit knowledge and understanding of the culture and the brand of HduV, was not feasible for all members of staff. Both Hutson and Warren questioned whether the expansion of the chain, both prior to and following its buyout by MWB, made this strategy less feasible. Speaking of the Harrogate and Brighton openings, Warren talked about having to employ key staff members such as sommeliers and reception managers from outside the company, and admitted that the essence of HduV got 'slightly diluted'.

The sale of the chain and its strategic implications

In moving to acquire the chain in 2004, MWB's strategic intention was to pair HduV with its own boutique hotel brand Malmaison, and to exploit the back-office synergies possible by merging the chains' duplicated functions such as finance and HR systems, purchasing, supply chains, and management of the two hotel brands. Both for the directors of HduV who sold out and for MWB who acquired the chain, the sale raised important strategic issues.

The challenge faced by its new owners following the merger of Hotel du Vin and Malmaison

The merger and subsequent expansion of both the HduV and Malmaison groups raised the serious challenge for MWB of managing two separate brands and workforces under a single senior management team. Robert Cook, former CEO at the joint group Malmaison Holdings, a subsidiary or MWB, described both the chains as having their own 'personality', and his central strategy of keeping each distinct from the other. He likened HduV as the 'shabby chic country cousin' to the 'sleek and glamorous' Malmaison, or alternatively as the Morgan car to the Maserati.[4]

Although initially Cook found the brand divide to be a potential impediment, as staff were unwilling to 'jump the fence' to work in the other hotel group, two to three years after the merger he felt that this trend had reversed and staff mobility, with the help of key 'trailblazing' individuals such as Warren, became as fluid between the two groups as it had traditionally been within: 'What we did do was . . . we created a sort of culture that we'd develop from within, so therefore, if you're a deputy in a Hotel du Vin, you'll then go and become a deputy in a big Mal, to then come back to being a number one in a Hotel du Vin.'[5]

Between 2004 and 2011 MWB rapidly expanded HduV by a further eight sites. Following minor adjustments to its operating model, the new owners were keen to continue to exploit the intangible assets of HduV, closely following the winning formula of the brand, namely hotels in historic buildings within essentially provincial towns and cities with year-round demand. It is clear from key individuals within both HduV and Malmaison that during this rapid expansion and consequent organisational restructuring there was a focused endeavour by the new owners and managers to simultaneously retain the 'culture' of both brands.

The key challenges faced by the two companies following the merger were as follows:[6]

- Ensuring the values and cultures of both Malmaison and Hotel du Vin were not diluted whilst bringing the two workforces together under the same operational leadership
- Managing significant growth from 11 hotels to 27 hotels in less than four years, creating over 1500 new jobs
- Creating a continuous learning culture while meeting the needs of the guest, the group, the local hotel and the different learning styles of the people in the business

- Protecting the 'DNA' of both groups (the people) to secure the groups' success.

In addition to the branding and human resources challenges posed by the merger, MWB was also faced with the task of marrying two managerial and operation styles. Talking of the differences existing between the two brands following the merger, Warren describes Malmaison as having more of a centralised corporate structure compared to HduV's management style:

> 'My view is that one of the brands was too systematic and too procedural and had too much bang-bang-bang-bang-bang, and the other didn't have quite enough. That was the big difference, you know, and . . . some of the systems and procedures in Malmaison were essential and were very good, you know, for managing . . . cost perspective and purchasing . . . but some . . . were not, and were less human, they didn't take account of, personality, you know?'[7]

Sustaining entrepreneurial innovative energy following the chain's sale

Following the sale to MWB in 2004, Hutson remained with HduV for a few months to oversee the transition and development of the Henley site. With the exception of the operations director, all the key directors from the board left the business. However, rather than being severed after the sell-off, the network ties of the directors were reworked and reformulated. Hutson, Basset, Chittick and Levett all pursued new entrepreneurial enterprises within the industry. These entrepreneurial relationships – based on reciprocal links between the new business ventures – meant that, with the exception of Basset, each has at some point been involved with no fewer than two companies founded by another member of the original HduV board.

Many of the new business ventures of the HduV directors are characterised by hybridisation – that is to say, they appear to straddle the divide between the original HduV concept and intimately related spin-off concepts. One example of this would be Hutson's new venture 'The Pig' proto-chain, envisioned as a 'Hotel du Vin for the country' and drawing heavily on its predecessor's core strategy, that is providing luxury without formality, shabby chic design and quirky idiosyncratic buildings set in locations which have the potential to offer year-long demand. This chain, which by 2013 was three hotels strong, has by common consent phenomenal potential to expand. Indeed, Peter Chittick, who was involved in the financial strategy of the chain, believes that, like HduV earlier, it could be 'easily rolled out in up to eight to ten locations in the UK'.

Table 1 **Key financial and performance data of HduV and Malmaison**

Year	Total revenue (£000)		Operating EBITDA (£000)		Occupancy rate (%)	
	HduV	Malmaison	HduV	Malmaison	HduV	Malmaison
2004	–	32,628	–	8,568	82	78
2007	37,074	58,198	9,143	14,761	83	78
2008	45,314	62,322	9,927	16,526	81	79
2009	50,763	60,271	11,221	15,366	81	78
2010	50,385	60,815	11,507	16,268	78	77

Hotel du Vin and Malmaison: future strategic challenges

By 2010–11 the combined turnover of the two hotel groups had exceeded £160 million and both chains shared similar high occupancy rates of around 77%. HduV continued to win critical acclaim and accolades after its sale to MWB, such as the *Guardian*'s and the *Observer*'s 'Best UK Hotel' title which it received between 2004 and 2009. See Table 1 for key performance indicators.

The successes of both the HduV and Malmaison chains have been paralleled by the acute financial problems faced by their parent company MWB Holdings, which collapsed into administration in November 2012 following a dispute between the group and its subsidiary, the office space provider of MWB Business Exchange, to which it owed £8 million. Shareholders Pyrrho Investments, the Hong-Kong-based fund which owns 24% of MWB Group Holdings, blamed the 'poor corporate governance' of former group CEO Richard Balfour-Lynn, who resigned from the company in March 2012.

Despite debts in the order of £230m, Malmaison and HduV Chief Executive Gary Davis stated that the collapse of the parent company would not impact on day-to-day operations and that, following strong business perform-ances from both hotel chains, the group plans to continue expanding both brands with the launch of 12 new hotels over the next 10 years, with a new Malmaison to open in Dundee in 2013.

Finally, in reviewing the growth of HduV post-sale, Hutson offers his thoughts on how the chain has been able to sustain its strong business performance and continue to expand, despite facing the strategic difficulties that follow a shift of governance towards a larger corporate structure:

'It's the graveyard of many a good entrepreneurial business, isn't it, sort of going from that small . . . small hands-on approach into something more corporate. With the Hotel du Vin I think because the concept was strong enough, it seems to have weathered [that transition] reasonably well.'[8]

Notes and references
1. £1 = $1.53 = €1.17.
2. R. Hutson, personal communication, 2011.
3. M. Warren, personal communication, 2011.
4. Robert Cook, *Directors Magazine*, June 2008.
5. Robert Cook, personal communication, 2011.
6. Sean Wheeler, Group Director of People Development at HduV and Malmaison, quoted in *Leader Magazine*, 2008.
7. M. Warren, personal communication, 2011.
8. R. Hutson, personal communication, 2011.

CASE STUDY

Going for growth: Teva's global strategy

Justin Boag and Sarah Holland

This case explores the growth strategies of Teva, an Israel-based pharmaceutical company and the world's largest 'generic' producer. Under the direction of Shlomo Yanai, Teva followed an aggressive growth programme. The company became a more diversified pharmaceutical company with markets all over the world using acquisitions and strategic partnerships. Investors, however, became uneasy about the lack of improvement in profitability, and at the end of 2011, Shlomo Yanai retired. In 2012 Teva appointed Jeremy Levin in the hope that he would be able to increase profitability by moving Teva towards mainstream pharmaceuticals.

● ● ●

In December 2011 Teva Pharmaceutical Industries ('Teva') announced the resignation of Shlomo Yanai, the 59-year-old President and CEO. He was to be replaced in June 2012 by the first non-Israeli in the role, the 58-year-old Jeremy Levin. Phillip Frost, Chairman of Teva, said: 'Jeremy is a highly regarded manager, but we are sad that Shlomo is leaving us, after doing great work. [Teva] has expanded and achieved growth in all financial parameters.' He added that if Mr Yanai 'chooses public service, the Israeli people will benefit'.[1]

At an investor call following publication of the annual results in February 2012, Shlomo Yanai declared: 'Our strategy is focused on growth and creating a highly diversified business, and on reducing our dependence on any one particular market or product. During the year, we took major steps towards reaching our strategic goals.'[2]

Investors may, however, have taken a different view, after Teva failed to achieve its planned EPS for 2011, and declared that it was unlikely to meet its target of $35 billion (£23bn; €27.3bn)[3] turnover by 2015. After peaking in 2010, the share price had plummeted (see Figure 1).

Teva built its success on manufacturing 'generic' drugs. These are identical copies of branded medicines that can be launched when the patent on the branded drug expires, typically at far lower prices. Ironically, despite being the world's largest generic drug manufacturer, the two most important contributors to Teva's turnover and profit were Copaxone, a widely used patented treatment for multiple

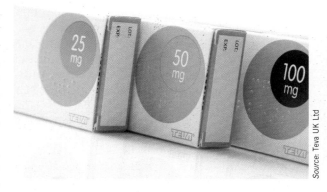

Source: Teva UK Ltd

sclerosis, and Provigil, a proprietary treatment for sleep disorders. These brands were themselves threatened with generic competition in 2013 and 2012 respectively.

Teva in a nutshell

- World's number one generic company
- World's 15th-largest pharmaceutical company
- Sales of $18 billion in 2011
- Product portfolio of over 1400 molecules
- Active in 120 countries
- Over 40,000 employees.

Figure 1 Teva's share price

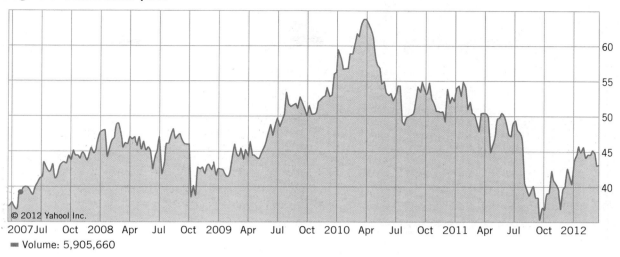

2007 Jul   Oct 2008 Apr   Jul   Oct 2009 Apr   Jul   Oct 2010 Apr   Jul   Oct 2011 Apr   Jul   Oct 2012
■ Volume: 5,905,660

Source: Yahoo Finance

Strategy

For the previous five years, under the leadership of Teva's President and CEO Shlomo Yanai, a former Israeli Army general with no previous pharmaceutical experience, the company had followed an aggressive policy of expansion and diversification. The company grew from an $8.4 billion business mainly focused on generics in 2006, to a more diversified pharmaceutical company reporting revenues of approximately $18 billion in 2011, with an expanded footprint in Europe, Asia and Latin America.

At the start of Mr Yanai's tenure, Teva's strategy was to acquire competitors in key markets to become, or to consolidate, a position as the dominant generic drug producer. However, by 2011, Teva was pursuing a diversification strategy, signalled by the purchase of Cephalon, a US-based research pharmaceutical company, and the announcement of a joint venture with the consumer health conglomerate Procter & Gamble to produce and promote over-the-counter (OTC) medicines.

Acquiring generic competitors in the USA, Europe and Japan

Generics win market share on price. Given the small margins, companies need to focus on economies of scale and ensure that they have a robust and cost-effective manufacturing capacity. The purchases of Barr in the USA, Ratiopharm in Europe, and Taisho and Taiyo in Japan, were all driven by these goals.

Teva purchased US-based Barr in 2008, at the time the fourth-largest generics company globally. On completion of the takeover Yanai commented:

'Acquisition of Barr will elevate Teva's market leadership to a new level . . . it will enhance our market share and leadership position in the U.S. and key global markets, further strengthen our portfolio and pipeline, and provide upside to our strategic plan, by allowing us to exceed our 20/20 goals for 2012.'[4]

Barr was acquired for a total consideration of $7.46 billion, plus the assumption of net debt of approximately $1.5 billion. Teva anticipated the transaction would generate at least $300 million in annual cost savings within three years and would continue to provide additional cost savings well beyond 2011. By April 2012 Denise Bradley, Vice President, Corporate Communications, Teva Pharmaceuticals-Americas, was able to tell JointMedia-News that: 'Today, one in seven prescriptions filled in the US are filled with a Teva drug.'

In 2010 Teva purchased ratiopharm, a German-based generic manufacturer with extensive reach in the EU and Eastern Europe. The price was approximately $4.95 billion and Yanai said:

'This is an exciting day for Teva and ratiopharm, with the acquisition of ratiopharm we will become the leader in key European markets and we are well-positioned to become the leader in many other European markets in the near future.'[5]

Following this acquisition, Teva became the number one generic company in Europe, holding the leading market position in 10 countries, as well as ranking in the top three in another seven. In addition, the transaction substantially increased Teva's sales in Canada.

Table 1 **The generic pharmaceutical market, 2010**

	Market size, 2010 ($bn)	Percentage volume penetration by generics of drugs no longer under patent protection
USA	312	75%
Japan	96	23%
Germany	45	68%
UK	22	63%

Source: IMS Market Progress

With the purchase of ratiopharm, Teva also gained significant 'bio-similar' manufacturing capacity and technical knowhow in Europe. 'Bio-similars' are copies of complex biological products such as monoclonal antibodies. A number of important blockbuster biological drugs were due to lose patent protection over the coming years. Bio-similars were expected to command substantially higher prices than traditional generics and represented an exciting prospect.

In the summer of 2008, when Teva acquired Barr Pharmaceuticals, Yanai commented that he was keen to forge a joint venture in Japan, arguing that the country was an important but difficult market to break into, and adding that it was ripe for generic development. For historical and cultural reasons, Japan had one of the lowest uptakes of generic drugs globally (see Table 1). In order to reduce the burden of prescription medicine costs on their healthcare system, the Japanese government introduced various measures aimed at increasing generic use from around 20% of prescriptions to a target of 40%. Words became actions a few months later, when Teva and the Japanese company KOWA Pharmaceuticals signed a definitive agreement to establish a 50:50 joint venture, Teva-KOWA Pharmaceuticals.

In December 2009, Teva-KOWA Pharmaceuticals acquired a majority interest in Taisho Pharmaceutical Industries Ltd, a Japanese generics company with over 200 products and annual sales exceeding $130 million. As a result, Teva-KOWA Pharmaceuticals became the fifth-largest generics company in Japan.

Teva-KOWA followed this with another acquisition in May 2011, of Taiyo Pharmaceutical Industry, in a deal worth $460 million in cash. Teva claimed that Taiyo, a privately owned company, was the third-largest generics company in Japan, with sales of $530 million in 2010, and brought with it significant manufacturing capacity in Asia. Teva now expected to reach its target of $1 billion in sales in Japan ahead of its 2015 schedule.

The move away from generics into research-based pharmaceuticals and over-the-counter medicines

In May 2011 Teva successfully trumped a rival hostile bid from Valeant Pharmaceuticals to acquire Cephalon, a research-based pharmaceutical company with around 4,000 employees located in Pennsylvania, in a deal worth $6.8 billion.

Cephalon posted sales of $2.76 billion in 2010, up 28%, and adjusted net income of $657 million, an increase of 40%. Growth was driven by the sleep disorder drug Provigil and its follow-up long-acting drug Nuvigil, the cancer drug Treanda and the cancer painkiller Fentora. Cephalon also boasted a large research portfolio in several key areas – Central Nervous System ('CNS'), Oncology, Respiratory and Women's Health, the most promising but highest risk being its proprietary stem cell technology.

Valeant, an aggressively acquisitive Canadian pharmaceutical company, had seen in Cephalon's established products an opportunity for further revenue growth and increased profitability, and had bid $5.7 billion, but had discounted the value of the therapies in development. The takeover by Teva was welcomed by the board of Cephalon, who saw Teva as an organisation that valued their pipeline and would support their ambitious research and development plans. As Cephalon CEO Kevin Buchi said at the time: 'Teva shares our strong commitment to R&D, and we believe our pipeline will thrive under their leadership.'[6] Mr Yanai added:

'Our newly-expanded portfolio in CNS, Oncology, Respiratory and Women's Health along with our robust pipeline of more than 30 late-stage products truly cements our position as a leader in speciality pharma. ... We are welcoming many of Cephalon's talented employees into the Teva family. The combination of our two winning teams will position Teva to create maximum value for our patients and customers.'[7]

Teva and Cephalon executives said they saw particular potential in a stem cell therapy for congestive heart failure under development with Mesoblast Ltd, in reslizumab for asthma, and in the lung-cancer treatment obatoclax. Ori Hershkovitz, a partner at Sphera Global Healthcare Fund in Tel Aviv, commented in an interview at the time: 'Teva's making four or five shots on goal with a very high-risk, high-reward kind of profile. If they pull off the stem-cell product, they're in the clear. But if they pull off two or three of the others, it would also be a very good deal.'[8]

In another diversification move in November 2011, Teva announced a joint venture with Procter & Gamble to create PGT Health headquartered in Geneva, Switzerland. Bob McDonald, Chairman of the Board, President and Chief Executive Officer of P&G, said: 'P&G's partnership with Teva creates a combined set of capabilities that is unmatched in the industry. Starting today our combined consumer health care business will now offer more branded OTC products to more consumers in more parts of the world.'[9]

The idea behind the joint venture was that P&G would bring best-in-class consumer understanding, branding, design and in-store merchandising, with brands such as Vicks, Metamucil and Pepto-Bismol, whereas Teva would bring deeper, broader pharmacy distribution, including a pharmacy sales force and strong pharmacy relationships, broader regulatory capabilities and new technologies and manufacturing capacity to P&G's leading brands. There was also the hope that the joint venture would be able to find synergies in the two research pipelines to bring novel approaches to areas such as allergy therapy. Teva became the manufacturer and supplier for the PGT Healthcare business and P&G's North American OTC business.

PGT Healthcare expected to accelerate growth for its parent companies and compete for leadership in the fast-growing, $200 billion consumer healthcare industry. The partnership started from a base of approximately $1.3 billion in annual sales, with the claimed potential to grow this to $4 billion towards the end of the decade.

2011 challenges for TEVA

Despite these bold acquisitions, 2011 proved to be a difficult year for Teva and for shareholders, with the share price nearly halving over the course of the year.

There were three major challenges. Firstly, problems following an FDA inspection at the former Barr plant led to a six-month closure of the main production line. As a consequence, Teva suffered a 48% reduction in US sales in the first three-quarters of 2011. Secondly, following a change of vial size for the anaesthetic propofol, some patients contracted hepatitis C due to alleged reuse of vials which were intended for single-patient use. In resulting litigation, it was argued that the increase in vial size led a number of centres to reuse the vials and so put patients at risk. Thirdly, the crucial profit generators Copaxone and Provigil were facing generic competitors earlier than expected.

December 2012: new strategy announced

Following the appointment of Jeremy Levine as CEO and Michael Hayden as President of Global R&D, Teva spent much of 2012 formulating its new strategy, which was unveiled to investors on 11 December. Levin promised to reshape the company into 'the most indispensable medicines company in the world' and provide significant value to shareholders. Levin said Teva would sustain 'profitable growth' through 2017. Analysts and investors were not convinced, as the share price fell sharply.[10]

Key elements of the new strategy included:

- Tailoring the product offering to address regional needs. With its diversified portfolio, Teva was well placed to focus on high-value generics in the USA and Japan but on consumer OTC products in Latin America and Russia, for example.
- Rationalisation of the marketed generic product portfolio. Less profitable products were culled, while price increases were implemented for others.
- Globalising key functions to streamline operations and gain economies of scale, cutting costs by $1.5 to $2 billion per year.
- New R&D focus on high-value generics called NTEs (New Therapeutic Entities). Teva planned to leverage its huge portfolio of over 1,400 medicines, and its extensive formulation and drug delivery expertise, to create new combination products that would be harder to imitate than traditional generics. These would offer medical value through improved efficacy or compliance, or reduced side-effects, in order to justify higher prices. For the first time, Teva would incorporate formal medical input to its generics business.
- Refocusing the R&D pipeline, with a strong emphasis on CNS and respiratory products. The oncology product obatoclax was discontinued.
- Formation of a drug discovery network comprising all the academic centres in Israel.
- Business development focused on smaller transactions to add pipeline and expand capabilities in key growth geographies.

Notes and references
1. Globes [online], Israel business news, www.globes-online.com, 2 January 2012.
2. 'Teva Pharmaceutical's CEO discusses Q4 2011 results', earnings call transcript, Nasdaq.com, February 2012.
3. $1 = £0.65 = €0.77.
4. Teva press release, 16 July 2008.
5. Teva press release, 2010.
6. Teva press release, May 2011.
7. Teva press release, May 2011.
8. Kresge, N. and Langreth, R. (2011) 'Teva bets on stem cells, cancer in $6.2 billion bid for Cephalon', Bloomberg online, 3 May 2011.
9. Procter & Gamble newsroom, November 2011.
10. 'Teva CEO promises to reshape, refocus company'. Reuters online, 11 December 2012.

CASE STUDY

CRH plc: dimensions of successful corporate strategy

Mike Moroney

Even with a small corporate headquarters in a challenging industry, corporate strategy can be the engine for growth and development, generating substantial value-added. However, such dimensions of this level of strategy remain arcane. These issues are explored in this case study on CRH, which is an exemplar of corporate management.

● ● ●

In February 2013, CEO Myles Lee announced full-year results for 2012 for CRH plc, an international leader in building materials. Since 2007, in common with its peers in the sector, CRH had been hit by the severe global recession in construction, unprecedented in its scale and synchronised nature since the 1930s. Between 2007 and 2010, CRH suffered a peak-to-trough decline in earnings of three-quarters. However, the outturn for 2012 confirmed a level performance over four years, tentatively indicating a cyclical floor. Moreover, by adapting its business and portfolio to new realities, CRH had positioned itself for cyclical recovery and to capitalise on acquisition and other opportunities arising from over-leverage in the industry. As ever, Myles Lee and his management team knew that success depended on CRH's own corporate-led strategy and actions.

The building materials industry

The industry involves the extraction, manufacture and supply of building materials, products and services for construction activity. These include primary materials (such as cement, aggregates, ready-mixed concrete and asphalt products), heavyside building products (e.g. concrete products, road vaults and bricks), lightside building products (e.g. plumbing, heating, electrical and lighting products) and distribution ('merchanting' and DIY). Sectors served are residential, industrial/commercial and infrastructure/public works. End-uses comprise early-cycle new construction work and late-cycle repair, maintenance and improvement (RMI).

Building materials are characterised by several distinguishing features. *Cyclicality* derives from the fact that construction cycles reflect general economic cycles. However, construction cycles are longer in duration and larger in amplitude, while their timing varies between countries. In developing economies, construction demand tends to lead GDP growth, in contrast to a lagged relationship in mature economies. In particular, capital-intensive, heavyside investment is characterised by long-term, large-scale commitments, significant lead times and, therefore, 'lumpy' additions to capacity.

In terms of structural growth, building materials manifest a dual *mature/dynamic* character. In developed (Western) markets, with most buildings and infrastructure already built, construction is stable and largely RMI-based, with population and public investment prime drivers of activity.[1] By contrast, in developing markets (Asia, Eastern Europe and Latin America) and in some Western countries at an earlier stage of economic development, long-term construction demand is closely linked to economic growth.

In general, building materials and products are *commodities*, have long life cycles, and are similar across markets and largely stable over time, with price-based competition predominant. Production processes are standard. Technology is non-proprietary and, for some products, relatively unsophisticated. Innovation centres on the enhancement of manufacturing processes, improvements in the ease of use and installation of products and the provision of value-added services and solutions to the customer.

Traditionally, the building materials industry has been *fragmented*. Production is linked to the location of appropriate reserves, with proximity to the end market being a key factor. Because building materials and products are characterised by a high weight to value ratio, high transport costs rapidly outweigh scale economies, with the result that the radius of economic activity and competition often can be

This case was prepared by Mike Moroney, Lecturer in Strategic Management at the J. E. Cairnes School of Business and Economics, National University of Ireland Galway. It is intended as a basis for class discussion and not as an illustration of good or bad practice. © Mike Moroney, 2013. Not to be reproduced or quoted without permission.

150 kilometres or less. In addition, markets are local in nature due to differences in building regulations, construction practices and product standards. Success is often determined by micro-market factors like locality, quality, reliability of service and price.[2] As a result, the industry developed over time as a large number of small and medium-sized firms, often family owned and run.

Structurally, consolidation is an ongoing trend (particularly in primary materials and merchanting) reflecting supply-side concentration and significant merger and acquisition (M&A) activity. During almost two decades to mid-2009, there were 20 large corporate deals involving total consideration of US$125 billion (£82.4bn; €97.5bn)[3] and an average value to EBITDA[4] multiple of 10.3 times.[5] In addition, large international building materials companies, including CRH, had over time leveraged strong local market positions and/or product competences to expand into other regions and areas of activity. Furthermore, local differences between geographic markets were eroding, driven by institutional harmonisation of regulations, standards and tendering, convergence in building practices, consolidation of customers and homogenisation of their needs. None the less, the underlying logic of fragmentation prevailed. Globally, the top five producers supplied only one-fifth of demand for cement, and one-twentieth for aggregates.[6] In the USA, while the top 10 concentration ratio was 75% for cement, in aggregates it was 30% and in asphalt 25%, with two-thirds of capacity privately held.[7]

Against the macro backdrop of weakening consumer and investor confidence in the Eurozone balanced by an improving outlook in the Americas, the outlook for building materials remained cautious. Notwithstanding cyclical falls of over a quarter in construction output in both the USA and Europe, the prospects were for an 'L-shaped' recovery of sub-trend growth.[8] Structurally, overcapacity and low utilisation rates prevailed in certain mature heavyside markets, particularly in Western Europe, with the prospect of consolidation, including closure of older, less efficient facilities.[9] Such restructuring was likely to be exacerbated by the hangover from the M&A boom, as heavily indebted firms sought to deleverage by selling assets.[10] Nor could it be assumed that developing markets would continue to provide a growth stimulus. Some China commentators were signalling a property correction in the short term and a peaking of cumulative cement consumption from mid-decade.[11]

Profile of CRH

Headquartered in Dublin, Ireland, CRH had annual revenues of €18.7 billion (£15.8bn; $24.0bn) in 2012 and employed 76,000 people in 3,500 locations in 35 countries worldwide. The Group enjoyed strong positions in developed markets in Europe and North America (85% of EBITDA)

and a growing presence in emerging economies in Asia, Central and Eastern Europe and Latin America (15% of EBITDA). CRH's prominence was recognised by many industry awards for corporate governance,[12] financial reporting, investor relations, and excellence/innovation in environmental and safety practices.

History, growth and development

CRH was formed in 1970 following the merger of two leading Irish public companies, Irish Cement Limited (established in 1936) and Roadstone (1949). At that time, CRH was sole producer of cement and principal producer of aggregates, concrete products and asphalt in Ireland, with Group sales of €26 million, 95% in Ireland. The Board of CRH set a clear strategy for the development of the Group: to seek new geographic platforms in its core businesses and to take advantage of complementary product opportunities in order to achieve strategic balance and to establish multiple platforms from which to deliver performance and growth. In 40-plus years of operation, the Group has undergone major growth through several phases of development, as described below. In general, change has been evolutionary, involving a managed, learning process of building, augmenting and layering competences.

- **Organic market penetration in Ireland** (from 1970). During the 1970s, Irish construction enjoyed a boom on the back of a modernising economy. The newly merged CRH capitalised on this favourable environment through its vertically integrated and leading positions in heavyside building materials and products.
- **Acquisition-led overseas expansion** (from the late 1970s). In the late 1970s, with a view to spreading risks and opportunities more broadly, CRH made a strategic decision to invest in familiar business areas overseas, through bolt-on acquisitions. Early expansion was in Western Europe (1973). The second domain of geographic growth was North America. In 1977, Don Godson (later Chief Executive, 1994–2000) went to the USA with 'a telephone and a cheque book'. By 2000, the Americas accounted for over half of Group turnover and profits. CRH's presence in emerging regions gathered pace from the mid-1990s. Initial steps in Latin America were followed by more substantial investment in Eastern Europe (notably Poland and the Ukraine) and, latterly, in Asia (China, India).
- **Product focus, larger acquisitions** (from the late 1990s). CRH also expanded in a limited, but highly rewarding, way into new product areas, including merchanting and DIY, security fencing, clay brick products and glass fabrication, evolving to a more product-based organisation. At the same time, leading industry consolidation,

the Group began to supplement its traditional mid-size deal flow with larger acquisitions.

- **Developing value-based growth platforms** (from the early 2010s). By the early 2010s, CRH's proven business model had established a global footprint and a diverse product template. The Group adopted a more nuanced and value-focused approach to strategy, emphasising accelerated integration, greater coordination, enterprise management and portfolio rationalisation. This approach combined the capabilities of large company disciplines with local company entrepreneurship.

Strategy

CRH'S strategic vision is to be 'a responsible international leader in building materials delivering superior performance and growth . . . through the business cycle'[13] with the focus on achieving superior long-term returns. Strategy was manifested through three core principles:

1 *Strategic balance.* CRH was assiduous in sustaining a diversified, broad-based exposure to all segments of construction demand (see Figure 1). This strategic balance encompassed dimensions of geography, product, sector, end-use, stage of the cycle and intensity of investment. This unique approach smoothed the effects of varying economic conditions and provided multiple platforms for growth. An indication of the severity of the industry downturn since 2007 is that, while CRH consistently outperformed peers through previous cycles, in the most recent down-cycle both balanced and single-product companies had been affected similarly.[14]

2 *Build and grow.* Particularly in developed markets, CRH's strategic emphasis was on creating clustered groups of businesses, encompassing vertically integrated material positions and scalable products and distribution networks.

3 *Value-based development.* Focusing on superior short- and long-term returns, CRH emphasised continued bolt-on and larger acquisitions combined with resource-backed market entry points in emerging economies.

CRH's strategy was underpinned by a proven business model providing a disciplined approach to long-term value creation, and by a supportive strategic architecture (structure, people and processes).

CRH served the breadth of construction activity, providing exposure to multiple demand drivers. Related core businesses spanned major primary materials (excluding steel and timber), building products and services for construction solutions (primarily heavyside concrete-based, with selected lightside) and specialist distribution (through builders' merchants and DIY stores). In the long term, CRH's businesses were underpinned by a high level of increasingly scarce reserves. In aggregates (sand and gravel, crushed stone) CRH's reserves of 15 billion tonnes were equivalent to over 80 years of production and were among the highest in the sector.[15] In 2011, CRH had 690 quarries/pits in the USA and 350 in Europe.[16]

A notable characteristic of CRH's product/market portfolio was leadership (Figure 2). Achieving product/regional leadership in its chosen markets was a deliberate core strategy of the Group. Reflecting the commodity and fragmented nature of the building materials industry, CRH focused on securing and maintaining leading positions in local or regional (and national) markets and in a number of product segments or niches. For certain product categories, CRH was a leading player on the global stage, ranking numbers two and three in aggregates and asphalt, respectively.[15]

Unlike its peers, CRH operated a federal structure, comprising a small central headquarters and four regionally focused product divisions (Figure 3). To capitalise on local market knowledge, a high degree of individual responsibility was devolved to experienced operational managers, within Group guidelines and controls. According to Dr Jack Golden, Human Resources (HR) Director: 'While the local operating units have operational autonomy, they do not have independence.' At the same time, a strong team emphasis and collective identity prevailed, reflecting a robust corporate culture.

Figure 1 **Products and markets**

2012: Sales €18.7 Bn . . . EBITDA €1.64 Bn

Region	Nth America 50%	Europe 35%	Emerging 15%
Product	Materials 59%	Products 22%	Distribution 19%
Sector	Infra 35%	Non-res 30%	Res 35%
End-use	New 50%	RMI 50%	

A balanced business by geography, product, sector and end-use

Figure 2 **Management and organisation**

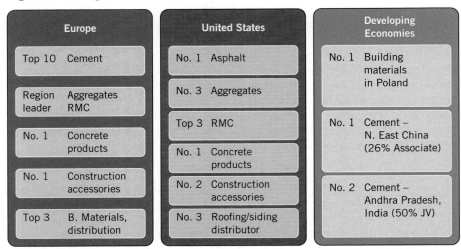

Europe	United States	Developing Economies
Top 10 — Cement	No. 1 — Asphalt	No. 1 — Building materials in Poland
Region leader — Aggregates RMC	No. 3 — Aggregates	No. 1 — Cement – N. East China (26% Associate)
No. 1 — Concrete products	Top 3 — RMC	No. 2 — Cement – Andhra Pradesh, India (50% JV)
No. 1 — Construction accessories	No. 1 — Concrete products	
Top 3 — B. Materials, distribution	No. 2 — Construction accessories	
	No. 3 — Roofing/siding distributor	

Figure 3 **Group organisation schematic**

CRH adopted a rigorous approach to evaluation, approval and review. The twin requirements of performance and growth were continually reinforced, with entities having to earn the right to grow. Planning was formalised and interactive, with stretch targets for financial and operational output measures. Performance measurement was timely, formal and rigorous, facilitating early critical review of underperformance, allowing appropriate corrective measures to be put in place and enabling senior management to draw broader lessons. Continuous improvement was relentless, as demonstrated by ongoing programmes of benchmarking and best practice. Products and processes were continually re-engineered to yield higher returns, primarily through greater efficiencies, but also from selective expansion into related products and regional markets. Ongoing development investment was roughly equivalent to the level of depreciation through the cycle[17] and incorporated new plant, capacity extensions and plant upgrades.

The value of CRH's rigorous management processes was evident in its internal response to the severe industry downturn post-2007. CRH put in place a broad-based, multi-year programme, focused on reducing the cost base, a sharpened commercial focus involving resizing businesses and resetting capacity, optimising cash generation and maintaining a strong balance sheet.[18] In the five years to 2012, CRH delivered industry-leading cumulative annualised savings of €2.2 billion across structural, process and procurement components, of which over 40% was permanent in nature.[19] These measures offset around half the adverse profit impact of volume declines and cost inflation over the period.[20]

CRH's management were characterised by experience, stability and continuity. In over 40 years, there had been only six chief executives, all of whom (like many senior managers) were internal appointments. In 2012, key corporate, divisional and operational managers numbered around 400. Managers were drawn from internally developed operating managers, highly qualified and experienced professionals, and owner–entrepreneurs from acquired companies, providing a healthy mix and depth of skills and backgrounds. Management turnover was low. Such constancy reflected long-term success through industry cycles, CRH's market-driven, performance-related remuneration policy (comprising variable compensation, manager share options and employee share participation) and a range of formal and informal mechanisms to promote integration (see below). Collectively, low turnover, rotation and promotion from within resulted in a wealth of in-house industry knowledge and expertise.

Finances

Finance was an important component of CRH's strategy across sector cycles. The Group was noted for its finance function, which was characterised by extensive business knowledge and operational contribution, as well as diligence, conservatism and prudence. Its contribution was evident in tight performance management, strong cash generation, a low Group tax charge, careful financial governance, diverse funding sources, and strategically timed equity funding to underpin subsequent development activity. CRH was widely recognised as having the best balance sheet in the sector, reflecting strong debt metrics, significant liquidity and a well-balanced profile of future debt maturities. With typical, healthy values of 6 to 7 times EBITDA/net interest cover and below 40% for net debt to equity, CRH possessed the highest long-term investment grade credit rating in the sector: BBB+ (Standard & Poors).[21]

Two hallmarks of CRH's financial management were a rigorous approach to capital allocation and a strong focus on cash generation. Operations were required to earn a mid-teen per cent return on invested capital (ROIC) through the cycle. Newly acquired businesses often found such financial rigour challenging. A cash-generative mentality pervaded all operations and was central to the Group's evaluation and control processes. Steady-state cash earnings were at least two-thirds higher than reported earnings per share (EPS). Such strengths enabled CRH to fund substantial development activity of reinvestment in existing assets and acquisition-led expansion without compromising its core financial principles.

Corporate strategy at CRH

Consistent with its federalist philosophy, CRH's corporate headquarters was small, employing fewer than 100 people in Dublin. Including support staff in the four divisions, around 250 people were engaged in headquarters-type activities. Central functions comprised finance, investor relations, corporate social responsibility, compliance and ethics, internal audit, HR and business development, the last of which also acted as a resource on cross-divisional deals, strategic planning and opportunities in emerging regions.

CRH's senior executive management team of eight was similarly small and tightly focused. It comprised the CEO, COO, finance director and HR director located in Dublin, together with the CEO and COO of CRH's Americas operations and the managing directors of CRH's European operations. Notwithstanding the centre's small size and limited range of functions, corporate strategy was pivotal to value creation, growth and development in CRH.

Scope and diversification

By 2012, CRH was a world-leading, diversified international building materials company with extensive and integrated exposure across the breadth of construction activity (Figure 4). CRH's main product concentration was in primary materials and heavyside products (cement, aggregates, asphalt, RMC and concrete products). Geographically, the Group had extensive operations in the developed markets of the USA and Western Europe. CRH also had a growing presence in emerging economies, some of which were highly prospective. Principal in this regard were Central and Eastern Europe (CEE), China and India, while Latin America and the Eastern Mediterranean also featured. In most cases, CRH occupied positions of market leadership, often with substantial market shares (ranging to the mid/high teens nationally and over 50% in the case of cement).

CRH's diversified scope had developed gradually over time. A preferred method of entering a new market involved an initial position in primary materials, backed by sizeable reserves. In developed economies, this was achieved primarily through bolt-on acquisitions which enhanced vertical integration, bolstered long-term reserves or filled out regional and product positions. In emerging markets, CRH targeted premium assets as an initial footprint, usually in cement and often in partnership with strong local established businesses.

Over time, the combination of acquisitions, development capital expenditure and selective product extensions resulted in an integrated, complementary and scalable cluster of businesses. The same process and outcome were

Figure 4 Balanced exposure to multiple demand drivers

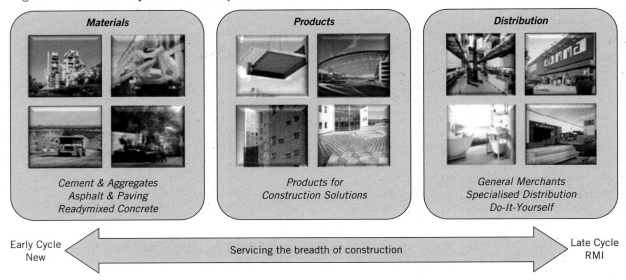

repeated across geographic markets, occasionally with additions to the product portfolio. In this way, CRH typically expanded from a local position to a regional presence and often a national profile.

Poland represented a classic and successful case study of diversified scope. In 1995, CRH acquired an initial market presence in cement, ranking first regionally and third nationally. Subsequent capital investment of €200 million added 1.8 million tonnes of cement capacity per annum. In 1998, CRH purchased an aggregates business, diversifying further over time into RMC, pavers, asphalt, aerated concrete, lime and bricks. By 2010, CRH was the biggest and most profitable building materials company in Poland.[22] Establishing an initial presence served another valuable function in emerging economies where a very different business and institutional context presented challenges. For a relatively low investment, the Group could learn about how the market functioned, the competitive environment, the nature of government–business relations and employee skills and expectations.

Corporate parenting

Senior management were active, externally and internally, in explaining and promulgating CRH's strategic stance, which was explicit, enduring and continually reinforced. Over time, the broad thrusts of the Group's strategy were progressively articulated and refined. Management training and meetings were used as opportunities to restate key messages, from reinforcing the performance-based 'right to grow' strategic mantra, to the minutiae of operational

best practice. Communications opportunities were exploited to the full. CRH's excellence in external relations was mirrored internally, utilising communications technologies such as the website, email, intranet and bulletin boards. Regular editions of the internal news magazine *Contact* were read avidly by managers and employees alike.

CRH operated a Group-wide management development system to develop the critical experience base of managers, particularly when they were more mobile, in their twenties and thirties. As CRH grew bigger, this system had become more formal and structured to ensure the systematic requisite exposure to the wide range of CRH's operations. A key element was the management database, on which the core 400 managers in the Group were formally profiled. In addition, there were a variety of formal development programmes for managers, many of which involved inputs and presentations on strategy from senior management, including the chief executive. These included the Management Seminar, Development Forum, Leadership Development Programmes (one and two) and Business Leadership Programme. Promotion, rotation and mentoring were also instruments of manager development. HR measures to ensure greater cohesion and consistency of policies were designed to foster coordination and a culture of interdependence.

At division level, integrated product management had become progressively strengthened over time, led by the USA. Coordinated divisionally, ongoing best-practice activities involved meetings by small teams of experts at local, regional and international levels facilitated by technical advisors. These resulted in highly innovative ideas and exchanges of products, delivering significant synergies. There were several best-practice programmes in each of the four product-based divisions. Best practice was supplemented by benchmarking exercises and the development of common systems platforms. In addition, divisions sponsored formal systematic programmes to improve operational performance and increase efficiency in a range of areas, including health and safety, recycling and energy recovery.

Informal mechanisms underpinned integration. Corporate culture was nurtured and sustained constantly. The supportive team orientation was evident in informal mentoring, hands-on assistance and individual and team coaching common within and across entities. Flexibility prevailed, particularly as regards hierarchy and job descriptions. HR Director Jack Golden was involved in Group issues pertaining to France, based on his previous experience as country manager there for another multinational. The Group continually reinforced its core values in formal statements of strategy, in external and internal communications and through corporate folklore. More subtle mechanisms also existed, including leading by example and clear norms of acceptable behaviour, such as the ethos of taking responsibility in internal reporting. Strong informal networks existed among managers, even between far-flung regions of the Group's activities, arising from organisational mechanisms of interaction and from a social dimension to formal events, notably the ceremonial occasion for inducting new managers accompanying CRH's AGM and the annual Management Seminar.

Finally, reflecting CRH's performance orientation, strategy was buttressed by formal and rigorous measurement, evaluation and control processes, ensuring early intervention and appropriate corrective measures.

Acquisition-led expansion

Acquisitions were the engine of corporate growth and development: 'CRH has the best track record of its peer group . . . of growing returns through acquisitions.'[23] Historically, acquisitions accounted for 70% of CRH's profit growth, with organic growth contributing one-quarter and currency movements the remainder.[24] In the 13 years to 2012, CRH completed almost 630 deals, spending €15.5 billion. Prior to the severe downturn from 2008, acquisition spending averaged €1.5 billion annually, falling to around €600 million per annum as the recession took hold.

Traditionally, CRH's acquisitions were bolt-on in nature (three to four deals per month at an average cost of less than €20 million), augmented from time to time with larger deals where there was compelling value and a strong strategic rationale. (No single deal amounted to more than 10% of the Group's capital base.) In general, CRH

acquired on favourable terms, reflecting the Group's 'valuation discipline'. Purchase price/EBITDA multiples ranged between 6 and 7.

CRH's rigorous and comprehensive acquisition strategy was singular in conception and execution and had 'proven very difficult to replicate'.[25] For identification of prospects, CRH resourced multiple development teams spread across the Group (including in India and China), seeking opportunities and maintaining contact with an extensive database of potential targets accumulated over 30 years. At any one time, a considerable number of acquisitions were under active consideration, ensuring a steady deal flow. Each purchase gave rise to further opportunities, in other (occasionally new) markets.

Courtship involved a patient and often long process of familiarisation and coaching. CRH took time to assess suitability and strategic fit, and to know management and their evolving needs. Much effort was spent appraising the target of CRH's strategy, management, values and expectations, including upfront clarity on post-acquisition priorities. It was not unusual for CRH to walk away from a deal, on grounds of timing, price or compatibility. Sometimes, acquisitions were completed at a later date.

To aid negotiation, CRH had codified, in a classified, proprietary document, the best practice, knowledge and processes involved in making an acquisition, gleaned from many years of experience. This was full of collected wisdom and practical advice on deal-making. An experienced operational manager guided each acquisition team. At the appropriate time, a senior-level 'ambassador' was introduced to close the deal. Before completion, each deal underwent rigorous evaluation, including qualitative operational review, due diligence, strict cash-flow testing and Board approval.

Traditionally, CRH's acquisitions shared many common characteristics:

- medium-sized, private, often family-run businesses
- geographic/product market leaders, with potential to enhance existing Group operations, fill a gap or provide a platform for growth
- careful structuring of deals, often involving initial stakes with buy options (and/or joint ventures) in new regions/product areas
- retention of owner–managers to ensure continuity and maintain human capital.

Post-acquisition integration to boost returns was rapid and well practised. From an estimated level of 10% on purchase, ROIC typically rose to 12% within the first year and to the benchmark level of 15% within two to three years.[26] Group financial, MIS and control systems were implemented immediately. Revenue and cost synergies were captured as benchmarking, best-practice programmes and (if warranted) targeted capital investment were put in place. The central expertise and coordination of CRH's super-structure delivered procurement economies of scale, enhanced customer access and greater network density and synergies. After three years, a formal look-back review was carried out. Although more complex and expeditious, the acquisition process for larger deals was similar in principle.

Outlook

As CRH grappled with the fifth year of a cyclical downturn, caution remained the watchword. On the other hand, progressive actions in recent years had adjusted the Group's cost base, sharpened its commercial focus and optimised cash-generating capacity, while maintaining a strong and flexible financial position. Moreover, as the Group had learnt during its 43-year history in a cyclical sector, collective crises presented individual opportunity. A protracted downturn would put pressure on over-leveraged peers, while CRH retained the capability to ramp up acquisition spending to €1.5 billion over an 18-month period[27] should appropriate value-enhancing opportunities arise. Fortune would favour the brave. The issue was the balance of caution and daring and, more pertinently, knowing when the tipping point came.

Notes and references
1. J.P. Morgan Cazenove, 'On the turn. We initiate on the Sector', 21 April 2011, p. 128.
2. Bank of America–Merrill Lynch, 'Cement Handbook: Time for more selective stock picking', 22 June 2009, p. 14.
3. $1 = £0.65 = €0.77.
4. Earnings before Interest, Tax, Depreciation, Amortisation and non-operational items (EBITDA).
5. J.P. Morgan Cazenove, 'On the turn. We initiate on the Sector', 21 April 2011, p. 27.
6. J.P. Morgan, *Building Materials*, 10 September 2008, p. 22.
7. Black, D. 'America's materials', CRH Investor Day 2010, slide 22.
8. Exane BNP Paribas, *Building Materials*, 12 January 2012, p. 10.
9. Deutsche Bank, 'Global cement trends: 2012–2015 outlook', 19 December 2011.
10. Credit Suisse, 'Building materials 2012: Another challenging year', 5 January 2012.
11. Deutsche Bank, 'How relevant is China for the European cement industry?', 27 January 2012.
12. UBS, 'European building materials: Significant upside to mid cycle valuations', 13 July 2009, p. 7.
13. CRH Annual Report on Form 20-F in respect of the year ended 31 December 2011, p. 10.
14. Lee, M. 'Introduction', CRH Investor Day 2010, slide 9.
15. J.P. Morgan Cazenove, 'On the turn. We initiate on the Sector', 21 April 2011, pp. 108, 109.
16. CRH Annual Report on Form 20-F in respect of the year ended 31 December 2011.
17. Goodbody Stockbrokers, 'CRH: Material upside', 28 June 2007, p. 16.
18. Lee, M. 'CRH plc Overview', Société Générale Premium Review Conference, 28 November 2012, slide 30.
19. CRH Full Year Results 2012, 26 February 2013.
20. Lee, M. 'CRH Presentation', Sanford C. Bernstein Strategic Decisions Conference, September 2012, slide 20.
21. Lee, M. 'CRH Presentation', Sanford C. Bernstein Strategic Decisions Conference, September 2012, slide 3.
22. Morris, H. 'Europe materials', CRH Investor Day 2010, slide 15.
23. Goldman Sachs, 'CRH', 18 October 2005, p. 3.
24. Goodbody Stockbrokers, 'CRH: Still to play its "Trump Card"', 13 July 2005, p. 7.
25. Merrill Lynch, 'Adding value or hot air?', 25 October 2005, p. 12.
26. Goodbody Stockbrokers, 'CRH: Still to play its "Trump Card"', 13 July 2005, p. 10.
27. Manifold, A. 'CRH Presentation', Pan European Building & Infrastructure Conference, Bank of America–Merrill Lynch, London, October 2010, slide 29.

CASE STUDY

SABMiller: from strength to strength

Duncan Angwin and Gerry Johnson

South African Breweries grew on the basis of its strength in developing markets, first in Africa and then in other parts of the world. SAB acquired Miller in 2002 to form SABMiller and acquired Foster's Group Australia in 2011, building its portfolio in developed markets and consolidating its position as the second-largest brewer in the world. This case study reviews the development of the company's strategy and the challenges it now faces as international competition intensifies.

•   •   •

In 2013 SABMiller announced growing sales for the first time in a decade at Foster's, its major Australian acquisition. This came after a strong set of half-year profits for the group announced at the end of 2012, with a 12% jump in pre-tax profits to $2.28bn (£1.49bn; €1.75bn).[1] Although shares had risen on the news, this was helped by an increase in dividend, and some analysts had commented that other parts of the business had performed below expectations, with the future having 'more downside than upside'.[2] At the top of the group there have been recent changes, with Graham Mackay (previously Chief Executive) and Alan Clark having been elevated to become Chairman and Chief Executive respectively.

Going forward, what options are there for the world's second-largest brewer to continue to grow from strength to strength? Might a different strategic direction be required

Source: Jason Alden/OneRedEye/SABMiller

in the future or should the group's previous strategy continue? Either way, SABMiller will be fiercely committed to continuing its long and successful history.

What began as South African Breweries had grown from a sprawling conglomerate under an isolated apartheid regime in South Africa to a listing on the London Stock Exchange in 1999. Since that time the company had moved from 88th to 7th in the FTSE 100 share index (see Figure 1) and had increased its capitalisation from US$5.5bn (£3.6bn; €4.1bn) to US$69.96bn (£45.8bn; €53.76bn). In 2013 SABMiller was the second-largest brewer by volume and profits in the world, following its acquisitions of the American brewer Miller Brewing Company in 2002, Grupo Empresarial Bavaria, South America's second-largest brewer, in 2005, and the Australian Beer Group Foster's in 2011. Its brand portfolio included international brands Pilsner Urquell, Peroni Nastro Azzurro, Miller Genuine Draft and Grolsch, along with local country brands such as Aguila, Castle Lager, Miller Lite, VB, Snow and Tyskie.

Figure 1 Five-year SABMiller share price vs. FTSE 100 and Beverages Indexes

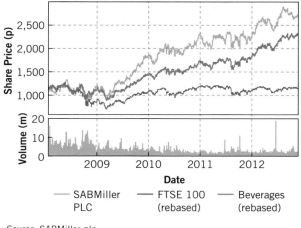

Source: SABMiller plc.

Table 1 SABMiller's strategic priorities

1. Creating a balanced and attractive global spread of businesses	'Our acquisitions in recent years have given us a wide geographical spread with good exposure to emerging markets without being over-reliant on any single region. This allows us to capture new growth in developing markets and "value" growth as consumers around the world trade up from economy to mainstream and premium brands. We also look to identify and exploit opportunities for growth within our existing business portfolio. This can involve a range of activities, from entering into local joint ventures or partnerships, to buying or building breweries, to acquiring local brands to help shape a full, local, brand portfolio.'
2. Developing strong, relevant brand portfolios in the local market	'Our aim is to develop an attractive brand portfolio that meets consumers' needs in each of our markets. In many markets, growth is fastest at the top end, as shown by the increasing popularity of our international premium brands. Another rising consumer trend is the shift towards fragmentation. Affluent consumers are varying their choices and becoming more interested in speciality brands, craft beers, foreign imports and other subdivisions of the premium segment. And a third trend is the growing importance of female consumers.'
3. Constantly raising the performance of local businesses	'In order to raise our performance, we need to become more efficient, especially in our manufacturing processes. Efficiency is part of our day-to-day management and the rise in commodity costs compels us to do whatever we can to counteract the squeeze on our margins. All SABMiller operations strive to improve our products' route to market, to remove costs and to ensure that the right products reach the right outlets in the right condition.'
4. Leveraging our global scale	'As a global organisation we are constantly seeking to use the benefits of our scale while recognising that beer is essentially a local business and that local managers are in the best position to identify and exploit local opportunities. Our aim is to generate maximum value and advantage from our size without becoming overcentralised and losing our relevance and responsiveness in each market.'

Despite these successes, challenges continued from the dramatic consolidation in the brewing industry. In the early 1990s the five largest brewing companies accounted for just 17% of global beer sales by volume.[3] By 2012 the four largest brewing companies accounted for 51%,[4] and analysts estimated they had captured around two-thirds of profits. Moreover, three of SABMiller's main global competitors, Anheuser Busch, Interbrew and Ambev, had merged in 2008 to claim market leadership with a consolidated 25% global market share, although by 2012 this had fallen to 21%.

The company had set out four strategic priorities in 2010 as summarised in Table 1. This can be seen as a synthesis of the learning the company had developed over its history, first weathering the political crises of twentieth-century South African history, then building its operations in emerging and mature markets, where it gained a reputation as 'a turnaround specialist' and now an acquirer of major breweries in mature markets.

Background

South African Breweries (SAB) predated the state of South Africa itself. It faced the challenge of doing business amidst the upheaval the country experienced during the twentieth century, including the 'apartheid' regime from 1948 to 1994. Worldwide opposition to apartheid included a campaign for economic sanctions on South Africa, aiming to restrict international business from investing in or trading with South Africa and restricting South African businesses

from trading in international markets. In 1950 SAB moved its head office from London to Johannesburg. Southern Africa became the focus of its business expansion during the subsequent four decades.

In this time SAB responded to business restrictions by focusing on leadership of domestic beer production through acquisition of competitors and rationalisation of its production and distribution facilities. It also expanded its product portfolio, obtaining control of Stellenbosch Farmers' Winery in 1960 and in the course of the rest of that decade obtained licences to brew Guinness, Amstel and Carling Black Label locally. Further expansions followed within the beverage sector, principally through acquisitions, leading to SAB controlling an estimated 99% of the market in South Africa by 1979, as well as commanding positions in Swaziland, Lesotho, Rhodesia (now Zimbabwe) and Botswana. SAB also diversified into hotels and gambling in 1978 by acquiring the Sun City casino resort.

The establishment of a multiracial democracy in South Africa in the 1990s eased SAB's expansion through the rest of Africa. By 2000 SAB's market strength in southern Africa provided a serious deterrent to potential competitors, but there remained little space for further local expansion, particularly in alcoholic beverages.

Emerging onto the global market

In 1993 SAB made its first acquisition outside Africa, purchasing Hungary's largest brewery, Dreher, and describing it as a 'beach-head move' into Central Europe. So began a strategy explained in the 1998 annual report: 'SAB's international focus has been on countries in which it believes it could use its expertise, which has been gained over 100 years in South Africa, to develop beer markets in emerging economies.'

The strategy of developing brewing capabilities in under-developed beer markets continued through the 1990s. SAB established a joint venture, China Resources Snow Breweries, with China Resources Enterprise Ltd, in 1994, adding China's biggest beer brand, Snow, to its portfolio. There followed further acquisitions in Eastern Europe, including the acquisition of Lech (1995) and Tyskie (1996) in Poland (these were merged in 1999) and acquisitions in Romania, Slovakia and the Czech Republic, and in 1998 SAB entered Russia by establishing a 'greenfield' brewery in Kaluga, near Moscow.

SAB's strategy was more fully spelt out in the 2000 report and this logic seems to prevail today:

'In the less developed world, Africa and Asia and much of Europe, brewing remained highly fragmented, with beer drinkers supplied by breweries which were never more than small-scale and localised, often producing low-quality beer . . . This fragmentation presented the opportunity for SAB from the mid-1990s to create a profitable and fast-expanding business in emerging markets with huge potential. This opportunity involves, generally, taking a share in a brewery with a local partner and transforming the business while retaining the brand, given drinkers' fierce attachments to their local brew. Transformation starts with upgrading quality and consistency to create a beer for which people are prepared to pay more and which can give us a healthy profit margin. Then comes improvement to marketing and distribution and improvement to productivity and capacity. In each country we have begun by acquiring an initial local stronghold from which we can advance into regions beyond the brewery's original catchment area. We then build critical mass in the region and progress, over time, to a national basis. This is often achieved by acquiring further brewing businesses and focusing the brand port-folio. An optimum brand portfolio gives us a better overall marketing proposition, increases total sales and delivers economies of scale in production and distribution.

This process demands, on one level, great political sensitivity in dealing with governments, partners, local communities and our workforce and, on another level, the deployment of expert operational management skills learnt in South Africa . . . Our management structure is de-centralised, reflecting the local nature of beer brand-ing and distribution.

Our businesses do not all advance at the same speed, nor have the same potential. It is characteristic of

emerging markets that growth can be variable, and we are accustomed to temporary setbacks. However, the spread of our international businesses provides a "port-folio effect", thereby reducing the impact of setbacks in one or two individual countries.'

SAB's history of buying local companies with strong mar-ket positions had worked very well for the group. The most successful acquisitions had domestic leadership positions in underdeveloped beer markets. It seemed unlikely that SAB would buy a business that was not number one or two in its market. Graham Mackay had commented that: 'We acquire reasonably priced assets, often severely neglected under public ownership in growing markets; establish market leadership and build local mainstream brands.' The way in which SAB could be successful with these acquisitions was through: 'operational improvement and efficiencies – to distribute beer more efficiently and drive down costs'. This could be achieved reliably through the use of sea-soned leaders with deep experience from the South African business drawing upon SAB's long standing strengths and capabilities in operational excellence in the beer indus-try and its distinctive people/performance management. Analysts' had also recognised, however, that SAB had had less success with its acquisitions in developed markets, where it seemed to have less strength.[5] This focus on local improvement was echoed in Mackay's comments: 'We are not top down. We are very locally driven.'

Beer is very much a local business with local taste, brands, heritage and economics. SABMiller can create winning brands that tap into deep local insights and win. One way in which SABMiller had been particularly effec-tive in boosting local sales was through advantaged execu-tion with the trade, where they worked alongside local beer retailers to help them grow their beer category, which would also help SABMiller sales. A good example of this has been the application of shopper marketing capabilities and insights by MillerCoors in the USA through working closely with customers such as Buffalo Wild Wings, 7-Eleven and Kroger.[6] Amongst its major competitors, SABMiller saw itself as the most local of the global brewers.

Going global

In 1999 SAB decided on a listing on the London Stock Exchange (LSE), justifying it in the following terms:

'Giving the group greater access to world capital markets and providing it with financial resources and flexibility so as to enhance the ability of SAB to take advantage of increasing consolidation in the inter-national brewing industry and to compete with other international brewers for development opportunities throughout the world.'

Initially SAB's share price lost over 15% relative to the FTSE 100 as analysts argued that this reflected a failure to make a major acquisition of a first-world (developed country) brand and its over-reliance on its developing markets.

SABMiller

In 2002 SAB succeeded in acquiring a significant position and brands in a developed market: Miller Brewing Company, the second-largest brewer in the USA. SAB paid Philip Morris Co. US$3.6 billion in stock and assumed US$2 billion of Miller's debt. The 2003 annual report claimed that this gave 'the group access, through a national player, to a growing beer market within the world's largest profit pool, and at the same time diversifying the currency and geographic risk of the group'. SAB became SABMiller following the acquisition and the second-largest brewer by volume in the world. However, the acquisition brought its own problems. James Williamson, an analyst at SG Securities in London, commented: 'They didn't buy it because they thought it was a strong growth business. They bought it because they needed a mature cash cow. Unfortunately it's been losing more market share than expected.'

Indeed, following the first full year of SABMiller operating Miller, its US market share had dropped from 19.6% to 18.7%, and by September 2003 the share price of the company had dropped from 530 pence on the day of acquisition of Miller, to 456.5 pence.

SABMiller appointed Norman Adami, previously Head of its South Africa Beer business, as President and CEO of Miller, and introduced the traditional SAB system of performance management that rewarded strong performers and focused on improving weaker performers. This was a considerable change from Miller's previous system of performance rating which routinely rated all staff at the highest level. SABMiller also announced that there would be a rationalisation of Miller's product portfolio from 50 brands to 11 or 12, meaning that market share would go down before it could go up again.

Continued acquisitions and international development

There followed a series of acquisitions. In 2003 the group made its first significant acquisition in Western Europe when it acquired Italy's Birra Peroni and subsequently developed Peroni Nastro Azzurro as a premium global brand.

In 2005 there followed a merger with Grupo Empresarial Bavaria, the second-largest brewer in South America, consolidating SABMiller as the world's number two brewer and making Latin America the largest contributor of profits in the group (32% of EBITDA in 2012, ahead of South Africa). The area has performed very strongly since the acquisition in terms of top- and bottom-line growth. Reviewing the Latin American operations at that time, the CEO confirmed that SABMiller saw these markets as offering 'exciting prospects for growth' and added:

> 'Although the Bavaria businesses are well managed and profitable, we plan to create further value by applying SABMiller's operating practices and management skills. The best opportunities lie in brand portfolio development, creating good relationships with distributors and retailers, and improving merchandising at the point of sale. The Bavaria acquisition brought very strong leader positions in its markets, with 90% market share – a huge advantage in a scale-driven industry.'

Table 2 summarises the other main acquisitions, joint ventures and plant investments. Amongst these the group saw Grolsch and Peroni Nastro Azzurro as other brands that could be developed internationally. Heineken taking back the rights to Amstel in South Africa may have prompted the Grolsch acquisition. SAB had been brewing Amstel there, as a premium Northern European beer, for 20 years, and the loss of Amstel meant that South African Breweries lost almost 10% of their business. Additionally, SABMiller was looking for a Northern European brand with heritage: hence Grolsch. Grolsch was not only a replacement for Amstel in the South African portfolio, but filled a larger gap in SABMiller's international brand portfolio. The group had some success in growing Peroni Nastro Azzurro but the Grolsch acquisition was not without its critics: SABMiller was forced to write off several hundred million euros.

In 2008 a joint venture, Miller Coors, was formed between Molson Coors, itself a merger of Molson Canada and Coors from the USA, and the SABMiller business in the USA. The benefits were said to include scale advantages and productivity improvements of US$500 million in the face of increasing cost pressures, improved logistics across the North American market and a complementarity of brands to compete more effectively against the dominance in the USA of Anheuser Busch. Commentators viewed the joint venture as a way of gaining market share in the profitable light beer category, which accounted for 40% of total US beer sales. The joint venture's brands could claim a 47.5% volume share of that category in US supermarkets. But they also pointed to the tendency for consumer preferences in terms of beer brands to move very slowly, and Trevor Sterling, of Bernstein Research, commented: 'Although Miller Coors appears to be trying to nibble Bud Light from two directions, it would be hard to convince consumers there was much difference between Miller Light and Coors Light which are priced at similar levels.' Nevertheless, even

Table 2 **Main acquisitions, joint ventures and brewery investments, 2001–12**

2001	A majority stake in the Sichuan Blue Sword Breweries Group in China. Pan-African alliance with Castel for investing in promising African countries. First international brewer to enter Central America when it acquired Honduran brewer, Cervecería Hondureña.
2002	Acquires 100% of Miller Brewing Company and changes name to SABMiller plc. Now the second-largest brewer (by volume) in the world.
2003	Acquired majority interest in Birra Peroni SpA.
2004	SABMiller associate, China Resources Breweries Limited, acquires two Chinese breweries.
2005	Buyout of joint venture partner in India, Shaw Wallace & Company.
	Acquired 71.8% of Columbian Grupo Empresarial Bavaria, the second-largest brewer in South America, for $7.8bn.
2006	Acquisition of the Foster's business and brand in India and in South Vietnam.
	Joint venture with Vinamilk to establish a brewery in Vietnam.
	SABMiller and Coca-Cola Amatil form Pacific Beverages Pty Ltd, a joint venture to market, sell and distribute SABMiller brands in Australia.
2007	Ten-year partnership with Foster's Group to brew Foster's lager in the USA. $170 million invested in a new brewery in Moscow.
	Pacific Beverages buys Australian premium brewer Bluetongue Brewery.
2008	Acquisition of Royal Grolsch NV for €816m ($1.2bn).
	Acquired the Vladpivo brewery in Vladivostok (Russia) and the Sarmat brewery in the Ukraine.
	Joint venture with Moulson Coors Brewing Co., named MillerCoors, to pool US interests.
2009	Acquisition of Bere Azuga, Romania.
	Acquired the remaining 50% interest in the Vietnamese business and the remaining 28% in the Polish business.
	Acquired three further breweries in China.
	Investment in new plant in Juba (South Sudan), Russia, Tanzania, Mozambique and Angola.
2010	Acquisition of Cervecería Argentina S.A. Isenbeck ('CASA Isenbeck'), the third-largest brewer in Argentina, from the Warsteiner Group.
	Building a US$34 million brewery in Namibia.
	A new US$105 million brewery begins operations in New South Wales, Australia
	Southern Sudan Beverages Ltd (SSBL) is doubling the size of its existing brewery operations.
2011	A new brewery in Nigeria.
	A new £3 million research brewery in the UK.
	CR Snow continues expansion in China with acquisition of the remaining equity interest in Hangzhou Xihu Beer and Huzhou Brewery and announces a new joint venture, Guizhou Moutai Beer, in partnership with China Kweichow Moutai Distillery Co. Ltd.
	SABMiller, Anadolu Group and Anadolu Efes agree a strategic alliance for Turkey, Russia, the CIS, Central Asia and the Middle East.
	SABMiller acquires Foster's Group, the number one brewer in Australia, for A$11.8bn.
2012	Strategic alliance with Castel to take over running of Nigerian businesses.
	Investment in doubling capacity in Uganda.

in the challenging environment of a recession, the profit performance of Miller Coors has been robust.

At the group level in 2009 profits dropped (see the financial summary in the Appendix), but this did not diminish top management interest in making further M&A. As CEO Graham Mackay stated via Bloomberg: 'Nothing is stopping us from the right acquisition . . . There is money available even if we have to raise capital. We think our shareholders would agree with it if it was the right acquisition.' He added, however, that: 'The right acquisition means something very different in an emerging market where a brewer can capitalise on growing volumes, than it does in the developed world where cost cuts and selling more premium beer is key.'

In 2011 SABMiller made a major acquisition of Foster's Group in Australia for A$11.8bn. Industry observers again remained to be convinced that this was the right move as Foster's, the number one brewer in Australia, was competing in a mature market and its beer volumes profits and market share were all in decline compared with its main rival Anheuser Busch InBev (ABInBev). In the year ended March 2012 Foster's volumes of beers were down 4% on the year, when SABMiller group saw an overall rise with African volumes growing as fast as 13% and Latin America by some 8%,[7] all against a backdrop of a weakening Australian economy and a poor summer. In the acquisition, Corona, Stella Artois and Asahi licences were lost, which analysts estimated as a loss of $70–100m in profits from Foster's.[8] The loss of Corona to Foster's main Australian rival, Lion Nathan, was a major blow, as it was the clear leader in the growing Australian imported beer sector. Analysts worried that SABMiller's Foster's deal mirrored its Miller purchase in 2002 when SAB bought into an effective duopoly in the low-growth US market and gave the brewer a long-term headache. As one investor remarked, 'SABMiller has turned around difficult situations before but those have often been from dominant market share positions.'[9] Australia was a tough market, effectively a duopoly.

The state of the world brewing market in 2012

In the five years prior to 2012 the world's brewing industry had racked up $142bn of M&A as global beer volumes (excluding China) recovered to about a 2% growth rate after the trough of 2008–10, though well below the 4–5% achieved in 2006–7. The growth rate by region varied considerably (see Table 3). Analysts expected flat beer volumes in North America and Europe and significant growth in Latin America, with China, India and Africa offering the best long-term volume prospects given their large populations and low per-capita consumption. Table 4 gives market profitability estimates by region.

In this context SABMiller's main competitors (see Figure 2) had different strategies. Heineken was increasingly centralising its brands in order to have a global brand design that it could then license, allowing global advertising and the use of a mass premium model. ABInBev was focused on cost reduction through a few very large acquisitions and had generally managed to achieve 10–15% improvements in margin in each one. Potential new competitors such as global spirits players were also increasingly encroaching on beer players' markets with greater focus on the same consumer occasions and needs (e.g. alcopops and ready-to-drinks). Companies such as Diageo, previously focused on developed markets, were now very active in

growing rapidly through M&A in key emerging markets. Some media commentators predicted this would lead to convergence in the wine, spirits and beer market and pointed towards increased innovation in mixing beers with spirits and flavours.

Where from here?

Certainly there are questions and strategic options to consider for SABMiller concerning the nature and scope of the portfolio of businesses, how profitability will be maintained and how SABMiller will continue to grow. It appears there is a continuing shift both towards global beer brands and towards consumer preference for premium beers and, as analysts such as Simon Hales of Evolution Securities Ltd have commented, further industry consolidation is likely. SABMiller might consider buying further assets in both developed countries and emerging markets, but there was a fundamental problem in that after a decade of consolidation, and given the importance of scale and market leadership (or number two in a market) for success in beer, there were relatively few attractive assets left. Many were held in private family, foundation or other hands and, even if available, would become increasingly expensive. Also, as Hales remarked, 'They have to be very careful how they play their hand. SAB's big deal record hasn't been great.'[10] The Miller acquisition took longer than expected to repay the cost of capital, and analysts believe the turnaround of Foster's will take some time.[11] It might also be that SABMiller would not want to be bigger at any price. It was already large enough to use purchasing power to force down ingredient prices. In the meantime the group would probably maintain its capital expenditure in areas where growth was steady, including Africa and China, and ease off where this was less evident, such as in Eastern Europe.

SABMiller has done extremely well since its listing in 1999, with 690% growth in total shareholder returns

Table 3 Compound annual growth rates, 2005–15 (per-capita terms)

Measure	Latin America	Middle East and Africa	Asia Pacific	World	North America	Western Europe
By value	13.5%	12%	6%	5%	3.75%	−0.5%
By volume	2.75%	3.75%	5.1%	2%	−0.25%	−1.35%

Source: Louise Lucas (2011) 'Thirsty for deal to seal consolidation', *FT Brewery Industry*, 11 May

Table 4 Market profitability estimates, 2010

Brazil	North America	South Africa	Other Latin America	Europe	Russia	Other Africa	Other Asia	China	India
$31/hl	$31/hl	$24/hl	$20/hl	$17/hl	$13/hl	$10/hl	$10/hl	$2/hl	$2/hl

Source: Merrill Lynch (2011) 'Investing in the global brewers', *Industry Overview*, 5 September

Figure 2 Market share of largest competitors by country

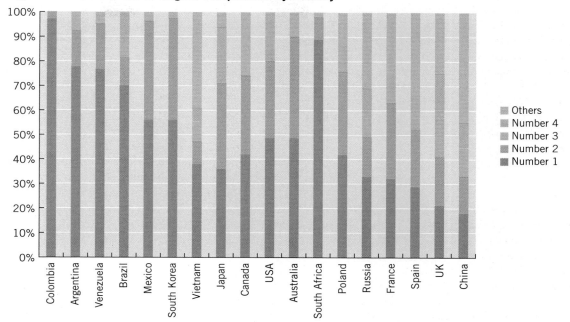

Source: 'http://www.google.do.uk/finance' \t '_blank' www.google.do.uk/finance. Google Finance™ is a trademark of Google Inc.

('TSR') to 31 March 2012 (compared with the FTSE 100 of 44%), and a goal stated in its 2012 annual report 'to deliver a higher return to our shareholders than our peer group over the longer term . . . in terms of total shareholder return (TSR), growth in adjusted EPS and free cash flow'. However, in 2012 SABMiller shares had increased in value by 20% compared with 70% for ABInBev, 50% for Carlsberg and 36% for Heineken.[12] In the global beer market, opportunities for expansion were shrinking: large transformational deals were fewer and with lower prospects of high financial returns. ABInBev was now the world's largest brewer, larger than the next two – SABMiller and Heineken – combined, and seemed to be focused on the Americas. The other global brewers were increasingly looking for growth from emerging markets, as beer growth seemed to be slowing in more developed consumer markets. Heineken was pursuing growth in Africa and Carlsberg was investing heavily in Russia. Japanese brewers were also becoming increasingly active in the Asian market. The added complication of the economic recession also impacted on all beer markets, albeit with different degrees of severity. SABMiller had always performed well, as its emerging market footprint had protected it from the declining beer volumes in the more mature markets such as Western Europe. The company was looking to drive organic growth across its portfolio of countries, but how would the portfolio of countries that SABMiller had built up through its acquisitions and joint ventures help it weather both the financial storm

and the competitive challenges? Did this require a change in the strategy of the company in terms of the emphasis on the 'local vs. global' brands in its portfolio? Should SABMiller consider entering into other beverage segments? Could there be yet another 'market changing' deal that could be shaped to win the battle in beer?

In considering options, it is also critical to remember the importance of heritage to SABMiller. The 13-member executive committee, consisting mainly of directors with considerable line experience from the South African business, has a strong appreciation of SABMiller's origins, and future strategies should factor in the lessons the business had learnt on its way to becoming the world's second-largest brewer.

Notes and references
1. $1 = £0.65 = €0.77 (April 2013).
2. Pablo Zuanic, at Liberum Capital, cited in Neville, S. (2012) 'FTSE continues its rise led by strong SABMiller results', *Guardian*, 22 November.
3. Merrill Lynch (2011) 'Investing in the global brewers', *Industry Overview*, 5 September.
4. Ibid.
5. Jones, D. (2012) 'Analysis: SABMiller faces long haul to turnaround Fosters', *Reuters*, 31 May.
6. Marketing at SABMiller PLC (2011) Investor Relations Quarterly Seminar Series, New York, 12 October 2012.
7. Jones, D., op. cit.
8. Ibid.
9. Ibid.
10. Cleary, A. (2009) 'SABMiller chief says he's ready for M&A, predicts slow recovery', *Bloomberg.com*, 11 August.
11. Jones, D., op. cit.
12. http://www.yahoofinance.com, October 2012.

APPENDIX SABMiller financial summary (US$m) for years ended 31 March

	2012	2011[1]	2010	2009	2008	2007	2006	2005
Income statements								
Group revenue	31,388	28,311	26,350	25,302	23,828	20,645	17,081	14,543
Revenue	21,760	19,408	18,020	18,703	21,410	18,620	15,307	12,901
Operating profit	5,013	3,127	2,619	3,148	3,448	3,027	2,575	2,547
Net finance costs	−562	−525	−563	−706	−456	−428	−299	−143
Share of associates' and joint ventures' post-tax results	1,152	1,024	873	516	272	205	177	148
Taxation	−1,126	−1,069	−848	−801	−976	−921	−779	−823
Minority interests	−256	−149	−171	−276	−265	−234	−234	−208
Profit for the year	**4,221**	**2,408**	**1,910**	**1,881**	**2,023**	**1,649**	**1,440**	**1,521**
Adjusted earnings	**3,400**	**3,018**	**2,509**	**2,065**	**2,147**	**1,796**	**1,497**	**1,224**
Balance sheets								
Non-current assets	50,909	34,870	33,604	28,159	31,947	25,683	24,286	12,869
Current assets	4,742	4,244	3,895	3,460	4,135	3,053	2,829	2,778
Total assets	**55,651**	**39,114**	**37,499**	**31,619**	**36,082**	**28,736**	**27,115**	**15,647**
Derivative financial instruments	−109	−135	−321	−142	−531	−209	−178	−
Borrowings	−19,226	−8,460	−9,414	−9,618	−9,658	−7,231	−7,602	−3,340
Other liabilities and provisions	−10,303	−7,760	−7,171	−5,746	−7,649	−6,295	−5,750	−3,552
Total liabilities	**−29,638**	**−16,355**	**−16,906**	**−15,506**	**−17,838**	**−13,735**	**−13,530**	**−6,892**
Net assets	**26,013**	**22,759**	**20,593**	**16,113**	**18,244**	**15,001**	**13,585**	**8,755**
Total shareholders' equity	25,073	22,008	19,910	15,375	17,545	14,406	13,043	8,077
Minority interests in equity	940	751	683	738	699	595	542	678
Total equity	**26,013**	**22,759**	**20,593**	**16,113**	**18,244**	**15,001**	**13,585**	**8,755**
Cash flow statements								
EBITDA	**4,979**	**4,502**	**3,974**	**4,164**	**4,518**	**4,031**	**3,348**	**2,736**
Net working capital movements	258	66	563	−493	−242	−13	−57	56
Net cash generated from operations	5,237	4,568	4,537	3,671	4,276	4,018	3,291	2,792
Net interest paid (net of dividends received)	610	271	175	−116	−410	−385	−248	−79
Tax paid	−893	−885	−620	−766	−969	−801	−869	−625
Net cash inflow from operating activities	**3,937**	**3,043**	**3,277**	**2,789**	**2,897**	**2,832**	**2,174**	**2,088**
Net capital expenditure	−1,522	−1,245	−1,483	−2,072	−1,927	−1,351	−984	−738
Net investments in subsidiaries, joint ventures and associates	−11,095	−183	−504	−555	−1,439	−429	−2,644	−897
Net other investments				−10	5	−2	−2	456

	2012	2011[1]	2010	2009	2008	2007	2006	2005
Net cash inflow/(outflow) before financing and dividends	−7,663	2,526	2,105	152	−464	1,050	−1,456	909
Net cash inflow/(outflow) from financing	8,819	−1,214	−804	620	1,240	−455	1,733	−271
Dividends paid	−1,324	−1,113	924	−877	−769	−681	−520	−412
Effect of exchange rates	−39	25	90	26	−113	−18	11	−56
(Decrease)/increase in cash and cash equivalents	−207	224	467	−79	−106	−104	−232	170
Per share information (US cents per share)								
Basic earnings per share	266.6	152.8	122.6	125.2	134.9	110.2	105	125.5
Diluted earnings per share	263.8	151.8	122.1	124.7	134.2	109.5	104.3	121.2
Adjusted basic earnings per share	214.8	191.5	161.1	137.5	143.1	120	109.1	101
Net asset value per share[2]	1,506.50	1,326.60	1,203.20	969.8	1,108.30	912	828	599.9
Total number of shares in issue (millions)	1,664.30	1,659.00	1,654.70	1,585.40	1,583.10	1,579.60	1,575.20	1,346.50
Other operating and financial statistics								
Return on equity (%)[3]	13.6	13.7	12.6	13.4	12.2	12.5	11.5	15.2
EBITA margin (%)	17.9	17.8	16.6	16.3	17.4	17.4	17.2	16.4
EBITDA margin (%)	23	22.9	21.7	22.3	21.1	21.6	21.9	21.2
EBITDA interest cover (times)	11.4	10.8	9.3	6.6	9.2	9.2	11.4	19.1
Total borrowings to total assets (%)	34.5	21.6	25.1	30.4	26.8	25.2	28	21.3
Cash flow to total borrowings (%)	27.2	54	48.2	38.2	44.3	55.6	43.3	83.6
Revenue per employee (US$000's)	305.9	280.4	256.9	272.5	309.8	278.1	284.7	315.5
Average monthly number of employees	71,144	69,212	70,131	68,635	69,116	66,949	53,772	40,892
Group revenue Primary segmental analysis								
Latin America	7,158	6,335	5,905	5,495	5,251	4,392	2,165	521
Europe	5,482	5,394	5,577	6,145	5,248	4,078	3,258	2,909
North America	5,250	5,223	5,228	5,227	5,120	4,887	4,912	4,892
Africa and Asia	7,196	5,280	4,457	4,132	3,367	2,674	2,221	1,937
South Africa:								
– Beverages	5,815	5,598	4,777	3,955	4,446	4,274	4,204	3,995
– Hotels and Gaming	487	481	406	348	396	340	321	289
	31,388	28,311	26,350	25,302	23,828	20,645	17,081	14,543

	2012	2011[1]	2010	2009	2008	2007	2006	2005
Operating profit (excluding share of associates and joint ventures)								
Primary segmental analysis								
Latin America	1,736	1,497	1,270	1,057	953	810	387	90
Europe	804	857	840	900	947	730	567	482
North America	–	16	12	230	462	366	454	487
Africa and Asia	546	343	280	352	330	272	257	249
South Africa: Beverages	1,091	997	826	704	962	1,043	1,011	906
Corporate	–190	–147	–139	–97	–94	–101	–86	–82
Group operating profit – before exceptional items	**3,987**	**3,563**	**3,091**	**3,146**	**3,560**	**3,120**	**2,590**	**2,132**
Exceptional credit/(charge)								
Latin America	–119	–106	–156	45	–61	–64	–11	–
Europe	1,135	–261	–202	–452	–	–24	–	–51
North America	–	–	–	409	–51	–	–	111
Africa and Asia	92	–4	–3	–	–	–	–	103
South Africa: Beverages	–41	–188	–53	–	–	–	–	–
Corporate	–41	123	–58	–	–	–5	–4	252
	1,026	–436	–472	2	–112	–93	–15	415
Group operating profit – after exceptional items	**5,013**	**3,127**	**2,619**	**3,148**	**3,448**	**3,027**	**2,575**	**2,547**
EBITDA								
Primary segmental analysis								
Latin America	1,865	1,620	1,386	1,173	1,071	915	436	90
Europe	836	887	872	944	952	733	569	482
North America	756	741	619	581	477	375	454	487
Africa and Asia	1,064	739	636	642	568	467	422	383
South Africa:								
– Beverages	1,168	1,067	885	764	1,026	1,102	1,062	956
– Hotels and Gaming	135	137	122	122	141	100	84	73
Corporate	–190	–147	–139	–97	–94	–101	–86	–82
Group	**5,634**	**5,044**	**4,381**	**4,129**	**4,141**	**3,591**	**2,941**	**2,389**

1 Restated for the adjustments made to the provisional fair values relating to the CASA Isenbeck and Crown Beverages Ltd acquisitions.
2 Net asset value per share is calculated by dividing total shareholders' equity by the closing number of shares in issue.
3 Calculated by expressing adjusted earnings as a percentage of total shareholders' equity.

Source: www.sabmiller.com/files/reports/ar2012/20012_annual_report.pdf

CASE STUDY

The internationalisation of Tesco – new frontiers and new problems

Neil Wrigley, Michelle Lowe and Katherine Cudworth

Tesco's international expansion until 2010 had seemed like a complete success despite the odd hiccough. This case re-examines Tesco's internationalisation in the context of harsher economic conditions, using a comparison of its operations in South Korea and the USA to draw out important strategic dimensions of the retail internationalisation process. It also explores the organisational consequences of that process for the firm, particularly when it is perceived to threaten the home market performance of the retailer.

● ● ●

In May 2013, Tesco, the UK's largest retailer and private sector employer of labour, announced annual sales for 2012–13 of £72 billion (~ $109bn ~ €85bn),[1] barely changed from the previous year. Profits were £3.4bn, down from £3.8 billion the year before. For Philip Clarke, Tesco's CEO since 2011, this was his second set of disappointing annual results. Sales across Europe were flat, and the company had had to decide at the end of 2012 to exit Tesco's business in the United States. The main source of encouragement seemed to be Tesco's growing Asian business. Philip Clarke declared: 'Building an international business, even when the global headwinds work against us, is the right thing to do . . . It has delivered a billion pounds in profit this year alone'.

Over a 15-year period since its entry into Eastern Europe in 1994, Tesco had progressively transformed itself from a purely domestic player to a major multinational corporation, with 65% of its operating space outside the UK and with store networks across countries in Central/Eastern Europe, Asia and the USA. Moreover, as signalled in the title of its 2009 Annual Report (*Value Travels*) and the prominence given in that report to its international profile, the firm publicly expressed its confidence that it had mastered the art of international expansion, so long a weakness of UK retailing. Tesco had emerged as one of the world's largest retailers, operating 3,255 stores and employing 216,480 staff outside the UK by 2011–12.

However, the end of the first decade of the twenty-first century marked something of a high-water mark for Tesco's international expansion strategy. The global economic crisis of 2007–9 significantly changed conditions across Tesco's international markets, placing important constraints on the firm's expansion plans at the very moment its market leadership in the UK came under the most intense pressure.

International expansion – Phase 1. From the UK to the emerging markets of Central Europe and Asia

In the early 1990s Tesco was the UK's second-largest food retailer, lagging behind the market leader Sainsbury's in terms of sales, turnover growth and profitability. Over the next decade its then CEO, Terry Leahty, managed a remarkable transformation, repositioning Tesco from its discount roots into a mass-market customer-focused retailer serving all segments of the UK market. One important innovation was the launch in 1995 of the Tesco Clubcard, the UK's first customer loyalty card, providing a platform to harvest customer information and sell additional customer services. Tesco also developed new store concepts such as Tesco Metro, a small city centre store format for local shoppers, and Tesco Express, originally a petrol station linked convenience store format, but during the 2000s freed of that linkage and increasingly the engine of Tesco's growth. By 2007, on a conservative definition of the UK grocery market, its share was 27.6% – almost twice as large as those of Asda/Walmart and Sainsbury's with 14.1% and 13.8% respectively.

As the increasingly dominant UK market leader in the late 1990s and early 2000s, Tesco began to face growing regulatory pressures relating to both market-competition requirements and land-use planning restrictions. In response, Terry Leahy, who was appointed CEO in 1997, strategically refocused the firm's operations and capital investment in an attempt to secure long-term growth, diversifying into non-food products and retail services (personal finance, telecoms, online shopping channels) and, most significantly, expanding out of the UK home market via one of the most comprehensive and sustained international diversifications ever attempted by a UK company.

After commencing that international expansion in Europe – entering the emerging post-Soviet consumer markets of Central Europe in the mid-1990s (see Table 1) – Tesco launched the next phase of its strategy in 1998. Leahy boldly committed the firm to an Asian expansion programme, initially entering Thailand and South Korea. The growth potential of the Asian markets had been extensively researched by Tesco for a number of years. However, the immediate catalysts for entry were the rapid liberalisation of previous restrictions on retail foreign direct investment across East Asia, and the opportunities presented by the Asian economic crisis of 1997–8 to make strategic majority-share acquisitions of fledgling but potentially market-leading retail businesses at discounted prices.

Tesco's subsequent expansion in the region was dramatic. Just 12 years later it had 1,719 stores, accounting for 46% of the total operating space (i.e. square footage of grocery sales area – see Table 1). Tesco had also signalled its commitment to develop businesses in two of the world's key twenty-first century economies, China and India. In China it was rapidly building the scale of its operation following entry in 2004, and in India it had successfully negotiated a partnership arrangement for entering a market in which ownership of retail businesses by international operators was on the cusp of being deregulated.

By the end of 2011, it is estimated that Tesco had invested a total of £6.9bn in Asia, achieving retail sales of £11.2bn (see Table 2). The market entries were far from being uniformly successful – Tesco struggled to build market share in

Table 1 Tesco's international operations

Region	Country	Year of entry	Number of stores, 2011–12	Regional total of operating space, 2011–12
Europe	Hungary	1994	212	27%
	Poland	1995	412	
	Czech Republic	1996	322	
	Slovakia	1996	120	
	Republic of Ireland	1997	137	
	Turkey	2003	148	
Asia	Thailand	1998	1092	46%
	South Korea	1999	458	
	Taiwan	2000	Exited market 2005	
	Malaysia	2002	45	
	Japan	2003	Exited market 2011	
	China	2004	124	
	India	Announced entry 2008		
N. America	USA	2007	185	2%
UK	UK	1919	2979	26%

Source: figures derived from Tesco Analyst Packs Preliminary Results 2011/12

Table 2 Tesco Asia: country summaries, 2011–12

Country	Population (m)	Grocery spend ($bn)	Tesco sales, 2011–12 (£m)	Tesco market share, 2012	Total invested capital, 2010–11 (£m est.)	Trading EBITDA return, 2011 (est.)	Total space (000 sq. ft), 2011–12	Numbers of hypermarkets and other stores, 2011–12	Club-card	Online
China	1,341.41	971	1,311	2.9%	801	3.9%	9,622	110, 14	Yes	Yes
Malaysia	28.23	31	981	10.2%	635	7.7%	3,778	45, 0	Yes	No
S. Korea	48.91	96	5,339	5.7%	3,600	13.7%	12,551	127, 286	Yes	Yes
Thailand	67.65	56	3,235	13.0%	1,375	19.6%	12,831	136, 956	Yes	Yes

Source: Wood, S., Wrigley, N. and Coe, N. (2013): 'Multi-scalar localisation and capability transference: exploring the Asian retail expansion of Tesco', submitted to Regional Sudies 2013

Table 3 **Tesco South Korea acquisitions**

Date	Capital investment	Price paid (£m)	No. of stores acquired	Sales on acquisition
May 1999	51% of Samsung–Tesco	85		
June 1999	Further 30% of Samsung–Tesco	57		
Feb. 2002	Further 8% of Samsung–Tesco			
July 2007	Further 5% of Samsung–Tesco	40–60		
July 2011	Further 5% of Samsung–Tesco			
Mar. 2005	Store acquisition from Aram Mart	49	3 HM, 9 SM	£111m in 2005–06
April 2008	Acquisition of Homever stores from E-Land	958	36 HM	Approx. £800m

Notes: SM – supermarket; HM – hypermarket

Source: Wood, S.M., Wrigley, N. and Coe, N. (2013) – see Table 2 on p. 658

Taiwan and Japan and was forced to sell or trade its store network assets and exit both markets. (The exit from Taiwan involved a swap of assets with rival market leader Carrefour: in return for Tesco's stores in Taiwan, Carrefour gave Tesco its stores in the Czech Republic and Slovakia.)

In contrast, the entries into South Korea, Thailand and Malaysia were built on far more successfully, and by 2011–12 South Korea provided Tesco with its second-largest market by sales after the UK, accounting for just over 8% of the firm's global revenues with sales of £5.3bn. Much can be learnt from considering the drivers of that success in more detail.

Success in South Korea

Tesco entered the South Korean market after the Asian economic crisis of 1997–8 via a partnership with Samsung, a major domestic conglomerate urgently seeking a cash injection. Tesco acquired a 51% stake in 'Homeplus', Samsung's retail chain, which at the time was in the initial start-up phase with just two stores trading and three sites in development. Retaining the original Samsung CEO, Tesco expanded Homeplus into a highly successful multi-format chain with more than 400 stores employing over 23,000 workers by 2008, in the process establishing itself as the strongly positioned, number-two-ranked chain in the market with potential in the future to displace domestic operator E-mart as market leader. During this period Tesco outperformed its multinational rivals to such an extent that Walmart and Carrefour were forced to exit the Korean market, leaving Tesco as the dominant international retailer.

Building on its 51% original stake, Tesco made substantial and continuous post-entry capital investments to build scale and to keep pace with the domestic market leader. This involved a substantial organic store development programme – one of Tesco's competitive strengths – together with strategic acquisitions. Notable among the latter were 36 ex-Carrefour 'Homever' hypermarkets for £950m in 2008 and 12 Aram Market stores for £49m in 2005. These substantial investments rapidly reduced Samsung's ownership share, first to 11% and then in two subsequent stages

to 1% (see Table 3). At the same time, Tesco transferred various practices from its UK business, for example the use of balance scorecard management measurement systems and techniques for developing own brand (rather than manufacturer brand) products.

Despite this rapid dilution of Samsung's share of the business, the partnership offered Tesco significant advantages. Firstly, Tesco gained knowledge of local business and regulatory conditions. In South Korea, local governments frequently work to protect traditional retailers from new discount stores such as Tesco's Homeplus, and Samsung could help with local politics and regulations. Secondly, they got an insight into local consumer culture and consumption practices, for example, Koreans prize being able to buy their fish live, unlike in Europe. Thirdly, the partnership helped Tesco maintain the impression of being a 'Korean' rather than a 'foreign' retailer, allowing Tesco to build Homeplus on the basis of a 'local' appeal and consumer image associated with the Samsung name (by 2010, there were only six Britons in the Korean business). In these ways, Tesco was able to blend centrally transferred operational and management practices with local knowledge and legitimacy. At the same time, the Korean business began to develop its own expertise relevant to Tesco's other businesses internationally. When Tesco launched its Homeplus non-food stores in the UK in 2005, it borrowed not only the brand but also much of the format from its Korean stores. In 2011, Samsung–Tesco launched the world's first 'virtual store', tapping into Korea's huge use of smartphones. The virtual store involved electronic displays of 500 popular products in a busy downtown Seoul subway station, which smartphone users could scan in order to obtain delivery at home the same day.[2]

International expansion – Phase 2. From success in emerging markets to the challenges of entering a mature market

In February 2006, after a year of intensive, but closely guarded, market research by a CEO-selected team of managers dispatched to Los Angeles, and building on more than a decade of in-depth investigation of the potential and characteristics of the market, Tesco announced its intention to commit £1.25 billion over five years to enter the western USA. The entry vehicle was to be a chain of convenience neighbourhood stores, later to be called Fresh & Easy Neighbourhood Markets. The decision represented a significant shift in Tesco's previous 'emerging market'-focused internationalisation strategy. As the British CEO of Fresh & Easy, Tim Mason, was to stress, the USA represented: 'The first mature, well-served market, that we have opened into, so actually [Fresh & Easy] is not filling a vacuum and has to earn its place.'

It was also, very clearly, a high-risk decision as the US market had a long record of proving to be the graveyard of overambitious expansion by UK retailers. As a result, the entry announcement generated widespread scepticism of Tesco's ability to succeed where so many others had failed. Indeed, even sympathetic analysts questioned Tesco's ability to achieve the targets (e.g. store productivity) implicitly set for the US venture. The consensus view in Crédit Suisse's (2007) terms was: 'It may be fresh, but it won't be easy.'

Tesco's decision to enter the USA also represented an important reversal of its previous view of the likelihood of success in the market. Indeed, it had consistently resisted many opportunities to enter the USA via acquisition of the regional food retailer chains of conventional large-format supermarkets, because of their track record of low profitability and the threat posed by Walmart (the largest retailer both in the USA and worldwide). The change in Tesco's assessment related to its growing skills in small-format store operations, its belief in the competitive potential of dense networks of convenience-focused neighbourhood stores providing an innovative retail offer, and evidence that the Walmart threat could be countered in the type of urban markets Tesco had targeted for its US expansion.

Tesco's small-format retail skills had developed in the UK as a competitive response to tightening regulation – both planning regulations which had made large-format out-of-centre stores increasingly difficult to develop, and competition regulation which blocked large-scale acquisitions but offered an opportunity for growth by acquisition in the convenience store market. In part, however, those skills had been developed proactively to gain competitive advantage in a rapidly expanding 'convenience culture' market. By the mid-2000s, the result was that Tesco had 700 'Express' convenience stores in the UK, supplemented by a range of other smaller-format stores (e.g. urban 'Metro' stores) and, additionally, had begun to export the Express format to its international subsidiaries.

Growing confidence in its ability to operate small formats profitably offered Tesco the opportunity to explore a US market entry focused around convenience. Additionally,

it recognised that the model of dense networks of high-visibility corner-location stores successfully used by US drug retailers (chemists) such as Walgreen could be used to structure a chain of smaller-format food stores on a mutually reinforcing network logic. In terms of retail offer, Tesco recognised that opportunities existed to exploit the extensive experience of UK food retailers in chilled prepared-meals development and operation of the cool-chain distribution/logistics systems required by those products. US food retailers, and in turn the US food manufacturing industry, had traditionally offered few of these products to customers, and the specialist distribution/logistics and quality control/traceability systems necessary to support extensive retail offers of that type were underdeveloped. As a result, opportunities existed to develop a chain focused on offering high-quality but affordable fresh and chilled prepared-meals products. Short lead times and a responsive distribution system, supplying higher levels of own-label products than were typical amongst US food retailers, could also be a competitive advantage.

None the less, Tesco recognised the threat posed by Walmart, in particular on the weaker US regional supermarket chains, driving significant consolidation of those chains. Additionally, it recognised that the supermarket sector was being squeezed between the Walmart-led supercentre operators and a new group of discount retailers operating smaller-format stores (and achieving much higher levels of profitability than the supermarket chains). However, the stores of the Albrecht family (Aldi on the east coast and Trader Joe's in the west) provided Tesco with reassuring evidence that the threat of Walmart could be faced. Moreover, it was exactly those urban markets which, as a result of escalating community resistance, Walmart was finding it most difficult to enter with its huge supercentres.

In November 2007, Tesco opened its first Fresh & Easy stores in Southern California. They averaged 10,000 square feet and carried a tightly edited range of 3,500 items with a focus on fresh and chilled prepared-meals products. Served by a short lead time, integrated food preparation and distribution system, they were based around entirely self-scanning checkouts. They were described by Fresh & Easy's Tim Mason as: 'designed to be as fresh as Whole Foods, with the value of Wal-Mart, the convenience of Walgreens, and a product range of Trader Joe's'. The stores were rapidly rolled out in Southern California, Phoenix and Las Vegas, and a year later exactly 100 had opened.

As Table 4 demonstrates, the subsequent pace of expansion was much slower than Tesco had achieved in South Korea and other emerging markets. Tesco's market entry into the USA coincided with the 2007–8 worldwide financial crisis and subsequent economic downturn. Previously high-growth western US urban markets like

Table 4 **Tesco US performance summary**

Year	Number of stores	Revenue (£m)	Trading profit (£m)
2007–8	61	16	(62)
2008–9	115	206	(142)
2009–10	145	349	(165)
2011	164	495	(186)
2012	185	652	(158)

Note: Parentheses represent net loss.

Source: figures derived from Tesco Annual Reports 2008–12

California were greatly affected by the sub-prime mortgage collapse and the deepening recession. American consumers were uncomfortable with some of Fresh & Easy's offer, for example , the lower levels of in-store service, use of self-scanning check-outs, the absence of freshly brewed coffee and the heavy reliance on own-brand products rather than manufacturers' brands. Fresh & Easy adjusted their offer, for instance introducing fresh coffee. However, slow store openings deprived the chain of necessary scale advantages. Start-up losses were much higher than planned.

Impact of the internationalisation process on the strategic possibilities of the firm

Tesco had made big steps in becoming an international operator, but it is worth noting that 66% of sales and profits are still generated from UK stores, so there is still some way to go before Tesco could truly describe itself as 'global'.

One of the defining characteristics of Leahy's 15-year strategic realignment of Tesco as a multinational operator was his ability to engineer that transformation largely under the radar of hostile public scrutiny and retain financial market support for the strategy. That was never likely to be possible with an entry into the USA. Despite the relatively modest scale of the £1.25 billion five-year US investment (compared to annual international capital expenditure of about £2 billion in 2010), Tesco was acutely aware of both the reputational risks and potentially transformational consequences of the US venture in the case of either success or failure. As Leahy noted in an interview for *The Economist* at the time of the US entry: 'We've carefully balanced the risks. If it fails it's embarrassing. It might show up in my career [but] it'll cost an amount of money that is easily affordable by Tesco – call it £1 billion if you like. If it succeeds then it's transformational.' Leahy was, in effect, required to publicly place his considerable 'reputational equity' on the line and subsequently found it necessary to repeatedly signal strategic commitment to the US venture.

In April 2011 Philip Clarke took over as CEO of Tesco after spending all his working life with the company latterly as director of the international businesses. It was an inauspicious time to step up, as Tesco's market share in the UK had dipped below 30% for the first time since 2005, with both Sainsbury's and Asda gaining market share at Tesco's expense. While the financial markets in general were climbing, the company's share price was more than 10 percent down from its 2010 peak. Clarke had the task of revitalising the UK offer as well as growing the international offer. In one of his first statements in 2011, Clarke emphasised the importance of internationalisation: 'Our international business is growing pretty fast and it's growing well. It's been my focus for the past six years and in some ways we're just at the beginning. We're going to globalise the best that we do.'[3] Yet by December 2012 Clarke had to admit defeat in America: 'The business has failed, let's face it'.[4] Tesco announced it wanted sell or close its Fresh & Easy stores and the US subsidiary's CEO, Tim Mason, had departed the company altogether.

Notes and references
1. £1 ~ \$1.53 ~ €1.17.
2. This section draws on N. Coe and Y-S Lee, 'We've learnt how to be local': the deepening territorial embeddedness of Samsung–Tesco in South Korea', *Journal of Economic Geography*, 2013, 13, pp. 327–56.
3. http://www.bbc.co.uk/news/business-13114113
4. *Financial Times*, 5 December 2012.

CASE STUDY

Gridsum and the Microsoft partner ecosystem: engaging in China and beyond

Shameen Prashantham

This short case looks at the network strategy adopted by Gridsum, a small and young entrepreneurial software firm in Beijing, China, in pursuit of internationalisation. Specifically the case describes how an ambitious entrepreneur in an emerging economy forged local links with a large multinational, Microsoft, and is seeking to transform them into a global relationship.

•　•　•

2006–8: foundation and origins

Gridsum is a software company that was founded in Beijing in December 2006 by CEO Qi Guosheng.[1] Qi was in his early twenties and had graduated with distinction from the School of Software in the prestigious Tsinghua University. (Tsinghua University and Peking University, both located in Beijing, are popularly referred to as 'the Oxford and Cambridge of China'.) As a student he had interned at the Microsoft Research facility in Beijing. This exposure perhaps influenced an early decision he made with respect to Gridsum, which was to develop its offerings on platform technologies from Microsoft. In the course of 2007 Gridsum initially focused on offering services in the areas of search engine optimisation and search engine marketing. By 2008 it had developed its own web analytic tool called the Gridsum Web Dissector.

2008–9: forming the Microsoft relationship

A major turning point for Gridsum was a formal relationship it forged with Microsoft. In 2008 Microsoft launched a worldwide initiative targeted at young firms. Called 'BizSpark', this programme was often referred to by Microsoft managers as the company's chief means of 'breadth' engagement with start-ups. Essentially, it was an offer of Microsoft software development tools free of charge for firms that were less than three years in operation and with less than $1 million annual revenue.[2] Microsoft's objective in making this generous offer was to encourage start-ups to build software solutions on its technology plat-

form, resulting in future revenue for Microsoft: when such a firm sells a licence of its own software it is likely to be bundled with a licence for the underlying Microsoft platform. Furthermore, this initiative was part of Microsoft's robust actions to counter the threat posed by 'open source' software.

In China, the roll-out of BizSpark was entrusted to a manager called Xu Yun. Xu was a computer engineer who, like Gridsum's Qi, had graduated from Tsingua University. Microsoft had previously not engaged meaningfully with start-ups and therefore Xu (much like his Microsoft BizSpark counterparts all over the world) had to start from scratch. He decided to make the Tsinghua alumni network his first port of call. He contacted his former classmates who in turn connected him with other contacts of theirs. Before long, he was made aware of Qi Guosheng and Gridsum. He invited Qi to a meeting, and right from their first interaction, Xu formed an impression that here was a young company – with fewer than 20 employees at the time – that would become a great success one day. Gridsum became one of the earliest companies that he signed up for the BizSpark programme in China.

From Gridsum's perspective, the BizSpark relationship gave it much more than free software: it was an opportunity to begin a formal process of relationship building with Microsoft. Notwithstanding the CEO's prior exposure to the Microsoft Research facility and his early decision to build the company's offerings on Microsoft technology, until then there had been no defined relationship.

Now, however, there was someone that Gridsum knew within Microsoft (Xu) who could be approached to discuss an idea or request some assistance. Xu was in a position to provide a pathway into a complex organisation that was not easy for any new venture to navigate. Having made this start to a formal relationship, Gridsum lost no time in seeking to convey the quality of its technology offerings and its commitment to working with Microsoft.

With the help of Microsoft's Xu, Gridsum was able to build connections with different 'product groups' within Microsoft (i.e. units that were responsible for generating sales revenue of specific proprietary technologies) and 'platform development units' (i.e. groups of managers who were tasked with encouraging software companies to adopt Microsoft technology as their underlying platform, and so typically did not have sales targets, unlike the product groups). Given the vast number of such groups, Gridsum's CEO Qi soon realised he would need to be somewhat selective, at least initially, in building links to these teams.

Silverlight was a Microsoft technology that had been launched at the time and was being promoted particularly aggressively. Gridsum had used this very technology in the most recent version of its core offering and Qi saw an opportunity to get the attention of the Silverlight team, in particular. As he expected, when he demonstrated Gridsum's user interface which had been built on Silverlight, the Microsoft team was enthused. This team began to showcase Gridsum's offering as part of its marketing activities in order to demonstrate Silverlight's capabilities in developing a user interface in software products. In this way, Gridsum got free publicity that was beneficial to its own marketing efforts.

Another way in which Gridsum made an early positive impression on Microsoft was by applying its technology to help Microsoft carry out a specific task in China. Again through Microsoft's Xu, Gridsum CEO Qi had got wind of a need within Microsoft China. This concerned the recent launch of free anti-virus software targeted at Chinese consumers and small businesses. Microsoft's Technology Market Division in China needed to capture important marketing metrics during the promotion period, which were proving difficult to obtain using conventional techniques that were not very effective in China. Qi saw an opportunity to make Microsoft a customer of Gridsum! Gridsum worked hard to understand the technological specifics of how Microsoft was going about the promotion of this anti-virus software, and then customised its Web Dissector technology to help Microsoft capture the information it needed.

So successful was this new technology that Microsoft recognised Gridsum with a special award. Kudos in the business media followed, and Gridsum had a blue-chip reference client that led to other high-profile customers such as Coca-Cola. Gridsum was now firmly on the radar of several Microsoft China managers.

2009–11: consolidating the Microsoft relationship

Gridsum's relationship with Microsoft moved to a new level in 2009. By then BizSpark had proved to be a great success for Microsoft, attracting tens of thousands of young firms around the world. A follow-up – but rather different – partner programme was introduced in late 2009 for young firms. Called 'BizSpark One', this programme was referred to as Microsoft's chief means of in-depth engagement with start-ups. The BizSpark One programme is highly selective. With a worldwide capacity of 100 members, the goal of the programme was to identify (through a rigorous selection procedure) and invite highly innovative start-ups that appeared most likely to make a significant impact, and whose technology was aligned with Microsoft's. In effect, Microsoft was seeking to foster the development of firms that could turn into significant partners in the future as exemplars for the thousands of other start-ups partnering with Microsoft through the generic BizSpark programme. The BizSpark One members had the opportunity to forge a relationship with Microsoft on a one-to-one basis by being given access to a named account manager. He or she frequently doubled as a mentor.

Microsoft's Xu Yun was given dual charge of the BizSpark and BizSpark One programmes in China. Given the successful relationship forged with Gridsum over the preceding 12 months, as indicated above, he had no hesitation in inviting Gridsum to be the first Chinese start-up to join BizSpark One.

A positive outcome of the deepened relationship was access to finance. This was especially welcome in an emerging economy like China where venture capital funding, although available, is not as well entrenched as in more sophisticated economies such as the US and UK. Although the BizSpark One programme did not directly provide venture capital, two major funding rounds were influenced by this relationship. In 2010 Gridsum received funding from Steamboat Ventures, an international firm, following an introduction made by Microsoft. In 2011 a further infusion of capital was obtained from the venture capital arm of Nokia, the Finnish multinational which by then had become a strategic partner of Microsoft in the mobile telephony market. This was partly responsible – along with a positive outlook for the data analytics industry in China – for the surge in growth that Gridsum witnessed between 2010 and 2011 when its headcount more than trebled from 33 to 111 employees, and then nearly doubled again to just below 200 by the end of 2012.

But what Gridsum's CEO Qi saw as the *real* opportunity was not the access to money (valuable though it was) but rather the scope to consolidate the relationship with Microsoft within the Chinese market in the first instance, and eventually beyond. He came to the view that it would no longer suffice to rely on one-off engagements with different teams, valuable though this had proved initially. Now, Gridsum's focus was to align its own product offerings even more closely to those of Microsoft in China. Gridsum began actively monitoring Microsoft's China strategy, in order to understand the likely product launches that were on the horizon. Gridsum's intention was to tailor its offerings in order to complement Microsoft's forthcoming offerings. Having a deep relationship provided a conduit to valuable information about forthcoming plans in advance of the market.

The launch of the Microsoft Windows Phone in China is a case in point. When Gridsum learnt of the imminent launch of Microsoft's Windows Phone in China, it dedicated significant resources (in relative terms) to develop a product, Mobile Dissector SDK, that would work on this platform. This proved to be of great interest to Microsoft – and, this time, not only within China. For the first time, corporate managers in Microsoft's US offices began taking notice of this Chinese start-up, because China had been identified as a key market for the Windows Phone. Thus by having done its homework diligently Gridsum had identified a global priority of Microsoft's: that is succeeding with the Windows Phone in the Chinese market. The venture then leveraged its unique sources of competitive advantage (expertise in online analytic software for the Chinese market) to develop a complementary offering to that of Microsoft's, resulting in substantial revenue growth for Gridsum.

Although Microsoft China's Xu Yun had left the company several months before, Gridsum had a new partner manager at Microsoft, and in 2010 Gridsum's relationship with Microsoft in the Chinese market was a well-established one. Reflecting on his company's relationship with Microsoft, Gridsum's CEO Qi observed:

> 'The fact that Gridsum has been successful in forming an effective relationship with Microsoft stems from two reasons. One is that Microsoft really wants to partner with potential partners from an early stage, so Microsoft allocates sufficient resources and dedicated people in cooperating with startups such as Gridsum. The other is that Gridsum has an innovation 'gene' – our cutting edge solution which is based on the Microsoft platform opens the door to cooperate with Microsoft.'[3]

And now Gridsum was seeing the beginnings of attention being paid to it by the US-based Microsoft office (in Silicon Valley) that managed BizSpark and BizSpark One. For Microsoft, it was important to identify examples of highly successful young ventures through these programmes (in particular, through BizSpark One) that could be showcased. Gridsum represented the most prominent example from China, a market of growing importance to Microsoft.

Source: www.gridsum.com

Gridsum CEO Qi Guosheng with Steve Ballmer, CEO of Microsoft in Beijing, May 2011

The head of the BizSpark One team in the USA decided to focus even greater attention on Gridsum, in order to illustrate to young firms around the world that partnering with Microsoft was desirable. To this end, he arranged for a high-profile event in Beijing to coincide with a different global initiative of Microsoft's (a worldwide competition for young software developers) at which there would be two speakers: Microsoft's CEO Steve Ballmer and Gridsum's CEO Qi Guosheng.

This event, in May 2011, represented the zenith of Gridsum's BizSpark One relationship with Microsoft, and its scale was unparalleled within that partnering programme anywhere in the world. The head of BizSpark One travelled to the event from California with his entire corporate team comprising eight members. For him, the importance of the Chinese market could not be overstated, and Gridsum was an invaluable success story that testified to the benefits of engaging with the Microsoft partner ecosystem. Predictably, the media attention that the event garnered was considerable. Gridsum's CEO Qi was excited at the prospect of building upon this unprecedented opportunity to transform what was essentially a local relationship into a global one over the coming months and years.

May 2011 onwards: extending the Microsoft relationship globally

An important development that Qi had initiated in the months leading up to the May 2011 event with Steve Ballmer was to persuade Xu Yun, the former Microsoft manager who had drafted Gridsum into the BizSpark and BizSpark One programmes, to join Gridsum as head of business development. Qi's thinking was that if the relationship with Microsoft was to develop beyond the China subsidiary, then he needed someone with a deep understanding of 'the vast ocean' that Microsoft represented. Xu, who knew Gridsum well and believed in the venture's potential, was attracted to the unexpected invitation. Qi was keen that Xu join Gridsum in time for the event with Steve Ballmer. Xu managed to accommodate this request – and his first day at work was the very day of the event! He knew all of the Microsoft people and played the role of 'a doubled-edged adhesive' – as he describes himself – or a bridge between Gridsum and Microsoft.

In the period since Xu became the business development director he has leveraged his wide array of contacts within Microsoft, especially in the USA. He accompanied Qi to Microsoft's Worldwide Partner Conference in Los Angeles in July 2011, the BizSpark One Summit in San Francisco in November 2011, as well as a follow-up business trip in March 2012 to the Microsoft global headquarters in Redmond, Washington (near Seattle) in a bid to explore possibilities for Gridsum to be part of global opportunities with Microsoft offerings such as, for instance, the search engine Bing.

In subsequent months Gridsum has continued to widen its base of relationships within Microsoft, in both China and the USA. Gridsum's Qi and Xu have continued to take advantage of visits by senior corporate executives from Microsoft headquarters in the USA to China by meeting them, and sustaining the dialogue about expanding the range of their joint activities with Microsoft, both in China and elsewhere. They believe that they must be proactive, yet patient, while dealing with the complex Microsoft partner ecosystem.

The outcomes of these efforts remain to be seen. As they seek to build on the successes in China to create a global partnership with Microsoft, there are multiple issues that Qi and Xu must ask themselves:

- How should we prioritise our efforts to form new links amongst the wide array of Microsoft businesses?
- How do we convince sceptics in the USA and elsewhere that China is capable of creating a world-class software company?
- How do we ensure that our ongoing partnering efforts in the USA do not jeopardise our strong standing in China?

Notes and references
1. Qi Guosheng is the CEO's full name as the surname comes first in China.
2. $1 ~ £0.65 ~ €0.77.
3. The quotation is from an interview with the author.

CASE STUDY

Severstal and the global steel industry

Eustathios Sainidis

The case study gives an overview of the global steel industry, a highly dynamic, volatile and fragmented sector. It describes how Severstal, one of the largest Russian steelmakers, has developed its international strategy through a number of overseas acquisitions. With a strong vision to become one of the major global players in its industry, the company has been successfully developing its strategic capability. However, the global economic crisis that began in mid-2007 proved a major test for Severstal and its future direction.

• • •

By the end of 2012 the World Steel Association (Worldsteel) was once more forecasting a difficult trading year for steelmakers around the world. Growth in demand for steel products in 2012 and 2013 would be lower than in earlier years. The forecast for 2013 global steel consumption was 1.4 billion mt (metric tonnes), almost the same as three years earlier in 2010. Worldsteel's Economics Committee Chairman Hans Jürgen Kerkhoff blamed the uncertainty arising from the debt crisis in the Eurozone and an unexpected slowdown of Chinese industrial output. As he put it:

'These factors have weighed heavily on business confidence and manufacturing activities around the world. As a result momentum in both developed and emerging parts of the world weakened considerably . . . Since the 2008 economic crisis, uncertainty and volatility has become the norm for the steel industry but it is worth noting that world steel demand has maintained positive growth despite all the headwinds and lingering difficulties.'[1]

By the end of 2011 Severstal, one of Russia's largest steelmakers (by production output), reported net profits of $2.2 billion (£1.45bn; €1.72bn)[2] on revenues of $15.8 billion (£10.39bn; €12.33bn), a much better year than the loss-making financial years of 2009 and 2010. Severstal's major shareholder and CEO, Alexei Mordashov, remained bullish and confident about the company's future despite the recent difficult years. His approach was to stay flexible and cautiously optimistic about Severstal's strategic direction. His goal was to place Severstal in the top five global steel producers by EBITDA[3] by 2015.

Source: Dr Eustathios Sainidis

Since 2004 Severstal has undertaken a number of successful overseas acquisitions in the USA, Europe and Asia, but the global economic downturn since 2008 has demanded a rethink of its international strategy. Alexei Mordashov's forecast is for further consolidation in the steel industry, a focus on emerging markets, and further diversification by the key players in the global steel sector.

A challenging and dynamic industry

Steel is an alloy made of iron and small amounts of carbon, and is one of the most widely used materials. Its main applications include the construction, shipping, automotive and energy markets. Its success as a product is based on its strong, resilient, versatile and recyclable properties.

Since the late 1980s the steel industry has become more global in terms of both competition and markets. Steel producers have also invested in production and energy efficiencies, leading to higher profit margins. Foreign direct investment opportunities and the rapid growth of the emerging economies of China, Eastern Europe, Russia and South America have created a financially rewarding business environment. Steel production in 2011 reached close to 1.4bn mt of crude steel, with China by far the largest consumer (624 million mt), followed by the European Union (153 million mt) and NAFTA[4] countries (121 million mt). Demand for steel has been increasing year on year since the 1990s until the third quarter of 2008 when the steel industry was one of the first to feel the severe impact of the longest global economic slowdown since World War II. Figure 1 shows the development of steel consumption by geographical regions from 1950 to 2010.

Major players in the industry include ArcelorMittal, which is by far the largest producer of steel products and is led by the Indian-born Lakshmi Mittal, followed by the Chinese Hebei Group in second place (2011 data). ArcelorMittal was the result of the acquisition of Luxembourg-based Arcelor by Mittal in 2006. The acquisition has become a milestone in the consolidation process of the steel industry. The newly formed company is nearly twice the size of the Hebei Group with a production capacity enough to supply the entire automotive market. Table 1

Figure 1 Steel consumption 1950–2010 by geographical region

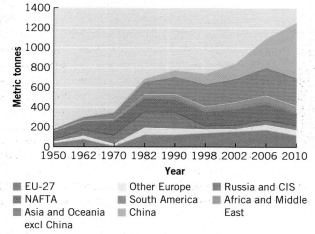

Source: World Steel Association

gives an illustration of how the competition has changed between 2000, 2008 and 2011, showing evidence of consolidation and the rise of steelmakers from emerging economies.

Although the industry has seen significant merger and acquisition activity, it still remains highly fragmented in comparison to other manufacturing sectors. Steel

Table 1 Leading world steel producers by volume

Company	Headquarters	2011 Rank	2011 Crude steel output (million mt)	2008 Rank	2008 Crude steel output (million mt)	2000 Rank	2000 Crude steel output (million mt)
ArcelorMittal	Luxembourg	1	97.2	1	103.3	4	22.4
Hebei Group	China	2	44.4	5	33.3	–	–
Baosteel Group	China	3	43.3	3	35.4	8	19.1
POSCO	South Korea	4	39.1	4	34.7	2	27.7
Wuhan Steel Group	China	5	37.7	7	27.7	26	6.7
Nippon Steel	Japan	6	33.4	2	37.5	1	28.4
Shagang Group	China	7	31.9	–	–	–	–
Shougang Group	China	8	30	22	12.2	22	8.0
JFE	Japan	9	29.9	6	33.0	9	29.0
Ansteel Group	China	10	29.8	17	16.0	20	8.8
Shandong Steel Group	China	11	24	11	21.8	64	3.0
Tata Steel	India	12	23.8	8	24.4	57	3.6
United States Steel	USA	13	22	10	23.2	14	10.7
Gerdau	Brazil	14	20.5	13	20.4	25	7.1
Nucor	USA	15	19.9	12	20.4	16	10.0
ThyssenKrupp	Germany	16	17.9	18	15.9	7	17.7
Evraz	Russia	17	16.8	15	17.7	59	3.6
Maanshan Steel	China	18	16.7	19	15.0	54	3.7
Benxi	China	19	16.5	–	–	–	–
Hyundai Steel	South Korea	20	16.3	–	–	–	–
. . .	. . .	...	. . .	. . .	. . .	. . .	. . .
Severstal	Russia	23	15.3	14	19.2	18	9.6

Source: World Steel Association

producers use mergers and acquisitions as their preferred strategy to achieve growth and market penetration. Organic development is expensive and environmental regulations can be a barrier to building new steel plants. Acquisitions act as a strategy to achieve synergies, achieving diversification and targeting niche markets.

The acquisition of the Anglo-Dutch steel producer Corus by Indian-based Tata Steel is one such example. Professor Phanish Puram from London Business School commented on the acquisition: 'The Tata–Corus deal is different because it links low-cost Indian production and raw materials and growth markets to high-margin markets and high technology in the West.'[5]

Such 'vertical' acquisitions (in other words, the linking of iron ore producers and steel producers) have resulted in increased negotiating power for steelmakers with regard to their suppliers and customers. Although prices for raw materials (iron ore and carbon) have continued to increase, steel producers see their supply chains as a source of creating value and reducing costs. This offers strong financial returns, allowing for investment in quality and service with the aim of differentiating steel products and charging a premium.

The most resourceful steel producers saw opportunities in investing in overseas operations in order to expand their product portfolio through related and unrelated acquisitions. The privatisation of government-owned assets in emerging economies such as Russia, Brazil, India, China and the Middle East allowed for foreign direct investment strategies. Owning a steel plant close to construction, shipping and automotive manufacturers in these locations offers a competitive advantage in the rapidly growing local markets. Exchange rates are also in favour of Russian and Chinese steel producers, with a weakening US dollar since the mid-2000s assisting cross-border acquisitions.

On the other hand, customers of steel producers are also pushing for structural changes in their own supply chain. Automotive manufacturers in particular would like to see steel producers having a greater role in the production of their vehicles, with the early stages of car assembly (e.g. stamping) taking place within the steel mills. Steel producers who have invested in such production facilities to fabricate custom-made parts can offer differentiated products attracting higher prices.

However, there were signs of the steel industry reaching a tipping point even before the 2007 global economic crisis arrived. Gradually increasing pricing pressures, gaps in product mix and asset concentration indicated that the industry had reached maturity by 2006. Industry analysts were already talking about evidence of 'hyper-competition' from as early as 2002. The industry was changing rapidly, with the dominant steel producers based in the USA, Japan and Germany now under attack from new players in South Korea and Russia and more recently China and India. The

Figure 2 World steel capacity utilisation

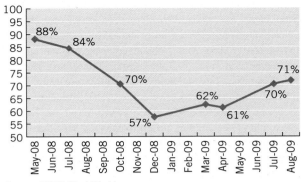

Source: HSBC Steel Weekly

industry has been experiencing a constant cycle of global consolidation and fragmentation and opportunistic short-term counter-attack strategies. The 2008 global economic downturn was a wake-up call for steel price speculators and investors, making shareholders of steel producers much more cautious and asking their CEOs to take more calculated risks and become more market-focused in their business ventures.

After eight years of good growth in the metals industry, September 2008 proved to be a turning point for steel producers. The global financial crisis and subsequent economic downturn had a severe effect on the industry and its markets. At the start of the economic recession in 2008, demand for steel had fallen by 60% and prices dropped to 2002 levels, a 70% fall relative to their peak in 2007. With many steel producers continuing to operate at full capacity, very soon oversupply resulted in plummeting steel prices (see Figure 2). In 2012, although some regional markets (China, India and South America) were still experiencing growth, the lack of credit available to industrial consumers meant orders for steel products were growing at a very slow rate. Banks and other financial institutions were still very risk averse, making funds available to businesses across the steel supply chains very difficult to come by. Steel producers were faced with difficulties in investing in their existing and future assets.

Global market opportunities

The emerging markets of South America, Asia and the Middle East are the main growth markets for steel. The expectation is that they will continue to grow at a faster rate than the mature markets of North America, Europe (EU-27) and Japan. The steel market is very cyclical with short 'peak-to-peak' periods. Huge demand variations exist between regional markets, which makes forecasting very difficult. Industry experts expect an annual increase of about 5% in global construction, automotive and other transport markets by 2021. Areas for growth for the future (2021) include Asia Pacific, Africa and the Middle East. The US and European (EU-27) markets are expected to stay at 2012 levels, if not decline. None of these markets is currently dominated by one single steel producer, but all the major international steel players have strategies in place to target these lucrative markets.

China has become not only a major producer but also the largest consumer of steel products. The country's domestic production has increased annually by 15%; however, there are only a small number of efficient Chinese producers capable of exporting steel, with a historical tendency to overproduce, putting further pressures on steel prices. Non-Chinese steel producers have used this weakness in Chinese steel production capabilities as an attractive proposition for market opportunities and acquisitions in the country.

The USA has a high level of steel consumption, mainly in the automotive, machine tool and construction markets, and at the same time has several steel-producing companies. As a market the USA is attractive for its high demand, and the low value of the US dollar has led to growing inward foreign direct investment. On the other hand, the main barriers to investment in the USA are the powerful trade unions and occasional federal protectionist measures.

South Korea has evolved as one of the major steel exporters, with an increasing market share in the USA, Japan and China. Significantly, South Korea is the biggest indirect exporter of steel, because of its increasing domestic demand for steel-based products supplying the country's rapidly expanding automotive, shipping and electronics industries. The country exports almost 60% of its automotive production, 90% of its shipping products and 60% of electronics. This is about 10 times more than the European Union countries and three times more than Japan.

Severstal Group

Severstal was founded in 1955 as Cherepovets Steel Mill and remained under Soviet government ownership until the collapse of the Soviet Union in 1991. It was privatised in 1993, under the ownership and leadership of Alexei Mordashov, when it was registered as the open joint stock company 'Severstal'. The city of Cherepovets in north-west Russia, 600 km north of Moscow, remains the global headquarters of the company under its latest form as the Severstal Group.

Severstal's core businesses are steel and mining products, but its portfolio also includes unrelated assets such as a domestic airline and the Cherepovets local port. Since its privatisation on the 1990s it has become one of the most internationally minded Russian companies with extensive overseas exports, activity and ownership of foreign assets. The company is listed on the Russian (RTS) and London (LSE) stock markets. Together with its Russian steel and mining operations, Severstal owns production facilities in the USA, Italy, Africa and the CIS countries. The range of products includes raw materials, such as iron ore, and coking coal which are supplied for in-house production of flat, rolled and long steel products as well as downstream products of steel pipes, wire ropes and metalware. Recent business ventures include the acquisition of a goldmining business (Nordgold) in West Africa, and a joint venture with Arcelor producing galvanised steel products (Severgal).

At the start of the global economic recession in 2008 Severstal produced 19.2 million mt of steel, becoming the third-largest producer by volume in Russia and number 14 in the world, with revenues reaching $22.4bn ($5.4bn EBITDA). The group employed over 100,000 staff with the majority based in its Cherepovets steel mill. In 2012, Severstal dropped to number 23 in the list of global steel producers, with an output of 15.3 million mt of steel and revenue of $15.8bn ($3.6bn EBITDA) by the end of 2011.

Since 2002 Severstal has shifted its focus towards high-value-added steel products and in particular the lucrative but also extremely demanding automotive steel market. To do so the company embarked on a series of acquisitions outside Russia, starting with the acquisition of Rouge in the USA, a long-established but by then bankrupt supplier to the automotive giant Ford. Rouge was rebranded as Dearborn, now part of the Severstal North America subdivision. The majority of Severstal North America Inc.'s assets are the outcome of acquisitions, although the steel plant SeverCorr was an organic development built in 2007 at a cost of $880m. The US steel facilities are all strategically located near major customers producing highly efficient, low-cost, high-margin products.

Severstal has a very good relationship with the Russian government, access to capital for upgrading and extending its production facilities, and a very positive public image in its home town Cherepovets. A lot of investment was also put towards promoting the international image of the company with a strong emphasis on corporate governance and sustainability. In addition, overdue investment in modernising existing assets was underway with a $1.5bn injection of cash to upgrade production facilities in its US facilities. This was reinforced by a statement made by Severstal's CEO Alexei Mordashov: 'We are committed to operating in North America, which is one of the world's most important long-term markets for steel, and will retain our most efficient units with a view to making them even more flexible and efficient.'[6]

Severstal Group divisions

The aim of reducing costs and at the same time allowing for a simplified and more efficient corporate reporting system led, in April 2008, to a major corporate restructuring of Severstal. The Severstal Group became the management holding company, built around three divisions: Severstal Russian Steel, Severstal Resources (mining assets) and Severstal International. The three divisions comprise a vertically integrated business entity with a global reach of related diversified products. Further reshaping and fine-tuning of the corporate structure of the Severstal Group occurred in 2012, including divestments of loss-making assets and a stronger focus on emerging markets where demand for steel products is expected to grow.

Severstal's global strategy

Since 2004 the Severstal Group has embarked on a number of international and domestic acquisitions. Alexei Mordashov is a strong believer in the consolidation of the steel industry and his vision is to make the company a globally recognised player, in particular in the automotive market and other high-value niche markets. Mordashov has pursued a number of aggressive and high-risk offshore acquisitions in the USA and Europe, taking over offshore loss-making steel mills with the objective of turning them into profitable businesses.

Although the company has had good experience of acquisitions as a method of pursuing its strategic direction, there is still a lack of a shared common practice within the business for integrating newly acquired assets. There is strong dependency on the skills and knowledge of a very few senior managers who are able to negotiate and manage newly acquired businesses, but at a broader organisational level there is a lack of shared understanding and culture on how to incorporate such management competences. The strong leadership in certain business units has contributed to their efficient and rapid growth, whereas other units that lacked similar management competences are underperforming. Moreover, the three Severstal Group divisions do not necessarily share the same business culture. Coordination of global activities is heavily centralised, allowing for moderate flexibility, although this is an area that Mordashov aims to improve with continuous investment in his managers' competences. The company has been investing in management development training programmes to act as enablers for a common 'Severstal thinking'. For a number of years now a proportion of senior Severstal managers have embarked on further training and upskilling; most notable were the collaborations with Northumbria University and Cranfield University in the UK, and with the Skolkovo School of Management in Moscow, as well as internal Severstal training programmes.

Severstal has continued to invest in its corporate governance, corporate social responsibility, and sustainability as part of its strategy to raise global awareness of the Severstal brand and attract investment capital. In Russia, Severstal and its leader Alexei Mordashov are seen as the modern face of healthy and transparent Russian enterprises that could stand as equals with Western companies. The investment into corporate governance and the LSE listing in 2004 have contributed to raising multi-billion-dollar funds by Russian and foreign creditors to support the company's global expansion strategy.

The future

The steel industry is under pressure to act upon environmental concerns and to improve energy efficiency and cut harmful emissions. Even though the Kyoto Protocol is unlikely to have the desired impact in Russia and China, the imperatives of dealing with climate change are bound to impact on the industry.

By the end of 2012 steel demand forecasters were expecting an extremely volatile market, at least in the short term. The automotive steel market, the biggest market for steel producers in the USA and Europe, has been undergoing recovery after several tough years. In early 2013 all of the Big Three (GM, Ford and Chrysler) were reporting 15% gains in sales compared with a year earlier. The Chinese steel market is expected to continue to grow, albeit at a slightly slower pace than in earlier years. Since Severstal exports two-thirds of the production from its Cherepovets steel mill to China, this represents another threat, as competition in the Chinese market will intensify. Severstal's stakeholders were nervous when the Board decided to sell the two loss-making European subdivisions Lucchini (Italy) and Carrington Wire (UK) during 2012. Concerns were raised amongst the company's shareholders about a possible sale of some of its US assets, although the management issued reassurances that Severstal has a long-term commitment to its US operations which serve as a vehicle for its global strategy. The divestment and restructuring was a response to industry investors limiting the borrowing capability of Severstal given its financial situation in the previous years. Would Severstal ride out the current problems and emerge as a successful player in a tough industry?

A video clip showing how steel is made by Severstal can be found at: http://youtube/KH97w_awy.

Main sources
HSBC Steel Weekly, 31 August 2012.
Severstal, *Annual Reports* (2011, 2010, 2009, 2008).
World Steel Association (http://www.worldsteel.org/).

Notes and references
1. World Steel Association (http://www.worldsteel.org/).
2. $1 = £0.65 = €0.77.
3. Earnings Before Profit, Interest and Tax.
4. North American Free Trade Agreement (USA, Canada and Mexico).
5. http://knowledge.wharton.upenn.edu/india/article.cfm?articleid=4109
6. Severstal, *Annual Report*.

CASE STUDY

FeedHenry – innovating in the cloud

James Cunningham and Clare Gately

This case describes the innovation and strategic dilemmas facing FeedHenry in providing platform technology to enable enterprises worldwide to develop mobile apps using cloud technology. The case explores the decisions the management team must make, with limited resources, in balancing the type, source and focus of their innovatory activities.

●　　●　　●

The company name, FeedHenry (Figure 1), is a fusion of the term RSS Feed and Henry Shefflin, a well-known Irish sports star of Ireland's national game of hurling. Follow FeedHenry on Twitter: @feedhenry

Think about how you find information. The chances are you have downloaded applications (apps) that open up the world of knowledge on your phone. This new social media are an increasingly important element of how we are informed, inspired and entertained. For businesses, the development of an app has become a necessary part of the marketing mix; 91 of the top 100 US brands had mobile apps by 2012.[1] The global mobile apps market is expected to be worth €27 billion (£22.8bn; $34.6bn)[2] by 2015, with over 5 billion mobile devices such as smartphones, iPhones, laptops and tablets enabling downloads at a rate of 2–3 apps per month per person.[3,4] These apps are delivered to users through the internet, using cloud computing. Cloud technology enables users to store data and run applications on a virtual internet-based server. Simply by using a web browser on any mobile device, users can access the software tools they need whenever and wherever they choose. Global demand for cloud-based apps has led to a surge in enterprises undertaking mobile apps development, eager to win a share of this emerging market.

FeedHenry, an Irish technology enterprise, entered the mobile apps market in 2010. Its entry marked a significant repositioning of the enterprise from its original start-up focus. For the previous two years, FeedHenry developed technology for the web-in-media and telecommunications markets. By 2010, however, management faced a tough decision to rethink their markets and technology focus. Led by their new CEO, Cathal McGloin, FeedHenry moved from the

Figure 1 FeedHenry logo

Source: www.feedhenry.com

slowly declining, investment-scarce media and telecoms industry to the emerging mobile apps market. Their market repositioning caused a rethink of how they used their proprietary technology and compelled them to rethink their technology focus too. The management team decided to move from web technology for media and telecommunications to mobile apps technology. They began this process by developing apps as a professional service. This paved the way for their platform technology innovation, which enables enterprises to build their own apps. This reconfigured platform technology model utilised their core technology to best advantage, widening the potential application of their software to an array of industries.

Their software enables businesses of any size to build and deploy mobile apps across operating systems such as Android, iOS, BlackBerry, Windows and Nokia as well as the mobile web. Cathal McGloin best summed up the opportunity as: 'This type of technology will disrupt markets; it's like the Internet all over again. The market will be huge.'[5]

Building and financing the ecosystem

FeedHenry's core software was originally developed at the Telecommunications Software and Systems Group (TSSG, www.tssg.com), a campus company of the Waterford

This case was prepared by Dr James Cunningham, Senior Lecturer in Strategic Management at the J.E. Carines School of Business Management and is Director of the Whitaker Institute at the National University of Ireland, Galway, Ireland, and Dr Clare Gately, Lecturer in Strategy and Entrepreneurship at the Waterford Institute of Technology, Waterford, Ireland. It is intended as a basis for class discussion and not as an illustration of good or bad practice. © James Cunningham and Clare Gately 2013. Not to be reproduced or quoted without permission.

Institute of Technology (W.I.T.; www.wit.ie) in the south-east of Ireland. Barry Downes, Executive Director of Innovation and Commercialisation at TSSG, founded FeedHenry as a campus company in 2008. Downes used his experience with technology start-ups to source key personnel and forge initial contacts with media and telecommunications companies such as Eircom and O₂. They in turn became early adopters of FeedHenry's technology. Cathal McGloin joined FeedHenry as Chief Executive Officer (CEO) in May 2010 and brought with him significant international contacts and technology start-up experience. Later that year, McGloin championed the spinout of FeedHenry from TSSG, taking the intellectual property rights for the platform technology software.

Over the next two years, FeedHenry's management team were developed and now comprise six executives. Micheál Ó'Foghlú, a lecturer in the Department of Computing, Mathematics and Physics at W.I.T., is the Chief Technical Officer (CTO), and Elaine Fennelly is the Financial Controller, having previously worked in start-ups and with multinational enterprises (MNEs) located in Ireland. Joe Blake was hired in 2010 to develop sales. The company has international sales offices in Dublin, the UK, Belgium, and Boston, MA. Joe Drumgoole joined in 2011 to focus on product management, and Javier Perez joined in 2012 to focus on the US market. Cathal McGloin (CEO) operates from FeedHenry's Boston office, while Barry Downes sits on the Board of Directors of FeedHenry but is not involved in the day-to-day running of the enterprise.

The company's headquarters is located in ArcLabs, a research and innovation centre at W.I.T. (www.arclabs.ie). By 2012, FeedHenry employed 30 people at this facility, principally in research and development activities. The campus incubator setting provides a rich environment of knowledge and technical experts, which has proved very important to FeedHenry in filling core skills gaps. Occasionally, FeedHenry contracts specific projects to other SMEs located at ArcLabs. FeedHenry maintains strong links with W.I.T. through undergraduate internship programmes and the recruitment of technical graduates. Barry Downes[6] commented:

> 'If you have a full life-cycle research centre, you have your academic programme on one side, and on the other you have people who are very market-orientated who might have a project management background or who might have run a company before. One of the key things we do is bring all these people together.'

FeedHenry secured its first funding as angel investment of €500,000, which helped capitalise the company as part of the spinout from TSSG in November 2010. Three months later, FeedHenry secured a further €500,000 in a syndicated venture capital investment backed by one of Ireland's leading banks (Bank of Ireland Seed and Early Stage Equity Fund). According to Cathal McGloin:

> 'The initial seed investment enabled us to push the frontiers of our operations and increase our workforce. We have more than 2,000 customers now using the FeedHenry platform, up from 500 at the start of 2011.'[7]

Following its successful venture capital backing, FeedHenry also received substantial investment from strategic partners.[8] As a high potential start-up, the company is supported by Ireland's indigenous enterprise development agency, Enterprise Ireland, in making the transition from research to the international marketplace. W.I.T. has a minority shareholding in FeedHenry.

FeedHenry's business model

Since its inception, FeedHenry's business model has evolved to match the enterprise's changing technology focus. FeedHenry offers a 'platform as a service' solution to which customers subscribe in order to build and manage apps. Subscribers can deploy these apps internally to staff or to clients and customers across a range of operating systems. FeedHenry generates revenue using a subscription-based business model. Mobile apps developers subscribe for a licence, for a negotiated timeframe, to use FeedHenry's secure platform technology.

In December 2011, 20% of FeedHenry's revenue was from licence revenue; by the end of the first quarter of 2012, 43% of revenue was licence revenue. The new platform technology model encourages longer buy-in from companies for a reduced annual licence fee. This helps build long-term relationships and locks in a consistent revenue stream. A longer-term licence agreement also drives down the cost per hit for signed-up app developers.

Life cycle of FeedHenry

FeedHenry has undergone two development phases and transitions to date. The first phase involved researching, defining and communicating the business problems it could solve. Management undertook a SWOT analysis to understand what FeedHenry was good at in the mobile apps environment. They then generated hypotheses about the type of apps and service required by potential clients and undertook early test marketing to validate these hypotheses and assumptions. This process convinced them of the high usability and market potential of their platform technology. Additionally, they realised the value in offering businesses and developers a cloud platform that would allow them to build apps that can securely integrate with back-end business systems. FeedHenry's cloud platform offers mobile application functionality which allows businesses to manage their apps and produce apps reports on consumer downloads. The second phase involved validating the concept and scaling the product to market. The ambition of FeedHenry, now in its third phase of development, is to lead and compete in both the apps and cloud industries, based on the marketing and technology strategy of providing 'simple, secure and scaleable' platform technology.

So far, this strategy has won clients and customers for three key reasons. Firstly, it drives down the development cost for enterprises of each app developed. The underlying technology is an open-source platform technology that enables users to develop, deploy and manage mobile apps solutions across operating systems using standard web technologies. FeedHenry's unique offering reduces the development lead time and expense of mobile apps development for enterprises. Secondly, FeedHenry trains and enables other companies to build apps using its simple-to-use platform. Apps can be developed using standard web technologies and languages, thereby decreasing the technical expertise and skills required.[9] Thirdly, FeedHenry provides secure features, using its private cloud technology, which can be managed and integrated across company activities such as its existing IT and communications systems. Crucially, data and information developed using FeedHenry's platform technology use its stable private cloud services to manage and store information securely (see Figure 2).

The end-to-end security features of FeedHenry's technology are critical for the enterprise market they serve, helping allay fears over confidentiality and data protection. This point was noted by Nichols of *imedia* magazine[10] in 2011:

'To me the significance of this company and what they are doing lies in the ability to bring simpler and faster app development to the most security-conscious industries in the world.'

Competition and competitive advantage

Competition in the mobile apps market is intensifying, with no clear market leader emerging. Some cross-platform competitors such as Appcelerator Inc. and PhoneGap are gaining market share in the end-user apps development market. Both companies concentrate mainly on consumer apps development rather than on the corporate market, although FeedHenry believes this may change as the growth in enterprise apps accelerates and attracts more competition. FeedHenry, on the other hand, searches for niches and market segments further up the value chain where it can compete using its existing technology, communication, distribution and sales channels. Core products are aimed at chief information officers (CIOs) or chief technical officers (CTOs) as key buyers of mobile systems. This approach allows FeedHenry to promote its technology, develop key relationships and make sales by convincing key corporate decision-makers.

FeedHenry's competitive advantage lies in the cloud-based mobile application platform it has developed, which makes it possible for enterprises and developers to build, integrate, manage and deploy their apps across platforms. This technology means that users can develop and run apps from any mobile device, with the assurance that their work is safe and secure on FeedHenry's private cloud.

Figure 2 FeedHenry's platform technology

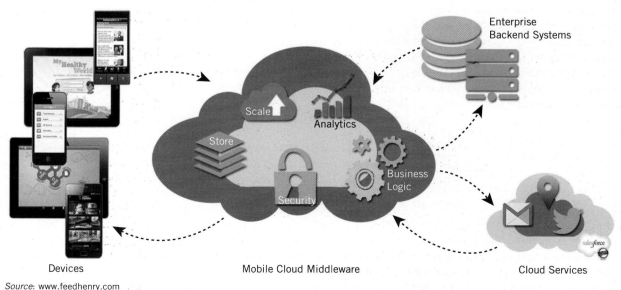

Devices   Mobile Cloud Middleware   Cloud Services

Source: www.feedhenry.com

FeedHenry's value proposition emphasises the secure and stable nature of its mobile platform technology, a key concern of cloud technology adopters. End-users pass through four security 'gates' (authentication, access control, auditing and logging/confidentiality) before gaining access to FeedHenry's private cloud. At the back-end, cloud service providers and enterprise IT systems pass through a similarly rigorous security check process. In 2012, the International Association for the Wireless Telecommunications Industry (CTIA), an international representative organisation, recognised FeedHenry's global appeal, awarding it first place in its category at the global CTIA emerging technology awards.[11]

Building credibility

From the start, FeedHenry's management were acutely aware that building early credibility and reputation in the enterprise market is very important, especially for a small start-up technology business. In building credibility they have adopted a dual approach. Firstly, they form strategic partnerships with international telecommunications organisations. The signing of a global deal with Telefónica Digital in January 2012 represented a major milestone. Telefónica offers FeedHenry's mobile app solution to its business clients as a value-added service, whereby client companies can build mobile apps using a standard web code such as HTML and Javascript. According to Matthew Key, Chairman and CEO of Telefónica Digital:[12] 'This partnership will be welcome news for any organisation that recognises the power of mobile apps and how they can drive increased revenue, boost employee productivity and enhance the overall customer experience.'

Secondly, by simultaneously developing partnerships with technology leaders such as Hewlett Packard, VMWare, EMC, Appfog, CloudFoundry and Tier 3, the company positions itself as a key technology innovator and adds an important channel to its go-to-market strategy.

In addition to its partnership strategy, FeedHenry has developed a direct market channel with business clients such as Aer Lingus, Glanbia, Diageo and Riverdance. The management of client relationships, however complex and time-consuming, is vital to its customer philosophy of solving customers' problems quickly and empowering them through dedicated training and continuous online and offline support.

FeedHenry's entrepreneurial culture – from college to corporate

As a campus spinout, the early organisational development of FeedHenry involved a transition 'from college to corporate'. This necessitated a cultural and mindset shift by the original founders and early employees towards more formal processes with corporate standards, rules and policies. Striking the right balance between an entrepreneurial culture and formal processes has fostered a vibrant yet efficient atmosphere at FeedHenry's headquarters at ArcLabs in Waterford, Ireland. Most of the technical employees are in their early twenties, predominantly sourced as graduates from W.I.T.'s computing degree courses. Employees are highly committed, hard-working and engaged. All full-time, permanent employees are offered share options in FeedHenry. Elaine Fennelly, the Financial Controller, tells of employees who regard their work at FeedHenry as a hobby as well as a job. All employees, regardless of position, are encouraged to work on their own ideas for the advancement of FeedHenry. The entrepreneurial organisation has a low hierarchy structure, with project managers leading cross-functional, skills-based teams on a project-by-project basis. Offices are bright and light-filled with an open-plan, modular layout. Round tables are set out to encourage small-group interaction and discussion. Elaine explains that one of the challenges facing FeedHenry is to sustain a nimble, 'fresh' organisation as it grows. FeedHenry will soon outgrow its campus incubation space and will need to find new premises while maintaining its vibrant work environment so carefully formed at ArcLabs. Furthermore, FeedHenry faces a challenge of recruiting an age/gender mix of talent that fits its entrepreneurial culture and can grow into key positions as the business grows.

Innovation strategy

As part of its repositioning in 2010, FeedHenry changed its innovation strategy towards the development and provision of platform technology to enable the design, development and management of apps by other firms. Management believe that this strategy best fits with the capabilities available to the firm and situates FeedHenry as a technology leader in this space. According to Cathal McGloin, the mobile apps industry is still evolving and FeedHenry's business and innovation strategy is evolving too. He believes FeedHenry needs to remain very fluid and not too planning orientated, given the dynamic, uncertain nature of the mobile apps environment.

In thinking about the next few years, management have a clear sense of direction about where FeedHenry is going. The challenge is to make the right calls on technology and market opportunities – sales and fit. There are hard decisions ahead for FeedHenry in terms of choosing the right types of platform and apps capability. Elaine Fennelly describes the difficulty in marrying what FeedHenry's technical experts want to do, in creating new or advanced technologies, with 'getting cash out' in building revenues from existing technologies. For a small company with limited resources, there is an opportunity cost for any option chosen. The fear among FeedHenry's management is that they will miss out on apps or misjudge the dynamics in consumer markets. There is also an element of firefighting in trying to keep up with demand while simultaneously forging ahead with the development of new technologies and remaining innovative with limited resources.

Their approach to date is to explore markets to 'find where the sweet spot is' in terms of generating revenues in the short term and to build market position over the medium term. Then, they build a prototype of the new app in-house, work hard with early adaptors in refining the prototype and do early test marketing to establish interest and demand. Thereafter they hope that the timing is right and consumers and clients realise a need for the technology. Further, Cathal McGloin carefully studies technology and market trends and spends a substantial amount of his time networking with peers and other industry players to gauge changes in mobile technologies and markets. Cathal describes this as a technology push model while keeping an eye on market trends in technology and apps evolution. His comment that 'the market is not divorced from technology' points to his philosophy in the development and commercialisation of new products. He is clear that with a disruptive innovation, the scale of which is unknown, the technology needs to be created and developed in-house. Once the technology has been developed, FeedHenry takes on a dual role as an educator and a promoter of the new technology to clients and consumers.

Cathal is convinced that as a disruptive innovator, FeedHenry is in a strong position to set industry standards and lead the development of platform technology in the mobile apps sector: 'By being early with leading technology we can shape the mobile applications platform and dictate to industry in terms of how it pans out.'[13]

Notes and references
1. *Forbes* online magazine, January 2012.
2. €1 = £0.85 = $1.31.
3. http://ec.europa.eu
4. http://www.research2guidance.com
5. For an overview of FeedHenry's mobile enterprise application platform, go to http://vimeo.com/34086215
6. *The Irish Times*, 27 June 2008.
7. *The Sunday Business Post*, 29 July 2012, p. M12.
8. Ibid.
9. For an overview of app development on FeedHenry's platform, go to http://vimeo.com/34513716
10. Nichols, J. *imedia*, 1 June 2011.
11. *The Sunday Business Post*, 29 July 2012, p. M12.
12. Telefónica (2012) 'Telefónica Partners with FeedHenry to support Business App Strategies', press release, 11 January 2012, available at: http://pressoffice.telefónica.com (accessed 12 January 2012).
13. This and all other quotes not otherwise attributed are from interviews with the case authors.

CASE STUDY

Flight Centre Limited

Kenneth Wiltshire

Flight Centre Limited is one of the world's largest travel agency groups, with a rapidly expanding network that extends throughout Australia, New Zealand, the USA, Canada, the United Kingdom, South Africa, Hong Kong, India, China, Singapore and the United Arab Emirates. This is a case of a successful entrepreneurial venture established despite considerable industry and government obstacles, operating in a highly competitive environment requiring constant innovation, with a staff- and client-focused global business model. However, it faces significant challenges in an intensely competitive industry, including the growing capacity for clients to make their own travel arrangements online, and questions arise as to whether Flight Centre can continue to operate with one business model for all regions and cultures.

● ● ●

It all began when a few young Australians living in the UK got the inspiration in 1973 to begin a travel company called 'Top Deck Tours' using old refitted London double-decker buses to take tour groups around Europe. Despite harrowing experiences with bus breakdowns, snarling officialdom in many countries, shortage of working capital, and backbreaking hours for the founders/drivers/operators, the tours proved very popular and the number of buses and tours grew. Along this journey the entrepreneurs, who had no experience in the industry, had to engage in improvisation, rule bending, fudging, and originality in marketing with no formal strategy.[1] But the lessons learnt stood them in good stead when they decided to explore the gap they perceived in discounted air travel and founded Flight Centre in 1981.

This turned out to be a formidable challenge. The practice of flight discounting was virtually unknown in the travel industry in Australia, which was characterised by heavy government regulation of the airlines which had long-established relations with existing travel agents. The industry was immediately hostile to these new upstarts, and they had to turn first to lesser-known airlines to obtain discount business, and also had to engage in intense lobbying of government to change the legislation to allow their kind of operation to be licensed.

The first retail shop was established in Sydney in 1981 and made a profit of A$93,000 (£63,911; $97,321; €75,833)[2] in its first year from a turnover of A$2.5m (£1.72m; $2.62m; €2.04m). By 2012 Flight Centre

Source: Julian Eales/Alamy

Limited (FCL) operated almost 2,500 shops in 11 countries, earning a profit of A$294m from a turnover of over A$13bn, with 34 different brands.

Although there were five key founders, the focus inevitably falls on Graham 'Skroo' Turner who has been CEO or Executive Chairman for all of the company's history. He began his working life as a vet in Australia and the UK. Turner has been described as a maverick, a larrikin, a plain speaker and an entrepreneur. A softly spoken, bearded, physical fitness fanatic (cycling 30 kilometres before breakfast most days), his business instincts are shaped by a keen understanding of human nature, and by constant reading of management and leadership literature. He espouses his philosophy regularly within the organisation, especially through an annual published collection of wisdom, seminal leadership and management articles, sayings, poetry, proverbs, anecdotes, and a raft of business principles practices and goals for all aspects of the business.

His strategies are based on conceptual and philosophical underpinnings which he constantly updates in a staff manual, combined with application of common sense to emerging challenges. An innovator himself by instinct and nature, he is prepared to admit to mistakes, and he operates by placing trust in the leaders within the organisation, decentralising much decision making to country and sectional managers, including decisions on the choice of new markets to be explored, experimentation with business systems, and arranging local partnerships with suppliers and contractors of travel packages. However, he closely monitors performance across the company and travels around the world, stepping in when necessary. This has occurred on a few occasions when senior managers have made wrong calls. Described often in the media as a charismatic leader, he is now a legend in all parts of the travel industry. Despite the publicity that follows his success, Turner endeavours to maintain a low profile, seldom venturing into public issues or politics, although he is an environmentalist with concerns about population growth. The company makes no political donations.

The foundation of Flight Centre's business strategy is very clear and revolves around its people. In essence, the message is 'look after your people and they in turn will look after your clients'. Structure and motivation are key, all based on the belief that people like to work in teams. Flight Centre's operational structure was modelled on anthropological principles inspired by Nicholson's work on hunter-gatherers, and so there is the family, the village, and the tribe.[3] The family is a team usually consisting of 3–7 people; the village is a group of 3–7 geographic families or teams who support each other; the tribe is a maximum of around 25 groups of villages with a single tribal identity that come together for celebration and interaction. Beyond this, the tribes come together to form a nation.[4]

Innovation and experimentation are encouraged and staff suggestions readily analysed and many acted upon. An egalitarian culture prevails, with very few special perks for senior executives, not even car parking, and all Flight Centre offices are open-plan – Turner himself has no executive assistant or personal office. Incentives figure very largely in staff motivation; remuneration is by a basic salary plus a commission, which can be very rewarding, and this is complemented by share ownership and debenture schemes. The total package can be lucrative, having produced a number of employee millionaires in a relatively short space of time. There is a highly sought-after prize and a recognition–reward programme for staff performance and improvement, which is celebrated at gala conferences held around the globe. Employees have access to in-house health and fitness and financial well-being services. Staff are carefully recruited but more for their personal qualities than for any deep knowledge of the travel industry. The incentive model ensures that those who are not performing move on fairly quickly. None of the staff at Flight Centre belongs to a trade union – according to Turner, if employees desire to join a union it is an indication that you are not looking after them.

When the company decided to float in 1995, the decision was largely based on a desire to facilitate greater staff ownership in the organisation to enhance motivation, loyalty and identification. Of course, the additional funds were welcome, as the existing owners (the original founders) could not have personally financed the desired expansion of the business and did not want to borrow. Some suggested the need to establish a potential personal exit path for the owners to leave the company, which a float would facilitate. Indeed, the company has always eschewed borrowing, has had relatively little debt during its existence, and has a firm policy of keeping healthy cash reserves. This has often meant that the directors have placed themselves in some tight personal financial situations to fund expansion or acquisitions along the way. A failed share buyback scheme was attempted in 2005, but only because the directors felt that the share price had fallen well below the true value of the company as a result of external conditions. Flight Centre has always operated with a small Board of 4–5 people comprising the original founders for most of the company's history.

Another key element of the strategy is the price guarantee. The advertising slogan originally said 'Lowest Air Fares Guaranteed' because the company's policy is to beat any other lower published price for a fare. However, this slogan ran into objections from regulators, and today the brand carries the slogan 'Lowest Airfares Guarantee'. This promise has caused plenty of headaches and some cost (A$10m in 2011 – the total cost of matching lower fares submitted by clients). It is made more precarious because of the airlines that now offer direct deals to the public themselves. However, Flight Centre has stuck religiously with this pledge and it is now a firmly entrenched part of the brand and the culture.

The fundamentals of Flight Centre's strategy were and always have been centred on organic growth and in this it has been highly successful. Some buyouts have occurred, and also slight diversification (e.g. hire of bicycles), but the company is firmly grounded in the travel business and its variations. Expansion into corporate and student travel as well as more upmarket luxury products have all been positive. Behind the retail presence is an 'engine room' of wholesale activity as deals are negotiated with a plethora of suppliers. Most travel agents operate their own wholesale sections which arrange deals and contracts with flight accommodation and ground travel package operators, and then make these deals available to their own retail agents. In an effort to achieve cost efficiencies through internal competition, Flight Centre introduced a purchaser–provider approach whereby its retail stores could opt not to choose to buy from the company's own suppliers if they can do better elsewhere – a cost centre concept which was fiercely resisted at first and caused some morale problems, but has gained acceptance and introduces healthy intra-company competition. However, more in-house transactions are now happening than ever before.

Growth takes place within a global business model (see below) which remains essentially the same in all countries where Flight Centre operates, with some variations to suit local circumstances. Challenges arise when trying to introduce FCL's egalitarian management practices in regions such as the Middle East whose cultures are hierarchical in nature. Also, business operations are not seamlessly global, since deals and contracts in each country have to be with that country's government, airlines and tour operators, and this is an area which the company is trying to address.

The FCL global 'replicable small business model' contains six elements:[5]

1 Ongoing growth (organic, acquisitions, startup) at every level of the business.
2 A flat team-based and decentralised decision-making structure and local ownership by individuals with clear roles and responsibilities.
3 Individual rewards/incentives which are outcome-based, fully relevant and consistently measured by accurate key performance indicators.
4 Teams decentralised, multi-skilled if possible, all members with directorships (alternated).
5 The team leader working in the team with the same technical job as the rest of the team.
6 All business and support teams operating under the 'one best way' brand guide, both business systems and operating systems (the Systems Manual). In FCL we have one set of values, one culture and one set of philosophies.

The business model is followed by a list of rules for running a project, which are process orientated. Perhaps the most interesting one is: 'Perfection is banned – near enough is good enough. We want action and progress – not perfection.'

The company has faced some major challenges, many of which were very threatening to the travel business, including wars, natural disasters, global health epidemics and the global financial crisis. The sudden collapse and liquidation of Australia's Ansett Airlines caught the company off-guard because of the loss of overrides and super-overrides and credit card reversals. The familiar closures of London Heathrow Airport owing to its inability to cope with snow and bad weather, with days of flight cancellations, is an interesting case in point in which Flight Centre's own emergency helpline gave its customers up-to-the-minute information and the certainty that someone was looking after them, by comparison with the lacklustre performance of the airlines and the airport on this score. Customer loyalty was further entrenched. Indeed, the company has always been prepared to sustain extra costs to retain customer loyalty and business. Maintaining a healthy level of cash reserves has been an important element of risk management in a precarious industry.

Throughout the whole of its history, Flight Centre has had to deal with a great deal of inflexibility and intransigence from government officialdom. In the beginning, this applied particularly to the gaining of licences to operate in almost all countries. Innovative ways were found around this, including using less popular airlines, operating under licences of associates, and even occasionally beginning operations before licences were obtained and adopting a crash-through approach which involved severe risk-taking. This has usually been successful in the end, although initial attempts to operate in Vietnam were given up at considerable cost in the light of bureaucratic inertia. The company has baulked at bribery and corruption proposals from officials in some countries. In the latest twist in 2012 the company is being investigated by Australia's Competition Regulator for allegedly trying to collude with airlines because of an attempt it made to have an airline reveal a cheap air fare it was offering directly to the public, which was lower than Flight Centre had been offering for the same fare. The case hinged on the question of whether travel agents are an extension of an airline or competitors for airlines. It will have significant repercussions for accommodation and ground tour operators as well.

Perhaps the biggest competitive challenge has come from the growth of people making direct internet bookings with airlines and accommodation venues. The Flight Centre strategy to confront this is the offering of a combined online and personal booking blended facility, in which online customers get the added advantage of personal attention and follow-up, along with the price guarantee, the emergency helpline, and faster refunds of cancelled bookings. Clients will book online through Flight Centre, be given the name of their consultant, look at the fare, book it, and then hand it over to the consultant who holds it for 24 hours and personally follows it up. This system was close to implementation in 2012.

In the light of the increasingly competitive environment, including the threat posed by the client's own online bookings, Flight Centre formalised a Strategic Long Term Planning system (2–5 years). There is a heavy emphasis on leadership development through training and recruitment, development of its own product, refining the 'one best way' of operation, improving systems for distributing product, and significant attention to ICT and its potential. The brand strategy is focused very much on consolidation, given that out of the 34 brands less than half of all business is conducted under the Flight Centre brand itself. Another goal is to create a smoother relationship between transactional, virtual and real presence to ensure smoother integration and consistency in the emerging different modalities of travel bookings in different global markets. (There are countries where Flight Centre operates with no physical presence.)

Currently, 'Skroo' Turner identifies one big strategic challenge for the company as achieving greater productivity per employee. A number of approaches are being taken in this regard, including revision of support to the shop front, clever use of ICT and an improved database, and the introduction of more realistic performance measurement. Another is the creation of more hyper-stores in some markets where various teams performing in different roles for the company will be accommodated together in the one location on different floors. Oxford Street in London has been a prototype. This will be a seven-days-a-week operation. The village ladder will be in the one place. There is also

a vertical integration strategy to overcome the problem that can occur when the purchaser–provider principle does not fit. One part of the company cannot choose whether to purchase from another part because the margins are not suitable or the product is unavailable elsewhere. The goal here is better and faster service to the customer.

The pre-tax profit for the 2012 financial year was a record A$290.4 million, with strong performance in corporate and leisure sales despite the European debt crisis and other external shocks.[6] The company's sights are set for an overall organic growth rate of 9% a year, and Flight Centre continues to win a succession of travel awards in all categories of its operations.

Notes and references
1. James Bill (1999) *Top Deck Daze*, Halbon, NSW: Avalon.
2. A$1 = £0.68 = $1.05 = €0.80.
3. Nigel Nicholson (2000) *Executive Instinct*, New York: Crown; and Nigel Nicholson (1998) 'How hard wired is human behavior?', *Harvard Business Review*, July–August.
4. Mandy Johnson (2005) *Family Village Tribe: The Story of Flight Centre Limited*. Sydney: Random House.
5. Graham 'Skroo' Turner (2011) *Business Directory and Articles, Edition No. 2*. Brisbane: Flight Centre Ltd.
6. *Australian Financial Review*, Friday 6 July 2012.

CASE STUDY

Strategic leadership and innovation at Apple, Inc.

Loizos Heracleous and Angeliki Papachroni

This case looks at the extraordinary success of Apple as an innovative company under the leadership of Steve Jobs. In August 2011 Jobs resigned as CEO due to ill health (and sadly died soon after) – he was succeeded by Tim Cook. Could the new CEO manage the transition to new leadership from Jobs' unique approach and maintain Apple's record of achievement in an increasingly competitive marketplace?

●　●　●

Back in 1997, when Steve Jobs returned to the company he founded, few would have thought that the failing, niche Apple Computers would one day be recognised as one of the most innovative companies in the world, transcending the barriers of the computer industry to compete in the consumer electronics, telecommunications and music industries. Since Jobs' return Apple has increased from a $2 billion (£1.32bn; €1.56bn)[1] company in 1997 to a nearly $472 billion (£312.2bn; €368.4bn) company in January 2013, having briefly overtaken Exxon Mobil to become the world's most valuable company by market capitalisation in August 2011. Apple was recognised as the most innovative company in the world by *Business Week* for seven years in a row (2005–11) and led *Fortune's* world's most admired companies for five consecutive years (2008–12). Building on innovative products that have redefined their markets, such as the iPod, the iPhone and the iPad, a consumer base as loyal as a fan club, and a business model characterised by integration and synergies that no competitor could easily imitate, Apple continued its extraordinary performance, reporting $156.5bn in revenues and $41.7bn net income in 2012.

Source: Tony Avelar

Jobs' turnaround and rebuilding an innovative organisation

Things have not always been that rosy for the company once known as the underdog of the computer industry. During the time when Steve Jobs was away from the organisation (1985–97) Apple progressively degenerated to the point of struggling for survival. Apple charged premium prices and its computers were based on a closed proprietary operating system that was not made available for cloning by other computer makers, at a time when less costly IBM-compatible PCs gained mass appeal. Its cost base was too high compared to its major competitors. This combination of factors led to shrinking market share and low profitability. Apple lost momentum in the PC industry, despite the efforts of three different CEOs to reverse the decline. Jobs took on the role of Interim CEO in 1997 and then became CEO during 2000. His return to Apple marked the beginning of a new era for the company. He worked for a salary of $1 per year (and plenty of stock options) for 30 months, leading Apple's successful turnaround.

His priority was to revitalise Apple's innovation capability. 'Apple had forgotten who Apple was',[2] as he noted in an interview, stressing that it was time for Apple to return to its core values and build on them. According to a former Apple executive who participated in Jobs' first meeting with the top brass on his return to Apple, Jobs went in with shorts, trainers and a few days' beard, sat on a swivel chair, spun slowly, and asked them what was wrong with Apple. Jobs then exclaimed that it was the products, and that there was no sex in them any more.[3] Upon taking charge, Jobs axed 70% of new products in development, kept 30% that he believed were 'gems', and added some new projects that he believed could offer breakthrough potential. He also revamped the marketing message to take advantage of the maverick, creative Apple brand, and employed stock-based incentives to retain talent.[4]

Upholding the value of user-friendliness, Steve Jobs led the launch of the first iMac in 1998, his first project after his return to the company. The iMac, or 'the computer for the rest of us' (its slogan when it was launched), revolutionised desktop computing by combining technological advancements and unique design. Following the iMac's success, the iBook was launched in 1999. In parallel, Jobs proceeded to simplify Apple's product mix in terms of four lines of desktop and portable computers designed for both the professional and consumer markets.

Whereas most of Apple's innovations led to even more closed Apple archipelagoes[5] (software and hardware integration), at the same time Jobs decided to loosen control in other areas, for example the use of standard interfaces such as the USB port. In the years to follow, a variety of innovative proprietary applications, developed in-house, supported the Apple Macintosh product lines. These include programs such as Apple's own web browser, Safari, developed in 2003, as well as those in the iLife package (iDVD, iMovie, iPhoto) that offered editing and creative opportunities to users.

Growing the Apple ecosystem: breakthrough innovation in the consumer electronics and entertainment industries

In 2001 Apple introduced its first iPod, launching a new era for the company as it entered the consumer electronics industry. Capitalising on the emerging trend of MP3 music, and despite being a relatively late entrant in this market (rival systems like Winamp and MPMan were released in 1997 and 1998 respectively), Apple introduced a break-through product in terms of design and user-friendliness that soon became synonymous with the MP3 music player category. A year later, in 2002, Apple released iPods with a larger memory that were compatible with Windows, a move that further pushed iPod sales. By the end of 2003 more than one million iPods were sold, marking the first substantial stream of revenues apart from the Macintosh. Since then the iPod product range has been renewed every 3 to 5 months, and the company announced in 2007 that it had sold the 100 millionth iPod, making the device the fastest-selling music player in history.

One of the most important innovations for Apple has been the launch of the iTunes Music store in 2003, a revolutionary service through which consumers could access and purchase online music for only $0.99 per song. The iTunes Music Store was compatible with all iPods (running both on Macs as well as on Windows-based computers) and served as Apple's Trojan horse to what Jobs had envisioned as the digital hub where digital content and Apple devices would be seamlessly interconnected. The downloaded songs had royalty protection and could only be played by iPods, bringing the interoperability between Apple's hardware, software and content to a new level and creating higher barriers to entry into this ecosystem (as well as exit from it). iPods had the capacity to display videos and through them Apple became a significant distributor of movies and TV shows.

Apple's next groundbreaking innovation was the iPhone, a device combining a phone, a music player and a personal computer. The iPhone redefined the mobile phone industry in the same way that iPod and iTunes revolutionised the music industry. Launched in 2007, six years after Palm's first smartphone in the USA, Apple's iPhone nevertheless redefined the mobile phone industry. In 2008 Apple launched the App Store, the only authorised service for loading programs onto the iPhone. The App Store was based on the same principle of seamless integration between hardware and software, giving Apple 30% of third-party developers' revenues along the way.

The Apple ecosystem was further reinforced in 2010 with the introduction of the iPad, a tablet computer that galvanised what had, for 10 years, been a commercially failure-ridden product category. Consumers could play games, read books, load all sorts of applications, and access the Internet through their iPad. By September 2012, Apple's iPad revenues had reached a total value of $58bn since its introduction, including $32bn over that financial year.

In October 2011, Apple introduced iCloud, a cloud service for storing music, photos, applications, calendars and documents that can be wirelessly transferred to multiple iOS devices, Macs and Windows-based computers. iCloud came with 5 GB of free space, while additional space could be purchased from Apple. By providing a means of integrating the use of multiple Apple devices, iCloud was a significant move towards a mobile Apple ecosystem.

Playing with different rules

Deep collaboration

Long before it was voted the world's most innovative company, Apple had placed its trademark on a long list of technological breakthroughs including the mouse, the graphical user interface, colour graphics, built-in sound, networking and wireless LAN, FireWire and many more. Some of these, such as the graphical user interface, were seen by Jobs on visits to research facilities such as Xerox's Palo Alto Research Center, and were adapted for broader use in Apple's offerings. Apple's approach over the years had been to make the use of a personal computer as easy and intuitive as possible through developing a highly responsive operating system, establishing standard specifications to which all applications' software packages were expected to conform, strict control of outside developers, and delivering computers with high performance.[6]

Apple practices what employees call 'deep collaboration', 'cross-pollination' or 'concurrent engineering'. This refers to products developed not in discrete stages but by 'all departments at once – design, hardware, software – in endless rounds of interdisciplinary design reviews'.[7] When asked about innovation at Apple, Jobs noted that the system for innovation is that there is no system:

'The reason a lot of us are at Apple is to make the best computers in the world and make the best software in the world. We know that we've got some stuff that [is] the best right now. But it can be so much better. . . . That's what's driving us . . . And we'll sleep well when we do that.'[8]

Sticking with a proprietary ecosystem

Apple's innovations have redefined existing product categories such as music players and mobile phones, and helped the company successfully enter hotly contested new markets such as the entertainment industry. Key to these achievements has been the focus on design, the consumer experience, and the seamless integration of hardware and software and content. The tight integration of its own operating system, hardware and applications has been a strategy followed diligently by Apple. As Steve Jobs says:

'One of our biggest insights [years ago] was that we didn't want to get into any business we didn't own or control the primary technology, because you'll get your head handed to you. We realised that for almost all future consumer electronics, the primary technology was going to be software. And we were pretty good at software.'[9]

Despite the obvious advantages of such an approach, there are also some potential risks when competing with a proprietary system in a networked, interoperable technology world. This is one reason why Apple's computers have remained a niche product in the personal computer market in terms of market share. Add to this the inevitable product failures (and Apple has had its fair share of these), and the potential downside of closed systems becomes apparent.

Apple is nearly unique among contemporary technology companies in doing all of its own design in-house, at its Cupertino campus.[10] Other companies have outsourced most or all of their product design function, relying on outsourced design manufacturers (ODMs) to develop the products that with minor adaptations will fit into their product lines. Apple, however, believes that having all the experts in one place – the mechanical, electrical, software and industrial engineers, as well as the product designers – leads to a more holistic perspective on product development; and that a critical mass of talent makes existing products better and opens the door to entirely new products. According to Jobs:

'You can't do what you can do at Apple anywhere else. The engineering is long gone in the PC companies. In the consumer electronics companies they don't understand the software parts of it. There's no other company that could make a MacBook Air and the reason is that not only do we control the hardware, but we control the operating system. And it is the intimate interaction between the operating system and the hardware that allows us to do that. There is no intimate interaction between Windows and a Dell computer.'[11]

Over the years, there have been some notable exceptions to this proprietary approach. In order to reach a broader consumer base, in late 2003 Apple offered a Windows-compatible version of iTunes, not only allowing Windows users to use the iPod but more importantly familiarising them with Apple products. Another milestone came with the company's switch from PowerPC processors made by IBM to Intel chips, a decision announced in mid-2005. This decision allowed Macs to run Windows software, implied lower switching costs for new Mac consumers and also allowed software developers to adapt their programs for Apple more easily. A previous alliance with Microsoft occurred in 1997 when Microsoft agreed to invest $150 million in Apple, reaffirming its commitment to develop core products such as Microsoft Office for the Mac.

Apple has also developed a series of strategic alliances in the course of its efforts to become the centre of the digital hub, where digital content would be easily created and transferred to any Apple device. Development of the iPod, iTunes and iPhone has necessitated this collaborative approach, since entry in the entertainment and consumer electronics markets would not have been as successful without some key strategic partners (e.g. the big record labels such as EMI, Sony BMG, Universal and Warner Brothers for iTunes, or YouTube for the iPhone). At the same time Apple has proceeded with a number of acquisitions of relatively small, innovative firms in fields such as video creation and microprocessor production intended to strengthen its own technological core competences.

Apple's corporate culture

Along with being recognised as one of the most innovative companies in the world, Apple has also gained a reputation of being among the most secretive as well. A T-shirt for sale at the company shop said: 'I visited the Apple campus. But that's all I'm allowed to say.' Few people know what happens behind closed doors, and Apple employees are bound by strict confidentiality agreements. New recruits not only were warned that the penalty for revealing Apple secrets would be swift termination of employment, but also were hired in so-called dummy positions, roles that remained unspecified until the hiring was complete. Before discussing a topic at a meeting, all members would need to verify that they were 'disclosed' on it, meaning they had been granted the permission to discuss it. The whole organisation was thus composed of smaller pieces of a bigger puzzle, which was in turn only known to the highest levels.[12]

In addition to secrecy and a start-up mentality, Apple's culture focused on intense work, creativity and perfectionism, combined with a rebel spirit. For many years, Jobs stimulated thinking 'out of the box' and encouraged employees to experiment and share with others 'the coolest new thing' they had thought of. It may not be accidental that Apple's emblem of corporate culture is a pirate flag with an Apple rainbow-coloured eye patch, designed after a famous Jobs quote: 'It's better to be a pirate than join the navy.' This flag was hanging over the Macintosh building as Apple's team were working on the first iMac, to act as a reminder of their mission.[13]

Along with the rebel spirit, Apple had a tradition of long working hours and relentless pursuit of perfection. Each manufacturing and software detail is worked and reworked until a product is considered perfect, aiming for seamless integration of software and hardware. Further, Apple's employees are not paid astronomically. They are not pampered, nor do they enjoy unique privileges beyond what most large companies offered. They are talented people with passion for excellence, proud to be part of the Apple community. This pride stems from a corporate culture that fosters innovation and a sense of Apple's superiority against competitors, as a company that can shape the future of technology. Apple recruits talent of the highest calibre, and Jobs often approached and recruited people known as the best in their fields. Specialisation and clear specification

of responsibilities at Apple is a way of employing the best people for particular roles, reflecting Jobs' aversion towards a general management approach.[14]

For Apple employees the culture has been experienced by employees as both daunting and fascinating: 'If you're a die-hard Apple geek, it's magical. It's also a really tough place to work.'[15] Contrary to Google's infamous relaxed atmosphere, Apple is known for being tough and perfectionist. If any product release does not meet expectations, Apple can be a 'brutal and unforgiving place, where accountability is strictly enforced'.[16]

Jobs' passionate but also combustive management style is legendary; he has been known to reduce employees to tears, or publicly fire them in fits of anger.[17]

Apple's organisation design was flat and simple. Even though Apple did not have an official organisation chart, one interpretation of its design was that the organisation radiated around the CEO, with 15 senior vice presidents and 31 vice presidents overseeing the main functions. In terms of this structure, the CEO would only be two levels away from any key part of the company; and financial management was centralised, with the only executive responsible for costs and expenses being the chief financial officer.[18] Apart from ensuring confidentiality, other aspects of Apple's organisational design provide the necessary agility and focus. Small teams bear responsibility for crucial projects, a characteristic that is reminiscent of start-up companies. Committees are not prevalent at Apple. As Jobs mentioned:

'We are organised as a startup. One person is in charge of iPhone Os software, one person is in charge of Mac hardware, one person is in charge of iPhone hardware engineering, another is in charge of worldwide marketing, and another person is in charge of operations. We are organised like a startup. We are the biggest startup on the planet. And we all meet for three hours once a week and we talk about everything we are doing, the whole business.'[19]

Steve Jobs' leadership

'Some leaders push innovations by being good at the big picture. Others do so by mastering details. Jobs did both, relentlessly.[20]

When Jobs returned to Apple in 1997 after an absence of 12 years, he arrived with much historical baggage. He was Apple's co-founder at the age of 21, and was worth $200 million by the age of 25. He was then forced to resign by the age of 30, in 1985, after a battle over control with CEO John Sculley which ended with Jobs losing all operational responsibilities. By 2007, however, Jobs was voted as one of the greatest entrepreneurs of all time by *Business Week* and by 2010 the World's Best CEO by *Harvard Business Review*, having restored Apple to a world-leading, innovative and influential company.

Many believe that Jobs' achievement of being regarded as one of the greatest technology entrepreneurs is based not so much on his knowledge of technology (he was not an engineer or a programmer, neither did he have an MBA or college degree) but on his innate instinct for design, the ability to choose the most talented team and 'the willingness to be a pain in the neck for what matters for him most', such as great design and user-friendliness.[21] Strategically speaking, Jobs understood that to be different as a company, you have to make tough choices; in Apple's case, this was clearly reflected in the product markets it decided to pursue, as compared, for example, to large competitors. Referring to Apple's focus, he noted: 'I'm as proud of what we don't do as I am of what we do.'[22]

According to insiders, Jobs was opposed to using any sort of unauthorised applications or external software in Apple products. Everything was to be designed by and follow Apple's standards of user-friendliness, excellence and simplicity. As Jobs explained: 'We do these things not because we are control freaks . . . We do them because we want to make great products, because we care about the user and because we like to take responsibility for the entire experience rather than turn out the crap that other people make.'[23]

Jobs could be inspirational, but also could be experienced by employees as scary. According to Guy Kawasaki:

'Working for Steve was a terrifying and addictive experience. He would tell you that your work, your ideas, and sometimes your existence were worthless right to your face, right in front of everyone. Watching him crucify someone scared you into working incredibly long hours. . . . Working for Steve was also ecstasy. Once in a while he would tell you that you were great and that made it all worth it.'[24]

The high praise as well as high criticism made people try harder, jump higher and work later into the night. Jobs has been credited with imposing discipline on Apple, a quality that the company had lacked for years.

After the onset of pancreatic cancer in 2003 and an operation to address it in 2004, by 2009 Jobs' health was again deteriorating. In January 2009 he announced that he was taking leave of absence from Apple until June, due to health issues relating to a 'hormone imbalance'. COO Tim Cook would handle day-to-day operations, and Jobs would stay involved in major strategic decisions. Commentators disagreed on the degree of impact Jobs' absence would have. Some said that the new products Apple would introduce over the following 18 months had already been developed, and that Cook would manage Apple effectively in Jobs' absence. Cook's leadership role in Apple's operations since 1998 had given him a deep understanding of the company and a prominent position, being the only person to have a vast area of responsibility apart from Jobs and the one who replaced him during his medical absences. An industry veteran prior to joining Apple, Cook served as Vice President of Corporate Materials at Compaq, and as Chief Operating Officer of the Reseller Division at Intelligent Electronics. Seen as a low-key, soft-spoken executive, Cook's focus on efficiency and operations has been laser-sharp.

Others, however, believed that Jobs' motivational role, negotiation skills and creative vision were crucial for Apple and therefore Jobs' absence would adversely affect the company. Another medical leave followed in 2011, and in August 2011 Jobs resigned from his position as CEO, when Tim Cook, former COO, was appointed as CEO. Jobs remained at Apple as Chairman until his death in October 2011.

Entering a new Apple era

Upon becoming Apple's CEO, Tim Cook maintained a low profile and focused on managing the transition to the post-Jobs era as smoothly as possible. He sent the following email to Apple employees to reassure them that he would remain faithful to Apple's 'DNA':

'I want you to be confident that Apple is not going to change. I cherish and celebrate Apple's unique principles and values. Steve built a company and culture that is unlike any other in the world and we are going to stay true to that – it is in our DNA. We are going to continue to make the best products in the world that delight our customers and make our employees incredibly proud of what they do.'[25]

Despite record profits during Cook's first year as CEO, Apple was facing new challenges. One was the effects of leadership transition, with many observers wondering whether Apple could retain its distinct culture and set of capabilities after Jobs. Further, in the smartphone market Apple was facing a strong alternative technology in terms of Google's Android system. High-quality hardware, which many believed to be as good as the iPhone, was available from Samsung. The release of Windows 8 for tablet PCs posed a threat to the iPad, as did Amazon's new Kindle, which had improved functionality and graphics. Apple was competing in a technology industry where many companies, inspired by Apple's own model, started to move away from single devices and specialisation towards mobile connectivity and interconnected service offerings.

Cook was faced with the challenge of leading the world's most valuable and proprietary company into uncharted waters. Would Apple be able to sustain its magic now that its chief architect had gone? Was Apple's operating model better understood by competitors and in danger or imitation? Was it making the best use of its enviable cash hoard? Could it keep delivering blockbuster products, which would result in the level of growth and profit performance that markets expected? Was Apple's huge size becoming a liability? What should Apple do differently, if anything, to address its strategic challenges and sustain its exceptional performance to date?

Notes and references
1. $1 = £0.65 = €0.77.
2. Burrows, P. (2004) 'The seed of Apple's innovation. Interview with Steve Jobs', *Business Week*, 12 October, http://www.businessweek.com/bwdaily/dnflash/oct2004/nf20041012_4018_db083.htm
3. Burrows, P. and Grover, R. (2006) 'Steve Jobs' magic kingdom', *Business Week*, 6 February, http://www.businessweek.com/magazine/content/06_06/b3970001.htm
4. Booth, C. (1997) 'Steve's job: restart Apple', *Time*, 18 August, http://www.time.com/time/magazine/article/0,9171,986849,00.html
5. Technology that makes Apple products separate from other companies' technologies and hence difficult, if not impossible, to integrate with non-Apple products.
6. Cruikshank, J. (2006) *The Apple Way*, New York: McGraw-Hill.
7. Grossman, L. (2005) 'How Apple does it', *Time*, 16 October, http://www.time.com/time/magazine/article/0,9171,1118384,00.html
8. Cruikshank, J. (2006), ibid.
9. Morris, B. (2008) 'What makes Apple golden', *Fortune*, 17 March, http://money.cnn.com/2008/02/29/news/companies/amac_apple.fortune/index.htm
10. Apple's corporate headquarters in California.
11. Morris, B. (2008), ibid.
12. Lashinsky, A. (2012) 'The secrets Apple keeps', *Fortune*, 18 January, http://tech.fortune.cnn.com/2012/01/18/inside-apple-adam-lashinsky/
13. Grossman, L. (2005), ibid.
14. Lashinsky, A. (2011) 'How Apple works: Inside the world's biggest startup', *Fortune*, 25 August, http://tech.fortune.cnn.com/2011/08/25/how-apple-works-inside-the-worlds-biggest-startup/
15. Lashinsky, A. (2012), ibid.
16. Lashinsky, A. (2011), ibid.
17. Elkind, P. (2008) 'The trouble with Steve Jobs', *Fortune*, 5 March, http://money.cnn.com/2008/03/02/news/companies/elkind_jobs.fortune/index.htm
18. Lashinsky, A. (2011), ibid.
19. Jobs, S. (2010) Interview at D8 Conference, http://allthingsd.com/20100607/steve-jobs-at-d8-the-full-uncut-interview/
20. Isaacson, W. (2011) 'American icon', *Time*, 17 October, http://www.time.com/time/magazine/article/0,9171,2096327,00.html#ixzz1kZBq5m00
21. Grossman, L. (2005), ibid.
22. Burrows, P. and Grover, R. (2006), ibid.
23. Isaacson, W. (2011), ibid.
24. Cruikshank, J. (2006), ibid.
25. Cheng, J. (2011) 'Tim Cook says "Apple is not going to change"', *Wired*, 25 August, http://www.wired.com/epicenter/2011/08/tim-cook-says-apple-is-not-going-to-change/

CASE STUDY

'Where's Irene and just exactly what is she up to?' The acquisition of Cadbury PLC by Kraft Foods, 2010

Eric Cassells

This case relates the hard-fought acquisition battle by Kraft Foods to acquire the large confectionery manufacturer Cadbury. Like many cross-border acquisitions, the bid battle was controversial and attracted considerable investor and wider stakeholder comment, often less than favourable. In the event, Cadbury's defence led to an increased offer and the bid was successful, but subsequent UK parliamentary proceedings later censured Kraft's senior management, warned against the role of short-term hedge fund investors in the bid, and raised numerous policy issues concerning large acquisitions. The case concludes by examining the subsequent demerger of Kraft in 2012, and the creation of the global snacks business of Mondeléz International.

● ● ●

'A commentator said that in the history of M&A activity there is no M&A deal that has made more people unhappy than the impending acquisition of Cadbury by Kraft.'[1]

The unhappy people included trade unions, employees, Cadbury investors, Kraft investors, senior government ministers and, perhaps most unusually, confectionery traditionalists and the heritage lobby, even though both corporations were already well over 100 years old, and both claimed a rich heritage and a history of growth by innovation and acquisition.

Cadbury's heritage

Cadbury was founded in Birmingham, England, in the 1820s by John Cadbury to sell tea, coffee and chocolate drinks, before becoming one of the first manufacturers of branded chocolate bars. The business was awarded a Royal Warrant in 1854 as manufacturers of high-quality cocoa and chocolate to Queen Victoria. As their product lines expanded, the family heirs to the business built a purpose-designed factory in 1878 on an estate they named Bournville. The Cadbury family were Quakers[2] by conviction, and their social interests led George Cadbury to build a 'model village' for his workers on adjacent land to 'alleviate the evils of modern cramped living conditions' and create an alcohol-free living community. This village was the foundation of Cadbury's image as a benevolent, enlightened and paternalistic employer, maintained in later years through the creation of the 'Cadbury Foundation'.

In 1905, Cadbury introduced its innovative 'Dairy Milk' chocolate bar, using a much higher proportion of milk than previous products in the market. This became the best-selling chocolate bar in the UK, and was followed by a range of other successful chocolate-based bars. The bars were packaged in a distinctive purple colour (see Figure 1) that became an important element of the company's branding.

In 1918 the company opened its first international plant in Australia, and in 1919 it acquired important brands in a merger with JS Fry. The most significant merger occurred, however, in 1969 when it joined with Schweppes to form a major international conglomerate spanning confectionery and soft drinks. More drinks brands were subsequently

Figure 1 Original Cadbury Dairy Milk packaging, showing the distinctive Cadbury colour

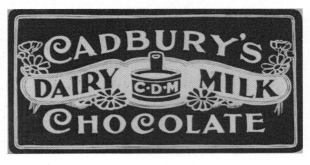

acquired and Cadbury Schweppes consolidated its position as the third-largest soft drinks company in the world behind Coca-Cola and Pepsi. By 2007, however, group management believed that shareholder value would be increased through a demerger of the businesses, and that the component parts may be worth more than the whole business. On 2 May 2008 Cadbury (focusing on chocolate and confectionery) demerged from the drinks businesses, which became 'Dr Pepper Snapple Group'. Cadbury then concentrated on the core chocolate and confectionery business, making a commitment to source all cocoa beans through Fair Trade channels in August 2009.

In October 2007, Cadbury announced the closure of its ageing Somerdale plant (located near Bristol in the UK) with over 500 jobs affected. Production from this plant was to be concentrated in other factories in the UK and Poland. A further step in focusing on the group's core was taken with the sale of its 'own-label' (non-Cadbury-branded) trading division for £58 million ($88.2m; €68.8m).[3] This strategy of focusing the group and driving cost efficiencies to produce shareholder value was overtaken by the unwanted acquisition bid from Kraft.

Kraft

Kraft has its origins in Chicago in 1903, originally established to sell cheese. By 1914, the Kraft family had moved into cheese manufacturing in Stockton, Illinois, and patented the production of processed cheese in tins in 1916. Demand for this product grew dramatically with the need to supply US forces in the First World War.

By 1924, the growth of the company had led to a listing stock exchange, and the opening of a sales office in London. Over the next 30 years, the company grew through a series of deals to sell dressings, dinners (such as macaroni cheese), coffee, and cheeses. By 1953 Kraft had 200 products in its portfolio sold throughout the USA, Canada, the UK, Germany and Australia. The corporation became an increasingly diversified business producing grocery foods, snacks and confectionery, and it continued to expand internationally.

Further diversification took Kraft beyond foods in 1980 through a merger with Dart Industries, maker of Duracell batteries and Tupperware plastic containers. However, by 1986, the company was refocusing on foods by spinning off most of these non-foods businesses. Deal-making continued, however, with the merger of Kraft and the General Foods business of Philip Morris, to form Kraft General Foods in 1989, the world's second-largest foods business.

Throughout the next two decades acquisition of brands continued apace, in snacks, general foods and drinks, and confectionery, with deals taking place in Italy, the UK, Sweden, Hungary, Norway, Slovakia, Lithuania, Poland, Ukraine, Bulgaria, Brazil, Romania, Australia, Germany, Russia, Turkey, France, Egypt and Morocco. In 1993, Kraft acquired the business of Terry's of York, a leading confectioner in the UK – an acquisition that would return to haunt the company in its pursuit of Cadbury.

Meanwhile, Kraft's independence from Philip Morris was started through the second-largest US IPO on the New York Stock Exchange in history in 2001, completed through a final spin-off in March 2007.[4] This left Kraft as the world's second-largest food company with revenues of $42 billion in 2008.[5]

The bid

On 28 August 2009, Irene Rosenfeld (CEO of Kraft) met Roger Carr (Chair of Cadbury) to discuss a possible friendly takeover, valuing each Cadbury share at £7.55. Carr rejected the offer, but news of Kraft's interest was leaked on the London stock market 10 days later. By this stage, the potential offer price had dropped to £7.45 per share, once again rejected by Cadbury's board.

In the period following this announcement, Cadbury wrote to the UK Takeover Panel on 21 September, asking them to issue Kraft with a 'put up or shut up' notice, whereby a formal offer is required to be made by a certain date, or the potential bidder must withdraw (and stay silent) for six months. This protects the target company from ongoing uncertainty, and discourages the use of informal 'speculative' offers to put a target 'in play'. This was done on 30 September, and Kraft was given until Friday 9 November to table a formal bid.

The bid came on 9 November, valuing each Cadbury share at £7.45 which consisted of £3 in cash plus 0.2589 new Kraft shares for every Cadbury share. Allowing for exchange fluctuations, Kraft valued its bid at £9.8 billion. The offer document[5] highlighted the following benefits:

- A 'substantial' premium of between 26% and 39% over the free-standing share price of Cadbury.
- An 'attractive multiple' of 13.9 times Cadbury's EBITDA.[6]
- Kraft's current trading and prospects were deemed 'strong', based on its third-quarter 2009 reporting data. Kraft stated that 'this provides evidence of its long-term sustainable business model and the attractiveness of Cadbury shareholders of holding Kraft Foods shares'.
- Kraft identified estimated cost savings of $625 million, in line with other historical transactions at 6.5% of revenues. The $625 million was to come from savings and scale economies in procurement, manufacturing, customer service, logistics and R&D ($300m), general and administrative costs ($200m) and marketing and selling costs ($125m). In addition, significant revenue-based synergy benefits would take 'time to be realised'.

Table 1 **Kraft's four priorities for long-term strategy**

Kraft priorities	The importance of the Cadbury acquisition
Focus on growth categories to transform Kraft into a leading snack, confectionery and quick meal company.	A combined global portfolio of 40 leading confectionery brands, each with sales in excess of $100 million.
Expand its footprint and scale in growing developing markets.	Cadbury offers Kraft a complementary presence in developing markets, with Kraft's strength and channels in Brazil, China and Russia, and Cadbury in India, Mexico and South Africa.
Increase presence in 'instant consumption' channels as they continued to grow relative to traditional grocery channels in the established US and EU markets.	Kraft's strength lay in traditional grocery channels, whereas Cadbury was well placed in 'instant consumption' channels.
Pursue margin growth, through improved portfolio mix, reducing costs and investing in quality.	The higher exposure to confectionery of a post-acquisition Kraft would provide Kraft shareholders with an improved portfolio of higher-margin growth products.

- The fit between Kraft and Cadbury was deemed 'unique' and was deemed to enhance Kraft's stated strategic priorities. 'Unique' was usually interpreted by analysts at the time as a reference principally to perceived complementary distribution channels in emerging markets.
- Kraft was committed to ongoing financial discipline.

Kraft also said it had built 'strong operating and financial momentum', strengthened its leadership team, invested in core brands, and built scale in its key marketplaces. Its four priorities for long-term strategy, which would be enhanced by the Cadbury acquisition, are listed in Table 1.

Those unhappy people – trade unions

Trade unions in the UK examined the bid and expressed their concern, predicting that up to 7,000 jobs would be lost.[7] Kraft commented that they hoped to reverse the closure, previously announced by Cadbury, of the Somerdale plant with the loss of 500 jobs. This may have been designed to win over employee or union backing, but drew suspicion instead as:

- The offer document laid out a significant cost savings target, which seemed more likely to lead to job losses than saved jobs.
- The historical precedent of Kraft's acquisition of Terry's of York in 1993 existed. In this acquisition, Kraft had promised to maintain production in York, but closed the York factories soon after the takeover.

Those unhappy people – the heritage and nationalist lobby

Like all cross-border takeovers, the bid raised protectionist fears for jobs, skills (such as R&D) and corporate control being stripped out of the UK. Additionally, Kraft had to contend with Cadbury's iconic status in the UK, in terms of its brands, its reputation for community involvement, and its heritage as a distinctive paternalistic employer.

In May 2012, Felicity Loudon, a Cadbury family heiress, sold her £48 million house to raise funds to start her own chocolate company. Angered by the acquisition of the company her great-grandfather had established by an 'American plastic cheese company', she intended her new company to be a 'memorial to her great-grandfather'.[8]

Those unhappy people – Warren Buffet

Kraft's bid did not attract the uniform support of its own investors. The largest shareholder in Kraft was Berkshire Hathaway, led by Warren Buffet, the influential investor and a favourite of the US financial news channels.

On 16 September 2009, Buffet warned that Kraft must not 'overpay' for Cadbury. This was ominous for Kraft, as Buffet was a long-term supporter of the corporation, holding 9.4% of shares precisely because he believed the shares were undervalued. More provocatively, on Bloomberg's business news channel on 19 January, while describing Kraft CEO Irene Rosenfeld as a 'good person', Buffet described an increased final takeover offer (together with the near-simultaneous sale of Kraft's US pizza business to raise necessary funds) as a 'bad deal'. He dismissed the potential synergy benefits identified in Kraft's offer document, saying he was distrustful of unrealised benefits. He stated: 'If I had a chance to vote on this, I'd vote no.' Referring to the proposed acquisition of Cadbury specifically, he concluded 'I feel poorer'. Kraft's shares fell 2% on his intervention.[9] Irene Rosenfeld was asked about Buffet's intervention by Bloomberg TV. Refusing to be drawn, she stated that she believed Buffet was evaluating the deal from the basis of existing cash flow, and ignoring the potentially transformational synergies which were at the heart of the strategy to acquire Cadbury.

The Cadbury defence

Cadbury published its formal defence document on 14 December 2009.[10] The four pillars of the defence were:

1 Cadbury is a strong pure-play confectionery business with iconic brands and excellent market positions:
   - Leading positions across the world in all confectionery segments.
   - Number one confectionery company in fast-growing developing markets outside the USA.
2 Cadbury has been transformed through an ongoing 'Vision into action' plan, which was delivering ahead of targets:
   - The initiative delivered a simplified portfolio of pure confectionery brands, a de-layered organisational structure, the renewal of manufacturing ability, improved distribution in emerging markets, and investment in marketing and R&D.
   - While 80% of the required investments of the programme had been made, only 45% of the anticipated benefits had been realised to date.
3 Kraft undervalues what Cadbury has created:
   - By 14 December, the effective value of the bid had dropped to £7.26, due to share price and currency fluctuations.
   - Cadbury's forecast for 2009 indicated the EBITDA multiple on offer was low (at 11.6 times.) This multiple compared to higher multiples expected in confectionery – 15.5 times proposed for Hershey by Wrigley, and 18.5 times paid by Mars for Wrigley.
   - The 60% majority of the consideration comprised Kraft shares, which had 'significantly underperformed against peers' in the previous eight years.
4 The next phase of 'Vision into action' would deliver further improved revenue growth, enhanced profitability and higher cash returns:
   - Long-term targets were revised upwards for organic revenue growth of 5–7% per annum, targeted margins of 16–18% by 2013, and operating cash conversion of 80–90% by 2010.
   - These revised targets would deliver incremental profits of £200m in 2013, the equivalent of around £1.30 per share of added value.

In addition, the document described Cadbury as 'performance driven, values led', claiming it obtained 'sustainable value from our values'. In particular, the company highlighted its commitment to Fair Trade sourcing and the Cocoa Partnership, its strong environmental emission and waste targets, its standards on healthy foods and nutritional labelling, and high employee workplace satisfaction benchmarks. In an interview with the *New York Times*, Cadbury CEO Todd Stizter suggested shareholders had to factor in these values when deciding on the bid: 'It's a culture that very much cares about how it conducts business. Shareholders will have to judge whether that little bit of magic that makes us special . . . what that's worth.'

The defence document did not deal explicitly with the hope of a counter-bid from a friendlier acquirer (a 'white knight'). Cadbury was, however, variously encouraging Hershey, Ferrero Rocher, Kohlberg, Kravis & Roberts (KKR) and Nestlé to consider a counter-bid. None of these bids materialised, however, strengthening Kraft's position with investors looking to realise value in the short term.

In the wake of the Cadbury defence document, analysts believed Cadbury had put up a robust defence and that Kraft would need to increase its bid to win, Sanford Bernstein Research and Nomura both suggesting a target price of £9.00, Crédit Suisse £8.50 and Kepler Capital Markets £8.00.[11] The *New York Times* noted Cadbury's line that:

> 'It is special and not just fodder for a . . . "low-growth" conglomerate like Kraft. So far, shareholders seem to be supporting Cadbury. The question that analysts and others have asked is the number of short-term investors – mainly hedge funds – that have taken up residence in Cadbury's stock betting that a deal will get done. It's a concern because Cadbury's stock is riding high now in part on hopes that a bidding war will erupt; the stock could easily plunge if none does.'[12]

What happened?

In the wake of the defence document, the Cadbury board felt that they had strengthened the case for a higher price. Unless they could persuade other bidders to join in, however, Cadbury shareholders all knew that the current value of their shares was only underpinned by the Kraft offer itself. The Cadbury defence team calculated that, to realise the gain from the bid, the majority of shareholders would sell at a price of about £8.30 – either to a higher offer from Kraft, or to 'short-term' hedge funds operating in the market.[13]

At the start of the bid, only 5% of Cadbury shares were held by short-term traders. CEO Stitzer had suggested that in early December short-term investors and hedge funds comprised about 15–20% of the shareholder base, 'a relatively modest level' for such battles. In the heat of the battle, and with limited information due to disclosure limits on acquisitions under the Takeover Code, it is difficult to be certain of the scale of such infiltration. In retrospect, however, it was noted that:

> 'The initial bid from Kraft sparked a 40% jump in Cadbury's share price which many shareholders took advantage of by selling stock, a large proportion of which was bought by short-term investors, such as hedge funds. Indeed 44 days after the initial bid, 31% of Cadbury was owned by these short-term investors who were motivated by the promise of a quick profit.'[14]

However, the interest of hedge funds in the shares during this period was governed by Kraft's perceived commitment to the deal. As long as they believed that Kraft would pay more to secure Cadbury, there was only limited downside risk for hedge funds and much upside potential in buying the shares.

As the battle raged, the role of the hedge funds attracted attention from the press and politicians, and was one of the aspects of the bid that was selected for investigation later by the UK Parliamentary Committee. One of the most vocal critics at the time was Vince Cable, Liberal Democrat opposition spokesman for Business, Innovation and Skills (BIS). Cable wrote to Lord Mandelson, the responsible government minister, stating that: 'This takeover . . . raises broader questions about how hedge funds, out to make a quick buck, can destabilise even the most established companies.'[15]

In a later speech Roger Carr, Chairman of Cadbury, acknowledged that, in fact, much of Cadbury's shareholding base was already held through the US stock market, and 'was simply not owned by a large number of mainstream UK institutions'. In fact, 49% of Cadbury shareholdings were held in the USA at the start of the bid.

As time wore on, and a counter-bid failed to appear, and due to the increasing participation of hedge funds, the defence document was more likely to produce a higher Kraft bid than the maintenance of Cadbury's independence. On 5 January 2010, Kraft altered the composition of its bid, but not its overall price, to include a further £0.60 of cash in place of new Kraft shares, thus reducing the balance of the acceptance risk for shareholders who might be reluctant to own shares in a 'lower-growth' US food conglomerate, or to hold $-denominated shares.

In turn, Cadbury's defence was boosted by the issue of its 2009 trading results on 12 January 2010. Operating profit and perceived forward value had risen by 27% to £808m, with like-for-like sales up 11% to £6bn. These improved results focused analysts' attention back on the perceived 'derisory' earnings multiple of the bid.[16] Chairman Roger Carr also focused on the bid price, stating 'our company value has grown'. He refused, however, to put a value on the company, because: 'The minute you put a price into the market then it becomes the ceiling, not the floor.'[17]

Price was settled on 18 January 2010 when the Cadbury's board agreed to recommend an increased offer of £8.40 per Cadbury share (with £5 of the consideration now being paid in cash), together with an added special cash dividend of £0.10 per share. This deal effectively valued Cadbury at about £11.5 billion. Within two weeks, Kraft was able to claim acceptances from 72% of Cadbury's shareholders, reaching the necessary level for the takeover.

Political and regulatory concerns – 'Where's Irene?'

The Cadbury takeover process caused consternation in the press and trade unions, and among politicians, regulators and the general public in the UK, so much so that the BIS

Committee of the UK's House of Commons issued a report on 6 April 2010 which stated that: 'The Kraft takeover of Cadbury has proved to be an event which is likely to shape future public policy towards takeovers and corporate governance.'[18]

The report hearings were highly critical of the behaviour of Kraft, and bloggers gleefully described MPs as 'fighting each other to lay into Kraft'. MP Lindsay Hoyle at one point queried whether Kraft was 'remote, smug, and . . . duplicitous'.

The measured tones of the Committee's report focus on two issues, primarily:

1 Kraft's promise during the heat of the takeover battle to reverse the decision of Cadbury to close its factory in Somerdale and move production to Poland was in fact reversed less than three weeks after Kraft took control of Cadbury. UK Secretary of State for BIS, Lord Mandelson, commented that 'this will confirm the worst fears of those who felt the takeover would result in job losses'. During the hearings, MP Peter Luff questioned Kraft's official claim to 'inspire trust and make a delicious difference . . .', while his colleague Lindsay Hoyle reminds Kraft's managers that Kraft closed the Terry's confectionery plant after it bought the company in 1993, despite promising to keep it open. The Committee found that 'Kraft's initial indications that it would keep the [Somerdale] factory open, which it reversed after gaining control of Cadbury, heightened the public's feelings of mistrust towards Kraft.' The Committee's formal conclusion was more measured but still opines that:

    'Kraft acted both irresponsibly and unwisely in making its original statement . . . [and] has left itself open to the charge that either it was incompetent in its approach . . . or that it used a "cynical ploy" to improve its public image during its takeover of Cadbury.'

2 The Committee expressed their 'extreme disappointment' that:

    'Irene Rosenfeld, the CEO of Kraft Foods Inc., did not give evidence in person. Her attendance at our evidence session would have given an appropriate signal of Kraft's commitment to Cadbury in the UK and provided the necessary authority to the specific assurances Kraft have now given to the future of Cadbury.'

    Indeed, during the proceedings, MPs simply demanded 'Where's Irene?' and lambasted Kraft's senior representative at the hearing, Marc Firestone, as an 'apologist' for her, and called her absence a 'sizeable discourtesy'. The *Daily Telegraph* quoted Mrs Rosenfeld's comment that: 'Attendance would not be the best use of my personal time.'

The UK's regulatory Takeover Panel were asked to consider the statements by Kraft in relation to Somerdale to determine whether there had been a breach of the Takeover

Code which legally governs acquisitions in the UK. Kraft was formally criticised for not meeting the standards of care in making its statement that was required by the code, which states: 'Each document statement made during the course of an offer must be prepared with the highest standards of care and accuracy and the information given must be adequately and fairly presented.'

These explicit reprimands for the most senior members of Kraft's management team were widely reported in the UK. Under pressure to show Kraft's commitment, Mr Firestone gave assurances that Kraft was committed to Cadbury and the UK in a number of specific areas:

- Cadbury products would continue to be managed from the UK, and Cadbury's brand names would not change under Kraft.
- To honour the commitments made by Cadbury to the workforce at Somerdale, prior to its impending closure.
- That there would be no further compulsory redundancies among manufacturing employees in the following two years. (Despite this assurance, the committee contrasted Irene Rosenfeld's mid-takeover battle statement that 'the UK would be a net beneficiary' of jobs from the deal against the reality of the Somerdale closure, redundancies in Cadbury's finance, legal and communications departments, and the lack of assurances to employees at Kraft's own UK headquarters. Kraft's senior management were urged to engage in a 'meaningful dialogue' with the unions and workforce at Cadbury 'as a matter of urgency in order to start to restore trust'.)
- To accept its obligation to support Cadbury's existing pension arrangements.

- To maintain Cadbury's Research & Development facilities in the UK. (Despite this, the Committee specifically noted Mr Firestone's 'careful use of words' and that Kraft have made no 'specific commitment to the current level of employment and world class skills in R&D at the centres of excellence'.)
- To continue support for the 'Cocoa Partnership' and uphold Cadbury's undertaking to extend its use of Fair Trade. (Concerns were expressed at whether Kraft's sustainability engagement model placed Fair Trade principles at the centre of business in the way that Cadbury had been perceived to have done.)
- To confirm the funding for the philanthropic Cadbury Foundation for the next three years, and to adhere to Cadbury's commitments to community engagement.
- To uphold Cadbury's commitment to the environment.

After taking evidence, the Committee wrote to Irene Rosenfeld asking her to endorse these undertakings that were in the public domain. The report concluded that 'if Kraft is serious about restoring its reputation in the United Kingdom, it is vital that it delivers on all of them'.

The policy context of the takeover

The Parliamentary Committee report, having reprimanded Kraft and extracted the specific assurances noted above, went on to identify general policy concerns that were part of the context of acquisition bids in the UK. Their report, therefore, asked the government's BIS Department to comment. The government duly did,[19] as set out in Table 2.

Table 2 **The Parliamentary Committee's issues and the government's responses**

Issue noted by Committee	Response by UK government
That Cadbury's 'world-class' Research and Development function and skills might be transferred to the USA, which would amount to a 'serious breach of trust'.	The government has limited powers to force Kraft to supply information and comply with its commitments.
The future of Cadbury was ultimately decided by Hedge Fund managers who purchased shares during the bid, concerned with short-term financial returns from a raised bid and, therefore, a successful acquisition. The Committee noted existing concerns in this area, but were 'sceptical about the extent to which . . . informal engagement alone can instigate fundamental change in institutional shareholder behaviour'.	The government quotes the Office of National Statistics (2008) that in 1969 institutional investors owned 24%, and foreign investors 7%, of UK quoted shares. By 2008, these figures had increased to 40% and 41%, respectively. The response further notes that market liquidity has increased, and the speed of change of ownership (often through the influence of hedge funds) is much faster than 30 years previously.
Noting the government's possible review of legislation governing takeovers, the Committee recommended that, whilst the government avoided 'protectionism against foreign takeovers', it nevertheless ensured that all takeovers (domestic or foreign) are conducted in the interests of the UK economy.	The government reiterated the belief that the UK benefited (through inward investment) from 'open markets' for corporate control internationally, and drew 'no distinction' between foreign and domestic ownership. It was noted that 'many takeovers . . . fail even by the criterion of shareholder value – with serious implications for people who work for firms on both sides'. The government stated, however, 'that does not mean we should return to the old-fashioned public interest test, which encouraged weak management to lobby for protection'.

Just where is Irene?

As to Kraft's commitments to the BIS, in December 2011 a plan to shed 200 jobs at Cadbury's Bournville plant was announced. At the same time, Kraft announced a £17m investment in research at its designated sole 'Centre of Excellence for Chocolate' globally, now located in Bournville. The BIS Committee revisited events in April 2011 to monitor Kraft's commitments. Concern was expressed at poor engagement between Kraft and the trade unions, and the perception that strategic decisions over the Cadbury brands were made in Kraft's European headquarters in Zürich. More personal criticism also followed for Ms Rosenfeld:

'In a repeat of our predecessors' experience, Irene Rosenfeld . . . refused to give evidence despite repeated requests from us that she should appear. Neither that refusal to attend, nor the manner of it, reflected well on Kraft, nor did Kraft's persistence in failing to acknowledge the seriousness of the Takeover Panels criticism – criticism which by its gravity would alone have merited Ms Rosenfeld's appearance before us, a committee of public scrutiny.'

What happened – post-acquisition

When the Cadbury board recommended the final offer of £8.40 to shareholders, the value represented an 'impressive 50% premium on the value of Cadbury at the start of the bid . . . yielding the highest such premium in recent history in the UK'.[20]

Warren Buffet reduced his holding in Kraft from 9.5% to nearer 6% in the aftermath. His comments reflected the belief that bidders often overpay to the detriment of their shareholders. In the immediate aftermath of the deal there was speculation that Kraft would suffer the 'winner's curse' (of having paid too much for synergies that would take much longer to deliver, or of ignoring the real costs of post-acquisition integration).

By Kraft's fourth-quarter results for 2010, commentators believed that shareholders were: 'Still wondering whether they bit off more than they could chew when they put up £11.5bn for Cadbury last year.'[21] Net profits had fallen 24% to $540m in the quarter, reflecting the scale of integration costs, and a 'disappointing' 2.2% rise in Cadbury's like-for-like sales, well behind the 5% sales growth that Cadbury had posted in its last period of independence. The deal had not yet shown itself to be the transformational move that Ms Rosenfeld staked her reputation on. Kraft's next move to transform itself was less expected.

On 4 August 2011 Kraft announced its intention to split into two separate corporations. Kraft said its two businesses: 'Now differ in their future strategic priorities, growth profiles and operational focus.'[22]

Figure 2 Mondeléz brand colours

The lower-growth North American grocery foods business was to include brands such as Kraft and Philadelphia cheeses, and Capri Sun, with revenues of $16bn. At the same time, a much more focused, globally spread snacks and confectionery business, including Trident gum, Oreo cookies and Cadbury, would have estimated revenues of $32bn. Within the confectionery arm of the global snacks business, Cadbury brands represented over 80% of revenues. The rationale for the global snacks business remained those that drove the Cadbury acquisition: to move into higher-growth segments, and to increase footprint and 'white space' synergy possibilities for iconic brands (see Appendix 2) in fast-growing emerging markets. When interviewed by Bloomberg TV on 16 September 2010, Ms Rosenfeld reaffirmed that Cadbury was: 'A critical piece of the puzzle we have been trying to complete.'

The demerger took place on 1 October 2012 when the North American grocery foods business started trading as Kraft Foods Group Inc., while the global snacks business (including Cadbury) became Mondeléz International, with Ms Irene Rosenfeld firmly at its helm. A list of Mondeléz 'heritage' brands is shown in Appendix 2. Mondeléz's principal brand launch colour was the same distinctive shade of purple as Cadbury had used for over a century (see Figure 2).

Notes and references
1. suite101.com, 2010.
2. Quakers (or 'Friends') are a non-conformist religious group with strong beliefs in social justice.
3. £1 = $1.53 = €1.17.
4. The demerger of Kraft from the Philip Morris empire was initiated by launching an Initial Public Offering (IPO) on the New York Stock Exchange, inviting investors to acquire shares directly in Kraft. The IPO was the second largest in US history and the scale of Kraft meant that it was not fully demerged (or 'spun-off') from Philip Morris, as an independent company with its own distinct shareholders, until a final offering in 2007.
5. Kraft Annual Report 2009.
6. Earnings Before Interest, Taxes, Depreciation and Amortisation.

7. Unite, quoted on BBC at http://news.bbc.co.uk/1/hi/england/west_midlands/8456737.stm/
8. *The Daily Mail*, 7 May 2012.
9. 'Buffett blasts Kraft bid for Cadbury', *Guardian*, 20 January 2010.
10. Cadbury PLC (2009) *Higher Performance, Higher Value: Reject Kraft's offer.*
11. Russell, M. (2009) 'Cadbury Defence Document – what the analysts say', just-food.com, 15 December 2009.
12. De la Merced, M.J. (2009) 'Valuing Cadbury's defense against Kraft', at http://dealbook.nytimes.com/2009/12/14/valuing-cadburys-defense-against-kraft/
13. Moeller, S. (2012) 'Case study: Kraft's takeover of Cadbury', at http://www.ft.com/cms/s/0/1cb06d30-332f-11e1-a51e-00144feabdc0.html
14. Gillingwater, L.-R.R. and Moeller, S. (2012) 'Hostile bids and chocolate bars: the takeover of Cadbury', at http://www.cass.city.ac.uk/news-and-events/news/2010/may2/hostile-bids-and-chocolate-bars-the-takeover-of-cadbury
15. Wood, Z., Carrell, S. and Wachman, R. (2010) 'Buffet blasts Kraft bid for Cadbury', at http://www.guardian.co.uk/business/2010/jan/20/buffett-blasts-cadbury-takeover?/
16. Cleary, A. (2010) 'Cadbury reports profit surge in defense against Kraft (update 3)', at http://www.bloomberg.com/apps/news?pid=newsarchive&sid=axJlz.50cxRY/
17. Ibid.
18. House of Commons BIS Committee (2010) 'Mergers, acquisitions and takeovers: the takeover of Cadbury by Kraft', 9th report of session 2009–10, London: The Stationery Office.
19. Gillingwater and Moeller, op. cit.
20. Gillingwater and Moeller, op. cit.
21. Webb, A. and Wilson, A. (2011) 'Was Cadbury a sweet deal for Kraft investors?', at http://www.telegraph.co.uk/finance/newsbysector/retailandconsumer/8471076/
22. BBC News business (2011) 'Kraft to split into two companies', at http://www.bbc.co.uk/news/business-14403616

APPENDIX 1 – Timeline of Kraft's bid for Cadbury

28 August 2009	Irene Rosenfeld, Kraft Chairman and CEO, meets Cadbury Chairman Roger Carr to outline a takeover deal in cash and shares which values Cadbury's shares at £7.55 each (£3 in cash, plus 0.2589 Kraft shares for each Cadbury share).
7 September	The London market is alerted to an offer of £7.45 per share (£10.2bn for the company), which is swiftly rejected by Cadbury's board.
12 September	Carr repeats his rejection in a letter to Irene Rosenfeld, with the comment that joining Kraft's 'low growth conglomerate business' was an 'unappealing prospect'.
16 September	Warren Buffet, CEO of Berkshire Hathaway (Kraft's largest shareholder with 9.4%), warns the group not to overpay for Cadbury.
21 September	Cadbury writes to the UK Takeover Panel asking them to request a formal offer from Kraft, under the 'put up or shut up' rules, which would put a deadline on Kraft's offer to be completed.
25 September	Cadbury CEO Todd Stitzer says Kraft's offer does not make strategic or financial sense.
30 September	Takeover panel rules that Kraft has until 17:00 on November 9 to make a formal offer ('put up'), or walk away from the bid ('shut up') for six months.
21 October	Cadbury posts strong third-quarter results for 2009, with sales up 7% and margins increasing. Cadbury's shares fail to react, amid market suggestions that another bidder is unlikely to come forward.
3 November	November results disappoint with weaker than expected results, and a cut in full-year sales forecasts.
9 November	Kraft meets the deadline, formalising a bid of £3 in cash and 0.2589 Kraft shares. Due to the intervening decline in Kraft shares, this now values Cadbury shares at £7.17 (£9.8bn for the company). Cadbury rejects this as 'derisory'.
18 November	Italy's Ferrero Rocher and US Hershey admit they are considering counter-bids for Cadbury. Both companies are purer confectionery plays than Kraft. There are suggestions that KKR may back a joint bid from both companies.
23 November	Cadbury's shares rise to all-time high of £8.195 amid speculation of a bid from Nestlé.
4 December	Kraft posts its formal offer document to Cadbury shareholders, which triggers a 60-day deadline to complete the deal under those terms.
14 December	Cadbury issues its formal defence document, raising its growth targets (sales and margins) further, promising higher dividends, and reminding shareholders of the possible counter-bids.
5 January 2010	Kraft 'sweetens' its bid for Cadbury by altering the bid to offer a further £0.60 in cash, whilst withdrawing an equivalent value of Kraft shares – the overall bid value stays the same, but risk of the offer to Cadbury shareholders is reduced.
6 January	EU Commission rules there are no significant competition grounds to review.
7 January	Cadbury meets Hershey informally, to encourage a friendly offer.
12 January	Cadbury posts a further defence, reporting robust trading in the fourth quarter ahead of its own targets.
18 January	Cadbury board recommend the improved offer from Kraft, offering shareholders the equivalent of £8.40 per share (£5 in cash and 0.1874 new Kraft Shares), with an extra £0.10 special dividend. The company is valued at just under £12 billion.
2 February	72% of Cadbury shareholders have approved the deal.

APPENDIX 2

Brand trademark	Country of origin	Year
Barnum's Animals	United States	1902
Bassett's	England	1842
Cadbury	England	1824
Canale	Argentina	1875
Christie	Canada	1853
Cote d'Or	Belgium	1883
Dentyne	United States	1899
Figaro	Czech Republic/Slovakia	1896
Fontaneda	Spain	1881
Freia	Norway	1898
Fry's	England	1761
Gallito	Costa Rica	1909
HAG	Germany	1906
Hall's	England	1893
Jacobs	Germany	1895
Kraft	United States	1903
LU	France	1850
Maxwell House	United States	1892
Milka	Switzerland	1901
Nabisco	United States	1901
Opavia	Czech Republic/Slovakia	1840
Oreo	United States	1912
Pavlides	Greece	1841
Peek Freans	England	1857
Petit-Beurre	France	1886
Philadelphia	United States	1880
Saiwa	Italy	1900
Suchard	Switzerland	1825
Terry's	England	1767
Toblerone	Switzerland	1908
Vizzolini	Argentina	1906
Ygeias	Greece	1863

Source: Mondeléz International website, December 2012

CASE STUDY

Gazprom and NIS: the oil and gas industry in Serbia

Vladan Hadzic

This case analyses the acquisition of Serbia's major oil company (NIS) by the Russian energy giant Gazprom. The deal was surrounded with controversy and the economic justification was criticised by many. The case study discusses the historical and political issues that influenced the acquisition as well as the economic and business rationale. Developments after the deal are also discussed.

●　　●　　●

The Serbian government initially planned to sell a 25% stake in NIS for $300 million (£197m; €233m)[1] and further to commit the acquiring company to invest another $250m. However, in 2009 Gazprom Neft, a division of Gazprom, acquired a 51% stake in Petroleum Industry of Serbia (Naftna Industria Srbije – NIS), the major oil company in Serbia, for a modest sum of $580m. While the Serbian government more or less achieved the expected price, some other companies (e.g. OMV from Austria) were prepared to offer much more. Deloitte & Touche estimated the value of NIS to be $3.2bn (see Appendix).

It was understood that Gazprom would invest a further €550m in modernising NIS refineries and constructing gas storage facilities in northern Serbia. In addition, the Serbian government would have a stake in the South Stream pipeline (discussed later in the case). Gazprom also agreed to take on NIS's debt of around €600m which was mainly owed to the Serbian government. There are many reasons that might explain the deal, some of which are rooted in history and politics.

Kosovo and strong ties between Serbia and Russia

There are traditionally strong ties between Serbia and Russia because of their common ethnic origins (they are Slavs) and religion (both are of Orthodox Christian faith). There are historic issues too: for instance, Russia entered World War I to protect its fellow Slavs in Serbia. During and after World War II, both countries were communist, although the Yugoslav communists, headed by Josip Broz Tito, managed to avoid the Russian model.

More recently, political reasons have been important, and in particular the Kosovo issue may have been a factor that influenced the Gazprom deal. Serbs have always regarded Kosovo as an integral part of their country – almost the cradle of their culture as it was a major part of the Serbian Empire in the fourteenth century. After the Battle of Kosovo in 1389, in which the Turks defeated Serbia, there followed 500 years of rule by the Ottoman Empire during which the Muslim/Albanian population of Kosovo grew. Even now, over 600 years later, the Battle of Kosovo is still seen as a symbol of Serbian patriotism.

Following the break-up of Yugoslavia in the early 1990s, the long-term ethnic and political unrest among the ethnic Albanian majority (mainly Muslim) in Kosovo gave rise to a resistance movement seeking independence. The levels of violence on both sides escalated and NATO intervened because of alleged atrocities against the Albanian population. The Serbian government turned to Russia for help. While military help never arrived, Russia supported Serbia and strongly objected to the whole NATO campaign; the ties between the Serbian and Russian governments grew even stronger.

Kosovo declared its independence from Serbia in February 2008, unilaterally, and the move was recognised by a majority of EU countries as well as the USA. However, the whole Kosovo issue still rankles with Serbs and they still remember that Russia was their ally in this dispute.

Despite this, the Serbian government is still publicly committed to pursuing entry to the EU – perhaps the economic benefits outweigh the political problems?

It often seems to Serbs that Russia is the only country that understands and backs the Serbian position on Kosovo.

Russian support over Kosovo may well have influenced the Serbian government in agreeing economic cooperation with Russia.

Economic downturn and investment

This deal between NIS and Gazprom was heavily criticised, but the fact is that the regional markets (in the Balkans) look rather risky to many investors from Western and Central Europe, mainly because of political and economic instability. For that reason most major players are withdrawing from the market, leaving Russian companies (e.g. Lukoil and Gazprom) as the ones most interested.

In the light of the economic crisis after 2008, foreign direct investment from the EU slowed drastically, leaving a void in the Serbian economy. Werner Weihs-Raabl, Head of Infrastructure Finance at Austria's Erste Bank, stated: 'There is a special need for infrastructure projects such as bridges and port extensions, which can be developed faster if EU funds are combined with private investments.'[2]

None the less, some EU-led infrastructure projects are continuing. Spanish, Austrian and Chinese companies are undertaking infrastructure projects. In addition, the Japanese government has been helping Serbia since 1999, by providing grants to address the basic and urgent needs of the Serbian population (healthcare, primary education, poverty reduction, social and environmental protection, and general well-being). However, more investment funds are required, and Serbia and Russia have been discussing loans. In 2012 the two sides negotiated a loan from Russia worth $800m to restore Serbia's shaky railways. The deal would guarantee contracts to Russian railway companies and the purchase of Russian-made locomotives. The deal was signed in Moscow on 11 January 2013 subject to Serbian government approval.

Closer ties are also evident outside the realm of business. Russia opened a promised Humanitarian Centre in Nis, southern Serbia (close to Kosovo), early in 2012.

Gazprom announced on 21 November 2011 that a working meeting took place between Alexey Miller (Chairman of the Gazprom Management Committee) and Boris Tadić (then President of the Republic of Serbia). The meeting reviewed the issues relevant to formulating the terms and conditions for long-term Russian gas deliveries to Serbia, developing local oil refining and petrochemical capacities, and establishing gas-fired power plants supplied by Gazprom on special terms. In 2011 Gazprom supplied Serbia with 1.4bn cubic metres of natural gas.

Access to affordable gas and income generation

Gazprom was the sole gas supplier to Serbia after the deal struck between Belgrade and Moscow under the regime of the former President of Serbia Slobodan Milošević (see Appendix).

NIS owed around $250m to Gazprom for gas used prior to 2002. Unable to repay the debt to Gazprom, the Serbian government offered stakes in some of the state-owned companies to their partners, including Gazprom. Companies were not named, but it is likely that NIS was one of them. Without the debt paid, the role of Serbia in the South Stream project would have been very different. It may be that the Serbian government, who were willing to play an important role in the project and secure a better gas deal, offered NIS to the Russians at a reduced price.

In December 2011 the Serbian government declared that it had negotiated a deal with the Russian government and Gazprom to secure gas at an 'affordable' price. Whether this is a 'fair' price is difficult to verify as fuel costs remain very high. One reason behind this, of course, is the global price, and the Serbian government thought that it may have secured a better deal from Russia than was available elsewhere.

Russia's newly proposed South Stream project, which is designed to bring Russian gas supplies, by a southerly route, into the EU, will pass through Serbia, delivering gas to European countries (Greece, Italy, Hungary, Slovenia and Austria) – see Figure 1. Construction started in 2012 and the first gas is scheduled to be delivered late in 2015. Once operational, South Stream should further reduce the cost of gas to Serbia.

The South Stream construction project will help increase the industrial potential of Serbia. In particular, the new project will create about 2,200 jobs in Serbia and attract up to €1.5 billion of direct investments. As a result of the project a joint venture company was set up – South Stream Serbia AG (51% owned by Gazprom, 49% by Srbijagas) – to construct the pipeline. On the other hand, the South Stream project will increase Serbian dependence on Russian gas.

Corruption in Serbia

Despite the changes in Serbian leadership since democracy was established in 2000, a number of 'businessmen' as well as politicians favoured by the ousted President Slobodan Milošević are still powerful. They own a significant proportion of private businesses. Verica Barać, former Head of the Anti-corruption Council in Serbia, said on 13 December 2011:

'The same collusion is taking place as in the 1990s, plus all the people and values have been reinstated. There are closed centres of power that consist of secret services, Milošević-era tycoons, many other influential people, and political parties, that are entirely a part of that system.'[3]

Figure 1 **South Stream**

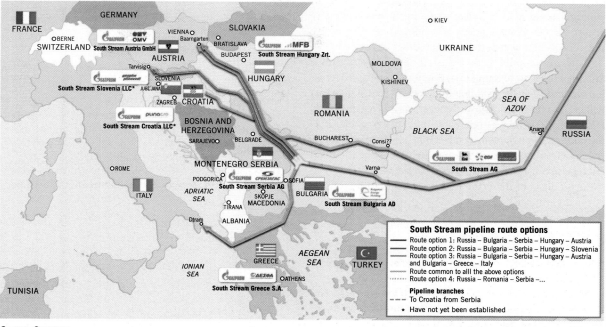

Source: Gazprom

Zoran Stojiljković, a board member of Serbia's Anti-Corruption Agency, told BalkanInsight: 'Political elites are champions of corruption in Serbia, with the president, church, and army being the least corrupt.'[4] He explained that political elites buy influence by rigging tenders for privatisation, influencing laws or directing budgetary funds to their own political interests. A report on perceptions of corruption in Serbia, which was drafted by the Anti-Corruption Agency and the UN Development Programme in Serbia, published in November 2010, shows that the level of corruption in Serbia had not decreased.

The Serbian government, elected in May 2012, announced that it will fight corruption. It seems that the government really intend to do so, as it has already arrested the most powerful person of all – Miroslav Mišković, a Serbian billionaire. While charging Mišković for a crime is not the same as convicting him, recent actions by the Serbian government have been positively received by voters and the public in general.

This issue is very important to the current government as it believes that the previous government lost the elections because it did not do enough to address corruption. In addition, the EU put Serbia under pressure to investigate a number of privatisations that took place in Serbia after 2000. The Anti-Corruption Agency is currently investigating 24 such privatisations; NIS is not one of these. Even so, many still believe that the NIS–Gazprom

deal was bad for Serbia and that corrupt politicians were behind it.

Deputy Prime Minister Aleksandar Vučić, who is also the government's coordinator for the fight against corruption, said that the government was already checking further suspicious privatisations:

'There will be many more investigative actions and no one will be protected . . . Serbia has only just begun forming real institutions for the battle against corruption, which is why I expect it will be supported by Russia, the US, Germany, the United Nations and others in the process.'[5]

The aftermath of the deal

Douglas Muir wrote:

'Gazprom was able to buy NIS for much, much less than its real value – €400m ($588.4m) for a 51% stake in a company whose value was estimated to be more than €2 billion. The reasons for this have never been made clear. It may have involved corruption and/or a political quid pro quo for Russia's support on Kosovo. Or perhaps the last Serbian government was just really bad at negotiating. The purchase was made without competitive bids, even though several other large oil companies expressed interest, and two publicly stated that they would bid at least €2 billion.'[6]

Douglas Muir further stated that after Gazprom took control of NIS it made 2,000 redundancies. NIS has not paid any taxes as it is unclear whether it has made any profit. As far as fuel prices are concerned, they were regarded as high before the deal and they still are.

It is questionable what sustainable benefits South Stream will bring to Serbia. Gazprom will sign up NIS customers and their gas will flow through its pipeline. Serbia will maintain the pipeline and collect transit fees of around €200 million a year. Any greater influence is unlikely, as has already been seen in Belarus and Moldova. However, there were some suggestions that Serbia may be the main energy-supply hub for south-east Europe:

'The route of the pipeline has been finalised. The output from the Black Sea is planned for Bulgaria, then it will be Serbia that serves as a manager for former Yugoslav republics of Bosnia and Herzegovina and also Croatia, where auxiliary branches of the pipeline will be built.'[7]

On 3 July 2012, NIS (now controlled by Gazprom) announced that it would invest €500m annually over the next three years, ramping this up to €1bn annually after 2015. In the first stage, some 30% will go into exploration and production, 30% into refining and 40% into sales and distribution. Thereafter, investment will focus on oil and gas production, with the aim of increasing output to 5m tonnes of oil equivalent, up from 1.7m tonnes in 2012.

The commitment was confirmed on 29 October 2012 when Gazprom reported that the final investment decision was signed between Gazprom and Serbia. Leonid Chugunov,

Head of the company's Project Management Department, made the following observation:

'A year ago we commissioned South Stream's first facility – the Banatski Dvor underground gas storage facility that shaved gas consumption peaks in Serbia during cold weather. Transitioning to the investment stage at the Serbian section, ahead of all the other countries, will provide new opportunities for national economy growth as well as secure a long-lasting benefit related to our participation in the project. According to provisional estimates, South Stream will create in Serbia approximately 2,200 work-places and attract up to €1.5 billion of direct investments.'[8]

Dusan Bajatovic, Director General of state-owned Srbijagas, replied:

'It is a pleasure to us that the Republic of Serbia is the first South Stream member country to adopt the final investment decision. The project is within schedule and enjoys the full backing of our government. We will be ready to start preparations for the South Stream in Serbia soon. It is obvious that South Stream is a project of national significance and we are elaborating relevant regulations on the project. Moreover, the project will assure energy security and additional budget revenues for Serbia, create the environment for new projects in the energy and chemical industries that will boost the inflow of investments and new jobs creation.'[9]

As far as the performance of NIS shares is concerned, given the overall state of the global economy, these have performed very well, especially in 2011 (see Figure 2).

Figure 2 **NIS share price (left, in Serbian currency RSD; right, by volume) from 31 August 2010 to 7 December 2012**

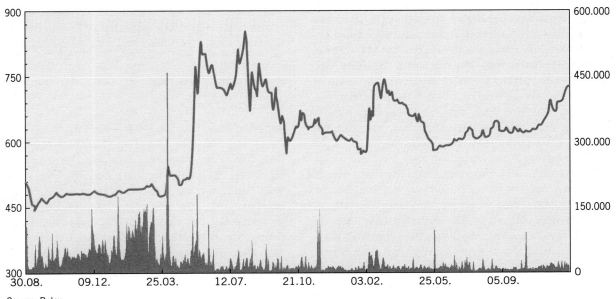

Source: Belex

The market reacted positively to the news that Gazprom Neft had launched a takeover bid (for an additional 19.12% of NIS shares) in January 2011. In addition, the company reported strong profits in 2010. Shares in NIS became part of the benchmark share index (Belex 15).

NIS shares gained 30% in one week in May 2011 after reporting excellent results for Q1 2011 (34% higher revenue) and demand for NIS shares rocketed.

So there is still a lot of debate within Serbia about the wisdom of this deal. Will it bring economic benefits to the people and government of Serbia or was it a 'political' deal? Will the new Russian owners deliver their promises? Did corruption have a part to play? It certainly looks as if there was a lot more to this deal than most joint ventures and acquisitions.

Notes and references
1. $1 = £0.65 = €0.77.
2. Blogs.ft.com, Beyond-BRICS, 20 December 2011.
3. B92, 13 December 2011.
4. BalkanInsight, 30 November 2010.
5. SETimes.com, 18 September 2012.
6. fistfullofeuros.net, 7 August 2009.
7. Pravda.ru report, 20 November 2012.
8. Gazprom.com, 29 October 2012.
9. Ibid.

APPENDIX

Gazprom

The Soviet gas industry dates back to 1943, but it was the large natural gas reserves discovered in Siberia and the Ural and Volga regions in the 1970s and 1980s that enabled the Soviet Union to become a major gas producer.

In August 1989 the Ministry of Gas transformed itself into the State Gas Concern (Gazprom) which became the country's first state-corporate enterprise. The company was still controlled by the state, but now the control was exercised through shares, 100% of which were owned by the state.

When the Soviet Union dissolved in 1991, Gazprom kept the assets located in Russia and was able to secure a monopoly in the gas sector. In 1993, Gazprom became a joint-stock company in which every Russian citizen received vouchers to purchase shares of the formerly state-owned companies. The state retained 40% of the shares. Trading of Gazprom's shares was heavily regulated and foreigners were prohibited from owning more than 9% of the shares.

In 1998 the Russian Prime Minister, Chernomyrdin, reduced the state control over Gazprom and subsequently there has been evidence of tax evasion and a poor return on investment to the state (the state did not receive a proper dividend). In addition, management launched a massive asset-stripping campaign, selling Gazprom's property at cut prices to themselves and their relatives.

In 2000 Vladimir Putin established state control in strategic companies, including Gazprom. As a result of this campaign, some 'stolen' assets were returned to Gazprom. In 2005 the state purchased a further 10.8% of Gazprom shares so that the Russian state had effective control over the company, owning just over 50% of the shares.

Gazprom Neft

In September 2005, Gazprom bought 72.633% of Sibneft (now Gazprom Neft) for $13.01 billion, aided by a $12 billion loan, which consolidated Gazprom's position as a global energy giant and Russia's biggest company. On the day of the deal the company was worth £69.7 billion.

Gazprom Neft is the fifth-largest Russian oil company by crude oil production and is ranked in the top 20 globally according to proven hydrocarbon reserves, with an oil equivalent in excess of 1 billion tonnes. Gazprom Neft's operations are focused on the exploration, development, production and sale of crude oil and gas, as well as oil refining and the marketing of petroleum products. The company refines more than 80% of the oil it produces.

Petroleum Industry of Serbia and NIS

NIS, in its present form, was established in 1991 as a public company for the exploration, production, refining and trade of crude oil, petroleum products and natural gas. This company gave rise to three other companies: NIS, Srbijagas and Transnafta. Srbijagas is an important player in the South Stream project and was established on 1 October 2005 following the restructuring of NIS.

In October 2005, NIS was transformed into a joint-stock company. In January 2010, 19% of the shares were owned by Serbian citizens and current/former employees of NIS. In June 2010 NIS was transformed into an open joint-stock company and has been listed on the Belgrade Stock Exchange (Belex) since 30 August 2010. In 2012 Gazprom Neft owned 56.15% of the share capital of NIS; 29.88% of NIS shares are owned by the Republic of Serbia. The remaining shares belong to citizens, employees, former employees and other minor shareholders.

Slobodan Milošević

Slobodan Milošević was President of Serbia from 1989 to 1997 and then the President of the Federal Republic of Yugoslavia until October 2000 when he was ousted from power. He was indicted for war crimes in May 1999 and later tried by the International Court of Justice in The Hague, where he died in 2006 before any verdict was reached.

CASE STUDY

International HIV/AIDS Alliance (B):[1]
a strategy for 2020

Gerry Johnson

The International HIV/AIDS Alliance is a network of organisations throughout the world dedicated to combating the spread and the effects of HIV and AIDS. Following the development of a strategy from 2010 to 2012, this case explains the issues the Alliance faced in 2012 as it sought to develop a strategy to take it forward to 2020.

• • •

Thirty-four million people live with HIV globally (69% in Sub-Saharan Africa). More than half do not know they are HIV positive. In 2011, 1.7 million people died of AIDS-related causes and there were 2.5 million new HIV infections. Most AIDS deaths can be prevented with antiretroviral therapy (ART) but only 54% of those eligible for treatment in low- and middle-income countries receive ART. These are the challenges that the International HIV/AIDS Alliance ('the Alliance') faces.

In mid-2011 Awo Ablo joined the Alliance as Director of External Relations, with responsibility for external stakeholders, including donor organisations and policy-makers. As part of her brief she was given responsibility for developing the Alliance strategy to 2020 as part of a small group led by the Executive Director. By the end of 2012 this process was nearing completion. The key drivers of the strategy had been discussed and agreed. What remained was to agree the future strategic direction.

The Alliance

The Alliance has its international Secretariat in Brighton, UK, which provides services to a global partnership of 41 nationally based, independent organisations working together to mobilise communities against HIV and AIDS. The Alliance is united around its mission: supporting community action on HIV, health and human rights to end AIDS. Its vision is a world in which communities have brought an end to HIV transmission and secured their health and human rights. Its actions are guided by their values which are that the lives of all human beings are of equal value, and everyone has the right to access the HIV

Source: Nell Freeman

information and services they need for a healthy life. The Board of Trustees is the Alliance's highest policy and decision-making body. It approves the Alliance's strategic framework and is responsible for ensuring that the organisation's policies and strategies are in keeping with its mission. It also selects and appoints the Executive Director.

The work of the Alliance

Since 1994, the Alliance and its partners have supported over 3,000 projects in over 40 countries, reaching millions of people. It works in six areas.

- *Prevention services.* Over 90% of Alliance Linking Organisations (LOs) have prevention programmes. In higher prevalence settings the Alliance supports prevention activities and services aimed at the general population, with care initiatives that reach people living with HIV and through sexual and reproductive health services. In lower-prevalence countries it supports prevention programmes focusing on relevant members of key population groups such as men who have sex with men, injecting drug users and sex workers – 'key' because they are the ones most affected but also because of the central role they play in breaking the back of the epidemic.

- *Care and support to orphans and vulnerable children.* In Africa and Asia the Alliance supports children orphaned by AIDS, living with HIV or caring for sick parents. This includes helping with school expenses, food, clothing and legal issues, as well as providing emotional and social support.
- *Care and support services.* The Alliance provides care and support services, including HIV testing and counselling, treatment, palliative care, support, and reducing the stigma and discrimination faced by people with HIV/AIDS.
- *Treatment adherence.* Even where ART becomes available, effective rollout requires people to understand how it works. So the Alliance works to ensure that community structures and leadership, especially from people living with HIV, support and endorse its introduction and use.
- *Technical support and capacity building.* HIV affects people most when they do not have access to information, services or protection for their rights, or when they can not act freely within their environment. The Alliance provides civil society organisations with technical support using expertise from the regions.
- *Policy and advocacy.* The Alliance aims to influence and improve the HIV policies of international policy-makers and donors using the experiences of LOs and the lessons learnt about successful responses to HIV.

To help deliver these services, the Alliance offices in Brighton are organised as three departments. The Programmes Department faces the LOs, the Corporate Services Department provides services such as HR and IT, and External Relations is concerned with external stakeholders, including donors.

Alliance funding and finances

Global funding for HIV/AIDS increased sixfold between 2002 and 2008 but has remained on a plateau since 2008. Of the \$7.6 billion (£5bn; €5.9bn)[2] from donor governments in 2011, the USA was the largest donor (59.2%), followed by the UK (12.8%), France (5.4%), the Netherlands (4.2%), Germany (4.0%) and Denmark (2.5%). Despite the economic downturn, donors have avoided major cuts in aid

budgets. The Alliance itself receives virtually no funding from the general public and is mostly funded by the foreign aid or assistance budgets of OECD countries, including: the UK's Department for International Development (DFID), the USA (USAID), Sweden (SIDA), Denmark (DANIDA), Norway (NORAD) and Australia (AusAID). Multilateral donors include the Global Fund to Fight AIDS, TB and Malaria, UN agencies, the European Commission and the World Bank. Private philanthropic donors are less prominent but include the Bill and Melinda Gates Foundation and the Levi Strauss Foundation.

Alliance income in 2011 reached \$100m, the majority of which went directly from donors to the LOs (see Figure 1). Most of the Alliance's funding is restricted to programme activities overseas, with a smaller amount of unrestricted funding to support overall delivery of a strategy and core functions such as support to LOs, business development, fundraising, knowledge sharing, marketing, communications, finance, HR and IT.

The 2020 Strategic Plan

The planning process

The planning process for the 2010 Strategic Plan that Awo inherited had been led by Sam MacPherson, as Head of Planning, who had subsequently left the Alliance. The process had involved extensive consultation with Board members, LOs and external stakeholders in helping develop and review both the key drivers of the strategy and the strategic options. Awo was extensively briefed on this process. Her approach was, however, different:

> 'The LOs have delegated responsibility for the global strategy formulation to the Secretariat. Sam had been here nine years and executed the strategy planning in a highly consultative fashion. I sometimes struggle to interpret the limits and freedoms of the delegated responsibility that we have as a Secretariat. We and the LOs are equal for sure, but how we execute the delegated responsibility is, I guess, the question . . . Consultation is absolutely part of the process but the drivers for this strategy were arrived at prior to consultation. The external game changers had to be the drivers for the strategy; so our approach was driven by this and my own approach was more "can we find some more evidence that's robust, before we take decisions?" It is what we do about those drivers that will be mapped out by consultation.'

The strategic drivers

The planning process described by Awo gave rise to a document that identified a number of 'strategic drivers' of future strategy. Extracts from the document are given in what follows together with Awo's comments.

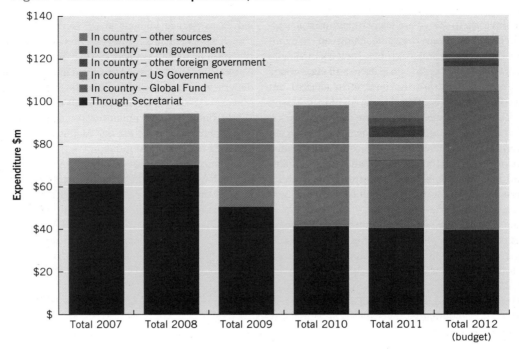

Figure 1 **HIV/AIDS Alliance expenditure, 2007–12**

1 Global and economic power dynamics

'By 2020 we envisage a world where the dominant global powers have changed significantly, with countries such as the BRICs[3] and the Gulf States exercising their economic and political strength on the national, regional and international stage. Economic recession and recovery will reduce the influence and international development resource flows from "old" powers like the US, the UK and Europe. Overseas Development Assistance (ODA) is likely to be concentrated in the poorest countries. In some regions, e.g. Latin America and the Caribbean, increasing violence, corruption and drug trafficking are likely to be stronger influences on society than economics alone.

International frameworks will weaken (UNAIDS, WHO and other UN agencies will see their influence reduced) as new powers assert national sovereignty. On the national stage new economic powers will be free to decide what, how, how much and who they fund. The main recourse for change to national priorities comes from the country's own citizens.

The emerging economies' differing attitudes to democracy and human rights will impact on their priorities for development assistance. Within regions the emerging economies will have a huge influence on their neighbours.

A weakening of international frameworks may also mean a strengthening of religious bodies, which for the most part are not dependent on international aid.

Changes in geopolitical power within the Gulf States, for example, may lead to even stronger and far-reaching religious forces in development.

Multinational corporations will continue to shape our lives. Despite the economic downturn there are likely to be more very rich people than ever before. Rich philanthropists and multinational corporations, some with CSR foundations, have enormous potential for funding, but they are shaped by personal politics and market interests.

What will this mean for the Alliance? Overseas Development Aid (ODA) from traditional donors will decrease and many LOs will see their ODA base dry up. The influence of new regional powers will increase. Understanding the motivations and interests of new donors (whether multinationals, rich philanthropists or religious institutions) will be key. International policy frameworks will become less influential as the importance of national actors and dynamics increases.'

Awo commented:

'Our relationship with domestic governments had been created as an instrument of Western donor goodwill. That framework – the development assistance model – struck me as one that was rapidly disappearing. In its place the governments in Africa, Asia and Latin America are having more responsibility for the welfare of their own citizens . . . So I asked why hasn't the Alliance got many relationships with the governments of the countries where we work? Why am I not hearing of contracting relationships where governments outsource some of their health provision to our LOs in X or Y country? The Global Fund for AIDS, TB and Malaria (GFATM) or the US government's foreign aid arm will give money to an NGO like the Alliance, parallel to government systems; it doesn't go into the local government budget. The accountability and results are not necessarily shared with the population even if they have a transparent government in that country, because it's separate; it doesn't necessarily sit as part of a government health system because of the emergency nature of the donors' response to AIDS . . . Maybe we need to focus our time with LOs on building their relationships with their domestic governments; making sure they have good programme models that are cost efficient so governments will buy them because these middle income governments aren't going to pay what the Bill Gates Foundation or the US government paid . . . In addition the private sector will have an increasing role as designers of programmes and as deliverers of programmes of work. Maybe we have a role there too.'

2 Shifts in HIV/AIDS population dynamics: from LICs to MICs

'Large numbers of the world's people living with HIV and the poorest live in countries now considered middle income countries (MICs). While in 2000 two-thirds lived in low income countries (LICs), by 2009 this dropped to just one-third. Looking at poverty rather than HIV, the dynamics aren't very different: 70% of the world's extreme poor now live in MICs. The total number of LICs has fallen and will continue to fall in the next decade and many of them will be fragile states.[4]

There is a clear agenda of "growth leads to development" and it is being demonstrated by donor withdrawal from MICs. As a result, international donor funding for HIV is not following the epidemic, nor is development assistance tracking the poor. Donors are focusing on poor countries, rather than poor people. As countries graduate from LICs to MICs they are becoming ineligible for donor assistance, irrespective of poverty indicators.

We expect inequality to increase as development assistance from MICs is withdrawn. Greater inequality may lead to increased numbers of sex workers and injecting drug users. Human rights programming may be difficult to support in MICs where national resources will be the main source of funding and in LICs and fragile states where civil society may be more nascent and donor funding more concentrated on reconstruction and emergency/humanitarian responses.

What will this mean for the Alliance? Funding from ODA will decline or disappear and will need to be replaced by other sources in MICs. Since 2005, eight countries where the Alliance has LOs have graduated from LIC to MIC status.[5] Most of our current programming (in terms of people reached and financial volume) currently takes place in MICs. By 2015, only 12 countries where we currently have LOs are likely to still have LIC status.[6] Human rights work will be more challenging within our current model.'

In relation to this, Awo commented:

'When we looked at World Bank indicators for the countries where we work we saw that since 2001 there has been a huge migration of "Alliance countries" from low-income status to middle-income status. So, Botswana, India and Nigeria are now middle-income countries. The US, the UK, the Nordic donors are the big ones for HIV funding and they have all said publicly that they are pulling out of MICs on a number of issues or entirely, though they may still help with infrastructure projects because that still helps trade links.'

She explained, however, that the increased wealth of these countries did not necessarily go hand in hand with enlightened policies on AIDS:

'Key populations in some countries often have difficulties in accessing HIV treatment, prevention and care services due to high levels of stigma, discrimination, violence and persecution. According to UNAIDS, only 22% of countries have laws protecting men who have sex with men from discrimination. Even fewer countries (15%) have laws to protect transgender people from discrimination. Over the last few years more than 100 countries have used criminal law to prosecute citizens who fail to disclose their HIV status to others.[7] These practices undermine access to HIV services for key populations. Increased efforts to strengthen health systems, especially but not only in low-income countries, is crucial.'

3 Increasing focus on measurable, quantifiable results

'Donors increasingly measure results and want to focus on and fund these rather than the activities or inputs that bring about these results. This results-led agenda is donor driven and often linked to satisfying taxpayers, even though there is little evidence that public support is greatly influenced by results as expressed by governments. Donors increasingly want to contract development services, rather than fund organisations to achieve shared goals. Taking this agenda to its logical conclusion, donors may change aid delivery models to provide payment by outcomes. When the thing being delivered is an outcome such as the number of additional people on HIV treatment or the number of infections averted, this becomes hugely problematic to measure and attribute to one agency. Private-sector donors are also likely to apply similar approaches.

Payment by results favours easily quantifiable results. Donors may not apply this principle to the significant proportion of funding they invest in fragile and post-conflict states. On the positive side, the results agenda is a natural impetus for greater cost efficiency and effectiveness.

What will this mean for the Alliance? Quantitative measures and payment by results favour commodities and biomedical approaches more than social enablers and approaches like community mobilisation; the strategic investment framework provides our advocacy platform to challenge this. The Alliance needs to focus on developing a shared methodology to measure value for money in response to this driver.'

4 The end of AIDS exceptionalism

'Apart from the US (decreasing) and AusAID (increasing), no bilateral donor currently has an HIV/AIDS specific budget line. This reflects the changing nature of the epidemic. Predominantly, HIV will be framed as a health systems issue, bypassing the crucial difference that AIDS, unlike many public health concerns, forces systems (government, clinicians, etc.) to confront sex, sexual minorities, drug use and society's moral and cultural norms.

AIDS exceptionalism also sits within a wider trend focusing on the interdependency of aid sectors; growth, health, livelihoods, governance, etc. USAID is already pushing for mergers of different organisations in the Caribbean for this reason. Yet opportunities still exist for AIDS to play a leading role and have a voice, for example with the non-communicable disease (NCD) agenda – the programmes, infrastructure and experience built by the AIDS response can be used for NCDs.

What will this mean for the Alliance? Voices questioning a primary HIV focus will continue. Some LOs will explore integration while others fully take on a broad health/human development agenda. There is a risk of distancing ourselves from key populations as we broaden the agenda.'

Awo commented:

'I went to the regional meeting held in Indonesia of all the LOs from our Asia and Eastern Europe region. They were there to discuss how they were doing against the current strategy. For a lot of them the name of the organisation is an acronym, a bunch of letters, and many have an "H" in it and an "A" which I assumed related to HIV and AIDS. But as they introduced themselves they would explain what their letters meant and a lot of them had turned the "H" into "health" and the "A" was for "and". Nonetheless they said "we still need to be tackling HIV in our communities because often we're the only ones doing it. We're not going to go into a country where HIV isn't a big problem and we want to continue working for those key populations where there are concentrated epidemics; but we also realise that the communities around us have needs other than HIV. So the conundrum for us is that we are focused on HIV but recognise the drive to deliver better health and wellbeing outcomes in other areas for our communities. So, it's a balancing act. . . . Another issue we identified was that we do not prioritise our resources systematically based on the burden of the epidemic and the impact we could have. The question is, should we?'

She also added:

'Not all money is created equal. An NGO has "unrestricted income" and "restricted income". Unrestricted means you can spend it on whatever you think you need to do to reach your mission and deliver an over-arching strategy. The Alliance sets a target of 20% unrestricted. But part of the donor trend is a reluctance to fund unrestricted.'

Awo also added further points on AIDS exceptionalism:

'The Millennium Development Goals (MDGs) run out in 2015. These are goals that UN Member States committed to in 2000 which focused the attention of the world on priority actions for reducing poverty in the developing world. They have been enormously influential. The MDGs include a goal to combat HIV/AIDS, malaria and other diseases. So, health issues were winners and HIV was a big winner. But we will be lucky if we get a mention in the next framework . . . There were also targets set in 2011 by all governments at the UN High Level Meeting on HIV/AIDS on how many people should be on treatment. We have reached eight million but the target is double that by 2015 and the analysis by the UN demonstrates that, given the current rate of programme work on HIV, we will not reach those goals by 2015. UNAIDS has also plotted and costed exactly what interventions and actions are needed to break the back of this epidemic. New infections will need to drop dramatically in order to attain the other MDG goal of reducing the rate of HIV infection by 50% by 2015.[8] The decline in new HIV infections has not been sufficient in areas where the epidemic is concentrated among key population groups with a higher risk of HIV infection, such as sex workers, people who inject drugs and men who have sex with men. There is a need for increased investments in prevention efforts targeted at groups that are highly vulnerable to HIV transmission . . . To achieve all this we mustn't take our foot off the pedal . . . And remember that the Alliance is respected for working with key populations.'

5 Improvements in biotechnology and ever-increasing use of ICTs

'There will be significant developments in biotechnology such as the expected availability of microbicides by 2019, the potential of a new TB vaccine, treatment as prevention and better ART. These present enormous opportunities and health benefits, but will have behavioural and social effects that are as yet poorly understood. Home HIV testing is likely to be made more available, which raises questions about how people access follow-on health services, along with questions about how those on treatment will understand themselves or be understood by their communities in terms of HIV transmission, sexual and injecting risk and social roles. Those who are marginalised will continue to be excluded from many of these developments.

Although there will still be a digital divide, new information and communication technologies (ICTs) such as telemedicine, the Internet and mobile phones have the potential to help improve access to services, For example diagnosis and prescriptions could be accessed remotely and even anonymously. Increased access to the Internet will provide greater availability of information on health and rights.

What will this mean for the Alliance? The ability to reach marginalised and high-need communities will be critical, along with protecting a reputation that ensures we continue to be a trusted provider of health and human rights information. There is a need to explore and understand what these new technologies mean for key populations; and what the role of community mobilisation is in increasing uptake and reducing the negative impacts. The Alliance will need to understand and work with online communities.'

Awo explained further:

'I was surprised that you could get diagnosed with HIV and wander off with no drug regimen until your CD4 cell count hits 350. But in 2011 at the Rome conference for HIV, highly significant clinical trial results were announced. If someone who is HIV positive starts taking the HIV regimen earlier than the current WHO guidelines (i.e. at a CD4 count between 350 and 550), then the viral load reduces to such a low that their transmission risk to somebody else can potentially be reduced by 96%. So, for the first time it has been shown that treatment is not only keeping people alive and healthy but can prevent them passing on the virus. So, the Alliance needs to rethink how much it does to support more

people getting treatment early and adhering to that treatment. However, we have been perceived as a much more traditional prevention organisation, distributing condoms, providing education, information and counselling about transmission risks, prevention behaviours, etc. It also means getting more people to adhere to their drug regimens, because if people don't, then the prevention effect doesn't work.'

Some key questions

Awo also issued a discussion paper that outlined some key questions that needed to be addressed. These included the following.

Strategic responses
How should we respond to the divergence becoming apparent between LICs and MICs?
Many LICs may continue to receive ODA. Here it seems appropriate to continue to invest in helping to scale up and maximise the impact of LOs. However, in states in which ODA may not continue (in the main MICs) we will have to shape new community responses.

What should we do to convince governments and donors that LOs are able to go beyond the project level to influence investment decisions at national level, particularly in MICs?
In non-ODA-assisted states, such as in Asia, Latin America and Eastern Europe, substantial volumes of funds are still misdirected to generalised programming and prevention activities for low-risk populations. There is also limited evidence that countries are substantially increasing domestic investments targeting key populations. This underscores the importance of generating political and social acceptance for policy and programming that targets key populations in the medium and long term, essential for long-term sustainable responses.

How might this be achieved?
In what ways might we work with the private sector as a provider of services?
We will need to develop new business models for MICs. Some emerging business models include the following:

1 **Service Delivery Commissioned Model:** delivering services and running clinics commissioned/funded by national governments. This will require defining standard packages of services and models with detailed (lower) unit costings; LOs going down this track will need to develop a better understanding of health systems and government budgeting and commissioning processes. A focus will be on facility-based service delivery.

2 **Government Development Partnership Model:** influencing health (and other) systems to improve access and quality for key populations and protect human rights. This would mean working with government to ensure the packages of services are high quality and comprehensive. It would involve providing training/education and workforce development for government providers or developing kitemarking for services for key populations. There could also be an advocacy role in influencing the spending priorities and budget allocation of national and local governments to ensure they meet the needs of key populations and provide a comprehensive package of services. Although some of this may be financed by government, prevention activities may be dropped compared with a focus on treatment for example.

3 **Watchdog Model:** holding governments to account and addressing structural barriers through legal processes. The ways of working here would be using the judicial system and litigation to improve access to health systems. The aims would be to influence equity of budget allocation and ensure that rights are being protected. If this was the sole or primary role of an Alliance LO, we would need to develop technical and legal expertise to scrutinise the work of public bodies. Funding for this kind of work will almost never come from national governments themselves, so alternative funding will have to be sought. LOs fulfilling this function are unlikely to be able to also deliver services for governments.

4 **Human Rights Defenders Model:** protecting human rights at the grassroots level. Here the focus would be on advocating change and a more enabling environment, using non-legal methods and advocacy to challenge violence, homophobia and transphobia, stigma and discrimination among communities. Funding for this role is highly unlikely to be provided by national governments, so alternative and innovative sources would be needed.

Which of these models is most appropriate and why? How would (a) the Secretariat and (b) support hubs need to change to support different business models?
Community action on HIV is often made difficult by hostile policy environments. Resource constraints, laws that perpetuate or exacerbate the marginalisation and stigmatisation of key populations, and a failure to enforce laws where they do exist, all undermine HIV efforts and leads to rights violations.

Given the importance of key populations, what role should the Alliance play: e.g. should it become a stronger, more challenging public campaigner or one that seeks to work more closely with governments?

A video featuring the work of the AIDS Alliance can be seen on: 'Someone's mother, someone's brother' at http://www.youtube.com/watch?v+jwDAiX2dut.

Notes and references
1. The first International HIV/AIDS Alliance case study appeared in the 9th edition of *Exploring Strategy*, deals with the 2010–12 strategic plan and is available at www.pearsoned.co.uk/mystrategylab
2. $1 ≈ £0.66 ≈ €0.78.
3. Brazil, Russia, India and China.
4. Such as Somalia, Sudan, Congo, Zimbabwe, Chad, Haiti and Afghanistan. Fragile states are *de facto* categorised as LICs.
5. Côte d'Ivoire, India, Mongolia, Nigeria, Senegal, South Sudan, Vietnam and Zambia. Figures from the World Bank (2011).
6. Bangladesh, Ethiopia, Burkina Faso, Burundi, Haiti, Kenya, Kyrgyzstan, Mozambique, Myanmar, Uganda and Zimbabwe, from World Bank (2011), 'Country and lending groups', http://data.worldbank.org/about/country-classifications/country-and-lending-groups
7. UNAIDS (2012), UNAIDS report: *Together We Will End AIDS*, July 2012.
8. Ibid.

The author wishes to thank the International HIVAIDS Alliance for their co-operation in the writing of the case study.

CASE STUDY

The Mexican narco-trafficking problem

Clive Kerridge and Sophia O. Kerridge

This case study looks at examples of 'successful' international crime organisations, namely Mexican drug trafficking cartels. These illegal businesses are often just as structured, organised and strategically managed as legal corporations. This case gives an opportunity to evaluate strategic options, from the point of view of Mexican government policy advisors, as the state attempts to understand the NTOs' strategies in order to counteract them.

●   ●   ●

The problem

The new President of Mexico, Enrique Peña Nieto (PRI Party), came to power in December 2012 with a big problem on his hands: spiralling violence associated with the notorious drug cartels.[1] During 2011, drug-related deaths rose to over 12,000, several regions were increasingly lawless and some of the country's highest-ranking military and police officials had been arrested over drug-related crimes. Then, in mid-2012, the US Congress found HSBC's Mexican branch guilty of laundering money for some of the nation's narco-trafficking organisations (NTOs). The new president was facing strong diplomatic pressure, the threat of declining international business investment (especially in the US border area), a serious threat to national security, and recognition that the NTOs were:

'. . . now posing a multi-faceted organised criminal challenge to governance in Mexico'.

Report to the US Congress, August 2012[2]

The problem had been inherited from his predecessor, Enrique Calderón of the opposing PAN Party. In an effort to tackle the growing strength of NTOs in his home state of Michoacán, Calderón had deployed the military onto the streets. Little did he know in 2006 that he would be unleashing a 'drug war' of huge proportions, destabilising the illegal narcotics trade and instigating violent battles, not only between the military and NTOs but also between the NTOs themselves. As a key part of his election campaign, Peña Nieto had promised to 'change strategy'. His policy advisors needed to analyse the NTOs' activities and to define the new government's strategic options – and quickly.

The business

The first part of solving any problem is to identify it: Peña Nieto's government was not just facing a problem of widespread violence. This was violence orchestrated by large, complex organisations that ran very profitable businesses in the trade of narcotics – an industry worth billions of dollars, employing thousands of people.

In 2010, the UNODC estimated the value of the illegal global drug trade at $320 billion per year (£210bn; €250bn),[3] indicating that profits from the US cocaine market alone constituted $35 billion. In comparison, immigrant smuggling from Latin America to the USA was valued at $6.6 billion a year and the arms trade from the USA to Mexico was worth just $20 million a year (see Figure 1).[4]

The cocaine trade is a particularly profitable undertaking due to its non-labour-intensive production, simple technology and compact transportation. The value added to cocaine at each stage of the manufacturing and distribution process reflects the varying levels of risk and complexity. For example, a kilo of cocaine that in Colombia would cost around $2000 has a value of $10,000 in Mexico and, after crossing the US border, would sell wholesale at $30,000. Once broken down, mixed and split among street dealers, the value per kg is $100,000.[5]

As can be seen in Figure 2, most of the profits from the drug trade are at distribution level (to final consumers).

The case was prepared by Clive Kerridge, Senior Lecturer in Strategy at the University of Gloucestershire and Director of consultancy KvH International Ltd, and Sophia Kerridge, who completed her Oxford University research thesis on Mexican and Colombian drug trafficking violence and government responses, and now works for Peace Brigades International in Colombia. It is intended as a basis for class discussion and not as an illustration of good or bad practice. © Clive Kerridge and Sophia Kerridge 2013. Not to be reproduced or quoted without permission.

Figure 1 Estimated annual value of some global criminal markets in the 2000s

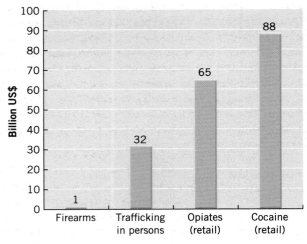

Source: UNODC World Drug Report 2010, Figure 4, p. 33

Figure 2 Distribution of gross profits (in %) of the $35 billion US cocaine market, 2008

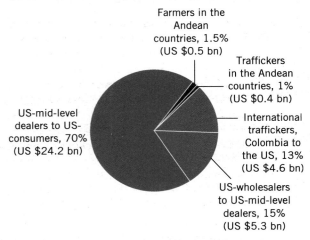

Source: UNODC World Drug Report 2010, Figure 39, p. 79

However, the fragmented and decentralised nature of end-level distribution means that *concentrated* wealth is at the international trafficking level. So, although 70% of gross income goes to dealers selling to consumers, there are thousands of street-level drug dealers in the USA who share those profits. In their celebrated 2005 book *Freakonomics*,[6] Levitt and Dubner encapsulate this fragmentation and low 'retail' profitability in the title of Chapter 3: 'Why do drug dealers still live with their moms?'. At production level, there are various supply sources and little value has yet been added, so gross profits are small compared to those made by the international drug trafficking organisations.

This smuggling or trafficking is undertaken by a select number of groups that specialise in complex operations, coordinating products from many sources and delivering them to numerous destinations. Through this bottleneck, wealth and power are concentrated. It has been estimated that the Colombian Cali and Medellín Cartels, which dominated the cocaine trade during the 1980s, each made close to $5bn annually just from cocaine trafficking.[7]

The illicit drug trade is not a static or stable industry. For decades, Latin America has been the main supply source for the US market, the world's largest consumer of marijuana, opiates, cocaine and ATS (amphetamine-type stimulants). However, the dominant criminal organisations and the types of drugs being trafficked have changed: whereas earlier traffickers primarily dealt with marijuana, Colombians became the world's principal cocaine traffickers. Colombia has continued to be one of the biggest cocaine producers in the world but Mexican NTOs are now the dominant traffickers, also involved in the marijuana, opiate and ATS trades. These evolutions in market control or dominance occur due to factors such as changes in an NTO's ability to operate or fluctuations in demand. For example, in 2012, ATS demand in the USA was increasing, whereas cocaine demand there was forecast to decrease; yet cocaine demand in Europe was predicted to rise.

Legal and illegal businesses: the law enforcement effect

The illicit nature of the industry means drug trafficking is always at risk of interruption by law enforcement. Therefore, NTOs are often organised to keep a low profile and avoid the state's attention. Yet they maintain the capacity for violence and to co-opt or corrupt state employees so they can guarantee impunity and protection over their activities. NTOs face additional operational costs because, unlike legal businesses, agreements cannot be enforced or arbitrated by the law. NTOs have to enforce their own contracts and settle their own disputes, with violence if necessary.

Like legal businesses, however, the drug trade benefits from economies of scale. Organisations seek to expand and integrate various stages of the industry, where possible monopolising the market, to maximise efficiency and profitability. Low barriers to entry, and the attraction of quick and high profits, ensure constant new competition that can potentially destabilise the market. Stability and control may be achieved via NTO alliances (though such alliances are often temporary) or with the division of territories and markets. The unpredictability of operating under such conditions inevitably requires NTOs to be adaptable: for example, if leaders are arrested it must be possible to substitute them quickly. This supports the observation by a high-level panel of the United Nations that: 'Organised crime is increasingly operating through fluid networks rather than more formal hierarchies. This form of organisation provides criminals with diversity, flexibility, low visibility and longevity.'[8]

Such adaptability can also be seen through novel trafficking mechanisms, which are introduced to remain ahead of the competition and law enforcement, for example via tunnels under (and catapults over) the US–Mexican border or small submarines operating in the Caribbean; also through the development of new generations of drugs which are easier to transport, less complex to produce, and harder to detect. As for longevity, life expectancy for the people involved in NTOs is often short (with prison as the most likely alternative), as the police and military attack the NTOs' organisational structures.

'Balloons' and 'mercury'

NTOs do not benefit from the legal and other protections enjoyed by legitimate businesses. However, they are not constrained by the legislation and state bureaucracy that can slow down business growth and development. In some senses, NTOs are operating in a completely 'free market'! To survive in such fast-changing environments, NTOs have to be dynamic, entrepreneurial organisations. For example, if the state suppresses drug production in a certain part of the country, NTOs will often transfer their activities to another area, or even abroad, where law enforcement is less effective (the 'balloon effect': squeeze a balloon and the air moves to the parts with less pressure).[9] When counter-narcotics efforts in Colombia during the late 1980s reduced NTO capacity to manage complex international smuggling routes, Mexican groups began taking over cocaine trafficking. Additionally, when the state puts pressure on the senior levels of large NTOs, these organisations tend to split into many smaller units (the 'mercury effect'). This occurred in Colombia once the Cali and Medellín Cartels had been destroyed. It is worth noting that none of these measures resulted in the termination of international trafficking or the illicit drug trade.

The growth of the Sinaloa Cartel

Perhaps most embarrassing for the Mexican authorities has been the continued dominance of the Sinaloa Cartel, often referred to as the world's leading organised crime or 'mafia' business. Its infamous leader, Joaquin 'El Chapo' Guzmán, heralded in various *narcocorridos* (modern Mexican folk songs) for his legendary outlaw status, amassed a personal fortune which in 2012 *Forbes* magazine valued at $1bn. Guzmán had been arrested in 2001 but managed to escape and had repeatedly eluded recapture, continuing to direct the Sinaloa Cartel, which went

on to dominate the illicit trafficking industry in Mexico and much of the Americas. Rumours about this NTO and its ability to influence and corrupt state officials were rife – to the extent that the PAN government felt compelled to release a statement in 2010 that it was *not* cooperating with the Sinaloa Cartel to bring down competing NTOs.

The Sinaloa organisation has strong local roots and was one of the original cartels, dating back to long before the 1980s. Based in Sinaloa State, it controlled marijuana production and trafficking in much of northwest Mexico, mostly destined for the US market. The political stability during the many years of the PRI Party's control, up until 2000, meant that the Sinaloa Cartel had embedded itself into the political structure, protecting its activities and members. As its leader, Guzmán was the local 'patrón', somewhat similar to the figure of *The Godfather*,[10] enforcing his own law among the local population and giving out favours, buying him a strong local support base that served to protect him during his many years as a fugitive.

This local support base and political protection network was typical of Mexican NTOs until the early 2000s when the situation began to unravel for two principal reasons:

- The democratisation and election of a new governing party (PAN) in 2000 destabilised the traditional political links – NTOs no longer had the same patronage and protection networks they had enjoyed under the PRI.
- Previously dominant Colombian NTOs, subjected to heavy government and US pressure, started to lose its ability to manage complex international trafficking operations. They were already working with Mexican crime gangs, so the Colombian groups started to sell cocaine directly to the Mexican NTOs, which then independently managed transportation and supply to the US market.

Although the Mexican state had previously been able to limit or informally manipulate NTO activity through its links with the cartels, Mexico's new PAN government was less able to do so, leaving NTOs to operate with more freedom. The US cocaine market was a huge opportunity for the cartels, with enormous profits to be made. Consequently, Mexican NTOs started to develop their structures to accommodate the international trafficking of cocaine, meaning new transport routes, connections and management of supply chains.

NTO diversification

After dramatic growth in the 1980s and 1990s, by the year 2000 US cocaine demand was reaching saturation so, while Mexican NTOs had the opportunity to take a dominant position in this billion-dollar market, there was not much opportunity to expand the market itself. An outcome was that the main Mexican NTOs were soon facing strong competition from each other over access to the lucrative US market. Competition was based on territorial control – access to trafficking routes in Mexico, border areas, production areas, places with corrupt law enforcement, and ports of entry and exit (including airports).

As the competition became fiercer, several NTOs looked for ways to diversify, moving into new markets, such as cocaine for Europe, or supplying new illicit drugs (principally methamphetamines) into North America via their established routes and contacts (Figure 3). Others took the opportunity to reinforce their local territorial control by developing the domestic consumer market, in this way involving more local people in their business model and increasing local dependency on (and thus loyalty to) that NTO.

The Sinaloa Cartel, for example, building on its existing dominance of the Mexican drug trafficking market and its relationships with US distributors and Colombian suppliers, expanded international operations to almost all of the Americas and started to develop trafficking networks through western Africa, as a route to penetrating the European market. Strategically located on the western US border, it also developed various complex but effective drug corridors for all types of illegal narcotics making their way into the USA. Such was their territorial dominance that anyone involved in any part of the drug trade in their territory had to do it under the watchful eye of the Sinaloa Cartel, paying 'taxes'. Although these groups were not directly affiliated, their activities got absorbed into the Sinaloa Cartel's network of 'interests'.

With the extra income generated from this new era of trafficking, the Sinaloa Cartel had to find new ways of investing and protecting its cash. One was money laundering, the creation of new legal businesses where the carbel could hide and reinvest its drug profits. Involvement in legitimate businesses presented new markets that the Sinaloa Cartel could seek to monopolise, using a mixture of legal and illegal methods. Looking to increase its market position further, the cartel also pursued an aggressive strategy of territorial expansion from 2005 onwards, seeking to control the entire west coast of Mexico from Guatemala up to California and the US border states. This brought it into direct territorial conflict with other NTOs, notably the Gulf Cartel, its main historical competitor on the East Coast, resulting in a series of bloody turf battles.

Figure 3 Cartel territories and drug–smuggling routes, 2008

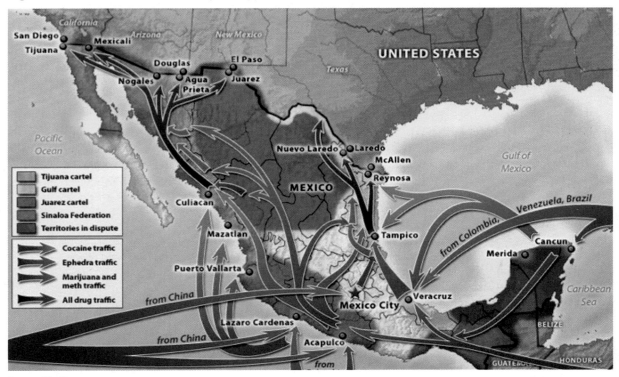

Source: Stratfor

A changing competitive landscape . . .

The Gulf Cartel had expanded in much the same way in the early 2000s but had also developed a new wing to its operations: a paramilitary section that came to be known as the Zetas. The Zetas served to enforce the Gulf Cartel's 'law', collect debts and generally ensure territorial control and protection of assets. Through violence, the Gulf Cartel achieved control of the entire eastern coast by 2008.

In response, and in order to expand into new areas, the Sinaloa Cartel did much the same, creating various armed groups or allying with local crime gangs. To build up those enforcement operations, the Sinaloa Cartel increased its investment in areas such as weapons procurement and trafficking, recruitment and corruption of military and police.

This led to further diversification in cartels' activities: to keep their paramilitaries busy, and, to enforce territorial control, these groups dedicated their time not only to supporting and protecting the narco-trafficking operations and assets, but also moved into extortion, human trafficking and other criminal activities that benefit from the presence of armed 'protection'. These new activities meant that the government of Mexico was faced with highly competitive and successful criminal business organisations, willing to compete violently and now developing military capabilities.

Although tackling the cartels with force became harder for the state, these more diverse NTOs also developed a weakness: they could not survive without the capability to deploy force against the competition, which in turn could not survive without the huge income from trafficking, which was needed to fund arms procurement and increased personnel numbers. Managing the multifaceted nature of these organisations (legal and illegal business, together with military elements) meant expanding management capabilities. Expansion inevitably implied more difficulty in keeping 'below the radar' of the state.

. . . and changing alliances

As the NTOs rapidly became stronger and more diverse, internal tensions and frictions increased, aggravated by frequent attacks from competing NTOs, causing constant changes in the NTO management hierarchies. This led to many clashes, such as a dramatic rupture within the Sinaloa Cartel in 2008 after a leadership dispute, resulting in a new splinter NTO that the Sinaloa Cartel immediately came into competition with. The same happened in other cartels, as the new paramilitary wings started to assert their own authority and undermine the parent organisations' traditional *modus operandi*.

From 2006 onwards, the Mexican police and military stepped up strikes against the cartels, while the NTOs increasingly attacked each other: violence levels exploded, resulting in thousands of deaths every year and huge organisational instability for many of the NTOs. While the aim for all of them was to manage successful international trafficking operations, for which they prefer a relatively stable environment, survival was now based on eroding their main competitors.

Despite the inter-NTO competition and the government's 'drug war' initiatives (Figure 4), the Sinaloa Cartel continued its strategy of aggressive expansion and attacking its rivals, including those with which it was once allied. While it suffered defections, deaths and arrests, its ability to maintain successful trafficking operations allowed it to continue dominating the market. Arguably, the continuing leadership and legendary status of *El Chapo* was the glue that held the Sinaloa Cartel together, giving it stability despite changes to the hierarchy below. The Sinaloa Cartel continued to successfully undermine lesser organisations, through street battles and bombings and by organising the arrest and death of their leaders – and through the successful corruption and co-option of state agents.

A threat to stability of the state?

The year 2009 saw a new dynamic, as the Zetas broke away from the Gulf Cartel and expanded control dramatically through eastern Mexico and into Central America, using extreme levels of violence and brutality when dealing with opponents. The Zetas are formed principally of military deserters or people with some form of military training, which is clearly reflected in their organisational structure. Their military chain of command and strict discipline have meant that when leaders are removed, there is a clear line of succession. The organisation's reputation for violence and lack of 'second chances' has allowed them to assert authority over new business activities despite their rapid organisational and operational expansion. The Zetas, unlike the more traditional NTOs, are more opportunistic: they have no need to win over the local population, and their principal motivation is income and gaining control over varied illegal industries in as large an area as possible.

The resulting clash between the Zetas and the Sinaloa Cartel is also a clash of business models. Sinaloa and the older drug cartels focus on exploiting their core competences (international trafficking capabilities) and maintaining their brand reputation (for quality and reliability) in the industry. Embedding their activities in local economies is central to their survival and, at the highest levels, family and personal ties reinforce the networks. In contrast, the Zetas are more involved across a range of local criminal businesses and are less dependent upon international trafficking operations. Although risks are spread

Figure 4 Evolution of the Sinaloa and Gulf Cartels, 2003–12

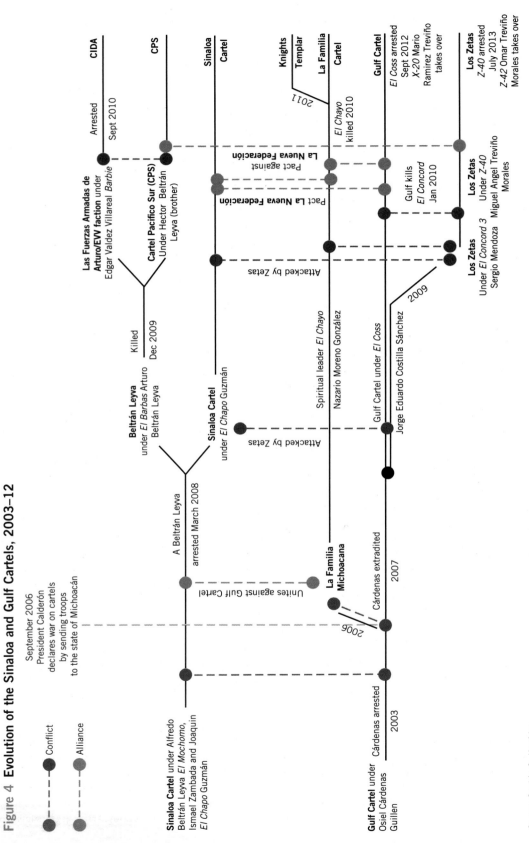

Figure 5 Mexican drug cartels' main areas of influence, 2012–13

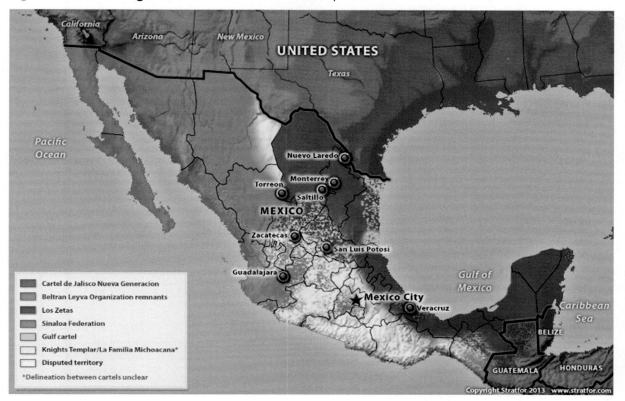

Source: Stratfor

across various operations, those local businesses have much lower barriers to competitive entry and are more susceptible to fragmentation. Furthermore, their rapid expansion and excessive use of violence have attracted the attention of various states and competitors, and forced Zeta units to adapt constantly. Blood, rather than political corruption, is their currency.

From 2010 to 2012 the violence continued: frictions caused divisions; divisions led to several new organisations and new alliances. Meanwhile the Mexican state, through police and military responses, continued trying to break the NTOs' power and influence (Figure 5) by attacking their organisational hierarchies. While this has served to destabilise the NTOs, it does little to limit the business of drug trafficking, as the organisations merely adapt and continue supplying drugs to their customers. As a sombre warning to the incoming President Peña, there was no pause in the levels of violence after his election in 2012: indeed the NTO violence was even reaching Mexico City, something many thought the cartels would never dare. The need for a new approach was evident. This was the challenge for President Peña Nieto and his policy advisors.

A new strategy in the war on drugs

By 2012 it was clear that the state's strategy was not having the desired results. If anything, quite the opposite: there was widespread anxiety about personal and public security, particularly in the main cities. A new presidency was an opportunity for a new approach in the war against the cartels, perhaps confronting them from an altogether different position.

In theory, a change in political leadership should affect NTOs negatively, since previous political linkages would end and fresh ones would have to be established within the new political system. With the election of the PRI in 2012, the party that had previously accommodated NTOs was returning to power. Although rumours of a return to the previous system of 'cohabitation' with the NTOs was fiercely denied, the pervasive violence meant that such options surely would be considered, if they might guarantee better public safety.[11]

At the same time, the Mexican state also has to respond to various national and international influences. In a democracy, where the president has just a few years to turn things around, there have to be visible improvements if there is any hope for re-election. There are also external influences that need to be considered, such as foreign investment, US political pressure, and impacts on neighbouring countries as the NTOs expand across beyond Mexico's borders.

Evidently, the previous administration's policy of armed attacks on the NTO hierarchies and short-term disruptions of certain drug routes had not produced the desired results. In part, this was because that strategy had not attacked the root of the problem, the *business* of drug trafficking.

To develop an effective strategy, the state needs to understand how the NTOs grew to be so large and wealthy; what strategies NTOs used to develop their markets and fight their competition. Much like other companies may look at competitors and try to evaluate their strategies as a means to improve or adapt their own, the state can also do this to identify the cartels' business weaknesses and vulnerabilities. By analysing how an NTO has developed its business model, the state can evaluate its likely strategy in future scenarios and try to act pre-emptively. Not least, instead of fighting the symptoms of the NTO problem, notably violence and the widespread influence of wealthy criminal families or organisations, it may be more productive to beat the NTOs at their own game: by changing conditions for the *business* of trafficking.

The new president's policy advisors were well aware that suitable counter-NTO strategies would have to be acceptable to a range of stakeholders, in Mexico and beyond. For implementation to be feasible, it would be imperative that the government had sufficient and appropriate capabilities. It was a tough but vital assignment.

For further information, see the following videos.

The business model

- CNN, 'How do Mexican cartels get drugs into the US?', http://www.youtube.com/watch?v=nO2AOQAeVJI
- DNA Info, 'DEA's New York Chief explains the "business model" of drug trafficking', http://www.youtube.com/watch?v=k2bFO-VY1ps
- Insight Crime, 'Drug gangs and human smuggling', http://www.youtube.com/watch?v=JH9GNd5ARmU&list=UUhEvdHcQEGdoKTsLFeNdb7g&index=3

The Sinaloa Cartel

- http://www.youtube.com/watch?v=4PEiOI6g9eg
- Stratfor, 'Mexican Cartels: Sinaloa Cartel', http://www.stratfor.com/video/mexican-cartels-sinaloa-federation

Zetas

- Reuters, 'Reuters investigate: Mexico drug cartel unleashes new levels of violence', http://www.youtube.com/watch?v=wcQDEexlkWc
- Insight Crime, 'Zetas in Guatemala', http://www.youtube.com/watch?v=STjiPvDtpb8&list=UUhEvdHcQEGdoKTsLFeNdb7g
- BBC, 'Mexico Zetas leader Z-40 captured', http://www.youtube.com/watch?v=QZswKWg-OaQ
- Stratfor, 'Mexican Cartels: Los Zetas', http://www.stratfor.com/video/mexican-cartels-los-zetas

Violence as a marketing strategy

- Al Jazeera, 'Mexican drug gangs' public relations campaign', http://www.youtube.com/watch?v=MFasg6qI1TY

Money laundering

- Al Jazeera, 'How Mexican drug lords spend their ill-gotten gains', http://www.youtube.com/watch?v=BY1dcqgEG2I

Notes and references

1. Note that the term *cartel*, used in reference to large drug trafficking organisations, does not necessarily mean that they control and determine market prices.
2. June S. Beittel (2012) CRS Report to the United States Congress, R41576, 3 August 2012.
3. $1 ~ £0.65 ~ €0.77.
4. UNODC (2010) *The Globalization of Crime: A Transnational Organized Crime Threat Assessment*, p. 16.
5. Patrick Radden Keefe (2012) 'Cocaine Incorporated', *New York Times Magazine*, 15 June 2012, http://www.nytimes.com/2012/06/17/magazine/how-a-mexican-drug-cartel-makes-its-billions.html?pagewanted=all
6. Steven D. Levitt and Stephen J. Dubner (2005) *Freakonomics: A Rogue Economist Explores the Hidden Side of Everything*, New York: William Morrow.
7. Sophia O. Kerridge (2011) *Drug Trafficking Organizations and the State in Colombia (1980–1995) and Mexico (1995–2011)*, MPhil Latin American Studies, Oxford University.
8. United Nations High-Level Panel on Threats, Challenges and Change (2004), quoted in UNODC (2010) *The Globalization of Crime: A Transnational Organized Crime Threat Assessment*, p. 27.
9. Michael Shifter (2007) 'Latin America's drug problem', *Current History*, February 2007, p. 62.
10. As epitomised in *The Godfather* mafia movies, based on a novel by Mario Puzo.
11. *El Mundo* (2012) 'Queremos tener tranquilo el pueblo. Todo está en su mano', Bogotá, 2 October 2012.

CASE STUDY

Dancing with the mouse: a strategic metamorphosis at Ocean Park, Hong Kong

Daphne Po May Wong

This case examines the strategic development route of strategy at Ocean Park, a maritime theme park located in Hong Kong (HK). Originally founded by the HK government, its strategy has had to change and adapt to a series of challenges in its environment – not least the competition created by the arrival of a Disney theme park in HK. Under new leadership a more distinct strategic path has been created through a 'Master Redevelopment Plan'. From the perspective of 2012, the planning process has paid dividends.

● ● ●

How the story began

The idea of building a marine theme park in Hong Kong was first suggested by J.D. Bromhall in 1957, then the Director of Agriculture and Fisheries in Hong Kong. In the 1970s, about 45% of Hong Kong's urbanised population lived in congested public housing estates and Bromhall dreamt of building a park for local people. He hoped that by providing an amenity where people could watch marine animals living in large open habitats it might give them a taste of space that they seldom experienced at home. The Hong Kong government provided land to realise Bromhall's aspiration. Initially the Hong Kong Jockey Club funded the HK$150 million (£12.7m; $19.3m; €15.1m)[1] for the construction of the park which operated as the Club's subsidiary. In January 1977, Ocean Park (OP) was formally opened. Located at the southern part of Hong Kong Island, it took up 169 acres of land spread over the Lowland and the Headland areas. The two sites are linked by a cable car system with panoramic views overlooking the South China Sea.[2]

In 1977, Sir Kenneth Ping-Fan Fung, the first Chairman of Ocean Park, proclaimed the Park as an education, entertainment and conservation provider and these have been the cornerstones of the Park's mission ever since. In July 1987, OP was separated from the Hong Kong Jockey Club and all its assets and the donations that had been bequeathed to the Park, including a HK$200 million grant by the Hong Kong Jockey Club, were transferred to the Ocean Park Trust Fund. The Park was re-established by statute as the Ocean Park Corporation and is a quasi-governmental organisation. It is entrusted with a high degree of autonomy in managing its own affairs but ultimately answerable to the Hong Kong goverment.

Its chairman is appointed by the government and its board of directors is composed of the Park's senior management staff, government officials, trade professionals and academics. The 1987 statute stipulated its purpose as 'a public recreational and educational park' and a 'provider of education and entertainment at affordable prices'. It can only use its income for education and research purposes, covering operational and development expenditure on park facilities.[3] In other words, Ocean Park has to be financially self-sufficient yet refrain from profit maximisation.

Those were the days

In the first decade up to the late 1980s management of OP focused on daily operations and maintenance, without much of a long-term strategic vision. A conforming and conservative mentality prevailed in management. When presenting its 1991 and 1992 Annual Report to the Legislative Council the Park's Chairman explicitly stated that: 'Financial viability has not been the Park's sole objective, but merely a means of achieving its broader corporate goals. . . . to supply these outstanding facilities at affordable prices.'[4]

This approach determined its admission charges policy as well. Entrance fees in the late 1980s were HK$140

(adults) and HK$70 (children), which correspond to about £12 for adults and £6 for children – virtually unchanged for years. There was even a fee reduction in 1993 to HK$130 (adults) and HK$65 (children) and children aged 3 to 11 could enter the Park for free.

From 1991 to 1995 Darrell Metzger was Chief Executive of the Park. He had previously worked in Disneyland and introduced more commercial expertise and the missing flair needed to manage a theme park. Until Metzger's time, the way the Park fulfilled its multiple roles was not distinctively clear. Perhaps its management expected that by watching sea lions and fish exhibited in pseudo-habitats and being entertained by whales and dolphins in shows, visitors would then become educated and more concerned about nature, thus discharging its triple duties in one go.

But Metzger did things somewhat differently. He adopted a five-year development plan to fulfil OP's mission in a more concrete manner. He enhanced the Park's contribution to oceanographic research by hosting international conferences, strengthening bonds with international research bodies, offering animal research facilities to students, breeding a wide variety of animals naturally and artificially, and launching research projects, such as saving the dolphins of the Yangtze River. Also, the Ocean Park Conservation Foundation (OPCF) was established in 1993 with the objective of improving attitudes and practices towards wildlife conservation in Hong Kong and Asia. Every year, 21 January is now designated as the annual Ocean Park Conservation Day with all the daily admission receipts being donated to the OPCF. For the educational role, workshops on marine mammals and conservation for teachers were developed and outreach programmes for schoolchildren began in 1992. As a result, annual school visitor numbers surged from 6,000 to well over 25,000 in 1995. When it came to entertainment, animal shows and rides were still the major attractions in those years, supplemented with other activities such as Chinese arts and crafts events every now and then.

Metzger also took a more aggressive marketing approach forming strategic alliances with, for example, Toys 'Я' Us, Fuji Film, radio stations, Lego, Caltex, the Hong Kong Cultural Centre and the Hong Kong Space Museum. New initiatives were launched to open up the Park as a venue for MICE (meetings, incentives, conferences and exhibitions) and weddings. At this time the visitors' mix to the Park was about 70% local residents and 30% tourists, but minimal efforts had been expended to penetrate into the local residents' market. So in 1995 the first loyalty programme for local visitors, the Ocean Park Fun Club, was introduced. Promotional activity was extended to mainland China, and collaborations with overseas theme parks in the form of reciprocal admission agreements were tried out. This five-year plan led to a considerable improvement in OP's revenues and attendance numbers. After his success at OP, Metzger left OP in 1995 to further his theme park career in Singapore.

The Dark Ages

After enjoying two decades of stability and relative prosperity, the period between 1997 and 2003 saw the Park hit hard by a series of external threats. First there was the avian influenza epidemic in 1997, followed by the Asian financial crisis in 1998. Not only did these events result in deficits for four consecutive years (1998–2001) with an accumulated loss of HK$222 million, but also the Severe Acute Respiratory Syndrome (SARS) epidemic in 2003 that followed nearly wiped out all tourism activities in Hong Kong. This devastated the Park's business and consequently extraordinary cost control measures were taken by restructuring employees' pension benefits, requiring staff to take four days' unpaid leave per month to cut wage costs, introducing other pay and concession cuts, reducing operating hours and show schedules and closing the Park every Monday. By the end of the financial year 2002–3 OP had recorded a cumulative deficit of HK$4 million.

Perhaps there were silver linings to these clouds. These crises forced the Park to abandon expensive capital-intensive projects and opt for less costly and creative attractions. Firstly it redefined its position as a more agile provider of 'edutainment' which actually meant introducing more low-cost initiatives such as the 'Physics in motion scheme' that taught students scientific principles behind the rides, and 'Animal close-encounter programmes' where visitors could feed and play with the sea animals. Also, during this period more entertainment events were introduced that capitalised on the Park's resources. The Halloween Bash made its debut in 2001 and has now turned into a very popular festive occasion. Eventually an annual pattern of entertainment attractions called the 'Big Five' was formed, which became key revenue drivers: the Summer Splash in July/August, the Halloween Bash in October, the Christmas Sensation in December, the Lunar Lucky Fiesta to celebrate Chinese Lunar New Year in January/February, and Animal Close Encounters in April/May. Unexpectedly, the threats had led to a rather belated realisation of OP's mission as an entertainment provider.

After SARS was over in July 2003, the government of mainland China made a timely decision to implement the 'Individual Visit Scheme' which allowed mainland citizens to travel more freely to Hong Kong. This relaxation in policy created an influx of tourists to Hong Kong, giving a swift bounce-back to the Park's business. Since then the mainland market has surpassed the local market, changing the demographic split of visitors to about 40% locals, 50% mainland China tourists and 10% others.

Disney – the ultimate challenger

In November 1999, the Hong Kong government[2] announced the building of a Disneyland theme park in Hong Kong (HKDL) in which it would have a 57% stake. This would become the fifth Disneyland theme park world-wide and the third of its kind outside the USA. The sheer size and overwhelming strength of Disney in brand power and resources dwarfed OP. There was widespread concern immediately after the news broke that a home-grown park like OP could not survive against this giant. In September 2005 HKDL was opened, located at Penny Bay on Lantau Island in Hong Kong, with access to the airport and downtown within 30 minutes via a special tailor-made rail line. The Disney Park is 310 acres in size, housing traditional Disney entertainment facilities, 2,100 rooms in themed resort hotels and a 2,800 square metre retail, dining and entertainment complex.

In OP's 1999–2000 Annual Report, the management showed a sudden change in tone from its traditionally administrative pitch to a bolder and more proactive one, and began to talk about anticipating customers' needs, responding to market shifts, exceeding expectations, living with uncertainty, transformational restructuring and stretching imaginations. Faced with a new rival, the Park resorted to some short-term actions to beef up its marketing muscle. Instead of simply relying on facilities to passively attract visitors to the Park, a stronger 'pull' marketing approach was introduced by reaching out actively to people through integrated and multiple marketing channels to create demand. In 2000, one year after the announcement to build HKDL, OP finally changed its ageing icon – a seahorse – which had represented the Park since 1977 and replaced it by the more interesting Mascot Family (Figure 1) as its new ambassadors. These are personified cartoon figures with Whisker the Sea Lion as the chief of the crew. It had taken the Park's management over two decades to realise the importance of re-energising its dated image.

Despite these efforts to pull in more visitors, by the late 1990s OP found itself standing at a strategic crossroads under the looming shadow of Disney. After all, to maintain a high-quality oceanarium while charging entrance fees at economy rates was financially very difficult. At that time the future of the Park was full of uncertainty.

A soul-searching journey and the White Knights

In 2002, an Ocean Park Task Force was formed to contemplate OP's future. In June 2003 the Hong Kong government appointed an Ocean Park Development Group under the Task Force to reconsider the Park's future. In July 2003 Allan Zeman was appointed by the government as

Figure 1 **The Ocean Park mascot**

Source: Daphne Po May Wong

Chairman of OP. He is in no way a theme park expert. He openly admitted that he had never been to OP before and had only visited a theme park once in the USA. So why choose a theme park novice to be the leader at such a critical moment? Somehow Zeman is gifted in turning losers into stars, the classic example being his successful conversion of a deserted corner in the central business district of Hong Kong into a world-famous social hub. His business know-how and creativity made him the ideal person for this position. Ever since his appointment, Zeman has been entertaining the public by appearing at press conferences in exotic costumes such as a panda, a jellyfish, a Sumba girl or a Chinese ghost – he has a flair for publicity.[5]

As Chairman of the Park, Zeman also became leader of the Ocean Park Development Group. Zeman and other members of the Group (who were drawn from Park staff, government departments, trade experts and consultants) reflected on a wide range of possibilities, including relocating or closing down the Park. They benchmarked OP against several international theme parks and concluded that OP did have a distinctive rationale and the show had to go on. But the question was 'how?'. To Zeman, upgrading facilities and adding new attractions was simply not good enough. He wanted a complete overhaul, something on a much grander and dramatic scale; putting this in his favourite terms, OP had to be 'world-class'. Though Zeman had a vision for the Park, he needed someone who knew the theme park business inside out to join him in reviving the Park. So he embarked on a global talent hunt for a new CEO. As a result, Tom Mehrmann was recruited and came on board in early 2004 (Figure 2).

Mehrmann had been in the commercial theme park business for over 30 years, occupying senior positions at Knott's Berry Farm in California, Marine World and Warner Brothers' Movie World in Madrid. His success in

Figure 2 Tom Mehrmann and Paul Pei

Source: Juan Manila Express

implementing large-scale capital projects for theme parks gave him the needed edge to take up the role of CEO. Aside from experience, perhaps it was his personality traits that really counted. He is known as a gregarious and industrious person. Zeman once described him as: 'Easy going, modest with a great sense of professionalism, sensitive and loyal to the staff.'[6]

Mehrmann sees himself as a coach and a confidante to his staff rather than just their boss. To him every day in the Park is unique, so he practises 'management by walking around' (MBWA). By interacting with guests and staff, he has a firmer grasp on what is happening at the front line.

Mehrmann knew his role was to develop an ambitious plan to give the Park new life, but he also knew that even the best plan would have to rely on its people for execution. The need to instigate changes in corporate culture and employee attitudes had to come before everything else and Mehrmann had to be the catalyst for such a change. Mehrmann described his own management style as 'participative, interactive and engaging'. Being autocratic and top-down is simply not him. Instead of barking out orders, he looked for ways to include people in the change process – how together they could revitalise the Park.[7]

When he first arrived, Mehrmann found that staff loyalty was high, the retention rate of its workforce was about 90% and 20% had an average tenure of more than 20 years. He described the staff as: 'Hard-working but not as engaged as he wanted them to be.' Given the unique background of OP, there were some entrenched norms among its staff. Typically there was conservatism and an aversion to change in order to avoid getting blamed personally.[8] Therefore before change could take place, first he had to gain the trust of his staff.

Mehrmann advocated a caring corporate culture and assured his staff that he would not remove anyone at the outset. He deliberately conveyed a message that more

latitude would be given to take risks, hoping to break down bureaucratic mindsets. To reinforce his message and align organisational values, a series of ice-breaking communication channels were instituted, including a staff survey to gather suggestions, open 'All Staff Communication Meetings' and the 'Chief Executive Exchange Sessions' for employees to express their views. Some motivational initiatives, such as career planning for staff to boost morale and deliver a promising message for job prospects, were introduced – a 'Shining Spot Scheme' and 'Competency Model' which recognised high-performing staff in the Star Award Presentation Ceremonies and the Annual Staff Appreciation Night. These new ideas gradually succeeded in building a spirited team.

Revival for the fittest – the Master Redevelopment Plan (MRP)

The process of developing a strategic plan for the Park was long and winding. Unlike the commercial sector, a governmental organisation's plan undergoes a much longer timespan in fermentation. The planning process actually dates back to 2000, when the Planning Department compiled a long-term strategic blueprint for the whole of Hong Kong called the 'Hong Kong 2030: Planning Vision and Strategy Study'. The overarching objective of this was to map out Hong Kong's long-term development direction. With broad directions being delineated, the planning actions then funnelled down sub-units and sub-plans for different industries, one of which was to study the tourism potential of different districts in Hong Kong.

One idea was to develop the Aberdeen harbour area (which is close to OP) as a tourism node. In 2001, the Planning Department hired consultants to study the prospect of transforming Aberdeen and they confirmed the Park's significance as a major catalyst for this urban renewal project. In 2004 Mehrmann inherited the leadership role of the Development Group from Zeman. The prime mandate to Mehrmann was to lead the Group in creating a Master Redevelopment Plan (MRP) to rejuvenate the Park. He hired 15 designers from around the world and produced a detailed blueprint for Ocean Park outlining its renewed vision, design concepts for new attractions and shows together with feasibility studies on the technical and financial aspects.

The planning process of the MRP was iterative, involving cross-disciplinary departments and consultations with key stakeholders and the public. Along the way comments from these parties were collated, studied and incorporated into action programmes. Extensive work by different departments was needed, such as legalising the decision, assessing environmental and sustainability issues, obtaining funding and monitoring the process so as to ensure its accountability.

After 18 months of planning work, the Group came up with a new vision for Ocean Park: 'To aspire to be a world leader in providing excellent guest experiences in a theme park environment connecting people with nature.'

OP would stick to its long-held mission as an education, conservation and entertainment provider, but this time these would be delivered with style and sophistication. The Park would aim to complement and supplement Disney's fantasies with an enhanced 'ocean flavour'. The Development Group adopted what it called a 'keep the best and improve the rest' approach. So after 30 years it was decided the Park needed a major facelift.

In February 2005, the Group submitted the MRP to the Task Force for consideration and in March briefings were given to members of the Legislative Council on the content of the plan. Meanwhile the MRP was widely distributed to different parties for consultation and feedback. In October 2005 it was formally endorsed by the Chief Executive of Hong Kong together with the Executive Council, and in December 2005 the MRP was formally approved by the Legislative Council.

The project would cost HK$5.5 billion in total. No government grant was required and the whole plan was funded by a mixture of government and commercial loans. The construction work was spread across eight phases from 2006 to 2013. New attractions were to be introduced in each phase, while normal operations of the Park ran in parallel with the construction. 'SkyFair Celebration', the helium air balloon ride, was the first to roll out in February 2007. In April 2009, the world's first integrated indoor and outdoor multi-Asian-species exhibit 'Amazing Asian Animals' was unveiled. In September 2009 'Ocean Express', a funicular train connecting the Headland and the Lowland, was opened. In January 2011 'Aqua City', a giant aquarium showcasing over 5000 marine animals, was launched. The 'Rainforest' and 'Thrill Mountain' featuring new rides also came into operation in June and December respectively in 2011. In July 2012, the final phase of the new attractions, the 'Polar Adventure' themed zone, was also completed. The number of employees had now increased to about 3,000, rides and attractions were increased from 35 to 70, and annual visitor numbers were projected to be well over 7 million by 2021–2.[9]

Furthermore, in 2008, the Executive Council of the HK government had given the green light to build a new rail line, the South Island Line, due to be completed in 2015. It would reduce travelling time between the Park and downtown to a matter of minutes. Given the rather suburban location of Ocean Park, a railway system passing its main gate would not only offer convenience to visitors but also improve its transportation network to put it on a par with HKDL.

To further raise the Park's potential as an overnight destination, Zeman believed that accommodation on site could prolong guest stay and thus spending. With only 70 acres out of the Park's 200 acres of land developed, this made the option to build hotels on the Park attractive and viable. The MRP proposed building three hotels of different classes to be completed in different stages, including 'The Ocean', a three-star budget hotel at the entrance, the four-star 'Fisherman's Wharf' at the lowland's bay area, and the 'Summit Hotel', a deluxe boutique hotel with a spa on the Headland. It was projected that visitor numbers would increase by 25% with average time spent in the Park increased from 3 to 8 hours. To contain investment risks in the hotel projects, a Build-Operate-Transfer Model (BOT) was proposed where OP would decide on the overall strategic direction of the hotels and charge an annual fee to the hoteliers who build and operate the hotels for 20 to 30 years, after which the properties will be handed back to OP. However, by 2013, the hotel project had not been rolled out.

From a city park to a regional park to a destination park

Initially OP had been designed as a local amenity for the Hong Kong people. Through the years it had evolved from its humble roots into a major tourist attraction in the Asia Pacific region. Ever since Zeman and Mehrmann took charge in 2004, it has been breaking attendance records continuously. In 2011–12 its visitor numbers were the 11th highest worldwide, fourth in Asia and first in Greater China.[10] In November 2012, OP received the Applause Award at the International Association of Amusement Parks and Attractions Expo, which recognised it as the best theme park worldwide.[11] Now with more supportive infrastructure, including hotels on site and the South Island Railway line in sight, OP can certainly aspire to be a destination park in its own right.

The World Tourism Organisation has predicted that China will be the world's leading tourism destination by 2020 and, being situated at the southern gateway to China, the Hong Kong tourism industry becomes a natural beneficiary. With the completion of the Hong Kong–Zuhai–Macao Bridge by 2015–16 and the China high-speed rail system being completed in the foreseeable future, travelling time among the major cities in China will be greatly shortened, making it more plausible for the main cities in South China such as Hong Kong, Macao, Zuhai and Guangzhou to further integrate into the so-called 'One-hour Living Circle'.[12] All these bode well for OP's future as a destination park.

The road ahead

The year 2011–12 has been fruitful for Ocean Park. Over 7 million people visited the Park, a 20.3% increase over the previous year, and it has achieved its own projection on attendance numbers 10 years earlier than predicted. The financial surplus from operations was HK$505.4 million with an impressive growth rate of 49% over the previous year. The new attractions, together with the staging of special events to celebrate OP's 35th anniversary, have created significant momentum in boosting business in 2011–12.

While Ocean Park has succeeded in rejuvenating itself and has reaped the rewards from the MRP, at the same time HKDL has launched new expansion projects. Other rivals such as Panyu in Guangdong Province, South China, completed a marine-theme park in 2010, and in 2012 Singapore completed expansion projects at Sentosa, gearing it up to become the world's largest oceanarium. Meanwhile, Macao has also indicated its intention to build a non-gaming theme park, and Shanghai has already begun to build a Disneyland 4.7 times the size of HKDL. In fact, the number of major theme parks in Asia has tripled during the last few years. The MRP has dramatically turned around the fortunes of Ocean Park, but it will have to continue to fight for the limited tourism time and dollar in an extremely competitive market. In the face of all this competition, what will be the next strategic path for the Park?

Notes and references
1. HK$1 = £0.08 = US$0.13 = €0.10.
2. Bloomfield, F. (10 January 1977) 'A dream comes true: Ocean Park – Hong Kong's magical sea garden', Hong Kong Standard.
3. Department of Justice. (1 July 1987) Ocean Park Corporation Ordinance (Chapter 388), Government of HK.
4. Ocean Park Corporation, Annual Report (1990–1 and 1991–2).
5. Kwok, V.W.I., (13 February 2007) 'Allan Zeman: Hong Kong's mouse killer', *Forbes*.com. Retrieved from http://www.forbes.com/2007/02/13/zeman-ocena-park-cx_vk_0213autofacescan01.html.
6. George, M. (7 December 2007) 'Ocean Park gets engaged', *South China Morning Post*.
7. Sharp, J. (September 2008). 'Tom Mehrmann, Ocean Park – from sweeper to CEO', *Hong Kong Business*, pp. 37–40.
8. George, M. (7 December 2007) 'Ocean Park gets engaged', *South China Morning Post*.
9. Legislative Council (September 2005) *Redevelopment Plans for the Ocean Park. Legislative Council Brief* (EDB CR1/6/2091/02), Hong Kong: Government of the HKSAR.
10. 2012 Theme/Museum Index Report. (2013) TEA /AECOM.
11. Ocean Park Corporation. *Ocean Park Hong Kong Recognized as World's Top Theme Park by Prestigious 'Applause Award'*, retrieved from http://www.oceanpark.com.hk/html/en/footer/corporate-information/press/press.php?id=583.
12. The Greater Pearl River Delta Business Council (2010) *An Overview of Recent Development in the Greater Pearl River Delta*, Government of the HKSAR.

APPENDIX Visitor figures at Ocean Park, Hong Kong

Years	Numbers (000,000)	Years	Numbers (000,000)	Years	Numbers (000,000) projection*
Jan–June 1977	1.3	1989–90	1.8	2002–3	3.6
1977–8	1.9	1990–1	2.0	2003–4	3.3
1978–9	1.9	1991–2	2.3	2004–5	4.4
1979–80	1.6	1992–3	2.7	2005–6	3.2
1980–1	1.5	1993–4	2.8	2006–7	3.2
1981–2	1.3	1994–5	3.0	2007–8	3.6
1982–3	1.1	1995–6	3.0	2008–9	2.75
1983–4	1.5	1996–7	3.8	2009–10	3.38
1984–5	1.6	1997–8	2.8	2010–11	3.0
1985–6	1.3	1998–9	2.9	2011–12	3.68
1986–7	1.4	1999–2000	3.0	2012–13	4.03*
1987–8	1.5	2000–1	2.8	2013–14	4.38*
1988–9	1.7	2001–2	3.4	2021–2	4.92*

Source: Ocean Park Corporation, *Annual Reports* (1987–2012).
Legislative Council (November 2005) *Proposed Funding Arrangement for Ocean Park Redevelopment Plans, Legislative Council Panel on Economic Services*, LC Paper no. CB (1) 339/05-06(03), Government of the HKSAR.
Ocean Park Corporation (2007) *Presentation to the Economic Services Panel of the Hong Kong Legislative Council*, CB(1)2164/06-07(02).
Retrieved from http://www.legco.gov.hk/yr06-07/chinese/panels/es/papers/es0718cb1-2164-2-ec.pdf

CASE STUDY

GMB: strategic leadership in a trade union

Phil Wyatt

This case explores how different general secretaries of the GMB trade union in the UK have responded over three decades to the leadership challenge posed by falling membership, financial strain and a conservative organisational culture.

● ● ●

Over six million members of the UK workforce, of about 30 million, are members of a trade union. Unions aim to protect people against unfair treatment at work, such as bullying or discrimination, by representing individual members or groups of members in talks with management. They negotiate collective agreements with employers covering pay and conditions, including health and safety conditions. They also campaign for government policies that benefit working people.

Each union is led by a general secretary who acts as chief executive officer. He or she is elected by the members and is responsible to a national council formed from union activists (volunteer workplace representatives and officers of local union branches) who are also elected. Unions employ full-time officers and staff to support activists in recruiting and representing members and to bargain with employers on their behalf. Unions' income comes mainly from contributions paid by members.

The GMB is the UK's third-biggest union with over 600,000 members. They work in the public services, manufacturing industry and private sector services like retail distribution and security firms. The letters GMB are a shortened version of the union's former name – the General Municipal Boilermakers' and Allied Trades Union.

Paul Kenny was appointed GMB Acting General Secretary and Treasurer on 23 March 2005, subject to approval from the union's national conference, the GMB Congress, in June. He accepted despite knowing that:

● The union had just endured 22 months of turmoil culminating in the suspension days earlier of Kevin Curran who had beaten him in the 2003 leadership election to succeed the previous general secretary John Edmonds.
● The union rulebook barred anyone who was acting temporarily as general secretary from standing for election as general secretary, whilst also requiring that an election be held 'forthwith in the event of a vacancy'.

Source: Stefan Rousseau

Paul Kenny

● Within weeks of Edmonds' retirement in June 2003 a financial crisis had erupted with the union's banks calling for spending cuts of £5 million ($7.6m; €5.9m).[1]
● The number of members had dropped by 15% from 676,000 in 1995 to 572,000 in 2004.

GMB had not adjusted well to a changing operating environment. It was not alone. Over the previous 25 years UK trade unions, taken together, had lost half their members and two-thirds of their workplace representatives for two main reasons.

Firstly, changes in employment law in the 1980s by the Conservative government led by Margaret Thatcher had effectively banned 'closed shop' agreements between unions and employers. These had required all employees to be members of the union(s) which management dealt with. Unions had enforced such agreements by threats to disrupt production unless management complied. The Labour government led by Tony Blair that was elected in 1997 kept the ban on 'closed shops', though it relaxed other restrictions on unions.

Secondly, UK manufacturing industry had been shrinking, with millions of job losses. Unions had proven unable to replace members lost in manufacturing with new recruits in the expanding service sector, despite huge opportunities to do so. Total UK employment had increased from 25 million at the bottom of recession in 1993 to over 28 million by 2005, yet total trade union membership had gone down.

Paul Kenny's predecessors had struggled with similar problems. Could he turn the situation around?

GMB strategy in the Edmonds era (1986–2003)

A turnaround strategy is what John Edmonds had sought since becoming General Secretary and Treasurer of the General Municipal Boilermakers' and Allied Trades Union in 1986 when membership was 816,000 but falling fast.

Edmonds' time in office was characterised by a series of leadership initiatives aimed at reversing a relentless loss of membership amidst ongoing financial pressure. They passed through three overlapping phases:

- 1986–94: mergers to shore up GMB's relative rank among Britain's unions.
- 1990–9: targets set by top management to focus action.
- 1997–2003: reorganisation to release resources for recruitment.

Edmonds began by convincing his executive council to shorten the union name to GMB, adopt a new union logo, and authorise a series of mergers with other smaller unions. By reorganising GMB into a section structure, Edmonds offered a safe haven to potential merger partners facing financial difficulty brought on by declining membership numbers. These mergers brought in over 100,000 members by 1994, helping to diversify GMB's membership base and to preserve its position as one of Britain's leading trade unions. They also brought property assets that could be sold off or redeveloped for union use.

However, membership continued to fall, mainly due to job losses in UK manufacturing industry. By 1991 GMB membership (including all its merger partners up till then) was below 800,000 and the union was reporting an operating deficit.

In 1990 Edmonds persuaded the union's executive council and the GMB Congress to adopt a fresh statement of GMB purpose. That statement included commitments to:

- Provide every GMB member with the opportunity to discover and develop their talents and to enjoy fulfilling and rewarding work.
- Boost recruitment, in part by providing outstanding service to working people and their families, building a reputation for GMB as the best trade union in Europe.
- Work 'in partnership with the more farsighted employers, negotiating constructive and beneficial agreements which help to achieve our purpose'.

- Create an atmosphere of teamwork and joint endeavour among all GMB office holders and employees.

The executive council also endorsed his proposal for a new broader bargaining agenda aimed at achieving a closer match between what GMB members wanted from work and union negotiating priorities with employers. Survey evidence suggested that a narrowly pay-related bargaining agenda fell short of workers' aspirations. Edmonds argued that job security, the opportunity to develop their abilities, flexible work arrangements, and jobs that allow workers to use their initiative and earn promotion all counted highly with working people but had not been pushed in negotiations with employers.

In 1991 Edmonds steered his colleagues into adopting a fresh approach to union strategy development. He invited what he called the GMB Senior Officers – an *ad hoc* group comprising the president, general secretary, deputy general secretary, 10 regional secretaries, 15 national officers and half a dozen departmental managers from the union's national college and national office – to conduct SWOT assessments of eight key performance areas over a four-year perspective matching the 1992–5 period of office of the GMB executive council.

The outcome was 40+ targets grouped into four priority categories, with seven top-priority targets and 15 second-priority targets. In most cases individual union officials were asked to coordinate action on targets among colleagues (see Table 1).

Table 1 GMB first priority targets, 1992–5

The seven top targets were concentrated in two of eight key performance areas:

1 Growth by organisation and recruitment:
   - Set recruitment priorities
   - Develop services and benefits for workplaces where GMB was not yet recognised for bargaining purposes by employers.
2 Growth by merger.
3 A representative, responsive, democratic and stable union.
4 Effectiveness in bargaining and representation.
5 Provision of attractive services to members.
6 Efficiency in managing resources:
   - Balance the budget
   - Bring in a new budget system
   - Introduce management training
   - Get members to sign their support for the check-off system (whereby employers transfer employees' union contributions from their pay to the GMB)
   - Investigate earnings-related union contribution rates.
7 Achieving a high public profile.
8 Expanding its influence in the 'corridors of power' (such as at the European Commission and European Parliament in Brussels in view of the increasing significance of EU law for rights at work in the UK).

Table 2 The 'Seven Key Elements for Success', 1996–9

- Confident activists.
- Focused and committed officers.
- A lay democracy (i.e. members who are not also GMB employees such as regional officers) that is involved.
- Relevant issues (relevant to whom was left open).
- Resources directed to recruitment.
- A teamworking approach.
- Information supporting recruitment.

The SWOT process was intended to give the executive council a stronger grip on GMB strategy. However, as membership continued to fall and operating deficits persisted, the SWOT approach was abandoned for the new executive council elected in 1995. Except for setting recruitment targets and collecting members' signatures in support of check-off arrangements, little more than lip service was paid to the previous priorities.

Instead Edmonds led his Senior Officer colleagues into recommending, and the executive council into adopting, a strategy aimed at changing the union's culture into one in which improving recruitment and organisation drove all GMB activity. Within this overall aim a series of key tasks were identified grouped under seven headings and all GMB decision-making bodies were called upon to support the executive council's strategy (see Table 2).

At Edmonds' prompting the executive council set every region the same challenge – to recruit 1,000 new members each month. Monthly league table reports showed regional results. Only two regions, London and Southern, consistently hit the target. A code of practice was introduced for all GMB officials requiring regular workplace 'health checks' based on practice in the GMB London region.

Worsening operating deficits prompted the 1997 GMB Congress to agree changes in the way the union was managed, to eliminate financial deficits and release resources for recruitment work. The changes included:

- Cutting the number of officers and staff employed at the union's national office from 87 in January 1997 to 66 by May 1999.
- Transferring GMB financial functions from national and regional offices to a new national administration unit near Glasgow, reducing relevant staff numbers from 112 in January 1997 to 71 in May 1999.
- Controversially, holding the GMB Congress every two years instead of annually, with section conferences in the alternate years.
- Requiring the GMB national college in Manchester, which ran training courses for over 5,000 union activists each year, to break even within three years.

- Shifting administration of the solicitors, cutting the direc' to members.

Following consultation, a proposal by the number of regions was abandoned and the structure remained the same as that adopted in 19 of the 10 regions enjoyed considerable autonomy. Region secretaries directed dozens of officers and staff and commanded substantial budgets. They also influenced elections for regional seats on the central executive council (including winning seats themselves) and influenced the way their elected regional members voted on critical issues. National officers enjoyed no such control over resources, nor had comparable influence. Regional secretaries were very powerful within the GMB, especially when they acted in concert.

Regions appointed 39 new recruitment officers between January 1998 and May 1999 and a further 20 organisers between 2001 and 2003. Recruitment rose, peaking at 99,900 in the year to October 2001 (equal to almost 16% of existing membership). Membership increased temporarily but fell back again. Operating deficits persisted.

In 1998, after 18 years of Conservative government and policies that made union activity more difficult, the new Labour government introduced laws more favourable to unions and new rights for unions to accompany employees in individual grievance and disciplinary cases. This should have boosted union membership. But by 2000 a GMB recruitment strategy dominated by consolidation in workplaces where the union was already present had not stemmed the loss of members.

In summary, from 1986 to 2003 GMB membership dropped from over 800,000 to 600,000 despite mergers with other unions that brought in more than 100,000 members. Between 1991 and 2003 the union reported 12 annual operating deficits, breaking even only once, in 1993. Those deficits exceeded £56 million and averaged over 11% of total income over the period. Allowing for investment income, gains on the sale of fixed assets and reorganisation costs, the overall financial deficit over the years 1991 to 2002 added up to almost £30 million, some 6.4% of total income.

In his last financial report John Edmonds presented accounts for 2002 showing an operating deficit amounting to 13% of GMB income. However, there had been a 15,000 membership increase during the year.

Turmoil under Kevin Curran (2003–5)

The retirement of John Edmonds led to a keenly contested election to succeed him. GMB Northern Regional Secretary Kevin Curran was declared the winner. He had campaigned for the return of 'closed shop' agreements, a shift balance of power within the union from London [to] the regions, and a review of the GMB's support for the [La]bour Party. Curran beat GMB London Regional Secretary [P]aul Kenny, the union's longest-serving regional manager, by a wide margin.

Both Curran and Kenny opposed privatisation of public services and both supported better employment rights for workers. Where they differed most was in their recruitment records. Since 1997 the Northern region had lost nearly 10,000 members in manufacturing and private sector services, increasing its public services membership by only 2,000. By contrast, the London region had lost 12,000 members in manufacturing but boosted its membership by 16,000 in public services and by 4,000 in private sector services.

Although he had lost the election, Kenny still had allies among the other regional secretaries and on the union's central executive council, its national governing body between meetings of GMB Congress. Curran's intention, declared within days of his election, to appoint an independent commission to examine the GMB, gave his rivals a reason to fear him and an issue with which to isolate him. Executive council members felt their positions threatened by outsiders. Regional secretaries feared the emergence of a dominant general secretary intent on abandoning decision making by consensus. Both groups felt their anxieties confirmed when a key adviser let slip Curran's interest in bypassing them and seeking approval for his decisions through referendums of rank-and-file GMB members.

The union rulebook made no provision for referendums and Curran could not rely on regional secretaries for support. By organising awkward questions at executive council meetings and adopting a common line at regional secretaries' meetings, Curran's critics set about undermining the authority of the new general secretary. He stayed the nominal leader, but Kenny and his supporters became the real decision-makers. Together Kenny's allies had effective taken control of the union by late 2003/early 2004 and began putting in place a turnaround strategy.

Their starting point was to restore financial stability. The call from the union's banks for big spending cuts had been prompted by annual operating deficits over the period 1998–2003 adding up to £29 million, a pattern the banks called 'a recipe for disaster'. The GMB's response to escalating deficits had been to sell assets each month in order to cover operating costs and stay within agreed bank overdraft limits. Now Kenny and his allies took drastic action to cut costs:

- In 2003–4 the union cut 138 of its 730 officer and staff posts, closed its national college, sold and leased back its head office, and slashed spending on campaigns and communications, conferences and fees paid to international trade union bodies.

- Changes to the GMB pension fund for union employees included raising the normal retirement age from 60 to 65 and increased pension contributions paid by officers and staff.

These measures transformed the 2003 operating deficit into a 2004 operating surplus, and the 2003 overall financial deficit of £16.7 million (after charging almost £10 million in rationalisation costs) into a 2004 overall surplus of £4.4 million. But membership fell again to a new low of 572,000 in 2004 (see Tables 3 and 4).

In July 2004 the executive council set up a task group to advise how the union could recruit and involve as many members as possible over the next 10 years. The creation of this task group confirmed de facto that Kenny and his allies now ran the union and not Kevin Curran. The executive council vetoed Curran's proposal for an independent commission consisting mainly of outside experts and selected GMB regional officers. Instead they founded a task group dominated by executive council members, including three

Table 3 **GMB membership, 1986–2012**

Year	Membership (000s)
1986	816
1991	<800
1995	676
2000	631
2002	659
2003	600
2004	572
2005	575
2008	601
2010	602
2011	610
May 2012	622

Table 4 **GMB finances, 1991–2011**

Year	Income (£ million)	Operating deficit (–) / surplus (+) (£ million)	Total deficit (–) / surplus (+)[1] (£ million)
1991	36.0	−1.8	+0.9
1995	35.5	−6.5	−4.7
2000	39.9	−4.6	−4.0
2002	43.0	−5.6	−5.2
2003	44.2	−6.6	−16.7
2004	45.8	+1.9	+4.4
2005	45.3	+0.3	+4.0
2010	55.8	+6.2	+8.1[2]
2011	57.4	+6.4	+8.6[3]

1 After allowing for investment income, gains on the sale of fixed assets and reorganisation costs
2 2010 before pension scheme actuarial gain of £13.5 million
3 2011 before pension scheme actuarial gain of £2.6 million

Table 2 The 'Seven Key Elements for Success', 1996–9

- Confident activists.
- Focused and committed officers.
- A lay democracy (i.e. members who are not also GMB employees such as regional officers) that is involved.
- Relevant issues (relevant to whom was left open).
- Resources directed to recruitment.
- A teamworking approach.
- Information supporting recruitment.

The SWOT process was intended to give the executive council a stronger grip on GMB strategy. However, as membership continued to fall and operating deficits persisted, the SWOT approach was abandoned for the new executive council elected in 1995. Except for setting recruitment targets and collecting members' signatures in support of check-off arrangements, little more than lip service was paid to the previous priorities.

Instead Edmonds led his Senior Officer colleagues into recommending, and the executive council into adopting, a strategy aimed at changing the union's culture into one in which improving recruitment and organisation drove all GMB activity. Within this overall aim a series of key tasks were identified grouped under seven headings and all GMB decision-making bodies were called upon to support the executive council's strategy (see Table 2).

At Edmonds' prompting the executive council set every region the same challenge – to recruit 1,000 new members each month. Monthly league table reports showed regional results. Only two regions, London and Southern, consistently hit the target. A code of practice was introduced for all GMB officials requiring regular workplace 'health checks' based on practice in the GMB London region.

Worsening operating deficits prompted the 1997 GMB Congress to agree changes in the way the union was managed, to eliminate financial deficits and release resources for recruitment work. The changes included:

- Cutting the number of officers and staff employed at the union's national office from 87 in January 1997 to 66 by May 1999.
- Transferring GMB financial functions from national and regional offices to a new national administration unit near Glasgow, reducing relevant staff numbers from 112 in January 1997 to 71 in May 1999.
- Controversially, holding the GMB Congress every two years instead of annually, with section conferences in the alternate years.
- Requiring the GMB national college in Manchester, which ran training courses for over 5,000 union activists each year, to break even within three years.

- Shifting administration of the union's legal service onto solicitors, cutting the direct cost of GMB legal support to members.

Following consultation, a proposal by Edmonds to reduce the number of regions was abandoned and the GMB regional structure remained the same as that adopted in 1936. Each of the 10 regions enjoyed considerable autonomy. Regional secretaries directed dozens of officers and staff and commanded substantial budgets. They also influenced elections for regional seats on the central executive council (including winning seats themselves) and influenced the way their elected regional members voted on critical issues. National officers enjoyed no such control over resources, nor had comparable influence. Regional secretaries were very powerful within the GMB, especially when they acted in concert.

Regions appointed 39 new recruitment officers between January 1998 and May 1999 and a further 20 organisers between 2001 and 2003. Recruitment rose, peaking at 99,900 in the year to October 2001 (equal to almost 16% of existing membership). Membership increased temporarily but fell back again. Operating deficits persisted.

In 1998, after 18 years of Conservative government and policies that made union activity more difficult, the new Labour government introduced laws more favourable to unions and new rights for unions to accompany employees in individual grievance and disciplinary cases. This should have boosted union membership. But by 2000 a GMB recruitment strategy dominated by consolidation in workplaces where the union was already present had not stemmed the loss of members.

In summary, from 1986 to 2003 GMB membership dropped from over 800,000 to 600,000 despite mergers with other unions that brought in more than 100,000 members. Between 1991 and 2003 the union reported 12 annual operating deficits, breaking even only once, in 1993. Those deficits exceeded £56 million and averaged over 11% of total income over the period. Allowing for investment income, gains on the sale of fixed assets and reorganisation costs, the overall financial deficit over the years 1991 to 2002 added up to almost £30 million, some 6.4% of total income.

In his last financial report John Edmonds presented accounts for 2002 showing an operating deficit amounting to 13% of GMB income. However, there had been a 15,000 membership increase during the year.

Turmoil under Kevin Curran (2003–5)

The retirement of John Edmonds led to a keenly contested election to succeed him. GMB Northern Regional Secretary Kevin Curran was declared the winner. He had campaigned for the return of 'closed shop' agreements, a shift in the balance of power within the union from London to the regions, and a review of the GMB's support for the Labour Party. Curran beat GMB London Regional Secretary Paul Kenny, the union's longest-serving regional manager, by a wide margin.

Both Curran and Kenny opposed privatisation of public services and both supported better employment rights for workers. Where they differed most was in their recruitment records. Since 1997 the Northern region had lost nearly 10,000 members in manufacturing and private sector services, increasing its public services membership by only 2,000. By contrast, the London region had lost 12,000 members in manufacturing but boosted its membership by 16,000 in public services and by 4,000 in private sector services.

Although he had lost the election, Kenny still had allies among the other regional secretaries and on the union's central executive council, its national governing body between meetings of GMB Congress. Curran's intention, declared within days of his election, to appoint an independent commission to examine the GMB, gave his rivals a reason to fear him and an issue with which to isolate him. Executive council members felt their positions threatened by outsiders. Regional secretaries feared the emergence of a dominant general secretary intent on abandoning decision making by consensus. Both groups felt their anxieties confirmed when a key adviser let slip Curran's interest in bypassing them and seeking approval for his decisions through referendums of rank-and-file GMB members.

The union rulebook made no provision for referendums and Curran could not rely on regional secretaries for support. By organising awkward questions at executive council meetings and adopting a common line at regional secretaries' meetings, Curran's critics set about undermining the authority of the new general secretary. He stayed the nominal leader, but Kenny and his supporters became the real decision-makers. Together Kenny's allies had effective taken control of the union by late 2003/early 2004 and began putting in place a turnaround strategy.

Their starting point was to restore financial stability. The call from the union's banks for big spending cuts had been prompted by annual operating deficits over the period 1998–2003 adding up to £29 million, a pattern the banks called 'a recipe for disaster'. The GMB's response to escalating deficits had been to sell assets each month in order to cover operating costs and stay within agreed bank overdraft limits. Now Kenny and his allies took drastic action to cut costs:

● In 2003–4 the union cut 138 of its 730 officer and staff posts, closed its national college, sold and leased back its head office, and slashed spending on campaigns and communications, conferences and fees paid to international trade union bodies.

● Changes to the GMB pension fund for union employees included raising the normal retirement age from 60 to 65 and increased pension contributions paid by officers and staff.

These measures transformed the 2003 operating deficit into a 2004 operating surplus, and the 2003 overall financial deficit of £16.7 million (after charging almost £10 million in rationalisation costs) into a 2004 overall surplus of £4.4 million. But membership fell again to a new low of 572,000 in 2004 (see Tables 3 and 4).

In July 2004 the executive council set up a task group to advise how the union could recruit and involve as many members as possible over the next 10 years. The creation of this task group confirmed *de facto* that Kenny and his allies now ran the union and not Kevin Curran. The executive council vetoed Curran's proposal for an independent commission consisting mainly of outside experts and selected GMB regional officers. Instead they founded a task group dominated by executive council members, including three

Table 3 GMB membership, 1986–2012

Year	Membership (000s)
1986	816
1991	<800
1995	676
2000	631
2002	659
2003	600
2004	572
2005	575
2008	601
2010	602
2011	610
May 2012	622

Table 4 GMB finances, 1991–2011

Year	Income (£ million)	Operating deficit (–) / surplus (+) (£ million)	Total deficit (–) / surplus (+)[1] (£ million)
1991	36.0	−1.8	+0.9
1995	35.5	−6.5	−4.7
2000	39.9	−4.6	−4.0
2002	43.0	−5.6	−5.2
2003	44.2	−6.6	−16.7
2004	45.8	+1.9	+4.4
2005	45.3	+0.3	+4.0
2010	55.8	+6.2	+8.1[2]
2011	57.4	+6.4	+8.6[3]

1 After allowing for investment income, gains on the sale of fixed assets and reorganisation costs
2 2010 before pension scheme actuarial gain of £13.5 million
3 2011 before pension scheme actuarial gain of £2.6 million

regional secretaries who were particularly close allies of Paul Kenny, one of whom chaired it. Kenny himself was not a member. He did not need to be.

Ever since 2003 claims about electoral malpractice had circulated within the union. In December 2004 the GMB executive council appointed an independent lawyer to inquire into allegations of breaches of union rules and ballot rigging during the 2003 election for general secretary. These stemmed in part from evidence at an employment tribunal hearing that unlawful acts had been committed. When Kevin Curran refused to apologise to the GMB executive council for allegedly attempting to put pressure on the person conducting the inquiry, he was suspended on 15 March 2005.

On 7 April 2005 the GMB announced that Curran would be leaving by amicable agreement. His formal departure on 6 May created a vacancy that, according to the GMB rulebook, required an immediate election for general secretary – one in which Paul Kenny was not entitled to stand.

However, the executive council judged that if the serious allegations of electoral malpractice were to be proven they would cast doubt on the integrity of GMB electoral procedures. It therefore decided that circumstances existed which were so exceptional that they justified *not* calling an election for general secretary and treasurer until it had received and considered the inquiry's report.

This stance was accepted by the June 2005 GMB Congress, which approved Kenny's appointment. It was also accepted in December 2005 by the Trade Union Certification Officer who regulates trade unions in the UK.

The inquiry established that serious wrongdoing had taken place in the 2003 election, including breach of union rules, abuse of procedure, misuse of union funds and acceptance of financial contributions from employers and suppliers towards campaign costs. It accused supporters of Kevin Curran of alleged criminal acts.

The executive council therefore recalled GMB Congress and on 11 March 2006 agreed new rules for future elections and called for an immediate election for general secretary and treasurer. The recalled Congress also abolished the rule banning an acting general secretary from standing for election as general secretary. With nominations from 201 union branches, Paul Kenny was elected unopposed as general secretary in May 2006, and confirmed as such by the June 2006 GMB Congress.

Kenny's framework for the future (2005–12)

Kenny and his supporters shared an agenda. They set it out in the report from the task group advising on the union's future which was endorsed by the 2005 GMB Congress. The thrust of that agenda was threefold:

- to restore financial stability
- to promote membership growth and a new recruitment strategy
- to increase accountability and membership involvement in union affairs.

To manage that agenda Kenny worked through the same group with which he had neutered his predecessor: his allies among the regional secretaries. He renamed this group as the Senior Management Team and they held meetings every couple of months with the regional secretaries and select managers from GMB national office under the chairmanship of the union president. He also delegated important tasks to Senior Management Team members. By 2008, in a report to GMB Congress abolishing the post of deputy general secretary, he referred to this team as 'akin to a board of directors'.

The measures taken by the Senior Management Team, and their results, were as follows.

1 Financial stability

The 2003–4 package of spending cuts was followed by a series of increases in contribution rates charged for union membership.

In 2007, following evidence of abuse of union rules, the central executive council forced out some senior regional officers and activists and cut the number of regions from 10 to nine by merging the Liverpool and Lancashire regions. In 2011 the boundaries between two other regions were moved. These were the first significant changes to the union's regional boundaries since 1936.

Again following evidence of abuse of union rules in two regions, Congress 2010 set new requirements to improve branch accountability. Branch costs fell from £7.2 million in 2010 to £6.5 million in 2011.

An operating surplus was achieved for eight years in a row from 2004 to 2011. The GMB balance sheet strengthened from net assets of £26 million in December 2003 to £54 million in December 2011 (before pension liabilities of £16 million). Kenny reported in 2010 that the union had begun building up its officer force again.

2 Membership growth and recruitment strategy

To promote recruitment the Senior Management Team set up a national organising team consisting of senior officers from each region and a national coordinator, supported by a small department at GMB national office. Regions agreed to back recruitment in three national target areas as well as their regional priorities. The earlier emphasis on monthly league tables comparing regions' results with each other was dropped. Instead each region was asked to contribute to increasing the national average recruitment by 2,000 per month.

It was agreed to focus more on workplace organisation where GMB membership was weak but where the union was recognised by employers, rather than pursue 'greenfield' sites – new workplaces where no union was yet present.

Officers and activists were encouraged to adopt a stance of always having a 'claim on the table' and constantly pressing issues of concern to the workforce. The 1986–2003 GMB logo that featured two figures holding hands over the strapline 'working together' was dropped. When the union adopted a rewritten, plain English rulebook, the chance was taken to delete the reference in the GMB purpose statement to working in partnership with employers. A more rigorous relationship became the order of the day, illustrated by Kenny's address to the 2012 GMB Congress when he used the words 'fight/fighting/fought' 11 times.

In the three years ending 2012 average annual recruitment of 77,000 included some 8,700 among the three national targets – school support staff, the Asda supermarket chain, and the National Health Service. From its low point in 2004 GMB membership rose in each of the next seven years. By May 2012 it had reached 622,000.

3 Greater accountability and involvement of lay members (i.e. members who are not also GMB employees)

GMB Congress: The Congress agreed in 2005 to return to holding annual meetings and in 2009 to increase by one-third the size of Congress delegations, to make the conference more inclusive. But a 2009 proposal to require regional delegations to contain at least 80% working members was dropped after consultations showed opposition among activists, many of whom were already retired.

Congress 2010 acknowledged that the number of branch nominations might fall short of that needed to ensure full delegations, and that action was needed to ensure that delegations fairly represented the balance of membership in each region. It authorised regions to select 10% of delegations as 'balancing' delegates such as extra women or young delegates, and to appoint 'top-up' delegates to ensure each region sends a complete delegation. Congress 2005 saw 294 elected and appointed lay delegates attending, of whom 65 were women delegates. By 2012 this had risen to 392 of whom 126 were women.

Central Executive Council: By 2007 Kenny had persuaded regional secretaries that they did not need to be elected members of the union's central executive council to retain their power and leadership status, and that their position on the council was provocative. So no regional secretary stood for election to the executive council in 2007 or 2011, making the executive council an all-lay-member body (except for the general secretary). However, they continue to attend and speak at executive council meetings.

Congress 2005 voted to keep the rule whereby only regional council members were eligible for election to the central executive council. In the 2007 elections 38% of seats were uncontested (21 of 55), falling to 33% (18 of 55) in 2011. But the proportion of members voting fell from 9% in 2007 to 7% in 2011.

Conclusion

Paul Kenny was re-elected unopposed in November 2010. In his report to the 2011 GMB Congress he summed up his achievements as follows: 'Our GMB has come a long way since 2004. Membership up, finances sound, accountability and transparency as standard behaviour instead of just meaningless words on election statements.'

His address to the June 2012 GMB Congress declared the 2005 agenda well under way or completed, and in December he announced his intention to retire in 2013, two years before his term of office expires. However, in the same week of February 2013 that the Bank of England forecast a slow recovery for the UK economy, Kenny withdrew that announcement, under pressure from GMB activists and officials to stay.

How should the union develop from now on? Has it found a winning formula since 2005, making continuity the key to a brighter future for GMB? Or should Kenny's successor, whenever he or she takes over, try to break free from a culture that has left one GMB official 'feeling like I am standing on an ice floe that is melting beneath my feet', learn from John Edmonds' experience and seek to lead the union in a fresh direction? If so, how?

Note
1. £1 ~ $1.53 ~ €1.17.

CASE STUDY

Academies and Free Schools

Kevan Scholes

The public sector continues to face dilemmas as to how far strategic management should be centralised or devolved. This case looks at one example – the extension of devolved control of schools in England and Wales through the creation of Academies and Free Schools. However, the principles and issues involved in this case would apply to many other public services and private sector organisations.

●   ●   ●

'The academies programme is not about ideology, it's a practical solution . . . The same ideologues who are happy with failure . . . also say you can't get the same results in the inner cities as the leafy suburbs so it's wrong to stigmatise these schools. Let's be clear what these people mean. Let's hold their prejudices up to the light. What are they saying? "If you're poor, if you're Turkish, if you're Somali, then we don't expect you to succeed. You will always be second class and it's no surprise your schools are second class." I utterly reject that attitude.'[1]

This was Michael Gove, the Secretary of State for Education in England and Wales, speaking in 2012 about the growing controversy about plans to turn most schools to 'Academy status' and to allow the establishment of more Free Schools. Both Academies and Free Schools receive state funding but are semi-independent and outside local authority control.[2] Disagreement over the political and management control of schools was certainly not a new issue. Indeed, there had been many significant changes over the previous 150 years.

Since 1833, when British governments first took a role in the provision of education, through financial grants to support the work of voluntary bodies, including churches, there had been a progressive involvement of the state in the policy, funding and management of education in the UK. From 1870 elementary education became compulsory and partially state-funded. The 'Balfour' Education Act of 1902 created Local Education Authorities (LEAs). The Act allowed for all schools, including religious denominational schools, to be funded by the LEA through local taxation.[3]

Mossbourne Community Centre Academy School, London

The 'Butler' Education Act of 1944 established the Ministry of Education, headed by a single minister responsible for education policy and delivering state education through LEA-funded schools. The most significant change in the following 50 years was the introduction of 'comprehensive' (as against 'selective') schools from the mid-1960s. By 2005 about 93% of English schoolchildren attended the state-funded school system.[4] This was financed from national taxation and was free between the ages of 3 and 18.

There were four main types of state-funded school in England:[5]

● *Community schools* (about 60% of the total), in which the LEA employed the schools' staff, owned the schools' lands and buildings, and had primary responsibility for admissions.
● *Voluntary controlled schools* (about 10% of the total), which were almost always church schools, with the lands and buildings often owned by a charitable

foundation. However, the LEA employed the schools' staff and had primary responsibility for admissions.

- *Voluntary aided schools* (about 20% of the total), linked to a variety of organisations. They could be faith schools (often the Church of England or the Roman Catholic Church) or non-denominational schools. A charitable foundation contributed towards the capital costs of the school and appointed a majority of the school governors. The governing body employed the staff and had primary responsibility for admissions.
- *Foundation schools* (about 10% of the total), in which the governing body employed the staff and had primary responsibility for admissions. School land and buildings were owned by the governing body or by a charitable foundation. The Foundation appointed a minority of governors. Many of these schools were formerly grant-maintained schools. In 2005 the Labour government proposed allowing all schools to become Foundation schools if they wished.

What *are* Academies and Free Schools?

Academies were first introduced by the Labour government in 2005 as secondary schools funded and monitored *directly* by the Department for Education. Academies could also accept funding from private sources such as individuals or companies. The policy of running schools with the types of freedoms to be offered to Academies and Free Schools was well established in other countries. They were often called Charter Schools. The English changes were inspired by the example of Sweden[6] which had 'charter' schools dating back to 1992. The Labour government thought such changes would be particularly important in areas of social deprivation where traditional schools were seen to be 'failing' – as reflected in the academic performance of pupils and through Ofsted[7] inspections. Following the general election of 2010 when Labour lost to a Conservative/ Liberal Democrat coalition, Academies became a main plank of government policy for *all* existing schools – not just as a replacement for failing schools. By 2012 almost 40% of secondary schools had converted to Academy status and there were about 80 Free Schools in England and Wales (out of a total of 22,000 state schools – about 18,500 primary and 3,500 secondary). Plans for primary school academies were also announced in 2012.

What is different about Academies?

The Department for Education (DfE) website[8] explains the similarities and differences between traditional state schools and Academy schools: 'Academies are publicly-funded independent schools that provide a first-class education.'

Freedoms

Academies benefit from greater freedoms to innovate and raise standards. These include:

- freedom from local authority control
- the ability to set their own pay and conditions for staff
- freedoms around the delivery of the curriculum
- the ability to change the lengths of terms and school days.

Sponsors

Some Academies, generally those set up to replace under-performing schools, have a sponsor. Sponsors come from a wide range of backgrounds, including successful schools, businesses, universities, charities and faith bodies. Sponsors are held accountable for improving the performance of their schools. They do this by challenging traditional thinking on how schools are run and what they should be like for students. They seek to make a complete break with cultures of low aspiration and achievement. The sponsor's vision and leadership are vital to each project.

Funding

Academies receive the same level of per-pupil funding as they would receive from the local authority as a maintained school, plus additions to cover the services that are no longer provided for them by the local authority. However, Academies have greater freedom over how they use their budgets to best benefit their students.

Academies receive their funding directly from the Young People's Learning Agency (an agency of the Department for Education) rather than from local authorities.

Governance

The principles of governance are the same in Academies as in maintained schools, but the governing body has greater autonomy. Academies are required to have at least two parent governors.

. . . and what's the same?

Admissions, special educational needs and exclusions

Academies are required to follow the law and guidance on admissions, special educational needs and exclusions as if they were maintained schools.

Collaboration

Academies have to ensure that the school will be at the heart of its community, collaborating and sharing facilities and expertise with other schools and the wider community.

All high-performing schools applying for Academy status are expected to partner a weaker school. Collaboration and partnership are now embedded in the school system, and this is also the case for Academies.

Selection

Schools which already select some or all of their pupils will be able to continue to do so if they become Academies, but schools becoming Academies cannot decide to become newly selective schools.

What additional differences do Free Schools have?

The DfE website[9] also explains the *additional* freedoms that Free Schools have (compared with Academies):

'Whereas Academies were mainly "conversions" from existing state schools . . . a Free School could be set up by any suitable proposer, where there is evidence of parental demand such as a petition or declaration from interested parents and a clear and compelling business case. This could include one or more of the following groups: teachers, charities, academy sponsors, universities, independent schools, community and faith groups, parents, businesses (on a not-for-profit basis) . . . Free Schools will have some additional freedoms. For example, teachers in Free Schools will not necessarily need to have Qualified Teacher Status. They will be subject to the same Ofsted inspections as all state schools and will be expected to maintain the same rigorous standards.'

Reaction of different stakeholders

Since education policy has always been a major political battleground and is close to the hearts of many individuals and groups, any changes tend to receive a mixed reaction from these 'stakeholders'. The plans to extend the number of Academies and Free Schools were not universally welcomed. Here are some reactions from different stakeholders as reported by the media:

Local Education Authorities, such as Leicestershire County Council, said that they would receive reduced funding because Academies got money directly from central government. Council leader David Parsons said he disagreed with the scheme because the county had 'some of the best schools' and 'some of the best results' in the country. 'Because of the academies programme, the government is effectively putting a tax on local authorities of about £100 per pupil, per year', the Conservative leader said.[10]

Head teachers of those schools which might be forced into academy status following a poor Ofsted report, such as Leslie Church at Downhills Primary in North London, were worried that the school's democratic rights would be affected as elected governors and local councillors would no longer be involved in decision-making.[11]

Some parents and teachers mounted public protests, such as those at Montgomery Primary School in the Sparkbrook area of Birmingham. They claimed there had been a lack of consultation and that academy status was being imposed by the government. They also claimed that parents would have less say in how the school was run and how money was spent if Montgomery gained academy status.[12]

Teachers' Unions, such as the National Union of Teachers, said that school communities and their local authorities, and not an external sponsor, were best placed to judge what support any particular school needed. They also expressed concerns that external sponsorship could be the beginnings of the privatisation of England's schools.[13]

School Leaders, through their Association of School and College Leaders, said that the key to success in schools remained excellent teaching and leadership, rather than their governance 'status'. There were many successful schools that remained working within the local authority system of governance.[14]

In turn, the Department for Education was keen to broadcast good news about Academies and Free Schools on its website:[15]

'Kevin Eveleigh, Head of Barnaby Road Academy [Primary and Nursery], Nottinghamshire said: "I couldn't figure out why I would want the money my parents had paid in taxes to be handled by [an LEA]. I was convinced we could do it better locally. We also wanted to protect our staffing, particularly a team of brilliant teaching assistants. We have more control over the allocation of our resources to meet our own needs. I choose the education initiatives I want to get involved in and can ignore those that aren't relevant – all my meetings are about the school I work in and the children I know. And we are genuinely giving hands on support to a local school in a very deprived area"'.

'Mark Lehain is the lead proposer for Kempston Academy (as a Free School). The proposal aims to establish a school with a rigorous approach to standards as an alternative to the existing schools in Bedford borough. The proposal is for a small secondary school with no more than 100 students in each year group, offering personalised learning, strong pastoral support, and daily sessions of games and extended learning. Mark Lehain said 'We believe every child, regardless of their background, should be able to get a really good set of exam results by the time they are 16. We feel the only way you can do that is to give parents more choice in the kind of schools their kids have and we think for a lot of kids, ours is the type of school their parents will want for them'.

International comparisons

As mentioned above, the policy of running schools with the types of freedoms offered to Academies and Free Schools was well established in other countries. For example, Sweden[16] had more than 1,000 such charter schools dating back to 1992. Indeed, in 2010 the Swedish Kunskapskolen became the lead sponsor in converting Hampton Community College in Richmond, Surrey, into an Academy.[17] In the USA the Charter Schools programme (started in 1991) was regarded as a major success[18] with more than 2 million pupils attending 5,600 charter schools across 40 states by 2011.[19] In Canada (from 1995) charter schools were established in Alberta but not in other provinces, and there were 22 schools by 2010.[20] In New Zealand, following the general election in 2011, the National–ACT coalition government announced plans to establish charter schools.[21] Interestingly, Chile had a long history of 'charter schools' dating back to the 1980s with about 50% of pupils studying in charter schools by 2011.[22]

Future developments

In March 2012 a group of City financiers announced plans for a chain of more than 2,000 schools (10% of the state system) – Clarendon Associates.[23] Schools would be expected to make a surplus, with half going to teachers as enhanced benefits and half to a central charity to fund school building projects.

So in the early 2010s the debate continued even as many Academies and Free Schools were being launched.

Notes and references

1. Angela Harrison (2012) 'Michael Gove: Academy school critics happy with failure', BBC website (www.bbc.co.uk), 4 January 2012.
2. Local authorities in the UK run local government at city or county levels. This includes both the political process of local councils and the provision of local services, including schools.
3. 'The history of education in England', *Wikipedia*, 2012.
4. Approximately 7% of schoolchildren in England attend privately run, fee-charging, Independent schools which do not have to follow the National Curriculum, and whose teachers are not required by law to have official teaching qualifications. However, they are registered with, and inspected by, the state.
5. 'Education in England', *Wikipedia*, 2012.
6. Liz MacKean, BBC website, 8 August 2010.
7. All state-funded schools are regularly inspected by the Office for Standards in Education (Ofsted) which publishes reports on the quality of education at each school. Schools judged by Ofsted to be providing an inadequate standard of education may be subject to special measures, which could include replacing the governing body and senior staff.
8. Department for Education website (www.education.gov.uk).
9. Ibid.
10. BBC website, 19 January 2012.
11. See reference 1 above.
12. BBC website, 25 January 2012.
13. See reference 1 above.
14. Ibid.
15. Department for Education website (www.education.gov.uk).
16. Liz MacKean, BBC website, 8 August 2010.
17. Richard Garner, *Independent*, 29 January 2010.
18. Department for Education website (www.education.gov.uk).
19. 'Charter Schools', *Wikipedia*, 2012.
20. Department for Education website (www.education.gov.uk).
21. Ibid.
22. Ibid.
23. Jack Grimston, *The Sunday Times*, 11 March 2012.

CASE STUDY

Paul Polman and the revitalisation of Unilever

D. Jan Eppink

This case focuses on the changes that Paul Polman initiated to make Unilever a much better-performing company than it was in the years before he took over as CEO. As a background to this, the case starts with a brief history of the company, followed by an analysis of the strategy followed and how the company's performance improved. The challenge is how to maintain and improve on this.

• • •

In the 2012 Annual Report, Paul Polman, Unilever's CEO since January 2009, announced that turnover for the year had been 10.5% higher than the year before. Underlying sales growth, a measure of organic growth, was 6.9%. Underlying sales growth in developing markets was 11.4%.

Commenting on the results, Paul Polman said:

> 'Despite deteriorating global economic conditions and a competitive environment which remains intense, we again delivered volume growth ahead of our markets and gained value share across the majority of our business. Our performance reflects continued investment in innovation, brand-building and people, whilst keeping discipline on both costs and execution.'

The challenge facing Unilever in 2012 was to maintain progress and improve on it.

History of Unilever

Although Unilever itself was not established until 1930, the two companies that formed Unilever were already well established before the start of the twentieth century. Unilever was created when Margarine Unie from the Netherlands and Lever Brothers from the United Kingdom decided to start working together. Legally, it still consists of two separate entities, Unilever NV in the Netherlands and Unilever PLC in the United Kingdom, with two headquarters, one in the centre of Rotterdam and one in the centre of London.

The origin of the Dutch branch lies in the butter trade, a company established by Simon van den Bergh in the nineteenth century. In 1872 the company started the production of margarine. A competitor in the margarine market was owned by the Jurgens family. To reduce competition, the two companies merged to form Margarine Unie in 1927. In the following two years Margarine Unie bought a company in the business of butchering, fat processing and margarine production and a company with slaughterhouses and meat processing facilities.

Lever Brothers in the UK started as a grocer and began to produce soap in 1884, initially as hard soap bars but later in the form of soap flakes. Later, the company acquired a food company and an ice cream company. The corporate mission of its founder, William Hesketh Lever, was: 'To make cleanliness commonplace; to lessen work for women; to foster health and contribute to personal attractiveness, that life may be more enjoyable and rewarding for the people who use our products.'

Both companies used vegetable oil as a resource for their production. In the course of 1929 the two companies decided it was more advantageous to 'merge' than to stay independent. Lever Brothers became what is now known as Unilever PLC; Margarine Unie became Unilever NV.

Strategy of Unilever before 2009

Product scope

The strategy of Unilever focused on having leading positions and being in high-growth markets.[1] The various brands in 2006 were in two categories: Foods, and Home & Personal Care. In Foods there were two sub-categories: Savoury, Dressings & Spreads; and Ice Cream & Beverages. Well-known brands included Knorr, Bertolli, Blue Band, Magnum, and Ben & Jerry's. The Home & Personal Care category also had two sub-groups: Personal Care and Home Care. Brands included Axe, Dove, Omo and Cif.

In 2011 the same four groups are mentioned, although with slightly different names in the Food category: Savoury, Dressings & Spreads is now called just Foods, and the Ice Cream & Beverages group is now called Refreshment.

Unilever sells its products to a variety of retailers. In the developed world there is an increasing reliance on supermarket groups, often multinational (e.g. Walmart (USA) and Carrefour (France)). In the developing countries its products are sold in smaller shops with no supermarkets in sight.

International scope

From the start Unilever has been an international company. Its two parent companies were already very active in sourcing raw materials and serving foreign markets. Early on, markets were often protected by trade barriers. Then as now, preferences in taste, in particular for food products, differ a great deal. These factors explain the historically high degree of decentralisation of decision making and also of production and marketing.

Business-level strategy

The 2006 Annual Report describes the ways in which Unilever will compete and deliver value. The three elements are:

- continuous product development and improvement
- sharing innovations and concepts with businesses around the globe
- lowering costs of sourcing, manufacturing and distribution, while maintaining and improving product quality.

Performance

The Appendix (p. 737) gives an overview of the most important financial data from 2004 to 2011. It shows that turnover from 2004 to 2008 grew far less than net profit. The data also show the difference in sales growth in the various regions that Unilever operates in.

Annual reports mention the Total Shareholder Return ranking of Unilever compared to its chosen peer group. This is summarised in Table 1 and shows that in 2006 Unilever was part of the lowest third of the group. In Fortune's 2008 global list of most admired companies, Unilever's competitors were ranked as follows: Procter & Gamble 5th, Nestlé 27th and L'Oréal 37th. Unilever was not ranked in the top 50.

There was a time when the market capitalisation of Unilever was more than twice as high as that of its major competitor Procter & Gamble. Around 2005, however, the value of Unilever was lower than that of P&G. Unilever was not on the list of most-desired companies to work for, which is a must if a company wants to attract the best employees. Furthermore, analysts suggested that the elements of business strategy mentioned above were more a wish than a reality. At that time questions were being asked about the

Table 1 Composition of peer group and ranking of Unilever, 2006–11

2006 Peer group		8/7/09 Peer group
Avon	L'Oréal	Same as in 2006[1]
Beiersdorf	Nestlé	
Cadbury Schweppes	Orkla	
Clorox	Pepsico	
CocaCola	Procter & Gamble	
Colgate	Reckitt Benckiser	
Danone	Sara Lee	
Heinz	Shisheido	
Kao		
Kimberly-Clark		
Kraft		
Lion		
	Rank 13th	Rank 8th/9th/5th
2010 Peer group		**2011 Peer group**
Avon	Kimberly-Clark	As in 2010
Beiersdorf	Kraft	
Cadbury	L'Oréal	
Campbell	Nestlé	
Coca-Cola	PepsiCo	
Danone	Procter & Gamble	
General Mills	Reckitt Benckiser	
Heinz	Sara lee	
Henkel	Shisheido	
Kao		
Kellogg		
	Rank n/a	Rank Top third

1 Cadbury Schweppes demerged into two separate entities. In 2009 only Cadbury was part of the peer group.

rationale for a company like Unilever. Were there any synergies between food and personal care products, and, if so, where were they? What did the corporate centre do to make these real? Was it better to split up the company?

At the AGM held in May 2005 there was criticism of Anthony Burgmans, Head of Unilever NV, from the Dutch shareholders' association (VEB) because of the disappointing performance of the company. VEB asked investors to vote against the appointment of Mr Burgmans as non-executive chairman. VEB mentioned the failure of Unilever's five-year growth strategy for which he was partially held responsible.[2]

Worries about such questions and a further decline in performance led the board of directors to decide that the new CEO should come from outside Unilever. Paul Polman, with a long history in the business of fast-moving consumer goods, was chosen. Polman had worked for many years at Procter & Gamble and was Nestlé's CFO and Head of the Americas division before joining Unilever.

Paul Polman's reforms

First few months

In his first speech at the Annual General Meeting of shareholders on 13 May 2009, Paul Polman said that in his first few months he had spent time understanding the portfolio of brands and categories, the businesses across countries and regions, the innovation capabilities and the organisational strengths while meeting many of the key people in the company.

He was encouraged by what he had seen. The elements were there to succeed consistently. There were great brands, leading global positions, strong innovative capabilities, a depth of organisational quality and great values on which the company had been built. Another statement at the AGM was:

> 'Although we will undoubtedly fine-tune and sharpen the strategy as we move forward, our main priority is now to put electricity through the wires, to get consistent business results. It requires making the company increasingly externally focused, with a passion for winning.'

Having worked for two of Unilever's largest competitors, he was in a very good position to make such a judgement.

In an interview for this case, Polman said his plans for the future had two stages: the aim of the first was to close the gap with better-performing competitors in the fast-moving consumer goods business, and the second was to bring Unilever into a leading position compared to those competitors. His approach had four elements: a change in strategy, a change in personnel, a change in organisational structure, and a change in culture. Polman's reasoning behind this sequence was that you first have to decide what the change in strategy should be, then find the right people that fit with the new strategy, align the structure with the strategy, and work on a change in culture from the start.

Change of strategy

Paul Polman said that a succesful strategy: 'must make clear choices, have an aligned activity system and is made possible by a high performance organisation. A good strategy also has a flywheel effect'.

Looking at the phrasing of the strategy in the Annual Report of 2011, compared with that in the report from 2006, one can see similarities. Both talk about growth and the importance of innovation in products, yet the results are quite different when looking at the regions and the categories.

The period 2008 until 2011 saw an increase in the sales of products in developing and emerging countries. This reflects the presence of Unilever in high-growth markets. Over this period turnover in Western Europe decreased by 4.7% from €12,853 million (£10,911m; $16,468m)[3] (32% of turnover) in 2008 to €12,269 million (26% of turnover). Turnover in the Americas rose by 15.5% from

€13,199m to €15,251m (33% of group turnover) with stronger momentum in Latin America. Turnover in Asia, Africa, Central and Eastern Europe increased by 31% from €14,471m (36% of group turnover) to €18,947m (41% of group turnover). Taken together, sales in emerging markets in 2011 stand at 54% of turnover. (For more details see the Appendix.) Part of the increase of turnover was the result of acquisitions. In this period Unilever acquired the personal care business of Sara Lee in Europe, the Russian personal care company Concern Kalina, and the US-based company Alberto Culver.

Looking at the change in categories, it is clear from the Appendix that turnover of Foods increased from 2008 to 2011 from €21,926m to €22,790m but percentage-wise dropped from 54% to 49%. In the same period turnover of the Home and Personal Care categories increased from €18,597m (46%) to €23,677m (51%).

The flywheel effect (see Figure 1) describes the interaction of revenue growth, operational leverage and reinvestment of free cash flow in the business, resulting in the 'virtuous circle of growth'. It starts with profitable volume growth which in turn creates operating cost leverage. Together with cost savings, created, for example, by closely managing indirect costs, it enables reinvestment in the business, into R&D and marketing as well as increasing margins.

Right from the start Polman stressed the importance of profitable volume growth. Until then, considering input cost inflation and disposals of non-core businesses, turnover of the company had remained at almost the same level for years. In contrast, other companies in the fast-moving consumer goods sector had shown considerable growth. Consequently, a priority among the nine objectives for 2009 was to return to profitable volume growth, as a prerequisite to return to improved performance.

Following his first year (2009) as CEO, Polman's new approach is summarised as the 'Compass Strategy', detailing how the company will win in four ways:

- *winning with brands and innovation*: superior products, widespread appeal, and bigger, better and faster innovation
- *winning in the marketplace*: lead market development, win with winning customers, be an execution powerhouse
- *winning through continuous improvement*: fast and flexible and increasingly competitive, advantages of global scale, best return on brand and customer investment
- *winning with people*: develop a team fit for growth, a place to succeed.

The launch of the 'Unilever Sustainable Living Plan' in 2010 introduced a galvanising business purpose which draws on Unilever's long history and values. Unilever's ambition to double its turnover without increasing the environmental footprint, whilst increasing overall social impact, requires a novel, sustainable and equitable approach. By 2020, the company aims to complete the three main objectives of the Unilever Sustainable Living Plan: to help a billion people take action to improve their health and well-being; to halve the environmental cost involved in the manufacture and use of its products; and to enhance the livelihood of hundreds of thousands of people while growing the business, for example by sourcing 100% of its agricultural raw materials sustainably. The corporate brand is growing fast and Unilever is again a prefered employer in most countries it operates in and is credited for driving a more responsible business model.

In an interview for *Harvard Business Review*[4] Polman answered the question about how sustainablility benefits the Unilever business:

> 'I always turn the question around: How would you make the case that not doing this could help society and mankind? For proper long-term planning, you've got to take externalities into account, in order to be closer to society. It's clear that if companies build this thinking into their business models and plan carefully, it will accelerate growth.'

Change of people

Just as the board of directors had looked outside Unilever for a new CEO, Polman extended this to some other positions as well. For a company that is admired for its excellent management development programmes, this was a remarkable step. Polman succeeded Cescau as CEO in January 2009. Jean-Marc Huët was recruited from Bristol-Myers Squibb as CFO and Pier-Luigi Sigismondi joined Unilever in mid-2009 as Chief Supply Chain Officer, after a career in Nestlé.

The changes not only affected the top levels in Unilever; there was also a 'management shuffle' after Polman's arrival. Polman remarked:

> 'Managers of major divisions and locations must deeply understand the power of bringing innovation to the marketplace. Increasingly a strong customer development and/or marketing background will be required from our cluster leaders to ensure that brand and category positions are built again and we constantly grow share.'

As far as total headcount is concerned, there was a reduction after 2008 (see Table 2). Then, total headcount was 174,000, whereas at the end of 2011 it stood at 169,000. Since 2008 turnover per employee has increased sharply.

Reduction in headcount affected all levels in Unilever. In the London headquarters only a part of the building is now used by Unilever; other floors are rented out, and headcount in the London HQ is now several hundreds lower. In the Rotterdam office some floors are also rented out.

Changing of organisational structure

In 2011, Unilever transformed its organisational structure. Following an earlier step to change from a highly decentralised structure to a multi-country organisation with 22 regional centres, operating in 11 categories, the change in 2011 puts the focus on four categories and eight geographical clusters. This will significantly speed up decision making and improve resource allocation. It also identifies business opportunities faster, allows trade-offs to be made more quickly and transfers best practices across regions and categories more rapidly, all supporting the key drivers of growth.

One of the themes of 'Winning in the marketplace' is to win with customers. One way of achieving this is through the introduction of 'Customer Insight and Innovation Centres' (CiiCs). The first one was opened in New Jersey, followed by the opening of a centre in London in 2009 and centres in Paris, Shanghai and São Paulo in 2010. The centres, now in 11 locations, enable Unilever to work directly with customers on issues such as merchandising, store layout, displays and packaging. New concepts can be designed and tested without the expenses of in-store pilots. In 2011, working very closely with customers in the drugstore segment resulted in underlying sales growth of 9.2% in that channel.

'Winning with people' requires providing staff with the opportunity to develop themselves, enabling them to reach their full potential. The top international high-potential personnel were traditionally trained at Unilever's International Management Training Centre in Kingston upon Thames, UK. In December 2010 the company announced the establishment of a Global Leadership Training Centre in Singapore, to be opened in 2013. The year 2011 saw the start of the Unilever Learning Academy, for e-learning and classroom courses. In its first year, 128,000 employees followed one or more of the 7600 training courses on offer. An industry observer remarked that he had the impression that in the years before Polman, budgets for employee development were an easy target when profit targets had to be reached. Recruiting was even outsourced but has now been brought in-house again. Moreover, he thought that morale was not as high as it should have been at that time for 'winning in the market place'.

Table 2 **Number of employees per region (average during the year, 000s)**

	2011	2010	2009	2008	2007	2006
Western Europe	29	29	29	32	35	38
The Americas	42	40	41	42	44	46
Asia, Africa, CEE[1]	98	96	98	100	96	105
Total	169	165	168	174	175	189

1 Central and Eastern Europe.

The history of Unilever, in common with other companies that were early to internationalise, shows that regional managers had a high level of decision-making power. National markets were so different that it was not always possible for managers at a central level to have the right information about local circumstances to make the best decisions. In Unilever geographical clusters have profit responsibility which may add to the desire for decentralisation in decision making. The changes in the composition of the Unilever (Leadership) Executive suggest a change to a more category-driven company, with decision making now more centralised than before. As decentralisation carries the risk of less coordination, it can, for example, lead to fragmented introduction of products in various countries and consequently higher marketing and production costs. This is especially relevant in categories where brands and products have a global reach, such as in parts of the personal care business.

Change in culture

Culture in Polman's words is 'how you bring the values to life in the company'. One aspect of this is how you change systems to change the behaviour of people at all levels in the organisation. In this section attention is paid to the changes in two systems: performance target setting, and remuneration.

Performance target setting

The board of directors is ultimately responsible for target approval. These targets are then cascaded throughout the Unilever organisation.

The main key performance indicators over the years 2006–11 are summarised in Table 3. They remain quite constant over the period, with few changes, some having been made in order to simplify definitions and communications. Polman mentioned in interview that the move from 'underlying operating profit' to 'core operating profit' at the beginning of 2012 introduced more discipline and rigour to restructuring spending with the objective of improving prioritisation of resources, between competing restructuring projects and other investments.

Targets are becoming more long-term, whereas operational control seems to be done more frequently. Early in his tenure as CEO, Paul Polman made the decision to abandon earnings guidance – he stopped quarterly reporting and changed the compensation system to encourage better 'long-term behaviours'. At the same time he sharpened the performance culture, putting focus on 'winning the consumer' squarely back into the business model with the ultimate goal that this will be to the benefit of the shareholders as well. He actively encourages shareholding with a longer-term focus, aligned with the business model and purpose.

In line with what Polman stated about being more cost-competitive, there is a focus on short-term performance indicators too, such as cash flow, cost levels and market share:

> 'For 2009, given the uncertainties, we have adjusted short-term targets, now on a six months basis to drive clear accountability/responsibility and to be responsive to fast-changing circumstances . . . We are driving speed with thirty days action plans to correct underperforming businesses and with simple managerial goals . . .'[5]

To support the objective of refocusing on consumers and customers and to make profitable volume growth the number one priority, the company has taken decisive steps. From 2009 to the end of 2011, Unilever spent around €300 million on improving product formulations. Now over 90% of its formulations are equal to, or better than, the competition in blind testing. This is reflected in market share gains across its businesses. Furthermore, the company invested €850 million more in advertising and promotion over the same period, despite reducing non-productive media spend by almost €100 million in 2011. It has also doubled capital spend from around 2% to 4.3% to support renewed growth.

Importantly, Unilever stepped up its innovation programme with fewer, bigger and better projects that are rolled out faster, globally. The company has also started to invest in supply chain capabilites and capital investment, creating from what was an underinvested, decentralised structure a highly efficient, consumer-focused, global supply chain.

Table 3 Key performance indicators, 2006–11

2006	2007	2008	2009	2010	2011
USG	USG	USG	USG, UVG	USG, UVG	USG, UVG
OM	OM	OM	OM, RDIs	UOM	UOM
UFCF	UFCF	UFCF	UFCF	FCF	FCF
ROI	ROI	ROI	ROI		
TSR rank	TSR rank	TSR rank	TSR rank		

Notes:

USG:	Underlying sales growth
UVG:	Underlying volume growth
OM:	Operating margin
UOM:	Underlying operating margin
RDIs:	Costs of restructuring, disposals and one-off items
UFCF:	Ungeared free cash flow (complex calculation to measure progress against goals for long-term value creation)
FCF:	Free cash flow
ROI:	Return on investment
TSR rank:	Total shareholder return (share price change + dividends, assuming these are reinvested) rank in peer group
Underlying:	based on continuing operations at constant exchange rates, excluding acquisitions and disposals

Remuneration arrangements

The Annual Report 2011 states that the remuneration systems:

> 'Support the longer-term objectives of Unilever and the longer-term interests of the shareholders. The fixed elements of the remuneration package must ensure that highly experienced and talented individuals can be attracted and the performance related elements are structured so that target levels are competitive, but Executive Directors can only earn high rewards if they exceed the ongoing standards of performance that Unilever requires.'

The performance-related elements are an annual bonus and two longer-term share plans. A claw-back of the performance-related elements is possible 'in the event of a significant downward revision of the financial results of the Group'.

In line with these objectives, the annual bonus measures for the executive directors for 2012 are underlying volume growth, core operating profit margin improvement and underlying sales growth. For the two share plans (the Global Share Incentive Plan and the Management Co-investment Plan), operating cash flow and relative total shareholder return are additional criteria.

Over two-thirds of the target remuneration for the executive directors is now linked to performance, with the majority of this linked to shareholder-aligned longer-term performance. The remuneration structure is generally consistent for the executive directors and senior management of Unilever.

Top executives are required to build and retain a personal shareholding in Unilever: 400% of salary for the chief executive officer, 300% for the chief financial officer and members of the Unilever executive, and 150% for the 'top 100' management layer below.

Targets are now set more strictly than before. In 2011, for example, the bonus payout was reduced by 25% as a result of underachievement on the margin target, even though growth was industry-outperforming and stock best-performing on the Amsterdam Stock Exchange. Targets are set realistically but are challenging.

As far as Polman himself is concerned, as he said in an interview for *Management Today*:

> 'My decisions are made for the long term interest of the company. It would be easy for me to jack up the share price, collect a bonus and go sailing in the Bahamas, but in five or 10 years Unilever would not be in good shape.'

Below top-executive level, historically there was little differentiation between top and mediocre performers and almost no opportunity for most managers to boost their income through sizeable bonuses. The organisational changes set out to improve focus, speed and efficiency. As a consequence, performance targets are clear, more aligned and differentiated. While performance rewards bring the opportunity to earn more than in the past, the percentage of fixed income is lower.

Every manager has three business targets and one developmental goal; each target is aligned to the Compass. Each manager is individually assessed, rated and ranked. Ranking results in the fact that only a quarter of senior management are judged as top-performing and paid accordingly.

What's next?

After three years at the helm, Polman had appeared to have transformed Unilever into a more successful company – certainly the share price had responded positively to the changes. Unilever's share price has consistently outperformed that of Procter & Gamble, Nestlé and the FT100 index between 2009 and 2013. Commentator Van Geest remarked that: '. . . it now seems that Unilever, after years of underperforming compared with Nestlé, Danone and P&G, is changing for the better'.[6] Another wrote that: 'after only one year at the helm of the company he has had what some in the investment community are calling an incredibly galvanising impact on the company'.[7]

However, in an article based on an interview with Paul Polman, Saunders observes: 'Unilever may be a big beast, but is a lumbering one whose inability to proceed at more than a walking pace has frustrated markets and shareholders alike for years.'[8]

These are some of the quite different observations about the same company, with the latest being the most sceptical. Some questions remain: Will the improvements that Paul Polman has achieved at a revitalised Unilever be sustained? How will competitors react to a more agressive Unilever? Are even tougher changes in strategy and execution necessary?

For the latest financial data, go to Unilever's annual report at: http://www.unilever.com/images/ir_Unilever_AR12_tcm13-348376.pdf

Main sources
Annual Reports Unilever, 2006, 2007, 2008, 2009, 2010, 2011.
Arnoldus, D. (2002) *Family, Family Firm and Strategy. Six Dutch familiy firms in the food industry 1880–1970*. Oegstgeest/Amsterdam: Aksant Academic Publishers.
The Economist (2012). 'Fighting for the next billion shoppers', 30 June.
The Economist (2012). 'Consumer goods in Africa. A continent goes shopping', 18 August, pp. 49–50.
Fortune (2008) 'List of global most admired companies', http://money.cnn.com/magazines/fortune/globalmostadmired/top50/index.html
Jones, G. (2005) *Renewing Unilever: Transformation and Tradition*. Oxford: Oxford University Press.
Ruddick, G. (2009) 'Unilever boss Paul Polman in management reshuffle', http://www.telegraph.co.uk/finance/newsbysector/retailandconsumer/474235/Unilever-boss-Paul-Polman-in-management-reshuffle

Notes and references
1. Unilever Annual Report 2006.
2. Muspratt, C. (2005) Unilever's Dutch head fends off rebel vote. *Telegraph*, May 11, 2005 (http://www.telegraph.co.uk/finance/2915500/Unilevers-Dutch-head-fends-off-rebel-vote.html).
3. €1 = £0.85 = $1.31.
4. Ignatius, A. (2012) Captain Planet. Interview with Unilever CEO Paul Polman. *Harvard Business Review*, Vol. 90, No. 6, pp. 112–118.
5. Unilever Annual Report 2008.
6. Geest, N. (2010) *Eindelijk, Unilever.* http://www.iex.nl/Column/59149/Eindelijk-Unilever.aspx
7. Russell, M. (2010) *In the spotlight – Paul Polman's first year at Unilever.* http://www.justfood.com/analysis/in-the-spolight-paul-polmans-first-year-at-unilever
8. Saunders, A. (2011) The MT Interview: Paul Polman of Unilever. *Management today.* March 1, 2011. http://www.managementtoday.co.uk/news/1055793/MT-Interview-Paul-Polman

APPENDIX 1

	2004	2005	2006	2007	2008	2009	2010	2011	
Financial data									
Group									
Turnover	37,168	38,401	39,642	40,187	40,523	39,823	44,262	46,467	(€ million)
Operating profit	3,981	5,074	5,408	5,245	7,167	5,020	6,339	6,433	(€ million)
Net profit	2,941	3,975	5,015	4,136	5,285	3,659	4,598	4,623	(€ million)
UngearedFree cash flow	5.3	4.0	4.2	3.8	3.2	4.9			(€ Billion)
Free cash flow						2.4	4.1	3.4	3.1 (€ Billion)
Share price NV year end	16.44	19.28	20.70	25.15	17.34	22.75	23.30	26.57	(€)
Region									
Europe									
Turnover	15,252	14,940	15,000						(€ million)
Operating profit	2,045	2,064	1,903						(€ million)
Western Europe									
Turnover			13,322	13,327	12,853	12,076	12,015	12,269	(€ million)
Operating profit			1,787.0	1,563	2,251	1,250	1,917	1,967	(€ million)
The Americas									
Turnover	12,296	13,179	13,779	13,442	13,199	12,850	14,562	15,251	(€ million)
Operating profit	896	1,719	2,178	1,971	2,945	1,843	2,169	2,250	(€ million)
Asia Africa									
Turnover	9,620	10,282	10,863						(€ million)
Operating profit	1,040	1,291	1,327						(€ million)
Asia, Africa and Cerntral & Eastern Europe									
Turnover			12,541	13,418	14,471	14,897	17,685	18,947	
Operating profit			1,443	1,711	1,701	1,927	2,2532,216		
Categories									
Savoury, dressings, and spreads									
Turnover	13,476	13,557	13,767	13,988	14,232	13,256	14,164	13,986	
Operating profit	1,880	2,026	1,993	2,059	3,216	1,840	2,846	2,693	
Ice cream and beverages									
Turnover	7090	7,332	7,578	7,600	7,694	7,753	8,605	8,804	
Operating profit	−30	609	900	809	915	731	724	723	
Foods									
Turnover	20,566	20,889	21,345	21,588	21,926	21,009	22,769	22,790	
Operating profit	1,850	2,635	2,893	2,868	4,131	2,571	3,570	3,416	
Personal care									
Turnover	9,780	10,485	11,122	11,302	11,383	11,846	13,767	15,471	
Operating profit	1,508	1,793	1,913	1,786	1,824	1,834	2,296	2,536	
Home care and other									
Turnover	6,822	7,027	7,175	7,297	7,214	6,968	7,726	8,206	
Operating profit	623	646	602	591	1,212	615	473	481	
Home and personal									
Turnover	16,602	17,512	18,297	18,599	18,597	18,814	21,493	23,677	
Operating profit	2,131	2,439	2,515	2,377	3,036	2,449	2,769	3,017	
Total									
Turnover	37,186	38,401	39,642	40,187	40,523	39,823	44,262	46,467	
Operating profit	3,981	5,074	5,408	5,245	7,167	5,020	6,339	6,433	

CASE STUDY

LEAX: managing growth in a volatile world

Anders Melander

Life is not dull! The thought came to CEO Roger Berggren when he reflected on the changes the LEAX Group had gone through in the last four years. The financial crisis in 2008–9 quickly changed into a very profitable 2010 and 2011. However, uncertainty increased and became more pronounced than ever. Volatility, flexibility and agility seem to be the words of the day! The challenge, Roger thought, was how to make the LEAX Group prosper from this volatility.

● ● ●

Even though there was a concern about the high market uncertainty, the overall position for the LEAX Group was good at the end of 2012. Decreasing slightly in the last year, margins were still higher than for most competitors and the profits from 2010 and 2011 made the balance sheet pleasant reading. The financial muscle was there again. However, the growth objectives had been difficult to achieve. In fact, after the fast recovery, with a growth of about 100% in 2010–11, growth was marginal in 2012 and profit margins suffered from the increasing market volatility. At this rate the '2215 objective' (where '2215' corresponds to a turnover of SEK 2 billion (£0.20bn; $0.30bn; €0.24bn)[1] and EBITDA of SEK 200 million (£20.3m; $30.9m; €24.0m) by the end of year 15 (2015)[2] is distant.

LEAX's history and business model

The LEAX business and concept was formed in 1982 by two mechanics, Lennart Berggren and Axel Seger. The idea was simple: LEAX would not have any products of its own but would produce other companies' products more effectively than they could do it themselves. Unlike other suppliers of production services, LEAX offered a broad programme including grinding, lathing and milling. LEAX quickly achieved a customer base, and because the founders were very talented craftsmen, the company was soon established as a proficient subcontractor of mechanical components.

By 1991, LEAX had around 18 employees and a turnover exceeding SEK 10 million. The next year, however, a deep recession caused the Volvo Group to temporarily stop purchasing LEAX's components. Given that around 80% of turnover derived from Volvo Trucks and that LEAX had invested SEK 10 million in a new factory, the company was now facing a severe crisis. As a result of the crisis, Lennart and Axel restructured the company. Drawing conclusions from the crisis, they also created four key strategic objectives to prevent similar occurrences in the future:

1 Reduce the dependence on individual customers – a single customer should not exceed 20% of the company's turnover.
2 Concentrate on manufacturing specific components – develop economies of scale by expanding operations on shafts, cogwheels and yokes.
3 Focus on quality and IT solutions – develop more accurate quality systems with efficient and reliable IT services.
4 Enhance long-term strategic work – build resources and competences to create new opportunities.

The focus on quality led to the identification of opportunities to help other companies build up their environmental, quality and management systems. This, in turn, emerged as the foundation of a growing consultancy operation, known as Leax Quality (founded as Q-Control), which proved vital to LEAX's growth in the coming years.

In 1997, Lennart and Axel handed over the ownership of LEAX to their four sons who had been involved in key positions within the organisation for several years. At the time, the company had a turnover exceeding SEK 60 million and employed 67 people. Nevertheless, in his new position as CEO of LEAX, Roger Berggren (Lennart's youngest son) announced that LEAX was going to expand even faster in the future. His stated vision for the company was to become a 'one-step partner' for their customers, comparable to a shopping centre with several specialist stores.

During Roger's first five years as CEO, LEAX achieved remarkable results as turnover increased by more than 300%. Although part of this expansion occurred on an international level, the company maintained its major production in Sweden, where all the main functions remained. Roger was, however, aware that globalisation was opening new doors. He believed that thinking ahead was crucial and stated the company's slogan: 'The day we cease getting better, is the day we stop being good.'

He summarised the financial objectives for the group by the numbers '5-5-5', meaning that in 2005 the turnover should be SEK 500 million with profits of SEK 50 million.

The results of 2005 exceeded these objectives and in 2007 LEAX had become 19 times larger than it was 10 years earlier. The company was now established as a leading service provider of mechanical and electromechanical solutions for the Swedish heavy vehicle, electromechanical and mining industries.

LEAX achieved its expansion by taking over factories from customers but also by growing organically in existing factories. The Group had further improved its managerial processes and was now producing larger components. In June 2007, LEAX took over Scania's production of propeller shafts and other driveline components. Through this large acquisition, LEAX further extended its production portfolio with competence areas such as assembly and painting. This opened up new possibilities for LEAX to continue to grow. The acquisition of the site made Scania by far the largest customer, generating 20% of the total turnover in 2007 (the maximum allowed for a single customer according to LEAX's strategic objectives).

The larger volumes developed LEAX into a more powerful player with the capability of offering cost-efficient solutions. At this time, the firm competed with 5–6 other subcontractors for its share of the target market, yet the most intense competitors were the customers themselves. As competition increased in the capital-intensive heavy vehicle industry, the OEMs were increasingly facing make-or-buy decisions, where LEAX competed with the OEMs' internal factories to produce their products more effectively than they could do themselves. LEAX was successful in doing this.

Despite a comprehensive investment programme of SEK 300 million in 2007, LEAX struggled to supply the increased quantities demanded by the market during the first half of 2008. Further investments were, therefore, announced to increase production capacity. In June 2008, a second production site in Latvia was inaugurated to allow further expansion in Eastern Europe. However, as we know, the prospects for future expansion changed radically in the autumn of 2008.

A sudden crisis

In October 2008 Volvo Trucks announced that orders for heavy trucks in Europe had fallen from 21,948 (Q2) to 115 (Q3).[3] In addition, Scania revealed a similar decline. Although Volvo Trucks had laid off around 1,400 employees the previous month, this came as a shock to the Swedish subcontractors. The common belief had been that the OEMs were making adjustments to 'normal' market conditions after a year of exceptional demand, but in reality the financial crisis had begun manifesting itself across the globe.

Among the Swedish heavy vehicle subcontractors, the severity and unpredictability of this demand shift caused alarming declines in cash flows and essentially paralysed production overnight. The troubles continued. Thus, in less than four months, the Swedish heavy vehicle industry went from enjoying the upside of operating leverage to facing the severe risk of carrying high fixed costs. At LEAX, the question was no longer whether there would be a downturn but rather how drastic it would be. Concerns spread quickly within the organisation as approximately 70% of turnover was derived from the heavy vehicle industry.

Facing the crisis

Early in November 2008, LEAX made a decision to cut 50 people from its Swedish-based workforce. However, the troubles continued; as cancellations of orders escalated, both Volvo Trucks and Scania – representing LEAX's two largest customers – declared that production facilities were to be shut down completely for one month during the first quarter of 2009. Regulations in the Swedish labour market, including a three-month period of notice for redundancies, required LEAX to act. Malena Bergenback, Human Resources Manager at LEAX, described how she tried to handle the situation:

> 'After a Board Meeting around Christmas, Roger approached me in the hallway saying "It is not enough, we have to do more!" We initiated negotiations with the union concerning adjustments in working hours. In January 2009, we reached an agreement in which personnel could be sent home with 48 hours' notice on the condition that their missed working time [a maximum of 370 hours] would be made use of in an economic upswing.'[4]

None the less, in less than six months, LEAX was forced to reduce the number of employees from over 600 (excluding temporary employees) to around 400 and to close one of its factories. LEAX was facing a paradox: every bit of pressure was pulling the company to do everything that was necessary to cut costs in the short term, yet Roger realised that focusing too much on short-term needs would undermine the company's success after the crisis. His view was: 'The demand in the automotive industry will return sooner or later. We have to deal with the short-term needs without forgetting about the long term. Our focus is trying to act so we strengthen what is unique about the company.'

At the beginning of April, LEAX reached an additional agreement with the union concerning reduction of wages. This contract involved 15% temporary reduction for all employees, including top management and the board of directors. In parallel, however, the European Union approved LEAX's investment project of SEK 4.6 million, which meant that employees could use some of their free time for education and training:

'The idea is to encourage employees to update their knowledge in order to raise the core competences of the company. If this project arouses enthusiasm among employees, we are likely to be in a better position when demand returns.'

Anna Wik, Project Manager at LEAX

Besides the main focus on production, middle management's competence development in financial analysis and marketing proved crucial for the future development of the Group.

Later in the spring, the mining industry followed the same development as the automotive industry, but, fortunately, the electromechanical industry still demonstrated a strong performance in the first half of 2009. LEAX also resumed its consultancy business to compensate for the lower production levels and temporarily moved some of the employees to this business area. In addition, LEAX had employed a rather conservative financial strategy, which helped the organisation maintain a better cash flow. LEAX does not use factoring (i.e. selling its accounts receivable to a third party). Roger Berggren's view was: 'A company that uses factoring will receive its customers' payments straight away. Whereas we get our money 60–90 days later. Consequently, when the market froze, we still received money three months forward whilst many of our competitors experienced a complete stoppage of cash inflow.'

A vital element of the LEAX organisation has always been its engagement in strategic planning. At the beginning of April 2009 long-term strategic planning was back on the agenda. New market opportunities were gradually presenting themselves as competitors struggled to deliver their orders. LEAX adopted a cautious approach. Frank Johansen, Head of Marketing, explained why LEAX did not rush into new projects: 'The orders we accept now will stay with us for a long time. Accepting lower prices to cover our fixed costs will undermine long-term success

when the market returns to normal. We need to be patient. The question, however, is how patient?'

In 2009 the annual turnover was less than half of that in 2008 and the Group made a loss of about 20m SEK (about 5% of turnover). In late 2009, however, the market improved and the Group was profitable once again. As the market improved LEAX's management's work on cutting costs and maintaining a sufficient cash flow was gradually leaning more towards increased efforts in marketing and sales. The increased ability to initiate and conclude business deals at the factory level, a result of the educational activities undertaken in the crisis, was promising for the future.

A vertical take-off

In 2010 the market recovery was 'as remarkable as the downturn in 2009'.[4] Turnover increased by some 75% and profit margins were higher than ever before. This achievement was reached even though the electromechanical factory was divested in mid-2010, the reason being that the nuclear power industry showed no sign of following the outsourcing trend in the automotive sector.

The profitable organic growth and the divestment of the electromechanical operations positioned the LEAX Group well for acquisitions. However, the market for suitable targets did not grow as anticipated in the crisis. The number of attractive targets was lower than expected and the decision-making processes were generally slow.

In the first three quarters of 2011 the market continued to improve. Margins increased substantially (excluding the divestment in 2010). Even though there was organic growth in all factories, the most remarkable increase was in the Latvian operations. The second factory in Latvia, close to the Russian border, more than doubled its turnover and employed about 80 people by the end of the year. In 2011 the decision was made to intensify marketing in Russia and to start a new factory in Brazil. This new factory represented the end of a process started in 2009. Alternative options considered had been the outsourcing of a factory from potential customers in South America and a joint venture with a Brazilian company. The logic was clear: the LEAX Group had a substantial export of components to customers operating in South America. Transferring these volumes to a South American production system would reduce costs and constitute a platform for organic growth in the region. In addition, the freed capacity in Europe could be marketed within that region. The Brazil factory was opened in spring 2012.

The Group now consisted of six factories, in Sweden (three), Latvia (two) and Brazil, organised in limited companies. The Group collectively offered an extensive range of services in flexible machining, assembly and testing of subsystems, as well as quality consultancy and measuring techniques. Yet, each subsidiary had the same generic business strategy: contract manufacturing. Customers were mostly from the vehicle industry, but mining and construction, agriculture and the general mechanical industry offered interesting growth prospects. Some of the largest customers include Scania, Volvo Trucks, Meritor, Atlas Copco, Sandvik, SKF and Dana.

The need for an agile production system became obvious at the end of 2012. Market growth slowed down and, even if the LEAX Group did not directly suffer from the financial crisis in Southern Europe, its customers became increasingly sensitive to market signals, and production forecasts were jumpier than ever. The difficulties in managing changing capacity demands obviously affected the profitability of the Group. Being privately owned, there was no immediate pressure to utilise accumulated financial resources by major investments or acquisitions. However, 2015 was quickly approaching and the present growth pace was not at all sufficient to reach the objective of 2 billion SEK in (profitable) turnover.

In April 2013 the LEAX Group acquired the business of Brinkmann GmbH in Detmold, Germany. Brinkmann is a well-known gear and gearbox specialist manufacturer with some 80 employees. In the press announcement from LEAX Roger Berggren concludes:

'Acquiring Brinkmann is of great importance for LEAX's growth in continental Europe. The German facility opens up new possibilities for us to grow our business. Our long term ambition is to grow in Germany. We want to increase the business with German companies both in Germany and globally.'

For a recent update visit www.leax.se

Notes and references
1. SEK 1 = £0.08 = $0.13 = €0.10.
2. In 2008, the (original) objective was 2212, i.e., the aim was to achieve the growth by 2012. Due to the crisis in 2008–9, realisation was postponed until 2015.
3. Volvo Group Report, 2008.
4. This and all other quotes are from the author's own research interviews, unless otehrwise stated.
5. LEAX Group Annual Report, 2010.

CASE STUDY

Changing tracks at Babcock Rail

Gerry Johnson

This case explains the changes that took place in the engineering services business, Babcock Rail, between 2009 and 2012. It provides an opportunity to consider how appropriate the leadership style and levers for change were, given the change context the company faced at the time.

● ● ●

Until 1994 British Rail (the nationalised, vertically integrated organisation that controlled the whole UK railway system) was responsible for all the UK's train services and railway stations, and also all rail support services, including track maintenance and engineering. British Rail was privatised in 1994 and 60 different businesses were established to deliver these services. What became known as First Engineering was established to undertake both track and signalling maintenance as well as upgrade and replacement work for the privatised rail system. It was then acquired by the Peterhouse Group and, in turn, this was acquired in 2004 by Babcock International PLC, the engineering support services group.

Following major rail accidents around that time, Network Rail, who were responsible for the railway infrastructure, including tracks and signalling, decided to take all the maintenance work back in-house. Babcock therefore lost the cash flow from that work. Together with its competitors, First Engineering, renamed Babcock Rail in 2006, was left with an infrastructure replacement and upgrade business. This involved the replacement of railway track, crossings and junctions using large, complex equipment to lift old track, scoop out the gravel, replace with new ballast and lay track. In addition, the business dealt with upgrades and modifications to signalling systems, PA systems in stations and railside telecommunications as well as providing consultancy services such as specialist geological surveys.

Kenny Douglas became Finance Director of Babcock Rail in 2008 and explained: 'This project work was relatively low value, so the business had started taking on larger projects which it did not have the systems and processes to manage.'[1] These were large, fixed-price, complex multidisciplinary projects of £50–£100 million ($76–$152m;

€59–€118m)[2] that required the coordination of a range of operations, often together with a civil engineering input. On the face of it, these projects simply combined the different activities undertaken by Babcock Rail – activities that the business did well – but when they were combined, the ability to manage them as multidisciplinary projects was lacking. The result was that they were unprofitable. Kenny explained:

> 'There was a failure to understand the resources required to manage such projects and a lack of project management skills and appropriate accounting systems. For example, in one review of a project, I was assured it was profitable, but subsequently found a £600,000 loss. The manager had not monitored the cost of the people involved. In addition the projects were being handled between project managers; so it was unclear who "owned" them. When I joined in 2008 the focus was, however, on reducing the overhead rather than getting these projects under control.'

Managers were also struggling to cope with a new information system that the Group had introduced in 2006. Combined with a number of change initiatives introduced during this time, Alan Mackie, the HR Director, recalled: 'We went into something approaching melt-down.' In 2009 Babcock Rail had budgeted for a healthy operating profit but turned in a major loss. It was becoming clear to Babcock International Group executives that, despite the efforts of two successive chief executives, the financial performance of Babcock Rail was stubbornly failing to meet group expectations. Peter Rogers, the Group CEO, had gone public in the press saying that unless the situation could be improved he was considering selling the business, or shutting it down.

This case was prepared by Gerry Johnson. It is intended as a basis for class discussion and not as an illustration of good or bad practice. © Gerry Johnson 2013. Not to be reproduced or quoted without permission. We are grateful for the co-operation and assistance of Babcock International in preparing the case.

Bobby Forbes, the Commercial Director, explained that the situation within the business was also getting worse:

'The managing director at the time had decided to stop bidding on projects on which we did not make money. So, turnover went through the floor: the business was restructured with the aim of delivering around £125 million turnover by 2009. It was also very difficult to recruit, not least because of declining performance and the word had got out that Babcock Group were not committed to the business, that they were looking for a buyer and that we had about six months maximum to survive. So we had good people leaving and a lot of agency staff brought in to meet demand when we couldn't recruit; and they had not gone through the same training as Babcock people.'

On top of this the relationship with the principal customer, Network Rail, which accounted for over 90% of the turnover, was deteriorating. This came to a head in 2009 over a safety audit undertaken by Network Rail that identified safety failings which it believed Babcock Rail was not taking seriously enough. It threatened to take Babcock Rail off its bidders list.

Babcock Group decided that the situation needed immediate attention and decided to install John Howie as Chief Executive. John Howie had a track record of managing change in BAE and other Babcock businesses, including the Rosyth dockyard and the nuclear submarine base at Faslane in Scotland. As Kenny Douglas explained: 'We knew John would bring a sense of realism. He also brought a level of confidence to the senior team and "headroom" from head office.'

The customer

On his arrival John Howie felt that:

'Most staff, senior managers and some of the board had got to the point where there was a growing recognition that the position was no longer tenable, that something was going to have to change, almost irrespective of what that change was. I think if you asked most people in the organisation it was obvious that things weren't right. For many I spoke to there was a recognition that they had got into a very bad place with the customer and when you've only got one customer, that's not a clever place to be. They could see that we weren't winning as many contracts as we needed and they could see a lack of cohesion in the management team.'

With regard to the problems with Network Rail:

'The reality was that when you looked at it, there were very few safety issues. They were issues about planning

and management. For example a core part of our work for Network Rail was the track replacement update programme and that was coming under pressure from their route directors for the number of times we were handing pieces of track back late and delaying and disrupting train services. Network Rail had got to the point where they decided something didn't smell right and they were looking for evidence to support that perception. The safety audit provided that.

What had happened over the years is that we had built a philosophy of "the customer is wrong, we're right". It didn't permeate the entire workforce but it was evident in fairly significant places. So, when the customer was telling us things we should have been listening to, we weren't hearing them. Some of this was the default assumption of all the contractors that "we know best; we are technically the experts and the customer really isn't". But even on safety, it was "the customer doesn't understand".'

This attitude was influencing decision making on commercial settlements, pricing and contract terms as well as day-to-day relationships with customers. It manifested in the inability to settle contract conflicts, pricing and situations where Babcock Rail was not recovering cash because contract agreements had not been signed.

Network Rail ran a set of supplier ratings. Preferred suppliers needed to be at the top of these ratings and in 2009 the feedback from Network Rail was that on all factors on which Babcock's performance was measured, Babcock Rail's performance was below that of its competitors.

Bobby Forbes, the Commercial Director, explained:

'A lot of people were protecting their own operations and their own knowledge. There was little transparency in the business and little trust. There was also what amounted to a fear culture; project staff were unwilling to give bad news to senior management. The result of all this often was that "surprises" emerged at close-out stage on a contract. This was partly due to the lack of sharing of information, generally.'

This relationship with customers was unusual for a Babcock business. John Howie:

'Babcock generally adopt a partnering ethos; it tries to work with customers. The rail business was much more about sticking a finger in the customer's forehead; it was more intolerant and demanding. The customer was rather the same but a situation where the customer and supplier are both throwing bricks at each other is never going to be effective or sustainable. Somebody had to break the cycle and you can't force customers to break the cycle.'

The relationship with Network Rail was complicated by the fact that in the technical and management disciplines, people tended to have long-term rail industry backgrounds. Indeed, prior to 1997 many managers within both Babcock and Network Rail worked in different departments of what was then the nationalised British Rail.

The change context

Despite the concerns at head office about the performance of the business, there was a recognition that, if it was to be turned round, the Group would have to invest in fixing the problem. It was also recognised that it could take time. John Howie had been given no timeframe by Peter Rogers. Within the business he believed there were different perceptions of the extent of the changes needed:

'There was a level of nervousness about what did all this mean? Could the business continue or couldn't it? There are always those in denial: "things aren't great but they've always not been great so life will just continue". There were a few at the upper end of the company who imagined that the axe was likely to fall.'

His own view was not wholly negative:

'The underlying business was relatively sound. There were gaps in ability around things like project management, but financial, commercial, technical and engineering capability and management disciplines were all there. The business was better than people were starting to think it was. So, in that sense the real challenge was getting the business onto the right financial footing without losing those things.

There was a philosophy in a company I used to work for that in these situations you get rid of the entire senior management team because it tells everyone else that change is coming. I think that's a foolish approach because you tend to waste good people. What came to light here was that there were some really good people who had just lost their way or weren't able to make their voice heard.'

In the years since privatisation, people in the business had experienced different sorts of change. For many there had been three different sets of owners and their physical locations had changed, as had many management processes. There had also been a series of change initiatives, but with little success:

'Previous change programmes comprised literally hundreds of initiatives written down on big lists, with every one of those initiatives owned by one of three people in the transformation team. So there was no buy-in from anyone in the business to implement them.'

The responses to these past initiatives varied:

'There were those who believed that the things you say have to change actually aren't broken. There were those who said, "we've been here before, we always have these change programmes but they never come to anything". And there were others who recognised that change was absolutely needed but were nervous about doing it effectively this time.'

He did not, however, encounter significant resistance to change:

'The senior management team had grown frustrated because they could see things were wrong and were not convinced that the right things were being done. At middle management level again there was recognition that change was needed. They had a less well rounded view of why that change was necessary; some pointed their finger at lack of management cohesion, lack of sense of direction, and others saw it all as the customer's fault. Of course, when you got into the detail everyone recognised the need to change providing it's the other guy who's doing it. And people found themselves juggling priorities and in my view were getting priorities wrong.'

Alan Mackie added:

'We had also got through the IFS problems,[3] so we had better quality of information by the time John arrived. If we had been in the middle of getting to grips with that that I am not sure the change programme would have worked. We would have been fighting on too many fronts.'

What was clear was that there was a lack of coherence on what changes were needed. John explained:

'It was quite obvious at my first meeting with them that the board were not joined up. It was not that there were factions – it wasn't political intrigue. They had lost their sense of togetherness. So, senior managers were getting wheeled into board meetings where directors were arguing with each other about what should get done and that's never helpful.'

'Fit for the Future'

The change programme was given a name: 'Fit for the Future'. John Howie had in mind a three-year plan with three phases: 'Six months to get the patient out of the operating theatre – phase 1. Phase 2: 12–18 months in intensive care and get the patient back onto the ward. And then, ultimately, back out onto the street – phase 3.'

It was a deliberate plan to get people to look at it in 'bite-sized chunks', because: 'What you need to do to get the patient out of the operating theatre are not the things you do when you're thinking about how to rehabilitate them for life in the real world.' His approach to managing change was informed by his experience in other Babcock businesses and in BAE. He explained:

'It's a combination of three things. One is having a methodology that you can articulate and sell of how you plan, manage and control change. Quite often change programmes involve a good deal of fire fighting and can appear haphazard to people, so having a methodology that says "this is the way we will employ change, and here's why it works; we've done it before" helps. The second part is about getting in front of people, talking to them in honest, simple terms about what the problems are, what needs to be done and what you might need from them to do it. That's all about personal interaction and communication to get "buy in". The third part is getting the organisation to function with a set of agreed goals which are clear and unambiguous, which everyone has bought into is working towards them.'

He added:

'What people generally get wrong is trying to be far too clever. They come up with incredibly intricate change programmes that deal with every problem from the lack of paperclips in the stationery cupboard right up to the fact that the customer is going to shut us down. People just can't comprehend the complexity of it all. What works best is to boil it down to the five or ten things that are going to make the biggest impact on the biggest problems. Get each of those initiatives owned by a named individual, give them authority, make it clear why it's being done and then focus them on delivering. And, when you've got those ten things done, come up with the next ten but keep the list short and meaningful so that it's clearly understood. If you start to make it too difficult the interaction between the problems gets in the way of ever solving any of them because every action has 47 unintended consequences and the whole thing just grinds to a halt.'

His diagnosis of the problems and required action began with consultations with key stakeholders: customers, senior management, key members of the staff, people in the workforce and regulators. This resulted in a 'candidate list' of key issues. These were then discussed and agreed with the board and key heads of department.

Cost reduction and restructuring

There was an early setback: the loss of the 'high output track renewals contract'. This had gone out to tender and, although Babcock Rail was the UK expert, it was awarded

elsewhere. It was the most profitable contract the business had. John Howie explained:

'That created an even bigger cliff edge, because it was a big chunk of profitability and overhead recovery. It meant that the business could not massage its way out of trouble: something radical was needed to reduce cost and reset the clock. We came to the conclusion that we needed to take about 25% of the head count out and re-engineer the backroom work to be done with far fewer people.'

The cost reduction started at board level. The size of the board was reduced by half. This was accompanied by a reduction in the layers of management.

'We redesigned the entire management organisation down to supervisor level. So, all the roles were, effectively, new. We sat down with every individual to understand their aspirations and take a view on where the opportunities and risks were in relation to the priorities we had set. The entire management population was at risk. We reappointed the ones that we thought were the best placed people to take the business forward. There were some who didn't get offered any of the roles because the things that they thought were important and the things we decided were important just weren't the same.'

There were additional benefits. The rail industry had a reputation for union militancy, but here, too, there was the acceptance of the need for change even though this involved the 25% reduction in head count – around 400 people – which Alan Mackie had prime responsibility to handle. He explained:

'We were able to show that we had started with the management. So when it came to reducing the industrial workforce, that helped get the unions' support. We also made it clear that unless if we didn't handle the redundancies right first time, there might not be a second chance; the whole business was at risk.'

The structure of the business was also streamlined. Some of the activities that had operated as business units in their own right lacked critical mass and could not sustain their own overheads. They were grouped together where there was a level of management, technical and customer compatibility. This resulted in just two operational output directors, one in charge of track and plant and one in charge of 'infrastructure': signalling, telecoms, power systems and consultancy. This, too, was challenging for some. For example as John Howie explained:

'The guy we put in charge of the infrastructure business was really a track expert and he was uncomfortable with the change, but the infrastructure part of the business was the bit that I thought was less well managed and he had all the traits of somebody who could get a grip of it. It but it took a few sessions to persuade him. I think he had got to the point where he believed the company was looking to exit him and he had sort of resigned himself to going so it took some persuading for him to stay and to step outside his comfort zone.'

The appointment had other implications:

'To get a track guy to be in charge of signalling was the ultimate heresy. I had deputations of people saying "there's no signalling representative on the board; who is looking after our interests?" So, there was that kind of residual technical culture, which was one of the things we had to dispel. My response was "sorry, it doesn't work that way".'

Customer relations

A major priority was to improve relations with Network Rail. John Howie was of the view that nobody in the senior teamed really believed that the approach to managing the customer that was being taken was sustainable. His approach was:

'I'm now going to stop you having to do things you were never comfortable with and make it ok for you to find ways of supporting the customer. For example it meant getting both sides not to default to blame in the first instance. So, if something looks like it's going wrong, pick up the phone and ask. Don't automatically assume failure on our part or blame the customer. I'll help by keeping Group off your back to allow deals to be done and I'll deal with the customer at a senior level to make sure they give us some train space to fix the problems.'

Here John Howie was able to help directly with Head Office: 'Head Office people were visiting the business on a near weekly basis. In the whole time I was there they didn't visit once. My approach to them was: "Let's only make commitments to Head Office that we can keep so that we under-promise and over-deliver".'

And with Network Rail: 'Fortunately, there were two main board directors on Network Rail who were key to this and one of them was an ex-colleague of mine from BAE systems. We had known each other for 15–20 years and there was a level of mutual respect. So, I was pushing an open door.' Again, the approach was to prioritise. For example:

'The response to the safety issue had been a 405 point plan. The customer doesn't want that. The safety audit told him that there are fundamental problems with site access, with planning, with control of plant and

equipment, etc. He wants to know what the handful of big things are that we are going to do against each of the main problems and how we will monitor them. So: here is an issue, here is what we are going to do to fix it and this traffic light will tell you whether it's going well, it's going badly, or it's fixed.'

There were outstanding contracts with Network Rail that also needed sorting out. Bobby Forbes took a lead in this:

'We had a lot of contracts which were not being converted into cash. After John had re-engaged at the top level, I was responsible for working with a Network Rail team to sort these out. It involved going through contracts worth £180 million to reach an agreement with them which released £30 million for Babcock Rail.'

It was also necessary to ensure that the tendering process was improved. Gerry Moy, the Infrastructure Director, explained: 'We made sure this was a process of review for every single tender by senior and experienced people. Decisions were rigorously debated. The result was that we no longer had contracts that didn't make money.'

John explained that there was also a shift in the control measures used:

'The business was very good at operational control measures because Network Rail drove them. So track quality and time, all that stuff was all measured to death. The bits that weren't getting measured were the management activities. So, if you take transformation activities, once we had identified those nine, ten priorities, we introduced a system of fortnightly flash reports, a one page PowerPoint with key milestones, a progress indicator and some risks and dependencies. And every two weeks the owner of that priority would report progress to a steering group'.

Kenny Douglas also worked on revising the information needed to run the business:

'People simply didn't know how to price a project. For example the bases of identifying labour costs were historic: they weren't using current cost information in bids. So we clarified the rates to be used. Of course this meant we became quite expensive for a while. But we needed to get to a situation where customers, partners and ourselves understood the real costs and risks of a bid.'

More widely, there was also a review of the business model: 'For example, should we just do work with a business of £100 million and a lower margin? Should we retrench to Scotland or should we expand, further, to London?' One consequence was that the geography of the business was changed. The decision was taken not to bid for any contracts south of Birmingham. John Howie:

'The decision was on the simple basis that we don't have the people, we don't know the local customer, we don't have a supply chain, so we were wasting money and effort bidding for things that, if we won, we would catastrophically fail at. That wasn't particularly well received in some quarters but it was a way of symbolising that things weren't going to be the same.'

Two-way communication

All of this required a widespread change of attitude in the business. John Howie believed that central to this was effective two-way communication:

'First, you have to work on the basis that people's mindsets are not incredibly deeply rooted; or at least that they have been overtaken by a view that something is fundamentally wrong and that they have developed a level of dissatisfaction with the status quo. If people believed that what the business was doing was fundamentally right and that they just needed to hold their nerve, it would have been much, much harder. People had realised that things were not good and something had to be done.

Second, face to face contact matters because people can read your face. Issuing lots of company newsletters and erudite memos isn't going to cut it. Half the people won't read them, of the people that read them many won't understand them and others won't care. What works is when you sit round a table with bacon butties and a cup of tea with a bunch of guys in boiler suits in their territory and talk with them about where we are and what the issues are in a language they understand, not in management speak. Invariably you get the initial drain down of how rubbish everything is. You've just got to take that on the chin. They have also got to think that the things they flag up to you, you are going to do something about. And you have to get them to buy into this view of a better way of doing things. The feedback out of those sessions was, generally, really positive.'

A business plan was also produced that was widely distributed to employees and to customers that clearly laid out the challenges and priorities. As John Howie explained, this helped internally and externally:

'It's the first time I've had a letter back from a customer about a business plan. The letter said: "I get loads of marketing junk over my desk every day and never read any of it. When yours said business plan I thought, I'm going to have a look at this. I've spent years trying to figure out what it is your business does and this is the first time, in this document, you have given me the answer".'

'Clear Signal', a monthly newsletter, was also introduced to report on progress against the agreed priorities. There were, however, more novel ways of communicating priorities, for example the Children's Calendar competitions on health and safety:

'The idea was to get children to draw a picture of their parent at work and put a caption on it saying why it's really important they come home safe at night. In other words, if we can't get you to be safe for your own sake, what if your kids never saw you again, how would you feel about that? We got all the kids in with their parents and I talked to the kids, saying "It's really important you explain to your mum and dad why we don't want them getting injured at work because I don't want to have to face you and explain they're not coming home." If you go into the Network Rail offices in Glasgow, on the Reception desk, there were three of our calendars lined up across the Reception desk.'

A boost to business

In March 2010 one of Babcock Rail's biggest competitors, Jarvis, collapsed. Babcock was responsible for track renewals on the west coast rail lines down as far as Birmingham. Jarvis was responsible for east coast lines from the Scottish borders down to London and into the Midlands. Network Rail immediately approached Babcock to ask if it could take over Jarvis's track renewals programme. It brought an additional £50 million a year turnover, effectively compensating for the loss of the high-output track renewals contract. Care was needed, however, to ensure it was profitable business:

'Jarvis had been in financial difficulty for many years and their reputation was badly damaged, not least because of rail accidents they had been involved in. In order to attract people, they were paying really high salaries. Had we simply replicated that, our business would have quickly become unsustainable. The unions recognised that problem at a senior level, so they worked with us on how we would deal with it. We hired a big chunk of the ex-Jarvis people but we didn't hire them all. And we took a strategic decision to close a couple of their depots. So, we ended up, effectively, taking from the ashes of Jarvis something that would be profitable and sustainable.'

There were other implications arising from taking over the Jarvis business. For example, as Bobby Forbes explained: 'It helped us consolidate the rebuilding of trust through maintaining openness and delivering consistently. When we took over Jarvis, we didn't let Network Rail down. It was fairly seamless.' But Gerry

Moy added: 'You always need an element of luck. We were lucky Jarvis presented itself at that time. But then, arguably, if you are managing things well, you make your own luck.'

The future

By the time the main part of the 'Fit for the Future' programme had been completed, the business was back up near the top of customer ratings, and by 2011 customer feedback was continuing to improve. In seven out of ten categories Babcock Rail was ahead of competitors. By 2012 it was named as net rail supplier of the year. With a 2011/12 turnover of over £160 million, the business was back in profit, and, for a rail business where margins are low, was doing well.

As Bobby Forbes saw it there were, however, further challenges: Network Rail had prompted a major change in the industry:

'Network Rail procurement strategy has changed. They have embarked on a partnership route which means we need to work with other suppliers as partners on a contract. To take an example we have been working on a freight diversion route. We originally tendered for the track work only at £25 million. We have ended up working with three other suppliers in a partnership contract worth £211 million. In 2010 the policy of our parent group didn't allow us to tender over £3 million. In the first place that shows you how much the trust and confidence in Babcock Rail has changed. But it has also meant that we are having to develop skills in collaborative working across the business. It has involved training, behavioural workshops and assessments of individuals' suitability.

Network Rail also invited commercial directors across the industry to get together in working groups to sort out various issues. I have led two of those groups. It's another indication of the level of trust and respect we have rebuilt; it wouldn't have happened three years ago.'

Notes
1. All quotes in the case are from the author's interviews.
2. £1 = $1.53 = €1.17.
3. IFS is the information system at Babcock.

CASE STUDY

In the boardroom at HomeCo[1]

Gerry Johnson

This case is concerned with how strategy might be determined in practice. It explains the strategic issues facing a (hypothetical) company producing plastic homeware products and the strategic options being advocated to tackle them. Profiles of the board members are provided, so the case lends itself to a role-play exercise in which they discuss the options as well as the underlying purpose of HomeCo and the objectives it should be pursuing.

● ● ●

HomeCo is probably best known for its range of plastic goods, such as buckets and bowls, sold through supermarkets and hardware shops throughout the UK where it has built a substantial market share. Its products can also be found in various countries in Europe to a lesser extent. It does not have much international presence beyond that. Recently, however, its growth has been challenged by an American multinational firm on the back of much higher marketing expenditure.

HomeCo was founded some 40 years ago as a family-owned industrial plastics firm. This original interest in industrial products was superseded by growth in consumer products sold through retailers, which now comprises the bulk of the turnover and profit of the Plastics Division of HomeCo. The family influence on the business gradually declined as the business raised capital from investors in 1995. Its ownership structure is now as shown in Table 1. Prior to 1995, the then family owner also sold shares to employees. This tradition has been continued, with an employee share ownership scheme now accounting for some 10% of the shares.

In addition to the Plastics Division, a second division was established in the late 1990s. This was based on two acquisitions: one of a business specialising in plastic storage units for offices and the second in sleeves for CDs and DVDs. Initially these businesses were run within the overall business, but in 2001 it was decided to set up a separate division to use the technology available from these business units to develop a wider range of plastic storage and leisure goods; and so a separate 'Homeware Division' was created. Table 2 shows the breakdown in turnover and profit contribution of each of the businesses.

After its flotation the company, then just a plastics business, grew rapidly and profitably, and this was reflected in its growth in share price. In 1998 the board decided that if future growth was to be maintained, diversification was necessary and this led to the acquisition of the other plastics businesses. However, financial analysts believe that the company paid too much for these acquisitions and their performance has never really justified the optimism voiced at the time. There is also scepticism as to just what HomeCo, as a corporate parent, can add to these businesses. In addition the growth in the plastics business, though continuing, has slowed down, and financial analysts believe that the growing interest of multinational

Table 1 Ownership structure of HomeCo

	Percentage of shares
Family	15
Employees	10
Institutional shareholding	60
Other individual (non-institutional) shareholders	15

Table 2 Turnover and profit contribution of each business

	Turnover		Percentage of total group operating profits
	£m ($m, €m)[1]	%	
Plastics Division:			
Consumer	205 (312, 242)	40	52
Industrial	80 (122, 94)	16	14
Homeware Division	210 (320, 247)	44	34
Total	495 (754, 583)	100	100

Note:
1 £1 ~ $1.53 ~ €1.17.

firms in this area will inevitably threaten nationally based firms with limited markets. The result has been a declining share price and disquiet amongst investors with interests in the firm.

However, there is a belief of some in the firm itself that inadequate attention has been paid in the past to the competences developed in retail markets. They argue that the lessons learnt in marketing to major retail chains could be transferred to the new Homeware Division more effectively than they have been. The argument here is that the company has not sufficiently sought for or managed synergies effectively.

Michael has been Chairman and Group Chief Executive for the last five years. He has announced that he intends to retire as Group CEO and become a part-time non-executive chairman. The board has decided that his successor will be Brian, the existing Chief Executive of the Plastics Division.

The board now has to decide what should be done. It appears to have a number of options:

1 Expand the international operations of the plastics business (i.e. focus on traditional strengths but grow internationally). If capital is required for this, arguably look for buyers for the industrial plastics business or for all or some of the Homeware Division, which some argue has failed to deliver against original expectations. Of course, this would mean a loss of jobs, something that the employee shareholders and perhaps family shareholders would object to considerably, as well as some management.

2 Realise capital from selling off some of the Homeware Division activities and absorb the activities with a more obvious retail plastics emphasis into an expanded consumer plastics business unit.

3 Pursue the strategy advocated by the Homeware Division, namely invest further in that division, expand its product range and its distribution.

4 Sell the whole company. A multinational plastics business has already expressed its interest in a potential takeover and at a price well above the existing share price.

However, prior to a discussion on such strategic options, Michael, the Chairman, has decided that there needs to be clarity on other issues:

'We have to be clear about our strategy: that is true. However, first we have to decide who the strategy is for. If we do not, then the debate on strategy will lack any clear focus. At the extreme it can just be an exercise in self-interest.'

With this in mind, the brief of the board is to discuss and decide upon what Michael sees as a set of related issues:

1 To whom are the board responsible in deciding future strategy and for the performance of the group?

2 Is there a rationale for the group? If so, what is it? As Michael puts it: 'It is becoming increasingly clear that some influential shareholders and industry analysts are unclear what the group is about, what its logic is and why it has the businesses it has: and this is depressing the share price.'

3 What business units should HomeCo have?

4 And what should their strategies be?

Members of the board

Chairman and Group CEO (Michael)
Group Finance Director (Paula)
CEO – Plastics Division and Group Chief Executive Designate (Brian)
CEO – Homeware Division (Charles)
Family Non-executive director (James)
Employee Non-executive director (Arthur)
Two Non-executive directors (Julia and Derek)

Michael: Chairman

Michael has been Chief Executive and Chairman of the HomeCo Group for five years; he is now relinquishing the post of Chief Executive and moving to a part-time Chairman's role. He was recruited into HomeCo at the time of its public flotation.

Michael has become convinced that some major changes have to be made at HomeCo and that 'they probably need someone other than me to do this'. He is open-minded about what should be done but within the last few years has become more and more convinced that, whatever the strategy, it has to be targeted towards increasing shareholder value. This conviction has come about for two linked reasons. The first is the sluggish profit performance, and the second is the consequent pressure he has come under from financial institutions to improve returns to shareholders and the long-term prospects for shareholders. Although he recognises the heritage of the company, its family traditions and its responsibility to employees, he has become convinced that, while their interests are important, it is the institutional investors who have to be the primary concern.

He sat on the board at the time of the acquisition of the businesses now forming the Homeware Division, though these were primarily driven by the previous chairman. He supported these acquisitions at that time, but is more questioning now about their worth and their future prospects. He acknowledges that this could be because he is by history a 'plastics man' and that his primary interest in the past has been the development of the consumer plastics business:

'I acknowledge that achieving greater synergies with the Homeware Division should be possible but, based on experience so far, they are more difficult to realise than was thought. Or to put it another way, do we really need different divisions? We have ended up with an infrastructure above our businesses – a corporate centre – and I am being asked what that adds to the businesses; what is it there for? If we aren't clear on that, then the centre is at risk of just being a costly overhead: and our investors would have every right to be unhappy about that.'

His overriding concern, however, is that there should be a full debate within the board on what should be done. He knows there are different views about the future strategy of the business. He believes strongly that the way forward, therefore, is to address an overarching question before details of the strategy are discussed: who is the strategy for? Michael puts it as: 'Who are we answerable to? I didn't think as a board we are clear enough. I don't see how we can discuss future strategy without being clearer. If we are not, debating strategy is unfocused.' He sees his primary role in the meeting as insisting on clarity on this issue and then ensuring that strategies are examined and evaluated in terms of that focus.

Brian: Chief Executive of the Plastics Division and Chief Executive Designate of the Group

Brian was recruited to HomeCo to run the Plastics Division when Michael took over as Group CEO. By background he is a consumer products man, having spent most of his time with Unilever, mainly in marketing jobs. He believes that, in the end, it is success in the marketplace that will provide the best return for shareholders. He sees the priorities as defending market share in the UK for the plastics business and growing it internationally.

He has had less direct exposure to pressure from the institutional investors than has Michael. His view is that Michael may be unduly concerned about such pressure and that it is likely to be a short-term reflection of a downturn in the growth rate of the business. The answer is to go for growth.

He understands concerns about the Homeware Division. His view is: 'If both Plastics and Homeware are growing and developing their markets profitably, then there is no issue. Shareholders and managers alike would be satisfied.' However, he is unsure of the current approach with regard to Homeware, though he believes the appointment of Charles as CEO of Homeware has been a good one.

'Charles has been recruited to grow the Homeware Division. If he is successful he will have done his job. And as Chief Executive of HomeCo I will be satisfied. But

I am less sure about the current structure. Now I am taking over as Group CEO, I can see an argument for pulling all retail plastics businesses together, selling off some of the non-retail businesses in Homeware, and just having two divisions – Consumer and Industrial. That seems much more clear cut: the two divisions would each have clearly different market focuses; and surely that makes sense.'

He then added: 'Could Charles run an enlarged consumer business? I don't know. I would like to see evidence of success in what he is doing just now.'

In the meantime, he sees that his new role as Chief Executive of the Group is to ensure that the growth and profit targets for each of the divisions and their constituent businesses are met: 'That is the primary role of the corporate centre. The businesses manage their strategy: the centre makes sure they achieve the results.'

As for the shareholders, particularly the institutional investors, he believes that the new and separate role of Group Chairman for Michael is primarily to provide an interface with them: 'My responsibility is the businesses: Michael's responsibility is the shareholders.'

As for the takeover interest by the multinational competitors, he is worried that this would result in his not getting the chance to manage the HomeCo Group – something he has been aspiring to for years.

Charles: Chief Executive of the Homeware Division

Charles was appointed just two years ago to take over the Homeware Division. He also has a background in consumer goods marketing. He believes that, paradoxically, HomeCo's plastics heritage has marginalised the businesses in the Homeware Division.

'HomeCo has never realised the potential of Homeware. The major reason for this is it doesn't know how to do so. Selling buckets and bowls to retail chains is not the most sophisticated marketing you can imagine. Sure, we could benefit from the contacts and the supply chain. But it's not the marketing expertise we need: its resources – investment in marketing and good people – that would help. The problem is the Group is too concerned with its buckets and bowls to see this.'

He acknowledges the logic of bringing together all the retail businesses together in one division but also has concerns:

'Okay, but there are two problems. First, I think it could end up just being an emphasis on the existing consumer plastics business – just buckets and bowls again. And there is no more growth to be had there. Second, although I think I could do a good job heading that enlarged business, I am not sure the rest of the board would back my appointment, so I would be out.'

Like Brian, he believes that the answer to the current problems is to build profitable growth by concentrating on the businesses. He wants to get down to discussing the strategies for achieving this. While he understands Michael's concern about shareholder pressure, he believes that this can be alleviated by ensuring improved performance of the businesses through growth. He also believes there is a good potential for cost savings in the businesses through greater efficiency. He knows this would mean losing jobs and believes that the company has been 'soft' on this issue because of the historical influence of both the family and the employees.

He would prefer that the Homeware Division stays as it is for the time being and is concerned about the takeover interest by the plastics multinational. As he sees it, a takeover from it would inevitably result in a break-up of HomeCo. Privately he will admit that whether this makes sense or not, this is his first job running a business at this level and he wants to make it work.

Paula: Finance Director

Paula was recruited as Finance Director of the firm eight years ago. She used to be with the auditors of HomeCo.

As well as being Finance Director of the group, Paula is the main contact, other than Michael, with the various investors and has a responsibility for maintaining good relationships with investment managers. She is, perhaps, the most exposed to current criticisms and concerns about the share performance of the firm. She summarises this as follows:

'There are three main issues that investors are concerned about. One is the disappointing return to them in recent years. The second reason is that they believe we paid too much for the acquisitions. The third reason is that they do not understand the acquisitions we have made. They believe that fundamentally this is a basic plastics business and wonder if we really understand some of the businesses we have got into. They want to see evidence that we can make them work. In the absence of such evidence they would prefer us to dispose of them. Indeed some argue that the Homeware businesses would benefit by being owned by a corporate parent would understand them better than us. In any case they want us to focus much more on answering the question of how we will provide greater value to our shareholders than currently.'

Paula is therefore 100% behind Michael in asking for clarity in the board about who the firm is answerable to before getting down to the details of the strategy debate. And she sees it starkly:

'It is the institutional investors: they are the majority shareholders. It is vital we all recognise that. If we do not, the destiny of the business may be removed from our hands by them. We have to start taking their interests much more seriously.'

Because of this she is determined to support Michael's insistence on a debate on this issue before moving on to a discussion of strategic options.

Personally Paula is neutral as to whether there should be a Homeware Division as well as a Plastics Division. She has some sympathy with Charles's view but the company has never really focused on the Homeware businesses and its markets. However, she has some sympathy with those who believe that HomeCo is inherently a fairly simple plastics business:

'There is an argument to say that we should focus on what we know best. That inherently HomeCo is a plastics business. That's where our capabilities lie. The danger, however, is that, as such, we may be even more vulnerable to a takeover. Ironically a buyer may be less attracted to us with our Homeware businesses than without. So in some respects I think the issue of the corporate logic of the business gets in the way of a real debate about how we act in the best interests of our shareholders. I suspect that if we do the numbers (and I have) the most logical answer of what is best for most shareholders is to negotiate the best offer we can for the sale of the business. I also think that we could probably maximise the price if we dispose of Homeware first. That is what I intend to argue.'

Arthur: Employee Director

At the time, when external investment was raised the family insisted that the employees should retain 10% of the shares and have the right to have a non-executive director on the board. For the last 10 years this non-executive director has been Arthur.

Arthur is now retired from HomeCo but used to be a senior trade union official for 25 years when he worked for the company. He was proud to build up good working relationships between the employees and the family in his time, and believes that that has been one of the strengths of the firm in the past. Indeed, he is concerned that some recent appointments at senior management level have eroded this strength.

He also takes seriously the legacy of what the family intended:

'It was always intended that HomeCo be a caring employer. The whole point of giving the employees the right to own shares was to give them an interest in the commercial success of the business. We have built that interest and have a good employee relations track record as a result. It is all very well the directors talking about maximising shareholders' returns: they need to remember we are shareholders.'

Arthur sees himself as representing the interests of the employees, and this is about getting a good return on their shares as well as ensuring job security.

As a director of the firm he is aware of the current take-over interest and opposes it because he believes that it would result, inevitably, in significant job losses and is a short-term rather than a long-term view.

Although he does not approve of Charles's attitude towards the employees, he does believe that developing Homeware, rather than disposing of it, is a good argument. Disposal would again result in job losses: development means job security.

He knows that he has a battle on his hands in the board but sees his role not only to fight on behalf of the employees as shareholders but to 'fight for the small shareholders who invest in businesses not just for short-term gain but because they believe in the viability of those businesses.

Julia: non-executive director

Julia is a non-executive director who joined the board four years ago at the request of two of the most significant investors. She sees her role as taking a measured view about the future of the business, with a priority interest in developing returns for shareholders. Her brief on appointment was to encourage the board to address some key issues which the investors found problematic. These were (and remain) the following:

● How to maximise long-term shareholder benefit?
● Whether this is best done by focusing on a plastics business alone or a diversified business?
● Within either option, how to minimise costs, including the costs of the corporate centre?
● Regarding the last point, to determine just what the corporate centre adds in terms of value to the businesses. On this issue her personal view is that the corporate centre is unclear on what it adds and, as a result, is destroying value and lowering returns to shareholders. Indeed, she wonders whether it is really needed.

She has tried to remain dispassionate and objective over the last few years in following this brief. She believes she has influenced Michael and Paula to take seriously the needs of shareholders. She is concerned that Brian and Charles have not really thought through the implications of this for the future of the business:

'Brian and Charles are, essentially, managers and see their responsibilities as being down into the businesses. I believe they need to lift their sights to look at the interests of the shareholders and then decide the strategies of the businesses in that light.'

She is delighted that Michael is asking that these issues, which she sees as central, need to be clarified and will give Michael support in ensuring this happens.

The recent expression of interest by the multinational plastics firm is one about which, again, she has tried to remain objective. Her focus is on wanting to be convinced about how growing returns to shareholders in the future can be achieved. Her intention is to challenge the executives to demonstrate they can develop a strategy that does provide such an increase in shareholder value:

'I want to hear from them how they expect to be able to create real value from these businesses. It is not good enough simply to say we should grow them. I want to hear a much more convincing story about building bases of competitive advantage. I don't see that as an easy matter in the market conditions they are facing. I am, however, open to being convinced. But if they don't convince me of this, I believe the sale of the company would be in shareholders' interests.'

Derek: non-executive director

Derek has a number of non-executive positions in firms related to plastics, oils and chemicals businesses. He is regarded as an industry expert in some of these sectors. He joined the board at the invitation of Michael whom he knows well. Derek has a clear view about what should now be done. He believes that the firm has done well in the past but made a mistake in acquiring the Homeware businesses, since the senior management at the time knew very little about them. He has a good deal of confidence in Charles and believes that, given time, Charles could sort them out and maybe achieve the sort of growth required. However, he explains the current situation as follows:

'The fact is we now have a choice. Do we go for a long-term strategy which could require a good deal of investment in Homeware as well as a plastics business faced with multinational competition? I can see why the management of the business might see this as a challenge they would like to take on: but I see it as a risk. The alternative is to try and maximise the offer price in a takeover. I think we should do this for two reasons. First, because I think there is a window of opportunity here. I think we can get a good price now; but I am not sure we will be able to do so in a year or so. Second, I think the Homeware businesses can be used to enhance that offer. I think our share price is depressed because of our Homeware businesses and that we should get rid of them. If we do, I think it will make us more attractive for a takeover, but at a higher offer price than currently. So I think we have a short-term opportunity that we need to be following which is in the best interests of most of the shareholders. The problem is it is not in the interest of all the shareholders or in the interest of some of the managers.'

He understands why Michael wants a debate about the centrality of shareholders but has his reservations on this:

> 'Look, Michael has come under a lot of pressure recently from investors; and he knows that Brian and Charles don't understand this entirely. I understand his concerns but I think he is being somewhat academic in all this. The fact is we have a short-term opportunity to get a really good price for this business and we should take it. If we don't I fear the time will pass. I also believe that if we follow Michael's logic and place the shareholder first we will come to the same conclusion anyway. It is in their best interest to take the short-term opportunity to maximise the value of their shares through a sale. I know there are those around the table who won't like that but I intend to push hard to get them to see the logic of such a sale.'

James: non-executive director

James is the grandson of the founder of HomeCo. He is a non-executive director. For some years he worked within the firm but left a few years after it went public. He was elected as a Labour Party Member of Parliament for a local constituency. He describes himself, politically, as 'New Labour, socially responsible and commercially aware'.

James takes seriously the family heritage of the firm and supports the strong belief of his father in the employee shareholder scheme, which he had set up. Indeed, he believes the interest of the family and employees are closely aligned. He explains:

> 'The family set up this firm with the long-term in mind. It was there to benefit the interests of the family over decades. I believe this is also the interest of the employees and, indeed, the wider shareholders. The family, employees and the ultimate shareholders are interested in the pros-

perity of this firm over decades, not a few years. The perspective I want to see this firm taking is to ensure its growth and prosperity over those time periods. I am well aware that since we external investors involved the board, and Michael in particular, have come under all sorts of pressure that might lead to short-term decisions. I am very much against these.'

James believes that it is the responsibility of the board to take a long-term view in the interests of all shareholders. In the board, and in Parliament, he is scornful of professional investment managers (who publicly he has referred to as 'wide boys') whose primary interest, he argues, is their own careers rather than the long-term interest of firms or the real shareholders.

> 'We have created an industry of financial advisers and investment houses that have created a reality of their own. The shareholder is virtually isolated from the firms they invest in. They know virtually nothing about them, they are not encouraged to know about them and have become reliant on sometimes spurious advice from so-called specialists.'

He does not have a firm view as to what should be done at HomeCo except that he is determined to oppose its sale. Beyond that he intends to listen to the arguments. He does have doubts as to whether the firm has really thought through its diversification programme, but is open to persuasion if there is a long-term future there. He is, however, concerned that a decision to dispose of the Homeware businesses might in turn expose the group to a takeover bid to which he would be opposed.

Note and reference

1. HomeCo is a fictitious name for the case study. The description of the business is not intended to represent or be based on any specific existing business.

CASE STUDY

QR National – Aurizon

Kenneth Wiltshire

Aurizon (formerly QR National) is currently Australia's largest national rail freight operator and an internationally competitive freight business. It had achieved this success, whilst remaining in government ownership, through strategic decisions on competition and investment and the formation of alliances. In response to problems in its public finances, the Queensland government announced plans to privatise the freight component of Queensland Rail. This gave rise to a protest campaign from unions, the media, the public, and some coal companies. The freight arm of the company was privatised in 2010 to become 'QR National', with the passenger arm remaining as a government-owned corporation. Because of brand confusion between QR National and Queensland Rail, a decision was taken in late 2012 to rename the company 'Aurizon'. After two years of privatisation its strategy is becoming clear.

● ● ●

Australia is an extremely large continent, larger than either the USA or Western Europe, but with a relatively small population. Consequently in the past governments had to provide the major transport and communication infrastructure, because private enterprise found the task uneconomic, especially as the population was very scattered across the nation. Another factor is the Australian belief, embedded in the nation's value system, that every citizen is entitled to the same standard of public services wherever they may live – a very costly goal for governments to deliver. Establishment of railways in the nineteenth century faced all of these challenges.

QR (Queensland Rail) began as a colonial-style railway, with the first train travelling from Ipswich to Grandchester on 1 July 1865. Queensland is the most decentralised state in Australia and the railways were a major element in opening up the vast frontier. Indeed, the railways were seen as the key element of land settlement policy. The Queensland track was built to a gauge of only 3 feet 6 inches (narrow gauge), rather than the standard gauge of 4 feet 8 inches, to save costs in the construction, and the railway remained the single largest cost item in the government's budget throughout the nineteenth century. Indeed, the wages of all public servants often depended on the financial situation of the railways.

Over time a number of community service obligations were forced upon QR, including concessional freight rates for particular commodities or regions, concessions to some passengers such as pensioners and schoolchildren, and free travel for politicians for life. Organisational change has been a constant theme. QR has been through several institutional forms. It began as a government department operating under its own piece of legislation, The Railways Act. In 1991 QR began the commercialisation process with the creation of an independent Board of Directors (non-executives), appointed by the government to set strategic direction. In 1995 the entity was corporatised as a statutory Government Owned Corporation (GOC) and on 1 July 1995 it became a company GOC with two ministers as shareholders – the State Treasurer and the Minister Responsible for Transport. In 2010 the company was split in two, with the freight arm being privatised to become 'QR National', and the passenger arm remaining as a government corporation, 'QR'.

In government ownership, QR had always confronted the classical governance dilemma of trying to run as a business but also remain a service to the public, with the main issue being how to maintain an 'arm's length' relationship with its owner, the Queensland government. The role of the Board had never been clear – it set strategic directions, which the government noted, but in reality there was a disconnection between plan and execution.

QR was required to pay an annual dividend to the government, which was set in a rather arbitrary fashion depending on annual results. It needed government approval for raising capital – a delicate aspect, since competitive strategies in rail require large outlays on track and rolling stock. For most of its existence QR was subject to the full array of public sector accountability, including Auditor-General, Parliamentary Committee scrutiny, Freedom of Information, etc. In its government corporate forms QR's Board comprised people with business expertise, but the discretionary areas for the Board have been somewhat limited, with the government retaining control over most aspects. QR was highly unionised, which caused tensions regarding the introduction of modern business practices and had been a major factor in keeping the railway in public ownership.

However, the dominant policy matter had been the need to cross-subsidise an unprofitable passenger network, especially in urban areas, from profitable freight operations, especially haulage of coal. QR was also subject to regulation of its network access prices, often a source of tension. The same regulator, The Queensland Competition Authority, also oversees the ports, which have become bottlenecks in recent times, hindering QR's own freight haulage operations. It had six operating divisions:[1]

- QR National: coal and bulk logistics, transport and general freight business
- Passenger Services: community, long-distance and tourist passenger network
- Network Access: managers of the Queensland railway network, including access to it and operations on it
- Infrastructure Services: construction, maintenance and management of the rail network
- Rolling Stock and Component Services: manufacture, heavy repair and overhaul of most of QR's rolling stock fleet
- Shared Services: internal business support across QR operations.

In the last part of the twentieth century, as a result of sweeping national reforms to Australian competition policy, the 'business areas' of the public sector lost their traditional protected positions and were forced to engage in open competition, including payment of full taxes, total transparency, and a requirement to provide third-party access to their infrastructure. This had a major impact on Australian railways, which now faced competition from private freight companies that had to be given access to the track for their rolling stock at competitive prices.

Rather than take a defensive stance, QR took strategic advantage of this situation and won contracts in other Australian states (e.g. coal contracts in the Hunter Valley of New South Wales), and overseas in competition with private bidders. This was quite an achievement for an organisation with a long-standing public service culture. A large part of the credit is given to the entrepreneurial skills of the CEO of the time, Bob Scheuber, who had a long career in QR, having worked his way up the ladder. He had always retained his union membership, and the trust he had generated with his staff is considered to have been a vital factor in

being able to introduce the new corporate and strategic focus, which required some job cutting. It was also a key aspect of his leadership of QR, which had the usual run of accidents that railways have the world over. He has commented that in his major media appearances during such crises he regarded the interviews as a key avenue for communicating to his own workforce, just as much as to the public.

In 2006, QR signalled a more commercial future with the appointment of former BHP CEO John Prescott as Chairman. In 2007, leading steel executive Lance Hockridge (formerly of Bluescope and BHP) was appointed CEO to replace Bob Scheuber whose contract had expired.

QR's success had been aided by a set of strategic partnerships it had formed with linked operators in the transport and logistics supply chain. It has also had active Corporate Social Responsibility programmes with several community, 'not for profit' organisations.

In 2008, in a shock announcement, the State Labor government revealed that the Global Financial Crisis had made a major dent in the State's finances, so much so that Queensland lost its long-standing Triple-A credit rating and was facing intense difficulties in raising loans in the face of mounting debt levels. In response to this crisis the government announced a privatisation programme which would include government forests, ports and parts of QR including its freight division and coal network. This immediately produced a public outcry, since privatisation had not even been mentioned during the election campaign. The unions immediately mounted a major protest campaign against privatisation in general but especially at the proposals for QR. This campaign gathered intensity and was backed by substantial media commentary, particularly when it became obvious that the government had not carefully thought through the privatisation goals or process and its likely ramifications.

Business generally welcomed the privatisation moves, citing various reasons why rail freight should be in private hands. The debate, it was argued, was about who is the best owner of QR's freight business, the government or the private sector – not an argument about individual managers but about structures and governance.

The question being asked was 'Do we want QR's freight business owned by a government, which has a complex array of political and policy objectives, or do we want it owned by an entity with only a commercial focus?'[2] Three reasons for privatisation were advanced:

1 The freight business is capital intensive and it is extremely important that the required investments are made to transport Queensland's growing coal exports. A commercial entity that is well capitalised will generally invest when it sees sufficient demand for the services, but a government owner must weigh the more

immediate political benefits of investing instead in possibly schools or hospitals.

2 It is more difficult for a government to run QR efficiently given that it is constantly lobbied by customers, unions and other stakeholders making demands that they would not do to a private operator.

3 QR needs to be responsive to commercial opportunities and such decisions with a customer, who might be prepared to pay, should not have to pass through a political filter.

On the other hand, a group of leading economists attacked the privatisation plan, saying that the measures of costing and return had overstated the financial returns, given the costs of dressing up the assets for sale, and undervalued the dividend stream that would have kept flowing to the government if the asset remained in public ownership. The coal industry expressed concerns at the plan to sell both QR track and rolling stock as one entity (i.e. an integrated operator like the Class 1 railways in the USA) which it claimed might lead to anti-competitive pricing and access decisions that would create inefficiencies and delay upgrades. The argument effectively complained that this would amount to replacing a public monopoly with a private one.

QR itself conducted a study of rail privatisations around the world and was unimpressed by experiences in the UK and New Zealand, but regarded Canadian experience more favourably. The British experience was believed to have brought some benefits, including possibly lower rail fares than might have been otherwise, but it also seemed that crowded trains, allegations of profiteering by the multitude of new rail service providers, paralysing crashes, and endless political friction had led to a bigger British government subsidy than had been the case when rail was in full British government ownership. Many argued that the splitting of the UK's train operating services from the track (i.e. 'above-rail' from 'below-rail' assets) was the source of many of the problems, because it led to a multitude of small train operators squabbling over access to lines that were controlled by a company that had no financial incentive to maintain or improve the infrastructure.

The main Australian competitor group to QR, Asciano, which operates the Pacific National group, an above-rail operator,[3] expressed concerns to the competition regulator that the sale of a vertically integrated QR would give it incentives to discriminate against above-rail competitors.

As the debate wore on it became clear that the government had not taken many of these factors into account, especially the question of which body would have responsibility for track maintenance. Some 5000 workers in QR currently had this responsibility. It was not clear what the interface between the newly privatised parts of QR and the rest would be, and particularly why a government would

continue to subsidise one part but not the other. The actual valuation of the assets and their split was another very difficult task. Moreover, QR had an enviable safety record, a reputation for good technical excellence, a sound customer/commercial balance, and sense of corporate responsibility; the damage which could be done to this brand needed to be considered.

In the event the government responded to union and public concerns about ownership by announcing that the sale of QR's freight operations and coal network would be by public float, with parcels of shares reserved for QR staff, and preferential access to shares for the Queensland public. The government offered QR National employees A$1000 (£685.40; $1041.90; €812.80)[4] worth of free shares, plus an additional A$4000 worth on a discounted basis. The government would also retain a 25–40% initial shareholding which would be sold down over time. The Rolling Stock Workshops, which service the freight rolling stock, and the track maintenance staff who build new track or maintain current track, will be included in the new privatised freight entity, called 'QR National'. Therefore QR National was planned to be a fully integrated freight operator and track owner.

With the split of freight from passenger operations, the plan also created a new entity called Queensland Rail, which would become a government-owned passenger business offering the suite of passenger services that were currently provided.

It is significant that the sale of QR National had been preceded by a worldwide trade show, since it was recognised that there was not sufficient interest in Australia, given the scepticism and uncertainty surrounding the government's intentions. In the event the privatisation could not have succeeded without overseas investment. The float was at A$2.40 and the share price quickly rose to A$4.00, then settled at A$3.40. The irony is that the Australian investors who had had little faith in the venture were now forced to buy in at a higher price than they could have had at the flotation. The fact that both the Labor government and the Opposition pledged eventually to sell down the government share gave some certainty, although it was reported that some potential investors in the company remained wary, given the government's retention of some ownership.

QR National became listed in the top 30 companies in Australia by market capitalisation at A$8.5 billion – bigger than Qantas, the largest airline. Unlike experience with other privatisations around the world, there were few staff redundancies, numbers falling from 9,500 to 9,000 through voluntary redundancies (staff have employment guaranteed for three years under the enterprise agreement). In the words of a senior official, 'Compulsory redundancy is the last resort of the bad manager.' QR National embarked on a policy of creating more indigenous employment and now employs more indigenous workers than was the case under government ownership. It has also tripled the number of apprenticeships it has offered.

The government retained 34% ownership but has no seat on the new board and has not issued any directions to the company. Some Community Service Obligations remain in place relating mainly to regional freight concessions, which are government funded. The rail freight operator owns 3,000 km of track, with the government retaining ownership of 7,000 km. Ownership of the track facilitates a focus on supply chains, and vertical integration means a strong incentive to maintain the track and address safety concerns, especially during natural disasters such as floods, which have caused severe damage. The company is recognised as having an excellent record in this domain.

Since privatisation, the company's activities have continued to be heavily associated with mineral haulage in Queensland, the intensely mineral-rich north-west region of Western Australia, and the Hunter Valley of New South Wales. It is the major Australian player in resource infrastructure. QR National also still carries general freight across Australia on the interstate freight node and provides consulting and technical services overseas. The philosophy is now one of growth, for it believes that without growth it will not have a strategy. That strategy can be summed up as 'supply chain management', which will be vital, both to address competition and to achieve innovation. Different strategies beckon, including ownership of track, using others' tracks and building new track. Competition comes in many forms, including:

● Other Australian rail operators also pursuing supply chain control
● Overseas interests currently receiving minerals and other freight who desire full and certain supply chain control
● Many mining companies who fancy establishing their own track and rail operations
● Gaining access to existing tracks owned by competitors under the access rules laid down by National Competition Policy, despite these existing operators claiming their track is fully utilised
● Opportunities presented by new, smaller mining companies amenable to suggestions of combining to establish new rail lines
● The perverse competition scenario created by the current Australian national government which has introduced the world's highest carbon tax and will apply it to rail but not to road haulage. (QR National became one of the biggest power users in Queensland.)

The strategy of supply chain control and management covers a broad spectrum of possibilities and alliances, including vertical integration of rail, suppliers such as miners and farmers, ports, and overseas purchasers. It also means the company will need to become closer to its customers, understand their industries and the factors unique to them, and closely follow the development of new and growing industries such as carbon capture and storage. There is also the matter of re-engaging with customers who were formerly 'at war' with the company before privatisation and who were trying to take over their track.

In other words, QR National decided to pursue a growth strategy based on its core business, with any diversification not straying too far away from its core business. It committed to maintaining its good corporate citizen record through employment policies, strategic sponsorships (including the Newcastle Knights football team), and other Corporate Social Responsibility programmes. This privatisation appears to have unleashed a new dynamic in performance and growth without much of the downside often experienced elsewhere. It has proven the sceptics wrong. QR National was launched from a strong base with a sound record and now 'feels grown up', but it has significant challenges to face to remain in the game for the long haul.

There was a strong performance in 2012, with growth of 52% in underlying earnings before interest and tax, reaching A$584 million. This was in spite of lower coal haulage volumes (due to the slowness of large coal projects coming on stream) and partly caused by losses to the USA during the Queensland floods. The company predicted modest growth and the cut of another 750 jobs through voluntary redundancies. With much debate occurring in Australia about the prospective length of the resources boom, CEO Lance Hockridge said: 'It is a more cautious world.'

Late in 2012, the Queensland government, as a result of a major Commission of Audit into State debt-laden finances, announced that it was going to progressively sell down its remaining stake in QR National. With the share price rising to A$3.30, up from the listing price of A$2.55, the media declared that the sceptics had been silenced as QR National had performed well.

Also late in 2012, as a result of continuing brand confusion between QR National and Queensland Rail, including among politicians themselves, the company announced that it was changing its name to 'Aurizon', clearly an attempt to combine the iconic word images of Australia and Horizon.

Notes and references
1. *QR Annual Report 2009.*
2. *Australian Financial Review*, 30 November 2009.
3. 'Above rail' refers to a rail organisation that operates passenger and freight operations but does not own or maintain the rail track.
4. A$1 ~ £0.69 ~ $1.05 ~ €0.80.

GLOSSARY

acceptability expected performance outcomes of a proposed strategy to meet the expectation of the stakeholders (p. 379)

acquisition when one firm takes over the ownership ('equity') of another; hence the alternative term 'take-over' (p. 331)

BCG matrix uses market share and market growth criteria to determine the attractiveness and balance of a business portfolio (p. 244)

Blue Oceans new market spaces where competition is minimised (p. 58)

business case provides the data and argument in support of a particular strategy proposal, for example investment in new equipment (p. 521)

business-level strategy how an individual business competes in its particular market(s) (p. 7)

business model describes how an organisation manages incomes and costs through the structural arrangement of its activities (p. 301)

CAGE framework emphasises the importance of cultural, administrative, geographical and economic distance (p. 274)

collaboration all those affected by strategic changes are active in setting the change agenda (p. 469)

collaborative advantage the benefits received when a company achieves more by collaborating with other organisations than it would when operating alone (p. 342)

collective strategy how the whole network of an alliance, of which an organisation is a member, competes against rival networks of alliances (p. 341)

competences the ways in which an organisation may deploy its assets effectively (p. 70)

competitive advantage how a strategic business unit creates value for its users which is both greater than the costs of supplying them and superior to that of rival SBUs (p. 193)

competitive strategy how a strategic business unit achieves competitive advantage in its domain of activity (p. 193)

complementor (i) customers value your product more when they have another organisation's product than if they have your product alone; (ii) it is more attractive to suppliers to provide resources to you when they are also supplying another organisation than if they are supplying you alone (p. 49)

configurations the set of organisational design elements that interlink together in order to support the intended strategy (p. 454)

corporate entrepreneurship refers to radical change in an organisation's business, driven principally by the organisation's own capabilities (p. 331)

corporate governance is concerned with the structures and systems of control by which managers are held accountable to those who have a legitimate stake in an organisation (p. 113)

corporate-level strategy is concerned with the overall scope of an organisation and how value is added to the constituent businesses of the organisation as a whole (p. 7)

corporate social responsibility the commitment by organisations to behave ethically and contribute to economic development while improving the quality of life of the workforce and their families as well as the local community and society at large (p. 127)

cost-leadership strategy involves becoming the lowest-cost organisation in a domain of activity (p. 194)

critical success factors those factors that are either particularly valued by customers or which provide a significant advantage in terms of costs. (Sometimes called key success factors (KSF)] (p. 58)

cultural systems these aim to standardise norms of behaviour within an organisation in line with particular objectives (p. 448)

cultural web shows the behavioural, physical and symbolic manifestations of a culture (p. 155)

deliberate strategy involves intentional formulation or planning (p. 404)

differentiation involves uniqueness in some dimension that is sufficiently valued by customers to allow a price premium (p. 197)

diffusion the process by which innovations spread amongst users (p. 305)

direction the use of personal managerial authority to establish a clear strategy and how change will occur (p. 470)

disruptive innovation creates substantial growth by offering a new performance trajectory that, even if initially inferior to the performance of existing technologies, has the potential to become markedly superior (p. 310)

diversification (related and unrelated/conglomerate) increasing the range of products or markets served by an organisation (p. 226)

divisional structure is built up of separate divisions on the basis of products, services or geographical areas (p. 436)

dominant logic the set of corporate-level managerial competences applied across the portfolio of businesses (p. 232)

dynamic capabilities an organisation's ability to renew and re-create its strategic capabilities to meet the needs of changing environments (p. 71)

economies of scope efficiency gains made through applying the organisation's existing resources or competences to new markets or services (p. 232)

emergent strategy a strategy that develops as a result of a series of decisions, in a pattern that becomes clear over time, rather than as a deliberate result of a 'grand plan' (p. 410)

entrepreneurial life cycle progresses through start-up, growth, maturity and exit (p. 312)

***Exploring Strategy* Model** includes understanding *the strategic position* of an organisation (context); assessing *strategic choices* for the future (content); and managing *strategy in action* (process) (p. 10)

feasibility whether a strategy can work in practice (p. 390)

first-mover advantage where an organisation is better off than its competitors as a result of being first to market with a new product, process or service (p. 308)

focus strategy targets a narrow segment of domain of activity and tailors its products or services to the needs of that specific segment to the exclusion of others (p. 199)

forcefield analysis provides an initial view of change problems that need to be tackled by identifying forces for and against change (p. 475)

functional structure divides responsibilities according to the organisation's primary specialist roles such as production, research and sales (p. 434)

game theory encourages an organisation to consider competitors' likely moves and the implications of these moves for its own strategy (p. 212)

gap analysis compares actual or projected performance with desired performance (p. 369)

global–local dilemma the extent to which products and services may be standardised across national boundaries or need to be adapted to meet the requirements of specific national markets (p. 270)

global sourcing purchasing services and components from the most appropriate suppliers around the world, regardless of their location (p. 268)

global strategy involves high coordination of extensive activities dispersed geographically in many countries around the world (p. 262)

governance chain shows the roles and relationships of different groups involved in the governance of an organisation (p. 113)

hypothesis testing a methodology used particularly in strategy projects for setting priorities in investigating issues and options; widely used by strategy consulting firms and members of strategy project teams (p. 521)

industry a group of firms producing products and services that are essentially the same (p. 41)

inimitable capabilities those capabilities that competitors find difficult to imitate or obtain (p. 77)

innovation the conversion of new knowledge into a new product, process or service *and* the putting of this new product, process or service into actual use (p. 296)

international strategy a range of options for operating outside an organisation's country of origin (p. 262)

leadership the process of influencing an organisation (or group within an organisation) in its efforts towards achieving an aim or goal (p. 466)

learning organisation an organisation that is capable of continual regeneration due to a variety of knowledge, experience and skills within a culture that encourages questioning and challenge (p. 411)

legitimacy is concerned with meeting the expectations within an organisational field in terms of assumptions, behaviours and strategies (p. 150)

logical incrementalism the development of strategy by experimentation and learning (p. 411)

market a group of customers for specific products or services that are essentially the same (e.g. a particular geographical market) (p. 41)

market segment a group of customers who have similar needs that are different from customer needs in other parts of the market (p. 56)

market systems these typically involve some formalised system of 'contracting' for resources or inputs from other parts of an organisation and for supplying outputs to other parts of an organisation (p. 452)

matrix structure combines different structural dimensions simultaneously, for example product divisions and geographical territories or product divisions and functional specialisms (p. 438)

merger the combination of two previously separate organisations, typically as more or less equal partners (p. 331)

mission statement aims to provide the employees and stakeholders with clarity about the overriding purpose of the organisation (p. 108)

objectives statements of specific outcomes that are to be achieved (often expressed in financial terms) (p. 109)

open innovation involves the deliberate import and export of knowledge by an organisation in order to accelerate and enhance its innovation (p. 300)

operational strategies these are concerned with how the components of an organisation effectively deliver the corporate- and business-level strategies in terms of resources, processes and people (p. 7)

organic development is where a strategy is pursued by building on and developing an organisation's own capabilities (p. 330)

organisational ambidexterity the ability of an organisation simultaneously to exploit existing capabilities and to search for new capabilities (p. 487)

organisational culture the taken-for-granted assumptions and behaviours that make sense of people's organisational context (p. 147)

organisational field a community of organisations that interact more frequently with one another than with those outside the field and that have developed a shared meaning system (p. 150)

organisational knowledge the collective intelligence, specific to an organisation, accumulated through both formal systems and the shared experience of people in that organisation(p. 80)

outsourcing activities that were previously carried out internally are subcontracted to external suppliers (p. 235)

paradigm is the set of assumptions held in common and taken for granted in an organisation (p. 153)

parenting advantage is the value added to businesses by corporate-level activities (p. 226)

participation elements of the change process are delegated by a strategic leader, who still retains authority over, and coordinates, the processes of change (p. 469)

path dependency where early events and decisions establish 'policy paths' that have lasting effects on subsequent events and decisions (p. 143)

performance targeting systems focus on the *outputs* of an organisation (or part of an organisation), such as product quality, revenues or profits (p. 449)

PESTEL framework categorises environmental influences into six main types: political, economic, social, technological, environmental and legal (p. 34)

planning systems plan and control the allocation of resources and monitor their utilisation (p. 447)

platform leadership refers to how large firms consciously nurture independent companies through successive waves of innovation around their basic technological 'platform' (p. 301)

Porter's Diamond suggests that locational advantages may stem from local factor conditions; local demand conditions; local related and supporting industries; and from local firm strategy structure and rivalry (p. 266)

Porter's Five Forces Framework helps identify the attractiveness of an industry in terms of five competitive forces: the threat of entry; the threat of substitutes; the power of buyers; the power of suppliers; and the extent of rivalry between competitors (p. 41)

portfolio manager he or she operates as an active investor in a way that shareholders in the stock market are either too dispersed or too inexpert to be able to do so (p. 240)

power the ability of individuals or groups to persuade, induce or coerce others into following certain courses of action (p. 126)

profit pools the different levels of profit available at different parts of the value network (p. 88)

project-based structure teams are created, undertake their work (e.g. internal or external contracts) and are then dissolved (p. 442)

rare capabilities are those capabilities that are possessed uniquely by one organisation or by a few (p. 77)

recipe a set of assumptions, norms and routines held in common within an organisational field about the appropriate purposes and strategies of organisational field members (p. 150)

resource-based view states that the competitive advantage and superior performance of an organisation is explained by the distinctiveness of its capabilities (p. 70)

resources assets possessed by an organisation, or that it can call upon (e.g. from partners or suppliers) (p. 70)

returns the financial benefits that stakeholders are expected to receive from a strategy (p. 380)

risk the extent to which the outcomes of a strategy can be predicted (p. 379)

S-curve the shape of the curve reflects a process of initial slow adoption of an innovation, followed by a rapid acceleration in diffusion, leading to a plateau representing the limit to demand (p. 306)

situational leadership successful leaders are able to adjust their style of leadership to the context they face (p. 468)

social entrepreneurs individuals and groups who create independent organisations to mobilise ideas and resources to address social problems, typically earning revenues but on a not-for-profit basis (p. 317)

staged international expansion model proposes a sequential process whereby companies gradually increase their commitment to newly entered markets as they build market knowledge and capabilities (p. 281)

stakeholder mapping identifies stakeholder expectations and power, and helps in the understanding of political priorities (p. 122)

stakeholders those individuals or groups that depend on an organisation to fulfil their own goals and on whom, in turn, the organisation depends (p. 107)

strategic alliance where two or more organisations share resources and activities to pursue a strategy (p. 341)

strategic business unit supplies goods or services for a distinct domain of activity (p. 192)

strategic capabilities the capabilities of an organisation that contribute to its long-term survival or competitive advantage (p. 71)

strategic choices involve the options for strategy in terms of both the *directions* in which strategy might move and the *methods* by which strategy might be pursued (p. 12)

strategic drift the tendency for strategies to develop incrementally on the basis of historical and cultural influences, but fail to keep pace with a changing environment (p. 162)

strategic groups organisations within an industry or sector with similar strategic characteristics, following similar strategies or competing on similar bases (p. 54)

strategic issue-selling the process of gaining attention and support of top management and other important stakeholders for strategic issues (p. 512)

strategic lock-in is where users become dependent on a supplier and are unable to use another supplier without substantial switching costs (p. 204)

strategic plan provides the data and argument in support of a strategy for the whole organisation (p. 521)

strategic planners (also known as strategy directors or corporate managers) managers with a formal responsibility for coordinating the strategy process (p. 503)

strategic planning systemised, step-by-step procedures to develop an organisation's strategy (p. 405)

strategic position is concerned with the impact on strategy of the external environment, the organisation's strategic capability (resources and competences), the organisation's goals and the organisation's culture (p. 11)

strategy the long-term direction of an organisation (p. 3)

strategy canvas compares competitors according to their performance on key success factors in order to develop strategies based on creating new market spaces (p. 58)

strategy in action this is about how strategies are formed and how they are implemented (p. 13)

strategy lenses ways of looking at strategy issues differently in order to generate many insights (p. 20)

strategy projects involve teams of people assigned to work on particular strategic issues over a defined period of time (p. 520)

strategy statements should have three main themes: the fundamental *goals* that the organisation seeks, which typically draw on the organisation's stated mission, vision and objectives; the *scope* or domain of the organisation's activities; and the particular *advantages* or capabilities it has to deliver all of these (p. 8)

strategy workshops (also called strategy away-days or off-sites) these involve groups of executives working intensively for one or two days, often away from the office, on organisational strategy (p. 518)

structures give people formally defined roles, responsibilities and lines of reporting with regard to strategy (p. 433)

suitability assessing which proposed strategies address the *key opportunities and restraints* an organisation faces (p. 372)

SWOT the strengths, weaknesses, opportunities and threats likely to impact on strategy development (p. 91)

synergy the benefits gained where activities or assets complement each other so that their combined effect is greater that the sum of parts (p. 233)

systems support and control people as they carry out structurally defined roles and responsibilities (p. 433)

three-horizons framework suggests that every organization should think of itself as comprising three types of business or activity, defined by their 'horizons' in terms of years (p. 4)

threshold capabilities capabilities that are needed for an organisation to meet the necessary requirements to compete in a given market and achieve parity with competitors in that market (p. 73)

tipping point is where demand for a product or service suddenly takes off, with explosive growth (p. 307)

transnational structure combines local responsiveness with high global coordination (p. 441)

turnaround strategy here the emphasis is on speed of change and rapid cost reduction and/or revenue generation (p. 484)

value chain and system the categories of activities within an organisation which, together, create a product or a service (p. 83)

value net a map of organisations in a business environment demonstrating opportunities for value-creating cooperation as well as competition (p. 49)

values statement concerned with the desired future state of the organisation (p. 108)

value of strategic capabilities are of value when they provide potential competitive advantage in a market and generate higher revenues or lower costs, or both (p. 76)

vertical (forward and backward) integration entering into activities where the organisation is its own supplier or customer (p. 235)

vision statement concerned with the desired future state of the organisation (p. 108)

VRIO four key criteria for assessing potential competitive advantage of capabilities: value, rarity, inimitability and organisational support (p. 76)

Yip's globalisation framework sees international strategy potential as determined by market drivers, cost drivers, government drivers and competitive drivers (p. 264)

INDEX OF NAMES

GENERAL INDEX

Page numbers in bold refer to definitions in the glossary

ACKNOWLEDGEMENTS

We are grateful to the following for permission to reproduce copyright material:

Figures

Figures 1, 2, 3 and 4 in Case Study 'CRH plc: dimensions of successful corporate strategy' from *CRH Annual Report*, 2011, reproduced with permission; Figure 1 in Case Study 'SABMiller: from strength to strength' from SABMiller plc., Courtesy MatteoPeccei, SABMiller; Figure 1 in Case Study 'Severstal: Growth strategies in a Russian steel company' from World Steel Association, reproduced with permission; Figures 1 and 2 in Case Study 'Innovating in the cloud' from www.feedhenry.com, reproduced with permission; Figure 1 in Case Study 'The pharmaceutical industry' from PhRMA, *Medicines in development – Biotechnology – 2006 Report*, p. 51, Pharmaceutical Research and Manufacturers of America; Figure 2 in Case Study 'SABMiller: from strength to strength' from www.google.do.uk/finance, Google Finance™ is a trademark of Google Inc.; Figure 2 in Case Study 'Gazprom and NIS: the oil and gas industry in Serbia' from Belex, belex.rx. Reproduced with permission; Figure 2 in Case Study 'The Mexican narco-trafficking problem' from Stratfor, reproduced with permission; Figures 2.4 and 6.9 adapted from *Competitive Strategy: Techniques for Analyzing Industries and Competitors*, The Free Press (Porter, Michael E. 1998) Adapted with the permission of Simon & Schuster Publishing Group from the Free Press edition. Copyright © 1980, 1998 by The Free Press. All rights reserved; Figure 2.5 from The Right Game, *Harvard Business Review*, July–August pp. 57–64 (Brandenburger, A. and Nalebuff, B. 1996), Reprinted by permission of Harvard Business Review. Copyright © 1996 by the Harvard Business School Publishing Corporation. All rights reserved; Figures 3.4 and 6.2 adapted from *Competitive Advantage: Creating and Sustaining Superior Performance* The Free Press (Porter, Michael E. 1998) Adapted with the permission of Simon & Schuster Publishing Group from The Free Press edition. Copyright © 1985, 1998 by Michael E. Porter. All rights reserved; Figure 3.5 adapted from *Competitive Advantage: Creating and Sustaining Superior Performance* The Free Press (Porter, Michael E., 1998) Adapted with the permission of Simon & Schuster Publishing Group from The Free Press edition. Copyright © 1985, 1998 by Michael E. Porter. All rights reserved; Figure on page 139 from www.moneycontrol.com, 28/12/2012, reproduced with permission; Figure 4.3 from David Pitt-Watson, Hermes Fund Management; Figure 5.5 adapted from *Turnaround: Managerial Recipes for Strategic Success*, Associated Business Press (Grinyer, P. and Spender, J.C. 1979) p. 203, reprinted with permission of Peter H. Grinyer and J.C. Spender; Figure 6.5 adapted from The US airlines relative positioning, *Tourism Management*, 26 (1), p. 62, Fig. 1 (Gursoy, D. Chen, M. and Kim, H. 2005), Copyright 2005, with permission from Elsevier; Figure 6.6 adapted from *The Essence of Competitive Strategy*, Prentice Hall (Faulkner, D. and Bowman, C. 1995) Reproduced with permission from Pearson Education Ltd.; Figure 6.7 adapted from *Hypercompetition: Managing the Dynamics of Strategic Maneuvering* The Free Press (D'Aveni, Richard with Robert Gunther 1994) Adapted with the permission of Simon & Schuster Publishing Group from The Free Press edition. Copyright © 1994 by Richard D'Aveni. All rights reserved; Figure 6.8 adapted from A framework for responding to low-cost rivals, *Harvard Business Review*, December (Kumar, N. 2006), Reprinted by permission of Harvard Business Review. Copyright © 2006 by the Harvard Business School Publishing Corporation. All rights reserved; Figure 7.2 from *Corporate Strategy*, Penguin (Ansoff, H.I. 1988) Chapter 6, with permission of The Ansoff Family Trust; Figures 7.5 and 7.9 adapted from *Corporate Level Strategy*, Wiley (Goold, M., Campbell, A. and Alexander, M. 1994) Copyright © 1994 John Wiley & Sons, Inc. Reproduced with permission of John Wiley & Sons Inc.; Figure 8.3 adapted from *The Competitive Advantage of Nations* The Free Press (Porter, Michael E. 1990) Adapted with the permission of Simon & Schuster Publishing Group from The Free Press edition. Copyright © 1990 by Michael E. Porter. All rights reserved; Figure 8.5 from In the eye of the beholder: cross-cultural lessons in leadership from Project GLOBE (GLOBE stands for 'Global Leadership and Organizational Behavior Effectiveness') *Academy of Management Perspectives*, February, pp. 67–90 (Javidan, M., Dorman, P., de Luque, M. and House, R. 2006); Figure 8.6 adapted from Global gamesmanship, *Harvard Business Review*, May (MacMillan, I., van Putter, S. and McGrath, R. 2003), Reprinted by permission of Harvard Business Review. Copyright © 2003 by the Harvard Business School Publishing Corporation. All rights reserved; Figure 8.8 adapted from *Managing across Borders: The Transnational Solution*, Harvard Business School Press (Bartlett, C.A. and Ghoshal, S. 1989) pp. 105–11, Reprinted by permission of Harvard Business School Press. Copyright © 1989 by the Harvard Business School Publishing Corporation. All rights reserved; Unnumbered Figure on page 303 from *Making the Transition to Cloud*, Fujitsu Services Ltd. (Gentle, David 2011) With permission from Fujitsu Limited UK; Figure 9.2 adapted from A dynamic model of process and product innovation, *Omega*, 3 (6), pp. 639–56 (Abernathy, J. and Utterback, W. 1975), Copyright © 1975, with permission from Elsevier; Figure 9.4 from *The Innovator's Solution* Harvard Business School Press (Christensen, C. and Raynor, M.E. 2003) Reprinted by permission of Harvard Business School Press. Copyright © 2003 by the Harvard Business School Publishing Corporation. All rights reserved; Figure 9.5 from *The Entrepreneurial Mindset* Harvard Business School Press (MacMillan, I. and McGrath, R.G. 2000) p. 176, Reprinted by permission of Harvard Business School Press. Copyright © 2000 by the Harvard Business School Publishing Corporation. All rights reserved; Figure 10.3

from *Managing Acquisitions*, The Free Press (Haspeslagh, P. and Jemison, D. 1991) reproduced with permission from the authors; Figure 10.5 from Strategic alliances: gateway to the new Europe, *Long Range Planning*, 26, p. 109 (Murray, E. and Mahon, J. 1993), copyright © 1993, with permission from Elsevier; Figure 12.1 adapted from Of strategies, deliberate and emergent, *Strategic Management Journal*, 6 (3), P. 258 (Mintzberg, H. and Waters, J.A. 1985), Copyright © 1985 John Wiley & Sons, Ltd.; Unnumbered Figures on pages 462 and 463 from www.sony.net; Figure 13.5 from *Managing Across Borders: The Transnational Corporation*, 2nd ed., Harvard Business School Press (Bartlett, C.A. and Ghoshal, S. 1998) Reprinted by permission of Harvard Business School Press. Copyright © 1998 by the Harvard Business School Publishing Corporation. All rights reserved; Figure 13.6 adapted from *Strategies and Styles*, Wiley-Blackwell (Goold M. and Campbell, A. 1989) Figure 3.1, p. 39, reproduced with permission; Figure 13.7 from Achieving strategy with scorecarding, *Journal of Corporate Accounting and Finance*, March–April, Exhibit 1, p. 64 (Lawson, R., Stratton, W. and Hatch, T. 2005) © 2005 Wiley Periodicals, Inc. Reproduced with permission; Figure 13.8 from Structure is not organization, *Business Horizons*, vol. 23, pp. 14–26 (Waterman, R., Peters, T.J. and Phillips, J.R. 1980), McKinsey & Company, reproduced with permission; Figures 14.2 and 14.4 adapted from *Exploring Strategic Change*, 3rd ed., Prentice Hall (Balogun, J. and Hope Hailey, V. 2008) Reproduced with permission from Pearson Education Ltd.; Unnumbered Figure on page 531 from Wychavon County Council, *Wychavon's 2012–16 Strategy 'One-Pager'*, reproduced with permission; Figure 15.3 adapted from An attention-based theory of strategy formulation: linking micro and macro perspectives in strategy processes, *Advances in Strategic Management*, 22, pp. 39–62 (Ocasio, W. and Joseph, J. 2005), copyright © 2005, with permission from Elsevier; Figure 2 in Case Study 'Severstal: Growth strategies in a Russian steel company' adapted from World Steel Association, *21st Century Steel: 2008–2009 Update*, figure on p. 8, reproduced with permission.

Maps

Map 4 in Case Study 'Gazprom and NIS: the oil and gas industry in Serbia' from Stratfor, reproduced with permission.

Tables

Table on pages 654–6 from www.sabmiller.com/files/reports/ar2012/20012_annual_report.pdf, Courtesy MatteoPeccei, SABMiller; Table 1 in Case Study 'The LEGO Group: Adopting a strategic approach' adapted from LEGO, *Annual Reports*, 2007 and 2012 © 2013 The LEGO Group, Used with permission; Tables 1, 2 and 3 in Case Study 'Vodafone: Developing communications strategy in the UK market' from Ofcom, *Communications Market Report 2012* © Ofcom Copyright 2012; Table 1 in Case Study 'Severstal: Growth strategies in a Russian steel company' from World Steel Association, reproduced with permission; Tables 1a, 1b and 1c in Case Study 'Ryanair: The low fares airline – future directions?' adapted from Ryanair, *Annual Report 2012*, reproduced with permission; Table 3 in Case Study 'The internationalisation of Tesco: new frontiers and new problems' from 'We've learnt how to be local': the deepening territorial embeddedness of Samsung–Tesco in South Korea, *Journal of Economic Geography*, 13 (2), pp. 327–56

(Coe, Neil M. and Lee, Yong-Sook 2013), reproduced by permission of Oxford University Press; Table 4 in Case Study 'Vodafone: Developing communications strategy in the UK market' from Pure Pricing, *UK Broadband, bundling and convergence update*, July 2009; Table 5 in Case Study 'Vodafone: Developing communications strategy in the UK market' adapted from Vodafone, *Annual Report 2012*, reproduced with permission; Table 14.1 adapted from *Exploring Strategic Change*, 3rd ed., Prentice Hall (Balogun, J. and Hope Hailey, V. 2008) Reproduced with permission from Pearson Education Ltd.; Table 15.1 from How to pick a good fight, *Harvard Business Review*, December, pp. 48–57 (Joni, S.A. and Beyer, D. 2009), Reprinted by permission of Harvard Business Review. Copyright © 2009 by the Harvard Business School Publishing Corporation. All rights reserved.

Text

Extract on pages 690–2 from House of Commons BIS Committee (2010), *Mergers, Acquisitions and Takeovers: The Takeover of Cadbury by Kraft*, 9th report of session 2009–10, London, the Stationery Office, Contains public sector information licensed under the Open Government Licence (OGL) v1.0. http://www.nationalarchives.gov.uk/doc/open-government-licence; Case Study 'International HIV/AIDS Alliance (B): A strategy for 2010' The author wishes to thank the International HIVAIDS Alliance for their co-operation in the writing of the case study; Extract on page 649 from SABMiller, *Annual Report*, 2000; Extract on page 650 from SABMiller, *Annual Report*, 2003; Extract on pages 728–9 from Department of Education, www.education.gov.uk, Contains public sector information licensed under the Open Government Licence (OGL) v1.0. http://www.nationalarchives.gov.uk/doc/open-government-licence; Case Study 'Changing tracks at Babcock Rail' The author wishes to thank executives of Babcock Rail and Babcock International PLC for their co-operation in the writing of this case study; Box 1.2 adapted from www.samsung.com reproduced with permission; Extract 3.1 from Tony Hall, Chief Executive of Royal Opera House in *Royal Opera House Annual Review*, 2005/6, p. 11, reprinted by permission of Royal Opera House; Extract on pages 172–3 from Barclays emails reveal a climate of fear and fierce tribal bonding among traders, *The Guardian*, 28/06/2012 (Joris Luyendijk), Copyright Guardian News & Media Ltd. 2012; Extracts in Box 7.4 from Berkshire Hathaway, *Annual Reports*, The material is copyrighted and used with permission of the author; Extract on page 492 from On organizational becoming: rethinking organizational change, *Organization Science*, 13 (5), pp. 567–82 (Tsoukas, H. and Chia, R. 2002), Copyright 2002, reproduced by permission of the Institute for Operations Research and the Management Sciences (INFORMS).

Photographs

Alamy Images: Julian Eales 676, Jeremy Hoare 629, Rob Wilkinson 559; **Corbis**: Michael Kim 583; **Rufus Curnow**: ii; **Daphne Po May Wong**: 717; **DK Images**: 544; **Getty Images**: Tony Avelar/Bloomberg via Getty Images 680, Simon Dawson/Bloombery via Getty Images 185, Alain Jocard/AFP 600, Neil Lupin/Redferns 24, Peter Macdiarmid 624, Jordan Mansfield 571, Alessia Pierdomencio/Bloomberg via Getty Images 496; **Gridsum**: 664; **International HIV/Aids**

Alliance: Members of People Living with HIV group in Nyimbwa, Uganda © Nell Freeman for the International HIV/AIDS Alliance 700; **iStockphoto**: © webphotographeer 357; Juan Manila Express: 718; **Dieter Mayr Photography**: 102; **Press Association Images**: Ng Han Guan/AP 290, Mark Lennihan 429, Chris Radburn/PA Wire 612, Stefan Rousseau 721; **Rex Features**: 171, Steve Bell 255, McPix Ltd 595, VIEW Pictures 727; **SABMiller plc**: Jason Alden/OneRedEye 647; **Dr Eustathios Sainidis**: 666; **Teva UK Limited**: 634.

All other images © Pearson Education

In some instances we have been unable to trace the owners of copyright material, and we would appreciate any information that would enable us to do so.